Racial and Ethnic Relations in America

Volume I

Ability testing - Ethnic enclaves

Editorial Board

Carl L. Bankston III
University of Southwestern Louisiana

Carole A. Barrett
University of Mary, North Dakota

Kibibi Mack
University of Maryland, Baltimore County

Franklin Ng
California State University, Fresno

William Osborne
Florida International University

Ranee K. L. Panjabi
Memorial University of Newfoundland

William E. Pemberton
University of Wisconsin, La Crosse

Maria E. Pérez y Gonzalez
Brooklyn College, CUNY

Gregory Walters
University of Ottawa

Managing Editor, **Christina J. Moose**

Project Editor, **Rowena Wildin**

SALEM PRESS, INC.
PASADENA, CALIFORNIA   HACKENSACK, NEW JERSEY

Managing Editor: Christina J. Moose   Project Editor: Rowena Wildin
Research Supervisor: Jeffry Jensen   Manuscript Editors: Rowena Wildin, Robert McClenaghan
Acquisitions Editor: Mark Rehn   Research Assistant: Jun Ohnuki
Photograph Editor: Karrie Hyatt   Production Editor: Joyce I. Buchea
Editorial Secretary: Andrea E. Miller   Design and Layout: James Hutson

Copyright © 2000, by Salem Press, Inc.

All rights in this book are reserved. No part of this work may be used or reproduced in any manner whatsoever or transmitted in any form or by any means, electronic or mechanical, including photocopy, recording, or any information storage and retrieval system, without written permission from the copyright owners except in the case of brief quotations embodied in critical articles and reviews. For information, address the publisher, Salem Press, Inc., P.O. Box 50062, Pasadena, California 91115.

Some of the essays in this work originally appeared in the following Salem Press sets: *American Indians* (1995), *American Justice* (1996), *Ethics* (1994), *Great Events from History: North American Series* (revised edition, 1997), *Identities and Issues in Literature* (1997), *The Sixties in America* (1999), *Survey of Social Science: Psychology Series* (1993), *Survey of Social Science: Sociology Series* (1994), and *Women's Issues* (1997).

∞ The paper used in these volumes conforms to the American National Standard for Permanence of Paper for Printed Library Materials, Z39.48-1992(R1997)

Library of Congress Cataloging-in-Publication Data

Racial and ethnic relations in America / editorial board Carl L. Bankston . . . [et al.].
   p.   cm.
   Includes bibliographical references (p.   ) and indexes.
   Contents: v. 1. Ability testing—Ethnic enclaves — v. 2. Ethnic entrepreneurship—Political correctness — v. 3. Politics and racial/ethnic relations in Canada—Zoot-suit riots.
   ISBN 0-89356-629-2 (set : alk. paper). — ISBN 0-89356-630-6 (vol. 1 : alk. paper). — ISBN 0-89356-634-9 (vol. 2 : alk. paper). — ISBN 0-89356-635-7 (vol. 3 : alk. paper)
   1. North America—Ethnic relations Encyclopedias.   2. North America—Race relations Encyclopedias. I. Bankston, Carl L. (Carl Leon), 1952-   .

E49.R33   2000
305.8'00973—dc21   99-29348
                                                                                                                                    CIP

First Printing

PRINTED IN THE UNITED STATES OF AMERICA

Racial and Ethnic Relations in America

Contents

LIBRARY
ALMA COLLEGE
ALMA, MICHIGAN

Photo Credits in Volume I

Pages 2, 30, 49, 246, 273, 334, 341, 348, 378: *James L. Shaffer*; Pages 4, 239: *Associated Publishers, Inc.*; Pages 13, 43, 54, 61, 68, 73, 109, 115, 136, 165, 168-169, 176, 182, 272, 287, 294, 303, 305, 332, 373: *AP/Wide World Photos*; Page 17: *Nicole Rosenthal/AP/Wide World Photos*; Page 21: *Alon Reininger/Unicorn Stock Photos*; Page 24: *Alfred A. Knopf*; Pages 28, 34, 58, 87, 97, 119, 132, 152, 157, 184, 203, 216, 234, 258, 315: *Library of Congress*; Pages 32, 47: *Lester Sloan/Columbia Pictures Industries*; Pages 36, 122, 146, 198, 212, 267: *Dick Hemingway*; Pages 39, 259: *Frances M. Roberts*; Pages 72, 80: *Ben Glass/Orion Pictures Corporation*; Pages 77, 117, 178, 205, 359, 362, 383: *Ben Klaffke*; Page 84: *Archive Photos*; Page 93: *Mike Derer/AP/Wide World Photos*; Pages 106, 125, 276, 289, 327: *Richard B. Levine*; Pages 112: *Museum of Modern Art/Film Stills Archive*; Page 139: *National Baseball Library, Cooperstown, N.Y.*; Page 143: *Ed Andrieski/AP/Wide World Photos*; Page 144: *Delicia Lopez/AP/Wide World Photos*; Pages 186, 350: *Mark Duncan/AP/Wide World Photos*; Page 189: *Eric Crystal*; Pages 192, 227, 229, 343: *National Archives*; Page 209: *Smithsonian Institution*; Pages 214, 268, 308: *Asian American Studies Library, University of California, Berkeley*; Page 218: *Beverly Taylor, Birmingham News/AP/Wide World Photos*; Page 223: *Ronald Reagan Library*; Page 252: *The Institute of Texan Cultures, San Antonio, Texas*; Page 298: *Lou Dematteis*; Page 364: *Robert W. Ginn/Unicorn Stock Photos*; Page 369: *The Korea Society*

Introduction: Editor's Note

People from all racial and ethnic groups have shaped the societies of North America, and an understanding of race and ethnicity is therefore essential to understanding our continent. The three volumes of *Racial and Ethnic Relations in America*, in 897 essays, deal with some of the most important topics, events, and issues surrounding relations between and among the peoples of North America.

Both the United States and Canada were created by the arrival of one set of people, the Europeans, in the lands of another set of people, indigenous or Native Americans, misnamed, from a European perspective, Indians. At the beginning of the seventeenth century, some of those early European settlers (or invaders, from some points of view) brought with them members of yet another group. The first Africans in the New World, indentured servants not yet clearly defined as slaves, are generally believed to have landed in Virginia in 1619. There were twenty of those early Africans. By the time of the American Revolution a century and a half later, nearly one in five people in the original colonies of what became the United States was of African background.

The Europeans themselves were heirs to a variety of ethnic traditions. Those Europeans who established themselves in the northern part of the continent, in what became Canada, were associated with two major ethnicities in their old countries. The French settled in the areas of Canada that became known as New France. Elsewhere in Canada, the British took control. Although New France came under the British in 1763, through the centuries Canada has continued to have a dual ethnic identity, as both French and English, in language and heritage. Many of the English speakers, moreover, actually came from Scotland or Ireland.

The central part of the continent, which became the United States, was also settled by diverse European ethnic groups. In the 1600's, Swedes and Finns settled in the Delaware River Valley, creating the colony of New Sweden. The Dutch took over the colony in 1655, establishing a substantial Dutch presence in North America, which continued to be reflected in the place-names and family names of the New York region even after the English took over the colony.

Although those from the British Isles—England, Ireland, Wales, and Scotland—furnished the majority of people in the central part of North America, there were also large numbers of Germans in the region. During the early years of the United States, Germans accounted for nearly one out of every ten new immigrants, and Germany continued to be one of the main countries of origin of immigrants to the United States throughout the nineteenth century. The German language, in fact, was widely spoken in the United States until World War I.

Spanish-speaking Europeans settled in the south and west of the territory that is now the United States, many of them with both Spanish and Native American ancestors. Much of the United States continues to have a strong Hispanic heritage today. Spanish is the second most widely spoken language in the United States, and Hispanic or Latino culture distinguishes many regions of Texas, New Mexico, Arizona, California, New York, Florida, and other states.

In the nineteenth century, new immigrants from around the globe brought new ethnic traditions to these nations founded on intergroup contacts. The Chinese put down roots in places like San Francisco, New York, Los Angeles, and Vancouver. Italians, Greeks, Poles, Yugoslavians, and other Southern and Eastern Europeans provided much of the workforce for industrializing America in the late nineteenth and early twentieth centuries. Relations between racial and ethnic groups literally made the nations of North America. These relations are not just a matter of history, either. An increase in the diversity of the American population makes these relations critical today.

The Rise of Diversity

Visitors to North American cities often experience surprise at the cultural variety of these cities. Toronto, a Canadian city close to the border with the United States, is home to large Chinese, Filipino, and Vietnamese communities, and many sections of Toronto are distinctly Asian in character. Miami, at the southern toe of the United States, has become a bilingual Spanish and English city as people from Cuba and other parts of the Caribbean and Central America have settled. Los Angeles, similarly, is multilingual—rich not only in Spanish speakers with which its ethnic subgroups have identified since the city's founding but also in an increasing multitude of Asian and other groups.

Moreover, the racial and ethnic diversity of North America is changing—increasing, rapidly. Although most immigrants to North America prior to the mid-twentieth century were Europeans (sometimes a result of strict immigration laws that favored those groups through quota systems), by the 1990's Latin America and Asia were the primary sources of immigrants. The 1990 United States Census revealed that the Hispanic percentage of the U.S. population had doubled between 1970 and 1990, from 4.5 percent to 9.0 percent; in the late 1990's, it stood at about 11 percent. The Asian percentage of the population more than tripled during those two decades to about 3 percent of the nation's people, and now it has surpassed 4 percent. At the same time, the percentage classified as "white" decreased from nearly 88 percent to just over 80 percent by 1990 and just over 72 percent by 1997; it appears that this trend will continue.

Along with this acceleration in ethnic and racial diversity has been an increased recognition, and celebration, of cultural pluralism. In the 1930's, the historian Marcus Lee Hansen proposed what has become known as the Hansen thesis, the principle that grandchildren of immigrants tend to rediscover the ethnic identities that the immigrants' children have sought to discard. Although this may not always be true, there does seem to have been an "ethnic revival" among the people of North America. People with Irish or Scottish surnames are discovering the joys of Celtic music. German Oktoberfests have become popular events in towns settled by Germans. And the trend is toward increasing diversity: Milwaukee, for example, boasts a multitude of German subcultures who see themselves as distinct from one another, and Asian Americans are hardly the monolithic culture that the U.S. Census's lumping of them into "Asian Americans and Pacific Islanders" would suggest. Similarly, Latinos are extremely diverse, not only culturally and ethnically but also politically, from the generally conservative Cuban Americans who fled Fidel Castro's 1959 revolution to the often liberal Puerto Ricans of the Northeast and the Mexican Americans, Guatemalans, Nicaraguans, Hondurans, and Salvadorans of the Southwest. The diversity multiplies. The trend seems spurred by a need to assert identity and individuality at the same time that there is a need to seek membership in a group—a group with its own history, heritage, and traditions *other than* those of a dominant and increasingly homogenous "melting pot" culture of minimalls and one-size-fits-all solutions to social problems.

Members of racial groups are showing a new pride of ethnicity. Across the United States and Canada, Native Americans are asserting their traditional rights and cultures. The slogan of singer James Brown, "I'm black and I'm proud," is alive among African Americans. In universities, departments of Latino studies, African American studies, Asian American studies, and Native American studies attest to the growing awareness of racial and ethnic identities in North America.

The Need for Reliable Information
This new and growing diversity makes a reliable and dispassionate source of facts and information on intergroup relations a vital and increasingly indispensable resource. It is this need that *Racial and Ethnic Relations in America* seeks to fill.

The demand for information is fed by the ethnic revival, but that is not its only source. North America's deepest injustices, most profound conflicts, and bitterest controversies have their roots in racial and ethnic tensions. The tensions between English-speaking and French-speaking Canadians, two separate cultural groups, pose some of that nation's greatest domestic political problems. In the United States, African Americans and whites often see the world differently, and continuing racial disparities in income, ownership of property, housing, education, and employment are troubling matters in a country that professes ideals of equality of opportunity for all individuals. Some of the most divisive and controversial issues in American society, such as affirmative action, concern how Americans should address questions of racial and ethnic inequality. During the late twentieth century, major riots sparked by racial issues rocked American cities such as Miami and Los Angeles.

The increasing ethnic diversity of North America has been a source of debates and controversy as well as celebration. California, home to large numbers of Latinos and Asians, has seen political movements and even legislation to end bilingual education, stop the supply of public services to illegal immigrants, and forbid affirmative action. Elsewhere in the United States, some writers and activists have claimed that even legal immigration is excessive and poses a grave danger to the identity of the nation. Both the United States and Canada have begun to rein in their once-liberal refugee policies. Controversial, divisive issues demand attention and require thorough, well-organized sources of facts and ideas.

The hope is that this encyclopedia will offer, through the voices of credentialed scholars in history, sociology, anthropology, and other appropriate disciplines, a basic and centralized resource from which to begin investigation into the many, and multidisciplinary, topics that have an impact on this timely, and timeless, subject. In this set, we attempt to introduce order into the complexity by approaching these subjects from three general perspectives.

Approaches to Coverage
First, we include topics that approach racial and ethnic matters from the point of view of *theory*. Theories are explanations. They may be explanations of how racial and ethnic groups are formed, how they change over time, how they relate to one another, or how they affect their members. For example, the assimilation theories described in these volumes detail the views of many scholars on how ethnic groups become more similar to one another with contact. The various theories of prejudice presented here consider how antagonism between members of racial or ethnic groups may be perpetuated or reduced.

Second, we include topics that approach racial and ethnic relations from the perspective of *history*. Understanding the contemporary ethnic makeup of North America requires a knowledge of the history of immigration, as well as the histories of different ethnic groups within the larger society—particularly as their histories influenced, and were influenced by, those of other groups, both dominant and minority. Grasping the notion of racial inequality and the strong feelings many Americans have about race necessitates, to take one of the most important and obvious examples, an examination of slavery as a historical influence on American society. This set gives readers easy access to a wealth of articles on the historical background of race and ethnicity.

Third, we include topics that approach the subject from the perspective of *current events and issues*. Racial and ethnic matters hit the headlines of newspapers and magazines virtually on a daily basis. What, if any, is the connection between race or ethnicity and welfare? See "Welfare reform." Is immigration to North America increasing? See "Racial and ethnic demographics: trends." Why do some support continued immigration while others feel that allowing immigration is a form of national suicide? See "Immigration 'crisis' " as well as the many entries on immigration acts and laws. Is our society becoming more or less racially segregated, and what might be some of the problems associated with racial segregation? See the many entries on segregation, desegregation, and hypersegregation. Here, readers can find details on the hot topics of today's American societies in a format that enables them to delve more deeply into many of the key issues affecting our ability to interrelate with peoples of different racial, ethnic, and cultural backgrounds.

Organization of This Encyclopedia

The comprehensive quality of these approaches to racial and ethnic relations is enhanced by an organization that makes the topics easy to access and thus helpful to both students and browsers. Topics have been carefully chosen for their relevance and importance to racial and ethnic relations. The essays—ranging in length from brief definitions of 200 words to comprehensive overviews of 2,500 words or more—present clear, detailed descriptions of ideas and theories, descriptions of people and events, and essential facts about court cases, laws, and movements.

All topics are arranged alphabetically, in encyclopedia style—from "Ability testing" and "Abolition" through "Zionism," "Zoning," and "Zoot-suit riots." For all but the shortest essays, a "Significance" section at the beginning of the essay summarizes the import of the topic for intergroup relations. Cross-references appear in a "See also" section at the end of each entry, so that readers can find related entries. Each of the longer entries provides a list of "Core Resources"—a briefly annotated bibliography of books and other materials that can help readers learn more about the subject of the entry. These bibliographic sections refer readers to both classic and up-to-date works.

The text is illustrated with more than 70 charts, graphs, time lines, and tables that demonstrate trends and bring events to life. More than 275 black-and-white photographs display the continent's diverse peoples in action.

At the end of each volume, a Categorized List of Entries will help users find entries by areas of interest, such as groups (African Americans, American Indians, Arab Americans, Asian Americans, Italian Americans, Latinos, etc.), issues (such as Discrimination or Immigration or Prejudice), and generic topics (such as Laws or Theories or Movements). This list will prove especially valuable for those users of the encyclopedia seeking a broad range of information on relatively large areas of interest, for any essay that is germane to a particular category is listed under it—as well as under any other category to which it pertains. There are, for example, fully 212 essays that relate to the African American experience, 128 to American Indians, 71 to Asian Americans, 49 to various Euro-American groups, 45 to Latinos, and 39 to Jewish Americans, along with 51 that specifically pertain to issues surrounding Canadian race relations. In addition, a plate of essays pertain to smaller or newer ethnic groups: 5 specifically to various Arab Americans, 6 to Caribbean Americans, 6 to Italian Americans, and 14 to Irish Americans, for example. Sociological theories, terms, and concepts form the basis of 100 essays. The arts are the subject of 16 essays; civil rights, 20 essays; key court cases are the topic of 73 entries; demographic and housing issues, 31 essays; discrimination, 14 essays; education, 37 essays; employment and workplace issues, 26 essays; ethnicity, 18 essays; family issues, 20 essays; government programs and policies, 30 essays; identity issues, 30 essays; immigration, 36 essays; laws and acts, 76 essays; movements, 28 essays; organizations and institutions, 81 essays; race and racism, 29 essays; religious topics, 31 essays; riots and other conflicts, 66 essays; treaties and agreements, 7 essays.

At the end of volume 3, an overall Time Line puts the issues into a historical context that can be seen at a glance, giving an easy-to-follow chronological structure for topics covered in the text. The Core Resources sections that accompany each individual entry are complemented by a final bibliography that presents works on race and ethnicity that will be key to students of the subject. A unique section, "Pioneers of Intergroup Relations," provides sketches of individuals who have been especially influential in shaping relations among racial and ethnic groups in North America. A personages index highlights the major individuals in the work, allowing readers to quickly find references to specific people. Finally, a comprehensive subject index provides access to the many events, laws, acts, persons, issues, theories, concepts, and other topics discussed throughout the three volumes.

The entries in these volumes have been written with the intention of making them comprehensible to younger readers without being patronizing, at the same time providing facts and ideas that will be of interest to the most advanced users. The work has been assembled with the advice of a panel of academic experts, in order to make it as accurate and reliable as possible; their names and academic affiliations appear on the title page. In addition, a list of the contributing writers, along with their academic affiliations, appears in the front matter to the first volume. Without the expertise of all these individuals, this publication would not have been possible.

Carl L. Bankston III
University of Southwestern Louisiana

List of Contributors

Nobuko Adachi
Illinois State University

McCrea Adams
Independent Scholar

Antwi A. A. Akom
University of Pennsylvania

William Allison
Bowling Green State University

Carl Allsup
*University of
Wisconsin—Platteville*

Thomas L. Altherr
*Metropolitan State College of
Denver*

Candace E. Andrews
San Joaquin Delta College

T. J. Arant
Appalachian State University

Mary Welek Atwell
Radford University

Tanya M. Backinger
Jackson Community College

James A. Baer
*Northern Virginia Community
College*

Barbara Bair
Independent Scholar

Thomas E. Baker
Texas Tech University Law School

Carl L. Bankston III
*University of Southwestern
Louisiana*

Rosann Bar
Caldwell College

Gregg Barak
Eastern Michigan University

Graciela Bardallo-Vivero
Berkeley College

Bernice McNair Barnett
University of Illinois at Urbana

Carole A. Barrett
University of Mary

Michael L. Barrett
Ashland University

Paul Barton-Kriese
Indiana University—East

Harry H. Bash
University of Missouri, St. Louis

Alvin K. Benson
Brigham Young University

S. Carol Berg
College of St. Benedict

Milton Berman
University of Rochester

Jon L. Berquist
Independent Scholar

Joseph M. Bessette
Claremont McKenna College

Tej K. Bhatia
Syracuse University

Cynthia A. Bily
Adrian College

Bette Blaisdell
Independent Scholar

George P. Blum
University of the Pacific

Steve D. Boilard
Independent Scholar

James J. Bolner
*Louisiana State University,
Baton Rouge*

Aubrey W. Bonnett
*State University of New York,
Old Westbury*

Cliff Brown
University of New Hampshire

Dallas L. Browne
*Southern Illinois University at
Edwardsville*

Fred Buchstein
*John Carroll University
Dix & Eaton*

Mary Louise Buley-Meissner
*University of
Wisconsin—Milwaukee*

Michael H. Burchett
Limestone College

Gregory R. Campbell
University of Montana

Malcolm B. Campbell
Bowling Green State University

Edmund J. Campion
University of Tennessee

Terri L. Canaday
Mississippi State University

Byron D. Cannon
University of Utah

Glenn Canyon
Independent Scholar

Richard K. Caputo
Barry University

Brenda E. Reinertsen
Caranicas
Fort Berthold Community College

Peter E. Carr
*Caribbean Historical &
Genealogical Journal*

Sharon Carson
University of North Dakota

Jack Carter
University of New Orleans

Paul J. Chara, Jr.
Loras College

Jessica M. Charbeneau
Independent Scholar

Frederick B. Chary
Indiana University Northwest

Cheryl D. Childers
Washburn University

Erica Childs
Fordham University

Balance Chow
San Jose State University

Ward Churchill
University of Colorado at Boulder

John G. Clark
University of Kansas

Lawrence I. Clark
Independent Scholar

Thomas Clarkin
University of Texas

Helena Antolin Cochrane
Widener University

Philip N. Cohen
*University of Maryland,
College Park*

Richard H. Collin
*Louisiana State University,
New Orleans*

Richard G. Condon
University of Arkansas

William H. Coogan
University of Southern Maine

Tom Cook
Wayne State College

William J. Cooper, Jr.
*Louisiana State University,
Baton Rouge*

Randall Coyne
*University of Oklahoma
Law School*

David A. Crain
South Dakota State University

Stephen Cresswell
West Virginia Wesleyan College

Gary A. Cretser
*California State Polytechnic
University, Pomona*

Norma Crews
Independent Scholar

Laura A. Croghan
College of William and Mary

Edward R. Crowther
Adams State College

Rochelle L. Dalla
University of Nebraska

Richard V. Damms
Mississippi State University

Mary Yu Danico
*California State Polytechnic
University, Pomona*

G. Reginald Daniel
*University of California, Santa
Barbara*

Sudipta Das
*Southern University at New
Orleans*

Jane Davis
Fordham University

Héctor L. Delgado
University of Arizona

Judith Boyce DeMark
Northern Michigan University

Ione Y. DeOllos
Ball State University

Thomas E. DeWolfe
Hampden-Sydney College

Ashley W. Doane, Jr.
University of Hartford

Frederick J. Dobney
St. Louis University

Davison M. Douglas
William and Mary Law School

Joyce Duncan
East Tennessee State University

Jennifer Eastman
Clark University

Craig M. Eckert
Eastern Illinois University

Paul Eisenhauer
Chestnut Hill College

Sharon Elise
*California State University,
San Marcos*

Robert P. Ellis
Worcester State College

Susan Ellis-Lopez
Heritage College

Dorothy Engan-Barker
Mankato State University

James B. Epps
University of South Florida

John L. Farbo
University of Idaho

James V. Fenelon
John Carroll University

Celestino Fernández
University of Arizona

John W. Fiero
*University of Southwestern
Louisiana*

Brian L. Fife
Ball State University

Michael Shaw Findlay
California State University, Chico

Alan M. Fisher
*California State University,
Dominguez Hills*

Roberta Fiske-Rusciano
Rutgers University

John H. Fleming
*University of Minnesota—
Minneapolis*

Karen Anding Fontenot
*Southeastern Louisiana
University*

Brenda Forster
Elmhurst College

Gregory Freeland
California Lutheran University

R. M. Frumkin
Center for Democratic Values

C. George Fry
*Lutheran College of Health
Professions*

Gloria Fulton
Humboldt State University

Lucy Ganje
University of North Dakota

John C. Gardner
*Louisiana State University,
Baton Rouge*

Keith Garebian
Independent Scholar

Karen Garner
University of Texas at Austin

Judith L. Gay
Chestnut Hill College

Phyllis B. Gerstenfeld
*California State University,
Stanislaus*

Louis Gesualdi
St. John's University

K. Fred Gillum
Colby College

Marc Goldstein
*University of Rochester
New York University*

Robert F. Gorman
Southwest Texas State University

Jennifer Lynn Gossett
University of Cincinnati

Lewis L. Gould
University of Texas, Austin

Roy Neil Graves
University of Tennessee, Martin

William H. Green
University of Missouri, Columbia

Johnpeter Horst Grill
Mississippi State University

Christopher Guillebeau
The University of Memphis

Michael Haas
University of Hawaii at Manoa

Peter J. Haas
Vanderbilt University

Marian Wynne Haber
Texas Wesleyan University

Frank E. Hagan
Mercyhurst College

Sam Ramsey Hakim
University of Nebraska at Omaha

Irwin Halfond
McKendree College

Timothy L. Hall
*University of Mississippi
Law School*

Susan E. Hamilton
Independent Scholar

Sheldon Hanft
Appalachian State University

Robert M. Hardaway
*University of Denver
College of Law*

Roger D. Hardaway
*Northwestern Oklahoma State
University*

Roxanna E. Harlow
Indiana University, Bloomington

Keith Harper
Mississippi College

William M. Harris, Sr.
Jackson State University

Stanley Harrold
South Carolina State University

Karen C. Hauser
Dominican University

Donald M. Hayes
Sam Houston State University

James Hayes-Bohanan
University of Arizona

Peter B. Heller
Manhattan College

Arthur W. Helweg
Western Michigan University

Eric Henderson
University of Northern Iowa

Diane Andrews Henningfeld
Adrian College

Howard M. Hensel
*United States Air Force
Air War College*

Steven Hewitt
University of Saskatchewan

C. L. Higham
Winona State University

Roseanne L. Hoefel
Alma College

Mary R. Holley
Montclair State University

Chalis Holton
Independent Scholar

Ronald W. Howard
Mississippi College

William L. Howard
Chicago State University

Eleanor A. Hubbard
University of Colorado at Boulder

Mary Hurd
East Tennessee State University

Charles C. Jackson
Augusta State University

John Jacob
Northwestern University

Robert Jacobs
Central Washington University

Joyce P. Jacobsen
Rhodes College

M. A. Jaimes
University of Colorado at Boulder

Duncan R. Jamieson
Ashland University

Kristine Kleptach Jamieson
Ashland University

Robert L. Jenkins
Mississippi State University

Albert C. Jensen
Central Florida Community College

K. Sue Jewell
Ohio State University

Bruce E. Johansen
University of Nebraska at Omaha

Craig Johnson
Syracuse University

Jonathan Kahane
Springfield College

Charles L. Kammer
The College of Wooster

Mathew J. Kanjirathinkal
Independent Scholar

Valli Kanuha
University of Hawaii

Ludmila Kapschutschenko-
Schmitt
Rider University

Mabel Khawaja
Hampton University

Debra A. King-Johnson
Clemson University

Peter Kivisto
Augustana College

Kathleen Odell Korgen
William Paterson University

Jeri Kurtzleben
University of Northern Iowa

M. Bahati Kuumba
Buffalo State College

Linda Rochell Lane
Tuskegee University

Lisa Langenbach
Middle Tennessee State University

Eleanor A. LaPointe
Ocean County College

Sharon L. Larson
University of Nebraska—Lincoln

Abraham D. Lavender
Florida International University

Sharon M. Lee
Portland State University

Eric M. Levine
Wurzweiler School of Social Work

Gregory A. Levitt
University of New Orleans

Thomas T. Lewis
Mt. Senario College

Patricia Lin
California State Polytechnic University, Pomona

James W. Loewen
Catholic University of America

Anne C. Loveland
Louisiana State University, Baton Rouge

William C. Lowe
Mount St. Clare College

Emma T. Lucas
Chatham College

David C. Lukowitz
Independent Scholar

Wei Luo
Southern Illinois University School of Law

Donna Echols Mabus
PLATO Associates

Kenneth S. McAllister
University of Illinois at Chicago

Richard B. McCaslin
High Point University

Grace McEntee
Appalachian State University

Robert E. McFarland
Truett-McConnell College

Susan Mackey-Kallis
Villanova University

Paul Madden
Hardin-Simmons University

Paul D. Mageli
Independent Scholar

Scott Magnuson-Martinson
Normandale Community College

Krishna Mallick
Bentley College

Bill Manikas
Gaston College

Robert D. Manning
Georgetown University

Cecilia G. Manrique
University of Wisconsin— La Crosse

Carl Henry Marcoux
University of California, Riverside

Martin N. Marger
Michigan State University

Jonathan Markovitz
University of California, San Diego

Grace Maria Marvin
California State University, Chico

Lynn M. Mason
Lubbock Christian University

Thomas D. Matijasic
Prestonsburg Community College

Hisako Matsuo
Southern Illinois University at Carbondale

Judith R. Mayo
Northeast Valley Health Corporation

Steve J. Mazurana
University of Northern Colorado

Edward V. Mednick
New Jersey City University

Daniel J. Meissner
University of Wisconsin— Madison

Scott A. Melzer
University of California, Riverside

Howard Meredith
University of Science and Arts of Oklahoma

Diane P. Michelfelder
Utah State University

David N. Mielke
Appalachian State University

Laurence Miller
Western Washington State University

Liesel A. Miller
Mississippi State University

Randall L. Milstein
Lansing Community College

Eli C. Minkoff
Bates College

Fathali M. Moghaddam
Georgetown University

Kesha S. Moore
University of Pennsylvania

William V. Moore
College of Charleston

Chris Moose
Independent Scholar

Brian Mullen
Syracuse University

Molly H. Mullin
Duke University

Gil Richard Musolf
Central Michigan University

Franklin Ng
California State University, Fresno

Burl L. Noggle
Louisiana State University, Baton Rouge

Eileen O'Brien
University of Florida

Carlota Ocampo
Trinity College

Oladele A. Ogunseitan
University of California, Irvine

Gary A. Olson
San Bernardino Valley College

Gwenelle S. O'Neal
Rutgers University

Patrick M. O'Neil
Broome Community College

Max Orezzoli
Florida International University

Amy J. Orr
University of Notre Dame

Martin Orr
Boise State University

William Osborne
Florida International University

Maria A. Pacino
Azusa Pacific University

Lisa Paddock
Independent Scholar

Martha I. Pallante
Youngstown State University

Ranee K. L. Panjabi
Memorial University of Newfoundland

William A. Paquette
Tidewater Community College

Jason Pasch
Independent Scholar

Craig S. Pascoe
University of Tennessee, Knoxville

Darryl Paulson
University of South Florida

Cheryl Pawlowski
University of Northern Colorado

Pedro R. Payne
University of California, Riverside

Thomas R. Peake
King College

William E. Pemberton
University of Wisconsin— La Crosse

Michael P. Perez
California State University, Fullerton

Marilyn Elizabeth Perry
Independent Scholar

Thomas F. Pettigrew
University of California, Santa Cruz

Julio César Pino
Kent State University

Mark A. Plummer
Illinois State University

Marjorie Podolsky
Penn State University—Erie

David L. Porter
William Penn College

John Powell
Penn State University—Erie

Steven Pressman
Monmouth University

Francis P. Prucha
Marquette University

Lillian M. Range
University of Southern Mississippi

Samory Rashid
Indiana State University

R. Kent Rasmussen
Independent Scholar

E. A. Reed
Baylor University

Thomas D. Reins
California State University, Fullerton

William L. Reinshagen
Independent Scholar

Jon Reyhner
Montana State University, Billings

Douglas W. Richmond
University of Texas, Arlington

Richard Robbins
Curry College/University of Massachusetts—Boston

Jaclyn Rodriguez
Occidental College

Mícheál D. Roe
Seattle Pacific University

Moises Roizen
West Valley College

Fred S. Rolater
Middle Tennessee State University

Courtney B. Ross
Louisiana State University, Baton Rouge

John Alan Ross
Eastern Washington University

John K. Roth
Claremont McKenna College

Joseph R. Rudolph, Jr.
Towson State University

Dorothy C. Salem
Cleveland State University/Cuyahoga Community College

Glenn J. Schiffman
Independent Scholar

Helmut J. Schmeller
Fort Hays State University

J. Christopher Schnell
Southeast Missouri State University

Kathleen Schongar
The May School

Todd J. Schroer
Western State College

Stephen Schwartz
Buffalo State College

Larry Schweikart
University of Dayton

Rebecca Lovell Scott
College of Health Sciences

Aristide Sechandice
University of Georgia

Terry L. Seip
Louisiana State University, Baton Rouge

R. Baird Shuman
University of Illinois, Urbana-Champaign

Robert Mark Silverman
Jackson State University

Malik Simba
California State University, Fresno

Donald C. Simmons, Jr.
Mississippi Humanities Council

Donna Addkison Simmons
Independent Scholar

M. W. Simpson
Eastern Washington University

Kevin F. Sims
Cedarville College

Rejoice D. Sithole
University of Wisconsin Centers, Waukesha

Andrew C. Skinner
Brigham Young University

James Smallwood
Oklahoma State University

Charles V. Smedley
Charleston Southern University

Christopher E. Smith
Michigan State University

William L. Smith
Georgia Southern University

Daniel L. Smith-Christopher
Loyola Marymount University

Christy Jo Snider
Purdue University

Robert Sobel
Hofstra University

John A. Sondey
South Dakota State University

Robert M. Spector
Worcester State College

James Stanlaw
Illinois State University

Sandra K. Stanley
California State University, Northridge

Glenn Ellen Starr
Appalachian State University

Francis C. Staskon
Independent Scholar

David L. Sterling
University of Cincinnati

Pamela R. Stern
University of Arkansas

Ruffin Stirling
Independent Scholar

Ruby L. Stoner
Penn State University College of Technology

Geralyn Strecker
Ball State University

Leslie Stricker
Park College

Irene Struthers
Independent Scholar

Susan A. Stussy
Independent Scholar

Glenn L. Swygart
Tennessee Temple University

Stephen G. Sylvester
Montana State University— Northern

James Tackach
Roger Williams University

Vanessa Tait
University of California, Santa Cruz

Robert D. Talbott
University of Northern Iowa

Harold D. Tallant
Georgetown College

Emily Teipe
Fullerton College

Nancy Conn Terjesen
Kent State University

Felicia F. Thomas
California State Polytechnic University, Pomona

Yonette F. Thomas
National Academy of Sciences

Vincent Michael Thur
Wenatchee Valley College

Harry A. Tiemann, Jr.
Mesa State College

Leslie V. Tischauser
Prairie State College

Brian G. Tobin
Lassen College

Derise E. Tolliver
DePaul University

Frank Towers
Clarion University

Paul B. Trescott
Southern Illinois University

Mfanya D. Tryman
Mississippi State University

Robert D. Ubriaco, Jr.
Spelman College

Jiu-Hwa Lo Upshur
Eastern Michigan University

Harry van der Linden
Butler University

Fred R. van Hartesveldt
Fort Valley State College

Lyn M. Van Swol
University of Illinois at Urbana-Champaign

Milton D. Vickerman
Bloomfield College

Mary E. Virginia
Independent Scholar

Randolph Meade Walker
Le Moyne-Owen College

Thomas J. Edward Walker
Pennsylvania College of Technology

Gregory Walters
Saint Paul University

Annita Marie Ward
Salem-Teikyo University

Claudia A. Pavone Watson
University of Hawaii, Hilo

Elwood David Watson
East Tennessee State University

Robert P. Watson
University of Hawaii, Hilo

William L. Waugh, Jr.
Georgia State University

Ashton Wesley Welch
Creighton University

Donald M. Whaley
Salisbury State University

Richard Whitworth
Ball State University

David A. Wilder
Rutgers University

David E. Wilkins
University of Colorado at Boulder

Raymond Wilson
Fort Hays State University

Richard L. Wilson
University of Tennessee at Chattanooga

Sharon K. Wilson
Fort Hays State University

Theodore A. Wilson
University of Kansas

Thomas Winter
University of Cincinnati

Michael Witkoski
Independent Scholar

Trudi D. Witonsky
University of Wisconsin, Madison

Karen M. Wolford
State University of New York College at Oswego

Eugene F. Wong
Voorhees College

Susan J. Wurtzburg
University of Canterbury New Zealand

Gene Redding Wynne, Jr.
Tri-County Technical College

George Yancey
University of Wisconsin at Whitewater

Philip Q. Yang
California Polytechnic State University, San Luis Obispo

Cynthia Gwynne Yaudes
Indiana University

Clifton K. Yearley
State University of New York at Buffalo

Paul J. Zbiek
King's College

Dorothy Zeisler-Vralsted
University of Wisconsin— La Crosse

Racial and Ethnic Relations in America

A

Ability testing

Significance: Ability tests are sometimes described as objective and fair tools for identifying individuals' strengths; however, many people have criticized them as being biased against African Americans, Latinos, women, and other groups. Because of the increasing use of ability tests in the decisions made about people's daily lives, it is critical to understand how they might be unfair.

Ability tests play a significant role in American society. Intelligence and achievement tests are used for many purposes in education: to evaluate a student's progress, to identify areas of weakness, and to help define teaching goals. They are a major component in the decision to place students in special classes or to admit students to universities and colleges. Some occupations also use ability tests to determine qualifications for employment, entrance into training programs, and promotions. With such widespread use, it is imperative that these tests be fair.

Test bias is a systematic error that disadvantages the performance of one group over another. Although lower scores are not always indicators of bias, various aspects of a test can affect performance and lead to incorrect beliefs about the abilities, knowledge, and characteristics of an individual or group.

Sources of Bias

Critics identify several sources of bias in test items. Most important, they note that tests are biased toward the culture in which they are developed. Those developed in the United States, for example, generally have been written by middle-class males who have had Anglo-American life experiences. Their attitudes, beliefs, and values are subtly built into their tests. The information that these individuals have acquired and used within their own cultural experiences will determine what they think is important to know. Therefore, the content presented in the test may be culturally inappropriate for someone who has not been reared in the same cultural situation as the test developer.

Psychologist Robert Williams believes that items on ability tests do not measure general abilities, aptitude, or intelligence for everyone who takes them but rather demonstrate the test taker's knowledge of the test producer's culture. Not only must the test takers know the "correct" answer; they also must respond in a specific way in order to get credit for their knowledge. The scores on these tests, then, will be as much measures of acculturation and income as they will be measures of ability or skills.

Language has been identified as a major source of bias in ability test items. Test takers may not adequately understand the wording of items because they are not written in their native language, or because items may be phrased in an unfamiliar way. Psychologist Ernesto Bernal points out that even with translated tests or the use of interpreters, the language bias is not always eliminated, because the meaning of a word in one language, dialect, or region may not directly correspond to a word or phrase in another language, dialect, or region. A related type of bias results from the differences in meanings of words, which may be related to cultural background, gender, or income.

Sometimes the type of question asked or task required may interfere with a test taker's performance. Researchers have discovered that people have different cognitive or information-processing styles. That is, they have preferences for the ways they learn, remember, and solve problems most effectively. Some do well with understanding bits of information that have meaning by themselves. Others will learn and remember things if they are related to other information. Researcher Asa Hilliard refers to these as analytical and relational styles, respectively. If the ability-test item is written in such a way that it restricts certain test takers from using their preferred ways of processing information, they are more likely to do poorly on the test. In fact, most tests assume that everyone will or should use the style that is seen primarily among middle-class or upper-middle-class white males. If they do not, they are penalized for using a "nonstandard" problem-solving approach.

Research also suggests that test takers tend to score better when they identify with the situations and subjects covered by the test items. Researcher Paula Selkow found that women and men sometimes respond differently to male-oriented and female-oriented content. The timed format of some tests may also be a source of bias.

An example of bias can be found in the section designed to measure social reasoning and knowledge of socially acceptable ways of behaving contained in some standardized intelligence quotient (IQ) tests. A child who has been taught different cultural values and/or has life experiences that do not mirror those of the test developer will be at a serious disadvantage when taking this part of the test. For example, consider the question, "What is the thing to do if you lose a ball that belongs to one of your friends?" The "best" answer, according to the scoring guidelines in the test manual, is to buy a new one and pay for it. A poor child, however, may not be able to buy a new ball, and may not see that as an option. The "next-best" answer is to look all over for the ball. Yet if the ball is really lost, would it not be a waste of time to continue to look for it? If it were possible to find it, however, it might very well be better to look for it than to buy a new one. A child may have been taught that it would be best to apologize for losing the ball. The test taker would not receive credit for this answer.

When value-based questions such as the one above are scored, an assumption is made that the test taker lacks the knowledge to answer the question correctly. It would not be clear, however, without further questioning, why an individual actually missed the question. Scoring procedures do not generally allow for the possibility of alternative correct answers. The test assumes a common cultural

Ability tests such as the one being taken by this African American student have been criticized as being biased against racial and ethnic minorities.

perspective that may not be shared by all test takers.

Some tests require that the examinee respond to or respond with information that is decontextualized. That is, the information is taken out of the situation that makes it relevant. This is consistent with an analytical cognitive style and is the type of training that is likely to be emphasized by middle-class whites and the traditional education system. For example, many vocabulary tests require a strong memory for specific facts and details. Relational learners may have difficulty defining words that are presented to them outside a meaningful context, such as a picture, a sentence, or a paragraph. They may "talk around" the definition and receive no credit for their knowledge.

Concerns about test bias have existed since the beginning of the psychological testing movement. At various points in history, European immigrants to the United States, African Americans, and Latinos have been discriminated against by those using results from ability tests as evidence of their supposed inferiority. Native Americans, Asian Americans, and Jews have also been affected by the misuse of tests.

IQ Tests

Alfred Binet developed the first usable IQ test in 1905, as a way to diagnose low-achieving French students. He argued against the notion that intelligence is a fixed quantity. Lewis Terman, however, who provided the major adaptation of Binet's intelligence test from French to English in 1916, stated that the questions on the test did indeed provide a measure of innate intelligence. He believed that his revised test proved that the Eastern European immigrants of the day, as well as people of African descent and the poor of all colors, were genetically inferior to whites. He did not include test items that were consistent with the language and other cultural experiences of these groups.

The personal and political views of social scientists have contributed to the biased use of tests. In the 1960's, psychologist Arthur Jensen published articles and books supporting the view that intelligence is an inherited trait. Most often cited as evidence were the large differences between the average IQ scores of whites and other groups. Jensen opposed the notion that these differences are attributable to item bias.

Most psychologists view the large differences in average IQ scores between whites and almost every other group as an indication of test bias. They note that many individuals who are not proficient in English have been subjected to IQ tests in that language. Also problematic for many psychologists are the social consequences for groups that have already suffered educational and vocational disadvantages, as well as discrimination. According to these psychologists, IQ testing often leads to further negative political and educational consequences.   *Derise E. Tolliver*

Core Resources
Leon J. Kamin's *The Science and Politics of IQ* (New York: Halsted Press, 1974) discusses the political nature of the role psychologists have played in support of IQ testing. Arthur Jensen, in his *Bias in Mental Testing* (New York: Free Press, 1980), challenges the criticisms against IQ tests and offers research to support his view that group differences in IQ test scores are not attributable to bias. Asa G. Hilliard III's "IQ Testing as the Emperor's New Clothes: A Critique of Jensen's Bias in Mental Testing," in *Perspectives on Bias in Mental Testing*, edited by Cecil R. Reynolds and Robert T. Brown (New York: Plenum Press, 1984), presents a critique both of Jensen's work and of the notion that IQ tests measure intelligence. Jensen's "Test Bias: Concepts and Criticisms," also in *Perspectives on Bias in Mental Testing*, responds to Hilliard's criticisms of his book.

See also: College entrance examinations; Intelligence and race; Intelligence testing; Standardized testing and IQ testing controversies.

Abolition

> **Significance:** The abolition movement attempted to apply the concepts of Christian brotherhood and democratic egalitarianism to race relations; it helped to end slavery in the United States.

By the mid-eighteenth century, American Quakers such as John Woolman and Benjamin Lay were denouncing slavery as un-Christian. The rationalism of the Enlightenment, with its stress upon natural law, added ammunition to the arsenal of critics of slavery.

The egalitarian rhetoric of the Revolutionary era illustrated the irony of slaveholders fighting for liberty. As a result, most Northern states abolished slavery by 1784. New York and New Jersey did so afterward. Southern whites felt that they could not afford to abolish slavery, yet they too felt the need to justify the institution on ethical grounds. They concentrated on humanizing the institution and argued that it was a "necessary evil."

Antislavery feeling receded after 1793 because of fear of slave revolts, the increasing profitability of slavery following the invention of the cotton gin, and new scientific theories that reinforced racism. The leading antislavery organization in the early nineteenth century was the American Colonization Society (ACS). The ACS attempted to resettle free blacks in Africa and encouraged voluntary emancipation without challenging the right to own human property. The colonization plan allowed liberal slaveholders and moderate members of the clergy to rationalize their guilt over slavery.

In 1825, a great Protestant religious revival swept the northeastern region of the country. Ministers such as Charles Grandison Finney preached a new perfectionist theology that sought to counter the growing worldliness of Americans. This revival sparked a host of humanitarian crusades designed to protect the rights of the disadvantaged and to cleanse American institutions of contamination.

By the early 1830's, many evangelical reformers began to view slavery and racism as sinful because racism violated the Christian ethic of equality. Known as immediate abolitionists, these reformers demanded the immediate and unqualified liberation of slaves and an end to racial discrimination. With the formation of the American Anti-Slavery Society in 1833, abolitionist speakers toured the Northern states attempting to rally support for their cause. Abolitionists were frequently attacked by angry mobs, and their literature was destroyed in Southern post offices.

The abolition movement failed to end racism in the North. It did, however, spark anti-Southern feelings, which led to increased controversy within the national government. This conflict led directly to the Civil War. During the war, abolitionists pressured the federal government to transform the conflict from a war to preserve the Union into a war to end slavery. Abolition advocates were disappointed by the Emancipation Proclamation because it was based upon military necessity rather than moral principle, but they accomplished their central purpose with the passage of the Thirteenth Amendment, which ended slavery in the United States.

Garrisonian Ethics
One major faction within the abolition movement was led by editor William Lloyd Garrison. In a real sense, the publication of the first issue of *The Liberator* on January 1, 1831, established Garrison as the foremost abolitionist in the country. Garrison's harsh attacks upon slaveholders and colonizationists caused a national sensation even though the circulation of his newspaper never exceeded three thousand.

Like all abolitionists, Garrison demanded that everyone recognize a personal responsibility to improve society. The three major tenets of his ethical philosophy were human liberation, moral suasion, and no compromise with evil. Garrison actively campaigned on behalf of legal equality for African Americans, temperance, and equality for women. Garrison rejected force and violence in human affairs. He sought the moral reformation of slave

William Lloyd Garrison, the editor of *The Liberator,* was an outspoken and uncompromising advocate of the abolition of slavery.

owners, not their destruction. He never advocated slave revolts, and he wanted the Northern states to allow the South to secede during the crisis of 1860-1861.

Garrison sincerely believed in all that he advocated, and he would not compromise his principles. He rejected any solution to the issue of slavery that involved a program that would delay emancipation. He also demanded that his followers reject participation in the American political system because the Constitution was a proslavery document. Other abolitionists, such as Gerrit Smith and James Birney, attempted to use the political system as a way to gain publicity for the cause of abolition.

African American Abolitionism
In a sense, there were two abolition movements. The white movement was based on a moral abstraction, but African Americans were forced to confront the everyday realities of racism in nineteenth century America.

Frederick Douglass emerged as the major spokesperson for African Americans during the antebellum period. Douglass self-consciously attempted to use his life as an example to repudiate racist stereotypes. Because of his eloquence, Douglass gained an international reputation as a public speaker, and in doing so, he proved the humanity of African Americans.

Like Garrison, Douglass strongly supported temperance and women's rights. He was, however, willing to use any means to achieve the liberation of slaves, including violence and political action. He approved of John Brown's idea of using the southern Appalachians as an armed sanctuary for runaways. He also supported the Free-Soil and Republican Parties even though neither advocated the emancipation of Southern slaves. He justified his positions as part of a larger struggle to advance the cause of racial equality in America. For Douglass, as for other African Americans involved in the cause of abolition, equality was the only acceptable ethical standard for a free society. *Thomas D. Matijasic*

Core Resources
Books that provide additional information on the abolition movement include Gilbert Hobbs Barnes's *The Antislavery Impulse: 1830-1844* (New York: Harcourt, Brace & World, 1964), *The Antislavery Vanguard: New Essays on the Abolitionists* (Princeton, N.J.: Princeton University Press, 1965), edited by Martin Duberman, Gerald Sorin's *Abolitionism: A New Perspective* (New York: Praeger, 1972), James Brewer Stewart's *Holy Warriors: The Abolitionists and American Slavery* (New York: Hill & Wang, 1976), and Alice Felt Tyler's *Freedom's Ferment: Phases of American Social History to 1860* (Minneapolis: University of Minnesota Press, 1944). Nathan Irvin Huggins's *Slave and Citizen: The Life of Frederick Douglass* (Boston: Little, Brown, 1980) looks at the African American abolitionist, and Russel B. Nye's *William Lloyd Garrison and the Humanitarian Reformers* (Boston: Little, Brown, 1955) examines the prominent white abolitionist.

See also: American Anti-Slavery Society; Emancipation Proclamation; *Liberator, The*; Slave rebellions; Slavery and race relations; Slavery: history; Slavery: North American beginnings; Thirteenth Amendment.

Aboriginal Action Plan

The Canadian Aboriginal Action Plan, released on January 7, 1998, focused on aboriginal communities and the tasks of reconciliation and renewal as recommended by the Royal Commission on Aboriginal Peoples. These tasks were to be accomplished primarily through an emphasis on partnerships, aboriginal self-government, and other recommendations of the Royal Commission. They included recognition of, apologies for, and reconciliation over past injustices and abuses suffered by many aboriginal Canadians, often at the hands of the federal government. The action plan sought to improve living conditions for aboriginal Canadians, particularly the young.

The plan had four main objectives: renewing partnerships, strengthening aboriginal governance, developing a new fiscal relationship, and supporting strong communities, people, and economies. The first objective, the renewal of partnerships, included a statement of reconciliation, community-based healing of sexual and physical abuse in the residential schools, public education to help nonaboriginals better appreciate aboriginal peoples, and a coordinated approach to addressing the problems of aboriginals living in urban settings. The second objective was strengthening aboriginal governance through such steps as affirming treaty relationships, commemoration of the historic treaties, a new independent claims body, cost-shared Metis enumeration, funding for aboriginal women's organizations, establishment of an aboriginal center of excellence to assist groups in promoting self-government, and professional development strategies in lawmaking, environmental stewardship, and resource management. The third objective was developing a new fiscal relationship through a more stable, accountable relationship that promotes greater self-reliance, new financial standards for governments to comply with generally accepted accounting procedures, support for development of First Nations sources of revenue including taxation, statistical training for aboriginal groups to promote data collection and information exchanges, as well as an aboriginal peoples survey following the 2001 national census. The fourth objective was supporting strong communities, people, and economies through a five-year strategy to develop aboriginal human resources, providing for an increase in the number of houses on reserves and a remedy for the shortage of water and sewer facilities. Other specific goals of the strategy included expanded aboriginal policing services, an aboriginal Head Start program available on reserves, reduced welfare dependence, increased access of aboriginal businesses to capital and markets, the creation of urban aboriginal youth centers, education reform, and greater focus on prevention, treatment, and care of diabetes. *Gregory Walters*

See also: Aboriginal Canadians; Royal Commission on Aboriginal Peoples.

Aboriginal Canadians

> **Significance:** The ancestors of First Nation, Inuit, and Metis peoples lived in North America long before explorers arrived on the continent. They enjoyed their own forms of government, language, culture, and spiritual beliefs. Attitudes of racial and cultural superiority led to a suppression of aboriginal cultures and values.

For several thousand years, aboriginal peoples, descendants of the original inhabitants of North America, have occupied what is now Canada as hunters and gatherers. Aboriginal or "Indian" peoples prefer to be known as First Nations, a term that came into common usage in the 1970's to replace the word "Indian." The Inuit (which means "people" in Inuktitut, the Inuit language) and Metis are the two other aboriginal peoples recognized by the Canadian Constitution. Inuit are Arctic people who have lived above the tree line in the Northwest Territories and in Northern Quebec and Labrador for thousands of years. Inuit has replaced the traditional term "Eskimo." Metis are of mixed aboriginal and European ancestry and identify themselves as distinct from First Nation people, Inuit, or nonaboriginal people. Their unique culture draws on diverse ancestral origins such as Scottish, French, Ojibway, and Cree.

Aboriginal peoples share a deep spiritual relation with the land and the various life-forms it supports. They believe that humans participate in a world of interrelated spiritual beings. Before the arrival of Europeans, the First Nations had developed systems of government that reflected their different cultures, spiritual beliefs tied to ancestral lands, social structures, and economies. In the eighteenth and nineteenth centuries, contact with Europeans and the introduction of firearms and diseases changed aboriginal ways of life. By the 1940's, First Nation leaders began fighting to preserve their cultures, forms of self-government, and rightful place in Canadian society. In November, 1996, the Royal Commission on Aboriginal Peoples proposed a twenty-year agenda to develop a new relationship between aboriginal and nonaboriginal people based on values of mutual recognition, respect, sharing, and responsibility.

Aboriginal peoples and their tribes must be understood in historical relation to six major cultural regions. A tribe is a large group of First Nation individuals who share a common language, environment, and culture. These cultural groupings and regions include the Woodland First Nations, the Iroquoian First Nations of southeastern Ontario, the Plains First Nations, the Plateau First Nations, the First Nations of the Pacific Coast, and the First Nations of the Mackenzie and Yukon River Basins.

The Woodland First Nations is the easternmost cultural area characterized by dense boreal forest and bordering in the north on a tundralike land. The eight principal tribes, who spoke languages belonging to the Algonquian family, include the now extinct Beothuk (Newfoundland), Mi'kmaq (Nova Scotia, Gaspé in Quebec, Prince Edward Island), Malecite (southwestern New Brunswick and Quebec), Montagnais and Naskapi (Quebec and Labrador), Ojibway (from the north shores of Huron and Superior Lakes north, to the edge of the prairies), Algonquian (Ottawa Valley), Odawa (Manitoulin Island), and Cree (flanking the Ojibway on the north and west).

The nine principal Iroquoian tribes (and languages) of southeastern Ontario include the Huron, Petun, Neutral, Erie, and the confederacy of the Mohawk, Oneida, Onondaga, Cayuga, Seneca, and Tuscarora south of Lake Ontario and extending to the upper St. Lawrence River.

Eight principal tribes of First Nations inhabited Canada's plains. The Blackfoot, Blood, Peigan, Gros Ventre, and Plains Cree spoke languages of the Algonquian family. The Assiniboine and Sioux spoke Sioux and the Sarcee spoke Athapaskan.

The First Nations of the Plateau area of interior British Columbia include the Interior Salish tribes (Lillooet, Thompson First Nation, Shuswap, Okanagan, Lake First Nation), the Kootenay, and three main Athapaskan tribes, the Chilcotin, Carrier, and Tahltan.

The six principal tribes of the Pacific Coast First Nations include the Haida (the most northerly tribe), the mainland coast Tsimshian, Gitksan, and Nisga'a, and the southernmost Nootka and Coast Salish. Modern-day British Columbia contains seven of Canada's eleven indigenous language families within its borders.

The twelve tribes of the Mackensie and Yukon river basins (Chipewyan, Beaver, Slaveys, Yellowknife, Dogrib, Hare, Kutchin, Han, Tutchone, Kaska, Mountain, and Sekani) all spoke Athapaskan. Their vast homeland occupied more than one-quarter of Canada's total land mass.

Although no precise statistics exist, it is believed that the West Coast languages of Haidan, Tlinglit, and Kutenaian have only a few hundred speakers. The only languages that seem assured of survival are the Cree, Ojibwa, and Inuktitut languages.

Demographics

Approximately 2,370 parcels of reserve land are divided among 608 First Nations, which represent fifty-two cultural groups (such as Haida, Cree, and Mohawk) and more than fifty languages. The estimated aboriginal population in 1997 totaled 1,333,700. Population projections for the year 2005 suggested that the aboriginal population would grow 1.7 percent per year overall and 2.3 percent per year on reserves. Manitoba and Saskatchewan are the two provinces with the largest proportion of aboriginal people (14 percent). In the territories, aboriginal peoples represent 67 percent of the population in the Northwest Territories and 29 percent in the Yukon. The average First Nation community population is 975 people; sixty-four First Nations, or "bands," have a population of more than 2,000. As of December 31, 1995, the total registered Indian population was 593,050, of which 245,131 lived off the reserve. Most aboriginal people live outside reserves, but less than half of the registered Indian population (41 percent) live outside reserves.

Administrative History and Legal Status

In 1755, the British crown established the Indian Department, a branch of the military set up to foster good relations and cultivate military alliances with the First Nations. In 1867, the year of confederation, the new federal government gave itself legislative authority over "Indians and lands reserved for Indians" through the Constitution of 1867. In 1876, the Canadian parliament passed the Indian Act, which set out certain federal gov-

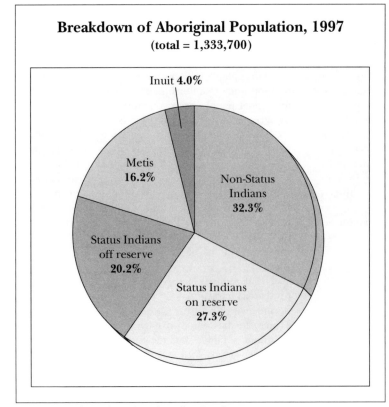

Breakdown of Aboriginal Population, 1997
(total = 1,333,700)

Inuit **4.0%**

Metis **16.2%**

Non-Status Indians **32.3%**

Status Indians off reserve **20.2%**

Status Indians on reserve **27.3%**

Source: Data are from Indian and Northern Affairs Canada.

ernment obligations and regulated the management of First Nation reserve lands. A key provision of the act was the concept of "enfranchisement" or the total assimilation of First Nation populations as citizens. In 1869, government surveyors plotting routes for incoming settlers met opposition by the Metis under the leadership of Louis Riel, Jr. The Manitoba Act of 1870 provided some land rights for resident Metis families, but the provisional Metis government was suppressed.

A 1933 amendment to the Indian Act extended enfranchisement of First Nation members who met the qualifications set out in the act. Any First Nation man over the age of twenty-one, literate in English or French, educated to an elementary level, of good moral character, and free of debt could be declared enfranchised or "no longer deemed to be an Indian." In this way, the distinction between him and other nonaboriginal citizens would be removed. Under the act, an Indian woman who married a non-Indian was no longer considered an Indian, nor were her children. The reverse was not true for non-Indian women who married Indian men. This blatant gender discrimination lasted until 1985 with serious consequences for dignity and well-being. Without their Indian status, women were no longer allowed to reside on or own land on their reserves. Often unaware that they would lose their status when they married non-Indians, these women were no longer eligible for housing and education benefits and programs available to Status Indians.

For more than one hundred years, the government was empowered to order the enfranchisement of First Nation people. It kept the First Nations in a state of wardship by regulating all aspects of their existence both on and off the reserve, such as an 1884 ban of the Pacific Coast potlatch ceremony. Until the mid-1950's, federal government Indian agents had effective control over such activities as reserve leave privileges and the residential school system, which denied children the rights to speak their own languages and practice their spiritual beliefs and rituals. The system frequently separated children from their families and communities. Tragically, some children were victims of physical and sexual abuse. Until 1960, when First Nation peoples were given the right to vote in federal elections, First Nation members could vote only if they became enfranchised. First Nation members were also involuntarily and automatically enfranchised when they joined the clergy or completed university. From 1867 to 1966—the date of the establishment of the Department of Indian Affairs and Northern Development (DIAND)—Indian and northern affairs administration was handled by various departments, including the Office of the Secretary of State, Citizenship and Immigration, Mines and Resources, and Northern Affairs and National Resources. Effective changes in the

relations between aboriginal and nonaboriginal Canadians would come only after 1966.

The Constitution Act of 1982 recognized existing aboriginal and treaty rights of the First Nation, Inuit, and Metis peoples of Canada. In June, 1985, Parliament passed Bill C-31, which became the Act to Amend the Indian Act, ending more than one hundred years of discrimination in the Indian Act. The major impact of Bill C-31 has been the elimination of gender discrimination. Since its passage, about 105,000 individuals have successfully regained their legal status. In 1985, 29 percent of Status Indians lived outside reserves, but by 1991, 40 percent lived outside reserves. This statistical change of relationships is most likely due to the reinstatement of Status Indians under Bill C-31.

Self-Government and Land Claims

In August, 1995, the government of Canada launched a process to negotiate the inherent right to aboriginal self-government that exists within the Canadian constitution. Aboriginal groups have a right to develop health care, child welfare, education, housing, and economic programs in negotiation with federal, provincial, and territorial governments or jurisdictions. The First Nations' rights in self-government take many forms because self-government arrangements for peoples without a land base differ from those for peoples with a land base. Self-government agreements have been negotiated in conjunction with land-claims settlements such as the Sechelt Indian Band Self-Government Act (British Columbia), the Cree-Naskapi (of Quebec) Act and the Yukon Self-Government Act. As of 1996, DIAND was negotiating self-government arrangements with ninety aboriginal groups throughout Canada. In addition to the new territory of Nunavut and the self-government aspirations of the Inuit, the Yukon has signed six self-government agreements, and eight more are being negotiated with Yukon First Nations. Self-government processes for Metis and "off-reserve" aboriginal groups (groups that are not part of a reserve but related to the First Nations) exist in most provinces. Enumeration is one of the key building blocks of Metis and off-reserve self-governments. The federal government and the province of Saskatchewan planned to share the development cost of an enumeration proposal with the Metis nation of Saskatchewan in spring, 1999. Self-government institutions, devolution of programs and services, and public government are initiatives that provide opportunities for aboriginal input into program design and delivery. These should ultimately lead to direct control of programming and new approaches to negotiation.

In 1993, after years of negotiations, the Nunavut land claim was settled. This is the largest land claim ever settled in Canadian history. It gives the Inuit control of more than 350,000 square kilometers of land, of which 36,000 square kilometers include mineral rights.

In February, 1996, a group of thirteen First Nation chiefs (leaders from the Westbank, Musqueam, Lheit-Lit'en, N'Quatqua, Squamish, Siksika, Muskoday, Cowessess, Opaskwayak Cree, Nipissing, Mississaugas of Scugog Island, Chippewas of Georgina Island, and Chippewas of Mnjikaning) signed the Framework Agreement on First Nation Land Management. This government-to-government agreement ensures that First Nations can pass their own laws to develop, conserve, protect, manage, and use their lands.

Social and Economic Development

DIAND's Indian and Inuit programs seek to improve living conditions on reserves and in northern Inuit communities. In 1997-1998, DIAND's total budget was $4.4 billion with $3.8 billion allocated for education, social services, and community infrastructure such as roads and sewer systems. During this same period, the First Nations managed more than 83 percent of DIAND's total expenditures on these services. In the late 1980's, the First Nations managed only 62 percent of program expenditures on community services. The data reveal that the relationship between the government and the First Nations is changing from one of service provider to one of an advisory funding agency.

Although living conditions in First Nation communities have markedly improved since the 1960's, living standards still fall far short of what other Canadians assume to be basic. The average income for Status Indians in 1997 was about $10,000, half the Canadian average. Moreover, of the approximately 73,000 families living on reserves, only 35,000 had adequate housing. The total number of housing units on reserves increased from 60,509 in 1989-1990 to 80,443 in 1996-1997. The demand for basic services such as education, social services, and health care in First Nation communities continued to grow in the late 1990's. This is partially because the on-reserve First Nation birthrate is more than double that of the Canadian population as a whole (twenty-seven births per thousand compared with thirteen births per thousand).

The gap in life expectancy between First Nation members and other Canadians was seven years in 1997. Sui-

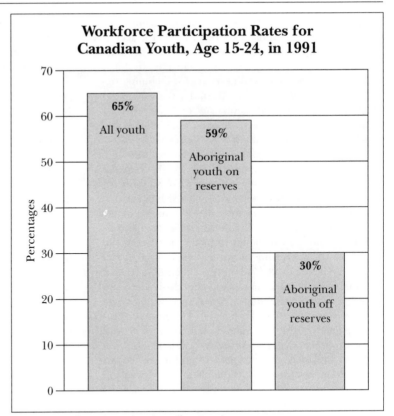

Workforce Participation Rates for Canadian Youth, Age 15-24, in 1991

65% All youth

59% Aboriginal youth on reserves

30% Aboriginal youth off reserves

Percentages

Source: Data are from Indian and Northern Affairs Canada.

cide rates of registered Indian youth age fifteen to twenty-four were eight times higher than the national rate for women and five times higher than the rate for men. Aboriginal people were more likely than other Canadians to have hearing, sight, and speech disabilities. Alcohol, drug, and solvent abuse among youth was a problem, and the reported incidences of AIDS (acquired immunodeficiency syndrome) and HIV (human immunodeficiency virus) infections were increasing in relation to the mainstream. Incarceration rates of aboriginal people were five to six times higher than the national average.

The aboriginal labor force (3 percent of the Canadian labor force) was young and growing at twice the Canadian rate in 1997. It was concentrated in government services (15.2 percent), wholesale and retail trade (14.6 percent), manufacturing (10.3 percent), and accommodation/food and beverage (9.4 percent). As a whole, aboriginal people were underrepresented in manufacturing and financial and insurance services but well represented in construction and natural resource industries. The lag in labor force participation was greatest for on-reserve Indians (participation rates were 47 percent for Status Indians living on reserves, 57 percent for off-reserve Indians, 57 percent for Inuit and 59 percent for Metis, compared with the national rate of 68 percent). On-reserve aboriginal youth participation rates were 30 percent compared with 59 percent for off-reserve aboriginal youth and 65 percent for all Canadian youth. The income gap between First Nation and non-aboriginal communities widened since the late 1980's.

Access to equity and debt capital, markets for their products and services, suitable work experience, access to lands and resources, and innovation in the workplace pose formidable challenges. Jobs and wealth creation are vital to prosperous aboriginal communities and meaningful self-government. Yet, in 1997, less than 1 percent of all Canadian businesses were owned by aboriginal people, and half of these were located on reserves. Community-owned enterprises averaged ten employees. Large enterprises such as Cree Construction International in Quebec and the forestry companies owned by the Meadow Lake Tribal Council in Saskatchewan were significant players.

Canada's Aboriginal Action Plan, released in January, 1998, set forth a five-year aboriginal human resources development strategy meant to create a broad-based partnership involving groups, governments, the private sector, and other relevant institutions. As part of its approach to strengthening economic development, the government was to participate in sectoral, national, and regional economic development forums to help identify priorities and shape new initiatives. Partnership was to be the basis for a new chapter in Canada's relationship with aboriginal people.   *Gregory Walters*

Core Resources

First Nations in Canada/Les Premières nations du Canada, published under the authority of Ronald A. Irwin, minister of Indian Affairs and Northern Development (Ottawa, Ontario: Minister of Public Works and Government Services, 1997), provides an excellent overview of aboriginal peoples and their cultures, prehistory, and historical developments as well as contemporary legislation, issues, and trends. *Indians and Inuit of Canada/Les Indiens et les Inuit du Canada* (Ottawa, Ontario: Indian and Northern Affairs, 1990), focuses on First Nation, Inuit, and Metis language families, differences between native and European languages, and the development of written aboriginal languages. The Inuit Tapirisat of Canada, founded in 1971 as a national organization dedicated to the needs and aspirations of all Canadian Inuit, has produced the beautiful text, *The Inuit of Canada* (Hull, Quebec: Inuit Taparisat of Canada, 1995), which describes Inuit perspectives on culture and history, environment and resources, and present-day issues and opportunities. An extensive catalog of First Nation art, claims, legislation and treaties, and northern re-

sources development is available from the Publications and Public Enquiries Kiosk, Corporate Services, Indian and Northern Affairs Canada, Ottawa, Ontario K1A 0H4, e-mail: InfoPubs@inac.gc.ca.

See also: Aboriginal Action Plan; Department of Indian Affairs and Northern Development; Indian Act of 1876; Indian-white relations: Canada; Nisga'a Agreement in Principle; Nunavut Territory; Riel Rebellions; Status Indians.

Accent discrimination

Significance: Under U.S. law, employers can discriminate against applicants for employment whom they believe to have accents that might impede normal business activities. Persons whose primary language is not English, therefore, may have to shed their accents to qualify for jobs that involve speaking with the general public.

A standard American English accent is commonly heard in schools and spoken on radio and television, but there are regional variations, especially in Hawaii, New England, and the southern states. Immigrants who learn English tend to speak the new language in accordance with the pronunciation and intonation patterns of their native tongues, which means that those unfamiliar with their accents may not understand them completely and may ask these immigrants to repeat what they are saying. At issue, therefore, is whether an employer can reject someone with an unfamiliar accent without discriminating against that person on the basis of ethnic group membership.

The Nature of Accents

Vocal muscles develop so early in life that it is difficult for an adult native speaker of one language to learn a second language without carrying forward the accents of the primary language. In the United States, composed as it is of immigrants and their descendants, English is spoken with many accents. Some schools teach adult immigrants to speak without a noticeable accent, but these classes are expensive and not always accessible to newcomers, whose time is usually preoccupied with material adjustments to life in a new country.

The United States does not have an official standard of speech, although the informal standard is the American English accent spoken by newscasters at the national level. Accent is the result of speech patterns that differ from region to region or country to country. For example, Cuban speakers of Spanish speak more quickly than do Mexican speakers of Spanish. Variations also exist within countries. Because one characteristic of an ethnic group in the United States is the manner in which its members pronounce English, ethnic group membership is often identified by or associated with accent. It is this connection that makes accent a key issue of racial and ethnic relations.

Antidiscrimination Legislation

In the Civil Rights Act of 1964, Congress banned discrimination on the basis of a person's color, ethnicity, or race in education, employment, government services, public accommodations, public facilities, and voting. The law regarding employment discrimination prohibits not only obvious discrimination, such as signs that say Blacks Need Not Apply, but also the use of neutral-sounding job qualifications that systematically place minorities or women at a disadvantage unless these qualifications are vital for the performance of the job. To refuse to hire a member of a minority group on the pretext that the person's accent is too strong, therefore, might violate the law unless the lack of a noticeable accent can be demonstrated to be necessary for the performance of the job.

Litigation on Language Discrimination

In *Carino v. University of Oklahoma Board of Regents* (1984), the federal appeals court ruled that Donaciano Carino, a dental laboratory supervisor, could not be terminated from his position because of his Filipino accent as his job did not involve communication with the general public.

In 1982, Manuel Fragante, a Filipino with a noticeable accent, applied for the position of applications intake clerk in the motor vehicle licensing division of the City and County of Honolulu. The hiring officer turned him down, claiming that Fragante's accent would make communication difficult; Fragante's lawyer argued that his client's accent was fully understandable and therefore was a mere pretext for a Japanese supervisor to discriminate against a Filipino. In *Fragante v. City and County of Honolulu* (1987), the federal district court in Honolulu upheld the right of the employer to refuse to hire someone with a "heavy accent," ruling that Fragante's accent was not an immutable part of his Filipino ethnic group membership. The court of appeals upheld the ruling in 1989, and the Supreme Court refused to review the case in 1990.

In 1985-1986, James Kahakua and George Kitazaki applied for the position of weather-service broadcaster. Although they were native speakers of English, they spoke "pidgin" English, a decided accent local to Hawaii. The position involved broadcasting marine weather reports to ships at sea, and most of the vessels in the area were based in California, so the National Weather Ser-

vice felt justified in refusing to hire the two men because their accents might prevent a clear transmission of information. Kahakua and Kitazaki sued the weather service for discrimination but lost.

Impact on Public Policy

In the 1964 Civil Rights Act, Congress did not explicitly forbid discrimination on the basis of accent. For the present, clarity in speech is recognized as a bona fide occupational qualification for jobs involving considerable oral communication with the general public. The standards for determining whether an accent is unclear tend to be subjective, so the issue may be resolved by use of the Test of Spoken English, a standardized test administered nationwide by the Educational Testing Service.

Michael Haas

Core Resources

Laughlin McDonald's *Rights of Racial Minorities: The Basic ACLU Guide to Racial Minority Rights* (2d ed., Carbondale: Southern Illinois University Press, 1993) is one of the publications sponsored by the American Civil Liberties Union that describes the laws governing employment discrimination. A more focused study is Rosini Lippi-Green's *English with an Accent: Language, Ideology, and Discrimination in the United States* (New York: Routledge, 1997). For an analysis of the legal issues, see Mari J. Matsuda's "Voices of America: Accent, Antidiscrimination Law, and a Jurisprudence for the Last Reconstruction," in *Yale Law Journal* (100, 1991), and Beatrice Bich-Dao Nguyen's "Accent Discrimination and the Test of Spoken English: A Call for an Objective Assessment of the Comprehensibility of Nonnative Speakers," in *California Law Review* (81, October, 1993).

See also: Civil Rights Act of 1964; Culture and language; Discrimination: racial and ethnic; Employment among Asian Americans; Filipino Americans.

Accommodationism

Accommodationism refers to the outward acceptance of racial inequality by African Americans to obtain concessions from a white-dominated society. This ideology is most commonly associated with black educator and activist Booker T. Washington. During Reconstruction, many blacks called for bringing about change through militant means, but Washington instead advocated downplaying white racism and focusing on black economic solidarity, racial pride, vocational education, and political passivity. In a speech delivered at the Atlanta Exposition in 1895, now commonly known as the Atlanta Compromise address, Washington declared that blacks and whites could remain socially separate while cooperating economically, and implored whites to be patient while blacks established a foothold at the bottom of the socioeconomic order. The address established Washington as the dominant African American political figure until his death in 1915.

By focusing on economic empowerment and separate community development, accommodationists managed to achieve modest successes in a violently oppressive sociopolitical climate. Nevertheless, institutionalized racism continued to encumber southern blacks, who migrated in increasing numbers to northern cities. Within a decade of Washington's Atlanta Compromise address, new ways of thought arose to challenge accommodationism. In 1905, W. E. B. Du Bois, a former ally who had become a critic of Washington, organized the Niagara Movement as a radical alternative to accommodationism. The Niagara Movement precipitated the establishment of the National Association for the Advancement of Colored People (NAACP) in 1909, ushering in a new era of protest through legalism and direct action.

"Accommodationism" remains in general use as an academic term among students of racial relations. "Accommmodation" suggests a necessity to assimilate or "melt" into the dominant society without a forthright willingness to do so, unlike "conformity," which suggests some level of willingness to blend into mainstream society.   *Michael H. Burchett*

See also: Atlanta Compromise; Conformity theories; National Association for the Advancement of Colored People; Niagara Movement.

Adarand Constructors v. Peña

In *Adarand Constructors v. Peña*, the U.S. Supreme Court held that broad affirmative action programs involving employment and contracts were unconstitutional but preserved the applicability of affirmative action to specific and limited circumstances of discrimination.

Randy Pech, a white contractor in Colorado Springs, Colorado, submitted the lowest bid for a federal road-repair project. The contract, however, was awarded to a company owned by a Latino man because of a 1987 law requiring that the Department of Transportation award at least 10 percent of its funds to companies owned by minorities or women. Pech took his complaint to the courts. The case was decided by the Supreme Court at a time when criticism of affirmative action had become widespread both among the public and in Congress. In addition, the makeup of the Court itself had changed since the last federal affirmative action case in 1990; notably, Thurgood Marshall, a staunch liberal, had re-

tired and been replaced by another African American jurist, Clarence Thomas, a conservative.

Overturning previous decisions offering support of federal affirmative action, on June 12, 1995, the Court voted 5 to 4 that the type of affirmative action program involved in the case was unconstitutional. In an opinion written by Justice Sandra Day O'Connor, the Supreme Court stated that the Constitution protects individuals but was not intended to offer special protections to groups. Treating "any person unequally because of his or her race" causes the person to suffer an injury that is not acceptable under the Constitution's guarantee of equal protection under the law. The law can treat people differently because of race "only for the most compelling reasons," and racial classifications by government agencies are "inherently suspect and presumptively invalid." The Court did say, however, that affirmative action programs could be acceptable to remedy specific, provable cases of discrimination.

The decision severely undercut all federal affirmative action programs, most notably those involving jobs or contracts required to go to minorities ("minority set-asides"). In addition, federal law at the time of *Adarand* required firms that did more than fifty thousand dollars of business a year with the federal government and had more than fifty employees to have a written affirmative action policy, which meant that the *Adarand* decision could affect the policies of nearly all major employers in the United States. Reaction to the decision was strong and immediate. A leader of the Anti-Defamation League called it a "sea change" in the law. Many civil rights leaders protested the decision and urged the government not to abolish all affirmative action efforts. Conservative Republican leaders in Congress, in contrast, vowed to pass legislation to eliminate all "racial preferences" in federal hiring and contracting.

McCrea Adams

See also: Affirmative action; *Bakke* case; *Fullilove v. Klutznick*; *Griggs v. Duke Power Company*; Set-aside; *United Steelworkers of America v. Weber*.

Adolescent ethnic identity

Significance: Racial or ethnic identity is awareness of belonging to an ethnic group that shapes a person's thoughts, feelings, and behavior. How an individual feels about himself or herself as a member of a racial or ethnic group and how the person perceives other groups significantly affect the successful interaction between and among racial/ethnic individuals and groups.

Sociologists Jean Phinney and Hari Alipuria contend that for all individuals, but especially those who are not part of North America's white majority, integrating a sense of ethnic identity into an overall sense of personal identity is an important task of late adolescence that may affect the establishment of a coherent occupational, ideological, or interpersonal identity. More is known about ethnic identity development among African Americans than among other ethnic groups, although research on Latinos, American Indians, and Asian Americans is rapidly increasing.

Ethnic identity has several components. The first is whether the individual identifies himself or herself as belonging to a racial/ethnic group. The second component is the individual's knowledge of and engagement in behaviors characteristic of a racial/ethnic group, such as celebrating holidays specific to that group, following the group's patterns of speech and dress, and preferring group-specific foods. Feelings about the individual's ethnic group membership make up the third component. Individuals may value and feel positively about their ethnic group or react negatively to belonging to a certain racial/ethnic group. The final component is the importance placed on racial/ethnic group membership.

Personal Identity
To understand how racial/ethnic identity is formed, it is necessary to understand the general process of identity development. Identity is referred to as a sense of self, including an individual's commitment to certain values, roles, and life pursuits. According to sociologist James Marcia, it is possible to determine an individual's identity status based on the degree to which he or she has made occupational, ideological, and interpersonal relationship commitments and the degree to which he or she has engaged in a sustained search or exploration in the process. Individual identity status varies and may be one of four types. *Identity achieved* youth are those who have established a coherent sense of self by making commitments after a period of experimentation. Such an individual might say, "It took me a while to figure it out, but now I really know what I want for a career." Individuals in the stage of *moratorium* are those who are in the process of exploration but who have not yet made certain commitments to values or ideological beliefs. Such a person might say, "There are so many different political parties and ideals; I need to figure it all out before I decide which to follow." *Identity foreclosure* describes those individuals who have made commitments without exploring alternatives. Such an individual might say, "I have never really questioned my religion. If it is right for my parents, it must be right for me." Finally, *diffused* individuals are those who have made no ideological

commitments and have not yet begun the process of exploration. Such an individual might say, "I have not chosen the occupation that I really want to go into, but I am working as a food server until something better comes along."

Sociologist Erik Erikson asserts that adolescence is a critical time for identity formation. However, identity is not static, and an individual's sense of self may shift and change over time. Nonetheless, most research suggests that identity achievement is the most mature resolution and diffusion the least, with foreclosure and moratorium being intermediate steps.

The Process of Ethnic Identity Development
Sociologists Jean Phinney and Doreen Rosenthal suggest that ethnic identity development parallels general identity development. They have identified three distinct stages of ethnic identity, which, like the identity statuses identified by Marcia, involve the processes of exploration and commitment. Adolescents with an *unexamined ethnic identity* (who resemble foreclosed adolescents) have simply internalized the values and attitudes of the dominant culture, with little understanding of issues related to their ethnicity. Such an individual might say, "I don't pay attention to ethnicity; I just try to fit in with the crowd." Those in an *ethnic identity search* (who are similar to those in the moratorium stage) are exploring the meaning of their ethnicity and may experience a growing conflict between the values of the dominant culture and those of their ethnic group. Such a person might say, "Sometimes I feel like I don't fit in; family and community mean more to me than individuality, but individuality is necessary for success in the larger society." Finally, adolescents with an *achieved ethnic identity* have a clear sense of their ethnicity. They feel a sense of belonging to their racial/ethnic group and emotionally identify with it. Such an individual might say, "I am proud to be a member of this group; I will pass the traditions and customs on to my own children some day."

Developmentalist Sheila Marshall notes that parental involvement may speed up the process of ethnic identity development among adolescents. Ethnic socialization is the process through which parents attempt to teach their children about their ethnicity and special experiences they may encounter within the broader society (such as discrimination), given their ethnic background. Ethnic socialization in minority families focuses on understanding the individual's own culture, getting along in mainstream society, and dealing with racism, according to sociologist A. Wade Boykin. Interestingly, although ethnic socialization speeds up the process of ethnic identity formation, it does not appear to lead adolescents to a stronger sense of ethnic identity.

Ethnic identity, an important component of personal identity, is formed partly through rituals such as this coming-of-age rite involving Little Cornflower (center), a thirteen-year-old Apache girl.

Ethnic Identity of Minority and Majority Youth

Although many people assume that only individuals in minority groups develop ethnic identities, white individuals also develop a sense of ethnicity. Research on whether racial/ethnic minority or white adolescents have more difficulty forming a stable sense of self has revealed more similarities than differences, with one exception. Having a strong ethnic identity is associated with higher self-esteem and stronger self-efficacy among minority youth, but not among white youth, according to Phinney and Alipuria. Therefore, the importance of establishing a strong, stable ethnic identity appears most significant for minority rather than majority group members.

Relations Between Minority and Majority Groups

Identity development is largely affected by social context. Therefore, minority adolescent identity development cannot be understood without an examination of the environmental and social contexts in which minority youth function. Often, these contexts include racial stereotypes, few role models, and rewards or punishments for identifying with one's ethnic group rather than the majority white group.

According to Phinney and others, minority youth have four possibilities for dealing with their ethnicity on a social context level: *assimilation* (trying to adopt the majority culture's norms and standards, while rejecting those of their own racial/ethnic group); *marginality* (living within the majority culture but feeling estranged and outcast); *separation* (associating with members of their own racial/ethnic group and rejecting the majority culture); and *biculturalism* (maintaining ties to both the majority and minority cultures).

Minority youth are often encouraged to assimilate into the dominant white culture, but those who do are sometimes ridiculed by members of their own group. Those who attempt to assimilate are often excluded from majority society based on physical appearance or other ethnic trait. This may lead to marginality, where minority youth feel that they are on the edge of mainstream society and will never be accepted as a full member. Separation is a strategy adopted by many minority youth, particularly African Americans, who may experience severe prejudice and discrimination. Biculturalism is often a more successful approach than separation or assimilation. Biculturalism occurs when youth know and understand the norms of more than one culture, and successfully move between them by selecting the appropriate norms depending on the situation. Mexican American and Asian American adolescents have been found to be more bicultural than African American or Puerto Rican American youth. *Rochelle L. Dalla*

Core Resources

Erik Erikson's *Identity: Youth and Society* (New York: Norton, 1968) provides the basis for understanding psychosocial development and identity formation. James Marcia's works on identity formation during adolescence include "Identity in Adolescence," in the *Handbook of Adolescent Psychology*, edited by Joseph Adelson (New York: Wiley, 1980), and "Common Processes Underlying Ego Identity, Cognitive/Moral Development, and Individuation," in *Self, Ego, and Identity: Integrative Approaches*, edited by D. K. Lapsley and F. C. Power (New York: Wiley, 1988). Jean Phinney reviews the ethnic identity literature in "Ethnic Identity in Adolescents and Adults: A Review of Research," in *Psychological Bulletin* 108 (1990), and she and Doreen Rosenthal describe impacts of the environmental context on ethnic identity formation in "Ethnic Identity in Adolescence: Process, Context, and Outcome," in *Advances in Adolescent Development*, vol. 4, edited by Gerald R. Adams, Thomas P. Gullotta, and Raymond Montemayor (Newbury Park, Calif.: Sage, 1992). A. Wade Boykin published "Black Child Socialization: A Conceptual Framework," in *Black Children: Social, Educational, and Parental Environments*, edited by Harriette Pipes McAdoo and John Lewis McAdoo (Beverly Hills, Calif.: Sage, 1985).

See also: Assimilation theories; Biracialism; Ethnic identities of women; Ethnicity and ethnic groups; Minority and majority groups; Separatism.

Affirmative action

> **Significance:** Since the 1960's, affirmative action has been considered a major strategy in the attempt to eliminate institutional discrimination in the areas of employment and education by providing minorities and women with greater access to opportunity; it has also been controversial and widely debated.

Affirmative action policies and programs, which are specifically designed to increase the numbers of minorities and women in employment and education where their representation has been sparse or nonexistent, have created tremendous controversy since their introduction in the 1960's under the John F. Kennedy and Lyndon B. Johnson administrations. Affirmative action programs involve strategies designed to increase the participation of women and minorities, particularly in the areas of employment and education. Typically, affirmative action programs are gender-conscious and/or race-conscious measures designed to assist minorities in overcoming past and present discrimination.

Purpose of Affirmative Action
Affirmative action policies have been applied to a host of situations involving discrimination in employment and education. The underlying purpose is to increase the prospect for equality of opportunity while eliminating systemic discrimination against specific populations. Equality of opportunity has historically been the social agenda pushed by civil rights organizations. They believe that affirmative action is an important strategy in the struggle for equal opportunity.

The enforcement of affirmative action is predicated on Titles VI and VII of the Civil Rights Act of 1964 (and to a lesser degree on Executive Order 11246, a 1965 order requiring equal employment opportunity clauses in all federal contracts). The U.S. Department of Justice, the Equal Employment Opportunity Commission, the Office of Federal Contract Compliance Programs (of the Department of Labor), and the federal courts have used Title VII to dismantle long-standing patterns of discrimination in employment and education. Affirmative action programs are actually considered remedial strategies.

Ideally, affirmative action is a twofold approach. First, it is an analysis of the existing workforce to determine if the percentages of "protected groups" in a given job classification are similar to the percentages of those groups in the surrounding community. Second, if it can be substantiated that certain practices have an exclusionary effect in the selection process, affirmative (race- and gender-conscious) measures may be required to remedy the situation. A number of steps may be taken to alter the existing selection process, including the establishment of goals and timetables for hiring, the development of recruitment programs, a redesigning of jobs and job descriptions, substantiation of the use of testing as a selection instrument, and attempting to improve the opportunity for advancement training for those in positions with limited career paths.

An affirmative action program may involve some or all of these steps. Additionally, affirmative action may be either voluntary or mandated by the courts. A court order or consent decree may force an offending enterprise to make restitution and to submit a detailed plan specifying its intentions to provide back pay and strategies for equitable promotion opportunities to those it has victimized. It may also include a provision on how it proposes to restructure its recruitment and hiring practices to come into compliance with federal guidelines. A primary concern of affirmative action is to encourage that additional measures be taken that go beyond the mere cessation of discriminatory practices.

Without the invoking of goals and timetables, the responsibility for providing equal opportunity would rest solely with the employer. Goals and timetables provide a type of indicator for employers; they are different from quotas, which are rigid and inflexible. Quotas do not allow for flexibility above or below the stated numbers.

Distributive and Compensatory Justice
Since the Supreme Court's decision in the "reverse discrimination" case of *Regents of the University of California v. Bakke* in 1978, the debate on affirmative action has been framed within interpretations of Title VI of the Civil Rights Act of 1964, the 1965 Executive Order 11246, and subsequent decisions by the Supreme Court. The Court's decisions have appeared to oscillate between limiting and expanding affirmative action. Two major questions are considered in such decisions: whether affirmative action is permissible and appropriate under the law and whether it should be limited to victims of discrimination or should include distributive remedies.

According to Kathanne W. Greene, in *Affirmative Action and Principles of Justice* (1989), affirmative action rests on two basic principles: distributive justice and compensatory justice. Distributive justice is concerned with the distribution of the benefits, rights, and burdens shared by members of society. These benefits and rights can be distributed in several ways; they may be based on equality of opportunity, for example, or based on need, effort, and utility. Therefore, there is no one best way to effectuate distributive justice.

Compensatory justice is essentially concerned with compensation (or reparation) for past injustices against individuals or groups by the government: A victim is entitled to fair compensation or entitled to be returned to a situation comparable to that which existed before the injustice. There is little debate that the U.S. government was a participant in the injustices perpetuated against certain groups (as in *Plessy v. Ferguson*, 1896).

Levels of Preferential Consideration

There are arguably three levels at which preferential considerations or affirmative measures may be accorded women and minorities in employment and education under affirmative action. First, an affirmative measure can be accorded minorities or women who are less qualified than their white male counterparts. Second, an affirmative measure can be granted to minorities and women when they and their white male counterparts are equally qualified. Third, minorities and women can be accorded an affirmative measure when they are more qualified than their white male counterparts.

The Controversy

Critics of affirmative action argue that it accords special privilege to entire categories of people whose individual members may or may not have experienced discrimination. Moreover, they maintain that affirmative action

Milestones in Affirmative Action

Year	Event	Impact
1965	Executive Order 11246	Requires firms doing business in excess of $50,000/year with the U.S. government to submit time tables and goals for diversifying their workforces.
1978	*Regents of the University of California v. Bakke*	Strikes down a policy that established a quota for minority admissions on grounds that it is unfair to a qualified white applicant ("reverse discrimination").
1979	*United Steelworkers of America v. Weber*	Upholds an agreement between an employer and a union, establishing goals for minority inclusion in a training program on grounds that any harm done to white employees is temporary and does not create an absolute barrier to advancement.
1986	*Wygant v. Jackson Board of Education*	Holds that right of seniority may take precedence over affirmative action plans when workforce is reduced.
1991	Civil Rights Act	Modifies effects of Supreme Court rulings that increased burden of proof on plaintiffs.
1995	*Adarand Constructors v. Peña*	Holds that broad affirmative action programs involving employment and contracts are unconstitutional, but preserves the applicability of affirmative action to specific and limited circumstances of discrimination.
1996	Proposition 209	California voters approve Proposition 209, a measure that ends state-supported affirmative action. Opponents of affirmative action in other states are encouraged by the passage of this measure.

policies establish rigid quotas and may therefore extend opportunities to individuals who are otherwise unqualified. The resulting argument is that affirmative action programs create "reverse discrimination" against white males. Proponents, on the other hand, argue that race-conscious and gender-conscious measures are needed because race and gender have long been bases for discrimination. Race and gender, they say, still limit opportunities for minorities and women in certain areas of society. Consequently, minorities and women will only be able to achieve equal opportunity through the use of race- and gender-conscious strategies.

Affirmative action and equality of opportunity have been inextricably linked in the minds of some Americans. Yet over the years affirmative action has become associated with concepts that have served to bias many others against it. For example, terms such as "preferential treatment," "minority set-asides," "quotas," "managing diversity," and "reverse discrimination" have caused many whites to become hostile to the concept of affirmative action. Few Americans would dispute the fact that minority populations and women have experienced widespread discrimination in the past. Many, however, disagree that they continue to experience discrimination. One reason has to do with the perception that there is already widespread application of affirmative action programs in both the public and private sectors.

"Reverse" Discrimination

Some opponents of affirmative action insist that such policies and programs amount to social engineering and violate the Constitution: They virtually sanction discrimination against white males, thereby simply reversing the object of discrimination. The reverse discrimination argument maintains that women and members of minority groups receive preferential treatment in employment (for example, in obtaining promotions) and in admission to institutions of higher education, particularly where a past history of discrimination can be documented. In such situations, white males who may demonstrate greater academic skill, may have accrued more seniority on the job, or may have scored higher on an entrance examination may be passed over so that the institution can increase the numbers of an underrepresented population. Consequently, and controversially, such decisions are not based on merit. It might be noted that very little objection has been heard concerning episodes of nepotism and widespread preferential treatment offered to veterans (which are clearly not based on merit).

In the well-known 1978 *Regents of the University of California v. Bakke* litigation, a white applicant with a higher score on a medical school entrance examination than some minority applicants was rejected because of the practice of reserving fifteen spaces for minority applicants. Tremendous controversy ensued. (Little was said about the sons and daughters of upper-level university officials who also happened to receive special consideration over more qualified applicants.) Although affirmative action policies are attempts to rectify past and present discriminatory practices, they do undeniably have a negative impact on the opportunities of some white males (as argued in *Weber v. Kaiser Aluminum and Chemical Corporation*). Opponents of affirmative action argue that all that can be hoped to be achieved legally is the eradication of discrimination. Nothing else, constitutionally, can be done. Any attempt to compensate victims of discrimination—especially if they are given preferential consideration in hiring, promotion, or admission to an institution of higher education—simply results in another form of discrimination. Compensation, if it were to be considered, should be offered only to the actual victims of discrimination, not to individuals simply because they belong to a particular group. Departing from its previous rulings on affirmative action, the Supreme Court gave support to this view in 1995 in its decision in *Adarand Constructors v. Peña.*

Limited Success of Affirmative Action

It has been argued that affirmative action programs have experienced only limited success, despite the fact that they have been an accepted strategy for many years. Augustus J. Jones, Jr., in *Affirmative Talk, Affirmative Action: A Comparative Study of the Politics of Affirmative Action*, suggests a number of reasons for this. First is poor communication between policymakers and those responsible for implementing the policies. If policies are not clearly delineated, they cannot be effectively administered. Second, a lack of adequate resources may prohibit successful implementation. Money, information, authority, and the necessary staff must all be in place. Third, those responsible for implementation may be antagonistic to affirmative action and may operate opposite to their directives. Fourth, dysfunctional organization structure may preclude the effective implementation of policies. Fifth, political leadership (especially at the national level) may sour the social climate for the acceptance of affirmative action. In particular, inflammatory rhetoric using such terms as "preferential treatment," "racial quotas," and "reverse discrimination" has helped to create reservation and even anger among some whites regarding the legitimacy of affirmative action. Presidents Ronald Reagan and George Bush, for example, consistently referred to affirmative action policies as reverse discrimination and quota legislation.

Reagan, in particular, was an outspoken critic of affirmative action policies and programs. He believed that they were unfair and that they led to rigid quotas, and during his administration he appointed men and women that shared his views. It has been noted that Reagan put together a conservative team of legal experts in the Department of Justice that shared his opposition to affirmative action. His administration also challenged the use of statistical data as a means of substantiating discriminatory patterns by employers.

Both Reagan and Bush appointed minority individuals who opposed affirmative action to posts in their administrations and in federal agencies. Reagan completely restructured the U. S. Commission on Civil Rights and selected Clarence Pendleton, an African American, to be chairman of the commission. Pendleton proved to be so extreme in his opposition to affirmative action that he was rejected by much of the African American community and rebuffed by black Republicans. Linda Chávez, a Hispanic, was selected staff director of the U.S. Civil Rights Commission. Criticizing affirmative action programs in a number of speeches, she argued that affirmative action actually endangered the progress made by African Americans since *Brown v. Board of Education* (1954) and that it was a new type of paternalism.

Clarence Thomas, as chairman of the Equal Employment Opportunity Commission (EEOC), applied a more restrictive interpretation of Title VII than his predecessors had. He decided that the EEOC would pursue only individual claims of discrimination that could be explicitly proved. Therefore, neither statistical data nor the underrepresentation of certain populations in the workforce would be sufficient to demonstrate systemic discrimination. The individual complainant had to provide undeniable proof of discrimination. This policy virtually eliminated the conception of "pattern and practice" discrimination for filing suit.

Congress and the federal courts also manifested some degree of retrenchment regarding affirmative action during the 1980's. Amendments were introduced in Congress to eliminate affirmative action, while the federal courts, in particular the Supreme Court, vacillated on the applicability of affirmative action policies. A number of decisions by the Court in the 1980's and 1990's, particularly *Adarand Constructors v. Peña*, called into question the use of broad affirmative action programs.

In the 1990's, affirmative action suffered some serious setbacks. In 1995, the Regents of the University of California decided to end affirmative action in admissions and hiring. Other states, including Texas, began dismantling affirmative action programs. The results were mixed, with some prestigious universities reporting a significant drop in minority admissions. The following year, California voters approved Proposition 206, the California Civil Rights Initiative, a proposal to amend the California state constitution. The proposition declared

In the 1990's, a number of institutions, including the University of California, began to dismantle their affirmative action programs. Students David Kim (left) and Pooh Mayo protest the end of affirmative action at the UC campus in Berkeley in 1995.

that the state should "not discriminate against, or grant preferential treatment to, any individual or group on the basis of race, sex, color, ethnicity, or national origin in the operation of public employment, public education, or public contracting." The proposition drew support from Ward Connerly, a black businessman from Sacramento, because it provided for equal treatment under the law, in accordance with a "color-blind" society, and opposition from organizations such as the American Civil Liberties Union and the National Association for the Advancement of Colored People, which believed the measure was designed to end state-supported affirmative action. Legal challenges against the proposition were for the most part unsuccessful, and California governor Pete Wilson implemented the proposition in March, 1998.

Charles C. Jackson

Core Resources

An excellent explanation of affirmative action goals and discussion of timetables versus quotas can be found in

Robert K. Fullinwider's *The Reverse Discrimination Contro-versy: A Moral and Legal Analysis* (Totowa, N.J.: Rowman & Littlefield, 1980). A discussion of the justification for reverse discrimination can be found in chapter 3 of Tom Regan and Donald VanDeVeer's *And Justice for All: New Introductory Essays in Ethics and Public Policy* (Totowa, N.J.: Rowman & Allanheld, 1982). An analysis of the effort to dismantle affirmative action is provided by Charles C. Jackson in "Affirmative Action: Controversy and Re-trenchment," *The Western Journal of Black Studies* 16 (no. 4, Winter, 1992). William G. Bowen and Derek Bok's *The Shape of the River: Long-term Consequences of Considering Race in College and University Admissions* (Princeton, N.J.: Princeton University Press, 1998) provides a defense of affirmative action. Black conservative Shelby Steele's *A Dream Deferred: The Second Betrayal of Black Freedom in America* (New York: HarperCollins, 1998) is sharply criti-cal of affirmative action, calling it redemptive liberalism meant to make whites feel better. A good look at the application of affirmative action programs at the local level can be found in Augustus J. Jones, *Affirmative Talk, Affirmative Action: A Comparative Study of the Politics of Affirmative Action* (New York: Praeger, 1991).

See also: *Adarand Constructors v. Peña; Bakke* case; Civil Rights Act of 1964; College admissions; Equality of op-portunity; *Griggs v. Duke Power Company;* "Reverse" rac-ism; Proposition 209; *Richmond v. J. A. Croson Company; Weber v. Kaiser Aluminum and Chemical Corporation.*

African American-American Indian relations

> **Significance:** Traditional American racial history, by focusing on American Indian-white or black-white relations, has ignored the important cultural contributions of American Indian-black interactions.

Since the 1960's, revisionist historians have shown great interest in the histories of American Indians and African Americans. The study of the history of the contact be-tween these two groups has been a logical development, and much new evidence has emerged. For example, significant contact between American Indians and Afri-cans occurred in Europe at the time of Portuguese encounters with Africans. In the sixteenth century, American Indians were traded for West African slaves, who were needed to work on Brazilian plantations.

The Spanish were the first major users of African slaves in the New World. An initial function of Africans,

because of their knowledge of Indian culture, was to aid in exploration as guides and interpreters. The first Afri-can in the New World known by name was Estevanico, a Muslim native of Acamor. He accompanied the expedi-tion of Pánfilo de Narváez, which was shipwrecked off the coast of Florida in 1529. Francisco Vásquez de Coro-nado was also accompanied by Africans as he explored central Kansas in 1541.

Indigenous forms of servitude were modified by the Spanish to serve the labor needs of their mines and plantations. Beginning with Hernando de Soto in 1538, the Spanish transported thousands of Indians from the Southeast to the West Indies. By 1540, however, Indian slavery was deemed unsuitable because of the Indians' susceptibility to disease; thereafter African labor began to be used. The mixing of Native American and African slave populations in sixteenth century Spanish America created a solidarity between the two groups, as seen in numerous revolts and insurrections.

American Colonization

Contacts among the races in the age of exploration were minor compared with those that occurred in the period of colonization. The main areas of interaction can be divided geographically into, first, New England, the Mid-dle Colonies, and the Chesapeake, and second, the Southeast and Indian Territory. Except for the case of the Seminole Wars in Spanish Florida, the relations between blacks and Indians were not as amicable in English North America as they were in Spanish America. This was attributable in large part to demographics. The numbers of Indian and African slaves from New England to the Chesapeake were small in the early seventeenth century. Over time the Indian population diminished, and the black population increased. Although the two groups were initially few in number and spread over a large geographical area, there was extensive intermin-gling, which served to modify the physical appearance of both in Massachusetts, Connecticut, New York, New Jersey, Delaware, Maryland, and Virginia. The main form of relationship during this time was intermarriage be-tween free blacks and reservation Indians. Reservations, in fact, were centers of racial fusion all the way from Cape Cod to the Chesapeake. Crispus Attucks, Paul Cuffe, and Frederick Douglass were famous men of mixed blood.

A mulatto named York, the first black to cross the continent, was critical to the success of the Lewis and Clark expedition of 1804-1806. The explorers would have turned back at the Rocky Mountains had not York be-friended the Shoshone, who provided needed supplies and horses. York, the son of two slaves, was known as Big Medicine by the Indians. He spoke several Indian lan-guages as well as French. The Indian woman Sacagawea was his constant companion during the expedition.

Indian Slavery

The most massive contact between Indians and African Americans arose within the system of slavery developed by the so-called Five Civilized Tribes of the Southeast—the Cherokee, Chickasaw, Choctaw, Creek, and Seminole. Predominant among the Five Tribes were the Cherokee, whose 12,395-member nation held 583 slaves in 1809. By 1824, the numbers had grown to 15,560 and 1,277 respectively. Although it seems that the Cherokee were not unduly harsh masters, they refused to allow intermixture with blacks. The Chickasaw and Choctaw tribes together counted 25,000 members, with 5,000 slaves. Believing, like the Cherokee, in racial separation, these two tribes were crueler masters. The Chickasaw, who on occasion murdered the slaves of other owners, were especially cruel.

The Creek and Seminole were considered the least civilized of the Five Tribes, partly because they had the least prejudice toward blacks. This was especially true of the Seminole, who allowed their "slaves" to live in separate farming communities while paying a small annual tribute. The Creek, a patriarchal society, had children by slave women. The Creek reared these children as equals to their full-blooded progeny. A famous Creek chief, Tustennuggee Emartha, or Jim Boy, was of such mixed breed. The Seminole, who numbered about 3,900 in 1822, owned 800 slaves. These slaves were "maroons"—they had escaped the plantations of Georgia and the Carolinas. It was the presence of the maroons that initiated the Florida Wars.

War and Politics

Native American and African American military cooperation occurred in two campaigns closely related in time, geography, and cause. The second decade of the nineteenth century saw, in the Southeast, the outbreak of the Creek War and the First Seminole War. Both were precipitated by the anger of white slave owners who sought the return of their runaways from neighboring reservations. Andrew Jackson led the assault that crushed the Creek Red Stick Revolt in 1814, and he ended the First Seminole War in 1818 by capturing a Seminole stronghold in Florida.

African Americans figured prominently in both of these wars, since they had the most to lose in the event of a defeat. In numerous battles, Indians and blacks fought and died together. Jim Bowlegs, who was a slave of Chief Billy Bowlegs and served as his interpreter and adviser, later became a Seminole maroon leader, organizing a resettlement for his group in Mexico in 1850. The Indians and blacks continued to fight for their independence in two successive wars until the Civil War broke out.

The participation of slave-holding Indians in the Civil War (1861-1865) was determined by their respective views on slavery. The Chickasaw and Choctaw tribes, who were the most prejudiced against blacks, supported the Confederacy; the Creek and Seminole opposed it. The Cherokee held a divided position; mixed-bloods (part Indian, part white) generally supported the South, while full-bloods tended to sympathize with the North. In the confusion of war, the slaves were left largely on their own, attacking both Unionists and Confederates. After the war some blacks sought incorporation into the various tribes. This action was resisted by the Choctaw and Chickasaw. After the tribes' removal to Indian Territory, the legacy of Indian slave-holding was clearly evident. By 1907, no Seminole family was free of black intermixing, and almost no Creek families were pure-blooded. The other three tribes, however, had practically no mixture.

Since the 1960's a new alliance has occurred between Native Americans and African Americans in the arena of political activity. The Black Power and Civil Rights movements inspired Red Power organizations such as the American Indian Movement (AIM). Black theology has been the model for the development of what has been called "red theology." Such political actions have spread to international bodies such as the United Nations and the Organization of Indigenous Peoples, in which African and indigenous New World peoples sustain positive contact.

William H. Green

Core Resources

Jack D. Forbes's *Black Africans and Native Americans: Color, Race, and Caste in the Evolution of Red-Black Peoples* (New York: Basil Blackwell, 1988) uses ethnohistorical and philological methods to break new ground in the study of American culture by stressing Native American contributions to the ethnic complexity of the nation. Gary B. Nash's *Red, White, and Black: The Peoples of Early America* (Englewood Cliffs, N.J.: Prentice-Hall, 1974) argues that American culture arose as the product of three centuries of intense mixing and contact between three cultures: red, black, and white. Dwight W. Hoover's *The Red and the Black* (Chicago: Rand McNally, 1976) presents a detailed history of Indian-black interaction from the fifteenth century, with special attention to the distinct development of each culture. William Loren Katz's *Black Indians: A Hidden Heritage* (New York: Atheneum, 1986) examines how European Americans sought to discourage contacts between Indians and blacks from the age of exploration to Reconstruction. R. Halliburton, Jr.'s *Red over Black: Black Slavery Among the Cherokee Indians* (Westport, Conn.: Greenwood Press, 1977) and Theda Perdue's *Slavery and the Evolution of Cherokee Society, 1540-1886* (Knoxville: University of Tennessee Press, 1979) look at slavery within the Cherokee Nation. Daniel F. Littlefield, Jr., examines the rise and development of Creek slavery from its beginnings to the aftermath of the

Red Stick Rebellion in *Africans and Creeks: From the Colonial Period to the Civil War* (Westport, Conn.: Greenwood Press, 1979) and shows the influence of African slaves on the Seminoles' activities as they fought and signed treaties with the federal government from the time of the removal policy to the Civil War in *Africans and Seminoles: From Removal to Emancipation* (Westport, Conn.: Greenwood Press, 1978). Kevin Mulroy's *Freedom on the Border: The Seminole Maroons in Florida, the Indian Territory, Coahuila, and Texas* (Lubbock: Texas Tech University Press, 1993) describes the long interaction between black Seminoles and their native masters as both sought to cooperate and survive destructive federal policies.

See also: Civil War; Indian slavery; Seminole Wars; Slavery: history.

African American Baptist Church

> **Significance:** An amalgamation of African and European forms of religious worship found expression beginning in the late 1700's.

The religious revivals of the 1730's collectively known as the first Great Awakening transformed the spiritual climate of British North America by the mid-eighteenth century. Church membership grew and evangelical religious ideas, which emphasized a person's own relationship with God, began to acquire hegemony over the religious values propagated by the established churches. Among those people who embraced evangelical ideals were African American slaves, who found attractive the notion of a personal God, the hope for salvation, and the less formal style of evangelical worship. This was especially true in the South, where African Americans benefited from a practice among some white evangelicals of allowing blacks to preach to other blacks and where African Americans were the targets of white missionary activity.

The Baptist Church

African Americans were particularly drawn to the Baptist faith, especially in the latter part of the eighteenth century. White Baptists, themselves often among the poorest in southern society, actively recruited African Americans. Furthermore, Baptists did not require formal education as part of ministerial training, and what learning they did encourage centered on mastering the contents of the Bible. Even African Americans held in

bondage and denied opportunities for formal education could fulfill these expectations, and more than a few became ministers. African American slaves not only joined biracial Baptist churches but also fashioned their own fellowships, where they blended the traditional folk religions they brought from Africa with the evangelical nostrums of the Europeans, thus creating a hybrid African American religion.

In the Savannah River Valley, which connected the hinterlands around Augusta, Georgia, with the port city of Savannah, evangelical revivals among whites and blacks bore organizational fruit among African Americans, who formed their own Baptist church at Silver Bluff, near Augusta, in 1773.

About that time, a slave named George Liele heard a sermon preached by the Reverend Matthew Moore, a white minister, and became convinced that he needed to respond to the gospel. Baptized by Moore, Liele became a preacher and began to exhort other slaves in the vicinity of Augusta to become Christians. Liele's master temporarily had to flee Georgia for his life and freed Liele. For the next several years, Liele and a colleague, David George, preached regularly at the Baptist church in Silver Bluff. George, who was born a slave in Virginia and had run away from a cruel master before coming to the Deep South as the slave of George Galphin, was converted after hearing sermons in the mid-1770's by several African American preachers, including Liele. George and Liele organized other churches, including the congregation at Yama Craw, outside Savannah, in 1777.

Among those who heard Liele preach at Yama Craw was Andrew Bryan, a South Carolina slave baptized by Liele in 1782. Bryan eventually purchased his freedom and devoted himself to his ministry. Although whites who feared an unshackled black man whipped Bryan twice and imprisoned him once, he continued to preach to ever-larger congregations, which often contained both blacks and whites. In 1788, his congregation constituted itself into the Savannah Georgia First Colored Church, commonly called the Savannah Church. At the time, it boasted 575 members, and it would grow to more than 800 by the time of Bryan's death.

A Fusion of Beliefs

The religious teachings of Liele, George, and Bryan fused the African concepts of a unitary universe where the sacred and profane are not segregated, the European mythologies of Heaven, Hell, and redemption, and their present reality of slavery. God would help Africans through their travail of slavery and would one day lead them out of bondage. In this melding process, certain African religious practices were proscribed. The church covenant of Liele's Yama Craw Church specifically banned the consumption of blood and strangled meat of animals offered to idols, which had been a part of some West African religious rituals. Other African practices were given an important place, such as moaning as part of religious singing. This practice originated in ecstatic African religious rituals, and moaning and wailing have been preserved in southern gospel singing. This hybrid religious ritual did not confine itself to African American communities. The emotional shouts and ritual cadences of African worship affected the rhythms of white discourse as well, especially the sermon form, in which the preacher and congregation engage in something of a dialogue.

Both Liele and George eventually fled the South for the British Empire, seeking to continue their ministerial work without the specter of slavery hanging over them. Liele went to Jamaica, establishing the first Baptist churches there. George went to Canada, where he worked with both blacks and whites before organizing a Back-to-Africa movement, in which a thousand Canadian blacks went with George to Sierra Leone in 1792.

Congregation members gather outside the Paradise Baptist Church. Baptist churches have played an important part in the lives of African Americans since the first African American Baptist Church was founded near Augusta, Georgia, in 1773.

Bryan, however, remained in the South, calling upon African Americans to lead better lives and, sometimes stealthily, urging whites to live out the Golden Rule in dealing with blacks. By establishing churches that counseled patience while teaching a theology of ultimate deliverance, African American leaders like Liele, George, and Bryan helped African Americans survive slavery by encouraging them to expect freedom soon.

Edward R. Crowther

Core Resources

LeRoy Fitts's *A History of Black Baptists* (Nashville, Tenn.: Broadman Press, 1985) presents a sympathetic and readable account of black Baptist leaders and churches. C. Eric Lincoln and Lawrence H. Mamiya's *The Black Church in the African American Experience* (Durham, N.C.: Duke University Press, 1990) is a well-written survey of African American churches since their earliest times and their meaning in the African American struggle in the United States. Editor Gayraud S. Wilmore's *African American Religious Studies: An Interdisciplinary Anthology* (Durham, N.C.: Duke University Press, 1989) contains a series of essays that may help readers interpret the fragmentary documentary record of early African American religious life. Milton C. Sernett's *Afro-American Religious History: A Documentary Witness* (Durham, N.C.: Duke University Press, 1985) contains letters from Bryan and Liele and many other representative documents of the African American religious experience.

See also: AME Church; AME Zion Churches; Black church; Slavery: history.

African American cowboys

Despite the predominantly white images in television and film Westerns, many cowboys were African American. Attracted by the high wages and the pull of the open range, the cowboys were a diverse lot that included former Civil War soldiers, former African American slaves, Mexicans, and American Indians. Evidence suggests that perhaps as many as 25 percent of cowboys were African American. Most of the African Americans were unable to read or write, so few records of their daily life exist, but like their peers, they spent as many as four months in the saddle, working the long drives. The cowboy's job was dangerous, hard, and lonely. Because the cowboys had to work together to herd the cattle up the trail, segregation was impractical, but African American cowboys were constantly reminded of the inequalities of the time. Pay for African American cowboys was frequently less than for their white counterparts, and segregation was common in cattle towns along the trail. Despite the discrimination they faced, however, the contribution of the African American cowboy to the westward movement and the settlement of the western United States is indisputable.   *Donald C. Simmons, Jr.*

See also: African American stereotypes; African Americans and film; Segregation on the frontier.

African American literature

> **Significance:** In the eighteenth century, the African American presence in the United States added a new dimension to the cultural identity of American literature. African Americans first wrote about their experiences as slaves; later, they infused new perspectives into the literary canon through experimentation and through revisions of existing conventions.

Personal accounts of slaves' journeys to and bondage in the United States produced a new genre, the slave narrative, in the eighteenth century. The genre borrows from the autobiography, travelogue, and captivity narratives that were already common forms of writing among the early settlers. While most Puritans and Pilgrims expressed faith in their God and hope in their journey to a new land, the African American narratives convey extremes of alienation and suffering.

Slave Narratives

Among the pioneer African American writers of slave narratives is Gustavas Vassa, who narrates his experiences in the United States. His account, titled *The Interesting Narrative of the Life of Olaudah Equiano, or Gustavus Vassa, the African, Written by Himself* (1789), contains a description of the terrible journey by sea. Although African Americans came from diverse regions of Africa, slaves were perceived as members of a single race, so their diversity of heritage was overlooked and their regional differences were ignored by slave owners, who defined them in terms of their functions.

From 1830 to 1865, with the exception of one poet, James H. Whitfield, all black authors wrote autobiographies or were subjects of biographical works. *Scenes in the Life of Harriet Tubman* (1869, revised as *Harriet the Moses of Her People*, 1886) is the biography of a runaway slave who became a conductor on the Underground Railroad; at great risk to her life, she assisted slaves in fleeing to the northern states and freedom.

The most famous African American in the antislavery movement was Frederick Douglass. He wrote three auto-

biographies during various phases of his life. He reports his early interest in learning how to read and write, his confrontation with his inhumane owners, and his ultimate freedom. Dedicated to a vision of transforming the oppressed state of his race, Douglass shared his story to inspire others.

Biographical Narratives

After the Civil War (1861-1865), biographical narratives remained a popular genre among African American writers. These narratives integrate the art of storytelling and history telling and allow the authors to address the theme of racial discrimination within personalized contexts of economic and social challenges.

The autobiography of Booker T. Washington, *Up from Slavery: An Autobiography* (1901), is a personal testimony of success that is in many ways comparable to Benjamin Franklin's famous autobiography. As a native son of Virginia, Washington realized the importance of education. Washington became an advocate of the development of practical and technical skills; many of his African American opponents criticized him for his excessive loyalty to whites in a laboring capacity.

W. E. B. Du Bois is another black author who was concerned about the survival of African Americans in America; he advocated democratic rights for his race. He was conscious of the diversity among African American cultural experiences. Unlike Washington, who was born a slave, Du Bois was born free and grew up in the cosmopolitan culture of Massachusetts. He attended Fisk University in Nashville, Tennessee, then went to Harvard and was graduated magna cum laude. He recorded impressions of his complex experiences in *The Souls of Black Folk* (1903). In this work, he makes a case for a racial bond among African Americans despite their varied backgrounds. He explains that Washington's advice in *Up from Slavery* stems from his rural agrarian background; however, the future of the African American race called for a more uniform approach to democratic rights. Du Bois was aware of the psychological tensions linked to segregation; therefore, he predicted the color line would be the problem of the twentieth century. He advocated that the talents and skills of African Americans must not be developed in contempt for other races, but rather in conformity to the greater ideals of the American republic. He proposed that double consciousness or pride in African heritage and pride in American citizenship was better than a divided self. There was no need for African Americans to seek assimilation in America at the cost of their African heritage.

Some African Americans resorted to collaborative writing for biographical narrative. An example is *The Autobiography of Malcolm X* (1964), written in collaboration with *Roots* author Alex Haley. It blends the dramatic conventions of narration with first-person reporting. The book captures America's cultural landscape of the 1950's and 1960's, while highlighting the turning points in Malcolm X's life. The biography records his criminal activities, prison experiences, and conversion to the Nation of Islam. After his release from prison, Malcolm X's pilgrimage to Mecca led to the realization that the message of religion is to foster peaceful relations among all races. Therefore, upon his return to the United States, he renounced his allegiance to Elijah Muhammad, who was preaching hatred toward the white race. Malcolm X remained active in the struggle for equality of African Americans and became a popular black leader; he was assassinated in 1965.

Poetry

African American writers have used the genres of poetry and fiction to express their identity. Folk literature became a vehicle for blending the reality of their experiences in America with their nostalgia for the African past. Slaves were not allowed to get a formal education and were generally perceived as unfit for intellectual activities. Only a few slaves had their owners' permission to read and write, and their literacy centered on the reading and interpretation of the Bible.

Among such privileged and literate slaves was the first African American poet, Phillis Wheatley, who was known as "a sable muse" among European educated circles. Wheatley was faced with the dual challenge of writing as an African American and as a woman. She blended the literary conventions of her time, such as heroic couplets, with innovative zeal. In many of her elegies, she addresses the subject of death in the metaphorical context of Christian hope for salvation, implying rescue from a state of bondage. It was her love of liberty that prompted her to write the poem "To His Excellency General Washington" for leading the forces of independence. Unfortunately, poverty and domestic hardship squelched her poetic voice. Wheatley's literary work was primarily accepted as testimony of African American ability to participate in American literature.

Paul Laurence Dunbar's poetry captures the African American voice in American literature. Dunbar's mixed use of oral and written conventions was also practiced by realists such as Mark Twain. It is not surprising that a renowned realist writer, William Dean Howells, praised Dunbar for integrating the African American voice into literature.

Harlem Renaissance

The 1920's marked the beginning of the Harlem Renaissance, when African American writers transcended the constraints of the European tradition to infuse an independent perspective into American literature. The Harlem Renaissance produced powerful works of poetry by, among others, Langston Hughes, who claims ties to the grandeur of ancient civilization through his African heritage and depicts the ravages of social and economic disparity.

A recurrent theme to appear in the fiction of African American writers is the identity of the mulatto in relation to an environment of rejection. African American fiction treats such rejection as a lingering social phenomenon. Toward the end of the nineteenth century novelist Pauline E. Hopkins addressed racism in her serial novels, exposing the hypocrisy within race relationships. Hopkins's fiction is prophetic in the sense that, as did Du Bois, she saw that the problem of the color line would be the great problem of the twentieth century. Later, Jean Toomer's collection of short fiction, *Cane* (1923), embraced the tensions of segregation and victimization of the mulatto from the male perspective. He makes powerful use of folk sound, imagery, and symbol to portray racial barriers that signal that a claim to an interracial heritage is a social taboo.

Novels

The Harlem Renaissance allowed for novels that captured the reality of African American experience. Richard Wright's novel *Native Son* (1940) remains a masterpiece that portrays the fate of a black man who is overpowered by economic oppression. The protagonist accidentally kills the liberal daughter of his employer. Wright pursues the prevailing conventions of naturalism to depict the helpless condition of African Americans. His novel resembles Theodore Dreiser's *An American Tragedy* (1925): Both writers were inspired by real trials. In response to Wright's fiction, there were some black writers who were not interested in depicting merely the helpless condition of the black man; they were also interested in probing the challenges and complexities of African American experience to understand their own cultural identity in America. Among the leading male novelists who focus on the quest for identity is Ralph Ellison, who wrote *Invisible Man* (1952). This novel combines realism with surrealism and draws upon black folklore and myth. James Baldwin was another African American novelist who investigated the archetypal theme of initiation and discovery of self in his novel *Go Tell It on the Mountain* (1953). This novel draws heavily upon the author's childhood experiences.

A contemporary leading black male novelist is Ishmael Reed. In his novel *Mumbo Jumbo* (1972), Reed experiments with the conventions of fiction to capture the complexity of African American identity as he integrates multiple layers of meaning in his prose. He parodies Western tradition and African American conventions. Reed decries any idealism that imposes unrealistic restrictions on the artist.

Among those African American writers whose style Reed parodies is Zora Neale Hurston, who grew up in the black community of Eatontown. Her work marks a major breakthrough for feminist literature. For example, in her novel *Their Eyes Were Watching God* (1937), she combines the voice of self-expression with the social challenges encountered by African American women. The Hurston legacy matures in Alice Walker's fiction. Walker uses a self-reflective voice in her epistolary novel *The Color Purple* (1982).

Probably the most memorable female African American voice in the twentieth century is that of Toni Morrison. In *Beloved* (1987, made into a film in 1998) she takes an innovative approach to a ghost story. She traces the historical context of slavery and exposes the hazards of allowing the past to override the present.

Mabel Khawaja

Core Resources
Claudia Tate's *Black Women Writers at Work* (New York: Continuum, 1983) surveys feminist African American

Best-selling African American author Toni Morrison wrote of slavery and ghosts in her award-winning 1987 novel *Beloved*.

scholarship and provides fifteen interviews with leading black women writers. Houston Baker's *Modernism and Harlem Renaissance* (Chicago: University of Chicago Press, 1987) claims that the Harlem Renaissance liberated African American authors from traditional literary constraints. Henry Louis Gates's *The Signifying Monkey: A Theory of Afro-American Literary Criticism* (New York: Oxford University Press, 1988) examines the influence of African folk tradition and the revisionist trends in African American literature. Toni Morrison's *Playing in the Dark* (New York: Vintage Books, 1990) criticizes the perspective of critical theory that treats African American presence in literature from a fixed viewpoint and disregards the symbiotic interracial relationships.

See also: African American music; African American stereotypes; African Americans and film.

African American music

> **Significance:** Throughout the course of North American history, black musicians have drawn from their African heritage and borrowed from outside sources to create a variety of musical genres that have generated interest from multiracial audiences, weakening interracial barriers while reinforcing negative or simplistic stereotypes of African Americans.

The history of African American music illustrates an ongoing cultural interaction between African Americans and European Americans from the colonial period through the twentieth century. Through a constant exchange of material, styles, and instrumentation, black and white Americans forged a pluralistic and distinctly American musical culture that survived despite a prevailing institutional racism that discouraged cultural interaction. The advent of mass media in the twentieth century resulted in a general breakdown of social, cultural, and regional barriers that exposed diverse audiences to black musical styles, catapulting African American music into the cultural mainstream.

Early African American Music
Africans transported to North America as slaves brought with them a rich musical heritage that included professional and common folk stylings. From the beginning, slaves from various tribal and linguistic backgrounds relied on music as a vehicle for communication and expression and as a means of coping with the physical discomfort and psychological despair of bondage. Distinctively African musical traits such as blue notes and

call-and-response patterns persevered in the music of plantation slaves. The scarcity of African instruments on Southern plantations encouraged the development of a cappella vocal music exemplified by the field song and the spiritual, which developed as increasing numbers of slaves became Christians. Both field songs and spirituals used rich imagery and emotional intensity to impart themes of joy, suffering, and longing, often employing double meanings and subtle metaphors as a means of "signifying" the Africans' true desires and poking fun at their white masters. Slave music often contained hidden social connotations; the cakewalk, an elaborate slave pageant with musical accompaniment held during plantation holiday celebrations, clandestinely ridiculed white mannerisms to the bemusement of both blacks and unwitting whites.

Popular Genres of Nineteenth Century Black Music

By the 1820's, white entertainers were performing parodies of slave songs and dances for white American audiences. Blackening their faces with burnt cork and affecting exaggerated "darky" behavior, these performers laid the foundation for the minstrel show, which peaked in popularity just before the Civil War (1861-1865). The minstrel show exposed white audiences to a diluted form of African American music and produced lasting works by composers such as Daniel Decatur Emmett (author of "Dixie") and Stephen Foster. Nevertheless, the vitality and poignancy of the best minstrel compositions were eclipsed by the negative images of childish, shiftless blacks that defined minstrelsy. The blackface minstrel show declined in popularity following the Civil War as the minstrel style became increasingly associated with black performers seeking to enter show business; as late as the 1920's, many black performers still called themselves minstrels.

Following the Civil War, black musicians made inroads into American popular culture, aided by increased attention from patrons of high art and the migration of black musicians into new geographical regions. Northern missionaries traveling south to minister to freed blacks sparked white interest in African American spirituals through publication in 1867 of a collection entitled *Slave Songs of the United States* and the organization of the Fisk Jubilee Chorus, a group of nine black youths who in 1871 embarked on a seven-year tour of the United States and Europe that would raise $150,000 to found Fisk University in Nashville, Tennessee. The Jubilee chorus was widely imitated throughout the South as black and white educators sought to raise money for black schools, establishing the place of spirituals in the American mainstream and further eclipsing the minstrel show as a cultural phenomenon.

The popularization of African American vocal music through spirituals coincided with the development of various styles of black instrumental music, the most influential of which was ragtime, a multiethnic mixture of folk stylings that rose to popularity in the 1890's. Although conceived by African Americans, ragtime was from its inception a multiethnic art form influenced by black interaction with urban immigrants. Early manifestations of ragtime combined modified Latin rhythms with a European march cadence. Black musicians, with a few notable exceptions such as Scott Joplin, dissociated themselves with ragtime before the turn of the century; nevertheless, ragtime continued to be associated with African Americans, partly because of the readiness of white music publishers and promoters to exploit popular interest in black American culture. By the time Joplin's "Maple Leaf Rag" was published in 1899, popular white composers were exploiting the ragtime style, and more often the name, for commercial gain. This trend culminated in the production of "coon songs" written by Broadway and Tin Pan Alley composers in a ragtime style with humorous lyrics about "negro life" that perpetuated the mythical stereotype of blacks as carefree, childlike, and rhythmic.

Jazz and Blues

In the late nineteenth century, as ragtime and spirituals defined high black culture and cultivated white audiences, new strains of music reflecting various degrees of African influence developed in the South. Emancipation of slaves after the Civil War created a new mobility among black musicians, who traveled throughout the United States playing in saloons, brothels, juke joints, medicine shows, and minstrel shows, often to white or mixed audiences. From this polyglot of styles emerged two distinct genres that would shape popular music through the twentieth century: jazz and blues. Blues, which flourished in areas with a high black population density such as the Mississippi Delta, set the field song to musical accompaniment by incorporating European and Hawaiian influences into a distinctly African musical framework; jazz, rooted in cosmopolitan New Orleans, resembled ragtime in its multiethnic nature and its emphasis on the African musical devices of syncopation, polyrhythm, and call-and-response.

Jazz and blues emerged in the midst of a growing white fascination with African American culture in the early twentieth century. Although jazz was conceived in an interracial environment, the first jazz recordings in 1917 featured the all-white Dixieland Jazz Band (the first popular all-black jazz band, the King Oliver Band, first recorded in 1923). By the mid-1920's, the United States and Europe had become obsessed with jazz. Blues, while less popular among whites than jazz, exerted considerable influence upon white folk musicians (such

Milestones in African American Music

Year	Event	Impact
1619	First African slaves arrive in colonial America	Slaves bring African musical styles to the New World. Their vocal tradition is preserved in work songs and spirituals.
1871	Fisk Jubilee Singers tour United States, Europe	Nine-member choir of black youth popularizes African American spirituals, raises $150,000 to found Fisk University.
1899	"Maple Leaf Rag" published	Ragtime peaks in popularity following the publication of this Scott Joplin composition.
1912	"St. Louis Blues" published	Classically trained musician W. C. Handy popularizes rural black folk music style.
1951	"Rocket 88" released	This recording, produced by Sam Phillips and performed by Jackie Brenston and his Delta Kings, is one of the earliest examples of rock and roll.
1959	Motown Records founded	Songwriter Berry Gordy, Jr., establishes what becomes one of the most successful black-owned record labels—and businesses—in U.S. history.
1984	*Purple Rain*, album and feature film by Prince, released	Self-produced project by black artist attracts a racially mixed audience, influencing the burgeoning music video industry.

as Jimmy Rodgers) and attracted the attention of progressive whites through its association with the Harlem Renaissance.

The Rise of "Race" Music

The commercialization of American music through radio and records in the 1920's exposed black and white audiences to a wide range of African-influenced musical styles, and promoters and performers of this music often sought to enhance their appeal by embracing racial stereotypes. Record companies marketed various black folk styles under the category of "race" music, and radio stations catering to black audiences (but attracting white ones as well) proliferated throughout the South and in urban areas in the North. Black migration to northern cities skyrocketed during World War II, resulting in a mixing of musical styles in urban ghettoes that produced a diverse body of music ranging from the gospel of Malhalia Jackson to the electric blues of Muddy Waters and John Lee Hooker.

The Commercial Era

The United States' ongoing obsession with jazz through World War II nurtured an ongoing white fascination with African American culture. In the late 1940's and early 1950's, black rhythm and blues enjoyed increasing popularity among white teenagers economically empowered by postwar prosperity. Less cerebral than bebop jazz and less "ethnic" than electric blues, this hybridized, dance-oriented music provided a sound track for the emerging youth culture of mobility and independence. From this culture emerged rock and roll, a culmination of generations of exchange between black and white southern folk music. The arrival of rock and roll in the American mainstream both symbolized and influenced the changing course of race relations in the United States of the 1950's: Many popular early rock-and-roll performers were African American, and white rockabilly artists such as Elvis Presley openly affected black speech and mannerisms; early rock-and-roll package tours were interracial and played to interracial audiences. White middle-class objections to the racial liberalism and subtle sexuality of rock and roll created a backlash against the music in the late 1950's that coincided with a white backlash against school desegregation. Yet rock and roll had already broken down barriers that had been weakening for generations.

The explosion of rock and roll in the 1960's catapulted African American music and artists into the mainstream of American culture. By mid-decade, Quincy Jones had become the first African American record label executive, and the distinctive sound of a black-owned record label, Motown, permeated the airwaves of AM radio. The atmosphere of experimentation that defined late-1960's popular culture encouraged a multicultural creative environment in which various styles clashed and merged and interracial groups such as the Jimi Hendrix Experience, Sly and the Family Stone, and Santana symbolized the openness and youth-oriented solidarity of the counterculture. The experimental mind-set of the 1960's combined with a new black consciousness brought new black musical genres to prominence in the 1970's, from rock-influenced fusion and funk to Afro-Caribbean styles such as dub (a precursor of rap), ska, and reggae, a mixture of calypso and New Orleans rhythm and blues that evoked millennialist religion and black separatism in its lyrics. Meanwhile, the mainstream of black music was dominated by vocal rhythm and blues, which retained much of its early style while incorporating contemporary musical and social themes. From the lighter side of funk and rhythm and blues emerged disco, a predominantly white cultural phenomenon that nevertheless reflected the social diversity of the urban club scene, garnering special appeal among Latino and gay American communities.

Late Twentieth Century

During the last two decades of the twentieth century, African American music continued to demonstrate an eclecticism and image consciousness reflected in its history and exacerbated by the ever-increasing power of mass media. The 1980's and 1990's witnessed greater financial and creative empowerment of blacks in the American music industry, as music videos brought increased exposure for African American music and artists. Nevertheless, the marketing of black music retained its historical penchant for stereotyping: Despite the professed realism of hardcore rap, its images of violence and misogyny exploited white apprehension of and fascination with inner-city blacks; the enormous popularity of hip-hop—itself a multiplicity of styles—encouraged commercial stereotyping that at times echoed past images of carefree, rhythmic black people.

The history of African American music is one of increased popular acceptance and exposure accompanied by a decreased sense of identity. Black musical expression, once regarded as an exotic but exploitable raw material, gradually became yet another entry in the diverse lexicon of American music. Black music in the late twentieth century reflected the general eclecticism of the age as well as the obsession with formulas characteristic of the popular music industry; nevertheless, it remained significant as both a reflection and a determinant of American popular culture.   *Michael H. Burchett*

Core Resources

Robert Palmer's classic *Deep Blues* (New York: Viking, 1981) traces the development of African American music from its West African roots to modern rhythm and blues, exposing the continuous exchange between black and white musicians that shaped early American popular music. Samuel A. Floyd, in *The Power of Black Music* (New York: Oxford University Press, 1995), offers fresh insight into the linkage between African culture and American popular music. John Rublowski's *Black Music in America* (New York: Basic Books, 1971) catalogs some African and early African American musical instruments and styles. Chapter 14 of Edward Ayers's *The Promise of the New South* (New York: Oxford University Press, 1992) describes the musical environment that spawned ragtime, jazz, and blues in the late nineteenth century. For a discussion of the cultural impact of ragtime, see Edward Berlin's *King of Ragtime: Scott Joplin and His Era* (New York: Oxford University Press, 1995). Griel Marcus, in *Mystery Train*, fourth revised edition (New York: Plume, 1997), uses case studies of various artists to discuss contributions of black and white folk music to the development of rock and roll.

See also: African American literature; African American stereotypes; African Americans and film; Great Migration.

African American stereotypes

> **Significance:** A number of stereotypes regarding African Americans, positive and negative, impair intergroup relations because they cause people to view all African Americans as being the same rather than possessing individual traits and characteristics.

Over the years, a number of stereotypes have developed concerning African Americans. Some of these stereotypes—earth mother/mammy, natural musician, and super athlete—have basically positive connotations; however, others—Sambo, Uncle Tom, sexual predator, smart-mouthed but clever adolescent, welfare queen—have primarily negative connotations. Negative stereotypes are obviously detrimental, but even their positive counterparts are destructive and dangerous because they create the expectation that all members of a group will be able to achieve certain feats or will act in certain ways. These sorts of expectations place excessive pressure on those who cannot or do not want to live up to the stereotype.

Early Stereotypes

During slavery, blacks were often viewed as "Sambos," or mentally inferior, lazy people, usually cheerful and childlike, a characterization that made slavery more palatable to its practitioners. Three other early stereotypes cast

African American men as sexual predators ("bucks") or Uncle Toms and women as mammies, or nurturing earth mothers. Both whites and blacks used the term "Uncle Tom" to refer to an African American man (occasionally a woman) who gives in readily to demands made by members of the dominant white group. This term is often said to have originated with Harriet Beecher Stowe's 1852 novel *Uncle Tom's Cabin*; however, the term probably entered popular culture as a result of George L. Aiken's *Tom Shows* (1852), a crude and violent traveling show that presented caricatures of both slaves and slave owners.

The stereotypical depiction of an African American woman as a mammy, a sort of earth mother selflessly caring for children, probably originated because so many African American women cared for the children of white plantation owners. The mammy figure was popularized by Margaret Mitchell's 1936 novel *Gone with the Wind*, which was made into an Academy Award-winning movie.

Another early stereotype was the portrayal of African American men as sexual predators, or black "bucks," who would attack any white woman they encountered. This stereotype, born of white fears about the mixing of races, forced many African American men in the Deep South to be very careful in their attitude toward and dealings with white women from shortly after emancipation through the second half of the twentieth century. The slightest suspicion of sexual relations between a black man and white woman could mean legal problems and even physical danger (lynching) for an African American man.

Modern Stereotypes

In the second half of the twentieth century, some of the early stereotypes diminished in intensity and others persisted in a somewhat altered form. For example, although the Sambo image faded, African Americans were still commonly believed to be mentally inferior to whites. These old stereotypes were, however, joined by new ones that were adopted and popularized by the media. Typically, the African Americans who appeared in films and television programs in the 1950's and early 1960's portrayed one-dimensional characters who embodied common stereotypes.

One stereotype that developed in this period was of the African American as a super athlete. The success of African American athletes such as baseball player Willie Mays, football star Jim Brown, and boxers such as Joe Louis and Muhammad Ali (Cassius Clay) led many Americans to believe that all African Americans possessed super athletic abilities.

Another common stereotype viewed all African Americans as having a superior sense of rhythm that produced excellent music and made them skillful dancers. Although much of the music regarded as American—jazz, blues, gospel, and rock—has its origins in African American culture and thus can be regarded as a product of African Americans, it is a mistake to project this level of musical talent onto all members of the group. Also, the stereotype ignores the historical and cultural reasons behind the creation of these musical genres. Likewise, although some African Americans possess an excellent sense of rhythm and are extremely skilled dancers, not all members of the group are similarly talented.

A common stereotype often exploited by the media is that of the street-smart, wisecracking, slightly goofy male adolescent (or young adult) African American. This cynical, know-it-all attitude is common among teenage boys or young men,

One popular and persistent stereotype of an African American woman was as a mammy who selflessly devoted herself to the care of her master's children.

but the stereotype turns it into an African American characteristic, often depicting the young black adolescent as a gang member. Of course some African American adolescents belong to gangs but adolescents from numerous other racial and ethnic groups also join gangs.

The welfare queen—a woman who refuses to work and maintains an "upscale" lifestyle through unfair use of welfare—is a new twist on the stereotype that African Americans are slothful, childlike people. Welfare queens, usually single mothers, are depicted as lazy, perhaps immoral women who are having babies to increase the amount of their welfare check and to avoid working. In fact, in 1993, more white women were receiving welfare benefits than were African American women.

Annita Marie Ward

Core Resources

Louise Kidder discusses stereotypes in *The Psychology of Intergroup Relations: Conflict and Consciousness* (New York: McGraw-Hill, 1975). Barbara Rollock discusses the portrayal of African Americans in *The Black Experience in Children's Books* (New York: New York Public Library, 1984). Well-known journalist Carl Thomas Rowan tells what it is like to deal with racial barriers and stereotypes in *Breaking Barriers: A Memoir* (Boston: Little, Brown, 1991). Other books that deal with the African American experience and stereotypes include Frank L. Keegan's *Blacktown, USA* (Boston: Little, Brown, 1971), Gordon Parks's *Born Black* (Philadelphia: Lippincott, 1971), and Louise Meriwether's *Don't Ride the Bus on Mondays: The Rosa Parks Story* (Englewood Cliffs, N. J.: Prentice Hall, 1973).

See also: African Americans and film; Black "brute" and "buck" stereotypes; Prejudice and stereotyping; Stereotype; Stereotyping and the self-fulfilling prophecy; "Welfare queen" stereotype; Welfare stereotypes.

African American women

> **Significance:** African American women, who constitute the largest segment of the nonwhite population in the United States, as a group have done much to effect greater social equality based on race, gender, and social class.

In spite of the many social and economic hardships that African American women have endured in the more than four hundred years since they were brought to America, as a group they have made significant contributions to the United States, both to the survival and progress of the African American community and to the social and economic development of the larger society. The challenges that African American women have faced include slavery, segregation, and institutional race, gender, and class discrimination. Nevertheless, they have made notable accomplishments in education, politics, government, the social sciences, entertainment, human services, journalism, law, medicine, business, sports, and the military. African American women have also played a key role in sustaining vital institutions within the African American community, such as the African American family, the black church, black colleges and universities, and black-owned businesses. A major factor that has enabled African American women to continue to survive and progress despite enormous structural barriers is their strong sense of community. Their belief in strong kinship bonds and reliance on mutual aid networks, consisting of family, friends, and neighbors, have helped African American women to function as agents of social change.

Sociodemographic Characteristics

According to the 1990 U.S. Census, there were 16,138,000 African American females in the United States, constituting 6.6 percent of the population. When African American males are included, the entire African American population makes up 12 percent of the U.S. population. As a group, African American women have made strides in education over the years. In 1990, they had a median of 12.8 years of education and made up approximately 60 percent of the nearly 800,000 African Americans enrolled in colleges and universities in the United States. In 1990, 14.5 percent of all African American women graduated from college.

Although the number of African American women represented in white-collar occupations increased from the 1960's to the 1990's, the majority work at the lower end of the pay scale in these positions. Generally, African American women are employed in clerical, technical, retail sales, and administrative support positions. They continue to be underrepresented in professional and managerial positions and to be overrepresented in low-paying service occupations. In 1990, only 18.8 percent of African American women worked in professional and managerial positions, while 27 percent were employed in service occupations. Their income remained relatively low. In 1990, the median annual income for African American women was $8,327, compared with $10,316 for white women, $12,867 for African American men, and $21,169 for white men.

In spite of the social and economic gains that African Americans experienced in the 1960's and 1970's, African American women, along with African American men and children, continue to be overrepresented in the impoverished class. In fact, in 1990 the percentage of African Americans with incomes below the poverty level was 33 percent, compared to 11 percent for whites. Among the primary factors contributing to an inordinate number of African Americans having incomes below the poverty level are social policies that have resulted in occupational displacement and an inequality in economic and educational systems that has destabilized families and contributed to an increase in the rates of marital disruption. In 1990, 43.8 percent of African American families were headed by women. An inordinate number of these families maintained by women were poor.

Social and Economic Issues

African American women continue to be confronted with social and economic factors that impede their upward mobility in the United States. In many respects, various laws, policies, and practices have contributed to the marginal status of African American women. In spite of the fact that they have increased their participation in the private sector and government, they remain largely outside decision-making positions. Therefore, as workers, African American women are not well positioned to influence policies and practices that limit their full participation in the workplace. Other factors that continue to prevent African American women from experiencing social equality in the United States include negative cultural images, factory closings, the relocation of factories to foreign markets, business development outside central cities, lack of adequate funding for inner-city schools, federal cuts to financial aid to higher education, employment discrimination, and housing discrimination.

Cultural images that portray African American women negatively and suggest that they are better suited for domestic service and other low-paying, service-related occupations contribute significantly to the societal perception that African American women are intellectually incapable of assuming meaningful and responsible positions.

The decline in old-line industries such as the automobile and steel industries beginning in the 1970's, in conjunction with the relocation of many factories to foreign markets where labor is cheaper, has meant the occupational dislocation of many African American

Although African American women continue to be underrepresented in managerial positions, many black women, including these women meeting at the University of Dubuque in Iowa, have enjoyed success in the business community.

women and men who once depended on these industries. Living primarily in central cities, African American women have also been adversely affected by the trend of businesses moving from the central cities to suburban communities and other areas peripheral to cities. Given the fact that many cities do not have adequate mass-transit systems, many African American women, and their husbands, have lost their jobs because of their inability to travel to these locations.

The traditional funding of public schools is also a factor that affects how well African American girls are academically prepared and skilled in marketable technologies. When inner-city schools are compared with suburban schools, the former have inadequate resources, including facilities, textbooks, equipment, and other educational materials. The fact that property taxes serve as the primary source of funding for public schools means schools within the inner-city are economically disadvantaged in comparison with suburban schools. Federal cutbacks in aid to institutions of higher education have also lowered the participation and graduation rates of African American students.

Employment discrimination adversely affects the participation rates and mobility of African American workers. Employment discrimination manifests itself most frequently in the refusal of employers to hire African American women. These women also experience glass ceilings, in which employers limit how far they can rise within the company or agency. In addition, they face tokenism, whereby employers set a limit on the number of African American women whom they are willing to hire in order to meet affirmative action requirements.

Housing discrimination continues to affect African American women. In many communities, financial institutions use various, often insidious methods to refuse property loans to African American women. In addition, discrimination is directed against African Americans who rent. In the past, the most common practice found among savings and loan institutions to prevent African Americans from purchasing property was to retain their applications in the pending file until their contract on the property expired.

The Response of African American Women
African American women have challenged unjust policies and practices in courts, in legislatures, and before school boards and other policy-making bodies. They have done so through voting and other forms of political participation and by establishing schools, businesses, and civic organizations within their own communities. African American women have also challenged the television, film, and music industries to eliminate their negative and nonrepresentative images and messages and to replace them with positive imagery and accurate information.

African American women have recognized that while they have concerns that are unique because of race, gender, and social class, they also share common interests with women who are members of other racial and ethnic groups. Some of these issues are the need for affordable child care and health care, pay equity, and the need for policies and legislation that can eliminate race, gender, and class inequities within societal institutions.

K. Sue Jewell

Core Resources
Books on African American women and the issues that surround them include Angela Davis's *Women, Race, and Class* (New York: Random House, 1981) and K. Sue Jewell's *From Mammy to Miss America and Beyond: Cultural Images and the Shaping of U.S. Social Policy* (New York: Routledge, 1993). Three articles dealing with African American women and economics are Elizabeth Higginbotham's "We Were Never on a Pedestal: Women of Color Continue to Struggle with Poverty, Racism, and Sexism," in *For Crying out Loud: Women and Poverty in the United States* (New York: Pilgrim Press, 1986), edited by Rochelle Lefkowitz and Ann Withorn, Julianne Malveaux's "The Economic Interests of Black and White

Women: Are They Similar?" in *The Review of Black Political Economy* (13, Summer, 1985), and Margaret C. Simms's "Black Women Who Head Families: An Economic Struggle," in *Slipping Through the Cracks: The Status of Black Women* (New Brunswick, N.J.: Transaction Books, 1986), edited by Simms and Malveaux.

See also: Affirmative action; Colored Women's League; Discrimination: racial and ethnic; Education and African Americans; Employment among African Americans; Ethnic identities of women; Women and racism; Women of color.

African Americans and film

> **Significance:** Cinematic representations of African Americans have been the subject of debate and contest since the inception of the film industry. Struggles over stereotypes within film and over who controls the production of images of African Americans are firmly linked to broad cultural understandings and conceptions of race.

The social and political stakes of film for African Americans were dramatically expressed early on, in the reception of D. W. Griffith's 1915 film *Birth of a Nation*. As the first full-length feature film, *Birth of a Nation* helped inaugurate the studio system, and Griffith's work as director supplied some of the basic elements of cinematic grammar. The film represented African Americans in purely stereotypical roles (as happy and loyal slaves, mammies, bucks, and brutes) while glorifying the Ku Klux Klan. Because the film was released while lynching was at its peak, the material it treated raised some concern, and the National Association for the Advancement of Colored People (NAACP) protested the film. As Ed Guerrero notes in *Framing Blackness* (1993), screenings of the film were often preceded by people dressed as members of the Klan riding through towns, and there was a march of twenty-five thousand Klansmen through Atlanta, Georgia, on opening night. Although the NAACP was not able to prevent the film from being shown, it did succeed in bringing enough political and economic pressure to make Hollywood executives think twice before producing a film that celebrated organizations like the Klan.

Although *Birth of a Nation* may have presented an unusually virulent form of racism, stereotypical cinematic representations of African Americans would predominate in mainstream films for decades to come. However, these films never existed without contest or debate. Some African Americans believed that the best way to counter stereotypical representations was to protest in the courtrooms and streets; others decided to produce their own images. In the late 1920's and 1930's, a series of "race films" that were produced, written, and directed by blacks attempted to present more realistic images of African Americans. Oscar Micheaux was the most famous of these filmmakers, releasing thirty-four films during a thirty-year period. Micheaux and the other independent black filmmakers who were his contemporaries had very limited resources, and it was not always clear that their representations were any less stereotypical than those of their mainstream counterparts. Nevertheless, they did manage to address black themes and to provide exposure for a large number of black actors while explicitly addressing a black audience.

Impact of the Civil Rights and Black Power Movements
Although this early independent black film industry started to decline in the face of increased competition from Hollywood studios and the economic toll of the Great Depression, some of its concerns were eventually addressed by mainstream cinema. From the end of World War II through the 1960's, the Civil Rights and Black Power movements increasingly targeted Hollywood and helped create an environment in which some of the earlier depictions of African Americans were increasingly untenable. Stereotypes such as "mammies" and "bucks" never disappeared from Hollywood films, but they were eventually supplemented with more nuanced images of blacks. Although mainstream films in the years immediately after *Birth of a Nation* tended to support the ideals of segregation, Hollywood films in the 1950's and 1960's had an integrationist ethic, which was marked most clearly by the growing stardom of African American Sidney Poitier in such films as *Edge of the City* (1957) and *The Defiant Ones* (1958).

At the height of the Black Power movement, African American audiences expressed dissatisfaction with integrationist narratives that failed to address the contemporary realities of racism. This, coupled with black political power and the severe financial problems that were facing the Hollywood studios, led to a new wave of black-centered films that were released in the late 1960's and early 1970's and were labeled "blaxploita-tion" films because they were cheaply made and generally relied upon the same kinds of sexuality and violence that Hollywood used in its "exploitation" films.

Some of the most famous blaxploitation films, including *Sweet Sweetback's Baadasssss Song* (1971), *Shaft* (1972), and *Superfly* (1972), featured supermasculine black heroes who often had to fight against an oppressive social system. Occasionally, these heroes were women, including Tamara Dobson and Pam Grier in films such as *Cleopatra Jones* (1973) and *Coffy* (1973), who were just as macho as their male counterparts, Fred Williamson and Jim Brown. Although the depictions of strong African American heroes who were able to confront the problems surrounding them appealed to many blacks, the films were criticized and protested for their tendency to reproduce stereotypical images of African Americans as prostitutes, pimps, and violent drug dealers. By the mid-1970's, the genre had died out, as Hollywood studios discovered that they could court African American audiences without relying on black-centered films.

Backlash and Beyond
In the late 1970's and the 1980's, a conservative backlash against African American protests and gains (in the

Influential and sometimes controversial filmmaker Spike Lee, shown directing the 1996 film *Get on the Bus*, employs fully developed African American characters in films that deal with black issues.

cinema as well as in the broader society) produced a series of films that openly relied upon racial stereotypes. However, films in which African Americans are presented solely as stereotypical or peripheral figures (such as the *Rocky* series, 1976-1990, or *Caddyshack*, 1980) were eventually joined by a series of new black independent films made by people such as Robert Townsend and Spike Lee. Townsend's *Hollywood Shuffle* (1987) was an explicit critique of Hollywood's representations of African Americans. It follows the career of a young and talented black actor who finds that there is plenty of work available in Hollywood, but only in stereotypical roles, as pimps, muggers, and so on.

The most powerful African American filmmaker to emerge in the 1980's was Spike Lee. Lee's first commercial film, *She's Gotta Have It* (1986), which was criticized for its depiction of black sexuality and its apparent acceptance of a black woman's rape, nevertheless presented African Americans as fully realized human beings in a black-centered world. However, it was Lee's 1989 film *Do the Right Thing* that established him as one of the most important and influential directors of the decade. The film, which follows events that lead to the death of a black man at the hands of white police officers, had tremendous box-office success although it was also the subject of immense controversy. It is widely credited with enabling the success of a variety of 1990's black filmmakers such as Matty Rich, the Hughes Brothers, and John Singleton.

The 1990's saw a proliferation of black-centered mainstream and independent films. Some of the most interesting of these films (such as Cheryl Dunye's *The Watermelon Woman*, 1997, and John Singleton's *Rosewood*, 1997) were intended, in part, to question or correct Hollywood's past treatment of African Americans. Others, such as Kasi Lemmon's *Eve's Bayou* (1997), depict African American social worlds without any apology for the omission of white characters. Of course, African American characters were also present in a wide variety of films in which they were not always central to the narratives, and black stereotypes resurfaced and were reconfigured in seemingly endless varieties. *Just Cause* (1995) and *A Time to Kill* (1996) in particular are remarkable for the ways in which they critique, reconfigure, and redeploy the figure of the black brute/rapist. The tension between and within films in the 1990's serves as a condensed history of the always contested cinematic representations of African Americans.

Jonathan Markovitz

Core Resources
Donald Bogle's *Toms, Coons, Mulattoes, Mammies, and Bucks* (New York: Continuum, 1992) provides the most thorough investigation of African American stereotypes in film. Ed Guerrero's *Framing Blackness* (Philadelphia: Temple University Press, 1993) is an excellent analysis of the ways in which blacks have been defined by film and have struggled to define themselves in that medium. Robert Lang's *The Birth of a Nation* (New Brunswick, N.J.: Rutgers University Press, 1994) and Fred Silva's edited collection *Focus on "The Birth of the Nation"* (Englewood Cliffs, N.J.: Prentice-Hall, 1971) provide extended discussions of the importance and legacy of *Birth of a Nation*. Lisa M. Anderson's *Mammies No More* examines changing cultural representations of black women.

See also: African American literature; African American music; African American stereotypes; African American women; Black "brute" and "buck" stereotypes; Ku Klux Klan; Lynchings.

African Americans in the Civil War

> **Significance:** Both the North and the South relied upon African Americans to support the war effort. In the South, African American service raised doubts concerning the role of blacks in Southern society, especially when many Southerners recommended the use of slaves as soldiers. In the North, blacks pointed to their military service as proof that they deserved equal treatment under the law.

President Abraham Lincoln initially regarded the Civil War (1861-1865) as a means to preserve the Union, so he rejected calls for African American military service. He feared that black troops would alienate the border states and harden the Southern commitment to the war. However, the advancing Union armies were magnets for escaped slaves, and officers soon used African Americans as laborers. In 1862, some officers began recruiting former slaves as soldiers without government permission. In July, 1862, Congress authorized the president to use black troops, but it was not until the release of the Emancipation Proclamation in January, 1863, that Lincoln allowed for the enlistment of African American soldiers.

Military Service
Approximately 180,000 African Americans served in the Union army during the war, with an estimated 37,000 losing their lives in combat or to disease. Another 29,000 African Americans served as seamen, making up a quarter of the Union navy. Because of Northern discriminatory attitudes, black soldiers and sailors often performed

Company E of the 4th U.S. Colored Troops assembles at Fort Lincoln in 1865. African Americans served in both the Union and the Confederate armies during the Civil War.

manual labor, releasing white soldiers for combat duty. Given the opportunity, however, African Americans fought valiantly. Black Union soldiers met the enemy in 449 separate engagements. They faced great risks from Confederate soldiers who were outraged at the sight of an African American in uniform. At Fort Pillow, Tennessee, and Poison Spring, Arkansas, rebel troops murdered African Americans who were attempting to surrender. At war's end, sixteen soldiers and four seamen had been awarded the Congressional Medal of Honor. Many black soldiers remained in the military, serving in western units. Native Americans soon dubbed them "Buffalo soldiers" because their hair resembled that of the buffalo.

Although the navy was integrated, African Americans who enlisted in the army served in segregated units, often under white officers who had little respect for them. African Americans were not permitted to become officers until 1865, and only about one hundred of them obtained commissions. Because they were regarded as laborers, African Americans received less pay than white soldiers. They received ten dollars per month minus three dollars for clothing, while whites earned thirteen dollars a month plus a clothing allowance. This situation led to increasing resentment in the later years of the war

as blacks saw more combat. When William Walker refused to report for duty until his pay was equal to that of white soldiers, he was court-martialed. Found guilty of mutiny, he was executed by a firing squad in March, 1864. Three months later, Congress approved the equalization of pay rates with retroactive pay through the beginning of 1864. Soldiers who could prove they were free as of April 19, 1861, were permitted retroactive pay for service in 1862 and 1863, which meant that many former slaves were not eligible for the back pay. Shrewd officers got around this unfair provision by having black soldiers swear that they did not owe anyone labor on that day, an oath that former slaves could honestly take.

In addition to military service, African Americans assisted the Union war effort by performing many other duties. Approximately 200,000 African Americans served as nurses, cooks, teamsters, or laborers. Slaves fleeing to the Union forces often provided valuable information regarding troop movement and terrain.

The Confederacy

When war broke out in 1861, a small number of free African Americans in the South, motivated by a sense of regional loyalty, volunteered to enlist in the Confederate army. Some of these men served in military units during the war. Although they never saw combat, two Louisiana regiments of African Americans called the Native Guards drilled with the state militia. However, the notion of African Americans serving in the military contradicted the belief in white superiority, and the Confederate government officially prohibited African Americans from military service until March, 1865. At that time, desperation prompted the government to approve the enlistment of 300,000 slaves in the army. Because the war ended only a month later, very few African Americans actually served in the Confederate army.

Despite the ban on military service, African Americans played a crucial role in the Southern war effort. They provided support for the military, cooking food, working in field hospitals, and performing manual labor such as digging trenches and building roads. Because African Americans completed these essential tasks, white soldiers were not diverted from combat duty. The Confederate navy also made use of African Americans, usually as firemen, cooks, and laborers. Moses Dallas, an inland pilot, guided a Confederate force in a successful attack on a Union gunboat in 1864. Robert Smalls, a slave who worked on an armed ship, the *Planter*, brought his family on board and sailed the vessel out of port while the officers were ashore. Smalls surrendered the ship to the Union navy and became a hero for his efforts.

African Americans also worked in the industries that supplied the army. They worked alongside whites in the iron mines, composing approximately half the labor force at the Tredegar Iron Works in Richmond, Virginia, and an estimated 20 percent of the workers in the Confederate Ordnance Department were black. Perhaps the most important role that African Americans played during the war was on the home front. As whites left the farms and plantations to fight in battle, the Confederacy became dependent upon African Americans for the production of agricultural products.   *Thomas Clarkin*

Core Resources

Benjamin Quarles's *The Negro in the Civil War* (Boston: Little, Brown, 1953) provides an overview of African American experiences during the war. Noah Andre Trudeau's *Like Men of War: Black Troops in the Civil War, 1862-1865* (Boston: Little, Brown, 1998), examines African American actions in specific battles. James M. McPherson's *The Negro in the Civil War* (New York: Vintage Books, 1965) includes documents and statements from the Civil War era.

See also: Civil War; Emancipation Proclamation; Military and racial/ethnic relations; Military desegregation.

African Canadians

> **Significance:** Although African-Canadians are a small minority in Canada, they have a long history that links at least three continents. Moreover, though they are a family tree with many roots and branches whose existence was long kept secret, they have played active roles defending English authority and protesting Canadian racism and continue to make significant contributions to society.

Canada's first black immigrant arrived in 1628, when a nameless six-year-old boy from Madagascar (later baptized Olivier LeJeune) became the property of David Kirke, an English privateer who conducted raids on the French colony of the Saint Lawrence. Institutional slavery accounted for the growth of blacks in what was New France before the English conquest. Blacks from the Caribbean plantations were bought and sold, and others entered the country during trade with Louisiana. Between 1628 and 1783, almost all blacks in Canada were slaves. By 1760, the slave population totaled twelve hundred. When the British took control in 1763, slave auctions in Nova Scotia were given prominent newspaper publicity, along with notices about slave runaways and rewards for their recapture. During the American Revolution, American blacks moved into Canada, attracted by promises of land, freedom, and equal rights in exchange for loyalty to the British cause. When some three thousand black Loyalists arrived in 1783, most settling in Nova Scotia and New Brunswick, some in Ontario and Quebec, the total black population reached five thousand (including fifteen hundred slaves). Though only a small percentage of the black Loyalists actually received land, and blacks were often sold as slaves to Canadian Indians, black loyalty ran high in the American Revolution. During the war, the Black Pioneers, a regiment from Shelburne, fought for the English in the belief that British North America was a safe haven.

In 1796, 600 Jamaican Maroons (escaped slaves) were brought to Halifax. They helped build the Citadel, but disenchanted with their poor financial lot, 550 of them (including about 60 children) set sail for Sierra Leone in 1800, right in the wake of the first Back to Africa movement in January, 1792, when approximately 1,196 blacks (chiefly from New Brunswick and Nova Scotia) left Halifax in sixteen ships. Neither these events nor a third, small exodus to Trinidad in 1820 of 95 refugee blacks affected Canada's reputation as a haven for blacks, especially during and after the War of 1812, when from her base in Saint Catherines, fugitive slave Harriet Tubman ran the Underground Railroad, an informal network of "safe" routes and sanctuaries for runaway slaves. Between 1815 and 1860, roughly 50,000 of these fugitives remained in Canada, and after the official abolition of slavery, some of them became sharecroppers or tenant farmers for the English Loyalists, and others served as tradespeople or apprentices.

West Indians

Between the Civil War and 1900, Canada accepted blacks only in emergency situations. Because the western provinces needed settlers, 1,500 experienced black Oklahoma farmers were allowed into the prairies between 1909 and 1911. With the outbreak of World War I, the nation was more interested in nationalism and patriotism than in black rights, prompting an exodus of 2,000 blacks after the war, chiefly to northern U.S. cities and Harlem, New York. This loss was partially offset by the arrival of small groups of West Indian immigrants who settled in the east, particularly Ontario, Quebec, and the Maritimes.

Up to the 1960's, West Indian immigration was only a small percentage of total Canadian immigration because of tight restrictions based on ethnic affiliation. For example, a law prevented the entrance of black Jamaicans but not white ones. After pressure from England (which had adopted an open-door policy in 1948) and the Caribbean, Canada, as a Commonwealth partner, had to relax its immigration policies. In 1955, the West Indian Domestic Scheme allowed 100 women to enter each year from Jamaica and Barbados to work as contracted domestics. By 1965, 2,700 had been admitted. In 1967, Canada fine-tuned a framework established in 1962, which became known as the points system, whereby all immigrants, regardless of country of origin, were to be assessed according to education and training, occupational skills, arranged employment, knowledge of French and English, family sponsorship in Canada, and employment opportunities in areas of destination. Subsequently, the black population more than doubled. The peak years of West Indian immigration were 1960 to 1990; this influx represented 3.34 percent of total Canadian immigration in the 1960's, 11.02 percent in the 1970's, and 9.49 percent in the 1980's. Most West Indians originated from Jamaica, Trinidad, Guyana, Haiti, and Barbados. The West Indians outnumbered expatriate blacks from England and the United States as well as immigrants from Africa.

Diverse Origins

Although the term "African Canadian" is used to describe all black immigrants to Canada, not all black Canadians wish to be collectively identified by the term: Jamaicans prefer not to be grouped with blacks from Africa; black immigrants from the United States or Britain have little in common with those from Trinidad or Guyana. Some Caribbean blacks prefer to be identified as Indo-Afro Caribbean Canadians, an unwieldy preference that has a revealing ethnological significance. In addition, some Africans do not like to see the word "African" applied to people born outside Africa.

Canadians from Africa include blacks from West, East, and South Africa, and Ethiopia; South African whites and Portuguese; and Asian Indians of Muslim, Hindu, and Christian backgrounds. Black Africans are a very small group in Canada, partly because Canadian immigration policy has not favored African or Asian applicants. By 1925, when Canada's population had nearly doubled, mainly because of an influx of whites from Europe and the United States, blacks were discouraged from entering. From 1946 to 1950, Africans made up only 0.03 percent of new immigrants, with the figure rising an average of only 1 percent to 2 percent over the next twenty years. From 1968 to 1970, following the White Paper on Immigration, the average rose to approximately 2 percent of total immigration, with Nigerians and Ghanaians preferred to other Africans because of their education and skills. The highest number of Africans came between 1972 and 1980, chiefly Ugandan Asians (7,000 in 1972-1973) fleeing Idi Amin's dictatorship, and Portuguese and English settlers from Angola, Mozambique, and Zimbabwe after these

Canadians celebrate their Caribbean heritage on this float in the Caribana festival. Many African Canadians trace their ancestry to the West Indies.

three countries achieved independence. Also, between 1973 and 1983, some 16,000 South Africans, mainly non-black, entered Canada, with an additional 321 arriving in 1984. The same year, Canada accepted 684 Ethiopian refugees, most sponsored by the federal government rather than private sources. The Green Paper on Immigration in 1976, which curtailed the entry of immigrants from the so-called independent classes, allowed those who were already in Canada to sponsor close relatives. Between 1950 and 1985, more than 100,000 immigrants entered Canada from Africa, including persons of European and Asian descent. Most African immigrants came from English-speaking colonies, and a smaller number from French-speaking regions, chiefly Mali, Senegal, Zaire, the Malagasy Republic, and the Ivory Coast. About one-third of all these people spoke African languages (such as Ashanti, Hausa, Yoruba, Ibo, Kru, Sotho, Tswana, and Zulu).

Economic Life

Early in African Canadian history, black Loyalists, Maroons, and refugees were extremely vulnerable to exploitation and discrimination in employment and wages. Lacking high education and professional skills, they were forced to perform manual labor. Those who had been promised free land discovered that the small plots allotted to them were inadequate to support their agricultural efforts, so these settlers were also compelled to find menial jobs in neighboring white towns. Those black immigrants who fled discrimination in California were able to settle in Victoria, British Columbia, because their savings and business skills enabled them to operate small businesses. The black Oklahoma farmers who migrated to the prairies were viewed as a "black problem." Until well into the twentieth century, most black immigrants from the West Indies, England, and United States performed low-paying services as unskilled laborers. During and soon after World War I, many blacks found work as industrial laborers in the Maritimes, and others were hired as railway porters in Montreal and Toronto. In 1955, the West Indian Domestic Scheme allowed one hundred women per year from Jamaica and Barbados to work as servants, a frustrating experience for most who had been successful professionals (teachers, nurses, office workers) in their home countries. However, their contracts as domestics allowed them to apply for landed immigrant status after a year, which enabled them to move around the country freely and sponsor family members. The points system (instituted in 1967) encouraged well-educated black West Indians to flock into the country. This economic history has produced very wealthy blacks, middle-class blacks, and extremely poor blacks, much the way Canadian society as a whole divides itself according to economic level.

Social and Cultural Life

In the nineteenth and early twentieth centuries, black Canadians were caricatured as minstrels or as pleasure-seeking, irresponsible, sexual beasts, incapable of cultural assimilation. Paradoxically portrayed as dependent yet threatening, they were compelled to retreat into ghettos. In Toronto, for instance, in 1851, about one thousand blacks lived in the northwest section, eight hundred of whom were fugitive slaves. City directories specified those residences and businesses that were owned by blacks, and interracial socialization was discouraged. The existence of black slavery and subjugation in Canada was largely denied or blamed on the Americans.

In the early days of the color bar, the chief means of support were the Christian churches that were segregated not only along sectarian lines but also along color lines. Many fraternal organizations, mutual-assistance groups, and temperance societies were formed, and almost all were associated with the churches, whose leaders often led demonstrations and made petitions to various levels of government on issues of racial inequality and injustice. Gradually, individual provinces took decisive action, as in the cases of Saskatchewan's first Bill of Rights (1947) and Ontario's Racial Discrimination Act (1944) and Human Rights Code (1961). By the mid-1970's, all major Canadian cities had active black groups such as the Congress of Black Women, the National Black Coalition, and the British Columbia Association for the Advancement of Colored People. However, despite considerable advances, blacks continue to view school boards and the police with suspicion. School segregation ended in 1965 when Ontario's last such school closed, but new immigrants from Africa and the Caribbean find that their strong dialects put them at a disadvantage in English and other subjects requiring strong language skills, so much so that many of them are improperly streamed into vocational subject areas rather than academic ones. As far as the law is concerned, blacks respect Canada's record of human rights while decrying many instances of police brutality, harassment, and racially motivated prosecution.

The sociocultural life of African Canadians is becoming increasingly entrenched through black municipal councillors, school trustees and administrators, urban multicultural organizations and carnivals (such as Toronto's annual Caribana Festival), and university chairs in black studies. Cultural styles (including those of worship, music, speech, and family structure) have developed in response to conditions in Canada. Urbanization and increasing secularization have changed the roles of the church and local community. Blacks have leaders in virtually all walks of life, from politics and the arts to pop entertainment and sports. Some famous

African Canadians include Lincoln Alexander (first black lieutenant-governor of Ontario), Donovan Bailey (sports—track), Salome Bey (music), Dionne Brand (poetry), Rosemary Brown (politics), Austin Clarke (fiction), Ferguson Jenkins (baseball), Dudley Laws (radical politics), and Oscar Peterson (music).   *Keith Garebian*

Core Resources

Ken Alexander and Avis Glaze, in *The African-Canadian Experience* (Toronto: Umbrella Press, 1996), note that Canadian society is changing quickly, although freedom, justice, peace, and equality can be taken away or redefined to frustrate black aspiration; they address the question of whether Canada's black community will be split along the lines of its American counterpart (West Indians and other African Americans). One of the best available sources for black Canadian history is Robin W. Winks's *The Blacks in Canada: A History* (Montreal: McGill-Queen's University Press, 1971); it is filled with statistics and useful sociological facts.

See also: African American stereotypes; Afro-Caribbeans; Immigration law: Canada; Jamaican Americans; Slavery: history; Slavery: North American beginnings; Underground Railroad; West Indian Americans.

African Liberation Day

In 1963, thirty-one African heads of state convened in Ethiopia for the Summit Conference of the Independent African States, with the overall goal of freeing African people from the yoke of European domination and white supremacy. On May 25, 1963, the Charter of the Organization of African Unity was signed, and it was decided to celebrate African Liberation Day (ALD) every year on May 25. Sponsored by the All African People's Revolutionary Party, ALD has led to the concerted action of the member states of the Organization of African Unity to pool financial aid to revive, strengthen, and intensify liberation movements throughout Africa. As much as possible, the goal is to end exploitation and oppression of Africans at home and abroad by finding peaceful solutions through deliberations and frank exchange of views among the nations that are involved.

ALD has become an institution throughout the African world, being a day when all African people rally for unity and denounce racism, capitalism, and Zionism. On ALD, African people focus on what they share—their common past, set of problems, and future—as they pause to think about the plight of their African brothers who are under foreign rule and who are seeking to win their freedom and fundamental human rights.

Alvin K. Benson

See also: All African People's Revolutionary Party; Black nationalism; Pan-Africanism.

Afro-Caribbeans

> **Significance:** African slaves imported to the Caribbean Islands developed a unique Creole culture, rich in African heritage but infused with European notions of white supremacy that encouraged internal racism among Afro-Caribbeans.

The Caribbean Islands were the birthplace of African slavery in the New World; between 1518 and 1860, millions of Africans were imported to the islands to work the extensive sugar plantations operated by European colonials. Around 43 percent of Africans transported to the Western Hemisphere were sold as slaves in the Caribbean; less than 5 percent of these Africans were imported to the United States and Canada. Africans greatly outnumbered whites and natives on most Caribbean islands and therefore were able to forge their own cultural identities. These Creole cultures, which varied from island to island, combined Old World African folkways and elements of European and native language, religion, and customs to create a common framework from which to unite the diverse tribes of transplanted Africans. The harshness of Caribbean plantation life and the resultant high death rate among Caribbean slaves necessitated a constant flow of human cargo from Africa, ensuring the continued presence of strong African elements in island Creole cultures. Nevertheless, the influence of dominant European colonial societies continued to permeate the social, spiritual, and economic lives of Afro-Caribbeans long after slavery ended in the 1860's.

Modern Afro-Caribbeans

The demoralizing effect of centuries of bondage and cultural alienation left Afro-Caribbean cultures susceptible to the influence of colonial value systems and social norms once the institution of slavery collapsed. Free Afro-Caribbean communities became structured along rigid lines of socioeconomic caste, based primarily upon the skin color and reputed ancestry of individuals and families. Many Afro-Caribbeans began to deny or downplay their African roots and to claim European colonial heritage and ancestry. Under this system, light-skinned Afro-Caribbeans of modest economic means were placed above their darker counterparts, and dark-skinned individuals who attained wealth often gained entry into the whiter upper castes.

The system of "shading" that defined social hierarchy in Afro-Caribbean societies often affected these societies' perceptions of fellow Caribbeans. For example, residents of the Dominican Republic, although clearly of mixed European and African descent, traditionally identified themselves as "Spanish" while invariably classifying neighboring Haitians as "black." Economic and social discrimination against Haitian immigrants to the Dominican Republic is exemplary of the internal racism that accompanied massive internal and interisland migration in the Caribbean during the first half of the twentieth century. Rural (and often darker-skinned) Afro-Caribbeans migrating to urban areas and immigrants from poorer (and more Africanized) countries were often consigned to the most squalid living conditions and the least desirable employment.

An Afro-Caribbean woman celebrates at the Caribbean Day Festival in New York City.

In the aftermath of World War II, a new black political consciousness, influenced by labor and Civil Rights movements in the United States, began to emerge in the Caribbean in opposition to the old colonial social order. By this time, many Afro-Caribbeans had been exposed to strains of racial and economic protest from the United States, most notably in the teachings of black separatist Marcus Garvey, who inspired the Rastafarian movement in Jamaica. By the postwar era, Afro-Caribbean workers and intellectuals had joined forces with Garveyites to form labor unions; by the 1960's, many of these unions had been transformed into black-dominated political parties, winning significant elections in Guiana, Trinidad, and Jamaica.

Afro-Caribbeans in the United States

Afro-Caribbean migration to North America predates the American Revolution. Slave trading between Caribbean and mainland colonies brought substantial numbers of Afro-Caribbeans to North American port cities and exerted a palpable Caribbean influence upon slave and free black cultures; free Afro-Caribbean immigrants to North America attained notoriety in the black communities of New Orleans and other port cities. However, the bulk of Afro-Caribbean immigration to the United States took place in the twentieth century, with more than five million people of African descent migrating from the Caribbean to the United States between 1945 and 1990. Among these immigrants were many thousands of "boat people" from Cuba and Haiti, who fled their native countries in search of political asylum or economic opportunity. Thousands more arrived by more conventional means, blending into the large Caribbean American communities in Eastern urban areas. Although many established permanent residence in the United States, it is estimated that around 80 percent of Caribbean immigrants to the United States in the latter half of the twentieth century were seasonal workers who returned to their home countries.

Afro-Caribbean immigrants have exerted a profound influence on the cities and labor force of the United States, posing challenges to its social structure, educational system, and notions of assimilation and diversity. Homegrown racial prejudices have formed the crux of many of these challenges; many light-skinned Afro-Caribbeans, regarded as whites in their home countries, experienced racial discrimination for the first time in their lives upon migration to the United States. Immigrants from relatively homogenous Caribbean societies often encountered ethnic groups with whom they had had little or no previous contact, such as Mexican, Asian, and African Americans, sparking occasional cultural clashes and social tensions. Groups of Afro-Caribbean immigrants have occasionally clashed with each other, as did Cuban Americans and Haitian Americans in Miami during the 1980's. Despite occasional difficulties, various groups of Afro-Caribbeans established thriving communities in major metropolitan areas of the eastern and southern United States after World War II—most notably the Cuban American enclaves of Miami and the

"Nuyorican" community of Puerto Ricans in New York City. These communities have contributed greatly to the cultural and political framework of eastern urban areas and the United States as a whole.   *Michael H. Burchett*

Core Resources
Peter Winn, in *Americas: The Changing Face of Latin America* (New York: Pantheon Books, 1992), provides ample information on Afro-Caribbean migration to the United States and its effect on American society. In *Africans in the Americas: A History of the Black Diaspora* (New York: St. Martin's Press, 1994), Michael L. Conniff and Thomas J. Davis compare and contrast the development of Afro-Caribbean and African American societies. Sidney W. Mintz and Richard Price discuss continuity between African and Afro-Caribbean cultures in *The Birth of African-American Culture* (Boston: Beacon Press, 1992). For a discussion of the political and cultural impact of Afro-Caribbean literature, see Patrick Taylor's *The Narrative of Liberation* (Ithaca, N.Y.: Cornell University Press, 1989).

See also: African Canadians; Cuban Americans; Dominican Americans; Haitians and Haitian refugees; Jamaican Americans; Puerto Rico; West Indian Americans.

Afrocentrism

A philosophy of historical analysis and education put forth by Molefi Kete Asante, professor of African American studies at Temple University, in his works *The Afrocentricity Idea* (1987), *Afrocentricity* (1988), and *Kemet, Afrocentricity, and Knowledge* (1990). In these works, Asante defines Afrocentrism as the perspective on history that allows students to observe the world from the point of view of the African and African American. Asante created Afrocentrism as a reaction to "Eurocentric" interpretations of history, which, in Asante's view, marginalize ethnic and racial minorities by portraying them as victims and passive participants in European-dominated history. Asante's philosophy advocates a "multi-centered multiculturalism" in which all racial groups are encouraged to write history from their perspective to replace the "monocentric," or European-dominated, historical perspective. Asante's philosophy does not advocate the elimination of the European perspective but rather invites the European perspective to be presented alongside the interpretations of other racial groups. Opponents of the Afrocentric model, however, accuse Asante and his supporters of historical inaccuracy and of using history to promote a racist political agenda. The philosophy of Afrocentrism borrows heavily from the writings of Carter G. Woodson, Asa Hilliard, and Cheikh Anta Diop.
Jason Pasch

See also: Ethnic studies programs; Eurocentrism; Multiculturalism.

Aid to Families with Dependent Children

By 1930, mothers' pension programs, which provided meager financial support to poor children in their homes, were in effect in most states for widows and divorced women with children. These programs were funded through counties or cities and served only a limited number of women, few of which were African Americans. Those women who received aid had to undergo a grueling and humiliating investigation to prove their character and "fitness" to have custody of their children.

In 1935, President Franklin D. Roosevelt signed into law the Social Security Act, part of which established Aid to Dependent Children (ADC). ADC shifted care for dependent children to the federal government and the states from the cities and localities. The original law provided aid for children up to the age of sixteen in families where the breadwinner was disabled or unemployed or even underemployed. ADC was limited, until 1961, to single-parent families. However, ADC entitlements often remained linked to the character and moral fitness of the primary caretaker, most often a single mother. As the program evolved, states created rules that denied aid to unwed mothers, African American women, or those women whose lifestyles did not adhere to the community's mores.

Congress, from the beginning, appropriated fewer funds and established lower matching and reimbursement rates for ADC than other public assistance programs. A 1962 amendment to the Social Security Act, Section 1115, gave the states free rein to experiment with the renamed program, Aid to Families with Dependent Children (AFDC). That same year, federal law allowed states to require adult recipients to work in order to qualify for aid for themselves and their children. Work and training programs became a focus of "helping the poor to help themselves" in the late 1960's and in the 1970's; these programs were limited in scope, however, and were often punitive rather than helpful. In the 1960's and early 1970's, the National Welfare Rights Organization, under the leadership of Johnnie Tillmon, a welfare mother, helped publicize the idea that AFDC was a basic, fundamental human right.

Although AFDC provided some money and services to mothers and children in desperate need, the bureaucracy and stigma attached to welfare cut deep into a woman's pride and self-esteem. Since every state provided only enough funds to AFDC recipients to help them exist below the poverty level, the program contributed to the "feminization of poverty."

Public attitudes toward the poor and destitute continue to be negative and punitive; many people believe that being poor in the United States has more to do with character than with economic and social issues. This often causes single mothers to be accused of being morally deficient and lazy.

In August, 1996, Congress passed the Personal Responsibility and Work Opportunity Reconciliation Act. The law, effective October 1, 1996, gave states authority over AFDC, food stamps, and Supplemental Security Income (SSI). Federal guidelines limited able-bodied welfare recipients to two years of benefits and five years over a lifetime.   *Candace E. Andrews*

See also: Poverty and race; "Welfare queen" stereotype; Welfare reform: impact on racial/ethnic relations; Welfare's impact on racial/ethnic relations; Work ethic.

AIDS conspiracy theory

Various media polls taken during the 1980's and 1990's showed that approximately one-third of African Americans believed in the AIDS conspiracy theory—that the acquired immunodeficiency syndrome (AIDS) is caused by a virus engineered to eliminate nonwhite populations. Another third of those polled were not sure, and the remainder did not believe in a conspiracy. Stories of accidental or deliberate development of the human immunodeficiency virus (HIV) and its dissemination among nonwhite populations have been dismissed by health officials and scientific researchers.

African Americans' suspicions were fueled, in part, by public scrutiny of the Tuskegee experiment (1932-1972), in which treatment for syphilis was withheld from poor black men in order to study the natural consequences of the disease. A leading doctor for the Nation of Islam has also promoted the idea that the U.S. government invented HIV/AIDS to eliminate blacks. In 1997, a black American biochemist attempted to stop a polio vaccination campaign in Ghana by claiming that the polio vaccine and other drugs being shipped to Africa from the United States might contain the virus. He claimed the West wanted to wipe out black Africans in order to obtain the many rich resources found on the African continent.

AIDS conspiracy theorists cite as evidence the similarities between HIV and other viruses and testimony by a Pentagon official to Congress in 1969 requesting funding for development of a biological warfare agent to attack the human immune system. One version of the conspiracy theory is that a new virus was developed and tested on prisoners who participated in the experiment in exchange for early release. The researchers did not recognize the long incubation period for HIV infection and released the apparently healthy prisoners. Many went to New York City, where they later became ill. The former prisoners passed the virus to others through homosexual activity. Another version of this story is that the virus was deliberately released among the poor and disenfranchised as a form of genocide.

HIV is, in fact, quite similar to a number of viruses, including HTLV-1 (a leukemia virus) and SIV (a virus that infects monkeys). Genetic and HIV/AIDS researchers refute the conspiracy theory on a number of grounds. First, they say it was not technologically possible nor was it practical to engineer as complex a virus as HIV in the late 1960's and early 1970's. Second, given what is known about the sequence of genes in HIV, it is not possible to splice known viruses together to produce this sequence. Finally, the thrust of research into biological weapons in the 1970's was not on splicing viruses but on other techniques.

Public health officials are concerned that people who believe in the conspiracy theory are less likely to get tested for HIV or to take appropriate precautions to avoid exposure to others' body fluids. Early identification of HIV carriers allows them to be started on medications that prolong the period before they develop symptoms of AIDS.   *Rebecca Lovell Scott*

See also: Genocide: physical; Tuskegee experiment.

Alaska Native Brotherhood and Alaska Native Claims Settlement

In Sitka in 1912, thirteen native Alaskans formed the Alaska Native Brotherhood (ANB) in order to obtain citizenship for Alaska natives. The founders, heavily influenced by Presbyterian missionaries, in addition to fighting for civil rights, urged the abandonment of traditional native languages and customs, a position the organization reversed in the 1960's.

The ANB was active in the pursuit of voting rights and citizenship for Alaska Natives. In 1922, an ANB leader and attorney, William Paul, successfully defended his great-uncle Chief Shakes against the felony charge of voting illegally, thus winning the right to vote two years before Congress passed the Indian Citizenship Act in 1924.

The brotherhood led a series of boycotts against businesses that discriminated against natives and in 1946 lobbied successfully for the passage of the Antidiscrimination Act by the territorial legislature. It also successfully lobbied Congress to extend the 1934 Indian Reorganization Act to include Alaska. This contributed significantly to economic development in southeastern Alaska by enabling several native villages to apply for federal loans to purchase fishing boats and canneries. The brotherhood's organized efforts to secure land rights for Alaska Natives were a precursor to the Alaska Native Claims Settlement Act of 1971.

Although Alaska had been part of the United States since 1867, treaties had established only six small reservations in southeastern Alaska. The vast majority of Alaska's eighty thousand natives continued to claim aboriginal title (and therefore fishing, hunting, and other land rights) to the 400 million acres that make up the state of Alaska. A number of land use and aboriginal rights controversies in the 1960's led to the creation of the Alaska Federation of Natives (AFN) in October, 1966. The AFN carried out most of the formal negotiations and lobbying leading up to the signing of the Alaska Native Claims Settlement Act (ANCSA) on December 18, 1971.

The act extinguished native title to all but 44 million acres of land in exchange for $962.5 million. The previously established reservations and the existing tribal governments were dissolved, and twelve regional and more than two hundred village corporations were created to replace them. The twelve regional corporations, corresponding to historical and cultural groupings of Alaska Natives, divided the land and the $962.5 million. A thirteenth corporation, established for natives living outside the state, received cash only. Of the land received, half was to be conveyed to the village corporations within each region. A portion of the cash settlement was also to be shared with the village corporations empowered to develop and operate community businesses. Because the regional corporations were expected to invest in more grandiose enterprises, they were given greater powers to develop land and to tax those operating within their zones. Both regional and village corporations were expected to make a profit for their native shareholders.

Initially, the act provided for stock ownership only for those natives born prior to the date of enactment. It also established a twenty-year period during which corporate lands and profits could not be taxed and individual stocks could not be sold. This moratorium was set to expire in 1991, creating fears that the corporations and the lands they held would become vulnerable to nonnative corporate raiders or be sold to satisfy debts. Congress responded by amending the act in 1988. The amendment provided for the establishment of "settlement trusts" to which corporate lands may be conveyed. The

trusts, and therefore the land held by them, cannot be transferred from native control. Congress also permitted the corporations to amend their own articles of incorporation in order to issue new stock to those born after 1971 and to prevent the sale of stock to outsiders.

See also: Indian Citizenship Act; Indian Reorganization Act.

Alcatraz Island occupation

During the turbulent 1960's, Native Americans began to demand self-determination, better housing, better medical care, more jobs and educational opportunities, and recognition of treaty obligations. Broken promises and delays in attaining these objectives fueled an activism among urban and rural American Indians. Alcatraz Island, site of a federal prison that closed in 1963, became an opportunity to expose and redress their grievances.

On March 9, 1964, five Sioux, led by a descendant of Crazy Horse, claimed the island under the terms of the Treaty of Fort Laramie of 1868, which allowed American Indians to claim abandoned federal property that had once been tribal land. They occupied the island for only four hours and left it under threat of arrest.

On November 9, 1969, under the leadership of Richard Oakes and Adam Nordwall (also known as Adam Fortunate Eagle), fourteen Native Americans landed on the island and held it for nineteen hours. Before their forced expulsion, the tribe members recounted their grievances and claimed the island on behalf of Indians of All Tribes.

On November 20, 1969, eighty-nine American Indians from a number of tribes took over the island for a third time. A much more organized and prepared group, they held the island for nineteen months. During their stay, they elected a council that assigned such daily operational duties as security, laundry, cooking, and sanitation to individuals. They established a preschool and day-care center and offered classes in Indian beadwork, leathercraft, and woodworking. Emotional and financial support for their cause grew, as well-known actors, writers, and others became involved. The population of the island fluctuated, ranging up to about one thousand.

The Indians met with federal negotiators and demanded recognition of their ownership of Alcatraz and establishment of an educational and cultural center for Native American studies. Federal negotiators rejected these demands and countered with offers that included providing appropriations to build a park that would contain a museum and trading post. The Indians re-

A group of American Indians stand under an altered property sign on Alcatraz Island, which they seized in 1969 and held until 1971.

jected these proposals as not meeting their demand for self-determination.

The Indians' frustration with the government's refusal to meet their demands, along with internal friction among the occupants, weakened their will. On June 11, 1971, U.S. marshals landed and removed the remaining fifteen American Indians in less than thirty minutes, without incident. Nevertheless, the occupation of Alcatraz had focused attention on tribal grievances on and off the reservation and had demonstrated a resurgence of Native American pride and the need for self-determination. *Sharon K. Wilson and Raymond Wilson*

See also: American Indian activism; American Indian Movement; Indian Reorganization Act; Termination Resolution; Trail of Broken Treaties; Wounded Knee occupation.

Alexander v. Holmes County Board of Education

In the late 1960's, a group of African American parents in Mississippi filed lawsuits challenging segregation in thirty of the state's school districts. In 1969, the U.S. Court of Appeals for the Fifth Circuit ordered the districts to file desegregation plans by August 11, 1969, to take effect by the beginning of the 1969-1970 school year. With the support of President Richard M. Nixon's Department of Justice, however, the school districts requested the court to allow them to postpone the submission of school desegregation plans until December 1, 1969. The court granted the request, and the parents who had filed the original suits appealed to the U.S. Supreme Court.

On October 29, 1969—only twenty days after deciding to hear the case and only six days after oral argument—the Supreme Court held that the court of appeals had erred in permitting the delay. The Court's decision stated that "the obligation of every school district is to terminate dual school systems at once." The Court ordered every affected school district to "begin immediately to operate as unitary school systems."

Courts throughout the South began to insist on immediate desegregation, in some instances in the middle of the school year. The *Alexander* decision, by rejecting the previous policy of "all deliberate speed," dramatically altered the time frame within which school boards were required to meet their desegregation obligations.

Davison M. Douglas

See also: Busing and integration; Desegregation: public schools.

Alianza Federal de Mercedes

Chicano activist Reies López Tijerina created the Alianza Federal de Mercedes in 1963. Born in Fall City, Texas, into a family of sharecroppers, Tijerina had become frustrated with migrant work. When he entered New Mexico in 1960, he was shocked by the poverty of the Hispanic community and concluded that the community's loss of land since 1848 was the real cause of their problems. After studying the Treaty of Guadalupe Hidalgo—the peace treaty that finalized the Mexican-American War in 1848 and established the guidelines for Mexico's losing the Southwest and the terms by which formerly Mexican property would be respected— Tijerina became convinced that the national forest in Tierra Amarilla belonged to the Hispanic community. This motivated him to establish La Alianza Federal de Mercedes.

La Alianza Federal de Mercedes soon became a notable, albeit short-lived, organization. With twenty thousand members, the Alianza marched on the state capital and occupied other lands. As the Alianza movement picked up momentum, it "arrested" New Mexico rangers for harassing the organization. Early in 1967, however,

New Mexico authorities arrested Tijerina for occupying a national forest. After being released on bond, Tijerina attempted to make a citizen's arrest of the district attorney of Rio Arriba County. A gun battle erupted, and Tijerina was subsequently charged and faced trial. Later arrests resulted in the demise of the Alianza by the end of the 1970's.   *Douglas W. Richmond*

See also: Chicano Movement; Guadalupe Hidalgo, Treaty of.

Alien land laws

> **Significance:** These state measures deprived Japanese Americans of their property rights.

Immigration from Japan to the United States increased significantly during the final decade of the nineteenth century, with most of the Asian immigrants settling in the Pacific states. As the number of Japanese laborers arriving in California increased substantially, however, a strong anti-Japanese sentiment developed: Their success threatened and antagonized the emerging labor unions. The Asian Exclusion League was formed in 1905, and a campaign to bar Japanese immigration was launched. Negotiations begun in 1906 between the United States and Japan resulted in the Gentlemen's Agreement of 1907, which limited immigration from Japan to nonlaborers and to families who were joining previously settled laborers. In 1907, an immigration bill was amended to prevent Japanese laborers from entering the United States via Hawaii, Mexico, and Canada.

The First Proposals
The California legislature's attempts to pass alien land bills began in 1907 when it appropriated funds to investigate Japanese agricultural involvement. The California State Labor Commission's report, which was favorable to the Japanese, resulted in a reprimand for the commissioner. In 1910, twenty-seven anti-Japanese proposals were introduced in the legislature. Enactment of the proposed anti-Japanese legislation was prevented that year by influence from the White House and, in 1911, by President William Howard Taft's direct intervention.

On April 4, 1913, a California bill that would prohibit Japanese and other foreigners ineligible for citizenship from holding or leasing land in California prompted the Japanese ambassador, Viscount Chinda, to make an informal protest to the Department of State. The proposed bill in California was modeled on an 1897 federal law barring ownership of land by aliens ineligible for citizenship. The federal law, however, contained a proviso that it would not be applicable where treaty obligations conferred the right to own and hold land. The California bill included a clause prohibiting the leasing of land to Japanese, but the Japanese contended that this right had been conferred previously by the Treaty of 1894 and reenacted in the Treaty of 1911.

In Washington, D.C., the introduction of the 1913 California Alien Land bill was viewed seriously. The prevailing opinion was that its effect could be more sweeping than the problems of 1908 and could lead once again to talk of war. When Secretary William Jennings Bryan and Ambassador Chinda exchanged mutual assurances of continuing friendship between the United States and Japan on April 4, the Department of State expressed confidence that the matter would be resolved amicably. The following day, Bryan met with the California congressional delegation, which emphasized the necessity of the proposed legislation. Members of the delegation described how, in many parts of California, more than half the farms were operated by Japanese, and neither U.S. nor Chinese workers could compete with Japanese labor. They asserted that despite the Gentlemen's Agreement of 1907, "coolie laborers" were arriving continuously. The feeling in California was so strong, they reported, that people who leased land to the Japanese were ostracized by their neighbors. Members of the delegation intimated that violent protests against the increase in Japanese competition were imminent.

In Japan, the Tokyo press vehemently opposed the legislation. The Japanese government filed a formal protest on April 7. President Woodrow Wilson's position was to remain outside the conflict because he believed that the proposed legislation lay within the rights of a sovereign state.

The final draft of the new law was adopted by the California Senate on April 12. Ambassador Chinda presented his government's formal protest against the bill to the Department of State. Because of agitation in Tokyo, where the bill was denounced by the press and where demonstrators were calling for war, the California legislature, despite overwhelming margins in both houses, delayed further action until May 20, when the Alien Land Law, known also as the Webb-Henley bill, was signed into law by Governor Hiram Warren Johnson. The statute barred all aliens ineligible for citizenship, or corporations with more than 50 percent ineligible alien ownership, from the legal right to own agricultural land in California, and it limited land-leasing contracts in the state to three years' duration.

Further Restrictions
To prevent the Japanese from circumventing the law, a more restrictive alien land bill was introduced in the

California legislature in 1920 to forbid the Issei (first generation Japanese Americans) from buying land in the name of their U.S.-born children, the Nisei. It also prohibited the transfer of land to noncitizens by sale or lease and established criminal penalties for aliens caught attempting to bypass the 1913 law. In a statewide ballot, California voters passed the 1920 Alien Land Law by a three-to-one margin. A number of cases to test the constitutionality of the new law were instigated by the Japanese. In 1923, the U.S. Supreme Court ruled against the Issei in four of these cases. Further restrictions also were passed in a 1923 amendment, which, together with the 1924 Immigration Act, effectively denied further immigration and determined the status of Japanese immigrants in the United States. The alien land laws in California were not repealed until 1956.

During 1917, an alien land law was enacted in Arizona. In 1921, Washington, Texas, and Louisiana followed suite, as did New Mexico in 1922, and Oregon, Idaho, and Montana in 1923. Other states followed: Kansas in 1925; Missouri in 1939; Utah, Arkansas, and Nebraska in 1943; and Minnesota in 1945.

Susan E. Hamilton

Core Resources

Frank F. Chuman's *The Bamboo People: The Law and Japanese-Americans* (Del Mar, Calif.: Publisher's Inc., 1976) and Charles F. Curry's *Alien Land Laws and Alien Rights* (Washington, D.C.: Government Printing Office, 1921) provide two perspectives on the alien land laws. Dudley McGovney's article, "The Anti-Japanese Land Laws of California and Ten Other States," in *California Law Review* (35, 1947) presents a detailed discussion of alien land laws in relation to state, federal, and English common law up to the time of publication. Gail M. Nomura's "Washington's Asian/Pacific American Communities," an article in *Peoples of Washington: Perspectives on Cultural Diversity* (Pullman: Washington State University Press, 1989), edited by Sid White and S. E. Solberg, gives specifics of Washington and Texas land laws. *Iron Cages: Race and Culture in Nineteenth Century America* (New York: Oxford University Press, 1990), edited by Ronald Takaki, provides insight into the origin of anti-Asian sentiment and its connection to legislation such as the alien land laws.

See also: Gentlemen's Agreement; Immigration Act of 1924; Japanese Americans; Yellow peril campaign.

Alienation

Alienation is one of several types of social dysfunction (others being anomie and relative deprivation) that may negatively affect individuals who feel estranged from their group. When individuals lose their association with a group (such as an ethnic or racial minority), invariably they lose their specific identities, which are necessary for their sense of security and stability. In some instances, people may attribute their alienation to the characteristics of urban society, which include submission to the mechanical control of industrial technology or a dependency on economic institutions.

Some sociologists subscribe to the following classification of alienation: *powerlessness*, which refers to individuals' expectations that their own behavior cannot bring about the desired social outcome; *meaninglessness*, in which individuals are uncertain about what they ought to believe; *isolation*, in which individuals feel an "apartness from society" and place low personal priority on the goals or beliefs typically valued in the given society; *self-estrangement*, which refers to individuals' conceiving of themselves as aliens or finding work unrewarding or unsatisfying; and *formlessness*, which signifies a breakdown or loss of effectiveness of social norms in regulating the conduct of individuals.

John Alan Ross

See also: Ethnicity and ethnic groups; Out-group.

All African People's Revolutionary Party

The All African People's Revolutionary Party (AAPRP) is a Pan-African socialist political organization for people of African descent. The party has chapters in the United States, Africa, Canada, the Caribbean, and Europe. The AAPRP was founded in 1968 in response to a call by Kwame Nkrumah, the first president of independent Ghana, for a political party that would unify independent African nation-states into a "United States of Africa" and link African people globally. The AAPRP is often associated with one of its founders, Kwame Toure (previously Stokely Carmichael), a key organizer during the Civil Rights and Black Power movements.

The AAPRP adheres to an ideology predicated on the philosophies of Nkrumah and Sekou Toure of Guinea. The party calls for unity among all people of African descent; a focus of efforts toward the liberation and empowerment of Africa; and opposition to colonial, capitalist, and imperialist relations. The party's approach thus runs directly counter to the racial integrationist philosophy of the era previous to its emergence.

The AAPRP is organized in work-study political education structures; it sponsors political events on college campuses and in the African descendant community. The AAPRP also has a women's wing, the All African Women's Revolutionary Union, and a youth component, the Young Pioneers League. The professed objective of the AAPRP is "the total liberation of Africa under scientific socialism." *M. Bahati Kuumba*

See also: African Liberation Day; Black nationalism; Black Power movement; Pan-Africanism.

Allotment system

> **Significance:** The allotment system, meant to assimilate American Indians by making them small farmers, instead led to a massive loss of Indian land.

Allotment—the division of tribal lands among individual American Indians—became the dominant theme in federal Indian policy between 1887 and 1934. During the 1880's many whites who regarded themselves as Friends of the Indian came to believe that Indians could be saved from extinction only by assimilation into American society. Tribal loyalties and cultures were seen as barriers to this end. Reformers hoped that by carving up reservations and making small farmers of the Indians, they could effectively detribalize and assimilate the Indians into American culture. This policy also attracted support from those who wanted to open up tribal lands for settlement or exploitation. There were precedents for this policy. In the first half of the nineteenth century, several eastern states had broken up state-recognized reservations by dividing land among tribal members, and a number of the removal treaties of the 1830's made provision for allotments to individual Indians who wished to remain east of the Mississippi.

In 1887 Congress enacted the General Allotment Act, also known as the Dawes Severalty Act (for Senator Henry Dawes of Massachusetts, one of its proponents). The act gave the president authority to allot reservation lands in "severalty" (to individual Indians). As a general rule, heads of families would receive 160 acres, single Indians less. Title to the allotments would be held in trust by the government for twenty-five years to enable allottees to acquire the necessary farming skills, and the land could not be sold during the trust period. Once an Indian took up an allotment, he became an American citizen. Land not required for distribution could be sold off or opened to white settlement, with the proceeds intended to support assimilationist policies. Planners believed that the Indians, freed from tribal domination, would develop as small farmers and become part of mainstream American society. The Five Civilized Tribes of Indian Territory, along with a few others, were originally exempted from the act, but in the 1890's, Congress

established a commission headed by Senator Dawes to negotiate allotment and thus the abolition of their tribal governments.

The actual process of allotment was complex and went on for more than forty years. Along the way Congress made several modifications: In 1900 the leasing of allotments before the end of the trust period was allowed; in 1902, heirs of allottees were permitted to sell their lands with the permission of the secretary of the interior; and in 1906 the Burke Act delayed citizenship until the end of the trust period.

The system did not work as intended. Many Indians came from nonagricultural tribal backgrounds and were reluctant to become farmers. Others found their allotments too small to support a family or of little agricultural value. Whites often encouraged Indians to lease or sell their lands, sometimes resorting to intimidation or outright fraud.

The foremost result of the allotment policy was a drastic reduction in the amount of land controlled by Native Americans, from 138 million acres in 1887 to 52 million acres when the policy ceased in 1934. Of the amount lost, 60 million acres had been declared "excess land" and disposed of by the government to non-Indians. By 1934, two-thirds of Native Americans were either landless or without enough land to provide subsistence. The policy weakened tribal cultures and fostered the growth of a large bureaucracy in the Bureau of Indian Affairs.

By the late 1920's, doubts about the allotment system were growing. An investigation led by Lewis Meriam shocked many when its findings were published in 1928 as *The Problem of Indian Administration* (better known as the Meriam Report). The report detailed dismal conditions and poverty among American Indians and identified the allotment system as the major source of Indian problems. In 1934, the Indian Reorganization Act stopped the process of allotment and allowed the reorganization of tribal governments. *William C. Lowe*

See also: Burke Act; General Allotment Act; Indian Reorganization Act; Indian-white relations: United States.

AME Church

> **Significance:** A radically distinct denomination becomes an advocate for the cause of abolition and a bulwark of the African American community.

Sixteen African Methodist delegates met in Philadelphia on April 9, 1816, to unite as the African Methodist

Episcopal Church. Delegates from Philadelphia and Attleborough, Pennsylvania, joined representatives from Baltimore, Wilmington, and Salem to elect a bishop. They elected Richard Allen, who was consecrated as the first bishop of the African Methodist Episcopal Church (AME Church) on April 11, 1816. From the original sixteen delegates in 1816, membership grew to 7,257 by 1822.

Allen, known as the father of African American religion, was born a slave in 1760 in Philadelphia. Sold to the Stokeley plantation near Dover, Delaware, Allen attended evangelical tent meetings and experienced a religious conversion when he was seventeen years of age. He joined the Methodist Society, which held classes in the forest under the leadership of a white man, Benjamin Wells. Allen became a convincing proselytizer, converting first his family and then his owner, who agreed to Allen's proposal to purchase his own freedom in 1777. Allen worked at many jobs and preached at his regular stops, developing broad contacts through his travels. As an aide to other itinerant preachers, he met Bishop Francis Asbury, who established the first General Conference of the Methodist Church in America in 1784. Allen declined to accompany Asbury on a trip through the South and returned to Philadelphia in February, 1786.

Allen joined such Philadelphia leaders as former slave clerk and handyman Absalom Jones and other members of the St. Thomas vestry: James Forten, William White, Jacob Tapisco, and James Champion. Allen and Jones became lay preachers throughout the city, including early-morning and evening services at St. George's Methodist Episcopal Church. As African American attendance increased, racial conflict became apparent. In November, 1787, African Americans worshiping at St. George's were ordered to the gallery. After mistaking the section of the gallery assigned for their worship, Allen, Jones, and White were physically removed while praying at the Sunday morning worship service.

The Free African Society

The humiliation of this incident led to a mass exodus of African Americans from this church and a movement to create a separate church. In the spring, these African American leaders established the Free African Society, the first mutual aid society established to serve their community. By 1791, they held regular Sunday services,

The First AME Church in South-Central Los Angeles serves as the starting place for a group of people bound for the Million Man March in the 1996 Spike Lee film *Get on the Bus*. AME churches have served black communities since the first one was established in Philadelphia in 1816.

assumed lay leadership positions, and made plans for construction of a church building.

The leaders differed over the issue of church affiliation, with the majority voting to unite with the Episcopal church. On July 17, 1794, the St. Thomas African Church was dedicated as the first African church in Philadelphia, a Protestant Episcopal church with Jones as pastor. Jones became the first African American priest in 1804.

Allen withdrew from the Free African Society to form a separate church, the Bethel African Methodist Episcopal Church, on July 29, 1794. Allen declared the church independent in management but did not sever all relations with the Methodist Episcopal Church. The articles of incorporation ensured independence by allowing membership only to African Americans. Allen became the first African American to receive ordination from the Methodist Episcopal Church in the United States.

A Force for Change

Such church independence helped African Americans resist the insults and subordination resulting from slavery and racial prejudice and reflected a growing role of the church in the community. Sermons underscored the need for the African American community to become self-reliant through the church, schools, and economic organizations in order to gain group solidarity and recognition. Christian character, in turn, depended upon Christian education.

In 1804, Allen established the Society of Free People of Color for Promoting the Instruction and School Education of Children of African Descent. In 1809, he helped Forten and Jones organize the Society for the Suppression of Vice and Immorality in Philadelphia, to provide community supervision of the morality of African Americans and to establish means for their moral uplift. These leaders recruited three thousand members for the Black Legion during the War of 1812. The successful functions associated with African American churches led to greater membership. By 1813, St. Thomas had a membership of 560, while Bethel Church had 1,272 communicants.

The movement spread to other cities and along the seaboard states. Church leaders continued their pioneering efforts for group solidarity. In January, 1817, the First Negro Convention met at the Bethel Church to protest the plans of the American Colonization Society for emigration of free blacks to Africa. Also in 1817, Allen and Tapisco published the First Church Discipline as well as a book of hymns compiled by Allen, Daniel Coker, and Champion.

The church continued to improve the conditions for African Americans. It supported the use of boycotts to protest the economic basis of slavery through the Free Produce Society of Philadelphia, which was organized at an assembly at Bethel Church on December 20, 1830, to advocate purchase of produce grown only by free labor. The First Annual Convention of the People of Color, convened in Philadelphia in 1831, elected Allen as its leader shortly before his death on March 26, 1831. The African Methodist Episcopal Church has survived as an integral part of the African American community and continued its strong leadership role.   *Dorothy C. Salem*

Core Resources
Katharine L. Dvorak's *An African American Exodus* (Brooklyn, N.Y.: Carlson, 1991) provides the history and theology of the nineteenth century African Methodist Episcopal Church. A number of books and articles describe Richard Allen and his life and work, including Allen's own *The Life, Experience, and Gospel Labors of the Right Reverent Richard Allen*, originally published in 1833 (Nashville, Tenn.: Abingdon Press, 1983), Carol V. R. George's *Segregated Sabbaths: Richard Allen and the Rise of Independent Black Churches, 1760-1840* (New York: Oxford University Press, 1973), *Richard Allen: The First Exemplar of African American Education* (New York: ECA Associates, 1985) by Mwalimu I. Mwadilitu (E. Curtis Alexander), Charles Wesley's *Richard Allen: Apostle of Freedom* (Washington, D.C.: Associated Publishers, 1935), and Gary Nash's "New Light on Richard Allen: The Early Years of Freedom" in *William and Mary Quarterly* 46 (April, 1989).

See also: African American Baptist Church; AME Zion Churches; Black church; Free African Society.

AME Zion Churches

The African Methodist Episcopal (AME) Zion Church is one of several black Methodist churches that originated in the northern United States in the late eighteenth and early nineteenth centuries. Organized in 1821, the AME Zion Church was conceived in the 1790's, when a handful of black congregations broke away from the predominantly white Methodist Episcopal denomination in search of greater autonomy and freedom of worship. These independent black Methodist churches eventually organized into three separate denominations: the Union Church of Africans; the African Methodist Episcopal (AME) Church; and the New York City-based AME Zion Church. Although largely similar in doctrine, these and other black Methodist churches operated separately, occasionally clashing over competition for membership and the question of which denomination was established first.

The AME Zion Church grew steadily before the Civil War, establishing congregations as far south as Louisville, Kentucky, and rousing white suspicion for its emphasis on abolitionism and religious self-determination. Emancipation and Reconstruction opened the postbellum South to black Methodist churches, sparking a dramatic expansion of AME Zion missionary activity in North America, the Caribbean, and Africa that increased AME Zion Church membership from 4,600 in 1860 to around 350,000 in 1896. In addition to missionary activity, the AME Zion Church has historically emphasized advancement of black citizenship rights, expanded roles for women in church government, and ecumenicism among black and white Methodist churches.
                                          Michael H. Burchett

See also: AME Church; Black church.

Amerasian Homecoming Act of 1987

When the United States withdrew all personnel from Vietnam in 1975, many Vietnamese wives of American citizens and their Amerasian children remained. The Amerasian children were excluded from the mainstream of Vietnamese society, and their mothers were unable to secure employment with the Vietnamese government or in government enterprises. The children were often placed in orphanages, awaiting adoption by unknown fathers in the United States.

In 1984, the U.S. State Department informed Vietnam that all Amerasian children and their qualifying family members would be admitted as refugees by the end of 1987 under the Orderly Departure Program (ODP) of the United Nations High Commissioner for Refugees. However, on January 1, 1986, Vietnam ceased cooperating with the program because of differences with the United States on other issues. When Vietnam resumed processing ODP applicants on October 19, 1987, the three-year deadline was running out. Accordingly, on December 22, 1987, Congress passed the Amerasian Homecoming Act as a part of legislation authorizing appropriations for the U.S. Department of State to establish the program on a more permanent basis.

Michael Haas

See also: Biracialism; Interracial and interethnic marriage; Orderly Departure Program; Vietnamese Americans.

American Anti-Slavery Society

> **Significance:** The American Anti-Slavery Society, which unified two centers of radical abolitionism, called for immediate eradication of slavery.

In December, 1833, sixty delegates gathered in Philadelphia to form the American Anti-Slavery Society, electing Arthur Tappan, a wealthy New York businessman, as president. They also approved a Declaration of Sentiments, drawn up by William Lloyd Garrison, Samuel May, and John Greenleaf Whittier, that called for immediate, uncompensated, total abolition of slavery through moral and political action. In signing the declaration, the delegates pledged to "do all that in us lies, consisting with this declaration of our principles, to overthrow the most execrable system of slavery that has ever been witnessed upon earth . . . and to secure to the colored population of the United States, all the rights and privileges which belong to them as men and Americans." The American Anti-Slavery Society organized a system of state and local auxiliaries, sent out agents to convert people to its views, and published pamphlets and journals supporting its position. The society grew rapidly; by 1838, it reported approximately 250,000 members and 1,350 auxiliaries.

Immediatism
Before the 1830's, most opponents of slavery advocated moderate methods such as gradual and "compensated" emancipation, which would reimburse former slave owners who released slaves, or removal of free African Americans to Liberia by the American Colonization Society, founded in 1817. The formation of a national organiza-

tion based on the principle of immediatism, or immediate and total emancipation, symbolized the new phase that antislavery agitation had entered in the early 1830's—radical, uncompromising, and intensely moralistic. The shift to immediatism was a result of several factors, including the failure of moderate methods; the example of the British, who abolished slavery in the empire in 1833; and, probably most important, evangelical religion. Abolitionists of the 1830's inherited from earlier antislavery reformers the notion that slavery was a sin. This notion, coupled with the contemporaneous evangelical doctrine of immediate repentance, shaped the abolitionist doctrine of immediate emancipation. Abolitionists emphasized moral suasion over political methods. They hoped to persuade people to emancipate the slaves voluntarily and to form a conviction of guilt as participants in the national sin of slavery.

The American Anti-Slavery Society represented the union of two centers of radical abolitionism, one in Boston, the other around Cincinnati. Garrison, the key figure among New England abolitionists, began publishing *The Liberator* in 1831 and soon organized the

Slave women and children gather near the doorway of a house. In 1833, the American Anti-Slavery Society called for the immediate abolition of slavery, terming it an "execrable system."

New England Anti-Slavery Society, based on the principle of immediate abolition. In the Midwest, Western Reserve College and Lane Seminary were seedbeds for the doctrine of immediate emancipation. Theodore Dwight Weld, a young man who had been converted to evangelical Christianity by Charles Finney, organized a group of antislavery agents known as The Seventy, who preached the gospel of immediatism throughout the Midwest.

Although the leadership of the antislavery movement remained predominantly white, free African Americans played a significant role in its ranks. Before 1800, the Free African Society of Philadelphia and black spokespersons such as astronomer Benjamin Banneker and church leader Richard Allen had denounced slavery in the harshest terms. By 1830, there were fifty antislavery societies organized by blacks, and African Americans contributed to the formation of the American Anti-Slavery Society in 1833. African American orators, especially escaped slaves such as Frederick Douglass and Sojourner Truth, moved large audiences with their impassioned and electrifying oratory. African Americans also helped run the Underground Railroad; Harriet Tubman led more than three hundred blacks to freedom. Generally, African American abolitionists shared the nonviolent philosophy of the Garrisonians, but black anger often flared because of the racism they found within the antislavery ranks. Influenced by tactical and race considerations, white abolitionist leaders such as Garrison and Weld limited their African American counterparts to peripheral roles or excluded them from local organizations.

Internal Divisions

The late 1830's marked the high point of the movement for immediate abolition through moral suasion. Abolitionism was hard hit by the Panic of 1837, which reduced funds and distracted attention away from reform. At the same time, abolitionists faced an internal challenge as the American Anti-Slavery Society divided into radicals and moderates. One issue causing the split was women's rights. Moderate abolitionists tolerated and even welcomed women in the society, as long as their activities were confined to forming auxiliary societies, raising money, and circulating petitions. They refused, however, the request that women be allowed to speak in public on behalf of abolitionism or to help shape the organization's policies.

The other issue that divided abolitionist ranks was that of political action. Some abolitionists, convinced that political action, not merely moral suasion, was necessary to effect emancipation, formed the Liberty Party in 1840. In the 1840's and 1850's, the majority of abolitionists moved gradually into the political arena, where they became involved in the Free-Soil movement and other aspects of the sectional conflict leading to the Civil War.   *Anne C. Loveland, updated by Sudipta Das*

Core Resources

Louis Filler's *The Crusade Against Slavery, 1830-1860* (New York: Harper & Row, 1960) is a comprehensive treatment of the people and groups who made up the antislavery movement and the relation of the movement to other reform activities of the period. Lawrence J. Friedman's *Gregarious Saints: Self and Community in American Abolitionism, 1830-1870* (New York: Cambridge University Press, 1982) presents a fresh, challenging analysis of the antislavery movement, written from a psychological perspective and focusing on the first-generation immediatists. *Antislavery Reconsidered: New Perspectives on the Abolitionists* (Baton Rouge: Louisiana State University Press, 1979) edited by Lewis Perry and Michael Fellman contains fourteen original, thought-provoking essays based on a variety of interpretive and methodological approaches. Richard H. Abbott's *Cotton and Capital: Boston Businessmen and Antislavery Reform, 1854-1868* (Amherst: University of Massachusetts Press, 1991) examines the activities and ideology of a group of Bostonian businessmen who fostered abolition. In *The Liberator: William Lloyd Garrison* (Boston: Little, Brown, 1963), John L. Thomas surveys not only the antislavery movement but also the many other reforms in which the well-known editor was engaged.

See also: Abolition; American Colonization Society; Free African Society; Free-Soil Party; *Liberator, The*; Underground Railroad.

American Civil Liberties Union

> **Significance:** This group, the most important civil liberties organization in the United States, uses the courts to protect the rights of controversial and ordinary individuals.

The American Civil Liberties Union (ACLU), founded January 18, 1920, has its origins in the movement to protect the right of pacifists to protest American entrance into World War I. The basic objective of the organization is to monitor and protect the constitutional rights of all American citizens and groups. Although the ACLU has earned notoriety by defending unpopular organizations and being involved in controversial court cases, it has over the decades taken thousands of routine cases as well, from the firing of a public librarian for refusing to remove a book from her shelves to the right of employees to join a labor union.

Methods

The ACLU uses the courts to achieve its objectives. Although it often petitions state courts, its main course of action takes place in the federal courts. Almost all its cases bear on constitutional issues, and some have led to landmark decisions by the U.S. Supreme Court.

Its critics accuse the ACLU of having a specific political agenda, but the organization claims to be neutral in politics and, in fact, has championed individuals and organizations from both extremes of the political spectrum. It has worked to overturn laws banning the Communist Party and defended the right of Nazis to march in Jewish neighborhoods. It has forced local communities to dismantle religious displays and defended the right of police officers to join the Ku Klux Klan and the ultraconservative John Birch Society. The organization has thus been strongly chastised by both the Left and Right. In general, however, the organization clearly has been part of left-of-center politics in the United States.

The ACLU's single purpose is an uncompromisingly rigid protection of civil liberties for all, no matter how unpopular, outrageous, or despicable the cause or individual. Its most controversial cases are the standard by which it measures its success. For the ACLU, opposition to all censorship means defending the rights of pornographers. Opposition to illegal searches means opposition to unannounced police sweeps of public housing to root out drug traffickers. Strict separation of church and state means absolute opposition to the most bland prayers in public schools and to the display of any religious symbol on public grounds or documents.

Structure

The ACLU is a private organization of volunteers whose membership in the mid-1990's numbered about 300,000. The organization relies on more than four thousand volunteer lawyers for its litigation; they are the heart of the organization. Its paid staff consists of fewer than a hundred people, but it has eleven paid lobbyists. Besides its two national offices in New York and Washington, D.C., it has affiliates in forty-six states and has eleven special project offices.

History

The positions of the ACLU have evolved over the decades of its existence. It has not always opposed censorship or the separation of church and state so rigidly. Some of its issues, such as the right of women to have abortions, have reflected changes in society rather than initiated them.

The ACLU was born out of the United States' entry into World War I. Wartime hysteria and widespread popular support for American participation led to the censorship of opposition to the war and harassment or imprisonment for individuals opposing American entry. To protect the right of free speech, members of the pacifist American Union Against Militarism (AUAM) formed the Civil Liberties Board (CLB). Because the AUAM and its branch CLB publicly embraced the radical left, a number of members resigned and formed the nonpartisan National Civil Liberties Board (NCLB).

The NCLB was unable to fight successfully the curtailment of civil liberties during the war or during the postwar Red Scare when the government harassed and prosecuted thousands of citizens suspected of harboring Marxist and other left-wing ideas. In 1920, its members created the restructured ACLU under the leadership of Roger Baldwin, a Boston attorney, who had been the guiding spirit of the NCLB. The broad base of the organization and its commitment to consider all violations of civil liberties distinguished it from other existing civil rights groups such as the National Association for the Advancement of Colored People (NAACP) and the Anti-Defamation League, founded by B'nai B'rith.

Over the next seven decades the ACLU was involved in some of the most renowned cases in American jurisprudence and issues in American society—the Scopes "monkey" trial, the internment of Japanese Americans during World War II, the rights of conscientious objectors, the Smith and McCarran Anti-Communist Acts, the Scottsboro case, abortion rights, antiwar protests, and many others.

The Skokie March Case

The organization's most unpopular cause among its membership was the defense of the 1976 proposed march by the American Nazi Party in Skokie, Illinois, a largely Jewish suburb of Chicago. The party planned the march after the city of Chicago refused them a permit for a rally there. Skokie also denied a parade permit on the grounds that it would cause a public nuisance. The ACLU took up the Nazis' petition, and although the controversy was resolved without a march through the suburb, the championing of the Nazis' cause split the organization almost to the point of extinction. This was not the first time the organization took on a case on behalf of the Nazis, but the reaction of its membership, the overwhelming majority of whom are leftists and many of whom are Jews, was unprecedented. The union suffered a 15 percent drop in membership renewal and found itself with a half-million-dollar deficit. The ACLU reorganized and cut its staff, and new leadership moved into position. In the years following Skokie, a new conservative era in the United

States, the organization faced the issues of the day: abortion rights, gay rights, the rights of sufferers of acquired immunodeficiency syndrome (AIDS), and the war on drugs. It became a favorite whipping boy of the Republican Party, but its function as the protector of the individual against the conforming impulse of society revitalized it as the country's leading civil rights organization.   *Frederick B. Chary*

Core Resources
The standard work on the ACLU is Samuel Walker's *In Defense of American Liberties: A History of the ACLU* (New York: Oxford University Press, 1990). Other good sources include *The Pulse of Freedom: American Liberties, 1920-1970's* (New York: W. W. Norton, 1975), edited by Alan Reitman, Paul L. Murphy's *World War I and the Origin of Civil Liberties in the United States* (New York: W. W. Norton, 1979), and Peter Irons's *The Courage of Their Convictions* (New York: Free Press, 1988). William Donohue's *The Politics of the American Civil Liberties Union* (New Brunswick, N.J.: Transaction Books, 1985) is a polemical attack on the ACLU. On Skokie, see Aryeh Neier's *Defending My Enemy* (New York: Dutton, 1979), David Hamlin's *The Nazi/Skokie Conflict* (Boston: Beacon Press, 1980), and James L. Gibson and Richard D. Bingham's *Civil Liberties and Nazis: The Skokie Free-Speech Controversy* (New York: Praeger, 1985).

See also: American Nazi Party; Civil rights; Japanese American internment; Red Scare.

American Colonization Society

Organized in 1816, the American Society for Colonizing the Free People of Color of the United States, commonly known as the American Colonization Society, attempted to resolve conflicts over slavery and racism by removing African Americans from the United States. Popular in many northern cities and in the upper South, it counted among its members national figures such as Henry Clay, Daniel Webster, and Francis Scott Key. The society planned to establish a colony in Africa to which free African Americans could voluntarily migrate. Although the society did not address the issue of emancipating enslaved African Americans, it hoped that the colonization scheme would prompt slaveowners to free their slaves, secure in the knowledge that the free blacks would not remain in the South. In 1822, the society helped to found Liberia, on the western coast of Africa, and supported a small settlement there. However, lack of financial support and the commitment to slavery in the lower South doomed the unrealistic plan to failure. Most important, almost all African Americans rejected the no-

tion of colonization, declaring the United States to be their rightful home. Only fifteen thousand made the journey to Liberia in the years before the Civil War (1861-1865).   *Thomas Clarkin*

See also: Abolition; American Anti-Slavery Society; Pan-Africanism; Transnationalism and ethnonationalism.

American Council on Race Relations

The American Council on Race Relations was founded by liberal whites in 1944, with the goal of obtaining justice for African Americans. Its first president was Charles Pickett of the American Friends Service Committee, supported by other white men of scholarly and religious background. The organization was committed to five strategies for working toward equality: calling for scientific study to dispel misinformation and misunderstanding about African Americans; working with public and private agencies to spread study results; assisting grassroots organizations in developing organizational skills; developing instructional materials for schools; and urging the popular media to use their influence to educate the general public about race.

The council soon became known for levelheadedness and organizational skill. In 1947, the council was asked by a group of city human relations commissioners to host a national conference in Chicago for leaders of groups working for racial justice, including the National Association for the Advancement of Colored People (NAACP), the Anti-Defamation League of B'nai B'rith, and the Japanese American Citizens League. At this conference a new group, the National Association of Intergroup Relations Officials, was founded. In the 1950's, the American Council on Race Relations worked actively in the Midwest to challenge segregation laws, especially in the public schools.   *Cynthia A. Bily*

See also: National Association for the Advancement of Colored People; Racial/ethnic relations: improving.

American Indian activism

Significance: In the mid-1960's, American Indians embarked on a new phase in their dealings with the U.S. government and its citizens, one marked by proactive insistence on rights that had been secured by treaty with the United States.

During the 1950's, the official U.S. government policy toward American Indians involved "termination" and "relocation." Termination was meant to end the special legal status of American Indians and to encourage the assimilation of native people into the U.S. citizenry. Through relocation, American Indians were to be taken off their traditional lands and relocated in urban areas for training and employment. The necessary complement to termination and relocation, in the government's view, was the abolishing of treaty rights for all the tribes. By the beginning of the Civil Rights movement, however, some American Indians were beginning to adopt some of the tactics and strategies used by civil rights protesters.

Northwest Fish-ins

In 1964, the National Indian Youth Council (NIYC) organized a fish-in in Washington State. Tribes there had increasingly been prohibited from fishing in waters granted to them by treaty. Sportfishers and commercial fisheries believed that Native American fishers were interfering with their ability to fish for profit and fun. The American Indian fishers, however, were most often fishing either in observation of tribal ritual or for subsistence. The fish-ins attracted widespread notice, drawing celebrities such as actor Marlon Brando and civil rights activist Dick Gregory. Case after case was adjudicated in the following years, from the Northwest to the upper Great Lakes. Many times the decision came down on the side of the tribal treaty rights. These successes, especially between 1964 and 1966, galvanized many young American Indians at a time when many of the tribal elders distrusted the course of activism. The success of NIYC leadership in the fish-in controversy legitimated more active protest.

Birth of the American Indian Movement (AIM)

In the Minneapolis-St. Paul area, in 1968, Native American residents had noted the extremely high rates of arrest of American Indians relative to other groups. They also heard many stories of rough and sometimes brutal police treatment of American Indians. Some Minneapolis Indians began to follow police cruisers on weekends to document what happened. During the next ten months, police arrests of American Indians dropped to almost zero, demonstrating at least that having witnesses and advocates on the scene helped matters. This was the beginning of the American Indian Movement.

The Taking of Alcatraz

In November, 1969, more than eighty American Indians landed on Alcatraz Island, formerly the site of a federal penitentiary, and declared it Indian territory under the 1868 Treaty of Fort Laramie, a treaty that granted federal land to American Indians if it was no longer in use by the federal government. The immediate reason for the taking of Alcatraz was that the San Francisco Indian Center had burned to the ground, leaving American Indians United, in town for a conference, without a place to stay. Though the island was empty two years later, the call for restoration of land by lawful treaty was once again established. Though there were successes in land restoration (for example, the return of Blue Lake to the Taos Pueblos and the return of Mount Adams to the Yakima), the issue of land and treaty rights brought into the spotlight the U.S. government's history of treaty abridgment and effectively ended the policies of termination and relocation.

Early 1970's

In 1970, more than 150 Pit River tribespeople occupied parts of Lassen National Park and Pacific Gas and Electric land in Northern California. Other demonstrators took over Ellis Island in New York to protest treaty violations. Lakota briefly occupied Mount Rushmore, a site sacred to their tribe.

Early in 1972, the Chippewa won back their rights to police fishing inside their reserve. That spring at Cass Lake, Minnesota, AIM convened to help decide how those rights would be allocated. During the convention, roads were blocked and guns were in evidence; the atmosphere was tense as AIM members battled what they saw as overly conservative traditionalists. The situation so unnerved local resort owners that they acceded to demands for absolute Chippewa control.

Shortly after the Cass Lake convention, an older Pine Ridge Sioux, Raymond Yellow Thunder, was murdered in Gordon, Nebraska, by five white men. Gordon officials did nothing about the situation, so AIM convened one thousand American Indians, who descended on the town in protest. After the apparent public relations successes of these protests, AIM leaders began to plan a caravan across the nation to Washington, D.C., the Trail of Broken Treaties, for the fall of 1972, before the presidential elections. It was hoped that the caravan would create favorable public sentiment for the cause of treaty enforcement and force the U.S. government to pay attention to the protesters' demands.

The group stopped in Minneapolis to release its list of demands, the Twenty Points, to the media. Among the demands was a repeal of the 1871 ban on further treaty making, the end of state court jurisdiction over American Indians, and a review of U.S. treaty violations of the past and redress for those violations. By the time the caravan arrived in Washington, D.C., on November 3, it had grown to numbers well exceeding expectations. A large number of reservation Indians turned out, although AIM was regarded primarily as an urban group.

Unfortunately, the unexpectedly large number of participants meant a shortage of accommodations. Eventually the Department of the Interior's auditorium was booked as a place for the activists to stay. As people began to leave the Bureau of Indian Affairs building, overzealous guards began to push people out through the doors. Believing that they might be turned over to a police riot squad, activists rushed back into the building and barricaded themselves in, breaking apart furniture in order to board windows and fasten doors. They remained inside for six days. Finally, on November 9, negotiators reached a settlement: Those involved would not be prosecuted, and $66,000 was appropriated for return transportation. The Twenty Points would be considered, and a response would be made.

The response to the Twenty Points issued by the administration of President Richard M. Nixon in January, 1973, disappointed the tribes. In essence, the administration rejected any notion of treaty enforcement or treaty reform although it promised more positive action.

Wounded Knee II

In January, 1973, a Sioux, Wesley Bad Heart Bear, was killed under uncertain circumstances. When a white man was charged with manslaughter instead of murder, Dennis Banks and Russell Means led AIM supporters first into Buffalo Gap, South Dakota, and then into Rapid City, demanding justice. Though tension filled the air for several days, a promise of justice was finally extracted, and Banks addressed the South Dakota legislature, promising a new era in race relations between whites and American Indians.

Banks and Means repaired to the Pine Ridge Reservation to celebrate. Unfortunately for them, Tribal Chairman Richard Wilson had declared (after the Raymond Yellow Thunder celebration and the occupation of the BIA office) that Means, Banks, and the AIM were never to celebrate on Pine Ridge again.

When they arrived, tribal police began to harass them. Tribal officials called in federal marshals to control the situation. On February 28, AIM occupied the Wounded Knee site on the reservation and announced political independence of Pine Ridge. More marshals arrived, and a number of AIM supporters from outside Pine Ridge arrived at the Wounded Knee compound, including a number of traditional holy people and a contingent from the Mohawk Nation.

The government issued several sets of ultimatums, culminating in an order during the second week that everyone leave Wounded Knee by six o'clock that day, or federal marshals would come in shooting. The National Council of Churches had representatives there, and they vowed that should such an order be implemented, they

During the occupation of Wounded Knee in 1973, a member of the American Indian Movement joyfully raises his rifle after receiving some good news regarding negotiations. In the 1960's, American Indians began to actively pursue their rights and interests.

would stand between the marshals' gunfire and the activists. The ultimatum was rescinded.

On March 11, Means announced on national television that the Oglala Sioux Nation had been formed and declared its independence from the United States. He promised to shoot anyone who crossed the nation's borders. Hank Adams, a fish-in veteran who had helped negotiate the BIA occupation, met with high-level administration officials to bring about some of the changes desired by AIM. The occupation lasted seventy-two days.

Legislative and Judicial Activism

The principle of tribal sovereignty was established between 1823 and 1832 in a series of cases: *Johnson v. McIntosh* (1823), *Cherokee Nation v. Georgia* (1831), and *Worcester v. Georgia* (1832). In all these cases, the operative phrasing was that tribes were "dependent, domestic nations." In *United States v. Kagama* (1886), the Supreme Court ruled that the federal branch of the U.S. government, specifically the Congress, held ultimate sovereignty over tribal nations. This solidified the "plenary power" of Congress, meaning that it could legislate American Indian affairs in any way it saw fit, without regard to constitutional review. Similarly, in *Lone Wolf v. Hitchcock* (1903), the Supreme Court ruled that Congress may abrogate at will any treaty with any tribe.

The tide in adjudication turned somewhat in the early 1900's. In *United States v. Winans* (1905), the Court recognized that tribes have rights reserved for them even if those rights are not specifically named in a treaty. In *Winters v. United States* (1908), the Court held that water rights are included even if not named in treaties.

The beginning of the modern era of American Indian law is the landmark case *Hitchcock v. Lee* (1959). In that case, the reserved rights by treaty were held to include the right of the Navajo to try a case in their own tribal courts. The state of Arizona's position, that it alone had the right to try cases, was rebuffed.

By the 1960's, there were numerous organizations that pursued the rights of American Indians through the courts. These included the Indian Rights Association, the Association on American Indian Affairs, the Legal Services Corporation, and the Native American Rights Fund. One of the persistent cases was the battle over fishing rights, which came before the Supreme Court three times during the 1960's. This series of cases became known as the Puyallup Series. In *United States v. Washington* (1973), the Supreme Court upheld the American Indian right to share equally in the salmon harvest in the Northwest. A subsequent case, *Washington v. Fishing Vessel Association* (1979), modified the earlier ruling somewhat by granting American Indians only a "moderate" fishing livelihood.

During the 1970's, American Indians increasingly won judicial approval for many tribal and self-determining activities. These included education, taxes, tribal governance, adoption, and revenue-generating operations of all kinds. Two particular landmark cases are *United States v. Mazurie* (1975), in which tribal courts gained the right to try a non-Indian, and *Fisher v. District Court* (1976), in which it was held that the state of Montana could not intervene in a Northern Cheyenne adoption. Finally, in 1977, the decision in *Delaware v. Weeks* ended the doctrine of plenary power, as the Court applied constitutional review to an act of Congress regarding American Indians.

Since then, three important congressional acts have been passed that seem to many to mark a new attitude toward American Indians. The 1978 American Indian Religious Freedom Act extended to American Indians the same religious freedom enjoyed by other Americans.

The 1988 Indian Gaming Regulatory Act opened the door to tribal generation of revenue through the gaming industry, a boon to many tribes' coffers. The 1990 Native American Grave Protection and Repatriation Act began finally to address a problem most American Indians believed to be a symbol of American lack of respect for the First Nations.   *T. J. Arant*

Core Resources
James S. Olson and Raymond Wilson's *Native Americans in the Twentieth Century* (Provo, Utah: Brigham Young University, 1984) is a comprehensive history with a chapter specifically devoted to activism. Alvin M. Josephy, Jr.'s *Red Power: The American Indians' Fight for Freedom* (New York: American Heritage Press, 1971) contains contemporary accounts of the Red Power movement. Vine Deloria, Jr.'s *Behind the Trail of Broken Treaties: An Indian Declaration of Independence* (2d ed., Norman: University of Oklahoma Press, 1987) examines the Trail of Broken Treaties and the siege at Wounded Knee in the context of American Indian history. Alvin J. Ziontz's "Indian Litigation," in *The Aggressions of Civilization: Federal Indian Policy Since the 1880's* (Philadelphia: Temple University Press, 1984), edited by Sandra L. Cadwalader and Vine Deloria, Jr., is an excellent review of judicial opinions relating to American Indians.

See also: Alcatraz Island occupation; American Indian Movement; American Indian Religious Freedom Act; Fish-ins; Indian Gaming Regulatory Act; Indian-white relations: United States; National Indian Youth Council; Pine Ridge shootout; Trail of Broken Treaties; Wounded Knee occupation.

American Indian agriculture

Significance: Although popular imagination sometimes stereotypes them solely as nomadic hunters, many, if not most, of North America's Native American peoples practiced agriculture, the domestication of plants for human consumption. At least half of the vegetable staples, including corn and potatoes, were first cultivated by American Indians, who often drew their sustenance from hunting, gathering, and agriculture.

At first sight, many immigrating Europeans did not recognize Native American agriculture because it did not resemble their own. Indians did not domesticate draft animals and only rarely plowed their fields. Sometimes crops were grown in small clearings in the forest.

Native Americans first cultivated many foods that are

taken for granted as everyday nourishment in the United States. For example, the main ingredients of caramel corn (peanuts and popcorn) are both indigenous to the Americas as are all edible beans except horse beans and soybeans, all squashes (including pumpkins), "Jerusalem" artichokes, the "Irish" potato, the sweet potato, sunflowers, peppers, pineapples, watermelons, cassava, bananas, strawberries, raspberries, gooseberries, and pecans.

Agriculture and Spiritual Life

The production of food is woven into Native American spiritual life. Among the Iroquois and many other native peoples, for example, festivals point to the role of the "three sisters" (corn, squash, and beans). Archaeologists believe that the food complex of corn, beans, and squash was transferred northward from Mexico as a set of rituals before it was an agricultural system. By practicing the rituals, Native Americans in the corn-growing areas of North America became farmers.

Many Native American peoples offer their thanks to the plants as well as the animals that they consume, out of a belief that the essence of life that animates human beings is present in the entire web of animate and inanimate life and objects. Long before a science of "sustained-yield" forestry evolved, Native American peoples along the coast of the Northwest harvested trees in ways that would assure their continued growth, as part of a belief that trees are sentient beings. Some Native Americans charted farming cycles through complicated relationships with the sun and moon. In addition to domesticating dozens of food plants, they also harvested the wild bounty of the forests for hundreds of herbs and other plants used to restore and maintain health.

Mayan Agriculture

Although the Maya are known for their temples in such places as Tikal, Copan, and Palenque, the Mayan commoners who supported the small elite who maintained the temples spent most of their time cultivating food, principally corn. Most of the Mayan ceremonial centers were surrounded by very large earthworks that were used for agriculture. These artificial ramparts were not discovered by modern archaeologists until they started using satellite images of the land because the earthworks often are submerged in jungle and thus very difficult to see from ground level. The earthworks included complex irrigation channels and raised fields, often hewn from reclaimed swampland. The Maya dredged nutrient-rich soil from the bottoms of the irrigation ditches to fertilize fields that they raised above the flood level of the rainy season. The fields were so rich that they produced several crops a year to feed the people in the urban ceremonial centers.

Pueblo Agriculture

About the same time that the Mayan civilization collapsed, the Pueblo Indians were building a corn-based culture in the area now known as Chaco Canyon in New Mexico. Culturally and economically, the Pueblo Indians of the Rio Grande have their roots in the Mogollon, Anasazi, and Hohokam communities to the west and southwest of the upper Rio Grande Valley. Cultivation of corn was introduced into the area about 3000 B.C.E. About 2000 B.C.E., beans and squash were added. Cotton later became a staple crop.

About 2,000 years ago, irrigation was introduced to supplement dry farming in the area. The Pueblo Indians used brief, heavy precipitation to advantage by constructing some of their irrigation works at the bases of steep cliffs to collect runoff. The residents of this area constructed roads that often ran for hundreds of miles to provide a way to share food surpluses—if one pueblo had a bad harvest, others would make it up. The cultivation of corn in Chaco Canyon supported a civilization that constructed the largest multifamily dwellings in North America. Such a high degree of agricultural organization supported a culture that dominated the turquoise trade in the area. Turquoise was important as a liquid asset, a medium of trade. Pueblos such as Pueblo Bonito became centers of trade, manufacturing, and ceremony.

The Role of Corn

Corn, the major food source for several agricultural peoples across the continent, enjoyed a special spiritual significance. Often corn and beans (which grow well together because the beans, a legume, fix nitrogen in their roots) were said to maintain a spiritual union. Some peoples, such as the Omahas of the eastern Great Plains, "sang up" their corn through special rituals.

Corn plays a role in the origin stories of many Native American peoples. The Pueblo Indians say that corn was brought to them by Blue Corn Woman and White Corn Maiden, who emerged to the surface of the earth from a great underground kiva, a sacred place. At birth, each infant is given the seed from an ear of corn as a fetish, to carry for life as a reminder that the Corn Mothers brought life to the Pueblo Indians. The corn fetish has a practical side as well: Should a harvest completely fail because of drought or for other reasons, the fetishes may become the seed corn for the next crop.

Bruce E. Johansen

Core Resources

William Brandon's *American Heritage Book of Indians* (New York: Dell, 1961) describes agricultural practices by a number of Native American peoples. William Cronon's *Changes in the Land: Indians, Colonists, and the Ecology of*

New England (New York: Hill & Wang, 1983) evaluates the role of agriculture among native peoples who met the earliest English immigrants. Vine Deloria, Jr.'s *God Is Red* (Golden, Colorado: North American Press, 1992) examines the spiritual roots of agricultural practices. Joe S. Sando's *The Pueblo Indians* (Santa Fe, N.M.: Clear Light, 1992) describes Pueblo agriculture. J. Donald Hughes's *American Indian Ecology* (El Paso: Texas Western Press, 1983) discusses ecological aspects of Native American agricultural practices.

See also: American Indian stereotypes; Indian-white relations: United States; Native American.

American Indian civil rights

> **Significance:** Indian activism, federal legislation, and tribal activities have all been important in the struggle of American Indians for equality.

Federal Indian policy in the United States has passed through three major historical phases. Before 1890, American Indians were either exterminated or forced onto reservations. Then, between 1890 and 1934, attempts were made to Christianize Indians and assimilate them into white culture. To this end, the policy during the 1940's and 1950's was to "terminate" federal relations with tribes. In the 1960's, federal policy began to change to direct assistance to the reservations to help them achieve self-determination. Many tribal governments have been reestablished and strengthened, and Native American cultures have been revived.

Activism

By 1961, termination had gone far enough to alarm many Indians, who believed that too much discretionary power over reservation Indians was being given to the states and that the answer to the problems of American Indians lay not in termination of federal services but in better legislation. Beginning in the late 1960's, American Indian activists began to call attention to the injustices still faced by Indians and to demand legislation to correct the situation. A group called Indians of All Tribes took over abandoned Alcatraz Island on November 9, 1969, and remained there for nearly nineteen months. Following a demonstration at Mount Rushmore in 1971, Indian interest groups organized the Trail of Broken Treaties march on Washington, D.C., to bring further attention to the American Indian situation. On October 2, 1971, march organizers stated their demands, which included fulfillment of treaty obligations, removal of Indian matters from the Bureau of Indian Affairs (BIA) and placement directly under the president of the United States, and no termination of federal services without a referendum.

More than fifteen groups supported the August, 1972, march, but the American Indian Movement (AIM), founded by Dennis Banks and George Mitchell in 1968, was the dominant participant. The march ended with the November, 1972, seven-day occupation of the BIA building in Washington. About six months later, on February 27, 1973, about two hundred armed AIM members seized the small town of Wounded Knee on the Pine Ridge Reservation in South Dakota. The occupation ended by peaceful negotiation seventy-one days after it began.

The Longest Walk started on February 11, 1978, when about 180 people set out from San Francisco to walk across the continent to Washington, D.C., to commemorate all the forced walks the Indian people had made in the past, such as the Trail of Tears in the 1830's. The organizers of the Longest Walk included such leaders of AIM as Vernon Bellecourt and Dennis Banks but no tribal leaders. About 5,000 to 10,000 people were estimated to have reached Washington by July 15, 1978.

Legislation

In mid-1994 there were 543 tribes that were "federally recognized" and received the services of the BIA. The Indian Reorganization Act (1934) delineated steps by which any "Indian tribe . . . residing on the same reservation" might formally organize for recognition. In 1978, the Federal Acknowledgment Program was established, delineating seven mandatory criteria for federal recognition. In the mid-1980's, about 125 American Indian groups whose relationship with the federal government had been terminated were trying to meet these seven criteria.

Indians, along with Latinos, African Americans, and other minorities, took advantage of the Voting Rights Act of 1965. The act banned many of the methods, such as literacy tests, that had been used since passage of the Fifteenth Amendment to the federal constitution in 1870 to prevent Native Americans from voting. Later, the 1975 renewal of the Voting Rights Act outlawed gerrymandering and required bilingual ballots and voting information.

The American Indian Civil Rights Act of 1968 extended many of the provisions of the Bill of Rights to members of Indian tribes in order to protect them from arbitrary actions of their own tribal councils. Although the government meant well, critics argued that the federal government unilaterally imposed the act despite its self-determination policy.

In July, 1970, President Richard M. Nixon presented a message to Congress requesting repudiation of the

In 1941, this Montana tavern posted its discriminatory policy of not selling beer to American Indians. The civil rights of American Indians were guaranteed by a well-meant but controversial act passed in 1968.

termination policy; legislative authority to empower any tribe to accept responsibility for the operation of federally funded programs in the Department of the Interior and the Department of Health, Education, and Welfare; authority to channel federal education funds to Indians in public schools through tribal governments rather than through local public-school districts; and authority for Indians to enter into long-term leases of their lands. These policies strengthened the right of the recognized Indian tribes to determine their own futures within the context of United States citizenship as well as the right of tribes to exist as tribes.

Self-Determination

Nixon's message produced the Indian Self-Determination and Education Assistance Act of 1975, which provided statutory authority to permit tribes to assume responsibilities formerly reserved for officials of the BIA and other departments of the government. Although theoretically sound, the Self-Determination Act did not operate efficiently. Conflict developed between tribes seeking full implementation of self-determination and the BIA, which was reluctant to surrender its dominance in Native American affairs. The BIA retained its position through measures such as increased bureaucratization, requirements that the BIA approve tribal contracts with non-Indian parties, and the vagaries of congressional appropriations.

The Indian Education Act of 1972, intended to make financial grants more available to school districts with

large numbers of Indian students, failed to define the beneficiaries sufficiently, and school districts that did not believe that they had a significant Indian student population soon found themselves besieged by students claiming Indian blood.

In 1978, Congress passed the Tribally Controlled Community College Act, which encouraged tribes to establish community colleges where native languages, culture, and history could be taught, and the American Indian Religious Freedom Act, which allowed Indians to worship in accordance with their ancestral beliefs. The federal government committed itself to "protect and preserve for Native Americans their inherent right of freedom to believe, express, and exercise the traditional religions" and directed federal agencies to make certain that Native Americans were not deprived of access to their sacred sites on federal land. However, the act did not contain provisions for enforcement.

Decisions in several Supreme Court cases recognized that tribes were sovereign entities that should be largely free from restrictions by both federal and state governments. *Santa Clara Pueblo v. Martinez* (1978), upheld the right of a tribe to be governed by its own traditional laws and to determine its membership, even if such procedures conflicted with the civil rights of individual tribal members or other Americans under the U.S. Constitution. Other significant cases include *Oliphant v. Suquamish Indian Tribe* (1978); *Merrion v. Jicarilla Apache Tribe* (1982); *Arizona v. California* (1983); *Nevada v. United States* (1983); *Montana v. Blackfeet Tribe of Indians* (1985).

The Indian Alcohol and Substance Abuse Prevention and Treatment Act (1986) was passed to develop a comprehensive coordinated attack on the illegal narcotics traffic in Indian country and the deleterious impact of alcohol and substance abuse on Indian tribes. It was to provide guidance through schools, tribal offices, the BIA, and the Indian Health Service (IHS) and to establish Indian Youth Programs, emergency shelters, and rehabilitation services.

On April 28, 1988, Congress passed two important acts. The Tribally Controlled School Grants Act assured maximum Indian participation in the direction of education services in order to make them more responsive to the needs and desires of Indian communities. The Indian Education Act (1988) was intended to provide financial assistance to local educational agencies to develop and carry out elementary and secondary school programs specially designed to meet the special educational and cultural academic needs of Indians. An Office of Indian Education was established in the Department of Education to encourage fellowships for Native Americans and adult education.

The Indian Gaming Regulatory Act of October 17, 1988, declared federal policy as promoting tribal economic development, tribal self-sufficiency, strong tribal government, and, if not specifically prohibited by federal law, as allowing gambling on Indian land under the supervision of a National Indian Gaming Commission. By the end of 1992, about 140 tribes maintained gaming operations.

Senate hearings in 1988-1989 on continuing Indian problems in the areas of health, education, religion, culture, employment, and tribal sovereignty led to considerable legislation. The Indian Child Protection and Family Violence Prevention Act (1990) sought to require reports of abused Indian children, establish reliable data on the topic for statistical purposes, authorize procedures to ensure effective child protection, establish an Indian Child Abuse Prevention and Treatment Grant Program for technical assistance, and provide for treatment and prevention of incidents of family violence. In 1992, Congress passed the Indian Higher Education Programs Act, providing financial aid for higher education.

Social Conditions

Senator John McCain of Arizona reported in 1992 that from 40 percent to 45 percent of reservation Indians and 22 percent of off-reservation Indians in the United States live below the poverty line. The BIA reported that as of 1985, Indians had a 39 percent unemployment rate, three times the rate for individuals in the United States as a whole. Twenty-five percent of Indian reservation households were receiving food stamps. Of the working-age population on Indian reservations, only about 40 percent were employed more than forty weeks out of the year, and the majority of those who worked earned less than $7,000 per year. The rate of alcoholism on reservations was 438 percent greater than the national average, tuberculosis 400 percent higher, diabetes 155 percent higher. There were 131 percent more accidents on reservations, 57 percent more homicides, 27 percent more suicides, and 32 percent more cases of pneumonia and influenza.

Education, Employment, and Housing

The 1991 Digest of Education Statistics reported that during the 1988-1989 school year, for every ten thousand bachelor's degrees awarded, only forty went to American Indian students; in that year, only forty-seven Indians in ten thousand were undergraduate students. More than 44 percent of Indian adults age twenty-five and older had not graduated from high school.

The BIA in 1992 estimated that an average of 48 percent of the available workers on or near reservation areas had no jobs, while the conditions of Indians in many urban areas was little better. In 1992, Congress passed the Indian Employment, Training, and Related Services Demonstration Act to demonstrate how Indian tribal governments can integrate to improve the effectiveness of employment and training services and to reduce joblessness in Indian communities.

Representative Doug Bereuter of Nebraska, taking his information from the U.S. Census Bureau, stated in 1992 that almost 24 percent of all Indians living in Indian communities or on reservations lacked adequate shelter. While the national average of homelessness was estimated at 6.4 percent, Indians had nearly four times the amount of homelessness of the general population. In addition, many houses on Indian reservations lacked running water or indoor plumbing of any kind. *Robert M. Spector*

Core Resources

Books that discuss U.S. policy toward American Indians include Theodore W. Taylor's *American Indian Policy* (Mt. Airy, Md.: Lomond, 1983), Christine Bolt's *American Indian Policy and American Reform* (London: Allen & Unwin, 1987), and *American Indian Policy in the Twentieth Century* (Norman: University of Oklahoma Press, 1985), edited by Vine Deloria, Jr. A general history of American Indians can be found in *The American Indian Past and Present* (4th ed., New York: McGraw-Hill, 1992), by Roger L. Nichols. Vine Deloria, Jr., and Clifford M. Lytle's *American Indians, American Justice* (Austin: University of Texas Press, 1983) examines the white justice system and its relationship with Native Americans as individuals and tribe members. *Native American Testimony: A Chronicle of Indian-White Relations from Prophecy to the Present, 1492-1992* (New York: Viking Penguin, 1991), edited by Peter Nabokov, is an anthology of Indian-white relations as seen by Native Americans from 1492 to 1992.

See also: American Indian activism; American Indian Civil Rights Act; American Indian Religious Freedom Act; Indian Act of 1876; Indian Act of 1951; Indian Act of 1989; Indian Citizenship Act; Indian Education Acts; Termination Resolution; Tribal sovereignty.

American Indian Civil Rights Act

A significant but controversial move toward the guarantee of individual American Indian rights came about in special Indian titles of the Civil Rights Act signed

April 11, 1968. The existence of tribal governments and tribal courts had raised the issue of protection of individual rights of Indian people living in a tribal context. Tribal governments are considered inherently sovereign since they predate the U.S. Constitution and do not derive their power to exist or to govern from either federal or state government. Further, federal recognition or regulation of tribes does not make them part of the United States government or guarantee constitutional protections. Even with the Indian Citizenship Act (1924), the Bill of Rights did not extend to situations involving tribal government.

In 1968, when civil rights legislation was proposed to remedy inequal protections of some groups in the United States, Senator Sam Ervin of North Carolina proposed bringing tribal governments into the constitutional framework of the United States. Largely because of tribal protests that the full Bill of Rights would severely upset traditional governing practices, however, a blanket extension of the Bill of Rights to tribal governments was replaced by a more selective and specific list of individual rights that were to be protected.

Title II of the act, often referred to as the Indian Bill of Rights, since it is very close to constitutional provisions, stresses the rights of individuals and so limits the authority of tribal governments. It specifically authorizes a writ of *habeas corpus* for anyone detained by a tribe. This bill does not prohibit "establishment of religion," which would have prevented continuation of the quasitheocracies that form the basis of government for some Indian communities, but it does guarantee "free exercise of religion." Also, persons are not guaranteed free counsel in criminal proceedings, and the right of indictment by grand jury is not guaranteed. Title III charged the secretary of the interior to draw up codes of justice to be used in courts of Indian offenses. Title IV repealed section 7 of Public Law 280, an act passed by Congress in 1953 that gave states authority to extend civil and criminal jurisdiction over reservations. This title also authorized the retrocession of jurisdiction already assumed by a state. Title V added "assault resulting in serious bodily injury" to offenses on reservations subject to federal jurisdiction. Title VI granted automatic approval of tribal contracts if the secretary of the interior did not act within ninety days.

The American Indian Civil Rights Act remains controversial: Many Indian people view it as a violation of tribal sovereignty. Congress unilaterally imposed the bill on tribal governments and people, and tribes have questioned the legality of permitting states to have a direct role in formulating and passing this law for tribes with no mechanism for tribes to accept or reject the legislation. Tribal culture is directly affected by this law because of the stress it places on individualism despite the fact that for most tribes, community needs take precedence over individual rights. Many Indian leaders believe the American Indian Civil Rights Act prevents tribes from exercising their inherent sovereignty.   *Carole A. Barrett*

See also: American Indian civil rights; Civil Rights Act of 1968; Indian Citizenship Act; Indian preference; Public Law 280; Tribal sovereignty.

American Indian dance and music

Significance: Native American dance and music, which incorporate and express cultural values, help people from other cultures understand the value that Indians place on nature and balance. Native people have also used dance and music to teach others that they share many motivations and needs.

Native American dance takes a number of forms, some of which are specific to the originating tribe and some that are more widespread. The Fancy Dance began in Oklahoma, where elders of the Ponca tribe called it the "crazy dance," and it rapidly spread throughout the country. Fancy Dances are characterized by elaborate costumes and intricate footwork and are one of the many attractions at most powwows. The dancers, usually Native American men, often compete, incorporating acrobatic moves into their steps.

Native American groups are also known for their social and ceremonial dances, which typically involve beautiful Indian costumes and headwear and often are derived from the ancient legends of the native tribes. In some native cultures, women dance a shawl dance, wearing a shawl to indicate respect for the drums, for the dancers, and for the singers. Most Native American tribes dance hoop dances. The hoop reflects the belief shared by many tribes that time is cyclical and that the cycle of nature has no beginning and no end and includes all creatures and all natural elements. Many tribes use the Ghost Dance to show respect for and to connect to ancient ancestors; others dance the Buffalo Dance, originally performed to ensure a good hunt. Many tribes have ceremonial dances, sometimes called spear-and-shield dances, that relate stories of famous hunts, preparation for war, and battles. The Pueblo Indians of the Southwest perform the Butterfly Dance, in which beautifully costumed women and men celebrate the fertility of the butterfly. The Eastern Woodlands tribes dance the Green Corn Dance; the Plains Indians perform the Sun

Dance, and the Hopis perform the Snake Dance, a kind of preliminary rain dance. Various forms of rain dances are common among many tribes including the Hopi, the Tohono O'odham, and the Pueblo Indians. The Tlinglits of Alaska dance raven dances, costumed like the raven, who serves as the trickster in many of this tribe's native myths and legends.

Many Native Americans believe that because ceremonial dances are part of a tribe's spirituality, people should dance them only if they are members of the tribe. However, others believe that anyone who can appreciate the spirit of the dances and who can learn them should be allowed to perform them. By learning the origins of the dances and by following the stories that some of them tell, members of other cultural groups can develop an appreciation for Native American culture.

Traditional Music

Traditional Native American music encompasses a wide range of sounds, from melodies played on wooden flutes to drums and chantlike singing to fiddle bands. One familiar sound is that of the Indian flute. In the Plains cultures, the wooden flute was used by a young man to attract a woman. Once the courtship was over, the young man usually put the flute away. In other native cultures, the wooden flute was used for meditation.

Drums are also a part of traditional Indian music and are often used to accompany dancers. Together the drums and the dancers tell stories of battles, hunts, and other events that teach the listeners and watchers of the history and legends of the tribes. Another aspect of the musical heritage of Native Americans are traditional songs. These songs, often accompanied by gourd rattles and basket drums, touch on topics such as fertility, hunting, honoring ancestors, and ceremonies. There are also traditional dance songs and creation songs. These traditional songs very clearly reflect the values and beliefs of the native tribes.

Another type of traditional music is played by the Indian fiddle bands of the Southwest. These bands were originally formed under the direction of Christian missionaries and usually consisted of violins, guitars, and sometimes the Apache fiddle. They played a variety of music including polkas, two-steps, Santiago dance tunes, and chicken scratch music. Musicologists and sociologists point out that the Native American musicians' capacity to develop tunes for these bands illustrates their ability to adapt and synthesize nonnative influences.

Since the beginning of the twentieth century, non-Indian composers have incorporated the sounds of native cultures in compositions that express the American identity. Some of the first composers to do this were Henry F. B. Gilbert, Arthur Farwell, John Powell, and Edward MacDowell, who is known for his 1897 composition *Indian Suite.*

Contemporary Music

In 1968, the American Indian Movement (AIM) was formed to further Native American interests and defend their rights. AIM encouraged Native Americans, particularly the young, to learn about their cultural heritage and to feel proud to be American Indians. Much of Native American contemporary music grew from this movement and from the effort of Native Americans to learn about and to understand their culture and their place within the larger American society. Native American Buffy Sainte-Marie gained recognition in the 1960's and 1970's with her protest

At a celebration at Santa Clara Pueblo in New Mexico, Pueblo Indians perform a traditional song.

songs, and she continued to write songs that reflected her Cree heritage in the 1990's. Many Native Americans combined the sounds and themes of their culture with rock, country, jazz, and blues to produce special strains of Native American contemporary music. Rock musicians Keith Secola and the Wild Band of Warriors were popular all across the United States and Europe as were the poet Joy Harjo and her rock band Poetic Justice. Popular singer Wayquay combined the natural sounds and chants of her Ojibway/Anishnabe ancestry with the rhythms of rock and blues to create music that made her popular in both the United States and Europe. John Trudell, an original leader of AIM, sang of his ancestors as well as of the plight of contemporary natives.

Contemporary Native American music helps non-Indians understand that although the Native American culture has special values and its members share a special heritage, Indians are essentially Americans who live within the same society and have the same needs, dreams, fears, and experiences as everyone else. All across the United States, Native American radio stations play contemporary native music so that a large number of Americans have an opportunity to experience the sound and to better understand the culture behind that sound.
Annita Marie Ward

Core Resources
Noted ethnomusicologist Charlotte Heath, director of the National Museum of the American Indian, edited two books on Native American dance and music: *The Music of the American Indian* (Los Angeles: University of California at Los Angeles Ethnomusicology Publications, 1980); *Native American Dance: Ceremonies and Social Traditions* (Washington, D.C.: National Museum of the American Indian and Fulcrum Publishing, 1998). James Cument edited *Encyclopedia of the North American Indian* (New York: Scholastic Reference, 1996), which includes more than four hundred illustrations from the legends, ceremonies, and dances of 149 Indian tribes.

See also: American Indian literature; American Indian theater; American Indians and film; Powwows.

American Indian Defense Association

The American Indian Defense Association (AIDA) was organized in New York City in May, 1923, by white reformers sympathetic to Indian causes. The organization, led by John Collier, AIDA's founder and first executive secretary, consisted primarily of wealthy, liberal Californians who joined hands in opposition to a proposed bill addressing land disputes in the Northwest that might have resulted in the loss of Pueblo lands. Members of AIDA were critical of the General Allotment Act of 1887, pleading for the maintenance of Indian tribal integrity.

In 1922, Collier explicitly stated AIDA's goals. The association was to aid in the preservation of Indian culture, including the revitalization of Indian arts and crafts. It sought to entitle Indians to social and religious freedoms and to rejuvenate tribal governments. Provisions were also made for safeguarding Indian civil liberties. Furthermore, Indians were to be entitled to federal aid in the form of Farm Loan Bank credits, public health services, and other federal assistance programs. To break its monopoly over Indian programs, Collier suggested reform of the Bureau of Indian Affairs. Through congressional lobbying, publication of pamphlets, and advice to Indian tribes, Collier and AIDA labored to influence federal Indian policy and to improve conditions on reservations.

In its first decade, AIDA grew to more than seventeen hundred members. Headquartered in Washington, D.C., the organization maintained branches in cities throughout the country. During the 1920's, Collier became the nation's leading advocate of Indian rights. After Franklin D. Roosevelt was elected president in 1932, Collier became a candidate for the post of commissioner in the Bureau of Indian Affairs. Despite Collier's Communist sympathies and confrontational nature, Roosevelt appointed him commissioner in 1933. Collier initiated an Indian New Deal whereby governmental Indian policy shifted away from assimilation and toward tribal revitalization. Collier's culminating triumph was passage in 1934 of the Indian Reorganization Act, the heart of the Indian New Deal. AIDA consistently supported Collier and the Indian New Deal, although the association was frequently critical of its application.

In 1936, AIDA merged with the National Association on Indian Affairs, becoming the Association on American Indian Affairs (AAIA). By the 1990's, AAIA was headquartered in New York City, where it maintained a staff of twelve employees and had forty thousand members nationwide with an annual operating budget of $1.5 million. AAIA provided legal and technical assistance in health, education, economic development, the administration of justice and resource utilization to United States tribes. In addition, the organization maintained the American Indian Fund, published the newsletter *Indian Affairs*, and occasionally published books.
Mary E. Virginia

See also: Allotment system; General Allotment Act; Indian New Deal; Indian Reorganization Act; Indian-white relations: United States.

American Indian demographics

> **Significance:** After European contact, most Native American nations experienced dramatic population losses, but by the 1990's, they represented one of the fastest-growing segments of American society.

When Europeans arrived on the shores of North America, they encountered an estimated 1.2 million to 18 million people. They were the "original Americans," descendants of people who journeyed to North America thousands of years before Europeans. Over the millennia, Native Americans evolved hundreds of unique cultural traditions with their own worldviews, perhaps two hundred languages (of several distinct families), ecological adaptations to every environmental situation, and a range of forms of governance. Native North America, before the arrival of Europeans, represented one of the most ethnically diverse regions in the world. Tragically, much of this cultural mosaic was extinguished by massive population declines after European contact. Yet Native Americans survived this demographic and cultural onslaught to represent one of the fastest-growing segments of American society in the 1990's.

Prehistoric Trends

The colonization of the Americas by Paleo-Indians (an anthropological term for the ancestors of Native Americans) was one of the greatest demographic events in global history. There has been considerable controversy regarding the dates for early migrations to North America. Some scholars have suggested that the earliest migrations occurred as far back as fifty thousand years ago; some have said that migration may also have occurred as recently as three thousand years ago. A more generally agreed-upon time frame for the migrations, however, is between twenty-five thousand and twelve thousand years ago.

Although many Native Americans reject the hypothesis that their ancestors immigrated from greater Eurasia, archaeological evidence suggests that some first Americans may have entered the Western Hemisphere during the many glacial periods that exposed Beringia, the Bering Strait land bridge. Beringia periodically linked Siberia with the Americas, allowing animals and humans access to both continents. Others may have made the journey using boats, following a maritime route or traveling down a coastal corridor. In any event, these irregular waves of colonizers represented the last great global movement of people into unoccupied land—a migra-tion hallmark in human history.

How many "first Americans" entered the Americas is unknown. Archaeologists note that the Late Wisconsin glacier's recession about fifteen thousand years ago allowed Native American people to migrate southward, eventually colonizing the remainder of the Americas. Before then, the glacier largely prevented further immigration and colonization. What specific routes they took and how rapidly people dispersed across both continents are topics of considerable archaeological debate. Firm evidence exists that by 9400 B.C.E. Native Americans had reached southern South America, indicating that Native Americans had dispersed widely across the New World's landscape. Despite hypotheses that argue for an accelerated population growth rate, it is likely that during this early colonization period, the Native American population's growth rates were slow to moderate, with cyclical rates of growth and decline. These population fluctuations reflected a complex array of changing social, demographic, and ecological conditions as local populations adapted to regional conditions.

In North America, Native American demographic distribution and redistribution paralleled closely the glacial retreat north, the trend toward regional and climatic aridity that altered local resources, and cultural innovations. The above factors, by 9000 B.C.E., eventually enabled the colonization of every available area on the North American continent. These hunter-gatherers and, later, the cultural traditions known as Archaic societies, developed a greater variety of lifeways, producing marked differences in population size, distribution, and vital events.

Paleopathological evidence indicates that prehistoric Native American populations faced a number of health risks. Documented cases of malnutrition, anemia, tuberculosis, trachoma, trepanematoid infections, and degenerative conditions occurred in pre-Columbian North America. These afflictions, coupled with periodic trauma, accidents, and warfare, affected the demographic structure of regional populations.

A cultural innovation that had significant demographic consequences was the invention and diffusion of agriculture. Sometime before 3500 B.C.E. in Mesoamerica, maize, beans, and squash were domesticated. As this cultural knowledge spread northward, many Native American societies east of the Mississippi River, in the Southwest, and along the major waterways of the greater Midwest adopted agriculture. Demographically, agriculture promoted the development of larger populations, residing in sedentary villages or cities. Near present-day Alton, Illinois, along the Mississippi River, for example, was the urban center of Cahokia. At its height about 1100 C.E., Cahokia extended over five square miles and had a population of perhaps thirty thousand people. Although regional population concentrations arose across native North America, by 1300 C.E. many areas containing high population densities began to decline. The causes of the decline and social reorganization in some regions are open to debate. It is clear that in a number of regions, high population densities and size remained until the European encounter.

By the time of European contact, native North America demographically contained a variety of population sizes and densities, ranging from fewer than one person per ten square miles in the Great Basin to the densely settled, resource-rich regions of the Pacific Northwest, Northeast, Southeast, and Southwest. These areas may have supported from five to more than one hundred people per ten square miles. By the time Europeans arrived, Native Americans already had undergone a number of profound demographic events.

Historical Trends
The European colonization of North America launched a series of catastrophic events for Native American populations. Native American societies experienced tremendous population declines. Native American populations periodically experienced mortality increases, decreases in their fertility performance, forced migration, as well as a deterioration of their societal health status.

Of all the factors that affected post-contact Native American societies, the accelerated death rates from the introduction of European diseases remain prominent. Europeans brought smallpox, measles, cholera, and other infections that were foreign to Native American people. It has been estimated that ninety-three epidemics of Old World pathogens affected Native Americans from the sixteenth to the twentieth centuries. Old World diseases, combined with warfare, genocide, and the introduction of alcohol, forced migration and relocation, and the overall destruction of indigenous lifeways resulted in the demographic collapse of native North America. One Native American scholar called it the "American Indian Holocaust."

Within decades of European contact, Native American populations declined. The colonization of the Spanish, French, and, later, English set in motion significant population changes. Between 1500 and 1820, Native American populations residing east of the Mississippi River declined to approximately 6 percent of their at-contact size. In the southeastern region, for example, the estimated Native American population in 1685 was 199,400. By 1790 their population was approximately 55,900—a decline of 71.9 percent. Paralleling this demographic collapse, the ethnic diversity of indigenous societies residing east of the Mississippi River declined between 25 and 79 percent, as distinct Native American

nations were driven to extinction or forced to amalgamate with other Native American nations.

In 1830, the remaining Native Americans in the East were forcibly removed to west of the Mississippi River under President Andrew Jackson's administration. Between 1828 and 1838, approximately 81,300 Native Americans were thus removed. For their relocation efforts, the U.S. government acquired 115,355,767 acres of Indian lands and resources. Furthermore, the Choctaw, Chickasaw, Cherokee, Seminole, and Muskogee lost between 15 and 50 percent of their population during the forced relocation. Other removed Native American tribal nations suffered similar demographic losses. By about 1850, the estimated Native American population stood at 383,000.

As Native American populations declined, the European, African American, and Latino populations grew, occupying the available lands acquired from Native Americans. Aside from losing their land and resources, the increasing contact with non-Indians had other important demographic consequences. Since contact, Native Americans have experienced an increased genetic exchange with European and African populations. The rise of people with Native American-European or Native American-African ancestry, or of all three ancestries, may have had significant implications for tribal survival and demographic recovery. Some scholars suggest that depopulation and the following demographic recovery resulted in certain physical and genetic changes in those who survived the epidemic. The incorporation of Europeans, African Americans, or other Native Americans promoted further those phenotypic and genotypic processes.

As the American population of European descent surpassed twenty-three million by 1850, Native Americans west of the Mississippi River began to experience directly the brunt of colonization and settlement. Before that time, western Native American populations had experienced introduced infectious diseases, intermittent warfare with Europeans, and an erosion of their resources. The Mandan, for example, boasted an estimated at-contact population of possibly 15,000. After the 1837-1838 smallpox epidemic, their population collapsed to between 125 and 1,200 individuals, forcing them eventually to merge, culturally and biologically, with the Arikara and Hidatsa. Western indigenous nations, from 1850 through 1880, witnessed continued demographic upheaval. Their population changes during those decades were affected by the dramatic social and economic changes in U.S. society. The United States economy was industrializing, American society was becoming more urban, and the federal government desired a link between the east and west coasts as a completion to its nation building. In addition, the United States experienced a dramatic influx of European immigrants. In three decades, from 1850 to 1880, the European population increased to 50,155,783. This prompted the federal government to alienate Native Americans from their remaining lands. To meet these economic and political demands, western lands and resources were needed. The continued demographic collapse of many Indian nations occurred under the guise of the nation's rhetoric of manifest destiny.

In an attempt to subdue the remaining indigenous populations and force them onto reservations, the U.S. government either negotiated a series of treaties or carried out military expeditions. The combined impact of war, disease, and the continued destruction of their lifeways resulted in further population decline. By the time Native Americans were relegated to reservations or rural communities in 1880, there were 306,543 Native Americans surviving in the coterminous United States.

The Twentieth Century

The indigenous population of the United States reached its nadir in 1890. The 1890 U.S. census recorded 248,253 Native Americans in the continental United States. Although most infectious diseases experienced during the pre-reservation era began to diminish, these acute infections were replaced with chronic diseases on reservations. Poor sanitation, poor nutrition, overcrowding, and severe cultural oppression resulted in the appearance of tuberculosis, trachoma, and intermittent measles and influenza outbreaks, as well as a rise in infant mortality. As these afflictions reached epidemic proportions, the Native American population between 1900 and 1920 remained rather static. Most Native Americans continued to live on reservations or in rural areas, isolated from society. In 1920, only 6.2 percent of Native Americans resided in urban areas.

After 1930, however, Native Americans began to experience a tremendous growth rate. With the passage of the Indian Reorganization Act (1934), cultural oppression lessened, health and sanitation conditions improved, and social programs began to affect Native American demography positively. Native American populations grew because fertility increased, infant survivorship improved, and the death rate fell. The result was a young age-sex structure.

The advent of World War II witnessed a migratory shift away from reservations and rural communities. Attracted by service in the armed forces and urban job prospects, many Native Americans migrated to major cities. The outflow of Native American immigrants to urban centers initiated a demographic trend that continued in the 1990's. The out-migration of Native Americans was stimulated further by the Bureau of Indian Affairs. In the mid-1950's, the federal government insti-

tuted a relocation program. The program assisted Native Americans through job training and support services in being placed in an urban center. In 1990, for the first time since indigenous people have been recorded by the U.S. Census Bureau, the census recorded that more Native Americans resided in urban than in rural areas. The greater Los Angeles metropolitan area, for example, had 87,500 people of Native American descent, an increase of 5 percent over the previous decade.

Since the 1950's, the Native American population has grown tremendously. In 1960, there were 523,591 Native Americans. By 1970, there were 792,730 people who identified themselves as Native American. The 1980 U.S. Census witnessed a 79.4 percent increase. The reasons for this growth are complex and multifactorial. First, after the transfer of the Indian Health Service from the Bureau of Indian Affairs in 1955, Native American health improved dramatically, especially infant and child health care. Second, Native American fertility increased and mortality decreased, adding significantly to the population. Finally, more Americans are identifying themselves as having Native American ancestry.

Contemporary Trends

The Native American population of the United States is young and growing. As a result, the Native American population suffers from social problems in which demography plays an important role. Native American health status lags behind that of the United States'

Population of American Indians and Total U.S. Population, 1890-1990
(thousands)

Year	American Indians	Total United States
1890	248	62,947
1900	237	75,994
1910	265	91,972
1920	244	105,710
1930	332	122,775
1940	333	131,669
1950	343	150,697
1960	523	178,464
1970	792	203,211
1980	1,420	226,546
1990	2,065	248,718

Sources: Data are from U.S. Bureau of the Census, *Statistical Abstract of the United States, 1997,* (117th ed.). Washington, D.C., U.S. Government Printing Office, 1997, and *Historical Statistics of the United States: Colonial Times to 1970, Bicentennial edition, Part 2.* Washington, D.C., U.S. Government Printing Office, 1975.

general population. Deaths by accidents, violence, suicide, tuberculosis, diabetes, and numerous other conditions exceed national averages. Unemployment, in both rural and urban areas, remains high, although the number of Native American-owned businesses increased by 64 percent between 1982 and 1987. Poverty also continues to plague Native American families. In the ten states with the most Native Americans, between 17 percent and 47 percent of Native American persons live in poverty. Finally, Native American people continue to report various risk factors associated with the above conditions. According to 1988 statistics, 31.1 percent of eighth-grade Native American children resided in single-parent households, 40.1 percent resided in households that earned less than $15,000 annually, and 18.6 percent spent more than three hours home alone every day. These factors conspire to promote continued poverty, low educational attainment, high unemployment, and ill health.

The 1990 census counted 1,878,000 Native Americans, an increase of more than 25 percent since 1980. Native American people reside in every state in the union, but the majority of the population is concentrated in the West. Also, a major portion of the population is concentrated in ten tribes.

The phenomenal growth rate among Native Americans exceeds the growth for African Americans and Americans of European descent but not the increase in the Latino or Asian American populations. Today, Native Americans and Alaska Natives compose approximately 1 percent of the United States population but continue to represent a higher percentage of the country's cultural diversity. *Gregory R. Campbell*

Core Resources
The demographics of American Indians are presented and discussed in several volumes, including Harold L. Hodgkinson's *The Demographics of American Indians: One Percent of the People, Fifty Percent of the Diversity* (Washington, D.C.: Center for Demographic Policy, Institute for Educational Leadership, 1990), *Statistical Record of Native North Americans* (Detroit: Gale Research, 1993), edited by Marlita A. Reddy, C. Matthew Snipp's *American Indians: The First of This Land* (New York: Russell Sage Foundation, 1989), and Paul Stuart's *Nations Within a Nation: Historical Statistics of American Indians* (New York: Greenwood Press, 1987). Books that examine the decline in the Native American population following contact with Europeans include David E. Stannard's *American Holocaust* (New York: Oxford University Press, 1992), Russell Thornton's *American Indian Holocaust and Survival: A Population History Since 1492* (Norman: University of Oklahoma Press, 1987), and *Disease and Demography in the Americas* (Washington, D.C.: Smithsonian Institution Press, 1992), edited by John W. Verano and Douglas H. Ubelaker.

See also: Disease and intergroup contact; Indian Removal Act; Indian-white relations: United States; Relocation of American Indians; Reservation system of the United States.

American Indian literature

Significance: In the latter part of the twentieth century, Native Americans began exploring their heritage and creating literature that reflects their experiences and culture. These writings help people from other cultural groups understand the values, beliefs, and traditions of Native Americans.

During the nineteenth century and the early part of the twentieth century, most works dealing with Native Americans were written by whites who visited the reservations and wrote about the people they found there and the stories they heard. These accounts may have led the American public to believe that American Indians were more exotic than they actually were. They offered information about the mythology and spiritual beliefs of Native Americans but did not always accurately portray their everyday life. One writer in the early twentieth century who did present a very accurate view of the Native American lifestyle was Charles A. Eastman (Ohiyesa), who wrote many books about Indian life and beliefs, including *The Soul of the Indian* (1911). Eastman was able to explain Native American life accurately because he himself was a Sioux who spent many years as the doctor on the Lone Pine Reservation in South Dakota. He could compare the Sioux culture to the white culture because he had been educated at Dartmouth College. At the end of the twentieth century, readers were still consulting Eastman's works for an understanding of Native American beliefs and values.

Civil Rights and Native American Literature
The Civil Rights movement of the 1960's encouraged all people of color, not just African Americans, to assert their right to self-determination and to demand that their cultures be respected. Such ideas and beliefs led to the development of a body of literature from various minority groups including Native Americans. In 1969, N. Scott Momaday, a member of the Kiowa tribe, became the first Native American to win a Pulitzer Prize. His book *House Made of Dawn* (1968) was about the identity formation of a twentieth century Kiowan who retraced the

earlier migration of his tribe from the mouth of the Yellowstone to southwest Oklahoma. Momaday's theme of identity formation was explored again and again by Native American writers in the following two decades. Momaday's success encouraged other Native Americans to explore their native cultures for literary themes.

Multiculturalism

In the 1980's and 1990's, the United States became increasingly multicultural. Just as the Civil Rights movement had encouraged people of color to think about their rights and identity, multiculturalism spurred people to explore their cultural values and beliefs and to write about them. Native American poets, novelists, essayists, and playwrights produced works that contained the writers' individual memories and experiences as well as those of the various tribes. Although each writer's works differed, certain rhetorical styles, themes, and elements emerged to characterize Native American literature. Because many of the stories and characters grow out of an oral tradition, Native American writers are likely to employ repetition and to produce stories that have morals rather than simply to tell stories in a linear fashion or to employ a problem-solving technique. The themes found in Native American literature often relate to those of oral storytellers and of Native American history. Tradition-based topics include tricksters, creation, encounters with death and with mystery, star spouses, and familial and other human relationships; history-based topics include migrations, abductions, betrayals, and colonization. Common elements such as buffalo, coyotes, spiders, minerals, weather, astrofigures, colors, directions, time, and dance also figure in Native American literature.

Hundreds of Native American writers from every tribe emerged in the 1980's and 1990's. Many of these writers became very popular and won literary prizes. Mary Tall Mountain of the Alaskan Athabascan tribe wrote poems about the discord that Western civilization created for Native Americans. Paula Gunn Allen, Joy Harjo, Louise Erdrich, and Leslie Marmon Silko wrote poems, stories, and novels whose themes were the traditional role of Native American women and reconciliation of that role in modern life. James Welch explored the meeting point of traditional values and the modern world. Many Native Americans dealt with social problems as they affected Native American life. Vincent L. Mendoza won the 1994 Native American Prose Award for *Son of Two Bloods*, which explored racism against people of mixed heritage. The poet Harjo and the playwright Drew Hayden Taylor explored alcoholism as it affected native peoples. Taylor, as well as writer Sherman Alexie, examined Native American stereotypes. Paula Underwood (Turtle Singing Woman), a member of the Seneca tribe and oral historian for the Iroquois nation, wrote the immensely popular *Who Speaks for Wolf* (1994), a compilation of traditional stories told to her by her father Sharp Eyed Hawk.

By the end of the twentieth century, many Americans had a much better understanding of Native American culture because its themes and values had been explored by numerous Native American writers in many very successful and popular works of literature. This literature helped non-Indians understand that American Indians had needs and desires that were very much like the needs and desires of other Americans. It also helped erase many of the negative stereotypes of Indians that had been created by American films and television shows.

Annita Marie Ward

Core Resources

Andrew Wight edited *Dictionary of Native American Literature* (New York: Garland, 1994). Two good anthologies of Native American literature are *American Indian Literature: An Anthology* (Berkeley: University of California Press, 1988), edited by H. David Brumble III, and *American Indian Literature* (Norman: University of Oklahoma Press, 1991), edited by Alan R. Vellie. *Harper's Anthology of Twentieth Century Native American Poetry* (San Francisco: Harper & Row, 1988), edited by Diane Niatum, provides an excellent overview of Native American poetry. Joseph Bruchac and Janet Witalec edited *Smoke Rising: The Native American Literary Companion* (Detroit, Mich.: Visible Ink Press, 1995).

See also: American Indian dance and music; American Indian stereotypes; American Indian theater.

American Indian Movement

The American Indian Movement (AIM) was founded July 28, 1968, in Minneapolis in reaction to police brutality and harassment of native peoples in the Minneapolis-St. Paul metropolitan area. Initially, efforts were made to unite the approximately twenty local American Indian organizations to provide victims with assistance in the form of foot and car patrols and witness reports. Although the names of some founders are unknown, several urban Indians from Minnesota Ojibwa reservations—among them Dennis Banks, Clyde Bellecourt, and George Mitchell—were prominent cofounders. By 1969, AIM was an organization in its own right with an agenda addressing the needs of American Indian peoples. In the mid-1970's, AIM maintained about eighty chapters, including eight in Canada and several overseas. Membership totaled five thousand in the early 1990's.

AIM's philosophy and goals identify the organization as a spiritual movement seeking to revitalize the traditional values that had long been a part of the lives of the American Indians. AIM's short-range goals for urban and reservation people included improving housing, working with youth, creating jobs, raising living standards, encouraging active involvement in community affairs, educating the dominant society about Native American culture, keeping Indian people informed about developments affecting them, and rendering active assistance where appropriate. To realize its goals, AIM established training sessions called "survival schools" in Minneapolis and other places to promote school curriculum development and to instill pride as an alternative to loss of identity.

Russell Means (left) and Dennis Banks, two leaders of the American Indian Movement, speak to reporters during the occupation of Wounded Knee in 1973.

In the early 1970's, AIM launched a series of actions that made it the best known and most controversial American Indian group. Confrontational measures intended to highlight Indian grievances, such as the seizure of Alcatraz Island in 1969, the brief takeover of the Bureau of Indian Affairs' Washington, D.C., headquarters in 1972, and the dramatic and sometimes violent 1973 standoff with federal authorities during a ten-week occupation of Wounded Knee on the Pine Ridge, South Dakota, reservation, focused considerable national attention on AIM and leaders such as Dennis Banks and Russell Means.

AIM's militant confrontational tactics have been condemned by some Indian leaders. These critics say AIM's actions have resulted in increased racial tensions, brutal crackdowns by federal authorities involving systematic violations of the civil rights of non-AIM members, and a retardation of potential economic investment on reservations. On the other hand, AIM and its supporters argue that the organization's efforts have served to awaken the dominant culture to legitimate Indian demands and civil liberties issues and to the consequences of not honoring them. Moreover, AIM can point to lobbying successes such as its sponsorship of international treaty conferences on various Lakota Sioux reservations, which led to the 1977 International Treaty Conference of the United Nations in Geneva.

David A. Crain

See also: Alcatraz Island occupation; American Indian activism; Pine Ridge shootout; Wounded Knee occupation.

American Indian Policy Review Commission

The American Indian Policy Review Commission (AIPRC) was established in 1975 as a follow-up to the Indian Self-Determination and Education Assistance Act, passed in the same year. The findings of the commission, chaired by Senator James Abourezk of South Dakota and also known as the Abourezk Commission, were published in 1977 in a multivolume report. The report opposed assimilationist policies and recommended continuing the 1968 initiative for the establishment of permanent government units in the federal system to protect and strengthen tribal governments.

Among the factors that led to the establishment of the commission was the activism and unrest sweeping American Indian communities in the early 1970's. According to Vine Deloria, Jr., and Clifford M. Lytle (*American Indians, American Justice*, 1983; *The Nations Within: The Past and Future of American Indian Sovereignty*, 1984), the 1973 occupation of Wounded Knee in particular was a catalytic event in the decision to create a commission to reexamine the government's Indian policy.

The AIPRC included Indian representatives selected according to partisan tribal politics of the time. Indians dominated the staff; a significant number of contracted consultants were also Native Americans. The commission included five American Indian commissioners and thirty-one (out of thirty-three) Indian taskforce members as well as six non-Indian members of Congress. Inevitably, complicated political dynamics plagued the commission.

The final report of the AIPRC generally followed the

line of Indian militants who had previously been excluded from positions on commissions and taskforces. The extensive document listed more than two hundred recommendations. The commission found that the relationship between American Indian tribes and the United States was political and was established via treaties, according to international law. It recommended that the following two fundamental concepts guide all future federal policy: Indian tribes are sovereign political bodies having the power to enact laws and enforce them within reservation boundaries, and the relationship between the tribes and the United States "is premised on a special trust that must govern the conduct of the stronger toward the weaker." The AIPRC report also stated that the right to choose a form of government is an inherent right of any Indian tribe.

No actual social reform directed toward improving the lot of American Indians actually took place following publication of the AIPRC report. Moreover, Congress soon afterward abolished the standing Indian Affairs Subcommittees that operated under the Department of the Interior. Eventually, a Senate Select Subcommittee on Indian Affairs was authorized by Congress to sort out the many AIPRC recommendations.

The commission received criticism from both ends of the political spectrum. Some criticized it for going too far, and others have argued that, although the commission had good intentions in its promotion of self-determination, its recommendations in reality represented a continuation of the paternalistic relationship between the U.S. government and the tribes.

M. A. Jaimes

See also: American Indian activism; Wounded Knee occupation.

American Indian Religious Freedom Act

The passage of the American Indian Religious Freedom Act in August, 1978, formally allowed Indian tribes the freedom to practice their religions. This law also allowed tribes to regain access to sacred sites on federal lands and the right to possess certain sacred objects such as eagle feathers. This joint resolution directs all federal agencies to examine their policies and procedures and to take appropriate measures "to protect and preserve for American Indians their inherent right of freedom to believe, express, and exercise traditional religions" and to allow them to maintain their practices and access their religious sites on government lands.

Until 1934, the Bureau of Indian Affairs had regula-

tions prohibiting the practices of Indian religion and actively pursued a policy aimed at Christianizing and "civilizing" the Indians. To accomplish this, the Bureau of Indian Affairs forbade the practice of most traditional religions. Violators, if caught, could be punished by fines or imprisonment. The goal of these policies, strongly supported by Christian churches, was to stamp out aboriginal religions.

The American Indian Religious Freedom Act is a key element in Indian self-determination and cultural freedom in the United States. Even with passage of this act, however, Native Americans continued to experience problems in access to sacred sites and the use of peyote. In 1994, the Native American Church's right to use peyote was an unsettled issue in both federal and state courts. Although peyote is subject to control under the Federal Comprehensive Drug Abuse Prevention and Control Act, a number of states allow its use in Native American Church ceremonies. Some courts uphold the right of Native Americans who are church members to possess and use peyote, while other courts do not grant the same recognition.

The 1978 federal statute affirms the right of Native Americans to practice their traditional religion, but it does not allow Indians to sue when federal agencies disregard Indian religious practices or when agencies pursue plans despite adverse impact on Native American religions. The extension of full religious freedom to Native Americans is an evolving concept, and the American Indian Religious Freedom Act is an important philosophical foundation.

Carole A. Barrett

See also: American Indian civil rights; Native American Church; Peyote religion.

American Indian slavery

> **Significance:** Thousands of American Indians were enslaved by European colonists in the early years of North American settlement.

The earliest known record of Carolina natives being captured and enslaved was in 1520, when Spanish explorers took them to provide slaves for sugar plantations in Santo Domingo. In 1663, William Hilton, an Englishman, also captured natives from the Carolina coast for Caribbean slave owners. In 1670, Charleston was settled by the English. In 1671, after the defeat of Kusso warriors and the taking of numerous captives, English colonists initiated the Indian slave trade when Henry Woodward was commissioned to open trade in Indian slaves with

Indians of rival tribes.

Carolina included what is now South Carolina and North Carolina until 1713, but between the 1670's and 1730, almost all of Carolina's American Indian trading was out of Charles Town, or Charleston, which was the hub of the area that became South Carolina. Agriculture and forest industries also were part of Carolina's economy, but trading with the natives became the most lucrative aspect of the Carolina economy. Deerskins, leathers, and furs were the most important exports from this trading, but slavery also became an important part of the trade. Although American Indian slaves existed in other areas (Virginia, for example), only South Carolina developed Indian slavery as a major part of its commerce. As a result, South Carolina enslaved more natives than any other English colony.

Despite some opposition, major factors encouraged slavery. The selling of captives into slavery in order to pay volunteer soldiers was an old custom in Europe, with military commanders and pirates routinely enslaving people on ships they captured. The idea that slavery was better than death, and that the natives would murder their captives if they did not have the option of selling them, was used as a moral justification for slavery. Although this rationale was accurate in some cases, it did not take into account the great increase in natives capturing other natives because a market existed for slaves—a market made by the Europeans. Prior to European contact, slavery had been practiced by some American Indians, who frequently sold captives as slaves, but not on a large scale and generally without the harsh treatment common to European slavery. In addition, the enslavement of both American Indians and Africans got strong support in Charleston because a large number of Charleston's political and economic establishment were from the Caribbean and brought a strong tradition of slavery with them to South Carolina.

Slave Trade

The trade in American Indian slaves became an important part of the national conflicts involving Great Britain, Spain, and France for control of the Americas. Indians were drawn into these conflicts, often allying with a European power against other natives allied with another European power. In 1680, for example, Indians allied with the British in Carolina began raids against Indians allied with the Spanish Catholic missions in Georgia and northern Florida. The British and Spanish had attempted attacks on each other, and the English feared that the natives in Georgia and Florida would ally with the Spanish to attack Carolina. At the same time, the availability of a large number of Indians who were easy to capture because of their sedentary village life was tempting to slave traders.

Although the Europeans actually kidnapped or captured American Indians in the early years of the slave trade, mostly from coastal areas, they soon began to rely on other Indians to do the capturing as the slave trade increased and moved farther away from the coast. Encouraging native allies to capture other natives for slavery became a major part of the strategy of the slave dealers. In 1712, for example, the Tuscaroras of North Carolina killed some English and German settlers who had taken their land. The governor of North Carolina announced the availability of Indian slaves to induce South Carolina officials to send him military help. South Carolina expeditions—consisting mostly of Indians—killed more than a thousand Tuscaroras, and more than seven hundred were sold into slavery. Peaceful natives along the route back to South Carolina also were captured and enslaved.

Native vs. African Slaves

Indians made up one-fourth of the slaves in Carolina in 1708, numbering fourteen hundred out of fifty-five hundred slaves, but the percentage generally decreased after that, for several reasons. Natives were more likely than Africans to try to escape. Although Indians had to beware of other hostile Indians, they frequently were successful in their attempts because they were in the same country as their original homes. For this reason, and because of the heavy demand for slave labor on the Caribbean sugar plantations, native slaves usually were sold to Caribbean traders. Some were also sold to New England. In addition, native slaves were more susceptible to European diseases and hence had a greater death rate than African slaves. For these reasons, native slaves usually were less desired than, and cost less than, African slaves. Because large numbers of native men were killed, a high percentage of Indian slaves were women, partly explaining a significant mixture of African and Indian genealogies.

Although some American Indian slavery continued for several more decades, the practice basically had ended by 1730 in Carolina, with the Carolina traders turning to other trades and the English turning their Indian slavery concerns to central America.

Abraham D. Lavender

Core Resources

Verner Crane's *The Southern Frontier, 1670-1732* (Ann Arbor: University of Michigan Press, 1929) is a classic work on relations between European settlers and American Indians in the South. Vicki Rozema's *Footsteps of the Cherokees: A Guide to the Eastern Homelands of the Cherokee Nations* (Winston-Salem, N.C.: John F. Blair, 1995) devotes several pages to American Indian slavery. Gene Waddell's *Indians of the South Carolina Lowcountry, 1562-*

1751 (Spartanburg, S.C.: Reprint Company, 1980) describes how enslavement was one of several major factors in the extinction of South Carolina's lowcountry tribes. J. Leitch Wright, Jr.'s "Brands and Slave Cords," in *The Only Land They Knew: The Tragic Story of the American Indians in the Old South* (New York: Free Press, 1981) gives details on the Carolina slave trade in American Indians, with emphasis on historical details.

See also: Indian-white relations: United States; Slavery: history; Slavery: North American beginnings.

American Indian stereotypes

> **Significance:** Outmoded stereotypes of Native Americans have long dominated various media; these stereotypes may affect public policy as well as individual perceptions.

Stereotypes are generalizations concerning groups of people. They are frequently inaccurate because they are commonly based on false or incomplete information. Stereotypical assumptions concerning groups may lead to individuals being penalized (or occasionally rewarded) for traits that they as individuals may not in fact possess. Such behavior is manifestly unfair, and for this reason it is important to understand stereotypes concerning Native Americans and to correct these misconceptions.

The first stereotyping of American Indians occurred among the various Indian tribes. Many Indian groups' names for themselves simply mean "the people" in their native tongues, but members of other tribes often gave them derogatory labels, some of which have become the name by which the tribe is generally known, such as Eskimo, believed to mean "eaters of raw flesh," or Atakapa, which means "eaters of people." Traditionally, many Indian tribes considered those who did not speak their languages or share their cultural norms to be less than human. Such behavior is called "ethnocentric," a reference to people's tendency to esteem their own culture and denigrate those of others, describing others' behavior as deviant or inappropriate.

Early European Stereotyping
With the arrival of Europeans in the Americas, additional stereotypes emerged and were soon recorded in various media. The earliest historic descriptions of New World cultures were written by the Spanish about peoples of the Caribbean and Central and South America. They did not describe the Aztec and Maya as possessing

different but worthwhile cultural traits; rather, Spanish narratives characterized them as lacking Christianity and "civilization." These distinctions allowed the Spanish to place native populations in a category apart from Europeans and to justify their own horrific treatment of aboriginal peoples.

The later colonization of North America by the English and French (among others) incorporated the assimilated Spanish preconceptions. The terms "Indian," "savage," "infidel," "barbarian," and "heathen" were widely used by the seventeenth century English to identify a large number of different Native American cultures and to treat them all as members of the same group. The French used the term *sauvage* for the same purpose. This collapsing of individual and cultural differences into broad generalizations was typical of the colonial period in North America. Such mental templates occasionally justified illogical policies such as plans to relocate different cultural groups onto the same tract of land. The planners did not seem to recognize—or did not care—that such policies often resulted in severe cultural conflicts.

It was common to describe Indians not simply as they were but in terms of their differences from Europeans, which were generally regarded as deficiencies. Europeans often evaluated Native Americans according to their own Christian moral code, dismissing as immoral behavior that which was perfectly appropriate and sensible within the culture in which it occurred.

"Good" and "Bad" Indians
Colonialism gave rise to two general categories of Native American stereotypes that, with variations and refinements, continued for centuries: the "good" Indian and the "bad" Indian. These categorizations had far more to do with intellectual currents among Europeans than with Indian cultures themselves. If Europeans wished to criticize their own society, they often turned to accounts of American Indians, supposedly unspoiled by the artificiality and constraints of civilization, to demonstrate the deplorable state of European culture. These conventions are most apparent in eighteenth century French literature and philosophy, as in the works of Jean-Jacques Rousseau and his notion of the "noble savage." Conversely, when Europeans wished to uphold the worth of their own social mores, they often called upon the stereotype of the Indian as dirty, wretched, and bloodthirsty to enhance, by comparison, the value of European society.

Among early English colonists, Puritan publications such as captivity narratives had didactic and social motives, namely to trumpet the virtues of Christianity, to support Christian conversion of Native Americans, and to justify colonial settlements on Indian lands. The "good" Indian motif was not prevalent in America until independence from England. At that time, American

Lt. John Dunbar, played by Kevin Costner, and Wind in His Hair, a Lakota played by Rodney Grant, hunt buffalo in a scene from the 1990 film *Dances with Wolves*, which revived the stereotype of the "noble savage."

literature with indigenous themes began to seem patriotic. American literary nationalism discovered the "proud and noble" Indian, and this theme was later incorporated into the works of painters and photographers. By the mid-1880's, authors had turned their frontier obsession to cowboys. Wild West shows became a popular form of public entertainment, combining stereotypical images of cowboys, soldiers ("Indian fighters"), and Indians.

Twentieth Century

With the arrival of the twentieth century, radio, films, and television continued to popularize various outdated views of Native Americans. A general misconception, still prevalent, is that Indian culture was timeless and unchanging until contact with the Europeans, at which time it was destroyed. This denial of both Native American history and survival suggests that the only true Indians existed before European contact and that their descendants somehow do not exhibit real "Indian-ness." This type of misconception underlies accounts of North American history that describe white settlement as progress advancing across a huge expanse of seemingly unoccupied vacant land and pushing the frontier west. Such accounts ignore native peoples as prime movers in their own right, and they deny the ethnicity and cultural diversity of a significant proportion of the North and Central American populations. Since the 1970's, American Indians themselves, in addition to non-Indian scholars, have confronted these and other stereotypes. Through publication and educational reform, they work to break the pattern of ongoing stereotyping. *Susan J. Wurtzburg*

Core Resources

The American Indian: Past and Present (4th ed. New York: McGraw-Hill, 1992), edited by Roger L. Nichols, and *History of Indian-White Relations*, edited by Wilcomb E. Washburn, volume 4 in *Handbook of North American Indians*, edited by William C. Sturtevant (Washington, D.C.: Smithsonian Institution Press, 1988) contain general historical accounts of American Indians and their interactions with Europeans. Images of Indians in literature, written accounts, and film are presented in Louise K. Barnett's *The Ignoble Savage: American Literary Racism, 1790-1890* (Westport, Conn.: Greenwood Press, 1975), Braulio Muñoz's *Sons of the Wind: The Search for Identity in Spanish American Indian Literature* (New Brunswick, N.J.: Rutgers University Press, 1982), *The Pretend Indians: Images of Native Americans in the Movies* (Ames: Iowa State University Press, 1980), edited by Gretchen M. Bataille and Charles L. P. Silet, Michael Hilger's *The American Indian in Film* (Metuchen, N.J.: Scarecrow Press, 1986), and Robert F. Berkhofer, Jr.'s *The White Man's Indian: Images of the American Indian from Columbus to the Present* (New York: Vintage Books, 1979).

See also: American Indians and film; Ethnocentrism; Prejudice and stereotyping; Stereotype; Stereotyping and the self-fulfilling prophecy.

American Indian studies

> **Significance:** American Indian studies programs, which began in the late 1960's, seek to preserve and understand American Indian history and culture.

Since the late 1960's, American Indian studies (or Native American studies) programs have served as the most important scholarly approach to knowing and understanding American Indian culture. Traditional teachings of tribal and village elders remain the solid foundation of American Indian and Native American studies. These culture bearers provide the understanding essential to legitimate study of the native peoples of the Americas.

Establishment of Programs

Dependence upon European American (notably Anglo-American) source materials has made for distortion in scholarly studies. As professor Henrietta Whiteman has stated, "Cheyenne history, and by extension Indian history, in all probability will never be incorporated into American history, because it is holistic, human, personal, and sacred. Though it is equally as valid as Anglo-American history it is destined to remain complementary to white secular American history." This specific difficulty led in large part to the creation of American Indian studies programs in existing institutions of higher learning. Despite limited funds, Native American programs began to emerge as interdisciplinary curricula. Most American Indian studies programs focus on long-term goals involved with cultural preservation, unlike Western, objective academic disciplines such as history and ethnology. American Indian studies use teaching, research, and service to cross cultural boundaries and create an atmosphere for understanding. In many instances, the American Indian studies degree programs are the only non-Western courses of study on campus.

American Indian or Native American studies programs vary considerably in method and subject matter. These also represent different degrees of institutional support, budget size, and quality of program leadership. In the late 1960's and early 1970's, various programs began to emerge at the University of California, Berkeley, and the University of California, Los Angeles. Other programs developed in the California State University system on campuses at Long Beach, Fullerton, and Northridge. At that time, California had the largest Native American population in the United States. Oklahoma had the second-largest native population. Two degree programs were created in Oklahoma in the early 1970's, one at Northeastern State University at Tahlequah, the capital of the Cherokee Nation, and one at the University of Science and Arts of Oklahoma in Chickasha. The Native American studies degree program at the University of Oklahoma was accepted by the higher regents in 1993. Other American Indian studies degree programs were created at the University of Minnesota, the University of Washington, Evergreen College, Washington State University, the University of Arizona, the University of Illinois (Chicago), Dartmouth College, the University of North Dakota, Montana State University, the University of New Mexico, and Cornell University, among others. By the mid-1980's, eighteen programs offered a major leading to a bachelor's degree. Of these, six programs also offered a master's degree.

Tribally Controlled Colleges

Tribally controlled colleges added new energy to American Indian studies. In 1968, the Navajo Nation created the first tribally controlled institution of higher learning. Navajo Community College was a success and led to the passage of the Tribally Controlled Community College Act of 1978. This act provides for some federal support for tribally controlled colleges initiated by tribes in the western United States. Initially, this helped support thirteen tribally controlled colleges. Since the act's passage, at least nine additional colleges have been initiated. Colleges that followed the creation of Navajo Community College include Sinte Glista College, Standing Rock College, Blackfeet Community College, Dull Knife Memorial College, Salish Kootenai College, Little Bighorn College, and Stone Child College, among others. Lummi College of Aquaculture in Washington has expanded to become the Northwest Indian College. Sinte Glista College on the Rosebud Sioux Reservation has grown to become the first fully accredited tribally controlled four-year institution of higher learning.

In all these examples, the tribally based community

Libby Chee, a twenty-year-old Navajo, attends college at Navajo Community College in the early 1970's. The school is one of a number of colleges and universities in the United States that offer programs in Indian studies.

colleges have not only aided the education of individual Indian young people but also improved the development of the tribal communities that they serve. Of primary importance is that Indian people are now controlling institutions that directly affect them. The tribally controlled colleges are far outstripping the state-supported and private colleges and universities in retention of American Indian students. The tribally controlled colleges have become important centers of research. These colleges are proving to be better suited to the needs of American Indian students and communities than their state-supported and private counterparts. The tribally controlled colleges offer hope to tribes that have, all too often, survived in a climate of despair.

Issues and Concerns

In the early 1990's, American Indian studies was in a period of questioning current methods and practices concerning spirit, philosophy, structures, roles, contexts, and intent. The quest for meaning appeared in many guises. The interest in the emotional component of community life, the expansion of traditional approaches to knowledge and wisdom, the acceptance of grammar and logic stemming from native languages, and the hope of differentiating Western-based interpretation from traditional knowledge all reflect the aim of uncovering purpose, meaning, and perspectives on truth in presentation. There is pervasive anxiety that the individual is being submerged in community. There is additional attention being given to the way people feel as well as the way they behave. There is also a movement in American Indian studies toward narrative storytelling in the literature. American Indian studies places human beings and the comprehensible societies in which they live into the story. These are real stories, however, not dry and forbidding pieces of analysis.

The quest for meaning only multiplies the pluralism of current research and teaching. The very process of recovering deeper motivations and attitudes, dragging the latent out of the manifest, requires such personal feats of imagination and use of language that questions about plausibility and proof are bound to arise. Senior faculty at one state-supported university in Oklahoma challenged the continuation of a bachelor's degree in American Indian studies, stating, "While the program is inessential to a liberal arts education, it is not inconsistent with one." This type of Euro-American bias makes it difficult to pursue knowledge and wisdom in an atmosphere with freedom of thought and feeling.

The obverse of the quest for meaning is an uneasiness with the material conditions of life that until recently seemed so compelling. A clear, single idea emerges from the doubts that have been expressed about the power of economic development. As American Indian studies

turns to more emotional content, the demand is for a more elusive process of comprehension. Analytical and technical research is increasingly limited, as mental patterns, attitudes, and symbolic acts become more prominent.

Questions of the use of quantification arise because of the almost exclusive use of United States and Western social science data. What is at stake is a profound epistemological question, not just a disagreement over collection of data. American Indian studies many times are very personal and intuitive. The insights are justified within a specific tribal context with powerful rhetorical and imaginative methods. They appeal to an interest in behavior that is very different from Anglo-American intellectual concerns, but never claim to be definitive.

The establishment of an agenda for American Indian studies, of a set of methods or purposes indigenous to the Americas, or of a special task for its practitioners, hardly seems plausible. American Indian studies is united in its respect of tribal traditions. There is observation of certain fundamental rules for using evidence so as to be intelligible across cultural boundaries. None of these skills is difficult to learn; neither is the telling of a sustained story, which is a special mark of scholars and teachers in American Indian studies. The one form of synthesis used most often by those in American Indian studies blends the disparate methods of current research in examinations of tribally specific localities. This synthesis convincingly links physical conditions, economic and demographic developments, social arrangements, intellectual and cultural assumptions, and political behavior, with mythic patterns and images.

Archives and Tribal Records

The most important repository of American Indian knowledge remains with the tribal elders. There is no substitute for this significant information. This knowledge and wisdom can be gained only with real commitment over a significant period of time. Tribal elders have become wary of "instant experts," whether Indian or non-Indian. All scholarship must access this wisdom and knowledge to reflect tribal tradition and history.

Once removed from this vital core of information are the tribal archives and records. These are held in a variety of ways. For example, the Wichita and Affiliated Tribes maintain their tribal archives as a part of the Wichita Memory Exhibit Museum at the tribal complex on reserve land north of Anadarko, Oklahoma. A second example is that of the Navajo Nation, which collects and preserves its records as a part of the Navajo Tribal Council Reference Library in Window Rock. A third example is that of the Cherokee Nation, which maintains a portion of its records in the Archives of the Cherokee National Historical Society in Tahlequah, while the records of the Cherokee Nation from 1839 through 1906 are held in the Indian Archives of the Oklahoma Historical Society, which functions as a trustee for the United States government. These records were placed in trust in 1906, just before Oklahoma statehood, before the National Archives of the United States was created. Each tribe maintains its records in an individual way. Contact with the tribes is the best means to understand their respective record-keeping systems.

U.S. National Archives

Large numbers of records about American Indian peoples are held by the National Archives of the United States. These are housed in the Washington National Records Center, Suitland, Maryland, and in eleven regional Federal Archives and Records Centers throughout the United States. Additional records holdings concerning American Indian peoples are contained at the presidential libraries administered by the National Archives and Records Service. The papers of the presidents and many of those of other high officials, including the files of individual members of Congress, are regarded as their personal property. These personal papers are collected in large part by state-supported university manuscripts collections.

The basic organizational unit in the National Archives collections is the record group. This refers to the records of a single agency, such as the Bureau of Indian Affairs and its predecessors. The National Archives endeavors to keep records in the order in which they were maintained by the respective agency. The agency filing system was designed for administrative purposes, not for the benefit of researchers. There are important guides to assist in research efforts, however. The two most important of these are *Guide to the National Archives of the United States* (1974) and *Guide to Records in the National Archives of the United States Relating to American Indians* (1981). Another useful volume is *Indian-White Relations: A Persistent Paradox* (1976), which includes papers and proceedings of the National Archives Conference on Research in the history of Indian-white relations.

Additional materials concerning Indian-white relations are contained in the United States Supreme Court decisions, the research that was used in the Indian Land Claims Act of 1946, and in the manuscript collections of major universities throughout the western United States.

American Indian studies has long been limited in perspective because of the heavy dependence upon documents generated by Euro-American policymakers, businesspersons, and military personnel. Scholarly works accepted many of the assumptions of those who produced these sources. American Indian people were perceived either negatively as an enemy or romantically as part of the environment. In the last decade, scholar-

ship in American Indian studies has changed significantly from this approach. More balanced efforts are being made by American Indian scholars utilizing native languages and tribal sources. All American culture and society is being shown in a new light as a result of the creative images and ideas of American Indian studies.

Howard Meredith

Core Resources

Charlotte Heth and Susan Guyette's *Issues for the Future of American Indian Studies* (Los Angeles: American Indian Studies Center, University of California, Los Angeles, 1985) looks at the field of American Indian studies. *Tribal Colleges: Shaping the Future of Native America* (Princeton, N.J.: Carnegie Foundation for the Advancement of Teaching, 1989) looks at the colleges that have been established for Native Americans. *Guide to the Records in the National Archives of the United States Relating to American Indians*, compiled by Edward E. Hill (Washington, D.C.: National Archives and Records Service, G.S.A., 1981) helps researchers find information contained in the archives.

See also: American Indian stereotypes; Education and American Indians; Education and racial/ethnic relations; Self-determination movements.

American Indian theater

> **Significance:** For hundreds and hundreds of years, Native Americans, through their oral stories, dances, and music have engaged in theater. In the latter part of the twentieth century, Native American dance groups and play groups were organized to express their cultural heritage and values and to share them with others throughout the United States and Canada.

Since the 1970's, Native American theater groups— dance theater groups, stage companies, and radio theater companies—have been performing throughout North America. In order to achieve their goal of familiarizing non-Indians with Native American culture and values, they often perform in schools and in smaller communities.

Dance Theater

Native American groups such as the American Indian Dance Theater travel throughout the United States, singing, dancing, drumming, and storytelling to express their native heritage. Some dance groups perform a wide range of Native American dances; however, other dance groups choose to specialize in the dance, music, and legends of only one of the four geographic groups of Indian nations: the Eastern Woodlands, the Northern and Southern Plains, the Northern Pacific, and the Southwest. A dance theater that specializes in the Eastern Woodlands tribes would present the music, dance, and legends of these tribes and wear the traditional clothing favored by groups such as the Seneca and Mohawks. Some dance groups specialize in the dances and legends of a single tribe or Indian nation.

Because Native American music and dances are part of the tribes' spiritual heritage, some Native Americans believe that only Native Americans should dance ceremonial dances. In fact, some purists believe that people should dance only the ceremonial dances of the tribe to which they belong and should follow tribal standards as to whether a man or woman should dance a particular dance. However, others believe that anyone who is interested in the spiritual aspects of the culture should be able to perform all Native American dances. Certainly the Native American dances serve as wonderful theater, illustrating both the stories and the spiritual concerns of that culture.

Stage Performances
The Civil Rights movement of the 1960's helped inspire Native Americans to strengthen their sense of identity and to preserve their right to self-determination. The multiculturalism of the 1980's and 1990's encouraged Native Americans and other people of color to identify the unique aspects of their cultures and to attempt to share them with other cultural groups.

In North America, theater groups were formed to give Native Americans a chance to appear on stage in productions that are written by Native Americans and that explore and convey Native American values. One such theater group, the Center for Indigenous Theater, was started by James Buller in Canada in 1974. The purpose of this theater is to train Native Americans in Western acting techniques that they can combine with native dance, song, and oral history to create original theater productions. Over the years, this theater has presented many original Native American plays. Each year, the James Buller Award is given to a Native American playwright for an original play that uses Native American culture and exhibits Native American values.

One of the best-known Native American theater groups is the Spiderwoman Theater, which offers story weaving and storytelling on themes relating to Native American women. Another well-known group is the Red Path Theater Company of Chicago, which produces the works of Native American playwrights who create original dramas from the history of and issues surrounding native people.

Other Native American theater groups include the Algonquian group in Connecticut and Albeza, the Native American Art and Film Institute Theater, in California, which dedicate themselves to the creation and production of plays about Native Americans. Albeza created the American Conservatory Youth Theater Company, which helps Native American youth create and present plays based on Native American legends in schools, on community stages, and in radio performances. One of the most popular of these plays, *Every Skin's Day in Court* (1998), uses the traditional mode of a trickster tale. However, in this modern-day tale, the coyote, the trickster, is a high-priced lawyer who has to face his own day in court. A 1997 play by Albeza director Diane Way, *Tiospe* (which means "extended family" or "band" in Lakota), explores the life of Indian children in a boarding school at the end of the nineteenth century. Way, of Lakota/Cheyenne heritage, won the Frank Silvera Writers' Workshop Award for this play. The Sin'Klip Native Theater performs in elementary schools throughout British Columbia, dedicating itself to passing on the cultural values and legends of native peoples and also to encouraging native youth to stay in school by giving them a sense of identity.

Radio Theater
The radio stations on Indian reservations are owned by the tribal governments. These stations play both traditional and contemporary Indian music and present radio plays, written and performed by Indians, that explore Indian themes and legends. They also present local programming and news. Their broadcasts present the Native American culture to everyone within their listening area.

Annita Marie Ward

Core Resources
Scholastic Encyclopedia of the North American Indian (New York: Scholastic References, 1996), edited by James Cument, offers four hundred illustrations relating to the legends, ceremonies, dances, theater, and customs of 149 North American tribes. Charlotte Heth, well-known ethnomusicologist and director of the National Museum of the American Indian, offers information about Native American ceremonies in *Native American Dance: Ceremonies and Social Traditions* (Washington, D.C.: National Museum of the American Indian and Fulcrum, 1998). Roger C. Echo-Hawk, Pawnee tribal historian, explores Native American oral traditions in *Hawk Kara Katit Pakutu: Exploring the Origins of Native America in Anthropology and Oral Traditions* (Boulder: University of Colorado, 1994).

See also: American Indian dance and music; American Indian literature; American Indians and film.

American Indian women

Significance: American Indian women's resiliency in the face of two hundred years of role changes and economic oppression caused by white encroachment manifests itself in women's creative, healing, and renewing power to restore balance.

White colonization and expansion have disrupted American Indian social systems and life patterns and necessitated varied personal and professional responses and adaptations to acculturation, Christianization, and economic change. Of crucial consideration are American Indian women's dynamism and diversity in terms, for example, of significant tribal variations and the centrality of the spirit world. Even ethnographers have subscribed to stereotypical myths and fantasies that reduce the rich variations to a squaw/princess duality. For these reasons, to improve the understanding of their contemporary experience, a better grasp of their historical context must be achieved.

History

Traditionally, women's identity as well as their harmonious role in the biological and social spheres as caretakers and culture bearers was grounded in spirituality, extended family, and tribe. Although not all women in all tribes shared equal power and status with men, many western North American tribes, such as the Klamath, rest on egalitarian systems of reciprocity in which separate and complimentary tasks assigned to each sex are equally valued. In the gynocratic tribal world, woman is the creator of existence; thus, the female principle inherent in the earth, minerals, crystals, stones, wood, water, sun, and moon is multitudinous, ever-generating, cyclic, and consistent. The welfare of the young and the complementarity of all life are paramount. Female spirits and mythological figures include the Keres Thought Woman, the Santa Clara Pueblo Clay Lady, the Navajo Changing Women, and the Sioux White Buffalo Calf Woman. Women in legends are honored for their powers of creation and their ability to provide harmony and balance in tribal life.

Roles and tasks are variable and lifestyles flexible enough to allow free sexual expression and nonconformity. For example, women in Plains tribes, such as the Canadian Blackfeet, inhabit a spectrum that includes the significant Sun Dance Woman, the sexually promiscuous woman, the submissive and obedient woman, and the independent and assertive woman. Among the Cheyenne are the daring horse riders. Lakota women participate in the Buffalo Ceremony. Indeed, widespread evi-

American Indian women such as this Creek woman sometimes have to work hard to achieve the right balance between the traditions of their ancestors and those of Americans of European ancestry in their everyday lives.

dence of the warrior woman exists in Apache, Crow, Cheyenne, Blackfeet, and Pawnee tribes. Also common in at least thirty-three tribes is the berdache, a cross-gender individual. Female berdaches, who may be lesbians, shift to male social and occupational roles, often earning high regard for their boldness, efficiency, status, and wealth.

Also unlike Anglo culture, American Indian women's status increased with age and the wisdom that comes with it. Especially revered were their opinions on sacred matters, herbal medicines, and tribal history. Tribes in which women of all ages played pivotal economic, political, and spiritual roles include the Cherokee, Montagnais-Naskapi, Navajo, Iroquois, Mandan, Hopi, Zuni, Northern Paiute, and Eastern Pueblo. For these cultures, matrilineal inheritance placed land, crops, houses, and tools in women's ownership and made men responsible for much of the labor and cultivation. Part of women's power came from their association with food and its supply. The precolonized Cherokee gynocracy is one example in which tribal decisions were largely influenced by the Women's Council, the head of which was believed to have an affinity with the Great Spirit. Before the influx of Catholicism, the Naskapi were gynocentric and, like the Huron, peaceful and nonhierarchical: Children and women, like men, were encouraged to be independent and decisive.

Acculturation

Acculturation to the European political, social, and religious order brought an increase in male dominance and control. Changes in traditional economic systems, even within America's largest Indian tribe (the Navajo), reduced women's status. Men's increased off-reservation work created a shift to independent rather than extended families, lessening women's support network in child rearing and eroding complementarity because men began to see their paychecks as theirs alone.

Another negative effect of white encroachment was the residue of so-called boarding school trauma: domestic labor "education," beatings for resistance, less classroom instruction for girls than for boys, and eventual shunning for their "white" ways by reservation residents. Accompanied by the Bureau of Indian Affairs field matron program, U.S. government efforts to "civilize" American Indian women into simulations of white women, including application of some Indian New Deal policies, neglected the import of their previous political roles. Nevertheless, women often became acculturated more successfully than men—for example, among the Oglala Sioux and Northern Paiute, women developed expertise as political leaders, landowners, and liaisons. Some also gained access to advanced training in the education and social welfare fields.

Generally, however, adapting to the mainstream has been fraught with conflict, stress, and vulnerability for American Indian women. At issue are the majority culture's value of a work ethic that emphasizes individual achievement, competitiveness, the accumulation of material wealth, and professional status, and that places family and cultural bonds second at best. These values conflict with the American Indian emphasis on communal concern, extended family responsibility, cooperation, and group-oriented identity. Because American Indian men without college degrees seldom marry college graduates, bicultural conflict for American Indian women desiring postsecondary education is compounded. Nor surprisingly, degree completion rates are low: 18 percent for Indian undergraduates, 1 percent for master's candidates, and 0.2 percent for doctoral candidates.

Demographics

The pre-Columbian Indian population ranged between twenty and forty-five million; by 1995, this figure was approximately two million, spread across 542 tribes. Among this population, 25 percent of women and 10 percent of men are sterilized without informed consent, life expectancy is fifty-five years and infant mortality is high, as are unemployment and poverty. Fifty percent of homes are female-headed households. The states with the largest American Indian populations are Oklahoma (formerly known as Indian Territory), Arizona, California, and New Mexico. The largest tribes are the Cherokee, the Navajo (which has most successfully preserved its language), the Chippewa (or Ojibwe), the Sioux, and the Choctaw.

Achievements

Many American Indian women are becoming social workers, psychologists, writers, artists, and political leaders dedicated to serving their tribes and communities. These women include Comanche LaDonna Harris, president and director of Americans for Indian Opportunity; Wilma P. Mankiller, former principal chief of the Cherokee Nation; and Laguna JoAnn Sarracino, developer of the Native American Mineral Engineering and Science Program; and contemporary writers who continue to communicate ancient knowledge and to tell the stories of their people and of survival, such as Paula Gunn Allen, Louise Erdrich, Rayna Green, Joy Harjo, Linda Hogan, Leslie Marmon Silko, Luci Tapahanso, and Roberta Hill Whiteman. Embodying success, autonomy, leadership, confidence, and emotional control, these women have attained professional recognition even as they have sustained cultural heritage and kinship connections, answering the demands of vital tribal needs with their leadership capacity. They contextualize their efforts at cultural preservation and restoration within family, nation, and sacred Mother Earth. Many have endured arrest rather than sacrifice treaty rights or forsake their sacred lands. Consistently redefining identities obscured by misconceptions, American Indian women remain a strong and vital force, perpetuating respect for the past with clear agendas for the future.

Roseanne L. Hoefel

Core Resources

Books that examine the American Indian woman include Paula Gunn Allen's *The Sacred Hoop: Recovering the Feminine in American Indian Traditions* (Boston: Beacon Press, 1986), Gretchen Bataille and Kathleen Mullen Sands's *American Indian Women: Telling Their Lives* (Lincoln: University of Nebraska Press, 1984), Rayna Green's *Native American Women: A Contextual Bibliography* (Bloomington: Indiana University Press, 1983), *Messengers of the Wind: Native American Women Tell Their Life Stories* (edited by Jane Katz, New York: Ballantine Books, 1995), and Steve Wall's *Wisdom's Daughters: Conversations with Women Elders of Native America* (New York: HarperCollins, 1993). Fred Hoffman's *The American Indian Family: Strengths and*

Stresses (Isleta, N.Mex.: American Indian Social Research and Development Associates, 1981) looks at the American Indian woman in the context of the family.

See also: American Indian demographics; Ethnic identities of women; Women and racism; Women of All Red Nations; Women of color.

American Indians and film

> **Significance:** Film images serve as a major source of information and misinformation regarding Native American history and culture for people who have no personal contact with Native Americans. Although these images often perpetuate damaging stereotypes, films concerning Native Americans can also be informative, educational, and entertaining.

Filmmakers in the early twentieth century relied upon the glories of the mythic Wild West as the basis for motion pictures involving Native Americans. Early films usually portrayed Native Americans as primitive people determined to wreak havoc on innocent white settlers. These films were so offensive that a delegation of Native Americans traveled to Washington, D.C., in 1911 to protest the misleading representations. Although there were some exceptions to these depictions, the stereotypes that appeared in these early films remained popular for many decades.

Stereotypes
Most films presented one of two stereotypical images: that of a bloodthirsty warrior or a noble savage. Under the first stereotype, Native Americans represented an evil to be eliminated. Brave cowboys or cavalry officers pursued and punished savage Indians who had committed some misdeed, in many cases either a massacre or the kidnapping of a white woman. Films ignored the diversity of Native American cultures, typically portraying American Indians of all regions and tribes in warbonnets and breechclouts, wielding tomahawks and living in tipis. Those Indians who did speak English inevitably did so badly, given to single-syllable words in short sentences. To compound the errors these films made, white actors usually played the parts of Native Americans, especially those with important roles in the film.

The extreme stereotype of the bloodthirsty warrior had its opposite in the noble savage, an image perhaps more sympathetic to Native Americans but still inaccurate. These Native Americans also lived in the nineteenth century West but were depicted as decent folk who had legitimate grievances against the white settlers. However, their dignity and their pride could not preserve their doomed cultures. This romantic image became increasingly popular after World War II. The noble savage stereotype reached new heights during the 1960's and early 1970's, when disenchantment with the war in Vietnam led to critical evaluations of American life. During this period, the treatment of Native Americans came to symbolize the failure of the United States as a liberal democracy. The noble savage theme was revived in the popular *Dances with Wolves* (1990), which contrasted a romantic image of the Lakotas against the barbaric actions of whites in the years after the Civil War. Once again, the film images of Native Americans expressed larger cultural issues that had little to do with the lives of American Indians. However, some filmmakers received credit for attempting to arrive at accurate depictions of Native American life, even though such efforts were usually flawed.

Changing Images
Westerns fell out of favor with audiences during the 1970's, and film images of Native Americans underwent significant changes. Although the character called Chief in *One Flew over the Cuckoo's Nest* (1975) was to some degree a noble savage stereotype alienated from the world, he was nonetheless a modern Native American. In addition, Creek actor Will Sampson played the role. The work of Sampson and Dan George, a Suquamish actor, marked the beginning of a promising new trend, the hiring of Native Americans as featured actors in motion pictures. Graham Greene, an Oneida Indian, received an Academy Award nomination for best supporting actor for his work in *Dances with Wolves*. Although the increase in Native American actors was laudable, perhaps the most encouraging development in regard to Native Americans and films was the appearance of Native American writers and directors committed to presenting accurate representations of Native American life. Critics hailed *Smoke Signals* (1998), the first major film written and directed by Native Americans, for its realism and honesty. The film won the Dramatic Audience Awards and the Filmmakers Trophy at the 1998 Sundance Film Festival.

Documentary films also offered insight into Native American life and into non-Indian perceptions of Native Americans. Early films purporting to accurately portray Native American life often took liberties with the truth. Performers in one of the earliest of these films, Thomas Edison's *Sioux Ghost Dance* (1894), were probably not actually performing the Ghost Dance. Director Robert Flaherty set higher standards with his study of life in the Arctic, *Nanook of the North* (1922), the first film ever referred to as a documentary. Although the film was

Lt. John Dunbar, played by Kevin Costner, rides alongside Kicking Bird (second from left), played by Oneida Indian Graham Greene, in the 1990 film *Dances with Wolves*. The film was laudable for its increased use of American Indian actors.

praised for its production values, some film historians contended that it romanticized native life and therefore fell into the noble savage stereotype.

During the 1970's, documentary films became an increasingly important form of artistic communication for many Native Americans. One film historian estimated that fourteen hundred documentaries concerning Native American life were made between 1968 and 1990, many of them produced by Native Americans. Sarah Osawa, a Makah filmmaker, produced *In the Heart of the Big Mountain* (1988), which examined the lives of Navajos forced to relocate from their homelands. Other documentary films examined the practice of traditional religious rites by Native Americans in prison, the struggle to preserve treaty rights, and memories of Wounded Knee. These and other works helped to preserve oral traditions and informed non-Indians about modern Native American life.   *Thomas Clarkin*

Core Resources
Gretchen M. Bataille and Charles L. P. Silet's *The Pretend Indians: Images of Native Americans in the Movies* (Ames: Iowa State University Press, 1980) offers several essays and reviews of specific films. Although it does not focus on films, Robert F. Berkhofer, Jr.'s *The White Man's Indian* (New York: Vintage Books, 1978) discusses the stereotypes that appear in Hollywood motion pictures. Raymond William Stedman's *Shadows of the Indian Stereotypes in American Culture* (Norman: University of Oklahoma Press, 1982) includes a chapter on film representations. Ralph E. Friar and Natasha A. Friar's *The Only Good Indian . . . The Hollywood Gospel* (New York: Drama Book Specialists, 1972) presents a critical but often humorous assessment of Native Americans in films.

See also: American Indian dance and music; American Indian literature; American Indian stereotypes.

American Indians in the justice system

> **Significance:** As members of distinct political communities with limited sovereignty, American Indian tribal people share a legal status unique among American citizens.

When Europeans first reached the Americas, they encountered native peoples whose ancestors had occupied the entire landmass for more than twenty thousand years. The numerous North American tribes used many different legal systems that functioned successfully under natural law without police, formal courts, or prisons. Decisions affecting individual rights were resolved in a manner that gave considerable weight to the best interests of the group and sought restoration of community harmony and balance. Around the fifteenth century, the indigenous peoples encountered Europeans holding different views of legal rights and posing a serious threat to native sovereignty and rights.

The Old Colonialism
English colonizers in North America generally pursued the treaty-making process as the chief means for acquiring land. Their diplomacy recognized Indian tribes as sovereign foreign nations. When the American Revolution ended British rule in the thirteen seaboard colonies,

the new American republic displaced England and continued the old colonialism in its diplomatic relationships with the tribes. The United States initially viewed American Indians as members of small nations who would remain permanently outside American political institutions.

Tribal Sovereignty and Indian Rights

Early American statesmen, including Thomas Jefferson, formulated ideal rules for the peaceful and voluntary extinction of Indian title through legal land purchases. Government policy encouraged Native Americans to enter the mainstream of the dominant culture and live alongside white settlers.

The United States abandoned this policy when it concluded that the tribal lands were too valuable to recognize Indian rights within them. Presidential administrations responded to pressure from anti-Indian frontiersmen and the desire of new southern states to appropriate Indian lands and dismantle tribal governments. Between 1815 and 1840, most eastern and southern tribes were removed—with great hardship and loss—west of the Mississippi, to the southern plains region designated Indian Territory.

As removal proceeded, a defining moment in the legal relationship between tribes and the United States came with the Cherokee court cases of the 1830's. The Cherokees, a highly advanced and acculturated southeastern tribe that was implementing Jefferson's advice, sought justice through the U.S. legal system, resisting impending removal from Georgia and the state's effort to dissolve their government and subject them to its laws. In *Cherokee Nation v. Georgia* (1831), Chief Justice John Marshall ruled that the case was not eligible to be heard by the Supreme Court because Indian tribes did not qualify as independent foreign nations. This decision characterized Indian tribes as "domestic dependent nations" whose relationship with the U.S. government was that of a ward to its guardian.

In a second case, *Worcester v. Georgia* (1832), Marshall reached different conclusions using the same legal background. He cited earlier treaties with the Cherokee recognizing their national character and right to self-government as distinct, independent political communities retaining natural rights as the original possessors of the soil. Georgia's actions interfered with the federal government's exclusive authority to make treaties with Indian tribes and were therefore invalid. The Cherokee legal victory was short-lived, as President Andrew Jackson refused to enforce the ruling, and the tribe was removed forcibly to Indian Territory within a few years. Yet on this important decision, cited frequently in later cases, hinged issues such as Indian title to lands, tribal independence, and the validity of treaty rights.

Dispossession and Warfare

Unexpectedly rapid American expansion westward beginning in the 1840's jeopardized the political autonomy and security of person and possessions that had been promised to removed tribes in their new lands. A final round of violent confrontation played out after 1860, as American movement into tribal lands of the West and Great Plains forced further cessions and destroyed the tribes' traditional economic base. Tribal sovereignty received a new setback in 1871, when the United States ceased negotiating treaties with tribal nations. Although previous treaties were to remain valid, from this point onward the federal government would unilaterally subject the tribes to congressional legislation and presidential orders.

The New Colonialism

Under this new colonialism, the situation of American Indians reached its lowest point. Tribal peoples were confined to reservations under authoritarian paternalistic control; there the government ruthlessly pursued assimilation goals through forced acculturation, while corrupt U.S. Indian agents plundered tribal resources. Furthermore, the General Allotment Act of 1887 forced tribal members to break up communal holdings by accepting 160-acre tracts and opened unallotted reservation land to sale. The eventual result was loss of both "surplus" land and many private allotments to whites.

By 1934, this process had reduced the tribal estate from 138 million to 48 million acres, half of which was desert. The Native American population, once numbering more than 10 million, fell to 250,000 toward the end of the nineteenth century. By the 1920's, tribal peoples suffered from impoverishment, poor health conditions, and lack of education—a situation from which they have not fully recovered.

After 1870, court rulings and congressional legislation upheld Marshall's legal precedents but further refined and narrowed the scope of tribal sovereignty. Moreover, the Bill of Rights did not protect tribal peoples' rights. In legal disputes with the government, Indians were denied freedom of choice of counsel (Sixth Amendment). The First Amendment right to assemble was violated through forced confinement on reservations, which Indians were unable to leave without permission. Cultural genocide and loss of property contradicted the Fifth Amendment.

The late 1870's and early 1880's witnessed the creation of tribal police forces and courts as instruments to enforce the government's determined assault on traditional Indian culture. The tribal courts' authority soon became controversial because of the Supreme Court ruling *Ex parte Crow Dog* (1883). Tribal magistrates on the Rosebud Reservation in South Dakota allowed a murder case to be handled in the traditional manner of restitution to the victim's family. Federal officials then arrested the assailant, Leonard Crow Dog, and convicted him of murder in the territorial district court. On appeal, the Supreme Court ordered him released on grounds that a federal court had no jurisdiction over crimes committed by Indians against other Indians on reservation land. In response, Congress passed the 1885 Major Crimes Act, which placed seven serious crimes under federal jurisdiction even when they were committed on reservation land. This list of crimes was further expanded in the twentieth century, leaving tribal courts with jurisdiction only over minor offenses.

A devastating blow to sovereignty came in the court case *Lone Wolf v. Hitchcock* (1903). This litigation involved the Kiowa tribe's attempt to halt the sale of "surplus" reservation lands based on a former treaty guarantee requiring the signed consent of at least three-fourths of male occupants. Ignoring the Constitution's Fifth Amendment protection of life, liberty, and property, the Supreme Court upheld lower court opinions that Congress had full authority over tribal land, an authority that superseded treaty guarantees.

In 1924, the government bestowed U.S. citizenship on American Indians. This gesture did not halt the loss of lands to whites or the campaign to suppress Indian culture. Moreover, some states successfully prevented these new citizens from voting.

The Indian New Deal
A major policy shift followed the election of President Franklin D. Roosevelt in 1932. The Indian Reorganization Act, or Indian New Deal, the inspiration of Roosevelt's Bureau of Indian Affairs chief, John Collier, ended allotment, helped tribes purchase some lost land, encouraged the recovery of traditional native culture, and attempted to revitalize the tribal system of self-government. The act improved conditions for Native Americans and gave them new hope; it is still considered the most important piece of Indian legislation in U.S. history. About half of the tribes refused participation, however, resisting Collier's paternalistic attempt to impose guidelines for U.S.-style constitutions. They preferred traditional forms of self-rule.

Termination
After World War II, a conservative Congress mounted the most serious threat to date against tribal sovereignty under the label "termination." This policy's most ominous components were congressional bills authorizing termination of various designated tribes, thereby liquidating federal treaty obligations and payments, and Public Law 280, which authorized states to assume jurisdiction over criminal and civil cases involving Indians.

Termination failed badly. States faced escalating welfare costs and were often reluctant to assume the added expense of policing or taking control of judicial matters in Indian country. As the injustice and impracticality of this policy became clear, it was put on hold after 1960. Congress eventually restored the status of most terminated tribes, and Public Law 280 was amended to the point where it ceased to be a threat to tribal sovereignty.

American Indian Civil Rights Act
Earlier rulings recognizing tribes as distinct political entities exempted their courts from external regulation. Concern that basic rights guaranteed to other Americans were sometimes violated in tribal judicial proceedings prompted passage of the American Indian Civil Rights Act. The legislation extended many (though not all) constitutional protections to tribal members. Some Indians welcomed this measure, and most tribal courts already adhered to its provisions. Traditionalists, however, saw it as another attempt to force the dominant white culture on tribal peoples with distinct sociocultural traditions. The legislation did give rise to some situations in which procedures consistent with Native American culture were challenged in court by both Indian and non-Indian litigants.

Post-1970 Developments and Issues
The period since the late 1960's has been marked by mixed success for Indian rights and tribal sovereignty. The late 1960's gave rise to political militancy among urban Indians who reacted against racism and sought to reconnect with their roots. Pride in being Indian and efforts to seek renewal through the recovery of language, religion, and other traditions, nearly eradicated by past U.S. policy, have contributed to a Native American cultural rebirth.

President Richard M. Nixon denounced termination and handed the Taos Pueblo tribe a major victory with the return of its sacred Blue Lake area. Renewed tribalism and self-determination empowered tribes by allowing them to contract with the government to assume management of numerous government programs and services on the reservation. Although contested at every step, tribes have also had some success in asserting control over natural resources.

During the presidency of Ronald Reagan, Indian rights suffered a setback in Supreme Court rulings that restricted First Amendment religious freedoms. In *Lyng v. Northwest Indian Cemetery Protective Association* (1988), the new conservative Court majority ruled against Native American efforts to protect sacred sites from development. A 1990 decision threatened the traditional use of the sacramental plant and drug peyote in religious ceremonies of the Native American Church, likened to the use of wine in the Christian Communion rite.

Since 1990, progress has occurred on the sensitive issue of repatriating the remains of tribal people from museums and private and government collections. Nevertheless, the exercise of tribal sovereignty and treaty rights continues to bring tribes into conflict with state and local interests. Also uncertain is the future of tribally owned gambling casinos on reservation land, a financially successful business venture for many tribes which is regulated under the Indian Gaming Regulatory Act of 1988. The long struggle of Native Americans to defend and preserve their rights in American society continues.

David A. Crain

Core Resources

A very useful source on the legal status and rights of tribal peoples and a historical account of Indian nations' struggle to maintain sovereignty is John R. Wunder's *Retained by the People: A History of American Indians and the Bill of Rights* (New York: Oxford University Press, 1994). Other good overviews are Vine Deloria, Jr., and Clifford M. Lytle's *American Indians, American Justice* (Austin: University of Texas Press, 1983); Wilcomb Washburn's *Red Man's Land, White Man's Law: A Study of the Past and Present Status of the American Indian* (New York: Charles Scribner's Sons, 1971); Charles F. Wilkinson's *American Indians, Time, and the Law: Native Societies in a Modern Constitutional Democracy* (New Haven, Conn.: Yale University Press, 1987). A relevant documentary collection of court cases, treaties, congressional legislation, government studies, and reports is *Documents of United States Indian Policy*, edited by Francis Paul Prucha (2d ed., Lincoln: University of Nebraska Press, 1990).

See also: American Indian Civil Rights Act; *Cherokee Nation v. Georgia* and *Worcester v. Georgia*; *Ex parte Crow Dog*; Gambling; General Allotment Act; Indian Citizenship Act; Indian Removal Act; Indian Territory; Indian-white relations: United States; *Lone Wolf v. Hitchcock*; Native American Church; Peyote religion; Public Law 280; Reservation system of the United States; Tribal courts; Tribal sovereignty.

American Jewish Committee

The American Jewish Committee was founded in 1906 by a group of prominent American Jews in response to a series of anti-Jewish riots (pogroms) in Russia. It was to be a defense and advocacy group dedicated to the prevention of any "infraction of the civil and religious rights of Jews, in any part of the world." During and after World War I, its efforts were concentrated on aiding refugees and combating anti-immigrant and anti-Semitic sentiment in the United States. In the late 1990's, the committee's work consisted mostly of analysis, advocacy, and legal action relating to issues such as immigration, civil rights, church-state relations, and social justice. In addition, it sponsors research in such areas as Jewish family life, intermarriage, and Jewish education, and the significance of Judaism in an age of modernity. Local chapters are encouraged to participate in legislative advocacy activities and involvement as *amici curiae* in litigation at the local and state levels. On the international scene, the committee has articulated a special commitment to Israel's security and to the support of democratic movements across the globe on the theory that the fate of Jews is inextricably bound to the fate of democracy.

Peter J. Haas

See also: American Jewish Congress; Anti-Defamation League; Anti-Semitism; Jewish Americans; Jewish Defense League.

American Jewish Congress

The American Jewish Congress began in 1918 as a coalition of Jewish groups interested in reviving Jewish life after World War I and in promoting Jewish interests at the Versailles peace conference. The original Congress was dissolved at the completion of its mission in 1920 but was immediately reformed as a self-standing community-relations organization, achieving independent status in 1928. At that time its chief interests were in aiding Jewish migration to Palestine and combating anti-Semitism in the United States. After World War II, it shifted attention to building coalitions with other groups so as to promote liberal social legislation, combat bigotry, and advance civil rights. Its current mission statement includes working "to protect fundamental constitutional freedoms and American democratic institutions, particularly the civil and religious rights and liberties of all Americans." In addition, it is dedicated to advancing social and economic justice, women's equality, and human rights at home and abroad. The Congress also has an abiding interest in the security of the State of Israel and maintains its founding interest in combating anti-Semitism and other forms of racism while at the same time enhancing Jewish religious, institutional, communal, and cultural life.

Peter J. Haas

See also: American Jewish Committee; Anti-Defamation League; Anti-Semitism; Jewish Americans; Jewish Defense League.

American Nazi Party

Significance: The American Nazi Party was the most notorious white supremacist organization during the first half of the turbulent 1960's. George Lincoln Rockwell, the leader of this small group, attracted considerable public attention by engaging in vicious verbal attacks on Jews and African Americans. After his murder in 1967, his message continued to inspire white supremacy politicians such as David Duke and small neo-Nazi groups of poorly educated white urban youths from Detroit to Los Angeles.

The person responsible for organizing a Nazi movement in the United States after World War II was George Lincoln Rockwell, a veteran of World War II and the Korean War. Rockwell was born March 9, 1918, in Bloomington, Illinois, and received a good education. During his Korean War service, he became interested in anti-Semitism and, according to his autobiography, he was entranced by Adolf Hitler's autobiography, *Mein Kampf.*

In 1958, Rockwell founded the National Committee to Free America from Jewish Domination with headquarters in Arlington, Virginia. In March, 1959, he renamed the organization the American Nazi Party and adopted the swastika and the Nazi flag as its symbols. The party never received much financial aid from supporters and had constant financial difficulties. Minor party branches appeared in Dallas, Los Angeles, Chicago, Boston, San Francisco, and Spotsylvania, Virginia. In 1962, Rockwell traveled to England to organize the World Union of National Socialists. However, as late as 1967, the party probably had no more than two hundred regular members. When Rockwell ran for governor of Virginia in 1965, he won only 1.2 percent of the total vote (6,300 votes).

Radical Racism

Even though his party was small, Rockwell attracted considerable public attention because of his radical racism. Like Hitler, he attacked both Jews and African Americans, and he called for white supremacy. The American Nazi Party blamed Jews for communism and race mixing. Rockwell also encouraged ties with the Christian Identity movement, an anti-Semitic organization founded in Britain in the 1920's that argues that God created only Christian whites. To demonstrate the depth of his hatred of Jews, he used a Jewish altar cloth as doormat to the party's headquarters, and he named his Doberman dog "gas oven," a reference to the Nazi extermination system at the concentration camp at Auschwitz-Birkenau, Germany.

Rockwell also directed his attacks toward African Americans who were attempting to desegregate the South. Rockwell painted the phrase "White man fight! Smash the black revolution" on the side of his house. In his autobiography, *This Time the World*, he attacked African American men's sexuality. He praised Hitler's goal of leading a white man's struggle against "racial suicide." On the other hand, Rockwell praised Elijah Muhammad, the leader of the Nation of Islam, for advocating African American separatism. Rockwell called the Muslim leader the "Hitler of the black men." Only after Rockwell discovered that the Nation of Islam's goals included gaining control over several Southern states did he advocate the return of all African Americans to Africa.

Shock Tactics

Rockwell used shock tactics to draw attention to his small group. In July, 1960, he caused a riot on the National Mall in Washington, D.C., by appearing in Nazi regalia. In May, 1961, he decided to attack both African Americans and Jews in the South by sending a Volkswagen "hate bus" to New Orleans. He planned to picket both the local headquarters of the National Association for the Advancement of Colored People (NAACP) and the premiere of the film *Exodus*. However, the American Nazis who picketed the theater were threatened by Jewish survivors of the Holocaust who lived in New Orleans.

American Nazi Party leader George Lincoln Rockwell speaks at a camp in Winchcomb, Gloucestershire, England, in August, 1962.

The local police intervened and arrested the American Nazis, but not before Rockwell had obtained considerable free publicity. Even after Rockwell's death, the American Nazis continued to use this shock tactic. In 1976-1977, the Chicago leader of the National Socialist Party of America, Frank Collins, threatened to march in the suburb of Skokie, where a considerable number of Holocaust survivors lived.

Legacy

Rockwell was a good organizer. He led outrageous demonstrations, but he also addressed college audiences to disseminate his views. After he was murdered in 1967 by a former American Nazi, John Patler, the party changed its name to National Socialist White People's Party. By the 1990's, the neo-Nazi movement had split into at least twenty-three organizations. Major racist groups range from Richard Butler's Aryan Nation in Idaho to Tom Metzger's White Aryan Resistance in California. Of the estimated twenty-five thousand dedicated militant white supremacists, perhaps one thousand are Nazis. However, the message has not changed. The various groups continue to demand white supremacy and target African Americans and Jews. Some white lower-class youths in Detroit, Michigan, and Los Angeles use Nazi rhetoric to compensate for their own failures in a changing society. In Louisiana, David Duke was initially inspired by Rockwell when he demonstrated against attorney William Kunstler in 1970 while wearing a Nazi armband. William Pierce, a former associate of Rockwell, wrote *The Turner Diaries*, which allegedly inspired a number of militant militia movements.

Rockwell did not invent the white supremacist movement in the United States, but he became a symbol to future neo-Nazis. The difficulty for many researchers is in explaining Rockwell's movement without giving him post-mortem publicity. Some major college textbooks on U.S. history ignore him completely. Certainly written coverage of his views gives exposure to American Nazism. For example, the small American Nazi Party in Chicago was ignored until a September, 1976, article in the *Chicago Sun Times* presented the Nazis to the city's population. However, ignoring the origin and the nature of the type of racist thinking that led to the Holocaust may be even more dangerous. *Johnpeter Horst Grill*

Core Resources

A good introduction to the Nazi movement in the United States is Leland V. Bell's *In Hitler's Shadow: The Anatomy of American Nazism* (Port Washington, N.Y.: Kennikat Press, 1973). For Rockwell's activities, two useful discussions are Lawrence N. Powell's "When Hate Came to Town: New Orleans' Jews and George Lincoln Rockwell," in *American Jewish History* (85, no. 4, 1997), and

Hate Groups in America: A Record of Bigotry and Violence, edited by Alan M. Schwartz (New York: Anti-Defamation League of B'nai B'rith, 1988). American Nazi activities in Chicago are described in Donald Alexander Downs's *Nazis in Skokie: Freedom, Community, and the First Amendment* (Notre Dame, Ind.: University of Notre Dame Press, 1985). Neo-Nazi activities, particularly in Detroit, are surveyed by Raphael S. Ezekiel's *The Racist Mind: Portraits of American Neo-Nazis and Klansmen* (New York: Viking, 1995). For a guide to neo-Nazi movements see Elinor Langer's "The American Neo-Nazi Movement Today," in *The Nation* 251, no. 3 (July 16/23, 1990), and Southern Poverty Law Center's Web site: http://www.splcenter.org/klanwatch/kw-2b.html.

See also: Anti-Semitism; Aryan Nation; Holocaust; Jewish Americans; Nation of Islam; White Aryan Brotherhood; White supremacist groups.

Amerind

The term "Amerind" is a neologism combining the words "American" and "Indian" that came into common usage during the 1970's. A result of tribal activism meant to counter racism toward native peoples, this term was chosen as an alternative to "American Indian" and "Native American."

The people to whom this term refers include members of any of the aboriginal peoples of North America, Central America, South America, and the West Indies. Europeans and European Americans have continually sought to lump all the original inhabitants of the Americas into a convenient single group. "Amerind" represents an attempt to refer to native groups collectively with a term that could be considered politically correct. Yet although the term may be descriptive and less inaccurate than others, it falls short of the redefinition needed when referring to the multitude of distinct original cultures of North America.

There are more than five hundred groups of indigenous peoples in the United States alone, each with its own name for itself, and each with a specific cultural heritage and political legacy. Who a people are can be defined only in terms of specific environment, language, customs, traditions, taboos, and other characteristics. Until modern Americans recognize the distinctive elements inherent in each indigenous community, any new terms such as "Amerind" will be viewed by scholars as empty generalizations. Such terms, although convenient, are more a reflection of American cultural bias than they are descriptive of the nature, quality, or diversity of the original inhabitants of the Americas.

Byron D. Cannon

See also: American Indian stereotypes; Indian; Native American.

Amistad slave revolt

> **Significance:** Abolitionists win a victory in the judicial battle that follows an illegal importation of Africans as slaves.

Although the British-Spanish Treaty of 1817 banned African slave trading as of 1820, a highly lucrative covert slave trade existed, especially between Africa and Cuba. In April, 1839, a Portuguese slave ship left West Africa bound for Havana filled with more than five hundred illegally purchased Africans, mostly Mendis. After a two-month passage in which one-third of the Africans died, the ship reached Havana. Government officials receiving kickbacks provided paperwork declaring these Africans to be *ladinos*, slaves residing in Cuba prior to 1820, which would make their sale legal. Within a few days, José Ruiz purchased forty-nine adult African men, and Pedro Montes bought four children, three girls and a boy.

The Uprising

The slaves were loaded onto the schooner *Amistad*, which set sail for Puerto Príncipe, a few days' journey away. The Africans, unable to communicate with the Spanish-speaking owners or crew, became convinced that they were to be eaten. On the third night out, Joseph Cinqué picked the lock on his iron collar and broke into the cargo hold, where he and others found cane knives. The Africans took over the ship, killing the captain and the cook. The two crew members disappeared, perhaps having jumped overboard. Ruiz, Montes, and Antonio, the captain's slave cabin boy, were spared.

The Africans demanded to be taken to Sierra Leone. For almost two months, Ruiz and Montes pretended to comply. During the day they sailed southeast, occasionally landing to scavenge for food and water, but at night they headed north and northeast, in hopes of finding help. The schooner's decrepit condition and the many blacks on board aroused suspicion. The *Amistad* came to the attention of the USS *Washington*, whose captain, Thomas Gedney, ordered the schooner boarded. The thirty-nine surviving slaves, by now almost starved and unable to resist, were taken into custody.

The Legal Battle

Ruiz and Montes filed suits to have their slave property returned to them; Gedney claimed salvage rights to the *Amistad* and its cargo, including the slaves; the Spanish government demanded the fugitives be handed over to it; U.S. abolitionists clamored for the Africans to be set free. Although African slave trade was banned, slavery in Cuba was legal, and Ruiz and Montes had paperwork documenting their ownership. Moreover, there were U.S.-Spanish relations to be considered in determining whether or not the United States should recognize Spanish property rights to the Africans. Precedents from an earlier slaver incident, the *Antelope* case, had to be analyzed also. Perhaps most important, the *Amistad* affair carried grave implications for the slavery issue in the United States—and President Martin Van Buren hoped to avoid that issue in his upcoming reelection campaign, knowing that his success depended on maintaining his coalition of Northern and Southern supporters.

Newspapers across the land kept an interested public informed of the status of the case. For the most part, Northerners were sympathetic toward the Africans, while Southerners felt they should be returned to the Spanish government to be tried for piracy and murder. The affair probably would have been handled quietly and quickly if the abolitionists had not recognized its potential to raise the public's awareness of the moral and legal issues at stake in the slavery question.

Abolitionists and other opponents of slavery quickly formed the *Amistad* Committee, made up of Simeon Jocelyn, Joshua Leavitt, and Lewis Tappan, to raise money for legal counsel and to appeal to President Van Buren to allow the case to be decided by the United States court system rather than turning the prisoners over to the Spanish government. The committee employed James Covey, a native African who could speak the Mendi language, to communicate with the *Amistad* blacks, for so far depositions had been given only by the Spaniards and the cabin boy.

The legal proceedings began in mid-September, 1839, in the United States Circuit Court convened in Hartford, Connecticut. The case worked its way over the next eighteen months from Circuit Court to District Court, back to the Circuit Court and finally to the Supreme Court. The abolitionists made sure that the case stayed before the public. The public, although ambivalent in its responses to the legal and moral questions, stayed interested.

The case also excited international interest, and the cause of the abolitionists was substantially aided when Richard Robert Madden, a British official living in Havana, gave a moving and informed deposition concerning the state of the slave trade in Cuba. He spelled out the means and extent of illegal activities and clarified the status of *ladinos*. He also stated that the children on board the *Amistad* were without doubt too young to be pre-1820 Cuban residents, and that he strongly believed

This illustration depicts the 1839 slaying of the captain of the *Amistad* by the African slaves being transported on his ship. The slaves were later freed and returned to Sierra Leone in 1841.

that all the *Amistad* captives were *bozales*, newly imported Africans, not *ladinos*.

The Conclusion

In January, 1840, Judge Andrew T. Judson of the U.S. District Court of Connecticut ruled that the Africans could not be counted as property in the calculation of salvage value, nor could they legally be held as slaves, because their initial purchase had been illegal. The government appealed the case, and a few months later, Judge Smith Thompson of the U.S. Circuit Court concurred in Judson's decision. The government again appealed, and the case came before the United States Supreme Court in early 1841. John Quincy Adams argued passionately on behalf of the defendants. On March 9, 1841, the Supreme Court also ruled that Africans brought to Cuba illegally were not property, that as illegally held free men they had a right to mutiny, and that they should therefore be released. In November, 1841, the Africans sailed to Sierra Leone, accompanied by a small group of New England missionaries.

The *Amistad* decision was a great victory for abolitionists and raised the public's awareness of the slavery issue. The case fed secessionist sentiments in the Southern states but helped opponents of slavery focus on legal attacks against the institution.   *Grace McEntee*

Core Resources

Christopher Martin's *The "Amistad" Affair* (New York: Abelard-Schuman, 1970) and Howard Jones's *Mutiny on the "Amistad": The Saga of a Slave Revolt and Its Impact on American Abolition, Law, and Diplomacy* (New York: Oxford University Press, 1987) describe the case and its effects. William A. Owens's *Black Mutiny: The Revolt on the Schooner "Amistad"* (Philadelphia: Pilgrim Press, 1968) is a dramatized but well-researched rendering of the incident that includes information on the fate of the Africans after the trial. *The "Amistad" Case: The Most Celebrated Slave Mutiny of the Nineteenth Century* (New York: Johnson Reprint, 1968) contains correspondence between the U.S. and Spanish governments concerning the *Amistad* case.

See also: Abolition; Slave rebellions; Slavery: history.

Ancient Order of Hibernians

The Ancient Order of Hibernians in America is a fraternal society of the Roman Catholics founded in 1836 to promote the interests and welfare of Americans of Irish descent and to promote unity, friendship, Christian charity, and education among its members. Although it is claimed that the Hibernians were originally organized in Ireland in 1565, when Rory O'Moore set up a protective association to oppose the English in Ireland, the actual origins are unknown. The order in the United States was established in New York City under a charter sent by officers of the parent organization in Ireland. In the late 1800's, secret Irish organizations associated with the Ancient Order of Hibernians encouraged Irish coal miners in Pennsylvania to protest low wages and poor working conditions. As a result, Irish Americans associated with secret societies were labeled as violent people and treated unjustly.

A unified constitution was adopted for the American order in 1908. The Ancient Order of Hibernians is dedicated to helping the people of Ireland achieve complete independence. The order has contributed millions of dollars for charitable purposes, including contributions to earthquake victims in the United States and Italy, and it has also contributed substantial amounts of money to Catholic educational and religious efforts. Headquarters of the American order are in New York City.

Alvin K. Benson

See also: Irish American stereotypes; Irish Americans; Labor movement.

Anglo-conformity

The tendency for those immigrating to North America to lose much of their native cultural heritage and conform substantially to an Anglo-Protestant core culture is conceptualized as the process of Anglo-conformity. In the late nineteenth and early twentieth century, Anglo-conformity was practiced by immigrant groups who came from eastern and southern Europe (Poles, Italians, Greeks). Although some of the individuals in those groups have maintained some of the distinctive elements of their native cultures, many others have become completely assimilated into the dominant American society. In the late twentieth century, many immigrant racial groups of non-European origin (Asian Americans, Hispanics) may also be experiencing Anglo-conformity. For example, in California, Proposition 227, which limits the time an elementary school student can spend in bilingual education, passed with a large amount of Mexican American political support. Therefore, immigrants from Mexico, and their children, now have strong social pressure to concentrate on English, the language of the dominant culture, at the expense of their own Spanish language. Anglo-conformity may also be experienced by nonimmigrant racial minorities since they are generally expected to follow European American styles of dress and speech patterns when operating in the dominant American society. *George Yancey*

See also: Anglo-Protestants; Conformity theories; European immigration to the United States: 1892-1943.

Anglo-Protestant stereotypes

Anglo-Protestant stereotypes began in early colonial times and include a variety of positive and negative images of the early settlers that reflect their contributions to American life. Because whole congregations and followers of influential preachers dominated most New England towns, religion and politics were closely connected. For this reason and others, Anglo-Protestants dominated the political, economic, and social life of America in colonial times and afterward, even though they constituted only a plurality of Americans by the end of the Revolution. Their ability to remain prominent in American political and financial affairs in the succeeding centuries contributed to their enduring stereotype as a "power elite."

Another stereotype is based on an image of early Anglo-Protestant settlers as self-disciplined, hardworking, pious men and women. Prominent among the early Anglo-Protestants were the Puritans in Massachusetts, who were befriended by Native Americans and thus able to survive the harsh conditions and celebrate the first American holiday, Thanksgiving. However, these same pilgrims tolerated little deviation from their religious and moral scruples and drove Roger Williams from their midst because of his religious views. They also supplied the English language with the term "puritanical," which reflects the popular belief that Anglo-Protestants are inflexible, intolerant, and given to a degree of hypocrisy.

A similarly negative stereotype, which was spawned partly by the Puritans' religious views and also by the Salem witch trials, depicts Anglo-Protestant religious leaders as harsh, overzealous, black-robed ministers who used the threat of an afterlife teeming with fire and brimstone to increase their power and influence and for their personal financial gain. Within this stereotype is an element of anti-intellectualism, in that these preachers and local officials used their education and eloquence to stir up communal anger and suspicion to divide and dominate those who relied on them for guidance and leadership. In Salem, the religious leaders were both victims and victimizers, having initially been misled by a vengeful group of "innocents" whose personal desires for power and revenge were unrecognized or ignored. In a frightening abuse of power, the town's religious leaders accepted the group's accusations as truth and exploited the fear that their theatrics and the trials fostered.

A more favorable stereotype is the popular caricature of the New England Yankee. The Yankee is an American version of the English rugged individualist who possesses a Calvinistic drive for hard work. He is as careful in dealings with his fellow man as he is with his religious conviction, because both are bound together in his perception that he will reap the profits of his moral convictions in this life and in the next.

These historical stereotypes combine in the modern image, which portrays Anglo-Protestants as hardworking, self-disciplined, God-fearing, powerful go-getters who at the same time are intolerant, puritanical, and overzealous in matters of church and state. *Sheldon Hanft*

See also: Anglo-Protestants; Power elite; Stereotype.

Anglo-Protestants

Anglo-Protestants are descendants of the early American settlers who were either members of the Anglican Church of England, which was the established (tax supported) church in six of the original colonies, or were members of the dissident English Protestant denominations that created churches in New England and the Chesapeake area and generally followed the religious precepts of the Westminster Convention held during the English civil war. American Anglicans, generally supportive of John Calvin's belief in the use of simple dress, observance of the Sabbath, and the use of legal means to prompt devout behavior, became Episcopals after the American Revolution, when the Anglican Church in America changed its name to note its maintenance of a structure of priests and bishops, the feature that made the Church of England most distinguishable from other Protestant churches. Throughout the nineteenth century, continued spurts of migration brought additional Anglo-Protestant groups to the midwestern and far western regions of the United States. Despite their decline as a percentage of the American population, Anglo-Protestants have retained a disproportionate amount of prominence in American political, economic, and social life, as demonstrated by the fact that all but one of the American presidents through Bill Clinton can be described as Anglo-Protestants.   *Sheldon Hanft*

See also: Anglo-Protestant stereotypes; Anglo-Saxon; Power elite.

Anglo-Saxon

From 410 to 500 c.e., after the Romans left what is now England, three ethnic groups—the Angles from the Schleswig region of northern Germany, the Saxons from northwest Germany and northeast Holland, and the Jutes from Denmark—migrated to England. These groups, which became known collectively as the Anglo-Saxons, mixed together and settled in such large numbers that they were able to impose their language and customs on the Celtic-speaking Britons, except in the Welsh mountains and the Scottish highlands. Under the most famous Anglo-Saxon king, Alfred the Great, the Anglo-Saxon kingdom expanded and became known as England, an Anglo-Saxon word meaning "land of the Angles."

In the United States and Canada, Anglo-Saxon refers to any person of English nationality, culture, or descent, and to anyone of the Anglican religion. More generally, the term is used to designate any white Gentile who speaks English. Many Anglo-Saxons have historically considered themselves superior to those of other races and ethnicities, with some white supremacist groups claiming ties to Anglo-Saxon ancestors. The Anglo-Saxons have left their mark on the grammar of the English language, as well as in thousands of English

words, including approximately one-fifth of the words spoken in the English language today.   *Alvin K. Benson*

See also: Anglo-Protestants; White "race"; White supremacist groups; Whites.

Anglophone

In Canada, which is a multicultural, multiethnic society, composed largely of immigrants, language is an important aspect of identity. Anglophones are Canadians whose mother tongue and dominant language is English. In contrast, the dominant language and mother tongue of francophones is French. Residents of Canada who have a mother tongue other than English or French are categorized as allophones. English is the dominant language of commercial, administrative, and social usage in all Canadian provinces except Quebec.

In 1991, more than fifteen million Canadians out of a population of more than twenty-seven million claimed English as their mother tongue, and more than six million were francophones. By 1996, more than seventeen million anglophones constituted about 60 percent of the population of Canada. The francophone proportion of the population was 24 percent in 1996 or nearly seven million. That year, nearly five million Canadians were allophones, an increase of more than 15 percent since 1991.

Although English dominates most facets and sectors of Canadian life outside Quebec, the government of Canada has adopted an official policy of bilingualism, endorsing a need for both French and English to be used in the federal administration of Canada. Extensive funding has been provided for bilingual education programs throughout the country.   *Ranee K. L. Panjabi*

See also: Bilingualism in Canada; Culture and language; Francophone; Official Languages Act; Visible minority allophones in Canada.

Annihilation of racial and ethnic groups

Significance: Annihilation and expulsion are two of six basic patterns of intergroup relations; the others are assimilation, pluralism, legal protection of minorities, and subjugation of one group by another. Annihilation and expulsion have been studied primarily since the 1960's, and scholars continue to debate how to define the concepts.

Annihilation of racial or ethnic groups is also called genocide, although other types of mass killing are sometimes included under that term; the expulsion of racial or ethnic groups is also called population transfer. Although these two phenomena are distinct, one can fade into the other. A government determined to expel a particular ethnic group at any cost may resort to genocide if expulsion becomes impractical, and the process of ethnic expulsion can lead to massive deaths from heat, cold, or hunger when it is carried out too abruptly.

Expulsion of an ethnic minority can assume three variants. One is the unilateral expulsion of an ethnic minority group across an international frontier. Classic examples are the expulsion of ethnic Finns from the part of Karelia annexed by the Soviet Union after the 1939-1940 Russo-Finnish War and the forcible transfer of ethnic Germans from Poland and Czechoslovakia after World War II.

In another variant, called the exchange of populations, two states agree to accept the minorities expelled by each other. The classic example is the expulsion of ethnic Greeks from Turkey and of ethnic Turks from Greece following the Greco-Turkish War of 1922-1923. When British India was partitioned in 1947, violence forced many Muslims to flee what became India and many Hindus to flee what became Pakistan. This process, too, could be called exchange of populations (although many Muslims remained in the new Republic of India).

In still another variant of ethnic expulsion, a government forcibly uproots a minority ethnic group and resettles it within the same state, but far from the group's homeland. Examples from American history are the deportation of the Five Civilized Tribes from Georgia to the Indian Territory in what is now Oklahoma in the 1830's and the rounding up of Japanese Americans of the Pacific Coast states into internment camps during World War II. Under Joseph Stalin, dictator of the Soviet Union between 1929 and 1953, many Estonians, Letts, and Lithuanians, from the Baltic states acquired by Stalin in 1940, were deported eastward to Siberia.

The Holocaust

During World War II, nearly six million Jews (German, Russian, Polish, Hungarian, Dutch, and French) were murdered by the Nazi regime. This mass extermination, called the Holocaust, differed from other acts labeled genocide: It aimed not merely to purify a single nation-state ethnically (as did the Turkish killings of Armenians in 1915-1923) but to eliminate an entire people, wherever in the world they lived. Reputable scholars agree that Nazi Germany was trying to exterminate all the Jews. The Nazis also targeted other groups for destruction; among them were the Gypsies.

Defining Genocide

Social scientists do not always agree about which incidents can be called genocide. It is difficult both to define genocide and to determine when it has occurred. The massive death toll among the Armenians of Turkey between 1915 and 1923, which reduced their numbers from a million to a little less than fifty thousand, is regarded as genocide by Armenians throughout the world and by many American social scientists (including sociologists Leo Kuper and Helen Fein and political scientist Robert Melson), but not (at least as of the late 1990's) by the Turkish government. Kuper also regards as genocide the bloody repression in Bangladesh during that country's 1971 struggle for freedom from Pakistan and the mutual killings of Hutus and Tutsis in Rwanda and Burundi in the early 1970's; Melson, however, sees both events as examples of massacre rather than genocide.

Many scholars regard as genocide only those mass killings undertaken by governments; many also argue that the intention to exterminate a group must exist. Such a definition would exclude many cases of the decimation of aboriginal peoples in North America; here, excess deaths often resulted from exposure to European diseases or from the violent acts of individual European settlers; governments did not always intend to exterminate the native peoples. All scholars agree that ethnocide—the deliberate destruction of aboriginal culture—was practiced. Melson carefully distinguishes between killings of members of a group with intent to intimidate and killings with intent to exterminate the group; the former, he argues, is not genocide. Scholars also argue about how innocent an ethnic group must be of secessionist aims or violent rebellious activity if it is to be seen as a victim of genocide rather than of arguably justifiable repression. Finally, some scholars, such as Judaic studies professor Steven Katz, insist that only the Holocaust deserves the label of genocide.

It is also sometimes difficult to determine if a dominant group is expelling an ethnic minority. After the Arab-Israeli War of 1948-1949, many Arabs fled Israel, and many Jews emigrated from the Arab states to Israel. Israel and the Arab states each accused the other of ethnic expulsion. Another ambiguous case is the exodus of the ethnic Chinese boat people from Vietnam in 1979. Although the Vietnamese government outlawed their livelihood as traders, it never explicitly ordered them to leave the country. Hence, some foreign scholars deny that ethnic expulsion occurred.

The causes of genocide are disputed. Kuper, who has studied ethnicity in Africa, sees the plural society, rigidly divided along ethnic lines, as a seedbed of genocide; it is difficult, however, to fit the German case into this theoretical framework. Sociologists of ethnicity Pierre Van den Berghe and Walter Zenner see so-called middleman (trader) minorities as especially likely victims of genocide; Kuper, seeing no utility in the middleman minority concept, disagrees. Political scientist Melson sees war and revolution as necessary preconditions for genocide. Political sociologist Irving Horowitz sees totalitarian regimes as the most likely to commit genocide; such a view, however, ignores all centuries prior to the twentieth.

Restitution

Some countries have made some form of restitution for past acts of genocide or ethnic expulsion. The government of the Federal Republic of Germany, created in 1949, decided to offer reparations payments to surviving Jewish victims of Nazism, wherever they happened to live; these payments, however, have been extremely modest. In the late 1980's, the United States Congress finally offered restitution payments to the survivors of the forced internment of Japanese Americans during World War II. Once a genocidal regime is gone, those who helped perpetrate genocide can be punished; in the early 1960's, Israel kidnapped, tried, and executed Nazi bureaucrat Adolf Eichmann.

Research

Although Americans first became aware of the Holocaust in 1945, serious research by sociologists on the subject of genocide did not begin until the 1970's. To many sociologists of the immediate post-World War II period, genocide must have seemed too emotionally charged an issue for objective social research; it may also have appeared to be an inexplicable aberration rather than a normal and recurrent social phenomenon.

Sociologists experienced a reawakening of interest in genocide because of the recurrent ethnic conflicts in post-World War II Africa and Asia, which seemed to worsen as the decolonization process accelerated in the 1960's. Another stimulus to research on genocide, particularly for younger sociologists, was the social and political turbulence in the United States in the 1960's and early 1970's, which shattered the illusion that violence and repression were faraway aberrations. Interest in the themes of ethnic conflict and the role of violence in politics was aroused by the Civil Rights movement, the urban riots, and the war in Vietnam. Among young Jews, the Arab-Israeli War of 1967 awoke both a new sense of ethnic pride and a new interest in the history of the Holocaust.   *Paul D. Mageli*

Core Resources

Michael Robert Marrus's *The Unwanted: European Refugees in the Twentieth Century* (New York: Oxford University Press, 1985) is a survey of refugee movements from 1880 to 1970 that devotes much attention to the Jews' flight from Nazism. *Genocide and the Modern Age: Etiology and Case Studies of Mass Death*, edited by Isidor Wallimann and Michael N. Dobkowski (New York: Greenwood Press, 1987) contains thirteen original essays, most on the Holocaust; one discusses the Armenian genocide, and another treats the decimation of the Australian aborigines. Robert Melson's *Revolution and Genocide: On the Origins of the Armenian Genocide and the Holocaust* (Chicago: University of Chicago Press, 1992) is a point-by-point, analytical comparison of the two genocides. Leo Kuper's *Genocide: Its Political Use in the Twentieth Century* (New Haven, Conn.: Yale University Press, 1981) provides new perspectives not only on the Holocaust and the Armenian genocide but also on a variety of post-World War II interethnic conflicts and atrocities unknown to the average American.

See also: Anti-Semitism; Ethnic enclaves; Genocide: physical; Holocaust; Immigration and emigration; Japanese American internment; Long Walk; Minority and majority groups; Racism as an ideology.

Anti-Catholicism

Anti-Catholicism is a feeling of dislike, hatred, and/or fear of people of the Roman Catholic religion. This feeling, produced by traditional antipathy between Catholics and Protestants based on fundamental differences between these two major Christian belief systems, can be found throughout U.S. history.

All the American colonies had laws directed against Catholics, but it was not until the 1830's, when the Irish began immigrating to the United States in large numbers, that anti-Catholic feeling became pronounced. From the 1830's to the Civil War, anti-Catholic feeling was expressed in pamphlets and books, in anti-Catholic and antiforeign organizations such as the Know-Nothing Party, and in violence against Catholic neighborhoods and churches. Although the Civil War (1861-1865) largely ended such attacks, anti-Catholic feeling flared in 1887 with the formation of the American Protective Association. This anti-Catholic organization enjoyed much success for a few years but died out in 1896. Anti-Catholic feeling, however, continued, expressed in the growing number of anti-Catholic publications found in the early part of the twentieth century and in the growth in popularity of the Ku Klux Klan, which emphasized anti-Catholicism as well as anti-Semitism. Anti-Catholic feelings became much less pronounced after World War II, although they surfaced again in the 1960 presidential race. Despite the anti-Catholic prejudices voiced by some, John F. Kennedy won the election to become America's first Catholic president.

Karen C. Hauser

See also: Irish Americans; Irish Catholic "race"; Ku Klux Klan.

Anti-Defamation League

B'nai B'rith was founded in New York in 1843 as a counterpart to the fraternal orders thriving in the United States in the nineteenth century. Its objective was to fulfill the traditional functions of Jewish societies in Europe that cared for the sick, elderly, and orphaned. In 1913, Leo Frank, a Jewish factory superintendent in Atlanta, Georgia, was arrested and charged with the murder of a thirteen-year-old female employee. After his trial and conviction, he was kidnapped from prison and lynched. Shortly thereafter, Frank was fully exonerated. The incident led B'nai B'rith to form the Anti-Defamation League to counter defamatory statements about Jewish people and to secure fair treatment for all people.

With a staff of more than four hundred and a $35 million budget, the Anti-Defamation League puts out a number of regular publications and supports studies involving anti-Semitism, racism, and other forms of bigotry. The group also maintains a speakers' bureau and gives annual awards that include a human rights prize and a First Amendment freedoms prize. Through its extensive publications, political lobbying activities, media campaigns, and education programs, the Anti-Defamation League wields considerable influence. Because the Anti-Defamation League also monitors the activities of hate groups and militias, the organization is often consulted by those seeking information and statistics on neo-Nazi groups and other hate groups in the United States. The Anti-Defamation League also collects and provides information on a broad range of First Amendment concerns.

The Anti-Defamation League is led by a National Commission, which consists of 151 members and meets once a year. In the interval between the commission's annual meetings, the National Executive Committee runs the organization. Membership in the Anti-Defamation League is by nomination or invitation. The organization has twenty-eight regional offices in major metropolitan areas, and each office has its own board of local Jewish leaders and prominent citizens.

Sam Ramsey Hakim

See also: American Jewish Committee; American Jewish Congress; Anti-Semitism; Frank, Leo, lynching; Hate crimes; Jewish Americans.

Anti-Semitism

> **Significance:** Anti-Semitism, discrimination or hostility by non-Jews against Jews as a group, whether expressed in words or in actions, has waned in the United States since the 1940's. However, it still influences interactions between Jews and others.

Anti-Semitism can be defined as hostility toward Jews, based on a belief in negative stereotypes concerning Jews. Anti-Semites commonly stereotype Jews as avaricious, excessively wealthy, overly aggressive, dishonest, hungry for power, clannish, and unpatriotic. Some anti-Semites see these characteristics as ineradicable racial traits. It is important to note that an individual may believe in one stereotype but not in others and that many non-Jewish Americans have positive stereotypes about Jews, seeing them as hardworking and intelligent. The term "anti-Semitism," which is not strictly accurate (Arabs as well as Jews possess a Semitic language), was coined in the 1870's to distinguish between the traditional Christian animosity toward Jews on grounds of religious difference and the newer animosity toward Jews on grounds of alleged racial difference.

Anti-Semitism can be expressed in words, in violent deeds, in political activism, or in discriminatory behavior. The political anti-Semite believes that Jews are excessively powerful and ascribes nearly all problems in the country to a Jewish conspiracy. Such a belief can be held by individuals who do not compete directly with Jews and who may have never even seen a Jew. The German Nazis, who killed six million European Jews during the Holocaust, represent the most extreme expression of political anti-Semitism. The White Aryan Brotherhood and the Ku Klux Klan are American examples. Most individuals who accept one or more anti-Semitic stereotypes never join such extremist movements.

The refugee social scientist Theodor Adorno and his American colleagues, in the pathbreaking *The Authoritarian Personality* (1950), argue that anti-Semitism and antiblack racism go together. The pioneering researchers Bruno Bettelheim (a psychologist) and Morris Janowitz (a sociologist), writing in the 1950 work *Dynamics of Prejudice*, disagree with that viewpoint. Antiblack racism, they find, is more prevalent among white non-Jews than is anti-Semitism. Anti-Semitic stereotypes, Bettelheim and Janowitz find, differ significantly from antiblack stereotypes. Jews are stereotyped as crafty, overly ambitious, and dishonest; blacks are most often stereotyped as lazy and sexually immoral.

Discrimination

It has traditionally been the more educated and affluent anti-Semites who have discriminated against Jews in employment, housing, and admission to universities and social clubs. According to sociologists Gertrude Selznick and Stephen Steinberg in the mid-1960's, even some college-educated people who were not especially anti-Semitic still condoned social club discrimination. Discrimination against Jews was much rarer by the end of the twentieth century than it had been between 1920 and 1945. Yet in the 1980's, sociologists G. William Domhoff and Richard L. Zweigenhaft still detected a pattern of exclusion from certain elite social clubs and underrepresentation in certain industries. Industrial psychologist Abraham K. Korman has seen a tendency among some large corporations to avoid recruiting at predominantly Jewish colleges and to confine Jewish hires to technical and scientific research jobs, and demographer Gary Tobin, sampling Jewish opinion in sixty American communities, heard some reports of discrimination on the job or in housing.

Conflict with Christians

Because Jews are both a religious and an ethnic group, precisely what constitutes anti-Semitism is not always clear. For example, some American Christians want their city governments to allow or sponsor creches (nativity scene displays) on public property and want public schoolchildren to sing Christmas carols at Christ-

mastime. Especially in parts of the United States that have almost no Jews (Jews were about 3 percent of the total population in 1980), such Christians are not necessarily anti-Semitic, although they are insensitive to Jewish feelings. Some Christians do not like Judaism as a religion but welcome individual Jewish converts to their own religions; such an attitude, while understandably offensive to many Jews, differs from the virulent racial anti-Semitism of Nazi Germany.

Sociologists Charles Y. Glock and Rodney Stark, in the 1966 work *Christian Beliefs and Anti-Semitism*, see a strong connection between adherence to Fundamentalist Protestant beliefs and acceptance of anti-Semitic stereotypes, but this conclusion is controversial. Two experts in public opinion polling, Gregory Martire and Ruth Clark, argue in *Anti-Semitism in the United States: A Study of Prejudice in the 1980's* (1982) that no relationship between Fundamentalism and anti-Semitism exists if differences in educational levels are taken into account. Nevertheless, many American Jews in the 1980's and 1990's feared the identification of Americanism with Christianity that they detected among some Fundamentalist Protestants.

Causes and Results

The reasons for anti-Semitism are disputed. The emotive theory, propounded by Adorno in 1950, argues that individuals become anti-Semitic to cope with the psychological frustrations engendered by a rigid and authoritarian upbringing. According to the cognitive theory, voiced by Selznick and Steinberg, lack of education leads individuals to accept the anti-Semitic stereotypes already found in the culture; psychological frustration, they argue, is beside the point.

In the 1980's, incidents of vandalism of Jewish synagogues revived the debate about how dangerous anti-Semitism is. Journalist Charles E. Silberman, in *A Certain People: American Jews and Their Lives Today* (1985), saw the threat as nearly nonexistent. Martire and Clark, in 1982, saw a decline in anti-Semitic attitudes since 1964 but conceded that much prejudice still existed. Gary Tobin reported, in *Jewish Perceptions of Anti-Semitism* (1988), that one out of every four interviewees claimed to have experienced some anti-Semitic incident in the year the survey was conducted; nevertheless, he viewed the danger of anti-Semitism as a controllable one. A

Bud Almassy applies paint remover to a swastika on the gate of the Jewish Passaic Junction Cemetery in Saddle Brook, New Jersey, in 1995. Although anti-Semitism declined after World War II, it still finds expression in acts such as cemetery vandalism.

public opinion survey released by the Anti-Defamation League in November, 1992, revealed that one-fifth of all Americans still harbored anti-Semitic beliefs or attitudes.

In 1945, many medical schools and Ivy League universities severely limited their enrollment of Jewish students by a quota system. Certain wealthy suburbs barred Jews from becoming residents; many resorts refused to admit Jews; and many corporate employers and elite law firms would not knowingly hire Jews. Nearly one-fifth of all Americans regarded Jews as a major threat to the United States, while fully one-half thought that Jews had too much power. In the decades since then, both anti-Jewish discrimination and anti-Jewish attitudes (as revealed to pollsters) have declined sharply.

The brunt of the effort to combat anti-Semitism was borne by such Jewish "defense" organizations as the Anti-Defamation League, the American Jewish Committee, and the American Jewish Congress. As late as the 1980's, they carefully monitored all anti-Semitic incidents. They sponsored much of the sociological research on anti-Semitism. Partly because of the pressure exerted by the Jewish defense organizations on the nation's colleges and schools of medicine, all quota restrictions on the admission of Jewish university students had been eliminated by the late 1960's. As the pressure of publicity was exerted on resort hotels, they too gradually opened up to Jews; access did not become a matter of law, however, until the passage of the Civil Rights Act of 1964. A Supreme Court decision of 1966 forced city clubs and service clubs to drop provisions excluding Jews by threatening to revoke the clubs' tax exemption; private country clubs were untouched by the ruling.

The post-World War II decline of anti-Semitism was only partly attributable to the efforts of Jewish organizations. The defeat of Nazi Germany and certainly revelations about the Holocaust helped discredit the United States' most rabid political anti-Semites. In the 1950's and 1960's, a booming economy that demanded technically trained workers reduced non-Jewish employers' motivation to discriminate. The rapid expansion of higher education during those years probably made it easier for universities to end discrimination against Jewish students and applicants for college teaching positions. Finally, the steady migration of African Americans to northern cities provided an alternative target for white bigots. *Paul D. Mageli*

Core Resources

Anti-Semitism in the United States: A Study of Prejudice in the 1980's (New York: Praeger, 1982) presents Gregory Martire and Ruth Clark's optimistic and somewhat controversial conclusions concerning trends in anti-Semitism, based on analysis of a 1981 opinion survey commissioned by a Jewish organization. Harold E. Quinley and

Charles Y. Glock's *Anti-Semitism in America* (New York: Free Press, 1979), the last volume produced by a twelve-year research project, summarizes the results for all the topics pursued during the project, including those of a 1964 nationwide survey. Gertrude Selznick and Stephen Steinberg's *The Tenacity of Prejudice: Anti-Semitism in Contemporary America* (New York: Harper & Row, 1969) is a study based on interviews of a nationwide sample of nearly two thousand non-Jews. *Jews in the Mind of America* (Charles Herbert Stember et al., New York: Basic Books, 1966) contains seventeen essays by sociologists, social psychologists, and historians. In *Jewish Perceptions of Anti-Semitism* (New York: Plenum Press, 1988), author Gary Tobin, who interviewed Jews across the United States in 1987, argues that anti-Semitic incidents (such as verbal slurs and discrimination) occur more often than is generally believed.

See also: American Jewish Committee; American Jewish Congress; Anti-Defamation League; Holocaust; Jewish Americans; Jewish stereotypes.

Antislavery laws of 1777 and 1807

> **Significance:** On July 2, 1777, Vermont became the first of eight northeastern states to end slavery. On March 2, 1807, a federal bill outlawed the slave trade but failed to condemn slavery outright, reflecting the young nation's moral ambiguity.

On July 2, 1777, Vermont became the first state to abolish slavery fully. Its 1777 Constitution outlawed "holding anyone by law to serve any person" as a servant, slave, or apprentice after he or she reached twenty-one years of age. In 1780, Pennsylvania passed a law gradually abolishing slavery. An attempt five years earlier had failed, partly because opponents argued that abolishing slavery would antagonize the South, where slavery was a deeply embedded institution, and break up the Union during the war for independence from England. Under the Pennsylvania law, any African American not registered as a slave by the end of the year would be considered free; however, children born slaves in 1780 would remain in service to their owners until they were twenty-eight years of age to compensate the owners for the cost of raising them. The law also enabled blacks to testify against whites in courts and legalized interracial marriage.

In Massachusetts, opponents defeated a gradual

emancipation bill in 1777, and three years later, voters rejected a constitution that declared all men free and equal and provided voting rights for free blacks. In 1781, however, a slave named Quork Walker sued for his freedom in a state court because his owner had severely abused him. The trial judge, Caleb Cushing, instructed the jury that the idea of slavery conflicted with state law, so Walker was ordered freed. Although the legislature refused to act, by 1790, slavery no longer existed in Massachusetts because of similar court actions in dozens of other cases.

During the American Revolution, the New Hampshire legislature gave freedom to any of the state's six hundred slaves who volunteered for the militia. Other slaves gained their liberty by running away and joining the British military. Thus, when the state's 1783 constitution declared all men equal and independent from birth, only fifty slaves remained in the state. Although slavery was never abolished legally, slave property was removed from tax roles in 1789 and eleven years later, only eight slaves remained in the state.

In 1783, Rhode Island passed a gradual emancipation bill after six Quakers petitioned the state assembly for immediate liberation for all human beings kept as property. The bill stipulated that all slave children born after March 1 would be apprentices; girls became free at age eighteen, boys at age twenty-one. After slaves were freed, their masters were required to post bonds with the state guaranteeing that the former slaves would never require public assistance.

Connecticut, the New England state with the largest population of African Americans, granted freedom to slaves who fought against England but three times—in 1777, 1779, and 1780—rejected gradual emancipation. In 1784, however, the legislature declared that all adult slaves would be free by the end of the year and that black and mulatto (mixed-race) children would become free at twenty-five years of age. The state also passed discriminatory laws forbidding free blacks to vote, serve on juries, or marry whites.

Both New York and New Jersey freed African Americans who served in the army, but these states were slow to enact antislavery laws. New York's legislature rejected gradual emancipation in 1777. Eight years later, a freedom bill supported by the New York Manumission Society, whose membership included Alexander Hamilton, John Jay, and Aaron Burr, was defeated. In 1785, New York prohibited the sale and importation of slaves and allowed masters to manumit (free) their slaves, but only if they guaranteed that they would not require public assistance. The next year, New Jersey passed similar laws. In 1788, New York declared that slaves would no longer be judged or punished under standards different from those used to judge whites. Although slave auctions

ended in both states by 1790, New York did not pass an emancipation bill until 1799. The bill allowed owners to free their slaves regardless of age or condition but permitted them to keep boys until twenty-eight years of age and girls until the age of twenty-five. In 1804, New Jersey became the last of the original Northern states to end slavery legally. Neither state allowed free African Americans the right to vote.

The 1807 Bill

Although these northeastern states had ended slavery, the invention in 1793 of the cotton gin by Eli Whitney had made cotton a more profitable crop by greatly increasing the speed at which seeds could be separated from the picked cotton, thus increasing plantation owners' desire for more cotton pickers. It has been estimated that no fewer than twenty thousand new slaves were imported in Georgia and South Carolina in 1803.

In December, 1805, Senator Stephen R. Bradley of Vermont introduced legislation that would prohibit the slave trade beginning in 1808, but the bill was stalled for some months. A similar bill was offered in the House of Representatives by Barnabas Bidwell of Massachusetts, again to no effect. Later that year, President Thomas Jefferson urged passage of the bill in his message to Congress. On March 2, 1807, Congress enacted a law specifying a twenty-thousand-dollar fine and forfeiture of ship and cargo for importing slaves, as well as other penalties for acts ranging from equipping a slave ship to knowingly buying an imported slave. The disposition of illegally imported slaves was left to the states, however. Enforcement of the law was delegated first to the secretary of the treasury and later to the secretary of the navy.

Antislavery forces rejoiced in this new and symbolically important law, but enforcement proved weak. An exhaustive census of the slave trade published in 1969 estimated that 1.9 million slaves were imported illegally between 1811 and 1870; more recent research has called that estimate low. Although more than one hundred slave vessels were seized and their officers arrested in the years between 1837 and 1862, and nearly as many cases were prosecuted, convictions were difficult to obtain, and judges often gave light sentences. Another weakness of the 1807 law was that it permitted the continuation of slave traffic between states. An owner could take his slaves into another slave state or, according to the Missouri Compromise of 1820, into a western territory south of 36°30′.   *Compiled from essays by Robert P. Ellis and Leslie V. Tischauser*

Core Resources

Books that discuss the end of slavery in the northeastern states include Gary B. Nash and Jean R. Soderlund's *Freedom by Degrees: Emancipation in Pennsylvania and Its*

Aftermath (New York: Oxford University Press, 1991), Arthur Zilversmit's *The First Emancipation: The Abolition of Slavery in the North* (Chicago: University of Chicago Press, 1967), and Robin Blackburn's *The Overthrow of Colonial Slavery, 1776-1848* (New York: Verso, 1988). John Hope Franklin's *From Slavery to Freedom: A History of Negro Americans* (5th ed., New York: Alfred A. Knopf, 1980), first published in 1947, is a pioneering study by an African American historian that contains a succinct summary of the enactment of the 1807 law and its aftermath. Warren S. Howard's *American Slavers and the Federal Law: 1837-1862* (Berkeley: University of California Press, 1963) is a copiously documented study of violations of the 1807 law during the quarter century before the outbreak of the Civil War. James A. Rawley's *The Transatlantic Slave Trade: A History* (New York: W. W. Norton, 1981) surveys the slave trade from its fifteenth century beginnings and places U.S. involvement in its international context.

See also: Abolition; Missouri Compromise; Proslavery argument; Slave codes; Slavery: history; Slavery: North American beginnings.

Apache Wars

> **Significance:** The incursion of white settlers into the Southwest leads to armed conflicts with indigenous Chiricahua Apaches.

After the signing of the Treaty of Guadalupe Hidalgo in 1848, large portions of northern Mexico were ceded to the United States. Numerous white settlers began moving into the newly formed Arizona and New Mexico territories. Much of this region was the traditional range of various Apache groups, particularly numerous bands of Chiricahua, Coyotero, and Mimbreño Apache. Many of these groups practiced raiding, taking goods from others as an extension of their traditional methods of subsistence. Raiding increased in frequency as more white settlers moved into Apache territory.

Cochise

In 1861, an Apache raiding party (thought to have been Coyotero Apache, not Chiricahua) kidnapped a boy who was part of a group of white settlers. The U.S. military quickly ordered Lieutenant George Bascom to investigate the incident and, if necessary, to take action against the "hostiles" that were thought to have committed the raid. On February 6, 1861, Bascom persuaded Cochise, the principal chief of the eastern Chiricahua, and some of his family and followers, to come in for a peace parley.

During the early stages of what has been termed the Bascom affair, Cochise tried to convince Bascom that it was not Chiricahua Apache who had conducted the raid. Bascom had Cochise and several of the chief's relatives arrested. Cochise later escaped. Bascom, as an act of reprisal for the kidnapping and Cochise's escape, ordered the execution of the chief's relatives.

This incident is generally viewed by historians as the starting point of what has come to be called the Apache Wars. Numerous armed conflicts involving various Apache groups occurred from 1861 to 1886 on both sides of the U.S.-Mexican border. For example, in retaliation for the execution of his relatives, Cochise organized a surprise attack on the Gidding party at Stein's Peak near Doubtful Canyon. Cochise killed nine of the settlers but lost sixty of his warriors in the attack. Numerous battles ensued in the years that followed.

In 1865, the Apache Wars reached a pinnacle. With the end of the American Civil War, the attention of the United States military shifted west to land traditionally occupied by Native American tribal groups. Action taken against the Apache by the Mexican military was also increasing. Mexican forces, combined with pressure exerted by U.S. military forces in the American Southwest, caused Cochise and other Apache leaders to remain constantly on the run. In 1866, Cochise was driven by U.S. forces into hiding in Mexico, where he continued to harass white settlers by periodically crossing the border to conduct surprise attacks. These skirmishes continued until October 10, 1872, when Cochise finally signed a truce with the Americans at Cochise's camp in the Dragoon Mountains in southern Arizona. Cochise died two years later.

Geronimo

Other Apache leaders, however, refused to abide by the truce of 1872 and continued their attacks on settler groups. Further west, Geronimo, a Bedonkohe/Chiricahua shaman from northern Mexico, was fighting his own wars against both Mexican and U.S. forces. By 1861, the U.S. Army was firmly established in southern Arizona. Forts Bowie and Apache had been built to assist the army in protecting the increasing numbers of settlers who continued to enter the Arizona territory. In 1871, an entire Apache camp was destroyed in the Camp Grant massacre.

In 1872, General George Cook, who had a reputation among Washington politicians for decisiveness in his dealings with Indian groups, took command of the Southwest operation. From 1872 until his dismissal in 1886, Cook's career was dominated by attempts to keep Geronimo in check. In 1877, Cook's men arrested Geronimo, along with family members and other Chiricahuas. Geronimo and his people were resettled on the

Chiricahua leader Geronimo (seated, fourth from left, arms outstretched) meets with General George Cook (second from right) in Arizona in 1886.

cal leaders in Washington, D.C., removed Cook and replaced him with General Nelson Miles. General Miles immediately sent out a force of approximately five thousand soldiers to seek out and capture Geronimo and his small band (estimated to be about twenty-four in number). On September 4, 1886, Geronimo, along with twenty-three members of his band of Chiricahuas (mostly women and children), surrendered for the final time at Skeleton Canyon—about sixty-five miles from Apache Pass, where the first skirmish of the Apache Wars had been fought. After Geronimo's surrender, Miles had all Chiricahuas in the immediate vicinity arrested, including the scouts that had been used by the army to track down Geronimo. Geronimo, his followers, and the former Apache scouts were placed in rail cars and transported east to a reservation in St. Augustine, Florida. With Geronimo's surrender and his removal to Florida, the Apache Wars ended.

Michael Shaw Findlay

Core Resources

D. C. Cole's *The Chiricahua Apache, 1846-1876: From War to Reservation* (Albuquerque: University of New Mexico Press, 1988) is a general history of Chiricahua with special attention to cultural conflicts with Euro-Americans. William B. Griffen's *Utmost Good Faith: Patterns of Apache-Mexican Hostilities in Northern Chihuahua Border Warfare, 1821-1848* (Albuquerque: University of New Mexico Press, 1989) summarizes historical accounts of hostilities between the Chiricahua Apache and Mexican military forces in Northern Mexico.

See also: Gadsden Purchase; Guadalupe Hidalgo, Treaty of; Popé's Revolt.

reservation at San Carlos. Sometimes referred to as "Hell's Forty Acres," San Carlos proved to be an inhospitable environment lacking sufficient water and game for Apache survival. Four years later, many Apache—including Geronimo—fled the reservation. From 1881 until his surrender at Skeleton Canyon in 1886, Geronimo fought numerous battles with both U.S. and Mexican forces and continued raiding white settlements. During this period of time Geronimo surrendered several times to the U.S. military. Late in the year 1881, for example, Geronimo was recaptured by Cook and taken to Fort Apache. Geronimo and his followers were again taken to the reservation but eventually fled to Mexico.

In April of 1882, Geronimo returned to San Carlos and conducted a raid, killing the chief of police and capturing several Mimbreño Apache, whom he forced to accompany him to Mexico. In May of 1883, Cook decided to pursue Geronimo into Mexico. On May 15, after several days of strenuous marching through Mexico's Sierra Madre, Cook attacked the camp of a group of Mimbreño Apache headed by Chato. Although the battle itself was indecisive, it had become evident that the military was not going to give up its pursuit of Geronimo. In the days that followed the battle, several chiefs of the Mimbreño Apache, including Chato, Loco, and Nana, surrendered to Cook. In March of 1884, Geronimo, by now a revered Apache leader, surrendered to Cook. This surrender and the subsequent confinement on the reservation, like the others, did not last. Geronimo fled and surrendered two more times.

Because Cook was unable to keep Geronimo under the purview of the U.S. government, military and politi-

Apartheid

Significance: Apartheid refers to the rigid system of total racial segregation, or, literally, "apartness," that evolved in South Africa between 1948 and the early 1980's. Its persistence until late in the twentieth century, in an otherwise "advanced" industrialized society, provoked world protest and elicited comparisons with racism in North America.

Apartheid can be defined briefly as the stringent policy of racial segregation and oppression that existed in the Republic of South Africa between the late 1940's and mid-1990's. Under apartheid, the government officially divided the country's population into "whites," "coloureds," and "blacks." The country was completely under the control of the white minority; other groups were restricted to certain areas of the country and had to obey an elaborate set of laws that mandated virtually every aspect of life, including where and how they could work.

The Development of Apartheid

The Dutch, who established Cape Town in 1652, were the first European settlers. In 1820, some five thousand English colonists settled Port Elizabeth. The British and the Boers united to form the Union of South Africa in 1910 (it became the Republic of South Africa in 1961). The first major African opposition movement, the African National Congress (ANC), was formed in 1912.

Blacks were subjected to a wide variety of oppressive measures after Europeans arrived. Asians and people of mixed ancestry also faced discrimination. In the 1930's and 1940's, growth in the cities drew tens of thousands of blacks looking for work. Black slums developed, and militant struggles erupted around the country. The National Party believed that the increasing black urban population presented a threat to its control, so it institutionalized and extended white supremacy and black oppression more than any previous regime had. In 1948, after the party was elected to power, apartheid became an all-encompassing system of racial stratification.

Prime Minister Daniel François Malan, the leader of the National Party, delineated four initial components of the apartheid program. Black representation to the House of Assembly would end; blacks would have limited self-government in their reserved lands; coloured voters would be removed from the voter rolls in Cape Province; and all schools and universities would be racially segregated. Many "petty apartheid laws" (for example, a law that made it illegal for blacks to use first-class railroad cars) were passed. In 1949, marriage between persons of different races was outlawed, and a 1950 act made sexual relations between the races illegal and punishable by up to seven years in prison.

Additional Restrictions

The Group Areas Act of 1950 established separate geographical areas for use by whites, coloureds, and blacks. Provisions were included for the forcible removal of blacks from areas where they were not wanted. The Population Registration Act required registration at birth as white, coloured, or African; an Asian category was added later. The Suppression of Communism Act made the expression of a number of ideas illegal, including anything that would promote hostility between people of European and African descent; in 1982, this was strengthened by the Internal Security Act. Pass laws and "influx control" laws mandated that all blacks sixteen years of age or older obtain a passbook (later called a "reference book"), which was to be carried at all times.

In 1951, the Bantu Authorities Act instituted a plan of "separate development" for the different groups in the country. Black "homelands" were established as the only areas where black South Africans could reside. Only within certain isolated and poor rural areas could blacks exercise any political freedom. Many men were forced to migrate to work in white parts of the country. Workers signed one-year contracts and were required to return to their homelands before being re-employed. Women, mostly domestic servants, were employed in the cities, and contact with their families was restricted. Violators were fined or imprisoned.

Protests and Violence

After the National Party rose to power, groups such as the ANC, led by Albert John Lutuli and Nelson Mandela, began to organize their followers in strikes and acts of civil disobedience to protest and to attract international attention. Church groups condemned apartheid, but their protests had no effect on government policies. Membership in the ANC soon grew to more than 100,000. In the "defiance campaign" of 1952, ANC leaders wrote to Prime Minister Malan requesting the repeal of the Bantu Authorities Act; they were rebuffed and were told essentially that the government would use any means necessary to enforce its new policies.

Indeed, through the years, protests and their violent, deadly suppression became a regular part of life for black South Africans. The infiltration of police informers led to arrests and the banning of the ANC's leadership. ANC leaders and other black leaders were thrown in jail for years; one, Steven Biko, died in jail under questionable circumstances. Mandela was sentenced to life imprisonment in 1964. In 1969, sixty-nine people who were protesting the pass laws died in the Sharpeville massacre; most were shot in the back. In its wake, the ANC and the Pan-African Congress, another antiapartheid protest group, were outlawed. The ANC went underground and into exile, eventually emerging with full force in the 1980's. In 1976, the Soweto riot saw many more black South Africans killed in the putdown of a protest begun by students over being required to use the Afrikaans language as their means of expression in school. In August, 1983, the United Democratic Front was formed as an umbrella organization of more than six hundred groups across racial and functional lines; it pressured the government to dismantle apartheid.

Apartheid Ends

In August, 1989, Frederik Willem De Klerk became president of South Africa. As a result of mounting internal, international, and global opposition to apartheid, he slowly began to dismantle the apartheid laws. In 1990, the government released Mandela from prison and lifted the ban on the ANC. These actions and others started South Africa on a course that would change its history forever.

After Mandela's release from prison, the black leader and De Klerk began a series of talks, the first of which took place in May, 1990, to move toward a democratic system of inclusion. In June, 1991, De Klerk ordered that the major apartheid laws be repealed, and formal negotiations to end apartheid began in December, 1991. Throughout the process, violent confrontations between South Africa's blacks and whites continued, with black leaders accusing the white government of continuing brutality. Negotiations were plagued by numerous roadblocks, but early in 1993, Mandela, De Klerk, and twenty-six other parties began the negotiating forum that set April 27, 1994, as the date for South Africa's first multiracial national democratic election based on adult suffrage and the "one person, one vote" principle.

Numerous world governments had had economic sanctions in place against South Africa for many years, and many investment companies and corporations had divested themselves of their interests in South African ventures or pulled out of South Africa. Sanctions and divestment were intended to pressure the government into repealing apartheid. By late 1993, because of the progress toward ending apartheid, Mandela and the ANC called for the removal of sanctions and called for new planning regarding investment in South Africa.

On November 17, 1993, South African negotiating parties ratified the new constitution which would bring an end to white domination by renouncing the country's racist past. Fundamental rights include such democratic basics as free speech, fair trials, prohibition against torture, a promise that people can live where they choose, an assurance that citizens cannot be stripped of their citizenship, and limitation on the president's power to declare a state of emergency. Discrimination based on race, gender, sexual orientation, physical disability, or age is also prohibited. The ten self-governing homelands that were established as reservations for blacks have been abolished. In December, 1993, the last white-dominated South African Parliament voted overwhelmingly to approve the new constitution.   *Emma T. Lucas*

Core Resources

J. D. Omer-Cooper's *History of Southern Africa* (Portsmouth, N.H.: Heinemann Educational Books, 1987) traces the development of the apartheid system, and Brian Bunting's "The Origins of Apartheid," in *Apartheid: A Collection of Writings on South Africa by South Africans* (edited by A. La Guma, New York: International Publishers, 1971) looks at its beginnings. Kenneth Grundy's *South Africa: Domestic Crisis and Global Challenge* (Boulder, Colo.: Westview Press, 1991) examines the role of international coalitions in the fight against apartheid. Ernest Harsch's *South Africa: White Rule, Black Revolt* (New York: Pathfinder Press, 1980) focuses on South Africa's black majority and its struggle for citizen rights. Oliver Tambo's "Armed Struggle Is the Way to Eliminate Apartheid," in *Problems of Africa: Opposing Viewpoints* (edited by Janelle Rohr, St. Paul, Minn.: Greenhaven Press, 1986) highlights the tactics and goals of the ANC.

See also: Discrimination: racial and ethnic; Discrimination: systemic.

Arab American intergroup relations

More than one million people of Arab origin are estimated to live in North America, 870,738 in the United States and 188,430 in Canada as of the late 1990's. Although figures for specific Arab national origin are not available for either country, they are available for the state of Michigan, which has a large population of Arab Americans. According to the 1990 U.S. census, 77,070 persons of Arab ancestry were living in Michigan. More than half of those people, 39,673, were of Lebanese background. Michigan was also home to 7,656 Syrians, 6,668 Iraqis, 2,695 Palestinians, 1,785 Egyptians, 1,441 Jordanians, 14,842 unspecified Arab Americans, and 2,310 other Arabs. In addition to these Arab Americans, the U.S. census reported the presence of 14,724 Assyrians (Chaldeans). Apparently in Michigan and other parts of the United States, most Assyrians do not, contrary to the opinion of most scholars, consider themselves Arabs.

Arab Americans come to the United States and Canada from the twenty-one countries of the Arab League. In addition to the countries in the Michigan breakdown, these nations are Algeria, Bahrain, Djibouti, Kuwait, Libya, Mauritania, Morocco, Oman, Qatar, Saudi Arabia, Somalia, Sudan, Tunisia, United Arab Emirates, and Yemen. Although the numbers of immigrants from most of these countries are too small for them to be separately counted, these subgroups have a significant effect on intergroup and intragroup relations. One Arab American group, the Arab Jewish Americans, part of the Sephardic Jewish population and believed to be sizable, is not counted by any official sources. They trace their ancestry predominantly to Syria, Egypt, Yemen, Iraq, Saudi Arabia, Tunisia, and Morocco. It is estimated that there are some 85,000 Arab Jews in the United States.

Demographics

According to the 1990 U.S. census, 48 percent of Arab Americans live in twenty metropolitan areas. The largest populations are in the Detroit, Michigan (61,065), New York City (58,347), and Los Angeles-Long Beach (56,345) areas. The table "Leading Metropolitan Hometowns of Arab Americans" shows their distribution in cities across the United States. In eight out of ten of the metropolitan areas with the highest Arab American populations, the median household income for Arab Americans exceeds that of the overall population. For example, in the Los Angeles-Long Beach metropolitan area, the median income for Arab Americans is 130 percent of that of the general population. The table "Arab American Median Household Income in Ten Metropolitan Areas" shows their relative prosperity.

Overall, Arab Americans are better educated than the average American. Arab Americans hold graduate degrees at a rate twice that of the general population. As might be expected given the level of educational achievement, in 1990, 80 percent of Arab Americans were employed versus 60 percent of all Americans.

Most Arab immigrants to the United States seek permanent status. One exception has been Yemeni temporary male workers, who often want to earn large sums of money to take back to their families in Yemen. Some Arab Americans of higher educational and occupational status look down on these Yemenis because they are less educated and poorer and have adopted the dress and lifestyles of young working-class American men. This violation of traditional manners is irritating to non-Yemeni Arab Americans, especially those striving for acceptance by American society. They fear that non-Arab Americans with ambivalent attitudes toward Arab Americans and who hold negative stereotypes of Arabs fostered by their unfavorable portrayal in the mass media will think less of them because of the behavior of some of the young Yemeni men.

Arab Americans' fears are intensified by hate crimes against them such as the one that took place in Dearborn, Michigan, in spring, 1976. In that incident, two young Yemeni immigrant workers who lived in one of the city's Arab American neighborhoods were murdered with shotguns for no discernible reason other than the fact that

Leading Metropolitan Hometowns of Arab Americans

Rank	Metropolitan Area	Population	Percentage of all Arab Americans
1	Detroit, Mich.	61,065	7.0
2	New York, N.Y.	58,347	6.7
3	Los Angeles-Long Beach, Calif.	56,345	6.5
4	Washington, D.C.-Md.-Va.	28,148	3.2
5	Chicago, Ill.	26,770	3.1
6	Boston, Mass.	22,391	2.6
7	Anaheim-Santa Ana, Calif.	15,662	1.8
8	Bergen-Passaic, N.J.	15,580	1.8
9	Houston, Tex.	15,389	1.8
10	Cleveland, Ohio	14,005	1.6
11	San Diego, Calif.	13,055	1.5
12	Pittsburgh, Pa.	12,141	1.4
13	San Francisco, Calif.	11,973	1.4
14	Miami-Hialeah, Fla.	11,344	1.3
15	Philadelphia, Pa.	10,345	1.2
16	Riverside-San Bernardino, Calif.	10,291	1.2
17	Nassau-Suffolk, N.Y.	8,837	1.0
18	Oakland, Calif.	8,668	1.0
19	Minneapolis-St.Paul, Minn.-Wis.	8,155	0.9
20	Phoenix, Ariz.	7,719	0.9

Source: Data are from U.S. Bureau of the Census, *Census of Population, 1990.* Washington, D.C., U.S. Government Printing Office, 1991.

Arab American Median Household Income in Ten Metropolitan Areas

Rank	Metropolitan Area	Median Income	
		Arab Americans	General Population
1	Washington, D.C.-Md.-Va.	$53,557	$46,884
2	Boston, Mass.	50,000	40,491
3	Bergen-Passaic, N.J.	48,050	45,040
4	Los Angeles-Long Beach, Calif.	45,750	34,965
5	Cleveland, Ohio	39,011	30,560
6	Chicago, Ill.	38,505	35,265
7	Houston, Tex.	36,700	31,473
8	Anaheim-Santa Ana, Calif.	36,000	45,922
9	New York, N.Y.	35,000	31,659
10	Detroit, Mich.	32,325	34,612

Source: Data are from U.S. Bureau of the Census, *Census of Population, 1990*. Washington, D.C., U.S. Government Printing Office, 1991.

they lived in an Arab neighborhood and "looked Arab." Fortunately, such incidents are rare, but they demonstrate the bigotry still present in some communities.

Arab American Women

Unlike their sisters in most Arab countries, Arab American women have become strong and courageous feminists. Carol Haddad, of Lebanese and Syrian heritage, founded the Feminist Arab Network (FAN) in 1983. It was composed of about one hundred women, about one-third immigrants and the rest born in the United States. FAN organized panels, wrote articles for progressive feminist newspapers, magazines, and journals, and spoke to numerous groups about what Arab American women wanted for themselves, non-Arab American women, and women throughout the world. Although FAN did not last for more than a few years, it nevertheless brought together activist Arab American women and Jewish, Latina, Asian American, and Native American women to further feminist and progressive causes. In 1994, the South End Press published an anthology by Arab American and Canadian feminists entitled *Food for Our Grandmothers*. Thanks to FAN's efforts, women have served as chairs and presidents of the American-Arab Anti-Discrimination Committee (ADC).

The Multicultural Immersion Program

The Arab American community is a diverse and successful one. Because of the turmoil in the Middle East, however, and the negative portrayal of Arabs in the mass media, Arab Americans have often felt the sting of prejudice and discrimination and the tragedy of violence and murder. At the 1984 Democratic National Convention,

African American Jesse Jackson expressed empathy for the plight of Arab Americans, saying that "Arab Americans, too, know the pain and hurt of racial and religious rejection. They must not continue to be made pariahs."

During the Middle East turmoil in 1989, Arab American businesses in Chicago's black neighborhoods were frequently boycotted by African Americans. The boycotts were motivated by the anti-Arab defamation with which the mass media showered the nation and the failure of Americans to distinguish between Arab Americans and overseas Arabs. All over the United States, Arab Americans became the targets of violence, property destruction, and even murder.

In 1996, to combat anti-Arab sentiment in Detroit, a social service agency called New Detroit launched the Multicultural Immersion Program. Directed by Sonia Plata, it consists of yearlong programs that bring together people from the major ethnic, religious, and racial groups in the metropolitan area to learn about one another through seminars presented by designated leaders from each of five major groups: African Americans, Arab Americans, Asian Americans, Latinos/Chicanos, and Native Americans. The key organizations that lend support to the groups are the Charles Wright African American Museum, the Arab Community Center for Economic and Social Services (ACCESS), American Citizens for Justice (an Asian American group), Casa de Unidad, and the American Indian Health and Family Services agency.

The first of the seven sessions in the annual program is an orientation, which is followed by five sessions that consist of seminars presented by members of each of the five major groups. Each group selects ten to fifteen of its leaders and members to organize and present an all-day, eight-hour program to members of the other four groups. These seminars feature lectures, discussions, presentation of audiovisual materials, dissemination of literature, and other creative efforts to foster communication, mutual understanding, and friendship among the program participants. The seventh session is a summing up of the program and graduation ceremonies. The program is underwritten by the Ameritech Corporation. Participants have access to Web sites that deal with multicultural issues, namely, www.webofculture.com and www.tenet.educ\academia\multi.html.

The Multicultural Immersion Program has become a model for all American communities intent on fostering positive relations among minority groups and intergroup peace based on justice, mutual respect, and understanding. In 1997, the program had seventy graduates.   *R. M. Frumkin*

Core Resources
A clear picture of Arab Americans and their struggles for an American identity is presented in *The Development of Arab-American Identity*, edited by Ernest McCarus (Ann Arbor: University of Michigan Press, 1994). This work deals with Arab images and stereotypes created by the mass media, anti-Arab racism and violence, including the murder of two Yemeni immigrant workers, and many other relevant topics. Arab American women are discussed in Evelyn Shakir's *Bint Arab* (Westport, Conn.: Praeger, 1997). Barbara Aswad edited *Arab-Speaking Communities in American Cities* (New York: Center for Migration Studies of New York, 1974). Her book deals with Chaldeans, Arab Christians and Muslims, Lebanese and Syrian Arab Americans, and other significant topics related to Arab Americans.

See also: Arab American stereotypes; Arab Americans; Arab Canadians; Sephardic Jewish Americans.

Arab American stereotypes

Arab Americans are from or trace their ancestry to a number of Arabic-speaking countries and profess belief in a variety of religions, usually Christianity or Islam. According to the U.S. census, most Arabic-speaking Americans are descendants of Lebanese immigrants, and about 90 percent are Christians rather than Muslims. Scholars suggest that Arabs have emigrated to the United States in three waves, from 1870 to 1940, just after World War II, and from 1948 to 1967, after the Israeli occupation of Jerusalem. Most of the Muslims in the United States were part of the latter two waves.

Social scientists have not studied stereotypes of Arab Americans in as much detail as those of some other ethnic groups, probably because of the relatively small number of Arab Americans in the United States (between one million and three million). Arab American stereotypes are revealed mostly through an examination of media coverage of events such as the Israeli-Palestinian conflict, the 1970's civil war in Lebanon, and acts of terrorism involving Arabs and the depictions of Arabic-speaking people in American films and books. Although many of the stereotypes are of Arabs, not Arab Americans, the characteristics that are found in them are often attributed to Arab Americans.

The Arab stereotype is predominantly a negative image, revolving around a number of overgeneralizations and falsehoods. Arabs have been portrayed in the media as oil millionaires buying up the United States, white slavers, and uncivilized rulers of kingdoms. Palestinians have been depicted as terrorists and called derogatory names such as camel jockeys, ragheads, and sandsuckers. Common misconceptions include the belief that Iranians are Arabs and that all Arabs are Muslims.

Before 1930, Hollywood studios frequently portrayed Arabs as members of the French Foreign Legion or royalty, Egyptians, and sheiks. Films from 1961 through 1970 depicted Arabs as royalty, murderers, sheiks, slaves, and slaveowners and often featured harems. Many of the roles incorporated elements designed to show the foreignness of the Arab culture and its supposed lack of civilization in comparison with mainstream American culture. In the 1980's and 1990's, acts of terrorism and conflicts in the Middle East caused Hollywood and the media to add violence and barbarism to the Arab stereotype. Arabs, particularly Arab men, were seen as anti-American, greedy, oil-rich, uncivilized foreigners who were abductors of Western women and, as Muslims, oppressors of women in general. In the media and in film, Islam has been equated with violence, terrorism, and suppression of women.

In order to counter the negative stereotyping, prejudice, and discrimination experienced by Arab Americans, numerous scholars have published papers on the topic, and several organizations such as the Association of Arab American University Graduates, the Institute of Middle Eastern and North African Affairs, and the American-Arab Anti-Discrimination Committee have been created to address these topics. One of the concerns about the negative stereotypes in the media is that they are not countered by positive portrayals. In particular, Arab American children are hardly present on television, and the Islamic religion is rarely depicted favorably.   *Francis C. Staskon*

See also: Arab American intergroup relations; Arab Americans; Arab Canadians.

Arab Americans

Significance: Arab Americans are an emerging group of U.S. citizens with an interest in the Middle East. The rise of Israel and Zionism have helped this group coalesce; however, Arab Americans have faced serious conflict with the influential American Jewish community.

Arab Americans are U.S. citizens who have roots in Arabic-speaking countries. Because Arab Americans are internally divided by religion and country of origin, reliable statistics on this group are difficult to obtain. Moreover, given the strong commitment of the United States to Israel, many individuals are reluctant to identify themselves as Arab Americans. Between one million and three million Americans are of Arabic or part-Arabic descent, but estimates vary greatly because of poor statistics.

Arab Americans are difficult to describe as a group because they often downplay or deny their ethnic origins in order to gain greater acceptance in an American mainstream that tends to stereotype them as "camel drivers" or probable terrorists and often compares their homelands unfavorably with the state of Israel. Arab Americans are generally included in the white category in Bureau of Census records, although on occasion some individuals may be classified as "other Asian." In key urban areas such as Detroit, Michigan, Arab American shopkeepers and entrepreneurs have experienced clashes with the African American community.

Definition and Overview

Arab Americans are all non-Jewish individuals claiming ancestral roots in Arabic-speaking countries from Morocco to Syria and Saudi Arabia or Yemen with minor exceptions such as Chaldean- and Kurdish-speaking individuals. Americans unfamiliar with the Middle East often assume that all Muslim natives of the region are Arabs. Therefore, Turkish and Iranian (Persian) Americans, who are Muslims but not ethnically Arabs, are often mistakenly believed to be Arab Americans. Arab Americans are far more likely to be Christian than are natives of their home countries, although a majority of Arab immigrants since the 1960's have been Muslim. In the late 1990's, the Arab American community was believed to be about half Christian and about half Muslim, with Christians being more acculturated and accepted in the United States. Arab American Christians often are indistinguishable from other Americans by the second generation, although Arab American Muslims form a more distinct group.

Middle Eastern problems such as the Lebanese civil war in the 1970's have pitted Arab American Christians against Arab American Muslims. However, since the Israeli victory in the Six-Day War in 1967, Arab Americans have begun to organize to confront hostile stereotypes in the press and discriminatory practices that often imperil their civil rights and employment opportunities. Arab American activists risk potentially serious conflict with the more established American Jewish community when they call on the U.S. government for an "evenhanded" (that is, less pro-Israel) Mideast policy. However, both Arab Americans and American Jews may be able to serve as constructive bridges between the United States and the Middle East and help them return to the generally good relations enjoyed before 1948.

Early History

Early Arab American immigrants came to the United States between 1870 and World War I. Most Arabic-speaking individuals who immigrated to the United States during this period were subjects of the Turkish Ottoman Empire, and immigration authorities often incorrectly called them Turks. Immigrants described as "other Asian" were in many cases Arabic-speaking.

Arab immigrants during this period were predominantly Orthodox or Eastern Catholic (Uniate) Christians. They often identified themselves by their religious loyalties or local origins, and very few of these pioneers stressed their Arab identity. Most came from the area that later became Israel, Jordan, Lebanon, and Syria, and they frequently called themselves Syrian. Some immigrants were urban artisans and skilled laborers, but most were peasants, less than half of whom were literate in their native Arabic.

Arab immigrants quickly became peddlers, and many participated very successfully in the free enterprise system. A minority among the Arab immigrant population turned to factory labor, but peddling allowed greater possibility for financial success and more opportunities to learn English and become acculturated. Some Arab American individuals established small businesses in cities and towns. Arab American communities grew in urban centers such as Boston, New York, and Detroit, and hard work produced success for many Arab Americans.

Early immigrants did not bring clergy with them from the Middle East. Therefore, Arab American community leaders worked to secure clergy to serve their compatriots. Most Arab immigrant clergy were marginally educated and prone to sectarian and ethnic factionalism. However, Maronite, Melkite, and Orthodox Christian churches were organized in New York toward the end of the nineteenth century.

Arab American newspapers thrived between 1892, when the first Arabic newspaper was established in New

York, and the 1920's. By the late 1920's, the number of Arabic readers was in decline because immigration had been limited by the Immigration Act of 1924, and the children of earlier immigrants spoke only English. The children of both Christian and Muslim immigrants frequently married outside their ethnic groups, and many lost their Arab identity.

Milestones in Arab American History

Year	Event
1870's	First Arab immigrants arrive in the United States.
1883	Kahlil Gibran, noted Lebanese immigrant and author, is born (dies 1931).
1892	First Arab American newspaper, *Kawkab Amerika*, is published.
1898	Maronites found newspaper called *Al Hoda* (the enlightener).
1948	The formation of the state of Israel creates a large Palestinian diaspora.
1961	Institute of Palestine Studies creates Maronite seminary (Our Lady of Lebanon) in Washington, D.C.
1967	Israeli victory in Six-Day War provides stimulus to Arab organizations to present their case to the American public.
1967	Professionals form Association of Arab American University Graduates.
1968	Sirhan Bishara Sirhan assassinates Senator Robert Kennedy.
1972	Lobbying group National Association of Arab Americans is founded.
Mid-1970's	Lebanese civil war divides Arab Americans.
1978	Lisa Najeeb Halaby marries King Hussein of Jordan and assumes the name Queen Noor.
1982	American Arab Antidiscrimination Committee (ADC), a civil rights activist group, is organized.
1985	West Coast ADC leader Alex Odeh is assassinated.
1989	Council of Lebanese American Organizations, umbrella organization lobbying for Lebanese freedom and sovereignty, is founded.
1991	Educational outreach group, Arab World and Islamic Resources and School Services, is created.

From the mid-1920's to World War II, immigration declined. After the passage of the Immigration and Nationality Act of 1965, the United States accepted significant although disputed numbers of Arab immigrants from all parts of the Arabic-speaking world. Most have been Muslims, and many have been educated professionals who originally entered the United States as students. New Arab groups, especially Egyptian Copts and Yemenites, have become important in the changing American cultural mosaic.

Arab American Organizations

Since the mid-1960's, an era emphasizing multiculturalism and the rediscovery of ethnic roots, Arab Americans have sought to foster pride in their Middle Eastern heritage. Significant Arab American organizations include the Association of Arab American University Graduates (formed in 1967), the National Association of Arab Americans (1972), the American-Arab Anti-Discrimination Committee (1982), Arab World and Islamic Resources and School Services (1991), the Council of Lebanese American Organizations (1989), the El Bireh Palestine Society of the USA (1981), and the Institute for Palestine Studies (1961).

Because the Arab American community includes many well-educated professionals, the Association of Arab American University Graduates (AAUG) has been very active since its founding in 1967. This tax-exempt educational and cultural organization promotes understanding between the American and Arab worlds through an annual convention, a strong publication program, speakers, and support of human rights in the Middle East and elsewhere. In its early years, the AAUG attracted post-1948 immigrants while the National Association of Arab Americans gained more U.S.-born individuals. By the 1990's, this distinction had largely disappeared.

The program of the twenty-ninth annual convention from October 18 to 20, 1996, in Anaheim, California, illustrates the diversity of concerns of

Arab Americans. Both Democratic and Republican speakers were present. The cultural and legal status of the Arab American community as well as its demographic makeup provided the focus for several sessions. The group also scheduled sessions on Palestinian issues and their connection to Arab Americans, the status of Arab American women, and studies of Arab American urban communities in the United States.

The National Association of Arab Americans (NAAA) lobbies Congress concerning issues of concern to Arab Americans. A February 27, 1996, statement by Khalil E. Jahshan, president of the NAAA, illustrates the group's public profile. Jahshan addressed the Near Eastern and South Asian Affairs Subcommittee of the Senate Foreign Relations Committee to request that the ban on the use of U.S. passports for travel to Lebanon be lifted for both humanitarian and business reasons. In his statement, Jahshan spoke with pride of the work of Lebanese Americans in Congress and praised Senator Spencer Abraham of Michigan and Representative Nick Joe Rahall of West Virginia for their support.

The American-Arab Anti-Discrimination Committee (ADC) confronts the civil rights issues facing the Arab American community. It has never had universal Arab American support because the head of the Maronite Catholic Church forbade its members from joining when the group did not support the Phalangist cause in the Lebanese civil war. However, since its founding by former South Dakota senator James Abourezk, a Lebanese American, the group has made significant progress on issues of concern to the Arab American community.

To protect the civil rights of Arab Americans, the ADC's department of legal services aids individuals who have experienced defamation and discrimination based on their Arab ethnicity. ADC wants the federal Office of Management and Budget to add a separate racial designation for Arab Americans to the record-keeping efforts of governmental agencies because it believes that Arab Americans are racially targeted and that anti-Arab hate crime is hard to document because it is difficult to separate relevant data regarding Arab Americans from data concerning other groups.

In an attempt to combat negative portrayals of Arabs in the media, the ADC media and publications department publishes a bimonthly newsletter, *ADC Times*, as well as special reports and "action alerts" on issues of concern. In addition, the organization's department of educational programs sponsors the ADC Research Institute, which encourages public school teachers to provide a balanced portrayal of Arab history and culture.

Arab World and Islamic Resources and School Services (AWAIR), founded in 1991, provides educational outreach at both the elementary and secondary school levels. To improve public understanding of the Arab world, this group conducts teacher training and provides a summer institute for teachers. To celebrate National History Day, this group donates an Arab and Islamic History Award. Book-length publications offer recommended curricula targeting both the elementary and the secondary school student.

The Council of Lebanese American Organizations (CLAO), an umbrella organization, lobbies for freedom and sovereignty for Lebanon and the withdrawal of all foreign troops, both Israeli and Syrian. It provides the monthly report *Adonis* as well as a monthly newsletter *Lebanon File*. In addition, this Lebanese American organization offers the annual Cadmus Award.

The El Bireh Palestine Society of the USA (EBPSUSA), founded in 1981, attempts to unite former residents of El Bireh now residing in the United States. It wishes to preserve traditional Arab culture and values in a new American environment and to facilitate contact among members. It offers educational and children's services. By focusing on remembered ties to a locality, this group strengthens the local allegiances of its members.

The Washington, D.C.-based Institute for Palestine Studies (IPS), founded in 1961, is a research-oriented, nonprofit, independent organization formed to study the Arab-Israeli conflict and status of the Palestinians. The best-known publication of IPS is the *Journal of Palestine Studies: A Quarterly on Palestinian Affairs and the Arab Israeli Conflict*. IPS also has an extensive list of publications in Arabic, English, and French.

Despite the existence of these organizations, Arab Americans still experience significant civil rights problems in education, employment, immigration law, and public accommodations. Whenever there is a crisis in the Mideast or a terrorist act such as the bombing of the World Trade Center in New York (1993) or the bombing of the Oklahoma Federal Building (1995), the Arab American community braces for significant hostility from the American population. In the latter case, for example, members of the news media and others immediately speculated that Arab terrorists were the murderers but were later proved wrong. Ironically, Arab American community ties have probably been increased by unfavorable portrayals of Arabs in the mainstream press and a political environment that makes criticism of Israel difficult to separate from traditional anti-Semitism.

Hate Crimes and Targeting Issues

The ADC uses the Federal Bureau of Investigation (FBI) definition of a hate crime. This definition states that a hate crime is "a criminal offense committed against a person or property which is motivated, in whole or in part, by the offender's bias against a race, religion, ethnic/national origin group, or sexual orientation group." Recent notable anti-Arab hate crimes include the September, 1996, arson of an Arab American mosque in Yuba City, California; the vandalization in September, 1996, and February, 1997, of a Santa Ana, California, statue of Alex Odeh, the West Coast ADC director assassinated in 1985; the slaying of a Jordanian tenant in May, 1997, by a Brooklyn, New York, landlord who expressed hatred for immigrants; an attack on a cashier in an Arab American-owned Detroit Mobil Oil station in an African American community in May, 1997; and repeated incidents of anti-Arab vandalism to the home of a Gaitherburg, Maryland, woman in September, 1997.

Perhaps more serious than these hate crime incidents is evidence of governmental targeting of individuals perceived to be Arab American or Muslim. Although the Federal Aviation Administration (FAA) denies targeting Arab Americans or including Arab descent as part of its terrorist profile, Arab American individuals repeatedly face detention and interrogation at airports, an experience not shared by members of many other groups.

An Arab American man proudly carries a flag during a parade in New York City. Arab Americans sometimes downplay their ethnicity because of anti-Arab sentiment.

Arab Americans are often deported by the Immigration and Naturalization Service (INS) under unusual legal provisions that allow the use of secret and unreliable evidence not subject to challenge. In a November 8, 1995, decision of the U.S. Ninth Circuit Court of Appeals, eight Palestinians won a significant civil rights victory over INS efforts to deport them for their alleged ties to the Popular Front for the Liberation of Palestine. The court held that aliens had the same freedom-of-expression rights as United States citizens. Despite this success, Palestinian immigrants who protest Israeli actions such as the 1982 invasion of Lebanon remain vulnerable to deportation threats.

Media Bias

The Progressive Magazine documents anti-Arab media bias in an August, 1996, article entitled "Up Against the Wall," detailing brutal U.S. Customs treatment of Arab women at the San Francisco airport. It also notes that both *U.S. News and World Report* and *The New Republic* incorrectly stated that the Prophet Muhammad advocated breaking treaties and broke the Treaty of Hudaybiah in 628. Only the first magazine retracted its error. Many Arab Americans see media bias against the Arab world and their poor treatment at the hands of U.S. government agencies as intertwined issues.

Prominent Arab Americans

From assassin to peacemaker, from author to queen, Arab Americans have achieved prominence in many fields. One of the best-known Arab Americans is Lebanese-born artist and author Kahlil Gibran, who made a difficult cultural transition between a mountain village in late Ottoman Lebanon and turn-of-the-century Boston. Although he was active in many cultural fields, Gibran is best remembered today as the author of *The Prophet* (1923).

Another well-known Arab American is Queen Noor of Jordan, widow of King Hussein. She was born Lisa Najeeb Halaby on August 23, 1951, in the United States to an Arab American family with Syrian roots. She received her B.A. in architecture and urban planning in 1974 as part of Princeton University's first coeducational class. When she married King Hussein on June 15, 1978, she converted from Christianity to Islam. They have had four children, two sons and two daughters. She has patronized many educational and cultural organizations in Jordan, and she has consistently exhibited an interest in work that enhances the welfare of women and children. Given her unique cross-cultural perspective, Queen Noor has attempted to serve as a bridge between American and Arab cultures. She supported the establishment of the Jordanian society in Washington in 1980 to promote better understanding and closer relationships between the United States and Jordan.

Two Arab Americans who have made their mark in politics are Spencer Abraham and George Mitchell. Abraham is a conservative Republican senator from

Michigan, first elected in 1994. The Lebanese American Abraham received his bachelor's degree from Michigan State University in 1974 and his J.D. from Harvard in 1979. After teaching at the Thomas J. Cooley School of Law from 1981 to 1983, he became Michigan Republican chair in 1983. He served as chief of staff to Vice President Dan Quayle from 1990 to 1991 and was cochair of the Republican National Committee from 1991 to 1993. Although he does not stress his Arab ancestry outside Detroit's Arab community, Abraham has a strong interest in the Middle East. He values his family's immigrant past and has worked hard to fight severe restrictions on new immigration. Mitchell, a Lebanese American born in Waterville, Maine, served as U.S. senator from Maine and Democratic majority leader in the 1980's. As a diplomat in Northern Ireland during the administration of Bill Clinton, he helped negotiate a peace agreement between Roman Catholics and Protestants in 1998.

Perhaps the most infamous Arab American is Sirhan Bishara Sirhan, born in Jerusalem on March 19, 1944. He became a resident of the United States in 1957 but remained an outsider who resented American economic and political aid to Israel. Angry over his family's losses in the War of 1948 and U.S. policy supporting Israel, Sirhan assassinated Senator Robert F. Kennedy on June 5, 1968, the day that Kennedy won the Democratic presidential primary in California. In addition to killing Kennedy, Sirhan assaulted five other people. After receiving a death sentence, Sirhan had his sentence commuted to life in prison. His assassination of Kennedy may have changed the course of U.S. political history because Kennedy appeared to have a realistic chance of receiving the 1968 Democratic presidential nomination. At the time, the press described Sirhan as a Jordanian because the term "Palestinian" had not yet come into use.

Arab American Churches

The Antiochian Orthodox Church is based in Syria, although it is now increasingly active in the United States. Metropolitan Philip heads the Antiochian Orthodox Christian Archdiocese of North America, headquartered in Englewood, New Jersey. Unlike most Arab Orthodox churches, the Antiochians do not focus solely on their own ethnic communities and Middle Eastern concerns. A notable example of Arab acculturation to life in the United States, this Arab-based church has sought and received the membership of many non-Arab Americans, including a significant number of former Episcopalians unhappy with what they perceive as liberal trends in belief and practice in the Episcopal Church.

The Coptic Orthodox Patriarchate-Archdiocese of North America, an Egyptian-based group, owes allegiance to H. H. Pope Shenouda III of Alexandria and Cairo, Egypt. The North American Bishop is H. G.

Bishop Surial, who resides in New Jersey, home to a Coptic seminary. The Egyptian Copts practice a form of Eastern Orthodoxy that dates from antiquity. They are generally considered the descendants of the ancient Egyptians because Egypt was Coptic Christian before it became Muslim.

Maronite Catholics are an Eastern Rite church that has been in full communion with Rome since the sixteenth century. Lebanese immigrants have brought the Maronite Church to the United States from its native Lebanon. The Maronites are notable for their married clergy. Maronite parishes exist in Austin, Texas; Detroit; New York; Washington, D.C.; and other U.S. cities. Our Lady of Lebanon Seminary in Washington, D.C., established in 1961, is the only Maronite Catholic seminary outside Lebanon. Priests from twenty-four American Maronite Catholic churches participated in the foundation of the seminary. During the Lebanese civil war in the 1970's, the Maronites in the United States and the Middle East allied with Israel. This caused severe conflict with other Arab American groups, especially those strongly supporting the Palestinian struggle for statehood. *Susan A. Stussy*

Core Resources

The Arab American Directory (2d ed., Alexandria, Va.: Arab Media House, 1997) provides a comprehensive view of the Arab American community in Washington, D.C. "Up Against the Wall" in the August, 1996, issue of *The Progressive* illustrates media bias against Arabs and Muslims. Michael W. Suleiman's "Arab Americans: A Community Profile," in *Islam in North America: A Sourcebook*, edited by Michael A. Koszegi and J. Gordon Melton (New York: Garland Publishing, 1992), surveys the nineteenth and twentieth century Arab American experience. "Ninth Circuit: Aliens Have First Amendment Rights," in *The National Law Journal* (November 27, 1995), describes the Palestinian Los Angeles Eight's fight against the Immigration and Naturalization Service. Jean Gibran and Kahlil Gibran's *Kahlil Gibran: His Life and World* (New York: Interlink Books, 1991) shows how an immigrant from an isolated and impoverished village in Lebanon became an important cultural figure in turn-of-the-century Boston. The authors are related to the author of *The Prophet*. Queen Noor's Web site, H.M. Queen Noor of Jordan (http://www.accessme.com/QNoorjo/main/resume.htm), contains official biographical information intended to present the queen and Jordan in a favorable light.

See also: Arab American intergroup relations; Arab American stereotypes; Arab Canadians; Immigration Act of 1924; Immigration and Nationality Act of 1965; Jewish-Arab American relations.

Arab Canadians

> **Significance:** Arab Canadians, who immigrated in two major waves, hail from a variety of countries and are affiliated with several religions. Despite their differences, they are unified by the Arabic language and by their cultural traditions, especially those affecting the family and social life.

The first wave of Arab immigrants to Canada were Syrian-Lebanese Christians in the late nineteenth century who were escaping from poverty and Ottoman Turk oppression. Located close to the Sublime Porte (the Turkish court and government in Constantinople), Syria could not resist Ottoman control. The Turks' *millet* system of administration divided the population into Christian and non-Christian groups, thereby creating hostilities and strengthening Turkish rule. Economic conditions were miserable, particularly in the mountainous region of Lebanon, where the silk industry and agriculture declined. A large number of European and American nationals and missionaries exposed the Syrian-Lebanese to Western influences, and Canada appeared to be a land of freedom and opportunity. By 1912, about 7,000 Arabs were in Canada, chiefly in Montreal, Quebec City, Three Rivers, Ottawa, Toronto, London, Windsor, Sault-Sainte Marie, and North Bay, with some immigrants in the Maritimes and prairies. Many of the immigrants began as peddlers; however, this type of work declined during and after the 1920's for three main reasons: the curtailment of Asiatic immigration, shifts in Canadian business practices (mail and telephone orders replaced door-to-door sales), and the stock market crash, which wiped out most Arab businesses.

The second wave of immigrants arrived in the postwar period, 1941-1951, after economic and political upheaval and the emergence of the Zionist movement. A broader mixture of Christian groups and a substantial number of Muslims and Druzes left their homelands, motivated by a desire to escape adverse conditions. Ontario and Quebec accounted for about two-thirds of the Canadian Arab population. Nova Scotia ranked third, followed by New Brunswick, Manitoba, Saskatchewan, and Alberta. Between 1961 and 1971, Ontario established itself as the province most favored by Arab Canadians. The postwar immigrants were more highly qualified, better educated, and more sophisticated than those in the first wave and were able to obtain white-collar and professional jobs.

Social, Cultural, and Religious Life

Arab Canadians make the family the focus of their social organization. Many have experienced, at some point in their family cycle, an extended family living arrangement, but even this underlines the patriarchal prerogative that emphasizes sex-role differentiation. Women are taught to be dependent on and submissive to men. Women's virginity is highly valued, and often extreme sanctions are levied against women who engage in premarital sex. Men are given greater freedom from domestic duties, and they are expected to be protectors of family honor. Although monogamy is characteristic, Muslim law does allow a man to have more than one wife; it also allows men to choose a spouse without requiring her to convert to his faith, largely because after divorce, the children traditionally remain with the husband's family and so are not lost to Islam. Traditional Arab husbands are loath to have their wives working outside the home because this gives women financial independence and removes them from under the family's surveillance. The ideal woman is the closely supervised homebody, though the wives of early Arab immigrants helped their husbands run small businesses either directly or behind the scenes.

Traditional Arab Canadian parents encounter a problem when their children have extensive contact with eligible young people of the opposite sex and so rebel against having their mate selected by their elders. Problems can also arise from prevailing teenage behavior patterns and nuclear family structures.

Islam is the fastest-growing religion in the world, and mosques and churches are being built in every major Canadian city. Religious institutions consolidate a group's identity by maintaining the Arab language and providing a link between Arabs in Canada and those in the United States.

Mass media (newspapers, magazines, books, radio, and television) have also consolidated Arab Canadian identity, along with food, music, dance, and group organizations. One of the most important means of cultural preservation is the Arabic language, which is taught in heritage language classes on weekends for those unable to attend Arab private schools. The federal government's multicultural policy enhances the development of ethnic identity without diminishing loyalty to Canada.

Ethnic Assertion

The immigrant generations are generally more likely than their Canadian-born counterparts to maintain links with their cultural heritage, but all Arab Canadians are aware of their origins. Relatives often enter into cooperative business ventures, and many nonrelated Arab Canadians form joint business ventures, with intermarriage occurring among the business partners' families.

Arab Canadians like Canadian justice, freedom, and respect for human rights. They also appreciate the Canadian political system and work ethic, along with technological sophistication and modern conveniences. However, Arab Canadians dislike weak Canadian family bonds, the relative absence of social controls over youth, the harsh climate, and the Canadian sense of social superiority. Overall, however, Arab Canadians have adapted successfully to the Canadian way of life, contributing with distinction to various fields. Although they acknowledge the value of the Canadian school and sociocultural system as factors of acculturation, they also show by their identity that Canada does not suffer from a melting pot syndrome.   *Keith Garebian*

Core Resources
The major study of Arab Canadians is Baha Abu-Laban's *An Olive Branch on the Family Tree: The Arabs in Canada* (Toronto: McClelland and Stewart, 1980), published in association with the Multiculturalism Directorate, Department of the Secretary of State, and the Canadian Government Publishing Centre, Supply and Services Canada. This is an exhaustively researched study of the meaning of Arab ethnicity, taking into account personal experiences of Arabs, Canadian perceptions of Arabs, and an assessment of the Arab Canadian community. Among its features are reports on Arab family life and conflicts with contemporary Western culture and morals.

See also: Arab American stereotypes; Arab Americans; Visible minority allophones in Canada.

Aryan Nation

The Aryan Nation represents the resurgence of white supremacy, a racial idea with a long and dishonorable history. This type of racism posits the absolute racial

Aryan Nation members met at Hayden Lake, Idaho, in April, 1989, to celebrate Nazi leader Adolf Hitler's one-hundredth birthday.

superiority of the white "race," often narrowly construed as Teutonic, and denies that peoples of various ethnic backgrounds can live together.

The Aryan Nation, a group of white supremacists centered in Hayden Lake, northern Idaho, was founded in 1973 by Richard Butler, self-styled pastor of the Church of Jesus Christ Christian, and is one of the largest white-separatist groups in North America. The group believes in the superiority of the white "race" and in the necessity of driving all nonwhites out of North America. It publicly denounces Jews and nonwhites, making a deliberate organizational outreach to disaffected, often dysfunctional youth, former Ku Klux Klan members, and marginalized white people. It has a paramilitary style of organization and holds an annual Aryan Nations congress. The group honors the memory of Nazi leader Adolf Hitler and preaches hatred of nonwhites, Jews, homosexuals, and those who disagree with its objectives. Particular virulence is directed against Jews, who embody evil in the eyes of this group.   *Gloria Fulton*

See also: American Nazi Party; Anti-Semitism; Aryan "race"; Christian Identity movement; Ku Klux Klan; Teutonic "race"; White Aryan Brotherhood; White "race"; White supremacist groups.

Aryan "race"

The term "Aryan" is used both for a group of Asian languages and for certain Asian peoples. Originally, it referred to the group of people from Persia who destroyed the Indus culture about 1500 B.C.E. and then developed their own culture in India and started the Hindu religion. These Aryans, known as Brahmans, were members of the highest Hindu caste.

In 1854, French writer Count Joseph-Arthur de Gobineau suggested that the white race was superior to all others and that the Aryan "race" was supreme among the whites. This theory gained interest in Germany and was promoted by composer Richard Wagner, among others. In the 1930's, it was espoused by the German dictator Adolf Hitler, who used the term "Aryan" to refer to Germans and certain other northern Europeans (the Nordic race) and indicated their racial superiority over all other peoples. Hitler used this theory to justify his persecution of the Jews, Gypsies, and other non-Aryans.

The racist use of the term has continued among certain white supremacist groups in the United States, and the Aryan Nation headquartered near Hayden Lake, Idaho, militantly advocates anti-Semitism and the establishment of a white racist state. However, the theory that there are pure or inherently superior human races or groups is rejected by modern anthropologists. *Alvin K. Benson*

See also: Anti-Semitism; Aryan Nation; Holocaust; Race as a concept; "Scientific" racism; White supremacist groups.

Ashkenazic and German Jews

In the second half of the seventeenth century, German and Ashkenazic Jews from the central and eastern European countries of Germany (Holy Roman Empire), Poland, and the Austro-Hungarian Empire came to the United States by a variety of routes. Ashkenazic Jews are Jews from Eastern Europe who spoke Yiddish and lived in separate enclaves, or ghettos, mainly in modern-day Russia and the Baltic countries outside Germany. Some came to America after the Dutch lost control of Brazil in 1654, and others came directly to New Amsterdam (present-day New York) before it was conquered by Britain's Duke of York. The city was the first to allow Jews to build a house of worship and purchase land for a cemetery. Although individual Jews and Jewish families can be found in the early colonial records of all of the thirteen original colonies, Charleston, South Carolina, was home to the largest Jewish community. Mediterranean Jews were predominant, although all of the colonial American Jewish congregations had large percentages of Ashkenazic and German Jews who came to the British North American colonies with the aide of London and Caribbean merchants.

After the American Revolution, immigration increased slowly, and by the 1830 U.S. census, the Jewish population had reached nearly 3,000, predominantly Ashkenazic and German Jews. The European Enlightenment, the passage of laws preventing Jews from entering professions and leaving their ghettos, and new taxes, combined with the unsuccessful revolution in Poland and throughout central and eastern Europe in 1836, brought a dramatic increase in emigration by German-speaking Jews throughout the 1840's and 1850's. By the outbreak of the Civil War in 1861, there were 150,000 Jewish Americans, more than 90 percent of whom were Ashkenazic and German Jews.

During this era, large numbers of trained rabbis came to the United States, and denominational divisions followed. In 1834, German Jews seeking to anglicize the liturgical service founded Charleston's Society of Re-

formed Israelites. Isaac Leeser, the promoter of the Jewish Sunday School movement, anticipated the Conservative Jewish movement that emerged later in the century. This era also saw the publication of several Jewish periodicals, including one by Rabbi Isaac Meyer Wise, which became a springboard for the creation of the first Jewish seminary and the establishment of the reformed Union of American Hebrew Congregations.

From the middle of the nineteenth century to its final decade, the influence of German Jews in business and in Jewish social, cultural, and religious life reached its apex. The German Jewish community began to seek recognition of its expanding economic success, creating a separation between the German Jews and the later-arriving Ashkenazic Jews from Russia, which led to more sectarian and social divisions within the Jewish religious and secular communities.

As new immigration expanded the number of American Jews beyond the four million mark, American "popularism" and the reemergence of the Ku Klux Klan during World War I led to the passage of a series of immigration acts, the last of which (Immigration Act of 1924) changed the base year for computing national immigration quotas from 1920 to 1890 and had the greatest impact on Jewish immigration. The decrease in new immigration meant that the German and Ashkenazic Jewish groups would continue to be the dominant group in the Jewish American population. Jewish Americans numbered nearly six million during World War II, and in the second half of the twentieth century, their numbers did not increase. *Sheldon Hanft*

See also: Immigration Act of 1924; Jewish Americans; Jewish ethnicity: definitions.

Asian American Legal Defense Fund

The Asian American Legal Defense Fund (AALDF) is the first organization on the East Coast of the United States to defend and promote the legal rights of Asian Americans through litigation, legal advocacy, community education, leadership development, and free legal assistance for low-income and immigrant Asian Americans. The organization is headquartered in New York City, and the executive director in 1998 was Margaret Fung, an Asian American lawyer. The AALDF was organized to help relieve the effects of racial prejudice and social discrimination experienced by Asian and Pacific Americans.

Many individuals from the diverse Asian American population have attained middle-class status, and a select few have entered upper-level management within major

United States corporations. However, in wages and career advancement, Asian Americans generally lag behind their white counterparts. The AALDF addresses these and other grievances by educating Asian American communities, particularly in the election process of the United States. Furthermore, to encourage voter participation, the AALDF has fostered the use of bilingual ballots and voter material in the United States. Asian Americans cast a significant number of votes in key electoral states such as California and major cities such as New York, Los Angeles, and San Francisco.

Alvin K. Benson

See also: Asian American movement; Chin, Vincent, murder.

Asian American literature

> **Significance:** Asian American literature is the fiction, essays, and other works written by Americans of Asian ancestry, usually on themes that touch on the authors' heritage. These works, which first appeared at the end of the nineteenth century, enable Asian Americans to identify with their own cultural heritage and help others better understand their culture and experiences.

The first published Asian American writers were two sisters, Sui Sin Far (Edith Maud Eaton) and Onoto Watanna (Winifred Eaton), the daughters of British planter Edward Eaton and his Chinese wife, Lotus Blossom. Critics have accused Sui Sin Far of presenting stereotypical descriptions of the Chinese and of Chinatown, but in fact, through her collection of short stories *Mrs. Spring Fragrance* (1912), she portrayed the discrimination and psychic pain that Chinese immigrants endured. In novels such as *Heart of Hyacinth* (1904), Onoto Watanna wrote of love affairs between Asian women and white men in which the Asian woman always accepted the superiority of a Western lover. She chose a Japanese-sounding name for her pen name because at the time, although the American public discriminated against the Japanese, they viewed them more favorably than the Chinese, stereotyping them as harder working and more intelligent.

Before World War II, several Asian American writers described their experiences growing up in the United States. One book, Younghill Kang's *East Goes West* (1937), offers a humorous look at the life of a young Korean American and pokes fun at white people's prejudices.

After World War II, several Japanese Americans published books about the internment camps and other wartime experiences. In *The Two Worlds of Jim Yoshida* (1972), Nisei (second-generation Japanese American) Jim Yoshida, who was in Japan when World War II broke out, relates how he was forced to serve in the Imperial Army and had to sue to regain U.S. citizenship after the war. In *No-No Boy* (1957), John Okada, another Nisei, wrote about the hysteria that he experienced in wartime America, and in the award-winning book *Obasan* (1981), Joy Kogawa described her life in a Canadian World War II internment camp.

The 1960's and 1970's

During the 1960's and 1970's, the Civil Rights and women's movements inspired many minority groups to become active politically and to become more aware of their heritage. This heightened activity and awareness resulted in the publication of more works by Asian Americans, which helped others understand and respect them.

In 1972, the first anthology of Asian American literature, edited by Kai-Yu Hsu and Helen Palubinskas, was published. This anthology included works from only three Asian American groups—Chinese, Japanese, and Filipino—and gave priority to writers born in America such as Frank Chin, Jeffrey Paul Chan, Lawson Fusao Inada, and Shawn Wong. However, other anthologies soon followed, broadening the spectrum of Asian American writers to include Americans of Korean, Southeast Asian, and Indian ancestry and immigrants such as Chitra Divakaruni.

In 1972, *The Chickencoop Chinaman*, was the first play by an Asian American, Frank Chin, to receive critical acclaim in New York. Asian American literature received widespread recognition with the publication in 1976 of Maxine Hong Kingston's *The Woman Warrior: Memories of a Girlhood Among Ghosts*. Kingston used ancient Chinese stories to develop her best-selling novel around the character of Fa Mulan, a woman warrior. This work, like many others by Asian American writers, incorporated elements of traditional Asian mythology and culture. It also illustrated the effect that the Civil Rights and women's movements had on literature produced by members of minority groups.

Common Themes

During the 1970's and 1980's, various demographic trends, such as increased immigration from Asia and Mexico, helped the United States become much more multicultural, and more Asian American writers felt encouraged to explore Asian themes. Although Asia is a large continent with many languages, cultures, and religions, certain themes and elements appear to be common in Asian American literature. These include the balance between dark and light and between masculine and feminine; conflicts between ancient heritage, familial obligations, and contemporary (often Western) lifestyles; and the effects of immigration. After Kingston's work became popular, there was widespread appreciation for novelists, poets, dramatists, and essayists of Asian ancestry.

Many Asian American women have written of the cultural conflicts that women experience when they move from traditional Asian cultures to the more liberal American culture. Velina Hasu Houston explored this theme in a 1985 trilogy, *Asa ga Kimashita, American Dream,* and *Tea,* whose main characters are Japanese war brides who have to cross traditional boundaries in order to survive in their new environment. In *Arranged Marriages* (1995), Indian-born poet Divakaruni presents images of the adjustment problems that many women from traditional Indian backgrounds have in American society.

Asian American writers also have explored familial obligations and tensions. In "Seventeen Syllables" (1994), Hisaye Yamamoto explored the tensions created within Japanese American families when traditional cultural expectations clash with contemporary lifestyles. In *Clay Walls* (1986), a novel by Korean American Kim Ronyoung, the issue of obligation to family is explored as the wife and mother ruins her eyes doing embroidery work to support her family after her husband loses all their money gambling.

Some Asian American writers based their stories on the immigrant experience, as did Wakako Yamauchi in her novel *And the Soul Shall Dance* (1977) and Fred Ho in the play *Chinaman's Chance* (1987). In *Honey Bucket* (1979), Filipino American Mel Escueta explored the issue of identity, attempting to deal with the guilt he felt after killing Asians during the Vietnam War. Frank Chin

used stereotypes in the humorous novel *Donald Duk* (1991), as did David Henry Hwang in his Tony Award-winning play *M Butterfly* (1988).

Perhaps after Kingston, who made the American public aware of Asian American literature, Chinese American Amy Tan is the writer who did most to popularize the genre. Tan rose to public attention with the publication of her novel *The Joy Luck Club* in 1989. She won both the National Book Award and the *Los Angeles Times* book award that year. Tan turned her novel into a screenplay for the 1993 film *The Joy Luck Club.* She has objected to having her work described as Asian American literature because she believes that the themes in her work, which include male-female relationships and family obligations, are universal. Still, Tan's themes arise from an experience that may be termed Asian American: the balance between male and female; clashes between traditional cultures and con-

> **A Short List of Asian American Literature for Young People**
>
> **Chinese American**
> *Child of the Owl,* by Laurence Yep
>   (Harper & Row, 1977)
> *The Star Fisher,* by Laurence Yep
>   (Morrow Publishing, 1991)
>
> **Japanese American**
> *A Jar of Dreams,* by Yoshiko Uchida
>   (Atheneum, 1981)
> *Farewell to Manzanar,* by Jeanne Wakatsuke
>   Houston and James D. Houston
>   (Houghton Mifflin, 1973)
>
> **Indian American**
> *Lights for Gita,* by Rachna Gilmore
>   (Tillbury House, 1994)
>
> **Cambodian American**
> *Children of the River,* by Linda Crew
>   (Delacorte Press, 1989)
>
> **Vietnamese American**
> *The Little Weaver of Thai Yen Village,*
>   by Khan Tuyet Tran
>   (Children's Book Press, 1992)

The eight actresses in the 1993 film *The Joy Luck Club,* based on Amy Tan's award-winning 1989 novel, pose in their mother-daughter roles. The film and book explore the daughters' relationships with their more traditional mothers.

temporary lifestyles; struggles with familial obligations; and identity and spirituality issues.   *Annita Marie Ward*

Core Resources
King-kok Cheung edited *An Interpretive Companion to Asian American Literature* (Cambridge, England: Cambridge University Press, 1996). Shirley Geok-lin Lim and Amy Ling edited *Reading the Literature of Asian America* (Philadelphia: Temple University Press, 1996). Judith Caesar explored Asian American themes in "Patriarchy, Imperialism, and Knowledge in *The Kitchen God's Wife*" in *North Dakota Quarterly* (62, no. 4, 1994-1995). Asian American literature is discussed in Sucheng Chann's *Asian Americans: An Interpretive History* (Boston: Twayne, 1991).

See also: Asian American movement; Asian American stereotypes; Asian American women; Asian Americans and film.

Asian American movement

Although Asian Americans generally have been considered a monolith by the wider American society, a great deal of ethnic diversity exists among the various groups of people with Asian ancestry. Until the post-World War II era, Asian Americans had remained fragmented, partly because of the ethnic divisions among them and the animosities between many Asian countries, which the immigrants had brought with them. Their experiences in the United States often served to reinforce those divisions. Farmworkers and other laborers were often divided into work groups according to their ethnicities and were urged to compete with each other. Also, when public opinion turned against a specific group of Asian Americans (as it did against the Japanese Americans during the "yellow peril" campaign of the late 1800's), other Asian Americans (including Chinese Americans) did not defend their fellow Asian Americans, but instead asserted their separate identities in fear of becoming mistaken targets of the persecution.

In the 1960's, these diverse ethnic communities, which included Chinese Americans, Japanese Americans, Korean Americans, and Filipino Americans, began joining together in an effort to make an impact on the educational, social, and political scenes of North America. This attempt at unity was the result of several factors: Barriers between the groups were diminished when second- and third-generation Asian Americans assumed leadership roles. Born in North America, they had become familiar with each other through schools and various social groups and did not share the inter-Asian animosities of the first generation. They also had not experienced the divisions between Asian American groups that occurred in the late nineteenth and early twentieth centuries. In fact, the wider society's tendency to lump all Asian Americans together forced them to associate with each other. Also, the injustice of the Vietnam War (1957-1975) communicated a general bias against Asians and Asian Americans.

Initially, the Asian American organizations were college-based. One of the first was the Asian American Political Alliance, founded at the University of California, Berkeley, in 1968. Similar organizations were formed at other campuses, and by the mid-1970's, "Asian American" had become a familiar term. Asian American professionals began forming groups, including the Asian American Social Workers, and Asian American caucuses developed in national professional associations such as the American Public Health Association. Asian American studies became part of the curriculum on college campuses, which helped create an awareness of Asian Americans as a group. As a result, publications began treating Asian Americans as a unit. Their relatively small numbers and lack of agreement on issues have kept Asian Americans from gaining a great deal of political influence, but they rank second behind Jewish Americans in political contributions.

Two incidents in the 1980's sparked Asian Americans to become an assertive political and social force. The first was the murder of Vincent Chin in 1982. His killers, who blamed the Japanese for the downturn in the automobile industry, mistook the Chinese American Chin for a Japanese national and bludgeoned him to death with a baseball bat. They were given light sentences and never spent a day in jail for their crimes. The second event was the discovery in the mid-1980's that the University of California, Berkeley, had instituted quotas that limited the number of Asian Americans admitted. After the Chin incident, Asian Americans formed the American Citizens for Justice, a watchdog group to prevent or rectify violence against Asian Americans.

In 1989, when five Southeast Asian elementary students were shot to death in Stockton, California, and Chinese American Ming Hai Loo was killed in Raleigh, North Carolina, an Asian American legal team and media people were there to see that justice was done. In addition, because of political influence exerted by Asian Americans, Japanese Americans who were incarcerated during World War II received some remuneration and recognition.

Other Asian American concerns have to do with the glass ceiling (Asians not being promoted to upper level positions for which they qualify), the Americanization of the younger generations (and accompanying loss of their culture), and intergroup relations in the inner city (such as between Korean shop owners and African

Americans). Due to the differing situations and cultures within the Asian American community, unity has not been fully achieved and overall goals have not been determined. In this way, the movement has not yet reached its full potential. *Arthur W. Helweg*

See also: Asian American stereotypes; Chin, Vincent, murder; Korean-African American relations; Loo, Ming Hai, murder; Orientalism; Yellow peril campaign.

Asian American stereotypes

Significance: The hard work and thriftiness that have contributed to the success of Asian Americans have, at times, caused members of other ethnic and racial groups to feel threatened. In the nineteenth and early twentieth centuries, Asian immigrants and their offspring were often called a threat to the American standard of living and were viewed by white Americans as a group that could not be assimilated. In the latter part of the twentieth century, there were millions of Americans of Asian ancestry in the United States; however, some of the old attitudes persisted: Many fourth-generation Asian Americans were identified as Asian (Chinese, Japanese, and so on) rather than as "American."

Prejudices Against the First Chinese Immigrants

The Chinese, who first immigrated to the United States in the mid-nineteenth century, were willing to work for low wages, which got them jobs but also made them the objects of white workers' jealousy and anger. On the West Coast, where many of the immigrants had settled, many white workers blamed Chinese immigrants for their economic woes. They called the Chinese laborers "coolies," a derogatory term, and claimed that they were of inferior character and could not be assimilated into American culture. This general climate of blame coupled with the desire of white nativists to limit immigration, and many discriminatory laws (such as the 1862 California law, an Act to Protect Free White Labor Against Competition from Chinese Coolie Labor) were passed against the Chinese immigrants. Many of these laws were later employed against immigrants from other Asian countries. As the Chinese immigrants moved beyond California, white workers in area after area spoke out against them, claiming that their willingness to work for meager wages would ruin all Americans' standard of living. In 1885, in Rock Springs, Wyoming, a white mob drove Chinese workers out of town and burned their homes, killing twenty-eight Chinese immigrants in the process.

Transfer of Prejudice

Although the Chinese were excluded from immigration by the 1882 Chinese Exclusion Act, other Asians—Japanese, Koreans, and Indians—did arrive in the United States. From 1900 to 1910, about 100,000 Japanese arrived on the West Coast. These immigrants tended to be better educated than the earlier Chinese immigrants had been. Nevertheless, white Americans on the West Coast, particularly in California, expressed alarm at their arrival, again claiming that the Japanese could never be assimilated into American society. The press and politicians claimed that a Japanese invasion was taking place and began to speak of the "yellow peril," which they said posed a threat to the American way of life and might result in the United States being taken over by the Japanese.

In 1924, Congress passed an Immigration Act that barred nearly all immigration from Asia. Only Filipinos were allowed to immigrate because as citizens of the Philippines, they could become U.S. citizens. However, during the late 1920's and during the Depression of the 1930's, trade unions wanted Filipino immigration banned, claiming the Filipino laborers' willingness to work cheaply was undercutting the American standard of living. Filipinos were called a "mongrel stream" that could not be assimilated. Union members urged the government to ship Filipinos back to the Philippines.

Japanese Americans During World War II

By the time Japan bombed Pearl Harbor in December, 1941, two generations of Japanese Americans were living in the United States and Canada: the Issei, the original immigrants, and their children, the Nisei. Some Japanese American families had been in North America for more than fifty years. Nevertheless, both the Canadian and the United States governments assumed that these Japanese Americans would not be loyal to them and placed 120,000 Japanese Americans in internment camps until the end of World War II.

Views of Asians After World War II

Immigrants who came to the United States under the quota system, established by the Immigration and Nationality Act of 1952, were often professionals, tending to be more affluent than earlier immigrants and far less likely to live in ethnic enclaves such as Chinatowns or Koreatowns. This new group of professional immigrants and their offspring gave the United States a new Asian American stereotype—the smart achiever.

In 1965, the quota system was abolished, allowing much more immigration from Asia. In the mid-1970's, large numbers of people from Cambodia, Laos, and Vietnam entered as refugees from the conflict in Southeast Asia. Many of these people, particularly the Hmong

A Korean shopping mall at Third Street and Vermont Avenue in Los Angeles burns during the 1992 riots. The stereotype of Korean shop owners as mercenary and racist was in part responsible for their stores becoming targets during the rioting.

universities in the University of California system, although the percentage of African American and Latino students fell from the early 1990's. This situation created resentment against Asian Americans and placed pressure on young Asian Americans to conform to the stereotype of Asian Americans as superior students.

Annita Marie Ward

Core Resources

William L. Tung's *The Chinese in America, 1820-1973* (Dobbs Ferry, N.Y.: Oceana Press, 1974) gives a detailed record and chronology of Chinese Americans' experiences from 1820 to 1973. Other useful books include *The Japanese Americans, The Korean Americans, The Chinese Americans, The Filipino Americans,* and *The Indo-Chinese Americans,* all part of the Peoples of North America series, edited by Nancy Toff (New York: Chelsea House Publishers, 1989). Senator Daniel Patrick Moynihan served as senior consulting editor to the series.

See also: Asian American women; Asian Americans and film; Asian Indians in the United States; Assimilation: cultural and structural; Cambodian Americans; Chinese Americans; Chinese Exclusion Act; Filipino Americans; Immigration Act of 1924; Immigration and Nationality Act of 1952; Immigration and Nationality Act of 1965; Japanese American internment; Immigration Reform and Control Act of 1986; Japanese Americans; "Model" minorities; Prejudice and stereotyping; Stereotype; Stereotyping and the self-fulfilling prophecy; Vietnamese Americans; Yellow peril campaign.

from Laos, were uneducated. Political leaders began to object to the entrance of refugees, claiming that their education and skill levels made it difficult for them to assimilate because they could not learn to read and write in English. It was also claimed that they took jobs away from Americans. Such stereotyping contributed to the English-only movement and passage of the 1986 Immigration Reform and Control Act.

Stereotypes and Resentment

In the last decade of the twentieth century, household incomes for Asian American families and educational levels for Asian American adults were generally higher than those of the general American population. New resentments and stereotypes emerged. In the cities, this resentment was often directed toward shop owners and landlords of Asian ancestry. These shop owners were often stereotyped as mercenary and racist, particularly by some blacks, such as the Nation of Islam's Louis Farrakhan, who likened the affluent Asian Americans to the Jewish landlords and shop owners of the mid-twentieth century. This resentment was portrayed in Spike Lee's movie *Do the Right Thing* (1989), which foreshadowed some of the violence directed toward shop owners of Korean ancestry during the Los Angeles riots of 1992.

Although people of Asian and Pacific Islander heritage represented about 4 percent of the U.S. population in 1999, they made up 8 to 10 percent of enrollment in Ivy League institutions. Students of Asian heritage made up 35 percent to 40 percent of the student bodies at some

Asian American women

> **Significance:** In the 1990's, Asian American women belonged to the fastest-growing group of minorities in the United States and Canada.

According to 1999 projections by the U.S. census, the total number of Asian Americans and Pacific Islanders in the United States more than doubled from the 1980 census figure of 3.4 million. Despite this rapid population growth, Asians in the United States, as in Canada, accounted for less than 5 percent of the population.

Demographics

There is growing awareness that Asian Americans come from many different backgrounds, not simply Chinese and Japanese ones. Although the 1990 census reported twenty-eight different Asian American groups, the focus of much of the literature has been on the eight largest or more recently controversial and influential groups: Chinese, Filipinos, Koreans, Asian Indians, Japanese, Vietnamese, Cambodians, and Hmong. Approximately 66 percent of Asian Americans in the United States live in five states: California, New York, Hawaii, Texas, and Illinois. They also have a tendency to congregate and concentrate in a few cities: Chicago, Honolulu, Los Angeles, New York, and San Francisco.

In general, Asian American men had higher rates of graduation from a high school or higher institution than women in 1990, 82 percent versus 74 percent. Among the various groups of women, however, disparities exist in terms of completion rates. A high school or higher educational level had been obtained by 86 percent of Japanese American women but only 19 percent of Hmong American women. Asian American women had a higher labor force participation rate than all women. In 1990, 60 percent of Asian American women were in the labor force, compared with 57 percent of all women in the United States.

The diversity in origins and cultural backgrounds of Asian Americans has made it difficult to speak of an Asian American culture that ties all these groups together. Nevertheless, common themes can be found in the experiences of women who must struggle constantly with the social burden not only of their race but also of their gender and their class.

Reasons for Coming to America

Historically, it is difficult to speak of Asian American immigrant women, because there were relatively few of them. Restrictions on Chinese and Japanese men bringing their wives to American shores led to the phenomenon of bachelor men and picture brides. In addition to legal restrictions, cultural deterrents kept Asian women from venturing abroad: "Respectable" women did not travel far from home; the only women to do so were maids and prostitutes. Those Asian women who were able to immigrate labored under hard physical conditions and were often callously treated. In many cases, however, leaving their home country was these women's only alternative to poverty, war, and persecution. Some of the most recent arrivals to the United States—Southeast Asians from Vietnam, Cambodia, and Laos—came as refugees of wars in their homelands. Still other Asian women came in search of adventure and the excitement of living in a new country, especially those from more affluent families and those who were well educated.

Yet, no matter what their original status in their native countries, Asian American women have often encountered a hostile society in the West. Even those who have been living in the United States or Canada for many years or decades have not been spared this hostility. Moreover, Asian American women born in the West are not guaranteed fair treatment. Many immigrant Asian women are faced with financial hardships, violence, and social ostracism, forcing them to learn survival skills in order to adapt to life in a new country. Some have adjusted quite well to the new environment, while others have not.

Issues of Concern

Asian American women have to some degree helped perpetuate the myth of Asian Americans as a model minority since, as wives and mothers, they socialize their families—using a cultural emphasis on education, hard work, and thrift—to excel in earnings, education, and occupational status. Such goals often set Asian Americans apart from other ethnic groups and can lead to jealousy, resentment, and discrimination.

Despite the hard work and self-sacrifice of many Asian American women, however, disparity often exists between striving and achievement. Many newer immigrants must contend with a lack of communication because of poor English-speaking skills. Asian American women have acquired a reputation for being conscientious and industrious but docile, compliant, and uncomplaining as well. The necessity of a paycheck relegates some to work as hotel room cleaners, waitresses, cooks, shop clerks, and electronics assembly-line workers. Some postpone learning English and as a result may never leave their entry-level jobs.

In general, Asian American women with a college education are concentrated in limited, less prestigious rungs of the professional-managerial class. Professionally, Japanese women typically become elementary or secondary school teachers and Filipinas become nurses. In 1980, Asian American women with four or more years of college were most likely to find jobs in administrative support or clerical occupations, such as cashiers, file clerks, office machine operators, and typists. They are overrepresented in these jobs, many of which not only have low prestige, low mobility, and low public contact but also offer little or no decision-making authority. Executive managerial status is limited to such occupations as auditors and accountants. Asian American women are least represented in the more prestigious professions: physicians, judges, dentists, law professors, and lawyers. Thus, Asian American women in general are poorly represented in higher-level management and leadership positions and experience the "glass ceiling," which often prevents women and minorities from rising above a certain job level. The fact that Asian American women do not reap the income and other benefits one might expect given their high levels of educational achievement raises questions about the reasons for such inequality. To what extent is this situation attributable to self-imposed limitations related to cultural modesty, the absence of certain social and interpersonal skills required for upper-managerial positions, institutional factors beyond their control, or outright discrimination?

The number of Asian American women turning to mainstream politics, running for office, or working in politics is increasing. The Civil Rights and antiwar movements motivated many younger Asian American women to become politically active over issues of discrimination because of race, sex, or place of origin. In the 1960's, the first wave of Asian American feminism focused on empowering these women economically, socially, and politically. The second wave of activism in the 1980's focused on working with specific women's groups as support networks for women of color. Some Asian American women became involved in assisting the homeless and the poor (many of whom are elderly immigrants), nuclear disarmament efforts, and the international issues of freedom in the Philippines and Korea and the sex trade in Asia.

Many conflicts still need to be resolved. Some tension exists in the Asian American community between new arrivals and long-term residents or citizens, between native-born and foreign-born members, and between the professional and working classes. New arrivals still look to Asia for reference, while the U.S.-born tend to view the world from an American perspective. The established working class views the new arrivals as competitors for the same scarce resources. The established professionals look askance at those with limited English proficiency and their culturally ill-at-ease immigrant counterparts. Professionals dissociate themselves from the residents of ethnic ghettos in Chinatowns, Koreatowns, and Japantowns. Working-class Asian Americans view the professionals' tendency to speak for the community with suspicion.

The chasm between traditional Asian familial values and mainstream values has brought conflict for Asian American women. In order to be effective, they must be aggressive, but such an approach is contrary to traditional Asian feminine values of passivity and subordination. They must be highly visible and public, contrary to the values of modesty and moderation. Thus, the Asian American woman pressured to conform to traditional female roles must overcome a number of barriers in the attempt to adjust to the American environment.

Cecilia G. Manrique

Core Resources

Additional sources of information about Asian Americans include Karin Aguilar-San Juan's *The State of Asian America* (Boston: South End Press, 1994), Harry H. L. Kitano and Roger Daniels's *Asian Americans: Emerging Minorities* (Englewood Cliffs, N.J.: Prentice Hall, 1988), Tricia Knoll's *Becoming Americans: Asian Sojourners, Immigrants, and Refugees in the Western United States* (Portland: Coast to Coast Books, 1982), Ronald Takaki's *Strangers from a Different Shore: A History of Asian Americans* (Boston: Little, Brown, 1989), and William Wei's *The

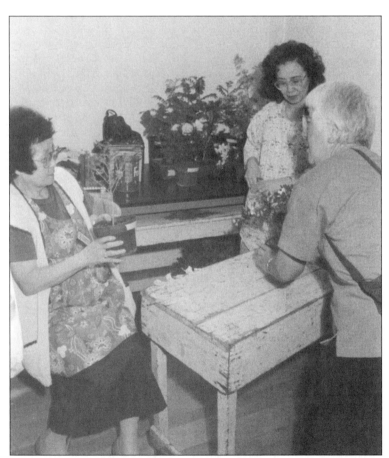

Three Japanese American women discuss plants and bonsai at a cultural gathering. Asian American women must reconcile traditional feminine values such as modesty and reserve with business and cultural practices in the United States.

Asian American Movement (Philadelphia: Temple University Press, 1993). *Making Waves: An Anthology of Writings by and About Asian American Women* (Boston: Beacon Press, 1989) is a collection of writings by Asian women edited by the Asian Women United of California.

See also: Cambodian Americans; Chinese Americans; Education and Asian Americans; Ethnic identities of women; Filipino Americans; Hmong Americans; Japanese Americans; Racism and women; Vietnamese Americans; Women of color.

Asian Americans and film

> **Significance:** Asian characters have been included in films from the earliest days of American film history. The evolution of how Asians have been, and continue to be, portrayed may be linked to a constellation of social, historical, and cultural factors.

Anti-Asian sentiments, buttressed by exclusionary legislations in the nineteenth century, resulted in stereotypical images that would permeate not only film but also literature and popular culture for much of the next century. In more recent times, American military engagements in Asia as well as challenges to U.S. global economic supremacy by Japan, Korea, and other nations of Asia have likewise shaped the cinematic characterizations of Asians.

Cinematic representations of Asians are also rooted in European theater and opera. By the seventeenth century, enthusiasm for *chinoiserie* made itself felt in theatrical and operatic productions. Dramas and operas with Asian themes were produced in France, Italy, Spain, and the Netherlands; Asiatic figures such as Tamerlane, Ch'ung-cheng, an emperor of the Ming Dynasty, and Aurangzeb the Mogul emperor were popular figures in several plays by Christopher Marlowe, John Dryden, and Joost van den Vondel. Voltaire's enthusiasm for the newly discovered wonders of Asia also resulted in *Ophelin de la chine*, a play about a Chinese orphan that had its American performance in 1767. The transference of representations back and forth across the Atlantic, coupled with the arrival of Asians in America, cumulatively evolved into a collection of cinematic human typologies. These typologies became formulas for the later "oriental" stereotypes in film.

Representations and Stereotypes
In the silent film era, the roles of Asians were dominated primarily by white actors of both sexes in "yellow face,"

a practice derived from earlier theatrical and operatic traditions. In D. W. Griffith's *Broken Blossoms* (1919), Richard Barthelmess played a Chinese laundryman who rescues an abused girl acted by Lillian Gish. The year before, Norma Talmadge was cast as a Chinese girl who is loved and abandoned by an American in *The Forbidden City*. During the silent era of film, several actors, including Lon Chaney, Nils Asther, Warner Oland, Sidney Toler, E. A. Warren, Peter Lorre, and Boris Karloff, became specialists in assuming Asian identities for their cinematic roles. Likewise, actresses such as Alla Asimova, Sylvia Sidney, Sigrid Gurie, Myrna Loy, and Gale Sondergaard were all considered sufficiently "exotic" in appearance to be cast on a regular basis as Asian women of one nationality or another.

Actors such as Warner Oland, however, were not simply identified with Asian roles; they also developed characterizations that became standard Asian stereotypes. One of Oland's earliest roles was that of Okada, a Japanese potato baron in the 1922 film *Pride of Palomar*, directed by Frank Borzage. His other roles as Chinese villains included the title role in *The Return of Dr. Fu Manchu* in 1930. His other "oriental" credits included *Mandarin's Gold* (1919), *East Is West* (1922), *Old San Francisco* (1928), *Daughter of the Dragon* (1931), in which he again played the evil Dr. Fu Manchu, *Shanghai Express*, opposite Marlene Dietrich, in 1933, and *Shanghai* in 1935.

Characters such as the evil Dr. Fu Manchu or Ming the Merciless in the popular *Flash Gordon* series established the stereotype of the ruthless Asian whose sole aim was to take over the Western world. This stereotype and its corollary notion of plots involving potential Asian world domination would continue into the 1960's and beyond. The theme of the "yellow peril" can be observed in the James Bond film *Dr. No* (1962). By the 1980's and 1990's, when Asian actors would be used in this particular characterization, the meglomaniacal Asian continued in films such as *The Year of the Dragon* (1985) and *Rising Sun* (1993).

Films depicting Asians as possessing violent propensities or as members of Asian secret societies have also been a standard theme in Hollywood movies. From the silent era on, Asians are routinely depicted as purveyors of opium, drugs, and sex. From *War of the Tongs* (1917) through *Chinatown Nights* (1929), *The Hatchet Man* (1932), and *The Year of the Dragon* (1985), Chinatowns or Asian milieus are consistently depicted as murky backdrops for crime, vice, and violence. Martial arts movies such as *Enter the Dragon* (1973), *The Big Brawl* (1980), *Enter the Ninja* (1982), *Revenge of the Ninja* (1983), and *The Protector* (1985) are all contextualized against the backdrop of Asian crime, vice, and violence. In these contexts, Asian men have for decades been portrayed as power-hungry, cruel, and lustful. In every instance, the object of their desires is a white woman who fights to retain her honor.

The stereotype of the Asian rapist had its early beginnings in silent films. One of the more sensational moments of film history may be seen in the 1915 film *The Cheat*, in which Sessue Hayakawa tears the gown off the shoulder of a white woman who refuses his advances and then brands her with a branding iron. Likewise, in films as varied as *Mr. Foo* (1914), *The Thief of Bagdad* (1924), *Old San Francisco* (1927), *The Bitter Tea of General Yen* (1933), *Daughter of the Dragon* (1931), and the the Fu Manchu and Flash Gordon movies (the latter featuring Ming the Merciless), Asian villains are depicted as rapists who delight in sadistic methods of torture.

The Hollywood tradition of the Asian villain has historically been matched with that of the "Dragon Lady" stereotype. In the silent era, Anna May Wong, née Wong Liu Tsong, became the first Chinese American actor to achieve international recognition for her portrayals of menacing "oriental vamps." She was first cast in the 1919 film *The Red Lantern*, which featured a cast of more than five hundred Chinese in supernumerary roles. Wong went on to the leading role of a Chinese woman who is deserted by her American lover in the first silent color movie, *The Toll of the Sea*, in 1922. In the next few years, she would star in films that ultimately cast her in the role of the mysterious and sinister counterpart to the male Asian villain. From the silent *Thief of Baghdad* (1924) through films such as *Daughter of the Dragon* (1931), *Shanghai Express* (1932), and *Java Head* (1934), Wong affected the remote yet seductive demeanor that suggested not only "the mysterious Orient" but also her characters' innate cruelty and deviousness.

These characterizations seldom represented Asian Americans as fully developed characters. Nevertheless, they came to be accepted by both the viewing public and filmmakers as realistic representations of Asians.

The evil villain had its counterpart in the Asiatic buffoon. This stereotype, identified usually by his ineptitude, had been a stock character in light theatricals and operas long before the advent of cinema. During the silent era, films such as *Chinese Rubbernecks* (1903), *The Yellow Peril* (1908), and *What Ho the Cook* (1921) depicted Asians as buffoons. *Chinese Rubbernecks* featured a slapstick chase scene through a Chinese laundry. In *The Yellow Peril*, a Chinese servant manages to disrupt a home and is subsequently thrown out a window, beaten up by a policeman, and finally set on fire. The comic Asian with quaint aphorisms and peculiar mannerisms also found expression in the proliferation of films featuring cinematic Asian detectives from Hollywood studios from the 1920's into the 1950's. The earliest movie featuring an Asian detective was the silent film *The Adventures of Boe*

Chinese American Anna May Wong achieved international recognition for her portrayals of menacing "Oriental vamps" in the 1920's and 1930's.

Kung (1912), featuring what was billed as "the Chinese Sherlock Holmes." Other films featuring Asian detectives included the 1926 film *House Without a Key*, with George Kuwa in the lead role, *The Chinese Parrot* (1928), starring Kamiyana Shojin, and *Behind That Curtain* (1929), with E. L. Park. In 1929, the silent film *The Peacock Fan*, starring Lucien Prival and Dorothy Dwan, dealt with the murder of a wealthy magnate. The detective who solved the crime was an "inscrutable" Chinese named Dr. Chang.

This genre did not become popular, however, until non-Asian actors were cast in the lead roles as Asian detectives. The best known of these was undoubtedly Charlie Chan, who was portrayed by a series of actors including Warner Oland, Sidney Toler, Roland Winters, Carol Naish, and Peter Ustinov. In their heyday from 1931 to 1941, the Charlie Chan films were produced by Twentieth Century-Fox. Monogram films also produced five films with Boris Karloff in the role of the Chinese detective James Lee Wong. Based on the character created by Hugh Wiley, the stories in the Wong series first appeared in *Collier's* magazine; the films included *Mr. Wong* (1938), *Mr. Wong in Chinatown* (1939), *The Mystery of Mr. Wong* (1939), *The Fatal Hour* (1940), and *Doomed to*

Die (1949). Mr. Wong, as played by Boris Karloff with taped eyes, was portrayed as a gentleman and a scholar educated at Oxford University and the University of Heidelberg. He was also represented as an authority on "Oriental" art and literature. In another of the Wong films, *The Phantom of Chinatown* (1941), a Chinese American actor, Keye Luke, was cast as Wong, becoming one of the few Asians to play a lead Asian character.

From the 1930's into the 1950's, more than fifty Charlie Chan movies were made. Warner Oland, the first of the three non-Asian actors to play Chan, made sixteen Chan movies before his death in 1938. Sidney Toler then played the role for the next three years. Toler starred in eleven Charlie Chan movies before his own death in 1947; he was replaced by Roland Winters. In all the Charlie Chan adventures, Chan's urbane if stilted "Chinese" ways were usually contrasted with the manners of highly excitable Irish police captain Flannery or of Chan's wide-eyed African American butler, played by Mantland Moreland. In addition, eight *Mr. Moto* films, based on the character featuring the Japanese spy/detective created by John P. Marquand, were produced between 1937 and 1939. The first seven films featured Peter Lorre as Mr. Moto; the last, made in 1965, featured Henry Silva as the Japanese detective.

Asian American Contributions to the Film Industry
Although non-Asian actors have long been used to play lead Asian characters in Hollywood films, Asians themselves have worked behind the scenes or as supernumeraries in film from the earliest days of the film history. The 1914 film *The Chinese Lily*, for example, boasted an all-Chinese cast. One of the pioneers of the silent film era was Leong But-jung, who was also known as James B. Leong. Leong began the Wah Ming Motion Picture Company, which was financed by Chinese American businesses. The intent of this company was to produce films with Chinese themes using all-Chinese casts. Leong and another Chinese American, Moon Kwan, were also involved in the D. W. Griffith film *Broken Blossoms* (1919). Moon served as the film's technical director, while Leong worked as Griffith's assistant director. Another Chinese American, James Wang, served as the technical director for the 1919 film *Red Lantern*, with its cast of hundreds of Chinese American extras.

As leading figures, the two Asian American actors who gained the widest attention in the early history of film were Anna May Wong and Sessue Hayakawa. Wong's film career spanned more than thirty years; Hayakawa's career, which began in silent films in 1914 with his appearance in *Wrath of the Gods*, extended into the era of sound with roles in *Tokyo Joe* (1949) and *The Bridge over the River Kwai* (1957). Few today, however, remember Hayakawa's wife Tsuru Aoki, who starred in several films including *The Courageous Coward* (1919). Aoki had both a film and a theater career and was known as an actress and director.

Several other Asian American actors have also had unusually long careers by virtue of their versatility in a range of supporting roles. Key Luke, who began his acting career in the 1930's in films such as *The Painted Veil* (1934), starring Greta Garbo, continued his acting career into the television era, during which he achieved renewed popularity for his role in the 1970's *Kung Fu* series. Other Asian American actors such as Philip Ahn, James Shigeta, Nobu McCarthy, Buelah Kwoh, James Soo, Mako, and Victor Sen Young have all enjoyed varied degrees of public visibility through their long careers.

The 1980's and 1990's may be characterized as the decades when Asian American actors came into increasing prominence. Actors from Asia such as Joan Chen, Jackie Chan, and Ming Na-wen, along with Asian Americans such as Russell Wong, Jason Scott Lee, and the late Brandon Lee, achieved levels of stardom that had not been possible in earlier times. Recent decades have also seen attempts to portray Asians as fully developed characters. The success of films such as *The Joy Luck Club* (1993), as well as the international recognition of films directed by Asian-born directors such as Wayne Wang, Ang Lee (*Eat, Drink, Man, Woman*, 1994), Zhang Yimou (*Red Sorghum*, 1987; *Raise the Red Lantern*, 1991), Chen Kaige (*Farewell My Concubine*, 1993), and Hung Tran Ahn (*Scent of Green Papaya*, 1993), have offered the viewing public a much broader and more complex perspective on Asians in North America and abroad.

Patricia Lin

Core Resources
Asian Americans in film are discussed in Renee Tajima's *The Anthology of Asian Pacific American Film and Video* (New York: Film News Now Foundation, 1985) and Mel Gussow's "Beyond the Dragon Lady and No. 1 Son" (*The New York Times*, September 3, 1990).

See also: African Americans and film; American Indians and film; Asian American stereotypes; Latinos and film.

Asian Indians in Canada

Significance: Asian Indians are representative of a new type of immigrant entering North America. They are generally highly educated professionals who are entrepreneurial, and transnational in their orientation. Their ongoing contributions to both Canada and their homeland continue to be significant.

Asian Indians, also known as East Indians, have a migratory tradition and are found in almost every part of the world. For statistical purposes, the people who claim India as their homeland are often lumped under the South Asian category, which includes people from India, Pakistan, Bangladesh, and Sri Lanka.

The Early Years

Asian Indians started entering Canada in significant numbers in 1903, a year after the coronation of Edward VII. On the way to the coronation pageantry, a small, multi-ethnic contingent from the Crown Colony of Hong Kong stopped in Vancouver. Among the party were twenty-three Sikhs from the Punjab, a butterfly-shaped region that covers part of India and part of Pakistan. The Sikhs, who wear *kirpan* and turbans and have uncut beards, were so well received in Canada that some of them, joined by other Sikhs, returned the next year as immigrants.

At the time, the Canadian Pacific Railroad needed laborers and steamship companies lacked passengers. Therefore, both recruited Japanese and Indians, first in Hong Kong and then in the Punjab. Punjabis mortgaged their land at interest rates of 10 percent to 12 percent to get the sixty-five-dollar passage to Vancouver, where they worked in lumbering and mining and for railroads, making twelve times what they could in Punjab. Forty-three South Asians entered in 1904-1905 and 2,623 in 1907-1908. By 1908, the Asian Indian population in Canada had reached about 5,000, mostly Sikhs residing in Vancouver, whose objective was to return to Punjab wealthy and to buy land.

Because the numbers of Japanese and Asian Indians increased so rapidly and the bearded and turbaned Sikhs were highly visible, anti-Asian sentiment quickly developed. An agreement was reached with the Japanese government to stop emigration to Canada. The Sikhs presented a problem because placing restrictions on them would foster anti-British sentiment in colonized India. To end the influx of Sikhs, the Canadian government raised the head tax on immigrants from $25 to $200 and required all immigrants to arrive in Canada direct from their country of origin, without any intermediate stops, which was not possible for anyone sailing from India.

Some Sikhs challenged the regulations by chartering the *Komagata Maru* and sailing directly to Vancouver on April 4, 1914. Upon arrival, entry was denied to all except for twenty-two passengers who had proof of return domicile. After a period of turmoil, the remainder returned to Calcutta on September 27, 1914. Canada's color bar for immigration was established.

The Quiet Period

From 1909 to 1943, only 878 South Asians entered Canada, which did not compensate for the thousand-plus

---

Population Distribution for Canada, 1996

South Asian	670,590
Total Visible Minority	3,197,480
Total Population	28,528,125

Source: Census of Canada, 1996.

---

that left during the economic downturns between 1920 and 1930. Canadian law allowed immigrant men to return home for long periods of time (for example, to get married) and to bring their wives and any children under eighteen years of age to Canada; however, the difficulty of registering and manipulating the bureaucracy prohibited many wives and children from actually entering. Sikhs from Punjab remained the dominant group, and most of them lived in Vancouver. Their concerns, however, increasingly began to focus on Canada rather than their native India. They branched out into agriculture, and an entrepreneurial class developed. Some owned sawmills; others ran small businesses. The community changed from a group of men doing hard physical labor so that they could return to Punjab a *bara sahib* (big man or important person) to a community of families establishing themselves in Canada, making it their permanent home. *Gurdwaras* (Sikh places of worship) and cultural and religious organizations were founded. Some immigrants maintained their interest in their homeland and supported India's struggle for independence. Although they made Canada their home, the Sikhs were a minority and were discriminated against by white Canadians. These "unwanted foreigners" were sometimes refused service in stores, were denied the right to vote, and were suspected of being disloyal; their children were taunted by their classmates. However, they were able to survive, even during the economic decline of the 1930's, because they helped one another—Sikhs were seldom on welfare. It was during this period that Sikhs won the right to vote.

Policy Changes

After World War II, Canada became a world player and not only took on responsibilities such as helping refugees but also became an example in such areas as human rights. Consequently, the nation began to change its immigration policy, starting with the Immigration Act of 1947. The 1966 White Paper on immigration led to regulations introduced in 1967 that abolished all types of discrimination, promoted family reunification, and set up a point system for unsponsored immigrants. The Immigration Act of 1976 made it clear that Cana-

Educational Level and Occupations
of South Asian Canadians
(percent)

	South Asians	Total Canadian Population
Educational Level		
Secondary certificate or less	46.1	57.2
Trade certificate, diploma	32.8	28.5
University degree	21.1	14.3
Occupation		
Clerical	19.1	17.2
Professional	17.0	16.0
Service	11.5	12.7
Manufacturing and related	11.3	7.3
Managerial, administrative	9.5	7.9
Sales	7.7	9.9
Other	23.9	29.0

Source: Ronald D'Costa's "Socio-Demographic Characteristics of the Population of South Asian Origins in Canada," in *Ethnicity, Identity, Migration: The South Asian Context.* Milton Israel and N. K. Wagle, eds. Toronto: University of Toronto, Centre for South Asian Studies, 1993.

South Asians became Toronto, and the population was no longer dominated by Punjabi Sikhs but included Hindus, Muslims, Christians, Jains, Gujaratis, Keralites, Pakistanis, Sri Lankans, and Bangladeshis. These new arrivals stepped into mid- and high-level positions or quickly rose up. They were politically and socially astute. They benefited Canada by giving it some of the best talent the world had to offer and aided their homeland by sending remittances to relatives and enabling a transfer of technology.

Anti-Asian sentiment and violence broke out in Canada, especially in Toronto and Vancouver in the 1970's, but by the 1990's, Asian Indians in Canada were a prosperous minority and enjoyed a much higher level of acceptance than in previous decades.

Arthur W. Helweg

dian immigration policies would facilitate family reunification, employ nondiscriminatory admission standards, and fulfill Canada's humanitarian obligation to refugees.

The South Asians responded to each legislative change. Between 1945 and 1955, 1,139 South Asians were admitted; from 1956 to 1962, 4,088; and from 1963 to 1967, 12,856. After the 1967 change in immigration law, 30,501 Asian Indians entered between 1968 and 1972 and 57,411 between 1973 and 1977. In 1996, 235,930 of Canada's 4.9 million immigrants, or 4.8 percent, had been born in India.

Changes in the Immigrant Population

Under the new immigration laws, the characteristics of the South Asian and Asian Indian population in Canada changed. The 1967 legislation established a point system, giving preference to those with education and skills needed in Canada. South Asia, particularly India, had many highly educated medical doctors, engineers, scientists, and managers who quickly emigrated. Most were urban-oriented, English-speaking individuals from Delhi, Bombay, and Ahmedabad. They had been educated in a British-oriented system and were familiar with Western ways. Many brought their families with them.

The majority of these new immigrants were not part of the Sikh network and saw Toronto as the place of opportunity. Therefore, the center for Asian Indians and

Two Asian Indian girls stroll down a Toronto street. Many of the Asian Indians who settled in Canada after World War II settled in Toronto and other cities.

Core Resources

Hugh Tinker's *The Banyan Tree: Overseas Emigrants from India, Pakistan, and Bangladesh* (Oxford: Oxford University Press, 1977) is a brief synopsis of South Asia's overseas communities. *Continuous Journey: A Social History of South Asians in Canada* (Toronto: McClelland and Stewart Ltd., 1985), by Norman Buchignani and Doreen M. Indra, with Ram Srivastava, is a comprehensive social history of South Asians in Canada focusing on their struggle, growth, and adaptation to diverse communities throughout the country. S. Chandrasekhar's *From India to Canada: A Brief History of Immigration, Problems of Discrimination, Admission, and Assimilation* (La Jolla, Calif.: A Population Review Book, 1986) is a collection of articles on subjects ranging from regional settlements to occupation distribution of Asian Indians in Canada. Hugh Johnston's *The Voyage of the Komagata Maru: The Sikh Challenge to Canada's Colour Bar* (Delhi, India: Oxford University Press, 1979) is a superb account of a group of determined Sikh peasants who challenged Canada's discriminatory immigration policies.

See also: Asian Indians in the United States; Immigration law: Canada; *Komagata Maru* incident.

Asian Indians in the United States

> **Significance:** The more than one million people of Asian Indian origin or descent living in the United States have contributed significantly to their adopted nation. The Asian Indian community contains a large proportion of well-educated, affluent, highly motivated people.

Emigration from South Asia has been a dominant behavioral pattern since the Indus Valley civilization (2500-1700 B.C.E.). The impact of merchants and Buddhist missionaries from India is evident today in Central and East Asia, where Indian mythology, dance, and theater have had lasting effects. Movement from western India to Africa dates back to the second century C.E. Small-scale movement changed to mass emigration as Indians provided cheap labor for British colonies, many becoming indentured servants. The result was a diaspora of nine million Indians scattered throughout the British Empire but concentrated in places with labor-intensive economies, especially plantation systems, such as Mauritius, Fiji, Trinidad, and East Africa. Wide-scale migration to the United States, Australia, and Canada developed in the 1960's, largely because changes in immigration regulations removed existing racial barriers. The oil-rich Middle East has become a focus for South Asian immigration since 1970.

Coming to America

Initially, Asian Indians came to the United States as sea captains and traders in the 1790's, actively pursuing trade between India and North America. A very few came as indentured laborers. By 1900, the nation was home to about two thousand Indians, including about five hundred merchants, several dozen religious teachers, and some medical professionals. Six thousand Indians entered the United States through the West Coast between 1907 and 1917, but another three thousand were barred entry. Many of these immigrants came from Canada, where they had faced hostilities, only to meet with the same sort of treatment in the United States. Most immigrants from India during this period originated from Punjab and were adherents of the Sikh faith.

As Indian immigration increased, anti-Asian violence on the West Coast began to target Indians. Discriminatory laws were passed, prohibiting them from owning land and being eligible for U.S. citizenship. In fact, the Immigration Act of 1917 is sometimes referred to as the Indian Exclusion Act. The hostile environment, along with the Great Depression of the 1930's, resulted in several thousand immigrants returning to India. Therefore, in 1940, only 2,405 Asian Indians were living in the United States, mostly around Yuba City, California.

After World War II, new legislation gave Asian Indians the rights to become citizens and own land and established a quota of 100 immigrants per year, allowing for family reunification. Between 1948 and 1965, 6,474 Asian Indians entered the United States as immigrants. The Immigration and Nationality Act of 1965 removed the national origins clause in U.S. immigration legislation and gave preference to highly educated and skilled individuals. India had a ready pool of such talent, and the mass movement from India to the United States began. Sixty-seven percent of the foreign-born Asian Indians in the United States have advanced degrees, as opposed to only 25 percent of the American-born. In addition, Asian Indians are highly represented in the managerial and sales/technical/clerical workers and have low representation in the service, blue-collar categories.

The post-1965 immigrants fall into three categories: initial immigrants, second-wave immigrants, and sponsored immigrants. The initial immigrants, who came soon after restrictions were lifted in 1965, are mainly very highly educated men—doctors, scientists, and academics—who migrated for better educational and professional opportunities. By the 1990's, most of these immigrants, now middle-aged, were earning more than

Profile of Asian Indians in the United States

	1980	1990
Total Population	387,223	815,447
Percent under age 5	11.1	8.5
Percent age 18 years and older	69.9	70.04
Percent age 65 and older	8.0	2.8
Median age	29.6	28.9
Males per 100 females	99.8	116.0
Family Structures		
Percent of married-couple families	91.0	89.2
Percent of female householder, no husband	5.7	5.2
Percent of male householder, no wife present	3.4	5.6
Persons per family, average	3.45	3.83
Nativity, Citizenship, and Language		
Percent foreign born	70.4	75.4
Percent naturalized citizens	39.6	34.3
Percent of persons age 5 and older who speak a language other than English at home	68.9	77.8
Educational Attainment Among Those Age 25 and Older		
Percent high school graduates	80.1	84.7
Percent with four or more years of college	51.9	58.1
Labor Force Status Among Those Age 16 and Older		
Percent in labor force	65.4	72.3
Percent unemployed	5.8	5.6
Occupational Distribution, Percent		
Managerial and professional	48.5	43.6
Technical sales and administrative support	28.0	43.6
Service	7.8	8.1
Farming, forestry, and fishing	0.9	0.6
Precision production, craft, and repair	5.2	5.2
Operators, fabricators, and laborers	9.5	17.8
Income		
Median family, dollars	24,993	49,309
Median household, dollars	20,598	44,696
Per capita, dollars	8,667	17,777
Percent of families below the poverty level	7.4	7.4
Percent of individuals below the poverty level	10.6	9.7

Sources: Susan B. Gall and Timothy L. Gall, *Statistical Record of Asian Americans.* Detroit, Mich.: Gale Research, 1993; Padma Iyers Rangaswamy, *The Imperative of Choice and Change: Post-1965 Immigrants from India in Metropolitan Chicago.* Doctoral thesis. Chicago: University of Illinois at Chicago, 1996; and U.S. Census Bureau, 1980, 1990 Census.

$100,000 annually. Their wives typically had little more than a high school education and did not work outside the home, and their children were in their late teens or early twenties. This first wave of immigrants were concerned about retirement and their children. The second-wave immigrants, who came in the 1970's, were also highly educated professionals. However, these professionals tended to be couples, both of whom worked. Their children were mostly college-bound teenagers, and one of their main concerns was getting their children through college. The third group of immigrants were those individuals sponsored by established family members. They generally were less well educated and more likely to be running motels, small grocery stores, gas stations, and other ventures. Their concerns were to establish themselves in a successful business.

Profile
The Asian Indian population in the United States—which consisted of about 7,000 people in 1970—grew to about one million by the late 1990's, making them the fourth-largest immigrant group. This group reached 815,447 in 1990, a 111 percent rise since 1980, when they numbered 387,000. The percentage of foreign-born was up from 70 percent in 1980 to 75 percent in 1990. The community is, on the average, getting younger; the median age dropped from thirty years in 1980 to twenty-eight years in 1990. However, over the same period, the size of the elderly population increased. The gender balance has become more equitable as well: In 1966, women made up 34 percent of the population; in 1993, they accounted for 53 percent. In the mid-1990's, the mean family income of Asian Indians reached $59,777, the highest of any Asian group. In the 1980's, the trend to sponsor relatives was very strong, thus lowering the overall education and income levels of the community. By 1990, the number of individuals at

the poverty level had doubled, but they still represented about the same percentage of the whole population of Asian Indians.

The post-1965 immigrants flocked to the major metropolitan areas, where their skills were most marketable. By the mid-1990's, 70 percent of the Asian Indian population lived in eight major industrial-urban states: California, Illinois, Michigan, New Jersey, New York, Ohio, Pennsylvania, and Texas. However, the Asian Indians in the United States generally do not live in concentrated areas but are dispersed throughout the city. The vast majority speak English and are familiar with American ways, so they do not need to rely on their compatriots for help. In addition, because many of them are professionals, they are affluent enough to live where they choose.

The educational attainment of the Asian Indian population is very high: 73 percent of those age twenty-five or older have at least a high school education. A 1984 study showed that Asian Indians had a mean high school grade-point average of 3.8 on a scale of 4. Therefore, they form sizable proportions of the student bodies at the elite colleges in the United States. In 1998, they held more than five thousand faculty positions in American colleges and universities.

The Asian Indian population uses lobbying and campaign contributions to promote its special interests, which range from revisions of immigration policy to

Two Asian Indian women perform a Sikh Kathar, or story-telling dance, during a parade in New York City. The numbers of Asian Indians in the United States increased greatly during the last quarter of the twentieth century.

efforts to prevent or minimize Pakistan's military buildup.

One of the best-known areas of South Asian entrepreneurial behavior is the hotel and motel business. Hindus from the Gujarat region in India, most with the surname of Patel, began arriving in California in the late 1940's. They bought dilapidated hotels and motels in deteriorating neighborhoods and, with cheap family labor, turned the businesses into profitable enterprises. In the mid-1980's, the newsstand business in New York City was dominated by Indian and Pakistani immigrants

Asian Indian Businesses in the United States, by Type and Receipts, 1987

Type of Business	Receipts
Services	$2,917,588,000
Retail trade	$1,935,454,000
Finance, insurance, and real estate	$182,676,000
Transportation and public utilities	$158,605,000
Wholesale trade	$879,785,000
Construction	$177,070,000
Manufacturing	$241,067,000
Agricultural services, forestry, fishing, and mining	$21,349,000
Other industries	$201,090,000
Total	$6,714,684,000

Source: Susan B. Gall and Timothy L. Gall, eds., *Statistical Record of Asian Americans*. Detroit, Mich.: Gale Research, 1993.

who controlled 70 percent of the kiosks. However, ten years later, the Indians and Pakistanis were being replaced by immigrants from the Middle East. South Asians have also been prominently involved in laundries, gift shops, and the garment industry. In the early 1990's, 40 percent of the gas stations in New York City were owned by Punjabi Sikh immigrants.

India has benefited tremendously from emigration to the United States. Remittances, sent by immigrants to remaining family, have made areas such as Gujarat and Punjab relatively prosperous. Large amounts of capital from abroad have been invested in high technology, and new ideas from the United States and elsewhere are also evident. By the mid-1990's, many Asian Indians had returned from abroad to set up industries or work for international companies establishing a presence in India. The bicultural knowledge and skills of these returnees have contributed to Hyderabad's becoming the Silicon Valley of India. However, the impact is not limited to Hyderabad; it can be seen in Bombay, Calcutta, and Delhi as well as Punjab's prosperous agricultural Doab region. *Arthur W. Helweg*

Core Resources

Arthur W. Helweg and Usha M. Helweg's *An Immigrant Success Story: East Indians in the United States* (Philadelphia: University of Pennsylvania Press, 1990) is a comprehensive study of the Asian Indian community in the United States. Hugh Tinker's *A New System of Slavery: The Export of Indian Labour Overseas, 1830-1920* (Oxford, England: Oxford University Press, 1974) and *Separate and Unequal: India and the Indians in the British Commonwealth, 1820-1959* (Delhi: Vikas Publishing, 1976) chronicle South Asian migration. Bruce La Brack's *The Sikhs of Northern California 1904-1974* (New York: AMS Press, 1988) sets forth the development of the Sikh community in California.

See also: Asian Indians in Canada; Immigration Act of 1917; Immigration and Nationality Act of 1952; Sikhs in Canada; Sikhs in the United States.

Asian Pacific American Labor Alliance

Significance: A new labor-activist organization forms to address the needs of a growing Asian and Pacific Islander community in the United States.

On May 1, 1992, the Asian Pacific American Labor Alliance (APALA) held its founding convention in Washington, D.C. That gathering drew five hundred Asian, American, and Pacific Island unionists and laborers from around the United States, including garment factory workers from New York City, hotel and restaurant workers from Honolulu, longshore laborers from Seattle, nurses from San Francisco, and supermarket workers from Los Angeles. The establishment of the APALA was the culmination of several decades of Asian American unionization activity.

Unionizing

Since the mid-1970's, Asian American labor activists in California had worked to strengthen unionization attempts by holding organizational meetings in the larger Asian American communities within San Francisco and Los Angeles. Through the efforts of such neighborhood-based organizations as the Alliance of Asian Pacific Labor (AAPL), stronger ties between labor and the community were forged, and Asian union staff members were united more closely with rank-and-file labor leaders. Those too-localized efforts of the Alliance of Asian Pacific Labor, however, failed to organize significant numbers of Asian American workers. In order to begin unionizing on the national level, AAPL administrators, led by Art Takei, solicited organizational aid from the American Federation of Labor-Congress of Industrial Organizations (AFL-CIO), a key U.S. labor collective.

Upon the invitation of the AFL-CIO executive board, AAPL vice president Kent Wong attended the 1989 national AFL-CIO convention in Washington, D.C., to lobby for the establishment of a national labor organization for Americans of Asian and Pacific Island descent. In addressing Wong's request, AFL-CIO president Lane Kirkland acknowledged the local accomplishments of the AAPL in California and recognized the organizing potential of the growing Asian American workforce. In 1991, Kirkland appointed a national Asian Pacific American labor committee. This group of thirty-seven Asian and American labor activists met for more than a year to create the Asian Pacific American Labor Alliance. In planning for the 1992 convention, the Asian Pacific American labor committee released a nationwide invitation for Asian, American, and Pacific Island unionists, labor activists, and workers to gather in Washington, D.C., to take on the responsibility for bridging the gap between the national labor movement and the Asian Pacific American community.

APALA Is Born

The response to that invitation exceeded the committee's expectations. At the May 1, 1992, convention, more than five hundred delegates participated in adopting an Asian Pacific American Labor Alliance constitution and in setting up a governmental structure with a national headquarters in Washington, D.C., and local chapters throughout the United States. Organized in this manner, the APALA could receive recognition and control from a national administration guided by the AFL-CIO, while still using its powerful techniques of community organization at the local level.

During the convention, APALA organizers and delegates recognized and honored Asian Pacific American labor pioneers whose achievements they believed had melded national and local unionization efforts successfully. Among them was Philip Vera Cruz, the eighty-seven-year-old former vice president of the United Farm Workers Union. Vera Cruz had worked since the 1930's to create local unions for farmworkers in the southwestern United States, and continuously lobbied for national support of farmworkers' unionization.

With an eye toward the future, APALA drafted a Commitment to Organizing, to Civil Rights, and to Economic Justice, which called for empowerment of all Asian and Pacific American workers through unionization on a national level; it also called for the provision of national support for individual, local unionization efforts. The APALA also promoted the formation of AFL-CIO legislation that would create jobs, ensure national health insurance, reform labor law, and channel financial resources toward education and job training for Asian and Pacific Island immigrants. Toward that end, the group called for a revision of U.S. governmental policies toward immigration. APALA's commitment document supported immigration legislation that would promote family unification and provide improved immigrant access to health, education, and social services. Finally, the document promoted national government action to prevent workplace discrimination against immigrant laborers; vigorous prosecution for perpetrators of racially motivated crimes was strongly supported. To solidify their commitment, APALA delegates passed several resolutions, which they forwarded to the AFL-CIO leadership. These documents decried the exploitative employment practices and civil rights violations alleged against several United States companies.

Convention delegates also participated in workshops that focused on individual roles in facilitating multicultural harmony and solidarity, enhancing Asian American participation in unions, and advancing a national agenda to support more broadly based civil rights legislation and improved immigration policies and procedures. From these APALA convention workshops, two national campaigns were launched. The first involved working with the AFL-CIO Organizing Institute to recruit a new generation of Asian Pacific American organizers, both at the national and local levels. The second campaign involved building a civil and immigration rights agenda for Asian Pacific American workers, based upon APALA's commitment document and its convention resolutions.

Through the legislative statement of its goals and in lobbying for their substantive societal implementation, the Asian Pacific American Labor Alliance was the first Asian American labor organization to achieve both national and local success. Although by the time of the 1992 APALA convention Asian Americans had been engaged in various forms of unionization activity for more than 150 years, establishment of APALA within the ranks of the AFL-CIO provided it with more powerful organizational techniques. The Asian Pacific American Labor Alliance was able to solidly unite Asian Pacific workers, simultaneously integrating them into the larger U.S. labor movement.

Thomas J. Edward Walker and Cynthia Gwynne Yaudes

Core Resources

Sharolyn Rosier's "Solidarity Starts Cycle for APALA," in *AFL-CIO News* (37, no. 10, May 11, 1992), summarizes the AFL-CIO conference report on the establishment of the Asian Pacific American Labor Alliance. Kent Wong's "Building Unions in Asian Pacific Communities," in *Amerasia Journal* (18, no. 3, 1992), assesses the difficulties of Asian American unionization and gives suggestions for overcoming those problems.

The State of Asian America: Activism and Resistance in the 1990s (edited by Karin Aguilar-San Juan, Boston, Mass.: South End Press, 1994) explores the connection between race, identity, and empowerment within the workplace and the community. Chris Friday's *Organizing Asian American Labor* (Philadelphia: Temple University Press, 1994) analyzes the positive impact of Asian Pacific immigration upon the formation of industries on the West Coast and in the Pacific Northwest between 1870 and 1942.

See also: Employment among Asian Americans; Labor movement.

Assimilation: cultural and structural

Significance: Sociologist Milton Gordon made a major contribution to assimilationist theory by clearly distinguishing two types of assimilation: cultural assimilation, sometimes referred to as acculturation, and structural assimilation, which refers to the integration of minority groups into all aspects of social life.

According to Milton Gordon in *Assimilation in American Life* (1964), the study of how groups are incorporated into American society has been plagued by two major problems. First, the American legal system does not distinguish groups on the basis of race, religion, or nationality. Instead, all individuals are simply considered Americans. In contrast, Gordon says, the social reality is that there are distinct subgroups in American society, organized and identified on the basis of race, religion, and nationality. Because the legal system ignores this, the reality is hidden.

The second problem that Gordon defined lies in the manner in which the social sciences have dealt with the reality of diversity in American life. Gordon claims that social scientists before him focused primarily on the cultural behavior of individuals and groups and on studying the extent to which various ethnic racial groups had adopted the values and behavior of the dominant group in society, Anglo-Americans. They also focused on studying the attitudes of the dominant group, examining the extent and basis of racial prejudice. This is problematic, according to Gordon, because it ignores the issue of how so many diverse groups are incorporated into the social structure. Furthermore, neither social scientists nor policymakers have made clear what the goals of assimilation are—whether the United States would like to see total assimilation into one culture (a "melting pot" composed of a blend of cultures) or whether groups should maintain distinct cultures (a view sometimes referred to as cultural pluralism). To Gordon, the major question is: What is the impact of racial, religious, and national diversity on social relations and social institutions in a democratic industrial society such as the United States? To answer this question, Gordon argued, sociologists must clearly define assimilation and the various types of outcomes that might emerge from intergroup contact. Consideration of both cultural issues and the social structure must be included.

Gordon was the first to distinguish assimilation from acculturation and to propose two distinct types of assimilation: cultural assimilation (or acculturation) and structural assimilation. Generally, acculturation requires a change of culture on the part of the out-group in order to adapt to the dominant group. Structural assimilation requires that the out-group enter into the clubs, groups, and social institutions of the core group, thereby establishing primary relationships with individuals in the core. Ultimately, total assimilation implies that there are no cultural differences and that out-groups can no longer be distinguished from anyone else.

Seven Steps of Assimilation

Gordon defines total assimilation as a process that may require seven steps toward its ultimate conclusion, the blended society. Step one is *acculturation*, in which an ethnic group changes its cultural patterns to those of the core group (also referred to as Anglo-conformity). Step two is *structural assimilation*, in which the out-group establishes primary relations with the core group and enters the social structure of the core. The third step is *marital assimilation*, in which the out-group intermarries with members of the core and produces children. Step four is *identification assimilation*, in which ethnic groups identify with the core instead of their ancestral ethnic group. The fifth step is *attitude-receptional assimilation*, in which the core is no longer prejudiced against members of the out-group. Step six is *behavior-receptional assimilation*, in which the core stops discriminating against members of the out-group, and step seven is *civic assimilation*, in which the out-group has no value conflicts with the core group over governance.

According to Gordon, although acculturation is likely to be the first step, it may take place without leading to the other steps toward total assimilation. A group may acculturate itself to the norms of the dominant group without that acculturation being followed by any further acceptance or integration for a prolonged period of time. In other words, a group's successful acculturation neither guarantees its entry into the subsociety of the core nor guarantees that the core group will stop being prejudiced toward them or discriminating against them. Thus, the process of total assimilation requires cooperation from both sides: The entering group must adapt itself to the core group, and the core group must come to accept the entering group and treat its members on the basis of their individual merit rather than on the basis of their ethnic, religious, or national heritage.

Anglo-conformity

Gordon applied his seven-stage theory of assimilation to an analysis of several diverse ethnic, religious, and racial groups in American society to examine variations in the assimilation process. Generally, he believed that the mode of acculturation in the United States is one of Anglo-conformity. In other words, if groups are to be considered acculturated, they must conform to the behavioral patterns and norms of those whose ancestors migrated from England. In fact, he believed that Anglo-conformity had largely been achieved in terms of acculturation. Gordon said that acculturation was very successful with the children of immigrants because of their immediate contact with public schools and the mass media. When acculturation was weak, as in the case of American Indians and African Americans, he claimed that factors existed that retarded the process of acculturation for these groups, that acculturation was still happening, but at a slower pace. In the case of American Indians, their ongoing ethnic identification with ancestral tradition, coupled with their isolation on reservations and special status as sovereign nations, mitigated against acculturation. Gordon said that, for African Americans in the rural South, slavery and the long years of exploitation and discrimination which followed had led to the development of a subculture whose behaviors and values were so distant from Anglo culture that prejudice and discrimination remained intense. For those African Americans who migrated to urban industrial centers, acculturation was also retarded because of prejudice and discrimination.

Generally, however, despite the failures of some groups to move speedily through the assimilation process, Gordon maintained the belief that assimilation would eventually occur. To the extent that he saw the development of a black middle class, he saw barriers breaking down, providing evidence that discrimination would have only a delaying effect on assimilation.

Education and Desegregation
Contemporary applications of Gordon's theory have diverged, in part, from the earlier ideological concepts that called for Anglo-conformity. This can be seen particularly in the area of education. Curriculum reform has been directed toward multicultural education, with its goal of appreciating diversity. Many educators argue that when individuals come to appreciate the contributions that various ethnic, racial, and religious groups have made to American society, they will come to appreciate and identify with one another. This is seen as an important step toward ending prejudice and discrimination. At the same time, however, many educators stress that it is important for immigrant children to learn English—an important step, Gordon acknowledged, toward acculturation on the basis of Anglo-conformity.

School desegregation programs also can be interpreted as applications of Gordon's concepts of acculturation and structural assimilation. Many—not all—social scientists argue that when children of different racial and ethnic backgrounds can go to school together, play sports together, and know one another intimately, they will grow up without prejudice and discrimination. Furthermore, school desegregation programs are expected to break down the isolation of groups. Residence has remained distinctly organized around race (in particular) and ethnicity. School busing programs, many of which were instituted in the 1970's and 1980's, promoted desegregation and structural assimilation by forcing children across the boundaries of their racial or ethnic communities. In many cases, these programs have operated without the support or cooperation of the core subsociety—Anglo-Americans.   *Sharon Elise*

Core Resources
Milton Gordon, in his *Assimilation in American Life* (New York: Oxford University Press, 1964), assesses previous

theories of assimilation and explains his own seven-stage theory of assimilation, distinguishing between cultural and structural assimilation as well as giving three models of assimilation outcomes: Anglo-conformity, the melting pot, and cultural pluralism. Robert Blauner, in his *Racial Oppression in America* (New York: Harper & Row, 1972), criticizes assimilationist theories and counters their focus on race prejudice with an analysis of racial privilege as embedded in a system of internal colonialism. David Wellman, in his *Portraits of White Racism* (New York: Cambridge University Press, 1977), presents an excellent critique of assimilationist perspectives on race relations, offering his own theory of white racism to counter the notion that prejudice is responsible for discrimination.

See also: Anglo-conformity; Assimilation: cultural and structural; Assimilation theories; Attitude-receptional assimilation; Behavior-receptional assimilation; Civic assimilation; Cultural pluralism; Discrimination: racial and ethnic; Identification assimilation; Marital assimilation; Melting pot theory; Prejudice and discrimination: Merton's paradigm; Race relations cycle; Racial/ethnic relations: theoretical overview; Structural assimilation.

Assimilation theories

> **Significance:** Assimilation refers to the process by which individuals or groups take on the culture of the dominant society, including language, values, and behavior, as well as the process by which groups are incorporated into the dominant society. The melting pot theory and Anglo-conformity are two models of assimilation.

Assimilationist theories suggest that the outcome of race and ethnic relations in society is assimilation: the ultimately harmonious blending of differing ethnic groups into one homogeneous society. A key question that emerges among assimilationist theorists concerns the basis of that homogeneity. The melting pot theory holds that distinct groups will each contribute to the building of a new culture and society that is a melting pot of all their differing values and behaviors, and the Anglo-conformity theory holds that (in North America) the varying groups will all adopt the values and behaviors of the dominant, Anglo-Saxon group.

Anglo-conformity
According to Milton Gordon in his book *Assimilation in American Life* (1964), assimilation involves both acculturation and structural assimilation, wherein groups are

fully incorporated into, and indistinguishable from, the larger society. Cultural assimilation, or acculturation, however, can proceed in either a melting pot pattern or an Anglo-conformity pattern. Gordon, who attributes the Anglo-conformity thesis to Stewart Cole, states that this pattern requires that immigrants completely abandon their cultural heritage in favor of Anglo-Saxon culture. According to Gordon, those who propose Anglo-conformity as a viable ideal of assimilation view the maintenance of the English language, institutions, and culture as desirable. Such views, in his estimation, are related to nativist programs that promote the inclusion of those immigrants who are most like the English as well as to programs that promote the acceptance of any immigrants willing to acculturate on the basis of Anglo-conformity. According to Gordon, those espousing the Anglo-conformity ideal cannot be automatically labeled racist although, as he puts it, all racists in the United States can be called Anglo-conformists. Furthermore, Anglo-conformists tend to assume that English ways and institutions are better than others. Even those who do not support that view argue that these ways and institutions, regardless of their relative merit, do predominate in existing American society. Therefore, newcomers must adapt to what is already in place. Anglo-conformists also assume that once immigrants have acculturated based on Anglo-conformity, they will be found acceptable and will no longer be the targets of prejudice and discrimination.

Melting Pot

Although the Anglo-conformity ideal has been the prevalent form of assimilation proposed, the melting pot ideal has also been an important and influential aspect of assimilationist thought. Particularly in the early twentieth century, those who viewed American society as a new experiment in which diverse peoples came together to forge a new culture saw Americans as a new "race" of people. In this view, the United States was a giant melting pot that received all immigrants, melting them—and their cultures—down into one homogeneous and unique group.

The melting pot theory of assimilationist theory was implied by sociologist Robert Ezra Park's theory of the race relations cycle, suggested in the 1920's. In that theory, Park presented the idea that assimilation involves both cultural and biological processes. In other words, Park conceived of assimilation as accomplished both by the "interpenetration" of distinct cultures, in which each group takes on some of the other's culture, and by amalgamation, or biological mixing through intermarriage and reproduction.

Gordon criticizes melting pot idealists for failing to discuss whether all groups can contribute equally to the final mixture. Furthermore, since Anglo-Saxons arrived chronologically before other immigrants, they were able to establish the social order into which newer immigrants are expected to "melt." Because of this difference in group influence on the American character and society, Gordon claims that the melting pot ideal masks the fact that non-Anglo-Saxons are the ones expected to change. Furthermore, although some differences, such as nationality, can be melted down among whites, other differences, such as race and religion, are either not willingly given up or cannot be melted away. Blacks and other people of color, according to Gordon, are prevented from melting down by racial discrimination.

Other Theories and Criticisms

In their book *Beyond the Melting Pot*, Nathan Glazer and Daniel Patrick Moynihan review the melting pot theory in the light of continuing ethnic diversity and conflict in New York City. Glazer and Moynihan believed that ethnic groups could join society if they were willing to change, to acculturate. Unlike Gordon, Glazer and Moynihan do not view prejudice as the major obstacle to assimilation. They view internal group weaknesses as the major obstacle; they also cite the lack of a single American identity for immigrants to adopt. Glazer and Moynihan think that ethnic groups develop a new ethnic identity, thus remaining distinct—neither melted down nor conforming to the Anglo model.

In his 1981 book, *The Ethnic Myth*, Stephen Steinberg states that the early rise of nativism in the United States implies that Anglo-conformity dominated assimilationist views. Nativism refers to the desire to maintain the given ethnic character of society or particular social institutions. Generally, nativists see themselves as the real Americans and are xenophobic, or fearful and hateful of foreigners. Anglo-Saxon settlers wished to preserve their cultural legacy in the face of massive immigration that labor shortages forced them to tolerate. Perhaps one of the greatest instruments for Anglo-conformity has been the centralized system of public education that was developed in the United States. Immigrants were and are taught English language skills, as well as citizenship, and are thus Americanized. According to Gordon, other forms of Anglo-conformity assimilation include political movements by nativists to exclude "foreigners" from social institutions, favoring immigration only by people similar in background and culture to Anglo-Saxons, and basing social inclusion on the adoption of Anglo-Saxon culture by immigrants.

Park, who supported the melting pot theory, held that the melting pot would emerge through amalgamation—accomplished through intermarriage across lines of ethnicity. Intermarriage then becomes an important measure of the extent to which groups are merging into one homogeneous group. Studies of intermarriage reveal that ethnic groups, in particular, are marrying across group lines, though not always across religious or racial lines. For example, intermarriage has increased substantially between Jews and non-Jews, although in-marriage is still strong for Italian Americans and Irish Americans. Intermarriage still tends to be culturally prohibited across racial lines, reflecting important differences between race and ethnicity that melting pot theorists tended to downplay in their analyses.

Assimilationist theorists generally have not distinguished race from ethnicity. They have not ignored the significant differences between the levels of assimilation of white ethnic groups and groups of other races; they explain them either as a product of the greater prejudice held against people who look different or as a product of the failure of nonwhite minorities to conform to and embrace the dominant culture. Assimilationist theorists view prejudice as the product of the differences that minority group members present to the dominant society. As group members acculturate, these differences diminish, and the people are accepted by the dominant society. They then no longer experience discrimination.

Sharon Elise

Core Resources

Milton Gordon's *Assimilation in American Life* (New York: Oxford University Press, 1964) presents the author's theory of assimilation, with chapters devoted to the Anglo-conformity model and the melting pot model. Stephen Steinberg's *The Ethnic Myth* (New York: Atheneum, 1981) reexamines ethnicity in the light of economic organization and the class structure. Nathan Glazer and Daniel Patrick Moynihan's *Beyond the Melting Pot* (2d ed., Cambridge, Mass.: MIT Press, 1970) is a controversial book that presents studies of blacks, Jews, Puerto Ricans, Italians, and Irish Americans in New York to re-examine the melting pot thesis. Robert Blauner's *Racial Oppression in America* (New York: Harper & Row, 1972) begins with a criticism of predominant trends in the sociology of race relations, particularly assimilationist theories, and counters their focus on race prejudice with an analysis of racial privilege as embedded in a system of internal colonialism. Joe R. Feagin and Clairece Booher Feagin's *Racial and Ethnic Relations* (4th ed., Englewood Cliffs, N.J.: Prentice-Hall, 1993) is an introductory text in the sociology of race relations that examines sociological theories against the background of extensive case history of both white ethnic groups and ethnic groups of other races.

See also: Anglo-conformity; Assimilation: cultural and structural; Attitude-receptional assimilation; Behavior-receptional assimilation; Civil assimilation; Ethnicity and ethnic groups; Identification assimilation; Interracial and interethnic marriage; Marital assimilation; Melting pot theory; Moynihan Report; Nativism; Race relations cycle; Racial/ethnic relations: theoretical overview.

Atlanta Compromise

Significance: Booker T. Washington's controversial advocacy of accommodationism had a major influence on African American political and economic strategies.

Booker T. Washington, born a slave on a small Virginia plantation, gained his freedom at the end of the Civil War in 1865. He learned to read by studying spelling books and occasionally attending a school for African American children. In 1872, Washington enrolled at Hampton Institute in Virginia, a technical and agricultural school established for emancipated slaves. After graduation, he taught in Malden, West Virginia, then later returned to Hampton Institute.

In May, 1881, Washington received an invitation to join a group of educators from Tuskegee, Alabama, to help establish a technical and agricultural college for African American students. Tuskegee Institute opened on July 4, 1881, with Washington as its principal. Washington raised funds, acquired land, supervised the construction of buildings, and recruited talented faculty members. Within a decade, the school had gained a national reputation for providing outstanding technical and occupational training for African American students.

In the spring of 1895, Washington was invited to join a planning committee for the forthcoming Atlanta Cotton States and International Exposition, which would highlight the South's most recent developments in agricultural technology. Washington was asked to deliver one of the key addresses during the exposition's opening ceremonies, a speech that would focus on the role of African Americans in the South's agricultural economy.

The Address

Washington delivered his Atlanta Exposition address on September 18, 1895, to an audience of several thousand listeners. He opened by thanking the directors of the Atlanta Exposition for including African Americans in the event and expressing his hope that the exposition would do more to "cement the friendship of the two races than any occurrence since the dawn of our freedom."

Washington went on to predict that the exposition would awaken among both white and black southerners

Booker T. Washington, a major African American leader during the late nineteenth century, delivered an address in Atlanta, Georgia, in which he advocated accommodationism.

"a new era of industrial progress." He illustrated his point by telling a parable of a ship lost at sea whose crew members were desperate for fresh water. The captain of another ship, hearing the pleas for water by the captain of the distressed vessel, urged the lost sailors, "Cast down your bucket where you are." When the captain of the lost ship followed that advice, his crew members brought aboard sparkling fresh water from the Amazon River.

Washington then urged his African American listeners to cast down their buckets "in agriculture, mechanics, in commerce, in domestic service, and in the professions." He said that African Americans would prosper "in proportion as we learn to dignify and glorify common labour and put brains and skill into the common occupations of life." He added that "no race can prosper till it learns that there is as much dignity in tilling a field as in writing a poem."

Washington also told his white listeners to cast down their buckets among the South's African Americans, "who have, without strikes and labour wars, tilled your fields, cleared your forests, built your railroads and cities, and brought forth treasures from the bowels of the earth, and helped make possible this magnificent representation of the progress of the South." He encouraged white Southerners to educate African Americans in "head, heart, and hand" so that they would remain "the most patient, faithful, law-abiding, and unresentful people that the world has seen." He asserted that in "all things purely social we can be as separate as the fingers, yet one as the hand in all things essential to mutual progress."

Washington concluded his speech by expressing his belief that the "wisest among my race understand that the agitation of questions of social equality is the extremest folly, and that progress in the enjoyment of all the privileges that will come to us must be the result of severe and constant struggle rather than of artificial forcing." He emphasized that African Americans must achieve economic self-reliance before they received "all the privileges of the law."

Washington's address was enthusiastically received by those present and the press. President Grover Cleveland wrote a congratulatory note. Washington received dozens of invitations to speak around the country and deliver his pragmatic message of economic self-reliance and political accommodationism.

Critics

Nevertheless, critics of Washington's philosophy soon surfaced, accusing Washington of making an unsatisfactory compromise by accepting an inferior social and political position for African Americans in exchange for economic opportunities. These critics argued that the tools for economic independence alone would not lead African Americans toward full citizenship and that the widespread segregation of and discrimination against African Americans in the United States, especially in the South, was proof of the flaws of Washington's reasoning.

Perhaps the most eloquent critic of Washington's message was W. E. B. Du Bois. In *The Souls of Black Folk* (1903), Du Bois, who would later found the National Association for the Advancement of Colored People (NAACP), asserted that Washington "represents in Negro thought the old attitude of adjustment and submission," that the ideas expressed in what he called Washington's "Atlanta Compromise" were merely "a gospel of Work and Money" that prompted African Americans to surrender political power, civil rights, and opportunities for higher education. In contrast to Washington, Du Bois advocated that African Americans receive the right to vote, civic equality, and opportunities for higher academic education, as opposed to the kind of occupational training offered at Tuskegee Institute.   *James Tackach*

Core Resources

Two biographies of Booker T. Washington that discuss the Atlanta address are Louis R. Harlan's *Booker T. Washington: The Making of a Black Leader, 1856-1901* (New York: Oxford University Press, 1972) and Arna Bontemps's *Young Booker: Booker T. Washington's Early Days* (New York: Dodd, Mead, 1972). Booker T. Washington's *Up from Slavery* (1901; reprint, New York: Bantam Books, 1970) contains the entire address and a discussion of the events surrounding it. In his *The Souls of Black Folk* (1903; reprint, New York: Penguin Books, 1989), W. E. B. Du Bois critiques the ideas expressed in Washington's Atlanta Exposition address.

See also: Accommodationism; Education and African Americans; National Association for the Advancement of Colored People.

Attitude-receptional assimilation

Attitude-receptional assimilation, as described by Milton Gordon in *Assimilation in American Life* (1964), is the fifth of his seven stages of assimilation of minority or immigrant groups into a host society's dominant culture. Attitude-receptional assimilation results in the lack of prejudice against a racial/ethnic subgroup or minority. This process occurs in varying degrees during the assimilation process. Gordon suggests that prejudice is a result of differences in extrinsic cultural traits such as manners, dialect, and expression rather than of differences in intrinsic cultural traits such as religion, historical language, and values. Lack of prejudice is mostly likely to precede the next stage of assimilation, behavior-receptional assimilation (lack of intentional discrimination), or this relationship can be opposite in direction. Gordon also suggests that attitude-receptional assimilation may occur during acculturation but not structural assimilation. For example, attitude-receptional assimilation is completed to a greater degree in the assimilation of certain European ethnic groups such as the Irish than it is in the assimilation of American Indians. One possible reason for this difference is that the latter group, in contrast to the Irish, maintains different extrinsic traits for political and demographic reasons, and that behavioral-receptional assimilation is less for American Indians than for the Irish because of the establishment of separate nation-states for American Indians.

Attitude reception, in Bill McGuire's reception-yielding model (*The Psychology of Attitudes*, 1993), is the likelihood of a change in attitude such as a reduction of prejudice. It is defined as a product of the probability of reception (how focused or distracted the person is) and the probability of the person's yielding to the information received (which is affected by the use of appeals involving fear and other factors). The relative weight of each variable depends upon the persuasion context, which involves elements such as the mode of communication. In addition, reception is related to the characteristics of the recipient such as verbal intelligence.

Francis C. Staskon

See also: Anglo-conformity; Assimilation: cultural and structural; Assimilation theories; Behavior-receptional assimilation; Civic assimilation; Identification assimilation; Marital assimilation; Prejudice: reduction; Structural assimilation.

Authoritarian personality theory

Significance: The theory that an identifiable personality type, termed the authoritarian personality by Theodor Adorno and his colleagues, was especially susceptible to racism gained popularity in the early 1950's. The study that produced the theory was trying to account for the rise of Nazism and the perpetration of the Holocaust in 1930's and 1940's Germany.

The idea of the authoritarian personality was conceived by a group of social scientists and was developed to try to explain behavior of extraordinary social importance. The behavior, a widespread German willingness, prior to World War II, to embrace an extreme form of fascism, was of intensely personal importance to two of the researchers: They had fled Germany and come to the United States to save their lives.

The personality that Theodor Adorno and his colleagues described in *The Authoritarian Personality* (1950) is a prefascist personality. Their choice of the label "authoritarian" could have been better made, since a dictionary definition of the term covers only a small part of the personality syndrome (collection of characteristics) they revealed. Through questionnaires and scales, Adorno's group studied their subjects' anti-Semitic ideology, politico-economic ideology, ethnocentrism, religious attitudes and practices, and other related topics. Through clinical interviews and projective testing, they evaluated their subjects' personalities in considerable depth. The personality type they came to call authoritarian is a complex one, and those who display it are troubled individuals, often coping with society's demands in ugly and dangerous ways.

F-scale

Adorno and his colleagues developed the F-scale to measure the degree to which respondents display authoritarianism. The person who measures high on the scale is extreme on many, if not all, of the following characteristics. The person may exhibit *conventionalism*, a rigid adherence to conventional middle-class values. The person may show both *authoritarian submission*, a submissive, uncritical attitude toward idealized moral authorities of the in-group, and *authoritarian aggression*, a tendency to look for and condemn, reject, and punish people who violate conventional values. *Anti-intraception* is opposition to the subjective, the imaginative, and the tender-minded. *Superstition and stereotypy* are the belief in mystical determinants of an individual's fate and a disposition to think in rigid categories. *Power and toughness* refer to a preoccupation with the dominance-submission, strong-weak, leader-follower dimension. This aspect of the authoritarian personality includes identification with power figures and an exaggerated assertion of strength and toughness. *Destructiveness and cynicism* mean a generalized hostility and vilification of the human. *Projectivity* is the disposition to believe that wild and dangerous things go on in the world; it represents the projection of unconscious emotional impulses. Finally, the authoritarian personality may show an exaggerated concern with the sexual activities of others. The *high authoritarian* is an anxious, often confused person who sees threats where others would see only minor concerns and who favors drastic actions to protect against those threats.

Researchers investigating the authoritarian personality in the 1950's found people in the United States who displayed the same authoritarian characteristics that were found among Nazis, a situation that prompted considerable concern. Individuals that test high on the authoritarian scale, in fact, can be found in virtually every society. It was the Jewish population that was the prime target of high authoritarians in Nazi Germany. In the United States, African Americans, Latinos, Asian Americans, and any other racial or ethnic group that can be identified may be the target of the high authoritarian.

Dogmatism

The syndrome labeled "the authoritarian personality" was identified originally as a basis for the development of fascism, but it soon became evident that political ideology was a coincidental factor. Racism, sexism, ethnocentrism, and other fanatical forms of behavior can flourish within almost any political framework. Milton Rokeach proposed an apolitical variation of authoritarianism, which he called "dogmatism," to address this issue.

Rokeach had noticed that members of Communist Party cells in the United States, at a time when communism was seen as the ultimate evil, scored low on authoritarianism. Seeking a reason for this counterintuitive finding, Rokeach concluded that because the communist political system was in many ways opposed to the fascist system, the extremism of the U.S. communists was concealed. Political references on the F-Scale had pushed respondents toward nonauthoritarian choices. Rokeach developed a test, the D-Scale, to measure a more general, apolitical version of authoritarianism he called "dogmatism." He found, as he expected, that communist extremists scored high.

An interesting question within authoritarianism theory remains unanswered: Do high authoritarians' dysfunctional personalities influence all that they do, or are they capable of dealing with some topics with average rationality? For example, is the racist whose actions are heavily influenced by authoritarianism capable of political or religious rationality? Research that correlates average F-Scale or D-Scale scores with measures of racism conceals individual differences of this sort. Anecdotal accounts and informal observation often suggest that some people can display strongly authoritarian characteristics in one circumstance and virtually none of them in another. The fanatical racist may have moderate religious views, the political fanatic may show no animosity toward minorities, and so on.

Criticism

Critics of the related concepts of authoritarianism and dogmatism have called attention to a seemingly simpler concept that may explain the behaviors of those who score high on the F-Scale. Most, perhaps all, of the characteristics identified in the early research on the authoritarian personality can be found in highly anxious people. Two of the characteristics or aspects of them—projectivity and identification—are identical to ego defense mechanisms stated by Sigmund Freud to be ways people combat anxiety. Although the terminology is a bit different, several of the other characteristics also accomplish the basic purpose of Freudian defense mechanisms.

Probably the most reasonable way to relate anxiety to authoritarianism is to suggest that developing these personally protective but societally damaging characteristics is but one of several ways people may cope with anxiety. Some resolve anxiety-producing conflicts directly; this is presumed by most psychologists to be the healthiest approach. Some develop neurotic, perhaps even psychotic, patterns of behavior. Probably a few withdraw from society or from life itself as suicides. Developing an authoritarian personality protects a person well, but at a high and often hidden cost to society.

Authoritarian personality theory offers an interesting, research-based explanation of racism to complement the many other explanations that the behavioral sciences have offered. Unfortunately, it provides few suggestions of how racism may be reduced or eliminated; those that have been proposed work in conjunction with other explanations of the phenomenon. The theory can offer a few suggestions because, at least in its original form, it indicates that individuals who can be identified as high authoritarians have developed their dysfunctional personalities over a lifetime. They are very unlikely to change, even with extended counseling. Further, they are unlikely to feel a need to change; their barely rational beliefs protect them to a much greater degree than they cause them discomfort. It is other people who experience the discomfort.

Stress and High Authoritarians
Most of the identified characteristics of high authoritarianism become more extreme under stress, and high authoritarians are likely to be seriously stressed by many circumstances that other people can tolerate. Some of the ways in which an understanding of the nature of the authoritarian personality can be used to moderate racism rely on minimizing stress in the potential racist. Too often, however, nothing can be done about the sources of the stress; at best, behavioral scientists can suggest ways to limit its consequences.

Because high authoritarians think in rigid categories, they especially need reassurance and rational direction by strong leaders during unsettling times to minimize the likelihood of their becoming involved in extreme actions. For example, during bad economic times for which there are no easy-to-understand causes, leaders ideally should state that the bad times will not last forever, that they are caused by factors that the nation can discover and correct, and that no villains are responsible—no one should be sought out and attacked. Such statements would offer some stress reduction and would discourage people from seeking scapegoats. All people would benefit from such leadership; high authoritarians require it. Unfortunately, agitation or irrational, emotional direction can prompt high authoritarians to extreme action. Some leaders, including Adolf Hitler, have gained considerable power by taking advantage of high authoritarians' vulnerability.   *Harry A. Tiemann, Jr.*

Core Resources
T. W. Adorno, E. Frenkel-Brunswick, D. Levinson, and R. Sanford's *The Authoritarian Personality* (New York: Harper Brothers, 1950) is the source of the concept of the authoritarian personality and of the F-Scale devised to measure it. Milton Rokeach's *The Open and Closed Mind* (New York: Basic Books, 1960) documents a decade of research since the publication of *The Authoritarian Personality* and provides broad coverage of extremist behavior, heavily overlapping that of Adorno and his colleagues. *Cracks in the Melting Pot: Racism and Discrimination in American History* (compiled by Melvin Steinfield, Beverly Hills, Calif.: Glencoe, 1970) covers topics such as racism and discrimination in other countries, anti-Indian policies, the Mexican War, and presidential racism.

See also: Anti-Semitism; Holocaust; Psychology of racism.

B

Bakke case

Allan Bakke had applied to the medical school of the University of California at Davis, but he was not among the one hundred applicants finally accepted by the school. Pursuant to university policy, sixteen of the hundred slots had been reserved for racial minority students. Bakke, who was white, claimed that since he was better qualified than some of the applicants accepted for the sixteen minority positions, the university had discriminated against him on the basis of race.

The California Supreme Court ruled in favor of Bakke, and the case was appealed to the U.S. Supreme Court. The case drew national attention, attracting a record-breaking number of *amicus curiae* briefs. On June 28, 1978, the Court, sharply divided, issued its decision in favor of Bakke. In a 5 to 4 vote, the Court held that the University of California at Davis' practice of reserving positions strictly on the basis of race violated Title VI of the Civil Rights Act of 1964. Title VI provides that "[n]o person in the United States shall, on the ground of race, color, or national origin, be excluded from participation in . . . any program or activity receiving Federal financial assistance." Davis did not contest the fact that it was receiving federal financial assistance. Although the decision was not based on constitutional grounds, Justice Lewis Powell, writing for the majority, noted that the guarantees of Title VI are grounded in principles found in the equal protection clause of the Fourteenth Amendment.

A different 5 to 4 majority, however, also declared that race could be considered as one of several criteria for admission to a university. One's status as a racial minority presumably could help one secure admission, but only if the position being contested were formally available to all, irrespective of race. The Court thus did not rule out affirmative action programs in general, only those provisions that amount to strict racial quotas. The decision can therefore be seen as a compromise between those who would abolish all forms of affirmative action as reverse discrimination and those who would guarantee outcomes based on race.

The narrowness of *Regents of the University of California v. Bakke* ensured the continuation of affirmative action programs in various forms. Less than a week after the *Bakke* decision, the Court let stand a lower court's ruling that permitted quantitative "goals" for the hiring and promotion of women and minorities. For almost fifteen years after *Bakke* the Court seemed to agree that the lingering effects of slavery, segregation, and blatant discrimination—and perhaps the continuation of more subtle biases—justified some institutionalized efforts to provide special assistance to racial minorities in employment and education. In the mid-1990's, however, those assumpions were challenged anew. The Supreme Court decision in *Adarand Constructors v. Peña* (1995), for example, ruled that a federal policy mandating that a certain percent-

Marchers take to the streets in New York City to protest the U.S. Supreme Court decision that the University of California, Berkeley, medical school erred in admitting less-qualified minority applicants and rejecting Allan Bakke, a better-qualified white man.

age of construction projects receiving funding from the Department of Transportation be set aside for minority-owned companies was unconstitutional. *Steve D. Boilard*

See also: *Adarand Constructors v. Peña*; Affirmative action; Civil Rights Act of 1964; "Reverse" racism.

Banking practices

> **Significance:** The extension of legally protected civil rights to minorities in the United States has intensified intergroup conflict over socioeconomic mobility. Bank practices regarding the extension of consumer credit—critical in purchasing a home, starting a small business, or obtaining a college education—have shifted from overt to covert forms of discrimination. This trend has helped create the two-tiered financial services system.

The Civil Rights movement of the 1960's provided the moral and legal impetus for redressing the disadvantaged conditions of racial and ethnic minorities in the United States. In the 1970's and 1980's, minorities made substantial progress in overcoming obstacles to socioeconomic mobility as mirrored in their rising educational and occupational levels. As middle-class minorities grew, however, overt discrimination began to be replaced by subtler but no less pernicious forms of racism. One of the most devastating—because of its long-term consequences—is the unequal access to consumer financial services from first-tier, or traditional, banks. This has contributed to the persistence of racial inequality through lower rates of minority home ownership, small business development, and college graduation. Furthermore, the concentration of minorities in urban communities and the consolidation of corporate banking operations in the late 1990's have led to the rapid expansion of second-tier, or fringe, banks that offer high-cost financial services. The second tier of the banking system features check-cashing outlets, rent-to-own stores, and pawnshops, all of which market expensive financial services to primarily poor and minority groups.

Overt Discrimination and First-Tier Banks
The institutionalization of race and class discrimination in bank lending practices dates to the inception of the Home Owner Loan Corporation (HOLC) in 1933. As Kenneth T. Jackson explains in his book *Crabgrass Frontier* (1985), the HOLC's goal of stabilizing the home mortgage market was based on appraising property values according to the general characteristics of the surrounding neighborhood rather than the specific properties to be mortgaged. This four-category, color-coded rating system devalued neighborhoods that were densely populated, racially mixed, or aging. Ratings ranged from first grade (green) homogeneous neighborhoods populated by white American (not Jewish) businesspeople and professionals to fourth grade (red) "declining" areas with deteriorating housing stock, low rents, and a racially or ethnically mixed population. This appraisal method is the historical basis of contemporary financial "redlining" or racially discriminatory lending practices, often employed against African Americans.

Overt discrimination by first-tier banks, prohibited by the Civil Rights Act of 1964 and other legislation, has disappeared. However, in subsequent decades, researchers have found that minorities continue to be more likely to be rejected for personal loans (mortgages, car loans, credit cards) than whites with the same socioeconomic characteristics. Although the negative consequences appear to be borne by individuals, the impact is much more profound in that these practices tend to concentrate minorities in declining urban neighborhoods where crime is high, jobs are scarce, and public schools are inadequate. Furthermore, as illustrated in Robert D. Manning's "Multicultural Washington, D.C.," in *Ethnic and Racial Studies* (1998), the postindustrial shift of economic activities away from the central city, which resulted in the exodus of the most successful urban minorities to the suburbs, creates a decline in investment in the inner city. In 1977, the Community Reinvestment Act was enacted to fight redlining policies by requiring banks to invest a small proportion of their loans in underserved areas. This legal commitment has been assailed by the banking industry, and because of the large numbers of corporate mergers in the late 1990's, regulatory enforcement is uncertain although members of minority communities continue to find it difficult to obtain loans.

Covert Discrimination and Second-Tier Banks
The deregulation of the U.S. banking industry beginning in 1980 has dramatically affected the cost and availability of consumer financial services. As bank mergers produce fewer branch offices in urban—especially minority—communities and higher fees for bank accounts, including substantially greater minimum cash balances, the numbers of alternative financial service facilities are increasing. John P. Caskey's *Fringe Banking: Check Cashing Outlets, Pawnshops, and the Poor* (1994) documents the rapid increase in the numbers of second-tier, or "fringe," banks that offer high-cost services to poor and minority clients. Second-tier financial service providers include regional and national chains of check-cashing outlets (which charge 1.5 percent to 3 percent for essentially a two- to three-day loan), pawnshops

(which charge 10 percent to 15 percent per month plus storage fees), rent-to-own stores (annual cost of credit from 150 percent to 450 percent), and finance companies (which charge 24 percent to 38 percent per year and require costly insurance). The most usurious loans are postdated, personal "payday" checks that typically cost 25 percent for a one-week loan or 1,250 percent per year.

The shift from overt to covert bank discrimination, which is manifest in the dramatic growth of second-tier financial services, generates billions of dollars in annual corporate profits. Michael Hudson, in *Merchants of Misery: How Corporate America Profits from Poverty* (1996), documents the direct and indirect linkages between second-tier banks and major financial corporations such as BankAmerica, Fleet Financial, Ford, NationsBank, and Western Union. These include providing profitable lines of credit, purchasing publicly traded stock, and "flipping" or buying high-interest loans from small companies for a small percentage or "finder's fee." In addition, the U.S. government's shift to paperless financial transactions at the end of the 1990's is likely to force those excluded from top-tier banks to cultivate new and more costly relations with second-tier financial services providers. The profit motive and linkage between the first- and second-tier banks have been suggested as the reason that "fringe" banks are more accommodating and hospitable to racial and ethnic minorities at the same time that first-tier banks are abandoning racial and ethnic neighborhoods. More disturbing, this subtle form of financial discrimination is creating a modern form of debt peonage that perpetuates economic inequality and therefore will exacerbate intergroup tensions.

Robert D. Manning

Core Resources

Kenneth T. Jackson's *Crabgrass Frontier: The Suburbanization of the United States* (New York: Oxford University Press, 1985) documents the historic role of the U.S. government in institutionalizing discriminatory bank lending practices as well as promoting the postwar boom in racially exclusionary suburban communities. *From Redlining to Reinvestment: Community Responses to Urban Disinvestment*, edited by Gregory D. Squires (Philadelphia: Temple University Press, 1992) illuminates the financial origins of the United States' urban decline and examines efforts to revitalize predominantly minority communities through a series of case studies. The historic transformation of the U.S. metropolis, guided by the postindustrial economy, and the changing patterns of racial inequality are the focus of Robert D. Manning's "Multicultural Washington, D.C.: The Changing Social and Economic Landscape of a Post-industrial Metropolis," in *Ethnic and Racial Studies* (volume 21, no. 2, March, 1998). David Caplovitz's sociological classic *The Poor Pay More: Consumer Practices of Low-Income Families* (New York: Free Press, 1963) explores the high cost of consumer credit to America's neediest citizens. Economist John P. Caskey's *Fringe Banking: Check Cashing Outlets, Pawnshops, and the Poor* (New York: Russell Sage Foundation, 1994) examines the exodus of corporate banks from minority neighborhoods and the accompanying growth of bottom-tier financial services. *Merchants of Misery: How Corporate America Profits from Poverty*, edited by investigative journalist Michael Hudson (Monroe, Maine: Common Courage Press, 1996), shows how the high cost of consumer credit for the poor generates huge profits for the United States' largest corporations.

See also: Culture of poverty; Housing; Poverty and race; Redlining; Segregation: de facto and de jure.

Baseball

Two brothers, Welday and Moses Walker, became the first African American baseball players in the major leagues. They played for the Toledo, Ohio, team in 1884. Integrated baseball, however, was poorly accepted, and by the 1920's, baseball's first commissioner, Judge Landis, prohibited black players. African American players, with the door to the major leagues closed to them, formed all-black teams in order to pursue their playing activities.

Initially black baseball teams were formed to play exhibition games against white teams or other black teams. The Cuban Giants, formed on Long Island, New York, in 1885, was the first all-black team. Although some short-lived black leagues were formed in the early twentieth century, the first successful one was the Negro National League, founded by "Rube" Foster in 1920. In 1923, a second black league, the Eastern Colored League, was formed. Because of the financial instability of the first black leagues, many teams survived by barnstorming—making exhibition tours—across the United States. A notable barnstorming was undertaken by the Kansas City Monarchs, who, beginning in 1931, traveled the country with a portable lighting system and played night games several years before the first white major league night game.

In 1936, the Negro American League was formed to replace its failed predecessors. The two most successful teams were the Kansas City Monarchs, who won seven championships, and the Homestead Grays (originally based in Pittsburgh, Pennsylvania), who won nine pennants. Several members of these teams, including catcher Josh Gibson, pitcher Satchel Paige, and infielder Jackie Robinson, were eventually elected to the Baseball Hall of Fame.

The beginning of the end for the all-black leagues came in 1945 when Branch Rickey of the Brooklyn Dodgers signed African American stars Jackie Robinson and John Wright to play on a Brooklyn farm team. Robinson broke the color barrier in 1947 with Brooklyn and was named rookie of the year. The door opened by Robinson was soon entered by Larry Doby, the first African American in the American League (Cleveland), and other black players. By the 1940's, the Negro American League, while retaining older stars such as Gibson, was losing most of its younger talent—Roy Campanella, Willie Mays, and Hank Aaron—to the major leagues. The drain of talent and subsequent declining attendance resulted in the folding of the Negro American League in 1960.

The impact of African Americans on major league baseball was dramatic: The sudden influx of talented players significantly raised the level of play. The composition of the Baseball Hall of Fame illustrates this impact. Even though black players were omitted from the hall from 1936 until 1962 (Robinson's induction), by the close of the twentieth century, more than 10 percent of inductees were African Americans. Progress in other areas of the game was slower. It was 1974 before an African American, Frank Robinson, became a manager.

Jackie Robinson, pictured in 1951, became the first African American baseball player in the modern major league in the late 1940's.

At the end of the twentieth century, few African Americans could be found in administrative positions.

Paul J. Chara, Jr.

See also: African American stereotypes; Sports.

Batson v. Kentucky

On the surface, *Batson v. Kentucky* (decided 1986) was one of a long string of efforts to eliminate discrimination from the judicial system. It departed from the Supreme Court's 1965 holding in *Swain v. Alabama*, in which the Court first considered the use of the peremptory challenge for discriminatory purposes.

In *Swain*, asked whether the equal protection clause of the Fourteenth Amendment prevented the total exclusion of blacks from a jury, the Supreme Court declared that the "presumption in any particular case must be that the prosecutor is using the State's challenges to obtain a fair and impartial jury . . .[even if] all Negroes were removed because they were Negroes." To overcome the presumption, the Court ruled, a defendant would have to demonstrate that the state followed a consistent pattern of discrimination in "case after case."

Swain prevailed until 1986. Challengers were unable to meet the standards of systematic exclusion established in the decision. State and federal courts alike refused to countenance presentation of evidence from only cases that involved black defendants. Over the repeated objections of Justice Thurgood Marshall, the Supreme Court waited to allow "states to serve as laboratories in which the issue receives further study before it is addressed by this Court" again. Marshall called the experimentation cruel, noting that "there is no point in taking elaborate steps to ensure Negroes are included in venires[pools of prospective jurors] simply so they can be struck because of their race by a prosecutor's use of peremptory challenges."

The reconsideration came in *Batson v. Kentucky*. Batson's counsel asked the Court:

> In a criminal case, does a state trial court err when, over the objection of a black defendant, it swears an all-white jury constituted only after the prosecutor had exercised four of his six peremptory challenges to strike all of the black veniremen from the panel in violation of constitutional provisions guaranteeing the defendant an impartial jury and a jury composed of persons representing a fair cross section of the community?

James Kirkland Batson had been charged with burglary and the receipt of stolen goods. The prosecutor used four of his six peremptory challenges to create, in his words, an "all-white jury." The defense counsel's motion to discharge the panel before it was sworn in on grounds that the panel did not represent a cross-section of the community and that to use it would be a denial of equal protection was denied by the trial judge. Tried and convicted, Batson appealed to the Kentucky Supreme Court, which upheld the conviction in 1984, based on the *Swain* doctrine. The U.S. Supreme Court disagreed. Reversing the conviction in April of 1986, it held that the impaneling of the jury resulted in a denial of equal protection. It ruled that when objection is lodged against an alleged racially discriminatory use of the peremptory challenge, the trial court must examine the validity of the claim. Thus, for the first time, a federal court agreed that an attorney can be forced to explain his or her reason for invoking a peremptory challenge.

Ashton Wesley Welch

See also: Criminal justice system; Jury selection.

Behavior-receptional assimilation

"Behavior-receptional assimilation" is a term coined by sociologist Milton Gordon to refer to one of seven stages of adaptation that a minority or immigrant group undergoes when entering a dominant host society. When assimilating groups reach a point where they encounter no intentional discriminatory behavior from the members of the host society, they have achieved behavior-receptional assimilation. In U.S. history, almost all immigrants, regardless of how they entered this society (through slavery, conquest, or voluntarily), have faced discrimination by the members of the host society, mostly the dominant white Anglo-Saxon Protestants (WASPs), because of national origin, religion, and racial and ethnic backgrounds. This discrimination takes various forms, such as verbal and physical attack, residential segregation, exclusion from the school system and employment, and avoidance of social and personal interaction. Irish, Italians, and Jews, who are now relatively integrated into the core society compared with non-European minority groups, experienced various types of severe discrimination because of religion until the mid-1900's. Although discrimination against these groups has not disappeared, the severity of this discrimination diminished in the second half of the twentieth century. Members of racial minority groups and newly arrived immigrants still face discrimination in housing and employment, which hinders the upward mobility of these groups. In that sense, these groups have not achieved behavior-receptional assimilation.

Hisako Matsuo

See also: Anglo-conformity; Assimilation: cultural and structural; Assimilation: theories of racial/ethnic relations; Attitude-receptional assimilation; Civic assimilation; Identification assimilation; Marital assimilation; Prejudice: reduction; Structural assimilation.

Bigotry

Bigotry is the obstinate and unreasonable attachment to one's own opinions or beliefs. Bigots are intolerant of beliefs that oppose their own. Often, such people are very emotional and may become stubbornly intolerant or even hostile toward others who differ with them regarding religion, race, sexual orientation, or other issues. This state of mind encourages stereotyping, overgeneralization, and other errors that suggest the absence of critical thinking.

Bigoted attitudes can be culturally transmitted as part of the education of children or adults. Bigotry is a learned prejudice that is founded on inaccurate and inflexible overgeneralizations. Bigots may believe, for example, that "all blacks are thieves," despite the fact that they have no experience on which to base this belief. Even if they know a very honest African American individual, they will state that this person is the exception to the rule or has yet to reveal his or her true character. When confronted with new information that contradicts their beliefs, bigots are unwilling to change but instead perceive the contradictory evidence as exceptional and may become excited and emotional.

Bigotry is not confined to race. Some bigots dislike fat people, redheads, or the elderly and discriminate against these populations without cause. However, bigotry, being a learned behavior, is not immutable but can be ameliorated through social policy.

Dallas L. Browne

See also: Prejudice and stereotyping.

Bilingual education

> **Significance:** Bilingual education usually involves the use of a minority and a majority language for teaching schoolchildren whose primary language is not English. Bilingual education combines language learning with teaching culture in meeting the educational goals of different minority groups.

Bilingual education in the United States has had a turbulent history. On June 2, 1998, voters in California ended the thirty-year-old tradition of bilingual education in California public schools by passing Proposition 227, which gives immigrant children only one year to learn English before they enroll in regular classes. The passage of this initiative and the courts' response to the new law (which almost immediately became subject to court litigation) were seen as a critical test of the United States' commitment to bilingual education; California, after all, represented the largest school system in the nation with the largest student population enrolled in bilingual classes. If California eliminated bilingual education, many other school systems in other states were hoping either to impose severe restrictions on bilingual instruction or to eliminate it totally by passing an English-only policy. In contrast, the Coral Way School in Miami, which became the United States' first successful bilingual school in 1963, continued to offer a strong commitment to bilingual education. Although support was eroding in other parts of the United States, Miami support for bilingualism was gaining strength. These examples best represent the roller-coaster history of bilingual education.

Over the years, bilingual education has experienced a series of ups and downs as various immigrant groups

Milestones in Bilingual Education

Period/Year	Event	Impact
1694-mid nineteenth century	Vernacular education schools	German-, French-, and Spanish-speaking schools in the East and South are common in spite of periodical attempts to replace German/Spanish with English.
1828	U.S.-Cherokee Treaty	Treaty recognizes language rights of the Cherokee tribe.
1848	Treaty of Guadalupe Hidalgo	Language rights of the new Spanish-speaking citizens of the United States are "guaranteed"—but rarely respected.
1868	Indian Peace Commission	Group concludes: "Their [native Indian] barbarous dialects should be blotted out and the English language substituted."
1889	American Protective Association proposal	Declares that English should be the sole language of instruction in all public and private schools.
1898	Spanish-American War	English becomes the medium of instruction in the new colonies, Puerto Rico, and Hawaii.
1917	World War II—Cox's bill	This bill, the product of anti-German sentiment, bans German from Ohio's elementary schools.
1930's	Decline of non-English languages	Bilingual education is wiped out, except in parochial schools in rural areas of the Midwest.
1964	Civil Rights Act	Language provision of this act becomes the legal basis for bilingual education.
1968	Bilingual Education Act	This act addresses the needs of students with limited English skills, promoting bilingualism and encouraging ways to help speed up children's transition to English.
1974	*Lau v. Nichols* decision	Establishes the principle that children have a right to instruction in a language that they can understand.
1998	Proposition 227	California voters pass Proposition 227, which gives immigrant children only one year to learn English before entering regular classes. Other school systems in other states watch this development with interest.

have arrived in the United States. One of bilingual education's most significant moments was the passage of the Bilingual Education Act in 1968. The act promoted bilingualism as a way to address the educational needs of children whose primary language is not English. In 1974, the Supreme Court ruled in *Lau v. Nichols* that a school district was required to provide bilingual education. Subsequent court decisions further highlighted the need for solid bilingual education programs as a means of providing equal access to education. However, many schools did not comply with this ruling. Bilingual education underwent a series of setbacks during the administrations of Ronald Reagan and George Bush. By 1990, the tide was turning in favor of the English-only campaigns. The passing of Proposition 227 in California was intended to deliver the most severe blow yet to bilingual education in the United States.

Maintenance vs. Transitional Bilingualism
The main problem that bilingual education attempts to address is how to respond to the need of minority children to learn the majority language, English. According to the U.S. Department of Education, more than five million children in public schools have limited English proficiency (LEP). If these children cannot understand what the teacher is saying, they obviously cannot learn academic subjects such as math, science, and reading. If their study of academic subjects is postponed until they are proficient in English, their progress in these subjects is seriously hampered. If the "sink-or-swim" approach is used and children are taught entirely in English, their performance in academic subjects will deteriorate. Bilingual education solves this problem by teaching academic subjects to LEP children in their native languages while teaching them English. Furthermore, studies show that improving cognitive skills in native languages further facilitates the learning of academic subjects. However, studies such as those by Jim Cummins show that at least four to six years of instruction in native languages (called Late-Exit to English) are needed before optimal results are registered both on proficiency in English and on other subjects in terms of achieving or exceeding national norms.

Most bilingual programs in the United States can best be characterized as transitional bilingual programs because they encourage the maintenance of the native language as a transition toward the learning of English. This process is called subtractive bilingualism. In the first stage, students are monolingual, learning only in their native language. Then students enter a stage of transitional bilingualism, in which they are functional in both their native language and English. Finally, they become monolingual in English.

Maintenance programs are additive bilingual pro-grams that maintain the students' native language as they learn English. At the beginning, students are monolingual, speaking only their native language, then they begin to become bilingual, adding English to their native language. In the end, the students become fully functional in English yet maintain their native language.

Proponents of additive bilingual programs claim that maintenance of the student's native language is critical for the child's linguistic and cognitive growth, school performance, psychological security, ethnic and cultural identity, self-esteem, and many other positive personality and intellectual characteristics. The supporters of transitional bilingual programs claim that these programs avoid unnecessary linguistic duality and confusion, which sometimes cause children to be unable to function well in either language; improve students' performance in school; and minimize social, ethnic, and political divisions. The latter view derives support from long-term bilingual programs that have been found to lack effectiveness. For example, in 1997, only 6.7 percent of LEP children moved into regular classes in California as compared with 15 percent in 1982. Other states exhibit the same trend, pointing to the low success rate of long-term bilingual programs aimed at maintaining both languages. Advocates of maintenance bilingual programs attribute these low success rates to factors that are not intrinsic to bilingual education, such as a lack of funding, trained teachers, and federal/state commitment to bilingual education; poorly structured classrooms (grouping large numbers of students with diverse and unrelated native languages); and not enough adequate pedagogical material. According to Jim Lyons, executive director of the National Association for Bilingual Education, a large number of bilingual programs are "not worthy of the name." Programs such as the Eastman school model (pioneered by Steven Krashen and Cummins), which is widely used in Los Angeles schools, have shown themselves to be effective. The model is notable for its effective use of the results of basic research in recent theories of language acquisition and its long-term bilingual and bicultural basis.

Alternatives to Bilingual Education
Alternatives to bilingual programs generally take the shape of programs to teach children English. Instead of simply placing LEP children in ordinary classes, children are placed in English as a second language (ESL) or English language development (ELD) programs. The ELD approach follows a strategy that encourages students to first comprehend and then speak English. The lessons are delivered in a low-anxiety, small-group, and language-conducive environment. Students' errors are tolerated, and the focus is on the acquisition of interactive communicative skills. The teacher provides what is

termed "comprehensible input" (expressions in English that make sense to children) by means of role-playing, modeling, and pictures. After about six to twelve months of ELD instruction, a shift is made to "sheltered English" instruction, which includes simplified language with common vocabulary, frequent paraphrasing, clarification, comprehension checks, and the use of simple sentence structures to teach context-rich subjects such as art and music.

Researchers Keith A. Baker and Adriana A. de Kanter suggest the structured immersion program modeled after the St. Lambert French immersion program in Quebec as an alternative to bilingual education programs. However, the success of the Canadian program is attributed to community and parent support; the fact that language-majority students (English speakers) were immersed into a minority language (French); and that the program goals included additive bilingualism. Similarly structured immersion programs failed in the United States because they involved language-minority children, neglected their native language, and were based on subtractive bilingualism.

Maria Ramirez, named teacher of the year in 1996 by the National Association for Bilingual Education, works with members of her second-grade class at Alsup Elementary School in Commerce City, Colorado. In the 1990's, bilingual programs and classes were criticized as being ineffective and costly.

As political battles are being waged all over the United States concerning bilingual education, the nation's schools are still being overwhelmed by never-ending waves of LEP children. However, the question of how best to teach these children English remains unanswered.   *Tej K. Bhatia*

Core Resources

James Crawford's *Bilingual Education: History, Politics, Theory, and Practice* (Trenton, N.J.: Crane, 1989) and Kenji Hakuta's *Mirror of Language: The Debate on Bilingualism* (New York: Basic Books, 1986) are two classic studies on the various facets (historical, political, and educational) of bilingual education. For the latest trends in bilingual education, see Duane E. Campbell's *Choosing Democracy: A Practical Guide to Multicultural Education* (Upper Saddle River, N.J.: Prentice Hall, 1996). James Cummins's *Empowering Language Minority Students* (Sacramento: California Association for Bilingual Education, 1989) deals with educational and other issues pertaining to minorities at risk. A detailed state-of-the-art treatment of language acquisition is presented in two volumes, *Handbook of Second Language Acquisition* (1996) and

Handbook of Child Language Acquisition (1998), edited by William C. Ritchie and Tej K. Bhatia (San Diego, Calif.: Academic Press). These two volumes contain several chapters dealing with the phenomenon of bilingualism, bilingual language acquisition, and bilingual education.

See also: Bilingual Education Act; Bilingualism in Canada; *Lau v. Nichols.*

Bilingual Education Act

Significance: In the face of a changing U.S. populace, legislation authorized bilingual education studies.

Bilingual education was thrust into the forefront of public attention in the 1960's, when Dade County, Florida, announced a successful experiment with a bilingual program for newly arrived Cuban refugees, most of whom were non-English proficient (NEP) or limited-English proficient (LEP). Citing Title VI of the Civil Rights Act of 1964, which prohibits discrimination in school districts receiving federal funds, Mexican advocacy groups supported the concept of bilingual instruction as a programmatic remedy for unequal educational

Tracy Callard, a bilingual education teacher from Kansas, visits an elementary school in La Joya, Texas. The passage of the Bilingual Education Act resulted in the formation of many programs designed to address the needs of children whose first language is not English.

attainments by Mexican Americans. The advocacy groups argued that without the ability to speak English, Mexican Americans could participate in neither the economic nor the political mainstream of the country.

Passage of the Bill

Responding to pressure from his constituents, Texas senator Ralph W. Yarborough championed the cause of bilingual education by introducing a bill in early 1967 that sought to assist schools with a high percentage of low-income Latinos. In the House of Representatives, the bill ultimately gained forty-nine cosponsors, notably George E. Brown, Jr., and Edward R. Roybal of California and James H. Scheuer of New York. As the bill received bipartisan support, attention broadened to consider the plight of LEP/NEP students of American Indian, Asian, French Canadian, French Creole, and Portuguese ancestries. During the debate, statistics were presented showing that 11 percent of U.S. residents had a mother tongue other than English, and 3 million school-age children spoke a language other than English, 1.75 million of whom spoke Spanish.

Public hearings on the proposed legislation were held in Los Angeles, New York City, and three cities in Texas (Corpus Christi, Edinburg, and San Antonio). In addition to Hispanic advocacy groups, support for the bill came from the National Education Association. Since professional educators had no consensus on which teaching strategy worked best in boosting achievement levels for LEP and NEP students, they lobbied Congress

to provide funding for research.

Congress passed the Bilingual Education Act of 1968 as an amendment to the Elementary and Secondary Education Act of 1965, and $400 million was authorized to be spent for research from 1968 to 1973, although much less actually was appropriated. Funds were to be used to remedy LEP/NEP problems in languages other than English spoken by a substantial number of students.

Subsequent Developments

On January 21, 1974, the Supreme Court ruled in *Lau v. Nichols* that failure to use special methods to enable language-minority students to enter mainstream English classes was impermissible. The court, however, refused to rule on what pedagogical method would be best for mainstreaming LEP and NEP students into English-only classes, leaving the choice of method to local school districts.

Subsequent to *Lau*, Congress held hearings to assess the impact, which was determined to affect five million schoolchildren. One result was the Equal Educational Opportunities Act in 1974, a provision of which requires "appropriate action to overcome language barriers that impede equal participation." A second statute was the Bilingual Education Act of 1974, which provided federal funds to finance efforts at compliance with *Lau* for all affected students, not just for low-income students. In 1978, when the law was extended, objections to experiments in bilingual education mounted, and Congress restricted funding to educational projects in which no more than 40 percent of the students were native English speakers.

Several alternative methods of language instruction were studied. Submersion, which entailed placing LEP/NEP students into English-only classes on a sink-or-swim basis, was the method outlawed by *Lau*. Teaching English to Students of Other Languages (TESOL) was designed to remove LEP/NEP students from the mainstream to take special instruction in English. Immersion involved employing bilingual instructors who could teach in either language. Transitional bilingual education, the most popular program, involved fast-track English instruction aimed at rapid mainstreaming. Bilingual maintenance programs were designed to enable LEP/NEP students to retain language proficiency in the native language while learning English. Bilingual/bicultural programs went beyond bilingual maintenance to provide instruction in aspects of both the root and U.S. cultures. Culturally pluralistic programs, as adopted later at Texas border towns, were designed to integrate LEP/NEP and English-speaking students into multilingual/multicultural classrooms, so that both majority and minority children could learn together.

When objective studies demonstrated that the various bilingual instructional programs did not improve achievement levels for Mexican Americans, Congress passed new legislation, providing funds for capacity building, that is, to train teachers from language minority groups and to develop instructional materials for use in the classroom. The first such law, the Bilingual Education Amendments of 1981, was followed by the Bilingual Education Improvement Act of 1983 and the Bilingual Education Acts of 1984 and 1988.

During the eight years that Ronald Reagan was president, civil rights compliance reviews on language and other forms of educational discrimination decreased by 90 percent. In 1991, after Congress held hearings on the matter, the U.S. Department of Education's Office for Civil Rights set equal educational opportunities for national-origin minority and Native American students as its top priority. Although the battle to recognize Spanish and other languages as legitimate languages of instruction succeeded in the 1960's and 1970's, efforts to abolish bilingual education gained momentum in the 1980's and 1990's.   *Michael Haas*

Core Resources

Stephen T. Wagner's "The Historical Background of Bilingualism and Biculturalism in the United States," in *The New Bilingualism: An American Dilemma* (edited by Martin Ridge, Los Angeles: University of Southern California Press, 1981) is the lead essay in a symposium that discusses pros and cons of bilingualism in many facets of U.S. society. Christine H. Rossell and J. Michael Ross's "The Social Science Evidence on Bilingual Education," in *Journal of Law & Education* (15, Fall, 1986), reviews scientific evidence concerning alternative methods for teaching English to limited-English-speaking and non-English-speaking students. Barry L. Bull, Royal T. Fruehling, and Virgie Chattergy's *The Ethics of Multicultural and Bilingual Education* (New York: Columbia University Press, 1992) contrasts how liberal, democratic, and communitarian approaches to education relate to bilingual and multicultural education. Rosalie P. Porter's *Forked Tongue: The Politics of Bilingual Education* (New York: Basic Books, 1990) presents an indictment of efforts to deliver bilingual education.

See also: Bilingual education; Bilingualism in Canada; *Lau v. Nichols.*

Bilingualism in Canada

Significance: Canada has committed itself to English-French bilingualism by supplying public funding for the teaching of official languages, encouraging the use of both languages in the federal civil service, and making bilingual fluency a criterion in government job opportunities. The ultimate aim is to make both languages equitable in representation and significant for work and various realms of public service. However, the language issue remains one of the most contentious political aspects of Canadian life and a serious threat to the fragile unity binding the provinces of the country.

It was perhaps inevitable that Canada would adopt English-French bilingualism in view of the strong French presence in the province of Quebec. The people of Quebec have expressed an interest in retaining a distinctive identity, albeit that of a minority in a predominantly English-speaking North American continent. This desire for distinctiveness has aroused considerable controversy in the rest of Canada because of a perception that all provinces must be viewed and treated as equals.

However, many Canadians are sensitive to the unique character of Quebec society and believe that the French aspect of Canada provides an important distinction between Canadian and American culture. They believe that bilingualism distinguishes Canada from its southern neighbor and gives a rich and varied quality to Canadian life.

The Canadian political agenda on race relations is dominated by the "Quebec issue," almost to the exclusion of the needs and desires of the other ethnic groups that are part of Canadian society. The so-called visible minorities (blacks, Chinese, Filipinos, Japanese, Koreans, Latin Americans, other Pacific Islanders, South Asians, Southeast Asians, West Asians, and Arabs, as defined by the Canadian government) constitute a significant and growing proportion of the Canadian demographic picture. The overwhelming emphasis of successive Canadian governments on Quebec and its francophone population has pushed the visible minority agenda to the background of Canadian political concerns.

Statistics

The 1996 census established that nearly 60 percent of Canadians were anglophones (people whose mother tongue is English), less than 24 percent were francophones (mother tongue French), and nearly 17 percent were allophones (mother tongue something other than English or French). In 1996, 86 percent of the francophones lived in Quebec, and the francophone population in other provinces declined to less than 1 percent.

Immigrants from Asia, Latin America, the Caribbean, and Africa have caused major demographic changes in Canada. The allophone percentage of the population rose from 12 percent in 1951 to 15 percent in 1991 and 17 percent in 1996, and the rate of increase was estimated by Statistics Canada to be two and one-half times faster than the overall growth rate of the Canadian population. Hence, although officially bilingual, Canada is in reality a multilingual nation with Chinese as its third most used language. Every province of Canada has significant allophone communities, and there is a vibrant ethnic media including national television programming and newspapers and books published in more than fifty languages.

Historical Background

Aside from its contribution to a richer, more diverse cultural heritage for all Canadians, the concept of bilingualism has played a crucial role in attempting to prevent secession by Quebec and its francophone majority from the Canadian confederation. In the late twentieth century, Canada dedicated itself to the concepts of multiculturalism and pluralism, in contrast to the "melting pot" theory that has dominated in the United States. Multiculturalism seeks to provide a Canadian identity that recognizes the importance of unity in diversity by encouraging immigrants to retain aspects of their heritage while acculturing themselves to Canadian society in practical ways such as developing linguistic capability and the proper skills for employment opportunities. Multiculturalism, however, functions within the overall societal and governmental framework of bilingualism, which emphasizes the predominance of English and French. It remains to be seen whether Canada will eventually recognize other languages as they acquire prominence.

In 1969, the Canadian government passed the Official Languages Act, which declared that English and French would enjoy official status and could be used equally in parliament, in federal courts, and in federal institutions. Federal bilingualism got a real boost as a governmental policy with the election in 1976 of the separatist Parti Québécois government in Quebec. This served as a wake-up call to the federal government, and some significant measures were taken to implement bilingualism in practice as well as in theory.

In 1978, the criminal code was amended to provide service to the accused in the individual's own official language. In 1982, the Canadian Charter of Rights and Freedoms constitutionally enshrined the policy of official bilingualism and provided extensive language guarantees that have been interpreted by legal scholars to provide equitable representation for French, to include French as a language of work, and to expand the coverage of bilingualism to Crown corporations and other governmental institutions. Although the 1982 constitutional accord was widely perceived as a move to gain the confidence of francophones, the Quebec government refused to accept it.

Canada also provides for mechanisms of enforcement for bilingualism and funding for Canadians who believe that their language rights have been violated and who wish to launch a legal challenge.

Section 23 of the Canadian Charter provides for minority language guarantees in the realm of primary and secondary education, a clause that has helped francophone minorities in various Canadian provinces establish their own schools but that has also generated much controversy, particularly in Quebec, where it has been perceived as conflicting with the Quebec Charter of the French Language.

Canadians encounter both languages every day of their lives. Canadian money and postage stamps are printed in both languages. All products sold in Canada, including imported products, must carry instructions and information in both official languages. Parliamentarians are shown on television flowing easily from one language to the other in their speeches. Prominent

This Coca-Cola advertisement in the Montreal, Quebec, subway system is aimed at the area's French-speaking population. Officially, Canada is a bilingual nation, using both French and English.

Canadian prime ministers such as Pierre Trudeau, Brian Mulroney, and Jean Chrétien are Quebecers.

Perspectives on Bilingualism

Bilingualism began with the premise that a solid nation can be built by enabling people to speak each other's language and communicate freely. The assumption was made that the ever-decreasing French minority would identify more with a Canada that had some appreciation of its language and its rich cultural heritage. Years and millions of dollars after its promulgation, there are as many contentious opinions about bilingualism as there are Canadians. Opinions range from great enthusiasm, particularly among those who are fluently bilingual, to total cynicism (largely prevalent in parts of western Canada, which is emphatically English-oriented). The Reform Party, which originated in western Canada, resolved in 1987 to prevent the expansion of bilingualism in the west. Citizens' groups (such as the Association for the Preservation of English in Canada) have sprung up to denounce the bilingual agenda and to promote an English-only policy in various towns and cities. Statistics Canada demonstrated that the proportion of Canadians speaking French at home declined in the provinces outside Quebec between 1991 and 1996.

The linguistic issue is both a bone of contention encouraging separatism and a foundation for unity within the country. Although schoolchildren across the country have flocked to French immersion programs funded by the government, the use of French outside Quebec shows no signs of reaching the level of English usage. The French-language television stations that exist across the nation do not draw a large anglophone or allophone audience, which they would if bilingualism were truly successful. Other measures to encourage French usage such as the insistence on French language on all products sold in Canada have resulted in higher costs to consumers, a reality that is often irksome to shoppers. In some western and eastern provinces of Canada, French enjoys at best a marginalized status simply because there is no real incentive to use it. However, in the realm of sports, interestingly, French, English, and all peoples of Canada have come together in that hockey stars from every province including Quebec command a nationwide admiration. Athletic endeavors have proven to be a significant unifier of Canadian people.

Detractors argue that bilingualism is expensive and that it fails because although people can be trained in a language for years, if they do not live in a French-speaking community, they rarely retain their linguistic ability. Critics also believe that bilingualism contributes to the weakening of Canadian unity by emphasizing the differences between people. New Brunswick remains the only officially bilingual province of Canada, having adopted that policy in 1969.

Critics also point to the fact that all the efforts by anglophone and allophone Canadians to learn French have not stemmed the separatist tendencies of Quebec, which has frequently elected provincial governments dedicated to independence or sovereignty of their region from the rest of Canada.

The most compelling critical argument points to the absence of bilingualism in most regions of Quebec because its government promotes the use of French at the expense of English via the implementation of the Charter of the French Language (1977). This document declared French the official language of Quebec. Formalized and official discrimination against English in Quebec in matters referring to store and restaurant signs and education for allophone children has proven to be a potent argument against bilingualism in the rest of Canada. Bilingualism is perceived as a hypocritical and unsuccessful form of appeasement of an ever-decreasing French minority that responds with greater assertiveness in stressing its distinctive French (rather than bilingual) identity. Such detractors question whether requiring the rest of Canada to learn French will ultimately prevent the separation of Quebec or have any impact on that issue.

Meanwhile, francophones in Quebec are increasingly alarmed at their isolated status in a world awash in the English language. The francophone population of Canada declined from 29 percent of the total population in 1951 to below 24 percent in 1996. Statisticians have attributed this decrease to the swelling immigrant population of allophones and to a declining birthrate among francophones. Quebecers point to the failure of various attempts at constitutional recognition of their status as a distinct society as proof of the lack of adequate acceptance of their unique presence. Viewing their entire culture as imperiled, the francophones (86 percent of whom lived in Quebec in 1996) have officially formalized the predominance of French in Quebec and have deliberately sought immigrants who can blend into French Canadian society more readily.

Results

Despite the critics, statistics prove that bilingualism has had some success in Canada. In 1971, 13 percent of Canadians (2.9 million people) were bilingual. By 1991, the figure had risen to more than 16 percent (4.4 million) and, by 1996, to 17 percent (4.8 million). Interestingly, in Quebec, despite the unilingual political context, bilingualism has increased dramatically, rising between 1971 and 1996 from 28 percent to 38 percent. This could be because most young Quebecers have to learn English to acquire good jobs, especially in the burgeoning information technology field, which English dominates globally, particularly on the Internet. In 1996, 41 percent of francophones throughout Canada were bilingual, a statistic in marked contrast to the mere 9 percent of anglophones who were bilingual.

The policy of bilingualism has provided Canadians with an awareness of diversity and possibly a greater tolerance of another culture. However, acceptance of bilingualism has not been enthusiastic or wholehearted in many parts of Canada. The goal of a fully bilingual population, fluent in both official languages, may never be achieved, but the tradition of accommodating two forms of communication within one society has now been established and has become a distinguishing feature of Canada as a political entity. *Ranee K. L. Panjabi*

Core Resources

Two sources of data on bilingualism and its history are Grant Purves's *Official Bilingualism in Canada* (Ottawa, Ontario: Library of Parliament, Research Branch, 1992) and Statistics Canada's *The Daily: 1996 Census—Mother Tongue, Home Language, and Knowledge of Languages* (Ottawa: Statistics Canada, 1997). Two books on bilingualism in Canada include *Language and the State: The Law and Politics of Identity,* edited by David Schneiderman (Cowansville, Quebec: Editions Yvon Blais, 1991) and *Language Rights in Canada,* by Michael Bastarache et al. (Montreal, Quebec: Editions Yvon Blais, 1987).

See also: Anglophone; Charter of Rights and Freedoms; Charter of the French Language; Francophone; French Canadians; Multiculturalism Act; Multiculturalism in Canada; Official Languages Act; Visibile minority allophones in Canada.

Biosocial theories

Significance: Biosocial theories of ethnicity were developed to explain the persistence of ethnic and racial divisions in society, which assimilationists had earlier predicted would become less significant over time. These theories emphasize similarities in the behavior of humans and other species and use certain concepts derived from evolutionary biology to analyze ethnocentrism, xenophobia, and racial inequality.

The pioneers of biosocial theories, especially sociobiology—which gained popularity in the 1970's—were William D. Hamilton, who introduced the concept of inclusive fitness, and Edward O. Wilson, who postulated that certain human behaviors such as aggressiveness and xenophobia are genetically determined aspects of human nature and therefore unchangeable. Other prominent authors within this perspective are Pierre L. van den Berghe, Vernon Reynolds, Richard Alexander, Richard Dawkins, and David Barash. Milton Gordon, who like van den Berghe had initially been an assimilationist, later adopted a biologically based conception of ethnicity that can be categorized as "primordialist" because it maintains that ethnic and racial group affiliation is an ascribed primordial identity rooted in human nature.

Assumptions and Conceptual Framework

Sociobiological theory is universalist because it asserts that all humans have a single, common nature, regardless of their social or historical circumstances. It is also individualistic because it attempts to explain social relations and institutions as the result of individual choices intended to maximize benefits and minimize costs.

The main tenet of this kind of theory is the principle of fitness maximization, or inclusive fitness (also called the principle of kin selection). According to this principle, human beings are genetically predisposed to favor and marry their kin (those with whom they share a common ancestry, physical characteristics and/or culture) in order to maximize the reproduction of their own genes.

In *The Ethnic Phenomenon* (1981), van den Berghe suggests that ethnic and racial classifications are extensions of kinship classifications, that is, groupings of individuals into categories of kin and nonkin based on "objectively reliable predictors" of common descent. Kin groups organize for the pursuit of selfish but common interests; this social practice is called nepotism and may lead to coercive social institutions when the dominant ethnic group establishes a hierarchy of positions (stratification) and allocates them on the basis of race and ethnicity. Some types of racial and ethnic stratification are slavery, colonialism, and imperialism.

The principle of inclusive fitness, however, does not mean that people will always behave nepotistically. In certain cases, individual fitness may be maximized by cooperating with nonrelatives, a practice called reciprocity. In societies in which a group is subject to discrimination or stigmatization, its members may maximize their fitness by associating and cooperating with unrelated people.

In *Human Nature, Class, and Ethnicity* (1978), Gordon adopted an approach that includes biosocial development and interaction variables. He argued that the sense of ethnicity (understood as racial, religious, or national origin identification), socially considered an ascribed status, becomes incorporated into the self during the process of socialization. Therefore, injury to the ethnic group is seen by individuals as an injury to the self, and these injuries or threats to the self evoke aggressive responses.

Stereotyping, reinforced by affective tendencies and lack of contact in primary groups between different ethnic groups, triggers aggression derived from social dissatisfaction and frustration, which is then directed toward the group perceived as the source of dissatisfaction or toward scapegoats. In cases of generalized ethnic conflict, the calculation by each group of its chances of success may bring about an escalation of the conflict.

Criticism of the Theories

In *Theories of Ethnicity* (1989), Richard Thompson argues that van den Berghe's theory fails at the substantive level because after asserting that ethnic solidarity is based on underlying biological drives, he admits that culture and genes are inextricably intertwined, and that culture has sufficient autonomy to mold social behavior. Therefore, Thompson observes, van den Berghe's "weak" version of sociobiology does not add anything to the explanation of ethnic relations already offered by cultural determinism and has no predictive power.

Besides, sociobiology cannot offer any evidence in support of its assertions. Existing studies from which a genetic tendency for fitness maximization might be inferred have been done on nonhuman animal species with long evolutionary and reproductive histories in which culture has played no part.

At the methodological level, van den Berghe's theory is reductionistic; that is, it subsumes other racial and ethnic relations theories under the fundamental principle of fitness maximization. However, this principle, Thompson argues, has not been proved to explain any existing or past forms of ethnic and racial organization, and he concludes that the reduction is improper.

Philip Kitcher criticizes sociobiology on the grounds of its misplaced reductionism and its tendency to make vague general predictions or to derive from its principles conclusions that cannot be empirically verified.

Edna Bonacich, an advocate of split labor market theory, observes that "primordialist" conceptions cannot explain the problem of defining the boundaries of ethnic and racial groups. Because of interbreeding, the population of most societies is of mixed ancestry. In order to define ethnic identity, a descent rule is necessary, and the historical variability in such rules indicates their social rather than biological origin. Another criticism is that ethnicity may be redefined as a consequence of contact with another society: This is the case with Asian Americans, who in spite of having very diverse national origins, are nevertheless defined as an ethnic group within the United States. Finally, she asserts that shared ancestry has not prevented intraethnic conflict,

and that primordialist theories cannot explain variations in the frequency and intensity of those conflicts.

In spite of criticisms, it must be noted that sociobiologists deny that their theory lends any support to racist claims about the alleged natural superiority or inferiority of any racial group.   *Graciela Bardallo-Vivero*

Core Resources

The Ethnic Phenomenon (New York: Elsevier, 1981), by Pierre L. van den Berghe, is considered a major work in sociobiological theory. The book's main arguments are summarized in his previous article, "Race and Ethnicity: A Sociobiological Perspective," *Ethnic and Racial Studies* (1,4, 1978). Milton Gordon's explanation of ethnocentrism is developed in part I of *Human Nature, Class, and Ethnicity* (New York: Oxford University Press, 1978). Richard H. Thompson reviews and criticizes racial and ethnic relations theories from a sociological point of view in *Theories of Ethnicity: A Critical Appraisal* (New York: Greenwood Press, 1989). Philip Kitcher's highly readable book is entitled *Vaulting Ambition: Sociobiology and the Quest for Human Nature* (Cambridge, Mass.: MIT Press, 1985).

See also: Genetic basis for race; Race as a concept; "Scientific" racism; Social Darwinism and racism; Sociobiology and race; Xenophobia, nativism, and eugenics.

Biracialism

> **Significance:** Mixed-race Americans occupy a hidden or virtually invisible place in society, partly because they are not identified under traditional, one-race categorization systems. They are increasing in number and influence and struggling for acceptance.

Mixed-race people have been called biracial, brown, interracial, mestizo, multiracial, mixed, and rainbow. Strictly speaking, the term's use of the prefix *bi-* indicates two races; however, the concept of race itself is open to debate. Between 1870 and 1920, people of black and white parentage were called "mulatto." Historically, people of racially mixed parentage have been considered to be of the same race as the nonwhite parent—if one parent is black, then the child is considered to be black. If both parents are nonwhite and one is a Native American, then the child is considered to be a Native American. Mixed-race people who appear to be white sometimes "pass" for white and hide their true racial makeup. However, some mixed-race Americans dislike one-race classifications and want to be considered as belonging to more than one race. They argue that generally accepted racial categories do not fit them.

The number of mixed-race births in the United States increased noticeably during the last quarter of the twentieth century. U.S. Census Bureau figures showed that the number of interracial marriages increased from 310,000 in 1970 to 994,000 in 1991. Between 1968 and 1989, children born to parents of different races increased from 1 percent to 3.4 percent of all births. About three-quarters of African Americans are multiracial, and perhaps as many as one-third have some Indian ancestry. Virtually all Latinos and Filipino Americans are multiracial, as are most American Indians. Millions of people who consider themselves white have multiracial roots.

History

The first recorded interracial marriage in U.S. history was between adventurer John Rolfe and Pocahontas, the North American Indian princess reputed to have saved Captain John Smith from execution. Fur traders, trappers, mountain men, and Indians often married and produced racially mixed children throughout the eighteenth and nineteenth centuries.

As more white settlers entered the Americas, laws defining an individual's race and against intermarriage began to be passed. In 1785, a Virginia law defined a black person as anyone with a black parent or grandparent. People were considered white if they were one-eighth black. In 1830, Virginia adopted the notorious "one-drop" law—defining as black anyone with one drop of African blood. Whether a person was black was determined by genealogy, physical appearance, claims to identity and heritage, and blood. In essence, the one-drop law excluded everyone with a black ancestry from white society.

Laws prohibiting sexual relations or marriage between a man and a woman of different races—called miscegenation laws—were in force from the 1660's through the 1960's. The laws, created shortly after African slaves were first brought to colonial America, were attempts to restrict mixing of the races and were among the longest lasting of U.S. racial restrictions and the most prominent examples of white supremacy in action. These laws criminalized mixed-race marriages and illegitimized the children. Legislators passed miscegenation laws, and judges and juries enforced them, because they believed setting racial boundaries and categories was crucial to the maintenance of an orderly society. They were determined to protect "white purity." These laws were issues in civil cases about marriage and divorce, inheritance, and child legitimacy and in criminal cases about sexual misconduct.

A state miscegenation law was first held to be unconstitutional in *Perez v. Lippold* in 1948. The laws prohibiting miscegenation began to fall in the western states in the 1950's and 1960's but persisted in the South until after the landmark *Loving v. Virginia* decision, ruled on by the U.S. Supreme Court in 1967. The Court declared the Virginia miscegenation law unconstitutional because it violated the equal protection and due process clauses of the Fourteenth Amendment. The justices said the Virginia statute was designed to maintain white supremacy through racial categories and argued that culture—not race—determined meaningful human differences. The Court's ruling made racial categories synonymous with racism. In its 1954 ruling on *Brown v. Board of Education*,

Milestones in Interracial History

Year	Event	Impact
1930	Virginia adopts "one-drop" law	Defines a black person as anyone with one drop of African blood
1948	*Perez v. Lippold*	Marks first time a state miscegenation law is held unconstitutional
1954	*Brown v. Board of Education*	Forces states to repeal statutes that define race through blood
1967	*Loving v. Virginia*	Sets precedent that state miscegenation laws are unconstitutional
1977	Statistical Directive No. 15	Creates racial categories for Americans
1993	Congress asked to consider a multiracial category on census and other government forms	Marks birth of a mixed-race rights movement

the Court took another step toward eradicating racism by its deliberate nonrecognition of race. Because of *Brown*, during the 1960's and 1970's, most U.S. states repealed statutes that defined race through blood proportion. The states then attempted to erase racial terminology from their laws.

As the U.S. Supreme Court was trying to limit or eliminate racial categories, the U.S. Office of Management and Budget began to emphasize racial categories. In 1977, it issued a directive that divided Americans into five major groups—American Indian or Alaska native, Asian or Pacific islander, black, white, and Hispanic. The categories were created because the government was mandated by new laws to monitor voting rights and equal access for minorities in housing, education, and employment. These categories and the statistics they generated helped determine everything from census data to eligibility for inclusion in affirmative action programs to the drawing of voting districts. During the biracial baby boom that began in the late 1960's, people who did not fit neatly into these categories were instructed to choose the category that most closely reflected how they were perceived in their communities.

During the late 1970's and 1980's, interracial groups were formed around the country to challenge the official one-category-only classification of multiracial, multiethnic people, particularly in public schools. Some multiracial parents complained that their children were being forced to favor one parent and his or her racial heritage over the other. They argued that forcing children to select one race was a denial of their right to choose who and what they were. In 1990, the U.S. Census Bureau came under mounting pressure to recognize multiracial as a distinct racial category. People who did not want to identify themselves or their children as monoracial led the lobbying campaign to add a multiracial category to the census form. Organizations such as the Association of MultiEthnic Americans argued that monoracial categories were a form of bigotry against racially mixed Americans. They wanted the federal government to establish a public policy that explicitly acknowledged the existence of multiracial/multiethnic people. The government decided against including a multiracial category on the 2000 census; however, it allowed multiracial or multiethnic people to check as many categories as applied.   *Fred Buchstein*

Core Resources

To understand the feelings and experiences of Americans who live in multiracial families, read *Of Many Colors: Portraits of Multiracial Families* (Amherst: University of Massachusetts Press, 1997) by Gigi Kaeser and *Black, White, Other: Biracial Americans Talk About Race and Identity* (New York: Morrow, 1994) by Lise Funderburg. The

cultural, psychological, and social development, identity, and heritage of mixed-race people are explored in *Racially Mixed People in America* (Newbury Park, Calif.: Sage Publications, 1992), edited by Maria P. P. Root, *The New Colored People: The Mixed-Race Movement in America* (New York: New York University Press, 1997), by Jon Michael Spencer, and *Race and Mixed Race* (Philadelphia: Temple University Press, 1993), by Naomi Zack. The culture and diversity of interracial people are treated in *Culture and Difference: Critical Perspectives on the Bicultural Experience in the United States* (Westport, Conn.: Bergin & Garvey, 1995), edited by Antonia Darder, *English Is Broken Here: Notes on Cultural Fusion in the Americas* (New York: The New Press, 1995), by Coco Fusco, and Naomi Zack's *American Mixed Race: The Culture of Microdiversity* (Lanham, Md.: Rowman & Littlefield, 1995).

See also: *Brown v. Board of Education*; Censuses, U.S.; Genetic basis for race; Hypodescent; Interracial and interethnic marriage; Miscegenation laws; Multiracial identity; Multiracial movement; One-drop rule; Passing; Race as a concept.

Bison slaughter

Significance: The mass killings of bison led to the near-extinction of the species and destroyed the lifeblood of the Plains Indians.

In 1853, the American bison population was estimated at between sixty and seventy million animals. It was reduced to a few thousand in thirty years. The bison's decline was the result of human greed, uncontrolled exploitation, and U.S. government policy. Also called the American buffalo, the bison ranged throughout North America from the Rocky Mountains to the Atlantic shoreline and from northern Mexico to southern Canada. Its greatest concentration was on the grasslands of the Great Plains. It was the basis for a total way of life for the Native Americans of that region. The animals provided food, clothing, and shelter. An important part of the nomadic plains tribes' culture was the buffalo-hide tipi, which could be collapsed quickly when the tribe was ready to move on. On the treeless plains, the herds' dried droppings were fuel for the cooking fires.

On the northern Great Plains, where the terrain was rugged, a herd feeding near a cliff would be driven over the precipice by Indian men and boys waving buffalo robes and shouting, an event known as a buffalo jump. The waiting tribe rushed in to butcher as many of the animals as they could. Frequently, many more animals

A train on the Kansas-Pacific line stops to let its passengers shoot bison. The mass killings of the bison in the mid-1800's destroyed the lifestyle of the Plains Indians.

were left dead or dying than could be handled. Contemporaneous writers described the slaughter of from two hundred to two thousand bison in such hunts. However, because of the relatively small population of Native Americans in North America and their primitive weapons, the impact on the bison was slight.

Buffalo Bill and Sport Hunting

With the end of the Civil War, in April, 1865, army troops traveled west to battle the Cheyenne, Lakota Sioux, and Crow. The army contracted with local settlers to supply the troops with "buffalo beef." Workers constructing the new transcontinental railroad also had to be fed. Contractors included William F. Cody, better known as Buffalo Bill, probably the best-recognized of all the bison killers. Hunters frequently skinned the bison, cut out the tongue, and took only some of the meat, leaving the remainder of the bison to rot on the prairie.

Dressed hides were shipped east as lap robes for winter sleigh and buggy rides or were turned into overcoats. Highly romanticized stories by eastern writers about the exploits of Buffalo Bill and other bison hunters quickly made buffalo robes a status symbol. Demand increased, and more bison were slaughtered. Often only the skin was taken, the carcass left to scavengers. Hundreds of thousands of bison were killed each year for food and hides.

Bison also were killed for sport, as it became popular for groups of people to travel to the Great Plains simply to shoot bison. The railroads that linked the East and West cut across the ancient north-south routes of the bison. The seemingly endless herds were an annoyance to the train crews and a temptation to the passengers.

When trains were delayed, passengers fired into the massed animals, killing some and wounding many more. The railroads encouraged this, with advertising to induce people to ride their trains.

It is difficult to obtain accurate data on the number of bison slaughtered. Few records were kept and the killing took place over a wide area. In 1872, in western Kansas, approximately two thousand hide hunters were each bringing down about fifteen bison a day. At that rate, hunters were killing thirty thousand bison per day. As soon as the herds in one area were reduced beyond the point of diminishing returns, the hunters moved elsewhere, seeking larger herds. An 1869 report notes that in a good year, about 250,000 hides were shipped to the New York market alone. Railroad shipments between 1872 and 1874 totaled 1,378,359 hides.

A peculiarity in the behavior of the bison made them easy targets for hunters. Although bison could be stampeded, hunters in ambush could pick off the animals one by one, because they simply stood as others were shot and dropped in place. Hide hunters called it "a stand." Some of the herd nosed at their fallen comrades and then calmly joined the rest of the animals in grazing. A good hunter could kill seventy-five to one hundred bison per day. One especially skillful hunter, in a bet with his fellows and shooting at a stand from ambush, killed one hundred twenty bison in forty minutes.

The slaughter of the bison was far from a managed or controlled affair. Hunters indiscriminately shot the adults and subadults. Calves were ignored except, possibly, for camp meat. Unweaned, orphaned calves, not yet able to graze the abundant grasses, were left to starve to death.

Government Involvement

The U.S. government took the position that the still-warring Native Americans could be subdued if the bison were denied to them. The U.S. Army began a program of interdiction of the herds. General Philip Sheridan spoke out strongly in favor of continuing the slaughter of the buffalo "to settle the Indian question." Sheridan's Civil War comrade, General William Sherman, echoed these sentiments. He stated that the only way to force the Native Americans to reservations and turn them into farmers was to clear the prairies of the bison. The government further supported the bison slaughter by providing free ammunition to any buffalo hunter on request.

Great Herds Are Gone

As early as 1873, fewer and fewer bison were encountered in western Kansas. Hide hunters moved to the northern Great Plains territories and continued the slaughter. The decline spread throughout the range of the bison, and it soon became obvious to most observers that the great herds were gone.

The intensive slaughter for hides was brief, occurring mostly from 1872 to 1874, but the activity extended from 1871 through 1883. Most herds were shot out in about four years, and the hunters then moved on to other areas. Although a few bison survived, undoubtedly the species' numbers had slipped below that level ecologists call the minimum viable population size. For many animals, more than one male and one female are required to begin a breeding population. The great slaughter left the prairies littered with bison skeletons. For years, farmers could gather a cartload or two of bones and sell them to processors for fertilizer. One bone buyer estimated that from 1884 to 1891, he bought the bones of approximately six million bison skeletons.

Neither the settlers nor the Native Americans could believe that the bison was no more. The settlers thought that the herds had migrated to Canada and would soon return. The Native Americans, drawing on their mythology, believed the animals had returned to a great cavern in the ground to reappear if the right prayers were said and the right supplications were made. The great herds were, however, gone. The impact of the hide hunters' indiscriminate slaughter and the U.S. government's interdiction policy eliminated not only the bison but also the Native Americans' traditional nomadic way of life. Reluctantly, but with resignation, they became farmers on reservations as the U.S. government had sought. Perhaps the worst blow to the plains Indians was their loss of the religious and cultural relationship with the bison. Their entire civilization and lifeways had been destroyed along with the animals on which they depended.

Only a few scattered bison and some in private herds escaped the slaughter. Today, brought together in national parks, preserves, and other protected areas, they have survived and multiplied.   *Albert C. Jensen*

Core Resources

David A. Dary's *The Buffalo Book: The Full Saga of the American Animal* (Chicago: Swallow Press, 1974) is a detailed account of bison in North America. *Buffalo* (Edmonton, Canada: University of Alberta Press, 1992), edited by John Foster, is a collection of papers by specialists in ecology and sociology detailing the relationship between the plains Indians and the bison. Anne Matthews's *Where the Buffalo Roam* (New York: Grove Weidenfeld, 1992) describes a plan to restore the Great Plains

to their natural condition and the bison to their former numbers. Don Russell's *The Lives and Legends of Buffalo Bill* (Norman: University of Oklahoma Press, 1960) is a detailed examination of the Army scout and bison hunter.

See also: Indian-white relations: United States.

Black "brute" and "buck" stereotypes

In an effort to curtail African American political power and civil rights in the years following Reconstruction (1863-1877), some southern whites justified a wave of terrorism and lynching by creating new stereotypes of black male brutality. The black "brute" (a figure who was inhumanly brutal) and "buck" (a figure who combined brutality and sexual monstrosity and who desired nothing more than to rape white women) found their clearest early expression in the novels of Thomas Dixon and in D. W. Griffith's 1915 film *Birth of a Nation*, which was largely based on Dixon's *The Clansman* (1905). Although rape was charged only in a minority of lynchings and many of those allegations were false, these stereotypes were of central importance for lynching's public defenders, who insisted that lynching was necessary to defend the supposed purity of white womanhood. One of the most important strategies for antilynching activists and organizations (including Ida B. Wells-Barnett and the National Association for the Advancement of Colored People) was to attempt to undermine the support for lynching by debunking the stereotype of the black rapist. Controversy surrounding the use of black "brute" and "buck" stereotypes in a variety of contemporary arenas (including media and national politics) remains an important area of racial discourse.   *Jonathan Markovitz*

See also: African American stereotypes; African Americans and film; Lynchings; Politics of hate; Prejudice and stereotyping; Stereotyping and the self-fulfilling prophecy.

Black cabinet

The black cabinet was formed by more than a dozen African American men and women who had been appointed to federal positions by President Franklin D. Roosevelt by the year 1935. Known as the Federal Council on Negro Affairs after 1935, it was an informal gathering of African American advisers from various New Deal agencies led unofficially by Mary McLeod Bethune, the director of the National Youth Administration's Division of Negro Affairs. Its members included Robert Weaver, the Negro Affairs adviser in the Public Works Administration, and William Hastie, assistant solicitor in the Department of the Interior. Several other cabinet members later became nationally prominent. They usually met at the home of Bethune or Weaver and informally had some impact on New Deal agencies. Eleanor Roosevelt often provided the impetus behind certain changes after meeting with Bethune.

The appointment of blacks to federal positions symbolized the attempt by some New Dealers to eradicate racial injustice in the United States and influenced some blacks to convert from the Republican to the Democratic Party. President Roosevelt, however, ultimately did not challenge the more intransigent elements of a still segregated society. Still, although the black cabinet did not dramatically alter federal government policies toward African Americans because the appointments were not at the highest levels and its membership was fluctuating, it made white New Dealers more responsive to African American problems.   *David L. Porter*

See also: Roosevelt coalition; Summit Meeting of National Negro Leaders.

Black church

> **Significance:** The term "black church" refers collectively to the many autonomous denominations of African American Christian churches. The black church evolved as a highly visible social institution in response to white racism in American society and racism in white-defined Christianity.

Although African American religious experience is diverse and social forms of religious life vary greatly, the black church has historically been the most visible religious institution in African American culture. As a visible institution controlled from within the black community, the black church has played a central role in African American social and political history. This history has evolved within the broader historical context of American racism and racial politics. The church, also evolving within that broader context, has been an important center for the development of African American Christian theology and for community identity. In fact, the black church originated as a formal institution when African American religious leaders in Philadelphia were forcibly removed from worshiping on the main "whites only" floor of St. George's Methodist Episcopal Church.

When Richard Allen and Absalom Jones were evicted from the church in 1787, they and their fellow black Christians concluded that the racism of white-defined Christianity precluded full Christian expression for blacks in white-controlled congregations. Their formation of the Free African Society that year paved the way for the later creation of the fully autonomous African Methodist Episcopal (AME) Church, one of the earliest black churches in the United States. An institutionalized form of distinct African American Christian theology began to emerge.

Lincoln/Mamiya Model

In their expansive sociological study entitled *The Black Church in the African-American Experience* (1990), C. Eric Lincoln and Lawrence H. Mamiya propose a dynamic model for interpreting the sociology of black churches in their diversity and complexity. Lincoln and Mamiya identify the major black denominations as the AME Church, the AME Zion Church, the Christian Methodist Episcopal (CME) church, the National Baptist Convention, U.S.A., Incorporated (NBCA), the Progressive National Baptist Convention (PNBC), and the Church of God in Christ (COGIC). These denominations, as well as many other smaller ones and local churches, provide institutional structure for the religious (and often political) life of millions of African American Christians.

Although sociologists and political historians debate the nature of the black church and its political role, Lincoln and Mamiya offer a "dialectical model of the black church" that encourages an open and ongoing analysis. The Lincoln/Mamiya model offers a way of analyzing the ongoing tensions, both theological and political, within African American Christianity as those tensions are embodied in the structure of the black church. The model proposes the following six "dialectically related" pairs, or opposites. With these pairs the focus is on the ways that human experience shifts back and forth between the two opposites, sometimes tending more toward one idea, sometimes tending more toward the other.

For example, the first dialectic is that between "priestly" and "prophetic" functions of the church. In other words, it concerns how the church balances its role as the center for worship (priestly) in relation to its role as an agent for social change in the community (prophetic). Second, there is a dialectic tension in the black church between the "other-worldly" and the "this-worldly." Does the church focus on individual spiritual salvation for the "life to come" or does it focus on social justice in the here-and-now? The third dialectic proposed by Lincoln and Mamiya is between "universalism" and "particularism": how the black church negotiates its role in Christianity, broadly speaking, and its very particular role in African American history. The black church is part of a universal religious institution but is also a very particular response to white racism in American Christianity. A fourth dialectic is between the "communal" and the "privatistic": How does the church address individual spiritual life in the context of the social realities of African American experience? The fifth dialectic is especially important politically; it is between the "charismatic" and the "bureaucratic." This involves how the church uses the power of personalized and local leadership in relation to developing larger-scale institutional structure and national leadership as well as how it handles the tensions inherent in doing both. Finally, Lincoln and Mamiya join many African American historians and cultural critics when they identify the dialectical tension between "accommodation" and "resistance." Given the realities of white racism and African American history's origins in the experience of slavery, how has a primary social institution such as the black church moved between accommodating and resisting white mainstream culture in the United States?

Politics and the Church
It is in this final dialectic that much of the debate over the role of the black church in the twentieth century Civil Rights movement evolved. It is debated, for example, whether the church served as an accommodationist spiritual escape that diluted the intensity of its members, whether the church served as a fundamental source of activism and militancy, or whether the black church did both.

During the 1950's and the 1960's, the Civil Rights movement accelerated and moved to the center of the national political stage. Beginning with efforts to integrate schools following the Supreme Court's *Brown v. Board of Education* decision in 1954 and continuing through the Montgomery bus boycott (1955-1956), the formation of the Southern Christian Leadership Conference (1957), the Freedom Rides summer (1961), and the March on Washington (1963), hundreds of thousands of African Americans confronted American racism and fought for fulfillment of the United States' stated commitment to freedom for all its people. The black church played a central role during these years, providing people and resources for grassroots organizing while cultivating leadership for the national movement.

During this period, tensions arose in the black community that illustrate the sociological complexity of the church as a social institution. From the perspective of the emerging Black Power movement, the church was suspect in its adherence to Christian principles of nonviolence in the face of white racial violence and was deluded in its emphasis on integration into mainstream American society. For black nationalists, this main-

stream society remained white-dominated and white-controlled. Some nationalists argued that African American Christianity itself was flawed because of its origins as a religion of enslavement.

From another perspective, political and religious leaders such as Martin Luther King, Jr., proposed that African American Christianity provided both the spiritual and material bases for a militant liberation theology, one that posed a radical challenge to the white-supremacist status quo of the mid-twentieth century United States. King was a nationally recognized Christian leader, but with him were thousands of African American Christian women and men who argued that the black church provided the path of most, rather than least, resistance to white racism. As Lincoln and Mamiya point out, the fact that white racists bombed several hundred black churches during the civil rights period indicates that the threat posed to white supremacy by the black church was substantial.

A second debate that highlights some of the issues from the Lincoln/Mamiya model concerns the role of women in the black church. During the Civil Rights movement, women provided the "rank and file" of many organizing efforts, working together with men to form the core of the movement. In the church, however, men still maintained a monopoly in terms of formal congregational leadership. On the national level, this trend was even more pronounced; the nationally recognized black leadership of the Civil Rights movement was almost exclusively male. Women such as Rosa Parks, Fannie Lou Hamer, and Mamie Bradley (Emmett Till's mother) were recognized on a national level, but the political leadership of black women in many key political battles, especially on the local level, went unacknowledged both in the national media and in the formal leadership structure of the church.

Gender politics are significant because they highlight tensions within the church when issues that are often expressed in secular political terms (such as women's oppression) are also engaged in theological and spiritual terms. This can result in significant structural change within a social institution such as the black church. In the case of women and the church, the political becomes religious and the religious becomes political, bringing into play the dynamic tensions between the "this-worldly" and the "other-worldly," between the "priestly" and the "prophetic."   *Sharon Carson*

Core Resources
E. Franklin Frazier and C. Eric Lincoln's *The Negro Church in America: The Black Church Since Frazier* (New York: Schocken Books, 1974) is an important sociological study that offers the comparative perspectives of two important scholars of the black church. C. Eric Lincoln

and Lawrence H. Mamiya's *The Black Church in the Afri-can-American Experience* (Durham, N.C.: Duke University Press, 1990) covers theoretical and historical issues as well as providing in-depth denominational histories and useful statistical data. Peter J. Paris's *The Social Teaching of the Black Churches* (Philadelphia: Fortress Press, 1985) is a very good source for more detailed discussion of the ways that the black church, as a social institution, has participated in African American culture. *African American Religious Studies: An Interdisciplinary Anthology* (edited by Gayraud S. Wilmore, Durham, N.C.: Duke University Press, 1989) offers both a wide range of readings in the subject of African American religion and an introduction to many important scholars in the field.

See also: African American Baptist Church; AME Church; AME Zion Churches; Church burnings; Civil Rights movement; Free African Society.

Black codes

In their broadest sense, black codes were laws aimed at controlling African American life in the nineteenth century. Some of these laws, the slave codes, applied only to slaves. As America's indigenous black population grew, free blacks became increasingly subject to discriminatory laws designed to ensure their acquiescence to white rule. For example, some states refused to allow black people to carry canes, a widely recognized symbol of authority, and free blacks in nearly all states could be sold into slavery for failure to pay their taxes. Moreover, fearing that free blacks might incite or assist slave insurrections, especially in the wake of Nat Turner's revolt (1831), antebellum black codes became increasingly severe. In most southern states, free black status was barely distinguishable from slave status on the eve of the Civil War.

The term "black codes" most commonly refers to laws passed by former Confederate state legislatures in response to the Thirteenth Amendment to the Constitution (1865). These laws bestowed certain civil rights on the newly freed black population. While these codes varied from state to state, all black codes legitimized African American marriages, recognized their right to own property, and permitted blacks to sue and be sued, enter into contracts, and testify in court cases involving other blacks. On the other hand, most black codes forbade interracial marriage, denied blacks the right to bear arms, and prohibited blacks from testifying against whites in courts of law. On an even more negative note, the black codes merely granted African Americans an apprentice-like status that in no way conferred genuine freedom. They also attempted to tie black employment to a socioeconomic system that closely resembled slavery. Most states required newly freed blacks to secure employment with a local landowner or face involuntary service in plantation labor. Free blacks were also subject to involuntary service for civil offenses ranging from vagrancy and derogatory gestures to "mischief" and preaching the Gospel without a license. Moreover, in some states white landowners were subject to a fine or imprisonment for attempting to hire black laborers who were already under contract to someone else.

Appalled by southern actions, northern congressmen began calling for legislation that would ensure civil rights for all African Americans. The result was the Fourteenth Amendment to the Constitution, which forbade denial of "life, liberty, and property without due process of law" and guaranteed citizenship to all persons born or naturalized in the United States. This amendment, ratified on July 28, 1868, constitutionally guaranteed civil rights that had been stipulated earlier in the Civil Rights Act of 1866. It would take nearly a century, as well as the 1964 Civil Rights Act, however, for African Americans to gain their full civil rights under this constitutional amendment. *Keith Harper*

See also: Civil rights; Civil Rights Act of 1964; Civil Rights Acts of 1866-1875; Fourteenth Amendment; Grandfather clauses; Jim Crow laws; Literacy tests; Miscegenation laws; Turner's slave insurrection.

Black colleges and universities

> **Significance:** Black colleges and universities are historic institutions of higher education that have targeted African American students. They have been a major education vehicle for African Americans, allowing them to become credentialed to interact with others at work and socially and have enhanced intergroup understanding and relations.

Lincoln University in Lincoln, Pennsylvania, established by Presbyterians in 1854, is the oldest black institution of its kind still in existence, and Wilberforce University in Ohio, established by Methodists two years later, is the second oldest. Both facilities have remained in their original locations. However, the first separate educational facilities for blacks were private African schools established by free blacks after the Revolutionary War. Like later black colleges and universities, the early schools provided a strong sense of black identity as well as a way in which students could prepare for employment. Work opportunities, however, were often limited to manual labor or two professions that the larger society felt were less threatening: the ministry and teaching.

Many private and public historically black colleges and universities were established during the post-Civil War era and became the primary means by which African Americans could obtain a higher education in a society that restricted them from attending white institutions, either by law or by social norms. When they were created, many of these colleges were called "universities" or "colleges" but were actually secondary-school-level institutions. When studies that led to the professions of minister and teacher were incorporated into their curricula, these institutions rose to a post-high-school level. In most cases, the post-Civil War historically black colleges and universities included a theological purpose for all students: the instilling of what were considered Christian values.

By the early part of the twentieth century, American philanthropic organizations had started to help support black colleges and universities through financial gifts. In the North and West, these gifts were not considered problematic, but in the South, many whites insisted that fiscal support go to institutions that emphasized vocational and industrial training. Two major black academics of that era, Booker T. Washington of Tuskegee Institute in Alabama and W. E. B. Du Bois of Atlanta University in Georgia, debated the type of education that African Americans, especially in the South, should receive. Washington emphasized the need for vocational and industrial training, while Du Bois focused on education that would lead to the professions. By the 1930's, however, the debate was moot: Most historically black colleges and universities had developed into full-fledged colleges that required a high school diploma for entrance, and many were increasing graduate studies. These developments began to be supported in the 1940's with the establishment of the United Negro College Fund, which pooled the fiscal resources of financially fragile private institutions. By the end of the twentieth century, enrollment at black colleges and universities had increased to its highest levels, which demonstrates that they retained their appeal to African Americans.

Demographics
Historically black colleges and universities are predominantly black academic institutions established before 1964 whose main purpose has historically been the educating of African Americans. Each must be state authorized to provide either a junior college education or a four-year bachelor's degree, and each must be accredited by an association recognized by the U.S. Department of Education or show progress toward achieving that accreditation.

There were 109 historically black colleges and universities in 1995. Fifty of these, or 46 percent of the total, were public institutions, and the remainder were private institutions. They were located in fourteen southern states, three northern states, and three midwestern states plus the District of Columbia and the U.S. Virgin Islands. The institutions offered more than 450 academic programs in the liberal arts, sciences, education, business administration, social work, law, medicine, dentistry, engineering, military science, theology, and other fields. Most of the institutions offered associate or bachelor's degrees. Thirty-eight of the schools offered master's degrees, and twelve offered doctorate degrees. Some offered professional degrees.

Enrollments in black colleges and universities represented about 3 percent of total higher educational institution enrollments in the United States in the mid-1990's. Black enrollments increased from the 1960's to 1980, decreased from 1981 to 1986, and then increased in the late 1980's and the 1990's. Generally, black male enrollment has slightly decreased over these periods, while black female enrollment has increased signifi-

Howard University in Washington, D.C., one of the historically black colleges in the United States, is a respected institute of higher learning.

cantly. Historically black colleges and universities welcome nonblack students. In 1976, white enrollment in these institutions was more than 18,000; by 1989, this had increased to more than 26,000. Some institutions in gateway cities, such as Florida Memorial College in Miami, have had as much as one-third of their total student enrollments come from Hispanic communities. The majority of faculty and staff at these institutions are black, and the remainder are white, Latino, and nonblack foreign nationals. Although the institutions enroll just 20 percent of all African American undergraduates, they produce 30 percent of those who graduate.

Impact

American higher education has always been pluralistic; certain institutions were created primarily to serve students of a particular gender, race, ethnicity, or religion. Black colleges and universities fit this national pattern, even though their histories and original needs may have differed. The impact of these institutions on the African American communities of the United States has been significant: Many of the local and regional African American leaders—ministers, educators, politicians, businesspeople, writers, artists—throughout the latter part of the nineteenth and the entire twentieth century have been graduates of black colleges. One of the more famous graduates is civil rights leader Martin Luther King, Jr. Black colleges and universities, first established from necessity, have continued to be prominent in American educational life because they have a purpose that appeals to their majority clientele, the encouragement and credentialing of an ethnically aware population. At historically black colleges and universities, many black students thrive academically in an environment they consider supportive and socially acceptable.

William Osborne and Max Orezzoli

Core Resources

Historically Black Colleges and Universities: Their Place in American Higher Education, by Julian Roebuck and Komanduri Murty (Westport, Conn.: Praeger, 1993), includes very specific data from studies of race relations among students on both black and white campuses. A fine, older anthology that considers many issues faced by black educational institutions is *Black Colleges in America: Challenge, Development, Survival*, edited by Charles Willie and Ronald Edmonds (New York: Teachers College Press, 1978). Many scholars have contributed to this volume, which includes discussions of the self-concept of the colleges, the role of the graduate, the interaction of black college faculty and students, and teaching in key areas of the sciences and humanities. The United Negro College Fund has edited studies of black colleges and universities that provide continuing statistics and chang-

ing data, such as B. Quarles's "History of Black Education," in *United Negro College Fund Archives: A Guide and Index to the Microfiche* (New York: University Microfilms, 1985). The American Council on Education's Office of Minority Concerns publishes *Minorities in Higher Education: Annual Reports* (Washington, D.C., various years), an annual document full of data and statistics.

See also: Atlanta Compromise; Desegregation: public schools; Education and African Americans; United Negro College Fund.

Black conservatism

> **Significance:** Black conservatives tend to oppose treating people as members of racial groups; therefore, they tend not to support programs that aim at improving the situations of disadvantaged groups by means of what they term "racial preferences," including affirmative action. They usually place little emphasis on discrimination as a cause of minority disadvantages and maintain that individual self-help is the best way to overcome these disadvantages.

Contemporary black conservatism is the product of two related historical developments, the elimination of legal discrimination and the rise of the black middle class. The Civil Rights movement of the 1950's and 1960's was successful in overcoming segregation and overt discrimination by law in the United States. By the end of the 1960's, laws enforcing segregation had been struck down almost everywhere in the United States, and blacks had registered to vote in large numbers. African Americans and whites who believed that racial justice could be achieved simply by the government's ceasing to maintain unequal laws concluded that the Civil Rights movement had achieved its goal of equality between the races. Some argued that any remaining inequality would disappear as individual African Americans achieved higher levels of education and acquired attitudes consistent with upward mobility.

With the disappearance of discriminatory laws, a substantial group of well-educated, financially successful black Americans began to appear. Between 1960 and 1981, the percentage of blacks in the middle class almost tripled, from 13 percent to 38 percent of the black population. In general, the higher the social and economic position of an individual, the more likely that individual is to hold conservative views on matters such as economics and the role of government in society. Black success, then, has tended to encourage black conservatism.

Conservative Black Intellectuals

Thomas Sowell, an economist with degrees from Harvard, Columbia, and the University of Chicago, was one of the earliest and most influential of contemporary black conservatives. From the early 1970's onward, Sowell produced a long string of books in which he argued that liberal attempts to help blacks had simply made them dependent and led them to see themselves as victims. He argued that success is a product of a culture of achievement and that blacks could create such a culture by striving for individual self-sufficiency.

Many of Sowell's themes were adopted by other black academics. Glenn Loury, an economist at Harvard who later moved to Boston University, became well known in the 1980's for his opposition to affirmative action and his advocacy of black self-help. Loury, who expressed discomfort with being labeled as a conservative, argued that many of the problems of inner-city blacks were the result of irresponsible behavior. English professor Shelby Steele sounded many of the same notes in his books, *The Content of Our Character: A New Vision of Race in America* (1991) and *A Dream Deferred* (1998). Steele argued that many African Americans had adopted a view of themselves as victims and that they should concentrate on getting ahead by their own efforts.

The ideas set forth by black conservatives influenced African Americans usually not considered conservative, such as sociologist William Julius Wilson. Wilson maintained that discrimination was no longer as responsible for black disadvantage. The lack of jobs, combined with attitudes and forms of behavior created by dependency, produced the black underclass in the inner city, according to Wilson.

Conservative Blacks in Politics

Conservative black public figures attracted a great deal of attention in the 1980's and 1990's. In 1991, President George Bush nominated Clarence Thomas, an outspoken opponent of affirmative action, to the U.S. Supreme Court. As head of the Equal Employment Opportunity Commission during the administration of President Ronald Reagan, Thomas had rejected lawsuits on behalf of minority members as a group and pursued only lawsuits regarding individual acts of discrimination. Thomas's nomination, despite charges of sexual harassment, was confirmed.

In 1991, Gary Franks of Connecticut became the first black Republican elected to the House of Representatives since 1932. Franks always maintained a conservative position and opposed the Civil Rights Act of 1991. Although Franks was defeated in his majority-white district in 1996, most observers agreed that race was not the reason for his loss.

In the 1996 presidential primaries, black Republican

Four Key Characteristics of Black Conservatives

1. Black conservatives generally oppose racial quotas, set-asides, and other forms of racial preferences. They argue that ending racial discrimination means ending governmental action on behalf of anyone simply on the basis of race. Preferences for members of minority groups, in this view, provoke hostility from whites and create racial conflict. The conservatives maintain that programs such as affirmative action actually undermine black achievement because these goals enable minority members with lower qualifications to obtain jobs or entry into schools. Further, they claim that such programs cast suspicions on the real accomplishments of blacks because many people will believe that those accomplishments are simply products of affirmative action.

2. Black conservatives tend to emphasize the importance of individual responsibility. Poverty may be a product of past discrimination, but it can be overcome only by responsible behavior by individuals and not by political action. Getting and staying married, developing stable work habits, and pursuing long-term goals are, from their point of view, the best responses to minority disadvantages.

3. Their individualism leads black conservatives to advocate programs that give individual blacks the opportunity for upward mobility rather than programs aimed at improving the situation of blacks as a group. Tenant ownership of public housing and vouchers enabling low-income minority members to send their children to private schools are among the programs advocated by black conservatives.

4. Black conservatives usually favor market approaches to the problems of minority members and to social problems in general. They often support tax breaks for minority-owned businesses. Welfare, according to most black conservatives, should be temporary in nature and closely linked to placing welfare recipients in jobs.

Alan Keyes sought the Republican presidential nomination. Keyes, a former U.S. State Department official with a doctorate in government from Harvard, had headed the conservative organization Citizens Against Government Waste. He had run unsuccessfully for U.S. senator from Maryland in 1988 and 1992. His presidential campaign, in which he opposed affirmative action and abortion, also failed to win him the nomination.

Ward Connerly, a former real estate investor who had been appointed by California governor Pete Wilson to the University of California Board of Regents, focused national attention on the campaign against affirmative action. Connerly led the attack on affirmative action programs in the state's university system. He became the foremost proponent of the state's Proposition 209, an initiative banning affirmative action in California that passed in 1997 and was later challenged in the courts.

Criticisms and Defenses

Critics of black conservatives have accused them of saying things that please whites in order to further their own careers and of turning against programs such as affirmative action after benefiting from them. They have pointed out that the majority of black conservatives in political office, including Thomas and Connerly, have been appointed and not elected. Civil rights activist Julian Bond has argued that black conservatives receive attention because they get corporate sponsorship. Critics have pointed out that Thomas was nominated as Supreme Court justice after serving as a federal appellate court judge for only sixteen months. Connerly has been accused of having used minority set-aside programs to make money during his career in real estate.

In response, black conservatives and their defenders have pointed to the continuing existence of a large, poverty-stricken black population in the United States. They have maintained that liberal programs have failed to improve the lives of those in this population. Further, they have accused their critics of stereotyping African Americans as monolithically liberal and of demanding intellectual conformity.   *Carl L. Bankston III*

Core Resources

The views of black conservatives are presented in *Black and Right: The New Bold Voice of Black Conservatives in America* (Westport, Conn.: Greenwood, 1997), edited by Stan Faryna, Brad Stetson, and Joseph G. Conti. This collection of twenty-five essays contains writings by Justice Clarence Thomas, Shelby Steele, and former Connecticut congressman Gary Franks. Many of the goals and arguments of black conservatives are presented in *A Conservative Agenda for Black Americans* (Washington, D.C.: Heritage Foundation, 1990), edited by Joseph Perkins. Stephen L. Carter presents the view that affir-

mative action is unnecessary and harmful to blacks in *Reflections of an Affirmative Action Baby* (New York: Basic Books, 1992), a book about his own experiences as a student at Yale law school. Another highly personal book that presents a perspective usually associated with black conservatism is Shelby Steele's *The Content of Our Character: A New Vision of Race in America* (New York: Harper Perennial, 1991) and *A Dream Deferred* (1998). The essays in Glenn C. Loury's *One by One from the Inside Out: Essays and Reviews on Race and Responsibility in America* (New York: Free Press, 1995) consider the problem of racial inequality in the United States. Although often classified as a conservative, Loury rejects this label and argues that Americans must move beyond the liberal-conservative categories in thinking about race. Economist Thomas Sowell's views on race are in *Race and Culture: A World View* (New York: Basic Books, 1994).

See also: Affirmative action; Black middle class/black underclass relations; Civil Rights movement; Poverty and race; Proposition 209; Set-asides; Thomas/Hill hearings; Wilson-Willie debate.

Black flight

Movement from urban to suburban areas is often thought of as occurring primarily among whites. However, middle-class African Americans have also been leaving cities for suburbs, often settling in primarily black suburbs.

In the decades following World War II, the United States became an increasingly suburban nation as Americans left cities for suburbs. During the 1940's, the federal government began guaranteeing mortgage loans in order to encourage Americans to become homeowners. These mortgage guarantees went primarily to those buying homes in the suburbs, and they frequently underwrote home ownership in neighborhoods that intentionally excluded blacks. At the same time, the growing use of private automobiles and the construction of the freeway network encouraged movement to the suburbs.

As whites became more suburban, blacks became more urban. Early in the twentieth century, the African American population had been primarily rural. As agriculture became more mechanized, blacks moved to urban areas. Black concentration in cities, like white concentration in suburbs, was encouraged by the federal government. The federal Public Housing Authority established public housing largely in central city areas and restricted residence in public housing to the most economically disadvantaged. Because blacks were proportionately much more likely to be poor than whites were, the availability of public housing in cities combined with housing discrimination in the suburbs to bring black Americans into urban areas.

By the 1970's, white movement from the cities to the suburbs had become known as "white flight." Many observers of current events believed that whites were fleeing the cities to get away from blacks. The racial integration of schools, and especially the busing of children to achieve racial integration, may have contributed to the movement of whites out of the cities, although social scientists continue to debate this point.

Whites, however, were not the only ones to move to the suburbs. After the 1960's, the middle-class African American population grew rapidly, and suburban housing became more widely available for them. During the 1970's, the African American suburban population of the United States grew at an annual rate of 4 percent, while the white suburban population grew at a rate of only 1.5 percent. African American movement to the suburbs, labeled "black flight" by some social scientists, continued throughout the 1980's and 1990's. It was driven by many of the same factors that had been driving "white flight": the concentration of the poor in central city areas, the deteriorating condition of urban neighborhoods and schools, and the availability of suburban housing.

Black movement to the suburbs did not, however, lead to fully integrated neighborhoods across the United States. Instead, as authors Douglas S. Massey and Nancy A. Denton maintained in their influential book, *American Apartheid* (1993), African Americans tended to move into majority black suburban neighborhoods. Thus, "black flight" further concentrated minority poverty in the inner city by removing the middle class from inner city neighborhoods, while largely failing to integrate the American suburbs. *Carl L. Bankston III*

See also: Black middle class/black underclass relations; Discrimination: racial and ethnic; Housing; White flight.

Black Is Beautiful movement

The Black Is Beautiful movement, part of a broader drive to change political, economic, and social conditions for African Americans, emphasized the importance of countering stereotyped representations. Originating in the Black Power movement of 1965-1975, the phrase "black is beautiful" appealed to large segments of the black community not directly involved with movement organizations. Music and visual arts were central to this appeal: James Brown's "Say It Loud, I'm Black and I'm Proud" and Aretha Franklin's "Respect" signified the change in spirit from earlier integrationist phrases of the movement. Movement theorists, including Kwanza founder

Ron (Maulana) Karenga, declared the necessity of an art connected with the African American community and committed to its well-being and proposed that black art should "praise the people" as well as "expose the enemy" and "support the revolution." The Black Is Beautiful movement initiated sustained investigations of African traditions and history and celebrated the distinctiveness of African American culture. The success of evocations of "soul" in black music, food, speech, physical beauty, body language, and clothing inspired the creation of independent presses and bookstores and student demands for African American studies departments. Though the Black Power movement lost most of its impetus by 1975, the Black Is Beautiful ethos exerts a continuing influence on the struggles for multicultural, feminist, and homosexual self-definition.

Trudi D. Witonsky

See also: African American stereotypes; Black Power movement.

Black Jews

In its broadest sense the term "black Jews" includes all persons of African descent in the United States who claim to practice Judaism. Not all such blacks call themselves Jews; believing that the word "Jew" implies whiteness, some prefer to label themselves "black Hebrews" or "Israelites." There are no authoritative figures on the number of black Jews in the United States. Estimates run from 40,000 to 500,000, but the sources do not reveal how these numbers were established. One scholar, using the narrow definition of Jewishness accepted by Orthodox rabbis, puts the number at no more than 5,000.

Accounts were occasionally printed in the nineteenth century of individual African Americans who attended Jewish congregational services, some of whom were said to have formally converted to Judaism. Not until the twentieth century were there reports of black Jewish congregations in the northern part of the United States. These were small synagogues or temples founded by African Americans and led by self-proclaimed black "rabbis." Many were trained and "ordained" by Wentworth Arthur Matthew, who founded the Commandment Keepers Ethiopian Hebrew Congregation in Harlem, New York, in 1919. Matthew was inspired by Marcus Garvey's Back-to-Africa movement and its celebration of the superiority of African civilization. Rejecting Christianity as a religion imposed on slaves by whites, he claimed to be reconstructing a proud African Jewish heritage, taken away from blacks during slavery, that traced its roots through Ethiopia to the Jews of the Bible. Matthew was convinced that the ancient Hebrews were a black people, a belief also held by black Jews who asserted that they were descended from the lost tribes of Israel.

Practices among black Jewish groups vary enormously. Congregations following the example of Rabbi Matthew attempt to observe Orthodox ritual traditions, though they might add their own dress and musical or liturgical forms. They eat only kosher foods, hold services on Fridays and Saturdays, and celebrate Jewish holidays, especially the Passover festival, which has particular resonance for African Americans. Others include Christian elements and symbols in their services. Some who call themselves black Hebrews or Israelites try to reconstruct the primitive Judeo-Christianity of the first century, asserting that Jesus is the Messiah of the Jews but rejecting most Christian theology.

Whether trying to reclaim a mythical African past or hoping to establish a new identity, blacks were not welcomed by most white Jewish congregations. Some did become fully accepted members of regular Orthodox, Conservative, or Reform synagogues if they satisfied the Orthodox definition of Jewishness by being a child of a Jewish mother. Other African Americans became Jews through formal conversions, often entered into because they were a partner in a mixed marriage. With few exceptions, black synagogues and leaders have not been accepted as legitimate by the formal religious or secular American Jewish community nor been admitted into national denominational groups or local rabbinical councils. Most black groups have never applied for such membership, and those that have applied have had their applications ignored. Few black leaders have ever received official rabbinic ordination, although all heads of black synagogues call themselves rabbis, using their title in its original meaning, that of teacher.   *Milton Berman*

See also: Jewish-African American relations; Jewish ethnicity: definitions; Judaism.

Black middle class/black underclass relations

Significance: Much scholarly debate has taken place on the extent and consequences of the interactions between the black middle class and black underclass, in particular the effect of middle-class presence on the lives of poor urban blacks. A number of theories of urban poverty identify the lack of a connection between the black underclass and black middle class as a factor in the perpetuation of poverty.

The first step in understanding the relationship between the black middle class and the black underclass is to examine the concept of the underclass. The meaning and usefulness of the term have been debated frequently among scholars; however, the concept is potentially beneficial because it describes the new form of poverty that exists in urban areas. This inner-city poverty, unlike that of earlier decades, is characterized by chronic and persistent joblessness, concentration in a particular geographic area, and racial segregation.

The Underclass
The term "underclass" implies a lack of social and economic mobility. Although considerable progress was made toward racial equality in the 1950's and 1960's, some researchers believe that this progress has stopped and perhaps even reversed itself since the early 1970's. As signs of persistent inequality, they cite a growing gap in the incomes of blacks and whites, lower economic rewards for higher educational attainments on the part of blacks, and greater segregation and isolation of the races rather than increased mobility. The concept of an underclass, therefore, they argue, is an appropriate portrayal of the urban poor.

However, regardless of its potential, the term "underclass" has been stigmatized to the point that it has lost much of its usefulness as an analytical tool. Much of the discussion about the underclass does not focus on the structural factors that have segmented this population and constrained its members' mobility. Instead, the discussion tends to focus on crime and other negative products of poverty. This negative image has diverted attention from scholarly analysis and instead produced racism-tinged discussions of the immorality of the poor. The idea that people are impoverished because of their immorality and unwillingness to work is deeply rooted in American ideology. Many people believe that the United States is a meritocracy, in which all people are rewarded for their hard work on the basis of merit, and that no inequities factor into this equation. Therefore, many Americans equate the underclass with the "undeserving poor." This emphasis on the supposed immorality and deviance of the poor stigmatizes the underclass and turns the urban poor into scapegoats for many of the nation's problems. For example, some people believe that economic strain is caused primarily not by changes in the economy or the effects of inflation but by the use of tax money to support the underclass.

The concept of the underclass also evokes images of poor, young, urban African Americans that often produce feelings of fear, anger, and disdain among members of the white middle and upper classes. Although it is no longer socially acceptable to speak of members of racial minorities in disparaging terms, some of the harsh criticisms of the supposed immorality and criminal tendencies of the poor inner-city African Americans mask lingering racist attitudes toward blacks. The moral and racist connotations of the term "underclass" have made it ineffective as a conceptual framework for understanding the truly disadvantaged and the structural forces that have produced their poverty.

Community

The degree of community believed to exist between the black middle class and the black underclass varies. Some scholars suggest that the African American community has diverged so much that the two groups share very little in common. In *The Declining Significance of Race* (1978), sociologist William Julius Wilson suggests that class, not race, is becoming the fundamental category of stratification in U.S. society. Therefore, he argues that members of the black middle class have much more in common with their white peers than with the poor and working-class members of their racial group.

The Declining Significance of Race produced heated debate among academics and numerous scholars who argued that race was still a primary determinant of life opportunities in the United States. They said that although no one could deny the increasing class differentiation within the African American community, the stratification could not be said to measure racial equality. Racial inequality could still be observed in differences between whites and blacks in income, education, mortality, housing, psychological well-being, and other measures of the quality of life. The black middle class still suffers from lingering racism and discrimination in spite of civil rights legislation and affirmative action policies. Its increasing prosperity, occurring as it does alongside the severe hardship of the black underclass, is not a sign of the amelioration of racial discrimination.

Wilson suggests that when segregation was legal, the black community experienced a much stronger form of class integration. The black middle class lived and worked among poor and working-class blacks. The black middle class provided valuable social and material resources to their less advantaged neighbors. However, with the post–World War II economic boom and the passing of legislation against racial discrimination and segregation, the black middle class expanded and separated itself from the rest of the community. The class structure within the black community became more differentiated and hierarchical.

However, researchers warn against forming too communal a view of the segregated ghetto. Closer inspection of historical studies of the black ghetto during segregation shows that the African American community evidenced a highly stratified society within a compact geographical space. Although they were not totally able to separate themselves from the rest of the black community, the black middle class continuously attempted to form discrete enclaves within the geographic area. Without the forced segregation resulting from white racism, the black middle class would probably have been more successful at separating themselves spatially from poor and working-class blacks. Although researchers agree that the black middle class lived in close proximity to poor blacks, almost no data exist about the frequency and quality of their interactions.

Implications

Many scholars as well as community activists are hoping that the black middle class will become more involved in improving the opportunities of poor African Americans. Through mentoring and youth development programs, members of the black middle class are encouraged to share their knowledge, social networks, and values with black urban youth. A strong political movement within the African American community is seeking resources to address its social needs. Specifically, the disillusionment with liberal politics has led many African American activists to emphasize themes of empowerment and self-determination. This new political agenda, known as black empowerment, places much more emphasis on the dimensions of class and community. It focuses on the control of land in urban communities, emphasizing the economic and cultural strengthening of African American communities. Such a political agenda requires a strong interclass coalition and a commitment of the black middle class to share material and social resources.

Kesha S. Moore

Core Resources

Numerous books address the issues of race, class, and community. These include Elijah Anderson's *Streetwise: Race, Class, and Change in an Urban Community* (Chicago: University of Chicago Press, 1990), Oliver C. Cox's *Caste, Class, and Race: A Study in Social Dynamics* (New York: Doubleday, 1948), Edward Franklin Frazier's *Black Bourgeoisie* (New York: Free Press, 1965), Douglas Massey and Nancy A. Denton's *American Apartheid: Segregation and the Making of the Underclass* (Cambridge: Harvard University Press, 1993), W. J. Wilson's *The Declining Significance of Race: Blacks and Changing American Institutions* (Chicago: University of Chicago Press, 1978), St. Clair Drake and Horace Cayton's *Black Metropolis: A Study of Negro Life in a Northern City* (1945; reprint, Chicago: University of Chicago Press, 1993), and W. E. B. Du Bois's *The Philadelphia Negro: A Social Study* (1899; reprint, Philadelphia: University of Pennsylvania Press, 1996).

See also: Class theories of racial/ethnic relations; Economics and race; Meritocracy myth; Poverty and race;

Racial/ethnic relations: race-class debate; Wilson-Willie debate.

Black nationalism

> **Significance:** Black nationalism is an identity movement that emphasizes the distinctiveness of black heritage and culture and a revitalization movement that seeks to empower black communities so that they direct their own futures and have more control over their relations with other racial and ethnic groups.

Black nationalism, a historical movement that dates back to the sixteenth century, first appeared as protests by enslaved blacks who were being transported to the Americas and continued in the form of organized slave revolts that lasted until the Emancipation Proclamation. These protests could be termed nationalistic because the participants attempted to reclaim historic identities and rejected the power that whites had over them. One of the earliest, best-organized black nationalist movements was started by Paul Cuffe between 1811 and 1815. Cuffe was a black sea captain who transported several dozen black Americans to Africa in an attempt to establish a colony in Sierra Leone. Although black nationalism took various forms in the history of the United States, blacks who emphasized their identity and power have always existed.

The International Aspect

Black nationalism has been most explicitly expressed and most broadly studied in the United States, but the movement is not limited to one nation. Black nationalists have asserted their distinctiveness and attempted to achieve self-empowerment in many postcolonial coun-

Milestones for Black Nationalist Movements

Year	Person Responsible	Event
1815	Paul Cuffe (1759-1817)	Makes the first attempt to establish a black American colony in Sierra Leone, creating a pan-black movement between the continents.
1831	Nat Turner (1800-1831)	This black bondsman leads the most effective and sustained rebellion among slaves in American history.
1909	W. E. B. Du Bois (1877-1965)	Helps create the National Association for the Advancement of Colored People with the larger intent of forming a pan-African movement.
1920	Marcus Garvey (1887-1940)	Recruits masses of black Americans into his Universal Negro Improvement Association, which attempts to create a black nation in Africa that would be controlled by African Americans.
1931	Elijah Muhammad (1897-1975)	This spiritual leader of the Nation of Islam for three decades increases its membership and disseminates its ideas of race pride and self-determination.
1964	Malcolm X (1925-1965)	The major spokesperson for the Nation of Islam forms a separate organization that emphasizes action by many oppressed communities throughout the world.
1966	Huey P. Newton (1942-1989)	Along with Bobby Seale founds the Black Panther Party for Self-Defense, which organizes black communities to protect themselves and offers black education.
1995	Louis Farrakhan (1933-)	Nation of Islam head minister correlates nationalistic themes with external groups in events such as the Million Man March in Washington, D.C.

tries in the world, including Caribbean basin nations such as Jamaica, the Bahamas, Trinidad and Tobago, and earlier in history, Haiti. Nationalistic feelings not only helped black people in these nations rid themselves of the European powers that had colonized them but also continue to affirm their distinctiveness. Black nationalist organizations have been active in Brazil, South Africa, and western Europe, particularly Great Britain. Many of the movements outside the United States have influenced blacks in America, and American black nationalists have had an effect on blacks in other countries, especially during the latter half of the twentieth century.

Black Nationalist Leaders

Throughout U.S. history, the black nationalist movement has been led by members of the clergy. In slave eras, some religious leaders would sing black spirituals that often had a political and social meaning in addition to their theological intent. Some of these songs, such as "Steal Away to Jesus," were used to gather plantation slaves who would escape to freedom. In post-slave eras, African American ministers often became the major organizers of nationalistic movements because they were the primary leaders of black communities. In their sermons, ministers often drew analogies between the enslaved people of Israel in the Old Testament and disfranchised African Americans. Some black theologians such as Joseph Washington have suggested that black churches functioned as political organizations whose main goal was freedom from white oppression. In the early twentieth century, African American sociologist W. E. B. Du Bois advocated a dual-consciousness for blacks that emphasized their distinctiveness while recognizing them as Americans. Eventually Du Bois became disenchanted with the limitations on black status in the United States and explicitly promoted a Pan-African movement that would coordinate freedom movements between blacks in America and Africa. Toward the end of his life, he considered Africa the national homeland for all blacks and encouraged them to migrate there.

Marcus Garvey, a West Indian who had immigrated to the United States, was the creator of the largest mass movement of nationalistic blacks in the history of the nation. Under the auspices of his Universal Negro Im-

Members of the Black Panthers Party, a leading advocate of black nationalism, gather at the Alameda County courthouse in Oakland, California, to protest the trial of party leader Huey P. Newton.

provement Association (UNIA), millions of American blacks were recruited to one of the institutions and businesses he set up as alternatives to white-dominated facilities. These included black capitalist enterprises such as restaurants, grocery stores, hotels, and entertainment centers and a steamship line that served to transport black Americans wishing to migrate to Africa. Most important, he also established the African Orthodox Church, a religious denomination that symbolized the highest values of a people seeking freedom and empowerment. White hostility and organizational mismanagement diminished the UNIA's influence, but Garvey had demonstrated how separate institutions could help African Americans maintain their group identity and be empowered to express it.

Contemporary Black Nationalism

Many black movements followed in Garvey's footsteps, but one, in particular, has been successful in continuing parts of his legacy while rejecting any notion of moving back to Africa. The Nation of Islam, whose members are sometimes called Black Muslims, flourished under the leadership of Elijah Muhammad between the 1930's and the 1960's, reaching a peak membership of more than 100,000. The group's membership, however, does not reflect the many African Americans who did not join the organization but admired its tenets. The Nation of Islam shared Garvey's insistence that African Americans have their own separate organizations in a white-dominated nation and claimed that the black nation in the United States had a right to be an independent nation with its own land. The Nation of Islam claimed that blacks were the original people of creation and, therefore, the pure race. Blacks were to remain separate from nonblacks because interacting with nonblacks could only make them less pure. The Nation of Islam emphasizes the central role of the man in the family, the importance of economic self-sufficiency, the necessity to abstain from degrading habits such as alcohol, drugs, and casual sex, and the worship of Allah, the creator. Their institutions are primarily mosques and religious houses of teaching and worship, but they also have agricultural areas in the South, small businesses in the North, and some educational facilities such as elementary schools in their headquarters, Chicago, Illinois.

The death of Elijah Muhammad and the division of his organization into several groups has not diminished the influence of some of his followers. Louis Farrakhan, the leader of the most important of these groups, has expanded membership, accepted some Latinos and other minorities into the Nation, and correlated the Nation of Islam's agenda with non-Muslim organizations including black Christian churches and black community-based political groups.

The Impact of Black Nationalism

The two major debates among black nationalists in the United States center on whether African Americans need to return to Africa or at least live separately and on what kind of alliances they should form with other organizations and people. Many people question whether a group can be seriously nationalistic without going back to Africa or establishing a separate territory within a previously white-dominated country. Malcolm X, who was Elijah Muhammad's primary spokesperson while he was a member of the Nation of Islam, first believed in setting up a separate nation within United States boundaries but later perceived nationalism as a commitment and act that did not require geographical separation. Huey P. Newton and Bobby Seale, cofounders of the nationalistic Black Panther Party for Self-Defense, interpreted existing African American communities as unofficial black "places" that should be allowed self-determination and the expression of racial pride. Farrakhan has played down the notion of a separate land and instead emphasized the idea of separate thought. The second debate involves how closely black nationalists should ally themselves with either blacks who are not nationalistic or nonblacks. Malcolm X's organization,

founded after he left the Nation of Islam, Newton's Black Panther Party, and even Farrakhan's organization have worked with nonblacks, and all three have interacted with African American Christian clergy, who remain important black community spokespersons and organizers.

In the 1960's, when the U.S. Congress passed a series of desegregation laws, some people believed it would result in the demise of black nationalism. However, because the legal changes did not substantially affect discriminatory customs and attitudes, and African Americans remained the object of subtler forms of racism in their economic, political, and social lives, nationalism survived and grew. African Americans, even if they do not belong to a black nationalistic organization, continue to feel nationalistic pride and to attempt to empower themselves. As long as the United States is not a racially blind nation, it is likely that black nationalistic thinking and acts will affect American life. Black communal pride and black self-determination, the marks of identity and revitalization movements, remain relevant as long as the social implications of black "inferiority" persist.   *William Osborne and Max Orezzoli*

Core Resources

Modern Black Nationalism: From Marcus Garvey to Louis Farrakhan (New York: New York University Press, 1997), an exceptional anthology, relates the major black power era leaders' ideas and discusses contemporary movements through the 1990's. The major academic proponent of black nationalism, W. E. B. Du Bois, traces his own evolving thinking and contradicts some of his earlier social ideas in *Dusk of Dawn: An Essay Toward an Autobiography of a Race Concept* (New York: Harcourt Brace, 1940). For interviews of major figures of the movement, see *The Negro Protest: James Baldwin, Malcolm X, Martin Luther King Talk with Kenneth B. Clark*, edited by Kenneth B. Clark (Boston: Beacon Press, 1963). An incisive interpretation of the changes in Malcolm X's life and thought appear in George Breitman's *Last Year of Malcolm X: The Evolution of a Revolutionary* (New York: Merit Publishers, 1967). One of the most important historical works on the Nation of Islam is C. Eric Lincoln's *The Black Muslims in America* (Boston: Beacon Press, 1961). The Black Panther Party's minister of information, Eldridge Cleaver, wrote the twentieth century classic autobiography evidencing black identity problems called *Soul on Ice* (New York: McGraw-Hill, 1968).

See also: Afrocentrism; Black church; Black Is Beautiful movement; Black Panther Party; Black Power movement; Nation of Islam; Transnationalism and ethnonationalism; Universal Negro Improvement Association.

Black-on-black violence

Black-on-black violence reached epidemic proportions in the United States in the 1990's. This particular manifestation of intraethnic violence is frequently miscast as a relatively recent (post-1960's) phenomenon. However, social historian James W. Clarke documents an increased prevalence of violence within African American urban and rural communities since the nineteenth century. What has changed is the rate of increase of such violent confrontations and the youth of the victims. In the late 1990's, homicide surpassed disease and accident as the number-one cause of death in male African Americans age fifteen to thirty-four, and the lifetime risk of death by homicide was six times greater for African Americans than for whites. Earlier notions of the causes of black-on-black violence were based on presumed racial (biologically/genetically based) differences in aggression. Later, more psychologically oriented views portrayed black-on-black violence as compensation for self-perceived inferiority, manifested as self-hate.

Such views, while persistent among the general population, have been largely discredited. Black-on-black violence may be more reasonably viewed as a cultural phenomenon rather than as a racially or psychologically based act. Contemporary theory on black-on-black violence is typified by that of sociologist William J. Wilson, who postulates that disadvantage in community structure predicts violence equally in both African American and white neighborhoods. The fact that more African Americans than whites live in the conditions that promote violent behavior results in the different rates of intraethnic violence between African Americans and whites. Isolation from the society at large, diminished access to traditional role models, and dimmer job prospects make systematic upward mobility a dream that is not likely to be visualized or attained. The result is an erosion in the ability of traditional social controls such as schools and community self-supervision to govern violent behavior.

The black-on-black violence witnessed at the end of the 1990's may be attributed to several factors. The number of poverty-stricken communities, along with the magnitude of poverty in the most disadvantaged neighborhoods, has risen steadily since the 1970's. The resultant increase in stressors, plus context-specific attitudes advocating extreme response to relatively minor infractions, has a synergistic effect, creating a vicious cycle in which young persons witness routinized violence as a problem-solving tool, come to view such violence as a norm, and adopt this behavior as teenagers and adults, effectively modeling this behavior for subsequent generations. If handguns are readily available, people may tend to settle perceived challenges using guns rather than their fists, with devastating consequences.

The single best predictor of aggressive behavior as an adult is aggressive behavior as a child or adolescent. It is likely, therefore, that the surge in black-on-black violence has not yet crested. Systemic problems require systemic solutions. Such solutions are aided by a rising reconceptualization of black-on-black violence as a major public health issue requiring societywide prevention and intervention techniques to stem the epidemic. According to sociologist William Oliver, steps in the solution include providing greater access to education and jobs, greater dispersal of African Americans into the society at large, more stringent gun-control laws, strategically placed violence-prevention programs, and renewed community dedication toward the functional socialization of African American youth.   *James B. Epps*

See also: Crime and race/ethnicity; Criminal justice system; Ethnoviolence.

Black Panther Party

> **Significance:** The Black Panther Party for Self-Defense was considered a militant organization of African Americans that grew rapidly in major U.S. cities between 1966 and the mid-1970's. The party's confrontational approach to race and ethnic relations marked a change in focus of the Civil Rights movement from nonviolence to self-defense and black power.

The Black Panther Party was founded in 1966 by Huey P. Newton and Bobby Seale, two African American college students, in Oakland, California. The organization grew rapidly in urban areas of the United States and is estimated to have increased to between two thousand and five thousand members in its first three years. The overall objective of the Black Panthers was political, economic, and social equality for the African American community. Their philosophy and strategies differed from the nonviolent and civil disobedience tactics of the earlier Civil Rights movement. From the Black Panther viewpoint, the African American community was exploited and dominated by the United States' capitalist power structure, which used the police as a controlling force. Emphasis was therefore placed on self-defense, black unity, and achieving equal rights "by any means necessary."

Party Philosophy

The Black Panthers promoted a "revolutionary nationalist" philosophy that called for African American liberation and black community empowerment through self-

Black Panther Party founders Bobby Seale (left) and Huey P. Newton pose wearing the hats, leather jackets, and guns that expressed the party's militant stance.

reliance and the destruction of capitalism. Their teachings combined the black nationalist philosophies of Malcolm X with Maoist socialist philosophy. The Black Panthers' philosophy is summarized in its Ten Point Program, called "What We Want, What We Believe":

1. We want freedom. We want power to determine the destiny of our Black Community.
2. We want full employment for our people.
3. We want an end to the robbery by the capitalist of our Black Community.
4. We want decent housing, fit for shelter of human beings.
5. We want education for our people that exposes the true nature of this decadent American society. We want education that teaches us our true history and our role in the present-day society.
6. We want all Black men to be exempt from military service.
7. We want an immediate end to POLICE BRUTALITY and MURDER of Black people.
8. We want freedom for all Black men held in federal, state, county, and city prisons and jails.
9. We want all Black people when brought to trial to be tried in court by a jury of their peer group or people from

their Black communities, as defined by the Constitution of the United States.
10. We want land, bread, housing, education, clothing, justice, and peace. And as our major political objective, a United Nations-supervised plebiscite to be held throughout the Black colony in which only Black colonial subjects will be allowed to participate, for the purposes of determining the will of Black people as to their national destiny.

Party Programs

The Black Panther Party, identified by the distinctive black leather jackets and berets worn by members, was best known for its confrontational activities. These included openly carrying guns (then legal in California if unloaded), directly challenging the local police, and espousing antigovernment rhetoric. One of the Black Panthers' earliest strategies was monitoring the activities of the police in the African American community. In their role of "policing the police," Black Panthers would observe police interactions with community residents and inform the community members of their rights.

The Black Panthers were also known for the "survival programs" that they initiated. The first and most popular of these programs was the Free Breakfast for School Children Program, which began in 1970. It provided breakfasts for children in the community with food donated by local merchants. The survival programs in various Black Panther chapters included free clothing programs, legal assistance, and preventive health care services. The Black Panthers also sought to distribute alternative newspapers within the community. The Black Panther newspaper, *Black Panther: Black Community News Service*, was established in 1967 to facilitate this goal. The Black Panthers joined with other radical organizations of that period, including the Students for a Democratic Society (SDS) and the Student Nonviolent Coordinating Committee (SNCC).

The Destruction of the Party

The Black Panthers were viewed with great apprehension and disdain by the larger American population. The media emphasized their criminality and portrayed them as a violent, antiwhite organization. From the federal government's perspective, the Black Panther Party was an internal threat to the country. As head of the Federal Bureau of Investigation (FBI), J. Edgar Hoover spearheaded systematic efforts to infiltrate, attack, and destroy the Black Panthers through the Counterintelligence Program (COINTELPRO) administered by the FBI. This strategy, which began in the late 1960's, fueled internal conflicts between Black Panther Party members and external tensions between the party and other African American organizations. Other tactics employed included police raids on Black Panther headquarters, killing and jailing of members, and the use of infiltrators and informers. These actions hastened the Black Panther Party's destabilization and demise in the mid-1970's.   *M. Bahati Kuumba*

Core References

Huey P. Newton, founder of the Black Panther Party, wrote two books, *To Die for the People* (New York: Random House, 1972) and *Revolutionary Suicide* (New York: Harcourt Brace Jovanovich, 1973). Bobby Seale's *Seize the Time: The Story of the Black Panther Party and Huey P. Newton* (New York: Random House, 1968) chronicles the emergence and philosophy of the Black Panther Party from an insider's perspective. Panther minister of information Eldridge Cleaver's version of the Black Panther philosophy and ideology appears in *Soul on Ice* (New York: Dell, 1968). Elaine Brown's autobiography, *A Taste of Power* (New York: Pantheon, 1993), provides an insider woman's perspective of the Black Panthers. The historical documents of the Black Panther Party have been compiled by Philip Foner in *The Black Panthers Speak— The Manifesto of the Party: The First Complete Documentary Record of the Panthers Program*. For an illustrated introduction to the Black Panther Party, see Herb Boyd's *Black Panthers for Beginners* (New York: Writers and Readers, 1995).

See also: Black Power movement; Civil Rights movement.

Black Power movement

In 1967, Stokely Carmichael (later Kwame Toure) and Charles V. Hamilton, in their book *Black Power* (1967), argued that "black power" as a concept rests on the premise that before a group can enter the open society it must first close ranks. Carmichael, head of the Student Nonviolent Coordinating Committee (SNCC), and Hamilton, a professor at Columbia University, captured the mood of many young blacks in 1966 who rejected the nonviolent, assimilationist, Civil Rights movement led by Martin Luther King, Jr. Carmichael, who had marched with King in the South, split with King to adopt a more militant approach to combating American racism. By the summer of 1966, black power became the rallying cry for angry young blacks. As a movement it demanded an end to social injustice and a redefinition of the black liberation struggle that would be shaped by blacks themselves.

Although the movement was first associated with Carmichael, other prominent leaders of the movement included H. Rap Brown (later Jamil al-Amin), who led a protest delegation to the United Nations, Huey P. Newton and Eldridge Cleaver, major figures in the Black

Black power advocate Stokely Carmichael, head of the Student Nonviolent Coordinating Committee, speaks at the University of California, Berkeley, in 1966.

Panther Party in Oakland, California, Bobby Seale of the Black Panthers, author-poet LeRoi Jones (later Imamu Amiri Baraka), author-professor Angela Davis, and Ron (Maulana) Karenga, founder of the black cultural holiday known as Kwanza.

Although united by their militant opposition to what they saw as injustice toward blacks, black power groups differed in their vision of the future and in the political strategies they embraced. For example, groups associated with Karenga redefined black culture in terms of Kwanza, while Jones and Brown redefined black culture in terms of Islam. Cleaver and Newton's Black Panthers gained notoriety for violent encounters, including shootouts with police. Regardless of their ideological differences, black power groups frightened many whites. Another aspect of the Black Power movement was the joining of some black militants with white radicals to forge a potent antiwar movement (members of the Black Panther Party, for example, worked with white radical groups such as Students for a Democratic Society).

Like many white radicals, black power leaders modified their political views over time, creating a decline in the movement. For example, Carmichael became a pan-Africanist and emigrated to the West Africa state of Guinea. Newton earned a Ph.D. degree but died violently in 1989 at the hands of drug lords in California. Karenga and Davis became college professors in California. Cleaver, who became a born-again Christian and a Republican, died in 1998. Jamil al-Amin became the leader of a large Islamic community in Atlanta, Baraka became a Marxist college professor in New York, and Seale wrote a cookbook in the early 1990's. The presence of blacks in various fields in the 1990's can be seen as a reminder of the legacy of both the Civil Rights and Black Power movements and their impact on social justice in the United States. *Samory Rashid*

See also: Black Panther Party; Civil Rights movement; Student Nonviolent Coordinating Committee.

Blackness and whiteness: legal definitions

The inconsistencies in racial categories over the course of U.S. history reveal the inherent social construction of race. The federal government has never legally defined "whiteness" and "blackness," but individual states have done so in myriad ways that have fluctuated with changes in racial attitudes.

The United States Census illustrates the fluidity of racial definitions on a national level. The Office of Management and Budget (OMB), which constructs the racial options on the census, continues to alter the number and description of these categories. These determinations are influenced by common usage in the population. For example, in 1790, the first U.S. Census divided the population into free white males, free white females, slaves, and other persons (these included free blacks and American Indians residing in or near white settlements).

Throughout most of the nineteenth century, the U.S. census broke African Americans down into black and mulatto (mixed-race) racial categories. The 1890 census created the categories of quadroon and octoroon (one-quarter and one-eighth black, respectively) to distinguish between various black-white biracial persons. Toward the beginning of the twentieth century, as the "one-drop rule" ("one drop" of black blood made the person black) became entrenched in U.S. society, the census no longer included any mixed-race categories. After 1920, the census classified persons with any African ancestry as black.

Through 1950, census enumerators determined the racial classification of the individuals they recorded. In 1960, the bureau collected data through a combination of observation, direct interviews, and self-classification. Since the 1970 census, the primary means of collecting data has been through self-administered surveys. Debate over methods of data collection escalated toward the end of the 1990's, with some advocating statistical sampling as a means of obtaining a more accurate count of U.S. residents.

Although the majority of Americans with African heritage also have American Indian and/or white ancestors, there was no significant change in the percentage of Americans racially classified as black when the census became self-administered. This indicates the internalization of the "one-drop rule" among Americans with African American ancestry and may also be attributed to the lack of a multiracial option and census instructions to choose only one racial category. In 1998, the OMB, in response to the requests of the growing multiracial movement, decided to include instructions to "check all that apply" among the racial category options on the 2000 census.

No national legal definitions of "white" and "black" exist in the United States. The race of Americans is determined by the legislation of individual states. The census describes white Americans as those "having origins in any of the original peoples of Europe, the Middle East, or North Africa" and black or African Americans as those persons "having origins in any of the black racial groups of Africa." It is unclear how much longer these categories will exist. The categorization of persons by race and the very concept of race are increasingly challenged throughout all levels of American society. Just as racial categories on the census face an uncertain future, states' legal definitions of "whiteness" and "blackness" may soon be under fire.   *Kathleen Odell Korgen*

See also: Biracialism; Censuses, U.S.; *Ozawa v. United States*; Race as a concept; Whites.

Bleeding Kansas

> **Significance:** A territorial war between free-soil and proslavery elements presages a national civil war.

With the opening of Kansas Territory to settlement in 1854 through the Kansas-Nebraska Act, a contest began between groups supporting slavery (mainly persons from Missouri) and settlers from the Northwestern states who were Free-Soilers in practice, if not ideology. The Missourians seized control of the territorial government and immediately enacted proslavery legislation. President Franklin Pierce and his successor, James Buchanan of Pennsylvania, accepted the proslavery Kansas government and committed the Democratic Party to the admission of Kansas as a slave state.

By September, 1855, enough Free-Soilers had entered the state to enable them to repudiate the territorial legislature, organize a Free State Party, and call for a constitutional convention to meet in Topeka. A free-state constitution was written in October and November, 1855, and in January, 1856, the party elected a governor and legislature. Kansas found itself with two governments—one supporting slavery and considered legal by the Democratic administration in Washington but resting upon a small minority of the population; and the other representing majority opinion in Kansas but condemned as an act of rebellion by President Pierce and Senator Stephen A. Douglas of Illinois. Douglas, who had drafted the Kansas-Nebraska Act of 1854 as a way to extend a railroad westward across the territories, favored the theory of popular sovereignty, letting the people decide the issue of slavery. That doctrine, however, was exposed—eventually by Abraham Lincoln in the Lincoln-Douglas debates—as unconstitutional: The will of the people could not be held above constitutionally protected rights.

The Violence Begins
Although proslave and free-soil groups moved into Kansas, actual bloodshed remained at a minimum through 1855; nevertheless, the territory quickly came to symbolize the sectional dispute. Violence became commonplace in Kansas through the spring and summer of 1856.

Armed free-soil and proslavery parties skirmished along the Wakarusa River south of Lawrence as early as December, 1855; but it was the sack of Lawrence in May, 1856, by a large band of proslavery Border Ruffians from Missouri, that ignited the conflict. Retaliation was demanded: John Brown, the abolitionist crusader, his four sons, and three others struck at Pottawatomie, where they executed five settlers who were reputed to be proslavers. That act of terrorism sparked further retaliation. Early in August, free-soil forces captured the slavery stronghold of Franklin; later that month, Free-Soilers, led by Brown, repelled an attack by a large party of proslavers at Osawatomie. Guerrilla warfare raged throughout the territory until September, when a temporary armistice was achieved by the arrival of federal troops and a new territorial governor, John W. Geary. However, a solution to the travail of Kansas could come only from Washington, D.C., and it would have to overcome the determination of the Democratic administration and its Southern supporters to bring Kansas into the Union as a slave state. Meeting at Lecompton in January and February, 1857, the proslave territorial legislature called for an election of delegates to a constitutional convention. The measure passed over Governor Geary's veto.

The Lecompton Constitution
The constitutional convention that met in Lecompton in September, 1857, hammered out a document to the electorate; the proslavery leadership would agree only to submit the document to the people with the choice of accepting it with or without the clause explicitly guaranteeing slavery. However, ample protection for slavery was woven into the fabric of the constitution. Opponents refused to go to the polls, and the proslavery Lecompton Constitution was approved in December, 1857.

The Free-Soil Party, meanwhile, had captured control of the territorial legislature and had successfully requested the new territorial governor, Frederick P. Stanton, to convene the legislature in order to call for another election. On January 4, 1858, the Lecompton Constitution met overwhelming defeat. Kansas was, by that time, free-soil in sentiment, but the Buchanan administration supported the Lecompton Constitution, which became a test of Democratic Party loyalty. Although Douglas came out against the administration's position, the Senate voted in March, 1858, to admit Kansas under the Lecompton Constitution. Public sentiment in the North opposed such a policy, and the House of Representatives voted to admit Kansas as a state only on the condition that the state constitution be submitted in its entirety to the voters at a carefully controlled election. That proviso was rejected by the Senate.

A House-Senate conference proposed the English Bill, a compromise measure that stipulated that the Lecompton Constitution should be submitted to the people of Kansas again: If the bill were approved, the new state would receive a federal land grant; if it were rejected, statehood would be postponed until the population of the territory reached ninety-three thousand. Although Congress passed the bill in May, the voters of Kansas rejected the Lecompton Constitution again, this time by a margin of six to one. In January, 1861, after several Southern states announced secession, Kansas entered the Union as a free state under the Wyandotte Constitution.

John G. Clark, updated by Larry Schweikart

Core Resources

Roy F. Nichols's *The Disruption of American Democracy* (New York: Macmillan, 1948) is a traditional, yet effective, analysis of the 1850's, emphasizing the destruction of the Democrats as the national party. William E. Gienapp's *The Origins of the Republican Party, 1852-1856* (New York: Oxford University Press, 1987) emphasizes the rise of the Republican Party as the crucial element in ending the earlier U.S. party system. Argues that the formation of the Republican Party represented a realignment that started with the demise of the Whigs, continued with the rise of the Know-Nothings, and culminated with the events in Kansas that galvanized the disparate elements.

See also: Compromise of 1850; Free-Soil Party; John Brown's raid; Kansas-Nebraska Act; Lincoln-Douglas debates; Proslavery argument.

Bloc Québécois

> **Significance:** A new political party was created to contest Canadian general elections on the exclusive issue of sovereignty for Quebec.

The creation of the Bloc Québécois was a direct result of the constitutional turmoil that gripped Canada in the 1980's. Canada had adopted a new constitution in 1982, but the French-speaking province of Quebec refused to accept its legitimacy. Quebec's refusal was mainly on the grounds that the Constitution failed to give Quebec adequate powers to protect its French language and unique Québécois culture. In order to secure Quebec's assent, Brian Mulroney, the Canadian prime minister, and all ten provincial leaders met at Meech Lake, Quebec, in 1987, and crafted a series of amendments favorable to Quebec. However, it became increasingly apparent that

not all the provincial legislatures would ratify the Meech Lake Accord by the deadline date of June 23, 1990.

Faced with impending defeat, a number of Members of Parliament (MPs) from Quebec, regardless of party affiliation, began to lose hope that the federal government would grant their province enough concessions to justify their remaining within the Canadian federation. If federalism would not work, then full political sovereignty for Quebec was the only plausible alternative. Lucien Bouchard, minister of environment in the Conservative government of Mulroney, resigned on May 21, 1990, citing a loss of faith in the way the government had handled the crisis. Other defections, from both the Liberal Party and the Conservative Party, followed.

Party Formation

On July 25, 1990, the newly formed Bloc Québécois (BQ) announced that its primary allegiance was to the nation of Quebec and recognized the province's legislature, the National Assembly, as the supreme democratic institution of the Québécois people. Its mission was to defend Quebec's interests in the federal parliament and to promote sovereignty within Quebec. In June, 1991, the BQ transformed itself into a political party.

The Bloc Québécois experienced a good deal of electoral success in its early years. In a federal by-election in east Montreal on August 13, 1990, BQ's candidate, Gilles Duceppe, captured 66 percent of the vote to become the first sovereignist candidate elected to the Canadian Parliament. In 1992, the Canadian prime minister and the provincial premiers hammered out a series of concessions to Quebec at Charlottetown, Prince Edward Island. Similar in scope to the Meech Lake Accord, these proposals had to be endorsed in referenda held in every province. The Bloc Québécois took the position that the Charlottetown Accord did not go far enough in meeting Quebec's minimum demands and campaigned against it. The accord was voted down in six out of the ten provinces.

When a general election was called for October, 1993, the BQ fielded candidates in all of Quebec's seventy-five constituencies. The Liberals and Conservatives in Quebec campaigned on the issues of jobs and employment, but the BQ was the only party to speak consistently on the sovereignty issue. The BQ won a stunning victory, capturing 49 percent of the vote in Quebec and winning fifty-four seats. The BQ did very well among former Conservatives, taking 60 percent of the French-speaking vote. Nationwide, the Liberal Party under the leadership of Jean Chrétien won easily, gaining 177 seats, but because of the complete collapse of the Conservative Party vote, the Bloc Québécois emerged as the second largest party in Parliament and therefore earned the formal status of Official Opposition.

Canadians understandably found it disconcerting that the Official Opposition was a party dedicated to the breaking up of Canada. Compounding the problem was that many MPs of the Bloc Québécois were new to Parliament and had little interest in pan-Canadian or foreign affairs. Although BQ never developed a detailed party program, it emerged as a party that tended to be fiscally conservative and left-of-center on social welfare issues. It gained popularity by opposing the cuts in popular benefit programs proposed by some economy-minded MPs.

Another Victory

In 1994, sovereignists in Quebec scored another victory when the Parti Québécois was elected to power in provincial elections. The victory was undoubtedly more a result of the unpopularity of the outgoing Liberal Party than any dramatic upsurge in sovereignist sentiment. Nevertheless, the new Parti Québécois premier, Jacques Parizeau, promised to hold a referendum on sovereignty during his term of office. In preparation for the forthcoming referendum, a new sovereignist alliance was forged that included the Parti Québécois, the Bloc Québécois, and the Action Démocratique Party, a small splinter party led by Mario Dumont. On June 12, 1995, they agreed that if the sovereignists won the referendum, there would be a year's time in which to negotiate a new political and economic arrangement with the rest of Canada. Should those talks fail, then Quebec would issue a unilateral declaration of independence.

The promised referendum was held on October 30, 1995. More than 92 percent of Quebec's electorate voted, with those opposed to sovereignty winning by a narrow margin of 50.6 percent to 49.4 percent. Fewer than 54,000 votes out of a total of 4,700,000 separated the two sides. On the day after the election, a disappointed Parizeau announced his intention to resign as Quebec's premier, and on January 29, 1996, he was succeeded by Bouchard. Because Bouchard had to resign his seat in the House of Commons, Michel Gauthier was chosen leader of the Bloc Québécois. Although the sovereignists were defeated, their response was one of total defiance, confidently believing that the next referendum would finally yield the desired result.

David C. Lukowitz

Core Resources

Lucien Bouchard, in his *On the Record* (translated by Dominique Clift, Toronto: Stoddart, 1994), discusses his career, the founding of the Bloc Québécois, and the aspirations of the Québécois people. Kimon Valaskakis and Angéline Fournier, authors of *The Delusion of Sovereignty* (translated by George Tombs, Montreal: Robert Davies, 1995), attempt to expose what they believe are the myths and fallacies held by sovereignists, arguing that sovereignty would be detrimental to Quebec's economy and culture. Robert Young's *The Secession of Quebec and the Future of Canada* (Montreal: McGill-Queen's University Press, 1995) is a thoughtful and scholarly analysis on the impact that Quebec's secession would have, concluding that it would not be catastrophic for either Canada or Quebec.

See also: Meech Lake Accord; October crisis; Separatist movement in Quebec.

Blue laws

Blue laws are statutes that prohibit or restrict individuals from participating in various acts on Sunday. Such laws are therefore also called "Sunday legislation" and "Sunday closing laws." Both the laws themselves and legal sanctions for violations are determined at the state level. The majority of the laws focus on deterring economic pursuits; however, recreational activities are also targeted. The "blue" in blue laws came from either the color of the paper on which these statutes were initially printed in the New Haven (Connecticut) colony or from the association of this color with constancy and fidelity. The latter explanation reflects the Puritans' strict practice of and devotion to these laws.

Historically, punishment for violation of Sunday closing laws has taken the form of mainly fines, sometimes imprisonment, and occasionally even death. Many individuals have battled both the punishments and the laws themselves through legal action. Orthodox Jews led legal battles in the 1950's and 1960's because the Jewish Sabbath falls on Saturday and prevents observers from doing business on this day. Many Jewish store owners opened on Sunday to replace business lost observing their Sabbath, but they found themselves in violation of the law. Two U.S. Supreme Court cases in 1961 that challenged blue laws were *Braunfield v. Brown* and *Gallagher v. Crown Kosher Super Market*. In both cases, Orthodox Jewish merchants argued that blue laws were a violation of the First Amendment and that they were being denied free exercise of religion. The Supreme Court has consistently upheld blue laws since 1884, and despite the religious foundations of Sunday closing laws, the courts have cited secular reasons for maintaining these laws. The results in 1961 were no different, with the Supreme Court ruling that states had the right to promote the well-being of their citizens by enforcing a day of rest, and that religious links to blue laws were nonexistent.

The imposition of Sunday closing laws was met with protest not only by Orthodox Jews but also by Muslims,

Buddhists, Seventh-day Adventists, and Seventh-day Baptists, all of whom observe a Sabbath (or other holy day) on a day other than Sunday. The interests and rights of these groups were downplayed during court decisions, and their appeals were denied mainly because of states' rights to promote the well-being of citizens by allowing them to increase time spent with their friends and families. It is exactly these blue laws, however, that disregarded non-Christians' attempts to bring together loved ones and still maintain the ability to survive economically. The financial justification of appeals (Sunday provided one-third of weekly profits for Crown Kosher) was negated on the grounds that competitors were closed on Sunday. Some countered that just to survive, many non-Christians had to forsake their own Sabbath by working and subsequently were forced to observe Sunday's commemoration of the resurrection of Christ, a religious tenet in which they did not believe. After strong and consistent challenges by religious groups, the 1980's saw most states with blue laws providing exceptions for those individuals observing a Sabbath on a day other than Sunday.   *Scott A. Melzer*

See also: Jewish Americans; Judaism; Religion-based ethnicities.

Body of Liberties

> **Significance:** The Body of Liberties of 1641 granted slavery in Massachusetts Bay Colony a formal status, making it an institution in the British colonies.

From its outset, the Massachusetts Bay Colony endorsed the idea of unfree labor. One hundred eighty indentured servants arrived with the original colonists. Food shortages led to the surviving servants' being set free in 1830. Unfree labor, however, continued on a private basis, and some white criminals were made slaves of court-appointed masters. Captives from the Pequot War of 1636-1637 were given over into slavery. Some of these captives were subsequently transported to a Puritan enclave off the coast of Nicaragua, and black slaves were introduced from there to the Massachusetts colony. The colony, however, remained without a formal endorsement of slavery until the promulgation of the Body of Liberties in 1641.

The Creation of the Document
The Body of Liberties evolved out of the gradually weakening authority of Governor John Winthrop and his first Board of Assistants, and the emergence of the General Court as a representative body of freemen. In 1635, the General Court had appointed a committee to draw up a body of laws for the rights and duties of the colonists. This committee stalled over the church-state conflict, and another committee was impaneled in 1636. John Cotton sat on this committee. Cotton was a devout churchman who drafted a document that derived much of its authority from scripture. Cotton did, however, believe in limitations on authority and resisted adopting biblical statutes wholesale. Winthrop, who was lukewarm to the entire idea, called Cotton's code, "Moses his Judicialls."

Cotton's counterpart in drawing up the code was Nathaniel Ward. Ward was a Puritan with a sense of humor and a literary bent. Like most Puritans, he was a friend to strict discipline, but he also was a foe to arbitrary authority. He agreed with Winthrop and Cotton that all law was the law of God, but he insisted that the code be based on English common law rather than on the Bible. He became the chief architect and intellectual godfather of the Body of Liberties. The Pequot War slowed deliberations, but by 1639, the committee had created a document that combined Cotton's and Ward's work. The final document was adopted in November, 1641.

The Slavery Issue
In many ways, the Body of Liberties was an enlightened document and certainly remarkable by seventeenth century standards. A compilation of one hundred laws, the Body of Liberties allowed for wide judicial discretion and for each case to be judged on its merits. It also effectively barred the legal profession from defending anyone for pay, and it protected married women from assault. It addressed the liberties of servants in humanitarian terms for those times, limiting the number of lashes given to servants to forty. The capital laws were more lenient than those of England. The one problem, however, was slavery. This bold document addressed the slavery issue thus:

> There shall never be any bond slaverie, villainage or captivitie amongst us unles it be lawfull captive, taken in just warres, and such strangers as willingly selle themselves or are sold to us. And these shall have all the liberties and Christian usages which the law of God established in Israell concerning such persons doeth morally require. This exempts none from servitude who shall be judged thereto by authoritie.

Although not a ringing endorsement of slavery, the Body of Liberties nevertheless admits of it, opening the way for the official sanction of slavery. Later and stricter codes would formalize the institution in New England on a colony-by-colony basis, largely because trading in slaves was profitable. Yankee traders found that slaves were more valuable as cargo to be sold to the plantation colonies or in the West Indies than as laborers in the northern economy.

By 1680, Governor Simon Bradstreet estimated the number of "blacks or slaves" in the Massachusetts colony at one hundred to two hundred. The equation of race ("blacks") with slavery here is important. Some special laws were passed restricting the movement of African Americans in white society, but the Puritans encouraged Christian conversion and honored marriages between blacks. The conditions of slavery were not as harsh as in the plantation colonies. Slaves needed to read and write to do their jobs. Although there were occasional isolated rebellions, the slaves benefited from the New England love for learning and the strong Puritan emphasis on marriage and family.

Slavery gradually faded away in Massachusetts, perhaps because of its vague legal status. In the aftermath of the American Revolution, a national clamor for a Bill of Rights led individual colonies to adopt their own. While none expressly forbade slavery, the institution seemed at odds with the rhetoric. By 1776, the white population of Massachusetts was 343,845 and the black population was 5,249. The census of 1790 showed Massachusetts as the only state in which no slaves were listed.

Despite the legalization of slavery in the Body of Liberties, slavery was never popular in Massachusetts except as incidental to trade—and the slave trade was an accepted practice by seventeenth century European standards. The Puritans themselves were products of a rigorous, harsh, isolated experience. They were humanists and intellectuals with contradictions. They prized sincerity and truthfulness, yet practiced repression and inhibition to steel themselves against life's ills. They had a strong element of individualism in their creed, believing that each person must face his maker alone. Puritan humanism therefore never squared with the institution of slavery.

Brian G. Tobin

Core Resources

Ulrich B. Phillips's *American Negro Slavery* (Baton Rouge: Louisiana State University Press, 1966) is rich in original source material about the development of slavery. John Hope Franklin's *From Slavery to Freedom: A History of Negro Americans* (3d ed., New York: Alfred A. Knopf, 1967) is a classic text on the evolution of American slavery that contains a chapter on "Puritan Masters." *The American Puritans: Their Prose and Poetry* (edited by Perry Miller, New York: Columbia University Press, 1982) includes selected writings from John Cotton, Nathaniel Ward, and John Winthrop. Samuel Eliot Morison's *Builders of the Bay Colony* (Boston: Northeastern University Press,

1981) contains chapters on the Elizabethan architects of Massachusetts, including John Cotton, Nathaniel Ward, and John Winthrop.

See also: Slave codes; Slavery: history; Slavery: North American beginnings.

Bolling v. Sharpe

In *Bolling v. Sharpe* (decided December, 1954), a companion case to *Brown v. Board of Education* (decided May, 1954), the issue of segregated public schools in the nation's capital, a matter of congressional jurisdiction, was treated in an opinion separate from *Brown* because the Fourteenth Amendment did not apply to the federal government and because the applicable Fifth Amendment did not include an equal protection clause. From the perspective of practical politics, it would have been highly embarrassing for the Court to allow segregated schools in Washington, D.C., while ruling them unconstitutional in the rest of the country.

Speaking for a unanimous Supreme Court, Chief Justice Earl Warren first noted that the petitioners were African American minors who had been refused admission to a public school "solely because of their race." He then declared that the Court had long recognized that certain forms of governmental discrimination violated the constitutional mandate for due process of law. For precedents, he looked to an 1896 *dictum* by Joseph M. Harlan and to *Buchanan v. Warley*, a 1917 decision that had defended the equal right of citizens to own property based on a substantive due process reading of the Fourteenth Amendment. Also, Warren referred to *obiter dicta* in the Japanese American cases that acknowledged that racial classifications were inherently suspect, requiring that they be "scrutinized with particular care."

Warren gave an expansive interpretation of the "liberty" protected by the Fifth Amendment, explaining that it extended to the "full range of conduct which the individual is free to pursue." The government could restrict liberty only when justified by a "proper governmental objective," and racial segregation in education was not related to such an objective. Thus, the Washington schools were imposing an "arbitrary deprivation" on the liberty of black children. In addition, Warren noted that it was "unthinkable" that the federal government might practice the kind of discrimination prohibited in the states.

Bolling v. Sharpe had major theoretical implications, for the case indicated that the Supreme Court continued to interpret the due process clauses as protecting substantive rights as well as procedures, although the substantive focus had shifted from property interests to liberty interests. Also, the decision affirmed that the ideas of liberty and equality are often overlapping and that constitutional due process of law prohibits government from practicing invidious discrimination.

Thomas T. Lewis

See also: *Brown v. Board of Education*; *Buchanan v. Warley*; Civil rights; Desegregation: public schools; *Hirabayashi v. United States*; Segregation.

Bracero program

> **Significance:** Labor shortages during World War II prompted a plan to import agricultural workers from Mexico.

World War II created an agricultural labor shortage in the United States. By 1942, U.S. farmers were complaining about the labor shortages farms faced and demanding that workers be brought in to help plant, harvest, and distribute their agricultural products. In response, the U.S. and Mexican governments created the bracero program, also known as the Mexican Farm Labor Program (MFLP). The program contained many provisions designed to protect both the farmers and the braceros (a term that comes from the Spanish word *brazos*, meaning "arms" or "helping arms"). Because many Mexicans were afraid of being forced into the United States' military upon arrival in the country (World War II was raging), one provision was that no Mexican contract workers could be sent to fight in the U.S. military. Another provision was that Mexican laborers were not to be subjected to discriminatory acts of any kind. The United States agreed that the contract laborers' round-trip transportation expenses from Mexico would be paid and adequate living arrangements would be provided for them in the United States. There was also a provision that the braceros would not displace local workers or lower their wages.

The braceros were to be employed only in the agricultural realm and on the basis of a contractual agreement (in English and Spanish) between the braceros and their employers. The farmers agreed to pay the braceros wages equal to those prevailing in the area of employment, and no less than thirty cents an hour, for a minimum of three-quarters of the duration of the contract. The braceros also were granted the right to organize. Ten percent of the braceros' earnings would be deducted and deposited in a savings fund, payable upon their return to Mexico. Finally, the braceros would be given sanitary housing conditions. In 1943, braceros would be granted the right to have a Mexican consul and Mexican labor inspectors intervene in disputes on their behalf. With these provisions and guidelines intact, on September 29, 1942, the first fifteen hundred braceros were transported to California by train.

Problems Arise

Braceros encountered a variety of problems in the United States. Although their contracts were explained to them before they signed them, many braceros did not have a basic understanding of the contract's terms and conditions. Workers often understood little beyond the fact that they were going to work in the United States. Despite the difficulties of moving from one country to another, when the braceros arrived in the United States, they were not given time to orient themselves to their new surroundings but were required to report for work the following day.

The bracero program, begun in the 1940's, brought Mexican workers to the United States to perform stoop labor such as that being performed by these workers on a California farm in 1964.

Farmers were skeptical of the MFLP because the farmers viewed it as infringing on their own welfare and traditional independence. The farmers wanted the federal government to provide workers, but they wanted it to be done on their own terms. However, the labor shortage crisis was so severe that the farmers consented to the government's program. Once the braceros were consigned to their employers, the binational agreement between Mexico and the United States was followed weakly, if at all, by the farmers. The farmers, who had much more power and control than the Mexican labor inspectors did, could basically do as they pleased with the workers and their contracts.

For example, as contract laborers, the bracero workers were expected to adapt to and stay on the job under adverse conditions from which local workers would have turned away. The bracero workforce was used for the heaviest and worst-paid jobs. This meant that the bulk of the imported workforce was used largely in the production and harvesting of crops that required large numbers of temporary, seasonal laborers for hard stoop work. The braceros were considered a blessing, because local workers refused to do stoop labor. The farmers used the argument that Mexicans were better suited for back-bending labor than were the local workers to justify their claim that they could not continue farming without the braceros. Braceros frequently were treated like and referred to as animals. Despite the ill treatment and harsh conditions, many braceros continued to migrate in order to find work and much-needed money.

Dependency Develops
By entering into an agreement with Mexican workers and the federal government in 1943, agriculture began a dependency on braceros that continued after World War II had ended. Within a year of the program's inception, braceros had in many areas become a mainstay in farm production.

After World War II ended in 1945, the Migratory Labor Agreement was signed with Mexico to continue encouraging the seasonal importation of farmworkers. Between 1948 and 1964, some 4.5 million Mexicans were brought to the United States for temporary work. Braceros were expected to return to Mexico at the end of their labor contract, but often they stayed. Although the United States government sanctioned this importation of Mexican workers, it shunned the importation of workers during times of economic difficulties. During the 1953-1954 recession, the government mounted a campaign called Operation Wetback to deport illegal entrants and braceros who had remained in the country illegally. Deportations numbered in excess of 1.1 million. As immigration officials searched out illegal workers, persons from Central and South America, as well as

native-born U.S. citizens of Central or South American descent, found themselves vulnerable to this search. Protestations of the violation of their rights occurred, but to little effect.

Although the jobs reserved for the braceros were generally despised, they were nevertheless essential first links in the robust war food production chain. In this capacity, the Mexican workers made a vital and measurable contribution to the total war effort.

Kristine Kleptach Jamieson

Core Resources
Nelson Gage Copp's *"Wetbacks" and Braceros: Mexican Migrant Laborers and American Immigration Policy, 1930-1960* (San Francisco: R and E Research Associates, 1971) provides detailed accounts of emigration and immigration policies affecting migrant agricultural workers from Mexico. Richard B. Craig's *The Bracero Program: Interest Groups and Foreign Policy* (Austin: University of Texas Press, 1971) discusses the political agreement between the United States and Mexico regarding migrant laborers. Erasmo Gamboa's *Mexican Labor and World War II: Braceros in the Pacific Northwest, 1942-1947* (Austin: University of Texas Press, 1990) presents a detailed history of the life, conditions, and social policy affecting migrant workers from Mexico in the United States.

See also: Immigration Act of 1924; League of United Latin American Citizens; Mexican deportations; Operation Wetback; United Farm Workers.

Brain drain

The term "brain drain" refers to the loss experienced by a country resulting from the emigration of highly educated or skilled individuals. The cost of educating doctors, scientists, and engineers who then leave their homeland for the United States is considerable. Emigration produces a financial loss for the countries of origin and a substantial gain to countries such as the United States that provide preferential admittance to the highly educated. The loss is worsened by the fact that those who leave are often the most innovative and hardworking. Therefore, some feel that reparations should be paid to those countries losing educated personnel.

However, the sending countries benefit in a number of ways. Emigrants promote their homeland and its policies in their new abode. They send remittances and invest in their homeland. They share ideas and technology learned in their new land with relatives and friends from their place of origin. Many even return and use the knowledge and contacts gained overseas to start up

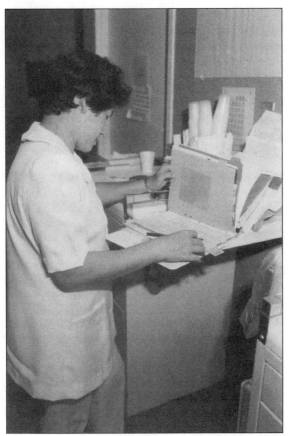

This Filipino nurse checks charts in a California hospital. The exodus of highly trained professionals such as this nurse from their native lands is sometimes termed a "brain drain."

international operations that create jobs and enhance the economy of their homeland. The brain drain concept is misleading because the emigration of the highly educated is not necessarily a loss to the sending nation.

Arthur W. Helweg

See also: Foreign professionals; Immigration and emigration.

British as dominant group

Beginning in the early seventeenth century and continuing unabated for more than three centuries, there was an immense flood of immigrants to North America from Britain. These people determined the linguistics, culture, religion, and politics of North America in ways that are still perceptible.

The 1600's were marked by a wave of English immigrants, including some who were indentured, to remote colonies in England's North American and Caribbean territories. These early arrivals were joined in the 1700's by Scotch-Irish and Scots settlers and, later, by Catholic Irish. In the first two centuries of settlement, African slaves were introduced to the New World. These later arrivals had an inestimable impact on North America, but certain factors help explain the British stamp.

The dominance of the English, both in the colonies and in Britain, was one factor. The British crown exerted control over immigration in the 1600's, with more than 70 percent of immigrants being English. Few Scots, Welsh, or Irish immigrated in the first decades of the colonial period, thus giving the English language and the Anglican (Episcopal) church a commanding position in everyday colonial life. When non-English groups arrived, they were confronted by a generally Anglicized society.

The changing dynamics of political and religious thought and the distance across the Atlantic Ocean helped make settlement a regional phenomenon. The land settled by various Britons was isolated and inwardly divided, often along religious lines. For example, in the northern colonies, where there was less arable land and farms were small, dissenters from within the Anglican church, known as Puritans, were the dominant group, along with a few Dutch- and German-speaking peoples. In the southern colonies, particularly in the tidewater regions, the traditional Episcopal faith was observed. Other Protestants, such as the Presbyterian Scotch-Irish, were pushed to the frontier, where they raised large families to work small farm plots. The dominant Anglo Americans with the best land settled onto large plantations.

It was in the coastal region, with its link to the Caribbean sugar centers, that African slavery took hold in British America. Slavery served as cheap labor that allowed for an almost aristocratic way of life that provided material benefit to the empire. Slaves contributed much to the way of life in the South but were in turn Anglicized. This continued until the British government made an effort to end the transatlantic (though not domestic) slave trade in the late 1700's.

British domination of North America was seemingly ensured when the British defeated the French in the Seven Years' War (1756-1763) and with the decline of the Spanish in eastern North America. Ironically, these events precipitated the end of direct British rule in the colonies. Though the colonies remained divided on many issues, grievances against the British crown led to the American Revolution. Drawing from the ideas of leading Enlightenment theorists, especially Englishman John Locke, the American revolutionaries succeeded in overthrowing British rule and establishing a fledgling republic.

North America did not, however, become less British as a culture. The United States, and later Canada, essentially continued the same patterns of commerce, Indian affairs, and settlement begun in the colonial period. Subsequent non-British immigrants to North America thus entered a society defined by British roots but open to contributions from elsewhere.

Gene Redding Wynne, Jr.

See also: Irish Americans; Irish Catholic "race"; Scotch-Irish "race"; Slavery: North American beginnings.

Broadcast media

> **Significance:** Television, films, and other broadcast media have often ignored minorities or portrayed them negatively. More diverse representations of American culture made their way onto the screen in the late twentieth century, but some stereotyping and Anglicizing of ethnic and racial groups still occurs.

American broadcast media have tended to reinforce popular stereotypes or simply ignore diversity issues rather than break new ground by offering realistic portrayals of racial and ethnic groups. For example, most of the films and television shows that portray the American West have ignored the existence of black cowboys.

Early Media
During the latter part of the nineteenth century, popular media tended to depict African Americans as simple-minded and slothful and Hispanics as dirty, devious, and lazy. Asian Americans typically were a mass of inscrutable, untrustworthy laborers, and Native Americans were usually shown as primitive savages. Media tended to either ignore racial and ethnic groups or portray them negatively.

During the early twentieth century, black entertainers began to perform in some radio programs and films. However, the depictions of African Americans tended to be stereotypical and unflattering; radio and film characters such as Buckwheat in the Little Rascals films, Jack Benny's sidekick, Rochester, and Stepin Fetchit were typically slow-witted, fearful buffoons. The media continued to depict blacks as lazy and dull-witted through the 1940's. For example, the popular radio program *Amos 'n' Andy* focused on the antics of two stereotypical black characters in Harlem, the conniving Kingfish and his gullible friend, Andy. The radio show featured an all-white cast, so when the program moved to television in 1951, the Columbia Broadcasting System scrambled to find suitable black replacements.

Another crossover from radio to television, *Beulah*

(1950), cast Ethel Waters and later Louise Beavers as the savvy, if inarticulate, black maid of a bumbling white family. Beulah routinely came to the rescue of her employers, but overall, the show did little to raise the status of African Americans. The lead character's signature line, "Somebody bawl fo' Beulah?" and her shifty boyfriend reinforced the notions that blacks were primarily uneducated laborers and domestics and were not to be trusted.

The media responded to the Japanese attack on Pearl Harbor in 1941 by portraying the Japanese—and by extension, all Asians and Asian Americans—as devious, cunning, and brutal people. Such depictions fueled wartime fears, contributed to the internment of Japanese Americans, and resulted in discrimination and harsh treatment of other Asian Americans.

The Late 1950's
African American singers such as Nat King Cole, Lena Horne, Sidney Poitier, and Harry Belafonte became respected and successful entertainers who were popular with both white and black listeners in the late 1950's. Some people believe that the relatively light complexions of Horne and Belafonte, and Poitier and Cole's "white" voices, made these entertainers more acceptable to white audiences and helped them break through the color bar. Whether or not this is true, these entertainers did help later African American singers and actors reach a wider audience, make more television appearances, and gain more (and better) film roles. Cole was given his own television program, *The Nat King Cole Show* (1956), but the popular singer raised the ire of some viewers when he appeared on stage accompanied by white female entertainers. The show was canceled after one season.

During the 1950's, Hispanics were rarely represented on television, despite growing numbers of Hispanic viewers. Characters such as Pepino Garcia on *The Real McCoys* (1957) reinforced prevailing stereotypes of Hispanics as farmworkers. The romantic and fiery-tempered characters played by successful and popular Latino actors such as Desi Arnaz and Cesar Romero were also somewhat stereotypical; however, the actors were able to achieve stardom. With the exception of Tonto (Jay Silverheels) on the *Lone Ranger* (1949), Native Americans were generally depicted as marauding savages in the 1940's and 1950's. Asian Americans were represented by *Bonanza*'s (1959) confused and deferential housekeeper, Hop Sing (Victor Sen Yung).

Changing Times
Perhaps the biggest changes in the media's perception of people of color occurred during the 1960's. The 1968 television show *Julia* featured Dihann Carroll as a widow and single mother working as a nurse. The show broke several stereotypes and was among the first programs to

depict a black character in a prestigious career field. It paved the way for several shows featuring African Americans in the subsequent decade. However, some people suggest that Carroll's light complexion and "white" diction enabled the show to become popular with white audiences and that acceptance of shows featuring African Americans was still somewhat lacking. On the big screen, films such as *Lilies of the Field* (1963) and *A Raisin in the Sun* (1961) tackled integration and prejudice, and *Guess Who's Coming to Dinner?* (1967) raised the issue of interracial relationships. The latter film featured some of the frankest discussion to date regarding race relations in general and had a profound impact not only on young people but also on their parents.

During the 1960's and 1970's, depictions of Asian Americans on television became more respectful although they remained stereotypical. On *The Courtship of Eddie's Father* (1969), for example, the Japanese house-keeper, Mrs. Livingston, was a frequent source of wisdom. *Kung Fu* (1972) depicted a Chinese American Buddhist monk who wandered the American West seeking peace and tolerance. Although the martial arts had been popularized in the United States by Chinese American actor Bruce Lee, the lead in the television show was given to a white actor, David Carradine.

Between 1965 and 1975, the proportion of African American characters on television reached 7 percent. *I Spy* (1965), *Mission: Impossible* (1966), and *The Mod Squad* (1968) all featured competent, well-educated African American characters. Movies such as *Cotton Comes to Harlem* (1970) and *Shaft* (1971) and television comedies including *The Flip Wilson Show* (1970), *Sanford and Son* (1972), *Good Times* (1974), and *The Jeffersons* (1975), eschewed assimilated characters in favor of those demonstrating black pride. African American film actors Billy Dee Williams, Richard Pryor, and Eddie Murphy also portrayed characters with an edge. Alex Haley's 1977 television miniseries *Roots*, based on his novel of the same name, found more than 130 million Americans tuning in to follow the history of four generations of black Americans. According to one survey, more than 90 percent of all blacks and 70 percent of whites watched at least some part of the eight-night series.

On-Screen Diversity

In the 1970's and 1980's, television programs and films began to portray racial and ethnic minorities in a more positive, realistic light. Depictions of African Americans were more positive and culturally diverse, and Hispanics also began to be portrayed as intelligent, competent members of American society. Hispanics also retained a distinct cultural identity with television programs such as *Chico and the Man* (1974) and *Tony Orlando and Dawn* (1974). Shows such as *Kojak* (1973), *Rhoda* (1974), *Baretta* (1975), and *Barney Miller* (1975) also celebrated ethnic diversity.

After playing an instrumental role in breaking African American stereotypes as a stand-up comedian and a star of the hit television series *I Spy*, Bill Cosby became one of the most beloved entertainers of the 1980's and the star of a popular weekly tele-

---

All in the Family

Norman Lear's 1971 hit television sitcom, *All in the Family*, changed the way television portrayed race and racism. The show's white, working-class lead character, Archie Bunker, freely voiced his prejudice against other racial and ethnic groups. Bunker, both lovable and excruciatingly closed-minded, was surrounded by African American neighbors, Hispanic and Jewish coworkers, and a Polish son-in-law. While poking fun at Bunker's futile attempts to maintain control of his world, the show also offered a measure of sympathy to those unable to cope with the complexities of a diverse society. Until *All in the Family*, no other television show dared broach bigotry in such frank terms.

All in the Family dealt with prejudice in a harshly realistic way, stirring controversy from its premiere. Some critics believed it legitimized bigotry and racial slurs. Others simply found the subject matter too uncomfortable to face. Eventually, however, *All in the Family* created its own niche, in part by satisfying two very diverse groups. Liberals took solace in the fact that the show demonstrated the folly and futility of prejudice, while many conservatives continued to identify with the main character's views.

Several spinoffs of *All in the Family* dealt with similar social and racial issues and also became hits. *The Jeffersons*, for example, created a black mirror image of Archie Bunker, equally intolerant of the white community.

Although *All in the Family* created an upheaval in the way television dealt with racial issues, the show and its offspring offered new levels of honesty and openness to a subject long ignored by popular media.

vision show, *The Cosby Show*, featuring a doctor and his family. His ability to entertain made him a superstar popular with both whites and blacks. The series not only undermined stereotypes for a mainstream audience but also was one of the first to celebrate African American identity as distinct from the dominant culture. However, some critics decried *The Cosby Show*, calling it a dark-skinned version of a white family program. Similarly, superstars of the 1990's whose popularity is not limited to black audiences, such as singer Whitney Houston and actor Denzel Washington, have been criticized for what some perceive as their similarity to white entertainers.

In the 1990's, race- and ethnic-specific programs, including *In Living Color* (1990) and *Martin* (1992), appeared on alternative networks such as Fox and UPN. Many of these programs, some with minority writers, directors, or producers, featured more realistic depictions of race and ethnic groups. Sometimes, however, in order to create humor or heighten drama, these programs exaggerated cultural and ethnic characteristics that bordered on stereotypes. The contributions of minority film directors and writers have helped bring a share of realism to the screen, as in the work of film director Spike Lee (*She's Gotta Have It*, 1986; *Do the Right Thing*, 1989; *Jungle Fever*, 1991; and *Malcolm X*, 1992). Lee, whose films often examine racism in the United States, has criticized Hollywood's stance toward black filmmakers. However, some critics have charged that his portrayal of black culture in the ghetto actually tends to perpetuate black stereotypes among white viewers.

Through the 1950's, television, film, radio, and other popular media reflected and reinforced stereotypes of race and ethnicity. Although writers and producers occasionally fall back on stereotypes and cliches for comedic or dramatic purposes, popular media since the 1960's have made a great deal of progress in presenting a more accurate picture of ethnic and racial groups.

Cheryl Pawlowski

Core Resources

Gender, Race, and Class in Media (edited by Gail Dines and Jean M. Humez, Newbury Park, Calif.: Sage Publications, 1995) offers a collection of discussions on the media's treatment of people of color and gender and class issues. George Hill, Lorraine Raglin, and Chas Floyd Johnson provide a compendium of television programs dealing with African American women in *Black Women in Television* (New York: Garland Publishing, 1990). Donald Bogle provides an illustrated encyclopedia of films and television shows featuring African American actors in *Blacks in American Films and Television* (New York: Garland Publishing, 1988). In *Prime Time: How TV Portrays American Culture* (Washington, D.C.: Regnery Publishing, 1994), S. Robert Lichter, Linda S. Lichter, and Stanley

Rothman discuss various aspects of television's depiction of American culture, including racial issues. Jan Nederveen Pieterse's *White on Black* (New Haven, Conn.: Yale University Press, 1992) delves into how Western popular culture portrays Africa and blacks.

See also: African Americans and film; American Indians and film; Asian Americans and film; Latinos and film; Stereotype.

Brotherhood of Sleeping Car Porters

A small group of men gathered in 1925 and organized the Brotherhood of Sleeping Car Porters in an effort to improve the Pullman Company's treatment of African American employees. Since the 1860's, black porters had been providing personalized service to rail passengers traveling in the finely furnished sleeping cars first introduced by George Pullman. Pullman cars, as they were known, were comparable to the nation's most luxurious hotels. The porters carried luggage, provided room service, made beds, and cleaned the cars. Despite their many duties, the porters were paid exceptionally low wages. In the summer of 1925, with assistance from magazine publisher A. Philip Randolph, leaders of the New York branch of Pullman porters met to organize a union, the Brotherhood of Sleeping Car Porters. For twelve years, the union struggled to reach a compromise with the Pullman Company, nearly abandoning the effort on several occasions. Finally in 1937, the Brotherhood of Sleeping Car Porters won the wage and work-hour concessions it was demanding, thus becoming the first African American labor union to sign an agreement with a major U.S. corporation. *Donald C. Simmons, Jr.*

See also: Employment among African Americans; Labor movement.

Brown v. Board of Education

> **Significance:** This landmark case struck down the "separate but equal" doctrine upheld by the U.S. Supreme Court in *Plessy v. Ferguson* (1896) and subsequent court decisions, ending legal racial segregation in public schools.

Oliver Brown et al. v. Board of Education of Topeka, Kansas, et al., usually referred to as *Brown v. Board of Education*, was but one case dealing with segregation in public schools that came before the Supreme Court in 1954. Similar suits were filed in South Carolina (*Briggs v. Eliot*), Virginia (*Davis v. County School Board*), and Delaware (*Gebbart v. Belton*). The cases all addressed the same basic problem: the exclusion of black children from all-white schools by state laws maintaining racial segregation.

Litigants and the District Court Ruling

The plaintiffs in the Kansas case were elementary schoolchildren in Topeka. The case was initiated in 1951, after the daughter of a black clergyman was denied admission to an all-white public school. As a class-action suit, it went before the U.S. District Court for the District of Kansas. Although the three-judge court found that public school segregation had a "detrimental effect upon the colored children," contributing to "a sense of inferiority," it denied them relief, upholding the separate but equal doctrine. The case then went to the U.S. Supreme Court, which reversed the lower court's decision unanimously.

In 1951, Linda Brown (now Smith, pictured in 1952 at the age of nine) was denied admission to an all-white school in Topeka, Kansas. The 1954 U.S. Supreme Court decision in her case ended legal segregation.

The Supreme Court's Argument

In writing the Court's decision, issued May 17, 1954, Chief Justice Earl Warren stated that "in the field of public education the doctrine of 'separate but equal' has no place" because segregated schools are "inherently unequal." The decision held that the plaintiffs were in fact "deprived of the equal protection of the laws guaranteed by the Fourteenth Amendment."

A second *Brown* opinion, generally known as *Brown II*, was issued a year later, on May 31, 1955. It remanded impending desegregation cases to lower federal courts, ordering them to issue equitable decrees in accordance with "varied local school problems." Although this decision directed the district courts and school boards to desegregate public schools "with all deliberate speed," it opened the door to judicial and political evasion at the local level. Thus, despite the fact that in *Cooper v. Aaron* (1958) the Court unequivocally reaffirmed the 1954 decision, strong resistance to the ending of both de jure (by law) and de facto (by custom) segregation delayed the implementation of the Supreme Court's ruling for many years.

Brown and the Civil Rights Movement

Although the *Brown* decision theoretically ended legal segregation in public education, it did not bring an immediate end to the segregation of schools or any other public facilities. In the South, change was particularly painful and slow, in both urban and rural areas. According to the U.S. Commission on Civil Rights, in 1963, nine years after the *Brown* ruling, less than half of 1 percent of southern black students were attending integrated schools. It would take marches, boycotts, sit-ins, and more aggressive racial agitation by blacks and sympathetic whites, plus growing media coverage and strong public pressure, to force change.

The Civil Rights movement took a dramatic turn in 1955, in Montgomery, Alabama, when Rosa Parks, a black woman, refused to surrender her bus seat and move to a section reserved for blacks. Her action began a boycott that led to other demonstrations throughout the South under the leadership of Martin Luther King, Jr. The movement culminated in the Civil Rights Act of 1964, the Voting Rights Act of 1965, and the Fair Housing Act of 1968.

However, the *Brown* decision was the most important legal precedent in the Civil Rights movement. It was also inevitable. In earlier cases, the Supreme Court, even while upholding the "separate but equal" doctrine, had begun to undermine it. As early as 1938, in *Missouri ex rel. Gaines v. Canada*, the Court rejected the practice of funding law schooling for blacks outside a state in lieu of providing equal facilities within the state. In 1950, in *Sweatt v. Painter*, the Court further determined that a separate public law school for blacks (in Texas) violated the equal protection clause of the Fourteenth Amendment because the school was not equal to the state's white law school in prestige or quality of faculty and facilities. Thereafter, by 1952, the Court had begun to review cases dealing with public schools, not only the professional schools.

Brown's Legal Legacy

Brown v. Board of Education set a legal precedent that would be used to overturn laws upholding segregation not only in public schools but also in other public facilities. The argument that separate facilities are "inherently unequal" is the cornerstone of much civil rights legislation that has effectively ended apartheid in the United States. New ground would be broken two decades later, in 1976, when the Supreme Court, in *Runyon v. McCrary*, ruled that even private, nonsectarian schools violated federal civil rights laws if they denied admission to students because they were black. Although some problems implementing these important rulings remain, the landmark decision in *Brown* made it clear that segregation would no longer be tolerated in a democratic society.   *John W. Fiero*

Core Resources

The role of the U.S. Supreme Court in school desegregation and the general impact of school integration are extensively covered in several studies, including Leon Jones's *From Brown to Boston: Desegregation in Education, 1954-1974* (Metuchen, N.J.: Scarecrow Press, 1979), *The Consequences of School Desegregation* (edited by Christine H. Rossell and Willis D. Hawley, Philadelphia: Temple University Press, 1983), *Shades of Brown: New Perspectives on School Desegregation* (edited by Derrick Bell, New York: Teachers College Press, 1980), and Larry W. Hughes, William M. Gordon, and Larry W. Hillman's *Desegregating American Schools* (New York: Longman, 1980).

See also: *Bolling v. Sharpe*; Busing and integration; Civil rights; Civil Rights movement; *Cooper v. Aaron*; Discrimination: racial and ethnic; Little Rock school desegregation; National Association for the Advancement of Colored People Legal Defense and Educational Fund; *Plessy v. Ferguson*; *Runyon v. McCrary*; Segregation: de facto and de jure; *Sweatt v. Painter*.

Buchanan v. Warley

In May, 1914, Louisville, Kentucky, passed an ordinance that made it unlawful for "any colored person" to move into a house on a block where the majority of houses were occupied by whites. Whites were similarly disqualified from moving to a block where the majority of the occupants were black. William Warley, who was black, contracted to buy a house lot from Charles Buchanan, a white man. Part of the contract between them was a proviso by Warley that said "I shall not be required to accept a deed to the above property unless I have the right under the laws of the state of Kentucky and the city of Louisville, to occupy said property as a residence." Warley refused to pay on the contract, alleging that the Louisville ordinance forbade him from living on the property. Buchanan sued Warley to force him to perform on the contract, attacking the ordinance as unconstitutional under the due process clause of the Fourteenth Amendment.

The U.S. Supreme Court unanimously held that the ordinance was unconstitutional. Justice William R. Day wrote that the Louisville law deprived both black and white people of the right to own and dispose of property in violation of the command of the Fourteenth Amendment that no person shall be deprived of life, liberty, or property without due process of law.   *Robert Jacobs*

See also: Discrimination: racial and ethnic; Fair Housing Act; Fourteenth Amendment; Housing.

Bureau of Indian Affairs

Attempting to centralize Indian administration, previously controlled by a bewildering array of government and military officials, Secretary of War John C. Calhoun on March 11, 1824, created the Bureau of Indian Affairs (BIA). Although authority over Indians initially resided in the Secretary of War, the fledgling bureau controlled all annuities and expenditures, managed funds for the civilization of Indians, mediated disputes between Indians under the trade and intercourse laws, and handled all correspondence. In 1832, the president was empowered to appoint a commissioner of Indian affairs.

In 1849, the BIA was transferred to the newly created Department of the Interior. Thereafter authority descended from the president of the United States to the secretary of the interior to the commissioner of Indian affairs. The coordination of field superintendents, agents, missionaries, traders, and local Indians was entrusted to a field superintendent who corresponded directly with the commissioner. The BIA grew rapidly, from its original three members to six thousand employees in 1911. By the late twentieth century, it had thirteen thousand employees and controlled a budget of nearly $900 million.

Designed to implement federal policy, the BIA has historically reflected prevailing government attitudes toward Indians. Initially, it oversaw funding under the

American Indians and others criticized the Bureau of Indian Affairs, created in 1824, for its apparent failure to address the native population's needs. In 1972, a group of Indian activists staged a sit-in at the bureau.

1819 civilization plan designed to aid assimilation through education. Similarly, under the General Allotment Act of 1887, the BIA was charged with the mammoth task of preparing a list of members of tribes as well as classifying and appraising Indian lands.

After World War I, responding to government economizing mandates, the BIA decentralized its operations. Regional offices were superimposed over the existing administrative structure, and further reorganization in 1946 provided for separate geographical divisions with regional headquarters.

Surveys and studies during the 1920's, including the scathing Meriam Report, revealed the appalling conditions of Indian life under the allotment plan, thereby giving impetus to fresh reforms. Between 1933 and 1945, during Commissioner John Collier's tenure, the BIA for the first time turned from its assimilationist policy. Because of Collier's influence, the Indian Reorganization Act (IRA) of 1934 provided for a revitalization of tribal government and social customs. The act also granted Indians priority hiring within the BIA. Indeed, by 1982, Indians accounted for 78 percent of BIA personnel.

Since the 1960's, the BIA's influence over Indian affairs has eroded, thereby favoring a shift of responsibility to Indians themselves. In 1975, for example, the Indian Self-Determination and Education Assistance Act encouraged Indians to assume control over pertinent government programs. In the 1990's, dispersion of BIA activities to states, to other agencies, and to Indians continued, yet the bureau remained a vast organization supporting twelve regional offices and eighty-two agencies headed by a commissioner. The BIA still oversaw several features of Indian life, including education, law enforcement, and the mobilization of public and private funds for economic development and natural resource management.

Mary E. Virginia

See also: General Allotment Act; Indian New Deal; Indian Reorganization Act; Indian-white relations: United States; Termination Resolution; Trail of Broken Treaties.

Burke Act

In 1887, Congress passed the General Allotment Act (or Dawes Severalty Act). This act sought to make small farmers out of American Indians by dividing tribal lands into individual allotments. Indians taking allotments received United States citizenship; the government held the title for the lands in trust for twenty-five years, during which time they could not be sold. At the end of the period, the Indian would receive a fee patent giving him full ownership of the land.

The administration of the General Allotment Act prompted considerable criticism. Many of those sympathetic to the Indians were concerned at the distinction between citizenship, which was taken up at the outset, and ownership, which came at the end of the trust period. The discrepancy became a source of worry in 1905 when the Supreme Court ruled that citizenship exempted an Indian from direct federal supervision, thus invalidating federal restrictions on liquor on allotments. Other people simply thought that the trust period postponed too long the time when Indians might sell their allotments.

In 1906, Congress passed the Burke Act, named for South Dakota congressman Charles Henry Burke. The act provided that the trust period could be extended indefinitely on presidential authority, though it also permitted the secretary of the interior to cut the period short if requested, provided an individual Indian could show competency to manage his or her own affairs. In either case, citizenship would not be granted until the end of the trust period, during which the Indian would remain subject to federal control.

The Burke Act had a major effect on the awarding of allotments, though not the one that some of its supporters had hoped. Though certificates of competency (and fee patents) were awarded cautiously at first, many allotments quickly passed out of Indian possession once they could be sold or mortgaged. During the act's first decade of operation, roughly ten thousand fee patents were issued, the vast majority of allotments passing out of Indian ownership. When the ardent assimilationist Fred K. Lane became secretary of the interior in 1917, the process speeded up. Competency certificates and fee patents were often given without the requisite individual investigation, sometimes to Indians who had not asked for them. In four years, twenty thousand fee patents were issued, again with much of the land quickly alienated.

During the 1920's, when Burke was commissioner of Indian affairs, the process slowed, but the overall trend of allotment lands passing into the hands of non-Indians continued. By 1934, when the Indian Reorganization Act finally stopped the allotment process, Indians had lost 86 million of the 138 million acres they had controlled in 1887. In the meantime the citizenship available under the Burke Act had been made redundant by Congress's grant of citizenship to all Indians in 1924.

William C. Lowe

See also: Allotment system; General Allotment Act; Indian Citizenship Act; Indian Reorganization Act; Indian-white relations: United States.

Busing and integration

> **Significance:** Busing as a tool for desegregating public schools has been controversial, and both Congress and the Supreme Court have dealt with the issue.

School desegregation has been the most controversial American educational issue of the twentieth century. Busing, one of the more feasible strategies for achieving school desegregation, generated tremendous controversy as desegregation plans were implemented during the late 1960's, 1970's, and 1980's. Consequently, school desegregation and busing have become inextricably linked in the minds of many people. Busing actually predates school desegregation by many decades, and it was originally simply a means of transporting students in rural areas to schools that were better equipped and staffed than traditional one-room country schools. In rural areas of the South, however, busing simultaneously served as a means of facilitating school segregation.

Busing to Facilitate Segregation

Many school districts in the South encompass entire rural counties, so transportation to school must be provided to students. Busing proved to be the most feasible means to transport large numbers of students. Until the Supreme Court's *Brown v. Board of Education* decision in 1954, segregated schools were legal in the South. Typically, segregation meant busing black and white children to different schools regardless of what school was closest to a child's house. Black children could be bused many miles even if a white school was right next door. Similar circumstances would apply for the white child if the nearest school was a black one.

The 1954 *Brown* decision was supposed to bring an end to de jure (by law) segregation, the practice of state-imposed segregation. A subsequent decision (*Brown II*) in 1955 addressed the issue of remediation and ordered that the elimination of segregated dual school systems proceed "with all deliberate speed." Yet thirteen years passed before the Supreme Court became disillusioned with the delay tactics and obstructions employed by many southern school districts and began enforcement of its desegregation decree. During that time, an entire generation of schoolchildren, both black and white, was subjected to the continuation of busing that facilitated segregation.

Busing to Facilitate Integration

Busing became an effective strategy for transporting students reassigned under desegregation plans. In *Swann v. Charlotte-Mecklenburg Board of Education* (1971), the Supreme Court established that busing was an acceptable strategy for desegregating school systems. In upholding the use of busing, the Supreme Court was aware that it might prove to be administratively awkward for school districts and that it might impose a degree of hardship on some districts. Although busing was sanctioned in the *Swann* decision, it was done so only in regard to de jure (by law) segregation. In *Keyes v. Denver School District No. 1* (1973), busing was ordered for the first time outside the South. In this case, the Supreme Court ruled on the issue of de facto segregation (segregation "in fact," generally resulting from discriminatory residential patterns) for the first time. In evaluating the Denver school system, the Court concluded that when segregative intent exists in a substantial portion of the school system, then a systemwide remedy to assure nondiscrimination is acceptable. A systemwide remedy necessitates the reassignment of significant numbers of students, which typically requires some degree of busing. In a number of desegregation cases, the federal courts used busing when forced to develop their own desegregation plans, especially when recalcitrant school districts refused to restructure long-standing dual systems of education.

A number of school districts in the South developed desegregation plans that were premised on voluntary integration strategies, such as freedom-of-choice plans, voluntary transfer plans, and magnet schools. The Fifth Circuit Court, in *United States v. Jefferson County Board of Education* (1966), argued that the only desegregation plans that would be acceptable to the federal courts would be those that work—those that are practical and that actually accomplish the goal of desegregation.

In *Green v. County School Board of New Kent County* (1968), the Supreme Court rejected the freedom-of-choice plan implemented by the New Kent County school board. The Court concluded that freedom-of-choice plans did not demonstrate significant levels of desegregation and did not remove the racial identification attached to specific schools. Although freedom of choice was rejected as the primary strategy in a desegregation plan, however, it was not precluded from being used as a supplemental component in a more comprehensive desegregation plan.

The federal courts came to a similar conclusion regarding voluntary transfer plans. White parents saw no benefit in having their children attend a segregated black school that was perceived to be educationally infe-

rior. On the other hand, many African American parents did not see the value in having their children attend segregated white schools where they were unwelcome. They were hesitant to expose their children to the physical threat posed by some segregated white schools.

Magnet schools have unquestionably been the most successful of the voluntary desegregation plans. Magnet schools have grown tremendously since their inception in 1972. Generally, these are racially integrated public schools that have innovative programs and activities that attract students from throughout a school district.

Freedom-of-choice, voluntary transfer, and magnet programs all required some degree of busing if they were to be properly executed. In some instances, voluntary desegregation plans involved a greater degree of busing than did the mandatory pupil reassignment plans initiated by the federal courts. Yet parents had little difficulty in accepting the notion of a voluntary desegregation plan. Voluntary plans permit parents and children who do not wish to participate in the desegregation effort to remain outside the process while remaining within the public schools. Many of the voluntary desegregation plans, however, proved to be unacceptable to the courts.

Resistance to Busing

Busing to achieve integration met with considerable opposition at the local, state, and federal levels. Although busing was merely a strategy to facilitate meaningful integration, it eventually became symbolic of all that some people found distasteful about the desegregation process. Opponents of desegregation characterized it as "forced busing." The issue of forced busing, for many, was associated with the reluctance of white parents to send their children to what had previously been inferior all-black schools. Actually, considerably more minority students (African American and Hispanic) than white students were bused for desegregation purposes. Over the decades of the 1960's, 1970's, and early 1980's, white parents took to the streets in their opposition to forced busing. The problem was exacerbated when some political leaders—instead of seeking to mollify and encourage the desegregation process—took advantage of the controversy for political gain.

During the time of the *Keyes* decision, when the use of busing was being established as a remedy in de facto segregation cases, there was substan-

On September 9, 1979, a Cleveland, Ohio, group protests a busing program slated to be instituted throughout the city the next day. The use of busing to integrate schools remains a very controversial issue.

tial political force growing in opposition to busing. According to Derrick A. Bell, Jr., in *Race, Racism, and American Law* (1980), Richard M. Nixon used an antidesegregation plank in his presidential campaign in 1968 to help defeat the Democratic presidential candidate, Hubert H. Humphrey. Nixon's opposition to forced busing assumed an even greater role in his reelection campaign for 1972.

Although the legitimacy of busing was upheld in the *Keyes* decision, the parameters for its use were questioned the following year in *Milliken v. Bradley* (1974). The Supreme Court failed to support metropolitan busing in Michigan that would have involved the city of Detroit and fifty-three surrounding suburban school districts. Detroit, at the time, was more than 63 percent African American, while the neighboring suburban districts were almost exclusively white. The Supreme Court reasoned that the plaintiffs did not demonstrate constitutional violations on the part of the suburban communities. The plaintiffs' request to include the suburban school districts in the desegregation effort was denied.

During this same period, Congress was reevaluating busing and its proper place in school desegregation. Congress attempted to pass legislation that would have either eliminated or limited the use of busing. It failed to pass antibusing legislation designed to reduce federal jurisdiction. It succeeded, however, in passing legislation that placed restrictions on the use of busing for desegregation beyond the next-nearest school. This permitted many students to remain at their neighborhood school, and since many neighborhoods were racially segregated, the legislation actually contributed to school segregation. Congress also passed legislation that prioritized remedies in school desegregation cases and prohibited the issuance of administrative or judicial orders requiring student reassignment at any time other than the beginning of an academic year.

Despite the guidelines established in the *Milliken* decision regarding metropolitan busing, the restrictive busing legislation passed by Congress, and other precedent-setting decisions in the federal courts, school desegregation continued to move forward. The responsibility of proof had changed, however—from demonstrating the mere existence of segregation in a school system to the more difficult to prove standard of segregative intent on the part of school officials.

Much concern surfaced in Congress and in the federal courts about "white flight," the movement of white families to areas outside racially mixed school districts as well as the increasing tendency of white parents to place their children in private schools. Although part of the decline in the number of white students can be attributed to desegregation and busing, white enrollment had actually begun to decline almost a decade before integration began. This decrease was a function of the declining white birthrate, departures to private schools, and departures to the suburbs. It should be noted that some suburban school districts not subject to desegregation actually lost more students proportionally than did city districts undergoing desegregation.

Although the phenomenon of white flight is generally associated with the desire to avoid school desegregation, technically the term is a misnomer. It would be more accurately characterized as middle-class flight. The African American middle class, along with other minority middle class populations, has continually sought to remove itself from the inner cities when presented with the opportunity.

Diminished Opposition to Busing

Opposition to busing appeared to diminish in the 1980's. The administration of Ronald Reagan tended to focus on other domestic and foreign issues. Nevertheless, the Reagan administration was firmly opposed to busing. It even threatened to reopen desegregation cases already settled through extensive busing if it believed that the remedy was too drastic. The Reagan administration argued that desegregation should occur on a voluntary basis. Consequently, it supported voluntary desegregation plans such as magnet schools, tuition tax credits, and school "choice" programs. Busing became a side issue as debates focused on the impact that tuition tax credits and choice programs would have on public schools. *Charles C. Jackson*

Core Resources

A thorough examination of busing can be found in *School Desegregation: Hearings Before the Subcommittee on Civil and Constitutional Rights of the Committee on the Judiciary, House of Representatives, Ninety-seventh Congress* (Washington, D.C.: U.S. Government Printing Office, 1982). Other excellent discussions are the Citizens Commission on Civil Rights, *"There Is No Liberty . . . "* (Washington, D.C.: Citizens Commission on Civil Rights, 1982); Derrick A. Bell, Jr., *Race, Racism, and American Law* (2d ed. Boston: Little, Brown, 1980); Harvard Sitkoff, *The Struggle for Black Equality: 1954-1992* (New York: Hill and Wang, 1993); and S. Alexander Rippa, *Education in a Free Society: An American History* (7th ed. New York: Longman, 1992).

See also: *Brown v. Board of Education*; Civil rights; Civil Rights movement; Desegregation: public schools; *Green v. County School Board of New Kent County*; *Keyes v. Denver School District No. 1*; *Milliken v. Bradley*; *Swann v. Charlotte-Mecklenburg Board of Education*; White flight.

C

Cable Act

On September 22, 1922, the Cable Act became law and reformed the rules by which women lost or obtained U.S. citizenship through marriage to foreigners. Representative John L. Cable of Ohio noted when introducing his bill that "the laws of our country should grant independent citizenship to women." By this act, the United States took the lead among nations in the world in acknowledging the right of a woman to choose her citizenship rather than to lose or gain it upon marriage. In the early twentieth century, under the laws of virtually all nations, a woman automatically lost her citizenship and took that of her husband upon marriage to a foreigner. The Cable Act, supported by all major women's groups at the time, was viewed as an important piece of reform legislation aimed at protecting a woman's right to choose her citizenship. As Representative Cable noted upon the bill's passage into law: "Justice and common sense dictate that the woman should have the same right as the man to choose the country of her allegiance."

The effects of the Cable Act were varied. Although aimed primarily at rectifying cases in which American women, under the 1907 Expropriation Act, automatically lost their U.S. citizenship upon marriage to an alien, it also revoked provisions of an 1885 act that automatically conferred U.S. citizenship on alien women who married Americans. Therefore, a foreign woman could not automatically become an American citizen upon marriage to an American, even if that were her desire. Instead, like any other alien, she would have to undergo an independent process of naturalization. One effect of this aspect of the law was to discourage Chinese American men from marrying immigrant women. For these reasons, the Cable Act has been considered anti-immigrant and anti-women by some latter-day observers. However, although an alien woman who married a U.S. citizen or whose husband became naturalized would no longer automatically be granted citizenship, she was not excluded from seeking U.S. citizenship. The act made the process of becoming an American citizen a matter of deliberate choice rather than an automatic effect of marriage. The Cable Act did not revoke the citizenship of any woman who before its passage had received American citizenship automatically by marriage.

The ultimate effect of the Cable Act was to treat women of all ethnic and racial backgrounds with complete equality insofar as the acquisition of U.S. citizenship was concerned. Modern human rights treaties generally follow this U.S. practice, recognizing that acquisition of citizenship should be a matter of free and independent consent.

Robert F. Gorman

See also: Chinese Americans; Women and racism.

Cambodian Americans

The migration of refugees from Southeast Asia created a fairly large population of Cambodian Americans during the 1980's. Cambodian Americans mostly live in urban areas, where they come into contact with members of other American ethnic groups. According to the U.S. census, there were about 150,000 Cambodian Americans in the United States in 1990. The largest concentration of Cambodian Americans was in California, where close to 70,000 lived. The largest Cambodian community was in Long Beach, California, where more than 17,000 made their home, and 4,250 people of Cambodian ancestry lived in nearby Los Angeles. Stockton, California, was home to the second largest Cambodian community, numbering more than 10,000. Outside California, the greatest number of Cambodian Americans were found in Massachusetts, where more than 14,000 lived, about half of them in the city of Lowell. Other states with large Cambodian populations include Texas, Pennsylvania, Virginia, New York, Minnesota, and Illinois.

Most of the Cambodians in the United States arrived as refugees. From 1975 until the end of 1978, Cambodia was ruled by the extremist Khmer Rouge. War between Vietnam and Cambodia broke out in December, 1978, and by January, 1979, the Vietnamese had conquered the Cambodian capital of Phnom Penh. Under the Khmer Rouge, virtually all of Cambodia had been turned into a collection of forced labor camps, and the war made it possible for thousands of Cambodians to flee to neighboring Thailand. The agonies of the Cambodian

A Cambodian father holds his son in Stockton, California, in 1985. Five years later, Stockton was home to more than ten thousand Cambodian Americans.

Although Cambodia is an overwhelmingly rural nation, most Cambodian Americans have settled in big cities, where they come into close contact with members of other ethnic groups. They have also brought their traditions and customs to their new homeland. By the early 1990's, for example, more than fifty Cambodian Buddhist temples had been established in Cambodian communities around the United States.

Carl L. Bankston III

See also: Education and Asian Americans; Employment among Asian Americans; Hmong Americans; Refugees and racial/ethnic relations; Refugees: U.S. policy; Vietnamese Americans.

Campus ethnoviolence

Ethnoviolence is defined by sociologists Fred Pincus and Howard Ehrlich as the intent to harm another individual because of that person's membership in a racial or ethnic group. Prejudiced views of that group—views that may range from subscribing to negative stereotypes to group hatred—must be a motivating force in ethnoviolence. Historically, researchers have used the term "ethnicity" to describe race, nationality/national origin, and religion. More recently, sexual orientation has been commonly included. Gender is less frequently included, despite compelling arguments for its similarities.

The harm inflicted through ethnoviolence may be psychological or physical, ranging from insults and hate-inspired graffiti to harassment, property damage, and assault. The conditions that breed this particular aggressive discriminatory behavior are summed up by social psychologists John F. Dovidio and Samuel L. Gaertner as simple extensions of common practices. First, in a world much too complex to consider every stimulus as novel, people impose structure by grouping and categorizing their experiences, including other people they encounter. In this process, people sometimes draw large conclusions from small bits of evidence, and bias begins. Second, motivation for control and power over limited resources prompts action. Third, the rules of a culture tell its members what behaviors are acceptable in expressing this bias.

One particular institutional "subculture" where such conditions for bias are especially problematic is the college or university campus. Most research indicates that the numbers of reported ethnoviolent events and racial tension on campus have increased since the 1980's. The following examples occurred in the late 1980's and the 1990's and are provided in separate sources by Mississippi State professor Mfanya Tryman, Evonne Parker Jones of Northern Virginia Community

people were widely publicized and aroused international sympathy. At the same time, the plight of refugees fleeing Vietnam also received media attention. In response, the U.S. government passed the Refugee Act of 1980, which led to the resettlement of thousands of refugees from Cambodia, Vietnam, and Laos in communities around the nation.

In the early 1990's, after Cambodian migration to the United States had largely ended, the Cambodian American population continued to grow. According to the U.S. census, Cambodian American families were much larger than the families of other Americans, averaging 5.03 people per family compared to 3.06 people per family for white Americans and 3.48 per family for African Americans. The youth of Cambodian Americans also contributes to their increase in numbers. The median age of Cambodian Americans in 1990 was only nineteen, while the median age for other Americans was thirty-four. People in this new and growing ethnic group tended to be economically disadvantaged, since 42 percent of Cambodian American families were living below the poverty level in 1990.

College, and sociologists Bradley Fischer and David Hartmann of Southwestern Missouri State University. At the Citadel, cadets dressed in Ku Klux Klan garb, entered the room of a sleeping black fellow cadet, engaged in racially oriented taunting, and burned a newspaper cross in front of him. At the University of Michigan, a campus radio station disc jockey allowed and encouraged the broadcast of racist jokes. At the University of Mississippi, the first black fraternity house on a previously all-white fraternity row was gutted by arson. At Stanford University, an initially peaceful protest yielded scrawled racial epithets in a black student's dorm room. A series of fliers proclaiming it to be "open season" on numerous minorities was slipped under doors at Northern Illinois University.

Such anecdotal evidence is supported by empirical studies. Sociologist Susan Hippensteele of the University of Hawaii indicated in a 1998 study that ethnic harassment, reported by 15 percent of a college population at large, was reported by 60 percent of lesbian, gay, or bisexual students. Fischer and Hartmann's 1996 study reports that 44 percent of black students at Southern Missouri State University (as opposed to 7.5 percent of white students) had experienced either racial slurs, written/graphic ethnic insults, or violent activity on campus.

Some people suggest that increases in campus ethnoviolence are the result of a backlash by nonminority students who perceive that minorities are receiving preferential treatment (through affirmative action and other programs). Others suggest that what is increasing is the number of reports, not the number of incidents, which could reflect an improvement, or greater openness, in the campus culture. Research into the prejudicial attitudes on campus that underpin ethnoviolence paints a dismal portrait, however. Typical research looks at majority college students' positive and negative stereotypes of ethnic groups. The frequency of acceptance of negative attitudes and rejection of positive stereotypes appears throughout the 1990's. The clearest evidence is seen when the views of students at one college campus are assessed over time. Lillian Phenice and Robert Grifore at Michigan State University did this in measuring attitudes of the student body about minority persons. The students read descriptions of character traits and tendencies and were asked whether these traits characterized black and Mexican American populations. Over a period of two years in the early 1990's, the number of positive attributes decreased and the number of negative attributes increased for both groups. These results are mirrored by a ten-year comparison at Iowa State University by sociologists Sue Crull and Brent Benton. These researchers indicated a diminishing majority tolerance for minority groups, manifest as increasing social distancing practices and attitudes.

Clearly, the problem of campus ethnoviolence requires response on at least two levels: the personal and the institutional level. On the personal level, colleges have begun to institute programs that attend to those who have been directly affected by ethnoviolence. Many, if not most, colleges in North America have created victim's advocacy programs. These programs provide considerable assistance to victims who come forward—assistance ranging from arranging access to medical or counseling facilities, to making victims aware of their rights and recourses, to social support. Hippensteele reports that in their early years, such programs were hampered by perceptions of limited legitimacy on the part of college administrations and that these programs remain limited by low rates of reporting.

At the institutional level, the conditions that prompt ethnoviolence need to change. Sociologist Thomas F. Pettigrew has outlined several steps that institutions such as colleges may use in promoting policies that help to defuse the conditions that breed ethnoviolence. First, promoting an attitude of seeing change as inevitable, rather than acceptable or desirable, seems to foster institutional cooperation and willingness to adopt unfamiliar behaviors. Second, it is necessary to accept that changing behaviors will change attitudes, and that behavioral changes must *precede* attitudinal changes. This process may evolve slowly, but the evidence is clear that strictly enforced sociobehavioral rules, whether formal or informal, not only foster compliance but also have the power to dispel myths—a goal poorly attained by "quick-fix" educational overviews of the cultures of others aimed at changing attitudes first in the expectation that behavioral changes will follow. Third, institutions need to engineer intergroup contact under optimal conditions. This entails, among other things, getting beyond tokenism in student and faculty recruitment and retention and encouraging equal access to campus resources, both formal (such as libraries) and less formal (such as clubs and fraternities). Finally, of the many emotional mechanisms that foster prejudicial aggressive behaviors, the most productive emotion to target may be fear. Many intergroup fears are born of deliberate or nondeliberate misinformation, lack of contact in conjoint activity, and simple ignorance. Dispelling such fears may help to lessen ethnoviolence, by reducing the prejudice and discriminatory behaviors that breed it.

Certainly colleges cannot be singled out as the predominant source of prejudicial attitudes. They draw students, faculty, and staff from the population at large and are subject to negative societal influences. They are, however, in a unique position for effecting change in a society in microcosm. Such a goal is in keeping with the perception of universities as architects of an improved social future, rather than recapitulators of a tarnished past.   *James B. Epps*

See also: Diversity training programs; Epithets and pejorative language; Ethnoviolence; Hate crimes; Hate speech; Racial/ethnic relations: improving; Stereotype.

Canarsie riots

In the 1960's, Canarsie—a neighborhood in southeast Brooklyn, one of the five boroughs of New York City— was home to some sixty thousand working-class and middle-class Jewish and Italian American people. Many of them had left other Brooklyn neighborhoods— Brownsville, East New York, and East Flatbush—because those neighborhoods had become racially integrated. For various reasons, these whites did not wish to live among African Americans. It was an unusual alliance: Many of the Italian Americans were politically and socially conservative, and many of the Jews were liberal and active in the Civil Rights movement. The two groups lived peaceably and orderly together until the late 1960's, when poor African Americans started to move into Canarsie.

With the influx of the new impoverished group came many inner-city problems: street crime, drug addiction, and erosion of families. The Jews and Italians blamed the welfare state and the African Americans for these problems and found confirmation for the racial stereotypes they had carried for years. They decided, individually and collectively, to drive out the African Americans. What followed was a series of violent protests and confrontations. The summers of 1966 and 1967 saw repeated racial clashes in Canarsie and throughout Brooklyn. White homeowners who considered selling their homes to African Americans were threatened. Firebombs were thrown into the homes of new black residents. After an eleven-year-old African American child was killed by a sniper, large groups of African American youths took to the streets, throwing rocks and bricks at white-owned businesses and at police. Young Italian men formed a group called the Society for the Prevention of Niggers Getting Everything (SPONGE), made random, violent attacks on black youths, and once crashed through police barricades to attack a group of twenty-five young African Americans. Thousands of extra police moved through Brooklyn to contain scattered outbreaks of violence and were attacked by white and African American groups. Eventually the police developed a plan that allowed groups to stage nonviolent protests, and the violence eased for a time.

Resentment continued to build among the white Canarsie residents. Then, in the fall of 1972, a desegregation plan was enacted to bus African American children from Brownsville to the Canarsie public schools. In protest of this "forced busing," white families boycotted the schools, keeping their ten thousand children home and staging public demonstrations of outrage under banners reading "Canarsie schools for Canarsie children." Black families responded by keeping their children out of school on November 6, then observed as Black Solidarity Day. The boycotts attracted national attention, and comparisons were drawn to the whites of Little Rock, Arkansas, blocking the schoolhouse door in 1957. Canarsie became a symbol of bigotry and prejudice and of the wide gaps that still existed between ethnic groups even in the seemingly integrated cities of the North.   *Cynthia A. Bily*

See also: Busing and integration; Crown Heights conflicts; Housing; Italian Americans; Jewish-African American relations; Little Rock school desegregation.

Carlisle Indian School

In 1879, a U.S. military officer, Captain Richard Henry Pratt, opened an Indian school in Carlisle, Pennsylvania, with the aim of assimilating Indian children into white society. Pratt belonged to a generation of policymakers working for what many believed to be a more humane, progressive approach to Indian policy. Unlike many of his predecessors, Pratt believed that Indian people were capable of being transformed into the European American model of the law-abiding, Christian, wage-earning citizen. According to Pratt, leaving behind everything that distinguished Indian people as "Indian," including language and spirituality was the only way for Indian people to survive.

Pratt first experimented with Indian education by training Plains Indian prisoners being held at Fort Marion in Florida. After persuading the federal government to allow eighteen male prisoners to attend Hampton Normal Institute, an all-black school in Virginia, Pratt recruited both male and female students from Indian communities across the country for enrollment in the Carlisle Indian Industrial School. At Carlisle, students were required to speak only English and to adopt middle-class European American ways of living. In addition to very basic academic skills, girls were trained in domestic skills such as ironing and cooking, while boys learned industrial skills. Such a curriculum did little to prepare students for life in Indian communities.

Students, however, proved much more able to maintain strong Indian identities than Pratt had expected,

Sioux boys line up after their arrival at the Carlisle Indian School in Pennsylvania. The school, opened in 1879, aimed to assimilate its students into Euro-American life by eliminating all vestiges of their heritage.

and many left Carlisle to return to their tribal homelands. Although Carlisle required a traumatic isolation from family and community, some students did, nevertheless, emerge from the experience with new skills and a determination to improve political and social conditions for other native people.   *Molly H. Mullin*

See also: Education and American Indians.

Caste model

> **Significance:** In contrast to assimilation theories, the caste model suggests that full acceptance of equal status and rights for a minority by the majority is never possible. Instead, in the United States, people will be assigned to separate and unequal castes according to their skin color.

Social scientist Allison Davis first proposed the caste model of race relations in *Deep South* (1941). A caste is different from a social class because caste membership is permanent. Generally, in a caste system, one caste is considered to be superior to the others. Castes may be divided into social classes by wealth and income, but the castes remain separate. Caste lines can never be crossed; rich members of one caste will not consider wealthy members of another caste to be their equals.

Caste and Class in the American South
John Dollard, a sociologist, supported the caste view after extensive research in a small, southern community.

The caste model he describes in *Caste and Class in a Southern Town* (1947) is based on the Hindu caste system found in India. In Dollard's view, a caste system had replaced the slavery system in the South after the Civil War. Two castes, separated by skin color, lived in the South. The white caste controlled most of the wealth and power, and the African American caste was impoverished, exploited, and terrorized. Members of the latter caste were placed in an inferior position where they would remain no matter what their accomplishments.

Social classes existed within each caste: There were many poor whites and a few wealthy blacks, but wealth or poverty mattered less than caste. Caste members could, through economic success or failure, move from class to class within the caste. However, members of the lower African American caste were forever denied equality with members of the white upper caste. Political and social equality were based on race, not wealth. The racial distinctions between the castes were critical and permanent.

Southerners were born into a caste; they had no choice as to caste membership, and they adopted the views of other members of their caste. According to the caste system, white Southerners were not racists because their feelings of superiority were just part of the social structure of their region.

Dollard identified two key differences between the Hindu and American caste systems. In India, the upper caste felt an obligation to defend or protect the rest of the community; however, the higher caste in the United States did not feel this obligation. In addition, members of the lower castes in India were exploited but did not feel abused because their status was assigned to them by tenets of the Hindu religion. African Americans in the South, on the other hand, were assigned second-class status for no reason other than traditional racist assumptions concerning their alleged inferiority. Their suffering and abuse had no origin in crime or sin. They were exploited and denied equality for no reason other than the color of their skin. A remedy or reasonable explanation for their problems did not seem evident.

Implications for Public Policy
If the caste model of race relations were accepted by political leaders and policymakers, little would or could be done to change social and economic conditions in a society. Efforts to increase social mobility, such as political action, union organization, or government programs, would have little impact on long-held racist customs and traditions. Attitudes concerning equality versus inequality could not be changed. The caste model implies that inequality is an inherent part of the system.

The caste model provided vivid descriptions of life in southern communities but had little to say about living conditions in the industrial North. Another weakness was its inability to describe the African American culture that was developing in reaction to the dominant views of white supremacists. The caste model implied that no links existed between whites and blacks and that each caste lived alone in almost complete isolation. It also offered few suggestions on how to change the system. It described and evaluated the white caste's domination of the black caste but did not examine the possibilities of change and progress in race relations. Under the southern caste system, there seemed to be no limit to the discrimination, and the immense amount of suffering seemed to have no significance or meaning. In this way, the American caste system bore little similarity to the model found in Hindu India.   *Leslie V. Tischauser*

Core Resources
Allison Davis et al., *Deep South* (Chicago: University of Chicago Press, 1941), and John Dollard, *Caste and Class in a Southern Town* (New Haven, Conn: Yale University Press, 1947), remain the classic works in this model of analysis. Also important is Oliver Cox's *Caste, Class, and Race: A Study in Social Dynamics* (Garden City, N.Y.: Doubleday, 1948), though the author is chiefly interested in class relationships. Another book that should be consulted, however, is Philip Mason's *Prospero's Magic: Some Thoughts on Class and Race* (London: Oxford University Press, 1962), which contains a thoughtful view of the caste model of race relations. Another interesting view of this model is found in C. Vann Woodward's *American Counterpoint: Slavery and Racism in the North-South Dialogue* (Boston: Little, Brown and Company, 1971).

See also: Class theories of racial/ethnic relations; Discrimination: racial and ethnic; Discrimination: systemic; Racial/ethnic relations: race-class debate; Social stratification theories.

Caucasian

"Caucasian" is a term used to describe people of the white (European) race. The term was first introduced by the German scientist Johann Friedrich Blumenbach in 1795. Blumenbach divided humanity into five races. He gave the name "Caucasian" to the European race because he believed that the ancestors of the Europeans originated in the Caucasus Mountains of southwestern Russia. He argued that the people of that area were the most beautiful humans, and because they were the ideal humans, they must have been the first ones created. Blumenbach then asserted that the Europeans were the ancestors of all the other races.

After Blumenbach's development of the term, Caucasian, and its variant, "Caucasoid," became the standard word used to refer to people of the white race. In common usage, this term, along with its companion terms "Mongoloid" (for people of Asian descent) and "Negroid" (for people of African descent), is popularly used to describe a group of people who share not only a common descent but also similar physical and sometimes psychological traits. In the second half of the twentieth century, however, scientists moved away from using these terms, or any terms describing racial categories, believing that humanity is too diverse to be described by the narrow concept of "races."   *Karen C. Hauser*

See also: Biosocial theories; Race as a concept; White "race"; Whites.

Celtic Irish

During the 1650's, the first immigrants from Ireland began to arrive in North America. These people were of southern Celtic Irish decent and brought to English colonies in North America as servants and laborers. It was not until the early 1700's that large numbers of people from throughout Ireland emigrated to North America. The majority of these immigrants were from northern Ireland and of Scottish ancestry; lesser numbers were from southern Ireland and identified themselves with traditional native peoples of Ireland and a Celtic heritage.

The Scotch-Irish immigrants to North America were fourth- or fifth-generation Scots in Ireland who had largely assimilated into the Irish culture except for their religious faith and their family names. The Scotch-Irish were predominantly Protestant rather than Catholic, and their family names revealed a Scottish heritage. Scotch-Irish living in northern Ireland considered themselves Irish, not Scottish. Immigrants to North America from southern Ireland were predominantly Catholic and usually bore family names of Celtic origin.

Despite the common heritage of Ireland, these two groups of immigrants were regarded quite differently upon their arrival in North America. The Protestant Scotch-Irish shared a common faith with the large numbers of established Protestant English settlers. The smaller numbers of southern Irish of Catholic and Celtic heritage became the focus of widespread ethnic discrimination.   *Randall L. Milstein*

See also: Irish Americans; Irish Catholic "race"; Scotch-Irish "race."

Censuses, U.S.

Significance: Every ten years, a federal census counts all the people residing in the United States. The information obtained includes each person's ethnic or racial background. This enables the size of each ethnic or racial group to be compared over time and allows governmental programs to take the size of an ethnic or racial group into account when determining policy.

The United States Constitution requires that population be the basis for determining the number of seats apportioned to each state in the U.S. House of Representatives. As the population of the country shifts, the decennial census permits a readjustment in the number of seats for each state. Census reports have also been used to calculate how many immigrants from particular countries are allowed admission into the United States as well as to determine what constitutes unlawful discrimination.

Censuses

A population census is a complete count of all persons residing in a particular area. A census differs from a population sample, which scientifically selects a percentage of persons in an area in order to estimate characteristics of the entire population of the territory.

To undertake a population census, census takers must identify the dwelling units in the area to be covered; then they must go to each abode and obtain information from all persons residing therein. Inevitably, census takers miss some people because not everyone is at home when the census taker arrives, some people choose to evade being counted, others are homeless or transient, and not all dwelling units are easy to identify. Censuses, thus, generally undercount population, especially in areas where less affluent minorities reside. That is why, some argue, a method known as "statistical sampling" may be more accurate than an actual headcount, provided that the census has identified all dwelling units.

Legal Requirements

The Constitution of the United States requires a population census every ten years. Because the Constitution requires that each state's representation in the federal House of Representatives be based on population, a major purpose of the decennial census is to increase or decrease the number of seats in the House of Representatives apportioned to each state in accordance with relative changes in the population of each state. The Constitution did not consider Native Americans to be citizens of the United States, so they were not originally counted in the census; those living on reservations did not affect the allocation of seats in the House of Representatives until after 1924, when they were granted American citizenship. Those of African descent were counted in each state, but before the Civil War (1861-1865), when they were not considered citizens, their number was multiplied by three-fifths for the purpose of reapportioning representation in the House of Representatives.

Beginning in the 1960's, affirmative action began to be applied to remedy employment discrimination in the United States. One aspect of the policy is that federal government employers and those with federal contracts are supposed to hire men and women of the various ethnic or racial groups in the same proportions as their relative availability in the workforce. To determine the composition of the workforce, employers usually rely on census data, which are disseminated by the U.S. Department of Labor.

Ethnic/Racial Categories

In the first federal census of 1790, each individual was assigned membership in one of two racial groups: white and colored. The colored population was divided into free colored and slaves, and both categories were divided into black or mulatto. These census categories were used until 1860, when the Asiatic category was added and a count was made of the people in various Indian tribes. The 1870 census used four categories: white, colored, Chinese, and Indian. In 1880, Japanese became the fifth category, and the term "Negro" replaced "colored." These five categories remained on census reports through 1900. The 1910 census added several new categories: Filipinos, Hindus, and Koreans. A footnote in the census report noted that Hindus were Caucasians but still were counted separately from whites. The 1920 census added Hawaiians and part Hawaiians, but these two categories were removed from the national enumeration in 1930 and 1940. Mexicans joined the category list in 1930 and 1940. In 1950, the only racial categories were white and nonwhite. In 1960, six categories were used: white, Negro, Japanese, Chinese, Filipino, and Indian. In 1970, Hawaiians and Koreans returned to the list, making eight categories. In 1980, the category black replaced Negro, and the list of Asian and Pacific races expanded to include Asian Indians, Samoans, and Vietnamese. In 1990, nearly every country in Asia was represented as a separate category.

Although Mexicans appeared as a category in 1930 and 1940, they did not reappear in national statistics for forty years. In 1970, the census counted "Persons of Spanish Heritage," but in 1980, the census counted Cubans, Mexicans, and Puerto Ricans separately. In 1990, the census reported the number of persons from almost all countries in the Caribbean, Central America, and South America.

Census reports on the territories of Alaska and Hawaii used unique category schemes. For Alaska, the census counted Aleuts, Eskimos, and Alaskan Indians; Aleuts and Eskimos became national categories in 1980 and 1990, but Alaskan Indians were pooled with all other American Indians in both years. For Hawaii, the indigenous Hawaiians were counted, although up to 1930, they were divided into pure Hawaiians, Asiatic Hawaiians, and Caucasian Hawaiians.

From the beginning, the census had separate subcategories for European ethnic groups (British, French, German, and so on), all of which were counted as white. The breakdown was made to record the number of foreign-born individuals in the population. Due to concerns among the earlier immigrants from western and northern Europe that too many eastern and southern Europeans were arriving, Congress passed the Immigration Act of 1924. This act replaced a temporary immigration law, passed in 1921, which had restricted immigrants to 3 percent of each admissible nationality residing in the United States as of 1910. According to the 1924 act, known as the National Origins Act, the maximum from each European country was calculated as 2 percent of the nationality group already inside the United States as determined by the federal census of 1890. Most Asians, effectively, were barred from immigration under the law with the exception of Filipinos, as the Philippines was an American possession as of 1898. The restrictive 1924 immigration law imposed no quota on immigrants from the Western Hemisphere. With the Immigration and Nationality Act of 1965, Congress established equal quotas for all countries, regardless of hemisphere.

With the advent of affirmative action, a five-category scheme was developed by federal civil rights enforce-

---

Racial Categories in the U.S. Census for the Year 2000

American Indian or Alaskan Native
Asian
Black or African American
Native Hawaiian or other Pacific Islander
White

---

ment agencies. The so-called COINS categories stood for Caucasian, Oriental, Indian, Negro, and Spanish. Later, the term "Oriental" was replaced by the term "Asian and Pacific Islander," and the term "Hispanic" replaced the term "Spanish."

Census for the Year 2000
During the 1990's, considerable pressure was brought to bear to change the categories for the census for the year 2000. Some blacks wanted to be called "African Americans." Hispanics wanted to be counted as "Latinos" and as members of a race rather than an ethnic group. Native Hawaiians wanted to be moved from the category "Asians and Pacific Islanders" and included with "American Indians and Native Alaskans." Middle Easterners, particularly those from Islamic countries, wanted separate status. Finally, some mixed-race or multiethnic people who spanned two or more of the categories wanted to be counted as "multiracial." Advocates of a society in which ethnic and racial distinctions would not be recognized officially wanted to drop all references to race and ethnicity in the census.

After many hearings and studies on the subject, the U.S. Office of Management and Budget decided to keep the previous categorizations with one modification: "Asians" would be counted separately from "Native Hawaiians and Other Pacific Islanders." The proposal for a separate "multiracial" category was rejected, but persons with multiracial backgrounds would be allowed to check more than one category. Thus, data on ethnic backgrounds of people in the United States have been collapsed into five racial categories: African American or black, American Indian or Native Alaskan, Asian, Native Hawaiian or Other Pacific Islander, and White. The census of the year 2000 permits a member of any of these five categories to also check "Hispanic or Latino."

Impact on Public Policy
The ethnic and racial diversity of the United States is best documented by the decennial federal census. The count of each ethnic or racial group is crucial in determining

whether discrimination occurs, but questions about ethnic group membership or race on a census deeply affect the identity of many persons, who in turn may support efforts either to abolish ethnic and racial counts or to change categories. *Michael Haas*

Core Resources
The best source on ethnic data in the census is the census report itself, which is found in most documents sections of university libraries, as well as on the Internet at www.census.gov. Bryant Robey's *Two Hundred Years and Counting: The 1990 Census* (Washington, D.C.: Population Reference Bureau, 1989) provides an overview of the census with a focus on the 1990 census. Margo J. Anderson's *The American Census: A Social History* (New Haven, Conn.: Yale University Press, 1988) is a historical account of the taking of censuses that includes many of the associated controversies. On the tendency to undercount minorities, see Harvey M. Choldin's *Looking for the Last Percent: The Controversy over Census Undercounts* (New Brunswick, N.J.: Rutgers University Press, 1994); Barbara Everett Bryant and William Dunn's *Moving Power and Money: The Politics of Census Taking* (Ithaca, N.Y.: New Strategic Publications, 1995). For the thesis that racial divisions have been artificially promoted by the census, see Michael Omi and Howard Winant's *Racial Formation in the United States: From the 1960's to the 1980's* (New York: Routledge & Kegan Paul, 1986).

See also: Affirmative action; Biracialism; Immigration Act of 1924; Immigration and Nationality Act of 1965; Multiracial identity; Multiracial movement; Quotas; Race as a concept; Racial/ethnic demographics: trends.

Certificate of Degree of Indian Blood

Of all the ethnic and racial groups in the United States, only American Indians are issued cards by the U.S. government stating their ethnic identity. The U.S. Bureau of Indian Affairs issues a card called a Certificate of Degree of Indian Blood, which indicates that the bearer is entitled to be called "Indian." It states the cardholder's tribal affiliation and blood quantum—the percentage of Indian blood the person possesses. One purpose of the Certificate of Degree of Indian Blood is to establish who is eligible for the various governmental services available to American Indians. State legislatures have also enacted laws that specify (with varying degrees of precision) who is considered an Indian in that state.

See also: Indian; Native American; Status Indians.

Charleston race riots

After the Civil War ended in 1865, South Carolina was controlled by Northern-born whites and Southern blacks with support from the U.S. federal government. Southern whites who were allied with some Southern blacks attempted to regain control of the local government. By 1876, a tense atmosphere had developed between the two forces as a gubernatorial election approached between Republican Daniel H. Chamberlain, the incumbent and a Massachusetts-born former Union army officer, and Democrat Wade Hampton, a former slaveowner and Confederate lieutenant general. Political corruption and intimidation characterized both sides. On September 6, black Democrats rallied in Charleston to support Hampton. A group of black Republicans attacked the black Democrats and their white escorts, and a riot ensued. The riot lasted for several days with black Republicans destroying property and attacking whites. One black man and one white man died, and about one hundred people were injured. Tensions remained high until the election on November 7, and the next day, as people were awaiting the election results, gunfire erupted in Charleston. Black police officers loyal to the Republicans began firing at the rioters. One black man and one white man were killed, and about a dozen other people were injured. Federal troops intervened and restored order. Both candidates claimed victory in the election, but by 1877, power had returned to white Democrats because of a political deal with the Republican presidential candidate. *Abraham D. Lavender*

See also: Civil War; Colfax massacre; Reconstruction.

Charter of Rights and Freedoms

Significance: Promulgated by the government of Prime Minister Pierre Trudeau and signed in 1982 by Queen Elizabeth II, the Canadian Charter of Rights and Freedoms quickly attained the distinction of being one of the world's most significant human rights documents. From the day it came into effect, April 17, 1982, the charter became the subject of intense discussion, analysis, and critique and subsequently was the focus of Supreme Court decisions that sought to interpret and clarify the meaning of its various clauses.

The Charter of Rights and Freedoms guarantees every Canadian fundamental freedoms—freedoms of conscience and religion, thought, belief, opinion and expression (including freedom of the press), and peaceful assembly and association. Members of visible minorities and other groups in Canada have a constitutional assurance and guarantee of their fundamental, basic rights. The rights and freedoms are, however, subject to reasonable limits, justifiable in a democratic society. The scope of the charter is broad because it was framed to provide a means of protection against the incursions of the state and to defend the rights of minorities against the dominance of the majority. The charter deals with democratic, equality, gender, legal, and language rights.

History

Although the government of Canada adopted the British parliamentary system, many people felt that Britain's emphasis on an "unwritten" constitution was not entirely appropriate in the Canadian context. Proponents of the charter preferred the system formulated in the United States, with its written constitution and the right of an independent judiciary to review the actions of government. The Canadian charter was an attempt to blend these two disparate democratic traditions while creating a dynamic document that could set the standard and provide clear guidelines for everyone in Canada. The most important of the charter's many contributions is that it enables the Supreme Court of Canada to rule on the validity of legislative action and oversee compliance with the human rights system established by the charter. However, it must also be emphasized that most of the rights that fall within the charter were previously protected via the British tradition of common law and by provincial and federal statute law as well as by Canada's adherence to the democratic concept of the rule of law.

The charter was necessitated by a need for unequivocal, written guarantees of human rights that were absent in earlier constitutional documents such as the British North America Act of 1867 (also called the Constitution Act). Although the earlier document assured Canadians of the rule of law and of parliamentary supremacy, it made no specific provision for the protection of human rights except to grant provinces the power to legislate property and civil rights. It did protect some linguistic and religious educational rights, but the courts did not have the effective mandate they needed to protect all Canadians in a rapidly expanding multicultural, multiethnic society.

Prime Minister John Diefenbaker sought a remedy with passage by Parliament of the Bill of Rights (1960), which assured fundamental freedoms in matters falling within the jurisdiction of the federal government. This legislation also prohibited discrimination on the basis of race, national origin, color, religion, and sex. However, this act did not enjoy the supremacy of constitutional status, and clearly the judiciary felt a need for further tightening of the human rights guarantees in Canada because it interpreted the act narrowly. Ironically, it was the enshrined British concept of parliamentary supremacy that hampered the development in Canada of a vibrant nationwide human rights system because the courts felt compelled to maintain legislative predominance, even at the expense of human rights.

The passage of the Canadian charter in 1982 provided the necessary constitutional foundation and legal underpinning to the entire system of human rights in Canada. Any law that is not compatible with the charter is invalid. The Canadian constitution precedes parliamentary supremacy, and the charter binds both federal and provincial governments.

International Interest in Human Rights

Following the end of World War II and the creation of the United Nations in 1945 as a forum for the resolution of international disputes, the issue of human rights acquired prominence and urgency. The extent of the human rights violations by Nazis against Jews and other minorities shocked people throughout the world and gave impetus to the creation of international treaties to protect and expand the realm of human rights. The Universal Declaration of Human Rights (1948) led the way, soon followed by the International Covenant on Civil and Political Rights (1966), an Optional Protocol to the Covenant (1966), and the International Covenant on Economic, Social, and Cultural Rights (1966). Canada played a significant role in the development of these international documents, which are known collectively as the International Bill of Human Rights.

Specific Provisions

Although most of the provisions of the Canadian charter are significant to members of any racial group, particularly the visible minorities, there are specific measures that are most relevant to the concerns of racial minorities. Section 15 guarantees equality and Section 27 protects the multicultural composition of Canadian society. Hence, discrimination is prohibited and cultural diversity is endorsed.

Section 15 guarantees equality before and under the law along with equal protection and equal benefit of the law without discrimination based on race, national or ethnic origin, color, religion, sex, age, and mental or physical disability. It also provides recognition for proactive programs to help the disadvantaged.

Andrews v. Law Society of British Columbia (1989) confined "discrimination" to the criteria established in Section 15 (race, color, and so on) or on analogous grounds. Further, the Supreme Court of Canada found in *R. v. Genereux* (1992) that to qualify, discrimination had to be against a member of a "discrete and insular minority." In *Benner v. Canada (Secretary of State)* (1997), the Court invalidated legislative provisions that granted or refused citizenship to children born abroad based on whether they had Canadian fathers or Canadian mothers and nullified the discriminatory treatment given to such applicants.

The extent of protection accorded by the charter to racial and ethnic minorities is extensive. However, establishing racial equality in Canada will require more than constitutional formulations. The ultimate challenge will be for community organizations, legislators, the media, and, when necessary, the courts to educate people and help spread a spirit of racial tolerance and recognition of the value of diversity to all sectors of the country.

Ranee K. L. Panjabi

Core Resources
Several good sources of additional information on the Charter of Rights and Freedoms in Canada are Kristen Douglas and Mollie Dunsmuir's *Charter of Rights and Freedoms: Fundamental Freedoms* (Ottawa: Library of Parliament, Research Branch, 1996), Kenneth Fogarty's *Equality Rights and Their Limitations in the Charter* (Toronto: Carswell, 1987), and the Canadian Human Rights Foundation's *Multiculturalism and the Charter: A Legal Perspective* (Toronto: Carswell, 1987).

See also: Bilingualism in Canada; Charter of the French Language; Human Rights Act; Multiculturalism Act; Multiculturalism in Canada.

Charter of the French Language

The Charter of the French Language was promulgated by the separatist government of Quebec, Canada, in 1977. Although it has been frequently amended, Quebecers remain committed to its goal of ensuring that French remains the dominant language in their province.

In its preamble, the charter recognized the significance and distinctiveness of the French language as articulating the identity of the majority francophone population of Quebec and dedicated itself to ensuring its wide usage in commerce, communication, education, and employment. While acknowledging that ethnic minorities and aboriginal peoples reside in Quebec, the charter is mainly concerned with the survival of French as the language of the legislature, the courts, the civil administration, and education.

Firms with more than fifty employees are compelled to engage in active francization of the workforce and are issued francization certificates when they have complied with the use of French in everyday work situations at management and employee levels, in communications internally and with external suppliers and clients, in company documents, in manuals and catalogs, on public signs and advertisements, in hiring, promotions and transfers, and in information technologies. There are penalties for noncompliance. Most controversial has been the provision for dominant French signs on commercial establishments, compliance being monitored by government inspectors. The charter limited access to English education for immigrant children, and this has been a point of contention. *Ranee K. L. Panjabi*

See also: Bilingualism in Canada; Francophone; French Canadians; Official Languages Act; Separatist movement in Quebec.

The Charter of the French Language, promulgated in 1977, contains a provision stipulating the use of French on commercial signage such as the marquee on this Cineplex Odeon theater in Montreal, Quebec.

Cherokee Nation v. Georgia and *Worcester v. Georgia*

> **Significance:** Two decisions rendered by the U.S. Supreme Court limited the sovereignty of Native American tribes by placing them under federal protection.

In 1823, the U.S. Supreme Court, with John Marshall as chief justice, made the first serious judicial effort to define the relationship between the federal government and Native Americans. The case, concerning disputed land titles, was *Johnson v. McIntosh*. The decision was that the federal government was, in effect, the Native Americans' ultimate landlord and they were the government's tenants. The Court judged the federal government to be responsible for Native American affairs, including the protection of Native American peoples against state actions that materially affected Native American lives and property.

Cherokee Nation v. Georgia

During a period in which the federal government and the states were locked in disputes about where the Constitution intended ultimate sovereignty to reside, Georgia contemplated removing Cherokee and Creek peoples from northern and western portions of the state. To legitimize its plans, Georgia charged that when it had agreed, in 1802, to cede its western land claims to the federal government, the latter had agreed to extinguish Native American titles to those lands and then to return them to the state. The federal government had not done so, and Georgia had been obliged to live since with a Native American state within a state. The land-hungry Georgians initiated steps to remove Native Americans, primarily the Cherokee. They denied the relevance of federal treaties with the Cherokee and threatened to use force against federal troops if they were dispatched to protect the tribe. Andrew Jackson's election as president in 1828 accelerated Georgia's actions to begin removal, because Jackson, a veteran Indian fighter who deemed Native Americans "savages," was a proponent of removal.

In December, 1828, the Georgia legislature added Cherokee lands to a number of Georgia counties. Far from being savages, the Cherokee who protested this action had become a successful farming people. Thanks to a syllabary produced by their own Sequoyah, they were literate and produced their own newspaper, the *Cherokee Phoenix*. They instantly assembled a distinguished delegation to appeal to Congress for assistance. This course was applauded by a host of congressmen and public officials—including Daniel Webster and William Wirt—who proclaimed Georgia's legislation unjust, on moral as well as legal grounds. Nevertheless, in December, 1829, Georgia's legislature enacted a comprehensive law that essentially nullified all Cherokee laws. Aggravating the Cherokees' plight was the discovery of gold in the following year in western Georgia, and a gold rush flooded their lands with gold seekers, in violation of Cherokee treaties. Under great pressure, Governor George Gilmer claimed the gold as state property and threatened to oust the Cherokees forcibly. Having failed in Georgia's courts, the Cherokees, as a last peaceful resort, appealed to the U.S. Supreme Court under Article III, section 2 of the Constitution, which gave the Court original jurisdiction in cases brought under treaties or by foreign nations.

In *Cherokee Nation v. Georgia*, Chief Justice Marshall, who had been sympathetic to Cherokee claims but also was aware of Jackson's hostility toward both Native Americans and Marshall's court, dismissed the case in March, 1831. Marshall asserted that the Court lacked the jurisdiction to halt Georgia's sequestration of Cherokee lands. In doing so, he defined the relationship of the Cherokee to the federal government as that of a "domestic, dependent nation" rather than a sovereign one.

Worcester v. Georgia

Marshall modified his decision in 1832, however, when deciding *Worcester v. Georgia*. *Worcester* resulted from a Georgia law enacted in 1831. The law, aimed primarily at white missionaries who were encouraging Cherokee resistance to removal, forbade whites from residing on Cherokee lands without a state license. Georgia arrested, convicted, and sentenced two unlicensed missionaries, Samuel Worcester and Elizur Butler, whom the American Board of Commissioners for Foreign Missions promptly defended, hiring William Wirt as their counsel. Wirt, running as a vice presidential candidate for the National Republican Party and as a presidential candidate for the Anti-Masonic Party, hoped for a decision that would embarrass Jackson.

Because the plaintiffs in *Worcester* were white missionaries and the defendant the State of Georgia, the Court had clear jurisdiction. Without overruling his *Cherokee Nation* decision, Marshall ruled in March, 1832, that the Georgia law was unconstitutional and therefore void, because it violated treaties as well as the commerce and contract clauses of the Constitution. Furthermore, Marshall declared, Georgia's laws violated the sovereignty of the Cherokee nation, and, in this case, the Court was constrained to define relationships between Native Americans and a state.

The Cherokee cases advanced two contradictory descriptions of Native American sovereignty. In *Cherokee Nation v. Georgia*, Marshall delineated the dependent relationship of Native American tribes to the federal government. In *Worcester*, sympathetically stressing historic aspects of Native American independence, nationhood, and foreignness rather than their domestic dependency, he defined the relationship of Native American tribes to the states. Together, these decisions suggested that although Native American tribes lacked sufficient sovereignty to claim political independence and were therefore wards of the federal government, they nevertheless possessed sufficient sovereignty to guard themselves against intrusions by the states, and that it was a federal responsibility to preserve this sovereignty. In subsequent years, these conflicting interpretations were exploited by both the federal government and Native Americans to serve their own purposes.

Mary E. Virginia

Core Resources

Ronald N. Satz's *American Indian Policy in the Jacksonian Era* (Lincoln: University of Nebraska Press, 1974) covers the Cherokee cases and clarifies the complex political climate in which the cases developed around conflicts between the Jackson administration, Georgia, and the Cherokees. Vine Deloria, Jr., and Clifford M. Lytle's *American Indians, American Justice* (Austin: University of Texas Press, 1983) and *The Nations Within* (New York: Pantheon Books, 1984) examine Native American sovereignty and the justice system. Francis Paul Prucha's *American Indian Treaties* (Berkeley: University of California Press, 1994) and *The Great Father* (vol. 1, Lincoln: University of Nebraska Press, 1984) analyze the relations between the federal government and Native Americans.

See also: Indian Removal Act; Trail of Tears; Tribal sovereignty.

Cherokee Tobacco case

In the *Cherokee Tobacco* suit, two Cherokee nationals, Elias Cornelius Boudinot and Stand Watie, challenged the imposition of an 1868 federal tax law on their tobacco factory, which had been established in the Cherokee nation under provisions of the Cherokee/U.S. Treaty of 1866. (This case was received by the Court in 1870, argued in 1871, and decided May 1, 1871.)

Article 10 of the 1866 treaty stated that Cherokee citizens had the right to sell any product or merchandise without having to pay "any tax thereon which is now or may be levied by the U.S." Two years later, Congress enacted a general revenue law that imposed taxes on liquor and tobacco products "produced anywhere within the exterior boundaries of the U.S." Justice Noah Swayne, speaking for a deeply fractured court (three

justices concurred with Swayne, two dissented, and three did not participate), said that the case boiled down to which of the two laws—treaty or general domestic—was superior. Swayne developed what has been termed the "last-in-time" rule. In effect, whichever is latest in time, be it treaty or statute, stands.

This was a catastrophic precedent for tribes, since the treaty termination law, which had been attached as a rider to the March 3, 1871, Indian Appropriation Act, had closed the door on Indian treaties, although preexisting ratified treaties were still to be honored by the U.S. This law effectively froze tribes in political limbo: They were no longer recognized as nations capable of making treaties with the federal government, yet they remained separate sovereignties outside the pale of the federal Constitution.

Tribes, as a result of this decision, were virtually bereft of legal or political protection. The federal government could thereafter explicitly or implicitly abrogate treaty provisions and tribes had little recourse, save returning to the corridors of the very Congress that had enacted the abrogating legislation.

This opinion ignored the historical and political reality that the Cherokee nation was a separate and autonomous political entity not subject to general domestic laws unless they had given their express consent; it denied the fact that Congress itself had not explicitly stated in the 1868 law that the revenue act applied to Indian Territory. Moreover, it disavowed the general principle that specific laws, such as treaties, which create special rights are not to be held "repealed by implication by any subsequent law couched in general terms."

David E. Wilkins

See also: Indian Appropriation Act; Treaties and agreements with Indians: United States; Tribal sovereignty.

Chicago Conference

This meeting of approximately five hundred American Indians from throughout the United States convened at the University of Chicago in 1961 to establish policy goals in Indian affairs for the presidential administration of John F. Kennedy. The conference brought together an eclectic mix of people and gave some voice to tribal groups, mostly from the eastern United States, that lacked federal recognition. Discussion of issues was impassioned and often pitted traditionalists against progressives.

This meeting marked the beginning of adamant, vocal, and sophisticated articulation of problems in Indian country and with federal Indian policy. The *Declaration of Indian Purpose*, a manifesto of sorts, came out of this meeting. The declaration called for abandonment of the termination policy and reorganization of the Bureau of Indian Affairs and for the government to address the need of tribes for better education, medical care, and economic development. The declaration was a statement of common needs. The National Indian Youth Council (1961), a split-off group of younger Indian people more willing to take a radical stance on issues, was inspired by this meeting. The Chicago Conference was a key event that began what is sometimes referred to as the Indian civil rights movement and marks a time when tribal groups often united to speak out on various common issues.   *Carole A. Barrett*

See also: American Indian activism; American Indian civil rights; American Indian Movement; National Congress of American Indians; National Indian Youth Council.

Chicano movement

> **Significance:** In the Chicano movement, Mexican Americans defined and took pride in their own identity, asserted their civil rights, and worked toward self-determination by improving their financial, social, and political circumstances.

The Chicano movement began in the early 1960's and peaked in the early 1970's. Many historians view the movement as a concise expression of the Chicano perspective on the Mexican American community's history. Chicano history begins with the indigenous peoples of what is now Mexico and the southwestern United States, proceeds with the Spanish conquest and colonization and the Mexican-American War (1846-1848), and continues during the subsequent expansion of European Americans into the American Southwest.

Chicano History
According to Chicano analysts, Chicanos are indigenous to the Americas, originating from Aztlán, the Aztec homeland in Central and North America. After the Spanish conquest and colonization in the 1500's of what is now Mexico and the Southwest, Chicano culture became a blend of Indian and Spanish customs and practices. Although the Spanish attempted to suppress the indigenous culture, the Indians' response to the influx of Spanish culture was to practice accommodation, outwardly accepting their "inferior" status to obtain concessions from the dominant group and occasionally rebelling.

In the eighteenth and nineteenth centuries, settlers from the United States began to arrive in the Southwest, then part of Mexico. These settlers, mostly of European ancestry, brought with them the concepts of white supremacy, patriarchy, Christianity, and capitalism. Under the 1848 Treaty of Guadalupe Hidalgo, which ended the Mexican-American War, Mexicans who remained in the new territories of the United States were designated as citizens with all constitutional rights and guarantees; land acquired under Mexican law was to be protected by U.S. law. However, by 1900, European Americans (called Anglos by Chicano historians) had seized 95 percent of Mexican-owned land.

The Mexican way of life gradually was replaced by the lifestyle of the Anglo settlers. Mexican farmers and ranchers were replaced by Anglos, who ran the farms and ranches differently, often along more capitalistic and less paternalistic lines. Some of the ranchers viewed Mexican Americans primarily as a reserve workforce. Across the Southwest, American businesses, courts, and law enforcement agencies replaced existing facilities. Schools were segregated; a triple system separated Mexican Americans, African Americans, and European Americans.

From approximately 1900 to 1930, millions of Mexican citizens migrated to the United States. Some fled to avoid the violent and economic dislocations of the Mexican Revolution; others came to fill the U.S. labor shortage caused by economic growth in industry and agriculture. Communities in the Southwest that historically had contained many Mexican Americans and industrial cities in the Midwest became destinations for those seeking employment, and migrant trails of Mexican and Mexican American workers developed throughout the United States.

Mexican, Mexican American, and Chicano Generations
In the 1930's, the political and nationalistic loyalties of members of the Mexican American community underwent profound change. The Mexican immigrants who arrived from 1900 to 1930 often did not think of themselves as citizens of the United States because of Mexico's geographic proximity and the ease of returning to their native country. Discrimination and anti-Mexican attitudes also made it hard for them to feel a part of their adopted country. However, in the post-World War I era, as millions of migrants moved into Mexican American communities and the U.S.-born generation began to grow up, more of the migrants began to think of themselves as Mexican Americans.

The Great Depression of 1930 resulted in the deportation of many Mexican immigrants. From 1930 to 1937, U.S. law officials and political authorities deported approximately 500,000 Mexican people (250,000 of which were children born in the United States and therefore

American citizens). The deportation demonstrates how many Americans viewed Mexican immigrants: as inexpensive and exploitable labor to be disposed of in times of economic distress.

This negative perception persisted even after World War II. From 1942 through 1945, several hundred thousand Mexican Americans were active in combat zones; several received the highest military honors. When the war ended and the veterans returned home, they discovered that their sacrifices had minimal effect on prewar attitudes toward and policies and structures affecting Mexican Americans. However, these veterans no longer accepted the status quo, and they joined with members of the community who had already rejected the ideas of gradualism and assimilation. From 1946 through 1963, Mexican American veterans, believing in the American ideal of equality and equal opportunity and having proved their patriotism and loyalty, created new organizations to address what they perceived to be barriers to their reform-oriented strategies. However, despite these organizations' numerous successful efforts against economic, political, and social discrimination (including the legal defeat of the triple school system and a significant role in helping elect John F. Kennedy to the U.S. presidency), many members of the Mexican American community became disillusioned at the lack of substantive improvement for communities and individuals. The most prominent problems were the continued exploitation of agricultural workers, immigration issues, low levels of educational achievement, and limited economic opportunities.

Chicano

The origin of the term "Chicano" is unclear; however, some experts believe that the word originated from an improper pronunciation or slang version of "Mexicano." Consequently, the user was viewed by middle-class Mexicans or Mexican Americans as uneducated, poor, and probably "Indian," a pejorative appellation from those of Mexican origin who rejected their indigenous roots. In the Chicano critique of Anglo society, the rejection of Anglo racial and ethnocentric designations also included the repudiation of those in Mexicano communities who accepted anti-Native American and capitalist belief systems. To call the self Chicano is to affirm that which is denounced by Anglo-created racial constructs and ethnocentric depictions. To be Chicano is to affirm and proclaim historic, indigenous origins and to understand that Chicano culture has Spanish-Indian roots in a land invaded and conquered by the European Americans.

Chicano Generation

In the Southwest, many Mexican Americans, particularly young people, began to reexamine their identity, especially their experience as a *mestizo* (mixed race) people in a culture and society dominated by white European Americans. The election in 1963 of five Mexican Americans to the town council of Crystal City, Texas, a town where the majority of the population was Mexican American, marked the birth of a new political generation. This new generation rejected European Americans' definition of "Mexican American"; they saw themselves as Chicanos, an indigenous people with roots in the Aztec homeland of Aztlán and possessing their own mestizo culture. The word *chicano* was appropriated from the denigratory use of *Mexicano* by whites who had stereotyped Mexican immigrants and citizens alike as lazy and dirty. *Chicano* came to connote ethnic pride, a defiant turning of the old hate language on its head. Members of the Chicano movement felt that to continue the previous (Mexican American) generation's strategy of reform was to practice accommodation and might even constitute an acceptance of European American constructions and a rejection of their mestizo-indigenous history.

Four individuals form the core of the Chicano generation and movement: José Ángel Gutiérrez, Rodolfo "Corky" Gonzáles, Reies López Tijerina, and César Chávez. During the 1960's, Gutiérrez of South Texas organized young Chicanos into the Mexican American Youth Organization, which emphasized their right to cultural self-determination and had the development of bilingual/bicultural education for all Mexican American children as one of its principal goals. In 1965, in Denver, Colorado, González founded the Crusade for Justice to improve education, job opportunities, and police relations for Chicanos. He also organized the first Chicano Youth Liberation Conference in 1969, which brought together representatives from a number of Chicano organizations. At the first conference, the delegates adopted El Plan Espiritual de Aztlán, a manifesto of political and cultural nationalism. Tijerina of New Mexico formed La Alianza Federal de Mercedes in 1963 in an effort to reclaim land he and many Chicanos felt had been taken from the Mexican owners in violation of the 1848 Treaty of Guadalupe Hidalgo. He led a 1967 raid on the courthouse in Tierra Amarilla, New Mexico. Chávez, prob-

One of the best-known activists in the Chicano movement was César Chávez, who led striking farmworkers in Delano, California, in the 1960's.

ably the best-known Chicano activist, led farmworkers in Delano, California, on a strike that developed into a grape boycott and lasted from 1965 to 1970. In many ways during these early years, the Chicano movement was integrated with Chávez's call for migrant farmworkers' rights because a huge proportion of the farmworkers were, and remain, Mexican or Mexican American.

These four men were the impetus for the Chicano movement and the core of its activities. Their concerns— improving the financial, social, and political status of Mexican Americans, gaining the respect due to Mexican Americans, claiming the right to self- determination, and building Chicano pride—were echoed in the goals of the many other Chicano organizations that were formed in the late 1960's and early 1970's. These and later organizations deal with additional issues such as the distinction between illegal workers and immigrants, legal problems involving the use of the Spanish language, the lack of mestizo-Chicano peoples in American history

instruction, police brutality, lack of health and education services, lack of education, and structural poverty.

The final politicization of the Chicano generation grew out of the Vietnam War. Many Chicanos saw the overrepresentation of Mexican Americans in the combat zones of Vietnam as proof of the veracity of the Chicano view of European American society and as a further betrayal of Mexican American World War II veterans' beliefs and sacrifices. The Vietnam War and the older and younger generations' differing feelings about it produced great tension within Mexican American communities; some older Mexican Americans were compelled to question and adjust their basic beliefs about patriotism and reform. The 1970 Chicano Moratorium was the largest Chicano antiwar demonstration and also the most violent police riot involving Chicano protesters.

All of these events, issues, and concerns fueled an attempt by Gutiérrez and others to organize a national political party, La Raza Unida, in the early 1970's. Although some of the party's local efforts favorably altered political relations between Chicanos and European Americans, the party was not successful at the national level. After 1975, the Chicano movement no longer was a cohesive force in Mexican American communities, although Chávez's widow, Helen Chávez, continued his leadership of the fight for the rights of farm laborers. However, during its heyday, the Chicano movement did engage a new generation of Mexican Americans with a much more comprehensive and complete vision and understanding of the Mexican American/Chicano experience in the United States.   *Carl Allsup*

Core Resources
Rodolfo Acina's *Occupied America: The Chicano Struggle for Liberation* (2d ed., New York: Harper & Row, 1976) presents the Chicano perspective on the Mexican American experience. Mario Barrera's *Race and Class in the Southwest: A Theory of Racial Inequality* (Notre Dame: University of Notre Dame Press, 1976) looks at both class and race. Arnoldo de Leon's *They Called Them Greasers: Anglo Attitudes Toward Mexicans in Texas, 1821-1900* (Austin: University of Texas Press, 1980) offers a history of the development of racial and ethnocentric constructs by European American society. David Montejano's *Anglos and Mexicans in the Making of Texas, 1836-1986* (Austin: University of Texas Press, 1987) demonstrates the complex interaction of race, ethnicity, and class and the evolving response by Mexican Americans toward European Americans' efforts to control Mexican American people.

See also: Accommodationism; Alianza Federal de Mercedes; Guadalupe Hidalgo, Treaty of; Latinos in the United States; Mestizo; Mexican deportations.

Children in the Civil Rights movement

Many African American children—from the very young to teenagers—were involved in the Civil Rights movement of the 1950's and 1960's in the United States. They participated in marches, demonstrations, boycotts, pickets, sit-ins, desegregation of schools, voter registration campaigns, and freedom rides. Some children accompanied their activist parents to organizing meetings, which were often held in black churches and conducted by members of the National Association for the Advancement of Colored People (NAACP), the Student Nonviolent Coordinating Committee (SNCC), the Southern Christian Leadership Conference (SCLC), the Council of Federated Organizations (COFO), and other civil rights organizations. The children were primarily involved in the movement in the South, especially Mississippi, Alabama, Georgia, Tennessee, Arkansas, Tennessee, and Florida, where both de jure (by law) and de facto (by custom) segregation existed. Although the movement was nonviolent, it elicited violent acts from angry white mobs who gathered around protests, local authorities trying to break up demonstrations and arrest protesters, and racist groups who bombed churches and attacked African Americans in an effort to intimidate them. In the course of the struggle to obtain civil rights, African American children were beaten, clubbed, gassed, threatened by lynch mobs, attacked by police dogs, blasted by high-power water hoses, arrested, jailed, and even killed.

In May of 1963, in Birmingham, Alabama, thousands of children marched for civil rights as part of the Children's Crusade. Birmingham police commissioner Eugene "Bull" Connor, a staunch segregationist, gave the order for police to attack the children with nightsticks, police dogs, and high-power water hoses. The police arrested the children, filling the city jails and then imprisoning children in a makeshift jail at the fairgrounds. In September, 1963, a bomb exploded in the Sixteenth Street Baptist Church in Birmingham, killing four young girls who had been attending Sunday school. The church had been selected as a target because civil rights activists gathered there and organized protests.

Children also played an important, and difficult, role in school desegregation. Their parents filed lawsuits on their behalf, but it was the children who attended these schools who bore the brunt of racially motivated attacks, verbal and physical abuse, and social isolation. Two of the nationally publicized cases occurred in Topeka, Kansas, and Little Rock, Arkansas. Topeka operated eighteen public elementary schools for white children only and four schools for black children. The Reverend Oliver Brown, on behalf of his daughter Linda Carol Brown, and twelve other black plaintiffs, on behalf of their children, filed a lawsuit to protest this segregation. After much expert testimony, the U.S. Supreme Court in 1954 issued a landmark decision that ended segregation of children in public schools solely on the basis of race because segregation deprived minority children of equal educational opportunities. In 1957, nine black youths (known as "the Little Rock Nine"), led by Daisy Bates, desegregated Little Rock's Central High School. President Dwight D. Eisenhower had to use state troopers to protect the children from physical violence by armed white adults opposed to desegregation.

Bernice McNair Barnett

See also: *Brown v. Board of Education*; Civil Rights movement; Desegregation: public schools; Little Rock school desegregation; Segregation: de facto and de jure.

Chin, Vincent, murder

In 1982, the U.S. automobile industry was in a slump. Many people believed that competition from Japanese automakers had caused the U.S. automakers' problems, and resentment against the Japanese was strong. On June 19, 1982, Vincent Chin, a twenty-seven-year-old Chinese American, went with three friends to a bar in Detroit, Michigan, to celebrate his forthcoming wedding. In the bar, two white autoworkers, Ronald Ebens, an automobile plant foreman, and his stepson, Michael Nitz, a laid-off autoworker and part-time student, who assumed that Chin was Japanese, taunted him. They called him "Jap" and used abusive language in blaming him for the loss of jobs at U.S. automobile-manufacturing plants. After a fistfight broke out, the manager evicted both groups of combatants.

Outside, Ebens and Nitz got a baseball bat from the trunk of their car and found Chin and his friends waiting for a friend to pick them up. Chin and his friends ran, but Ebens and Nitz hunted and trapped Chin in front of a McDonald's restaurant. There Nitz held Chin while Ebens bludgeoned him with the baseball bat. Four days later, Chin died of head injuries.

The two men were initially charged with second-degree murder but were later allowed to plead guilty to manslaughter. On May 16, 1983, Wayne County circuit court judge Charles S. Kaufman, after hearing only the arguments from the defense attorneys and not those of the prosecuting attorneys, sentenced the two men to three years' probation and fined each $3,000 plus $780 in fees. They were allowed to pay the debt in monthly payments of $125.

People across the country responded with disbelief

and outrage. Asian Americans in Detroit formed the American Citizens for Justice and, along with several California congressmen, demanded a review of the light sentences. They also asked the U.S. Department of Justice to investigate whether Ebens and Nitz had violated Chin's civil rights. The Justice Department had the Federal Bureau of Investigation (FBI) look into the matter. The FBI's investigation resulted in the convening of a federal grand jury in September, 1983, which indicted Ebens and Nitz on two counts, one of violating Chin's civil rights, the other of conspiracy. The following year, the Wayne County U.S. district court convicted Ebens of violating Chin's civil rights but acquitted him of the conspiracy charge. Ebens was sentenced to twenty-five years in jail and told to undergo treatment for alcoholism. He was freed after posting a $20,000 bond. Nitz was acquitted of both charges.

Ebens's attorney appealed the conviction, and the federal appeals court overturned the conviction in September, 1986, on the grounds that the attorneys for the American Citizens for Justice had improperly coached a prosecution witness. The Justice Department ordered a retrial, which took place in Cincinnati, Ohio. Ebens was acquitted of both charges. Neither Ebens nor Nitz spent a day in jail for murdering Chin.

The Chin incident—in which resentment against one Asian nation translated into violence against an Asian American whose ancestors were from another nation—convinced members of the Asian American community that to receive justice, all Americans of Asian descent, although from very distinct traditions, would have to unite and organize. In this way, the Chin murder led to the founding of the Asian American movement.

Arthur W. Helweg

See also: Asian American movement; Asian American stereotypes; Chinese Americans; Japan bashing; Orientalism.

Chinatowns

A Chinatown is an ethnic enclave outside Chinese homelands where the Chinese are concentrated. A China-

town can be found in almost every major city with a high clustering of Chinese throughout Southeast Asia, South and North America, Europe, and Oceania.

San Francisco's Chinatown was the first in the United States. It began to take shape in 1850 as large numbers of Chinese immigrants were lured there by the California gold rush. Initially called Little Canton, it was christened Chinatown by the press in 1853. In the next several decades, more than two dozen Chinatowns were established in mining areas, railroad towns, farming communities, and cities of California, as well as Nevada, Utah, Colorado, Montana, Wyoming, Idaho, Oregon, and Washington. As the Chinese diaspora accelerated, especially after the 1882 Chinese Exclusion Act, Chinatowns gradually emerged in New York, Boston, Chicago, Philadelphia, Washington, D.C., Baltimore, Maryland, and other cities.

San Francisco's Chinatown, formed in the 1850's, remains a center of Chinese American commerce and culture although most Bay Area Chinese Americans do not reside there.

The formation of Chinatowns in the United States was an outcome of both voluntary and involuntary forces. In a foreign land and with language barriers, the Chinese needed their own communities for information sharing, lifestyle preservation, business transactions, cultural maintenance, kinship networking, and psychological support. Externally, hostility and violence against the Chinese, housing and employment discrimination, and institutional exclusion forced them to establish their own enclaves for self-protection and survival.

Over time, some Chinatowns have survived and continued to grow, whereas other Chinatowns, such as Pittsburgh's, have faded. Many important demographic, economic, social, and geographical factors have contributed to the growth or decline of a Chinatown, including the size of the city in which the Chinatown is located; the number of Chinese residents in the city; the sex and age distribution of the Chinese population in the Chinatown; the demand for Chinese labor in the area; the demand of the Chinese in the Chinatown for goods and services; the continuation of new Chinese immigration and settlement into the Chinatown; land-use patterns and land values in the Chinatown and its surrounding areas; changes in the socioeconomic status of Chinese residents; relationships between the Chinese and other groups; and adaptation strategies of the Chinatown.

In the 1990's, there were more than two dozen Chinatowns in the United States, of which New York's Chinatown was the largest. Contemporary Chinatowns have been transformed into tourist centers and Chinese shopping bazaars. They also serve as living Chinese communities, Chinese cultural meccas, commercial cores, suppliers of employment and entrepreneurial opportunities, historical education hubs, and symbolic power bases for political office holders and seekers. Nevertheless, there is some evidence that injustice and the exploitation of new Chinese immigrants also take place in some Chinatowns. Despite the existence of the three types of traditional social organizations in Chinatowns (*huiguan* or district associations, *zu* or clans, and *tongs* or secret societies), they have much less influence on the lives of Chinese residents than they did in the past.

Historically, all Chinatowns were located in urban centers, and residents tended to have a lower socioeconomic status. However, in the late 1970's, the first suburban Chinatown emerged in Monterey Park, located east of Los Angeles. Also dubbed the Chinese Beverly Hills or Little Taipei, it is home to mainly middle-class people. Chinese Americans are the dominant economic, social, and cultural force in the city. In November of 1983, Monterey Park elected the first Chinese American woman mayor, Lily Lee Chen. There are signs that suburban Chinatowns are multiplying in the San Gabriel

Valley east of Los Angeles and in Silicon Valley, south of San Francisco, and they are likely to grow in the foreseeable future as a result of an influx of high-status Chinese immigrants.

Philip Q. Yang

See also: Chinese Americans; Chinese Exclusion Act; Ethnic enclaves.

Chinese American Citizens Alliance

Significance: This organization became a major social and political force in the Chinese American community.

Chinese began arriving in the United States in the mid-nineteenth century. Most of the immigrants were young men who left their families behind in China and who intended to return to China once they secured sufficient money to support their families comfortably. To secure passage to the United States, most of these men indentured themselves to a merchant or a labor agent, a system called the credit-ticket arrangement whereby merchants advanced Chinese money for passage to the United States and kept collecting payments for years. Some Chinese left less willingly, emigrating because of famine and political and social unrest in southern China or falling victim to the so-called "Pig Trade," which replaced slavery after it was outlawed following the Civil War. They chose the United States because of exaggerated tales of wealth and opportunity spread by traders and missionaries.

Chinatowns Formed

Once the Chinese landed in the United States, labor agents, under the credit-ticket arrangement, gained almost complete domination of their indentured workers and kept them in isolated communities that became known as Chinatowns. Many Chinese ultimately were unable to secure sufficient money for return passage to China; however, because they did not want to remain permanently in the United States, they had little incentive to assimilate. Their unwillingness or inability to become acculturated into the American "melting pot" became an indictment against all Chinese.

Life in California in the late 1800's was difficult at best for most Chinese. The Chinese communities organized *huiguan* (merchant guilds) that served as welcoming committees, resettlement assistance services, and mutual help societies for newly arrived immigrants. Chinese immigrants were also organized by the Chinese

Consolidated Benevolent Association (the Chinese Six Companies), originally agents of Chinese firms in Hong Kong that had established the "coolie trade" to San Francisco. The Six Companies kept traditional Chinese rules, customs, and values as the basis for appropriate behavior, helping protect Chinese from an increasingly anti-Chinese atmosphere.

Violence—External and Internal

Anti-Chinese sentiments and violence against Chinese began almost as soon as they arrived in North America. These attitudes existed at the top levels of government and labor unions as well as being held by local citizens. During the mid- to late 1800's, various political parties, including the Know-Nothing Party, the Democratic Party, and the Republican Party, promoted anti-Chinese platforms. During this time, workers' unions organized anti-Chinese activities and anti-Asian sentiments were propagated by newspapers in western states. In 1871, twenty Chinese in Los Angeles were killed and their homes and businesses looted and burned. In 1877, a similar incident occurred in San Francisco. In Chico, California, five farmers were murdered. Anti-Chinese riots broke out in Denver, Colorado, and in Rock Springs, Wyoming. In 1885, Chinese workers, employed as strikebreakers, were killed at a Wyoming coal mine. Chinese residents in Seattle and Tacoma, Washington, were driven out of town, and thirty-one Chinese were robbed and murdered in Snake River, Oregon. In 1905, sixty-seven labor organizations, in order to prevent employers from hiring Asians, formed the Asiatic Exclusion League.

In the early 1890's, the Chinese Six Companies influenced Chinese not to sign documents required by the Geary Act (1892), an extension of the Chinese Exclusion Act of 1882, which required all Chinese residing in the United States to obtain a certificate of eligibility with a photograph within a year. When the Geary Act was ruled legal, thousands of Chinese Americans became illegal aliens in the United States. The Tongs, secret societies of criminals that originated in China, used this opportunity to take control of the Chinatowns. The result was a vicious and bloody civil war among Chinese Americans. Few first-generation Chinese Americans actively opposed the rule of the Tongs.

Native Sons of the Golden State

Many young American-born (second-generation) Chinese opposed these "old ways" of doing things. They accepted the idea that they were never going to return to China and wanted to adopt American ways and fit into American culture. These young, second-generation Chinese formed the Native Sons of the Golden State in San Francisco in an effort to assimilate into American mainstream culture. The Native Sons of the Golden State emphasized the importance of naturalization and voters' registration. All members were urged to become American citizens and to vote. The organization also encouraged active participation in the civic affairs of mainstream American life. The leaders thought that some of the anti-Chinese sentiments and discriminatory actions were, in part, caused by the traditional attitudes and behaviors of the Chinese immigrants who remained isolated, did not learn English, and did not take part in politics.

As the organization grew, it established chapters in Oakland, Los Angeles, San Diego, Chicago, Portland, Detroit, Pittsburgh, and Boston, eventually changing its name to the Chinese American Citizens Alliance (CACA). In 1913, CACA defeated a California law designed to prevent Chinese from voting. The group fought against the National Origins Act, or Immigration Act of 1924, and sought the right for Chinese males to bring their wives to the United States. CACA helped defeat the Cinch bill of 1925, which attempted to regulate the manufacture and sale of Chinese medicinal products such as herbs and roots. By promoting numerous social functions, CACA also helped keep Chinese American communities together and moved them toward assimilation. CACA fought against the stereotyped portrayals of Chinese in films, newspapers, and magazines as heathens, drug addicts, or instigators of torture. In 1923, for example, the organization attempted to block publication of a book by Charles R. Shepard, *The Ways of Ah Sin*, depicting negative images of Chinese. CACA has also supported other community organizations, such as Cameron House, Self-Help for the Elderly, and the Chinese Historical Society of America.

Gregory A. Levitt

Core Resources

Ronald Takaki's *Strangers from a Different Shore: A History of Asian Americans* (Boston: Little, Brown, 1989), an account of Asians coming to live in America, provides some discussion of the Chinese American Citizens Alliance in the 1940's and the late 1980's. Shih-Shan Henry Tsai's *The Chinese Experience in America* (Bloomington: Indiana University Press, 1986) also looks at the immigration experience. Richard H. Dillon's *The Hatchet Men: The Story of the Tong Wars in San Francisco Chinatown* (New York: Coward-McCann, 1962) is a dated but interesting account of the violence in San Francisco early Chinatown under the rule of the Tongs.

See also: Chinese Americans; Chinese Exclusion Act; Chinese Six Companies; Immigration Act of 1917; Immigration Act of 1924; Immigration Act of 1943; Yellow peril campaign.

Chinese Americans

> **Significance:** The Chinese first came to the United States as laborers in the early to mid-1800's, finding considerable prejudice and discrimination, which diminished after World War II.

The Chinese began to immigrate to the United States in 1820, but their numbers remained small until the late 1840's, when the decaying empire of China was defeated in 1848 by Britain in the First Opium War. In 1849, gold was discovered in California, and the gold rush began. When word of the gold rush reached Canton, in the southeastern province of Kwangtung, many Cantonese peasants, who had made their living as laborers, farmers, and fishermen for centuries, began to leave their impoverished homeland for the chance of riches just across the Pacific.

Most of these early Chinese immigrants worked with exceptional diligence, industry, and enterprise and led a reticent existence in the mining camps and cities. These positive qualities earned the early Chinese immigrants acceptance among the California business community. Although their appearance set them apart from the rest of the townspeople, they were warmly welcomed as a valuable and respected segment of the citizenry. That goodwill wore thin as increasing numbers of Chinese arrived. In 1852 alone, more than twenty thousand Chinese landed at San Francisco, bringing the total number of Chinese on the coast to approximately twenty-five thousand. The flood of new arrivals severely taxed the city's resources, particularly in Chinatown, where most settled, at least temporarily. The white settlers' attitude toward the Chinese and Chinatown began to shift from curiosity to contempt.

Under the slogan "California for Americans," nativists began demanding legislation to restrict Chinese laborers and miners. In 1852, the California legislature re-

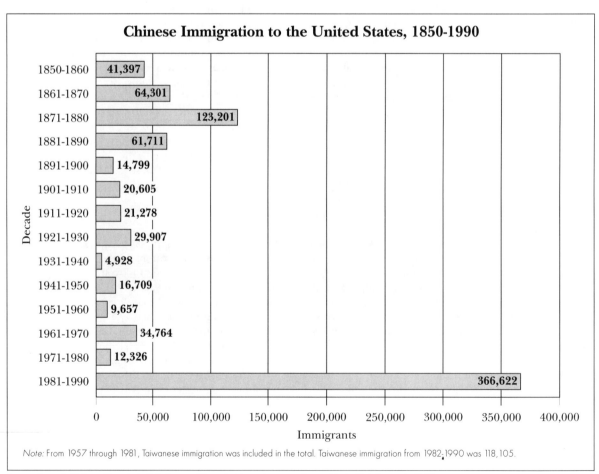

Chinese Immigration to the United States, 1850-1990

Decade	Immigrants
1850-1860	41,397
1861-1870	64,301
1871-1880	123,201
1881-1890	61,711
1891-1900	14,799
1901-1910	20,605
1911-1920	21,278
1921-1930	29,907
1931-1940	4,928
1941-1950	16,709
1951-1960	9,657
1961-1970	34,764
1971-1980	12,326
1981-1990	366,622

Note: From 1957 through 1981, Taiwanese immigration was included in the total. Taiwanese immigration from 1982-1990 was 118,105.

Source: Susan B. Gall and Timothy L. Gall, *Statistical Record of Asian Americans.* Detroit, Mich.: Gale Research, 1993.

sponded by passing the state's first discriminatory tax law, the Foreign Miners' Tax. This law required all miners who were not citizens of the United States to pay a monthly license fee. Because the Chinese were the largest recognizable group of foreign miners and already were concentrated in easily accessible mining camps, they constituted the majority of those taxed. California governor John Bigler also began a crusade against Chinese immigration on the grounds that it constituted a danger to the welfare of the state. The efforts of California nativists culminated in the Chinese Exclusion Act of 1882, one of the earliest federal laws restricting immigration to the United States. Other legislation followed, including the alien land laws (1913-1923), the Cable Act (1922), and the National Origins Act (1924).

This Chinese American family runs the New East Broadway Market in New York City. Many Chinese immigrants operate small businesses with the help of family members.

As a result of the exclusion, and because males far outnumbered females, the American Chinese population remained stable until the 1950's.

Chinese American Experience, 1942-1965

The image of Chinese Americans improved during this period, which ranges from 1942, the first full year of U.S. war against Japan, to 1965, the year of the Immigration and Nationality Act. This improvement was in part the result of China's being an important ally of the United States in World War II. A public awareness of the difference between Chinese Americans and Japanese Americans began to develop, at the expense of the latter. The Chinese American literature of this period is dominated by two sentiments, a diplomatic sentiment, which seeks to explain the values and virtues of the Chinese heritage to the general reader, and a sentiment of belonging, of claiming America as home.

Chinese American Experience Since 1965

After 1965, the Chinese population of the United States rose from 250,000 in 1966 to 1.6 million in 1990. This gave rise to a debate over what, if any, distinctions should be drawn between the native-born and the foreign-born. Frank Chin and the other editors of *Aiiieeeee! An Anthology of Asian-American Writers* (1974) and *The Big Aiiieeeee! An Anthology of Chinese American and Japanese American Literature* (1991) attempt to differentiate between the native-born and the foreign-born, implying that Chinese American identity should be determined on the basis of an American, rather than Chinese, mindset. Newcomers

(sometimes derided as "fresh off the boat," source of the title of David Henry Hwang's *FOB*, 1979) and more recent arrivals have brought with them significant resources and skills. These conditions render moot the American-centered definition of Chinese American identity. The increased diversity of the Chinese American community has made the issue of identity complex.

A common theme in twentieth century Chinese American literature is the critical representation of social issues. Cultural conflicts, generation gaps, and gender troubles are common to the experiences of many Chinese Americans from diverse backgrounds. This literature, including Maxine Hong Kingston's *The Woman Warrior* (1976) and *Tripmaster Monkey: His Fake Book* (1989), is essential to Chinese American identity and tends to problematize rather than resolve its dualities. This exploration of social issues has given rise to critiques of the American Dream (for example, Gish Jen's *Typical American*, 1991), of Western ideology regarding Asia (Hwang's *M. Butterfly*, 1988), and of the intricate complicities between American and Chinese ideologies. These thoughtful works epitomize the complex maturity of the Chinese American identity.

Compiled from essays by Balance Chow and Daniel J. Meissner

Core Resources

Gunther Barth's *Bitter Strength: A History of the Chinese in the United States, 1850-1870* (Cambridge, Mass.: Harvard University Press, 1964) describes the early years of Chinese immigration, providing a good examination of the development of anti-Chinese sentiment in California. Stuart Creighton Miller's *The Unwelcome Immigrant: The American Image of the Chinese, 1795-1882* (Berkeley: University of California Press, 1969) examines Chinese immigration in terms of coolie labor and the fear that Chinese laborers would undermine labor and revive slavery. Ronald Takaki's *Strangers from a Different Shore: A History of Asian Americans* (New York: Penguin Books, 1989) provides thorough coverage of the Asian immigrant experience. Two anthologies edited by Frank Chin et al. provide a look at Chinese Americans through their literature: *Aiiieeeee! An Anthology of Asian-American Writers* (Washington, D.C.: Howard University Press, 1974) and *The Big Aiiieeeee! An Anthology of Chinese American and Japanese American Literature* (New York: Meridian, 1991).

See also: Chinese American Citizens Alliance; Chinese Exclusion Act; Chinese Six Companies; Immigration Act of 1917; Immigration Act of 1924; Immigration Act of 1943; Immigration and Nationality Act of 1965; Page Law; *Wong Kim Ark v. United States*.

Chinese Canadians

Significance: There were close to a million people of Chinese ancestry living in Canada at the beginning of the twenty-first century. Though their struggle has been long and sometimes arduous, Chinese Canadians have come to play an important role in modern Canadian society.

In 1858, when gold was discovered in the lower Fraser River region of British Columbia, thousands of miners—including a few hundred Chinese—rushed in from California. Soon, many Chinese migrated from China to join these gold seekers, and by the summer of 1861, nearly 4,000 Chinese miners were working in the area. These Chinese were seasonal workers who returned to either California or China during the winter after mining in the spring.

After the failure of one of the largest banks in the region in 1864, an economic recession hit the West Coast. To reduce government expenses, British Columbia was combined with another British colony, Vancouver Island, in 1866. This unification caused further unemployment, and the Chinese were blamed for the lack of jobs.

In 1871, the colony of British Columbia became a province of Canada and needed a transcontinental railway to link it with the rest of the country. The construction of the railway led to a second wave of Chinese immigration, and by 1881, 4,350 Chinese were reported to be residents of British Columbia, the largest ethnic minority in the province. However, because of official government discrimination—and daily prejudice even sometimes to the point of physical violence—Chinese lived together for safety and ran businesses such as grocery stores, restaurants, and lodges in small sections of towns.

The discrimination against Chinese was typical of that in all parts of North America at that time. In 1882, the U.S. government passed a law suspending entry of Chinese laborers to the states and issued identity certificates to Chinese immigrants already in the country. Because this law went into effect immediately, Chinese who had lived in the United States but were working on the railway in Canada had no time to return. As a result, many Chinese from the United States were stranded in British Columbia. This led white people in the province to organize anti-Chinese societies and propose further federal restrictions on Chinese immigrants (such as forbidding them to work more than eight hours a day).

The federal government in Ottawa, however, was not concerned about Chinese issues. White people in British Columbia claimed that because there were almost no Chinese in Ottawa, the federal government did not understand the social problems of the province and kept lobbying for more restrictions. This struggle, lasting from 1874 to 1883, was called the Fight Ottawa campaign. After Noah Shakespeare, the president of an anti-Chinese organization, was elected to parliament from Victoria in 1887, the House of Commons established a Select Committee to study the "Chinese problem."

Exclusion: 1885 to World War II

In 1885, a federal head tax of $50 per person was imposed for the annual entry and departure of Chinese over twelve years of age. In 1901, it increased to $100, and only two years later, it became $500. In those days, the average annual income of Chinese workers in Canada was $225. This incredibly high tax was to discourage and restrict Chinese entry into Canada. However, even during this time, many Chinese came to Canada because of economic woes in China.

The Qing government of China signed the Treaty of Nanking with Britain in 1842, after losing the Opium War. Territorial concessions and huge indemnities crippled the Chinese economy, especially when the United States and France also forced the Qing government to sign similar treaties. Moreover, in 1894, China lost the Sino-Japanese War. The resulting enormous taxations caused many Chinese to look for jobs outside the country.

Because of the cost of travel, many male workers left their families behind in China and crossed the ocean by themselves, hoping to make enough money in Canada to send for their families or return to China with lots of money. However, both these hopes were soon shattered.

A Brief History of Chinese Canadians

Year	Event Involving Chinese Canadians	Germane World Event
1788	Chinese arrive in Canada.	
1849		The first English colonists arrive in British Columbia.
1858	Gold rush begins near Fraser River. Chinese come to the area from San Francisco and establish a Chinatown on Victoria Island.	
1882		Chinese Exclusion Act passes in the United States.
1885	Chinese Tax Act levies departure and entry tax on Chinese of $50 per person per year.	
1886	The United Colony of British Columbia is established, with the colonies of Vancouver Island and British Columbia.	
1886	British Columbia enters the Confederation as a province of Canada.	
1894		Sino-Japanese War occurs.
1901	Revision of Chinese Tax Act raises entry-departure tax to $100 per person per year.	
1903	Revision of Chinese Tax Act raises entry-departure tax to $500 per person per year.	
1908		The Leminux Agreement between Canada and Japan limits Japanese immigration.
1913		California Alien Land Act prohibits Japanese from owning land.
1923	The Exclusion Act virtually eliminates Chinese immigration to Canada.	
1924		The Immigration Exclusion Act is passed in the United States, preventing Chinese and Japanese immigration.
1941		World War II starts.
1945		World War II ends.
1947	The Exclusion Act is repealed.	
1967	The Immigration Act is passed, allowing increased immigration from Hong Kong, India, and the Caribbean.	
1997		Hong Kong returned to China by Great Britain.

Falling into despair, some hopeless men congregated in the opium dens and houses of prostitution in various Chinatowns, serving to reinforce white stereotypes of the "decadent Chinese."

The head tax ended in 1923, but that year the Exclusion Act was passed. This act prohibited all Chinese from coming to Canada (except certain consular officials, students, or merchants). Also, Chinese who had been absent from Canada for more than two years would lose their Canadian residency. Although there were about 45,000 Chinese in Canada during the exclusion period, they never constituted more than 0.5 percent of the total population. However, until World War II, almost 99 percent of Chinese Canadians were concentrated in British Columbia. The Great Depression led to even more restrictions regarding Chinese in the province. Even Canadian-born Chinese had to get visas from the Chinese consulate just to step across the border to Seattle. Canadian-born Chinese could not practice law, open a drugstore, teach in school, or work in the post office, even though they had been educated in Canada, many at universities. The new generation took trains—which ironically their parents or grandparents had built—and crossed the Rocky Mountains to settle in places where there was little discrimination, such as Toronto and Montreal.

The Younger Generation, Vietnamese Chinese, and Hong Kong Expatriates

After World War II, multiculturalism became an important issue in Canada. Diversity and ethnic awareness became the commonly expected standard of social behavior. As a result, attitudes toward Chinese have changed rapidly for the better in postwar Canadian society.

Yet, assimilation has often corresponded to a decrease in cultural awareness. For example, attendance at Chinese language schools has been decreasing as Chinese Canadian parents prefer piano or dance lessons to language maintenance. Chinese Canadian cultural participation is often limited to such activities as celebrating the Chinese New Year Festival or taking Chinese painting classes.

Because of increasing job opportunities, members of the younger generation have left the Chinatowns and live in all parts of the cities. As a result, Chinatowns have largely become the residences of poor or elderly single men and the sites of ethnic markets and restaurants. During the weekend, many tourists come to purchase inexpensive and exotic products and foods.

The post-World War II Chinese community in Canada became more diverse in the last quarter of the twentieth century. Several thousand Chinese Vietnamese landed in Canada after North Vietnam took control of South Vietnam in 1975. These new Chinese are gradually expanding their business influence in the Chinatowns. In

These shops in Chinatown in Montreal, Quebec, are evidence of the area's Chinese American community.

addition, Hong Kong Chinese are becoming the largest minority in Canada. From 1983 to 1993, almost 170,000 Hong Kong Chinese came to Canada. After about a hundred years of English occupation, in 1994, Britain agreed to return Hong Kong to China in 1997. In the year that the treaty was signed, 41,524 Hong Kong Chinese landed in Canada (18 percent of the total immigrants that year). As members of the British Commonwealth, Hong Kong residents could migrate to Canada relatively easily, especially as the Canadian government gave special consideration to those who were financially secure or could bring in new business.

The Present and Future Generation

Established Chinese Canadians and new Chinese immigrants are now a significant part of Canada's diverse and multicultural population. Many have been recognized nationally and locally for their achievements and contributions. Harvey Lowe, also known as the boy-wonder world yo-yo champion, broadcast the first Chinese Canadian radio program, *The Call of China*, in 1951 on CJOR Radio in Vancouver. This program was on the air for fourteen years. Novelist Paul Yee has been introducing the history of Chinese Canadians to the world through novels, historical academic works, and works for young people. Fred Wah is a well-known poet, and Thomas Ming Swi Chang is one of the best-known biotechnologists in the world, especially famous for his research on artificial cells and blood. Alexina Louie is not only one of the few Chinese Canadians who composes music for a living but also is a world-famous musician. In 1986, she was named composer of the year by the Canadian Music Council.   *Nobuko Adachi*

Core Resources

Probably the best place to start studying the history of Chinese Canadians is *From China to Canada: A History of the Chinese Communities in Canada*, edited by Edgar Wickberg (Toronto: McClelland & Stewart, 1982). It describes in detail the history of Chinese settlement in Canada in relation to the severe racial exclusion laws. *Chinatowns: Towns Within Cities in Canada*, by David Chuenyan Lai (Vancouver: University of British Columbia Press, 1988), is also a good first book. It provides a history of Chinese Canadians though changes found in the Chinatowns. Anthony Chan's *Gold Mountain: The Chinese in the New World* (Vancouver: New Star Books, 1983) tells the remarkable story of the gold-mining period of Chinese life in Canada. This work also depicts Chinese occupational changes from miners to merchants, the major occupation of the Chinese immigrants. Some original stories and pictures of early Chinese immigrants in British Columbia can be found in Paul Yee's *Saltwater City* (Vancouver: Douglas & McIntyre, 1988). James Morton's *In the Sea of Sterile Mountains* (Vancouver: J. J. Douglas, 1974) also depicts Chinese immigrants in British Columbia. *Inalienable Rice: A Chinese and Japanese Canadian Anthology*, edited by Garrick Chu (Vancouver: Intermedia Press, 1980), is a unique study that compares the historical differences and similarities of discrimination in Canada of two ethnic groups, Chinese and Japanese. Ted Ferguson's *A White Man's Country* (Toronto: Doubleday, 1975) studies Chinese exclusion in relation to Japanese and East Indians in Canada.

See also: Chinatowns; Immigration law: Canada; Vietnamese Canadians.

Chinese Exclusion Act

> **Significance:** This act represents the first time the United States sought to exclude immigrants by race and nationality; it marked a turning point in what had been, until then, an open door to immigrants from around the world.

The Chinese Exclusion Act of 1882 suspended immigration by Chinese laborers to the United States for a period of ten years and prohibited Chinese residents in the United States from becoming naturalized citizens. Merchants, students, and tourists, however, were still permitted to enter the United States for visits. Although the Chinese Exclusion Act of 1882 was established as a temporary suspension of immigration by Chinese laborers, it was only the first of many laws designed to exclude Asians from entry into the United States.

This law was both a political and social reaction to increasing non-European immigration in the second half of the nineteenth century. As the country became more industrialized and its frontier began to disappear, Americans became increasingly apprehensive about employment and the role of immigrants. American labor organizations objected to what they perceived as unfair competition by Chinese laborers.

Background

Chinese immigration to the mainland United States began in earnest after the Taiping Rebellion in 1848. Most Chinese immigrants headed for California, where the gold rush of 1849 led to an increased need for labor. In 1854, 13,100 Chinese came to the United States. This immigration, regulated by the Burlingame Treaty in 1868, was unrestricted; by 1880, the number of immigrants had risen to 105,465. The majority remained in California, where they were hired as laborers by the railroads, worked as domestics, and opened small businesses. San Francisco was the port of entry for many Chinese; the population of its Chinatown grew from two thousand to twelve thousand between 1860 and 1870.

The size and nature of this early Chinese immigration brought a long-lasting prejudice. Californians thought of Chinese laborers as "coolies"—that is, as cheap labor brought to the United States to undercut wages for American workers. Chinese workers were also accused of being dirty. Authorities in San Francisco suspected that crowded areas of Chinatown were the focus for disease and passed the Cubic Air Ordinance, prohibiting rental of a room with fewer than five hundred cubic feet of space per person. This municipal ordinance was later declared unconstitutional.

Discrimination and violence increased during the 1870's. In 1871, a mob attacked and killed nineteen Chinese people in Los Angeles. Dennis Kearney, a naturalized citizen from Ireland, organized the Workingmen's Party in 1877 to oppose Chinese immigrants. Shouting, "The Chinese must go!" Kearney threatened violence to all Chinese immigrants. In July, 1877, men from an "anti-coolie club" led workers into San Francisco's Chinatown on a rampage that lasted several days.

Because most local ordinances against the Chinese

This political cartoon from the late 1800's portrays the kind of anti-Chinese sentiment that played a part in the passage of the Chinese Exclusion Act.

had been declared unconstitutional, people who opposed Chinese immigration turned to Congress for new legislation. Congress responded in 1879 with a bill to limit Chinese immigration by prohibiting ships from bringing more than fifteen Chinese immigrants at a time. The bill was vetoed by President Rutherford B. Hayes on the grounds that it violated the Burlingame Treaty. With popular sentiment against continuing Chinese immigration, however, the treaty was amended in 1880, allowing the United States to limit the number of Chinese immigrants.

Exclusionary Legislation

The Chinese Exclusion Act of 1882 was a response to the intensity of anti-Chinese feelings in the West and to close political elections that made western electoral votes critical. As signed into law by President Chester A. Arthur, the act suspended immigration by Chinese laborers for ten years. The vote in the House of Representatives reflected the popularity of the measure. There were 201 votes in favor, 37 against, and 51 absent. Representatives from every section of the country supported the bill, with southern and western House members voting unanimously for the legislation.

Later laws were even more draconian. An amendment in 1884 excluded all Chinese and Chinese residents living in other countries from entering the United States except as students, merchants, or tourists. The Scott Act of 1888 prohibited outright the entry of Chinese laborers and denied reentry to those who traveled abroad, even if they held reentry visas. The law also placed additional restrictions on those who were still permitted to come to the United States. In 1892 the Geary Act extended for an additional ten years the exclusion of Chinese immigrants,

prohibited the use of *habeas corpus* by Chinese residents in the United States if arrested, and required all Chinese people to register and provide proof of their eligibility to remain in the United States. The act was renewed in 1902, and Congress made permanent the exclusion of Chinese immigrant laborers in 1904.

These exclusionary laws reflected a bias in American attitudes toward immigration by non-Europeans and increasing racial discrimination. Restrictions on intermarriage and land ownership by Chinese in many western states in the early 1900's led to a reduction in the number of Chinese residing in the United States from more than 100,000 in 1890 to 61,639 by 1920.

On December 17, 1943, the Chinese Exclusion Act was repealed. By then the threat of competition by Chinese labor was no longer an issue, and China was an ally of the United States in the war with Japan. *James A. Baer*

Core Resources

Corinne K. Hoexter's *From Canton to California: The Epic of Chinese Immigration* (New York: Four Winds Press, 1976) looks at Chinese immigration specifically; Maldwyn Allen Jones's *American Immigration* (2d ed., Chicago: University of Chicago Press, 1992) takes a broader view of immigration issues and history. Other valuable works include Tricia Knoll's *Becoming Americans: Asian Sojourners, Immigrants, and Refugees in the Western United States* (Portland, Oreg.: Coast to Coast Books, 1982), Ronald Takaki's *Strangers from a Different Shore: A History of Asian Americans* (Boston: Little, Brown, 1989), and *The Tarnished Golden Door: Civil Rights Issues in Immigration* (Washington, D.C.: U.S. Government Printing Office, 1980) by the United States Commission on Civil Rights.

See also: Chinese Americans; Immigration Act of 1943; Immigration and emigration; Immigration and Nationality Act of 1965; Nativism.

Chinese Six Companies

Significance: Rising anti-Asian nativism prompts Chinese immigrants to organize for political representation, social services, and physical protection.

News of the California gold rush of 1848-1849 was the first catalyst for large Chinese emigration across the Pacific to the United States. Most of the immigrants were young men who worked as laborers, often on the transcontinental railroads. The completion of the railroads and the Panic of 1873 had caused great economic difficulties in the West, and many white Americans and elements of organized labor began to blame the Chinese for the lack of jobs and the economic recession. Violence against Chinese became widespread. In October, 1871, crowds of whites burned and looted the Los Angeles Chinatown after two white policemen were killed by Chinese assailants. Nineteen men, women, and children were killed and hundreds injured as angry whites randomly attacked crowds of Chinese.

Anti-Chinese Laws

Under intense political pressure from white voters in the West, Congress moved to exclude Chinese and other foreign-born Asians from obtaining citizenship. The 1870 Nationality Act denied the Chinese the possibility of becoming naturalized U.S. citizens. In 1878, California convened a constitutional convention that prohibited further Chinese immigration and granted local municipalities the right to exclude Chinese immigrants or confine them to specified areas.

Chinese immigrants were prohibited from owning property, obtaining business licenses, procuring government jobs, and testifying in any legal proceedings. At the urging of white voters in California, Congress in 1882 passed the first of a number of Chinese exclusion acts that prohibited the entrance of Chinese into the United States. The Supreme Court upheld the exclusion acts, ruling in 1889 that the Chinese were "a race that will not assimilate with us[and] could be excluded when deemed dangerous to peace and security."

In San Francisco, anti-Chinese laws were supplemented to isolate its large Chinese community. Local laws and hostility from whites forced newly arrived Chinese to settle in Chinatown. Segregated by these discriminatory laws, Chinatown began to establish structures to govern and protect its residents. San Francisco's Chinatown, made up primarily of men as a result of the immigration control acts, had developed a reputation as a center of vice. Chinatown leaders moved to control the small criminal element that had begun to define Chinese society to the non-Chinese residents of San Francisco.

The Six Companies Form

Most of the early Chinese immigrants to San Francisco's Chinatown came from the southern provinces of Guangdong and Fujian. Early on, wealthy merchants in Chinatown had organized around clan groups and district associations in their hometowns in China. By 1854, there

were six main associations in Chinatown. The first, formed in 1849, was the Gangzhou Gongsi, named after the district in Guangdong province that was the source of most of its members. The second, the San Yi Gongsi, consisted of immigrants from the administrative districts of Nanhai, Panyu, and Shunde. Immigrants from the districts of Yanging, Xinning, Xinhui, and Kaiping made up the third association, the Si Yi Gongsi. Immigrants from the Xiangshan area formed the fourth association, the Yang He Gongsi. The fifth, the Ren He Gongsi, was made up of the so-called Hakka peoples from Guanxi province.

The formation in 1854 of the sixth association, the Ning Yang Gongsi, marked the informal beginnings of the Chinese Six Companies Association. The Six Companies served as a public association for leaders of the major associations in Chinatown to mediate disputes between its members and serve as a representative of the Chinese community as a whole. Newly arrived immigrants from China who were in need of assistance sought out these family or district associations. When business or personal disputes developed between members of different associations, the Six Companies would provide a forum for peaceful mediation of disputes.

The Role of the Companies

The anti-Chinese legislation of the 1880's forced the Six Companies to move toward a more overt role as representatives of Chinese interests in San Francisco. On November 19, 1882, the group formalized its existence by establishing an executive body drawn from members of the existing associations. The Six Companies, formally known as the Chinese Consolidated Benevolent Association (CCBA), adapted some of the representative principles of U.S. political culture. The CCBA was recognized by the state of California in 1901. At the time, the Six Companies sought to create a body above family clans or associations that would resist the growing anti-Chinese movements in California and the western United States and would assume a more public role in its resistance to anti-Chinese legislation.

The Six Companies in San Francisco had limited success in challenging anti-Chinese legislation as violations of the Fourteenth Amendment to the Constitution. The Six Companies supported the 1896 case of *Yue Ting v. Hopkins*, which forced the Supreme Court to overturn San Francisco safety ordinances designed to harass Chinese laundrymen. Anti-Chinese attitudes in San Francisco and across the United States did not diminish after 1900. In 1902, an amendment to extend the Chinese Exclusion Act indefinitely was passed by Congress without debate.

In the first half of the twentieth century, the Six Companies in San Francisco supported measures to improve the quality of life in Chinatown. In 1905, the Six Companies established a school in Chinatown to teach children Chinese culture and language. In the 1920's, it helped raise funds to construct the Chinese Hospital to serve the Chinatown community. The Six Companies also established block watch programs and night patrols to prevent crime in the Chinatown area. The group still worked to overturn anti-Chinese sentiment and was an increasingly powerful political force, able to deliver votes to local politicians sympathetic to the views of Chinatown citizens.

In 1943, Congress passed an Immigration Act that repealed the exclusion laws, and barriers to Chinese Americans in the United States began to fall. In California, many Americans of Chinese ancestry moved to white neighborhoods after anti-Chinese laws were overturned. In this period, one of the major activities of the Six Companies was the promotion of the Nationalist government in Taiwan. Because most of the residents of San Francisco's Chinatown had immigrated from mainland China, significant opposition to the historical leadership of the group appeared.

The Six Companies' promotion of social isolation from white society was very divisive in the 1960's. A longtime opponent of federal social programs to aid the poor, the Six Companies eventually embraced government assistance and even administered federal job training programs in the 1970's. As Chinese Americans became more involved in Chinese politics and gained access to higher-paying jobs, participation in Chinatown affairs decreased significantly. The Six Companies became less of a force in Chinese American politics on a national scale, but it continued to work from its base in San Francisco.   *Lawrence I. Clark*

Core Resources
Victor Nee and Brett de Barry Nee's "The Establishment," in *Longtime Californ': A Documentary Study of an American Chinatown* (New York: Pantheon Books, 1973), examines the founding of the Six Companies and its role in Chinatown in the twentieth century. Thomas W. Chinn's *Bridging the Pacific: San Francisco Chinatown and Its People* (San Francisco: Chinese Historical Society of America, 1989) provides a detailed look at San Francisco from its founding to the late 1980's, by the cofounder of the Chinese Historical Association of America.

See also: Chinese American Citizens Alliance; Chinese Americans; Chinese Exclusion Act; Immigration Act of 1943; Page law.

Christian Front

Founded in 1938 by the "radio priest of Royal Oaks, Michigan," the Reverend Charles E. Coughlin, the Chris-

tian Front consisted of a group of neighborhood clubs that emerged as a major American pro-Fascist, anti-Semitic organization. For the previous five years, millions of Americans, worn down by the Great Depression, had listened to Coughlin's powerful, demagogic voice attack bankers, Jews, and communists while offering religious sermons and quick-fix solutions to the economic despair that gripped the nation. His appeal was particularly powerful among poor city dwellers who also followed his widely circulated publication *Social Justice*. Coughlin urged his followers to form neighborhood platoons to battle Jewish and communist enemies. In 1940, a Brooklyn gang of eighteen members of the Christian Front was indicted for planning to bomb public buildings and kill important government officials (although Coughlin himself disavowed any connection with this plan).

Although he did not hold an official position in the Christian Front, Coughlin served as an adviser and recruiter. A Federal Bureau of Investigation (FBI) investigation into the Christian Front brought increased church response. Finally, the U.S. entry into World War II caused the Catholic Church to order Coughlin to stop broadcasting and return to simple parish life. The war also caused *Social Justice* to be banned from the mails

The Reverend Charles E. Coughlin, a radio priest from Michigan, founded the anti-Semitic, pro-Fascist Christian Front in the late 1930's.

under the Espionage Act. Nevertheless, during the war, scattered Christian Front gangs still operated; in one notable incident in 1944, a Christian Front gang attacked Boston Jews in Dorchester. The Christian Front was in many ways symptomatic of racial and ethnic relations in the Depression years leading up to World War II—a time when many Americans were open to accepting scapegoats such as Jews and immigrants as the cause of their economic woes.   *Irwin Halfond*

See also: Anti-Semitism; Hate crimes; Hate speech.

Christian Identity movement

The term "Christian Identity" refers to religious beliefs expressed by a variety of churches, political organizations, and biblical study groups scattered around the United States. These religious beliefs are based on three points of doctrine. First, followers of Identity hold that white people, especially Anglo-Saxons, are the true Israelites and therefore the true chosen people of God. Second, they hold that modern Jews are not descendants of the ancient Israelites but children of Satan. Third, they maintain that the world is about to plunge into a final struggle between good and evil. In their teachings, whites are on the side of good in this ultimate battle and Jews and nonwhites are on the side of evil.

Christian Identity emerged from a religious movement known as British-Israelism or Anglo-Israelism that appeared in the late nineteenth century. Adherents to Anglo-Israelism maintained that the British and nations related to the British were descendants of the lost tribes of Israel. Anglo-Israelism won a number of followers in the United States, notably the attorney Howard Rand and William J. Cameron, a public relations officer for automobile manufacturer Henry Ford. Although Anglo-Israelism was generally not antagonistic to Jews, many of the American Anglo-Israelites were strongly anti-Semitic. Cameron, for example, was involved in producing a series of anti-Jewish articles that appeared in Ford's newspaper, *The Dearborn Independent*. Some anti-Semitic political extremists, including Gerald L. K. Smith, established close connections with the American Anglo-Israel movement.

From the late 1930's to the 1960's, individuals influenced by Anglo-Israelism created Christian Identity as a belief system entailing both religious faith in the superiority of the white race and political extremism. Two of the most notable of these individuals were Wesley Swift, a former Methodist minister, and William Potter Gale, a retired army colonel who had studied for the Episcopal ministry. Swift founded the Church of Jesus Christ Christian, a church name that was later taken by white su-

premacist leader Richard Butler, who claimed to be Swift's successor. Butler, who became the best-known Identity leader after Swift's death in 1970, also founded the racist organization Aryan Nation as the political wing of his church. Gale, together with Swift, established the Christian Defense League, which dedicated itself to promoting the Identity ideal of white Christian patriotism. Gale was also one of the founders of the extremist organization Posse Comitatus, which denied the constitutionality of all government except local, county government.

The Identity movement received national attention in 1992, when Identity believer Randy Weaver and his family were besieged for eleven days by federal authorities seeking to serve a warrant for firearms violations. However, many less well known racial extremists, such as the members of the heavily armed Covenant, Sword, and Arm of the Lord, are Identity believers. In addition, a number of non-Identity American political figures, including former Ku Klux Klansman and Louisiana politician David Duke, maintain close ties to Identity followers.   *Carl L. Bankston III*

See also: Anglo-Saxon; Anti-Semitism; Aryan Nation; Aryan "race"; White Aryan Brotherhood; White church; White supremacist groups.

Church burnings

During the mid-1990's, specifically between January 1, 1995, and June 1, 1997, the southeastern United States experienced a rash of arsons, fire bombings, and attempted fire bombings of African American and multiracial houses of worship. Leaders in the African American communities targeted by the arsonists were quick to compare the activity to similar events during the Civil Rights movement of the 1960's. Churches, they noted, had historically been the targets of hate groups because they were so closely associated with the black unity of the civil rights struggle. Several organizations, most notably the National Council of Churches, held press conferences calling on the Bureau of Alcohol, Tobacco, and Firearms (ATF), a section of the Treasury Department, and law enforcement agencies to be more aggressive in investigating the suspicious fires. President Bill Clinton responded to the public outcry with a call for federal oversight of the arson investigations.

The U.S. Congress unanimously passed legislation that expanded the circumstances under which the federal government could prosecute for damage to religious property. The measure extended the statute of limitations for prosecution of church arson cases from five to seven years and increased penalties for church arson from ten to twenty years. Despite criticism from

The Reverend W. D. Lewis stands in front of the burned rubble that was the Little Zion Church in Green County, Alabama, in January, 1996. This church burning and others in the area were suspected to be racial hate crimes.

Church of the Lukumi Babalu Aye v. Hialeah

Believers of the Santería religion perform animal sacrifices for the cure of the sick and, at certain ceremonies, cook and eat the animal's flesh. In 1987, the Hialeah, Florida, city council responded to a public outcry against a Santería church by passing a series of ordinances that had the effect of outlawing the killing of animals in religious rituals.

Church attorneys attacked the ordinances as a violation of freedom of religion under the First and Fourteenth Amendments. After federal district and appellate courts upheld the ordinances, the church appealed the case to the Supreme Court, where the justices voted 9 to 0 that the ordinances were unconstitutional. The Court ruled that when a law is plainly directed at restricting a religious practice, it must satisfy two tests: justification by a compelling state interest and use of the least restrictive means to promote that interest. However, Justice Anthony Kennedy also reaffirmed *Employment Division, Dept. of Human Resources of the State of Oregon et al. v. Smith* (1990), a ruling that a neutral law of general applicability would not be required to pass the two tests when the law burdened religion incidentally. General and neutral laws might proscribe cruelty to animals or require the safe disposal of animal wastes; however, Hialeah could not place a direct burden on unpopular religious rituals without a secular justification.

Thomas T. Lewis

See also: *Employment Division, Dept. of Human Resources of the State of Oregon et al. v. Smith*; Santería.

many African American leaders that the Justice Department and the ATF were not moving quickly enough in their investigations, a special church arson task force arrested nearly two hundred suspects by mid-1997. More than one hundred of those arrested were eventually convicted in federal and state courts on charges related to the destruction of more than seventy churches. Those arrested were overwhelmingly white and nearly half were juveniles. Most of those found guilty of federal offenses were convicted of civil rights violations as a result of evidence that the crimes were racially motivated. Federal officials could find no evidence that the arson activity was coordinated or directed by a group of individuals or an organization.

The national response in support of the victims of the church burnings was equally impressive. A joint effort by the U.S. Department of Housing and Urban Development, the National Council of Churches, Habitat for Humanity, and many other groups rebuilt most of the churches. The Congress of National Black Churches also established a fund to prevent future arsons and to rebuild churches that had been burned. The Eli Lilly Foundation contributed six million dollars to efforts to rebuild and repair the churches that had been destroyed. Even the sometimes controversial hotelier and philanthropist Leona Helmsley donated one million dollars to assist in the rebuilding effort.

Donald C. Simmons, Jr.

See also: Civil Rights movement; Hate crimes; Hate speech; Racism: history of the concept.

Citizens' Councils

Citizens' Councils, prosegregation organizations of white southerners that flourished in the 1950's and 1960's, began with a single council in Indianola, Mississippi, in July, 1954. The council was created in reaction to the United States Supreme Court's ruling in *Brown v. Board of Education* in May, 1954, which found school segregation unconstitutional. During the next two years, as anger with the Court's decision mounted, Citizens' Councils appeared across the South from Virginia to Texas. The greatest concentrations of support appeared in the lower South. Membership, drawn primarily from the middle and upper classes of the region, reached 250,000 during the heyday of the Councils. The Councils' goal was to maintain white dominance through economic coercion and intimidation of blacks and political opposition to integration. The Councils were in the forefront of the growing resistance to the Civil Rights movement. In states such as Mississippi, they controlled the political agenda and sometimes even the machinery of government itself. The influence of the organization waned in the 1960's, but the Councils' legacy of bigotry and dislike for African American aspirations for justice remained strong. The Citizens' Councils represented the vehicle that many whites used to express southern unhappiness with the end of segregation.

Lewis L. Gould

See also: *Brown v. Board of Education*; Civil Rights movement; Segregation; White supremacist groups.

Citizenship Act

> **Significance:** The first legal definition of Canadian citizenship, reflecting a growing Canadian nationalism.

Before passage of the 1947 Canadian Citizenship Act, Canadians were British subjects. British subjects born outside Canada, unless specifically prohibited, became Canadians upon establishing permanent residence in Canada without need of any formalities.

The only legislation defining Canadian nationality was in various immigration and naturalization acts, a situation that failed to satisfy the growing nationalism of twentieth century Canada. Non-British subjects had to meet the provisions of laws and bureaucratic decisions designed to implement a "white Canada" policy. Canada's Chinese Exclusion Act of 1885 barred immigration from that country. The Immigration Act of 1910 continued and extended that policy by authorizing the cabinet minister responsible for immigration control to exclude any race deemed unsuitable to the climate or requirements of Canada. Although the 1952 act would substitute "ethnic group" for "race," not until 1962 did Canada finally end racial discrimination in admissions.

Canada left it to ministerial and bureaucratic discretion to reject or approve applicants for admission. Pre-World War II immigration policy encouraged immigration from Britain, the United States, and the countries of Western Europe. Italians, Slavs, Greeks, and Jews were thought of as less assimilable and less desirable; their access to Canada was limited or denied. Asians were barred. By government policy, all blacks appearing at Canada's border with the United States were refused admission on medical grounds, a decision that could not be appealed.

Non-British subjects lawfully admitted to permanent residence in Canada who were more than twenty-one years of age and had resided in Canada for five years could apply to the nearest court for naturalization, where they would be asked to produce evidence that they were of good character and met the requirements of the immigration laws. If the court agreed, the candidate would, upon renouncing all foreign allegiances and taking an oath of allegiance to the monarch of Great Britain, be naturalized as a British subject and Canadian national.

Citizenship Is Defined

This situation failed to satisfy the feelings of Canadian nationalism that had been growing from the time Canada became a self-governing dominion in 1867 and that intensified as Canada began to develop its own foreign policy and sent an army to fight in World War II. Nationalists wanted a definition of Canadian nationality that expressed the country's uniqueness and removed all vestiges of the colonial past. Paul Martin, the son of an Irish father and a French Canadian mother, had been powerfully affected by the sacrifices of Canadian troops during World War II. When he became secretary of state in the Liberal Party administration of William Lyon Mackenzie King in 1945, the first piece of legislation he undertook to move through Parliament was a law that would define Canadian citizenship specifically. He clearly hoped that a Canadian citizenship separate from that of Great Britain would serve as a unifying symbol for the nation. With the strong support of King, the bill became law on July 1, 1946, to take effect on January 1, 1947.

All persons who had been born in Canada or on a Canadian ship, except for children of foreign diplomats, were declared to be natural-born citizens of Canada, entitled to a certificate to that effect. Children born outside Canada before January 1, 1947, to fathers who had been born in Canada, or were British subjects with permanent residences in Canada, or had been naturalized under Canadian law, also would be considered to be natural-born Canadian citizens. A person born outside Canada after December 31, 1946, would be a natural-born citizen if the father were a Canadian citizen, the child's birth were registered with the appropriate authorities by the age of two years, and the child either established residency in Canada or filed a declaration of retention of Canadian citizenship before reaching twenty-one years of age.

The act provided that all who had been included in a certificate of naturalization before January 1, 1947, as well as all British subjects with a permanent residence in

Canada, were now Canadian citizens. The new act treated citizenship as a personal and individual right of women. A woman who was a Canadian citizen would no longer lose her nationality upon marriage to an alien, nor would marriage to a Canadian citizen confer Canadian nationality. Previously, women had gained or lost nationality by marriage.

Aliens, as well as British subjects who were not already Canadian citizens, had to fulfill certain requirements to be naturalized. The person had to be twenty-one years of age, have been lawfully admitted to permanent residency, and have lived in Canada for at least five years, be of good character, have an adequate knowledge of either English or French, and demonstrate knowledge of the responsibilities and privileges of Canadian citizenship. A certificate of citizenship would be issued when the applicant, in open court, renounced all conflicting allegiances and took an oath to bear true allegiance to the monarch of Great Britain, to uphold faithfully the laws of Canada, and to fulfill all duties of a Canadian citizen.

Later Developments

Not until the Citizenship Act of 1976, which came into effect on February 15, 1977, was the 1947 act replaced. Distinctions between the citizenship status of men and women were eliminated; children born abroad to Canadian mothers, as well as Canadian fathers, would now count as natural-born Canadian citizens. Persons born outside Canada to a Canadian mother and a non-Canadian father between January 1, 1947, and February 14, 1977, who had not been able to claim Canadian citizenship under the previous act, could apply for citizenship certificates under the 1976 act. Other provisions permitted persons to apply for naturalization after they had been residents legally for at least three of the previous four years and as early as eighteen years of age.

Milton Berman

Core Resources

Paul Martin's *Far from Home*, vol. 1 in *A Very Public Life* (Ottawa, Ont.: Deneau, 1983), the autobiography of the 1947 Canadian Citizenship Act's sponsor, contains a detailed description of the passage of the act. Freda Hawkins's *Canada and Immigration: Public Policy and Public Concern* (2d ed., Kingston, Ont.: McGill-Queens University Press, 1988) examines changes in immigration regulations that reflect changing concepts of who is acceptable as a Canadian. Robert Bothwell, Ian Drummond, and John English's *Canada Since 1945: Power, Politics, and Provincialism* (Rev. ed., Toronto: University of Toronto Press, 1989) includes valuable information on the development of Canadian nationalism and Quebec separatism. Alan Cairns and Cynthia Williams's *Constitutionalism, Citizenship, and Society in Canada* (Toronto:

University of Toronto Press, 1985) explores the relationship between citizenship, social change, and the evolution of political communities in Canada.

See also: Immigration law: Canada.

Civic assimilation

"Civic assimilation" is the seventh and final stage of the assimilation process outlined by sociologist Milton Gordon in his influential book *Assimilation in American Life* (1964). The term refers to the absence of value and power conflict concerning public or civic life between the members of the host society and the assimilating group. Because this condition is related to groups' cultural values and norms, not only race and ethnicity but also religion and social class are important factors in achieving civic assimilation. Although both ethnic and racial minority groups in the American middle class have adopted the values of the core culture to a certain extent, those in the lower class are still at a considerable distance from the American cultural norms because of segregation, unemployment, and poverty in both rural and urban areas. Public policies regarding education and welfare systems are largely divided into two groups that represent opposing views. This division, because of race and social class, hinders American society from achieving civic assimilation of minority groups. Religion is another significant factor that generates value and power conflict among peoples. For example, there is an association between pro-life opinion and Catholic values regarding the abortion debate in the American political arena. *Hisako Matsuo*

See also: Anglo-conformity; Assimilation: cultural and structural; Assimilation theories; Attitude-receptional assimilation; Behavior-receptional assimilation; Identification assimilation; Marital assimilation; Structural assimilation.

Civil liberties

> **Significance:** Civil liberties represent one of the most basic of all conceptions of individual human rights.

There is a critical distinction between civil liberties and civil rights. Civil liberties are seen as negative promises by (or negative commands to) the government not to do certain things. The U.S. Constitution's Article I, sections 9 and 10 (the prohibitions against the federal and the state governments respectively) and the entire Bill of Rights (the first ten amendments) are clearly lists of negative commands. The First Amendment, "Congress shall make no law respecting an establishment of religion," is only one of a long list. Other negative commands in the Bill of Rights include "No soldier . . . shall be quartered in any house. . . . No person shall be held to answer for a capital . . . crime, unless on indictment. . . . Excessive bail shall not be required."

Still, negative commands would not help much if a government did not also act positively to protect its citizens from improper acts by others. Purely negative commands need to be balanced with certain affirmative obligations, and these are properly known as civil rights. These become particularly important to members of groups that suffered discrimination in the past, such as African Americans, Asian Americans, Hispanic Americans, or women in the United States. Naturally, civil liberties and civil rights also overlap: A negative promise that the government will not interfere with free speech implies an affirmative promise that it will protect individuals who express their opinions, even in the face of majorities that wish to silence them. Still, distinguishing between the affirmative and the negative characteristics of two concepts is useful.

The Need for Negative Promises

The best way to understand the distinction between negative promises and affirmative guarantees is to compare the mainly negative wording of the U.S. Constitution with the constitution written by Joseph Stalin for the Soviet Union in 1936. The Soviet constitution was revised a number of times before the collapse of the Communist regime in the early 1990's, but each version followed the general provisions of Stalin's 1936 draft. At the time of writing, Stalin had already defeated all rivals and stood at the height of his power. Apparently, he wanted a constitution for propaganda purposes. It would be easy to dismiss this document by saying that Stalin never intended to live up to it, but it is still instructive to see how its provisions were worded.

Stalin's constitution contained a "Bill of Rights and Duties"—affirmative promises of numerous material benefits not provided by the U.S. Constitution. Among these were "the right to work," or guaranteed full adult employment, and a "right to rest and leisure," including a maximum forty-hour workweek, lengthy paid vacations, and resorts for working people. Also guaranteed were rights to education, medical care, and maintenance in old age. Women were granted "equal rights"—a promise still not explicitly included in the U.S. Constitution.

Stalin's constitution also promised religious freedom and free expression, typically called "civil liberties." Unlike the U.S. Bill of Rights wording, "Congress shall make no law . . . ," Stalin's promise is affirmatively worded: "In conformity with the interests of the working people, and in order to strengthen the socialist system, the citizens of the Soviet Union are guaranteed by law: (a) freedom of speech; (b) freedom of the press; (c) freedom of assembly, including the holding of mass meetings; (d) freedom of street processions and demonstrations. These civil rights are ensured by placing at the disposal of the working people and their organizations printing presses, stocks of paper, public buildings, the streets, communications facilities, and other material requisites for the exercise of these rights."

Stalin's free-expression promise is remarkably generous, providing for an unrestrained right to "street processions and demonstrations," while the U.S. Constitution limits its protection only to those who "peaceably assemble." Still more generous is the promise to supply paper and printing presses. This is in stark contrast to the situation in the United States, where exercising "free" speech can cost considerable money for media advertising. Yet the extensive record of persecution of dissident Russian writers belies Stalin's promises. Why did Stalin's constitution not protect individuals? In fact, the innocent-sounding, presumably nonbinding introductory clause, "In conformity with the interests of the working people, and in order to strengthen the socialist system," acted as a limit on the promise of free expression that followed. Only press or speech that was in the "interests of the working people" or "strengthen[ed] the socialist system" was ever allowed in the Soviet Union.

Stalin's constitution promised a whole range of economic benefits, far beyond the financial ability of even the wealthiest government to provide for all citizens. Clearly, this document was a mere wish list for the future, not a constitution.

Although the U.S. Bill of Rights contains only negative promises, those promises are far more effective, for it costs nothing for Congress *not* to pass a law. Under Stalin, speech was declared "free," but one could not even buy it. In the United States, speech may cost money, but it is freely available in the marketplace. Starting with a broad affirmative promise, the Soviet Union ended with no free speech at all. The United States began with a limited, negatively worded promise of free speech and has found itself with an overwhelming flood of information.

Historical Trends in Court Cases

Originally, the most important purpose of the U.S. Bill of Rights was to protect the states from the danger of an overly powerful national government. The period from the adoption of the U.S. Constitution in 1789 to the Civil War (1861-1865) was devoted to protecting the state governments (and only indirectly the citizens) from the federal government. During this period, perhaps the most important of the entire Bill of Rights was the Tenth Amendment's promise that "the powers not delegated to the [national government] by the constitution, nor prohibited by it to the states are reserved for the states respectively, or to the people." The First Amendment begins with the phrase "Congress shall make no law," clearly making the federal government its only target; none of the other nine original amendments, however, includes this language. One might assume that the intention was for the entire Bill of Rights to apply to only the federal government, but, given the doubt, it was natural for someone to test this assumption.

Perhaps the most important test case to determine to which level of government the Bill of Rights applied was the case of *Barron v. Baltimore* (1833). The city of Baltimore paved a number of streets and dumped leftover construction materials into the water near a wharf that Barron owned. The floor of the bay was raised so high that ships could no longer use Barron's Wharf; thus he was deprived of his property interest in his livelihood without due process or just compensation. Barron decided to sue the city of Baltimore to recover damages. Baltimore was a subunit, however, under the "sovereign" state of Maryland, which did not provide the same guarantee against eminent domain actions which the federal constitution included. Because Barron could not succeed in the Maryland courts, he turned to the federal courts, only to discover upon reaching the Supreme Court that it regarded the Fifth Amendment as applying only to the federal government. In effect, Barron was told that if the Maryland constitution did not offer him protection, he could not receive it from the federal government. With this decision, the Supreme Court declared that the first ten amendments to the Constitution applied only to the federal government and not to the states. This reflected the reality of the situation before the Civil War, especially with regard to the slavery of African Americans in southern states. No slave could claim the right of free speech by citing the First Amendment.

After the Civil War, Congress sought to reverse the *Barron* decision with the Fourteenth Amendment, which begins: "All persons born or naturalized in the United States, and subject to the jurisdiction thereof, are citizens of the United States and of the State wherein they reside." The point was to undo the notion of citizenship established in *Barron*. The language of this amendment certainly appears to mean that all persons, regardless of race, were to be citizens of both the United States and the state in which they lived and that citizenship could not be denied to African Americans as it had been in southern states. Thus the U.S. Constitution was to penetrate the boundaries of each state and extend to each individual citizen.

Then the Fourteenth Amendment, in negative language, states, "No State shall make or enforce any law which shall abridge the privileges or immunities of citizens of the United States; nor shall any State deprive any person of life, liberty, or property, without due process of law." Arguably, this section of the Fourteenth Amendment applies the negative commands contained in the Bill of Rights and elsewhere in the Constitution to the citizens of each state. Once the Fourteenth Amendment was ratified, it would appear that *Barron* had been overturned by an act of the American people.

The Changing Composition of the Supreme Court

Though the Supreme Court did not initially interpret the Fourteenth Amendment in this way, it started to do so beginning in the 1920's. The Court has been guided by the so-called doctrine of selective incorporation, which holds that parts of the Bill of Rights are so basic to the notion of due process that the states cannot deny them to any persons residing within their borders. Thus, the words "Congress shall make no law" now mean that no government within the United States shall make any law that abridges the freedom of speech or of the press.

For most civil liberties, the process began in 1925 with the case of *Gitlow v. New York*, in which the Court applied the free-speech section of the First Amendment to the states. This act of selective incorporation set in motion a set of cases that applied most of the rest of the First Amendment to the states. In *Near v. Minnesota* (1931), the Court applied the free press section, and *Hague v. Congress of Industrial Organizations* (1939) applied the assembly section to the states. Free exercise of religion came partly in *Hamilton v. Regents of the University of California* (1934) and more completely in *Cantwell v. Connecticut* (1940). The nonestablishment of religion followed in *Everson v. Board of Education of Ewing Township* (1947). These cases maintained that the First Amendment (at least) had such a crucial relationship to due process that states could not deprive the citizens of its benefits without denying them due process.

The Court did not advance much toward incorporation until Earl Warren was named chief justice in 1953, for only portions of the First Amendment and a single clause of the Fifth Amendment had been applied to the states by then. Warren joined Associate Justices Hugo L. Black, William O. Douglas, and (partially) Tom C. Clark, who had long argued for a much fuller incorporation, in support of the application of more sections of the Bill of Rights. Later, the appointment of William J. Brennan (and others) made it possible for the Court to incorporate eventually nearly all of the Fourth, Fifth, Sixth, and Eighth Amendments— that is, nearly all the important sections of the Bill of Rights. Thus, the civil liberties familiar to U.S. citizens against the actions of both the federal and state governments are a rather recent addition to the understanding of civil liberties in the United States.   *Richard L. Wilson*

Core Resources

A general study of the subject, such as Henry J. Abraham and Barbara A. Perry's *Freedom and the Court* (6th ed., New York: Oxford University Press, 1994), is a good place to begin. For one view of incorporation, see Raoul Berger's *The Fourteenth Amendment and the Bill of Rights* (Oklahoma City: University of Oklahoma Press, 1989). *The Bill of Rights: Original Meaning and Current Understanding* (edited by Eugene W. Hickok, Jr., Charlottesville: University of Virginia Press, 1991) examines each element of the Bill of Rights. The 1936 Soviet constitution and Stalin's defense of it are found in *Readings in Russian Civilization* (edited by Thomas Riha, Chicago: University of Chicago Press, 1964).

See also: Civil rights; Fourteenth Amendment.

Civil Liberties Act of 1988

During World War II, Japanese residents on the West Coast and Aleuts in Alaska were interned by the U.S. military. In effect, American citizens—merely because they shared a national or ethnic heritage with the Japa-

nese enemy—were imprisoned and forced to live under harsh conditions in isolated camps for the duration of the war. Although after the war the Evacuation Claims Act of 1948 provided some compensation, the amounts were not enough for those displaced to recover the resulting wartime losses. Pressure from the affected groups prompted Congress on August 10, 1988, to pass the Civil Liberties Act, which authorized the Attorney General of the United States to pay $20,000 in damages to each interned Japanese or his or her immediate family heirs, with a ceiling of $1.25 billion. The law also provided payments of $12,000 to each Aleut who was similarly relocated (up to a ceiling of $5 million); $1.4 million for wartime damage to Aleut church property; $15 million for the loss of Aleut lands that resulted from designating part of Attu Island as part of the National Wilderness Preservation System; and $5 million to aid elderly, disabled, and seriously ill Aleuts, to provide scholarships for Aleuts, to improve Aleut community centers, and to provide for Aleut cultural preservation. No funds were appropriated until November 21, 1989. The first letters of apology were sent out October 9, 1990. Recipients, in turn, gave up all claims for future recovery of damages.   *Michael Haas*

See also: Japanese American internment; Japanese Americans.

President Ronald Reagan addresses the crowd at the signing ceremony for the Civil Liberties Act of 1988, which provided compensation to Japanese Americans placed in internment camps during World War II.

Civil rights

> **Significance:** Civil rights are among the most basic of all conceptions of human individual rights, but must be paired with civil liberties to be effective.

Civil rights are typically paired with civil liberties; together they constitute the realm of human individual rights. Civil liberties are negative limits on government's treatment of private citizens. In the United States, civil rights are affirmative obligations that various levels of government have to protect citizens from coercion (often called discrimination) by the government or by private citizens. In Canada, civil rights are exclusively defined as the government's obligation to protect one person from actions by another individual. Both are important parts of human rights, particularly for democratic governments, since how well a regime protects its citizens individually is of paramount concern.

Civil liberties have a longer, clearer relationship to U.S. government than do civil rights, given that U.S. history began with the Constitution's negative commands. From the country's founding in 1787 to the Civil War (1861-1865), constitutional theory protected state governments (and only indirectly their citizens) from the federal government's power. During this period, the provision considered to be the most important of the Bill of Rights was the Tenth Amendment: "The powers not delegated to the United States by the constitution, nor prohibited by it to the states are reserved for the states respectively, or to the people."

The argument that the Bill of Rights restrained only the national government stemmed from the wording of the First Amendment, which begins: "Congress shall make no law." Although this phrase was omitted from the other nine amendments, the unwritten assumption was that the word "Congress" should be applied to all ten. It was natural for this assumption to be tested, as it was in *Barron v. Baltimore* (1833). Barron's livelihood came from a wharf that was rendered useless when the city of Baltimore dumped paving debris in the water, raising the bottom of the bay too high near the wharf. Barron decided to sue for money to recompense himself for his loss of livelihood. Baltimore was a subunit under Maryland State, whose constitution did not provide for the guarantee against such losses which the federal constitution's Fifth Amendment did. Thus, aware that he could not succeed in the Maryland courts, Barron turned to the federal courts; however, the Supreme Court regarded the Fifth Amendment as applying only to the federal government. The court told Barron that if the Maryland constitution did not offer him protec-

tion, he could not receive it from the federal government. This decision made it clear that the first ten amendments to the U.S. Constitution applied only to the federal government and not to the states.

The pre-Civil War conception of civil rights showed clearly in the case of *Scott v. Sandford* (1857). Dred Scott was an African American slave sold to a new owner who took him into a free state, into a free territory, and then back into a slave state. Since the U.S. Constitution's language did not include the word "slavery," it was not clear whether Scott's time in free areas meant that he had become free. In the highly politically charged pre-Civil War atmosphere, the Supreme Court might well have found that Scott was still a slave on narrow technical issues, but it went far beyond that by declaring unconstitutional the 1820 Missouri Compromise. This was the first congressional enactment to be invalidated since *Marbury v. Madison* (1803). Since the 1820 compromise had prevented a clash between North and South over slavery, the decision had explosive consequences leading to the Civil War. Another critical effect of the *Scott* decision was to reinforce the notion that one had citizenship in one's home state as well as another set of rights acquired only through that state in the national government, and that the limits on the national government did not necessarily apply to the state government.

The Fourteenth Amendment

After the Civil War, Congress sought to insert language into the Constitution that would at least potentially reverse both *Barron* and *Scott*. The Fourteenth Amendment's first section has four parts, the first of which reads, "All persons born or naturalized in the United States, and subject to the jurisdiction thereof, are citizens of the United States and of the State wherein they reside." This first statement seeks to undo the notion of citizenship established in *Barron*, whereby persons are primarily considered citizens of the state in which they reside and only secondarily, through that state, citizens of the United States. The Fourteenth Amendment's constitutional language certainly appears to mean that all persons, black or white, were to be citizens both of the United States and of the state in which they lived simultaneously, and that African Americans could not be denied citizenship as they had in southern states. This allowed the U.S. Constitution to reach through the boundaries of the state to reach each individual citizen.

The Fourteenth Amendment then states, "No State shall make or enforce any law which shall abridge the privileges or immunities of citizens of the United States; nor shall any State deprive any person of life, liberty, or property, without due process of law, nor deny to any person within its jurisdiction the equal protection of the laws." From a reading of the "plain meaning of the text," these words would seem to reverse the Court's decision in *Barron* by insisting that in subsequent comparable cases, those who found themselves in situations like Barron's could not be denied their property without "due process of law."

The Supreme Court's Response

The Supreme Court, however, did not initially respond as if such were the case; instead, it seemed to resurrect the pre-Fourteenth Amendment constitutional understanding. In one important case, hundreds of butchers in New Orleans, operating as small individual businesses typical of nineteenth century America, were thrown out of business after what is widely regarded as the corrupt passage of a law in the Louisiana legislature granting a state franchise (monopoly) to one company. The butchers sued, arguing that they had been deprived of their property (their livelihood) by the state "without due process of law." In what seems a very curious decision today, the Supreme Court ruled (in what are known as the *Slaughterhouse* cases (1873) that the Fourteenth Amendment sought only to make African American citizens equal with white citizens and did not affect the relationships between white persons (that is, butchers as butchers).

A few years later, in the *Civil Rights* cases (1883), the Supreme Court invalidated the 1875 Civil Rights Act. This act had made it a federal crime for public conveyances, hotels, restaurants, or amusement halls to refuse admission to anyone because of race, color, or previous condition of servitude, but the Court found that the Fourteenth Amendment stopped only government discrimination, not that of individuals or businesses. The Court's outlook was even more damaging to civil rights when it confronted a case of governmental discrimination in *Plessy v. Ferguson* (1896). Homer Plessy, only one-eighth African American in descent, was classified as an African American and was denied the opportunity to ride in the segregated first-class sections of public transportation in Louisiana. He sued on grounds that segregation in public transportation denied him "equal protection of the laws" under the last clause in the first section of the Fourteenth Amendment. The Court ruled, however, that Plessy was provided "equal protection" as long as the state provided him with "equal" facilities, even if the facilities were separate. By this means, the doctrine of "separate but equal" came to be the binding interpretation of the equal protection clause. This seems even more curious (if not outrageous) in view of the Court's contention in the *Slaughterhouse* cases that the Fourteenth Amendment solely protected the rights of blacks.

The end result of these cases was that the late nineteenth century Supreme Court treated the Fourteenth Amendment as if it did not exist for ordinary citizens. If an individual was a white butcher in New Orleans, that person was not covered by the Fourteenth Amendment, because the Court said that the "original intent" of those who proposed the amendment was merely to bring blacks to the level of whites. If an individual was an African American citizen, that person could claim no protection from the amendment if a state provided any kind of remotely comparable separated facilities, even if they were quite unequal in fact. From a current perspective, the Fourteenth Amendment seems not to have provided much protection for U.S. citizens.

Applying the Equal Protection Clause

For nearly sixty years, the Court did not go very far toward reversing itself on civil rights, but it did chip away at *Plessy* around the edges. It had still not gone very far when Earl Warren was named chief justice in 1953, but his leadership made it possible for the Court to move toward protecting civil rights by applying the equal protection clause. The first decision in this direction was the famous *Brown v. Board of Education* (1954), which overturned the *Plessy* case by deciding that "separate but equal" was an impossibility because segregated schools were inherently unequal.

By overturning *Plessy*, the Court was announcing a new jurisprudence with revolutionary implications. Perceiving this, some legal scholars wrote searching challenges to *Brown*, but the Court won, not simply because it was the highest court in the land but because its interpretation of the Fourteenth Amendment rang truer to the original language than did the earlier view. In fact, segregated schools had not been equal to integrated schools, and the "separate but equal" doctrine had been used fundamentally to discriminate against African Americans by maintaining grossly unequal facilities.

State action was the principal focus toward which *Brown* was directed. Southern states had been taxing all of their citizens, black and white, but had been using that tax money to benefit whites far more than blacks. Since African American citizens had no effective way to vote in most southern states, they had no political remedy against discrimination. The states' abusive use of coercive power gave the Supreme Court its greatest moral justification for ending segregation in schools and other facilities.

The Supreme Court, the least powerful of American national institutions, must lead largely by persuading citizens that its decisions are correct. American courts do have sufficient legitimate strength so that the national and state executive branches will respond to court orders, and individuals who defy the courts will find themselves in great difficulty. In *Brown*, however, the Court was seeking not to influence an individual but to persuade large masses of people who had the force of the state on which to counterpoise their power against the courts. Many southern states responded to *Brown* by erecting legal and constitutional barriers against the Supreme Court decision, continuing to use their coercive power to deny African Americans "equal protection." At the same time, they failed to protect African Americans from private racist groups such as the Ku Klux Klan.

Lacking support from the executive and legislative branches, the Court was unable on its own power to achieve the end of segregation. In the decade between the 1954 *Brown* decision and the passage of the 1964 Civil Rights Act, the courts decided case after case striking down discriminatory laws in southern states, a process that was so slow and tedious that only 1 percent of southern students were attending integrated schools by 1964. Only with the passage of the Civil Rights Act of 1964 and Voting Rights Act of 1965 did all three branches of the national government begin to act in concert for equal protection. Only when these acts were enforced by a sympathetic administration in the 1960's did the country begin to make real progress toward eliminating the improper use of southern state governmental power.

The problem was enormous because it was a question of striking down not only a handful of specific laws giving preference to whites over African Americans but also a whole fabric of law that protected privileges acquired over years of discrimination. The U.S. Constitution is designed to protect minorities that already have legal protections. Within the nation as a whole, white southerners became a minority who used the legal system to maintain their previous benefits. Although legislation should not be retroactive, the legal system should also benefit citizens equally, or the system's legal legitimacy will erode.

The attempt to redress all the problems caused by segregation was yet more difficult because many discriminatory acts were in the domain of activities long regarded as private and beyond the legitimate scope of government activity. Given their past benefits, citizens could rely on the constitutional and legal structure to resist integration. The Supreme Court could strike down statutes and state constitutional provisions one after the other, but once it had rendered the legal system presumably neutral, schools would still be largely segregated because of private decisions made by citizens without any overt governmental support. This became especially clear in the pattern of segregation in northern schools, which proved to be based on residential housing patterns. When the Court could find deliberate decisions made by local authorities to bring about the segregation of schools, it could strike them down; it could do far less, however, when discrimination was not the result of de-liberate governmental action.

However, the notion of civil rights entails affirmative guarantees that the government will act to provide fairness for all individuals. Moreover, other groups besides African Americans claim to have suffered discrimination in the past (no group more obviously so than women) and were not granted equal protection of the laws in the late 1800's, despite their pressing claims at that time. For some such groups the case for relief from past discrimination is not so clear. They will need to advance their claims carefully and persuasively if they are to win the support of a broad segment of fellow Americans.

Richard L. Wilson

Core Resources

An excellent book of general scholarship in this field is Henry J. Abraham and Barbara A. Perry's *Freedom and the Court* (6th ed., New York: Oxford University Press, 1994). A cogent statement of the case against the Court's current understanding of civil rights is made by Raoul Berger in *The Fourteenth Amendment and the Bill of Rights* (Oklahoma City: University of Oklahoma Press, 1989). Ronald J. Fiscus's *The Constitutional Logic of Affirmative Action* (Durham, N.C.: Duke University Press, 1992), presents a tightly logical argument in support of the concept of affirmative action as a part of the package of rights known as "civil rights." An opposing view can be found in Kent Greenwalt's *Discrimination and Reverse Discrimination* (New York: Alfred A. Knopf, 1983).

See also: Affirmative action; *Brown v. Board of Education*; Civil liberties; Civil Rights Act of 1960; Civil Rights Act of 1964; *Civil Rights* cases; Civil Rights movement; Discrimination: racial and ethnic; Fourteenth Amendment; Missouri Compromise; *Plessy v. Ferguson*; *Scott v. Sandford*; Segregation: de facto and de jure; Voting Rights Act of 1965.

Civil Rights Act of 1957

During the mid-1950's, the Civil Rights movement gathered momentum as it challenged racial segregation and discrimination in many areas of southern life. One area where progress proved slow was voting rights. Intimidation and irregular registration procedures limited electoral participation by African Americans. By 1957, support for legislation to protect voting rights was growing among Northern Republicans and Democrats in Congress. Yet Congress had not passed a civil rights bill since 1875, and there was strong southern opposition to any change in the status quo. It was, however, Senator Lyndon B. Johnson of Texas, the Senate majority leader, who took the lead. Not known at this point in his career as an advocate of civil rights, Johnson used his considerable legislative ability to shepherd the new bill through Congress. It passed just as the Little Rock school integration crisis was breaking.

The bill had several major provisions. It created a new body, the Civil Rights Commission, to investigate complaints of violations of civil rights. It raised the Civil Rights Section of the Department of Justice to the status of a division, to be headed by an assistant attorney general. It also made it a federal crime to harass those attempting to vote and allowed the attorney general to initiate proceedings against those violating the law.

The law's short-term effects were modest. Though the number of African American voters did grow, many impediments to voting remained, especially in the rural South. Many criticized the act's weak enforcement procedures: The Civil Rights Commission could gather information and investigate complaints, but it could take no action to protect those trying to vote. Not until the Voting Rights Act of 1965 would effective machinery for ensuring voting rights be established.

On the other hand, in the early 1960's, the administration of President John F. Kennedy did use the act's provisions (which were strengthened by the 1960 Civil Rights Act) to proceed against some of the worst cases of harassment. Also the act broke a psychological barrier by putting the first national civil rights law in eighty-two years on the books. It also highlighted the importance of voting rights to the overall civil rights struggle.

William C. Lowe

See also: Civil rights; Civil Rights Act of 1960; Civil Rights Act of 1964; Civil Rights Act of 1968; Civil Rights Act of 1991; Civil Rights Acts of 1866-1875; *Civil Rights* cases; Little Rock school desegregation.

Civil Rights Act of 1960

As the Civil Rights movement progressed in the 1950's, efforts to desegregate led to a backlash in the form of bombings and burnings of black churches, homes, and other property. African Americans, otherwise fully qualified, were still denied the right to vote by many local officials, often under implicit threat of violent reprisals.

During 1959, the Civil Rights Commission made its first report, minutely documenting a massive denial of the right to vote in the South and recommending that the president appoint federal voting registrars in response to citizen complaints. Attorney General William P. Rogers proposed instead that complaints should be filed with federal courts, which would appoint voting referees. In the House, a bill favoring the referee plan passed. Majority Leader Lyndon B. Johnson and Minor-

ity Leader Everett Dirksen then maneuvered passage of the bill in the Senate. Southern conservatives were pleased that the bill was so weak that no major change occurred; civil rights proponents had to accept half-a-loaf in order to advance their cause.

According to section 6 of the act, the procedure for those deprived of the right to register or to vote is to complain to the U.S. attorney general to file suit in a federal court, which has ten days to respond. If the court finds that a pattern or practice of exclusion has existed in a voting jurisdiction for at least one year, the judge appoints one or more voting referees. Within a second ten-day period, the voting referees then screen applicants to determine whether they meet statutory requirements for voting; if an applicant is found qualified to vote, the judge then issues a voting certificate to the applicant, who can vote in the next election, provided that the initial application was filed twenty days before the election.

To ensure enforcement of the right to vote, section 6 provides that election officials who refuse to honor the federal voting certificate can be found in contempt of court. The U.S. attorney general, in filing a motion to find an election official in contempt of court, can also sue the state in which the voter resides in case the voting official is later fired.

President Dwight D. Eisenhower signs the Civil Rights Act of 1960. Two more civil rights bills would be signed during the decade.

Since voting records were often destroyed in cases of this sort, section 3 requires all election officials to keep records of votes cast in federal elections for twenty-two months.

The law did not challenge voting requirements, such as the literacy test, only the unequal application of voting requirements to blacks and whites. Later voting rights acts repealed various artificial voting requirements. Other provisions of the 1960 Civil Rights Act empower the Civil Rights Commission to administer oaths and permit U.S. government property to be used for desegregated schools when facilities for locally desegregated schools are unavailable.   *Michael Haas*

See also: Civil rights; Civil Rights Act of 1957; Civil Rights Act of 1964; Civil Rights Act of 1968; Civil Rights Act of 1991; Civil Rights Acts of 1866-1875; Voting Rights Act of 1965.

Civil Rights Act of 1964

> **Significance:** The Civil Rights Act of 1964 outlawed the exclusion of African Americans from hotels, theaters, restaurants, and other public accommodations; barred federal funds to any activity that involved racial discrimination; warranted the Justice Department to initiate school desegregation suits; and forbade racial discrimination in employment and union membership policies.

The legislation that became the Civil Rights Act of 1964 was originally proposed by President John F. Kennedy on June 19, 1963, following a confrontation with Alabama governor George Wallace over the admission of black students to the University of Alabama. Kennedy declared that the bill should be passed "not merely for reasons of economic efficiency, world diplomacy and domestic tranquility—but above all because it is right." The act was forcefully advocated by President Lyndon B. Johnson after Kennedy's assassination. Its passage was facilitated both by pressure from civil rights advocates and by segregationist responses to those pressures. Events that helped rouse the public to support civil rights included the March on Washington in August, 1963, the bombing of black churches, the "battle of Oxford" that ensued when James Meredith sought to enter the University of Mississippi, the mistreatment of freedom marchers and freedom riders, and the murder in Mississippi of three civil rights workers.

Passage of the act came only after senators voted to end a filibuster on June 19, 1964, exactly one year after Kennedy had proposed the bill. Republican senator Everett Dirksen, the Senate minority leader, shared credit for passage of the act. Traditionally an opponent of civil rights legislation, Dirksen implored Republicans to support the bill as "an idea whose time has come."

Major Provisions of the Act
Unlike the first two civil rights acts of the modern period—those of 1957 and 1960, which were limited principally to ensuring the right to vote—the 1964 act attacked segregation on a broad front. The final bill was stronger than Kennedy's proposal to Congress. Its main provisions are found in the first seven of the act's ten titles. Title I, concerned with voting, was intended to create more effective enforcement of the right to vote in federal elections without consideration of color or race. It expedites the procedure for settling voting rights suits and mandates that uniform standards be applied to all individuals seeking to register and vote. To diminish the discriminatory use of literacy and comprehension tests, it equates completion of the sixth grade with literacy. Finally, it empowers the U.S. attorney general to bring suit if there is a "pattern or practice" of voting discrimination.

Title II forbids discrimination on the basis of race, color, religion, or national origin in places of public accommodation. Privately owned or operated facilities, such as country clubs, are exempted from the Title II prohibition. Title III deals with public facilities such as municipally owned or state-owned or operated hospitals, libraries, and parks. It authorizes the attorney general to bring a civil suit to order desegregation of any such facility whenever the attorney general receives a written complaint of discrimination from an individual or individuals unable to take the necessary legal actions themselves.

Title IV's concern is public education. Its main provision authorizes the U.S. Office of Education to organize training institutes to prepare school personnel to deal with desegregation; to assist school districts, states, and other political subdivisions in implementing school desegregation plans; and to offer financial assistance to school boards to facilitate their hiring of specialists for in-service training.

Title V reauthorized the U.S. Commission on Civil Rights, created by the Civil Rights Act of 1957, for four years and gave it the additional responsibilities of serving as a national clearinghouse for civil rights information and investigating allegations of fraud in voting. Under Title VI, any federal body that offers contracts, grants, or loans is required to bar discrimination on the grounds of race, color, or national origin from programs it supports financially.

Title VII established a federal right to equal opportunity in employment and created the Equal Employment Opportunity Commission (EEOC) to assist in imple-

President Lyndon B. Johnson signs the Civil Rights Act of 1964, a landmark piece of legislation that would have a dramatic effect on race relations in the United States.

menting this right. Under Title VII, employers, employment agencies, and labor unions are required to treat all persons without regard to their color, race, religion, sex, or national origin. Equality or nondiscrimination was mandated in all phases of employment, including hiring, firing, promotion, job assignments, and apprenticeship and training. Gender was inserted into the bill at the insistence of Senator James Eastland, a Democrat from Mississippi, in the vain hope that its inclusion would weaken support for the entire bill. The final three sections of the act confer no rights. They provide structures for federal authorities to operate while mitigating possible conflicts with communities under pressure to comply with other provisions of the act.

Subjected to judicial scrutiny, the 1964 legislation survived several challenges to each of its main sections. Many of its provisions were later strengthened by subsequent legislation, including the Voting Rights Act of 1965 and the Civil Rights Act of 1968.

Ashton Wesley Welch

Core Resources
Among the many fine sources for information on the Civil Rights movement and the 1964 Civil Rights Act are Derrick A. Bell, Jr.'s *Race, Racism, and American Law* (2d

ed., Boston: Little, Brown, 1980), Charles S. Bullock III and Charles M. Lamb's *Implementation of Civil Rights Policy* (Monterey, Calif.: Brooks-Cole, 1984), Anthony Lewis's *Portrait of a Decade* (New York: Bantam Books, 1965), and Sig Synnestvedt's *The White Response to Black Emancipation* (New York: Macmillan, 1972).

See also: Civil rights; Civil Rights Act of 1957; Civil Rights Act of 1960; Civil Rights Act of 1968; Civil Rights Act of 1991; Civil Rights Acts of 1866-1875; Civil Rights movement; Equal Employment Opportunity Commission; Voting Rights Act of 1965.

Civil Rights Act of 1968

Significance: The Civil Rights Act of 1968 banned racial discrimination in the sale or rental of most types of housing; it also extended most of the protections of the Bill of Rights to Native Americans.

After 1965, the Civil Rights movement devoted increasing attention to conditions in the North. It found much segregation there, a condition that was rooted in residential patterns rather than in Jim Crow laws. The prevalence of segregated housing determined the composition of schools and other aspects of urban life. Martin Luther King, Jr.'s Chicago campaign in 1966 focused national attention on the housing issue. His lack of success showed that white resistance to opening neighborhoods to minority residents was strong and would be difficult to overcome. Urban riots in northern and western cities provoked a "white backlash," as many northern whites ceased their support for further civil rights reform. In 1966 and 1967, President Lyndon B. Johnson tried and failed to persuade Congress to pass civil rights bills outlawing discrimination in housing.

Passing the Act

In 1968, liberal Democrats in the Senate brought forward a new civil rights bill containing a fair housing provision. Heavy lobbying by Clarence Mitchell, of the National Association for the Advancement of Colored People (NAACP), helped to marshal a majority of senators in support of the bill. As with earlier civil rights measures, southern senators attempted to talk the bill to death with a filibuster. However, in return for some relatively minor modifications in the bill, the leader of the Republican minority, Senator Everett Dirksen of Illinois, agreed to support an attempt to cut off the filibuster. This succeeded, and the bill passed the Senate on March 11, 1968.

In the House of Representatives, passage was far from sure. The assassination of Martin Luther King, Jr., on April 4, however, shocked the country and dramatically altered the political landscape. Support for the bill grew; it passed easily and was signed by President Johnson on April 11.

Fair Housing

The main thrust of the 1968 Civil Rights Act was to outlaw discrimination on the basis of race, religion, or national origin in the sale and rental of most forms of housing in the United States, as well as in the advertising, listing, and financing of housing. Exempted from the act's coverage were single-family houses not listed with real estate agents and small apartment buildings lived in by the owner. (About a month after the act became law, the Supreme Court ruled, in the case of *Jones v. Alfred H. Mayer Company*, that the Civil Rights Act of 1866 prohibited racial discrimination in housing and other property transactions.) Two other provisions of the act also grew out of the racial turmoil of the 1960's. One enumerated specific civil rights whose violations were punishable under federal law. Another sought to make the act more acceptable to the growing number of Americans concerned about urban riots by specifying stiff penalties for inciting or engaging in riots.

As a housing measure, the act proved disappointing. Its enforcement provisions were weak. Those with complaints of discrimination were directed to file them with the Department of Housing and Urban Development (HUD), which would then attempt to negotiate a voluntary settlement. If this failed, complainants would have to file their own lawsuits; the federal government would intervene only in cases where there was a clear pattern of past discrimination. In addition, white resentment at attempts to integrate neighborhoods remained high. Banks often found ways to avoid the law's provisions, making it difficult for many African American families to secure necessary financing. By the late twentieth century, it was clear that the act had not ended the country's dominant pattern of racial segregation in housing.

The Indian Bill of Rights

The Civil Rights Act of 1968 contained another provision unrelated to concerns over fair housing: the Indian Bill of Rights. This was grounded in the fact that Indians on reservations, as members of tribal communities, were not considered to be covered by the Bill of Rights. In 1896, the Supreme Court had ruled, in the case of *Talton v. Mayes*, that the Bill of Rights did not apply to Indian tribes or to their courts. In 1961, Senator Sam Ervin, a North Carolina Democrat, was surprised to discover the fact. Over the next several years, he held hearings on the subject. In 1968, he was able to amend the civil rights bill moving through the Senate to include coverage of Indian rights.

The Indian Bill of Rights extended a variety of constitutional protections to Native Americans with regard to the authority of their tribal governments. Among these were freedom of speech and religion, as well as protections for those suspected or accused of crimes. In fact, all or part of the First, Fourth, Fifth, Six, and Eighth Amendments were held to apply to reservation Indians, as was the Fourteenth Amendment's guarantee of due process. Some parts of the Bill of Rights were not included, however; the First Amendment's ban of religious establishments was not included, in deference to tribal customs, nor were the Second Amendment's right to bear arms or the Third's prohibition against the quartering of troops. Most important to most Indians was a provision that required tribal permission before states could further extend jurisdiction over tribal land.

William C. Lowe

Core Resources

Useful views of the 1968 Civil Rights Act may be found in James A. Kushner's *Fair Housing: Discrimination in Real Estate, Community Development, and Revitalization* (New York: McGraw-Hill, 1983), Lyndon B. Johnson's *The Van-*

tage Point: Perspectives of the Presidency 1963-1969 (New York: Holt, Rinehart and Winston, 1971), Donald G. Nieman's *Promises to Keep: African-Americans and the Constitutional Order, 1776 to the Present* (New York: Oxford University Press, 1991), and John R. Wunder's *"Retained by the People": A History of the American Indians and the Bill of Rights* (New York: Oxford University Press, 1994).

See also: American Indian Civil Rights Act; Civil rights; Civil Rights Act of 1957; Civil Rights Act of 1960; Civil Rights Act of 1964; Civil Rights Act of 1991; Civil Rights Acts of 1866-1875; Civil Rights movement; *Jones v. Alfred H. Mayer Company.*

Civil Rights Act of 1991

To many supporters of the Civil Rights movement, the 1980's was a decade of disappointment, when earlier gains seemed threatened by unsympathetic presidents and a conservative political atmosphere. Especially troubling from this viewpoint was the direction taken by the U.S. Supreme Court. In 1989, the Court issued a number of decisions that seemed to endanger past protections against employment discrimination by making the position of voluntary affirmative action programs less secure (*Richmond v. J. A. Croson Company*), making it more difficult for women and minorities to sue for job discrimination (*Wards Cove Packing Company v. Atonio*), and reducing protection against racial harassment on the job (*Patterson v. McLean Credit Union*).

Reaction against these decisions, especially the last two, made it easier for liberal Democrats to create a bipartisan coalition in Congress in support of an effort to pass a new civil rights bill. Though the administration of President George Bush did not initially support the bill, the president did sign the bill when it finally passed after two years of congressional consideration and debate.

The Civil Rights Act of 1991 took the form of a series of amendments to Title VII of the Civil Rights Act of 1964. Among its many sections were three important provisions. One sought to overturn the *Wards Cove* decision, which had required those claiming employment discrimination to prove that a specific employer practice had created a discriminatory effect and allowed employers to justify such a practice as a "business necessity." The act eliminated the latter claim as a defense against a charge of intentional discrimination. Another provision counteracted the *Patterson* decision by extending the 1875 Civil Rights Act's ban on racial discrimination in contracts to cover protection from harassment on the job. Finally, the act allowed victims of discrimination to sue for larger monetary damages in cases brought under the 1964 Civil Rights Act and the 1990 Americans with Disabilities Act.

Though rather technical and legalistic in character, the 1991 Civil Rights Act did make it easier for those who considered themselves victims of various types of discrimination to bring their cases to court.

William C. Lowe

See also: Civil rights; Civil Rights Act of 1957; Civil Rights Act of 1960; Civil Rights Act of 1964; Civil Rights Act of 1968; Civil Rights Acts of 1866-1875; *Richmond v. J. A. Croson Company; Wards Cove Packing Company v. Atonio.*

Civil Rights Acts of 1866-1875

After the Thirteenth Amendment abolished slavery throughout the United States in 1865, almost all freed blacks were without property or education, and most white southerners bitterly opposed any fundamental improvement in their political and social status. In 1865-1866, southern legislatures enacted the highly discriminatory black codes, and proponents of racial equality responded by calling for new federal laws.

Congress, using its new authority under the Thirteenth Amendment, overrode President Andrew Johnson's veto to pass the first Civil Rights Act on April 9, 1866. This law conferred citizenship on African Americans, a measure necessitated by the Supreme Court's Dred Scott decision (*Scott v. Sandford*, 1857). The law included a list of enumerated rights, including the right to make and enforce contracts, to sue and give evidence in court, and to purchase and inherit all forms of property. It also punished public officials if they used their legal powers to deny equality to blacks. Since the law's constitutionality was questionable, many of its major provisions were incorporated into the Fourteenth Amendment.

On July 16, 1866, Congress again overrode President Johnson's veto, this time to enlarge the scope of the Freedmen's Bureau. Among other items, this law authorized the bureau to use military commissions to try persons accused of violating the civil rights of freedmen.

Again voting to override a presidential veto on March 2, 1867, Congress passed the First Reconstruction Act. Dividing the South into five military districts, the act required southern states to call new constitutional conventions elected by universal manhood suffrage and to ratify the Fourteenth Amendment. Under the act, 703,000 blacks and 627,000 whites were registered as voters, with black majorities in five states.

As the Ku Klux Klan conducted a wave of terrorism against African Americans and Republicans in the South, Congress responded with the Ku Klux Klan Acts of 1870 and 1871, which provided police protection to enforce the rights guaranteed in the Fourteenth and

Fifteenth Amendments. In several decisions, such as *United States v. Cruikshank* (1876), the Supreme Court ruled that key parts of the statutes exceeded the constitutional powers of Congress.

Finally, on March 1, 1875, President Ulysses S. Grant signed into law the Civil Rights Act of 1875. This far-reaching act, largely the work of Senator Charles Sumner, outlawed discrimination based on race in public accommodations (inns, businesses, theaters, and the like) and made it illegal to exclude blacks from jury trials. In the *Civil Rights* cases (1883), however, the Supreme Court struck down most of the 1875 law, holding that the Fourteenth Amendment did not authorize Congress to prohibit discrimination by private individuals. This decision ended almost all federal attempts to protect African Americans from private discrimination until the passage of the Civil Rights Act of 1964.

Although the Civil Rights Acts of the Reconstruction era failed to guarantee any long-lasting equality for blacks, they did provide points of reference for the Civil Rights movement of the 1950's and 1960's. The Civil Rights Act of 1866 was resurrected in *Jones v. Alfred H. Mayer Company* (1968), when the Supreme Court upheld its use to outlaw private racial discrimination in economic transactions as a "badge of slavery."

Thomas T. Lewis

See also: Black codes; Civil rights; Civil Rights Act of 1964; Civil Rights Act of 1968; *Civil Rights* cases; Fourteenth Amendment; Freedmen's Bureau; *Jones v. Alfred H. Mayer Company*; Ku Klux Klan; Reconstruction; *Scott v. Sandford*; Thirteenth Amendment; *United States v. Cruikshank*.

Civil Rights cases

In the aftermath of the Civil War, the U.S. Constitution was amended three times in five years. The three amendments, taken as a whole, were designed not only to end slavery but also to eliminate its "badges and incidents." Each of the amendments contained a clause empowering Congress to pass implementing legislation. In 1875, Congress passed a Civil Rights Act that made it illegal for anyone to deny access to places of public accommodation—including inns, public transportation, and theaters—on account of race, color, or previous condition of servitude. Five cases claiming violations of the public accommodations provisions were consolidated for decision by the Supreme Court.

The Court ruled that Congress did not have the authority to prohibit discrimination by private individuals. Justice Joseph P. Bradley's majority opinion analyzed the congressional authority granted by two of the Civil War Amendments. The Fourteenth Amendment, he said, gave Congress authority to provide relief from state action which interfered with a person's rights to due process of law and to equal protection of the laws. The amendment did not allow Congress to legislate against an invasion of rights by private individuals. Such power belonged to the state alone. Since the Civil Rights Act purported to provide a remedy for private discrimination, it exercised a congressional power not granted by the Constitution.

In regard to the Thirteenth Amendment, the Supreme Court conceded that Congress had been empowered to abolish "all badges and incidents of slavery"; however, the "badges and incidents" included only legal disabilities, such as the inability to make contracts, hold property, and have standing in court. They did not include the "social rights of men and races in the community." The Court concluded that it was time for the former slave to "take the rank of a mere citizen, and cease to be the special favorite of the laws."

In his dissent, Justice John Marshall Harlan argued that since state governments established and maintained the roads, highways, and harbors used by public conveyances, and since the states licensed theaters, inns, and other places of public accommodation, state tolerance of discrimination amounted to state action that furthered discrimination in violation of the Fourteenth Amendment.

The significance of the *Civil Rights* cases is twofold. First, the Court ruled that Congress could not outlaw discrimination by private parties under the authority of the Civil War Amendments. Therefore, the victims of racial discrimination could expect relief only from state governments, which, in the South, had by 1883 reverted to the control of white supremacists. Second, the *Civil Rights* cases prevented Congress from legislating against private discrimination in public accommodations for nearly one hundred years. In 1964, Congress passed a Civil Rights Act that drew its authority not from the Civil War Amendments but from the "commerce clause" in the U.S. Constitution.

William H. Coogan

See also: Civil rights; Civil Rights Acts of 1866-1875; Fourteenth Amendment; Thirteenth Amendment.

Civil Rights movement

Significance: The quest for political equality in the second half of the twentieth century transformed the face of American politics; the pursuit of economic equality has met with greater opposition and has had less success.

Although the modern Civil Rights movement began with the Montgomery bus boycott in 1955, the struggle for civil rights has been an ongoing battle. The founding of the National Association for the Advancement of Colored People (NAACP) in 1909 was one of the first attempts to organize in the pursuit of civil rights. With the exception of some legal victories under the leadership of the NAACP, there was little progress in the field of civil rights until the end of World War II.

Voting Rights

With the end of Reconstruction after the Civil War, all the southern states developed devices to eliminate black voters. Each of the southern states adopted new state constitutions between 1890 and 1910 and employed devices such as the grandfather clause, the white primary, the poll tax, and the literacy test to strip blacks of their right to vote. These devices were enormously successful. There were more than 130,000 black voters in Louisiana in 1896. By 1900, only two years after Louisiana adopted a new constitution containing many discriminating features, there were only 5,320 black voters left on the rolls.

For several reasons, African Americans made securing the right to vote their number-one objective. First, the U.S. Constitution, particularly the Fifteenth Amendment, contains specific guarantees against voter discrimination. Second, blacks believed there was less social stigma involved in granting the right to vote than in integration. Integration meant race mixing, which was feared by white southerners. Giving blacks the right to vote did not mean that whites would have to intermingle with blacks. Finally, African Americans believed that securing the right to vote would bring about other changes. Black voting would result in the election of black politicians, and it would force white politicians to moderate their racial views.

The grandfather clause was the first major barrier to fall. Grandfather clauses said that if a person had a relative who voted before the Civil War (before 1861), then the person was exempt from other voter qualifications. Because blacks were not allowed to vote before the Civil War, they had to meet voter qualifications such as poll taxes and literacy tests. The U.S. Supreme Court unanimously struck down grandfather clauses in *Guinn v. United States* (1915).

The next major barrier to fall was the white primary election. As the term implies, only whites were permitted to vote in primaries. Since southern politics was dominated by the Democratic Party, whoever won the Democratic primary would win the general election. If blacks could not participate in the primary selection process, then they had no real input into the selection of political candidates.

In 1924, the Texas legislature passed a law prohibiting blacks from participating in that state's primary election. A unanimous U.S. Supreme Court struck down the Texas law in *Nixon v. Herndon* (1927). Immediately, the Texas legislature passed another law delegating authority to the executive committee of each party to determine who could participate in the primaries. As expected, they excluded blacks from participation. In a 5 to 4 decision, the U.S. Supreme Court once again threw out Texas' white primary in *Nixon v. Condon* (1932). Undaunted, Texas made a third effort to ban blacks from the primaries. In 1932, the state convention of the Texas Democratic Party, without any authorization from the state legislature, limited primaries to white voters. A unanimous U.S. Supreme Court, in *Grovey v. Townsend* (1935), upheld the action of the state convention, concluding that there was no state discrimination involved. Political parties were voluntary associations that had the right to determine their membership. It was not until *Smith v. Allwright* (1944), some twenty years after the first Texas white primary law was passed, that the U.S. Supreme Court finally declared white primaries to be unconstitutional. The NAACP had brought most of the white primary cases, including the *Smith* case, to the U.S. Supreme Court.

The third major voting barrier to fall was the poll tax, which was the payment of a fee in order to vote. Blacks were less able to afford the tax, and poor whites could always find someone to pay or waive their tax. Opponents of the poll tax tried to get Congress to abolish the fee. Five times the House of Representatives passed legislation to ban poll taxes, but each time the legislation was filibustered by southern senators. In 1964, the Twenty-fourth Amendment, which eliminated poll taxes in federal elections, was approved. Two years later, in *Harper v. Virginia Board of Elections*, the U.S. Supreme Court abolished poll taxes in state and local elections.

The last barrier to fall was also the most significant barrier in keeping blacks from voting: the literacy test. Most literacy tests required the voter to be able to read, write, and understand sections of the state or federal constitution. Although many blacks could pass the reading and writing portion of the test, almost all failed the understanding portion, primarily because white voter registrars had the sole authority to determine if a person understood a section of the constitution.

Attempts to get the courts to ban literacy tests were unsuccessful. The U.S. Congress passed the Voting Rights Act of 1965, which prohibited literacy tests in areas that were covered by the law. In 1970, an amendment to the Voting Rights Act banned literacy tests in all fifty states, and another amendment in 1975 permanently banned literacy tests.

School Desegregation

Before the Civil War, most states prohibited blacks from getting an education. After the Civil War, schools were established for black education, but on a segregated basis. In many areas, education for blacks ended at the sixth grade. High schools, vocational schools, and colleges and universities were often unavailable for black students.

In 1890, the Louisiana legislature passed a Jim Crow law requiring "separate but equal" accommodations for white and black passengers on the railroads. The railroads backed a challenge to the law because of the additional expense they would encounter. Homer Plessy, one-eighth black, was selected to test the law; he sat in the whites-only coach and was arrested. In *Plessy v. Ferguson* (1896), in a 7 to 1 decision, the U.S. Supreme Court upheld the Louisiana law. The Court found no violation of the "equal protection clause" of the Fourteenth Amendment because whites were as separated from blacks as blacks were from whites. Although the *Plessy* decision had nothing to do with education, the doctrine of "separate but equal" was quickly adopted to justify segregated schools.

The NAACP led the legal attack against segregated schools. The first strategy of the organization was not to seek to overturn *Plessy* but, on the contrary, to seek enforcement of *Plessy*. African American schools were indeed "separate," but were they "equal"? Black schools received far fewer dollars per student to operate, and black teachers were paid a fraction of what white teachers received. Black schools had a limited curriculum, few textbooks, no transportation for students, and often the buildings were no more than one-room shacks. In a series of Supreme Court cases involving higher education in the South, the NAACP time and again demonstrated that black schools were not equal. In fact, in many of the cases, there were no law schools or professional schools available to blacks. The Supreme Court consistently ordered the enrollment of black students where "separate but equal" was not being met.

By the late 1940's, the NAACP was ready to mount a direct challenge to *Plessy v. Ferguson*. Cases were brought in South Carolina, Delaware, Virginia, Kansas, and the District of Columbia. In 1954 the U.S. Supreme Court overturned *Plessy* and the "separate but equal" doctrine in *Brown v. Board of Education*. Chief Justice Earl Warren, speaking for a unanimous Court, wrote: "We conclude that in the field of public education the doctrine of

One of the most dramatic protests of the Civil Rights movement was this August, 1964, march on Washington, D.C., to demand equal rights for African Americans.

'separate but equal' has no place. Separate educational facilities are inherently unequal."

Many southern states invoked the doctrine of states' rights and argued that the federal government was usurping the power of states to control education. Massive resistance to the court's decision became the standard policy throughout the South. Some school districts closed their schools rather than integrate, while other communities exploded in violence. When a large, unruly mob prevented the integration of Central High School in Little Rock, Arkansas, President Dwight D. Eisenhower was forced to send in federal troops to protect the nine black students.

Token integration was the policy during the 1960's, but in 1969 the U.S. Supreme Court finally declared that the time for delay was over. Fifteen years after *Brown*, the Court declared that school districts were ordered to comply "at once" with the *Brown* decision. School districts increasingly relied upon busing as the means to desegregate the schools, and opponents of busing in both the north and south argued that it was leading to the destruction of neighborhood schools.

Public Accommodations

On December 1, 1955, a racial incident in Montgomery, Alabama, transformed the face of the Civil Rights movement. On that day, Rosa Parks, a black seamstress, refused to give up her seat on a Montgomery bus to a white passenger. Parks was arrested, and her arrest ushered in the Civil Rights movement. Blacks, led by a new resident to the community, the Reverend Martin Luther King, Jr., organized one of the most effective mass movements and boycotts in the nation's history, a boycott of the city's bus system. Almost a year after the boycott began, Montgomery officials reluctantly desegregated the bus system after a decision from the Supreme Court.

King emerged from the bus boycott as a national political figure, and in 1957, he and his supporters established the Southern Christian Leadership Conference (SCLC). Combining his Christian beliefs with the precepts of nonviolent resistance, King led several mass protest movements against what he perceived to be the moral injustices of a segregated society. In 1963, King wrote his famous "Letter from Birmingham Jail," in which he outlined his views on just and unjust laws. That same year, King led more than 200,000 civil rights supporters on a March on Washington, D.C. In 1965, King led one of the last major protests of the Civil Rights movement when he and his supporters marched from Selma to Montgomery, Alabama, to pressure Congress to pass a voting rights bill.

Another significant phase of the Civil Rights movement was characterized by "sit-ins." Triggered by four black college students seeking service at the "white" lunch counter of the local Woolworth's in Greensboro, North Carolina, within days similar sit-ins took place in more than sixty communities. Two months after the sit-in started in Greensboro, the lunch counters were integrated.

Many of the student leaders in the sit-in movement came together in 1960 and established the Student Nonviolent Coordinating Committee (SNCC). SNCC played a major role in voter registration drives throughout the South. By the mid-1960's, tired of the violence against them and the slow pace of change, SNCC became one of the most militant of the civil rights organizations and a key exponent of "black power."

In 1960, the Congress of Racial Equality (CORE) initiated the "Freedom Rides." Thirteen riders—some white, some black—boarded buses in Washington, D.C., on a trip through the heart of the deep South. Attacked and viciously beaten by white mobs outside Anniston, Alabama, and in Birmingham, the Freedom Riders focused the attention of the nation on the failure of southern states to protect passengers in interstate travel.

Realizing the difficulties blacks experienced in seeking service in public accommodations such as hotels, restaurants, and theaters, Congress passed the landmark Civil Rights Act of 1964, which made it illegal to discriminate in public accommodations on grounds of "race, color, religion or national origin." Another section of the law banned discrimination in employment and established the Equal Employment Opportunity Commission (EEOC) to enforce the law. The section on employment discrimination established "affirmative action," an approach that has been blamed by some for eroding white support for the Civil Rights movement.

The Collapse of the Civil Rights Movement

After 1965, the Civil Rights movement fell into disarray and decline. There were numerous reasons for the decline of the movement. To begin with, the broad base of public support for civil rights began to erode. Many Americans believed that Congress had passed enough legislation to deal with the problem of discrimination (most notably the sweeping 1964 Civil Rights Act) and that now it was time to let those laws work. Another factor was the nationalization of the push for civil rights. Until the mid-1960's the civil rights issue was widely viewed as a southern problem. When the movement moved northward, some white northerners withdrew their support. With the institution of busing for school desegregation and the attempt to integrate housing, many white Americans felt threatened.

The controversy over affirmative action policies also divided support for the movement. To many Americans, affirmative action meant quotas and programs that unfairly threatened their own job security. Another factor was the diffusion of the movement as it was broadened to include discrimination based on age, gender, physical disability, and sexual orientation. Fewer Americans were willing to support what they viewed as special privileges for women, the disabled, and homosexuals than to support civil rights, particularly voting rights, for African Americans.

The urban riots of the 1960's shattered white support for civil rights. White voters and politicians—President Lyndon B. Johnson among them—felt betrayed by the riots. They thought that the nation was trying to deal with the problems of racism and discrimination. Congress had passed three civil rights laws and one voting rights law within an eight-year period. When the Watts riot in Los Angeles broke out within a week after passage of the Voting Rights Act of 1965, the "white backlash" against civil rights essentially brought the movement to a halt. The riots represented the chasm that still existed between black and white, and they frightened many whites into thinking of "law and order" first and civil rights gains second. On the national scene, the escalating war in Vietnam drew attention away from the Civil Rights movement. When Martin Luther King, Jr., openly opposed the war, he was widely criticized by many civil rights leaders, as well as by President Johnson. In the late 1960's, the Vietnam War displaced the issue of civil rights.

Ideological disputes among black leaders of the movement also led to its collapse. Major disputes arose among civil rights organizations such as the NAACP, SCLC, CORE, and SNCC with respect to tactics and objectives. Younger blacks, particularly those in SNCC, were dismayed by the slow pace of change and, as a result, favored more militant tactics. The emergence of the Black Power movement in 1966, led by young leaders such as Stokely Carmichael of SNCC, was a direct assault on the approach of King and other moderates.

Accomplishments

The Civil Rights movement forever altered the political landscape of the United States. Perhaps the greatest accomplishment of the movement can be seen in the thousands of African Americans who hold elective office. The number of black members of Congress was at a record high in the mid-1990's. African Americans have been elected to virtually every political office in all areas of the country. The Civil Rights movement also ended the humiliating practice of segregation and abolished the laws which attempted to create two classes of citizens. Finally, the Civil Rights movement created a sense of pride and self-esteem among those who participated in the movement.   *Darryl Paulson*

Core Resources

Good overviews of the Civil Rights movement include Fred Powledge's *Free at Last? The Civil Rights Movement and the People Who Made It* (Boston: Little, Brown, 1991) and Robert Weisbrot's *Freedom Bound: A History of America's Civil Rights Movement* (New York: Plume, 1991). An excellent source on the major barriers to black voting and the struggle to overturn those barriers is Steven Lawson's *Black Ballots: Voting Rights in the South, 1944-1969* (New York: Columbia University Press, 1976). On school desegregation, the best single source is Richard Kluger's *Simple Justice: The History of Brown v. Board of Education and Black America's Struggle for Equality* (New York: Alfred A. Knopf, 1976). The legislative battle over the Civil Rights Act of 1964 is splendidly told by Charles and Barbara Whalen's *The Longest Debate* (Washington, D.C.: Seven Locks Press, 1985). The major civil rights organizations are described in Clayborne Carson's *In Struggle: SNCC and the Black Awakening of the 1960's* (Cambridge, Mass.: Harvard University Press, 1981) and Taylor Branch's *Parting the Waters: America in the King Years, 1954-63* (New York: Simon & Schuster, 1988).

See also: Affirmative action; Black Power movement; Busing and integration; Children in the Civil Rights movement; Civil Rights Act of 1964; Congress of Racial Equality; Discrimination: racial and ethnic; Freedom Riders; *Grovey v. Townsend*; *Guinn v. United States*; *Harper v. Virginia Board of Elections*; Jim Crow laws; King, Martin Luther, Jr., assassination; Little Rock school desegregation; Montgomery bus boycott; National Association for the Advancement of Colored People; *Nixon v. Herndon*; *Plessy v. Ferguson*; Poll tax; Race riots of the twentieth century; Segregation: de facto and de jure; Southern Christian Leadership Conference; Student Nonviolent Coordinating Committee; Voting Rights Act of 1965.

Civil Rights Restoration Act

> **Significance:** In 1987, Congress required recipients of federal financial assistance to uphold nondiscriminatory requirements of the 1964 and subsequent civil rights legislation in all respects, not merely in activity aided by federal funds.

Title VI of the Civil Rights Act of 1964 mandated that federal funds could not be used to support segregation or discrimination based on race, color, or national origin. The law did not affect a number of other civil rights problems, however. At Cornell University's School of Agriculture, for example, women could not gain admission unless their entrance exam scores were 30 percent to 40 percent higher than those of male applicants. Epileptics were often barred from employment, and persons in their fifties were often told that they were qualified for a job but too old. To rectify these problems, Congress extended the scope of unlawful discrimination in federally assisted schools in Title IX of the Education Amendments Act of 1972 to cover gender; the Rehabilitation Act of 1973 expanded the same coverage to the disabled; and the Age Discrimination Act of 1975 added age as a protected class.

Enforcement of the statute regarding education was initially assigned to the Office for Civil Rights (OCR) of the U.S. Department of Health, Education, and Welfare, which later became the U.S. Department of Education. OCR ruled that the statute outlawed not only discrimination in the particular program supported by federal funds but also discrimination in programs supported by nonfederal funds. All recipients of federal financial assistance were asked to sign an assurance of compliance with OCR as a condition of receiving a federal grant.

Grove City College

From 1974 to 1984, Grove City College in western Pennsylvania received $1.8 million in tuition grants and guaranteed student loans but refused to sign an assurance of compliance. The college argued that the funds were for students, not the college, but OCR insisted that the financial aid was administered as a part of the college's financial aid program and, therefore, the college must pledge as a whole not to discriminate on the basis of race, color, national origin, or gender. OCR instituted enforcement proceedings against Grove City College, and an administrative law judge ruled in 1978 that the college could no longer receive federal student loan moneys.

Grove City College and four students desiring financial aid then sued. In 1980, when the case was first tried, the federal district court ruled in favor of Grove City College on the grounds that no sex discrimination had actually occurred. On appeal, the court of appeals reversed the lower court's decision, and the matter was taken up by the Supreme Court of the United States, this time with Terrel H. Bell, head of the newly created federal Department of Education, as the defendant.

In *Grove City College v. Bell* (1984), Justice Byron R. White delivered the majority opinion of the Court, which held that OCR did not have sufficient congressional authority to withhold funds from Grove City College for failure to sign the assurance of compliance. Moreover, according to the Court, violations of Title VI could occur only in the specific program or activity supported directly with federal funds, a judgment that went beyond the question raised by the case. Justices William J. Brennan, Jr., and Thurgood Marshall dissented.

A New Bill

Shortly after the Supreme Court ruling, OCR dropped some seven hundred pending enforcement actions, resulting in an outcry from civil rights groups over the decision. Representative Augustus F. Hawkins authored the Civil Rights Restoration Act in the House, and Senator Edward "Ted" Kennedy sponsored the bill in the Senate. Their aim was to amend all the affected statutes—Title VI of the Civil Rights Act of 1964, Title IX of the Education Amendments Act of 1972, the Rehabilitation Act of 1973, and the Age Discrimination Act of 1975. According to the bill, any agency or private firm that wanted to receive federal financial assistance would have to comply with the nondiscrimination requirement as a whole, even if the aid went to only one subunit of that agency or firm.

Although Hawkins's version quickly passed in the House of Representatives, the measure was caught up in the politics of abortion, and the bill died in the Senate. Opponents advanced more than one thousand amendments over a period of four years, and representatives of the administration of President Ronald Reagan testified against passage of the law. A group known as the Moral Majority broadcast the fear that the bill would protect alcoholics, drug addicts, and homosexuals from discrimination, although there were no such provisions in the proposal.

More crucially, the Catholic Conference of Bishops, which was traditionally aligned with the Civil Rights movement, wanted two amendments to the bill. One proposed amendment, which was unsuccessful, would have exempted institutions affiliated with religious institutions from complying with the law if religious views would be compromised thereby. The other proposed amendment, which was opposed by the National Organization for Women, was an assurance that no federal funds would be spent on abortion. Congress delayed finding a compromise.

In 1987, leaving out references to abortion, Congress finally adopted the Civil Rights Restoration Act. By vetoing the measure, Reagan became the first president to veto a civil rights bill since Andrew Johnson. Supporters of the act sought to override the presidential veto. Opponents in the Senate tried to destroy the bill by various amendments in debate on the floor of the Senate on January 28, 1988. Senator John C. Danforth proposed an amendment that would disallow federal payments for abortion. This amendment passed. With the passage of the act by the Senate on March 22, 1988, Congress overrode Reagan's veto, and the law went into effect immediately.

Michael Haas

Core Resources

The law is explained and analyzed in Veronica M. Gillespie and Gregory L. McClinton's "The Civil Rights Restoration Act of 1987: A Defeat for Judicial Conservatism" in *National Black Law Journal* (12, Spring, 1990), Robert K. Robinson, Billie Morgan Allen, and Geralyn McClure Franklin's "The Civil Rights Restoration Act of 1987: Broadening the Scope of Civil Rights Legislation" in *Labor Law Journal* (40, January, 1989), and Robert Watson's "Effects of the Civil Rights Restoration Act of 1987 upon Private Organizations and Religious Institutions" in *Capital University Law Review* (18, Spring, 1989). Mark Willen's "Congress Overrides Reagan's Grove City Veto" in *Congressional Quarterly Weekly Review* (46, March 26, 1988) explains the parliamentary maneuvers required to get the law passed.

See also: Affirmative Action; Civil Rights Act of 1964.

Civil War

> **Significance:** The Civil War of 1861-1865 established the primacy of the federal government over the states in the administration of justice, and it elevated the ethical system of free-labor capitalism as the national standard. Its most profound effects on race relations in the United States resulted from its ending of slavery and emancipation of enslaved African Americans.

The Civil War redefined relationships both between the U.S. government and the individual and between the federal and state governments. During the course of the conflict, the Union and Confederate governments pursued aggressively nationalistic policies that undermined states' rights, civil liberties, and property rights.

The Slavery Issue

By the mid-nineteenth century, the free-labor ideal had taken hold in the states of the North. It was believed that economic opportunity should be open to all. To many in the North, the slave system in the South appeared to be the antithesis of the free-labor ideal. Northerners believed that slavery was inefficient, that it degraded labor as a whole, and that it created economic stagnation. Though most were willing to tolerate slavery where it existed, they wanted the western territories reserved for free white labor. They interpreted the Constitution as a document that made freedom national and slavery local.

Southerners shared a belief in the positive benefits of economic opportunity, but they identified it with the acquisition of land and slaves. Southerners dreamed of extending the slave system into the territories, arguing that the territories were the common property of all Americans; to prohibit slavery within them deprived Southern people of their right to share in the nation's bounty.

The Republican victory in 1860 brought to power an administration pledged to restrict slavery in the territories. Fearing that the new administration would undermine slavery, seven Southern states asserted their right to secede from the federal union and form a new government. Abraham Lincoln's administration denied the right of secession and refused to relinquish federal property in the South to the new Confederacy. When the state of South Carolina fired on a federal fort in Charleston harbor, President Lincoln called upon the states to supply troops to suppress the rebellion and preserve the federal union. Four additional states believed Lincoln's action to be an unjust usurpation of federal power and joined the Confederacy.

For the Lincoln administration, the highest good was the preservation of the Union. All issues of justice were considered in relation to that objective. The Confederacy was dedicated to the proposition that human property was an unalienable right and must be preserved. For the first year of fighting, the Lincoln administration took no action to destroy slavery. It enforced the provisions of the Fugitive Slave Law, and Lincoln rebuked Union general John C. Frémont when he issued a proclamation freeing the slaves of Confederate sympathizers in Missouri. Lincoln's Emancipation Proclamation did not take effect until January 1, 1863. When he issued the proclamation, Lincoln justified his action in terms of military necessity. The proclamation freed only the slaves behind Confederate lines, but after the Emancipation Proclamation was issued, the Union Army became a force for liberation.

Civil Liberties

Both the Union and Confederate governments restricted traditional civil liberties during the conflict. In early 1862, the Confederate Congress authorized President Jefferson Davis to suspend the writ of *habeas corpus* and to declare martial law in areas in danger of attack. That same year, President Davis ordered the first military draft in North America and established a Conscription Bureau to carry it out. Even more striking, the Confederacy never established a Supreme Court and allowed the attorney general to judge the constitutionality of laws. That omission seriously undermined the notion of judicial independence and gave the executive branch unprecedented powers over the administration of justice.

Thousands of civilians were arrested by the Union government during the war, and many were tried by military courts. In response to civil disturbances in Baltimore, Lincoln suspended the privilege of *habeas corpus* on April 27, 1861, along the rail line from Philadelphia to Washington. The suspension was later extended to other areas of the North and gradually became general in certain types of cases.

Most military arrests by the Union government were not political. The vast majority of civilian prisoners were blockade-runners, residents of Confederate states, army deserters, draft dodgers, foreign nationals, people who dealt in contraband goods, or fraudulent war contractors. A loyal opposition continued to function in the North throughout the war and actually won control of several state legislatures.

Among those arrests early in the war was John Merryman. Merryman was a member of a pro-Confederate Maryland cavalry unit that had damaged railroad bridges in April, 1861. Merryman's attorney successfully petitioned a federal circuit court for a writ of *habeas corpus* to show just cause for his arrest. The commander of Fort McHenry, where Merryman was being held, refused to honor the writ on the grounds that President Lincoln had suspended the privilege in Maryland. Judge Roger B. Taney responded by issuing a circuit court ruling stating that only the Congress had the power to exercise such a suspension (*Ex parte Merryman*, 1861). In spite of the ruling, Lincoln continued to maintain his right to suspend the writ as an essential power necessary to suppress the rebellion.

For purposes of election propaganda, unscrupulous Republican politicians and military officers attempted to exploit fears that traitorous secret organizations existed in the Midwest. Recent scholarship has demonstrated that the major "Copperhead" societies, such as the Knights of the Golden Circle and the Sons of Liberty, were little more than paper tigers. In the wake of Democratic victories in the state elections of 1862, Republican newspaper editors frequently printed tales of treasonable Democratic activities.

When Ohio Democrat Clement L. Vallandigham declared that the war was being fought to free blacks and enslave whites, General Ambrose Burnside ordered his arrest. A military commission convicted Vallandigham of attempting to hamper the government's efforts to suppress the rebellion and recommended imprisonment. President Lincoln altered the sentence to banishment, and Vallandigham was escorted to Confederate lines. Lincoln justified his action by arguing that it made no sense to shoot a simple-minded deserter and do nothing to the man who induced him to desert.

Later in the war, Democratic activist H. H. Dodd of Indiana organized the Sons of Liberty to protect the civil liberties of those opposed to the Republican administration. Acting on rumors that the Sons of Liberty had aided Confederates, Union general Henry Carrington arrested Indiana Democrats linked to the Sons of Liberty, including editor Lambdin Milligan. A military commission sentenced three of the defendants to death. Others received prison terms. The death sentences were never carried out, but it is clear that the men were tried on questionable evidence by military commissions in areas where civil courts were functioning. After the war, the Supreme Court ruled in *Ex parte Milligan* (1866) that such trials were illegal.

This Civil War drawing portrays an African American regiment being attacked by Confederate forces and bloodhounds in South Carolina.

Treatment of Black Troops

When the conflict began, neither the Union nor Confederate governments would sanction the use of African American soldiers. As the Union government moved toward an acceptance of emancipation, however, it also began to organize African American regiments.

In spite of the large-scale recruitment of black soldiers during the last two years of the war, the Union army discriminated against African Americans in a wide variety of ways including pay, chance of promotion, and the amount of fatigue duty black units were expected to perform. Although a few blacks did receive commissions, the vast majority of officers in the United States Colored Troops (USCT) were white combat veterans. The men of the USCT proved their courage at the battles of Port Hudson, Milliken's Bend, and Fort Wagner, where they took heavy casualties. Generally, however, the prejudice of many commanding officers led to the use of USCT regiments for fatigue or guard duty while saving white units for combat.

The Confederacy reacted harshly to the use of black troops by the Union army. President Davis approved of the execution of black prisoners of war in South Carolina in November, 1862. Later, Davis ordered that all former slaves captured while serving in the Union army be returned to the states for trial. The massacre of black prisoners by Confederate troops on several occasions forced Union authorities to threaten retaliation in order to stem the injustice.

The use of large numbers of black troops by the Union war effort helped pave the way for universal emancipation. Throughout his political career, Lincoln consistently asserted that slavery was morally wrong. Though emancipation began as a military tactic, it became a war aim. The courage of black soldiers allowed Lincoln to secure passage of the Thirteenth Amendment, providing for an end to slavery throughout the country.

Military Justice

The system of military justice employed within the army was seriously flawed. At least 267 soldiers were executed by the Union army during the Civil War era. More than half of those executed were either foreigners or African Americans. A number of black soldiers were convicted of mutiny for protesting unequal pay in the Union army. Racial tensions accelerated during the final months of the conflict. A high number of black soldiers were executed for alleged sexual offenses against white women. The Confederacy had an incomplete record of military justice. Since many Southern officers had received their training in the prewar U.S. army, the procedural flaws of courts-martial were similar in both armies.

The Civil War moved the United States toward a more perfect application of its ideals of equality and justice. The United States entered the war as a federal union with contrasting standards of justice, one based on free-labor ideals, the other on the slave system of the Southern states. Property rights took precedent over human rights, and equal justice was denied African Americans in virtually every section of the country. The Union government, through its policy of emancipation and the enlistment of African Americans into its armed forces, transformed the war from a crusade to preserve the Union into a war of liberation. In doing so, it expanded the nation's concept of justice to include equality for African Americans.   *Thomas D. Matijasic*

Core Resources

The most comprehensive source for military records on the Civil War is the U.S. War Department's *The War of the Rebellion: A Compilation of the Official Records of the Union and Confederate Armies* (130 vols., Washington, D.C.: U.S. Government Printing Office, 1880-1901). An excellent overview of all aspects of the war condensed into readable form is James M. McPherson's *Battle Cry of Freedom: The Civil War Era* (New York: Oxford University Press, 1988). Robert I. Alotta's *Civil War Justice: Union Army Executions Under Lincoln* (Shippensburg, Pa.: White Mane, 1989) argues that the military justice system was hopelessly flawed. Joseph T. Glatthaar's *Forged in Battle: The Civil War Alliance of Black Soldiers and White Officers* (New York: The Free Press, 1990) chronicles discrimination within the Union army. Frank L. Klement's *Dark Lanterns: Secret Political Societies, Conspiracies, and Treason Trials in the Civil War* (Baton Rouge: Louisiana State University Press, 1984) explodes the myth of vast treasonable societies operating in the North during the war. Mark E. Neely, Jr.'s *The Fate of Liberty: Abraham Lincoln and Civil Liberties* (New York: Oxford University Press, 1991) defends Lincoln's record on civil liberties and disputes the notion that arbitrary arrests were common. James G. Randall's *Constitutional Problems Under Lincoln* (rev. ed. Urbana: University of Illinois Press, 1951) blames Lincoln's subordinates for violations of civil liberties. Emory M. Thomas's *The Confederate Nation: 1861-1865* (New York: Harper & Row, 1979) is a brief, readable overview of the functioning of the Confederate government.

See also: African Americans in the Civil War; Civil liberties; Emancipation Proclamation; Slavery: history.

Class theories of racial/ethnic relations

> **Significance:** Class theories of racial and ethnic relations argue that prejudice and racism are inextricably linked with economic exploitation in a capitalist society.

Oliver C. Cox, an African American sociologist, described one of the earliest class-based theories of intergroup relations in *Caste, Class, and Race: A Study in Social Dynamics* (1948). Cox argued that African American workers in the United States were in the same position as exploited workers in any capitalist system. They were underpaid, abused, and exploited by employers who made huge profits. In Cox's view, exploitation of African Americans in the Old South had begun during slavery, but it persisted even after the death of slavery in 1865. Racial prejudice and discrimination were very advantageous in terms of money and wealth to the ruling white community. White workers, although they also received low wages, were not in the same position as African American workers because they had the advantage of being members of what they believed was the superior race. Cox's central point was that capitalist exploitation led to the subordination of Africans and that racism was used to justify the inferior status of black workers.

Exploitation as a Method of Control

Relations between whites and blacks have been based on a totally unequal exchange virtually from the time of the first contacts between Europeans and Africans. The nature of the relationship changed over time, from master and slave to capitalist and wage earner, but the motive remained the same, to make as much money as possible for the dominant white class. Economic exploitation, accomplished first through the use of force and enslavement, created a new underclass. As slaves, the Africans were controlled completely and for their entire lives by their masters. They were without power to control their own development, education, or working conditions. Those who exploited the Africans came to believe that only a backward and inferior people would allow themselves to become slaves, and they rationalized their acts by saying that the Africans were meant to become slaves. Although the slaves gained their freedom in the 1800's, the economic exploitation of African Americans did not end.

The earliest advocate of the class theory of race relations was W. E. B. Du Bois, the great African American educator, historian, and sociologist. Beginning with a series of essays published in 1903 as *The Souls of Black Folk*, Du Bois presented his view that economic exploitation was at the root of white American prejudice. According to Du Bois, whites had held on to their view of African inferiority for so long because they benefitted financially from it. White American workers and business executives prospered because blacks were forced into low-wage, low-prestige jobs. African Americans worked for less than half the wages of white workers because low-paying jobs were all that was available to them. Du Bois argued that the stability of the economic system was based on keeping African Americans badly paid, badly educated, and living in a state of almost constant fear through actual and threatened beatings and lynchings. The exploitative nature of American race relations was also shown by the many laws passed in states throughout the country, but especially in the South, that separated people by skin color in every area of life, from education to housing to employment opportunities.

Class and the Colonial Model of Race Relations
Advocates of the class model, such as sociologist Robert Blauner, distinguish between "external" and "internal" colonialism. As occupants of an internal colony, African Americans find themselves in the same position as people in a country subjected to a long period of imperial domination by an outside group (traditional, or external, colonialism). In both cases, the ruling class dominates, exploits, and degrades the people it has conquered economically, socially, and politically. It destroys the culture of its victims, leaving nothing except despair and degradation. All power transfers to a small economic elite of wealthy landowners and businesspeople from the dominant class. In the internal model, exploited people, excluded from full participation in the new economy, form a "colony" within the dominant society.

Members of the excluded population have little wealth, health, or happiness; however, their exclusion enables them to create a separate history and culture, sometimes based on memories of what it was like before "colonization." According to proponents of the colonial model of race relations, this culture of opposition, sometimes called the culture "behind the veil," was developed in slave quarters in the American South and still exists in American inner cities. Members of the oppressed class hate and despise the ruling class so much that they want to avoid contact with it at all costs.

The dominant and subordinate classes conflict with each other on many issues, not only economic questions such as wages and jobs. Generations of exploitation and second-class treatment create vastly differing views of everything from education to religion and crime control to politics. Conflicting worldviews are a basic characteristic of exploitative systems of racial and eth-

nic relations including colonialism. Capitalism divides society into social classes, and if that society is not homogeneous, it also divides the working class along racial and ethnic lines that prevent workers from seeing themselves as a unified class of exploited people. A working class divided by racial and ethnic hostilities cannot come together to push for economic justice for its members. In this way, the major beneficiary of a racially divided lower economic class is the dominant wealthy class. Marxist theories of race relations make exactly this point.

A newer Marxist perspective described in historian Eugene Genovese's *Roll, Jordan, Roll: The World the Slaves Made* (1974) incorporates earlier Marxist theories but adds another factor. Genovese notes that a racial consciousness develops among the exploited class and enables it to challenge the supremacist views of the ruling class. This spirit of nationalism helps the underclass develop a sense of purpose and dignity that enables the group to challenge the economic and political power of the dominating elite.

Impact on Public Policy
Under the class theory of race relations, exploitation can have two different results. Because conflict between the oppressor and oppressed involves more than just economic issues, it can lead to violence and revolution or to an extreme degree of separation between the classes, a separation so great that one group can barely understand the thinking, customs, and morality of the other. Anthropologist Oscar Lewis found evidence of this separation among minority groups in the United States in the 1960's. Lewis called the separate culture developed by the underclass the "culture of poverty." Many minority groups had experienced poverty and prejudice for so long that they had come to think differently than the white majority about the meaning of their lives and their futures. Work, love, survival, crime, happiness, and contentment meant different things to the poor from what they meant to middle-class Americans. Lewis argued that because of years of discrimination and abuse, African Americans, Latinos, and Native Americans had become so different from whites that only an act of violent revolt could restore them to lives of dignity and value.

Sociologist William J. Wilson shares some of the views held by advocates of class theories of racial/ethnic relations, although he disagrees with the more revolutionary implications of the "culture of poverty" concept. In *The Declining Significance of Race* (1978) and several other works, Wilson argues that something similar to a culture of poverty does exist. He also notes that white workers and business leaders benefited economically from racial exploitation, for a long time using U.S.

inner cities as a source of cheap labor. Problems began, however, when low-skilled jobs began to disappear from urban communities in the 1960's and 1970's as corporations began to move their manufacturing facilities to the suburbs where land was plentiful and inexpensive or to Asia and Latin America where labor was cheaper. Unemployment increased because many of the poor had no way to get to jobs in the suburbs. The loss of industry led to lower city tax bases and a subsequent decline in the city's schools. Those African American families who had become middle class, often through education, abandoned the old neighborhoods and headed for the suburbs. The most exploited class, the poorly educated, underskilled, low-wage earning, sometimes welfarereceiving inner-city poor, were left behind. The culture of what Wilson termed the "truly disadvantaged" stressed violence, escape, pessimism, and a lack of value for life.

Wilson's solutions—to improve schools and encourage corporations to return to inner cities—seemed rather meager, but they had a major impact on social policies adopted in the 1980's and the 1990's. The concept of "enterprise zones," aimed at encouraging businesses to relocate in inner cities, and the campaign to improve the quality of education found in inner-city schools are both in line with Wilson's ideas. However, these reforms do not address the question of economic exploitation nor do they consider the problem of how racial prejudice has been used to justify economic inequality. Those problems, which theories of the class origins of racial and ethnic relations seek to address, remain unresolved.

Leslie V. Tischauser

Core Resources

Robert Blauner's *Racial Oppression in America* (New York: Harper & Row, 1972) provides an overview and detailed analysis of the social class model. Oliver Cox's *Race Relations: Elements and Social Dynamics* (Detroit, Mich.: Wayne State University Press, 1976) presents the basics of class theories of racial/ethnic relations, as does Cox's older survey, *Caste, Class, and Race: A Study in Social Dynamics* (Garden City, N.Y.: Doubleday, 1948). William J. Wilson's views are found in *The Declining Significance of Race: Blacks and Changing American Institutions* (Chicago: University of Chicago Press, 1978). For an interesting critique of the view offered by Wilson, see sociologist Charles Vert Willie's *Oreo: On Race and Marginal Men and Women* (Wakefield, Mass.: Parameter Press, 1985).

See also: Black flight; Caste model; Colonial model of racism; External colonialism; Internal colonialism; Marxist models; Racial/ethnic relations: race-class debate; Wilson-Willie debate.

"Classless" society

Debates over the possibility of a classless society are central to the social scientific analysis of the nature of social inequality generally, and therefore specifically with racial and ethnic relations. These scholarly debates have occurred within specific social contexts—that is, they reflect larger political struggles between those who defend the alleged harmony and stability of the status quo and those who advocate social change toward the goal of equality. If, as many argue, a classless society is impossible (as all societies have had some level of inequality), then egalitarianism is utopian and misguided and acceptance of existing inequities is more "realistic." Critics of existing social orders, on the other hand, have generally argued that equality is both desirable and attainable, and the experience of innumerable preliterate societies is offered as anthropological evidence for the possibility of a classless society. In the social sciences, most theoretical traditions hold that social inequality (usually thought of in terms of "socioeconomic status" rather than class) exists in all societies and will presumably continue to exist in the future.

Social scientists known as structural functionalists define inequality in terms of "status" and—given the universality of status distinctions based on age and gender—argue that social stratification (the division of members of a society into hierarchical levels) is universal and necessary. Inequality in society serves to ensure that the most critical functions in society are performed by the most talented individuals. Society cannot do without inequality.

Sociobiologists, on the other hand, see social inequality as rooted in biology. Economic, racial, and gender inequalities are the function of variation in the genetic endowment of individuals. Those able to secure wealth, prestige, and power owe their success to the biological inheritance of intelligence, ambition, attractiveness, size, and other attributes. Because genetic variation within populations is universal, so too is social inequality.

Elitists, in contrast, argue that all societies require bureaucracies to conduct the affairs of state; those who occupy the command positions in these organizations—the elite—have the means to preserve their position and privilege. Throughout history, when elites have been overthrown, they were simply replaced with a new elite. The necessity of elites, according to this argument, precludes the emergence of classless society.

Marxists retain a concern with "class." Class is understood, in an economic sense, as a relationship to the means of production. Therefore, "class societies" are those in which a tiny minority own the major means of production and the vast majority are dispossessed and pressed into the service of the propertied class. Societies of this kind appear in the historical record only within the last ten thousand years. Although status inequalities are more universal, this was not a basis for the denial of access to productive property in classless societies. Marxists argue that most of human history is the history of classless societies. The emergence of classless societies in the future is made possible by the efforts of capitalists to homogenize the vast majority of the world's population. The success of the Soviet Union, Cuba, and other socialist states in reducing inequities (both economic and ethnic) is offered as evidence of the potential for classlessness.   *Martin Orr*

See also: Class theories of racial/ethnic relations; Marxist models; Social stratification theories; Sociobiology and race.

Clinton massacre

In 1875, widespread resentment of Congressional Reconstruction (the effort to rebuild and rehabilitate the South after the Civil War) mounted among whites in Mississippi. White Democrats began coordinating efforts to carry the fall statewide elections. The dominant issue for Democrats in the 1875 electoral campaign was the threat or fear of race war. Several race riots had already occurred throughout Mississippi during the summer. Democratic political solidarity was still in question, however, until the Clinton massacre of September 4. Clinton, a town in Hinds County, was the site of a political rally to which both Democratic and Republican speakers were invited. The rally was disrupted by gunfire, and both blacks and whites were killed and wounded. Confusion followed. News of the Clinton massacre, as it is now known, quickly spread throughout the state. Bands of armed whites converged on Clinton, and a reign of terror followed. Officials estimated that twenty to fifty blacks were killed by the angry white mobs. Many blacks fled to other towns, and some sought refuge in the woods. The Republican governor of Mississippi, unable to convince the president to send troops, watched helplessly as an undeclared race war waged throughout the state. Freedmen were denied access to the polls or were forced to vote for Democratic candidates. The Clinton massacre had served as the spark that inspired white Mississippi "redeemers," as they were called, to do whatever necessary to take control away from the Republicans and force black submission.   *Donald C. Simmons, Jr.*

See also: Disfranchisement laws in Mississippi; Race riots of 1866; Race riots of 1943; Race riots of the twentieth century; Reconstruction.

Clinton's Initiative on Race

On June 14, 1997, President Bill Clinton unveiled the Initiative on Race in his "One America" speech, delivered at the University of California at San Diego's commencement ceremony. The Initiative on Race promoted a national dialogue on race relations in the United States. This dialogue was to take place largely through open meetings around the country and was designed to produce a plan to calm racial tensions and promote economic opportunities for all Americans.

By executive order, Clinton created an Advisory Board of seven individuals representing diverse perspectives on the race issue: historian John Hope Franklin (chair); Linda Chavez-Thompson, executive vice president of the AFL-CIO; the Reverend Susan Johnson Cook; former New Jersey governor Thomas Kean; Los Angeles attorney Angela Oh; Robert Thomas, chief executive officer of Nissan, USA; and former Mississippi governor William Winter. The board was charged with promoting a constructive national dialogue to confront and work through concerns on race, increasing understanding of both the history and course of the country with respect to race relations, encouraging community leaders across the nation to develop initiatives to soothe racial tensions, and producing solutions to racial problems. The Department of Justice was to provide financial and administrative support, and the board was to disband on September 30, 1998, unless extended by presidential authorization.

In his speech, President Clinton called race relations the nation's "greatest challenge" and "greatest opportunity." He spoke of the United States' complicated history of race relations, which has been marked by both progress and division. The challenge, he said, was to "break down the barriers in our lives, our minds and our hearts." For this to happen, the country had to engage in "a candid conversation on the state of race relations today." Clinton promised to help lead the American people "in a great and unprecedented conversation about race." In addition to the dialogue on race, Clinton's speech focused on expanding opportunities to all people—which included using affirmative action "in the right way" and ensuring educational opportunities—and demanding that each individual as well as the justice system take responsibility for respecting the rights of all citizens and enforcing each person's civil rights. Clinton also called on the advisory board to examine problem areas of "substantial impact," including education, economic opportunity, housing, health care, and administration of justice.

The Initiative on Race was not meant to seek a quick or easy fix. The multicultural democracy envisioned by President Clinton would require commitments from government, businesses, communities, and individuals. In his speech, Clinton suggested that the ultimate solution must come from the human spirit.

Robert P. Watson and Claudia A. Pavone Watson

See also: Racial/ethnic relations: improving; Racism: changing nature of.

Code switching

Code switching is a meaningful form of language, interaction, and identity among individuals who are more proficient in separate languages than they are in a common, or shared, language. It is often an in-group device typically restricted to those who share the same expectations and rules of interpretation. For example, when Latinos do not know certain Spanish words, they communicate by substituting, or switching to, either English words or a combination of English and Spanish words, producing a mixture of the two languages that is known as Spanglish. Similarly, pidgin English is a dialect of mixed words and slang that serves the needs of millions of people who would be unable to communicate without it.

Occasionally, a pidgin language form becomes firmly established; when it is acquired by children and becomes the primary language of a linguistic community, it is referred to as a creole language, taking on all the characteristics of a normal language. Certain forms of pidgin English, loaded with negative connotations, are used among some impoverished and socially disadvantaged groups, particularly among ethnic minorities, gang members, and in the ghettos of New York and Los Angeles. To distinguish themselves from "outsiders," participants often use code switching to establish their identity with a particular social or ethnic group.

Alvin K. Benson

See also: Culture and language; Rap music.

Colegrove v. Green

Three voters who resided in Illinois districts with much larger populations than other congressional districts in the state filed an action to challenge the unequal sizes of Illinois legislative districts. In Illinois and other states, state legislatures had marked out legislative districts of unequal size or else had failed to draw new district boundaries when population patterns changed. One congressional district in Illinois, for example, contained 914,000 people while another district contained only 112,000. The effect of such maldistribution was to dilute

the voting strength of voters in larger districts and enhance the power of voters in smaller districts. In Congress, two representatives from districts containing fewer than 150,000 people could outvote a representative from a district containing more than 900,000. Thus government was more responsive to and controlled by people from smaller districts rather than representative of the wishes of the majority of voters, whose votes would be diluted in larger districts. Rural interests in many states controlled political power and the development of public policy, despite the fact that a majority of citizens lived in urban and suburban areas.

In an opinion by Justice Felix Frankfurter, the Supreme Court on June 10, 1946, declined to decide whether unequal legislative districts violated the equal protection rights of voters in larger districts. On behalf of a five-member majority, Frankfurter declared that issues concerning legislative districting were "beyond [the] competence" of courts because such issues were "of a peculiarly political nature and therefore not meant for judicial determination." By labeling legislative districting a "political question" unsuited for judicial resolution, the majority of justices avoided any examination of questions about discrimination and voting rights that were raised by the existence of unequal districts.

Three dissenting justices, Hugo L. Black, William O. Douglas, and Frank Murphy, complained that the Court was improperly permitting state legislatures to violate the rights of voters in larger districts. One justice, Robert H. Jackson, did not take part in the case.

The Court's decision left districting temporarily in the hands of state legislatures. Justices Black and Douglas were still on the Court two decades later, however, when a new set of justices revisited the issue and decided that districts must be designed with comparable populations in order to avoid violating citizens' equal protection rights. In *Baker v. Carr* (1962), the Supreme Court decided that such legislative districting questions were not reserved for the legislative branch alone but could also be examined by the judiciary. In the subsequent cases of *Wesberry v. Sanders* (1964) and *Reynolds v. Sims*, the *Colegrove* precedent was completely eliminated when the Court mandated that federal and state legislative districts be of equivalent sizes. *Christopher E. Smith*

See also: Reapportionment cases; Redistricting; Representation: gerrymandering, malapportionment, and reapportionment; *Reynolds v. Sims*.

Coleman Report

The *Equality of Educational Opportunity* study, known as the Coleman Report, was released in 1966. This study, conducted by James S. Coleman, focused on the effect that school desegregation had on the academic attainment of black and white students. After controlling for students' family background characteristics, the report concluded that the strongest influence on the individual achievement of both black and white students was the educational proficiency of their peers. In upper grades, this influence was found to be two to three times greater for black students than for white students.

Increased diversity in the racial composition of schools was also found to have a positive effect on the achievement of African American students, decreasing the achievement gap between African American students and white students by nearly half, despite findings of lower self-esteem among African American students in racially diverse classrooms than among racially isolated African American students. For white students, increased racial diversity in the classroom, especially during the first three grades, was found to decrease their preference for white peers. Data provided by the Coleman Report were analyzed in 1967 by the U.S. Commission on Civil Rights and again in the 1969 McPartland study to provide a more comprehensive analysis of the effects of desegregation.   *Terri L. Canaday*

See also: Desegregation: public schools; Education and African Americans; Education and racial/ethnic relations; Integration.

Colfax massacre

The terrorist group known as the White League formed across Louisiana during the Reconstruction (1863-1877) to keep African Americans out of the political arena. The league's activities led to the Colfax massacre, the bloodiest single instance of racial violence in the Reconstruction period in all the United States. Disputes over the 1872 election results had produced dual governments at all levels of politics in Louisiana. Fearful that local Democrats would seize power, former slaves under the command of African American Civil War veterans and militia officers took over Colfax, the seat of Grant Parish, Louisiana.

On Easter Sunday, April 13, 1873, a series of brutal acts were carried out by the White League in Colfax, resulting in the deaths of more than sixty African Americans. After the African American men had laid down their weapons and surrendered, many were flogged, mutilated, and murdered, and African American women were also raped and murdered. A pile of more than twenty bodies was found half-buried in the woods. Monroe Lewis, an elderly black gentleman, was dragged from his bed, forced to say his prayers, and then shot. After

being forced to cook food for a party of more than ninety white men, Charles Green was executed. Petitions to President Ulysses S. Grant requesting that justice be rendered were ignored.   *Alvin K. Benson*

See also: Charleston race riots; Civil War; Reconstruction.

College admissions

In North America, a degree from a college or university has long been viewed as an important means of attaining a measure of financial and social success. For a combination of reasons, however, certain ethnic and racial groups matriculate at considerably lower rates than whites and Asian Americans. Certain minority groups are even more underrepresented among graduating students. This phenomenon is commonly viewed as one reason that certain minority groups experience higher levels of poverty and lower social standing.

In the 1960's and 1970's, many colleges and universities implemented affirmative action components in their admissions processes. Such programs frequently included provisions that allowed applicants from targeted minority groups to be admitted with lower test scores than those in nontargeted groups. Some programs set quotas for certain categories of students, essentially dividing the available slots into blocks defined by race, gender, or ethnicity. Such outright quota setting was ruled unconstitutional by the U.S. Supreme Court in its 1978 *Regents of the University of California v. Bakke* decision.

For the next two decades, race and ethnicity continued to influence college admissions decisions, albeit not as the sole criterion. The practice became increasingly controversial, however. Many whites, like Allan Bakke, believed that affirmative action discriminated against them. Affirmative action was attacked on other grounds as well. Some minority students resented the fact that, irrespective of their actual abilities, it was assumed that they were accepted to college under a lower standard. Other minority leaders chafed at the very notion that certain groups of people, by simple virtue of their skin color, required special accommodations to enter college. Also some qualified nontargeted minority applicants, such as some Asian Americans, were denied admission to make way for targeted minority applicants.

Another controversial effect of affirmative action in college admissions was the presence of large numbers of minority students who, being admitted under lower standards, were underprepared for the rigors of college. As a result, many minority groups have experienced disproportionately high failure and dropout rates. Some

Asian and African American students study together on a grassy lawn. Affirmative action has played a controversial part in increasing the numbers of minority students admitted to institutes of higher learning.

See also: Ability testing; Affirmative action; *Bakke* case; College entrance examinations; Intelligence and race; Intelligence testing.

College entrance examinations

Significance: College entrance examinations are one of several measures used by U.S. colleges and universities to select candidates for admission. Criticism of these tests revolves around possible bias in the tests and how they are used.

American colleges and universities consider a variety of factors when selecting students for admission. These factors may include, but are not necessarily limited to, high school grades, class rank, difficulty of courses taken, personal interviews, letters of reference, and samples of students' written works. In addition, most colleges and universities require students to submit test scores from one or more of several nationally administered standardized tests. Known collectively as college entrance examinations, the most commonly used tests in the United States are the American College Test (ACT) and the Scholastic Aptitude Test (SAT). Some students also may take Achievement Tests (ATs) and the Preliminary Scholastic Aptitude Test/National Merit Scholarship Qualifying Test (PSAT/NMSQT).

The Tests

According to the American College Testing Assessment Program (ACTAP), which created and administers the ACT, the test does not ask students to recall specific information learned in high school but rather asks students to demonstrate their reasoning ability in four fields: English, mathematics, reading, and scientific reasoning. Students receive scores on a scale of 1 (low) to 36 (high) for each of the four skill areas, and a composite score. In addition, students receive scores on a scale of 1 (low) to 18 (high) for each of the seven subsections of the test. Student scores are also presented as percentiles.

The SAT, created and developed by Educational Testing Service (ETS), is administered in cooperation with the College Entrance Examination Board. Like the ACT, the SAT is designed to measure skills necessary

see such failures as evidence of curricula and standards biased against minorities. Others have charged that underprepared students do not belong in college and that efforts to retain these at-risk students have essentially lowered standards in curricula and graduation requirements.

As the academic and social consequences of affirmative action in college admissions became more openly debated in the 1990's, efforts to end the practice became more vigorous. Affirmative action suffered a number of blows in the late 1990's, including a 1995 decision by the Regents of the University of California to end affirmative action in admissions and hiring. The following year, the state's voters passed Proposition 209, the California Civil Rights Initiative, which placed the Regents' ban on affirmative action in state law and extended it to all public hiring and admissions. Similar actions were taken in other states, notably Texas. The immediate effects were mixed, with some of the more prestigious universities experiencing sharp drops in minority admissions. Conservatives have viewed these results as proof that racial preferences had been allowing unqualified applicants to be admitted simply on the basis of skin color or ethnicity. Liberals decry the resultant lack of racial and ethnic diversity on some campuses. By the end of the 1990's, efforts were under way at some campuses to reintroduce diversity by using a different criterion, such as socioeconomic status, in processing admissions. *Steve D. Boilard* for college-level work. The SAT tests two basic skill areas, verbal ability and mathematical reasoning, using a multiple-choice format.

The version of the SAT in use until the mid-1990's had two verbal sections containing questions involving antonyms, analogies, sentence completion, and reading comprehension. It also had two mathematical reasoning sections containing questions involving problem solving and quantitative comparisons. Each of these skill areas (verbal ability and mathematical reasoning) was scored on a scale of 200 (low) to 800 (high). Composite and percentile scores were provided. This version of the SAT also contained a fifty-question test of standard written English and a series of experimental questions. The experimental questions are not included in the student's score but are used in the development of future test questions.

ATs, administered by the College Board, were examinations based on specific knowledge of subjects including American history, European history, French, German, Hebrew, Latin, Spanish, mathematics, biology, chemistry, physics, English composition, and English literature. Some colleges required students to take these tests in addition to the SAT.

In the 1990's, Educational Testing Service developed new tests, the SAT I and SAT II, to replace the SAT. Like the SAT, the SAT I tests two basic skill areas: verbal and mathematical reasoning and is scored similarly. The SAT I verbal reasoning section focuses on analogies, sentence completion, and critical reasoning and contains a new critical reading section that tests vocabulary in context, analysis and synthesis, interpretation, and evaluation. The mathematical reasoning section allows the use of calculators, and a proportion of examination questions require students to enter the answer they calculate.

The SAT II was designed to replace the ATs and the test of standard written English. Content areas are expanded, and the test of standard written English is combined with the English composition test (an AT). The new writing test of the SAT II contains a series of multiple-choice questions testing grammar and usage and an essay section.

The Preliminary Scholastic Aptitude Test/National Merit Scholarship Qualifying Test, administered primarily during the junior year in high school, contains two sections testing verbal skills and mathematical reasoning in a multiple-choice format. Test scores are used to award National Merit Scholarships, National Achievement Scholarships, and Achievement Scholarships.

Criticisms of the Tests

Despite their importance and wide use, college entrance examinations are not without their flaws or their critics. The two main organizations that create college entrance examinations, Educational Testing Service and the American College Testing Assessment Program, work to maintain and improve the validity and reliability of the tests and to avoid bias. Nevertheless, the tests have been subjected to some serious criticisms, and it is because of the tests' importance that such criticism must be considered. Criticisms focus on the existence of bias and flawed questions, testing procedures, and accusations of lack of due process, violation of privacy, and misuse of test results. Critics have argued that standardized college entrance examinations are biased against women, the poor, minorities, students from rural areas, and students whose first or primary language is not English.

Other things being equal, high test scorers should perform better in college than low test scorers. National SAT test score averages have consistently showed that men perform better on the test than women. The gender gap in test scores varies by year but is generally 50 to 60 points. Gender differences on the SAT are greater on the mathematical reasoning section than on the verbal

College Freshmen, Fall, 1997, by Race and Ethnicity
(percent)

	Total	Men	Women
American Indian	3.1	3.0	3.2
Black	10.6	9.9	11.1
White	80.7	80.7	80.7
Mexican American	1.5	1.4	1.6
Puerto Rican	1.1	1.2	1.0
Other Latino	1.6	1.7	1.6
Chinese American	1.4	1.6	1.2
Filipino American	0.8	0.8	0.8
Japanese American	0.4	0.4	0.4
Korean American	0.7	0.7	0.7
Southeast Asian American	0.6	0.7	0.6
Other Asian American	1.4	1.5	1.3
Other	2.9	2.9	2.8

Note: Figures may not add up to 100 percent because of rounding.

Source: The Chronicle of Higher Education Almanac Issue, Vol. XLV, No. 1, August 28, 1998.

ability section. A similar pattern exists regarding PSAT/NMSQT scores. Men also score higher on the mathematics, reading, and scientific reasoning sections of the ACT. If standardized college entrance examinations accurately predict future academic success, men should have higher average grades in college than women. Yet, at least during the first year of college, women have higher average grades than men.

Educational Testing Service states that women's scores are lower because greater numbers of women have been taking the test since 1970 than took it in previous decades. Consequently, the test pool for women is increasingly less selective and includes a greater number of low scorers, reducing the overall average. Ruth Ekstrom, Marilane Lockheed, and Thomas Donlon, however, have found that the structure of test questions influences gender performance. Women are less likely to answer a test item correctly if the question contains only, or refers primarily to, male characters. A survey of the reading comprehension passages contained in SAT examinations showed that 93 percent of the characters to which the passages refer are male. In addition, evidence indicates that college entrance examinations place more emphasis on subject areas such as science and mathematics in which men have traditionally outperformed women. Accordingly, test content selection may account for some of the gender differences in test scores.

Students from wealthier families score higher on college entrance examinations. In the case of the SAT, students whose family income is more than $70,000 a year have test-score averages of 996. Students whose family income is under $10,000 a year have test-score averages of 780. ACT test scores and family income show a similar correlation. These patterns may stem from differences in educational opportunities rather than differences in aptitude. Additionally, less affluent students may be unable to afford test preparation courses.

Minority students score lower on college entrance examinations than whites. Differences vary by group and over time. For example, 1989 SAT scores show that average combined test scores for African Americans were 200 points lower than those of whites. Of all minority groups, Asian Americans performed the best. The 1989 SAT average combined score for Asian Americans was 934, compared to 937 for whites. ACT average composite scores follow similar patterns.

There is also evidence that college entrance examinations may contain bias against students from rural areas and students whose first or primary language is not English. James Loewen found that incoming University of Vermont students from rural areas have SAT scores that average 100 points lower than those of students from urban areas; however, the actual academic performance

of the two groups is similar. Alicia Schmitt found that Hispanic students who take the SAT are much more likely to answer incorrectly questions that contain cognates and/or homographs. Consequently, differences in test scores between Latinos and whites may be partially the result of language differences, not differences in aptitude for college work.

In addition to bias, critics have charged that college entrance examinations contain flawed questions (questions that have more than one meaning or more than one answer), which may unfairly penalize test takers. Critics have also charged ETS with using unethical testing procedures, lack of due process protection, and invasion of privacy. John Weiss, Barbara Beckwith, and Bob Schaeffer claim the experimental questions on the SAT are fundamentally unfair because they violate the principle of informed consent and are flawed. In addition, no due process protection exists for students who are accused of cheating on the examination. Students may appeal to ETS, but ETS has sole discretion in determining guilt or innocence in cases of suspected cheating.

Finally, college entrance examinations have been criticized for being misused by scholarship agencies and colleges and universities. Many scholarships are awarded primarily on the basis of PSAT/NMSQT, SAT, or ACT scores, though college entrance examinations are not specifically designed for this purpose. The National Merit Scholarships, awarded by the National Merit Scholarship Corporation, are given on the basis of PSAT/NMSQT scores. Roughly 62 percent of National Merit Scholarship are awarded to men. Critics claim that gender, economic, racial, geographic, and language biases in the PSAT/NMSQT place women, the poor, minorities, rural Americans, and individuals whose first or primary language is not English at a competitive disadvantage for these awards.

Standardized testing has become an established feature of American life. More than 100 million standardized tests are administered each year. Despite their flaws, college entrance examinations provide a systematic and relatively objective means to select candidates for admission. For schools that receive large numbers of applications for admission each year, test scores provide a relatively inexpensive and time-effective way to screen candidates. Realizing the flaws in standardized testing and the danger of overreliance on test scores, some institutions have developed alternatives to the traditional selection process. *Charles V. Smedley*

Core Resources

The Uses and Misuses of Tests (San Francisco: Jossey-Bass, 1984), edited by Charles W. Daves, provides a good discussion of critical issues regarding the use of standardized tests. Books that criticize standardized tests include James Crouse and Dale Trusheim's *The Case Against the SAT* (Chicago: University of Chicago Press, 1988), Banesh Hoffmann's *The Tyranny of Testing* (New York: Crowell-Collier, 1962), John G. Weiss, Barbara Beckwith, and Bob Schaeffer's *Standing Up to the SAT* (New York: Arco, 1989), and Phyllis Rosser's *Sex Bias in College Admissions Tests: Why Women Lose Out* (3d ed., Cambridge, Mass.: The Center, 1989).

See also: Ability testing; College admissions; Intelligence testing; Race and intelligence; Standardized testing and IQ testing controversies.

Colliflower v. Garland

In 1964, Madeline Colliflower was arrested and held in jail over a minor dispute with the Fort Belknap (Montana) tribal council and tribal court about renewal of a land lease. She was an enrolled member of the tribe. She objected to being jailed and sued the tribe in federal court on a writ of *habeas corpus,* claiming she was illegally imprisoned, was denied the right to counsel, was denied a trial, and was never confronted with witnesses against her. She charged that her constitutional rights had been violated.

The federal district court denied Colliflower's petition, stating that tribal governments were not bound to protect constitutional rights of enrolled members living on the reservation. The U.S. Court of Appeals overturned that decision and ruled in Colliflower's favor. It ruled that federal courts do have the right to determine the validity and legality of tribal court orders of detention. This decision was a blow to tribal sovereignty and brought forth issues of civil rights in Indian country. Among others, this case influenced the U.S. Congress to pass the American Indian Civil Rights Act (1968), which extends certain protections to individuals living under tribal government. *Carole A. Barrett*

See also: American Indian Civil Rights Act; American Indians in the justice system; Tribal councils; Tribal courts; Tribal sovereignty.

Colonial model of racism

As various European powers colonized the globe beginning in the fifteenth century, their agents encountered many peoples with ways of life markedly different from their own. The images of other peoples available in the accounts of merchants and travelers acquired a concrete reality as Europeans, aided by advances in navigation and military technology, went out to explore and then conquer the world.

It is more appropriate to speak of multiple colonial models of racism than of a single model because each of the colonizing powers brought different assumptions and practices to the enterprise. Britain adopted the policy of informal empire, whereby indigenous chiefs or rulers continued in power under the tutelage of British colonial administrators. Although *indigenes* might occupy positions within the British administration or army after suitable education or training, a rigid distinction between the British and natives existed. In India, for instance, the *sepoys,* or native soldiers, were segregated both administratively and personally from the British regulars, whose relations with the Indians were typically characterized by aloofness founded upon a sense of racial and cultural superiority.

Like the British, the French asserted their superiority over native peoples. They saw themselves as civilizers who had come to raise up Africans and Asians to their own level of culture. The French, however, conceived their superiority primarily in cultural rather than racial terms. The *evolué,* the native who had assimilated to French standards of culture that entitled him or her to formal equality with citizens of metropolitan France, had no counterpart in the regimes of other colonial powers.

Other imperial nations, such as Belgium and Portugal, implemented a harsh, exploitative regime that likened other races to beasts of burden for use in railroad construction, mining, and other economic activities. For the Belgians and the Portuguese, skin color supplied an index of social worth. Brazil, a former Portuguese colony, illustrates the legacy of the colonial model of racism through its social hierarchy: The correlation between lightness and darkness of skin and social position is nowhere else so pronounced. Racial conflict is also more severe in Brazil than in the contemporary United States.

The common element in these various approaches to colonial peoples was a conception of them as the "other," fundamentally different from Europeans. In fact, it was the African and Asian "other" who helped to define the European "self." Europeans gained a clearer sense of their own identity by juxtaposition of the "white" with the "black" and the "yellow" races. Though the process of decolonization has freed African and Asian peoples from domination by colonial powers, the impact of forced diffusion and assimilation of Western ways of life remains. When the president of an African nation wears a Western-style business suit instead of a traditional *dashiki,* his choice is evidence of historical patterns of interaction whereby colonists defined traditional attire as immodest and "savage." The colonial model of racism was the crucial factor in the movement from contact to conquest. *Aristide Sechandice*

See also: Caste model; Class theories of ethnic/racial relations; External colonialism; Internal colonialism; Racial/ethnic relations: race-class debate.

"Color-blind" society

The idea of a "color-blind" society is one response to the question of how a society with peoples of diverse races can live together in justice and racial harmony. More specifically, a color-blind society can be defined as a society where racial differences among people would be largely irrelevant with respect to both the laws that govern people in that society and the judgments that members of one race make about those of another.

The idea that society should be color-blind received widespread attention during the Civil Rights movement of the 1960's as an antidote to the legacy of slavery in the American South. Although slavery was officially made illegal with the ratification of the Thirteenth Amendment to the U.S. Constitution in 1865 and all American citizens were given equal protection under the law by the ratification of the Fourteenth Amendment in 1868, new laws legitimizing segregation, typically known as Jim Crow laws, quickly arose in states where slavery had been practiced. These laws established separate schools, voting places, and other facilities for whites and blacks, so they had the effect of sustaining a racially divided society. In 1896, the Supreme Court further legitimated racial segregation when it decided in *Plessy v. Ferguson* that such laws did not intrinsically discriminate against blacks. In dissenting from this decision, Justice John Marshall Harlan wrote: "Our Constitution is color-blind, and neither knows nor tolerates classes among citizens."

When the Supreme Court reversed *Plessy v. Ferguson* with its decision in *Brown v. Board of Education* (1954), the question of how to create a racially integrated society based on the color-blindness of the Constitution became a pressing issue. In the 1960's civil rights leaders such as Martin Luther King, Jr., called for the color-blindness of the Constitution to be accompanied by color-blindness on the part of American citizens. In his most famous public address, the "I Have a Dream" speech delivered to a crowd of thousands before the Washington Monument on August 28, 1963, during the March on Washington, King expressed the hope that one day his children would be able to live in a society where others would judge them not "by the color of their skin but by the content of their character." Behind King's belief in the desirability of a color-blind society was the idea that people should not be oblivious to the race of others, but that race, much like eye or hair color, should be largely irrelevant in their interactions with other human beings. Public policies resulting from the Civil Rights movement

such as the 1964 Civil Rights Act, which made it illegal for employers to discriminate against job applicants on the basis of their race and other characteristics, and the Voting Rights Act of 1965, which outlawed literacy tests as a condition for voter registration, were influenced by the ideal of a color-blind society. Their intent was to create a racially integrated society in the United States in which all people, regardless of race, would be treated equally under the law.

By the early 1970's, it was obvious that legislation had not brought about a color-blind society. Evidence of lingering discrimination could be found in the rate of employment and the level of the average annual yearly income for African Americans, which continued to lag behind those of white Americans. Yet, in a 1994 Louis Harris poll, a majority of whites responded that minorities—blacks, Latinos, and Asian Americans—by and large had equal opportunity with whites, that the nation was basically color-blind. These same minority groups, when polled by Harris, did not feel their opportunities were equal to whites.

In addition, an increase in racial and ethnic pride made many people doubt the wisdom of color-blind measures, which seemed to require a homogeneous society, with basically white values. Minority leaders began to argue that color-blindness was a white goal, symptomatic of white people's inclination to measure or value all cultures according to their own and to ignore or fail to acknowledge differences. They instead sought a pluralistic society, where racial and ethnic minorities would be free to live under their own value systems and respected by members of other groups.

Diane P. Michelfelder

See also: *Brown v. Board of Education*; Civil Rights Act of 1964; Civil Rights movement; *Plessy v. Ferguson*; Race-neutrality; Voting Rights Act of 1965.

Color coding

Color coding is social stratification based on skin color. Under this system, skin color and other physical characteristics as well as behaviors associated with particular racial groups are used to place people in specific social classes.

Most color coding is based on stereotypes of racial phenotypes. As Michael Omi and Howard Winant suggest in *Racial Formation in the United States* (1986), the concept of "race" in contemporary American life—whether a person is black, white, or Asian—is based largely on phenotypical, and therefore readily observable, characteristics such as skin color, hair color and texture, and body shape and size. Secondarily, color coding draws on stereotypical behaviors and characteristics associated with a particular race.

In the United States, color coding involves using a set of physical and social attributes associated with "whiteness" and white people to which all other nonwhite groups are compared. Light-skinned people are generally given higher social status, largely because of the privileges attendant on Caucasian heritage—to being and to appearing white. Both literary and social science sources indicate that social and economic access and mobility are strongly influenced by whether or not a nonwhite person is able to "pass" for white. The ease with which a person passes for white depends not only on the individual's physical appearance—the lightness of the skin—but also on whether that person possesses certain mannerisms and character traits associated with being white. These include the person's manner of speech, circle of friends and associates, educational status, occupation, and culture. Social status and privilege are accorded to those who are able to "pass" for white or to associate themselves with whiteness through social networks, occupations, or educational achievements that are typical of white people. *Valli Kanuha*

See also: African American stereotypes; Black "brute" and "buck" stereotype; Discrimination: racial and ethnic; Passing; Prejudice and stereotyping; Prejudice: racial; Race as a concept; Racial formation theory; Racial hierarchy; Social stratification theories.

Colored Women's League

The Colored Women's League (CWL), also known as National League of Colored Women and Washington Colored Woman's League, emerged in Washington, D.C., when black women active in education, benevolent, and literary societies joined together in June, 1892, in an effort to improve conditions for African Americans. Helen A. Cook, wife of the Honorable John T. Cook, served as president, and the recording secretary was Charlotte Forten Grimké, a teacher from Port Royal, South Carolina. Other founders included Coralie Franklin Cook, wife of a Howard University administrator; teachers Anna J. Cooper, Mary Jane Patterson, Mary Church Terrell, and Anna E. Murray from M Street School; and Josephine B. Bruce, the first black teacher in the Cleveland schools, who later married Senator Blanche K. Bruce.

As Chicago prepared to host the World Columbian Exposition of 1893, the Board of Lady Managers rejected the petitions of these Washington women to participate in the planning process because they did not represent a national organization. In response, the Washington Colored Woman's League issued an invitation to black women throughout the country to affiliate as a national league. Women's clubs responded from the state of South Carolina and from the cities of Philadelphia, Kansas City, Denver, and Norfolk, Virginia. In January, 1894, they incorporated, becoming the Colored Women's League. In October, the CWL received an invitation for membership in the National Council of Women (NCW). Its members accepted and sought to expand representation for the NCW convention in the spring of 1895. Instead, the competition between women's clubs in New York and in Boston resulted in the creation of a second national organization, the National Federation of Afro-American Women. The two national organizations merged in July, 1896, to form the National Association of Colored Women (NACW) to promote for self-protection, self-advancement, and social interaction. In 1896, Terrell became the first president of the NACW. *Dorothy C. Salem*

See also: African American women; National Association of Colored Women; Women of color.

Columbus's voyages

> **Significance:** Columbus's arrival signified the beginning of major European colonization of the Western Hemisphere, which resulted in the decline of indigenous peoples.

Although not the first European to set foot in the New World, Christopher Columbus is credited with opening it to European settlement. His first voyage brought the area to the attention of Europe, and his second began the colonization by Spain.

Columbus was probably born in Genoa, Italy, in 1451. About 1476, he went to Portugal and settled in Lisbon, the center of Portuguese maritime activities. There Columbus received an education, sailed on several voyages, married a Portuguese lady of the lower nobility, and became a prosperous ship captain.

Columbus became convinced that the East Indies could be reached by sailing west. The idea was not new, but most experts agreed that the voyage was too long and difficult. When Columbus offered the plan to King John II of Portugal in 1484, the king rejected it in favor of the route around the tip of South Africa. In 1485, Columbus moved to Spain and was introduced to King Ferdinand and Queen Isabella. Isabella showed interest in Columbus's ideas but would not consider the project at the time because she was fighting an expensive war with the Moors. Columbus returned to Portugal to try a second time to persuade King John II. While Columbus was in Lisbon, Bartolomeu Dias returned from his trip around the Cape of Good Hope, the voyage that gave Portugal her route to the spice wealth of India. King John had no interest in another route. Columbus then returned to Spain and sent his brother Ferdinand to King Henry VII of England and King Charles VIII of France to seek support. Both kings rejected the project.

The First Trip

In January, 1492, Granada, the last Moorish stronghold, fell. Isabella signed an agreement with Columbus on April 17, 1492. Three ships were readied, the *Niña*, the *Pinta*, and the slightly larger *Santa Maria*. Ninety men and boys were enlisted. The expedition sailed on August 3, 1492, stopping in the Canary Islands, then proceeding west. On October 12, Columbus discovered an island that he named San Salvador. Because he believed he had reached the outer islands of the East Indies, Columbus gave the natives there the name Indians. He described them as without clothes, friendly and loyal, guileless and unwarlike, and ready for conversion to the true faith.

Martín Alonso Pinzón left in the *Pinta* on a private gold-hunting expedition. The remaining two ships sailed to the north coast of Haiti. Columbus named the island La Isla Española, later called Hispaniola. On Christmas morning, the *Santa Maria* was caught on a reef and wrecked. With help from the native Arawaks, led by their chief, Guacanagarí, the crew and most of the sup-

plies were saved. Guacanagarí was a paramount chief, who trusted Columbus and exchanged gifts with him, thinking they were trading as equals. Columbus, however, interpreted Guacanagarí's gifts as a gesture of submission to the Spaniards.

Because of the gold ornaments worn by the Arawaks, Columbus determined that the island was suitable for settlement and decided to return to Spain. Before sailing, Columbus had a fort built at a site he called La Navidad, and the forty-four men of the wrecked *Santa Maria* were left with orders to seek more gold. In mid-January, 1493, Pinzón rejoined Columbus, and the two ships sailed for Spain, reaching it on March 15, 1493. Columbus was greeted joyously by the people and with honors by Isabella and Ferdinand. No one questioned the tales he told.

The Second Voyage

To assure Spanish control of the new lands, Columbus was sent on a second voyage on September 25, 1493, with seventeen ships and twelve hundred to fifteen hundred men, including soldiers, artisans, nobles, and five priests. They took with them horses, cattle, sheep, seeds, fruits, tools, and shoots of sugar cane, which would later become the chief crop of the Caribbean Islands.

Columbus sailed on a more southerly route, sighted Dominica in the Lesser Antilles, and turned north to Hispaniola, where he learned that the men he had left had disappeared and Fort Navidad had been destroyed. Greed for gold and women had led the Spaniards to mistreat the Arawaks, who finally killed the Spaniards and destroyed the fort. Columbus founded a second settlement, La Isabela, farther east on the same coast.

To maintain support in Spain, Columbus had to deliver gold. He sent an expedition into the interior under the leadership of Alonzo de Ojeda, who forced the Arawaks to mine gold under penalty of death. The Arawaks turned against the Spaniards, running off or killing themselves. To satisfy the demand for wealth, Columbus sent five hundred Arawaks as slaves to Spain. More than half of them died on the voyage; Isabella, who opposed enslavement of the natives, freed the rest.

Columbus discovered Jamaica and Cuba, which he thought were the mainland. Upon returning to La Isabela, he found the colonists in rebellion. To defend himself, Columbus

This 1869 engraving depicts Columbus's landing in America in 1492. The explorer's arrival marked the start of a long, often conflict-filled relationship between Europeans and American Indians.

sailed to Spain in June, 1496, leaving his brother Bartolomé as governor.

The Third Trip

After some delay, Ferdinand and Isabella received Columbus but refused to provide any further support. Most Spaniards, disappointed with the financial returns from the Spanish colony, also denied him support, but after two years, Columbus was able to finance a third voyage (1498-1500). This time he sailed to Trinidad and continued along the Venezuelan coast. He became convinced that this area was Paradise and that the Oronoco River was one of the four rivers of Paradise.

Columbus decided to go to the new capital of Hispaniola, Santo Domingo, which Bartolomé had founded in 1496. When he arrived, he found the colony in civil war. Columbus appealed to the Crown for reinforcements. In 1500, Isabella sent Francisco Bobadilla to Santo Domingo as governor. After an investigation, Bobadilla arrested Columbus and shipped him to Spain in chains. Six weeks after he arrived in Spain, Columbus was received by the monarchs, who treated him affectionately and assured him of his rights, but sent a new governor, Nicolás de Ovando, to Hispaniola.

Isabella decided to give Columbus one last chance. She provided him four ships for his fourth and last voyage (1502-1504). Passing through the Lesser Antilles, he headed for Santo Domingo, but Governor Ovando refused him permission to land. Columbus sailed to Central America and for eight months explored the coast, convinced that it was the Malay Peninsula. Storm damage, diseases, and fights with hostile natives forced Columbus to sail back to Santo Domingo. His unseaworthy ships had to be beached in Jamaica, where he was stranded for one year and five days before rescuers arrived. Columbus returned to Spain in 1504 a broken man. He died on May 20, 1506, in Valladolid, believing he had actually found the route to the east by sailing west.

Robert D. Talbott

Core Resources

Fernando Colon's *The Life of Christopher Columbus by His Son Ferdinand* (New Brunswick, N.J.: Rutgers University Press, 1959), translated and annotated by Benjamin Keen, is an important source of information. Other books about Columbus's life include Felipe Fernandez-Armestro's *Columbus* (New York: Oxford University Press, 1991); Gianni Granzotto's *Christopher Columbus* (Garden City, N.Y.: Doubleday, 1985), translated by Stephen Cartarelli; and Samuel Eliot Morison's *Admiral of the Ocean Sea: A Life of Christopher Columbus* (Boston: Little, Brown, 1942).

See also: Slavery: history; West Indian uprisings.

Competition theory and human ecology

> **Significance:** The competition theory attempts to explain why and when racial and ethnic conflicts emerge. Competition and changes in status, rather than inequality or segregation, are said to be behind most racial and ethnic conflicts. Besides offering a model for intergroup relations, these insights have fruitfully been used to explain various specific trends in North American and world history.

The competition and ecology tradition owes its formation to the work of early American sociologist Robert Ezra Park. Park described race relations in ecological terms. Plants and animals may thrive in close symbiotic relationships, they may develop and evolve on their own in isolated niches, or they may violently conflict over scarce resources. For Park, modern race relations were largely the result of a process by which human races that had evolved in isolated areas of the world came together, meeting in the urban areas of the modern world economy.

In the ecological theory, different groups compete for relatively scarce resources. However, racial and ethnic conflict also requires a collective sense of racial or ethnic boundaries and definitions that serve to organize competition along racial or ethnic lines. For example, a major migration of a new group into the territory occupied by another can lead to the development of definite ethnic identities on both sides. If sudden competition for scarce resources results, an ethnic conflict is likely.

Migration and Human Ecology

For Park, the city was a human ecological environment where the market brought different racial or ethnic groups together—as racial groups—each determined to satisfy its own needs, sometimes at the expense of others. If the city was a primary location of human ecological struggles, migration and modernization were the engines that drove the process forward.

Park's particular focus was on African Americans, including the process of their migration from the rural South to the urban areas of the North. The brutal waves of southern lynching in the late nineteenth century and the explosive race riots of the North in the early twentieth century led to the observation that some of the bitterest conflicts occurred not when slavery was most entrenched but when it was coming apart, and not when inequality between blacks and whites was most pronounced but when barriers to opportunity for blacks appeared to be weakening.

Park reasoned that prejudice between racial groups is a given, a natural outcome of human psychology. What leads to pronounced racial and ethnic conflict, however, is *changes* in the relative status of groups. Societies that are relatively static may have severe inequality but still relatively peaceful relations between racial groups, Park argued. The breakdown of the established social order—for example, the end of American slavery and the erosion of the racial caste system—releases previously latent animosities.

Labor Market Competition

As Susan Olzak explained in *The Dynamics of Ethnic Competition and Conflict* (1992), the conventional wisdom is that poverty and inequality cause racial and ethnic conflict, while equality of opportunity and desegregation lead to reduced conflict. However, the historical evidence is not consistent with this assumption. The worst inequality has not always produced the most conflict, and the most marginalized group has often not suffered the most vicious attacks. Instead, Olzak argued that *reducing* inequality and segregation precipitate conflict and protest. That is because desegregation and the expansion of opportunity increase rather than decrease direct economic competition between racial and ethnic groups.

Reduced segregation or expanded opportunities for disadvantaged minorities throw different groups into competition for the same resources in the same way that the immigration of a competing labor force does. In the new urban ecology, for example, African Americans competed with other racial and ethnic groups for jobs and secure niches. A zero-sum game appeared—whether real or merely perceived—in which the improving fortunes of one racial or ethnic group were identified as the cause of declining fortunes for another.

Racial and Ethnic Identities

An interesting question is why modern conflicts are organized primarily around race and ethnicity instead of economic class or other political affiliations. Many theorists of modernization, from the Marxist to the neoclassical tradition, had assumed that ethnic or racial solidarity was a premodern phenomenon that would be replaced by the rise of class identities or other political interest groups. Class-based movements and political parties have emerged in the modern era, but they have not eclipsed ethnic solidarities, movements, and conflicts. As modern societies have seen increased competition for key resources, the resulting conflicts have often demarcated along ethnic or racial lines.

As sociologist Joane Nagel has explained, the devel-

opment of the modern state—and its attempt to mediate racial or ethnic conflicts—has established a political terrain that leads to mobilization along racial and ethnic lines. For example, U.S. civil rights laws encourage people to identify employment discrimination against them as race-based if they want recourse from the government. So, laws intended to help minorities serve to strengthen racial and ethnic mobilization through the recognition and formalization of these identities.

Researchers dealing with the competition or human ecology theory have brought methodological advances to the study of racial and ethnic relations. First, they describe racial and ethnic relations in relatively universal terms instead of narrowly concentrating on the unique qualities of American race relations. Second, because of their emphasis on change as the prerequisite for conflict, they insist that theories be tested using data over time. Examining society at a fixed point in time prevents consideration of the dynamics of change in determining the nature of racial and ethnic relations.

Philip N. Cohen

Core Resources

Robert Ezra Park's *Race and Culture* (Glencoe, Ill.: Free Press, 1950), collects his most influential work from 1913 to 1944, which laid the foundations for much of contemporary competition and ecological theory. *Competitive Ethnic Relations*, edited by Susan Olzak and Joane Nagel (Orlando, Fla.: Academic Press, 1986), provides an overview of this theory and offers specific investigations applied to various situations in the United States and around the world. Olzak's *The Dynamics of Ethnic Competition and Conflict* (Stanford, Calif.: Stanford University Press, 1992) is an in-depth study that uses ecological theories of competition to explain U.S. ethnic conflicts around the turn of the nineteenth century.

See also: Assimilation: cultural and structural; Lynchings; Race relations cycle; Race riots of the twentieth century; Race/ethnic relations: race-class debate.

Compromise of 1850

Significance: A last national attempt to resolve the question of slavery in the territories brought the nation closer to civil war.

The U.S. Constitution, while creating a mechanism for the addition of states and acknowledging the right of each state to permit and even encourage slavery within its boundaries, made no mention of slavery's status in future states. Congress, when it admitted a state, could impose any condition it wished. The national government had first addressed the issue of slavery in territories and new states when the Confederation Congress passed the Northwest Ordinance of 1787. This ordinance excluded slavery from the unsettled area north of the Ohio River to the Mississippi River's eastern bank, the edge of the United States' holdings.

The Missouri Question
The issue reemerged in 1817, when Missouri, where between two thousand and three thousand slaves lived, applied to join the United States as a slave state. The question came before the Congress in 1819, and sectional tensions erupted. The U.S. Senate had eleven states each from the free North and the slave-owning South, but the North's growing population gave it a decisive advantage in the House of Representatives, so proslave forces committed themselves, at the minimum, to maintaining a balance between the regions in the Senate.

A temporary solution emerged in 1820, when Senator Henry Clay of Kentucky brokered a solution to the crisis. The Missouri Compromise stipulated that Missouri would be admitted to the Union as a slave state, while Maine, which had petitioned for statehood in late 1819, was admitted as a free state. The compromise also prohibited slavery from the remainder of the Louisiana Purchase in the area north of 36°30′ north latitude, while permitting it south of that line. Between 1820 and 1848, this solution maintained national peace, and the Senate remained balanced.

The Southwest and California
The Mexican-American War disrupted the relative peace. The United States received millions of acres of land spanning the area from the Continental Divide west to the Pacific Ocean and south from the forty-ninth parallel to Mexico. Before the war ended, David Wilmot, a member of the House of Representatives from Pennsylvania, attached an amendment to an appropriations bill stipulating that any territory acquired from Mexico must exclude slavery in perpetuity. Although the bill failed to win passage, the Wilmot Proviso fueled the smoldering fires of sectionalism, as many assumed that any additional western lands would be governed by the Missouri Compromise.

In 1849, just a year after the discovery of gold in California, the young California Republic petitioned the Senate for admission to the Union. Besides disrupting the balance between slave and free states, California straddled the 1820 compromise's line and threw the prior agreements into chaos. In both houses of Congress, the question of slavery became paramount:

Southerners rejected any attempt to exclude the practice from the West by nearly unanimous margins, while Free-Soilers from the North rejected the possibility of losing equal economic competition by similar percentages. Left in the middle were some elements of the national Whig Party, which struggled to preserve the Union while remaining a national party. The idea of disunion grew. Senator John C. Calhoun of South Carolina, long a firebrand for states' rights, proposed the formation of a sectional party to guarantee the practice of slavery. William Seward, an abolitionist representative from New York, also rejected the possibility of a compromise, citing the immorality of slavery. President Zachary Taylor, a hero of the Mexican-American War and a southerner, supported California's admission as a free state while rejecting the extreme position of persons such as Calhoun.

Five Resolutions
The first concrete proposal for compromise came from Senator Clay on January 29, 1850. Clay proposed a series of five resolutions: that the California Republic join the United States as a free state; that the rest of the territory acquired in the Mexican Cession be organized without any decision on slavery; that Texas receive monetary compensation in exchange for giving up its claims to parts of contemporary New Mexico; that the slave trade within the District of Columbia be abolished (although the actual practice of slavery would not be affected); and that a more rigorous fugitive slave law be enacted.

On February 5 and 6, Clay presented his resolutions and spoke for the Union's preservation. One week later, Mississippi senator Jefferson Davis rejected Clay's proposals, using bitter language that also attacked northern intentions. On March 4, the ailing Calhoun, in a speech delivered by Virginia's James Mason, rejected compromise on the principle of slavery in the territories. On March 7, Daniel Webster acknowledged that both sides had just grievances and urged support for Clay's whole plan, calming some tensions with his eloquent plea that the Union be preserved. On March 11, Seward stated the abolitionist's opposition to the compromise because of the immorality of slavery.

In April, the Senate referred Clay's resolutions to a select committee. The committee reported back to the full Senate an omnibus bill that contained the substance of the five original resolutions and sparked another four months of debate. Two major stumbling blocks to the compromise disappeared in July, when President Taylor and Calhoun both died. Millard Fillmore, who supported the compromise's ideas, replaced Taylor, who had bitterly opposed the omnibus bill. While Clay was vacationing, Stephen A. Douglas broke the omnibus bill into five parts and steered them through the Senate, and the House of Representatives followed suit. By September 20, Congress had adopted the five bills that made up the Compromise of 1850.

In 1854, the attempts at balancing the competing interests of the Free-Soil North with the proslave South ended when Senator Douglas proposed that the Kansas and Nebraska areas be organized using the concept of popular sovereignty. Congress adopted the Kansas-Nebraska Act that year, triggering the formation of a national political party dedicated to the idea of an exclusively free-soil policy in the West. The new Republican Party immediately became a force on the national political landscape, and its candidate, John C. Frémont, came within four states of being elected president in 1856. Ultimately, the election of Abraham Lincoln in 1860, a man committed to both the preservation of the Union and the free-soil doctrine, drove the South to secession.

John G. Clark, updated by E. A. Reed

Core Resources
Works that examine the forces and events preceding the Civil War include Bruce Collins's *The Origins of America's Civil War* (New York: Holmes & Meier, 1981), editor Eric Foner's *Politics and Ideology in the Age of the Civil War* (New York: Oxford University Press, 1980), Hamilton Holman's *Prologue to Conflict: The Crisis and Compromise of 1850* (New York: W. W. Norton, 1966), David Potter's *The Impending Crisis, 1848-1861* (New York: Harper & Row, 1976), and editor Kenneth Stampp's *The Causes of the Civil War* (rev. ed., Englewood Cliffs, N.J.: Prentice-Hall, 1974).

See also: Bleeding Kansas; Fugitive slave laws; Kansas-Nebraska Act; Missouri Compromise; Northwest Ordinance; Proslavery argument.

Compromise of 1877

The Compromise of 1877 represents the attempt toward equality that failed during Reconstruction (1863-1877) when newly elected President Rutherford B. Hayes ended efforts to establish a biracial democracy in the South. During his presidential campaign, Hayes favored "home rule" for the South as he campaigned against New York governor Samuel J. Tilden, a Democratic reformer. Although Tilden won the popular vote, Hayes claimed victory in South Carolina, Florida, and Louisiana. Republican Reconstruction governments still controlled these states, and it was doubtful that a former Union general could carry them by any other means than fraud.

Many southern Democrats, particularly scalawags, accepted Hayes's election, particularly if he would leave the South alone after taking office. Ohio Republicans

and southern Democrats met in a Washington, D.C. hotel and reached an agreement that if Hayes could assume the presidency, he would remove federal troops from South Carolina and Louisiana so that Democrats could regain control. Hayes consented after being sworn in. Race relations worsened because the Democrats ignored their promises to treat southern blacks fairly and Hayes forgot his pledge to ensure the rights of freedmen. Reconstruction had allowed African Americans to reconstitute their families, participate in government, and enjoy equality in dealing with whites, but the 1877 Compromise engendered a hatred of reform throughout the South for nearly one hundred years. African Americans would suffer social restrictions until the 1960's.

Douglas W. Richmond

See also: Reconstruction.

Confiscation Acts of 1861 and 1862

In August, 1861, the United States Congress passed a law confiscating all property, including slaves, used in the Confederate war effort. The law required judicial proceedings before any property could be appropriated, and it left unclear whether any confiscated slaves would be freed. The following July, Congress passed the Second Confiscation Act. The 1862 law, which also required a judicial hearing, declared that rebels were traitors whose property could be seized for the lifetime of the owner. The only property that would not be returned to the rebels' heirs was slaves, who were regarded as captives of war and set free after a period of sixty days. President Abraham Lincoln doubted that Congress possessed the constitutional authority to free slaves in the states. When he signed the bill into law, he included a statement of objections to its provisions. Although the power to confiscate rebel property was rarely used during or after the war, the difference between the first and second acts revealed the growing determination in the Union to end slavery and set the stage for the Emancipation Proclamation, which Lincoln issued in January, 1863.

Thomas Clarkin

See also: Emancipation Proclamation; Slavery: history.

Conformity theories

Conformity is yielding to group pressure to act as others do, even when no direct request has been made. People conform because they want to be liked by others or because they are simply using other people's behavior as a guide to what is normal or acceptable. Conformity theories of prejudice assert that people notice that others have prejudices and they then adopt these attitudes.

Many prejudices appear to be handed down from an individual's parents. This transmission of prejudice across generations presumably depends to some extent on observational learning. For example, if a child hears her parents ridiculing Martians, she is likely to conform to the same attitude toward Martians. If she then goes to school and makes disparaging remarks about Martians that are reinforced and approved by peers, her prejudice will be strengthened. In this way, prejudice is passed from generation to generation and reinforced by culture.

In some quarters of society, people may be pressured to express agreement with racist or sexist remarks. Even if they tell themselves that they are merely going along with others to avoid arguments, overtly agreeing with prejudicial attitudes can lead to subtle shifts in their attitudes because people tend to adopt attitudes that are consistent with their behavior. In this way, prejudice is further maintained.

A classic study of conformity was conducted by social scientist Solomon Asch in 1956. He asked college students to participate in an experiment involving visual perception. The students (the real subjects) were placed in groups with other student "subjects," all of whom were actually Asch's confederates. Each of the groups was shown four straight lines, and the students were asked to tell which of the three lines on the right side matched the line on the left. The confederates answered first, one by one choosing the wrong answer in this intentionally easy task. The real subject, the last one in line to answer, became distressed and, in an amazing 74 percent of cases, conformed to the pressure of the group and gave the wrong answer at least part of the time. Asch showed that social norms can be important not only in matters of style but also in matters of hard physical reality, and he illustrated the difficulty that people have in overcoming prejudicial attitudes in a group.

Other work by Asch and others shows that conformity is highest when people believe that they are the sole deviant in the group. When someone else disagreed, subjects were more likely to stick with their own opinions. When a minority of individuals gave a consistent but wrong answer, they were treated respectfully. When people holding minority views are consistent in and certain of their position, they can induce members of a majority to rethink their views and see issues in a new way.   *Lillian M. Range*

See also: Anglo-conformity; Dominant group; Minority and majority groups; Prejudice and stereotyping; Somatic norm theory.

Congress of Racial Equality

> **Significance:** The Congress of Racial Equality helped to eliminate discrimination in interstate travel on buses and trains and to end discrimination in both the public and private sectors of society, especially in housing and employment.

The Congress of Racial Equality (CORE) was founded in Chicago in the spring of 1942 by fifty young people who were committed to nonviolent direct action in their opposition to segregation and racial discrimination. Although James Farmer, the first national director of CORE, is often given credit for the founding of CORE, George Houser, Bernice Fisher, Homer Jack, Joe Guinn, and James Robinson also played substantial roles.

Initially, CORE was a volunteer organization. Along with the Fellowship of Reconciliation, CORE began the Freedom Rides in 1947. These early rides were called "journeys of reconciliation." They consisted of integrated teams of young adults traveling throughout the upper South on interstate buses testing the 1946 Supreme Court ruling that outlawed segregation in interstate travel.

CORE gained much of its reputation for its participation in the student sit-ins and the Freedom Rides of the early 1960's. The Freedom Rides were a response to the 1960 Supreme Court ruling expanding its 1946 decision. The Court decreed that train and bus terminals used by passengers engaged in interstate travel must also be desegregated. Arrests and violence followed the two integrated CORE teams in 1960 as they sought to force the hand of the federal government. With the assistance of the Student Nonviolent Coordinating Committee (SNCC) and the Southern Christian Leadership Conference (SCLC), they were successful in forcing the Interstate Commerce Commission to institute new penalties for noncompliance with the decreed desegregation.

During the first half of the 1960's, CORE carried on a number of concurrent campaigns around the country. While the national office focused on voter registration, local CORE chapters concentrated on desegregating lunch counters and roadside restaurants and fighting for fair housing practices, equal employment opportunities, and school integration. CORE participated in demonstrations, boycotts, and marches with the SCLC, SNCC, and the National Association for the Advancement of Colored People (NAACP). CORE took a leadership role in the 1963 March on Washington and was one of the ten civil rights organizations that met with President John F. Kennedy before the march.

In 1964, CORE began to move away from nonviolent

direct action and political neutrality, and by 1966, it had developed a political action program and was active in community organizing. CORE eventually broke with the nonviolent integrationist philosophy and joined the ranks of the more radical activist groups. CORE embraced "black power" and replaced James Farmer with Floyd B. McKissick as its national director.

The anti-integration posture assumed by CORE tended to push it more and more to the fringe of the Civil Rights movement. Membership in CORE dwindled during the 1970's and 1980's, and by the 1990's, it had experienced such a drop in membership and support that it was only a shell of its former self. Many attribute its decline to a change in philosophy and to the black nationalist position it took in the 1960's.

Charles C. Jackson

See also: Civil Rights movement; Freedom Riders; National Association for the Advancement of Colored People; Southern Christian Leadership Conference; Student Nonviolent Coordinating Committee.

Congressional Black Caucus

The Congressional Black Caucus, a group comprising African American members of the U.S. Congress, was established in 1970 by thirteen members of the House of Representatives who joined together "to promote the public welfare through legislation designed to meet the needs of millions of neglected citizens." Before that year, the House had never had so many African Americans among its 435 members, yet thirteen was still a small minority. The founders of the Congressional Black Caucus hoped that they could gain more visibility and power working together than they could acting alone.

In 1971, the Congressional Black Caucus was granted a meeting with President Richard M. Nixon, during which its members presented a document describing sixty actions the government should take on domestic and international issues. The president promised to promote desegregation by seeing that civil rights laws were more stringently enforced (later, caucus members came to believe that he did not work hard enough to fulfill his promise). Media coverage of the meeting helped the group gain recognition. Over the next quarter-century, members of the caucus built and strengthened ties with other influential members of the black community, including educators, community and religious leaders, and local and state legislators, which enabled the group to influence public policy at all levels of government.

Although originally formed to promote the concerns of African Americans and other members of minority groups, the caucus also worked to ensure that the government assisted others in need, including children, the elderly, and the physically and mentally ill. The group asserts that it is possible and desirable to develop a

Members of the Congressional Black Caucus, founded by thirteen African American members of the House of Representatives in 1970, meet with President Richard M. Nixon in 1971.

national African American position on matters of federal policy, and it has sought to direct that effort. Since its founding, the group has introduced and supported legislation concerning domestic issues such as employment, welfare and health care reform, education reform, small business development, urban revitalization, and federal disaster relief. In 1981, members of the caucus spoke out against the budget proposed by President Jimmy Carter, believing that it devoted too much funding to the military and too little to social programs. At House Judiciary Committee hearings in 1996, following a rash of firebombings of black churches across the South, the caucus criticized the federal government's apparent failure to prosecute those guilty of the crimes. Many of the group's positions have been unpopular, even among some African Americans; in the late 1990's, for example, the caucus strongly endorsed the work of the controversial leader of the Nation of Islam Louis Farrakhan, who was accused by many of teaching anti-Semitism.

As the visibility and influence of the caucus increased, the group called for action on international issues of special concern to African Americans, including human rights. It was one of the earliest and strongest voices urging that the United States use pressure against apartheid in South Africa and to call for increased attention and aid to other African nations.   *Cynthia A. Bily*

See also: Black nationalism; Church burnings.

Congressional Hispanic Caucus

The Congressional Hispanic Caucus (CHC) is an organization dedicated to improving the condition of Hispanics and Latinos through the legislative process. The caucus monitors policies of the executive and judicial branches of the U.S. government and seeks to strengthen the role of Hispanics and Latinos at all levels of government. In addition to the eighteen members of Hispanic descent in Congress in 1998, the caucus included approximately sixty associate members of the Senate and the House of Representatives.

The CHC has three main goals: significant progress toward fair representation of Hispanics and Latinos in federal government positions, the utilization of the talents and strengths of Hispanics and Latinos in the federal government, and the naming of Hispanics and Latinos to government positions at all levels but particularly to high-ranking, policy-making positions that can affect the daily lives of people. In 1995, the CHC requested that the United States General Accounting Of-

fice (GAO) prepare a study on the status of Hispanic and Latino underemployment in the federal civilian workforce, including its nature and adverse impact. In June, 1996, the GAO released a report confirming that Hispanics and Latinos were proportionately the most underrepresented group in the federal workforce.

By 1997, the CHC had been joined by numerous Hispanic and Latino advocacy groups in bringing attention to the low number of Hispanics and Latinos in both career and appointed positions in the federal civilian workforce. The chair of the caucus, California Democratic congressman Xavier Becerra, discussed the situation on numerous occasions with President Bill Clinton, asking what was being done about the problem. Led by the CHC, Hispanic and Latino communities became unified in holding the Clinton administration accountable to its pledge to assemble a government that truly represented all of the nation. The caucus called upon President Clinton to give this matter priority status with an aggressive plan to name more Hispanics and Latinos to high-level governmental positions.

Congressman José E. Serrano, a New Yorker of Puerto Rican background and member of the Congressional Hispanic Caucus, takes part in a parade in New York City.

Although it had been an unwritten rule to keep Cuba out of any official CHC business, Becerra made a trip to Cuba and met with Fidel Castro in late 1996. Reportedly, Becerra called for free elections and the liberation of political prisoners in Cuba. However, in 1997, Congress members Ileana Ros-Lehtinen and Lincoln Diaz-Balart, two Cuban American Republicans from Florida, left the CHC in protest over Becerra's violation of CHC policy. Consequently, for a period of time, the only Republican left on the CHC was Texan Henry Bonilla, making it impossible for the caucus to present itself as a bipartisan, pan-Hispanic organization and making it difficult for the CHC to be effective on issues involving immigration and English-only efforts. Becerra eventually persuaded Ros-Lehtinen and Diaz-Balart to return to the CHC, restrengthening the caucus in its drive to improve conditions in the United States for Hispanics and Latinos.

Alvin K. Benson

See also: Cuban Americans; Cuban Revolution; Latinos in the United States.

Conquest and annexation

> **Significance:** Conquest and annexation are two processes by which one group may be subordinated to another following contact. To maintain social stability, the subordinate or minority group must either be excluded from or integrated into dominant society.

The types of relations that exist between racial or ethnic groups in culturally diverse societies depend on how the various groups are brought into contact with one another and on how their cultural distinctiveness relates to gaining access to resources and power. Race or ethnicity is often the basis for social stratification. Barriers to the full societal participation of racial or ethnic subordinate groups include attitudes of prejudice, the practice of discrimination, and the existence of institutional structures and norms that limit the options of subordinate groups. Such systemic barriers are referred to as institutional discrimination.

Functionalist vs. Conflict Theories

Sociologists attempt to explain the maintenance of such stratification through *functionalist* theories and *conflict* theories. In the former, the focus is on how stratification systems maintain stability and social order. In the latter, the focus is on the struggle for power and resources and the means by which the powerful maintain and enlarge control. These two types of explanation are not mutually exclusive. They can reflect different points in historical time or different perspectives on the same experience of social inequality. In South Africa, for example, dramatic social stratification called apartheid existed, with the dominant white society (a numerical minority) controlling most of the land and mineral resources, technology, and the military until 1989, when apartheid ended. Elaborate laws controlled the freedom of movement of black South Africans and ensured the availability of a black labor force. From the dominant white perspective, a stable system existed, one that was justified by an ideology that was grounded in a belief in white superiority. From the black South African perspective, the structural injustices maintained unequal access to food, health care, education, and jobs; this lack of access prohibited social mobility. Both nonviolent resistance and violent confrontation resulted as blacks struggled for access to resources and self-determination.

Processes of Subordination

A variety of processes can lead to the formation, annexation, or conquest of racial or ethnic subordinate groups. These subordinating processes can be distinguished from one another according to the degree to which the racial or ethnic group participates voluntarily and according to whether migration is involved. *Voluntary migration* characterizes immigrant groups that may be seeking greater access to personal freedoms and economic resources. It also characterizes refugee groups that may be fleeing armed conflicts, persecution, or natural disasters. *Involuntary migration* characterizes the experience of slaves or indentured servants. In *annexation*, once-dominant peoples may become subordinate without migrating from their homelands. This occurs when nations expand their borders to incorporate neighboring lands and their inhabitants. Finally, *colonization* occurs when a foreign power usurps and maintains political, social, economic, and cultural domination over land and peoples without annexing them into its national structure. Even following a country's independence from a colonial power, it may be controlled by that power because of economic and social dependence on the former colonizer. This is referred to as *neocolonialism*.

Subordinate-Dominant Group Relations

Racial or ethnic groups can relate to the dominant group in a society in a number of ways. These ways can be characterized according to the degree to which the racial or ethnic group maintains a distinct identity and the degree to which these subordinate groups experience intergroup contact with the dominant group. *Genocide* is the ultimate loss of racial or ethnic identity coupled with separation from the dominant group. This may be a deliberate and systematic killing of group members with the intent of obliterating them, as was Adolf Hitler's policy toward Jews in Nazi Germany. Genocide also may be less intentional but no less complete. Disease and brutal treatment by the Spanish in the fifteenth and early sixteenth centuries wiped out the indigenous Indians of what is now the West Indies. This loss of a forced labor pool required that the Spanish begin to import African slaves.

Expulsion describes the subordinate form in which a racial or ethnic group's identity is maintained but the group is completely forced from the lands conquered by the dominant group. The Bosnian Serb "ethnic cleansing" of Bosnian Muslims during the early 1990's is a contemporary example of expulsion. Through massacre, rape, and the razing of villages, Muslim people were forced to flee their country.

Segregation describes the subordinate form in which group identity is maintained and separation from the dominant group occurs; however, complete removal of the racial or ethnic group from its homeland does not necessarily follow. Segregation may be voluntary, as with Amish Christian communities in Pennsylvania. It may be involuntary and enforced by law as was the case for African Americans in the southern United States until the 1960's, or it may be involuntary and enforced by social norms, as continues to be the case for African Americans, particularly for those living in poverty in urban settings.

Sometimes, substantial interaction occurs between members of subordinate and dominant groups. In *assimilation*, racial or ethnic groups relinquish their distinct identities to take on characteristics of the dominant group. In cultural assimilation, a racial or ethnic group adopts the cultural patterns of the surrounding society without necessarily being fully accepted into that society. In structural assimilation, a racial or ethnic group enters into close relationships with members of the dominant group and full participation in mainstream society.

Amalgamation or *fusion* describes the combining of a racial or ethnic group with the dominant group to form a new group. The mestizos of Latin America are an amalgamation of Spanish and indigenous Indian peoples. Societies in which this is a predominant occurrence are sometimes described as melting pots.

Finally, *cultural pluralism* describes societies in which ongoing intergroup contact occurs but ethnic or racial groups maintain distinct identities.

The Cowlitz Indians

One example of a subordinating process involves the Cowlitz Indians of what is now southwestern Washington State. Before the arrival of the "white man," this tribe was a powerful and independent dominant group. In the early 1800's, explorers, trappers, and traders provided the Cowlitz with their first contact with whites, who were moving westward and annexing more and more land. By the 1830's, the white settlers' numbers, technology, and access to military support (as well as the effects of their diseases on the native population) permitted them to become the dominant group, while the Cowlitz were transformed into a subordinate group. Land and other natural resources were no longer adequate to support both the dominant white economy and the Cowlitz aboriginal economy. A struggle for power and resources now characterized the relationship of the Cowlitz (and other American Indians) to the white settlers. This struggle led to armed conflicts, with white society ultimately retaining control. A plethora of treaties followed in the 1850's, with some tribes being segregated on reservations located in their ancestral lands. All treaties presented to the Cowlitz, however, required that they be expelled from their lands. Consequently, the Cowlitz refused all treaties. With continued encroachment of white society, the Cowlitz lost their land base and could no longer maintain their aboriginal economy. They were forced to enter the mainstream economy of the white society to survive.

The early 1900's was a time in which the dominant white society, both formally through law and informally through social norms and social censure, attempted to force assimilation on the Cowlitz. The Cowlitz were pressured to change their names, to cease practicing their cultural ways, and to speak English. In the mid-1900's, the Bureau of Indian Affairs of the United States government administratively terminated the tribe on the grounds that the Cowlitz people were completely assimilated and no longer constituted a distinct cultural group. This termination cut off the Cowlitz from those services and resources reserved for American Indians by the United States government.

In reality, the Cowlitz have not assimilated. Although their lack of a land base forced them into the economy of the dominant society, they have retained their ethnic identity and tribal government. They still gather socially as a tribe, own acreage on the Cowlitz River as a tribe, and regularly represent Cowlitz perspectives on local and state issues relevant to their ancestral lands. They and the white society within which they live form a plural culture. The Cowlitz have petitioned the United States government for recognition of their tribal status.

Mícheál D. Roe

Core Resources

John W. Berry's "Psychology of Acculturation: Understanding Individuals Moving Between Cultures," in *Applied Cross-Cultural Psychology* (edited by Richard W. Brislin, Newbury Park, Calif.: Sage Publications, 1990), presents the author's widely cited model of acculturation. Milton M. Gordon's *Assimilation in American Life: The Role of Race, Religion, and National Origins* (New York: Oxford University Press, 1964) presents a multidimensional view of assimilation. Books examining the American Indian experience include Dee Brown's *Bury My Heart at Wounded Knee* (New York: Pocket Books, 1981) and Bartolomé de Las Casas's *The Tears of the Indians* (translated by John Phillips, Stanford, Calif.: Academic Reprints, 1953), first published in the 1500's.

See also: Annihilation of racial and ethnic groups; Apartheid; Assimilation: cultural and structural; Genocide of American Indians; Indian-white relations: United States; Internal colonialism; Minority and majority groups; Pluralism vs. assimilation.

Conservatives and racial/ethnic relations

> **Significance:** The subject of race relations is one of the primary axes whereby American conservatism and liberalism are distinguished. Conservative theorists frequently downplay the significance of race in determining an individual's opportunities in life. They tend to view racial tensions as a product of misunderstandings or cynical manipulation by self-appointed minority leaders.

The terms "conservative" and "liberal" in U.S. political ideology are somewhat ambiguous, having changed over time. This is especially true with regard to racial issues. Early in the country's history, "conservatism," which tends to oppose radical change, could be used in defense of slavery. After the abolition of slavery, some conservatives defended segregation and other racist institutions. Therefore, it should not be surprising that conservatives traditionally have resisted programs to further advance the interests of minorities, such as affirmative action and racial quotas. By the 1990's, however, a combination of societal and cultural changes had brought about a situation in which conservatism was strongly associated with positions once championed by civil rights leaders such as the Reverend Martin Luther King, Jr.

Conservative Philosophy

Modern conservatism, sometimes called "neoconservatism," emphasizes the rights and interests of individuals over the interests of groups. This fundamental principle was at the center of King's calls for a "color-blind society." King sought the elimination of racial discrimination, which was prevalent in the 1950's and 1960's. Conserva-

tism in the late twentieth century embraced that same notion and used it against some of the governmental programs created to advance minority rights. The premier example of this is affirmative action. Although the term applies to a range of programs, in principle, affirmative action targets underrepresented minority groups for jobs, promotions, college admissions, political office, and other social goods. Affirmative action's goals are advanced through quotas, preferences, set-asides, and special outreach. Conservatism opposes most of these manifestations of affirmative action because they treat individuals according to their race or ethnicity. Although proponents of affirmative action claim that this "reverse" discrimination is necessary to compensate for the legacy of past discrimination, conservatives counter that this is still a form of discrimination and thus is harmful.

The conservatives' argument against affirmative action presumes that racial discrimination is not a significant factor in contemporary society. It implies that a level playing field has been achieved in economic and social relations. Such beliefs are vigorously challenged by advocates of affirmative action.

Individualism

Conservatives' attitudes toward discrimination stem in part from conservatism's philosophy of individualism. Conservatism holds that the interests of the individual should be the most important target of government policy. This contrasts with modern American liberalism, which allows for a greater emphasis on group interests. In other words, conservatives reject the idea of African American interests or Latino interests and, in fact, may reject the popular notion of African American or Latino communities. They believe that all of these are reducible to individuals, each of whom is unique and possesses his or her own set of interests.

Conservatism's emphasis on individual interests depoliticizes the issue of race. Although certain minority populations experience a higher degree of poverty, drug addiction, homelessness, incarceration, out-of-wedlock births, or other social and economic ills, conservatism prescribes actions that focus on root causes and do not specifically use race as a criteria for assistance. For example, conservatives believe that programs to create job opportunities for minorities living in depressed areas should be available to all unemployed persons in depressed areas, regardless of race. Similarly, policies that happen to affect one minority group more than others—for instance, imposing higher penalties for possession of illegal drugs that are preferred by a particular minority group—should be evaluated on their merits and not according to their relative impact on racial groups.

Overall, conservatism has come to take a rather academic and idealistic view of race. It has largely embraced the principles advocated by the Civil Rights movement of the 1950's and 1960's.

Conservatism and Race

Although earlier conservative views on race—such as those that defended slavery and segregation—were unlikely to be held by racial minorities, modern conservatism has been espoused by a growing number of African Americans, Latinos, and other minority members. Politically, this fact has been used by white conservatives to defend themselves against charges of racism.

One of the better-known black conservatives is Shelby Steele, of the Hoover Institute at Stanford University. Steele has written extensively about affirmative action, charging that it has the effect of reinforcing blacks' exclusion from the American mainstream. He has repeatedly argued that African Americans need to let go of the culture of "racial victimization," which he views as a self-defeating strategy. He also has decried the "divisive politics" of most of the liberal minority-advocacy groups who claim to speak for African Americans. Steele refers to the leadership of such groups as "the anointed" and argues that they are out of touch with the actual interests and desires of African Americans.

A number of other African American conservatives became highly visible in the late 1980's and 1990's. Among these was Stanley Crouch, who began as a writer on jazz and culture, then increasingly turned to matters of race and politics. Crouch's views are eclectic, and more than anything, he has earned a reputation as an iconoclast. However, he shares many of modern conservatism's views about race, especially its skepticism about liberal prescriptions on the subject. Thomas Sowell, an African American economist at Stanford University, takes a conservative view on racial issues, especially as they relate to welfare and economics. Sowell's work in the mid-1990's sought to explain the importance of ethnicity to socioeconomic outcomes. By using case studies from around the world, Sowell drew distinctions between culture (which is malleable) and race.

The linkage between race and conservatism took another interesting turn in the 1990's with the election of J. C. Watts, Jr., to the U.S. Congress. As an African American Republican, Watts was something of an anomaly, and his outspoken conservatism on matters of race earned him considerable publicity. For conservatives, the presence of Watts on their side helps to weaken their opponents' claims that conservative views on race are racist, or at least ethnocentric. Interestingly, Watts, like many of the conservative theorists listed above, has been criticized by some other African Americans as being somehow untrue to his race. For example, in 1990, the executive director of the National Association for the Advancement of Colored People (NAACP), Benjamin Hooks, said that "these people have nothing to offer except a conservative viewpoint in black skin." The notion that the color of one's skin should be relevant to one's political ideology riles black conservatives. As Watts has stated, "My father raised me to be a man, not a black man."

Steve D. Boilard

Core Resources

More and more conservative theorists are writing books on race. Shelby Steele's books include *The Content of Our Character: A New Vision of Race in America* (New York: HarperPerennial, 1991); *The Vision of the Anointed: Self-Congratulation as a Basis for Social Policy* (New York: Basic Books, 1995); and *A Dream Deferred: The Second Betrayal of Black Freedom in America* (New York: HarperCollins, 1998). Steele also helped produce a Public Broadcasting Service (PBS) television special about the racially motivated murder in Bensonhurst in 1990, "Seven Days in Bensonhurst." William Julius Wilson's *When Work Disappears: The World of the New Urban Poor* (New York: Random House, 1996) offers a black conservative's view of the problems facing inner-city African Americans and others. The range of Stanley Crouch's writings on race is illustrated in his early and recent works. See his *Ain't No Ambulances for No Nigguhs Tonight* (New York: R.W. Baron, 1972) and *The All-American Skin Game: Or, The Decoy of Race* (New York: Pantheon, 1995). Amy Waldman has written a somewhat critical overview of J. C. Watts's relationship with the Republican Party in "The GOP's Great Black Hope," in *Washington Monthly* (vol. 28, no. 10, October, 1996).

See also: Affirmative action; Civil Rights movement; "Color-blind" society; Discrimination: racial and ethnic; Quotas; "Reverse" racism; Set-asides; Wilson-Willie debate.

Constitutional racism

Three provisions of the Constitution of the United States, as adopted at Philadelphia in 1787, legalized slavery. These provisions, which provided a constitutional basis for treating those descended from Africans as inferior to those descended from Europeans, form the basis of what has come to be known as constitutional racism.

Some delegates at the constitutional convention wanted to abolish slavery, but the southern states, driven by economic dependency on the institution, insisted on retaining it. To ensure that the newly drafted constitution would be adopted by both northern and southern states, a compromise emerged between proslavery and antislavery delegates, and three specific clauses were included.

One provision, Article I, section 9(1), allowed the slave trade to continue until 1808. The part of the Constitution dealing with amendments, Article V, stipulated that this provision could not be amended.

Another compromise involved the status of slaves. Because the number of seats allocated in the House of Representatives for each state were to be apportioned on the basis of population, southern states might have considerable power in the new national legislature. However, a segment of the southern states' population was made up of slaves, who were not considered to have any civil rights and therefore could not vote. The compromise, provided for in Article I, section 2(3), was to calculate the number of persons in each state based on the decennial census, with each slave equal to three-fifths of a white person. Native Americans, who were not considered American citizens, were counted in the census, but their numbers were not used in calculating how many congressional seats were to be apportioned to the states.

A third provision, Article III, section 2(3), enabled slave owners to retrieve runaway slaves even from states that had abolished slavery. Congress later implemented this provision by passing the Fugitive slave laws (1793, 1850), which in turn were held to be constitutional by the U.S. Supreme Court in *Scott v. Sandford* (1857). In this case, a slave owner moved from Missouri to Illinois, taking along his property and his slaves. Because Illinois law prohibited slavery, Dred Scott, one of the slaves, sued to gain his freedom. The court ruled, however, that descendants of Africans, even those who obtained freedom from their former masters, were not citizens of the United States, had no civil rights, and therefore could not file a lawsuit or vote in an election. *Scott v. Sandford* provoked a constitutional crisis because laws in northern states that disallowed slavery and granted some civil rights to descendants of Africans were in effect nullified. The court's decision did much to infuriate opponents of slavery and sowed the seeds for the Civil War.

With the adoption of the Thirteenth Amendment to the Constitution in 1865, slavery was abolished. The Fugitive slave laws, accordingly, were nullified. Southern states obtained additional seats in the House of Representatives, as they could count every former slave as one person instead of three-fifths of a person. Reapportionment based on the 1870 census gave equal weight to black and white citizens but still excluded Native Americans.

The doctrine of "reason of state" has been used to discriminate against various minorities on several occa-sions. Under this doctrine, the preservation of the state is held to have priority over constitutional rights. Recent instances are associated with World War II, when the U.S. Supreme Court upheld the constitutionality of military rule of Hawaii and the incarceration of Japanese Americans.

Michael Haas

See also: Censuses, U.S.; Fugitive slave laws; Japanese American internment; *Scott v. Sandford*; Slavery: history; Thirteenth Amendment; Three-fifths compromise.

Contact and adaptation patterns

Significance: Although no two histories of contact between different racial or ethnic groups are identical, all such histories can be conceptualized in terms of several primary patterns of intergroup interactions over time. An understanding of these patterns enables the application of appropriate measures to deal with any problems or to facilitate interactions.

Much sociological analysis of race and ethnic relations consists of defining, categorizing, and conceptualizing initial contacts between racial and ethnic groups and mutual adaptations to the geographic and social proximity that follow the initial contact. The following is an examination of some of the better-known theories and analyses.

Assimilation
In sociologist Milton Gordon's now classic *Assimilation in American Life* (1964), he defined assimilation as "the process by which groups with diverse beliefs and behavior patterns become absorbed into another culture." He also coined the term "cultural pluralism" to describe the contrasting pattern of intergroup relations in which diverse groups retain important elements of their own cultures and coexist without assimilating into a single dominant culture.

Two-dimensional Perspective
Researcher Stanley Lieberson analyzed race and ethnic contacts along two dimensions: migrant/indigenous and superordinate/subordinate. All possible combinations of these two dimensions occur and result in very different processes of adaptation. When an indigenous group is subordinated (as when Native American tribes were subordinated by Europeans who arrived in New England and moved westward to California), warfare is

endemic; the indigenous group struggles to retain its territory and its power in the face of foreign aggression. When an immigrant group is subordinated, as when Irish and Italian immigrants arrived to labor in the major cities of the Northeast and Midwest, the immigrant group usually assimilates into the dominant culture in order to survive economically.

Social Psychologies

Scholar Rose Stegner stressed psychological variables such as emotional intensity, polarization of thinking, and realism versus revolution in her analyses of race conflicts in the United States. Similarly, Herbert Blumer focused on psychosocial variables in his description of the development of prejudice. He viewed prejudice as a function of the extent to which the minority group is experienced as "different," the degree of fear of economic competition, and the extent to which the minority group is viewed as inferior.

Integration Versus Segregation

Scholars Joan Moore and Marta Tienda both addressed the processes of integration and segregation of various groups of Latino migrants into U.S. communities. Puerto Ricans in Chicago and New York, Cubans in Miami, and Mexicans and Central Americans in Los Angeles experience degrees of economic integration and housing integration that vary depending on the characteristics of the cities in which they live, the educational and economic resources they bring with them, and the period in history during which they migrate. Although relatively affluent and well-educated Cubans may experience considerable economic integration, impoverished Puerto Ricans and Central Americans may be relegated to urban barrios. Sociologist Louis Wirth, in *The Ghetto* (1929), also described the process of segregation of economically and politically oppressed groups into separate areas of cities where they were confined by a variety of means, such as workplace discrimination that kept their incomes low, redlining of neighborhoods for nonservice by insurance and financial institutions, and inferior public education that limited the opportunities of their children to advance economically.

Multivariate Analyses

Sociologist William Julius Wilson, in *Power, Racism, and Privilege* (1972) argued that stratification into separate and unequal classes is a means by which the dominant group can exploit the labor of the minority group. Prejudice and pejorative attitudes toward the minority group develop from biological or cultural stereotypes. Conflict often results when the expectations or aspirations of the minority group for economic or political justice are frustrated by the actions of the dominant group, particularly if a sudden gap opens between their expectations and their gratification. Conflict caused by such a gap is called a "revolution of rising expectations" and could be seen in the African American protests during the late 1960's, which many believe resulted from African American frustration caused by a rapid shifting of the domestic policy agenda for social justice into foreign policy priorities, particularly the Vietnam War.

Racial Protest

Protest in a host of different forms is always a part of the response of a minority group to economic discrimination, segregation, and the development and expression of racial and ethnic prejudice by dominant groups. In the United States, the African American community has produced one of the world's richest literatures on racial protest. Historian John Hope Franklin, chair of the 1998 Presidential Commission on Race Relations, described the revolts and other protests of black slaves in the American South in his monumental *From Slavery into Freedom* (1947). Historian Kenneth Clark analyzes the Civil Rights movement of the 1960's in his book *The Negro Protest: James Baldwin, Malcolm X, Martin Luther King Talk with Kenneth B. Clark* (1963), and Lerone Bennett and his colleagues describe the most militant black protest groups that were also part of this broader social movement in *Pioneers in Protest* (1968).

Protest also took the form of organizations. The National Association for the Advancement of Colored People (NAACP), founded in 1909 by W. E. B. Du Bois, and the Urban League, founded in 1910, are two formal organizations committed to fighting legal and economic discrimination.

Multicultural History of the United States

Ronald Takaki's *A Different Mirror* (1993) traces the histories of native peoples, African slaves, "white ethnics" from Europe, Jews fleeing persecution in Russia and Europe, Mexicans whose lands were overrun and who later migrated to the United States, and immigrants from the many countries of Asia. Each group has a unique experience of contact and adaptation in the United States. The history and characteristics of each group interact with the times and places and ways in which they arrived in the United States or were subjugated by white Americans of European descent.

Judith R. Mayo

Core Resources

William Julius Wilson's *Power, Racism, and Privilege* (New York: Macmillan, 1972) is a sophisticated theoretical analysis of black-white relations in the United States that is well grounded empirically, as is all of his work. Joan Moore and Raquel Pinderhugh edited an excellent collection of papers on diverse Latino experiences of integration and segregation in American communities, *In the Barrios: Latinos and the Underclass Debate* (New York: Russell Sage, 1993). Marta Tienda's work consists of high-quality demographic analyses of trends in various Latino population groups, such as her book written with Frank Bean, *The Hispanic Population of the United States* (New York: Russell Sage, 1987). Ronald Takaki's *A Different Mirror: A History of Multicultural America* (Boston: Little, Brown, 1993) is an evenhanded yet particularistic treatment of the histories of the major ethnic and racial groups in the United States.

See also: Assimilation: cultural and structural; Assimilation theories; Contact hypothesis; Integration; Segregation vs. integration; Social stratification theories; Subordinate group.

Contact hypothesis

> **Significance:** According to the contact hypothesis, intergroup bias (prejudice, stereotypes, and discrimination) arises, in part, from ignorance and misinformation; favorable face-to-face contact between members of different groups will foster more accurate perceptions, greater intergroup attraction, and less bias directed at one another.

Intergroup bias manifests itself in three interrelated yet distinctive manners: feelings and attitudes (prejudice), generalized beliefs (stereotypes), and behaviors that favor one group over another (discrimination). In general, persons who are biased against members of another social group dislike those persons (prejudice), believe that they possess unpleasant or negative characteristics (stereotypes), and actively avoid or denigrate them (discrimination). Social psychologists have studied how intergroup bias arises and what tactics may be employed to ameliorate it. They have observed that persons generally feel a sense of self-investment and identification with groups to which they belong (in-groups) rather than with groups to which they do not belong (out-groups). Consequently, they may associate with fellow in-group members more than with out-group members and obtain a more accurate and complete knowledge of the in-group than of the out-group.

Ignorance of the out-group may contribute to intergroup bias, as persons are motivated to maintain a positive view of themselves by assuming the best about their in-groups and the worst about out-groups. Accurate information about an out-group that disconfirms negative expectations (prejudice and stereotypes) should improve intergroup relations, and accurate information may be obtained through face-to-face contact with members of the disliked out-group.

The Hypothesis

The contact hypothesis refers to the proposition that bias between groups can be reduced by bringing members of different groups together for face-to-face interaction. The contact hypothesis rests on two assumptions. First, intergroup bias is frequently based on ignorance or misinformation. Contact between group members provides the opportunity to disconfirm their erroneous beliefs and feelings about the groups. Second, the contact experience(s) will be sufficiently positive or pleasant to preclude exacerbation of existing bias.

Gordon Allport, in *The Nature of Prejudice* (1954), most clearly articulated the contact hypothesis when he argued that bringing members of disliked groups together can have a beneficial impact on intergroup relations, provided that the contact occurred under what have been termed favorable conditions. These include cooperative interaction, common goals, support from authorities or institutions outside the groups, and some degree of personal (as opposed to formal or superficial) contact. Research has generally supported these criteria as important in fostering contact that reduces bias between groups. Cooperation between groups produces more pleasant intergroup experiences than competition in which one group's gain comes at the expense of the other. Pursuit of a common goal, in particular a superordinate goal, encourages cooperation. Support for the contact from authorities and institutions helps to maintain it. Personal contact between members of the different groups can foster interpersonal attachments and reveal similarities and common interests between members of the different groups. Following Allport, the most influential voices in the area of the contact hypothesis have been Stuart Cook and Thomas F. Pettigrew.

Much of Cook's influential research has focused on the benefits of intimate contact with out-group members. Using laboratory groups engaged in cooperative tasks, Cook has found that contact is most effective in disconfirming stereotypes when it has "acquaintance potential." In other words, contact is most helpful when the different groups interact individually and get to know one another as unique persons, rather than as representatives of their groups. Unfortunately, Cook's research also indicates that while intergroup contact can improve relations among those involved in the contact experience, generalization of the positive experience to the out-group as a whole or to specific out-group members not present during the contact experience is often problematic.

Students of various cultures and backgrounds gather at a Toronto, Ontario, schoolyard. According to the contact hypothesis, contact such as this familiarizes people with other cultures and races and decreases prejudice, discrimination, and bias between groups.

tion of the favorable contact experience to the out-group as a whole should suffer. For contact to be most effective, therefore, the contact persons must be judged to be very typical of their respective groups while behaving in an unexpectedly positive manner.

A related difficulty with the contact hypothesis is the assumption that contact will be effective to the extent that it reduces assumed differences between the groups. Yet reducing differences between groups may threaten each group's sense of uniqueness and identity. Social identity researchers argue that contact will be most successful if it focuses on diminishing negative beliefs and feelings between the groups yet still perpetuates some distinctive differences between the groups. Ideally, then, the contact experience should not strive to eliminate all differences between the groups but rather should reduce unfavorable and inaccurate beliefs while preserving those differences that cast both groups in a positive light.

Finally, the success of contact depends in part on the measurements used to assess its impact. Although contact may foster a change in beliefs or feelings about an out-group, it may not always yield a change in behavior. For example, one may feel more positively toward a group following a favorable contact experience but may be reluctant to act differently toward members of that group because of social pressure from prejudiced members of one's own group. On the other hand, one may feel obligated to behave positively toward members of an out-group who have treated one well but may still harbor prejudice and unfavorable stereotypes of the out-group as a whole. For contact to be effective in producing the broadest change in intergroup bias, it not only must be favorable (involve cooperation in pursuit of common goals) but also should occur frequently across many situations and with many members of the out-group.

Pettigrew has argued that to be successful, favorable contact with an out-group member must be interpreted positively by the parties. The attributions that group members make about the contact experience will determine the success of the experience. Thus, favorable contact with an out-group member may be ineffective if that experience is discounted as an atypical event, one that does not reflect the true intentions or dispositions of the out-group members. For the experience to be most effective, out-group members who behave positively in a contact setting must be seen as having behaved voluntarily (not forced to act pleasantly) and as being typical of others in their group (not exceptions to the rule). Laboratory research has found support for this conclusion.

Criticisms

Proponents of social identity theory have raised some criticisms of the contact hypothesis. Factors that maximize the success of intergroup contact in promoting positive relations among persons in the contact setting may yield the least generalization to the out-group as a whole. As mentioned, contact that involves positive, intimate experiences with out-group members is likely to create friendship bonds and reveal interindividual similarities that cut across the different group memberships, thereby diminishing the importance of the group categories for one's self-identity in that setting. Yet the contact person(s) may be perceived to be less representative of others in their group, with the result that generaliza-

The Theory and Desegregation

The contact hypothesis has served as an argument for school and residential racial desegregation within the United States. The argument has been that part of the prejudice between blacks and whites can be attributed to the ignorance and misinformation that is the legacy of segregation. In American society, interracial contact experiences have usually been characterized by unequal status, with whites occupying a superior role (employer or landowner). Consequently, much of the contact has not met the equal-status, cooperative, and intimate conditions that maximize the probability that contact will dispel negative stereotypes and modify prejudice. Following the 1954 United States Supreme Court ruling that outlawed racial segregation in public schools, researchers have looked at the schools as a testing ground for the contact hypothesis.

Evidence indicates that contact is effective only under the limited conditions already discussed. Merely throwing black and white students together in classrooms is not sufficient to reduce intergroup bias. Indeed, forced contact can exacerbate bias when community and institutional support is absent. Moreover, contact situations may fail because persons feel uncomfortable in the unfamiliar position of interacting with the out-group, preferring to seek out fellow in-group members. At many integrated American colleges, a visitor can see how blacks mainly interact with blacks and whites with whites.

Interracial contact in the classroom appears to work best when students are placed in integrated work groups in which all members are peers with equal status. The groups are given tasks to solve as a team so that cooperation is reinforced, rather than the interpersonal competition that characterizes many traditional classrooms. Under these circumstances, where contact is of equal status, is cooperative in pursuit of a common goal, and is sanctioned by authorities (a teacher), the contact experience produces a marked improvement in interracial relations. *David A. Wilder*

Core Resources

Gordon Willard Allport's *The Nature of Prejudice* (Cambridge, Mass.: Addison-Wesley, 1954), the classic social psychological study of prejudice, reviews early conceptualization and research on the contact hypothesis as well as theories of how prejudice develops and what techniques can be used to reduce it. Yehudi Amir's "The Role of Intergroup Contact in Change of Prejudice and Ethnic Relations," in *Towards the Elimination of Racism* (edited by Phyllis A. Katz, New York: Pergamon Press, 1976), is a omprehensive review of empirical studies examining the contact hypothesis. *Contact and Conflict in Intergroup Encounters* (Oxford, England: Basil Blackwell, 1986), edited by Miles Hewstone and Rupert Brown, examines the success and limitations of the contact hypothesis. *Groups in Contact: The Psychology of Desegregation* (Orlando, Fla.: Academic Press, 1984), edited by Norman Miller and Marilynn B. Brewer, assesses the consequences of intergroup contact in a variety of settings.

See also: Desegregation: public schools; Discrimination: racial and ethnic; Prejudice and stereotyping; Prejudice: effects; Prejudice: reduction.

Coolies

"Coolie" derives from a Tamil word meaning hireling and was adapted by the British to refer to unskilled laborers in India and the Far East in the seventeenth century. The word was also used to describe unskilled five-year contract laborers, usually Indian or Chinese, working for low wages in exchange for free passage to

The pejorative term "coolies" was applied to workers such as these Chinese immigrants using a handcar to reach their gold claims in the mid-1800's.

British or Dutch colonies. Conditions were abysmal in the depots where the passenger waited and even worse on the ships, producing death rates comparable to those during the former slave trade. Horrid work conditions awaited the survivors.

With the influx of Chinese to the United States following the California gold rush of 1849, the pejorative term "coolie" was adapted to refer to any Chinese immigrant, creating the fiction that Chinese were all slave laborers brought to the United States as part of a conspiracy to avoid paying decent wages to American workers. The racist coolie stereotype also connoted spreaders of disease, gambling, opium, prostitution, and heathenistic religious practices. As Chinese laborers helped build the railroads and worked in mines (often during strikes), this dehumanizing stereotype encouraged anti-Chinese riots and lynchings during the 1870's. Although only 105,000 Chinese had come to the United States by 1880, pressure from labor and western politicians resulted in the Chinese Exclusion Act of 1882, banning all Chinese immigration. *Irwin Halfond*

See also: Asian American stereotypes; Chinese Americans; Chinese Exclusion Act.

Cooper v. Aaron

In *Brown v. Board of Education* (1954) the Supreme Court ordered an end to segregated schools and overturned the "separate but equal" doctrine established in *Plessy v. Ferguson* (1896). The ambiguity about how to implement school desegregation, however, created the opportunity for school boards to delay and defy the court's order.

After the *Brown* decision, the Little Rock, Arkansas, school board approved a plan calling for the desegregation of grades ten through twelve in 1957, to be followed by the desegregation of junior high schools and, finally, the elementary schools. The plan was to be completed by the 1963 school year.

Nine black students, carefully selected by the National Association for the Advancement of Colored People (NAACP), were to begin integration of Central High School on September 3, 1957. The day before desegregation was to begin, Governor Orval Faubus ordered the Arkansas National Guard to prevent the black students from enrolling. Governor Faubus claimed that he acted to prevent violence from occurring. After three weeks, a federal court injunction forced the National Guard to withdraw. On September 23, the nine black students entered Central High School and were met by an unruly mob. President Dwight D. Eisenhower was forced to dispatch federal troops to Little Rock to enforce the Court's desegregation order. In the face of the civil unrest, the school board asked for and received a two-and-a-half-year delay in their desegregation plan. The NAACP appealed the delay in *Cooper v. Aaron*.

Two primary issues confronted the U.S. Supreme Court. First, could the desegregation plan be postponed because of the fear of civil unrest? On September 12, 1958, a unanimous Supreme Court emphatically said no: "The law and order are not here to be preserved by depriving the Negro children of their constitutional rights." Second, were the governor and legislature bound by decisions of the federal court? Invoking the supremacy clause of the Constitution, the Court said: "No state legislative, executive or judicial officer can War against the Constitution without violating his undertaking to support it."

Although Governor Faubus lost the legal battle, he became a political folk hero in Arkansas and was elected to six consecutive terms (1955-1967). President Eisenhower was both praised and condemned for his actions. He was praised for sending in federal troops to enforce the Court's decision and condemned for failing to endorse personally the *Brown* decision and lend the weight and prestige of the White House to the Court's ruling. The *Cooper* case was the first legal confrontation over the enforcement of *Brown v. Board of Education*. The courts stood alone in this enforcement effort until Congress passed the 1964 Civil Rights Act. The Civil Rights Act endorsed the *Brown* decision and cut off federal funds to school districts refusing to comply with the Court's desegregation decision. *Darryl Paulson*

See also: *Brown v. Board of Education*; Civil Rights Act of 1964; Discrimination: racial and ethnic; Little Rock school desegregation; *Plessy v. Ferguson*; Segregation: de facto and de jure.

Cooperative learning

> **Significance:** Cooperative learning refers to a variety of ways that individuals work together to produce or obtain some defined goal. Teaching methods in general, and cooperative learning techniques in particular, have implications for different racial and ethnic groups and for intergroup relations.

Cooperative learning involves working in small groups toward some desired end. Groups, in and of themselves, do not have to be cooperative, but in cooperative learning, group members depend on one another to receive benefits. Cooperative learning methods can be contrasted with competitive methods, which have individuals work against one another to reach a goal, and individualistic methods, which encourage each person to work toward a goal without regard for the performance or behaviors of others.

Jigsaw

One of the first structured cooperative learning techniques, termed "jigsaw," was developed by social psychologist Elliot Aronson and his colleagues. Aronson envisioned an academic environment in which a heterogeneous mix of students could achieve success and learn to appreciate one another through equal-status contact. In jigsaw, students are placed in small groups that mix characteristics such as race, gender, and ability. The teacher assigns a common task, such as learning about Christopher Columbus, to the entire class. The assignment is broken down into subtopics. For example, the assignment on Columbus might include a review of Columbus's early life, information on his voyages, a description of life in and around America when Columbus set sail, and a review of Columbus's later life. Each student in a group assumes responsibility for one of the subtopics of the assignment. Students then meet with members from other groups who share the same subtopic. At this point, students have formed new, specialized groups in which individuals with the same information can help one another master the subtopic. Afterward, the members of the specialized groups return to their original groups to teach the material they have mastered and to learn the information on the other subtopics from other group members. Achievement is measured by testing students individually on all the information for the assignment. Jigsaw also includes extensive team-building and communication-training activities.

Although Aronson and his colleagues had high expectations for the cognitive and social benefits of jigsaw, reviews of the effects have been mixed. Cooperative learning methods that have emphasized group rewards over the individual rewards associated with jigsaw have shown more consistent benefits for learners. For example, Robert Slavin and his colleagues at The Johns Hopkins University have developed several successful group-reward cooperative learning methods including STAD, student teams-achievement divisions, and TGT, teams-games-tournament. In STAD, the teacher presents a lesson, and students study worksheets in small, heterogeneous groups. Afterward, students take individual quizzes. Group scores are computed based on how much each group member improves over previous performance and are reported in a class newsletter. TGT differs by having group members compete against members of other teams with similar records of past performance; group scores are based on the competition.

Other Methods

Two techniques developed by other research teams, learning together and group investigation, also use group rewards. Learning together emphasizes the development of social skills such as trust, conflict resolution, and accurate communication. Students work together to complete a single piece of work and are rewarded for working cooperatively and for task performance. In group investigation, small groups of students choose topics from a unit the class is studying. Group members then choose a subtopic for each member to investigate. Like jigsaw, group investigation uses task specialization. Unlike jigsaw, in group investigation, group members work together to prepare a presentation on their work for the entire class and are rewarded for group work.

Taken together, the various cooperative learning methods illustrate that there are benefits to cooperative learning methods over traditional competitive or individualistic approaches to instruction. Cooperative learning is also credited with increasing positive social interactions. Researchers report greater interaction between members of different racial or ethnic groups, greater acceptance of mainstreamed students, and greater friendship among students. Teachers and students in cooperative classrooms report more positive attitudes toward school. Finally, students in cooperative learning studies often show increased levels of self-esteem.

Racial Differences: The Riverside Project

Because of the clear relevance of cooperative learning techniques for the education of children, cooperative strategies have been investigated in a number of long-term school projects. A good example is the Riverside Cooperative Learning Project. One part of the project involved training student teachers in cooperative learning techniques and evaluating the effects of the training on their students. Elementary school student teachers were randomly assigned to either a traditional classroom structure, a STAD-structured classroom, or a TGT-structured classroom. STAD was considered the purest example of cooperative learning in the study because TGT contains a competitive element; in that group, members compete against members of other groups in order to gain points for their own group (team). Thus, TGT is more like a combination of cooperation and competition. TGT is still considered to be more of a cooperative method than the traditional classroom, which is oriented toward competitive and individualistic activities.

The gains that students made academically under the three classroom structures varied in the Riverside project based on the race of the students. African American students made the greatest gains in the STAD classroom, the classroom considered to be the clearest example of cooperative learning. Students of European descent did best in the TGT (cooperative-competitive) structured classroom. Mexican American students made the most gains in the traditional classroom. These results are important because they add support to the belief that some of the racial differences that occur in performance in schools may be related to culturally different preferences for one type of classroom structure over another.

In this study, the authors were surprised that the Mexican American students did not do better in the cooperative classrooms, since studies on ethnic differences suggested that Mexican American culture is oriented toward cooperation over competition. The Mexican American children in the Riverside project, however, were third-generation Americans with little knowledge of Spanish. Before the study began, they tested like the Euro-American students in terms of cooperation; the African American students, on the other hand, tested higher than the Mexican American and the Euro-American students on cooperation. Knowing which classroom structure will be best for a student, then, is not as simple as determining the student's racial or ethnic heritage.

Classroom climate was more positive in the cooperative classrooms than in the traditional classroom, particularly for the Mexican American and African American students. Cooperativeness was higher among students in cooperative classrooms, and students in cooperative classes were more democratic in choosing friends. Schools that want to emphasize social change, then, might prefer cooperative learning methods. Yet although cooperative techniques seemed better overall, the Riverside project also demonstrated that a variety of classroom structures may be necessary in schools to optimize performance for a majority of students.

Workforce Implications

Cooperative learning methods have also been investigated in laboratory studies with adult learners. Such studies are important for understanding the extent of the effects of cooperative learning methods and for evaluating whether they might be useful with older students and with materials that might be found in work environments. If the effects of cooperative methods on achievement transfer to work environments, employers might begin to train people differently and increase job performance. If the effects of cooperative methods on social interactions transfer, employers might improve organizational climates and also enhance job performance. Since the workforce is becoming more diversified, information on reactions to cooperative learning methods by different groups of people should be beneficial. A diversified environment also puts increased pressure on organizations to determine the best ways to get people to work together for increased productivity.

Preliminary studies on adults suggest that cooperative learning benefits can be obtained with dyads; individual accountability and external rewards may not be as critical as they are in the school setting, and personality differences and the type of material being learned may be more important.

Judith L. Gay

Core Resources

The Jigsaw Classroom, by Elliot Aronson et al. (Beverly Hills, Calif.: Sage, 1978), discusses the rationale for developing this cooperative learning method, explains the jigsaw technique in detail and presents the research findings. Robert E. Slavin's *Cooperative Learning: Theory and Research* (Englewood Cliffs, N.J.: Prentice-Hall, 1990) reviews various cooperative learning methods, some in detail, and the cognitive, social, and personal benefits associated with cooperative learning. More information about the Riverside project can be found in "Classroom Structural Bias: Impact of Cooperative and Competitive Classroom Structures on Cooperative and Competitive Individuals and Groups," by S. Kagan et al., in *Learning to Cooperate, Cooperating to Learn* (edited by Robert E. Slavin et al., New York: Plenum Press, 1985).

See also: Contact hypothesis; Prejudice: reduction; Psychological theories of intergroup relations.

Council of Federated Organizations

The Council of Federated Organizations (COFO) was developed in 1962 as a coalition of civil rights groups to coordinate voter registration in the southern regions of the United States. The COFO's president was Aaron Henry and its director was Robert Moses. More than 90 percent of COFO funding was provided by the Student Nonviolent Coordinating Committee (SNCC), which received money from the Voter Education Project. The COFO worked closely with SNCC and other civil rights organizations on its projects. Though the organization lost its funding in 1963, its most significant endeavor was the 1964 Freedom Summer project in Mississippi. This project arose from a mock election held in Mississippi in 1963 that showed that African Americans would vote if given the opportunity. Moses devised a new strategy of bringing white college students to Mississippi over the summer break to work on the voter registration project along with black activists. COFO workers were beaten and arrested, and some were shot at and even killed for assisting in registering black voters. They also operated freedom schools for African American children and helped organize the Mississippi Freedom Democratic

Party. The COFO made Americans aware of the discrimination that African Americans experienced in Mississippi at the hands of its white residents.

Jennifer Lynn Gossett

See also: Civil Rights movement; Freedom Summer; Mississippi Freedom Democratic Party; Student Nonviolent Coordinating Committee.

Crack cocaine

Crack cocaine, also known as freebase, rock, french fries, and ready rock, is a drug made by chemically removing the hydrochloride base of cocaine hydrochloride (a white powder which its users snort) with highly dangerous solvents, thus producing cocaine free of its base, or freebase (a paste that is smoked). Crack cocaine, so called because it makes a cracking sound when it is heated for smoking, can also be made less dangerously by heating cocaine hydrochloride with ammonia or baking soda, which also removes the base and produces a hard paste that resembles rock salt. Introduced in the 1970's and commonly used by the 1980's, crack became popular both because it produced a more intense high than regular cocaine and was much cheaper.

The question of whether African Americans and Latinos have been discriminated against in the U.S. criminal justice system's War on Drugs and specifically in the campaign against crack cocaine arises on several fronts. Critics claim, first of all, that enforcement generally targets minority communities and their inhabitants while allowing the major traffickers from the outside to go largely unpunished. More particularly, critics assert, laws dealing with powder cocaine, which is favored by whites, tend to be more lenient, whereas legislation concerning crack cocaine, preferred by some minorities, is apt to be harsher. Moreover, since 1986, when tougher laws were passed for crimes involving crack cocaine, minorities made up more than 97 percent of all crack defendants in federal courts, where severe sentences predominate, whereas typically whites arrested for crack violations, being able to afford legal counsel, ended up in state courts, which characteristically handed down more moderate punishments. More radical critics further charge that drugs—as well as acquired immunodeficiency syndrome (AIDS) and guns—are being foisted on minority communities to kill them off. The 1991 film *Boyz 'n' the Hood* was a prime illustration of such an argument.

That depiction acquired further credibility with the publication of *San Jose Mercury News* reporter Gary Webb's "Dark Alliance" series in August of 1996, which strongly suggested that Nicaraguan drug dealers had plied their crack cocaine trade in South Central Los Angeles in order to finance the Contras, who were fighting the leftist government of Daniel Ortega. Moreover, the U.S. government, especially the Central Intelligence Agency (CIA), was fully aware of such trafficking but did nothing, since the U.S. government also supported the Contra cause. The Reverend Jesse Jackson, political activist Dick Gregory, and congresswoman Maxine Waters reflected prominent black opinion, which found these judgments not only plausible but accurate as well. Waters said that "People in high places[knew] about it, winking, blinking, and in South Central Los Angeles, our children were dying" (quoted in Daniel Pipes, *Conspiracy*, New York, Free Press, 1997, p. 5).

Replies to these allegations came in the form of editorials, investigations by Congress and the administration of President Bill Clinton, and court decisions. *San Jose Mercury News* executive editor Jerry Ceppos admitted that there were "shortcomings" in Webb's articles, and this conclusion

Florida law enforcement agents hold a press conference in August, 1987, to discuss the 2,200 pounds of cocaine seized in Hollywood, Florida. The legal system has been criticized as being more lenient with powdered cocaine offenders (largely white) and tougher on crack cocaine offenders (mostly black).

was echoed by such newspapers as *The New York Times*, *The Washington Post*, and the *Los Angeles Times*. The Justice Department and the CIA inspector general both undertook investigations of the assertion that the CIA had participated in such drug trafficking, either directly or indirectly, and concluded that the agency had not done so. The House Intelligence Committee also investigated the question and found no connection. The case is not thereby closed, but until evidence can be introduced to make a connection between Nicaraguan drug dealers and the CIA, it will remain a weighty issue, particularly in African American communities. In any event, the fact that there are those who see crack cocaine as a conspiracy of a dominant group against people of color underscores the state of racial and ethnic relations in many communities in the United States.

As for the charge that blacks and other minorities are unfairly singled out for drug infractions and subject to harsher penalties, the Supreme Court in 1996 ruled that African Americans had not been targeted for drug prosecution in crack cocaine cases. However, an editorial that appeared in the May 15, 1997, issue of the *Los Angeles Times* (p. B-8) opined: "Putting aside the defendants' race, the blatant inequality exercised under these [federal] laws now looms large, seen by all but acknowledged by few." Notwithstanding the frequent frayed relations between inner-city neighborhoods and the police, few residents complain when drug pushers who terrorize their parks, public housing, streets, and stores are removed by the criminal justice system.   *Thomas D. Reins*

See also: AIDS conspiracy theory; Crime and race/ethnicity; Criminal justice system; Drugs and racial/ethnic relations.

Creole

The term "Creole" is an ethnic term that was originally used between the sixteenth and eighteenth centuries in Latin America to distinguish the offspring of the European colonizers from Indians and blacks as well as from any resident who had been born in Europe. During the colonization of Latin America, intermarriage between races was common, with Europeans marrying Indians and occasionally blacks, Indians intermarrying with blacks, and these couples' descendants with Europeans. The mixing resulted in a great variety of racial and ethnic types and led to a caste system in society. Europeans and their descendants formed the highest class of society, the European-born ranking above the native-born Creoles, and the Creoles ranking above those of mixed descent. As a result, Creole education and economic and political opportunities were quite limited.

The term "Creole" has been used to describe a variety of peoples. In Latin America, it was generally used to describe people of mixed Indian, black, and European ancestry.

After Mexico and other Latin American nations gained their independence, Creoles entered the ruling class. By the second half of the twentieth century, all the people in the West Indies were commonly referred to as Creoles, although in French Guiana, "Creole" refers to anyone who has adopted a European lifestyle. In the United States, the Creoles of Louisiana are the French-speaking white descendants of early French and Spanish settlers, and these people have their own culture and customs and even a composite language derived from French.   *Alvin K. Benson*

See also: Caste model; Mestizo; Social stratification theories.

Cress theory

The Cress theory of color confrontation is a controversial race relations theory that defines racism as a system of white supremacy designed to create worldwide domination of nonwhite peoples in order to ensure genetic survival of the white "race." Developed by pediatric psychiatrist Frances Cress Welsing, the theory was first presented in a 1970 paper entitled "The Cress Theory of Color-Confrontation and Racism (White Supremacy): A Psychogenetic Theory and World Outlook" and later appeared in her collection *The Isis Papers: The Keys to the Colors* (1991). The theory postulates that white-skinned people are genetically inferior to people of color because they do not produce melanin, a pigmenting hormone responsible for brown and black skin tones. Welsing notes that only a small minority of the world's people lack melanin, and that in reproduction, genes producing white skin are recessive (the offspring of whites and nonwhites have melanin pigments in their skin). Based on this evidence, Welsing attributes white skin to a genetic defect.

Welsing further states that the inability to produce melanin causes white people to experience a profound numerical and genetic "inferiority complex," which manifests as neurotic anxiety. This anxiety is transformed into intense fear of nonwhites, whose genes could annihilate the white race, and results in a psychological need to dominate and destroy nonwhite peoples. Welsing's ideas were influenced by the psychological theories of Sigmund Freud, a late nineteenth and early twentieth century Austrian physician credited as the founder of psychoanalysis. This influential psychiatric movement was based on the existence of the ego and unconscious motivation, and theorized that defense mechanisms evolved to protect the ego from psychological threat.

Welsing believed that the hostility and aggression exhibited by white people toward people of color developed from the operation of several of Freud's ego defense mechanisms. These defensive responses included repression of the sense of genetic inadequacy; reaction formation, where something desired (pigmented skin) is converted into something despised; and projection, where people project their own unacceptable feelings onto the recipients of their feelings (this would result in a white person who hates nonwhites developing the perception that nonwhites hate him or her). These defenses are thought to reduce uncomfortable feelings of guilt and anxiety.

Welsing wrote that the resulting hostility and fear explained the negative attitudes and oppressive behavior historically exhibited by whites toward nonwhites. Welsing believed that black people are the biggest targets of this unconscious envy, hatred, and maltreatment because among all melanin producers, their genes possess the greatest potential to transmit melanin. White supremacy therefore evolved as a worldwide social, po-

litical, and economic system designed to repress people of color and to prevent the genetic annihilation of the white race. Critics of the theory state that it is scientifically simplistic and empirically untested, focuses overly on biopsychological factors and ignores sociological contributions to the development of racism (such as class and economics); and is a form of "reverse" racism toward white people. Defenders of the theory point out that it is no more scientifically unsound and "racist" than long-standing theories of African American genetic inferiority.

Carlota Ocampo

See also: Afrocentrism; Biosocial theories; Genetic basis for race; "Reverse" racism; Sociobiology and race; White "race."

Crime and race/ethnicity

> **Significance:** One of the major issues associated with criminal justice in the United States is the relationship between race and crime. A large disparity exists between the numbers of African Americans, Hispanics, and other minorities in the general population and their numbers among those incarcerated in jails and prisons.

Although approximately 12 percent of the population of the United States is African American, blacks represent more than half of those imprisoned. In the mid-1990's, the Bureau of Justice Statistics of the U.S. Department of Justice reported that blacks were incarcerated at a rate six times that of the white population. In addition, four in ten of those on death row are black, and young black men are far more likely than whites to be the victims of police brutality. Blacks are also disproportionately represented among victims of crime. African Americans are three times more likely than whites and others to be victims of robbery and more than twice as likely to be victims of aggravated assault.

Data on Hispanics are often unreliable because many criminal justice agencies use only the classifications white and black. When Hispanics are included as white, statistics for both non-Hispanic whites and Hispanics are questionable. The practice inflates the number of whites in the system and creates the impression of fewer disparities than actually exist. Bureau of Justice Statistics reports on incarceration, however, indicate that in the mid-1990's, Hispanics accounted for 17 percent of prisoners, while they made up approximately 9 percent of the general population.

Statistics indicate that Asian Americans are underrepresented in both federal and state prisons. Although they constitute about 4 percent of the U.S. population, they are only 1 percent of those incarcerated. The majority of Asian American offenders are associated with nonviolent crimes such as gambling or prostitution.

Reliable Native American crime statistics are virtually nonexistent because such data are not gathered consistently in Indian country. Different tribes have different relationships with U.S. government agencies, contributing to problems both in defining and in reporting crimes among Native Americans.

Regardless of differences of experience among minority groups, it is impossible to examine crime and punishment in the United States without addressing whether these disparities are the result of discrimination, and whether such discrimination is a feature of the criminal justice system or if criminal justice simply mirrors the racism and inequality that exist in the larger society.

Stereotyping Crime

For many white Americans, "crime" means violent crime and the typical offender is young, black, and male, and the typical victim is white. In some communities, the image of the criminal is the Latino "gangbanger" or the violent "drunken Indian." In fact, based on arrest statistics collected by the Federal Bureau of Investigation (FBI) in the Uniform Crime Reports, for all crimes except murder and robbery, the typical offender is white. As the National Crime Victimization Survey repeatedly confirms, the majority of crimes are intraracial, involving offenders and victims of the same race. However, politicians and the mass media have used sensationalism and misinformation to intensify the public's fears and to lead to policies that promise to be "tough" on crime but that tend to ensnare poor, minority youths in the criminal justice system.

Popular policies, such as three-strikes-and-you're-out laws that mandate life sentences for three-time offenders, the abolition of parole, and mandatory sentences for relatively minor drug crimes, help account for the disparities between the percentage of minorities in the population and their percentage among prisoners. Although such policies may not have overt racist intentions, they result in perpetuating inequality based on race. Most of the three-strikes laws allow prosecutors to exercise tremendous discretion in determining which offenses qualify as a strike. Although

many citizens may imagine that such policies will catch violent career criminals, they have often been used against small-time criminals who are arrested on property crimes and drug offenses. Rand Corporation research and 1994 data from the Los Angeles Public Defender's office suggest that blacks were being charged under the law at a rate seventeen times that of whites.

Law Enforcement

Discussions of race and criminal justice often focus on confrontations between police and members of minority groups. Incidents such as the 1991 beating of Rodney King and its aftermath or the assault on Alfred Louima in a New York City police station in 1997 seem to represent entrenched prejudice in the criminal justice system. Historically, the poor and minorities have commonly been victims of "curbside justice" at the hands of law enforcement officers, and until the 1980's, when in *Tennessee v. Garner* the Supreme Court ruled the fleeing-felon rule unconstitutional, they were likely to be shot by the police as "fleeing felons." Studies published in the 1994 edition of the *Sourcebook of Criminal Justice Statistics* show that African Americans and Hispanics consistently have less favorable attitudes toward the police than do white Americans. These negative perceptions are based not only on incidents of police brutality or misconduct but also on a belief that police departments will not discipline the officers who are guilty but will instead form a wall of silence to protect them. Thus, for many minorities, misconduct goes beyond the actions of individual

---

Juvenile Arrests by Race, 1995
(percent)

	White	Black	American Indian	Asian American
U.S. population, ages 10-17	79	15	1	4
Most serious offense charged:				
Aggravated assault	56	42	1	1
Burglary	73	24	1	1
Drug abuse violations	64	35	1	1
Forcible rape	54	45	1	1
Larceny-theft	70	27	1	2
Motor vehicle theft	59	38	2	2
Murder	39	58	1	1
Robbery	38	60	1	2
Running away	77	19	1	3
Weapons charges	63	34	1	2

Note: Whites includes Hispanics. Figures may not add up to 100 percent because of rounding.

Source: Federal Bureau of Investigation, *Crime in the United States,* 1995.

Puerto Ricans protest against police brutality on the streets in New York City. Many police departments are instituting sensitivity training and community policing and increasing the number of minority members on their forces to prevent unfair treatment of blacks, Latinos, and other minorities.

racist police officers and extends to the institutional policies that refuse to make such officers accountable for their actions.

Many cities have adopted community policing strategies to address hostile relations between law enforcement officers and citizens, particularly those who reside in minority neighborhoods. Such programs use foot patrols to place police officers closer to the citizens in nonconfrontational situations. Officers work with community groups to deal with neighborhood problems and to reduce victimization. In some cases, minority police officers are assigned to minority neighborhoods.

Nationwide, the number of minority police officers has increased since the early 1970's when the 1972 amendments to the Civil Rights Act of 1964 prohibited racial or gender employment discrimination by state or local governments. The 1990 census indicated that 10 percent of police in the United States were African Americans and 5.2 percent were Hispanic. The percentages are far higher in cities such as Cleveland and Miami, where aggressive efforts have been made to recruit minority officers.

Race Issues in the Courts

In the courts, the connection between race and bail decisions, charges, jury selection, legal representation, and juvenile processing is ambiguous. Overt discrimination is seldom seen in most U.S. courtrooms, partly because in the 1960's, the Supreme Court repeatedly ruled that the constitutional rights of the accused must be respected by the state courts. On the other hand, such factors as the economic status of defendants and the quality of legal representation are indisputably linked. Research published in the *Journal of Quantitative Criminology* demonstrates that factors such as unemployment, a prior criminal record, and pretrial detention (the inability to make bail) have an impact on the probability of conviction. Members of minority groups, who are also more likely to be poor, suffer double disadvantages in the court system.

Race and Sentencing

Many observers of the U.S. criminal justice system have claimed that racial discrimination is clearly observable in sentencing. They charge specifically that African Americans are liable to receive harsher sentences than whites who are convicted of similar crimes. Others argue that blacks receive heavier sentences because they commit more and graver crimes. Mandatory federal sentences that impose penalties that are fifty times heavier for distribution of crack cocaine (used mostly by African Americans) than for powdered cocaine (used mostly by whites) seem to symbolize the disparity.

Studies of sentencing discrepancies such those conducted by Cassia Spohn, John Gruhl, and Susan Welch (1982) and Joan Petersilia (1983) reveal a complex situation in which blatant racism is seldom a factor but some judges take race into account by imposing harsher sentences on African Americans and other minorities who commit violent crimes against whites and more lenient sentences when victims are members of minority groups. In some jurisdictions, in marginal cases, whites are more likely to get probation, and blacks are more likely to be sent to prison. With respect to juvenile processing, white youths are more apt to be released to their parents, while a juvenile facility is a more probable destination for minority youths.

Examinations of the correlation of race with the death penalty show one consistent pattern. As the widely respected and frequently quoted studies done by David Baldus, George Woodworth, and Charles Pulaski, Jr., in 1990 showed, those who murder whites are more likely to receive a capital sentence than those who murder African Americans. On several occasions, the Supreme Court has been asked to rule on the constitutionality of the death penalty given the racial disparity in its use. Although the Court acknowledged in *McCleskey v. Kemp* (1987) that there was statistical evidence of race as a factor in the application of capital punishment, it refused to find the discrimination unconstitutional.

Implications

The United States has one of the highest rates of incarceration in the world, and minorities are disproportionately included among those confined. Although minorities have always been overrepresented in U.S. prisons, the disparity has increased dramatically since the 1980's. During the 1990's, more African Americans were under the supervision of the correctional system (in jail or prison, on probation or parole) than were enrolled in college. Hispanics were imprisoned at twice their representation in the general population. It is impossible to ignore the implications for the future, if sizable numbers of young people receive their higher education in a correctional institution rather than on a college campus.

Most observers attribute this growth in incarceration to the war on drugs. Law enforcement agencies at both the federal and state levels have focused their efforts on visible and open drug trafficking, the sort that occurs in poor, minority neighborhoods. They make more arrests in such communities than in affluent or suburban areas, where drug use is likely to be less obvious. The numbers of arrests, coupled with mandatory sentences for drug offenses, help to account for the expanded minority populations in prisons.

In examining the issues of race and criminal justice, many scholars have concluded that less overt racial discrimination occurs in the system than did in the past. Changes in the legal status of minority groups, Supreme Court decisions protecting the rights of the accused, and political action by African American, Hispanic, and other ethnic groups have helped to reduce discrimination. However, discrimination remains a factor in accounting for the disparate experiences of whites and minorities at all stages of the criminal justice system, from encounters with the police to charging to sentencing. Coupled with the economic biases inherent in the system, race and color continue to influence Americans' experiences of crime and punishment.

Mary Welek Atwell

Core Resources

The Color of Justice: Race, Ethnicity, and Crime in America, by Samuel Walker, Cassia Spohn, and Miriam DeLeone (Belmont, Calif.: Wadsworth, 1996), is an excellent introduction to contextual discrimination in the criminal justice system. Jerome G. Miller's *Search and Destroy* (New York: Cambridge, 1996) finds systematic discrimination in all facets of criminal justice. In *Unequal Justice: A Question of Color* (Bloomington: University of Indiana, 1988), Coramae Richey Mann focuses on how minorities experience the criminal justice system. She maintains that the system reflects the racism prevalent in American society. In *The Myth of a Racist Criminal Justice System* (Monterey, Calif.: Brooks/Cole, 1987), William Wilbanks reviewed literature on the system and concluded that charges of racism within criminal justice are false. Andrew Hacker's *Two Nations: Black and White, Separate, Hostile, Unequal* (New York: Ballantine, 1992) examines inequality throughout American society and looks especially at the relationship between interracial crime and inequality. Studies of sentencing patterns include Cassia Spohn, John Gruhl, and Susan Welch's "The Effect of Race on Sentencing: A Re-examination of an Unsettled Question," in *Law & Society Review* (vol. 16, 1981-1982), Joan Petersilia's *Racial Disparities in the Criminal Justice System* (Santa Monica, Calif.: Rand Corporation, 1983), and David C. Baldus, George Woodworth, and Charles A. Pulaska, Jr.'s *Equal Justice and the Death Penalty* (Boston: Northeastern University Press, 1990).

See also: Crack cocaine; Criminal justice system; Discrimination: racial and ethnic; Drugs and racial/ethnic relations; Jury nullification; Jury selection; King, Rodney, case; *McCleskey v. Kemp*; Police brutality.

Criminal justice system

Significance: The apparent unequal treatment of members of racial minorities by criminal justice officials contributes to tension and conflict in racial and ethnic relations. Members of racial minorities become angry and distrustful, and stereotyped images about the criminal tendencies of African Americans and Hispanics are reinforced in white people's minds.

Members of racial minority groups are overrepresented among those arrested, charged, convicted, and incarcerated for crimes. Although some commentators claim that the overrepresentation of minorities reflects their greater tendency to commit crimes, other analysts see disparities providing evidence of racial bias in the actions of legislators, police officers, prosecutors, and judges. Certain criminal laws, especially those concerning drug offenses, target minority neighborhoods for investigations and arrests. Police officers, prosecutors, and judges use discretion in arresting, charging, and sentencing offenders. When these discretionary decisions are affected by racial bias, unequal treatment will result. The appearance of unequal treatment in the justice system produces conflict in racial and ethnic relations as minorities express anger at white officials and many whites continue to believe that minorities are prone to commit crimes.

Historical Racial Bias

For most of U.S. history, the justice system openly discriminated against racial minorities, especially African Americans. Following the Civil War, the Fourteenth Amendment was added to the Constitution in 1868 to guarantee "equal protection of the law" for all people. However, African Americans and other minorities were still victimized by unequal treatment throughout the country. For example, they were often excluded from service on juries. As a result, all-white juries controlled verdicts in criminal cases, frequently punishing innocent minority group members for crimes they did not commit while freeing white offenders who committed crimes against African Americans and other minority citizens. Cities refused to hire minorities as police officers, and their all-white police forces used arrest and search powers in discriminatory ways to intimidate and harass African Americans, Hispanics, and others. In prisons, minority prisoners were sometimes kept separate from white inmates and subjected to harsher conditions.

The long-term legacy of racial bias in the criminal justice system had destructive consequences for racial and ethnic relations. The Civil Rights movement of the 1950's and 1960's led many minority group members to question racial discrimination in all spheres of society and demand equal treatment as promised by the equal protection clause of the Fourteenth Amendment. The criminal justice system was affected by the growing sense that minority groups were no longer willing to accept second-class treatment. In the late 1960's, cities throughout the United States exploded in full-scale riots, frequently precipitated by a shooting, arrest, or other action by a white police officer directed against an African American. Investigations into the causes of these riots recognized that the virtually all-white police forces in many cities contributed to the tensions underlying the civil disturbances. Many cities began to recruit minority police officers and train their officers to have greater understanding of racial and ethnic relations, either because they recognized that such actions would benefit their cities or because judges ordered such ac-

tions as a result of discrimination lawsuits. Similar problems were revealed in prisons, especially after the 1971 uprising at Attica prison in New York.

Intentional racial discrimination is much less of a problem than it was before the 1970's. Changes in the 1970's and 1980's reduced but did not eliminate the problems of racial bias in the criminal justice system. As indicated by the Los Angeles riots of 1992, which were sparked by the acquittals of white police officers who were videotaped beating an African American motorist repeatedly, unhappiness about perceived racial bias and discrimination in the criminal justice system continues to produce significant conflict within American society.

Racial Bias in Criminal Laws

Criminal laws are enacted by legislatures, either state legislatures or Congress. Although criminal laws are written in a race-neutral fashion so that they apply equally to everyone, the actual motivation for and consequences of some criminal laws may reflect subtle racial or ethnic biases. For example, as described by Richard J. Bonnie and Charles H. Whitebread II in *The Marihuana Conviction: A History of Marihuana Prohibition in the United States* (1974), drug laws outlawing marijuana were initially created because of bias against Mexican Americans who used the drug. By contrast, alcohol, used by the affluent whites who controlled legislatures, remained legal except during the brief period of Prohibition (1920-1933).

Apparent bias in the creation of criminal laws is not evident only in marijuana laws enacted in the first half of the twentieth century. The latter decades of the century saw a parallel development in the enactment of laws concerning crack cocaine. In the 1980's, Congress responded to concerns about the dangers of crack cocaine by increasing the punishments for selling and possessing it. Therefore, under federal sentencing guidelines, much more severe punishments are imposed on crack cocaine offenders than upon offenders who sell and possess the powder form of cocaine. In fact, despite the fact that crack and powder cocaine laws concern the same drug, an offender would need to sell or possess one hundred times as much powder cocaine in order to receive as severe a sentence as a crack offender. The 100-to-1 powder-to-crack ratio that determines prison sentences has a significant racial impact because the vast majority of those prosecuted for crack offenses are African Americans, and powder cocaine is the form most usually involved in the prosecution of whites.

The disparities caused by this sentencing law are evident in the average drug sentences received by African Americans and whites in the federal courts. For example, according to the *Compendium of Federal Justice Statistics, 1994*, the average sentence for white drug offenders was 66.4 months and for Hispanic drug offenders 70.6 months. By contrast, the average sentence for African American drug offenders was 106.7 months. This disparity was produced, in part, by the racial and ethnic impact of cocaine sentencing laws because, as reported in the U.S. Sentencing Commission's 1995 annual report, 88 percent of offenders sentenced for crack offenses were African Americans, and nearly 71 percent of offenders sentenced for powdered cocaine offenses were white and Hispanic. Several African American defendants alleged that prosecutors targeted minority group members for crack cocaine prosecutions while ignoring unlawful activities by whites, but the U.S. Supreme Court refused to let them request access to prosecutors' files in order to seek evidence of racial discrimination (*United States v. Armstrong*, 1996). Whites who learn about the higher rates of convictions and longer sentences for minority defendants may become distrustful of African Americans and Hispanics, whom they may stereotype as lawbreakers, if they do not know how the design of drug laws and choices made by police and prosecutors create disparities in convictions and sentences.

Racial Bias in Law Enforcement

Police officers use discretion in making stops and arrests. If individual officers presume that minorities tend to commit crimes, then those officers will use their discretion to stop and question African Americans, Hispanics, and other nonwhites. Some police agencies instruct their officers to stop members of racial minority groups because they use "profiles" to identify possible drug suspects. Profiles are a list of characteristics that the police believe are associated with drug trafficking. Included among these characteristics are membership in a racial minority group and operation of an expensive motor vehicle. Police officers sometimes stop drivers, claiming that the driver committed a minor infraction such as failure to use a turn signal, when in fact the drivers have been stopped because they fit the profile for drug traffickers. The use of such profiles has led police to detain and question many innocent African Americans and Hispanics, especially successful middle-and upper-class people such as doctors, lawyers, and business executives, because these people often own expensive cars. The use of profiles based on race and ethnicity has caused tremendous anger against police officers on the part of many innocent minority group members who feel targeted for police harassment because of their race and financial success.

Racial Bias in Courts

Prosecutors and judges make various discretionary decisions that determine the fates of defendants drawn into the criminal courts. If those decisions are influenced by racial biases, then the seriousness of charges, amounts set to gain release on bail, frequency of convictions, and severity of sentences may adversely affect members of racial minority groups. In addition, if minority group members are poor, their fates may be adversely affected by the inadequate or unenthusiastic representation provided by some defense attorneys who are appointed to represent poor defendants.

Prosecutors must decide whether to charge suspects and which charges to pursue. In some cases, prosecutors may decide to divert suspects out of criminal prosecution by dropping charges and sending people into various programs focused on education, substance abuse, job training, or psychological treatment. Prosecutors have historically favored middle-class suspects in sending people to these diversion programs, which spare suspects from having criminal convictions on their records. Because racial minority group members are overrepresented among poor people, in many counties they are less likely to benefit from diversion programs and instead receive criminal convictions and punishment. Prosecutors' decisions to offer favorable plea bargains or sentence recommendations similarly disadvantage poor minority defendants because such arrangements more frequently favor middle-class offenders, especially when defendants can afford to pay for private attorneys to provide vigorous representation. By contrast, public defenders and other attorneys appointed to represent poor people may handle hundreds of cases simultaneously. As a result, they may spend little time on each case and poor defendants may not receive equal treatment in plea bargains and sentence recommendations. Thus, the close links between race and poverty in the United States can produce racial impacts on the treatment of defendants in the court system.

Research on prosecutors' charging decisions, especially in death penalty cases, indicates that prosecutors often value the lives of white victims more than those of black victims. In *Equal Justice and the Death Penalty* (1990), for example, David Baldus, George Woodworth, and Charles Pulaski found that Georgia prosecutors were most likely to pursue the death penalty when African American defendants were accused of killing white victims and least likely to pursue the death penalty in cases with African American victims. Prosecutors' extra concern for cases involving white victims may reflect subconscious biases rather than open racial prejudice, yet the ultimate impact is to impose more serious charges and harsher punishments against minority offenders.

Racial discrimination may arise in decisions about bail. Bail is the amount of money that a defendant must supply to gain release while awaiting trial. If the defendant does not appear in court, the money is forfeited.

Some studies indicate that judges set higher bail amounts for minority suspects than for white suspects. As a result, these minority suspects are less likely to gain their freedom pending trial and less able to make contributions to the preparation of a defense by locating witnesses and providing other assistance to defense attorneys. In addition, the families of jailed suspects suffer significant harm because they lose income and may even be evicted from apartments when a family breadwinner is unable to work while in jail awaiting trial.

Discrimination may also occur during sentencing. Some studies have found that white judges are more likely to sentence African Americans than whites to prison, even when the whites are convicted of similar charges. Whenever judges have discretion in sentencing, there will be disparities between the punishments received by similarly situated offenders. If a judge's decision is affected by either deliberate or subconscious racial biases, then members of racial minority groups may receive harsher treatment. Some states have attempted to combat such discrimination by creating sentencing guidelines that instruct the judges on how they must sentence offenders for each charge. Although such guidelines have reduced the possibility of racial discrimi-

nation in sentencing decisions, they have not eliminated the possibility of racial bias because prosecutors still use discretion in setting the original charges that determine the path each case follows.

The U.S. Supreme Court
If individual prosecutors and judges possess racial biases, those biases may lead to discriminatory decisions in charging and sentencing defendants. If such discriminatory practices occur, it is up to higher courts to stop them. The U.S. Supreme Court earned a reputation as the governing institution responsible for stopping discrimination and injustice because of its actions in school desegregation cases. However, the U.S. Supreme Court has failed to guard against the continued existence of racial bias in many aspects of the criminal justice system. For example, extensive studies established that racial bias affects death penalty sentencing in Georgia by imposing capital punishment much more frequently against African American killers of white victims than either African American or white killers of African American victims. Rather than recognize this systemic discrimination as a violation of the right to equal protection, the Supreme Court simply declared that defen-

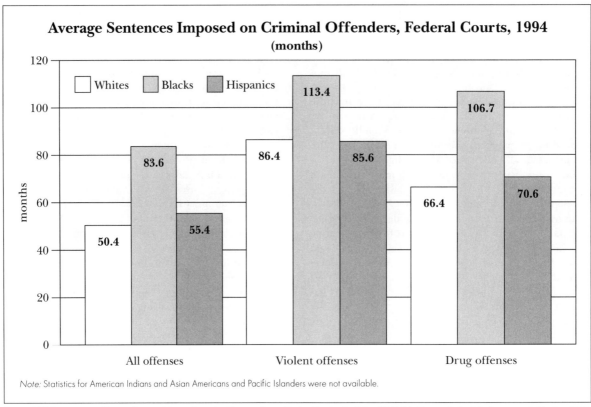

Average Sentences Imposed on Criminal Offenders, Federal Courts, 1994
(months)

Whites ☐ Blacks ☐ Hispanics ☐

All offenses: Whites 50.4, Blacks 83.6, Hispanics 55.4
Violent offenses: Whites 86.4, Blacks 113.4, Hispanics 85.6
Drug offenses: Whites 66.4, Blacks 106.7, Hispanics 70.6

Note: Statistics for American Indians and Asian Americans and Pacific Islanders were not available.

Source: U.S. Department of Justice, Bureau of Justice Statistics, *Compendium of Federal Justice Statistics, 1994.* Washington, D.C.: U.S. Department of Justice, 1997.

dants cannot use statistical studies to demonstrate the existence of racial discrimination (*McCleskey v. Kemp*, 1987). Although the Supreme Court says that prospective jurors cannot be excluded from jury service because of their race, the Supreme Court permits prosecutors to evade the rule by presenting other reasons—when jurors may actually be excluded because of their race. Such exclusions may be permitted, as long as the prosecutors do not admit that the exclusions are based on race (*Purkett v. Elem*, 1995). In the prison setting, the Supreme Court relaxed rules for the protection of inmates' religious freedom in order to permit prison officials to keep Black Muslim prisoners from attending an important weekly prayer service (*O'Lone v. Estate of Shabazz*, 1987).

Although the Supreme Court asserts that it has neutral justifications for these and other decisions, the adverse consequences for minorities drawn into contact with the criminal justice system led many observers to conclude that the Supreme Court sometimes ignores unequal treatment within the criminal justice system. As a result, white officials and citizens continue to employ racial stereotypes, such as the use of profiles previously discussed, assuming that minority group members are prone to commit crimes. Minorities are becoming increasingly frustrated and angry about the racial bias they experience in the justice system.   *Christopher E. Smith*

Core Resources

Gunnar Myrdal's *An American Dilemma: The Negro Problem and Modern Democracy* (New York: Harper Brothers, 1944) describes widespread racial bias in the criminal justice system during the first half of the twentieth century. An analysis of racial bias underlying sentencing for cocaine offenses is presented by Michael Tonry in *Malign Neglect: Race, Crime, and Punishment in America* (New York: Oxford University Press, 1995). Two books provide thorough reviews of scholarly studies on the existence of racial bias and discrimination in the criminal justice system, Coramae Richey Mann's *Unequal Justice: A Question of Color* (Bloomington: Indiana University Press, 1988) and Samuel Walker, Cassia Spohn, and Miriam DeLeone's *The Color of Justice: Race, Ethnicity, and Crime in America* (Belmont, Calif.: Wadsworth Publishing, 1996). In contrast, in *The Myth of a Racist Criminal Justice System* (Monterey, Calif.: Brooks/Cole, 1987), William Wilbanks argues that apparent racial disparities in sentencing and other aspects of the criminal justice system are not caused by racial bias. In his comprehensive survey of the justice system in *Race, Crime, and the Law* (New York: Pantheon, 1997), Randall Kennedy seeks the middle ground by highlighting biased aspects of the criminal justice system but noting improvements in the system and concluding that not all racial disparities necessarily stem from policies that were intended to cause discrimination.

See also: Crack cocaine; Crime and race/ethnicity; Discrimination: racial and ethnic; Drugs and racial/ethnic relations; Jury nullification; Jury selection; *McCleskey v. Kemp*; Police brutality; Race card; Simpson, O. J., trial.

Critical race theory

Critical race theory was a response to the mid-1970's conservative, reactionary attack on the achievements of the civil rights struggle and the failure of liberalism to stave off this attack, both ideologically and in public policy. This response was initially led by scholars of color such as Derrick Bell, Mari Matsuda, Charles Lawrence, and Kimberle Crenshaw, as well as white theorist Alan David Freeman.

Critical race theory argues that white racism is a hegemonic, socially and historically constructed cultural force in American society. This racism expresses itself in popular culture by believed myths, stories, legal rules, and the institutional disposition of prestige and power via the concept of whiteness. Critical race theorists use popular culture to deconstruct this hegemony (ideological, cultural, and political domination) by developing a broader, alternate reality through writing fiction and nonfiction. They also combine critical legal theory with an analysis of how law constructs race and gender and thus reveal how liberal legalism (rule of law/equal protection) advances white domination and interests at the same time that it purports to advance the civil rights of minorities and women. In fact, Bell and Freeman argue that white power is solidified by the narrow constraints of civil rights law as it has been interpreted by the courts. According to critical legal theory, too many justices in black robes, either consciously or unconsciously, subscribe to myths of white supremacy, and in this context fact-sensitive evidence makes formal equality a mask that hides how "whiteness," both unintentional and intentional, contours legal doctrine.

Critical race theory's major goal is to be antithetical to both liberal and conservative scholarly assumptions about neutral and objective, discursive, detached intellectual inquiry. Critical race theorists reject these values and see themselves as politicized, counterinsurgent scholars who create oppositional worldviews aimed at the liberation of all oppressed societal groups. For example, these "race crits" argue that the concept of meritocracy is fallacious—that whether discrimination is intentional or unintentional is immaterial in a society in which wealth, education, and power are distributed and affirmed by the workings of a hierarchy of white over black. By revealing, through a process called "internal critique," the internal contradictions of the concept of meritocracy, race crits hope that this clarification will create a "crisis of logic," or demonstrate the lack of logic in treating rich and poor alike, as both can be potentially prosecuted for violating a neutral/objective law against begging for bread in the streets.

In demonstrating the intersectional contexts of race, class, and gender, race crits seek to challenge the legitimacy of white supremacy and its most potent tactic of using the powerful ideology of "color blindness." This idea is powerful because of its varied sources, one of which is Justice John M. Harlan's dissent in the 1896 *Plessy v. Ferguson* case (in which Harlan touted the ideal of a color-blind society) and the other being the Reverend Martin Luther King, Jr.'s often-quoted clarion that one should be judged by the content of one's character and not by the color of one's skin. Race crits argue that race consciousness is so hegemonic that to ignore what one's optic processes immediately perceive and automatically connect to value judgments is actually to perpetuate white supremacy. The perpetuation of this myth is effected by ignoring the fact that every minority individual is forced by whiteness into a dual consciousness. The social and historical context of this duality is faced every day by blacks and other racial and ethnic minorities, such as when a person of color must decide whether to buy "flesh-colored" bandages or when he or she is recognized as the "first" black, Chicano, or female judge, lawyer, or prosecutor. The falsity of color blindness is exposed in such situations.

The development of critical race theory has experienced some major turning points: In 1980, students of color at Harvard University confronted the administration over the teaching of an alternative course on race and law; future race crits, including Lawrence, Matsuda, Crenshaw, and others, were involved in this incident. Another turning point was the rise of critical legal studies conferences and the insurgency by feminist crits and race crits within this movement by the 1986 and 1987 conferences. The 1987 conference, coordinated by a consortium of Los Angeles area law schools, was entitled "The Sounds of Silence." The unsilenced voices of the race crits were heard in a plethora of workshops at this conference, and selected papers presented were published in a special edition of the *Harvard Civil Rights and Civil Liberties Review* (spring, 1987). Another major event was a critical race theory conference at Mills College in Oakland, California, 1993, where various scholars met to discuss critical race theory. Out of this conference two different volumes on critical race theory were produced: *Critical Race Theory: The Cutting Edge* (1995), edited by Richard Delgado, and *Critical Race Theory: The Key Writings That Formed the Movement* (1995), edited by Kimberle Crenshaw, Neil Gotanda, Gary Peller, and Kendall Thomas. *Malik Simba*

See also: "Color-blind" society; Color coding; Meritocracy myth; *Plessy v. Ferguson*; White supremacist groups.

Crown Heights conflicts

Crown Heights, a racially mixed section of Brooklyn, New York, began to experience civil unrest in the late 1980's. Many of the residents are either poor black immigrants from Caribbean countries or Lubavitchers, Orthodox (Hasidic) Jews who maintain a strong religious identity that is reflected in their dress and their insularity. Both groups have been subject to stereotyping and victimized by discrimination, from both within and without the Crown Heights community. African American leaders charge that the Lubavitchers have received better treatment from local authorities than that accorded black residents, and Hasidic leaders have countered that black anti-Semitism has made Lubavitchers victims of street crimes and subject to continual harassment.

The racial unrest erupted into full-scale rioting in the summer of 1991, on the heels of the accidental killing of a seven-year-old Guyanese American youth named Gavin Cato. On the evening of August 19, a car carrying the Lubavitcher Grand Rebbe and Menachem Schneerson, a Hasidic spiritual leader, ran a red light at the intersection of President Street and Utica Avenue, striking and killing Cato and injuring his cousin, Angela. As a crowd gathered at the scene, a private Jewish ambulance whisked away the Hasidic driver, Yosef Lifsh, and his two passengers. Their departure spurred an angry reaction, leading, three hours later, to the fatal stabbing of Yankel Rosenbaum, a visiting Hasidic professor from Australia, and the arrest of his alleged attacker, a sixteen-year-old Trinidadian American and Brooklyn resident, Lemrick Nelson, Jr.

In the predawn hours of August 20, after Rosenbaum's death at Kings County Hospital, protests escalated into mob violence, with blacks and Hasidic Jews fighting with words, stones, and bottles, ignoring police efforts to stop the rioting. The violence continued through the next two days, fed by the rumor (later shown to be true) that the Hasidic driver, Lifsh, had left on a plane bound for Israel. Black leaders, including the Reverend Al Sharpton and Alton Maddox, demanded the arrest and return of Lifsh, and their followers rebuffed the efforts of New York mayor David Dinkins and police commissioner Lee Brown to restore peace, especially after learning that Nelson had been charged with second-degree murder in Rosenbaum's death. By August 24, rioting finally gave way to protest marches and an uneasy peace maintained by auxiliary police units that had been sent into Crown Heights to restore order.

In the months following the demonstrations, both groups complained that the police and city officials did little to solve the community's problems. In September, the Brooklyn grand jury refused to indict Lifsh in the death of Cato, angering the black citizens and their leaders. More unrest followed in October, 1992, when Nelson was acquitted of all charges in Rosenbaum's death. The Hasidic Jews protested and within a month filed a class-action suit against the city government on the grounds of unfair treatment in the 1991 riots.

The disturbances led to investigations at both the state and national levels. One major New York report issued in July, 1993, by Richard Girgenti, state director of criminal justice, was highly critical of both Mayor Dinkins and Commissioner Brown. The report, forwarded to the U.S. Attorney General, also led to ongoing Justice Department investigations of possible civil rights violations.

John W. Fiero

See also: Canarsie riots; Jewish-African American relations.

Cuban-African American relations

> **Significance:** The tension that arose between African Americans and post-1959 Cuban refugees in the Miami area of Florida (Dade County) represents an illuminating case study of the effects of immigration on urban racial and ethnic relations in the late twentieth century.

In the late twentieth century, the attitude of African Americans and their organizations to immigration was one of ambivalence. As a minority group, African Americans could not consistently oppose immigration as a threat to some imagined American cultural or ethnic purity. Yet many African Americans, struggling against discrimination and disadvantage, feared immigrants as competitors for scarce jobs and public services. In Dade County, Florida, unrestricted immigration from Cuba after Fidel Castro took power in 1959 fed Miami blacks' anxieties about economic displacement and political disempowerment. The black riots that erupted in Miami in 1980, 1982, and 1989, although ostensibly sparked by police brutality, were widely ascribed by contemporary commentators to resentment against Cuban refugees.

Racial Identity of Cuban Refugees
Tensions between African Americans and black immigrants from Jamaica and Haiti have been mitigated somewhat by a shared African heritage; with the refugee flow from Cuba, however, this factor did not come into play as much. When Castro took power in Cuba in 1959, people of full or partial African descent constituted nearly 40 percent of the total population of Cuba; yet 90 percent or more of the Cuban refugees of the 1960's and early 1970's were white. It was not until the Mariel boatlift of May-September, 1980, that the proportion of Afro-Cubans in the refugee flow came to approximate that of the island's population.

The Federal Government and Cuban Refugees
By the beginning of 1980, many of the Cuban refugees of the 1960's and early 1970's, who had arrived nearly penniless, had grown prosperous. Such success was due to the relatively high proportion of professionals and entrepreneurs among the earliest refugees, the refugees' hard work, and the generous assistance (about $2.6 billion between 1972 and 1976) that the refugees, as defectors from a communist regime, received from the federal government to help defray the costs of vocational training and retraining, transportation, and resettlement. African Americans complained that the refugees received more assistance than either other immigrants or poor native-born Americans did. The Mariel boatlift refugees of May to September, 1980, and refugees who arrived after that year did not, however, receive as much government help as the earlier waves of immigrants.

African Americans also complained about the way refugees benefited from federal programs not specifically targeted at refugees. When affirmative action policies were implemented in the late 1960's to provide set-asides for minority businesses, Hispanics were considered to be a minority and Cubans were Hispanics; hence, refugee-owned businesses were judged to qualify as minority-owned businesses. Local blacks resented what they saw as poaching by white newcomers on an entitlement originally intended for African Americans.

Cubans' Immigration Status as Bone of Contention
From 1959 to 1980, hardly any Cuban reaching U.S. shores was deported. The Cuban Adjustment Act of 1966 enabled all Cuban refugees to change their status to that of permanent resident after one year of living in the United States; other immigrants did not enjoy this privilege. After 1972, more and more Haitians, like Cubans, tried to reach the United States. Cubans fleeing by boat were always welcomed. In contrast, Haitians fleeing by boat were unceremoniously sent back to Haiti if intercepted at sea, detained in prison if they reached Florida, and often deported. Although the official justification for the disparity in treatment was ideological (Cuba was communist; Haiti was not), many Miami black activists

perceived racism. Many Cuban escapees were white; almost all Haitian escapees were black. In May, 1995, U.S. president Bill Clinton officially ended the privileged status of Cuban refugees. When the first Cuban escapees were sent back to Cuba, on May 10, Miami Cubans staged a four-day action of civil disobedience; Miami's native-born blacks stayed away from the protest.

Anti-Cuban Animosity and Urban Rioting

Between 1968 and 1989, there were several episodes of rioting by black Miamians, the bloodiest of which took place in 1980. The riots of 1980, 1982, and 1989 were widely attributed by journalists and scholars to the resentment of Miami blacks against Cuban refugees, although this was only one reason. All the riots stemmed from responses to alleged police misuse of force. In 1982 and 1989, the officers who used force were Hispanic, and Cubans did tend to rally around Hispanic police officers accused of brutality. Yet conflict between blacks and police officers had existed even before the mass arrival of Cuban refugees. Although one victim of black violence in the 1980 riot was a Cuban refugee, other victims were non-Hispanic whites: The mob was as much anti-white as anti-Cuban. Nor were native-born blacks the only ones to complain about police brutality. In 1992, an incident of police violence against a Haitian in a Cuban-owned store aroused protest; and in 1990, Miami's Puerto Ricans also rioted against an alleged police abuse of force.

Job Displacement

Whether Cuban refugees gained occupationally at the expense of Miami's blacks is a controversial issue, although local black leaders lodged complaints about such displacement as early as the early 1960's. Allegations that Cubans ousted blacks from service jobs in hotels and restaurants were met by counterallegations that blacks were themselves leaving such jobs voluntarily and that the percentage of Miami blacks in white-collar jobs had increased by 1980. By founding many new businesses, Cuban refugees created jobs; many such jobs, however, went to fellow refugees rather than to African Americans. As the Hispanic population grew and trade links with Latin America expanded, native-born blacks were hurt by the job requirement of fluency in Spanish. Although the Miami area economic pie grew during the 1960's and 1970's, blacks' slice of that pie, scholars concede, was stagnant; compared with pre-1980 Cuban refugees, they suffered in 1980 from greater poverty and unemployment and had a lower rate of entrepreneurship.

Black-Cuban Conflict in Local Politics

From 1960 to 1990, the Hispanic percentage of Dade County's population (most, but not all of it, Cuban) rose from barely 10 percent to 49 percent; the black percentage of the county's population never rose above 20 percent. By the late 1970's, more and more Cuban refugees were becoming naturalized U.S. citizens, gaining both the right to vote and a decisive weight in local politics. In 1983, the Puerto Rican-born mayor dismissed the black city manager, replacing him with a Cuban. Cuban American candidates defeated African American candidates for the posts of mayor of Miami in 1985, Dade County Schools superintendent in 1990, Dade County district attorney in 1993, and mayor of Dade County in 1996. The Cuban influx into elective politics prevented a black takeover of city hall (as had taken place in Atlanta, Georgia, and Detroit, Michigan), thereby reducing the chances for black businesspeople to benefit from municipal contracts. Yet African Americans' powerlessness was relative: They could vote and affect the outcome of elections.

The Nelson Mandela Affair and the Miami Boycott

In spring of 1990, Mayor Xavier Suar persuaded the Miami city government to withdraw its official welcome to Nelson Mandela, the leader of the black liberation struggle in South Africa, who was then touring the United States. Mandela, in a television interview, had praised Castro. Partly in response to this slap at Mandela, a Miami black civil rights leader, H. T. Smith, called for a nationwide boycott by black organizations of Miami-area hotels; this boycott was remarkably effective. It was ended in 1993 with an agreement promising greater efforts to employ blacks in Miami's hospitality industry.

Complexities of Miami-area Interethnic Relations

Dade's County's politics were not simply a Cuban-African American struggle. Sometimes blacks saw non-Hispanic whites as allies against the Cubans: In his losing bid for Congress against a Cuban American in 1989, the non-Hispanic white candidate won most of the black votes. Sometimes blacks saw both Cubans and non-Hispanic whites as oppressors of blacks. In a lawsuit that met with success in 1992, blacks and Cubans cooperated in an effort to make the Dade County Commission more representative of ethnic minorities. Blacks did not always form a united front against the Cubans: In a 1980 referendum ending the provision of Spanish-language documents and services by the Dade County government, black voters split, 44 percent for the proposition and 56 percent against. (Bilingualism was restored in 1993.) Haitians and native-born blacks did not agree on all issues; among non-Hispanic whites, white ethnic migrants from the North did not always agree with white Anglo-Saxon Protestants of southern background; and some of Miami's non-Cuban Hispanics resented Cuban predominance.

Comparison with Overall Black-Hispanic Relations

In other major U.S. cities, Cubans were, if present at all, a smaller part of the larger Hispanic group. Only in Miami did Hispanics build up a powerful political machine; hence, black resentment of Hispanic political power played little role in race relations elsewhere. The police brutality issue also operated differently: in Compton, California, Washington, D.C., and Detroit, Michigan, for example, there were complaints, in the early 1990's, about alleged brutality by black police officers against Hispanics.   *Paul D. Mageli*

Core Resources

In *Imagining Miami* (Charlottesville: University Press of Virginia, 1997), the best introductory study, Sheila Croucher attacks the notion that either the black or the Cuban community is a monolith. Her analysis of the Mandela affair and the subsequent boycott is especially enlightening. Marvin Dunn's *Black Miami in the Twentieth Century* (Tallahassee: University of Florida Press, 1997) is informative on the riots. On the politics of bilingualism, consult Max Castro's essay in Guillermo J. Grenier and Alexis Stepick's *Miami Now!* (Tallahassee: University Press of Florida, 1992). The displacement thesis is presented most clearly in historian Raymond A. Mohl's "On the Edge: Blacks and Hispanics in Metropolitan Miami Since 1959," *Florida Historical Quarterly* (vol. 69, no. 1, July, 1990). For rebuttals of this thesis, consult chapter 3 of Alex Stepick and Alejandro Portes's *City on the Edge: The Transformation of Miami* (Berkeley: University of California Press, 1993) and Alex Stepick and Guillermo Grenier's "Cubans in Miami," in *In the Barrios: Latinos and the Underclass Debate*, edited by Joan Moore and Raquel Pinderhughes (New York: Russell Sage Foundation, 1993). *City on the Edge* is also informative on Miami's Haitians.

See also: Afro-Caribbeans; Cuban Americans; English-only and official English movements; Haitians and Haitian refugees; Mariel boatlift; Miami riots of 1980; Refugees and racial/ethnic relations; Refugees: U.S. policy.

Cuban American National Foundation

The Cuban American National Foundation (CANF), an association of Cuban American exiles founded in 1981, has as its professed purpose the collection and dissemination of information on issues of interest to the Cuban people, grassroots lobbying on behalf of its Cuban American membership, and the promotion of freedom and democracy in Cuba and the world. CANF maintains offices in Miami and Washington, D.C., a library, and a speakers' bureau; supports education and research; publishes a newsletter; and hosts lectures, symposia, and an annual conference.

Although CANF's stated function is to provide a valuable cultural function on behalf of the Cuban exile community in the United States, this powerful organization is known for adopting a hardline extremist stance against Cuba and the regime of Fidel Castro. Miami multimillionaire Jorge Mas Canosa, who headed the group until his death in November, 1997, prided himself on supporting wide-ranging terrorist activity directed at the Castro regime, including assassination attempts, and boasted of dictating foreign policy to the U.S. government, claiming that he frequently edited White House briefings on Cuba. A right-wing Republican, Mas Canosa was a favored client of the administration of Ronald Reagan, which supported his anti-Castro program. Proud of his Central Intelligence Agency ties, the multimillionaire was infamous for his arrogance toward anyone who did not bow to his will, and he engaged in retribution and litigious vendettas against these people and their families. In 1992, he successfully lobbied the Democratic presidential campaign of Bill Clinton, gaining backing for his extremist political program in return for financial and political support.

CANF was the result of an initiative passed by the National Security Council intended to found an organization that would popularize Reagan's Latin American policy. CANF has become a nonprofit organization and thus is exempt from taxation. It garners major government grant funding, which it uses to fund its political supporters and programs. In 1987, CANF was successful in obtaining millions of dollars in governmental support from Congress for Television Marti, an anticommunist television broadcast, although its programs do not reach Cubans in Cuba. It was behind the Cuban Democracy Act of 1992, aimed at restricting trade with Cuba, and successfully blocked the nomination of Cuban American lawyer Mario Baeza as assistant secretary of state for inter-American affairs in 1993 because he was not sufficiently critical of Castro. However, most Cuban Americans no longer share CANF's extreme opposition to the Castro regime and would like to explore peaceful alternatives to the organization's past uncompromising position. It has been frequently observed that CANF duplicates the least attractive attributes of the Castro regime, which include suppression of free speech, oppression of political dissidents, human rights violations, and political elitism. United States policy toward Cuba, as it has been promulgated by CANF, is increasingly seen as anachronistic.   *Gloria Fulton*

See also: Cuban Americans; Cuban Revolution.

Cuban Americans

> **Significance:** Large numbers of Cuban refugees entered the United States in the second half of the nineteenth century and in the 1960's and 1980's. Their tightly knit, prosperous communities, and later, their sheer numbers, caused racial tension and conflict, particularly with African American communities in Miami.

In 1959, Fidel Castro led a popular revolt that toppled the government of Fulgencio Batista y Zaldívar in Cuba. A small number of Cubans who had sympathized with the Batista government fled to the United States. This tiny trickle of wealthy Cubans grew to torrential proportions as more and more people became dissatisfied with the new regime. The immigrants who came in this migratory wave, like those who came in the two that preceded it, met with discrimination and racial tensions in their new home.

Early Immigrants

Twice before, large numbers of Cubans had sought refuge from war by traveling to the United States and various Latin American nations. The first group left Cuba between 1868 and 1878 during the battle for independence known in Cuba as the Ten Years' War. Most of the Cubans went to the Florida cities of Key West and Tampa, although some located in New York City and New Orleans.

After the peace accord was signed in 1878, many Cubans returned to the island, although quite a large number remained in both Key West and Tampa (actually Ybor City) to work in the newly established tobacco factories.

These early immigrants—whose descendants still live in the area—formed tightly knit communities that revolved around the Catholic Church and Spanish culture. Because the principal reason for the migration had been political, not economic, most Cubans viewed their time in the United States as temporary. Perhaps for this reason, they assimilated to a lesser extent than most immigrant groups and did not adopt many American norms or much of the culture. This was a major cause of tension between Cubans and the established population.

The end of the nineteenth century brought another large influx of Cubans. When the Cuban War of Independence started in February, 1895, and as conditions on the island deteriorated, large numbers of Cubans migrated to the United States and Latin America. As in the previous migration, Cubans settled mostly in Florida and other large eastern American cities. This time, the immigrants did not suffer as much culture shock because the Cubans who remained behind after the end of the Ten Years' War provided a ready-made Cuban American community where they could locate.

Milestones in Cuban American History

Year	Event
1492	Explorer Christopher Columbus lands in Cuba.
1514	Settlement of Cuba begins.
1868-1878	The Ten Years' War is fought in Cuba, causing a large Cuban migration to the United States.
1895-1898	The Cuban War of Independence/Spanish-American War occurs. Many Cubans seek refuge in the United States.
1959	Fidel Castro takes control of Cuba through a revolution. Many supporters of Fulgencio Batista y Zaldívar leave.
1960	In January, the United States and Cuba sever diplomatic relations. A large migration of Cubans to Florida begins.
1961	The Bay of Pigs invasion takes place in April.
1962	The Missile Crisis occurs in October.
1964	President Johnson authorizes Freedom Flights from Cuba. Many more Cubans flee the island.
1980	The Mariel boatlift occurs. More than 125,000 Cubans leave the island on makeshift rafts and in boats rented by their relatives. Many criminals are included in these groups.
1989	The Soviet Union collapses.
1994	A smaller boatlift occurs, but President Bill Clinton puts an end to it by not granting the preferred status of refugee to future arrivals.

Twentieth Century

The Cuban War of Independence, which in the United States became known as the Spanish-American War (1898), lasted three years, during which Cuban exiles lived in communities separated in many ways from the local population. Then, in 1953, Fidel Castro began a revolt against the corrupt government of Fulgencio Batista y Zaldívar that resulted in the Cuban Revolution and Castro's socialization of the economy under a communist-allied government. By the early 1960's, when the wave of Cubans fleeing the Castro regime arrived, many of the Cuban Americans were second- or third-generation Americans and did not have a lot in common with the newer arrivals. Therefore, the post-Castro Cubans had to contend with the criticisms of the older, established Cuban Americans.

The first wave of post-Castro Cubans arrived immediately after Castro took over. Shortly after the United States and Cuba broke diplomatic relations in January, 1960, the next migratory wave began. In this wave were more than fifty thousand children without their parents, who were brought to the United States by a former president of Cuba and other Cubans, the U.S. Catholic Welfare Bureau, and Senator George A. Smathers of Florida.

The next large wave was made up of refugees who arrived on the Freedom Flights initiated by President Lyndon B. Johnson in the mid-1960's. Two daily flights brought thousands of Cubans, straining the economy of Florida, where most of them settled. Working-class Americans, especially African Americans in Miami, suffered when jobs were lost to workers willing to work for any wage simply to have employment. During this time, many Cubans, formerly professionals, worked menial jobs while they attended night school in order to perfect their English and perhaps return to their chosen professions.

In the 1970's, the number of Cuban refugees fell, and many earlier arrivals began to move away from Miami's Little Havana to its suburbs or to other southern cities. By the time the Mariel boatlift of 1980 started, the early refugees were enjoying a high standard of living and were able to help the new arrivals establish themselves. However, the boatlift strained the public resources of southern Florida and created racial tensions. A riot broke out in the African American community in Miami after the acquittal of a Hispanic police officer who shot an African American. After much destruction, order was restored although the underlying tension did not go away. Congress passed the 1980 Refugee Act, which substantially lowered the number of Cuban refugees that could be admitted each year.

Cuban Americans constitute the third largest Hispanic group in the United States, after Mexican Americans and Puerto Ricans. Because the earlier waves of

Cuban refugees row toward the USCG *Confidence* in August, 1994, about twenty-five miles off the coast of Cuba. Most Cuban Americans migrated for political reasons and were classified as refugees.

Cuban refugees were composed of middle- to upper-class Cubans, the south Florida area has experienced tremendous growth. Studies suggest that significant differences exist between refugees—like the Cubans—who migrate for political reasons and those who migrate for economic reasons.

The Cuban American community is very tightly knit, although its members vary greatly in their cultural affiliations: Some members follow Cuban customs and traditions; others tend to live more or less typical American lifestyles. One attribute that separates Cuban Americans from other immigrant groups is their staunchly anticommunist stance. Although other immigrant groups have softened their stance on communists in China or Vietnam, the Cuban American community, especially in Miami, has tended to view this change in stance as a weakness. This attitude is likely to prevail until the community is predominantly second- and third-generation Cuban Americans.   *Peter E. Carr*

Core Resources

For a very thorough review of Cuban Americans, see Thomas D. Boswell and James R. Curtis's *The Cuban American Experience* (Totowa, N.J.: Rowman & Allanheld,

1983). Other informative sources include John Crewdson's *The Tarnished Door: The New Immigrants and the Transformation of America* (New York: Times Books, 1983), Raul Moncarz and Jorge Antonio's "Cuban Immigration to the United States" in *Contemporary American Immigration,* edited by Dennis Laurence Cuddy (Boston: Twayne, 1982), Norman Zucker's "Contemporary American Immigration and Refugee Policy: An Overview," in *Journal of Children in Contemporary Society* (vol.15, no.3, Spring, 1983). For other useful sources, see Lyn MacCorkle's *Cubans in the United States: A Bibliography for Research in the Social and Behavioral Sciences, 1960-1983* (Westport, Conn.: Greenwood, 1984).

See also: Cuban-African American relations; Cuban Revolution; Mariel boatlift; Miami riots of 1980.

Cuban Revolution

Significance: A successful attempt to overthrow a corrupt regime institutes land reform, socialism, and a new dictatorship that threatens U.S. interests.

The Cuban Revolution of 1953 to 1959, led by Fidel Castro and culminating in the consolidation of the first communist government in the Western Hemisphere, came as a profound shock to most Americans. Cuba, ninety miles from the Florida shores and therefore of great strategic importance, first aroused U.S. interest at the start of the nineteenth century, when the administration of Thomas Jefferson expressed a desire to buy the island from Spain. The 1898 Spanish-American War, in which the United States intervened on the side of the Cuban rebels, resulted in the occupation of Cuba by the U.S. Army. The U.S. Congress granted Cuba independence in 1902, but the sovereignty of the new Cuban republic was restricted severely by the so-called Platt Amendment, which guaranteed the United States the right of military intervention and permanent ownership of the Guantanamo Bay naval base. U.S. economic influence in Cuba was protected as well. Because of favorable tariff and customs treaties, U.S. business came to dominate many areas of the Cuban economy, notably the sugar industry. This strong North American presence on the island provided the basis for a visceral Cuban nationalism that helps to explain the clash between Castro's revolutionaries and the United States.

Castro's Program
Castro's original goals were not explicitly hostile to the U.S. government. When on July 26, 1953, he launched his rebellion to overthrow the dictator Fulgencio Batista y Zaldívar, Castro had promised to restore constitutional civilian rule, hold free elections, and respect foreign property in Cuba. Through interviews with the U.S. media, Castro expressed a desire for continued good relations between the two countries. The administration of President Dwight D. Eisenhower, repelled by Batista's repeated violations of human rights, had placed an arms embargo on Cuba in 1958, signaling to Castro that the United States would not actively intervene to save the dictatorship.

The triumph of the Cuban Revolution in January, 1959, made it evident, however, that Castro's political and economic program was not compatible with U.S. interests. The execution of several hundred soldiers and policemen who had served Batista and the incarceration of thousands of political supporters of the old regime caused an angry outcry in the U.S. media. Castro's assumption of the premiership of the revolutionary government in February, with near-absolute powers, led the State Department to accuse him of betraying his promise to the Cuban people that he would restore democracy. His appointment of Communist Party members to key ministries seemed to confirm to the U.S. government that Cuba was drifting away from its traditional alliance with the United States. The flight of thousands of Cubans to Florida, and Castro's accusation that the U.S. government was harboring counterrevolutionaries bent on the overthrow of his regime, doomed any chance of reconciliation.

The economic reforms launched by Castro further strained relations with the United States. Laws limiting the size of rural and urban property resulted in the expropriation of United States-owned sugar estates without compensation to their owners. U.S. investments in Cuba's railroad, telephone, telegraph, electricity, and mining sectors were also nationalized. The swank American-owned hotels along Havana's shoreline were turned over to the state. Two years after the revolution, nearly all U.S. property in Cuba, estimated by the State Department at a value of one billion dollars, had passed into the hands of the Cuban government.

Cuban foreign policy underwent a radical shift in the first year of the revolution. The revolutionary government expressed solidarity for rebel forces plotting to oust pro-U.S. regimes in the rest of Latin America, and it sent supplies and Cuban advisers to guerrilla fighters in the Caribbean and Central America. Diplomatic and commercial relations were restored or established with the Soviet Bloc countries and China. The Cuban leader also announced that Cuba no longer felt bound by military treaties signed in the past with the United States and would buy arms and strategic goods from whichever nation would provide them. In June of 1960, the Cuban government seized U.S. petroleum companies that had refused to process Soviet crude oil coming to Cuba. The Eisenhower administration responded by cutting off the Cuban sugar quota and secretly preparing an invasion of the island by Cuban exiles trained in Guatemala by the Central Intelligence Agency (CIA). That December, Castro gained a pledge from Soviet premier Nikita Khrushchev to support Cuban independence in case of aggression from the United States. On January 2, 1961, Castro called on the United States to reduce the size of its diplomatic mission in Havana, which he accused of espionage activities. The United States broke off diplomatic relations with Cuba the next day and stepped up sabotage and covert aerial bombings of Cuban military facilities.

American Response

John F. Kennedy was even more committed than Eisenhower had been to reversing the Cuban Revolution and preventing the loss of Cuba to the Soviets. When he took office as president on January 20, 1961, Kennedy substantially altered the nature of the planned exile invasion. Whereas Eisenhower had instructed the CIA to train a small guerrilla army to infiltrate Cuba and harass Castro's military, the Kennedy administration mobilized a full-scale brigade to land at the Bay of Pigs on the southern end of the island and form the nucleus of a counterrevolutionary government backed by the United States. The invasion, launched in April of 1960, was doomed by bad planning, infighting among the exiles, and the failure of the Cuban people to rise up against Castro as the CIA had predicted. Castro used the defeat of the exile brigade as the occasion for his proclamation of the revolution as socialist. He then signed a treaty with the Soviet Union to protect the island from any future invasion through the installation of Russian nuclear missiles in Cuba. The United States, by attacking Castro, had brought about what it wanted most to avoid: the implantation of a communist regime and Soviet ally ninety miles from the U.S. mainland.

The Cuban Revolution profoundly altered U.S. foreign policy toward Latin America. The fear of a "second Cuba" appearing in the Western Hemisphere led to the U.S. invasion of the Dominican Republic in 1965 and U.S. covert operations against Marxist regimes in Chile and Nicaragua in the 1970's. The U.S. government also tried to undermine Castro's appeal to the rest of Latin America by channeling massive amounts of economic aid to the region through the Alliance for Progress, launched by Kennedy in 1961. A complicating factor in the U.S. response to the Cuban Revolution was the presence in the United States after 1959 of thousands of Cuban refugees who had been granted political asylum. They went on to transform Miami into a thriving financial center linking North and South America, and were hostile to any rapprochement between Washington and Havana, which limited the ability of the United States to offer Castro any incentive to abandon his commitment to socialism. *Julio César Pino*

Core Resources

Michael J. Mazarr's *Semper Fidel: America and Cuba, 1776-1988* (Baltimore, Md.: Nautical & Aviation Publishing Company of America, 1988) provides a good discussion of Cuba as an issue in U.S. politics. Morris H. Morley's *Imperial State and Revolution: The United States and Cuba, 1952-1986* (Cambridge, Mass.: Cambridge University Press, 1987) features a Marxist analysis of the formulation and implementation of the U.S. effort to reverse the Cuban Revolution. Thomas J. Paterson's *Contesting Castro: The United States and the Triumph of the Cuban Revolution* (New York: Oxford University Press, 1994) discusses how the Eisenhower administration's early embrace of Batista legitimized Castro's violent anti-Americanism. Hugh Thomas's *Cuba: Or, The Pursuit of Freedom* (New York: Harper & Row, 1971) offers an encyclopedic look at Cuban history from the eighteenth century to its alliance with the Soviet Union.

See also: Cuban Americans; Miami riots of 1980; Mariel boatlift; Platt Amendment.

Veterans from the failed 1960 Bay of Pigs invasion stage an anti-Fidel Castro rally in New York City.

Cultural citizenship

The concept of citizenship first arose in towns and city-states of ancient Greece, where it generally applied to property owners but not to women, slaves, or the poorer members of the community. The notion of citizenship has changed throughout the ages, most recently to one of national citizenship. Thomas M. Marshall described three central rights granted by citizenship: *civic rights*, which entitle individuals to freedom of speech and to information about what is going on, to assemble and organize without restrictions, and to be treated equally in law; *political rights*, which include the right to vote and run for office in free election; and *socioeconomic rights*, which include the rights to welfare and social security and to unionize and participate in collective bargaining. In an increasingly diasporic world, the notion of citizenship has been expanded to include those who claim to be a citizen of a culture rather than a nation. Those groups who feel that they are denied one or more of the three types of right described by Marshall may opt for cultural citizenship. These groups may regard themselves as part of various cultures and feel that they have citizenship in each country they have experienced. For example, a Vietnamese laborer who worked in Vietnam, then migrated to Australia, and then to Canada may claim three-way cultural citizenship. This person may identify with each of the three cultures' norms, values, beliefs, and traditions yet cannot claim one over the other. Such individuals are borderless citizens who have few geographic boundaries. *Mary Yu Danico*

See also: Cultural pluralism; Diaspora; Transnationalism and ethnonationalism.

Cultural pluralism

The concept of cultural pluralism has its origins in a 1915 essay by educator and social philosopher Horace Kallen, who argued—in an era rife with xenophobia, nativism, and anti-immigrant attitudes—that ethnic groups had a right to exist on their own terms, retaining their unique cultural heritage while enjoying full participation in, and the benefits of, a democratic society. *Beyond the Melting Pot* (1970), a controversial book by Nathan Glazer and Daniel Patrick Moynihan, expanded Kallen's early concept and revived the intense debate over the degree to which immigrant customs should, or would, survive with passing generations. In a new nation, Moynihan and Glazer argued, few vestiges of the immigrant culture would remain. Decades later, opinions of *Beyond the Melting Pot* still run a broad spectrum from praise to condemnation, but the book probably introduced one

of the most important social science dialogues of the twentieth century.

Much of the debate over cultural pluralism has focused on the issues of bilingual (and multicultural) education in public schools and universities. The high point of disagreement appears to be over the concept of assimilationism versus multiculturalism. Arthur Schlesinger, Jr., and others have argued that different ethnic groups in the United States share a common culture, and that cultural pluralism is not a model for which the United States should strive. Critics respond that the melting pot paradigm is a fantasy, and that "vegetable soup" or "tossed salad" might be more accurate models. They also point out that if society blends itself into one culture, the cultural values of that finished product will probably be strongly European. Asiatic, African, and Hispanic cultures would not survive the meltdown. *Christopher Guillebeau*

See also: Assimilation: cultural and structural; Assimilation theories; Melting pot theory; Multiculturalism.

Cultural relativity vs. ethnocentrism

Sociologists generally seek to understand the role of an individual cultural element, such as a particular ritual or religious belief, within an entire cultural system and to avoid making a judgment about it without taking the entire sociocultural system into account. This attitude, called cultural relativism, arose partly because social scientists have seen how the social and cultural characteristics of different cultures and subcultures often can be explained by those cultures' very different historical, environmental, economic, and political conditions. Maintaining such an attitude also suggests that one will not be quick to judge one culture as superior or inferior to the culture of any other group.

This open-minded attitude is assumed to be the opposite of ethnocentrism, a normal tendency to believe that the values, beliefs, norms, and customs of one's own culture are superior to those of others. Most people unwittingly are socialized into becoming ethnocentric; for example, they are not aware of how strongly they may have become influenced by their parents and schools to believe that their own society's culture is the one against which all others should be judged. Moral absolutism often is a part of ethnocentrism. Moral absolutists believe that their culture's definition of good and bad behavior sets the standard by which anyone else's behavior should be judged. The ethnocentric person is less likely than a cultural relativist to try to understand how the wider sociocultural context of another group may help explain its particular beliefs, behaviors, and values.

Grace Maria Marvin

See also: Ethnocentrism; Tolerance.

Culture and language

> **Significance:** Culture and the language that expresses it are intertwined, making it hard to determine which has more influence over the other. Whether a culture's perception and ordering of the world is determined by its language or a culture's language is solely a result of the way the society orders its world is still a matter of debate.

Language and culture are expressions of the world that are found in all societies. The nature of their interrelationship and influence on each other is not easily grasped. For the social scientist, the study of language within a culture is a means of looking at that culture's social structure and interpersonal relationships, since it is language that expresses the various aspects of culture, such as labeling, kinship, actions, and beliefs.

Definitions of Language and Culture
Language, the spoken communication of a cultural group, is the means by which most human thought is communicated. Also, much of social and cultural behavior is expressed by the means of the spoken word. Language is a cultural universal, and within each language are universals: greetings, farewells, formal language, and politeness. Language is an oral expression of concrete forms that also carries symbolic meaning; what one says may not be what one means. Thus, in addition to naming the world, language expresses relationships among things. This means that although a word such as "tomorrow" may be translatable from one language to another, it may not have the same meaning in both languages. In one, "tomorrow" may mean "the next day," while in another "tomorrow" may mean "some time in the future."

Culture is the overt and covert expression of the behavior and beliefs of a group of people. It is expressed in the traditions and customs of that people. It includes but is not limited to knowledge of the physical world, beliefs and rituals, moral direction, law, and artistic expression. One of the most important aspects of culture is that it gives order to the world in which its participants live. Colors, actions, kinship, and familial relationships are all a part of culture. These relationships are expressed by language, although they may be expressed differently in each cultural setting. In one setting, cats and snakes may be grouped together, since both have similar eye types, large mouths with fangs, and slithery bodies, and both make hissing sounds. In another setting, there may be no relationship between the two creatures.

Language, as a means of communication, has a two-fold role in a society. Language is a source of information about a culture and a society, and it is a means by which members of a society socialize or interact. Linguist Irving M. Copi discusses the three basic functions of language within a culture as being, first, to communicate information; second, to express emotion (to communicate feelings); and third, to give commands or requests. He states that these three groups of expression are not necessarily mutually exclusive. The interaction that is facilitated by language use enables individuals in a society to work together more effectively and eases social pressure.

The Relationship Between Language and Culture
The nature of the relationship between language and culture is not entirely understood. Ronald Wardhaugh has suggested at least four possible correlations of language and culture: (1) social structure may influence linguistic structure (for example, there may be gender-based differences in speech); (2) linguistic structure may determine social structure (it is the language itself, not the speakers of the language, that is gender-biased); (3) language and societal influences are bidirectional—that is, they may influence each other; (4) there is no relationship between language and culture. Most ethnolinguistic studies have eliminated the possibility that the last relationship is valid. They hold that there must be some relationship between language and culture.

Language has many functions within each culture. It is the primary means of the retrieval of sociocultural knowledge for each group. Language is also the agent of socialization within a culture, teaching each member his or her place within that society. In addition, language is used as an agent of power, distinguishing social rank, which is slightly different from simple socialization. Finally, as world communication develops and languages become less isolated, language planning is coming into prominence as a means of adaptation to increasing lingual and cultural encounters.

The study of the relationship between language and culture is valuable in leading to an understanding of the cognitive processes of various societies. Since each language is the medium by which its speakers express their organization of the world, each language system must be equally valid. One language is not "better" than another. Each language is valid because it expresses complex relationships in the world of its speakers. The "simple, primitive" language does not exist.

A child in any society usually grasps the main aspects of the primary language before the age of five years. The babbling of infants includes the sounds of many human languages, some of which do not occur in the language of the child's family or society. Positive reinforcement encourages the child to continue certain sounds and delete others from the babbling repertoire. Later learning extends to grammar, meaning, and symbolism. All this is achieved without formal instruction. Language, however, is not culturally bound. A person is not born with a genetic tendency to speak a language. A person of Yakima Indian ancestry does not "naturally" speak the Sahaptin language. If he or she has learned English as a primary language, his or her genetic structure does not make the learning of Sahaptin any easier.

In addition to rules of grammar, a child learns the appropriate social use of language, including his or her place in society. Often this relationship is indicated by "honorifics." Honorifics include terms of address to others that vary by gender, age, and family position, and terms that indicate social distance to those persons outside one's family. In English, social distance is indicated, for example, by the use of Mr., Mrs., and Ms. in combination with the surname of the addressee. A person addressing a close acquaintance would generally use a given name or nickname to identify the person. Social distance may be maintained by persons of differing age groups, social status, duration of acquaintance, or kinship. In Spanish and other languages, other formal terms of address are used in addition to a formal or informal version of the language. As one increases in age and/or social status, one's linguistic patterns change in accordance with the culture's standards.

While power as expressed in verbal communication in society may be related to social distance and rank, it also has a broader application. Language as a means of social power occurs in groups that use "jargon," or a specialized vocabulary or way of speaking. Black English is sometimes included in such a category; persons outside the "in" group may not be able to understand what is being said.

During the 1960's and 1970's, British sociologist Basil Bernstein suggested that although the relationship of language and culture is reciprocal, culture has the greater influence on language. According to this theory, it would be the speakers of the language, not the language, who were gender-biased.

Linguist Noam Chomsky asserted that language is a universal innate facility. He produced some seminal works in the field of ethnolinguistics (*Reflections on Language*, 1975). More recently, British sociologist Basil Bernstein has been interested in the role of language in the socialization process. He examines the ways in which members of various social groups develop language dialects as a means of communicating with one another. He suggests that it is culture that has the greater effect on language.

Implications for Intergroup Relations

Ethnolinguistics seems to be moving toward a concern for language planning and political correctness. Issues of bilingual education—the adoption of English as the official language in the United States, the use of French in Quebec, the acknowledgment of formerly low-status languages in Africa—are coming to the fore as studies in ethnolinguistics. Such issues as these affect the view that each individual in the societies involved has of himself or herself, and they may direct the focus of ethnolinguistics. *Susan Ellis-Lopez*

Core Resources

Nancy Bonvillain's *Language, Culture, and Communication* (Englewood Cliffs, N.J.: Prentice-Hall, 1993) discusses not only the relationship between language and culture but also means of communication between individuals, communities, and nations. Leslie A. Spier, Irving Hallowell, and Stanley S. Newman's *Language, Culture, and Personality: Essays in Memory of Edward Sapir* (Menasha, Wis.: Sapir Memorial Publication Fund, 1941) is a collection of essays that are considered classics in the field of ethnolinguistics. *Language in Use: Readings in Sociolinguistics* (Englewood Cliffs, N.J.: Prentice-Hall, 1984), edited by John Baugh and Joel Sherzer, presents a selection of classic papers in sociolinguistics from the 1970's and 1980's. Noam Chomsky's *Reflections on Language* (New York: Pantheon Books, 1975) is a general and nontechnical summary of some of the basic questions regarding language and human activity.

See also: Accent discrimination; Bilingual education; Bilingualism in Canada; Ebonics; English-only and official English movements; Epithets and pejorative language; Hate speech; Politics of hate.

Culture of poverty

Significance: The term "culture of poverty" has been used to describe the values, principles, and lifestyles associated with people living at the lowest economic levels of society. Because many minorities and immigrants grow up in a culture of poverty, it has profound implications for intergroup relations.

"Culture of poverty" is a term that refers to the pattern of life, the set of beliefs, and the typical behavior found among people who live in an environment dominated by economic deprivation. Culture is the way in which people live their lives and includes all the habits learned by an individual from other members of the community. In its broadest sense, a culture contains the essential information one needs to live in a given environment. Because the environment found in impoverished communities is built upon deprivation, isolation, discrimination, poor education, lack of jobs, crime, drugs, alcohol abuse, and welfare dependence, these negative forces shape the attitudes, expectations, and behavior of residents.

Oscar Lewis, an American anthropologist famous for his description of the effects of poverty on human lives in *La Vida: A Puerto Rican Family in the Culture of Poverty—San Juan and New York* (1966), believed that the values children learn from their parents about how to survive in such desperate circumstances make them less able to move out of poverty. Lewis suggested that only a violent revolution overturning capitalist society would enable the poor to find dignity and equality. Working within the system would not solve any problems because the values poor people learn include hatred for education (which rarely helps to get a person out of the slums), self-indulgence (since alcohol and drugs offer a quick way out of misery), and unwillingness to save or sacrifice for the future well-being of one's self or family (since the future offers little hope for improving one's economic circumstances). None of these values leads to educa-

tional or occupational advancement. The culture learned by the poor works against their ever getting out of poverty. For things to change, according to Lewis, the environmental conditions need to change.

Defining Poverty

Poverty takes three forms: social poverty, which is defined as economic inequality, or the lack of means to provide a minimally adequate standard of living; pauperism, a word that signifies an inability of individuals to take care of themselves; and voluntary poverty, which includes those who for religious and philosophical reasons give up material possessions to pursue prayer, meditation, or art. In the United States, most of the poor fall into the first two categories and include the unskilled, the uneducated, and a large number of children. As of 1993, the government defined as poor nonfarm families of four with incomes under $12,500, about half the income of an average American family of four. Farm families qualify as poor with slightly less income.

According to government figures, in 1992, about 32 million Americans, or 13 percent of the population, lived below the poverty level. That figure represented an increase of almost 4 million people since 1984, the largest proportion reported by the U.S. Bureau of the Census since the 1950's, when 22.4 percent of the nation lived in officially declared poverty. In 1988, the bureau issued a report on the American poor that showed that 10 percent of whites, 31.6 percent of blacks, and 26.8

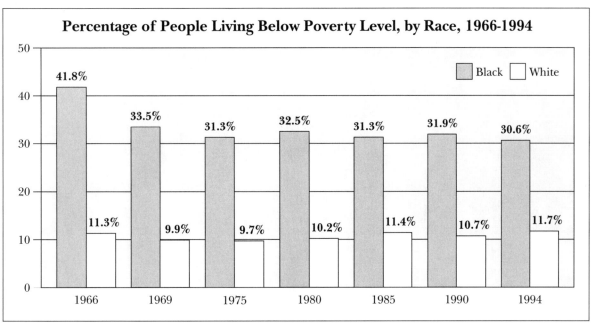

Percentage of People Living Below Poverty Level, by Race, 1966-1994

Source: Data are from the U.S. Bureau of the Census, *Statistical Abstract of the United States, 1996* (116th ed.). Washington, D.C.: U.S. Government Printing Office, 1997.

percent of Hispanics were impoverished; 20 percent of American children lived in poverty. More than half the families labeled poor were headed by single mothers, and those numbers were growing. Many of the poor, almost 45 percent, worked full-time but in jobs that required few skills, offered no opportunities for advancement, and generally had no benefits such as health insurance. For the "working poor," jobs themselves seemed to offer no opportunity for moving up the economic ladder. Working hard for forty hours a week or longer did not guarantee success.

Sources of Poverty

Race itself is not a cause of poverty; however, the American tradition of racial segregation and discrimination has guaranteed that large numbers of African Americans—almost two out of every five—live under the poverty line. The major causes of poverty in the United States include chronic unemployment resulting from low levels of education and lack of skills; low wages in unskilled entry-level occupations as well as in agricultural labor; old age; and catastrophes such as floods, fires, or large medical bills.

Poverty is seen by many as a sign of wickedness and moral degeneracy: People are poor because they are lazy and corrupt. These attitudes must be faced and absorbed into a poor person's consciousness every day, and

they only increase a sense of frustration and hopelessness. In a society that exalts the work ethic such as the United States, not working becomes a sign of individual worthlessness and insignificance. This attitude represents one of the most devastating nonmaterial effects of being poor.

According to the culture of poverty thesis, ending employment discrimination, raising wages, and increasing employment opportunities through job training programs would all help to reduce poverty, but the attitudes of the poor would change only very slowly because a whole way of life would need to be transformed. Education is the key to changing attitudes, especially by reducing the sense of despair frequently experienced by poor people. Yet dropout rates approach 45 percent in high schools in slum districts, and a majority of impoverished adults are functionally illiterate; a major change in educational outcomes thus would be required before schools could be accepted as a way out of poverty.

In American society, more than 71 percent of the African American poor live in large cities or surrounding suburbs, while most poor whites (almost 68 percent) are found in small towns, suburbs, and rural areas. In his book *The Truly Disadvantaged: The Inner City, the Underclass, and Public Policy* (1987), University of Chicago sociologist William J. Wilson observes that many African Americans live in neighborhoods with high concentra-

Emma Lee, a welfare recipient, and her six children live in two rooms in a hotel in New York City in January, 1971. Some sociologists believe that the culture of poverty makes it more difficult for the poor to escape their situation.

tions of people in similarly desperate economic circumstances, with average incomes of less than $5,000 a year. Poor black people, especially, tend to live in areas surrounded by other poor blacks and thus have little opportunity to meet or learn from individuals with more secure economic futures. These are the truly disadvantaged members of American society, the people who feel most cut off from the American mainstream, and the people most influenced by the culture of poverty.

Tough Environments

In the environment of the slum, cultural patterns emerge that promote survival in the midst of dangerous and violent conditions. Crime rates, murder rates, and levels of drug addiction, alcoholism, mental illness, hypertension, and other measures of social disintegration, including divorce, child abuse, and spouse abuse, are far higher in inner cities than in any other parts of the United States. Survival in these circumstances requires a toughness of spirit and a distrust of others. Because slum residents usually do not get adequate city services such as garbage collection and police protection, distrust of government grows, leading to increased levels of hopelessness and helplessness. Not even the schools, historically the institutions most used by immigrant and minority groups as the path to success, typically offer the type of skills and training necessary to make it out of the ghetto. The dream of college seems very distant to people without enough money to buy food.

The goals of the poor may be similar to those of the more well-to-do in terms of better jobs, improved educational opportunities, and a more pleasant future for their children, but the experience of the poor does not provide evidence that such dreams will ever come true. In many impoverished and racially segregated neighborhoods, crime, usually involving drug sales, offers a far quicker route to material success. Welfare payments, whether through Aid to Families with Dependent Children (AFDC), general assistance, or other aid programs, are another source of survival for the truly poor, although the welfare reforms of the late 1990's significantly curtailed these resources as long-term options. Such help, inadequate as it usually is, increases dependency and tends to reduce self-respect, as it is considered a sign of personal weakness to receive welfare.

Leslie V. Tischauser

Core Resources

Andrew Hacker's *Two Nations: Black and White, Separate, Hostile, Unequal* (New York: Charles Scribner's Sons, 1992) is a thorough analysis of racial issues in the United States. *A Common Destiny: Blacks and American Society*, edited by Gerald D. Jaynes and Robin M. Williams (Washington, D.C.: National Academy Press, 1988) attempts to refute the idea of a distinct culture of poverty, seeing discrimination and racism as the only impediments to full equality. William J. Wilson's *The Truly Disadvantaged: The Inner City, the Underclass, and Public Policy* (Chicago: University of Chicago Press, 1987) shows the devastating impact of poverty and the culture of poverty on millions of Americans. Charles Murray's *Losing Ground: American Social Policy, 1950-1980* (New York: Basic Books, 1984) saw a culture of poverty developing from American welfare programs and called for eliminating welfare and increasing incentives to work.

See also: Economics and race; Poverty and race; Welfare's impact on racial/ethnic relations.

Curanderismo

Curanderismo is a syncretic form of both faith and herbal medicine that is practiced by some Mexican Americans, particularly in treating such medical syndromes as *mal ojo* (evil eye), *susto* (spirit loss), *mal puesto* (hex), *caída de mollera* (fallen fontanel), and *chîlpil* (sibling rivalry). Folk healers, herbalists, spiritualists, and medical practitioners are men (*curanderos*) and women (*curanderas*) who are invariably shamans, people who possess sometimes specific religious powers for curing various types of maladies, even those caused by a sorcerer (*bruja*).

Curanderismo tends to integrate the rural or urban community, particularly through group ritual, which invariably emphasizes and fulfills the spiritual needs of the patient in sometimes dramatic rituals that are essentially psychodramas. *Curanderismo* provides traditional social and behavioral mechanisms for the release of unbearable pressures as perceived by the individual or group. This system of medicine also provides effective explanations for personal failure, and on occasion, it may serve to reinforce an established moral order. Although many maladies are believed to be the result of an individual's moral transgressions, illness may be manipulated as a means of gaining social control or even attention and is therefore beneficial to the patient.

John Alan Ross

See also: Latinos in the United States.

D

Declaration of First Nations

Canadians generally regard their country's multiethnic heritage with pride. Multiculturalism is applauded in a variety of ways, but special recognition is accorded to the "founding nations" of Canada. Unfortunately for Native Canadians, the term "founding nation" is usually reserved for only two groups—the French and the English.

Public and government recognition that Aboriginal Canadians (Canadian Indians) as a group had suffered economically, socially, and educationally became widespread in the 1960's. In order to engage natives in a dialogue regarding the issues that most affected them, the federal government encouraged the development of both regional and national native political organizations. The National Indian Council, which was formed in 1961, represented treaty Indians, non-treaty Indians, non-status Indians, and Metis. In 1968 this group divided into the Canadian Metis Society, representing Metis and non-status Indians, and the National Indian Brotherhood as the organization of Status Indians (both treaty and non-treaty).

Politicization grew, particularly following introduction by the government of its White Paper on Indian Affairs in 1969. In 1975, the various Dene bands sought Canadian recognition of the Subarctic Athapaskans as a distinct nation. The National Indian Brotherhood became highly involved in Canadian constitutional reform. The Declaration of First Nations, issued in 1981, was a concise statement of native sovereignty meant to influence the constitutional reform process. Following the Declaration of First Nations, the National Indian Brotherhood was dissolved and reconstituted as the Assembly of First Nations. They were ultimately successful in inserting language that affirmed "existing aboriginal and treaty rights," though these were not explicitly defined, into the Constitution Act of 1982.

Natives have continued to pursue the recognition of their cultures as distinct societies and as "founding nations" of Canada by defeating the Meech Lake Accord and by working for a form of native self-government apart from the provinces and the federal government.

Pamela R. Stern

See also: Aboriginal Canadians; Indian Act of 1876; Indian Act of 1951; Indian Act of 1989; Indian-white relations: Canada; Meech Lake Accord; Multiculturalism Act; Multiculturalism in Canada; Sovereignty; White Paper of 1969.

Deference rituals

Reinforced by larger systems of class, race, ethnicity, and gender, people who lack power are often expected to act deferentially when in the presence of higher-status individuals. Although the accordance of deference may involve a respectful regard between status equals, when relations are asymmetrical and unequal, people who act deferentially may be yielding to the wishes or opinions of others in an overly obsequious, servile manner because such behavior is expected of them.

According to the sociologist Erving Goffman in *Interaction Ritual* (1967), deference rituals can take two forms, presentational and avoidance. Presentational rituals provide guidelines on how a person should act in the presence of another individual by, for example, concretely depicting appreciation through compliments and minor services. Avoidance rituals are the most common forms of deference between status unequals. They lead to social distance between the recipients of deference and nonrecipients. For example, to avoid skin contact and give the appearance of "whiteness," African American domestic servants during the 1800's and early 1900's were often expected to wear white gloves when serving white masters or employers. Maintaining proper spatial distance and avoiding the use of a superordinate's first name are other examples.

Deference does not necessarily involve the blind obedience of authority figures by minority members. Deference rituals can also become sources of control by providing a way to cope with everyday discrimination and degradation. A person who renders deference to another may do so not because of what he or she thinks of that individual personally but in spite of it. When deference is feigned, minority members are able to preserve a sense of inner autonomy and may even insinuate disregard by modifying and exaggerating intonations, pronunciations, and gestures.

Eleanor A. LaPointe

See also: Discrimination: responses to; Minority and majority groups.

Delano Grape Strike

> **Significance:** The success of this strike brought gains in farmworkers' rights and coincided with Chicano activism and pride.

Delano, California, a small grape vineyard community in the southern San Joaquin Valley, was the scene of a historic farmworkers' strike that changed the course of Latino history in the United States. The strike began on September 8, 1965, when farmworkers walked off the fields protesting low wages and poor working conditions; it ended on July 29, 1970. This strike was coordinated by César Chávez and the National Farm Workers Association (NFWA). Half the world's table grapes were produced in the Delano area, which thus attracted thousands of vineyard workers.

The seeds of the Delano strike emerged on September 30, 1962, when Chávez and a few hundred workers met and founded NFWA. Workers began to formulate their agenda. Incentives were provided to encourage members to remain in the union. NFWA member benefits included a co-op store, a gas station, and a service center. By mid-1965, the union had twelve hundred members.

The Strike Begins

NFWA became involved in striking against Delano vineyards when Larry Itliong, a Filipino organizer, and another union, the Agricultural Workers Organizing Committee (AWOC), called a strike against grape growers in the Delano area. AWOC, founded in 1959 by the AFL-CIO, convinced a large group of farmworkers to walk out of the vineyards. Between six hundred and eight hundred mostly Filipino workers demanded the right to bargain with their employers for fair wages and just working conditions. Many strikers were aware of better wages, having worked in California's Coachella Valley, where the grape harvest is earlier than in Delano. Workers were paid $1.40 an hour in Coachella; Delano growers were unwilling to pay more than $1.25 an hour.

AWOC asked NFWA to join their strike, and five days later, after much deliberation, NFWA members voted unanimously to join the strike, which had spread to nine ranches and involved two thousand workers. The strike meeting was called on Mexican Independence Day, symbolically linking their struggle to the one 145 years past. Al Green, leader of AWOC, did not like NFWA's propo-

sition for a joint strike. NFWA called its own strike against the area's thirty other major grape growers. Chávez sent letters and telegrams to the growers, offering to negotiate contracts setting minimum pay at $1.40 per hour and specifying several other conditions of work.

AWOC concentrated demonstrations within the Delano area. Small picket groups demonstrated in front of vineyards and packing sheds. NFWA used other tactics, such as marches, fasts, and the grape boycott. In fall, 1965, Chávez visited several campuses, where rallies were held to garner student support. This effort resulted in hundreds of volunteers and supporters from the students and faculty. Their inclusion helped publicize the movement beyond the Delano area.

A feud between NFWA and the International Brotherhood of Teamsters, which began competing with NFWA for union membership, threatened the success of the strike. NFWA was being undercut by the Teamsters, who were making deals with local growers. This feud was settled temporarily in 1966, when the two groups merged to become the United Farm Workers Organizing Committee (UFWOC). Chávez became director and Itliong became associate director.

The Delano Grape Strike was waged primarily against a group of growers who refused to recognize or deal with NFWA. One of the tactics used to encourage the growers to negotiate a contract was fasting, which Chávez and others used on several occasions. One of Chávez's fasts lasted from February 15 to March 10, 1968. The march was another useful tactic. A 1966 march (the Pilgrimage), went from Delano to Sacramento, the California state capital. This well-publicized march ended with a large rally at the Capitol Building on Easter Sunday. The United States, Mexican, and Philippine flags, along with a banner of Our Lady of Guadalupe, flew at the front of this march, which began March 16. Hats with the union's red hatbands displaying the black eagle and *huelga* (strike) flags were well represented among those gathered at the capital. The national director of organizing for the AFL-CIO, Bill Kircher, marched with the farmworkers. This resulted in a period of lasting cooperation and support between Chávez and the leaders of the AFL-CIO. Union members throughout the United States and Canada voiced support for the farmworkers.

Grape Boycott

Calling the boycott against grape growers proved to be the most effective tactic. The boycott succeeded in reaching the middle class in the United States. In addition, Chávez was a charismatic leader, which blended well with the excellent press coverage of the boycott activities. Chávez stressed nonviolence as the union's guiding principle. Following the Civil Rights movement, in which Martin Luther King, Jr., had espoused nonviolence as a

The Delano Grape Strike developed into a grape boycott and spawned many later demonstrations such as this protest by the United Farm Workers in Modesto, California, in 1975.

technique for peaceful protest, this tactic was viewed as acceptable by large segments of the U.S. population. Nationwide focus on the farmworkers' movement compelled farmworkers to visit major cities in the United States and Canada seeking support for the grape boycott. Usually churches, unions, or universities provided venues for farmworker presentations.

The boycott originally was directed against the Di Giorgio Corporation, whose Sierra Vista Ranch covered forty-four hundred acres, and Schenley Industries, whose product lines, S&W Fine Foods and Treesweet juices, were nationally known. Consumers were urged to stop buying these brand names. Schenley became the first winery to settle a contract. Several small wineries run by Catholic religious orders also settled with a contract. Most of the growers in the Delano area were 1920's immigrants from southern and eastern Europe. John Giumarra, Jr., spoke proudly of how his family came from Sicily and built the largest of the vineyard operations, a twelve-hundred-acre complex that grossed $5.5 to $7.5 million annually. Their cultural backgrounds were of economic struggle to success, where workers needed little beyond what the patrons granted them. This background left most of the growers with little tolerance for farmworker demands.

The Giumarra Vineyards became the target of a nationwide boycott in the spring of 1967. Consumers could identify Giumarra grapes, because they arrived at the store in clearly labeled boxes. By late summer, 1967, Giumarra, feeling negative effects of the boycott, coun-terattacked. He persuaded other Delano growers to allow the use of their labels on Giumarra grape boxes. This was designed to prevent consumers from identifying Giumarra grapes in the market.

In January, 1968, the union expanded its boycott to include all table grapes. In October the focus shifted from the products themselves to their outlets. Stores that handled table grapes were faced with mounting pressure, as farmworker union members and supporters began distributing leaflets at stores and publicizing stores that handled the grapes. The boycott was bolstered by picketing at large stores. The boycott grew, and consumers increasingly refused to buy grapes. By 1969, more than seventeen million U.S. consumers had stopped buying grapes. Growers began to feel the financial impact of these tactics and slowly began the move toward granting union demands. This boycott was a major factor in achieving acceptance of the union, collective bargaining, and the signing of contracts. In 1970, 140 grape growers signed contracts with the UFWOC as a result of the Delano Grape Strike. This was a major victory for the farmworkers, but not the end of the struggle. The 1970's and 1980's were punctuated by numerous protests between growers and farmworkers. In 1984, Chávez was compelled to call another strike. Despite these setbacks, the Delano strike remains one of the most important events in the struggle for farmworker, and by extension Latino, rights.   *Gregory Freeland*

Core Resources

John Gregory Dunne's *Delano: The Story of the California Grape Strike* (Rev. ed., New York: Farrar, Straus & Giroux, 1971) offers a clear, concise history of the Delano strike. Paul Fusco and George Horowitz's *"La Causa": The California Grape Strike* (New York: Macmillan, 1970) is useful to anyone seeking the causes and effects of the strike. Craig Jenkins's *The Politics of Insurgency: The Farmworker Movement in the 1960's* (New York: Columbia University Press, 1985) provides an excellent analysis of the strategies and consequences of the farmworker movement. Jacques Levy's *César Chávez: Autobiography of "La Causa"* (New York: W. W. Norton, 1975) is a detailed account of Chávez's life and work. Consuelo Rodriguez's *César Chávez* (New York: Chelsea House, 1991) is a brief but informative book that captures Chávez's activities after 1970.

See also: Bracero program; Chicano movement; Immigration and Nationality Act of 1965; Immigration Reform and Control Act of 1986; Labor movement; Latinos in the United States; Mexican deportations; Operation Wetback; United Farm Workers.

Delgamuukw v. British Columbia

This landmark case involving the Supreme Court of Canada, decided in December, 1997, conceivably revolutionized aboriginal affairs in Canada—particularly land claims—as well as jurisprudence in some fundamental ways. The high court overturned the decision of the British Columbia Court of Appeal in the matter of land claims by the House of Delgamuukw. The House, speaking on behalf of fifty-one hereditary chiefs, claimed ownership and jurisdiction over fifty-eight thousand square kilometers of land in northwestern British Columbia as native lands whose title dated back before confederation. The group further argued that aboriginal title had not been extinguished when British Columbia entered the confederation. The group attempted to use oral tradition to argue the first claim and section 35 of the 1982 Constitution Act to argue the latter point. Justice Alan McEachern of the British Columbia Supreme Court threw out the aboriginal case after one of the longest trials in Canadian history, rejecting the use of oral evidence and agreeing with the British Columbia government's position that title had been extinguished with entrance into the confederation.

The case then went to the British Columbia Court of Appeal, which, by a three-to-two decision, overruled Judge McEachern on the question of extinguishment. The court did, however, agree with him on rejecting claims of ownership although it did not entertain questions of the fiduciary duties of the Crown in relation to lands claimed. The case then went before the Supreme Court of Canada, which issued a unanimous landmark decision in December, 1997. The Court ordered a new trial, largely for two reasons. First, it ruled that Judge McEachern had erred in rejecting oral tradition as evidence. Noting that the laws of evidence typically work against the rights and customs of aboriginal people, the Court argued that "notwithstanding the challenges created by the use of oral histories as proof of historical facts, the laws of evidence must be adapted in order that this type of evidence can be accommodated and placed on an equal footing with the types of historical evidence that courts are familiar with, which largely consists of documentary evidence."

Second, it ruled that the question of aboriginal title had to be dealt with more closely and clearly. The court therefore spelled out eight core components of aboriginal title. Title is a collective right, it is inalienable, it is a legal right to the land itself, it arises from aboriginal occupation of the land before colonial assertion, it is an exclusive right to use the land for a variety of purposes, it includes mineral rights, it is to protect aboriginal relationship to the land, and lastly it is a right but not an absolute right.

To prove aboriginal title, the Supreme Court set out a threefold test. First, the land must have been occupied by aboriginal peoples before Crown assertion of sovereignty (for British Columbia, that means before 1846); second, there must be continuity between present occupancy of the land extending back prior to 1846 (that is, occupancy must not have been interrupted or given up); and third, at the date of Crown assertion of sovereignty, the occupation of the land by aboriginals must have been *exclusive.*

The case presented many issues unaddressed by the Canadian Supreme Court, issues largely outside its competency, so it ordered a new trial in which the foregoing principles were to have been taken into account. The high court thus urged all parties to serious negotiations in "good faith," which it hoped would result in compromises but ultimately a settlement because, as the majority decision concluded, "let us face it, we are all here to stay."

Gregory Walters

See also: Aboriginal Canadians; Nisga'a Agreement in Principle; Nunavut Territory; Oka crisis.

Department of Indian Affairs and Northern Development

The Department of Indian Affairs and Northern Development (DIAND) has the mission of "working together to make Canada a better place for First Nation and Northern peoples." To fulfill its mission, the department has changed its role over the years from caregiver and administrator to adviser and supporter. This change reflects the ongoing evolution of relations in Canada between aboriginal and nonaboriginal peoples as colonial and paternal models are replaced with the self-government that aboriginals had before the arrival of settlers and the early federal policies of assimilation.

The history of DIAND extends back to 1755, when the British Crown established the Indian Department as a branch of the military. The 1867 British North American Act, which made Canada a confederacy, gave the federal government control over Indians and their lands. The twentieth century saw the increase of departmental administration through a variety of channels. DIAND was created in 1966 by an act of Parliament and in 1998 administered an annual budget of 4.4 billion dollars covering four principal areas of Indian and Inuit programs, land claims, northern affairs, and administration. More than 83 percent of the first three areas are managed by the First Nations.

The department has two primary goals: to improve living conditions in First Nation communities and to settle aboriginal land claims. In 1973, the government recognized two classes of claims, specific and comprehensive. Specific claims refer to grievances about the fulfilment of treaties or other matters governed by the Indian Act. Comprehensive claims recognize that there are continuing aboriginal rights to parts of the country where aboriginals originally held title.

DIAND is essentially an advisory, funding, and supportive agency in its relations with the First Nations, Inuit, and northerners. It supports the efforts by the First Nations, Inuit, and northerners to achieve self-determination and self-government to become full partners in Canada.   *Gregory Walters*

See also: Aboriginal Canadians; Royal Commission on Aboriginal Peoples.

Desegregation: defense

> **Significance:** The 1941 desegregation of the U.S. defense industry was a major step in the advancement of African American civil rights and black-white relations.

Ever since the Revolutionary War, the United States had experienced difficulty in bringing African Americans into its military. Although one of the victims of the Boston massacre, Crispus Attucks, was an African American, and black soldiers were with George Washington when he made his famous 1776 Christmas crossing of the Delaware River to attack the Hessians at Trenton and Princeton, it was not until the Civil War (1861-1865) that African American troops were recruited officially into the United States Army. Even then, however, a rigid policy of segregation was maintained. In the two wars that followed, the Spanish-American War (1898) and World War I (1917-1919), both the Army and Navy had black troops, but largely in supporting roles, and always as separate, segregated units. In addition, black troop strength was kept deliberately low, partly to avoid offending white soldiers and partly because the military establishment had a low opinion of the abilities of African American troops.

Roosevelt's Role

During the 1930's, however, under the presidency of Franklin D. Roosevelt, these prejudiced traditions began to change. Roosevelt's New Deal, which had been put into place to fight the ravages of the Great Depression, also addressed a number of social conditions, including civil rights. Although civil rights were never at the forefront of Roosevelt's agenda, his administration was more committed to them than any previous presidency had been, and his wife, the redoubtable Eleanor Roosevelt, was an especially strong and capable advocate for racial equality and justice. In addition, the shrewdly realistic president, who foresaw the coming struggle with Nazi Germany, realized that the U.S. military needed every capable citizen, of whatever color or background. The policy of "Jim Crowism," or rigid segregation of blacks and whites, remained largely in place, however.

Correctly estimating the extent and depth of prejudice against African American participation in the military, especially in positions of responsibility, Roosevelt moved cautiously. He had been assistant secretary of the Navy under President Woodrow Wilson during World War I; now, Roosevelt prodded and encouraged the Navy high command to enlist additional African Americans and to place them in positions of greater responsibility than stewards or mess servers. Gradually and slowly, the Navy responded. A similar broadening took place in the Army in 1935, when the president insisted that African American medical officers and chaplains be called up from the reserves. On October 9, 1940, Roosevelt announced a revised racial policy for the armed forces; its intent was to bring more African Americans into the military and to place them in positions of trust and responsibility. At a glacial but perceptible pace, the United States military was becoming more receptive to African Americans.

The progress was not sufficiently rapid for many African Americans, among them A. Philip Randolph, president of the Brotherhood of Sleeping Car Porters, one of the strongest and most effective African American unions in the country. Randolph, who well understood that black voters had become an essential part of the Democratic Party's electoral base, calculated that Roosevelt would need to respond to African American demands, especially as the 1940 presidential elections approached. Randolph's logic and timing were correct.

In 1940, Roosevelt ran for an unprecedented third term as president. Randolph, along with former Republican city councilman Grant Reynolds of New York City, began a campaign against the Jim Crow practices still prevalent in the United States military. Randolph and Reynolds also called for greater opportunities for African American workers in the rapidly growing defense industries, which had arisen as the United States rearmed against the threat from Nazi Germany and imperialist Japan. As the campaign intensified, Roosevelt faced a difficult situation that threatened his southern, conservative support at the same time that it endangered his urban, liberal allies. When Randolph announced plans for a march on Washington, scheduled for July 1, 1941, Roosevelt knew he must act. His determination was steeled by the resolve of his wife, Eleanor, who had long been a champion of equal rights for African Americans, and whose contacts with the black community were strong and deep.

On June 25, 1941, Roosevelt issued Executive Order 8802, which enunciated a broad policy of racial equality in the armed forces and the defense industry. The order was clear and sweeping in its intent:

> In offering the policy of full participation in the defense program by all persons regardless of color, race, creed, or national origin, and directing certain action in further-ance of said policy . . . all departments of the government, including the Armed Forces, shall lead the way in erasing discrimination over color or race.

President Roosevelt backed up the policy by establishing the Fair Employment Practices Committee, which was charged with monitoring and enforcing compliance among civilian contractors. It is estimated that Roose-velt's executive order, combined with the work of the commission, helped to bring fifty-three thousand Afri-can American civilians into defense industry jobs they otherwise would not have held.

The timing of the policy was impeccable. Randolph and the other campaign leaders, satisfied that the Roose-velt administration was sincere in its commitment to civil rights, called off the march on Washington. Political conservatives, who otherwise might have challenged the president's order, had to admit that it would not be proper to expect African Americans to serve in the military without allowing them to hold responsible posi-tions and achieve corresponding rank. Black voters re-sponded enthusiastically to the Roosevelt reelection cam-paign, helping him to sweep to victory in the November balloting.

Inevitably, there were racial tensions and outbreaks of violence, especially in lower- and middle-class northern neighborhoods. In 1943, for example, tension between black and white workers led to open violence at a park on Belle Isle near Detroit; in the end, federal troops had to be called in to restore order, and twenty-five African Americans and nine whites had been killed. Similar, if less bloody, events took place in other cities. Still, the transition to a more equitable situation continued in both civilian and military life.

However, the traditional segregation remained. Dur-ing World War II, black units still were kept separate and apart from white troops, and were generally reserved for support and logistical duties rather than combat. When the difficulties and emergencies of battle required it, African American units were brought into the fighting line; generally, they acquitted themselves well. By the end of the war, African Americans had distinguished themselves as ground soldiers, sailors, and pilots in both combat and noncombat situations. After the surrender of the Axis powers in 1945, there was a sense of inevitable change ahead for the United States military. The ques-tion of whether it would be a peaceful, productive change remained.

Post-World War II

Harry S Truman, who assumed the presidency in 1945 after the death of Franklin D. Roosevelt, was determined to make the change in a proper fashion. He assembled a special Civil Rights Committee which, on October 30, 1947, issued its report, *To Secure These Rights*. Clearly and unhesitatingly, the report called for the elimination of segregation in the United States military.

As the 1948 presidential elections approached, the issue of African Americans in the military affected the political atmosphere. Truman and the national Demo-cratic Party, as heirs of the Roosevelt New Deal, had strong connections with the Civil Rights movement and its leaders; at the same time, much of the traditional Democratic strength was in the South, where civil rights issues were strongly opposed by the entrenched estab-lishment. Southern politicians, such as Strom Thur-mond of South Carolina, threatened to bolt the party if the Democrats adopted a strong civil rights platform at their convention; however, inspired by the passionate appeal of Mayor Hubert H. Humphrey of Minneapolis, the Democrats did indeed adopt a positive plank on civil rights. The southerners stormed out, nominating Thur-mond to run on the "Dixiecrat" ticket, and Truman went on to win a come-from-behind victory in November.

One element of that victory was his own Executive Order 9981, issued on July 26, 1948, just after the Demo-cratic Party convention. Truman's order was similar to but stronger than Roosevelt's: It required equal oppor-tunity in the armed forces of the United States, regard-less of race, and called upon the military services to move immediately to implement the directive. The Air Force reacted promptly and soon achieved remarkable inte-gration of black and white troops; the Navy and Marines were more hesitant in their acceptance. In the end, however, all branches of the armed forces responded, making them among the most egalitarian and equitable of U.S. institutions.   *Michael Witkoski*

Core Resources

Richard Dalifiume's *Desegregation of the U.S. Armed Forces: Fighting on Two Fronts, 1939-1953* (Columbia: University of Missouri Press, 1969) emphasizes the role of African Americans as soldiers, sailors, and airmen and sheds additional light on Roosevelt's order and its impact. Bernard C. Nalty's *Strength for the Fight: A History of Black Americans in the Military* (New York: Free Press, 1986) provides a comprehensive narrative of the relationship between African Americans and the U.S. armed forces. Richard Stillman's *Integration of the Negro in the U.S. Armed Forces* (New York: Frederick A. Praeger, 1968) provides an especially good discussion of the Roosevelt and Truman policies regarding blacks in the military. The U.S. Department of Defense's *Black Americans in Defense of Our Nation* (Washington, D.C.: Government Printing Office, 1991) is a pictorial documentary that covers all branches of the armed forces and include defense- and military-related occupations as well. C. Vann Woodward's *The Strange Career of Jim Crow* (2d rev. ed., New York: Oxford University Press, 1966) has remained a definitive work on legal and official segregation in American life.

See also: African Americans in the Civil War; Military and racial/ethnic relations; Military desegregation; Race riots of 1943.

Desegregation: public schools

> **Significance:** School desegregation, mandated by the Supreme Court's 1954 *Brown v. Board of Education* decision, involved first the dismantling of legally required separate schools for whites and blacks and later "affirmative action" to produce genuine integration.

School desegregation refers, in the narrowest sense, to the policy of dismantling the legally enforceable system of separate schools for black and white Americans that prevailed in southern and border states from the late nineteenth to the mid-twentieth century. The Fourteenth Amendment to the Constitution of the United States, ratified in 1868, proclaimed the "equal protection of the law" for all citizens of the United States. In 1896, the Supreme Court held in the case of *Plessy v. Ferguson* that separate public facilities for African Americans were legal as long as they were "equal." Since that time, black plaintiffs had sometimes won cases by arguing that inadequate schools for blacks were unequal in public funding or physical facilities with the corresponding schools for whites. In the landmark *Brown v. Board of Education* decision in 1954, however, the doctrine of "separate but equal" was itself challenged. The African American plaintiffs argued, and the Supreme Court agreed, that such a legally mandated, separate school system for blacks was inherently unequal and hence denied African American citizens the equal protection of the law.

Brown's Impact

The logic of this decision assumed a crucial importance. Written by Chief Justice Earl Warren and unanimously endorsed by the nine justices, it established the framework for a chain of later decisions. The Court maintained, first, that education had become essential to the exercise of citizenship and was entitled to such equal protection. Second, it maintained that intangible factors must be considered in the assessment of equality. A lack of opportunity to interact in discussions and exchange views with those of the majority culture might itself handicap a minority. Among these intangible factors, the court borrowed heavily from a brief submitted by social scientists as "friends of the court." Segregation, this brief maintained, was construed by both whites and blacks to imply black inferiority. This feeling of inferiority had depressed the motivation of black children to learn and hence depressed their educational progress. Implied by the decision was a third strand of the social science argument: that stereotyping by whites in their views of blacks (and hence, prejudice) was promoted by racial segregation.

For a decade following this decision, the courts were lenient, white resistance was high, and only token desegregation occurred in most southern states. While it was held that school districts should proceed to desegregate "with all deliberate speed," the truly operative principle was "freedom of choice." No black child who wished to attend a previously white school could be refused, but blacks were inhibited by custom and by social and economic pressures, and only a small number chose to go to traditionally white schools. Many whites opposed any desegregation whatsoever. An influx of black students, they argued, would "ruin" the public schools by flooding them with students who were functioning at a level behind that of their white age-mates. Various strategies were employed to avoid large-scale integration. New private academies for whites were constructed, and states provided tuition grants to assist students to attend such academies; in a few locations, public schools were closed. In 1964, a decade after the *Brown v. Board of Education* decision, fewer than 2 percent of all southern black students were attending integrated schools.

Push for Integration

In the mid-1960's, however, an era of federal activism began. The Civil Rights Act of 1964 provided for the mandatory suspension of federal aid to school districts shown to be practicing racial discrimination. In 1966, this antidiscrimination clause was invoked, and federal funds were withdrawn from some of the more resistant school districts. In 1968, the Supreme Court in *Green v. County School Board of New Kent County* reinterpreted the *Brown* mandate to require whatever "affirmative action" was necessary to achieve an integrated school system. In later cases such as *Swann v. Charlotte-Mecklenburg Board of Education* (1971), the court elaborated that such affirmative action could require the transportation of students between schools, the reassignment of teachers, and a consideration of the white-black student ratio in evaluating the success of such affirmative action. Although controversial, the activist approach obtained results. By 1975, 44 percent of the black students in southern states were in schools with a white majority.

By the late 1970's, however, patterns of social separation became more complex. Many cases of racial segregation that attracted the attention of the courts were in northern cities. Racial separation was imposed not by the law but by economic and social factors such as housing patterns. Much of the middle class, including most whites, either moved to suburban communities or placed their children in private schools. Court orders to desegregate seemed only to encourage "white flight" and resegregation. Public opinion also became more complex. While the public continued to support racial integration, it became strongly opposed to the use of forced busing to achieve integration. Some former supporters of integration now championed the alternative of black separation and empowerment. Political leadership and the Supreme Court grew more conservative. In a series of legal challenges, the courts held that remedies such as busing between school districts could not be prescribed unless each of these school districts was guilty of deliberate segregation. Prosecutions by the Justice Department for violations of Title VI of the Civil Rights Act slowed to a trickle. Although blacks continued to become part of an increasing variety of society's institutions, legal and political pressures to desegregate diminished greatly.

Sociological Support

The jurists who decided *Brown v. Board of Education* were informed by social science findings that were both critical of the present and optimistic about the future. Sociologist Gunnar Myrdal, in his influential *An American Dilemma* (1944), interpreted the incompatibility be-

Paratroopers escort African American students from the Central High School campus in Little Rock, Arkansas, in 1957. Desegregation efforts met opposition in a number of southern towns.

tween the American ideal of equality of opportunity and the continuing presence of a legally sanctioned, race-based caste system as a chronic source of embarrassment to the national psyche. The research that was presented to the Court in *Brown v. Board of Education* suggested that the isolation of one group from another in a competing environment could breed mutual antagonisms and unflattering stereotypes. Once formed, such stereotypes become self-fulfilling prophecies influencing both the responses of others and one's perception of oneself. A famous study by psychologist Kenneth Clark showing that black children select white dolls as prettier was submitted as evidence that black children often adopt a negative, prejudiced view of themselves. This thesis—that segregation breeds prejudice, which in turn breeds mutual hostility, self-hate, and failure—was explicitly cited in Chief Justice Warren's opinion. It could be inferred that Warren also agreed that closer contact between blacks and whites would result in more equal opportunity by reducing prejudices, raising black self-esteem, and increasing academic success by African Americans.

Studies of the short-term effects of desegregation in schools have concentrated on changes in academic performance, changes in black and white attitudes toward each other, and changes in black self-esteem. More often than not, black academic achievement tends to be modestly improved after desegregation, and white academic achievement is not adversely affected. Attitudes of whites about blacks sometimes become more positive, sometimes become more negative, and sometimes change not at all. A crucial factor in increased positive attitudes is the existence of relationships that are both equal-status and cooperative in the pursuit of common goals. Black self-esteem has shown little change. Four decades later, at least 65 percent of black children still preferred white dolls, just as in Clark's pre-1954 studies.

An examination of the broader, long-term social and economic effects of desegregation also suggests a mixed picture. The resegregation of cities offers to inner-city black children opportunities that are dramatically unequal. Fear of changes in the quality of education following desegregation has in urban areas exacerbated white flight and the flight of middle-class blacks from urban areas. Indeed, many minority children of the inner city seem trapped in areas of crime, drugs, and violence in schools that are underfunded, underheated, undertaught, and overcrowded; the students have few middle-class black role models. These children seem to have little more opportunity than segregated black children did in 1954. For them, the net effect of the many social changes has been, at best, to break even.

There are, however, winners. Many graduates of the more successfully desegregated schools report cross-racial friendships of a quality that would have been rare before 1954. The highest-ranking black graduates of southern high schools are admitted to highly selective colleges with a regularity that would once have been astounding. The bottom line is that the *Brown v. Board of Education* decision was historically inevitable. That a constitutional democracy such as the United States would have approached the twenty-first century with a legally mandated caste system is almost unthinkable.

Thomas E. DeWolfe

Core Resources

Gordon W. Allport's *The Nature of Prejudice* (abridged ed., Garden City, N.Y.: Doubleday, 1958) describes much of the theory and research included in the social science brief in the *Brown* decision. Harold B. Gerard's "School Desegregation: The Social Science Role" (*American Psychologist*, August, 1983) reconsiders predictions made by psychologists in *Brown*, arguing that they were too optimistic. Jennifer L. Hochschild's *The New American Dilemma: Liberal Democracy and School Desegregation* (New Haven, Conn.: Yale University Press, 1984) argues that desegregation is resisted because racism is as firmly rooted in the United States as is the ideal of equality. Jonathan Kozol's *Savage Inequalities* (New York: Crown, 1991) is an impassioned account of underclass children in large U.S. cities and of the underfunded, overcrowded schools they attend. George R. Metcalf's *From Little Rock to Boston: The History of School Desegregation* (Westport,

Conn.: Greenwood Press, 1983) is a detailed history of the federal government's efforts to desegregate schools. Gunnar Myrdal's *An American Dilemma: The Negro Problem and Modern Democracy* (New York: Harper, 1944) highlights the incompatibility between core American ideals and the treatment and segregation of blacks. Raymond Wolters' *The Burden of Brown: Thirty Years of School Desegregation* (Knoxville: University of Tennessee Press, 1984) gives a detailed account of how five communities responded to the necessity of desegregating schools between 1954 and 1984. *Desegregation and the Supreme Court* (Boston: D. C. Heath, 1958), edited by Benjamin Ziegler, contains the text of the *Brown* decision and other related decisions.

See also: Affirmative action; *Alexander v. Holmes County Board of Education*; Black colleges and universities; *Brown v. Board of Education*; Civil Rights Act of 1964; Discrimination: direct institutionalized; Education and African Americans; Education and racial/ethnic relations; Equal educational opportunity; Jim Crow laws; Ole Miss desegregation; *Plessy v. Ferguson.*

Determined Residents United for Mohawk Sovereignty

Determined Residents United for Mohawk Sovereignty (DRUMS) was established at the Akwesasne Mohawk reservation in 1974. The Akwesasne Mohawk reservation (also called the Saint Regis Mohawk reserve) straddles the United States-Canadian border near Massena, New York, and Cornwall, Ontario. Beginning in the early 1970's, Akwesasne residents established DRUMS to combat increasing smuggling across the border. In the late 1970's and early 1980's, DRUMS's main focus turned to "speakeasies"—small, illegal drinking establishments that were contributing to an increasing number of traffic accidents on the reservation.

By June, 1989, DRUMS members were beginning to talk of blockading Route 37, the reservation's main highway, to keep away the clientele of several illegal casinos that had been constructed with smuggling profits. If the New York state police refused to close the gaming houses, many people believed civil disobedience to be their only option. DRUMS planned a blockade for June 9 but abandoned it in favor of a peaceful march. On July 20, two hundred FBI agents and New York state troopers raided seven casinos on the reservation, arresting thirteen people and seizing cash and financial records. DRUMS continued to oppose the casinos until May 1, 1990, when two Mohawk men, Mathew Pyke and "Junior" Edwards, were shot to death in firefights. After that, New York, Ontario, and Quebec police occupied the reservation, and the gaming houses were closed.

Bruce E. Johansen

See also: Gambling; Indian Gaming Regulatory Act; Reservation system of the United States.

Detroit riot

> **Significance:** The Detroit riot of 1967 was among the costliest race riots in U.S. history. Forty-one people died, nearly two thousand were injured, and damage estimates ranged from a quarter to a half billion dollars.

Urban race riots, which had taken place in Harlem in New York City in 1964 and 1967 and Watts in Los Angeles in 1965, had become part of the social upheaval of the decade. The urban unrest peaked during the summer of 1967. From Omaha, Nebraska, to Washington, D.C., riots took place in nearly 150 U.S. cities. In a July 12-16 riot in Newark, New Jersey, twenty-seven people died, more than eleven hundred were injured, and property damage reached fifteen million dollars.

The Riot

Detroit, Michigan, was a curious place for violence to erupt. Many African Americans commanded high wages in the automobile factories and high positions in the liberal United Automobile Workers union. About 40 percent of Detroit's 550,000 African Americans owned or were buying their own homes. Community leaders, both black and white, had made a civics lesson of the city's bloody race riot of 1943, which had left thirty-four dead and moved President Franklin D. Roosevelt to send in federal troops. Detroit's mayor, Jerome Cavanagh, had been elected with the support of the African American community.

However, a minor police incident on July 23, 1967, provided the spark that ignited the Detroit ghetto. An early-morning raid of a speakeasy on a run-down street resulted in knots of African American onlookers taunting the police. A brick crashed through the window of a police cruiser. At this point, the police could have either pulled out or used force to break up the crowd. They did neither. They dispatched cruisers but did nothing else; consequently, mobs gathered and started fires, then looting began. As the fires spread, so did the looting, creating a carnival atmosphere in the ghetto. Children joined adults in racing from stores with their arms full of groceries, liquor, or jewelry. Cars pulled up to businesses and their occupants filled them with appliances and other goods.

Both the mayor and the governor seemed paralyzed. Mayor Cavanagh ordered more swimming pools opened, and Governor George Romney suggested seeding rain clouds above the ghetto. Neither police nor peacemakers could stop the riot.

In order to quell the riot, Governor Romney deployed the National Guard, and President Lyndon B. Johnson sent in U.S. Army paratroopers. Although the Army troops were able to secure their sector of the ghetto, events went badly elsewhere. The National Guard and the police seemed to assume a license to kill. A subsequent investigation by the *Detroit Free Press* found that most of the official reports about the forty-three riot-related deaths (all but eight of them African Americans) had been pure fabrications. Three African Americans were shot as they sat in a car. A deaf man was killed because he couldn't hear a warning. A child holding a broom was gunned down. Finally, on the sixth day, July 28, the riot just burned itself out.

Impact

President Johnson moved quickly to appoint a commission to study the roots of urban racial unrest. The Kerner

With no police or National Guard nearby, looters freely carry away merchandise during the riot in Detroit in July, 1967.

Commission, named for its chairman, Governor Otto Kerner of Illinois, operated on the twin premises that the nation must ensure the safety of its people and that the nation must get at the root causes of racial strife.

The commission, which released its report in 1968, determined that the riots were not directed at white Americans but instead at their property and authority. It described a causal chain of "discrimination, prejudice, disadvantaged conditions, . . . all culminating in the eruption of disorder at the hands of youthful, politically aware activists." The frustration experienced by African Americans living in the ghetto was found to have long historical roots. The commission noted that the historical pattern of black-white relations had been "pervasive discrimination and segregation," which had resulted in whites leaving the inner cities and thus creating black ghettos. Young African Americans, alienated by the conditions produced by discrimination and segregation, had flocked to the banner of black power.

The commission concluded that the United States was moving toward separate and unequal societies, white and black. It called for increased national communication among races in order to end stereotypes and hostility. *Brian G. Tobin*

Core Resources
Richard N. Goodwin, a former speechwriter for President Johnson, fits the 1967 Detroit riot into the context of the times in *Remembering America: A Voice from the Sixties*. Journalist William Serrin's article "The Crucible," in the January/February, 1991, issue of the *Columbia Journalism Review*, is a firsthand account of the riot.

See also: Kerner Report; Newark race riots; Race riots of 1943; Race riots of the twentieth century; Watts riot.

Diaspora

"Disapora" comes from a Greek word meaning dispersion and refers to the dispersion of people outside their historic homelands. Historically, the term has been used mostly to refer to Jewish communities outside Israel. About 65.2 percent of the world's thirteen million Jews live outside Israel, and the concept has been very important in the Jewish community. The term began to be popular only in the last part of the twentieth century, however, and its usage has not spread to all applicable groups.

In the twentieth century, Pan-Africanism and the Civil Rights movement increased attention to the African origins of blacks outside Africa, and subsequently the term "diaspora" increasingly was applied to blacks living outside Africa. As the term became more popular, more references were made to the Irish diaspora. Other nations that have large diasporas include Asian nations, especially people with origins in China, Japan, and India.

Unlike the Jewish, African, Irish, and some other diasporas, the Asian diasporas have largely been products of the late nineteenth and twentieth centuries and have largely developed voluntarily for economic reasons. Japan is the best example. With a high population density and an oversupply of educated people, a lack of resources to maintain the population, a lack of hinterland or colonies to supply markets or resources, and a strong sense of racial solidarity, Japan developed numerous diaspora communities to provide needed jobs, resources, and markets. The Chinese diaspora communities are more diverse in origin than the Japanese but played a major role in China's emergence as a world economic power. The Indian diaspora communities are diverse, reflecting the caste system of India, and are created by small intragroup relations as well as by an Indian identity.

Important to the maintenance of groups in diaspora are a strong sense of identity with the homeland and with other diaspora communities of their group, group self-help, and a strong drive for self-preservation as a distinct group. The concept of diaspora has led to several controversial issues relating to intergroup relations. Questions have been raised about the national loyalty of people living in one nation but identifying with another. Whether the diaspora group should assimilate or be multicultural frequently is controversial. Conversely, the homeland of the diaspora group frequently expresses concern that its people in diaspora will lose contact or identity with the homeland and tries to maintain the loyalty of the diaspora communities. Some diaspora communities such as the Jewish and the Irish provide significant political and economic support to the homeland.

Some ethnic groups such as Italian Americans do not hope to return to the homeland nor do they consistently interact with it in any significant way; therefore, they are not considered to be in diaspora. Ethnic groups not generally referred to as diasporas include the Cuban Americans, who left their homeland to escape political oppression in large numbers in the 1960's. In 1991, *Diaspora: A Journal of Transnational Studies* was founded to study "diasporas and other transnational and infranational phenomena that challenge the homogeneity of the nation state" and to analyze relations of diasporas with real and imagined homelands. *Abraham D. Lavender*

See also: Cuban Americans; Ethnicity and ethnic groups; Immigration and emigration; Japanese Americans; Japanese Canadians; Japanese Peruvians in the United States.

Discrimination

Significance: Discrimination in one form or another appears to be endemic to all societies. In the United States, various groups have experienced various forms of discrimination, including racial discrimination, sexual discrimination (denial of certain rights to women), religious discrimination, cultural discrimination, age discrimination, discrimination against the disabled (both physically and mentally), and discrimination on the basis of sexual orientation.

Discrimination is the unequal treatment, whether intentional or unintentional, of individuals or groups on the basis of group membership that is unrelated to merit, ability, or past performance. The two most pervasive types of discrimination are legal discrimination and institutional discrimination. Legal discrimination is unequal treatment that is sustained by law. Institutional discrimination is a subtle form of unequal treatment based on race or ethnicity that is entrenched in social custom (that is, social institutions). Institutional discrimination may include segregated housing patterns, redlining by financial institutions, and the practice of minority group members being forced continually into low-paying jobs. Prejudice, which is often confused with discrimination, is the prejudgment of people, objects, or even situations on the basis of stereotypes or generalizations that persist even when facts demonstrate otherwise (for example, the majority of women on welfare are white, yet the stereotype of a female welfare recipient is that of a black woman with a brood of children).

The most pernicious acts of discrimination in the United States have been directed against racial and ethnic minorities. The history of racial and ethnic relations in the United States demonstrates that differential treatment has been accorded to all minority groups. A minority group is sometimes defined any group in a disadvantaged or subordinate position (in this sense, a minority may actually constitute a numerical majority; for example, blacks in South Africa). Minority populations have experienced the entire range of race relations, including assimilation, pluralism, legal protection, population transfer, continued subjugation, and extermination. While all minority populations have experienced some degree of discrimination, perhaps the most cruel and enduring discrimination has been experienced by those of African descent.

Africans were first brought to North America in 1619, and they proved to be an excellent source of inexpensive labor for the developing European colonies. In its early development, slavery was not rationalized by attitudes of racial superiority but simply by the need for cheap labor. Racial justification for slavery came later, as a strategy for maintaining the continued subjugation of blacks. Depicting blacks as subhuman, irresponsible, promiscuous, and lazy helped to stave off, for many years, groups (for example, abolitionists) bent upon ending slavery. The development of racist ideology during slavery has—over the years—continued to influence the relationship between blacks and whites in the United States.

The end of slavery in the United States did not, and could not, bring an end to discrimination. Discrimination had become institutionalized; it was embedded in social custom and in the very institutions of society. Initially, the Thirteenth, Fourteenth, and Fifteenth Amendments to the Constitution, along with the Civil Rights Acts of 1866 and 1867, did much to eliminate legal discrimination against the newly freed slaves. Yet many of those gains were abrogated by state legislatures in the South following the abrupt end of Reconstruction in 1877. The states of the Old Confederacy were able to circumvent much of the legislation passed during the Reconstruction period. They were able to sanction discrimination and deny civil rights by means of a set of laws called the black codes. The black codes virtually reintroduced many of the conditions that existed during slavery. Although the Fourteenth and Fifteenth Amendments guaranteed citizenship and the right to vote, these rights were abridged through intimidation, the poll tax, the grandfather clause, and literacy tests. Beginning in the 1880's, a more comprehensive set of laws—referred to as Jim Crow—gave rise to a system of legal segregation in South. This system of legal segregation was sanctioned by the "separate but equal" doctrine established in the *Plessy v. Ferguson* decision of 1896.

Legal Remedies

Substantial progress against Jim Crow did not occur until fifty-eight years later, with the *Brown v. Board of Education* decision (1954). In the *Brown* decision, the Supreme Court overturned *Plessy*, arguing that the concept of "separate but equal" was "inherently unequal." The *Brown* decision spurred many African Americans to exercise the rights and privileges guaranteed to all citizens under the Constitution. Beginning in the 1960's, the underlying legal, political, and economic context of race relations changed in the United States. Demonstrations, sit-ins, and marches by African Americans and their supporters caused America to begin addressing the second-class citizenship of minority groups. As a consequence, epoch-making legislation was passed in the form of the 1964 Civil Rights Act, affirmative action (in employment and education) was introduced, and governmental agencies actively tried to stamp out discrimination against minorities.

Yet riot after riot erupted across the nation in the 1960's. A combination of economic frustration, police brutality, resistance to desegregation, and assassinations of such leaders as the Reverend Martin Luther King, Jr., contributed to the eruptions. The Kerner Commission, which was commissioned to study the conditions leading up to the riots, concluded that "white racism" and discrimination were responsible for the outbreak of violence. Joseph S. Hines suggests in *Politics of Race* (1975) that African Americans have operated in a caste-like racial structure in the United States that has relegated them to inferior status, relative powerlessness, material deprivation, and sociopsychic resentment. Segregation and discrimination have been used as mechanisms for maintaining the sociopolitical structure (status quo). Within this structure, African Americans are members of a racial category for life; they are generally consigned to marry within their group; they are often avoided, both as ritual and as custom; and they experience limited opportunities.

Discrimination remains embedded in the social, political, and economic fabric of the United States. Employment and promotional opportunities are still strongly influenced by race. Consequently, minorities typically earn only a fraction of what white males earn, they tend to hold political office far less often than their numbers in the general population should warrant, and they are still excluded from membership in certain elite clubs because of their race. *Charles C. Jackson*

Core Resources

Hernan S. Cruz's *Racial Discrimination* (rev. ed., New York: United Nations, 1977), Joe R. Feagin and Clairece B. Feagin's *Discrimination American Style* (Englewood Cliffs, N.J.: Prentice-Hall, 1978), and Vernon Van Dyke's *Human Rights, Ethnicity, and Discrimination* (Westport, Conn.: Greenwood Press, 1985) survey various aspects of discrimination. Richard Kluger's *Simple Justice: The History of Brown v. Board of Education and Black America's Struggle for Equality* (New York: Alfred A. Knopf, 1976) focuses on one of the central episodes in the history of American discrimination.

See also: Bigotry; Civil Rights movement; Discrimination: behaviors; Discrimination: direct vs. indirect; Dis-

Discrimination played a part in the treatment of Chinese immigrants in the late 1800's, as this anti-Chinese cartoon demonstrates.

crimination: intentional vs. unintentional; Discrimination: overt/expressed vs. covert; Discrimination: racial and ethnic; Discrimination: responses to; Discrimination: spatial dimensions.

Discrimination: behaviors

Discrimination is perpetrated in many ways, including negative self-fulfilling prophecies, selective perception, avoidance of specific groups, denial of access (to jobs, housing, and the voting booth), tokenism, harassment, and violence. Many groups have been discriminated against in the United States, including women, Jews, Catholics, African Americans, Native Americans, Latinos, Asian Americans, Arab Americans, homosexuals, people with disabilities, people with mental illnesses, and the elderly.

Self-fulfilling prophecies are expectations that evoke behavior that makes the originally false conception true. Under this insidious process, the person who is the target of prejudice and therefore is expected to act or to be a certain way, responds to the prejudice by beginning to behave in a way that confirms the prejudice. For example, if an individual believes that all women are delicate and vulnerable, that person will tend to treat women this way, and women in turn will tend to act more helpless when interacting with that individual.

Selective perception, in which people's perceptions of the same incident differ, is another type of discriminatory behavior. For example, in one classic study, white college students watched a videotape of an argument between a white and black student. The argument grew heated, and in one version, the white student shoved the black student; in another version, the black student shoved the white student. White students described the white student who shoved as "playing around" or "dramatizing," but they described the black student who shoved as "violent."

Avoiding members of minority groups, even minor interactions such as making eye contact, is a passive form of discriminatory behavior that typically occurs in work, business, or recreational settings. It produces a subtle harmful effect by overlooking or minimizing the contributions of minority groups.

Another form of discriminatory behavior is denying equal access. For example, historically in the United States, fewer job opportunities have been available to women than men, especially at higher levels of government, business, and academics. Related to job discrimination is pay discrimination—women continue to receive lower pay for work similar or equal to that of men.

In tokenism, prejudiced people engage in positive but trivial or relatively insignificant actions toward members of a group they dislike. For example, a manager may make a token kindly gesture toward a minority member on staff (buying the person lunch at an expensive restaurant) or hire a minority member into a predominantly white work environment. Through this positive but insignificant gesture, the manager intends to avoid or at least delay more important actions such as promoting the individual or integrating the workplace. Having made this gesture, the manager feels that he or she has done something for the minority group. Tokenism has negative consequences for the minority member and perpetuates discrimination.

Discrimination can also take the form of overt actions such as harassment. For example, about 20 percent of women report that they have been sexually harassed on the job. In 1986, the U.S. Supreme Court ruled that sexual harassment violates civil rights, giving women a legal way to fight this behavior.

Aggressive behavior, which includes verbal abuse, vandalism, and crimes of violence, is another way in which discrimination is practiced. When taken to an extreme, this kind of behavior leads to intergroup warfare. It can also undermine the ability of members in diverse groups to interact positively and productively in their daily lives. *Lillian M. Range*

See also: Discrimination: direct vs. indirect; Discrimination: intentional vs. unintentional; Discrimination overt/expressed vs. covert; Discrimination: racial and ethnic; Tokenism.

Discrimination: direct institutionalized

Discrimination is an overt act directed toward an individual or group because the individual is a member of a specific ethnic group. Direct institutionalized discrimination involves one or more social systems (education, the economy, religion) and is used to oppress an entire ethnic or racial group. Joe R. Feagin and Clairece Booher Feagin in *Racial and Ethnic Relations* (5th ed., 1996), state that "direct institutionalized discrimination is organizationally prescribed or community-prescribed action that by intention has a differential and negative impact on members of subordinate racial and ethnic groups." Two examples will provide further clarification of direct institutionalized discrimination.

According to Dorothy Newman et al. (*Protest, Politics, and Prosperity: Black American and White Institutions, 1940-1975*, 1978), the National Association of Real Estate Boards "openly supported racial discrimination as a basic moral principle." The association's 1924 code of ethics states: "A realtor should never be instrumental in introducing into a neighborhood . . . members of any race or nationality, or individual whose presence will clearly be detrimental to property values in that neighborhood." Subsequently, this policy was supported by the Federal Housing Authority. Levittown, developed by the late William Levitt, was built for World War II veterans, yet black American soldiers were denied the opportunity to purchase these homes. The consequence of this discrimination has been high levels of residential segregation between blacks and whites.

Past legal segregation of educational institutions in the southern United States and de facto segregation in northern states also illustrate direct institutionalized discrimination. The vestige of this type of discrimination has remained and has contributed to the ongoing disparity in academic performance, facilities, and curriculum among schools. *Mary R. Holley*

See also: Discrimination; Discrimination: direct vs. indirect; Discrimination: indirect institutionalized; Discrimination: intentional vs. unintentional; Discrimination: overt/expressed vs. covert; Housing.

Discrimination: direct vs. indirect

Discrimination against racial and ethnic groups limits the life chances and choices of its victims in comparison with a society's politically dominant group. It is not, as some think, simply the accumulation of individual acts of unfairness. Rather, it is a social system embedded in a society's institutions that produces intergroup inequities in social outcomes.

A useful distinction can be made between direct and indirect forms of group discrimination. Direct discrimination is usually blatant and unambiguous. It occurs at the precise points where intergroup inequality is generated, and it is usually intentional. Therefore, direct discrimination involves unfair decisions explicitly based on group membership—racial, ethnic, religious, gender, and so on.

By contrast, indirect discrimination is subtle, often ambiguous and unintentional. It involves the perpetuation and magnification of the original restrictions imposed earlier by direct discrimination. Hence, indirect discrimination occurs when the inequitable results of direct discrimination are used as a basis for later decisions—concerning jobs, housing, education, and other central institutions of modern society. In other words, discrimination is indirect when an ostensibly nongroup criterion serves as a proxy for group membership in limiting social opportunities.

Although forms of direct discrimination are usually readily perceived as unfair, some observers deny that indirect forms constitute group discrimination. Yet the results of the two forms are the same and meet the general definition of group discrimination: Both direct and indirect discrimination restrict a group's access to the society's resources.

Examples clarify the distinction further. Direct discrimination exists when equally qualified blacks and women are paid less than whites and men for the same work. Indirect discrimination exists when the groups are paid unequally because prior discrimination in employment, education, or housing created apparent differences in qualifications or channeled the groups into differentially rewarded jobs. Hence, the direct-indirect distinction parallels the American legal distinction between disparate treatment and disparate impact. Although intentional direct discrimination typically triggers the causal chain, the original injury is often made worse by unwitting decision makers. Consequently, if remedies were limited only to instances where discrimination is *intentional*, much of indirect discrimination would go uncorrected. Worse, the legacy of past direct discrimination would continue to fester and be perpetuated further.

Forms of direct intergroup discrimination remain throughout North America, but they have declined over the past half century. Increasingly, however, indirect forms have taken their place. Less recognized and more difficult to combat, indirect discrimination has effectively limited the advances made by such groups as African Americans and First Canadians in spite of the decline of direct forms of restriction.

The difficulties inherent in establishing effective remedies for indirect discrimination are illustrated by the intensity of the controversy in the United States over affirmative action programs. Made necessary by the growing importance of indirect forms and one of the few methods that demonstrably remedies such discrimination, affirmative action has met with a series of political challenges. Virtually none of this debate, however, recognizes the critical distinction between direct and indirect discrimination.   *Thomas F. Pettigrew*

See also: Affirmative action; Discrimination: direct institutionalized; Discrimination: indirect institutionalized; Discrimination: intentional vs. unintentional; Discrimination: overt/expressed vs. covert; Disparate impact theory; Racism: changing nature of.

Discrimination: indirect institutionalized

Sociologists who study intergroup relations use the term "indirect institutionalized discrimination" to refer to the unintended denial of opportunity and inequitable treatment of individuals or groups in society caused by the established policies and practices of social institutions, such as the government, the economy, and education. This subtle yet damaging form of discrimination can be difficult to detect. It is often the result of policies being defined according to norms of the majority group and not with the intended purpose of carrying out individual or societal prejudices. Individuals and groups are not targeted because of their minority status; rather they are adversely affected because of certain characteristics or circumstances that are not consistent with the adopted norms of the institution in question.

In employment, for example, jobs with arbitrary height or weight requirements modeled after white males exclude certain ethnic groups. Asian Americans and some Hispanic ethnic groups are on average shorter than white Americans. Subsequently, they fail to meet such entrance requirements and are denied the opportunity of employment regardless of their ability to perform the job. Seniority requirements for advancement in the workplace also limit opportunity when minority group members enter jobs that are predominantly held by members of the majority. Despite the alleviation of structural barriers that prevent minority access entirely, minority group members are often not given promotions as a result of their comparatively shorter length of employment.   *Jessica M. Charbeneau*

Discrimination: intentional vs. unintentional

Four forms of discrimination have been identified by sociologists. The first form is intentional individual discrimination, which is an isolated act of discrimination performed by an individual on the basis of personal prejudice: for example, a male personnel officer who routinely passes over females for supervisory positions because he believes and consciously acts on the belief that "female supervisors mean trouble." The second form is unintentional individual discrimination, which is an isolated act of discrimination performed unconsciously by an individual. For example, if the personnel officer were unaware of why he was passing over females for supervisory positions, he would be performing an act of unintentional individual discrimination.

The third form, intentional institutional discrimination, occurs when discrimination is based on the personal prejudices of the members of an institution: for example, a male personnel officer who passes over women for supervisory positions because "boys in the company do not like to take orders from women." The fourth form, unintentional institutional discrimination, is discrimination that is part of the routine behavior of an institution that has unknowingly incorporated sexually or racially prejudicial practices into its operating procedures: for example, a construction company that routinely avoids hiring women because of its assumption that women are incapable of doing heavy construction work.

Recent discussions of discrimination have focused on unintentional institutional discrimination by suggesting different measures for correcting this form of discrimination in the workplace. Some people believe that this form of discrimination can be corrected only by affirmative action programs. Others argue that these programs are inherently unjust and that workplace discrimination can be corrected through antidiscrimination laws.

Krishna Mallick

Discrimination: overt/expressed vs. covert

Overt discrimination is discrimination that is visible and open. During the Jim Crow era in the United States, African Americans were publicly denied opportunities expressly on the basis of race. For example, they were denied membership in labor unions and equal access to public facilities, schools, and housing *because* they were black. Discrimination during this time was legal and was viewed as justifiable.

Attitudes toward overt discrimination have changed dramatically since the Jim Crow era. In 1964, Congress passed the Civil Rights Act, which banned discrimination in publicly owned facilities and in any programs that received federal aid on the basis of race, religion, national origin, color, or gender. Subsequent legislation has banned discrimination in areas such as housing.

Because overt discrimination is visible, it is usually easy to document and remedy, and it has become much less likely to occur than it was at the beginning of the twentieth century. However, overt discrimination is still practiced by many individuals and groups. It is expressed through harassing remarks and through racial and ethnic violence. It is also practiced by various private social clubs. For example, Tiger Woods, a multiracial prominent golfer during the 1990's, was forbidden to play at several golf courses in the United States because of his racial makeup.

Covert discrimination differs from overt discrimination in that it is often concealed. It refers to actions that may appear to be nondiscriminatory but are discriminatory in intent and nature. Sabotage, the deliberate but covert undermining of an individual's ability to do his or her job simply on the basis of prejudice, is one form of covert discrimination. Tokenism, the symbolic admission or hiring of an individual of color to mask otherwise discriminatory practices, is another.

Covert discrimination is often rationalized as being fair or necessary, when it actually denies equal opportunity. Poll taxes and literacy tests are examples of covert discrimination. In the late 1800's and early 1900's, individuals in some areas were not allowed to vote unless they passed a literacy test and/or paid a poll tax. Although the policies may have appeared to be rational or at least not blatantly discriminatory, they were discriminatory in intent and in their results. The policies were intended to exclude African Americans from participating in the political process because many of them could not afford to pay the tax or were unable to read. The policies were successful. Within years of implementation, the number of blacks registered to vote fell drastically.

Poll taxes and literacy tests were banned in 1965 when

the U.S. Congress passed the Voting Rights Act. Although legislation such as this has helped stop incidents of covert discrimination, it has not eliminated it. For example, some companies and institutions have stringent job requirements such as a minimal level of educational attainment or previous job experience. Some require applicants to pass tests to ascertain whether or not they are capable of performing the job. Although these practices appear to be nondiscriminatory, and they may in some cases be completely justified, they become discriminatory when the standards are set higher than deemed necessary for "business necessity" in order to prevent minority applicants from obtaining the job. Although steps have been taken to alleviate practices such as these, it is often difficult to prove that covert discrimination has occurred, and individuals are often unaware that they are victims.   *Amy J. Orr*

See also: Civil Rights Act of 1964; Discrimination: behaviors; Discrimination: direct institutionalized; Discrimination: direct vs. indirect; Discrimination: indirect institutionalized; Discrimination: intentional vs. unintentional; Discrimination: racial and ethnic; Literacy tests; Poll tax; Voting Rights Act of 1965.

Discrimination: racial and ethnic

> **Significance:** Responding to racial and ethnic discrimination and conflict has been particularly challenging for the U.S. government, given the immigrant nature of American society and the long-standing commitment to the principle of equality before the law in the country's political culture.

Within the founding documents of the United States are contradictory statements on equality and freedom—and hence on people's right not to be discriminated against. The Declaration of Independence calls it self-evident that "all men are created equal" and have "unalienable rights." Yet prior to the Thirteenth Amendment (1865) the Constitution upheld the institution of slavery, notably in a provision that fugitive slaves must be returned to their owners. Any new country proclaiming equality while allowing slavery and thinking of an entire race as inferior is founded on an impossible contradiction, one that many of the founders undoubtedly realized would have to be faced in the future. Until the mid-twentieth century, however, the federal government generally avoided becoming involved in attempts to legislate

against discrimination, allowing the states to establish their own policies. Many of the states, being closer to the people and their prejudices than the federal government was, were inclined to condone discrimination and even actively encourage it through legislation.

Discrimination existed in many different areas of life, including education, employment, housing, and voting rights. Two major pieces of legislation of the 1960's were designed to attack discrimination in these areas: the Civil Rights Act of 1964 and the Voting Rights Act of 1965. The primary avenue for fighting discrimination is through the courts, a fact which causes problems of its own. The Equal Employment Opportunity Commission (EEOC), for example, has the power to bring lawsuits involving employment discrimination; however, a huge number of charges of discrimination are brought before the agency. For that reason, as of the mid-1990's it had a backlog of many thousands of cases awaiting its attention. In discrimination cases the courts have sometimes applied a standard of discriminatory intent and sometimes relied on a standard of discriminatory impact.

Some types of discrimination are easier to see and to rectify than others. A number of activists and legal experts had shifted their attention by the 1980's to a type of discrimination generally known as "institutional discrimination." Institutional discrimination refers to discrimination that is built into social or political institutions, frequently in nearly invisible ways. Institutional discrimination is sometimes not even intentional.

Development of the American Nation
The framework for the development of the United States and its treatment of ethnic minorities was established during the first half century of the nation's history. When the American Revolution ended in 1783, there were few people in the thirteen colonies who considered themselves "Americans," as opposed to Virginians, Pennsylvanians, New Yorkers, and so on. Nevertheless, the people who joined under the Articles of Confederation had much in common. They shared a common language, ethnic stock, and history as well as a philosophy of government that stressed individual rights over group rights. Given time and interaction, one would expect these former colonials to develop a common sense of national identity.

To a substantial extent, that integration occurred during the nineteenth century via such common endeavors as the successful wars against the Spanish in Florida, against Britain in 1812, and against various Indian tribes. As people moved westward to the frontier, the conquest of the continent itself also became a unifying national purpose.

Yet a major challenge to the development of this emerging sense of national identity also arose during the nineteenth century. Between 1830 and 1910, while the country was absorbing new territory, approximately forty-four million immigrants entered the United States, mostly Europeans with backgrounds differing from the white Anglo-Saxon prototype of the founders. Moreover, the Civil War resulted in the freeing of millions of African American slaves, who suddenly became American citizens. There was also a trickle of immigrants arriving from Asia. Finally, there were Jewish immigrants, primarily in the Northeast, and Hispanics, primarily in the Southwest. The country's citizenry was becoming multiethnic and multiracial.

Native Americans
Adopted in 1789, the U.S. Constitution made Native Americans wards of the federal government. Treaties with the tribes, like all treaties, were to be federal affairs, and the Supreme Court has repeatedly affirmed the exclusive nature of this power of Congress (*Cherokee Nation v. Georgia*, 1831; *The New York Indians v. United States*, 1898). The Supreme Court has also repeatedly upheld the federal government's right to rescind—by ordinary legislation or the admission of new states to the union—those rights accorded the tribes by prior treaties (the *Cherokee Tobacco* case, 1871; *United States v. Winans*, 1905). Even the rationale for the guardian-ward relationship existing between the federal government and the tribes has been elucidated in the opinions of the Court. Essentially, it involves three elements: the weakness and helplessness of Native Americans, the degree to which their condition can be traced to their prior dealings with the federal government, and the government's resultant obligation to protect them. Few of the federal policies adopted before World War II, however, can be described as protective or even benign toward Native Americans.

Policies toward Native Americans traditionally built on the pattern of relations with the tribes established by Europeans prior to the ratification of the Constitution. For hundreds of years, the French, Portuguese, Spanish, English, and Dutch subdued the tribes they encountered, denigrated their cultures, and confiscated their lands and wealth. Early U.S. actions continued the pattern, especially where tribes physically hindered western expansion. During the 1830's, the concept of Indian Territory (land for the Native Americans territorially removed from European settlers) gained favor among European Americans.

When even the most remote of areas were eventually opened to European immigrants, the Indian Territory policy was abandoned in favor of a reservation policy: relocating and settling tribes within contained borders. Meanwhile, contact with European diseases, combined with the increasingly harsh life forced on Native Americans, had devastating effects on the tribes in terms of disrupting their societies and dramatically reducing their numbers. Beginning in the 1880's, reservation policies were frequently augmented by forced assimilation policies: Many young Native Americans were taken from their reservations and sent to distant boarding schools. There, tribal wear and ways were ridiculed, and speaking native languages in class could mean beatings. Only with World War I did these policies soften.

Significant changes in government attitudes toward Native Americans did not come until the Indian New Deal was instituted by reform-minded commissioner of Indian affairs John Collier in the 1930's. In the late 1960's, another chapter opened as Indians began to demand their own civil rights in the wake of the predominantly African American Civil Rights movement. More enlightened federal policies toward Native Americans began to emerge, and since the 1960's considerable legislation has appeared, including the 1968 American Indian Civil Rights Act and the 1975 Indian Self-Determination and Education Assistance Act. A number of factors have worked against Native Americans in advancing their own cause, among them the small number of Native Americans (less than 1 percent of the American population), the assimilation of their most educated members into the general population, and the fact that Native Americans generally think of themselves not as "Indians" or "Native Americans" but as members of a specific tribe.

Discrimination in Immigration Policy
Fulfillment of the United States' self-determined manifest destiny to spread from the Atlantic to the Pacific Ocean required people, and early in the nineteenth century the government opened its doors wide to immigrants from Europe.

Yet even during this period, the door was open to few beyond Europe. Hispanic immigrants could enter the country fairly easily across its southern border, but American memories of Texas's war with Mexico made the country inhospitable toward them. More conspicuously, immigration policy was anti-Asian by design. The Chinese Exclusion Act, for example, passed in 1882, prohibited unskilled Chinese laborers from entering the country. Later amendments made it even more restrictive and forced Chinese people living in the United States to carry identification papers. The law was not repealed until 1943. Beginning with the exclusion laws of the 1880's, quotas, literacy tests, and ancestry requirements were used individually and in combination to exclude Asian groups. Indeed, even after the efforts during the 1950's to make the immigration process less overtly discriminatory, preferences accorded to the kin of existing citizens continued to skew the system in favor of European and—to a lesser extent—African immigrants.

Meanwhile, Asians who succeeded in entering the country often became the targets of such discriminatory state legislation as California's 1913 Alien Land Bill, which responded to the influx of Japanese in California by limiting their right to lease land and denying them the right to leave any land already owned to the next generation. The most overtly discriminatory act against Asian immigrants or Asian Americans was perpetrated by the federal government, however, which under the color of wartime exigencies relocated tens of thousands of U.S.-born Japanese Americans living on the West Coast to detention camps during World War II. The Supreme Court upheld the relocation program in *Korematsu v. United States* (1944).

It was not until the 1960's and 1970's, during and following the Vietnam War and the collapse of a series of United States-supported governments and revolutionary movements in Asia and Latin America, that the United States opened its doors to large numbers of immigrants and refugees from Asia and the Hispanic world. The government went so far as to accord citizenship to children born of foreigners illegally living in the country.

African Americans
Nineteenth century European immigrants generally were able to make the transition to American citizenship effectively. The urban political machines found jobs for them and recruited them into the political process as voters who, in turn, supported the machines. The prosperity of the country, manifested in the land rushes of the nineteenth century, the industrial revolution, and the postwar economic booms of the twentieth century, enabled the vast majority of these immigrants to achieve upward mobility and a share of the good life.

The citizens who were unable to fit into this pattern, apart from the reservation-bound American Indian tribes, were the African Americans. Enslaved in thirteen states prior to the Civil War (1861-1865) and kept in subservience by state laws and various extralegal arrangements for generations afterward, African Americans remained a social, economic, and political underclass with little expectation of progress until nearly eighty years after the Civil War Amendments were added to the Constitution to free and empower them.

The Thirteenth Amendment (1865) abolished slavery, the Fourteenth Amendment (1868) was designed to prevent states from interfering with the rights of former slaves, and the Fifteenth Amendment (1870) constitutionally enfranchised African Americans. By the end of the nineteenth century, however, Supreme Court opinions and state action had combined to minimize the impact of these amendments. In the *Slaughterhouse* cases (1873), the Supreme Court crippled the Fourteenth Amendment. The Court's decision limited the amendment's privileges and immunities clause only to those rights a citizen has by virtue of national citizenship, not state citizenship. Second, it interpreted the due process clause as a restraint only on how a state may act, not on what it can do. Only the equal protection clause of the Fourteenth Amendment, which the Court limited to issues of race, continued to offer protection to the newly freed slaves, and in two subsequent cases even that protection was substantially reduced.

First, in the *Civil Rights* cases of 1883, the Supreme Court ruled that the equal protection clause applies only to state action, not to private discrimination. Then, in the pivotal case *Plessy v. Ferguson* (1896), the Court held that states could satisfy the requirements of the equal protection clause by providing "separate-but-equal" facilities for blacks and whites. In the meantime, the states began to employ literacy tests, poll taxes, and other devices and arrangements to restrict the ability of African Americans to vote.

Inclusion Policies
Between 1896 and 1936, not only did the separate-but-equal doctrine legitimize racial discrimination, but also the Supreme Court persistently sustained separation schemes as long as facilities of some kind were provided to a state's black citizens—even if the facilities were woefully inferior to those provided to the white community. In the mid-1930's, however, responding to cases being appealed by the National Association for the Advancement of Colored People (NAACP), the Supreme Court began to shift direction. Between 1936 and 1954, it began to demand that states provide equal facilities to both races and to adopt more demanding tests for measuring the equality of segregated facilities. A Texas system providing separate law schools for blacks and whites, for example, was ruled unconstitutional in 1950 in *Sweatt v. Painter* because the black law school lacked the "intangibles" (such as reputation and successful alumni) that confer "greatness" on a law school and hence was unequal to the long-established school of law for white students at the University of Texas. Likewise, during the same period the Supreme Court began to remove some of the state-imposed obstacles to African Americans voting in the South and to limit the use of state machinery to enforce private acts of discrimination. The separate-but-equal test itself was finally abandoned in 1954, when, in the landmark case *Brown v. Board of Education*, the Supreme Court ruled that segregated facilities are inherently unequal in public education.

The *Brown* decision led to a decade-long effort by southern states to avoid compliance with desegregation orders. With the Supreme Court providing a moral voice against segregated public facilities, however, these state

Overt racial discrimination, as evidenced by the "white ladies only" sign on the women's restroom door, was common in the South until Supreme Court decisions and the Civil Rights Act of 1964 made it illegal.

efforts failed when challenged in court. Moreover, a powerful multiracial Civil Rights movement emerged to demand justice for African Americans in other areas as well. In response, Congress enacted such landmark legislation as the 1964 Civil Rights Act (outlawing discrimination in employment and in places of private accommodation), the 1965 Voting Rights Act, and a series of affirmative action laws designed to benefit groups traditionally discriminated against in American society.

As a result of these laws, the profile of the United States as a multiracial society was irrevocably altered. This change occurred almost entirely as a result of action within the country's legal and constitutional channels. To be sure, prejudice cannot be legislated away even though discrimination can be made illegal. In the mid-1990's, most American cities continued to possess a large African American underclass even as affirmative action and Head Start programs were becoming controversial and being canceled. On the other hand, the policies that had been adopted during the 1950's and 1960's enabled a sizable African American middle and professional class to develop, and many American cities had elected African Americans to govern them by the 1990's. It has been argued that the growing prosperity of a subgroup of the African American community undercut the power of the Civil Rights movement. By the 1990's, a number of successful and affluent African American leaders, such as Supreme Court justice Clarence Thomas, were themselves opposing further affirmative action plans as well as further efforts to finance welfare programs perceived as primarily benefiting a heavily minority urban underclass.   *Joseph R. Rudolph, Jr., and McCrea Adams*

Core Resources
For good short discussions of government policies toward Native Americans, see Edward H. Spicer, *The American Indians* (Cambridge, Mass.: Belknap Press of Harvard University Press, 1980), and Francis Paul Prucha, *Indian Policy in the United States: Historical Essays* (Lincoln: University of Nebraska Press, 1981). Immigration and discrimination is well treated in Nathan Glazer, ed., *Clamor at the Gates: The New American Immigration* (San Francisco: Institute for Contemporary Studies, 1985); Ronald Takaki, ed., *From Different Shores: Perspectives on Race and Ethnicity in America* (2d ed., New York: Oxford University Press, 1994); and Nathan Glazer and Daniel Patrick Moynihan's classic, *Beyond the Melting Pot: The Negroes, Puerto Ricans, Jews, Italians, and Irish of New York City* (2d ed., Cambridge, Mass.: MIT Press, 1970). Interesting works within the vast literature on the Civil Rights movement include Leon Friedman, *The Civil Rights Reader: Basic Documents of the Civil Rights Movement* (New York: Walker, 1968); Anna Kosof, *The Civil Rights Movement and Its Legacy* (New York: Watts, 1989); and Dennis Chong, *Collective Action and the Civil Rights Movement* (Chicago: University of Chicago Press, 1991).

See also: Affirmative action; American Indian civil rights; Anti-Defamation League; Black Power movement; *Brown v. Board of Education; Civil Rights* cases; Civil Rights movement; *Griggs v. Duke Power Company; Heart of Atlanta Motel v. United States;* Immigration and emigration; Jim Crow laws; *Jones v. Alfred H. Mayer Company, Korematsu v. United States; Plessy v. Ferguson;* Race riots of the twentieth century; *Swann v. Charlotte-Mecklenburg Board of Education; Sweatt v. Painter; Wards Cove Packing Company v. Atonio.*

Discrimination: responses to

Significance: Racial or ethnic groups or individuals who are discriminated against can respond to discrimination in a variety of ways. The specific response selected, and how the dominant society responds to the behavior, have important consequences for intergroup relations.

Responses to discrimination can range from self-hatred to direct confrontation of those who discriminate. The specific response used, and the likelihood of success for that response, vary according to time and place.

Self-Hatred, Ghettoization, and Stigma Redemption
From the perspective of a racial or minority group, the most negative response to experiencing discrimination is self-hatred. The person discriminated against internalizes the negative evaluations of the discrimination and hates himself or herself for having the negative characteristic. In some cases, this can lead to allying with the discriminator against other members of the individual's group. Also, a person might simply adopt a defeatist attitude and withdraw from society. In extreme cases, an individual might commit suicide because of feelings of inferiority internalized from the discriminator. However, self-hatred does not necessarily mean that a person hates himself or herself; the hatred can be directed against the group to which the person belongs and which is the object of discrimination.

Another response to discrimination, one that usually has negative consequences for the person discriminated against, is ghettoization. The person limits himself or herself to living in a limited part of the larger society, associating mostly with other members of the discriminated-against group. In many cases, as has been true for blacks in the United States, ghettoization is forced on the person by discriminating restrictions based on race, religion, or another aspect of ethnicity. In some cases, as with many Jews historically, individuals choose to live in a ghetto in order to avoid daily or frequent incidents of discrimination and to maintain ethnic identity. However, whether forced or voluntary, a ghetto usually has negative consequences in that it limits a person's life opportunities in such areas as education and jobs. Ghettos usually lack facilities available elsewhere. Some activists have argued for ghettoization on a larger scale by supporting, for example, an all-black state or nation.

With stigma redemption, another way of responding, the victim of discrimination accepts the discrimination but comforts himself or herself with the belief that in the next world (heaven or hell, the afterlife, a reincarnation, and so on), the victim will be rewarded for being a good person and the discriminator will be punished for being a bad person. Historically, the version of Christianity taught to black slaves in the United States encouraged this perspective, and many African Americans followed this perspective into the twentieth century. This response has led to some blacks accusing other blacks of being "Uncle Toms" for not opposing discriminatory treatment.

Passing, Covering, and Correction
The person who uses passing as a response to discrimination is able, because of a lack of characteristics identifying the person as a member of the discriminated-against group, to be accepted by members of the discriminating group as a member of their group. The classic example in the United States is the person who is legally or socially classified as black but who, because of light color, can move to another area where the individual is unknown and be accepted as white. Passing can be permanent, ended by exposure, or ended temporarily (for example, during a visit to relatives). In the United States, at least until the Civil Rights movement in the 1950's and 1960's, several thousand people are estimated to have passed each year. Members of other ethnic groups, for example, Jewish Americans and Italian Americans, frequently can pass by changing such characteristics as their names, religions, or mannerisms.

Covering can be defined as temporary passing and is much more common than passing. The member of the discriminated-against group can successfully hide, in selected areas of life, such as the workplace, the characteristics that lead to experiencing discrimination. Covering is likely to be used by lifestyle groups that suffer discrimination, such as homosexuals, but also can be used by some ethnic groups.

Another way of responding to discrimination is trying to correct the behavior that leads to discrimination. This is more likely to be used for lifestyle groups regarding sexual or drug-using behavior, but some members of racial and ethnic minorities advocate changing behaviors for which their group is stereotyped negatively. For example, a number of black leaders, usually referred to as conservative blacks, argue that some of the negative stereotypes that lead to discrimination are based on behaviors that should be changed, such as teenage pregnancies, drug usage, and dependence on welfare. Others argue that this is blaming the victim.

Stigma Conversion and Confrontation
In the 1960's during the Civil Rights movement, a major effort was initiated to replace negative evaluations (stigmas) of blackness with positive evaluations. The slogan Black Is Beautiful and similar phrases such as I'm Black and I'm Proud emphasized pride in being black and converted blackness into a positive term. Similar slogans of self-acceptance and power became popular among other groups, including Sisterhood Is Powerful for women, Gray Panthers for the elderly, and Lavender [mixture of blue for males and pink for females] Power for gays.

Throughout history, racial or ethnic groups have resorted to direct confrontation to stop discriminatory treatment, frequently resulting in war. In the United States, the black Civil Rights movement was the major racial or ethnic confrontational movement in the twentieth century. Opinions differ on whether confrontations should be violent or nonviolent. Native Americans, Mexican Americans, and others also have confronted discriminatory behavior through mass protests.

Abraham D. Lavender

Core Resources
Erving Goffman's *Stigma: Notes on the Management of Spoiled Identity* (Englewood Cliffs, N.J.: Prentice-Hall, 1963) discusses several ways of responding to stigmatization including tribal stigmas of race, nation, and religion. Shirlee Taylor Haizlip's *The Sweeter the Juice* (New York: Simon & Schuster, 1994) is based on a personal story of racial passing. *Indians in American History* (Wheeling, Ill.: Harlan Davidson, 1988), edited by Frederick E. Hoxie, describes activities of the struggle for Native American civil rights. Ralph Abernathy's *And the Walls Came Tumbling Down* (New York: Harper & Row, 1989) discusses responses to discrimination followed by African Americans during the Civil Rights movement.

See also: African American stereotypes; Black Is Beautiful movement; Civil Rights movement; Conservative blacks; Jewish Americans; Passing.

Discrimination: spatial dimensions

> **Significance:** The consideration and pursuit of racial, ethnic, and gender equality have led to investigations of the spatial aspects of discrimination: the negotiation of public and private spaces, access to institutional resources and privileges, and intergroup relations and conflict.

Since classical antiquity, the distinction between public and private space has served as an entry point into issues of social and political analysis, legal and economic debate, and the ordering of everyday life. Different versions of this distinction have attained new or renewed prominence in a wide variety of disciplines ranging from neoclassical economics to legal studies and feminist scholarship. However, the distinction between "public space" and "private space" is not rigid, both because the two terms lack definitional clarity and because there is significant overlap between the two categories.

Public and Private: Basic Orientations
Research on spatial discrimination has been confusing, in part, because the dimensions of spatial discrimination have not been clearly defined. For social scientists, the public/private distinction is generally used to delineate

different kinds of social action occurring in various physical and social spaces. For example, for the eighteenth century philosopher and social theorist Jean-Jacques Rousseau, "public space" referred to the practice of citizenship—a metaphorical political realm characterized by discussion, deliberation, and debate. However, for modern scholars such as Jane Jacobs or Erving Goffman, public space is not only conceptual but also physical, characterized by face-to-face interaction and sociability. According to these scholars, "public space" can refer either to a city's built environment (spaces that have form, location, and structure) or to interactional and experiential space (rules, conduct, and conventions, displayed within spaces between strangers). In practice, the distinction between public and private space is often used to demarcate boundaries between the private world of family and the public world of sociability or between the public sector of state administration and the private sector of the marketplace. Historically, however, public/private distinctions have been used for social stratification purposes: to assign men and women to different spheres of social life on the basis of "natural characteristics" and to confine women to positions of economic inferiority with respect to men. Thus, differences between public/private distinctions not only point to different assumptions about how the social world operates but also are motivated by different problems, generate different issues, and raise very different concerns.

Dimensions of Discrimination
In the social sciences, the word "discrimination" refers to actions or practices carried out by members of dominant groups or their representatives that have a differential and negative impact on members of subordinate groups. For discrimination to occur, there must be a discriminator, an act having differential and harmful effects, and a victim. In regard to these three dimensions, similarities between spatial and traditional discrimination become evident and even intertwine and overlap. However, although both spatial and traditional approaches recognize variations in the number of discriminators, an important difference between these two perspectives is that the traditional approach tends to view discrimination as more individualistic, sporadic, and episodic than the spatial approach which—while recognizing microlevel discriminatory activity—emphasizes the social patterning of discriminatory actions on the institutional level, especially their presence in large-scale bureaucratic organizations.

Defining Spatial Discrimination
Spatial discrimination refers to the size, complexity, and organizational environment of groups or individuals

carrying out discriminatory activity in public or private settings. The size can vary from individual action to very large numbers of individuals engaged in routine practices in a large organization such as the finance division of a large corporation that regularly denies loans to minority individuals. Individual and small group actions may not be embedded in large organizations; however, discriminatory practices may still occur in normative contacts between acquaintances and strangers (such as a derogatory remark that reveals a prejudicial viewpoint against a loan applicant). From this perspective, spatial discrimination is not only the imposition of barriers at a given point in time but also entails a process of constantly defending any group privileges (such as access to housing in desirable areas) gained at the expense of another group. Thus, spatial discrimination can be viewed as a behavioral process aimed at maintaining the privileges of the dominant group.

Impact on Public Policy

Social scientists are not the only researchers who have contributed to broadening the concept of spatial discrimination. Legal research in which "the object of litigation is the vindication of constitutional statutory policies" has also contributed to blurred lines between public and private distinctions. For example, a doctrine known as *parens patriae* sometimes allows the government to enforce private rights, and private individuals may sometimes enforce public rights in what is referred to as a *qui tam* action. The concerns driving legal scholarship have led to sharp reformulations of how spatial discrimination and the public/private distinction are defined.   *Antwi A. A. Akom*

Core Resources

Joe R. Feagin, "The Continuing Significance of Race," in *American Sociological Review* (56, February, 1991), discusses antiblack discrimination in public places. Gunnar Myrdal's *An American Dilemma: The Negro Problem and Modern Democracy* (New York: Harper Brothers, 1944) attacks segregation for its deprivation of individuals' personal rights and narrow, provincial views of the world and future. Philip Kasinitz's *Metropolis: Center and Symbol of Our Times* (New York: New York Press, 1995) examines the social and psychological nature of urbanism and includes sections on the built environment and public space. Gordon Allport's *The Nature of Prejudice* (New York: Doubleday Anchor, 1958) examines prejudice as a useful tool for understanding ethnic relations in the social sciences.

See also: Discrimination; Discrimination: racial and ethnic.

Discrimination: systemic

Systemic discrimination refers to the unjustified differential treatment of categories of people across multiple social institutions: educational, economic, medical, and so on. The cumulative impact of this discrimination can negatively affect the life chances of targeted groups. In *Discrimination American Style: Institutional Racism and Sexism* (1978), sociologist Joe Feagin distinguishes between individual and institutional discrimination, noting that unlike the former, which can be attributed to one person and/or may be sporadic, institutional discrimination is a continual pattern of discrimination inherent in the operation of a social institution. He explains that this discrimination may be intentional or unintentional. For example, throughout the early to mid-twentieth century, Jim Crow laws were intentionally created to enforce racial segregation. The separation of facilities into "white" and "colored" meant poor schooling, poor health care, and poor housing for African Americans. On the other hand, unintentional or indirect discrimination does not involve intent to harm. Due to a history of discrimination, the norms of an institution may function in a way that can create unfair advantages for dominant group members while negatively affecting the life chances of subordinate group members. The interplay of discrimination across multiple social institutions produces systemic discrimination, or discrimination that is an integral part of the entire social system.   *Roxanna E. Harlow*

See also: Discrimination: direct institutionalized; Discrimination: intentional vs. unintentional; Jim Crow laws.

Disease and intergroup contact

Significance: Within decades after contact with Europeans, Native American societies experienced rapid population declines; although the reasons for the demographic collapse of native North America are complex, a prominent factor in that decline was Old World infectious diseases, introduced by European explorers and settlers.

After the arrival of Europeans, the estimated aboriginal population of native North America began to decline. The Spanish intrusion first into the Caribbean and then into the Southwest and Southeast, circa 1520, launched a series of lethal epidemics that infected various Native American people. The epidemiological conquest of native North America accelerated after the early seventeenth century with English and French colonization along the Atlantic seaboard. The dramatic population

North American Epidemics and Regions Affected, 1520-1696

Date of Onset	Epidemic	Regions Affected
1520	Smallpox	All regions
1531	Measles	Southwest
1545	Bubonic plague	Southwest
1559	Influenza	South Atlantic states, Gulf area, Southwest
1586	Typhus	South Atlantic states, Gulf area
1592	Smallpox	North Atlantic states, South Atlantic states, Old Northwest, Great Lakes states, Midwest east of Mississippi River, Southwest
1602	Smallpox	Southwest
1612	Bubonic plague	North Atlantic states, South Atlantic states, Gulf area, Southwest
1633	Measles	North Atlantic states
1637	Scarlet fever	North Atlantic states
1639	Smallpox	North Atlantic states, South Atlantic states, Old Northwest, Great Lakes states, Midwest east of Mississippi River
1646	Smallpox	Gulf area, Southwest
1647	Influenza	North Atlantic states
1649	Smallpox	North Atlantic states, South Atlantic states, Gulf area
1655	Smallpox	Gulf area
1658	Measles, diphtheria	North Atlantic states, Gulf area, Old Northwest, Great Lakes states, Midwest east of Mississippi River, Southwest
1662	Smallpox	North Atlantic states, Old Northwest, Great Lakes states, Midwest east of Mississippi River
1665	Smallpox	South Atlantic states, Old Northwest, Great Lakes states, Midwest east of Mississippi River
1669	Smallpox	North Atlantic states
1674	Smallpox	Gulf area, southern Plains
1675	Influenza	North Atlantic states
1677	Smallpox	North Atlantic states
1687	Smallpox	North Atlantic states
1692	Measles	North Atlantic states, Old Northwest, Great Lakes states, Midwest east of Mississippi River
1696	Smallpox, Influenza	South Atlantic states, Gulf area

Sources: Data are from Dobyns, Henry F., *Their Number Became Thinned.* Knoxville: University of Tennessee Press, 1983; Thornton, Russell, *American Indian Holocaust and Survival: A Population History Since 1492.* Norman: University of Oklahoma Press, 1987.

decline of indigenous people continued until the early twentieth century. By 1920, 270,995 Native Americans remained after the epidemiological onslaught of European colonization. They were the survivors of perhaps 1.2 million to 18 million Native Americans who inhabited North America at the time of the arrival of Europeans.

Increased mortality among Native Americans as a result of introduced European diseases such as smallpox is not attributable to a lack of sufficient immunological response to infections in general but to the fact that Native Americans had no prior exposure to these pathogens. The "new" pathogens therefore not only created a high degree of physiological stress but also engendered cultural stress. Epidemic episodes often resulted in a breakdown in the social system, elevating mortality levels.

Although European infectious diseases devastated many Native American societies, precontact native North America was not a disease-free paradise. Biological and archaeological evidence documents the fact that precontact Native American populations suffered from a number of afflictions. Malnutrition, anemia, and a variety of tuberculoid, trepanematoid, and other degenerative, chronic, and congenital conditions plagued indigenous populations. The general state of health, in combination with ecological and cultural factors, therefore, greatly affected the postcontact disease experience of Native American societies.

Sixteenth and Seventeenth Centuries

No Old World pathogen was more lethal than smallpox, which was unleashed in the Americas during the Spanish conquest. For four years, 1520-1524, the disease diffused across Central and North America. Whether smallpox reached pandemic proportions is debatable, but in populations with no prior exposure, mortality could be as high as 60 percent. The infected native populations experienced high death rates. Florida's Timucua population may have once had 772,000 people, but by 1524 the group was reduced to 361,000.

Throughout the 1500's and into the next century, twenty-three European infectious diseases appeared in native North America. Smallpox, measles, influenza, and the bubonic plague affected Native American populations largely east of the Mississippi and in the Southwest. European populations grew and expanded geographically as declining indigenous populations relinquished their lands and resources. Those Native Americans who resisted white encroachment were vanquished through genocidal warfare or reduced to mission life.

Eighteenth Century

By the eighteenth century, the European population had reached an estimated 223,000 people. Although Europeans were not the demographic majority, epidemics continued to pave the way for further colonization. Throughout the Atlantic coastal region and into the interior westward, native populations were decimated through genocidal warfare and diseases. In the southeastern region of North America, for example, the estimated Native American population in 1685 was 199,400. By 1970, the population was reduced to approximately 55,900—a decline of 71.9 percent. By contrast, Europeans and African Americans in the region increased their population to 1,630,100 or 31.4 percent.

In sum, European expansion during the three first centuries of colonization produced a demographic collapse of Native American populations. Introduced European infectious diseases, combined with periodic genocidal warfare and the destruction of indigenous lifeways, reduced Native Americans to approximately 600,000. By contrast, the European population grew to more than 5 million.

Nineteenth and Twentieth Centuries

During the nineteenth century, twenty-four epidemics affected Native American populations. Smallpox continued to appear every 7.9 years among some segment of the Native American population. Between the smallpox episodes, Native Americans contracted measles and cholera every 22.5 years. According to Henry Dobyns, an anthropologist and authority on Native American historical demography, more epidemics occurred during the nineteenth century, with more frequency, than during any other.

One of the most devastating epidemics during this century was the 1837-1838 smallpox epidemic. The disease diffused across most of native North America, but the northern Plains region was hit especially hard. It is estimated that seventeen thousand Native Americans on the northern Plains died before the epidemic subsided. Such acute infectious diseases continued to plague Native American communities into the early reservation period. Only then did these infections give way to the twentieth century epidemics of influenza, tuberculosis, and trachoma—chronic conditions that would infect Native Americans until the 1950's.

The placement of Native Americans on reservations or in rural communities did not mark the end of epidemics. Acute infectious diseases have been replaced by "diseases of poverty." Many of these afflictions reach epidemic proportions in some Native American communities. Deaths from tuberculosis, type II diabetes mellitus, violence, suicide, accidents, and alcoholism exceed the national average. In addition, Native Americans now have to contend with another epidemic—the threat of human immunodeficiency virus (HIV) infection—a disease that has made its presence felt in some Native American communities.
Gregory R. Campbell

See also: American Indian demographics; Genocide of American Indians.

Disfranchisement laws in Mississippi

> **Significance:** In August, 1890, the Mississippi legislature passed laws that effectively eliminated the black vote in the state.

At the end of the nineteenth century, Mississippi and South Carolina had the largest black populations in the United States. In 1890, fifty-seven of every hundred Mississippians were black. The Fifteenth Amendment to the U.S. Constitution (ratified in 1870) provided that no state could deny the right to vote on account of race; thus, Mississippi had a large black electorate. During the early 1870's, Mississippi voters elected hundreds of black officeholders, including members of Congress, state legislators, sheriffs, county clerks, and justices of the peace. In the mid-1870's, white Democrats launched a counteroffensive, using threats, violence, and fraud to neutralize the African American vote. After 1875, very few blacks held office in Mississippi.

By 1890, many politicians in Mississippi were calling for a convention to write a new constitution for the state. They complained that although only a small number of African Americans were voting, this small number could prove decisive in close elections. Many white leaders feared that black votes could decide close elections and worked toward a new constitution with provisions that effectively would disfranchise black voters. It would be difficult to draft such provisions, however, without running afoul of the Fifteenth Amendment.

The state's two senators illustrated the divisions of opinion that were so widespread among white Mississippians. Senator Edward C. Walthall argued against a constitutional convention, warning that it would only excite political passions for no good purpose. He felt certain there was no way to eliminate black political participation without violating the Fifteenth Amendment, and that if Mississippi made such an attempt, the U.S. government would show new interest in enforcing African American voting rights. On the other hand, Senator James George attacked the old constitution, claiming that it had been drafted by carpetbaggers and ignorant former slaves. George urged that the "best citizens" should now take the opportunity to draft a new state constitution. He warned that black voting could revive unless the state took measures to reduce the black

electorate by provisions of the state's highest law.

A bill calling a constitutional convention passed both houses of the state legislature in 1888, but Governor Robert Lowry vetoed it, warning that it was better to accept the state's existing problems than to run the risk of creating new ones by tampering with the state's constitution. Two years later, a similar bill passed both houses of the legislature, and the new governor, John M. Stone, signed the law. Election for delegates was set for July 29, 1890. The voters would elect 134 delegates, 14 of them from the state at large and the rest apportioned among the counties.

The state's weak Republican Party (to which many African Americans adhered as the party that had freed them from slavery) decided not to field a slate of candidates for at-large delegates. In heavily black Bolivar County, Republicans did offer a local delegate slate with one black and one white candidate. In Jasper County, the white Republican candidate for delegate, F. M. B. "Marsh" Cook, was assassinated while riding alone on a country road. In two black-majority counties, the Democrats allowed white conservative Republicans onto their candidate slates. In several counties, Democrats split into two factions and offered the voters a choice of two Democratic tickets. As it turned out, the constitutional convention was made up almost exclusively of white Democrats. The membership included only three Republicans, three delegates elected as independents, and one member of an agrarian third party. Only one of the 134 delegates was black: Isaiah T. Montgomery of Bolivar County.

The Mississippi Plan

Delegates elected the conservative lawyer Solomon S. Calhoon as president of the convention and immediately set about their work. Convention members had no shortage of ideas on how to limit the suffrage almost exclusively to whites without violating the Fifteenth Amendment. Some suggested that voters must own land, which few African Americans in Mississippi did. Others favored educational tests, since African Americans, only a generation removed from slavery, had had fewer educational opportunities than whites and therefore were often illiterate.

As finally devised, the Mississippi plan for disfranchisement had a number of parts, the most important of which were a literacy test and a poll tax. Under the literacy test, the would-be voter must either be able to read or to explain a part of the state constitution when it was read to him. This latter provision, the so-called "understanding clause," was included as a loophole for illiterate whites. Delegates knew that voting registrars could give easy questions to white applicants and exceedingly difficult ones to African Americans. The poll tax provision stated that a person must pay a poll tax of at least two dollars per year, for at least two years in succession, in order to qualify to vote. The voter would have to pay these taxes well in advance of the election and keep the receipt. The tax was quite burdensome in a state where tenant farmers often earned less than fifty dollars in cash per year. Because Mississippi's African Americans were often tenant farmers, poorer than their white counterparts, it was thought they would give up the right to vote rather than pay this new tax.

The Effect
In a notable speech, the black Republican delegate, Isaiah T. Montgomery, announced that he would vote for these new suffrage provisions. He noted that race relations in the state had grown tense and that black political participation in the state had often led whites to react violently. His hope now, Montgomery explained, was that black disfranchisement would improve race relations and as the years passed, perhaps more African Americans would be permitted to vote. The new constitution passed the convention with only eight dissenting votes; it was not submitted to the voters for their ratification.

The new suffrage provisions went into effect just before the 1892 elections. The new voter registration requirements disfranchised the great majority of African Americans in the state; they also resulted in the disfranchisement of about fifty-two thousand whites. The new registration resulted in a list of seventy thousand white voters and only nine thousand African American voters. The predominantly black state Republican Party had won 26 percent of the vote for its presidential candidate in 1888; after the new registration, in 1892, the Republican standard-bearer won less than 3 percent.

Under the Constitution of 1890, Mississippi had an almost exclusively white electorate for three-quarters of a century. This constitution served as a model for other Southern states, which eagerly copied the literacy test, the understanding clause, and the poll tax into their state constitutions. Only after passage of new laws by the U.S. Congress in 1964 and 1965 would African American voters again make their strength felt in southern elections. *Stephen Cresswell*

Core Resources
Stephen Cresswell's *Multiparty Politics in Mississippi, 1877-1902* (Jackson: University Press of Mississippi, 1995) discusses the drafting of the 1890 constitution and its role in limiting the success of the Republican and Populist Parties. Albert D. Kirwan's *Revolt of the Rednecks: Mississippi Politics, 1876-1925* (Lexington: University Press of Kentucky, 1951) remains the basic political history for the period before, during, and after the state's 1890 constitutional convention. J. Morgan Kousser's *The Shaping of Southern Politics: Suffrage Restriction and the* *Establishment of the One-Party South, 1880-1910* (New Haven, Conn.: Yale University Press, 1974) is a detailed explanation of how new constitutions in Mississippi and other southern states led to a homogeneous electorate, essentially a small clique of middle-class whites.

See also: Black codes; Civil Rights Acts of 1866-1875; *Civil Rights* cases; Fourteenth Amendment; Freedmen's Bureau; Ku Klux Klan; *Plessy v. Ferguson*; Reconstruction; Thirteenth Amendment.

Disidentification

The notion of disidentification stems from a racial or ethnic group's not wanting to be associated with the group with which the dominant group identifies them. For example, a Chinese American may not want to be identified with other Asian Americans or Chinese Americans but be seen as an "American." Disidentification, which has also been referred to as dissonance and disassociation, stems from ethnic group members' needs to distance themselves from negative stereotypes of their ethnic or racial group. Claude M. Steele, a psychologist at Stanford University, states that negative stereotypes about the intellectual abilities of women and ethnic minorities cause academic disidentification. Women and ethnic minorities distance themselves from their own groups for fear of being harmed by damaging stereotypes. Yen Le Espiritu and Mary Danico in separate studies respectively found that continued exposure of second-generation Filipino Americans and Korean Americans to negative ethnic stereotypes created a sense of ethnic shame that caused them to distance themselves from other Filipino and Korean Americans. A negative image or stereotype of an ethnic or racial minority group can create a need for members of the group to distance themselves from their group and subsequently no longer identify themselves as a part of the group.

Mary Yu Danico

See also: Ethnic identities of women; Self-identification among Asian Americans; Self-identification among Latinos.

Disparate impact theory

The 1964 Civil Rights Act covered two categories of employment discrimination liability: disparate treatment and disparate impact. Disparate treatment refers to discrimination against individuals, and disparate impact treats discrimination against an entire class of workers. Disparate treatment or impact cases involve an employer's discriminating against an individual or a group because of race, color, religion, sex, or national origin. Despite the 1964 legislation, discrimination has not disappeared from American society; citizens are still being prevented from enjoying the full benefits of equal opportunity in a number of areas, including employment, hiring, termination, and compensation or other employment conditions. The 1991 Civil Rights Act modified the 1964 act to facilitate discrimination litigation.

Disparate impact theory, instead of focusing on employer intent, examines discrimination caused by specific employer practices. The U.S. Supreme Court case of *Griggs v. Duke Power Company* (1971) provided the basis for the concept of disparate impact. In this case, the central issue was whether Duke Power, the defendant, used a test not relevant to job performance to screen out black applicants. The court ruled that the plaintiff must show that he or she applied for an available job, was rejected based on the employer's customary practice, and that this practice discriminated against a protected class (that it had a disparate impact on a protected class). If the plaintiff established this, then the defendant had to prove that the practice was required by business necessity. If the defendant met this requirement, the employee could still prevail if he or she could show that some other less discriminatory employment practice would serve the employer's business interest.

The 1971 Supreme Court ruling was incorporated into the Civil Rights Act of 1991 so that it could not be weakened by subsequent Court decisions. The 1991 act allows the plaintiff to treat the employer's entire decision-making process as an entity in cases in which the plaintiff cannot show separately which requirement caused the discrimination.

Under the 1991 act, the employer carries a greater burden of proof in establishing a reason for rejecting a potential employee. The act still allows the use of employment tests but limits how the scores can be used and prohibits race norming. According to this act, if race, color, religion, sex, or national origin were motivating factors in an employment decision, then unlawful discrimination exists, even if lawful factors were also used.

Gloria Fulton

See also: Civil Rights Act of 1964; Civil Rights Act of 1991; Discrimination: direct institutionalized; Discrimination: indirect institutionalized; *Griggs v. Duke Power Company*.

Distinct society concept

The concept of a "distinct society," as applied to the province of Quebec, became important in Canada in the 1980's. It was part of an effort to symbolically return the province of Quebec, the home of the vast majority of Canada's French-speaking citizens, to the constitutional fold. As a former British colony, Canada had its constitution, the British North America Act (1867), held by the mother country. A significant impediment to the constitution's being repatriated to Canada was Quebec, which saw itself as different from the other nine provinces and therefore deserving of special powers. In 1982, the Canadian government finally managed to get the provinces, with the notable exception of Quebec, to agree to the return and amending of the constitution. Quebec, however, remained symbolically opposed to the new constitution.

This situation continued until 1987, when the Canadian government of Prime Minister Brian Mulroney made a renewed effort to bring Quebec back into the constitutional fold. After intense bargaining, all of the provinces, including Quebec, agreed to what became known as the Meech Lake Accord.

The Meech Lake Accord was a process that would have amended the Canadian constitution, chiefly to satisfy the requirements of the province of Quebec. As part of the amendment process, a recognition that Quebec constituted within Canada a "distinct society" would have been added to the constitution. Many Canadians believed that Quebec was different from the rest of Canada and should be recognized as such. This distinction was primarily based on language, since a large majority of the province's citizens were French-speaking. Quebec's legal system was also significant to this argument, since the province, with its French roots, followed the Civil Code as opposed to English Common Law, the system in place in the rest of the country. Being recognized as "distinct" was important in Quebec, which had been seeking greater autonomy within the Canadian federation for a good portion of the twentieth century. The 1960's saw the creation of a democratic separatist movement, which sought to turn the province through peaceful means into an independent country. Many argued that recognition of Quebec as a "distinct society" was one way of defeating the separatist option and keeping Canada intact.

The "distinct society" concept became, however, the focus of those opposed to the Meech Lake Accord. Many of the agreement's opponents interpreted "distinct" as meaning superior instead of simply different. They also argued that since "distinct society" was nowhere defined, court interpretations of the phrase could have provided Quebec with powers not available to other provinces. In reply, the defenders of Meech Lake argued that calling Quebec "distinct" simply recognized reality.

Opposition to the agreement grew, especially among aboriginal Canadians and in the provinces of Manitoba and Newfoundland. The phrase "distinct society" but not the continuing controversy surrounding the issue died when these two provinces failed to ratify the Meech Lake Accord by the deadline of June, 1990.   *Steven Hewitt*

See also: Meech Lake Accord; Separatist movement in Quebec.

Diversity

When Allan Bakke applied to the School of Medicine of the University of California, Davis, his application was placed into a pool with other individuals of his race (white), and the screening criteria for his pool were different from those for other racially identifiable applicant pools. Accordingly, a majority of the Supreme Court of the United States ruled five to four in *Regents of the University of California v. Bakke* (1978) that he was discriminated against because the admission process was segregated by race. The justices also ruled five to four that a diverse student body is a "constitutionally permissible goal for an institution of higher education," and one of the judges in the majority, Lewis F. Powell, Jr., declared that "the nation's future depends upon leaders trained through wide exposure to the ideas and mores of students as diverse as this Nation of many peoples."

Thereafter, the term "diversity" was used in personnel decisions of many businesses, government agencies, and schools to justify selecting members of underrepresented groups. The term has never acquired a precise meaning, however, and could be applied to select disabled persons, gays, Hungarians, or any group not represented among existing employees at a job site or among students at an educational institution. In general, the term has assumed positive connotations, suggesting everything from tolerance to cultural pluralism.   *Michael Haas*

See also: Affirmative action; *Bakke* case; College admissions; "Reverse" racism.

Diversity training programs

> **Significance:** Diversity training programs are intended to improve relations between groups in a number of settings, most often schools and workplaces. These programs teach participants about the history and culture of different groups, improve participants' sensitivity to other people, and encourage people from different backgrounds to interact with one another in order to improve mutual understanding and respect.

The goal of diversity training programs is to improve intergroup relations in a number of different contexts, including schools, workplaces, and communities at large. The idea behind these programs is that people can be taught to understand one another better and that better understanding will result in improved communications, increased fellowship, and reduced hostilities.

History of Diversity Training
Diversity training programs (a term used here to refer to a variety of programs and other organized efforts to improve intergroup relations) were created toward the end of the twentieth century and are the result of several interrelated phenomena in American society. One driving force behind the creation of these programs was the increasing diversity of the American population. Although the United States has long had a reputation as a country of immigrants, never was this more true than in the 1980's and 1990's. Immigration rates in the 1990's surpassed historical records. Many of these immigrants settled not in traditional locales such as New York City and Los Angeles but in smaller towns across the country. As a result, existing residents of these towns were exposed to many cultural practices that were new to them. Furthermore, perhaps as a result of the Civil Rights movement, many ethnic minorities in the United States felt less pressure to assimilate into "mainstream" American culture and more freedom to retain their cultural identities and practices. Thus, throughout the United States, many people were in frequent contact with groups whose backgrounds were different from their own.

The late twentieth century also saw an increase in the number of laws protecting people from discrimination and harassment (the most prominent being the Civil Rights Act of 1964) and in the willingness of people to sue under these laws. Companies and institutions could be held civilly liable under these laws and therefore felt the need to protect their assets by aggressively promoting good intergroup relations.

Finally, in the 1980's, a rapid increase occurred in the number of hate crime laws and in the notoriety and number of hate groups. It is arguable whether the number of actual hate crimes increased, although certainly public awareness of these events did expand. Diversity training was believed by many to be a way to reduce these incidents and to reform the offenders.

Program Participants
Although diversity training has been used in a number of contexts, it is most common among three groups: students, employees, and offenders.

Diversity training is frequently used among students from the primary grades through college. Young people,

Selected Internet Resources on Diversity Training

Program/Organization	Web Address
American Institute for Managing Diversity	http://www.aimd.org
Diversity Resources	http://www.execpc.com/~dboals/div-gen.html
Just Cause	http://www.webcom.com/~justcaus/
National Coalition Building Institute	http://www.ncbi.org
National Conference for Community and Justice	http://www.nccj.org
Skin Deep (Public Broadcasting Service)	http://www.pbs.org/skindeep/
Teaching Steps to Tolerance (Simon Wiesenthal Center)	http://tst.wiesenthal.com
Teaching Tolerance (Southern Poverty Law Center)	http://www.splcenter.org/teachingtolerance.html

it is thought, are less set in their ways and more open to new ideas, so training at this stage may be the most effective. Furthermore, schools offer the ideal setting in which to expose large numbers of people to this sort of instruction. Many states have included multiculturalism in mandated statewide curricula for kindergarten through twelfth-grade students, and some schools have created special "brotherhood" clubs. Many colleges and universities have also encouraged or required courses on diversity.

It is commonplace for employers to require employees to attend diversity workshops. These workshops might be conducted by outside consulting firms or by specially trained employees. They have been offered in a wide variety of professions ranging from blue collar to white, in both the public sector and private. Sometimes they are offered in response to existing problems within a company or institution, and sometimes they are offered proactively in order to avoid the emergence of such problems, or to assist employees with interactions in new milieus.

Diversity training has sometimes been required as part of the sentence for those who have been convicted of hate crimes or similar offenses. The idea is that rehabilitating offenders through education is preferable to simply punishing them, especially considering the already overburdened correctional system and the prevalence of racism in U.S. prisons and jails.

General Program Goals

The precise characteristics of these programs vary a great deal depending on their audience and context. However, most of them share the same basic goals. A primary goal is usually education. Participants learn about the history, culture, and values of other groups, which might include a wide variety of ethnic and religious groups as well as gays and lesbians and people with disabilities. Lack of knowledge can lead to misunderstandings, which may increase tensions between groups, so education is believed to be a vital factor in fostering good relations between people. Furthermore, mutual knowledge may help lead to mutual respect. This aspect of diversity training is particularly important when a group of people is either little known or widely misunderstood.

A second goal of diversity training is to improve people's sensitivity toward each other. A particular individual may not know, for example, that a member of another group is likely to find certain words or practices offensive. Training attempts to make people aware of these issues, as many incidents that cause friction between people are probably inadvertent.

Third, many diversity training programs aim to increase people's interaction with members of other groups. Human beings have a tendency to stick with people very like themselves, but psychologists believe that the best way to reduce prejudice is for people to work together toward common goals. Furthermore, frequent interaction with others may help dispel myths and encourage people to view others as individuals rather than as stereotypes. Therefore, diversity training programs often offer a structured and supervised format for participants to interact with each other.

Examples of Programs

There are a wide variety of diversity programs offered, in numerous contexts. One example of a program for students is the Brotherhood-Sisterhood Camp, offered annually in Southern California by the National Conference of Christians and Jews. Los Angeles high school students from a variety of ethnic groups spend time exploring such topics as discrimination and stereotypes, trying to understand each other better, and discussing methods of improving discourse and relations.

The Southern Poverty Law Center has created a program aimed primarily at young people, called Teaching Tolerance. Interested teachers throughout the country can receive a free biannual magazine full of ideas for incorporating diversity awareness into the curriculum. The program also distributes such teaching aids as videos and lesson guides, and there is a Teaching Tolerance site on the Internet. This program encompasses all of the primary and secondary grades.

The Simon Wiesenthal Center in Los Angeles has a diversity program aimed primarily at older students and adults. The center operates the Museum of Tolerance, which has sophisticated, high-tech exhibits on intolerance in general and specifically on the Holocaust. In addition to the exhibits, the museum has a large library of books and videos and an interactive multimedia center and sponsors a variety of lectures and special exhibits. School groups are encouraged to tour the museum. The center also has created a Web site and curriculum guide for teachers, entitled *Teaching Steps to Tolerance.*

There are many diversity programs intended for adults in the workplace. Companies such as the American Institute for Managing Diversity and the National Coalition Building Institute specialize in offering workshops. In addition, many organizations have created specialized programs for their employees and constituents. For example, in 1998, the National Association of Realtors created a program called "At Home with Diversity: One America." This program was meant to help agents serve home buyers from a variety of backgrounds and to encourage more ethnic minority members to become agents. Diversity training is particularly common in large corporations and among law enforcement agencies. Many police departments require it for new recruits and provide ongoing training for experienced officers.

Diversity training has also sometimes been required for people who have been convicted of hate crimes and similar acts. In 1993, for example, a group of skinheads was convicted of committing several violent crimes against blacks and Jews and of plotting several more. As part of their plea agreement, the skinheads and their relatives were required to attend a three-day workshop led by Holocaust survivors, members of a black church the group had targeted, and an African American federal judge. In 1994, five men who participated in the murder of a homosexual man in Houston were ordered to attend therapy sessions to deal with their hatred and increase their sensitivity. Other programs have been created in jails and prisons, where racial hate groups are frequently endemic and bigotry is commonplace.

Phyllis B. Gerstenfeld

See also: Civil Rights Act of 1964; Cultural pluralism; Diversity; Hate Crime Statistics Act; Hate crimes; Hate speech; Prejudice: reduction; Stereotype; White supremacist groups.

Dominant group

"Dominant group," along with its reciprocal concept of "minority group," serves as a central orienting concept in the sociological study of racial and ethnic relations. These two structural concepts are so closely linked that "dominant group," while appearing extensively in the literature, is rarely formally defined: More typically, it assumes its meaning in antithesis to the widely accepted and more formally specified notion of "minority group." Accordingly, "dominant group" denotes a privileged social stratum that commands a disproportionate share of society's resources, including wealth, prestige, and political influence.

Some persisting ambiguities and several implications attending the usage of the concept of "dominant group" must be noted. Fairly trivial is the technicality that dominant and minority groups, strictly speaking, are not "groups." Because the members of either stratum do not all interact with one another on the basis of their respective designations, they are better regarded as societal "categories." More seriously misleading can be the tendency to use the term "dominant group" interchangeably with "majority group." What marks part of a population as a dominant group is not its relative number, but its relative power. Therefore, dominant group members may constitute only a small fraction of the society's population and be substantially outnumbered by the relatively powerless constituents of a minority group.

Another misleading tendency equates the notion of dominant group with that of "superordinate group." Here again, the notion of power—this time as distinct from authority—becomes vital. The German sociologist Max Weber defined "power" as the ability to realize one's will against the resistance of others; power wielded in accord with established norms is legitimated and represents "authority." Any society affords a distinction between superordinate and subordinate groups, based simply on an unequal distribution of valued resources. However, dominant and minority groups are a special case of such a disparity in which the inequality persists on nonnormative grounds. It applies only in societies that proclaim universal norms of status achievement yet selectively inhibit their realization. As the Swedish sociologist Gunnar Myrdal observed, such disjunctions between established principles and prevailing practices pose a dilemma for American society, one that marks the power (but hardly the authority) of one social stratum to maintain its privileges through nonnormative means while ascribing second-class citizenship to another.

This raises the seeming paradox that dominant (and minority) groups can exist only in societies that proclaim an essentially democratic ethos. However, in such a society, privileges (not rights) claimed by one group have yet to be effectively challenged, and rights denied another group still have not been redressed. This conceptualization also sharpens the distinction between discriminatory and merely differential treatment. Although in superordinate/subordinate situations, status disparities reflect legitimized differential and unequal treatment, in dominant/minority situations, such inequalities of treatment are deemed nonnormative and therefore discriminatory. A dominant/minority group situation may therefore be regarded as a transitional stage in an extended sociohistorical evolution from permanently ascribed statuses characteristic of caste systems toward a genuine class system of inequality where statuses are universally allocated by achievement criteria.

Harry H. Bash

See also: Majority and minority; Subordinate group.

Dominican Americans

> **Significance:** Dominican Americans are among the fastest-growing immigrant populations in the United States. In 1995, they were ranked sixth among those who had arrived in the country between 1990 and 1994, and they are the largest immigrant group in New York City according to the 1994 figures from the city's Department of City Planning. Their significant presence there has led to the emergence of a Dominican American community.

Situated between Cuba and Puerto Rico in the Caribbean Sea, the Dominican Republic shares the island of Hispaniola with its neighbor Haiti. The country is known primarily for its warm tropical climate, its sugarcane and tobacco exports, and its contributions to the international community in the personages of fashion designer Oscar de la Renta, musician Juan Luis Guerra, and major league baseball players such as Sammy Sosa, Juan Marichal, George Bell, and Pedro Guerrero.

In the early 1960's, after the assassination of Dominican dictator Rafael Léonidas Trujillo, the Dominican Republic was affected by political and economic turmoil. The ensuing unrest resulted in the outbreak of civil war on April 25, 1965, which led to a U.S. military occupation of the country in an effort to protect American economic interests. Following the U.S. intervention, many political activists were granted visas to the United States in an effort to stem political dissent against the new U.S.-sponsored right-wing government of Dominican president Joaquín Balaguer. This marked the beginning of a continued pattern of Dominican emigration to North America that was fueled by political as well as economic reasons.

Following a brief period of industrial growth under the new leadership of President Balaguer, Dominicans saw their country's economy worsen. The middle class all but disappeared in the wake of escalating oil prices, a massive foreign debt, and a decline in exports that resulted in a 23 percent unemployment rate as of 1990. This factor, coupled with the increased sentiments of frustration by Dominicans toward the leadership of the country, led to a Dominican diaspora in search of a place in which to obtain political and economic freedom. Like other immigrant groups in the United States, Dominicans have tended to settle in only a few states. According to the 1990 U.S. census, 70 percent of all Dominicans in the nation resided in New York, followed by New Jersey with 11 percent, Florida with 7 percent, and Massachusetts with 5 percent.

A New Community
The Dominican American community is made up of people who have obtained U.S. citizenship after their arrival to North America as well as those that are born in the U.S. of Dominican parents. So salient is the

Dominican Americans express pride in their heritage at this New York City parade.

Dominican migratory pattern to the New York City area that it has earned Dominican Americans the nickname of Dominicanyorks. Mass migration into New York City has resulted in the "Dominicanization" of neighborhoods such as Washington Heights. However, Dominican Americans have found some challenges in adapting to their new environment. Some resistance from the established residents, as well as political challenges in their local community, has led many Dominican Americans to become more actively involved in the political and economic activities of their community.

Part of the acculturation of Dominican Americans into mainstream society has been brought about through active participation in their neighborhood schools. In the early 1980's, a campaign was mounted to gain greater control over the schools in Washington Heights in order to make them more responsive to the needs of the local community. In 1980, the Community Association of Progressive Dominicans confronted the school board to demand bilingual education for newly arrived immigrants. Their presence in the political arena was also established in 1991 with the election of Guillermo Linares, the first Dominican ever to sit on the New York City Council. However, as is often the case with newly arrived immigrant groups to the United States, the moderate success of Dominican Americans has been considered by some as a challenge to the established residents of Washington Heights (mainly Jews, Puerto Ricans, and African Americans).

Ethnic Relations

As Steven Lowenstein explains in his 1989 work entitled *Frankfort on the Hudson: The German-Jewish Community of Washington Heights, 1933-1983*, the move by Dominican Americans to gain greater control over the local schools came at the expense of the established Jewish population in that area. Some see this as a source of tension between the two groups. One Jewish leader is quoted as saying: "In order to save our own congregation, we have to live with our neighbors, even if they are different from us, even if we don't like them. But we cannot help it. We have to live with the Blacks, with the Spanish." In the initial migration years, Dominicans rented apartments in the mostly Jewish-owned tenements; however, as the years progressed, the Jewish population became increasingly sparse in the Washington Heights area.

The newly arrived Dominican immigrants found acceptance within the Puerto Rican community in the early 1960's. Many Dominican immigrants were able to find housing and employment through friendships with Puerto Ricans. Some argue that the preexisting presence of the Puerto Rican community was helpful to the newly arrived Dominicans in that it led both Jewish and African Americans to come to terms with the unavoidable reality of a Latin American presence in New York City. However, as more and more Dominicans began migrating to the area, tensions arose within the Puerto Rican community. The growing sentiment was that Dominican Americans were accepting low-wage jobs and undercutting the Puerto Ricans in the job market. Likewise, as the Dominican population grew, many Dominican Americans began to feel that the Puerto Rican agenda followed by most of the Latino community leaders was not representative of the ever-growing Dominican population.

Similarly, African Americans have found themselves in competition with Dominican Americans for jobs and housing. Some African American business owners have complained about the aggressive tactics of some of the Dominican business owners. According to Linda Chavez's study entitled *Out of the Barrio: Toward a New Politics of Hispanic Assimilation* (1991), Dominicans own 70 percent of all Hispanic small businesses in New York. Although sociable relations between these two groups continue, they tend to reside in slightly segregated neighborhoods, perhaps because of racial and ethnic preconceptions held by both groups. Not unlike their African American neighbors, Dominican Americans have also been subject to racial discrimination based on physical appearance. As Patricia Pessar points out in her 1995 book *A Visa for a Dream*, often Dominicans who are perceived as "white" by Caucasians are treated better and offered better jobs than Dominicans who are dark-skinned.

The mixture of races found among Dominicans has frequently led to many dark-skinned Dominican Americans being misidentified as African Americans and subsequently being subjected to the same kind of racism experienced by American blacks. In Sakinah Carter's 1994 work entitled *Shades of Identity: Puerto Ricans and Dominicans Across Paradigms*, a twenty-two-year-old Dominican is quoted as saying:

> All we see on television when we arrive is how bad blacks are, so we cling to our difference, our Latino-ness, in order to say we are not those blacks that you hear about in the streets or see on the news. We aren't bad. But at the same time, it feels ridiculous not to embrace our blackness because many dark Dominicans do live as other blacks, treated as blacks by white people, and other Latinos who act like there is one Latino phenotype, like there's a way to look Latino. . . . I'm black and Latino, a black Latino—we exist, you know.

However, dating back to the initial wave of Dominican immigrants in the 1960's, and in spite of some social challenges, Dominicans, Puerto Ricans, Jews, and African Americans have all been able to coexist as productive members of their respective communities despite their cultural differences and racial preconceptions.

Pedro R. Payne

Core Resources

For an in-depth analysis of the history of the Dominican Republic, see Frank Moya Pons's *The Dominican Republic: A National History* (New Rochelle, N.Y.: Hispaniola Books, 1995). Luis E. Guarnizo writes a chapter on "Dominicanyorks" in *Challenging Fronteras*, edited by Mary Romero, Pierrette Hondagneu-Sotelo, and Vilma Ortiz (New York: Routledge, 1997), which explores the "binational interconnection" that has resulted from Dominican immigration into the United States. Another good source for issues pertaining to Dominican migration and adaptation to American society is Ramona Hernandez and Silvio Torres-Saillant's chapter in *Latinos in New York*, edited by Gabriel Haslip-Viera and Sherrie L. Baver (Notre Dame, Ind.: University of Notre Dame Press, 1996). Patricia Pessar, in *A Visa for a Dream* (Boston: Allyn and Bacon, 1995), manages to capture the Dominican immigrant experience as well as the cultural factors that affect Dominican acculturation into American society. For a historical account of the African and European ancestry of Dominicans and other Latin Americans, see *Afro-Latin Americans Today: No Longer Invisible* (London: Minority Rights Group, 1995).

See also: Afro-Caribbeans; Latinos in the United States; Puerto Rico.

Dot-busting

In 1987, the Asian Indian community of Jersey City, New Jersey, became the target of racial violence. People were beaten and property vandalized. Kaushal Sharon suffered permanent brain damage and Navroze Mody died of injuries. The attackers were called dotbusters (a reference to the dot worn by Hindu women on their foreheads), and they vowed to drive all Asian Indians (called dotheads) out of the area by violence. Local officials were slow to prosecute. Some Indian community leaders blamed New Jersey officials, calling them clannish and indifferent, while others feared that denouncing the authorities' apathy as racism would link them with despised minority groups.

After Mody and Sharon were attacked, fifteen Asian Indian students at Columbia University and Bernard College, joined later by Asian Indian students at the University of Pennsylvania, formed Indian Youth Against Racism (IYAR). In spite of being ostracized and patronized by their own elders, they helped organize demonstrations, helped the parents of Mody and Sharon obtain justice, and pressured officials to prosecute.   *Arthur W. Helweg*

See also: Asian Indians in the United States; Hate crimes; Hate speech.

Draft riot

> **Significance:** In 1863, The United States' first conscription act prompted wide-scale racial disturbances in New York City.

The firing on Fort Sumter on April 12, 1861, at the beginning of the Civil War, came at a time when the regular U.S. Army numbered only about 16,000 officers and troops. The traditional method of increasing the size of the army was to expand the state militias and to form a volunteer emergency national army recruited through the states. The immediate response of President Abraham Lincoln to the firing on Fort Sumter was to call for 75,000 militia volunteers for three months' service. This call was exceeded, and some volunteers were turned away because the expectation was that a show of force would be sufficient to defeat the South. Congress and the president subsequently found it necessary, however, to call for more volunteers. Repeated defeats of the Union army and the resultant loss of men caused President Lincoln to call for 300,000 volunteers in the summer of 1862. The difficulty of obtaining volunteers was soon apparent; bounties were increased, and the threat of the draft was invoked. Congress passed the Militia Act of July, 1862, which allowed the states to draft men into the militia and encouraged enlistments. President Lincoln called for another 300,000 men to be enrolled into the militia. Although the Militia Act of 1862 gave the federal government power to enroll men in situations where the state machinery was inadequate, the short-term (nine-month maximum) nature of the militia draft and the inequities of the system made it less than satisfactory.

Conscription Begins

Spurred by the loss of 75,000 men, by news of a conscription law passed by the Confederacy, and by the failure of the states to provide men promptly for the various calls, Congress passed its own Conscription Act on March 3, 1863. Henry Wilson, chairman of the Senate Committee on Military Affairs, was responsible for the introduction of a bill that eventually was passed and labeled "An Act for Enrolling and Calling Out the National Forces and for Other Purposes." This act was the first national draft law in the history of the nation. It called for the creation of the "national forces," which were to consist of all able-bodied male citizens and alien declarants between twenty and forty-five years of age, including African Americans. White opposition to blacks in federal army uniforms noticeably lessened as a result of the draft. In all, more than 168,000 African American recruits were drafted. Certain high officials, medically unfit persons, and hardship cases were exempted. Exemption could also be obtained by paying three hundred dollars or by securing a substitute.

The system was operated by the War Department under the direction of Colonel James B. Fry, provost-marshal-general. Provost-marshals were appointed in districts similar to the congressional districts and enrollments began. Quotas were established, and credit was given for enlistments. If the quotas were not met, drawings were held to determine who should be drafted. Small cards were placed in sealed envelopes in a large trunk, and the names were drawn in public by a trustworthy citizen wearing a blindfold. The system of paying three hundred dollars for exemption from service subsequently was abolished, but the privilege of hiring a substitute was continued. The names of more than three million men were gathered, but only about 170,000 were drafted, and 120,000 of those produced substitutes. The primary intent for passage of the law was to speed up voluntary enlistment, and more than one million men enlisted. The chief motivation for these enlistments was probably the threat of the draft.

Opposition

The draft brought President Lincoln and Secretary of War Edwin McMasters Stanton into conflict with state governors. Those governors who were unenthusiastic about the conduct of the war openly criticized the president and the draft, while governors who favored a more vigorous prosecution of the war often complained that their states had not been given full credit for previous enlistments. Lincoln and Stanton often temporized with the governors by granting postponements or additional credits as the end of the war drew near.

There was considerable resistance to the draft. Pennsylvania, Illinois, Indiana, and Kentucky had considerable problems with enrollment, and draft offices and officers were attacked in those states. The Irish in New York and New Jersey were particularly incensed by the draft, many viewing the conflicts as a rich man's war and a poor man's fight. With fifty-one categories of diseases qualifying men for medical exemption, the system was fraught with medical resistance problems. Surgeons administering medical qualifying exams were confronted by faked hernias (the most widespread cause of exemption), eye problems caused by applying eye irritants, and pretended deafness. Giving incorrect birth dates, claiming false dependents, and even the enrollment of dead people were other methods of noncompliance. Finally, there were the runaways. Given time to settle their affairs before departing for camp, a considerable number of draftees either relocated or fled to Canada.

With the public generally hostile to the draft, the best way for a community to avoid it was to fill the quota with volunteers. Consequently, bounty taxes were implemented to raise revenues to attract foreigners, new immigrants, and the poverty-stricken to enlist. The paying of bounties corrupted the draft system. It produced bounty jumpers who, attracted by lump-sum payments, were willing to jump off trains or boats to escape conscription.

Riots

Notorious resistance to the draft instigated the draft riots in New York City. Governor Horatio Seymour's speech of July 4, 1863, attacking the Lincoln administration for violations of individual liberty, did nothing to decrease the hostility of the New York Irish toward African Americans and the abolitionists. Antidraft rioting, which took place between July 13 and 15, destroyed property and physically harmed many African Americans. Some New York militia units that had been engaged at Gettysburg were hastily ordered back to New York to stop the rioting. Estimates of the casualties in the violence range up to more than one thousand. In spite of the violence, the federal government was determined to enforce the draft with even more fervor.

Confederacy and Conscription

The Confederacy's calls for volunteers and its national conscription law antedated those of the Union. Jefferson Davis's call for 100,000 volunteers came before the firing on Fort Sumter, and the Conscription Act was passed on April 16, 1862, almost a year before similar legislation was passed by the United States. The Confederate act conscripted men from eighteen to thirty-five years of age; later the same year, it was extended to include those between seventeen and fifty years of age. The Confederate law included a substitute system and a controversial list of exempted persons held to be essential at home. The category that caused the most discussion was that which exempted one slave owner or overseer for each twenty slaves. The Confederate draft was also controversial because it was a national levy; it made no concession to the doctrine of states' rights for which most Southerners claimed to be fighting.

It appears that the Confederacy's early use of a conscription law enabled General Robert E. Lee's armies to continue their general success in the Civil War well into 1863. It was only after the North also began drafting men that President Lincoln could be confident of victory. The North, with a much larger population, was able to sustain its losses and to continue the war indefinitely; the Confederacy could not. Continuance of the draft underscored Northern determination to continue the war to its conclusion. The result was Lee's surrender at Appomattox and the restoration of the Union.

Mark A. Plummer, updated by Irwin Halfond

Core Resources

Iver Charles Bernstein's *The New York City Draft Riots: Their Significance for American Society and Politics in the Age of the Civil War* (New York: Oxford University Press, 1990) is a detailed, highly readable study of the Civil War's worst draft riot. James W. Geary's *We Need Men: The Union Draft in the Civil War* (Dekalb: Illinois University Press, 1991) is an extensively footnoted study of the draft law's origins, operation, and effects. Stephen M. Kohn's *Jailed for Peace: The History of American Draft Law Violation, 1658-1985* (New York: Praeger, 1987) is a thorough study of resistance to compulsory conscription from colonial to recent times.

See also: African Americans in the Civil War; Emancipation Proclamation; Race riots of 1866.

Drugs and racial/ethnic relations

> **Significance:** Because much of the drug trafficking and use in the United States involves ethnic gangs and communities and because the criminal justice system has been accused of disproportionately targeting certain ethnic groups and neighborhoods, the relationship between illegal drugs and ethnic background will remain an impassioned political topic.

Some of the groups involved in drug trafficking and consumption include majority (Italian American and Irish American) and minority (Latino and Asian American) ethnic groups, native-born (African American) groups and foreign-born (Russian) groups, and largely foreign-born minority groups such as Jamaicans. Nonethnic groups include motorcycle gangs and white Americans. Patterns of use and trade differ in the various ethnic and nonethnic communities. For example, white Americans tend to use powder cocaine whereas African Americans commonly prefer crack cocaine; Asian Americans typically prefer to trade in opium and heroin while whites usually deal in marijuana and amphetamines. Although these generalizations are essentially valid, exceptions of course exist. All of these trafficking and consumption patterns constitute illegal behavior, which inevitably results in the prosecution of many offenders. From the start of the war on drugs in the early 1970's, questions began to arise regarding possible civil liberties violations that occurred in the criminal justice system's zeal to win the war.

Caucasians and Drugs

No single ethnic or racial group completely monopolizes any particular aspect of the illegal drug trade; however, it is possible to draw broad boundaries within which particular groups specialize and control "market share." Caucasian traffickers can be divided into three major categories: La Cosa Nostra (commonly known as the Italian Mafia), found in all major metropolitan areas; the Irish mafia, especially the Winter Hill gang in the Boston/New England area; and the Russian mafia, which is most prominent in New York City (Brighton Beach) and Los Angeles (the Fairfax district). All deal chiefly in heroin, although cocaine, marijuana, and other illicit drugs make up an important part of their business. The Italian and Irish gangsters have been around for decades, the former being identified with organized crime to the point of stereotyping. The Russian mafia became a larger factor in the late 1980's after the collapse of the Soviet Union, which resulted in widespread open corruption in that nation and abundant migration from its former republics to the United States. Many of these migrants were members of, or drawn to, Russian organized crime.

The Russians, like the Soviets before them, obtain illegal drugs from the opium-producing nations of the Golden Crescent (Iran, Afghanistan, and Pakistan) and have strong connections in the Muslim areas through which much of the opium and heroin pass on their way to Russia, from where the drugs are transported to Western Europe and North America, usually to New York City. Italian traffickers, who controlled the trade in opiates until the 1970's, also use Golden Crescent sources as well as those in the Golden Triangle (Myanmar, Laos, and Thailand). By the late twentieth century, Nigerian smugglers moved much of the opium from Asia and the Middle East to Europe, where Sicilian and Corsican traffickers shipped the drugs, usually from Marseilles or Amsterdam to New York City.

The majority of marijuana is planted by individual whites, principally in the rural parts of the American West or South and often on public land, largely owing to marginal incomes derived from the growing of traditional crops. A considerable part of methamphetamine production occurs in private white residences, though this enterprise is truly a cottage industry that knows no ethnic or racial boundaries. Street and motorcycle gangs distribute methamphetamines and other drugs.

Latinos and Drugs

Most of the world's cocaine is produced in Peru, Bolivia, Ecuador, Chile, and Colombia, and control of the drug's shipment to the United States is usually in the hands of cartels, either Colombian (Cali or Medellin) or Mexican (Tijuana, Sinaloa, Ciudad Juarez, and Gulf). The Mexi-

Although gangs such as the Crips, a Los Angeles street gang whose members flash signs for the camera, are among the groups believed to be involved in the trafficking and use of drugs, the drug trade involves people of various racial, ethnic, and socioeconomic backgrounds, not just minority members.

can traffickers, who account for approximately three-fourths of all cocaine sold in the United States, became major factors in cocaine distribution when the U.S. government began to close off traditional points of entry for the drug in south Florida and the Caribbean in the late 1980's. The Colombian cartels farmed out distribution to the Mexicans, who moved the drug up the Pacific corridor. The Mexican cartels also funneled opium, obtained from Asian traffickers, from Mexico to the United States, where the illegal drugs were distributed by the Mexican mafia (composed of Mexican Americans and Mexican nationals), other ethnic gangs, and street dealers of all backgrounds.

Asians and Drugs
Asian gangs became major players in the drug trade during the last three decades of the twentieth century. Like Russian organized crime, Asian criminal activity grew along with migration generated by politics and poverty and tended to victimize members of the Asian American community. Asian organized crime became heavily involved in drug traffic by the 1980's, challenging Italian predominance. Of the numerous Asian gangs (Chinese secret societies, Vietnamese or Vietnamese-Chinese gangs, the Japanese yakuza) the ethnic Chinese groups control the lion's share of the drug enterprise, largely because they have connections throughout the world, particularly in Southeast Asia, where Golden Triangle opium is produced and shipped to Bangkok,

where it awaits shipment to North America. Opiates are smuggled into the United States either from the south by ethnic Chinese gangs in cooperation with the Mexican mafia or from the north by Vietnamese-Chinese gangs in Vancouver, Canada, who carry contraband across the border into Montana and North Dakota.

African Americans and Drugs
African American participation in drug dealing tends to involve crack cocaine and street gangs, including the rival Bloods and Crips, which originated in Los Angeles and had established branches in many major urban centers west of Chicago by the mid-1980's. Jamaican gangs (also known as posses) originated along the East Coast and moved west, introducing crack cocaine to Kansas City, St. Louis, Dallas, and Houston by the mid-1980's. All of these gangs have been linked to extremely violent behavior, stemming partly from turf wars. The U.S. Attorney General's office has compared their paroxysms of brutality to the battles between legendary gangsters Frank Nitti and Al Capone. The office found that in contrast to these violent and visible gangs, many drug enterprises in African American communities involved "men and women who operated like successful business people with small or no criminal records."

Ethnic Groups and Drug Consumption
By the early 1990's, the war on drugs, especially the Just Say No campaign, had succeeded in making drugs less appealing, and drug use declined from the levels reached during the 1960's and 1970's but hardly disappeared. Among ethnic groups, Latinos in Los Angeles dipped cigarettes in PCP (phencyclidine, or angel dust), Iranian Americans smoked heroin, African Americans favored crack cocaine, and many ethnic groups consumed marijuana, which was gradually becoming more potent. White Americans also continued to use marijuana and other drugs, and LSD (lysergic acid diethylamide) enjoyed a resurgence among college students. By the late twentieth century, people were beginning to use drugs at a younger age, and the array of available drugs had grown significantly.

A December, 1994, *Los Angeles Times* series on crack cocaine focused on the drug's destructive impact on the city's minority communities. However, drug problems were hardly limited to poor, ethnic communities, as was pointed out in a late 1990's antidrug commercial. The spot began with the statistic "Forty-six percent of minors using marijuana are found in the inner city," then asks the question "Do you know where the other 54 percent reside?" as a young white in the suburbs skateboards up to a friend, who hands him a joint. In short, drugs cut across all racial, ethnic, income, and neighborhood barriers. One drug treatment executive put it this way: "When it comes to drugs, there is a complete democracy." Some communities and ethnic groups are clearly more negatively affected than others by drugs, which give rise to gangs, violence, illnesses, family ruptures, and job losses. However, the 1998 arrest, conviction, and lenient sentence given a Newport Beach, California, socialite for cocaine possession, the arrests of such movie stars as Charlie Sheen and Robert Downey, Jr., and the gang-related killings of musician Tupac Shakur and an undercover teenage drug informant for the Brea, California, police department demonstrate that drug usage and violence cut across racial, ethnic, and class lines.

Ethnic Groups and the Criminal Justice System

The question of whether the state and federal governments' antidrug activities violate people's civil rights finds citizens from all backgrounds—liberal and conservative, black and white, rich and poor—responding affirmatively and negatively. Those who believe that violations have occurred claim that the war on drugs gives government more power than is prudent, resulting in invasions of privacy (such as drug testing), needless confiscations of property, and misuse of the military to enforce drug laws (such as assigning military personnel to border patrol duty). Those who believe that civil rights have not been violated assert that these antidrug actions are both necessary and proper. In either case, the laws designed to stamp out illegal production, distribution, and consumption of illicit drugs need to be applied fairly, and many people maintain that a disproportionate number of minorities end up in the criminal justice system and, once there, are more likely to be convicted and more likely to receive harsher sentences. Critics note that under federal law, the possession of one gram of crack cocaine (favored mainly by African Americans) involves the same penalties as possession of one hundred grams of powder cocaine (the type used primarily by whites). They assert that this, along with the fact that since 1986 more than 97 percent of crack cocaine defendants in federal court are minority members, represents discrimination. The counterargument is that the wealthy can afford the legal advice that minimizes or eliminates encounters with the criminal justice system. A 1996 U.S. Supreme Court decision decreed that such disparities did not constitute unequal treatment. However, a *Los Angeles Times* editorial took issue, arguing, "These federal drug laws are not only unfair on their face but pernicious in their application."   *Thomas D. Reins*

Core Resources

The best introduction to debates surrounding late twentieth century drug problems in the United States is found in Neal Bernards's *War on Drugs: Opposing Viewpoints* (San Diego: Greenhaven Press, 1990), which devotes considerable attention to the connection between ethnicity and drugs. Physician David F. Musto provides the historical background to the War on Drugs in *The American Disease: Origins of Narcotic Control* (New York: Oxford University Press, 1987), which discusses racial minorities and drugs. Psychiatrist Thomas Szasz's *Ceremonial Chemistry* (New York: Doubleday, 1974) explores the drug issue as it relates to Asian Americans and to Malcolm X. Daniel K. Benjamin and Roger L. Miller recommend how to deal with users, dealers, and the criminal justice system in *Undoing Drugs: Beyond Legalization* (New York: Basic Books, 1991). Ronald Hamowy's *Dealing with Drugs: Consequences of Government Control* (San Francisco: Pacific Research Institute for Public Policy, 1987) contains articles that scrutinize the nature of addiction, drug-related crime, and government antidrug activities. For a good picture of Asian drug activities, consult *Asian Organized Crime*, by the U.S. Senate Committee on Governmental Affairs (Washington, D.C.: Government Printing Office, 1991).

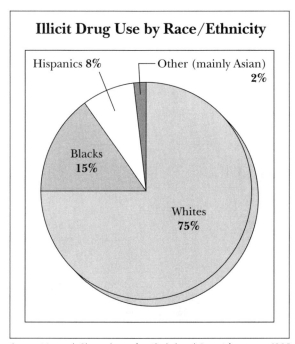

Illicit Drug Use by Race/Ethnicity

Hispanics **8%**

Other (mainly Asian) **2%**

Blacks **15%**

Whites **75%**

Source: National Clearinghouse for Alcohol and Drug Information, 1995 National Household Survey. http://www.health.org/pubs/95hhs/any.htm

See also: Crack cocaine; Crime and race/ethnicity; Criminal justice system; Irish Americans; Italian American stereotypes; Italian Americans; Jamaican Americans; Latinos in the United States.

Duro v. Reina

In 1984, while living on the Salt River Pima-Maricopa Reservation in Arizona, Albert Duro, an enrolled member of another tribe, shot and killed an Indian youth within reservation boundaries. Under the Major Crimes Act (1885 and amended), Duro was charged with murder, but eventually, federal charges were dismissed. Duro then was placed in the custody of the Pima-Maricopa police and was charged in tribal court with illegally firing a weapon on the reservation. Tribal courts' powers are regulated by a federal statute that limits tribal criminal penalties to misdemeanors.

After the tribal court denied Duro's motion to dismiss his case for lack of jurisdiction, he brought a petition before the federal court to dismiss. Duro's case was accepted on the basis that the Pima-Maricopa tribe's attempt to assert jurisdiction over a nonmember Indian would constitute discrimination based on race, a violation of equal protection guarantees of the American Indian Civil Rights Act (1968). Ultimately, in 1990, the U.S. Supreme Court determined that Indian tribes lack jurisdiction over persons who are not tribal members. Therefore, the Pima-Maricopa tribe had no criminal jurisdiction over Duro, a nonmember. The Court's decision set boundaries on the concept of tribal sovereignty in criminal cases and limited tribes to controlling internal relations among their own tribal members.

Carole A. Barrett

See also: American Indian Civil Rights Act; American Indians in the justice system; Tribal courts; Tribal sovereignty.

Dyer antilynching bill

After World War I, the National Association for the Advancement of Colored People (NAACP) sought congressional sponsors for federal antilynching legislation. More than three thousand people, mostly African Americans, had been lynched between 1889 and 1918. Of sixty-nine lynchings in 1921, 92 percent involved African Americans. In April, 1921, President Warren Harding requested that Congress pass antilynching legislation. Representative L. C. Dyer of Missouri introduced a bill that made lynching a national crime subject to federal prosecution and penalty. The House in January, 1929, easily adopted the Dyer bill, 220 to 119.

The Dyer bill languished in the Senate Judiciary Committee. Southern senators opposed the federal government's interference with the police powers of the states. The Dyer bill finally reached the Senate floor at a special session on the ship subsidy bill in November, 1922. The NAACP intensified its efforts to secure passage of the Dyer measure, sending senators a memo, signed by numerous professionals, urging adoption. Southern and border senators, led by Oscar Underwood of Alabama and Pat Harrison of Mississippi, filibustered the Dyer bill for a week. Republican senators at a December caucus abandoned their efforts to secure approval of the Dyer bill, clearing the way for Senate consideration of the ship subsidy bill. Other antilynching bills, including the Costigan-Wagner bill of 1935 and the Wagner-Gavagan bill of 1940, likewise failed.

David L. Porter

New York rioters hang an African American. The Dyer bill was designed to combat lynchings such as this.

See also: Frank, Leo, lynching; Lynchings; *United States v. Cruikshank.*

E

Eastern European Jews

The major emigration of Eastern European Jews to the United States did not begin until the 1880's. Jews began to emigrate when the services they performed as small-scale merchants and artisans were rendered obsolete by the modernization of agriculture and the early impact of industrialization on the peasant economy of Russia, Austria-Hungary, and the Polish territory held by Germany. The migration became a mass movement, however, when deadly state-sponsored riots left hundreds dead and thousands homeless in Russia and Russian Poland following the assassination of Czar Alexander II in 1881. About 250,000 Jews lived in the United States in 1880; by 1920, more than 2 million Eastern European Jews had joined them.

They were not given a warm welcome. The American Jewish community reacted with alarm, fearful that the upsurge in immigration would stimulate anti-Semitism and undermine the relatively comfortable position that Jews had attained in the country. Only as the magnitude of the problem became clear did the established Jewish community begin to organize an array of philanthropic institutions and establish defense organizations to combat anti-Semitism. The migration's size and the tendency of the new arrivals to cluster within the nation's largest cities, especially New York, made them particularly conspicuous. Crowded into slum areas where they transformed whole neighborhoods into regions where no English could be heard, they seemed particularly threatening to native-born Americans.

Many of the men, possessing few skills valuable to an industrial economy, became peddlers pushing carts or carrying packs filled with merchandise until they accumulated enough cash to open small retail stores. Many of the women and a significant proportion of the men found work in the garment industry. A few had previous experience in the needle trades, but of more importance was the willingness of owners to hire them. Manufacturing ready-to-wear clothing was a relatively new and risky industry that attracted Jewish entrepreneurs who were open to hiring and training Jewish workers.

Eastern European Jews settled in dense concentrations in their own neighborhoods and rarely interacted with other ethnic groups. Those whom they displaced, especially the New York City Irish, often responded with small-scale street violence. In addition, the Jewish community experienced sharp internal divisions. Jews from a given area of Europe tended to settle near each other, build separate synagogues, and create self-help and burial societies designed to serve migrants from the specific city or region from which they had come. A hierarchy of prejudice separated Jewish groups and influenced the choice of marriage partners. German Jews looked down on Polish and Russian Jews. Russian Jews were reputed to view marriage with Galician Jews, who came from the most poverty-stricken region of the Austro-Hungarian Empire, as equivalent to marrying a Gentile, which was taboo.

Economic success increased the interaction of the Eastern European Jews with the larger American society. In the affluent post-World War II years, they moved into the suburbs. Their children, fluent in English and increasingly college-educated, entered the professions as teachers, doctors, and lawyers. As the descendants of the Eastern European Jews merged with the American middle class, relations with other ethnic and religious groups became easier and less antagonistic. *Milton Berman*

See also: Anti-Semitism; Ashkenazic and German Jews; Frank, Leo, lynching; Jewish Americans; Jewish Americans as a middleman minority; Jewish ethnicity: definitions; Soviet Jewish immigrants.

Ebonics

On December 18, 1996, the Oakland School Board unanimously passed a resolution declaring black English, or African American English, to be "the genetically based" language of African American students. Public reaction was swift and remarkably explosive. *The New York Times* (December 24, 1996) declared that "black slang is a distinct language." The news media were filled with stories and editorials, and black English was the topic on numerous talk shows, serious and entertainment-oriented. However, the media largely ignored the findings of at least two or three decades of research done by sociolinguists about the structure of black English vernaculars and the learning difficulties experienced by children who speak black English, or Ebonics. This research was employed in the historic 1974 *Lau v. Nichols* U.S. Supreme court ruling, the passing of the Equal Educational Opportunities Act (1974), and the 1979 Supreme Court case involving black-English-speaking students at Ann Arbor, Michigan's Martin Luther King, Jr., Elementary School.

The Oakland board members used several terms for the language spoken by African Americans; however, "Ebonics" was the term adopted by the media and the public. The term "Ebonics" was introduced by Robert Williams in 1957 and is based on the blending of "ebony" (black) and "phonics" (sounds). Other terms such as "African American English" and "black English," which are used in linguistic studies, better capture the characteristics of this distinct American speech variety and its users.

There is some question as to whether Ebonics is a separate language or a dialect of English. Because the term "dialect" can be viewed as derisive, linguists prefer to use the neutral term "variety." Ebonics is a variety of English that is as distinct and as colorful as Irish English or Australian English. Ebonics has its own complex rules. For instance, an Ebonics speaker might say "She hungry" for the standard English "She's hungry," deleting the present tense of the verb "to be." The Ebonics speaker might substitute "Not no more" for the standard "Not any more," using multiple negation. Ebonics uses the word "be" to mean "sometimes" or "often," as in the sentence "She be tired," which in standard English is rendered "She is tired sometimes."

The rules that govern Ebonics are commonly found in many languages of the world. Therefore, characterizing Ebonics as structurally weak, somehow defective, or ungrammatical, or labeling it as slang is incorrect and reflects deeper social and racial problems in U.S. society. The Linguistic Society of America passed a resolution in January, 1997, stating that the variety of English known as Ebonics is "systematic and rule-governed like all natural speech varieties."

Ebonics is not a separate language, as first was claimed by the Oakland School Board and others. Proponents of Ebonics as a separate language claim that it has the vocabulary of English, but a grammar based on Niger-Congo or West African languages; however, this is incorrect. In spite of some structural differences, Ebonics much more closely approximates the structure and the lexicon of standard English than that of the West African languages.

Tej K. Bhatia

See also: Accent discrimination; English-only and official English movements; *Lau v. Nichols.*

Economics and race

> **Significance:** Racial differences, especially in earnings and employment, are of ongoing empirical and theoretical interest to economists. Racial differences in labor markets are caused by demand-side factors, such as discrimination in hiring and pay, by supply-side factors, such as different levels of education and work experience, or by a combination of supply and demand factors.

There are many differences between races in the sphere of economic activity. Differences appear in earnings, wealth, and income; employment patterns within and across occupations, industries, and geographical regions; unemployment rates; educational and job experience attainment; and socioeconomic factors such as family structure, crime rates, and life expectancy. In the United States, non-Hispanic whites have the most favorable economic status by all the measures listed above, while blacks generally have the least favorable status; Asians, Hispanics, and Native Americans fall in between on most economic measures. Unemployment rates are higher among nonwhites than whites, especially for the young. Whites generally earn higher wages and salaries and, therefore, generally have higher family incomes than nonwhites. Additionally, whites command a larger than proportionate percentage of national wealth, which includes investment income as well as earnings; they are disproportionately represented in the more desirable jobs such as the managerial and professional occupations.

Socioeconomic factors tend to compound the relatively unfavorable economic status of nonwhites. Nonwhites have higher average household and family sizes, so their smaller family income is divided among more people than is the family income of whites. Nonwhites are more likely to reside in female-headed households, which have lower incomes than do male-headed households.

Race and Income
The study of the role of race in determining income is a topic which can be approached from both the demand and supply sides of the market for labor. For example, measurement of earnings differentials by race falls under the areas of human capital theory and discrimination theory. Human capital theory, a supply-side argument, argues that a person's wages are determined in large part by his or her productivity, and that an individual's productivity can be increased by investment in education or on-the-job training; therefore, differences in earnings by race can be linked to differences in

human capital attainment. Discrimination theory, a demand-side theory, says that the wages paid to workers reflect the preferences of employers, employees, or customers as to the race of the worker. In any of these three cases, the workers in the preferred group or groups receive higher wages than equally productive workers receive in the other, disliked groups. Discrimination may affect the acquisition of human capital as well as its effective utilization on the job. If nonwhites are denied full access to educational opportunities, then they will enter the workforce possessing fewer marketable skills than whites and will command a lower wage. Also, if a worker believes he or she is likely to encounter discrimination in the workplace, he or she may invest less in human capital than otherwise and earn even less than he or she would in the absence of labor market discrimination.

There are many other possible sources of racial differences relating to differential labor productivity and differential access to productive assets. Acquisition of English is a crucial step in achieving higher earnings for immigrants. Additionally, nonwhites who have strong networks of members of their racial group to tap for job opportunities will prosper relative to isolated nonwhites. Nonwhites may have imperfect access to capital markets because of discrimination by lenders and a lack of accumulated family assets.

A more controversial source of racial earnings differences is different valuations of labor relative to leisure for different racial groups. If one group has a relatively high valuation of leisure, this is reflected both in a high reservation wage and a lower probability of being employed and in a lower number of hours worked by those members of the group who are employed.

Programs and Effects

Various policies have been enacted which attempt to influence either supply-or demand-side forces in order to lessen racial economic differences. The civil rights legislation passed in the United States in the 1960's attacked many forms of discrimination, such as segregated schools. In such systems, white and nonwhite schools were separate but not equal, and the goal was to make a quality public education available to all races. Legislation attacking discrimination in hiring has been passed in an attempt to ensure that jobs are open to all qualified applicants regardless of racial origin. Job training programs targeted at nonwhites have been set up by private and public groups. Finally, affirmative action policies have attempted to counter years of hiring discrimination by setting formal hiring quotas for nonwhites in large firms and governmental units.

Much research has focused on measuring the effects of antipoverty and antidiscrimination programs. There

has been an increase in the nonwhite/white earnings differential. Data from 1960 show an earnings differential for workers employed full-time (thirty-five or more hours per week, at least forty weeks per year) of 0.66, or 66 cents earned by a nonwhite male to every dollar earned by a white male; this ratio had risen to 0.80 by 1980. How much of this earnings increase can be attributed to the civil rights legislation passed in the 1960's and how much is attributable to independent societal forces is a hard question to answer, especially since discrimination can affect both investment in productive skills and the return obtained on those skills.

Another topic of continuing interest to economists is the effect of the minimum wage on minority employment. Black youth unemployment hit record levels in the 1970's and 1980's; if discouraged workers are included, then nonworking rates for black males can be as high as 75 or 80 percent in many urban locales. A question that arises is whether the minimum wage keeps employers from hiring some of these youths. It appears that rises in the minimum wage affect black workers, especially the young, disproportionately. If young blacks experience difficulty in their initial entry into the labor force, their subsequent work history may be altered unfavorably relative to a situation where they can enter a job which is low-paying but may lead to more lucrative subsequent employment.

Interest also focuses on assessing the success of various microeconomic policies, such as job training initiatives, which disproportionately serve nonwhites. Concern with the high nonwhite unemployment rates led to the use of job creation programs at the federal and local government levels in the 1970's. Researchers have attempted to determine if enrollment in a job training program improves earnings for participants relative to those not enrolled (or relative to what they would have earned without receiving the training). Generally, gains in earnings appear to be modest for participants.

Controversial Programs

The extent of poverty among different races and the effects of welfare programs on racial groups have also been studied. One controversial topic is whether the Aid to Families with Dependent Children (AFDC) program created more poor black female-headed households than would have existed otherwise. Critics of AFDC argue that it encouraged poor young females to have more children out of wedlock than they would otherwise have had and to remain out of the labor force while receiving support in the form of AFDC benefits.

Another controversial topic is the effect of affirmative action policies on racial earnings and employment differences. While workplace race segregation has been declining over time, it continues to persist. Using the

Duncan index to measure race segregation by occupation, researchers showed that in 1960, 45 percent of nonwhite men and 50 percent of nonwhite women would have had to move into white-dominated occupations in order to achieve workforce desegregation for each sex. By 1986, only 29 percent of nonwhite men and 26 percent of nonwhite women would have had to change jobs in order to achieve complete racial desegregation. While affirmative action programs combined with antidiscrimination laws appear to have increased hiring and promotion rates for minorities, critics argue that there may be costs in decreased productivity if less qualified minority applicants are hired instead of more qualified white applicants.

Comparative Studies

Government, through legislation and implementation of programs, has had a large influence on racial differences, and government agencies hire large numbers of minorities. Nonwhites tend to make higher hourly earnings relative to whites in the public sector: In 1960, the earnings differential in the public sector for nonwhite versus white males was 0.64; the private-sector differential was 0.79. This trend continued, although the difference narrowed: By 1980, the public and private sector differentials were 0.79 and 0.86, respectively. It is unclear whether these differences are the result of less discrimination in hiring and pay in government than in the private sector.

Another use of economic concepts in studying racial issues is to compare economic variables, mainly earnings, for different immigrant groups. The United States has experienced many waves of immigrants. While nineteenth century and early twentieth century waves of immigration were from Europe, immigration in the 1970's and 1980's consisted primarily of an influx of Southeast Asians and a mass of mostly illegal immigrants from Mexico and Central America. It is interesting to examine earnings differences for immigrant groups over time: A general pattern is that immigrants make low earnings relative to natives when they first arrive, and subsequently improve their earnings status; their descendants then make even higher earnings than did their parents. Whether newer waves of immigrants will experience this same pattern of steady improvement in economic status or will constitute a permanent underclass in American society is debatable.

Another puzzle for economists is why some immigrant groups prosper in the labor market relative to others. Asian immigrants, especially Chinese and Japanese, have higher earnings and employment rates than do other immigrant groups. An interesting pattern is that immigrant black groups, such as West Indians, have higher earnings than do native blacks. A large part of these differences appear to be attributable to the higher education of the successful groups.

U.S. Historical Patterns

Interest in racial differences in the United States stems from two historical phenomena: the forcible introduction of a large number of blacks into the country through the institution of slavery, and the basic fact that the U.S. population has been fed throughout American history by large waves of immigrants.

The main focus on racial differences in the United States has been on black-white differences. Blacks comprise the largest racial minority in the United States and occupy a unique position in the historical legacy of the country as the only racial group to have been forced to enter the country in large numbers through the institution of slavery. Their pattern of assimilation into the economic mainstream appears to differ substantially from those of all other groups of immigrants.

There has been much debate about whether this unique historical position is responsible for the subsequent lack of success on the part of blacks to improve their socioeconomic status as rapidly as other racial groups, such as the Chinese and Japanese, have done. In the 1980's, several "neoconservative" economists, including George Gilder and Thomas Sowell, argued that social class is a more important determinant of racial differences than is discrimination. Other economists, however, including Thomas Boston, argue that class is the product of racial discrimination and, therefore, it is not useful to draw a distinction between class and discrimination as possible causes of blacks' low socioeconomic status.

While much research has focused on identifying the sources of economic differences between racial groups, many economic researchers are more interested in evaluating and improving social programs aimed at narrowing these differences. There are many issues revolving around use of appropriate methodology for achieving both research agendas. One basic problem is how to measure the relative contributions of labor supply and demand factors to an individual's wage rate. Another problem is how to evaluate a program by comparing participants to a control group's experiences: If the participants are not carefully matched to appropriate controls, results may be attributed to differences in the groups rather than the program's effects. Also, the widespread use of nonexperimental data to evaluate program effects is inherently problematic because so many influences occur simultaneously: Changes in the non-white/white earnings differential between 1960 and 1980 may have been caused by increased governmental antidiscrimination efforts, by erosion of prejudice in society regardless of governmental actions, or by increased productivity of minority workers. Ongoing debates over appropriate use of research tools ensure the continuing role of economists in the discussion of societal racial differences. *Joyce P. Jacobsen*

Core Resources

Thomas D. Boston's *Race, Class, and Conservatism* (Winchester, Mass.: Unwin Hyman, 1988) aims to rebut the central propositions of neoconservative economists on the role of racial discrimination in black economic advancement. Robert Cherry's *Discrimination: Its Economic Impact on Blacks, Women, and Jews* (Lexington, Mass.: Lexington Books, 1989) covers black youth employment problems, black-Jewish relations, and the impact of social welfare programs. Ronald G. Ehrenberg and Robert S. Smith's *Modern Labor Economics: Theory and Public Policy* (3d ed., Glenview, Ill.: Scott, Foresman, 1988) contains an excellent chapter on the economics of discrimination. *A Common Destiny: Blacks and American Society* (Washington, D.C.: National Academy Press, 1989), edited by Gerald David Jaynes and Robin M. Williams, Jr., provides a comprehensive report on the socioeconomic status of blacks in the United States since 1940. Sar A. Levitan, Garth L. Mangum, and Ray Marshall's *Human Resources and Labor Markets* (2d ed., New York: Harper & Row, 1976) includes a clear description of the main economic theories of racial discrimination. Thomas Sowell's *Markets and Minorities* (New York: Basic Books, 1981) covers the experience of racial and ethnic minorities in America in various economic settings.

See also: Employment among African Americans; Employment among American Indians; Employment among Asian Americans; Employment among Latinos; Employment in Canada.

Edmonson v. Leesville Concrete Company

Thaddeus Edmonson, an African American construction worker, sued his employer, the Leesville Concrete Company, in 1988, claiming compensation for injuries suffered in a workplace accident. Edmonson invoked his right to a trial by jury. During the pretrial examination of potential jurors, the company's lawyers used their peremptory challenges to excuse two of the three black members of the panel. Edmonson asked the district court to require the company to provide a race-neutral explanation of the dismissals of the black panelists. Under *Batson v. Kentucky* (1986), racial motivation for juror challenges was held unconstitutional in criminal cases. In *Batson*, the U.S. Supreme Court had reasoned

that the use of race as a criterion in jury challenges by the prosecution violates the equal protection clause of the U.S. Constitution. Edmonson's case presented the issue of whether such dismissals are improper in civil cases. The trial court denied Edmonson's request and, after conflicting decisions in the court of appeals, he appealed to the Supreme Court.

In 1991, Justice Anthony Kennedy wrote for the Court in a 6-3 decision holding that racially based juror challenges are unconstitutional even in civil cases. Because the juror challenges use the power of the government to select jury members, the discrimination becomes "state action" even though invoked by a private litigant. All state action must be consistent with constitutional rules forbidding racial discrimination.

Justice Sandra Day O'Connor dissented, arguing that only governmental discrimination is forbidden by the equal protection clause and that the act of Leesville Concrete's counsel was not state action. *Robert Jacobs*

See also: *Batson v. Kentucky*; Jury selection.

Education and African Americans

Significance: Since the emancipation of the slaves in 1863, the debate has raged over the role of education and educational institutions in the African American community in the United States. After the Civil Rights movement of the 1950's and 1960's, the importance of an equal education and performance on standardized testing led the educational community to reevaluate the impact of education and its significance for African American students.

The Civil War (1861-1865), Reconstruction (1863-1877), and the Thirteenth Amendment (1865) ended slavery. Although free African Americans had attended schools in some northern states long before the Civil War, southern states had prohibited the teaching of either slave or free African American children. Emancipation in 1863 brought with it the challenge of providing educational opportunities for the freed men and women and their children, particularly in the former Confederate states.

In 1865, Congress created the Freedmen's Bureau to help former slaves adjust to freedom. The bureau continued to function until 1872 and, under the leadership of General O. O. Howard, established schools throughout the South. At their peak in 1869, these schools had about 114,000 students enrolled. The schools taught reading, writing, grammar, geography, arithmetic, and music through a curriculum based on the New England school model. A small number of African American teachers were trained in these schools, but the schools were usually staffed by northern schoolteachers, who brought with them their values, their educational ideas, and their methods. These white educators from northern states promoted the stereotypical idea of the kind of education African Americans should receive. Samuel C. Armstrong and many like-minded educators stressed industrial training and social control over self-determination. Many believe this philosophy was designed to keep African Americans in a subordinate position.

Washington to Du Bois
Booker T. Washington was the leading educational spokesperson for African Americans after the Civil War. Washington, who was born a slave, experienced the hectic years of Reconstruction and, in a speech delivered at the Atlanta Exposition in 1895, painfully articulated the outlines of a compromise with the white power structure, a policy later known as accommodationism. A student of Armstrong, Washington believed that industrial education was an important force in building character and economic competence for African Americans. He believed in moral "uplift" through hard work. At the Tuskegee Institute, which he helped establish in 1881, Washington shaped his ideas into a curriculum that focused on basic academic, agricultural, and occupational skills and emphasized the values of hard work and the dignity of labor. He encouraged his students to become elementary schoolteachers, farmers, and artisans, emphasizing these occupations over the professions of medicine, law, and politics.

Although revered initially, Washington has become an increasingly controversial figure. Some people say he made the best of a bad situation and that, although he compromised on racial issues, he can be viewed as a leader who preserved and slowly advanced the educational opportunities of African Americans. Critics of Washington see him as an opportunist whose compromises restricted African American progress.

W. E. B. Du Bois was a sociological and educational pioneer who challenged the established system of education. Du Bois, an opponent of Washington's educational philosophies, believed the African American community needed more determined and activist leadership. He helped organize the Niagara Movement in 1905, which led to the founding in 1909 of the National Association for the Advancement of Colored People (NAACP). Du Bois was a strong opponent of racial segregation in the schools. Unlike Washington, Du Bois did not believe in slow, evolutionary change; he instead demanded immediate change. Du Bois supported the NAACP position that all American children, including African American children, should be granted an equal educational opportunity. It was through the efforts of the NAACP that the monumental U.S. Supreme Court case *Brown v. Board of Education* (1954) outlawed segregation in U.S. public schools. Du Bois believed in educated leadership for the African American community and developed the concept of the Talented Tenth, the notion that 10 percent of the African American population would receive a traditional college education in preparation for leadership.

Post-Civil Rights Era
Du Bois's educational and political philosophies had a significant influence on the Civil Rights movement of the 1950's and 1960's. Out of the effects of public school desegregation during the 1950's and 1960's and the Black Power movement of the 1970's grew a new perspective on the education of African Americans. Inspired by historians such as Cheikh Anta Diop and Basil Davidson, educational philosophers such as Molefi Kete Asante formed the Afrocentric school of education. Asante and his followers maintain that a curriculum centered on the perspective of African Americans is more effective in reaching African American youth than the Eurocentric curriculum to which most students are exposed. Low test scores and historically poor academic records could be the result, according to Afrocentrists, of a curriculum that does not apply to African American students.

Statistics
According to *The African American Education Data Book* (published in 1997 by the Research Institute of the College Fund/United Negro College Fund), in 1994, approximately 43.5 million students were enrolled in public elementary and secondary schools, and nearly 5 million students were enrolled in private elementary and secondary schools. African Americans represented 16.5 percent of all public school enrollments. African Americans were underrepresented at private elementary and secondary schools, where they constituted only 9.3 percent of all enrollments. The number of African Americans enrolled in public schools declined as grade level increased, a finding that supports the evidence that African Americans leave school at higher rates than children of the same age in other racial groups. African Americans represented only 12.5 percent of those who received regular high school diplomas in 1994.

In schools made up primarily of African American students and located mainly in economically depressed urban centers, nearly a quarter of all students participated in remedial reading programs, and 22 percent participated in remedial math. By comparison, schools with less than 50 percent African American students had 14.8 percent of students enrolled in remedial reading and 12 percent enrolled in remedial math. Furthermore, only 87 percent of African American high school seniors graduate on time compared with 93 percent of non-African American seniors.

Test Scores

African American students have historically scored far below whites in geography, writing, reading, and math. The National Educational Longitudinal Study of 1988 reported that the average seventeen-year-old African American student had a reading score only slightly higher than that of the average white thirteen-year-old. Compared with whites, African American Scholastic Aptitude Test (SAT) takers had lower high school grade-point averages, fewer years of academic study, and fewer honors courses. Data collected by the National Assessment of Educational Progress, however, reveal that African Americans had registered gains in reading, math, and other subjects between the 1970's and the 1990's. Despite these gains, African Americans are underrepresented among high school seniors applying for college and represented only 9 percent of the college population in the 1990's (a decrease from 10 percent in the 1970's).

It is not surprising that many African Americans see no value in postsecondary education. Regardless of socioeconomic status or whether they had received a high school diploma, a higher percentage of African Americans who were eighth-graders in 1988 were unemployed and not in college than their white counterparts in 1993, a year after their scheduled high school graduation. Despite affirmative action legislation, African Americans still are less likely to be hired for a job when competing against equally qualified white applicants.

Socioeconomic Status

In both 1980 and 1990, African American high school sophomores were concentrated in the lowest two socioeconomic status quartiles. The proportion of African Americans in the lowest socioeconomic status quartile declined from 48 percent in 1980 to 39 percent in 1990. In both 1980 and 1990, African Americans were underrepresented in the upper two socioeconomic status quartiles. In addi-

tion, African Americans often attend schools with fewer resources in poorer neighborhoods of large, urban areas. Fifteen percent of schools that have primarily African American students have no magnet or honors programming, as opposed to only 1.6 percent of schools with a majority of white students. Also, a higher percentage of schools with a majority of African American students participated in the National School Lunch Program. The poverty level in the African American community is one of the factors believed to be responsible for consistently low scores on standardized testing. Along with poverty, the African American community has also experienced a greater amount of violence and delinquency among high-school-age youths. The homicide rate among African American men increased by more than two-thirds in the late 1980's, according to a study by Joe Schwartz and Thomas Exter (1990).

Parental Attitudes

Although much of the effort of public policymakers goes into integrating schools and creating more diversity in inner-city schools, African American parents seem more interested in developing a stronger academic program in their children's schools. A survey taken in 1998 by Public Agenda, a nonpartisan public-opinion research firm, showed that 80 percent of African American parents favored raising academic standards and achievement levels in primarily African American schools over emphasizing integration. Eleven percent of the parents polled said they would like to see the schools both

A father and son enjoy reading a book. In a 1998 Public Agenda survey, African American parents expressed a great deal of interest in their children's education.

integrated and improved. Of the white parents polled, 60 percent expressed a fear that discipline and safety problems, low reading scores, and social problems would result if African American students were transferred to a mostly white school. The Public Agenda survey demonstrates the differences in opinions on education based on racial background. For example, nearly 50 percent of African American parents felt that teachers demanded too little of their children because of the children's race. Despite the difference in opinion on these public issues, both African American and white parents expressed a great interest in their children's school success and the quality of their children's education.   *Jason Pasch*

Core Resources

A good introduction to the topic can be found in *The Encyclopedia of African American Education* (Westport, Conn.: Greenwood Press, 1996), edited by Faustine C. Jones-Wilson. *Issues in African American Education* (Nashville, Tenn.: One Horn Press, 1991), by Walter Gill, provides good background on the issues surrounding education. Booker T. Washington's *Up from Slavery* (New York: Doubleday, 1938) is a classic text on Washington's educational philosophy and life story. W. E. B. Du Bois's ideas can be found in *The Philadelphia Negro: A Social Study* (Philadelphia: University of Pennsylvania Press, 1899) and *Dusk of Dawn: An Essay Toward an Autobiography of a Race Concept* (New York: Harcourt, Brace & World, 1940). The Afrocentric philosophy is described in Molefi Kete Asante's *Kemet, Afrocentricity, and Knowledge* (Trenton, N.J.: Africa World Press, 1990). Statistics covering every aspect of African American education can be found in *The African American Education Data Book* (Research Institute of the College Fund/UNCF, 1997), by Frederick D. Patterson, Michael T. Nettles, and Laura W. Perna.

See also: Ability testing; Accommodationism; Afrocentrism; Atlanta Compromise; *Brown v. Board of Education*; College admissions; College entrance examinations; Employment among African Americans; Freedmen's Bureau; National Association for the Advancement of Colored People; Niagara Movement; Talented Tenth.

Education and American Indians

> **Significance:** Christian missionaries, the federal government, and public school systems have assumed responsibility for educating American Indians under policies that often have emphasized assimilation over tribal identity.

As more and more European settlers entered that part of the Americas now known as the United States, education was seen as a way of assimilating young Native Americans into the dominant white culture. The history of Europeanized Indian education over four centuries tells a story of cultural genocide.

Missionary Activity and Paternalism, 1568-1870

The first school specifically founded for the education of Indian youth in the New World was established by the Jesuits in Havana, Florida, in 1568. For the next three hundred years, Catholic and Protestant religious groups dominated non-Indian attempts to educate Indians. In 1617, King James asked Anglican clergy to collect money for building "churches and schools for ye education of ye children of these Barbarians in Virginia." One of the earliest of these religious schools was founded by the Reverend John Eliot in 1631 in Roxbury, Massachusetts. He developed a plan to bring Indians together in small, self-governing "Indian prayer towns" where they could be instructed in Christian ethics and arts. In order to become accepted by the Puritans in these prayer towns, Indians had to give up their old way of life completely, including long hair for men and short hair for women.

A common method of providing educational assistance during this period was by treaty stipulation. From the first treaty in 1778 until 1871, when treaty making with the Indians ended, the United States entered into almost four hundred treaties, of which 120 had educational provisions. The terms usually called for teachers, material, and equipment for educational purposes.

The first specific appropriation by Congress for Indian education was the Act of March 30, 1802, which allowed $15,000 per year "to promote civilization among the aborigines." The money went mostly to missionary groups. In 1819, Congress established a civilization fund, which lasted until 1873, to provide financial support to religious groups and other interested individuals who were willing to live among and teach Indians. The Act of March 3, 1819, which established this fund, also gave the president complete authority over Indian education and remained the basic authorization for the educational activities carried out by the government on behalf of Indian people.

Manual labor schools had their beginnings during the period when the tribes were being moved out of the East and Northeast. Usually these were located in Indian country or at a site convenient to several tribes and, for that reason, were agreeable to the Indians. They also drew support from the government, which believed that it was a waste of effort to provide only academic training. The first manual labor school, the Choctaw Academy, was organized in 1837 by Colonel Richard Johnson in Scott County, Kentucky. This school, and others that came later, offered religious, academic, and practical instruction. Six hours were spent daily in the classroom and six at work on farm and shop detail. By 1840, the U.S. government was operating six manual labor schools with eight hundred students and eighty-seven boarding schools with about twenty-nine hundred students.

Several Indian tribes, with the help of missionaries and educators, built and supported their own schools. The Mohawks did this as early as 1712 under the influence of the Reverend Thomas Barkley, an Anglican missionary. This school, with one temporary suspension, operated until the end of the American Revolution. The Choctaw and Cherokee, before their removal from their original homelands, had instituted common schools, supported with funds obtained from the United States for land cessions. After the removal of these tribes to lands west of the Mississippi, the Cherokee, in 1841, and the Choctaw, in 1842, reestablished their schools. (A number of states had not yet provided for a system of common schools in 1842.) The Cherokee system, by 1852, included twenty-one elementary schools and two academies. The enrollment in that year was given as 1,100. The Choctaw had nine schools, of which seven experimented with teaching reading and writing to

Five boys wear the uniform of the Carlisle Indian School in Pennsylvania. The school's aim was the complete assimilation of American Indians.

adults. Teachers were brought from the East to be in charge of advanced academic work, and the course of study included music, astronomy, Latin, botany, algebra, and elocution. Within ten years, however, the majority of their teachers had changed from eastern-educated missionaries to locally trained teachers. The Chickasaw, Creek, and Seminole tribes, also members of the Five Civilized Tribes, followed the example of the Cherokee and Choctaw within a few years and established school systems. In all cases, the schools were tribally supported, and they operated without federal supervision until 1906, when the tribal governments of these five tribes were destroyed by an act of Congress.

In 1851, the period of reservation settlement began and did not end until the 1930's. Schools established on reservations were designed to devalue the traditional culture and religion of Indian people. One of the most significant ways of undermining Indian culture was the government's attempt to suppress native language. In 1880, the Indian Bureau issued regulations that "all instruction must be in English" in both mission and government schools under threat of loss of government funding. In 1885, some teachers and administrators, recognizing the small utility of standard educational training and methods, suggested that special materials be created for Indian children. No special textbooks were developed, however, until well into the twentieth century.

Government Control and Dependence, 1870-1923
In 1865, under President Ulysses S. Grant, Indian boarding schools had their birth. After studying conditions among some of the western tribes, a congressional committee suggested that "boarding schools remote from Indian communities" would be most successful in solving the "Indian problem." Grant, believing that the only solution lay in "the civilization" of Indians into white culture, supported the move. In 1878, the boarding school system was launched when the Carlisle Indian School in Carlisle, Pennsylvania, was founded by General Richard Henry Pratt. Pratt, alarmed at the "gross injustices to both races[Indians and blacks]" which he had observed, believed that true equality could come to the Indians only if they learned to feel at home in the white world, where they deserved both "the opportunities and . . . safeguards of our Declaration and Constitution." At Carlisle, which enrolled children from the midwestern and western tribes, students were required to speak, read, and write English and to assume the clothing and customs of white people. They were taught skills which would later help them become employed in trades such as blacksmithing, carpentry, tailoring, and farming. Girls were taught domestic skills. After completing school, students were placed with white families for three years;

Major Events in Post-contact Education

Year	Event
1568	Jesuits establish a school at Havana, Florida.
1617	King James asks Anglican clergy to collect money for the erecting of "churches and schools for ye education of ye children of Barbarians of Virginia."
1631	The Reverend John Eliot establishes a school in Roxbury, Massachusetts.
1636	Harvard College is founded in part to provide education for Indian youth.
1755	Eleazar Wheelock founds Moor's Charity School in Connecticut.
1775	The Continental Congress makes a conciliatory gesture toward Indians by appropriating $500 to educate Indians at Dartmouth College.
1802	In the Act of March 30, Congress appropriates $15,000 per year to "promote civilization among the aborigines."
1819	In the Act of March 3, Congress establishes a fund to provide financial support to individuals and religious groups who are willing to live among and teach Indians.
1832	The position of commissioner of Indian affairs is created.
1837	Choctaw Academy, the first manual labor school, is organized by Colonel Richard Johnson in Scott County, Kentucky.
1867	A Peace Commission appointed by President Ulysses Grant calls for assimilation and specifically for the extinguishing of Indian languages.
1879	The establishment of the U.S. Indian Training and Industrial School at Carlisle, Pennsylvania, begins era of large off-reservation boarding schools.
1884	Haskell Institute is established at Lawrence, Kansas.
1900	All direct government funding of missionary schools is ended.
1924	Passage of the Indian Citizenship Act makes all Indians citizens of the United States.
1924	The Committee of One Hundred Citizens recommends better facilities and better-trained personnel for teaching Indian students.
1928	The Meriam Report criticizes government policies and services for Indians; it calls for dramatic reforms.
1931	John Collier becomes commissioner of Indian affairs and immediately seeks to implement the recommendations of the Meriam Report.
1934	The Indian Reorganization Act and the Johnson-O'Malley Act are passed.
1953	Six termination bills are passed; according to the bills, states are to assume the responsibility for the education of all Indian children in public schools.
1959	The Center for Indian Education is established at Arizona State University.
1967-1971	The National Study of American Indian Education is carried out at the University of Chicago; results are summarized in *To Live on This Earth*.
1968	The first tribally controlled college, Navajo Community College, is founded.
1969	A Special Senate Subcommittee on Indian Education produces a report entitled *Indian Education: A National Tragedy, a National Challenge*.
1971	The Coalition of Indian Controlled School Boards is formed.
1972	The Indian Education Act is passed.
1989	Twenty-four tribally controlled colleges exist in ten states.

they worked in exchange for their upkeep. The families were paid fifty dollars a year to cover costs of clothing and health care.

Forts no longer needed by the army were converted into boarding schools. Between 1889 and 1892, twelve such boarding schools were established. Little attention was paid to tribal differences in language and customs. It was assumed—rightly—that if children could be taken at a young enough age and moved far enough away from the influences of family and tribe, the odds against their ever again becoming a part of their original environment were remote. Children as young as five years old were sent to the boarding schools. The shock, fear, and loneliness which these children faced upon being uprooted from everything familiar and known can only be imagined. Pratt, operating under the noblest of intentions, had unwittingly contributed to one of the saddest chapters in Indian history.

By 1887, Congress was appropriating more than a million dollars a year for Indian education. About half the appropriations went to missionaries who were contracted to educate Indians. Feuding between Protestants and Catholics, however, aggravated because the Catholics were much more successful in establishing schools, led the Protestants to support funding only government-run schools. With the appointment in 1889 of General Thomas J. Morgan, a Baptist minister, as commissioner of Indian affairs, the Republicans made a systematic effort to stop government funding of all missionary schools. By 1900 all direct funding to these schools was ended. Tribes continued to receive a portion of the dollars which the federal government had previously provided the churches for funding of the mission schools. Some tribes maintained these schools in spite of the reduced resources; most used the funds for other needs.

Moves to Reform Indian Education, 1924-1944
As the new century began, the continued inability of boarding schools and English-only education to transform Indians into white people led to disillusionment and lowered expectations for Indian education. Increasingly, Indians were viewed in the same light as blacks at that time: as a permanent underclass for whom an inferior, nonacademic, vocational education was appropriate and adequate.

At the same time, because of the staggering loss of land and the inefficiency of education, the total Indian situation was growing progressively worse. In 1902, the Bureau of Indian Affairs (BIA) was operating twenty-five boarding schools in fifteen states for 9,736 students. By 1912, there were more Indian children in public schools than in government schools. As government schools lost ground, efforts to increase Indian enrollment in public day schools did not include examining the ability of

these schools to meet Indian needs.

In 1924, a "Committee of One Hundred Citizens" was called together by the secretary of the interior to discuss how Indian education could be improved. The committee recommended better school facilities, better-trained personnel, an increase in the number of Indian students in public schools, and high school and college scholarships. These recommendations helped establish reservation day schools up to the sixth grade and reservation boarding schools up to the eighth grade.

In 1928, a government-sponsored study, *The Problem of Indian Administration* (the Meriam Report), claimed that the Bureau of Indian Affairs was providing poor-quality services to Indians; it particularly pointed to the shocking conditions found in boarding schools. The committee recommended that elementary children not be sent to BIA boarding schools at all. Shortly after publication of the study, John Collier, one of the BIA's leading critics, became commissioner of Indian affairs and immediately sought to implement the recommendations of the Meriam Report. The Johnson-O'Malley Act (1934) allowed the federal government to pay states for educating Indians in public schools.

The Termination Era, 1945-1970
In the 1950's, under President Dwight D. Eisenhower, six "termination" bills were passed. They were intended to end all federal involvement with the Indians, leaving policy issues in health, education, and welfare up to the states. Conditions improved little as states, for the most part, failed to provide adequate services in any of these arenas. Another program aimed at "relocation" helped Indians move from reservations to cities, where, presumably, educational and employment opportunities were better. Indian children in cities showed improved academic achievement, but many felt displaced and unhappy.

Between 1967 and 1971, Robert J. Havighurst of the University of Chicago directed a research project entitled the National Study of American Indian Education. Its recommendations called for greatly increased Indian participation in goal setting and in implementation of programs. During this same period, a report compiled by a Senate subcommittee on Indian education revealed that Indian school dropout rates were twice the national average, that Indian students lagged two to three years behind white students in school achievement, that only 1 percent had Indian teachers, that one-fourth of teachers of Indian students preferred not to teach them, and that "Indian children more than any other minority group believed themselves to be 'below average' in intelligence."

During this time, Indian educators had become increasingly active, and, by the end of the decade, the

National Indian Education Association had been formed. In 1968 the first tribally controlled college, Navajo Community College, was founded, and in 1971 the Coalition of Indian Controlled School Boards was established.

The Move Toward Self-Determination Since 1970

The Senate report on the plight of Indians led to the passage of the Indian Education Act in 1972. This act provided for special programs benefiting Indian children in reservation schools as well as those attending urban public schools. It was amended in 1975 to require that Indian parents be involved in the planning of these programs. The amended version also encouraged the establishment of community-run schools and stressed culturally relevant and bilingual curricular materials. The Office of Education, after a two-year study, recommended that tribal history, culture, and languages be emphasized, using the students' native tongues as the language of instruction. During 1977, President Jimmy Carter created the new post of assistant secretary of the interior for Indian affairs and named a member of the Blackfoot tribe, Forrest J. Gerrard, to the position.

In spite of efforts to improve educational opportunities for Indians, in the last decade of the twentieth century Indian students still struggled for visibility in the education market. High school dropout rates for Indian students continued to be the highest for all minority groups, with only about half completing a high school education. Some reservation schools reported a yearly teacher turnover rate of 90 percent. In 1990, bachelor's degrees earned by Indians made up less than 0.5 percent of all degrees conferred. Numbers of doctorates earned by Indians between 1980 and 1990 actually dropped, from 130 to 102.

In the 1990's, several public school districts with relatively large Indian populations began to experiment with schools that focus on Indian culture along with traditional academic curricula. One of these, the American Indian Magnet School at Mounds Park All-Nations School in the St. Paul, Minnesota, public school system, declared the goal of "placing education into culture instead of continuing the practice of placing culture into education." Three centuries of national educational policy must take at least partial responsibility for the tragic decline of tribal cultures in the United States, but perhaps it will also take the lead in providing a vehicle for the land's original citizens to assume their rightful place in American society.

Dorothy Engan-Barker, assisted by Bette Blaisdell

Core Resources

Edgar S. Cahn and David W. Hearne's *Our Brother's Keeper: The Indian in White America* (New York: New American Library, 1975) chronicles the plight of American Indians and actions of the Bureau of Indian Affairs. Harold Fey and D'Arcy McNickle's *Indians and Other Americans: Two Ways of Life Meet* (rev. ed., New York: Harper & Row, 1970) includes first-person accounts by Indians regarding attempts by whites to "civilize" them. Theodore Fischbacher's *A Study of the Role of the Federal Government in the Education of the American Indian* (San Francisco: R & E Research Associates, 1974) discusses the role of the federal government in Indian education. Estelle Fuchs and Robert Havighurst's "Boarding Schools," in *To Live on This Earth* (Garden City, N.Y.: Doubleday, 1972), summarizes events leading up to and including the establishment of Indian boarding schools. Richard H. Pratt's *Battlefield and Classroom: Four Decades with the American Indian, 1867-1904*, edited by Robert M. Utley (New Haven, Conn.: Yale University Press, 1964), contains memoirs of General Richard Henry Pratt, chronicling his work in the establishment of Indian boarding schools. Also useful is *Indian Education: A National Tragedy, a National Challenge* (Washington, D.C.: Government Printing Office, 1969), by the U.S. Senate Committee on Labor and Public Welfare's Special Subcommittee on Indian Education.

See also: American Indian studies; Carlisle Indian School.

Education and Asian Americans

> **Significance:** Asian Americans have gained a reputation for high educational achievement. To some extent, this reputation reflects actual performance, and this performance has been part of the debate about why ethnic and racial groups vary in education.

The educational achievements of Asian Americans have attracted a great deal of scholarly and popular attention. Popular interest in Asian American educational performance often involves comparing this group with members of other minority groups, heightening the perception of Asian Americans as members of a "model" minority, a stereotype that often makes Asian Americans uncomfortable. Scholars interested in immigrants, minority groups, and influences on education have studied the educational performance of various Asian American groups in order to obtain insight into how immigrant membership and minority group membership may be related to achievement in school.

Levels of Achievement

Although it is difficult to discuss the educational performance of such a diverse group, Asian Americans do seem to show overall levels of achievement that are quite high. Moreover, they begin to distinguish themselves educationally at fairly early ages. In an analysis of 1980 U.S. census data presented in their book *Asians and Pacific Islanders in the United States* (1993), Herbert Barringer, Robert W. Gardner, and Michael J. Levin noted that Asian Americans showed high rates of preschool attendance. This was particularly true for Japanese, Chinese, Koreans, and Asian Indians. The 1990 U.S. census showed this pattern continuing. About 24 percent of all Asian American children under six years of age were enrolled in school, compared with 21 percent of white children. Among Chinese, Taiwanese, Japanese, and Thai American children, rates of early school attendance were particularly high, with 27 percent of Chinese, 31 percent of Taiwanese, 31 percent of Japanese, and 30 percent of Thai children under six years of age enrolled in school.

School enrollment, of course, is not the same thing as school performance. However, data from the 1988 National Educational Longitudinal Study show that as early as the eighth grade, Asian American children display higher levels of educational aspiration than other American children. According to these data, 43 percent of Asian American children reported that they aspired to education beyond a bachelor's degree, while only 25 percent of white eighth-graders wanted to pursue postgraduate education.

Asian American children are more likely than other American students to reach high school and stay in high school. Less than 6 percent of Asian Americans age sixteen to nineteen were high school dropouts in 1990, compared with nearly 7 percent of white Americans and 16 percent of African Americans. There were substantial variations among Asian groups; however, only the three most economically underprivileged Southeast Asian refugee groups (Cambodian, Hmong, and Laotian Americans) showed dropout rates that were higher than those of white Americans, and all of the Asian American groups had dropout rates that were lower than those of African Americans.

College entrance examinations are among the most commonly used indicators of high school performance. Although breakdowns by particular Asian groups are not available, the scores of Asian Americans in general were as high as the scores of any other racial group or higher. On the American College Test (ACT), for example, the average Asian American score was 21.7, equal to the average score for whites and higher than the average score for African Americans (17.1). The average Scholastic Aptitude Test (SAT) score for Asian Americans, 1056, was higher than that for members of any other racial or ethnic group, including white Americans (1052). Asian Americans tended to score much higher than white Americans on the math part of the test (560 for Asians, compared with 536 for whites) and substantially lower on the verbal part of the test (496 for Asians, compared with 526 for whites). This suggests that Asian

Early School Attendance, Dropout Rates, and College Attendance Rates Among Whites, African Americans, and Major Asian American Groups

Racial/Ethnic Group	Percentage under 6 years of age in school	Percentage age 16-25 not in school, not graduates	Percentage age 18-25 enrolled in college
White	21.4	8.6	28.9
Black	24.2	15.9	22.7
Chinese	27.0	4.8	51.3
Taiwanese	30.8	0.9	60.1
Filipino	21.1	5.5	44.4
Japanese	31.2	3.2	47.2
Asian Indian	24.3	5.0	51.0
Korean	25.4	4.3	43.8
Vietnamese	18.1	7.4	42.5
Cambodian	17.5	11.9	29.9
Hmong	16.8	10.9	27.4
Laotian	16.9	12.5	26.3
Thai	30.0	6.8	37.1
All Asian	23.8	5.5	45.7

Source: 1990 Census of Population and Housing, 5 percent Public Use Microdata Sample

American scores would have been even higher had many of them not been hampered by relatively weaker English proficiency.

Asian Americans were more likely than either white Americans or African Americans to be enrolled in college in 1990. Although 29 percent of whites and 23 percent of African Americans age eighteen to twenty-five were attending college in that year, 46 percent of Asian Americans in this age category were enrolled in higher education. Once again, there were substantial variations among Asian American groups, but only the Hmong and the Laotian Americans, two of the most recent and most economically underprivileged Asian American groups, showed lower rates of college enrollment than the majority white population.

Theories of Asian American Educational Achievement
According to researchers Stanley Sue and Sumie Okazaki, in their 1990 article "Asian American Educational Achievement," published in the *American Psychologist*, theorists have usually attributed Asian American school achievement either to innate, genetic characteristics of Asians or to cultural characteristics. Genetic explanations address the problem by citing the performance of Asians on intelligence quotient (IQ) tests and other measures of ability as evidence of higher levels of innate intellectual ability among Asians. Psychologist Richard

Lynn has argued that Asian scores on aptitude tests and IQ tests provide evidence for a genetic explanation of Asian academic achievement.

Cultural explanations of Asian American scholastic success have received wider acceptance than genetic explanations. From this point of view, Asian American families pass on cultural values that stress hard work and educational excellence. Looking at Vietnamese American children, Nathan Caplan, Marcella H. Choy, and John K. Whitmore maintained that Vietnamese families passed on cultural values to their children that enabled the children to do well in school. One difficulty with applying this explanation to Asian Americans in general is that the different Asian groups come from a variety of cultural backgrounds.

To address the difficulties raised by both the genetic and cultural explanations, Sue and Okazaki put forward the theory of "relative functionalism" in their 1990 article. According to this theory, Asian success is to be explained by blocked mobility: As a result of barriers to upward mobility by other means, such as social networks, Asians tend to focus on education. Although blocked mobility may influence the life choices of Asians, it would not account for trends in other groups that also experience blocked mobility but do not show the levels of academic performance characteristic of Asians.

Sociologists Min Zhou and Carl L. Bankston III have argued that Asian American educational success may, to some extent, be a consequence of the types of social relations found in Asian American communities. They have claimed that tightly knit ethnic communities, such as Chinatowns or Southern California's Little Saigon, can promote the upward mobility of young people by subjecting them to the expectations of all community members and by providing them with encouragement and support from all community members. This explanation, though, does not tell us why Asian Americans who do not live in ethnic communities may sometimes be high achievers in school.

The precise causes of Asian American educational achievement, then, remain a matter of debate. In all likelihood, some combination of existing theories may account for the scholastic performance of this group, with some theories applying more to some specific groups than to others.

Carl L. Bankston III

This young Asian American man receives his high school diploma. Many theories have been put forth in an attempt to explain the high level of educational achievement attained by Asian Americans as a group.

Core Resources

James R. Flynn's *Asian Americans: Achievement Beyond IQ* (Mahwah, N.J.: Lawrence Erlbaum Associates, 1991) provides an overview of the phenomenon of Asian American academic achievement and provides a useful introduction for those interested in this subject. *My Trouble Is English: Asian Students and the American Dream* (Portsmouth, N.H.: Boynton/Cook, 1995) offers insight into the importance of education as a means of upward mobility for Asian American students and into the challenges faced by many of these students. Stacey J. Lee's *Unraveling the "Model Minority" Stereotype: Listening to Asian American Youth* (New York: Teachers College Press, 1996) investigates the motivations and problems of contemporary Asian American students. The educational achievements of children of refugees from Southeast Asia are described in *Children of the Boat People* (Ann Arbor, Mich: University of Michigan Press, 1991). In *Growing Up American: How Vietnamese Children Adapt to Life in the United States* (New York: Russell Sage, 1998), Min Zhou and Carl L. Bankston III examine the experiences of Vietnamese children in American schools and compare Vietnamese American students with students of other Asian and non-Asian ethnicities.

See also: Asian American stereotypes; Education and African Americans; Family and socialization: Asian Americans; Intelligence testing; "Model" minorities.

Education and racial/ethnic relations

Significance: Educational reform has been a focal point for improvement of racial and ethnic relations since 1954. This movement began with attempts to integrate the public schools and has since extended to the expansion of the school curriculum.

The purpose of educational reform is to improve the educational status quo. In the area of race relations, it has involved the push to integrate public schools. Some education experts suggest that integrated educational facilities are far more advantageous than segregated ones. In 1954, segregated educational facilities—historically associated with discrimination and racism in the United States, as made official with the U.S. Supreme Court's decision in *Plessy v. Ferguson* (1896) that "separate but equal" facilities were permissible—were challenged by the Supreme Court's decision in *Brown v. Board of Education* (1954). In the latter case, the Supreme Court determined that segregated educational facilities for African Americans were "inherently" unequal, placing black students at an educational disadvantage that they were unlikely ever to overcome. Although racial and ethnic relations were a major focus of educational reform even before the *Brown* litigation, the real push for school integration began only after *Brown*.

School Integration

The 1950's witnessed massive social changes; chief among these was a renewed consciousness among people of color in general, and African Americans in particular, of their second-class place in society. Nowhere was this discrimination more evident than in racially segregated facilities, from public restrooms and restaurants to public schools. That segregation only echoed the deeper social and economic divisions between the races. In the wake of the *Brown* decision, however, the latter part of the decade began to witness a push for integrated schools.

Segregationists, particularly in the South, fought school integration at every step with a campaign of intimidation and delays called "massive resistance." At the same time, Cold War fears of Soviet technological superiority—which came to a head with the 1957 launching of the first artificial satellite to orbit Earth, the Soviets' *Sputnik*—spurred a drive toward the production of new math and science curricula in the schools. The goal was to produce more mathematicians, scientists, and engineers to combat the perceived Soviet threat. Conservative pressures to maintain the status quo therefore joined with postwar fears of a Communist takeover to mitigate against social equality in the classroom. At the same time, in the wake of *Brown*'s official denunciation of segregation, African Americans began taking bold steps to secure their civil rights: In December, 1955, Rosa Parks refused to sit at the back of a Montgomery, Alabama, bus and spawned the Montgomery bus boycott; in September, 1957, a plan to integrate a high school in Little Rock, Arkansas, was met by white resistance that extended to the level of Governor Orval E. Faubus, who resisted the entry of nine African American students with the National Guard. Racial strife would increase over the next years as the Civil Rights movement bloomed and liberal politicians stepped up their efforts to desegregate public schools.

Reform in the 1970's proved to be both prescriptive and reactionary. It was prescriptive in its call for more "effective schools" and reactionary as a strategy for helping to quell student activism during the period. Busing also emerged during this period as a controversial measure to integrate schools. Busing actually predates the effort to desegregate the public schools. For many years in the South, busing was used to facilitate segregation by

School children board a bus in Cleveland, Ohio, on the first day of court-ordered busing in September, 1979. Busing is a very controversial means of achieving integration.

transporting black youth to segregated black schools and transporting white students to segregated white schools. It became controversial when the federal courts decided that buses could be used for the opposite end—to bring black youth into white communities. Part of the controversy concerned objections that busing required extended periods of time traveling to and from school; however, given that such objections were rarely voiced when busing was used for purposes of segregation, many civil rights activists saw these objections as a smokescreen masking resistance to integration. Busing was the most feasible strategy for transporting large numbers of students and would remain the primary method for implementing mandatory pupil reassignment for purposes of desegregation.

A Nation at Risk?

The 1980's and 1990's witnessed a renewed call for the production of more mathematicians, scientists, and engineers. Much of this reform was initiated by the 1983 report *A Nation at Risk*. The report focused on what was seen as the failure of the public schools, the failure of public schoolteachers in their professional preparation and in their classroom instruction, and a prescription for strengthening the public school curriculum. In many school districts, many of the reform measures proffered by *A Nation at Risk* have been implemented. The number of academic core courses has been increased in high schools, teacher preparation programs at most of the major institutions of higher education have undergone restructuring, assessment tests at grades four, eight, and twelve have been implemented, and most public high schools have introduced requirements for computer literacy.

However, desegregation has not fared as well. Many school districts still remain segregated. Strategies such as schools of choice, magnet schools, and mandatory busing have all had varying degrees of success in the desegregation effort. Some school districts have been released from their obligation to enforce desegregation, a few because they had achieved a degree of "racial balance," particularly via magnet schools. The release for some, however, was not a function of successful desegregation but rather an artifact of white flight to the suburbs and to private schools.

White Flight

School desegregation has therefore never been fully achieved. As the mandate to desegregate was issued by the federal courts, the incidence of white flight increased. Initially a movement of middle-class whites to escape the decay and dangers of life in the city, white flight turned into a flight to avoid desegregation. As a result, many inner-city white schools initially forced to desegregate became predominantly black and Latino over time. In some large urban districts, desegregation became a feeble attempt to reshuffle the remaining white students into predominantly black and Latino schools. In the late 1990's, more than one-third of the states had African American and Latino students attending schools with minority populations exceeding 65 percent. In Illinois, New York, and Michigan, more than 80 percent of the African American student population attended segregated schools; in New York, Illinois, Texas, and New Jersey, more than 80 percent of the Latino student population attended segregated schools. A number of school districts once considered desegregated have become resegregated. Additionally, some have developed "second-generation segregation," which involves the sorting of students into academic tracks based on ability grouping. Disproportionately, African American and Latino students are placed into the lower academic tracks (especially in special education programs) while whites and Asian Americans are placed in the higher tracks. This phenomenon occurs even in schools said to be racially balanced.

Curriculum Reform and Multicultural Education

Beginning in the late 1960's and early 1970's, educational reform began to address racial and cultural differences not only through school integration but also through the curriculum. Much of this reformation emerged in the form of three new curriculum approaches: multicultural education, bicultural education, and centric education. Innovative and revolutionary, these new approaches have generated substantial controversies. Much of the debate stems from the fact that each approach makes race or ethnicity a focal point of the curriculum.

Multicultural education has been by far the most sweeping educational reform designed to deal with the issues of racism and discrimination. In the broadest sense, multicultural education is an extension of the Civil Rights movement, for the elimination of discrimination is not merely an issue of school attendance—of a black or Latino or Asian youth's right to sit next to white youth—but, more important, a struggle for equity in the pursuit of equality of opportunity.

Joel Spring argues that multicultural education programs have four primary goals: to build tolerance of other cultures, to eliminate racism, to include curricular content on other cultures, and to enable students to perceive the world from more than one cultural perspective. In their book *Multicultural Education: Issues and Perspectives* (1998), James A. Banks and Cherry A. McGee Banks suggest that multicultural education is not merely an idea but also an educational reform movement and a process. Its primary goal is to change the structure of educational institutions so that racial and cultural makeup, gender, and exceptionalities do not influence the opportunity to achieve academically.

In practice, multicultural education has taken a variety of forms, from the early grades to higher education, manifesting itself not only in choices to teach the culture and history of nondominant peoples such as African Americans, American indigenous populations, and Latino peoples but also to consider different interpretations of the causes of historical events and different evaluations of their outcomes. Even in science—and particularly with advances in the discipline of genetics—advances have radically altered nineteenth and early twentieth century explanations of racial and ethnic differences: Where once these were seen as a product of heredity, it is now known, for example, that variations in DNA (the genetic material that determines human traits, from eye and skin color to intelligence) are virtually identical across all groups of human beings and thus have no impact on their social, economic, and other potentials.

Bicultural Education

"Biculturalism" literally means operating in two different cultures simultaneously. The premise of bicultural education is to implement educational strategies that help members of subcultures—such as African Americans, Asian Americans, Native Americans, and Latinos—to function in the dominant (Eurocentric) culture without having to forsake their own cultures. All too often, individuals from subcultures have been expected to give up their native cultures if they were to experience a measure of success in the dominant culture. Many successful members of subcultures have articulated resultant feelings of alienation—both from the dominant culture and from their own native culture. A bicultural curriculum is structured in ways to help subcultures deal with the effects of racism and discrimination. Learning styles associated with particular subcultures are integrated into the curriculum. In addition, the teachers and other personnel are recruited from educators possessing a certain attitudinal posture that helps rather than hinders learning among subcultures. Some researchers suggest that the bicultural education environment should be warm, should employ a greater latitude of interpretation with respect to written material, and should use the child's own language for initial instruction to achieve the most positive results—for example, Spanish for Latino students, native tongues for American Indians, and even Ebonics for African Americans when such an approach proves to facilitate learning.

Centric Education

Centric education is often also referred to as ethnocentric education. Supporters of centric education take a more radical position relative to Eurocentric education than either multicultural or bicultural educators. In predominantly Latino schools that focus on Latino culture, centric teachers often use Spanish during informal interaction with students. This has proven to ease the acculturation process. Latino-centered education has gained a tentative foothold in the southwestern United States, although by far the most controversial centric approach has been Afrocentric education.

Afrocentrists (advocates of Afrocentricity) argue that an Afrocentric education has major implications for both the lifestyle that many African Americans have chosen to pursue and the type of education that they desire for their children. Although Afrocentric education is considerably more radical than multicultural education, some educational scholars actually view it as a single-group study under the broad rubric of multicultural education. Single-group studies are said to provide students from subcultures with a sense of their history and identity and, more important, with a sense of direction and purpose in their lives. An Afrocentric curriculum includes units or courses about the history and culture of African Americans, focusing particularly on how African Americans (and other subcultures) have been victimized and on their social, political, and cultural struggles for liberation. Pedagogy is also predicated on the ways that African American youth learn best.

Impact on School Curriculum

Multicultural, bicultural, and centric education do not merely advocate for the addition or deletion of certain types of material but also challenge the very existence of the curriculum that has historically been used in the public school—and therein lies much of the controversy over these various modes of educational reform. Longstanding distortions about European American traditions, heroic figures, and culture are often exposed and open to criticism under the multicultural, bicultural, and centric traditions. Hence, these approaches, while valuing the cultures and contributions of people of color, have been perceived by some whites as concomitantly devaluing European contributions. Such a perception is generally false; most efforts at educational reform have as their goal the amelioration, not the aggravation, of intergroup relations. *Charles C. Jackson*

Core Resources

James A. Banks and Cherry A. McGee Banks's *Multicultural Education: Issues and Perspectives* (Boston: Allyn & Bacon, 1998) provides an excellent description of the nature of multicultural education and the types of curricula that can be found under the multicultural rubric. Molefi Kete Asante introduced the term "Afrocentric" in his classic *Afrocentricity* (Trenton, N.J.: Africa World Press, 1988) and laid the foundation for the discussion of the centric perspective in education. Joel Spring's *American Education: An Introduction to Social and Political Aspects* (4th ed., New York: Longman, 1989) and *Deculturalization and the Struggle for Equality* (Boston: McGraw-Hill, 1998) provide an intriguing discussion of the educational struggles of dominated subcultures in American society, focusing on the historical struggles of African Americans, Asian Americans, Mexican Americans, Native Americans, and Puerto Ricans.

See also: Afrocentrism; *Alexander v. Holmes County Board of Education*; Bilingual education; Bilingual Education Act; *Brown v. Board of Education*; Busing and integration; Campus ethnoviolence; Carlisle Indian School; College admissions; College entrance examinations; Cooperative learning; Desegregation: public schools; Diversity training programs; Education and African Americans; Education and American Indians; Education and Asian Americans; Equal educational opportunity; Ethnic studies programs; Indian Education Acts; Multiculturalism; *Plessy v. Ferguson*; *Swann v. Charlotte-Mecklenburg Board of Education*.

Egalitarian symbiosis

When people of different races, religions, and ethnic origins peacefully coexist, sharing equally in the social, political, and economic rights of their society and contributing to the mutual benefit of all, the relationship is referred to as egalitarian symbiosis. Although the United States is perceived by many people as a successful experiment in racial and ethnic mixing, resistance to the efforts of people of different races, religions, and ethnic backgrounds to participate fully in the society has sometimes been pronounced and long-lasting, requiring the passage of minority and civil rights laws in order to avoid racial and ethnic conflict. Since the civil rights battles of the 1960's, many Americans have advocated a policy of multiculturalism, in which people of diverse ethnic origins live together in unity and still maintain their own cultures. Although problems involving prejudice and discrimination continue to be prevalent in the United States, people from a diverse mixture of racial and ethnic backgrounds generally live together in harmony, working toward a state of egalitarian symbiosis. *Alvin K. Benson*

See also: Contact and adaptation patterns; Equality.

Elk v. Wilkins

In 1884, John Elk, an American Indian, was refused permission to register to vote in a local election in Omaha, Nebraska. When he later appeared at the polls, he was again refused the right to vote. Elk lived apart from his tribe and met all residence and other requirements of the city of Omaha and the state of Nebraska but was turned away on the basis that he was an Indian and, therefore, not a United States citizen. Elk filed a lawsuit charging the state of Nebraska with violation of his Fourteenth Amendment rights by denying his right to vote.

As an Indian born in the United States, Elk argued he was a United States citizen as well as a state citizen. Nebraska courts ruled Elk ineligible to vote, and on November 3, 1884, the U.S. Supreme Court found Nebraska correct in denying Elk's right to vote. The majority of the Court determined that an Indian who was born a member of a tribe was not a United States citizen but a member of a distinct nation that was separate and apart from the United States. Therefore, the Court determined, a specific act of Congress would be required to make Indian people citizens of the United States. *Carole A. Barrett*

See also: Indian Citizenship Act; Voting rights of American Indians.

Emancipation Proclamation

> **Significance:** The Emancipation Proclamation of January 1, 1863, extended the legal state of freedom to most American slaves.

Although the American Civil War (1861-1865) was the result of sectional conflict regarding the issue of slavery, both the Union and the Confederate governments initially denied that slavery was a war issue. The Confederate government claimed that it was fighting only to defend the principle of states' rights. The Union government claimed that it was fighting to preserve the Union of states against Confederate efforts to destroy it.

Lincoln's Cautious Approach to Emancipation

From the very beginning of the war, abolitionists, Radical Republicans, and black activists urged President Abraham Lincoln to use the war as an opportunity to strike down slavery. Lincoln, though, acted in a cautious manner in the early months of the war. Until September, 1862, Lincoln refused to include the abolition of slavery as one of the Union's war aims. Furthermore, when radical commanders in the Union Army ordered the emancipation of slaves in parts of the occupied South in 1861-1862, Lincoln countermanded the orders.

These actions caused reformers to question the depth of Lincoln's own commitment to antislavery. In Lincoln's defense, it must be noted that Lincoln both publicly and privately often expressed a heartfelt abhorrence of slavery. Yet Lincoln knew that a premature effort to turn the war into a crusade for emancipation would be counterproductive to the cause of freedom. An early act of emancipation would prompt loyal slave states such as Kentucky, Maryland, and Missouri to join the Confederacy and probably cause the defeat of the Union. From a practical point of view, the Union government could not abolish slavery in the South if it lost the war.

The Origins of Lincoln's Emancipation Policy

Lincoln was finally encouraged to seek emancipation because of the actions of the slaves themselves. During the war, some 600,000 slaves—about 15 percent of the total—escaped from their masters. Slaves understood that the advance of the Union army through the South presented them with an unprecedented opportunity for escape. Most escaped slaves sought shelter with the Union army.

The presence of large numbers of slaves within Union army lines presented Union commanders with the question of whether the slaves should be returned to their rebellious masters or allowed to stay with the army and use up its scarce resources. Most Union commanders allowed the slaves to remain with the army, justifying this decision out of military necessity. Pointing to the right of armies under international law to seize or destroy enemy property being used to sustain the war effort, Union commanders claimed the right to seize the Confederacy's slave laborers as contraband of war.

The actions of Union commanders shifted the focus of emancipation from human rights to military necessity, thereby encouraging Lincoln to adopt a general policy of emancipation and giving Lincoln an argument with which to win public support for this policy.

The Proclamation and Its Limits

Lincoln's Emancipation Proclamation, which was issued January 1, 1863, declared that slaves in areas in rebellion against the United States were free. Slaves in the loyal slave states and slaves in areas of the Confederacy already under Union control were not freed by the proclamation. Because of this fact, some commentators have criticized the proclamation, claiming that the proclamation had little impact because it sought to free the Confederate slaves who were beyond Lincoln's control and neglected to free the slaves within his control. This criticism ignores several facts regarding Lincoln's action. The Emancipation Proclamation amounted to an announcement that henceforward, the Union army would become an army of liberation. Whenever the Union army captured an area of the Confederacy, it would automatically free the slaves in that region.

Additionally, the limited scope of Lincoln's proclamation was prompted by the limited powers of the president under the Constitution. Lincoln pointed out that, as president, his only constitutional power to emancipate slaves was derived from his power as commander in chief to order the military destruction of property that supported the enemy's war effort. Slaves belonging to masters in states loyal to the Union and slaves belonging to masters in areas of the Confederacy previously captured were not currently being used to support the enemy's war effort. In making this argument, Lincoln was not being evasive or cautious in seeking the emancipation of all American slaves. One month before he issued the Emancipation Proclamation, Lincoln proposed to Congress the passage of a constitutional amendment that would have freed all slaves living in the loyal border states and in currently occupied portions of the Confederacy.

The Effects of the Proclamation

In the end, perhaps two-thirds of American slaves were freed by the Emancipation Proclamation. The remain-

The Emancipation Proclamation
January 1, 1863
By the President of the United States of America

A Proclamation Whereas, on the twenty-second day of September, in the year of our Lord one thousand eight hundred and sixty-two, a proclamation was issued by the President of the United States, containing, among other things, the following, to wit:

That on the first day of January, in the year of our Lord one thousand eight hundred and sixty-three, all persons held as slaves within any State or designated part of a State, the people whereof shall then be in rebellion against the United States, shall be then, thenceforward, and forever free; and the Executive Government of the United States, including the military and naval authority thereof, will recognize and maintain the freedom of such persons, and will do no act or acts to repress such persons, or any of them, in any efforts they may make for their actual freedom.

That the Executive will, on the first day of January aforesaid, by proclamation, designate the States and parts of States, if any, in which the people thereof, respectively, shall then be in rebellion against the United States; and the fact that any State or the people thereof, shall on that day be, in good faith, represented in the Congress of the United States by members chosen thereto at elections wherein a majority of the qualified voters of such States shall have participated, shall, in the absence of strong countervailing testimony, be deemed conclusive evidence that such State, and the people thereof, are not then in rebellion against the United States.

Now, therefore, I, Abraham Lincoln, President of the United States, by virtue of the power in me vested as Commander-in-Chief, of the Army and Navy of the United States in time of actual armed rebellion against the authority and government of the United States, and as a fit and necessary war measure for suppressing said rebellion, do, on this first day of January, in the year of our Lord one thousand eight hundred and sixty-three, and in accordance with my purpose so to do, publicly proclaimed for the full period of one hundred days, from the day first above mentioned, order and designate as the States and parts of States wherein the people thereof, respectively, are this day in rebellion against the United States, the following, to wit:

Arkansas, Texas, Louisiana (except the parishes of St. Bernard, Plaquemines, Jefferson, St. John, St. Charles, St. James, Ascension, Assumption, Terrebonne, Lafourche, St. Mary, St. Martin, and Orleans, including the City of New Orleans), Mississippi, Alabama, Florida, Georgia, South Carolina, North Carolina, and Virginia (except the forty-eight counties designated as West Virginia, and also the counties of Berkeley, Accomac, Northampton, Elizabeth City, York, Princess Ann, and Norfolk, including the cities of Norfolk and Portsmouth); and which excepted parts are, for the present, left precisely as if this proclamation were not issued.

And by virtue of the power, and for the purpose aforesaid, I do order and declare that all persons held as slaves within said designated States, and parts of States, are, and henceforward shall be, free; and that the Executive government of the United States, including the military and naval authorities thereof, will recognize and maintain the freedom of said persons.

And I hereby enjoin upon the people so declared to be free to abstain from all violence, unless in necessary self-defense; and I recommend to them that, in all cases when allowed, they labor faithfully for reasonable wages.

And I further declare and make known, that such persons of suitable condition, will be received into the armed service of the United States to garrison forts, positions, stations, and other places, and to man vessels of all sorts in said service. And upon this act, sincerely believed to be an act of justice, warranted by the Constitution, upon military necessity, I invoke the considerate judgment of mankind, and the gracious favor of Almighty God.

In witness thereof, I have hereunto set my hand and caused the seal of the United States to be affixed.

Done at the City of Washington, this first day of January, in the year of our Lord one thousand eight hundred and sixty-three, and of the Independence of the United States of America the eighty-seventh.

ABRAHAM LINCOLN, By the President

WILLIAM H. SEWARD, Secretary of State

der of American slaves were freed by the laws of state governments in loyal slave states and by the Thirteenth Amendment (1865), which abolished slavery in the United States.   *Harold D. Tallant*

Core Resources

Slaves No More: Three Essays on Emancipation and the Civil War (Cambridge, England: Cambridge University Press, 1992), by Ira Berlin et al., LaWanda Cox's *Lincoln and Black Freedom: A Study in Presidential Leadership* (Columbia: University of South Carolina Press, 1981), Eric Foner's *Nothing But Freedom: Emancipation and Its Legacy* (Baton Rouge: Louisiana State University Press, 1983), John Hope Franklin's *The Emancipation Proclamation* (Garden City, N.Y.: Doubleday, 1963), and James M. McPherson's *Ordeal by Fire: The Civil War and Reconstruction* (2d ed., New York: McGraw-Hill, 1992) discuss the proclamation and its effects from a variety of viewpoints.

See also: Abolition; African Americans in the Civil War; Civil Rights Act of 1866; Civil War; Reconstruction; Slavery.

Employment among African Americans

> **Significance:** African Americans have historically been discriminated against in both hiring and promotion. Race relations will improve as African Americans become more prominent in positions of high responsibility.

African Americans continue to be confronted with the historical factors that produce racial discrimination in employment. Three salient factors contributing to racial discrimination in employment are trends in historical antecedents, educational level attainment, and employment and unemployment rates. Much excellent scholarly research provides data on these factors. In James Blackwell's *The Black Community: Diversity and Unity* (1975) and Talmadge Anderson's *Introduction to African American Studies* (1994), the authors provide historical and empirical data that more fully explain these areas.

Historical Antecedents

The first African American laborers were indentured servants who were brought to Jamestown, Virginia, in 1619. From the beginning, African Americans were not afforded a level playing field in employment. The seminal work by John Blassingame, *The Slave Community* (1972), offers a very good account of this period. Because the contemporary notion of rates of employment and unemployment is not relevant for slave labor, it is not possible to compare the work of African Americans and that of whites during the period of institutional slavery in America, which lasted from the mid-seventeenth century through 1865, more than two centuries.

Following slavery, most African Americans were involved in farm labor at very low wages. The majority lived in the South and often worked as sharecroppers or day laborers. In the first quarter of the twentieth century, in an effort to escape the rigid de jure (legal) segregation that restricted their opportunities for employment in the South, African Americans began moving to the North in search of better jobs in record numbers. Finding themselves in the midst of the rapidly growing Industrial Revolution, African Americans began to acquire jobs that paid wages that far exceeded those they could receive as farm hands in the South.

After World War II, more African Americans acquired skilled and professional jobs. Although in the 1990's, the wages earned by African Americans are still below those of white workers, they have slowly but steadily increased relative to those of whites. According to the U.S. census, the African American median family income was 72 percent of that of whites in 1969. By 1993, that percentage had increased only to 81 percent. For female-headed households, the median family income has remained unchanged, at about 81 percent that of whites. It is this trend that best reflects an important relationship between the races in the area of employment.

Educational Attainment Levels

The most pervasive trend in African American and white employment is that the former has always lagged behind the latter. In both percentage of employed and earnings, African Americans compare poorly with whites. Analysis of employment data from the 1960's into the 1990's shows that African American unemployment rates were double those of whites. As reported by Claudette E. Bennett in *The Black Population in the United States*, the unemployment rate for African American men in 1994 was 14 percent; the rate for white men was 6.7 percent. In that same year, African American women were unemployed at 12.1 percent while white women had an unemployment rate of 5.5 percent. Two factors substantially contribute to this disparity: educational differences and discrimination in hiring and promotions.

Educational attainment is perhaps the highest social goal among Americans. It is generally believed that success in life, especially employment, is directly correlated to the level of education a person obtains. Since 1940, the disparity between African Americans and whites in educational attainment for grades K-12 has

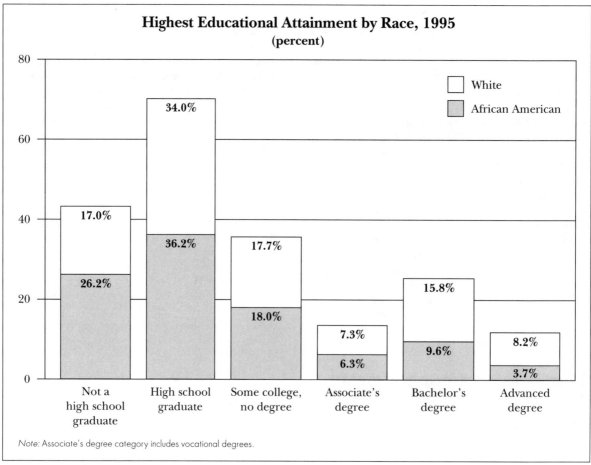

Highest Educational Attainment by Race, 1995
(percent)

Note: Associate's degree category includes vocational degrees.

Source: U.S. Bureau of the Census, *Statistical Abstract of the United States, 1996* (116th ed.). Washington, D.C.: U.S. Government Printing Office, 1997.

narrowed greatly. By 1990, the median years of education among the two groups was about equal. Although the percentage of whites having some high school (30 percent) far exceeded that of African Americans (19 percent), the percentage having completed high school for both groups in 1990 was 36 percent.

However, the percentage of whites with advanced degrees is nearly three times that of African Americans. The educational inequality at the post-high-school level places African Americans at a disadvantage when attempting to qualify for professional jobs. The World Future Society predicts that the average job in the United States in the year 2000 will require about fourteen years of education, and African Americans are predicted to remain behind. Some of the needed improvements in the educational system that will better prepare African Americans are offered by Charles V. Willie and Inabeth Miller in their book *Social Goals and Educational Reform* (1988). Additional proposals are made in the book edited by Gerald David Jaynes and

Robin M. Williams, Jr., *A Common Destiny: Blacks and American Society* (1989). Some of the proposed remedies include improving physical facilities in urban and rural schools, providing equivalent educational resources for all students, improving teacher quality and teacher training, enhancing school-community relations, and hiring and promoting substantially more African American faculty and administrators.

Unemployment Rates
Two factors stand out in any description of the African American experience in hiring and promotion in the United States. The unusually high rates of unemployment (official and hidden) and a modest presence in senior management positions point to major disparities between blacks and whites. Hidden unemployment refers to those persons discouraged in seeking employment and those who are involuntary part-time workers. The National Urban League estimates that the hidden unemployment rate for African Americans may be nearly

double that of the official reported rate.

Independent of gender, the unemployment rate for African Americans has continued to be more than double that of whites. This reality has held despite affirmative action, set-asides, and minority hiring policy programs. Similarly, the median per capita income for African American households and families has remained greatly below that of whites. Wealth owned by African Americans is less than 1 percent of that owned by whites. In the area of median worth of household, the U.S. Bureau of the Census reported in 1988 that African American worth was only 23 percent that of whites for families consisting of married couples. For female-headed families, African American families' worth was only 3 percent that of whites. Three times as many African American female-headed households live in poverty as those headed by white women.

Even within the corporate structure, African Americans have faired poorly. The federal Glass Ceiling Commission reported in 1995 that African Americans experienced disproportionately high resistance to advancement to high-level decision-making positions when compared with whites with similar education and training. Many of the experiences faced by African Americans in the corporate business environment are presented by George Davis and Glegg Watson in *Black Life in Corporate America: Swimming in the Mainstream* (1985). In a capitalist system in which employment and maximum fulfillment of human potential are vital to the accumulation of wealth, unfair employment practices have denied African Americans full opportunity to develop and maintain favorable conditions of wealth when compared with whites. With increasing national public policy that severely dampens affirmative efforts to level the playing field in hiring and promotion, the need for better education and employment seems less likely to be met.

Joe R. Feagin and Melvin P. Sikes argue in their book *Living with Racism: The Black Middle-Class Experience* (1994) that African Americans have been adversely affected by the racist hiring and promotion practices in the area of employment. However, most critical has been a failure of the nation to capitalize on an opportunity for a productive investment in African American human capital.

William M. Harris, Sr.

Core Resources

James Blackwell's *The Black Community: Diversity and Unity* (New York: Harper & Row, 1975), Talmadge Anderson's *Introduction to African American Studies* (Dubuque, Iowa: Kendall/Hunt, 1994), and John Blassingame's *The Slave Community* (New York: Oxford University Press, 1972) examine slavery and various historical factors that contribute to workplace discrimination against African

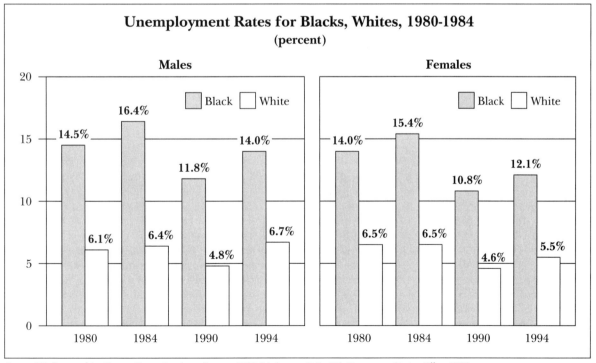

Source: U.S. Bureau of the Census, *Current Population Reports, 1993.* Washington, D.C.: U.S. Government Printing Office, 1997.

Americans. Statistics on African Americans and employment are found in *The Black Population in the United States* (Upland, Pa.: Diane Publishing, 1995). Two books dealing with African Americans in the workplace are George Davis and Glegg Watson's *Black Life in Corporate America: Swimming in the Mainstream* (New York: Doubleday, 1985) and Joe R. Feagin and Melvin P. Sikes's *Living with Racism: The Black Middle-Class Experience* (Boston: Beacon Press, 1994). *Social Goals and Educational Reform* (Westport, Conn.: Greenwood Press, 1988), edited by Charles V. Willie and Inabeth Miller, and *A Common Destiny: Blacks and American Society* (Washington, D.C.: National Academy Press, 1989), edited by Gerald David Jaynes and Robin M. Williams, Jr., suggest education reforms.

See also: Affirmative action; Discrimination: racial and ethnic; Economics and race; Education and African Americans; Glass ceiling; Great Migration; Poverty and race; Quotas; Set-asides; Sharecropping.

Employment among American Indians

Significance: Traditional means of making a living radically changed for Native Americans after contact with Europeans.

In the pre-contact period, prior to the arrival of Europeans in North America, Indians had extensive trading networks throughout Canada, the United States, and Central and South America. Agricultural goods, manufactured items such as jewelry, pottery, and tanned hides, and natural resources such as seashells were bartered or sold.

Traditional Labor
Labor was required to sustain this extensive trade network, but little is known about how the labor systems were organized. Tribal groups in the Mississippi River area, the southwestern United States, and Central and South America had highly specialized labor forces in which both men and women participated. Division of labor was determined in part by gender, talent, and social position. These societies were organized hierarchically and sometimes incorporated slaves (captives from other tribes), who performed undesirable labor.

Much of North America and Canada was inhabited by nomadic hunting and gathering societies and semi-sedentary agriculturalists. In these societies, division of labor was based primarily on gender and was less complex, with most tribal members working toward the common goal of providing food, shelter, and clothing for survival. In these subsistence economies, there was little opportunity for members to specialize in any one area, such as art or medicine. Such cultures stressed sharing and egalitarianism as a way to ensure the well-being of the people. Everyone worked for the common good.

The Fur Trade
European migration to North America was primarily motivated by economic interests. The first phase of European-Indian relations revolved around the fur trade, which required the incorporation of Indian labor. The early period of the fur trade is marked by relative equality among Europeans and native people. Indian men and women labored to supply processed hides and pelts for the fur trade. In return for their labor, Indians were paid with European trade goods—metal pots, needles, knives, guns, and a variety of domestic goods. During this period, those Indian people who obtained European trade goods would redistribute them among tribal members, thus maintaining the tribal ideal of generosity and sharing. The trade goods changed the work patterns of both Indian men and women. Guns and traps permitted more men to hunt and kill more game, and, in turn, women were required to tan more hides for trade. Indian labor during this period was still directed toward the good of the tribe, but increasingly tribal welfare depended on sources outside the tribe.

The fur trade was an important source of labor for American Indians, but the fur trade period ended as animal populations decreased and as European fashion changed. The decline in the fur trade coincides with the emergence of the United States and marks a period of change in the economic position of Indians. Indians were no longer needed as laborers in the new economy. The European American population was rapidly increasing and there was an increased desire for land. Indians became a hindrance in this emerging economic system. The relative lack of demand for Indian labor, coupled with the high demand for Indian land, caused the U.S. government to remove Indians from areas coveted by European Americans and resettle them on poor lands.

The Reservation System
The reservation system was firmly in place by the late nineteenth century, and it caused considerable change in the work patterns of tribal groups. For the most part, hunting and fishing were no longer possible on the restricted land base, and traditional agricultural practices were not viable or were discouraged. The reservation system afforded little opportunity for Indian people to provide adequately for their families, and it is directly linked to contemporary reservation poverty.

During the early reservation period, some Indian men worked for federal agents as freight haulers, policemen, and laborers. Indian women sometimes sold pottery, beadwork, baskets, or other small items. Income from these sources was small. Government policy largely confined Indian people to their reservations, so they were unable to sell their labor for wages off the reservations. Federal Indian policy, most notably the General Allotment Act (1887), reduced the Indian land base and subdivided the land among many heirs so that productive use of reservation lands became nearly impossible. High Indian unemployment rates caused gradual loosening of federal policies of confinement to reservations, and by the early twentieth century Indians commonly worked in off-reservation jobs as laborers on farms and ranches, and in mines. The 1930 census indicates that 80 percent of Indian men were working for wages, mostly in agricultural jobs. Most of this work was unskilled, seasonal, and off-reservation.

Many reservations cannot provide enough jobs for their residents. This member of the Hupa tribe in northwestern California is working as a museum curator.

The 1930's

In the 1930's, federal Indian policy sought to address the problem of high unemployment and poor economic opportunity on the reservations. A 1928 study, *The Problem of Indian Administration*, commonly known as the Meriam Report, criticized federal Indian policy that intentionally removed Indian control over lands and resources and contributed to the widespread poverty and unemployment that characterized reservations. Partly in response to this study, the Indian Reorganization Act was passed in 1934. This act was intended to enable tribes to consolidate severely checkerboarded reservation lands, take out low-interest loans to establish economic ventures on reservations, and increase farming and ranching opportunities on reservations. The Great Depression prevented any significant business development on reservations; however, a fair number of Indian people benefited through various New Deal programs, particularly the Indian Division of the Civilian Conservation Corps, which employed and trained more than eighty-five thousand Indians in nine years. During the same period, the Bureau of Indian Affairs organized a division to place Indians in off-reservation jobs.

Changes in the Mid-Twentieth Century

Thousands of Indians joined the wage labor force during World War II. Many Indian men and women joined the armed services or moved to urban areas to work in war industries. After the war, many Indian people remained in urban centers, while those who returned to reservations began to focus on reservation economic development and employment. Reservations remained poor and unemployment high, however. Few jobs came to the reservations, tribes had difficulty securing loans, reservation laws made business investments difficult, and many reservations were distant from markets. Additionally, off-reservation seasonal farming jobs became scarce with increasing technology. As a result, large-scale Indian urban migration continued after World War II and was encouraged by the federal policy of the 1950's known as relocation. Through the relocation program, Indians were removed to urban areas where jobs could be found. They received job training and housing assistance. The lack of any meaningful jobs on reservations, coupled with federal Indian policy, contributed to unprecedented Indian migration to urban areas from 1950 to 1980. By the 1980 census, more than half the Indian population resided in urban areas. Indians continue to move to cities because of poor economic opportunities on reservations. Urban Indians experience higher employment rates and per capita incomes than reservation Indians. They remain poor, however, with per capita income slightly ahead of urban African Americans and well behind urban whites, and unemployment rates more than double those of the urban white population.

The federal government abandoned relocation programs in the late 1960's and turned its attention to revitalizing reservation economies. Concurrently, tribal governments were strengthened and tribes began pursuing economic development initiatives independent of the federal government. Success has been mixed, and reservations still have high unemployment and poverty rates.

Modern Labor Force Participation
On the majority of reservations, the largest single source of jobs is government, either tribal or federal. Despite many sincere efforts, there has been little economic investment or growth on reservations, primarily due to lack of resources, capital, location, and a skilled labor force. Few businesses locate on reservations, and unemployment rates are in the 80 to 90 percent range on some reservations. U.S. census figures on the labor force report only those who are employed or are actively seeking employment. According to the 1990 census, 62 percent of Indians sixteen years and older were in the labor force (69 percent of the males and 55 percent of the females). Many of the jobs held, however, were seasonal or part-time. A larger number of American Indians than the total population were employed in service jobs: farming, fishing, forestry, construction, or manufacturing. Fewer Indians, as compared to the total population, were employed in managerial or professional specialty occupations. In 1990, the median income of Indian workers was considerably less than that of the total population, and 31 percent of American Indians were living below the poverty level, compared with 10 percent of all American families. According to the 1990 census, 51 percent of the reservation population was living in poverty.

American Indian labor force participation on reservations continues to be low because of a lack of economic opportunities. The Indian population is young and lacks job experience. More significant, however, is the education deficit among Indians. Only 56 percent of American Indians graduate from high school, compared to 69 percent of the white population. Urban areas offer more job opportunities, but male Indian labor is largely confined to manual occupations, which are subject to fluctuation because of economic downturns, weather, and other factors. Female Indians are employed primarily in low-skilled, nonmanual service jobs both on and off the reservation.

During the 1980's, some tribal governments managed to attract businesses and increase employment opportunities, but overall, success was limited. Indian gaming, sometimes referred to as "the new buffalo," is being explored by many tribes both as a source of income for the tribe and as a way to provide jobs. The gaming operations have brought jobs to many reservations, but these tend to be low-wage service positions such as cashiers and waitresses. Tribal governments look to gaming as a way to strengthen reservation infrastructures and improve the lives of the people while they search for other means to address the dual need for Indian employment and real economic development on the reservations.

Indian participation in the labor force has increased as Indians have moved off reservations; however, even in urban settings, Indian unemployment remains high. Job opportunities on the reservations are scarce. Tribal governments are increasingly asserting their sovereign status and distancing themselves from the federal government in the hope of creating viable economic institutions that will bring job opportunities to the reservations. Federal law continues to frustrate these efforts.

Carole A. Barrett

Core Resources
Marjane Ambler's *Breaking the Iron Bonds: Indian Control of Energy Development* (Lawrence: University Press of Kansas, 1990) focuses on the potential for energy development on reservations as a source of economic revitalization for tribes. Thomas Biolsi's *Organizing the Lakota: The Political Economy of the New Deal on the Pine Ridge and Rosebud Reservations* (Tucson: University of Arizona Press, 1992) examines what happened to the political and economic life of the Lakota people when the Indian Reorganization Act was implemented on two western reservations. Stephen Cornell's *The Return of the Native: American Indian Political Resurgence* (New York: Oxford University Press, 1988) takes a broad look at the complexity of Indian-white relations, allowing the reader to see why reservation economic development has been so bleak and why it is so vital for the continuation of tribal governments. Michael Lawson's *Dammed Indians* (Norman: University of Oklahoma Press, 1982) explores the devastating economic impact of dams along the Missouri River to Sioux reservations. *The Problem of Indian Administration* (Baltimore: The Johns Hopkins University Press, 1928), by Lewis Meriam et al., is a seminal work that explores in depth the poor economic conditions on reservations in the 1920's and the reasons for them. Much of the analysis is still meaningful.

See also: Indian Reorganization Act; Relocation of American Indians; Reservation system of the United States; Reserve system of Canada; Urban Indians.

Employment among Asian Americans

> **Significance:** Asian Americans have generally reaped benefits from both human capital (skills, education, training) and social capital (networks of kin and friends) in regard to employment.

Employment among Asian Americans can be examined along several dimensions. Statistics consistently indicate that Asian Americans are generally well educated in comparison to other racial and ethnic groups. Asian Americans might thus be expected to have high labor-force participation rates and to be concentrated in occupations that require high levels of schooling. At the same time, the Asian American population is quite diverse. Some ethnic groups—for example, Asian Indian and Japanese Americans—have generally high levels of schooling and incomes, while others, such as Cambodian and Vietnamese Americans, have high poverty rates and lower incomes.

Labor Force Participation and Unemployment Rates

Data based on the March, 1997, Current Population Survey (CPS) show that the Asian American labor-force participation rate is slightly higher than the national rate. For the U.S. population in general, 66.8 percent of people aged sixteen and older were in the civilian labor force. More than 68 percent of Asian Americans sixteen years and older were in the civilian labor force. More than 95 percent of Asian Americans in the civilian labor force were employed, compared with 94 percent of all Americans. Therefore, the unemployment rate of Asian Americans was slightly lower: 4.7 percent compared with a national rate of 5.6 percent.

Labor-force participation rates by gender are consistent with the overall patterns. Asian American men and women are slightly more likely to be in the labor force, and their unemployment rates are also lower. For example, 62 percent of Asian American women are in the labor force, compared with 60 percent of all American women.

Data on labor-force participation rates for specific Asian American groups based on the 1990 census reveal that, among persons sixteen and older, Filipinos and Asian Indians have the highest labor-force participation

rates (more than 70 percent), while Cambodians, Laotians, and Hmongs have the lowest.

Class of Employment

Class of employment is an important dimension of employment for the Asian American population because of the large numbers of foreign-born Asian Americans (more than 60 percent of Asian Americans are foreign-born). Research shows that immigrants are more likely than natives to be self-employed, because lack of English proficiency and knowledge of the general job market make it more difficult to secure employment in the private and public sectors. Surprisingly, data from the March, 1997, CPS indicate that Asian Americans are as likely as other Americans to be employed as private wage-and-salary workers: 78 percent of employed Asian Americans aged sixteen years and older were in this class of employment, as were 77.5 percent of all employed Americans aged sixteen and older. The main differences are in the percentages employed in the public sector and the percentages who are unpaid family workers. For all employed Americans, more than 14 percent worked as federal, state, or local government workers, compared with 12.7 percent of Asian Americans. Slightly more Asian Americans were self-employed workers (9 percent versus 8 percent), and nearly 1 percent of Asian Americans were unpaid family workers, compared with just 0.1 percent of all employed Americans.

Education Levels and Occupational Categories

Forty-two percent of Asian Americans have a bachelor's or higher degree, compared with 26 percent of U.S. whites, 13 percent of U.S. blacks, and 10 percent of U.S. Hispanics. About 15 percent of Asian Americans and U.S. whites have less than a high school education, compared with 25 percent of U.S. blacks and 45 percent of U.S. Hispanics. The types of occupations in which Asian Americans are employed reflect these educational attainment patterns. According to the March, 1997, CPS data, more than 35 percent of employed Asian Americans work in managerial and professional specialty jobs, compared with the national figure of 29 percent. There are no significant differences in the percentages employed in technical, sales, and administrative support jobs (29.8 percent of both Asian Americans and all Americans) or in service jobs (13.8 percent of Asian Americans and 13.5 percent of all Americans). However, fewer Asian Americans (1.2 percent) work in farming, forestry, and fishing jobs in comparison with all Americans (2.5 percent) and in high-skilled blue-collar jobs (6.5 percent of Asian Americans compared with 11 percent of all workers).

Gender differences in employment patterns also exist. A higher percentage of Asian American men (38

As of 1997, more than one-third of employed Asian Americans worked in managerial and professional specialty jobs. This Chinese American woman is employed as a bank manager.

percent) work in managerial and professional jobs compared with all U.S. men (28 percent), while Asian American women are as likely as all U.S. women to be employed in this occupational category. Asian American men are less likely to be employed as skilled or unskilled workers (25 percent versus 38 percent of all U.S. men), but Asian American women are more likely to work as unskilled workers. More than 12 percent of Asian American women work as operators, fabricators, or laborers, compared with 7 percent of all U.S. women workers. These statistics are consistent with research on the employment of many immigrant women (primarily Asian and Hispanic) in such industries as garment manufacturing.

Data from the 1990 census provide information on occupational differences across Asian ethnic groups. Almost 44 percent of Asian Indians worked as managers or professionals, as did about 37 percent of Chinese and Japanese Americans. In contrast, almost 40 percent of Cambodians, Laotians, and Hmongs worked as low and unskilled operators and laborers, compared with less than 10 percent of Asian Indians, Japanese, and Chinese. These ethnic group variations reflect educational differences and other factors associated with each group's history in the United States.

Earnings Disparity and the Glass Ceiling

Although Asian American participation in the labor force and occupational distributions suggest an overall picture of a minority group that is firmly integrated into the U.S. labor market and economy, there is compelling evidence indicative of unequal treatment of Asian Americans by employers. Unequal treatment can be observed in two important ways. First, Asian Americans may be paid less than whites in relation to such factors as education, experience, and occupation. Second, Asian Americans may not be promoted as quickly or as highly as white co-workers, a phenomenon known as the "glass ceiling." In the words of one scholar, the glass ceiling metaphor refers to "artificial barriers based on attitudinal or organizational bias that prevent qualified individuals from advancing upward in their organization."

Evidence of unequal pay comes from an analysis of 1990 census data that compared median annual earnings of Asian and white American engineers and scientists. The researchers chose to compare these two groups because Asian Americans made up less than 3 percent of the 1990 U.S. population but made up almost 6 percent of the total engineering workforce. The findings showed that at all levels of education, Asian Americans had lower median annual earnings than whites. For example, white engineers with a bachelor's degree had median annual earnings of $40,800, while for Asian American engineers with similar education, the level was $37,000. For those with doctoral degrees, median annual earnings were $57,200 for white engineers and $54,000 for Asian Americans. Other researchers have reported similar evidence of earnings disparity, underlining a persistent pattern of lower rates of return on education and occupation among Asian Americans.

It is more difficult to document glass ceiling experiences and to demonstrate racial discrimination in regard to promotions and career advancements. Nevertheless, recognition of a glass ceiling and its effects on racial minorities and women resulted in the creation of the federal Glass Ceiling Commission in 1991. The commission's report was published in 1995 and provided evidence that Asian Americans, like other racial minorities and women, were less likely to advance into high-level management positions than were white men. Often, white men with less experience would be promoted over Asian Americans. Some researchers suggest that top-level managers (almost all white men) do not view Asian Americans as potential managers, regardless of their educational attainment or experience. Thus, an important reason for Asian Americans' experiences with the glass ceiling may lie in employers' attitudes and their acceptance of stereotypes of Asian Americans. Additionally, because a high percentage of Asian Americans are foreign-born, their employment experiences may also be affected by employers' attitudes toward immigrants for whom English is a second language.

Asian Americans are participating in the labor force at levels equal to or higher than national rates. Because of their generally high levels of educational attainment, a relatively high percentage of Asian Americans are employed in managerial and professional jobs. Because of the diversity of the Asian American population, however, some Asian ethnic groups are not as well educated and are clustered in blue-collar occupations requiring fewer skills. Finally, there is evidence suggesting that all Asian Americans, including the most well-educated and those who work in professional and managerial jobs, experience earnings inequality and other glass ceiling effects. Thus, while Asian Americans are unlike other racial minorities in their educational and occupational profiles, they may share similar obstacles in employment.

Sharon M. Lee

Core Resources

Information on Asian Americans and employment may be found in Sharon M. Lee's "Asian Americans: Diverse and Growing" (*Population Bulletin* 53, no. 2); *Global Production: The Apparel Industry in the Pacific Rim* (Philadel-

phia: Temple University Press, 1994), edited by Edna Bonacich et al.; Miriam Ching Louie's "After Sewing, Laundry, Cleaning, and Cooking, I Have No Breath Left to Sing" (*Amerasia Journal* 18, no. 1); the U.S. Department of Labor's *A Report on the Glass Ceiling Initiative* (Washington, D.C.: Government Printing Office, 1991); Paul Ong and Evelyn Blumenberg's "Scientists and Engineers," in *The State of Asian Pacific America: Economic Diversity, Issues, and Policies* (Los Angeles: LEAP Asian Pacific Public Policy Institute and UCLA Asian American Studies Center, 1994), edited by Paul Ong; "Education, Occupational Prestige, and Income of Asian Americans," by Herbert Barringer et al. (*Sociology of Education* 63, 1990); the federal Glass Ceiling Commission's *Good for Business: Making Full Use of the Nation's Human Capital* (Washington, D.C.: U.S. Department of Labor, 1995); Deborah Woo's *The Glass Ceiling and Asian Americans: A Research Monograph* (Washington, D.C.: Glass Ceiling Commission, U.S. Department of Labor, 1995); Joyce Tang's "Caucasians and Asians in Engineering: A Study in Occupational Mobility and Departure" (*Research in the Sociology of Organizations* 11, 1993); Marilyn Fernandez's "Asian Indian Americans in the Bay Area and the Glass Ceiling" (*Sociological Perspectives* 41, no. 1, 1998); and Timothy P. Fong's *The Contemporary Asian American Experience: Beyond the Model Minority* (Upper Saddle River, N.J.: Prentice-Hall, 1998).

See also: Asian American movement; Asian American stereotypes; Asian Pacific Labor Alliance.

Employment among Latinos

> **Significance:** Latino Americans occupied a comparatively disadvantaged position in the U.S. labor market relative to the white population and to other minorities throughout the twentieth century. This overall trend, however, varied over time in response to changes in the economy.

Latino Americans were the fastest-growing minority group in the United States during the last quarter of the twentieth century. In 1980, they made up 6.5 percent of the civilian population, and by 1996, they had increased to 10.6 percent. The Bureau of the Census projected that this group would reach 14 percent by the year 2010. Empirical research on their employment situation has lagged behind such rapid changes, and it is difficult to discern patterns and trends when the available statistical information is not broken down into national-origin subgroups.

Historical Background

In the late nineteenth century and early twentieth century, Mexican laborers (mainly displaced peasants) began to cross the border into the American Southwest to find work. Throughout the twentieth century, U.S. immigration policy alternatively encouraged and restricted the entry of Mexicans, but the net result has been essentially a steady stream of immigrants. Their numbers, along with the descendants of earlier Mexican immigrants, have made Mexicans the largest subgroup of Latinos in the United States.

During World War I, Puerto Ricans were granted citizenship to ease U.S. labor shortages. By 1920, nearly 12,000 Puerto Ricans had left their home for the United States, settling mostly in New York City and finding employment mainly in manufacturing and services. Their numbers have grown, making them the second largest Latino subgroup.

Cubans constitute the third most numerous subgroup. From 1959, the year when Fidel Castro assumed power following the Cuban Revolution, to 1990, the Cuban population in the United States—which had pre-viously numbered only about 30,000—grew to 1,044,000 people.

The Latino American Labor Force

The Latino American share in the civilian labor force was 5.7 percent of the total in 1980, but it had almost doubled by 1996, to 9.6 percent. The Bureau of Labor Statistics projected further growth to 11 percent by the year 2005 (*Statistical Abstract of the United States: 1997*, 117th ed., U.S. Bureau of the Census: Washington, D.C., 1997).

In the 1980's and 1990's, the labor force participation rates (that is, the percentage of persons who are employed) for the Latino population age sixteen and older approximated those of the non-Latino white population in the same age group (66.5 percent for Latinos and 67.2 percent for non-Latino whites in 1996). However, the rate for Latino men (79.6 percent) was higher than that for non-Latino white men (75.8 percent) in the same year, while Latinas had a lower rate (53.4 percent) than non-Latino white women (59.1 percent).

The occupational distribution of the Latino population reflects both the traditional background of the

Although many Latinos, including these harvesting celery in Oxnard, California, are farmworkers, many earlier immigrants have become successful, trained professionals.

subgroups and the economic changes of later decades. According to the *Statistical Abstract*, in 1996, Mexicans were mostly operators, fabricators, and laborers (24.5 percent); they also had the highest percentage of workers in farming, forestry, and fishing among all the other subgroups (8.4 percent). Cubans had the highest proportion in managerial and professional occupations (21.7 percent) as well as in technical, sales, and administrative support positions (32.7 percent). The advances made by Puerto Ricans were evidenced by the fact that their concentration in the latter positions (32.1 percent) and in managerial and professional occupations (19 percent) closely approximated those of the Cubans. However, this advance may be more apparent than real because of changes in the occupational structure that have reduced the availability of lower-level, high-paying blue-collar occupations in favor of low-paying white-collar occupations.

Comparison with Non-Latino Whites

A comparison of the occupational distribution of Latinos with that of non-Latino whites reveals that the former are concentrated in lower-level occupations and that white men are concentrated in managerial and professional occupations. In the late 1980's, Mexican American men were concentrated in skilled and semiskilled blue-collar jobs, although they were advancing to better jobs; Puerto Rican men were in service and lower-level white-collar jobs. Latinas were more likely than white or black women to be semiskilled manual workers.

Regarding the evolution of Latino earnings and incomes, Gregory DeFreitas reports that in 1949, U.S.-born men of Mexican and Puerto Rican ancestry had incomes that were 55 percent and 76 percent, respectively, of the white non-Latino level. During the 1960's, both groups improved relative to whites; but in the 1970's, the Puerto Ricans experienced a decline and the Mexicans remained at the same level. Latinos generally suffered decreases in income during the 1970's. Median Latino incomes declined in absolute and relative terms after the 1970's. By 1987, Latino income was still almost 9 percent lower in real terms than it had been in 1973 and, when compared with the income of non-Latino whites, even lower than it had been fifteen years earlier.

According to the *Statistical Abstract*, the median income of Latino households, at constant 1995 dollars, was $25,278 in 1980; it rose later to $26,037 in 1990 but fell to $22,860 in 1995. It was 64 percent of the white non-Latino median income, which in 1995 was $35,766, and practically equal to that of blacks, which stood that year at $22,393.

Since the 1950's, Latinos have made progress in occupational mobility and earning levels, especially during periods of economic expansion. Cuban Americans are nearly equal with non-Latino whites in educational and economic achievement; Mexican Americans and Puerto Ricans, however, are still the most disadvantaged.

Unemployment

Unemployment has been a long-term problem for Latinos. Their actual unemployment rates reflect structural factors such as business-cycle fluctuations, industrial restructuring, and changes in demand as well as individual characteristics such as educational level and previous work experience. As indicated in the *Statistical Abstract* (1997), in 1980, the total unemployment rate was 7.1 percent, while it was 10.1 percent for Latinos. By 1992, these rates had risen to 7.5 and 11.6 percent, respectively. In 1996, both had decreased; the total rate stood at 5.4 percent and the Latino rate at 8.9 percent.

The rates, however, vary among the national-origin subgroups. Cuban Americans' unemployment rates have been almost as low as those of non-Latino whites, largely because of their above-average educational levels and accumulated work experience. By contrast, Mexican Americans and Puerto Ricans have generally experienced above-average unemployment. Puerto Ricans' unemployment rates are usually twice as high as those of Cuban Americans. Some scholars claim that Puerto Ricans' history of "circular migration" (their frequent returns to the island) tends to destabilize their employment.

Factors That Influence the Latino Labor Market

Education is one of the main factors that affect the labor market situation for Latinos. DeFreitas, after analyzing the trends in earnings of Latinos and non-Latinos from 1949 to 1979, found that those Latinos who were better educated were able to approximate the earnings of non-Latino whites in the 1960's.

Limited English ability is another relevant factor. Several empirical studies carried out in the 1980's found that language limitations could account for up to one-third of wage differentials between Latino and non-Latino white men. Other research has established that Puerto Rican and Cuban American men, who are concentrated in urban areas, tend to have lower participation rates in the labor force than men from the same national-origin subgroups with better English language skills. Mexican Americans, who are mainly operators, fabricators, laborers, and agricultural workers, have higher participation rates because those occupations do not require a good command of English.

Empirical studies have tried to establish the extent of discrimination suffered by Latinos in the labor market. According to the findings of a major study undertaken by the General Accounting Office (1990) to evaluate the effects of the Immigration Reform and Control Act of 1986, discrimination in hiring is practiced against "foreign-looking" or "foreign-sounding" applicants. In particular, an audit carried out as part of the study found that Hispanic job seekers were more likely than similarly qualified Anglos to be unfavorably treated and less likely to receive interviews and job offers. Consequently, discrimination could partially account for the higher Latino unemployment rates.

Self-employment may be a way to escape unemployment, low wages, and obstacles to promotion. However, capital is required to start a business, and many poorer Latinos find it difficult to accumulate savings and are not likely to receive loans from credit institutions. Cuban Americans, who have a higher status background, have opened many small businesses, creating an "ethnic enclave" of Latino businesses in Miami. The benefits of this type of social and economic arrangement have been highly debated. Some contend that it is an avenue of economic mobility for new immigrants; others argue that it may hinder their assimilation into the larger society. However, given the small proportion of self-employed Latinos and the level of their earnings, it is not likely that this type of employment will soon become a prevalent means to reduce inequality for Latinos in the labor market.   *Graciela Bardallo-Vivero*

Core Resources

The Hispanic American Almanac (New York: Gale, 1997), edited by Nicolás Kanellos, includes a chapter on labor and employment. The *Statistical Abstract of the United States,* published annually by the U.S. Bureau of the Census, Washington, D.C., is the standard source for statistical information. Two very good books are *Inequality at Work: Hispanics in the U.S. Labor Force* (New York: Oxford University Press, 1991), by Gregory DeFreitas, and *Hispanics in the Workplace* (Newbury Park, Calif.: Sage Publications, 1992), a collection of articles edited by Stephen B. Knouse, P. Rosenfeld, and A. L. Culbertson.

See also: Cuban Americans; Economics and race; Immigration Reform and Control Act of 1986; Latinos in the United States; Poverty and race.

Employment Division, Dept. of Human Resources of the State of Oregon et al. v. Smith

In this April 17, 1990, decision, the U.S. Supreme Court adopted a narrow interpretation of the free exercise clause, allowing Oregon to apply its drug laws to prohibit Native Americans from using peyote in religious ceremonies. Alfred Smith and Galen Black, two members of the Native American Church, were fired from their jobs in a drug rehabilitation clinic after their employer discovered that they used the hallucinogenic drug peyote during religious rituals. They applied for unemployment compensation, but Oregon's Department of Human Resources denied their claims based on a state law that disqualified employees who were discharged for work-related "misconduct." A state appellate court and the Oregon Supreme Court ruled that the denial of benefits was a violation of the free exercise clause of the First Amendment. Oregon appealed to the U.S. Supreme Court, contending that Smith's free exercise of religion had to be balanced by the state's interest in preventing the use of harmful drugs. The Supreme Court's first judgment was to remand the case to the Oregon Supreme Court to decide whether state law made an exception for the religious use of peyote. Oregon's court responded that state law provided no exception and that the only issue was the religious freedom of the First Amendment. The Supreme Court accepted the case for a second time.

The Supreme Court's major precedent, *Sherbert v. Verner* (1963), suggested that Oregon could prevail only if it could defend its policy with the "compelling state interest" test combined with the "least restrictive alternative" test. From this perspective, it appeared difficult for Oregon to justify the refusal of unemployment benefits to Smith and Black. The Court had upheld the *Sherbert* tests in at least seven cases since 1963.

In the *Smith* case, however, the Court voted six to three that Oregon had no constitutional obligation to make a religious exception for illegal drugs, provided that the law was reasonable, neutral, and generally applicable to all persons. Writing for the majority, Justice Antonin Scalia argued that in enforcing valid criminal laws not specifically directed at religious acts, government had no obligation to make a religious exemption. Such matters were generally left to the legislature's discretion, even if an "unfortunate consequence" was an incidental burden on unpopular religious practices. The three dissenting justices maintained that Oregon had not shown a compelling state interest to refuse to allow peyote for religious usage.

The *Smith* decision appeared to limit the extent to which religious minorities might claim constitutional protection for unpopular practices. Religious leaders and civil libertarians were outraged at the ruling, and Congress responded to the anti-*Smith* movement by passing the Religious Freedom Restoration Act (RFRA) of 1993, which was designed to restore both the compelling state interest test and the least restrictive means test against any incidental burden on religious practice.

Thomas T. Lewis

See also: American Indian Religious Freedom Act; *Church of the Lukumi Babalu Aye v. Hialeah.*

Employment in Canada

Significance: In 1991, nearly two million visible minority adults (blacks, Chinese, Filipinos, Japanese, Koreans, Latin Americans, other Pacific Islanders, South Asians, Southeast Asians, West Asians, and Arabs, as defined by the Canadian government) were in Canada, 78 percent of them immigrants. This population was expected to triple by 2016, raising concerns about the racial barriers that block these minority groups' access to employment.

Statistics Canada found in 1986 that visible minority men made up 3.4 percent of the available Canadian labor force and visible minority women constituted 2 percent. According to the 1991 census, 70 percent of visible minority adults considered themselves part of the labor force. Although systematic discrimination has largely been eliminated, anecdotal evidence demonstrates that racial minorities encounter a variety of employment problems ranging from unfair hiring practices (such as provisions that previous work experience must have taken place in Canada); stereotyping of entire ethnic groups and their disparagement by coworkers; racial harassment if they are too dedicated and hardworking in their jobs, causing anxiety and jealousy among colleagues; isolation from employee socializing; marginalization in the decision-making process; artificial hindrances to promotions and higher classifications; confinement to low-paying basic jobs; racial slurs and epithets, name calling, and at times hostile confrontation.

Background

As Nan Weiner points out in her book *Employment Equity: Making It Work* (1993), "Canada has been a nation of immigrants since the 1700's." Until the 1960's, because of the existence of numerous race-based immigration barriers, the overwhelming majority of immigrants to Canada were from Europe. In 1961, 90 percent of incoming immigrants were white. With the rescinding of racist policies in the 1960's, increasing numbers of Asian, African, Middle Eastern, and Latin American immigrants came to Canada. The racially neutral immigration points system enabled applicants to be judged on their qualifications rather than by their race. By 1988, 43 percent of immigrants were from Asia. The number was projected to reach approximately 140,000 visible minority immigrants per year by 2006.

The Visible Minority Labor Force

Visible minority members are inclined to settle in Canada's large urban centers such as Toronto and Vancouver. In 1991, 93 percent of visible minority adults over the age of fifteen lived in a metropolitan area, with 40 percent in Toronto, 15 percent in Vancouver, and 14 percent in Montreal. The visible minority population is younger than the Canadian average. In 1991, 75 percent of the adult visible minority population was under forty-five years old, compared with 66 percent of the general population.

Canadian statistics establish that visible minority members, both immigrants and Canadian-born, are usually more educated than the general Canadian population yet less likely to be employed in professions or management positions. According to Statistics Canada, in 1991, 11 percent of the adult Canadian population held university degrees compared with 18 percent of visible minority adults. A study of clerical workers in Ontario found that 20 percent of minority men and 14 percent of minority women clerks had university degrees. The comparable educational figure for the general population of Ontario was 4 percent for women and 7 percent for men.

Educational attainments do not necessarily translate into higher-paying positions. Statistics Canada figures for 1986 demonstrate that only 4 percent of upper management positions were held by racial minority employees. The comparable figure for white men in senior management was 77 percent, although they constituted only 48 percent of the labor force. At the middle levels of management, racial minorities held 4.7 percent of the positions, while white men occupied 61 percent. Visible minority women fared worse than visible minority men: In senior management, the female figure was 0.8 percent versus 3.3 percent for men. At the middle-management level, visible minority women held only 1.5 percent of the positions and men 3.2 percent. Interestingly, white women were well ahead of visible minority women, holding 16 percent of senior management and more than 30 percent of middle-management positions.

The 1991 census demonstrated some improvement: 8 percent of visible minority adults were managers compared with 10 percent of other adults. In the professions, there was definite improvement: 14 percent of visible minority men held such positions compared with 11 percent of men in the general population. However, 13 percent of visible minority women held professional positions compared with 16 percent of other women.

These figures varied significantly depending on the ethnic group. Seventeen percent of Korean Canadian adults were in management positions compared with less than 5 percent of Filipino Canadians. Although 19 percent of Japanese Canadian adults had professional positions, only 8 percent of Latin American Canadians enjoyed this status.

The aforementioned figures notwithstanding, Statistics Canada also found in 1991 that university-educated visible minorities did not enjoy the same access to higher-paying professional or management positions. A comparative study of university-educated visible minority members age twenty-five to forty-four found that more than 50 percent were in the professions and management, 39 percent in professional work, and 13 percent in managerial positions. The comparable figures for the general adult population were 70 percent overall with 52 percent professionals and 18 percent managers.

Karen Kelly, an analyst with Statistics Canada, stated that "Manual labor jobs were relatively common among highly educated Southeast Asians and Latin Americans." On the basis of 1991 statistics, she found that only 2 percent of the general adult population with university degrees were manual laborers, with a comparable figure of 4 percent for visible minorities. Eight percent of other adults with postsecondary education were manual laborers, although 12 percent of similarly educated visible minorities worked as laborers.

The situation regarding employment income had not improved significantly during the 1990's. Statistics Canada found in 1995 that visible minority Canadians earned approximately $22,498 (Canadian) per year, 15 percent below the national average. Significantly, the lower earnings affected both immigrants and Canadian-born visible minority members.

Confinement to low-paying positions is another problem affecting visible minority workers, both men and women. In 1986, only 3 percent of racial minority women and 4 percent of men were in professional positions. Thirty percent of visible minority men were in semi-skilled and other manual labor jobs. Twenty-seven percent of visible minority women were in clerical positions. According to the 1991 census, the proportion of manual laborers in the visible minority population compared with the general population was 16 percent to 13 percent. The figures for service workers were visible minority members 13 percent, general adult population 10 percent. There are significant variations among different ethnic groups. Thirty-two percent of South East Asian Canadians and 29 percent of Latin American Canadians were engaged in manual labor, but only 8 percent of Koreans and Japanese and 10 percent of West Asians and Arabs were so employed.

Visible minority members continue to earn less than their white counterparts in equivalent positions. In one of Weiner's studies, visible minority women were found to earn only 69 percent of what men earned. Visible minority men fared better, earning 97 percent. Hence, visible minority women were subjected to two forms of discrimination, racial and gender-based. Racial minority women earned 2 percent less than white women.

Unemployment and underemployment continue to affect visible minorities more than the Canadian general population. According to Statistics Canada, in 1991, racial minority unemployment was higher, at 13 percent, than in the general adult population, at 10 percent. Certain visible minority groups suffered more severely. Latin American Canadians and South East Asian Canadians experienced the highest unemployment rates at 19 percent and 17 percent respectively. The unemployment rate for South Asian Canadians and Arab Canadians was only slightly lower at 16 percent.

Employment Equity

Canada is officially a multicultural nation, recognizing the significance and contribution of all ethnic groups to the mosaic of Canadian life and society. One vital area of personal contribution is in the realm of employment. The Canadian government has passed legislation regarding employment equity in order to ensure equal treatment of all citizens regardless of race, color, gender, national origin, and religion. Employment equity legally provides for equal treatment in hiring, compensation, and training of employees to enable all workers to be as productive as possible in the workplace. The equity system in Canada has designated four groups that fall under employment equity legislation: women, aboriginal people, persons with disabilities, and visible (racial) minorities. The aim is to redress past discrimination by providing fairness in employment to these designated groups.

The Employment Equity Act of 1986 (which applied to the 5 percent of the labor force working for institutions employing one hundred persons or more and that are federally regulated) addressed many of these concerns. The federal Interdepartmental Working Group on Employment Equity Data was formed to assemble data to define the various ethnic groups. With employer awareness programs, enumeration of visible minorities, and education about diversity, it was hoped that the employment situation for racial minorities would improve. One aim was more recruitment of qualified individuals to diversify the Canadian workforce in various sectors of employment because visible minority members entering nontraditional work arenas have encountered discrimination.

The Employment Equity Act was extended in 1996 to incorporate the military, and in line with this, the Canadian Forces sought to recruit more visible minority members. In 1998, only 1,100 visible minority members were in a regular force of 63,000 military personnel. Federal regulations stipulated that a fully integrated workplace would consist of 9 percent (about 5,700) visible minority membership.

Racism in employment continues to affect thousands of visible minority Canadians despite the plethora of laws, statutes, and commissions formulated to prevent discrimination. Although the statistics provide ample evidence of discrimination, they cannot elucidate the human toll on victims of racial prejudice in emotional and psychological distress, hurt, anger, and frustration. Whether Canadian racial minorities someday achieve equal status and treatment in the workplace will depend on the degree of tolerance, acceptance, awareness, and sensitivity demonstrated by the white majority. Maxwell Yalden, Canadian human rights commissioner said, "Diversity is a fact of life in Canadian society at large. It only stands to reason that it should be a fact of life in the workplace as well."   *Ranee K. L. Panjabi*

Core Resources

Two sources of additional information on employment and racial relations in Canada are Nan Weiner's *Employment Equity: Making It Work* (Toronto: Butterworths, 1993) and Karen Kelly's "Visible Minorities: A Diverse Group," in *Canadian Social Trends* (1995).

See also: Multiculturalism in Canada; Racial/ethnic relations in Canada; Visible minority allophones in Canada.

Enclave economies

In an enclave economy, entrepreneurs from a single minority group cluster together and form a market that supplies others in the same group with goods, services, and jobs. The emergence of an enclave economy is attributed to the existence of a high level of social cohesion among members of a given racial or ethnic group. This solidarity generates loyalty to businesses owned and operated by people from the same ethnic group, insulating them from outside competition. As a result, enclave economies are able to expand and diversify over time, generating wealth and upward mobility for members of a given racial or ethnic group. In fact, enclave economies are considered to offer minority group members an alternative route to economic attainment, allowing for economic mobility outside the mainstream economy.

Scholars have examined economic activity and entrepreneurship in various racial and ethnic communities in order to better understand enclave economies. Some of the most pivotal

research in this area has focused on the Cuban community in Miami. For example, in *Latin Journey: Cuban and Mexican Immigrants in the United States* (1985), Alejandro Portes and Robert L. Bach examine the development of the Cuban enclave economy. Portes and Bach describe how Cuban refugees initially found low-paying jobs at the bottom of the U.S. economy; however, the concentration of Cubans in Miami allowed many to move up the job ladder by pursuing employment and entrepreneurship within the Cuban community. Portes and Bach argue that the presence of an ethnic market in Miami allowed many Cuban refugees to make economic gains that would have otherwise been impossible.

Like research focusing on the Cuban community, studies of the Chinese community in the United States have also expanded understanding of enclave economies. For example, in *Chinatown: The Socioeconomic Potential of an Urban Enclave* (1992), Min Zhou describes how the agglomeration of businesses owned by ethnic Chinese in New York City's Chinatown has generated economic opportunities for Chinese Americans. Zhou points out that although Chinatown's residents have origins in Taiwan, Hong Kong, mainland China, and Southeast Asia, a common ethnic identity stabilizes the enclave economy. Her analysis highlights the central role of ethnic solidarity in the production and maintenance of economic enclaves, arguing that group cohesion among ethnic Chinese stabilizes Chinatown's enclave economy.

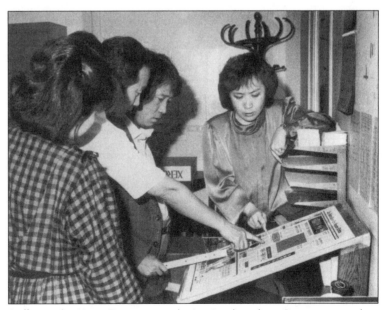

Staffers at the *Korea Times* prepare the Los Angeles edition. Businesses in enclave economies such as Koreatown in Los Angeles provide each other with goods and services.

Notwithstanding, a great deal of scholarly debate remains concerning enclave economies. For example, in *The New Chinatown* (1987), Peter Kwong describes how the perceived prosperity of an enclave economy can mask the extent to which its success is dependent on the exploitation of members of the group, particularly where employee-employer relations are concerned. Other scholars question the permanence of individual enclave economies. For example, in *Entrepreneurship and Self-Help Among Black Americans: A Reconsideration of Race and Economics* (1991), John Sibley Butler points out that in the past, minority groups have developed enclave economies only to see them decline as subsequent generations abandon the ethnic enclave for opportunities in the mainstream economy. *Robert Mark Silverman*

See also: Chinatowns; Cuban Americans; Economics and race; Ethnic enclaves; Ethnic entrepreneurship; Little Havana; Little Italies; Little Tokyos.

English-only and official English movements

> **Significance:** English-only movements are attempts by federal and state governments, lobbyists, organizations, or private citizens to make English the "only" or "official" language in the United States. Although some Americans see these movements as patriotic or well-intended, other Americans perceive such efforts to be anti-immigrant or racist.

Determining how many Americans cannot or do not use English for everyday activities is very difficult. According to the 1996 *Statistical Abstract of the United States*, more than thirty-two million Americans, or more than 13 percent of the population, speak a language other than English at home. Of these, around 44 percent, or about fourteen million people, do not speak English "very well." Figures such as these are cited by many Americans as evidence of national unity eroding under a wave of linguistic diversity and cultural strife. Since the 1980's, organizations such as U.S. English have pressed for state, local, and federal legislation to make English the only official language in various parts of the country. Several attempts have been made to pass a U.S. constitutional amendment mandating English as an official national language, but they have all failed. However, eighteen states have passed some form of official English legislation. In response to these activities, other organizations, such as English Plus, have worked to maintain linguistic and cultural pluralism in the United States. Four states have passed some kind of mandate supporting such sanctions.

Historical Precedents

Although two-thirds of Americans believe that English already is the official language of the United States, the Founders did not establish an official language, perhaps because they felt no need to address the issue. Although the United States has always had a large number of non-English speakers on its soil, English has been the dominant language in the land since the first settlements in the original thirteen colonies. In 1790 after the Revolutionary War—when the nation was perhaps at its height of linguistic diversity—the population was still 76 percent English-speaking (excluding slaves). The second most commonly spoken language in the new nation was German, spoken in states such as Pennsylvania, originally a bilingual English and German state. However, by 1815, the German speakers had largely merged linguistically and culturally with the English-speaking majority. English became the de facto national language. Although some of the nation's leaders occasionally complained about non-English speakers (for example, Theodore Roosevelt once said that Americans should not be "dwellers in a polyglot boarding house"), and the issue was occasionally raised, the official language debate did not receive much thought until the mid-1980's. The debate reached the national level in 1986 when California's Proposition 63, which made English the official state language, passed with 73 percent of the vote.

The Debate

Those who argue for an official language policy say that to live successful and fruitful lives in the United States, immigrants and non-English speakers must learn English: Without fluency in English, they will forever remain in a linguistic underclass, economically and educationally deprived. They believe that bilingual education and multilingual voting ballots and driver's license exams serve only to foster and perpetuate these people's dependence on other languages. They say that the situations in pluralistic countries such as Canada, India, or Belgium, where linguistic wars have been fought, demonstrate the need for a single language to unify the country. English-only supporters cite statistics showing that immigrants want to learn English and argue that, therefore, their efforts are not anti-immigrant.

Probably the most organized and outspoken English-only group is U.S. English, which was established in 1983 and by the late 1990's had a membership of four hundred thousand. The original board of directors and advisers included many well-known and respected individuals, including Nobel Prize-winning author Saul Bellow, social critics Alistair Cooke and Jacques Barzun, university president and former U.S. senator S. I. Hayakawa, actor Arnold Schwarzenegger, and newscaster Walter Cronkite (who resigned in 1988). The organization argues that English is the common bond that unites all Americans and that the United States shoud take active steps to avoid language segregation to avert some of the bitter linguistic conflicts that have plagued many pluralistic nations. They advocate adopting a constitutional amendment establishing English as the official language in the United States, restricting or eliminating bilingual education programs, requiring English competency for all new citizens, and expanding opportunities for learning English.

The storm over official English surprised many people when Senator Hayakawa, a Republican from California, in the mid-1980's introduced a constitutional amendment to make English the official language. The amendment also would have eliminated many foreign-language supplementary materials in both the public and private sector and, therefore, appeared to be aimed at ending bilingual education. Many people perceived the English-only movement as an attempt to disfranchise immigrants or nonnative English speakers by depriving them of access to basic social services and education. Many people felt that the amendment would only splinter the country into even more divisive interest and ethnic groups and foster xenophobia and intolerance.

One of the groups that formed to combat English-only initiatives was English Plus, established in 1987. The group is a coalition of more than fifty prestigious educational and civil rights organizations, including the American Civil Liberties Union, the Center for Applied Linguistics, and the National Council of Teachers of English. The organization's stated goals are to strengthen the vitality of

State Language Policies, 1998

State	Year	Action
States Where English Has Become the "Official" Language		
Alabama	1990	by constitutional amendment
Arizona	1988	by constitutional amendment
Arkansas	1987	by legislative statute
California	1986	by constitutional amendment
Colorado	1988	by constitutional amendment
Florida	1988	by constitutional amendment
Georgia	1986	by legislative statute
Hawaii	1978	by constitutional amendment
Illinois	1969	by legislative statute
Indiana	1984	by legislative statute
Kentucky	1984	by legislative statute
Mississippi	1987	by legislative statute
Nebraska	1920	by constitutional amendment
North Carolina	1987	by legislative statute
North Dakota	1987	by legislative statute
South Carolina	1987	by legislative statute
Tennessee	1984	by legislative statute
Virginia	1981	by legislative statute
States Supporting "English Plus," Official Linguistic Pluralism		
New Mexico	1989	by legislative resolution
Oregon	1989	by legislative resolution
Rhode Island	1992	by legislative statute
Washington	1989	by legislative resolution
Other Policies		
All U.S. states	1990	Native American Language Act gives American Indian languages special rights and status.
Arizona	1999	Grade 1 through 8 foreign-language instruction is mandated by statute.

the United States through linguistic and cultural pluralism. English Plus recognizes that English is, and should be, the primary language of the United States; however, the group argues that the equal protection clause of the U.S. Constitution requires that language assistance be made available to all who require it in order for them to enjoy equal access to essential public services, education, and the political process. Their efforts include advocating the acquisition of multiple language skills to foster better foreign relations and U.S. competitiveness in the global economy, encouraging people to retain their first language, working to develop and maintain language assistance programs such as bilingual education in elementary and high schools, and launching campaigns against legislative initiatives or actions that would make English the official language.

The Future
Many Americans feel threatened by rising immigration and changing demographics. Others see little reason to oppose English-only or official-English amendments or statutes since English is so necessary to life in the United States. Some Americans, however, believe that these amendments and statutes are really a form of racism. These people ask why proponents of English-only want to pass a law to enforce what is already in effect, unless they have a hidden agenda. However, regardless of what legislators or voters do, American identity, culture, and intellectual achievement will continue to be influenced by immigrants, who no doubt will be making their contributions in English.   *James Stanlaw*

Core Resources
Fernando de la Peña's *Democracy or Babel: The Case for Official English* (Washington, D.C.: U.S. English, 1991) makes the argument that English should be the official language in the United States. S. I. Hayakawa, the most influential spokesperson for the English-only movement, argues for amending the U.S. Constitution in *The English Language Amendment: One Nation . . . Indivisible?* (Washington, D.C.: Washington Institute for Values in Public Policy, 1985) and states his case in "Why English Should Be Our Official Language" in *The Educational Digest* (52, 1987). Arguments against official English are found in *Not Only English: Affirming America's Multilingual Heritage*, edited by Harvey Daniels (Urbana, Ill.: National Council of Teachers of English, 1990), and *Official English/English Only: More than Meets the Eye* (Washington, D.C.: National Education Association of the United States, 1988). Bill Piatt's *¿Only English? Law and Language Policy in the United States* (Albuquerque: University of New Mexico Press, 1990) discusses the legal downsides to making English the national language. Political scientist Raymond Tatalovich's *Nativism Reborn? The Official En-*

glish Language Movement and the American States (Lexington: University of Kentucky Press, 1995) examines the state legislatures and legislators who passed English-only measures and suggests that such sentiment is closely tied to anti-immigration politics. *English: Our Official Language?*, edited by Bee Gallegos (New York: H. W. Wilson, 1994), and *Language Loyalties: A Source Book on the Official English Controversy*, edited by James Crawford (Chicago: University of Chicago Press, 1992), present articles on the English-only controversy that appeared in the popular media and scholarly journals.

See also: Bilingual education; Bilingual Education Act; Equal educational opportunity; Pluralism vs. assimilation.

Entitlement programs

> **Significance:** In the United States, entitlement programs such as Old-Age, Survivors, and Disability Insurance (OASDI), Medicare, Supplemental Security Income (SSI), Unemployment Compensation (UC), and Temporary Assistance for Needy Families (TANF) embody the idea of the right to a minimum level of economic welfare and security according to standards prevailing in society. A question of fairness arises since contributors to and beneficiaries of such programs vary in race and ethnicity.

The Social Security Act of 1935 established a two-tiered system primarily of cash benefits. The higher-benefit tier comprised old-age insurance, more commonly known today as the Old-Age, Survivors, and Disability (OASDI) program, and unemployment compensation for the industrial labor force. The lower-benefit tier included two income- or means-tested assistance programs, Aid to Dependent Children (which became Aid to Families with Dependent Children, or AFDC) and Old-Age Assistance (later incorporated into the Supplemental Security Insurance, or SSI, program), which provided minimal support to those poor considered to be outside the wage labor pool. An examination of two programs, OASDI, commonly known as Social Security, and Temporary Assistance for Needy Families (TANF), the successor to AFDC, illustrates the relationship between race and ethnicity and entitlements; these programs challenge prevalent notions of fairness and, thereby, work against harmonious racial and ethnic relationships.

Old-Age, Survivors, and Disability Insurance
The Social Security Act of 1935 excluded agricultural workers and domestic servants—who were mostly Afri-

can Americans—from both old-age insurance and unemployment compensation. More than three-quarters of African Americans, many of whom were sharecroppers, lived in the South in 1935, and the federal old-age insurance benefit of fifteen dollars per month would have provided more cash than a cropper family would typically see in a year. Because of southern opposition, the act was written so that agricultural workers and domestic servants were eligible only for means-tested assistance programs.

Although coverage was expanded to most of the workforce by 1960 and benefits were indexed to inflation and maximum taxable wages were indexed to future wages in 1972, pockets of old-age poverty remained, primarily among minorities and women. Although poverty rates among white males over age sixty-five dropped from 10.4 percent in 1972 to 5.7 percent in 1996 and among elderly women from 16.5 percent to 12.1 percent, the decline among African Americans, from 39.9 percent to 25.3 percent, still left significant numbers of poor black people.

Social Security also distributes costs and benefits un-

evenly. African American women are less likely than white women to qualify for a spouse benefit because only women who have been married for at least ten years are eligible. In 1970, 73.5 percent of white women aged forty-five to sixty-four were married, compared with 54.1 percent of black women; 20.4 percent of black women were separated, divorced, or had an absent husband, compared with only 7.3 percent of white women. Moreover, in 1970, only 39.5 percent of all married white women with a husband present were in the labor force, compared with 50 percent of married, nonwhite women with a husband present. Thus, Social Security taxes of black working women have historically subsidized the spouse benefits of white housewives.

Issues regarding the fairness of Social Security also extend to ethnic groups with high concentrations of working legal immigrants. Such immigrants contribute to the payroll tax that supports the present generation of retirees, but they are ineligible for future Social Security benefits (unless they become citizens) even though they might have the requisite earnings history. The Im-

Coretta Scott King (to the right of the traditionally clad Indian man) leads a group of marchers in a call for increased welfare benefits on Mother's Day, 1968. Entitlement programs have been criticized as being unfair, costly to maintain, and a disincentive to work.

migration Reform and Control Act of 1986 promoted family reunification. As a result, many Latinos and Asian Americans encouraged their able-bodied relatives to come to the United States from such countries as Cuba, the Dominican Republic, Mexico, Peru, Cambodia, Korea, Laos, Japan, and Vietnam. These ethnic Americans may be denied the economic protections of Social Security in the event their working immigrant relatives retire in the United States with little or no savings.

Temporary Assistance for Needy Families

Temporary Assistance for Needy Families (TANF), formerly Aid to Families with Dependent Children (AFDC), was nearly federalized in the early 1970's and turned over to the states in 1996. In both instances, race and ethnicity played pivotal roles. Coming off the Civil Rights movement and related urban riots in the late 1960's, President Richard M. Nixon's proposed Family Assistance Plan (FAP) would have provided a federally guaranteed income for the working and nonworking poor. FAP sought to quell urban disturbances and decrease welfare dependency by providing incentives for African American men to become family breadwinners and for African American women to stay home with their children, while also paradoxically promising to encourage women on welfare to work more.

In effect, however, FAP would have nearly tripled the welfare rolls and would have had its greatest impact on the South. In 1971, about ten million people were AFDC recipients; FAP would have made twenty-eight million people eligible for assistance. Overall, 52 percent of those covered by FAP would have been southerners and two-thirds of poor African Americans in the South would have received some payment. Because family size determined benefit levels, FAP would have doubled or tripled household incomes. It would also have increased wage levels to nearly triple a farm laborer's income. Southerners joined members of organized labor, who opposed the FAP requirement of working at jobs paying the prevailing rather than the minimum wage, and welfare mothers, who thought the FAP benefit too low, to defeat the measure in the Senate in 1972.

Between the 1970's and 1990's, an increasing proportion of welfare benefits went to young, single mothers. Trends in out-of-wedlock births were such that in 1993, white illegitimacy rates approached 24 percent, close to the rate that led many in the 1960's to believe that the black family was near collapse, and the black illegitimacy rate was 69 percent. In addition, by the early 1990's, immigrant welfare participation was, on average, higher than that of native-born Americans—9.1 percent versus 7.4 percent respectively. Some Latino and Asian immigrant groups used welfare at a rate far above that of American-born blacks (13.5 percent). Dominican and Cuban immigrants had welfare rates of 27.9 percent and 16.0 percent respectively, and Cambodian and Laotian immigrants had rates of 48.8 and 46.3 percent respectively.

Most white Americans came to see welfare recipients not as equal citizens with justifiable needs but increasingly as the undeserving poor and began to view welfare not as deserved support for the needy but as handouts for shirkers. By the mid-1990's, the political climate regarding the role of government had changed so that increased reliance on market forces eclipsed income maintenance and other interventionist strategies designed to ensure a modicum of income equality and economic well-being. Over the objection of many African American and ethnic congressional leaders, the Personal Responsibility and Work Opportunity Reconciliation Act of 1996 ended the federal mandate for welfare and set a five-year outside limit on the amount of time a family could receive cash assistance. In addition, the law barred future legal immigrants from receiving food stamps, Medicaid, disability benefits, and most other forms of federally funded social services for the first five years they were in the country. Because of their disproportionate participation in these programs, poor African American, Latino, and Asian American women and their children were thought to be most adversely affected by the legislation.   *Richard K. Caputo*

Core Resources

Increased racial tensions associated with the politics of entitlement programs are addressed in Richard K. Caputo's *Welfare and Freedom American Style II: The Role of the Federal Government, 1941-1980* (Lanham, Md.: University Press of America, 1994), Jill Quadagno's *The Color of Welfare: How Racism Undermined the War on Poverty* (New York: Oxford University Press, 1994), and Linda Faye Williams's "Race and the Politics of Social Policy" in *The Social Divide: Political Parties and the Future of Activist Government*, edited by Margaret Weir (Washington, D.C.: Russell Sage Foundation, 1998). Ethnicity and entitlements are discussed in Peter Brimelow's *Alien Nation* (New York: Random House, 1995) and Robert Suro's *Strangers Among Us* (New York: Alfred A. Knopf, 1998). William Julius Wilson's *The Truly Disadvantaged: The Inner City, the Underclass, and Public Policy* (Chicago: University of Chicago Press, 1987) is a benchmark study in the relationship between race and public policy. The Urban League Web site, which follows social policy legislation bearing on race relations, can be found on the Internet at www.urban.org.

See also: Aid to Families with Dependent Children; Poverty and race; Welfare reform: impact on racial/ethnic relations; Welfare's impact on racial/ethnic relations.

Environmental racism

Significance: Environmental racism is the disproportionately high allocation of environmental disease factors to underprivileged racial and ethnic groups through biased public policy and industrial practices associated with urban and regional planning or environmental design.

Activist Benjamin Chavis is credited with coining the phrase "environmental racism" in 1987 during a demonstration against the placing of a toxic-waste landfill in an African American community in Warren County, North Carolina. The systematic segregation of neighborhoods by race and ethnicity enables governments and other agencies to practice environmental racism. The economic and political inequalities that arise from such segregation create impoverished regions with lower environmental awareness and little political power. This makes it easy for governments and businesses to choose these regions as places to locate externalities of industrial development that are likely to have a harmful effect on the environment. Three specific biases—remediation, situational, and judicial—are evident in environmental racism.

Remediation bias leads to the preferential cleanup of pollutants from an area inhabited by white Americans while polluted areas in minority communities are left untouched. An often-cited example of remediation bias is the case involving the Anacostia and Potomac Rivers in the Washington, D.C., region. More than one billion dollars was spent to clean the Potomac, which travels along white neighborhoods, but no efforts were made to clean the equally polluted Anacostia, which flows through African American neighborhoods.

Situational bias is the location of industries known to produce hazardous environmental pollutants, such as incinerators and landfills, in neighborhoods inhabited by minority races and ethnic groups. For example, Kettleman City, California, a community that is 95 percent Latino, is home to the largest toxic-waste dump in the western United States. Despite the already heavy burden of environmental pollution from agricultural chemicals and toxic industrial waste, Chemical Waste Management proposed building a new toxic waste incinerator in the city in 1988. The local county government approved the plan on the basis of a 1,000-page environmental impact report that was not accessible to the general population and without direct consultation with any of the area's residents until a lawsuit was filed to remedy the situation.

Judicial bias causes polluters of environments occupied by white Americans to suffer significant punitive repercussions, while those who pollute areas occupied by racial minorities and ethnic groups receive no punishment or only minor penalties. Studies have found that companies found guilty under existing hazardous-waste laws suffer 500 percent more severe penalties at sites populated by white Americans than at sites populated by minority groups. This leads to the perception that the threat of punitive action deters polluters only in predominantly white neighborhoods, leading to further resistance against integration of residential areas. Another form of judicial bias affects Native American communities. In 1986, the Western Shoshone National Council began to contest the authority of the United States to use the Nevada test site, which includes the southern Newah homelands, for explosion of nuclear weapons and other hazardous bombs. The U.S. Department of Energy sponsored proposals to build nuclear waste dumps within Shoshone lands without Newah permission. Cases involving Native Americans are often complication by the question of who has jurisdiction over the affected regions.

Environmental racism can be reduced or eliminated through political empowerment of minority communities and vigilant activism by community organizations. The establishment of a national center to approve proposed sites for pollution-prone industries would nullify tendencies toward environmental racism fostered by biases in regional politics.   *Oladele A. Ogunseitan*

See also: Criminal justice system; Discrimination: racial and ethnic; Racism: changing nature of.

Epithet transfer

Epithet transfer is the process whereby derogatory language initially applied to a particular racial or ethnic group is transferred to another group. Usually, it is an established, dominant group that will use epithets when referring to newcomers. The term "epithet" derives from the Greek, meaning "something that is put on or added." Within the context of race relations, however, the words added to a group's identity usually have a negative connotation. Epithets demonstrate the fear that dominant groups have of newcomers, the desire to subordinate them in much the same way that the original targets of the epithet were, and the intensity of intergroup conflict. Hostility is especially pronounced when a dominant group feels threatened, as occurred at the beginning of the twentieth century, when large numbers of immigrant groups entered the United States and competed with established group members for jobs. Epithets and their transfer encourage stereotyping of groups and therefore become contributing factors in both prejudice and discrimination waged at newcomers.

Epithet transfer can be illustrated by reference to two ethnic epithets, *dago* and *guinea*. *Dago*, an altered version of the Spanish name Diego, or James, was initially applied to Spaniards and the Portuguese. With the arrival of a new wave of Italian immigrants in the United States around the beginning of the twentieth century, this epithet—with its connotation of "foreigner"—was transferred to them and became a frequently used, highly insulting ethnic slur. It described Italians, their language, their food, and Italy itself. One definition given for *dago* was macaroni, a food closely associated with Italians. Likewise, during Prohibition, inexpensive red wine was called *dago red*. Italy became *Dagoland*. More generally—in what can be seen as another transfer of the epithet—*dago* was used to refer to anyone of darker complexion who was of Mediterranean ancestry and even of Cubans.

Skin color also was an underlying issue in the transfer of the *guinea* epithet. During the eighteenth century, *guinea* referred to African Americans whose heritage was linked to the Guinea coast of Africa. Once again, Italians became subject to epithet transfer and were categorized as *guineas*. This enabled established groups to distance themselves from Italian newcomers by perceiving them to be dark-skinned and, therefore, equal in status to African Americans, who historically had been relegated to a subordinate position in society. As Irving Allen in his 1990 work *Unkind Words* suggests, Italians were "no better than blacks." *Guinea gangplank*, a name referring to the Verrazano Bridge in New York, is an example of the term being used in a disparaging manner. Not only did the bridge honor an Italian, Florentine navigator Giovanni da Verrazano, but it connected the largely Italian Staten Island with Long Island, New York.

Just as Italians have experienced the process of epithet transfer, so, too, have words associated with Italians been extended disparagingly to other groups. The term *wop* is a shortened form of the Italian *guappo*, which comes from the Latin *vappa*, or "wine gone flat." Although at one time used as a greeting, gradually *wop* took on a pejorative connotation: *wop house* for Italian restaurant and *wop special* for spaghetti. The word *wop* has been interpreted as an acronym standing for "without passport/papers," in reference to Italian immigrants who were deported because they did not have documentation, and "working on pavement," reflecting the work done by many Italian immigrants. *Wop* was extended to refer not only to Italians but also to any dark-skinned person of southern European descent.

On the structural level, epithets and their transfer reflect the pervasiveness of discrimination in society. On the individual level, those subject to ethnic slurs are vulnerable to stigmatization and psychological harm.

Rosann Bar

See also: Epithets and pejorative language; Hate speech; Italian American stereotypes; Stereotype.

Epithets and pejorative language

> **Significance:** Most people can remember times when they were hurt by being on the receiving end of a pejorative label. In racial relations, this hurt may be compounded almost infinitely because the racial slur is a form of one-way communication that completely invalidates the humanity and individuality of the person at whom it is directed, and the racial slur transmits racial hatred and misunderstanding from one generation to another.

Every minority group, and many nationalities, may be the victim of some form of invective directed toward them by members of hostile or rival groups. On occasion, these epithets may be intended humorously, but more frequently, the intent of such a term is to cause hurt or embarrassment to the target group. These epithets are most damaging to the minority and ethnic groups that have been most severely marginalized in a given society. For a white American, being called a "Yankee" is hardly likely to cause undue pain, even when slogans such as "Yankee, go home" are scrawled on the walls of Western European capitals, because this term has a positive connotation as well (at least in the minds of the majority group). Other terms may be used as epithets for certain minorities or nations but are not universally regarded as slanderous. For example, the term "Pollock," attributed to a Polish American, may not be well-intentioned, but it is based on *polak*, the name Polish people use to call themselves, and it may be the manner of delivery rather than the epithet itself that is offensive.

The most damaging form of pejorative language, however, is that which is directed toward groups that have suffered repeatedly in the wider society just for being who they are or who have been exploited and shunned by the dominant group. African Americans, Jewish Americans, Asian Americans, and Native Americans are often subject to abusive language that dwells on physical, socioeconomic, and historical qualities that single them out as groups seemingly eternally on the receiving end of ethnic hatred. The terms themselves carry a semantic load that evokes painful associations in the target group. The abuse is not restricted to personal encounters but can become pervasive in the culture through the media of cartoons and caricatures, film, comics, graffiti, popular literature, mass mailings, and the Internet. This ensures that the negative stereotype will perpetuate itself to future generations.

According to the First Amendment to the U.S. Constitution, freedom of speech is an inalienable right of American citizens. However this right, when exercised without regard to the effect speech has on others, can come into conflict with the Fourteenth Amendment, which was designed to provide "equal protection of the law" to all citizens, born or naturalized. The right of an individual citizen to say what he or she thinks thus comes into direct conflict with the right of every citizen to be free from prejudicial treatment. Among the issues that this debate raises is the relationship between words and actions, because violence directed against minority groups is often preceded by verbal abuse.

Critical race theorists, who have assessed this question from a legal and moral standpoint, view racial relations in the United States as having a history of repeated injurious outcomes that must be recognized as torts and redressed legally. The damage that is done by racial invective is well documented and ranges from hurt feelings to such serious social ramifications as social isolation, physical manifestations of fear, self-hate, and suicide. The injury is not only to the victim but also to the perpetrator and to the society as a whole, because racial invective violates the fundamental egalitarian principle upon which the Constitution of the United States is based and which forms the moral underpinnings of the society.

For these reasons, critical race theorists would support a public sanction against racial invective that would recognize the harm done to those members of society least able to resist this type of assault. The key issue in such legal redress would be the balancing of First Amendment rights of freedom of speech with the right of the individual to be free from racial slander.

Gloria Fulton

Core Resources

Philip H. Herbst's *The Color of Words: An Encyclopaedic Dictionary of Ethnic Bias in the United States* (Yarmouth, Maine: Intercultural Press, 1997) is a dictionary of racial and other pejorative language that traces the origin of these terms and how they are used. *Words That Wound: Critical Race Theory, Assaultive Speech, and the First Amendment*, edited by Mari J. Matsuda (Boulder, Colo.: Westview Press, 1993), Harry M. Bracken's *Freedom of Speech: Words Are Not Deeds* (Westport, Conn.: Praeger Publishers, 1994), Monroe H. and Eric M. Freedman's *Group Defamation and Freedom of Speech: The Relationship Between Language and Violence* (Westport, Conn.: Greenwood Press, 1995), and Catharine A. MacKinnon's *Only Words* (Cambridge, Mass.: Harvard University Press, 1993) treat various aspects of the conflict between the

First Amendment issue of free speech and the issue of the danger posed by unregulated hate speech.

See also: African American stereotypes; Critical race theory; Hate crimes; Hate speech; Stereotype.

Equal educational opportunity

> **Significance:** "Equal educational opportunity" refers to the right of everyone to receive an equal chance for access to a good education, not to an "equal" education. The latter is impracticable; the former, if not completely achievable, can be approximated and, to the extent it is achieved, can ameliorate intergroup relations.

Americans have long believed that schools could solve most social problems. Schools were used to Americanize immigrants during the latter part of the nineteenth century and the early part of the twentieth century. They were viewed as the most appropriate institution for fighting childhood diseases and combating the advantage that the Soviets had in aerospace technology during the 1950's. During the 1960's, schools were the point of entry into fighting the War on Poverty. In the 1970's, schools were seen as instruments in solving the problem of unemployment. Schools, in the 1980's, were perceived as instruments to help the United States increase its competitiveness in global markets. Essentially, in each decade since World War II the schools have been expected to solve one or more social problems. Above all, schools have been expected to provide equal educational opportunity.

Definitions

"Equal educational opportunity" has been assigned a variety of meanings by a number of educational scholars. It is complex; its meaning often shifts, depending on the context in which it is used. According to Charles A. Tesconi, Jr., and Emanuel Hurwitz, Jr., in their book *Education for Whom? The Question of Equal Educational Opportunity* (1974), "equal educational opportunity" does not describe a state of affairs but suggests what ought to be—what should be, or what is desirable. Joel Spring, in *American Education: An Introduction to Social and Political Aspects* (1989), contends that equal educational opportunity cannot be achieved. The best that can be offered is the opportunity to an education. Factors such as intellectual ability, social class, and property value within specific school districts all affect access to education and the quality of education received. Consequently, the argument persists that the only way to approximate equal educational opportunity is to equalize educational "input": Equalization in access, curricula, facilities, staff, administration, and management must be approximated across schools. Conversely, if some schools provide significantly less in terms of facilities, staff, or curricular offerings, students attending such schools do not receive equal educational opportunity. These issues have prompted litigation, by poor school districts in many areas of the United States, which challenges traditional methods of financing schools. The assumption is that equalizing funding will help foster greater equal educational opportunity.

A different approach emphasizes educational "output," which is at odds with educational "input." Propo-

nents of this approach hold that equal educational opportunity must be measured by how well students demonstrate achievement in school. Such a position maintains that whatever mechanisms (resources, staffs, or facilities) are necessary to assist primarily lower-income and minority students to achieve should be utilized in the effort to equalize educational opportunity. There is a prescriptive function to the notion of educational output. Educational output arguably could be viewed as the approach upon which the compensatory programs and legislation of the 1960's and 1970's were premised, including the Vocational Education Act of 1963, the Civil Rights Act of 1964, the Economic Opportunity Act of 1964, the 1965 revision of the Na-

Two girls, black and white, consult with their teacher. The concept of an equal educational opportunity played a part in the desegregation of U.S. schools.

tional Defense Education Act, the Elementary and Secondary Education Act of 1965, Public Law 93-380 of 1974, and Public Law 94-142 of 1975.

School Desegregation

The concept of equal educational opportunity was the basis upon which African Americans, through the National Association for the Advancement of Colored People (NAACP), were able to argue successfully before the Supreme Court (*Brown v. Board of Education of Topeka, Kansas*, 1954) to end the system of segregated schools in the South. The Supreme Court affirmed that racially identifiable African American schools did not provide equal educational opportunity. Chief Justice Earl Warren argued in the unanimous opinion of the Supreme Court that to separate black children from white children solely on the basis of race not only was unconstitutional discrimination but could generate a feeling of inferiority as well—one that might affect the hearts and minds of black children in ways unlikely ever to be undone. While the implementation of the mandate to desegregate the public schools in the South was delayed (in some instances by more than sixteen years), de jure segregation was constitutionally ended with the *Brown* decision. Still, desegregation of the public schools was only the first step in the effort to achieve equal educational opportunity for all.

Segregated schools were viewed as responsible not only for the disparity in facilities, the lower level of curricular offerings, and the overall lower qualifications of school personnel which were characteristic of black schools but also for the disparities in academic achievement between black and white students. Such beliefs contributed to an already growing body of research suggesting that minority students were culturally disadvantaged, or culturally deprived. Investigation into the beliefs and causes of the lower academic achievement of minorities (especially on standardized and IQ tests) became known as "deficit theory" research and functioned as the driving force behind many of the compensatory education programs of the 1960's and 1970's.

Many of the strategies suggested for remedying low academic achievement by African Americans (and poor students in general) were premised on deficit theory. Deficit theory inferred that the child, the family, or the culture of the child (which was much more palatable) made that child socially and intellectually unprepared for success in school. Arthur K. Spears, in "Institutionalized Racism and the Education of Blacks" (in *Readings on Equal Education*, 1984), later suggested that deficit theory was, in practice, more damaging than helpful because it failed to focus attention on the structural problems in public education. Nevertheless, much of the educational and social policy during the 1960's and

1970's looked to deficit theory to help explain educational, social, economic, and even political inequality. Beginning in the 1960's, educational policy began to address the perceived deficiencies of specific populations through compensatory education and early intervention programs.

The Coleman Report

One of the principal components of the 1964 Civil Rights Act was a call for the investigation into the suspected racial inequalities in educational opportunities. Researchers led by James Coleman collected data from approximately 60,000 teachers and approximately 570,000 students. The research findings suggested that social class background accounted for the variation in black and white academic achievement. Given that a significantly greater proportion of African Americans come from lower-class backgrounds than do whites, this fact was proposed as the rationale for their lower academic achievement. Based on this research, many social scientists and educators began to suggest that the minorities themselves were not intellectually deficient, as some earlier scientists had argued, but that these groups suffered from "cultural deprivation." Their homes, families, neighborhoods, and in general their culture made them disadvantaged. The solution proffered by some social reformers was early intervention programs and compensatory education. Early intervention programs, it was argued, would give disadvantaged youth a "head start" in preparation to enter school. Such programs would provide the proper cultural exposure and the intellectual stimulation missing from the child's normal environment. Compensatory education would provide the remediation (of skills and knowledge) for students already in school.

The War on Poverty

The Coleman Report (*Equality of Educational Opportunity*, 1966), along with liberal advocates (in and out of education), had a tremendous impact on U.S. education policy. President Lyndon B. Johnson initiated one of the most comprehensive domestic campaigns in U.S. history to eradicate poverty. Referred to as the War on Poverty, it was proclaimed to end poverty and inequality by destroying the "cycle of poverty" that tended to entrap the poor, generation after generation. Poor housing, inadequate health care, poor diet, and inequality of educational opportunity were thought to contribute to the cycle of poverty. Education was, by far it was thought, the most critical component in the cycle. If a link in the cycle were ever to be broken, it would best be accomplished through education.

Most of the educational programs created as a result of the War on Poverty were unsuccessful. Some proponents argued that inadequate funding and mismanagement were the reasons the programs failed to live up to expectations. A number of opponents argued that the programs were ill-conceived and were doomed to failure because they could not change the home environment of the child. One program, however—Head Start—did prove to be somewhat successful and has continued to assist low-income, pre-elementary youth in preparation for school.   *Charles C. Jackson*

Core Resources
Equality of Educational Opportunity (Washington, D.C.: U.S. Government Printing Office, 1966), by James S. Coleman et al. (the Coleman Report), had far-reaching ramifications regarding public opinion and government policy. John U. Ogbu's "Class Stratification, Racial Stratification, and Schooling," in *Class, Race, and Gender in American Education*, edited by Lois Weis (Albany: State University of New York Press, 1988), demonstrates the relationship between race and class stratification in schooling in America. Myra P. Sadker and David M. Sadker's *Teachers, Schools, and Society* (2d ed., New York: McGraw-Hill, 1991) details the barriers that minorities have encountered in attempting to achieve equal educational opportunity. Joel Spring's *American Education: An Introduction to Social and Political Aspects* (4th ed., New York: Longman, 1989) gives an excellent overview of the forces that affect equal educational opportunity. Charles A. Tesconi, Jr., and Emanuel Hurwitz, Jr.'s *Education for Whom? The Question of Equal Educational Opportunity* (New York: Dodd, Mead, 1974) takes a dialectical approach to the issue.

See also: *Brown v. Board of Education*; Education and African Americans; Education and American Indians; Education and Asian Americans; Education and racial/ethnic relations; Equality of opportunity; *Plessy v. Ferguson*.

Equal Employment Opportunity Act

The Equal Employment Opportunity Act, which became law March 24, 1972, stipulated that government agencies and educational institutions could not discriminate in hiring, firing, promotion, compensation, and admission to training programs; it also allowed the Equal Employment Opportunity Commission (EEOC) to bring discrimination lawsuits directly rather than referring them to the attorney general.

Equal employment opportunity issues emerged in the 1960's as a result of changes in societal values, the changing economic status of women and minorities, and the emerging role of government regulation in the area of civil rights. The enactment of the 1964 Civil Rights Act occurred at a time when African Americans were fighting for equal treatment and protection under the law with respect to voting rights, employment, fair housing, and better educational facilities. A provision of this act was the prohibition of discriminatory hiring practices on the basis of race, color, religion, sex, or national origin. The 1964 act, however, lacked major enforcement and punishment provisions. It also failed to include all aspects of employment within government, labor, and the private sector. Almost ten years after the passage of the Civil Rights Act of 1964, Congress was lobbied to provide amendments to the act which would enhance employment opportunities for minorities.

The passage of the Equal Employment Opportunity (EEO) Act of 1972 amended Title VII of the Civil Rights Act of 1964 by expanding the protection of individuals with regard to hiring, firing, promoting, and other human resource functions to all persons without regard to race, color, religion, sex, or national origin. The EEO Act strengthened the enforcement powers of the 1964 Civil Rights Act by allowing individuals who believed that they were being discriminated against to file suit in court for legal recourse to remedy the discriminatory employment practices.

The EEO Act of 1972 tied previous employment legislation (the Civil Rights Act of 1964, Executive Order 11246 of 1964, and the Intergovernmental Personnel Act of 1970) together and required federal and state agencies, government subcontractors, small businesses with more than fifteen employees, and labor organizations to establish affirmative action programs to remedy past discriminatory practices and to prevent future discriminatory employment problems.

Donna Echols Mabus

See also: Affirmative action; Civil Rights Act of 1964; Equal Employment Opportunity Commission; Equality of opportunity; *Griggs v. Duke Power Company*.

Equal Employment Opportunity Commission

Created by the Civil Rights Act of 1964, the Equal Employment Opportunity Commission (EEOC) takes an active role in monitoring workplace compliance with civil rights legislation; it investigates complaints of discrimination based on race, ethnicity, sex, age, religion, national origin, or disability. The increasing numbers of cases being brought under the Civil Rights Acts of 1866 and 1871 and the Fourteenth Amendment in the 1950's and 1960's encouraged passage of the Civil Rights Act of 1964 to provide protection for workers against discrimination in the workplace. The Equal Employment Opportunity Commission (EEOC) was created to investigate complaints and to provide legal remedy to those victimized.

Initially, the EEOC focused on cases of racial discrimination in the private sector. The landmark Supreme Court decision in *Griggs v. Duke Power Company* forced employers to show the job-relatedness of employment requirements. In 1972, the Civil Rights Act of 1964 was amended to include the public sector as well as the private. Affirmative action programs were created during the 1960's and 1970's, and the EEOC monitored their implementation and operation. EEOC regulatory efforts were very broadly focused and, through consolidation of complaints into class actions, the agency was able to address broad categories of discrimination.

Judicial interpretation of the Civil Rights Act of 1964 expanded the focus of the commission to include sex discrimination and sexual harassment cases. EEOC guidelines addressed issues such as sex-based job classifications ("pink collar" occupations) that limited employment opportunities for women. The concept of comparable worth was addressed by the EEOC in the 1970's. A lack of presidential support for equal employment opportunity during the 1980's, however, slowed the process of reducing sex discrimination and addressing issues of sexual harassment. In 1978, the *Regents of the University of California v. Bakke* case challenged the validity of affirmative action programs, and the status of such programs was being hotly debated as the decade ended.

Under Presidents Ronald Reagan and George Bush, the EEOC was much less active than it had been during the 1960's and 1970's. Under the direction of Clarence Thomas, who was appointed chairman by President Reagan, the commission was much less aggressive in investigating complaints and declined to pursue sex discrimination complaints based on the concept of comparable worth. The imposition of quotas to rectify cases of long-term discrimination and the consolidation of broad classes of discrimination were effectively ended. The handling of cases one by one severely limited the effectiveness of the EEOC. The Civil Rights Act of 1991 reaffirmed the principles of equal employment opportunity and affirmative action, although the use of quotas was discontinued.   *William L. Waugh, Jr.*

See also: Affirmative action; *Bakke* case; Civil rights; Civil Rights Act of 1964; Civil Rights Act of 1991; Equal Employment Opportunity Act; Equality of opportunity; *Griggs v. Duke Power Company.*

Equality

Equality is the balanced or equal distribution of resources, opportunities, and rewards provided by a society, regardless of an individual's race, color, gender, age, sexual orientation, religion, or previous condition of servitude.

Historically, Karl Marx and Friedrich Engels, in *The Communist Manifesto* (1848), argued that the most important source of inequality within a society relates to the control or ownership of the means of production. They believed that after a prolonged struggle between two social classes they termed the bourgeoisie (the merchant class) and the proletariat (the worker class), a classless society and equality would emerge. The primary characteristic of this society would be the distribution of resources based on an individual's needs. Because some individuals will need more and therefore receive more, this proposed method of distribution does not develop perfect equality within a society. However, Marx and Engels contended that resources would be in abundance, and all individuals within the society would have their needs met, so the slight inequality that would exist would be acceptable.

However, Kingsley Davis and Wilbert Moore, in their article "Some Principles of Stratification" (*American Sociological Review*, 1945), argued that inequality is necessary. They contended that certain positions within society are of greater importance than others to the well-being of society. If all individuals received equal shares of societal resources regardless of their position, there would be no motivation for an individual to attempt to achieve the rigorous training necessary to fill the important positions. Consequently, important activities might not be completed, resulting in damage to or the demise of society. Theorists such as Gerhard Lenski, Max Weber, and Talcott Parsons viewed stratification of society as inevitable and equality as potentially counter to the social forces at work within society.

Legally, equality has been an evasive goal for racial and ethnic minorities throughout the history of the United States. In an effort to acquire equal access to societal resources, minority group members have appealed to the Supreme Court of the United States on several occasions. In *Brown v. Board of Education* (1954), the Supreme Court rejected the argument of *Plessy v. Ferguson* (1896) and several lower courts that equality could be measured by such tangibles as condition of buildings, transportation, curricula, educational qualifications of teachers, quality and extent of teacher training, pupil-teacher ratio, extracurricular activities, and time and distance involved in travel to school. The Court ruled that equality involves qualities that are intangible and incapable of being measured. In addition, the Court stated that separate educational facilities were inherently unequal because of these intangible qualities. Through court cases such as *Brown*, the Supreme Court attempted to lend its power to minorities, thereby making it possible for them to become more successful in their efforts to acquire valuable resources and gain equality with the majority white group. However, these Supreme Court rulings, while being of assistance, have not completely alleviated social inequality in the United States.

Ione Y. DeOllos

See also: *Brown v. Board of Education*; Inequality; Marxist models; *Plessy v. Ferguson*; Social stratification theories.

Equality of opportunity

Minimally, equality of opportunity involves a situation in which individuals are not excluded from competing for desirable positions because of their race, sex, or class background. More broadly, this ideal of justice requires that race, sex, and socioeconomic background do not negatively influence one's chances for economic success. Thus equality of opportunity calls for hiring processes, including recruitment and screening practices, free of discrimination against minorities and women. To make the competitive race for desirable positions fair, it is also necessary that men and women, people of different races, and the economically advantaged and disadvantaged all have equal educational opportunities for developing their abilities. The same applies to groups such as visually impaired individuals and people with physical disabilities.

During the 1950's and 1960's it became widely acknowledged that American society did not offer equal opportunity to all its citizens, and judicial and legislative action was undertaken to correct this situation. In *Brown v. Board of Education* (1954), the Supreme Court mandated racial integration in public schools, arguing that segregated schools deprive minority children of equal educational opportunity. Title VII of the Civil Rights Act of 1964 prohibits discrimination in employment. During the 1970's the federal government initiated affirmative action programs, requiring that employers not only refrain from intentional discrimination but also actively recruit women and minorities for underrepresented positions and eliminate bias in job criteria. These programs might involve that qualified minorities or women are hired or promoted instead of equally or seemingly more qualified white males. Critics view these programs as violating the equality of opportunity of white males, and of the population in general; their defenders maintain that such programs only eliminate the undeserved competitive advantage that white males have acquired be-

cause they are not subject to institutional discrimination, as minorities and women are. Critics succeeded during the 1980's in curtailing but not eliminating affirmative action programs. Since the 1960's, various laws have been adopted that improve the educational and job opportunities of individuals who are physically impaired. Much less political attention has been given to addressing inequality of opportunity caused by economic poverty as such.

Harry van der Linden

See also: Affirmative action; *Bakke* case; *Brown v. Board of Education*; Civil Rights Act of 1964; Equal Employment Opportunity Act; Equal Employment Opportunity Commission.

Ethnic cleansing

Ethnic "cleansing" is the forced expulsion of a specific population from a territory. Because ethnic cleansing is predicated on the idea that a particular group of people is undesirable, it brings into focus many ethical issues in the areas of bigotry, prejudice, and human rights. The term is often a euphemism for murder and land theft sanctioned by a state government. It usually refers to the expulsion of an "undesirable" population from a given territory for political, strategic, or ideological reasons, or because of religious or ethnic discrimination. Forced emigration and population exchange are elements of ethnic cleansing. Forced population removal or transfers have occurred repeatedly throughout history, most often to create or secure an ethnically homogeneous homeland or state.

The Assyrian king Tiglath-Pileser III (745-727 B.C.E.) carried out the first recorded case of ethnic cleansing. One-half of the population of any land that he conquered was forcefully removed and replaced by settlers from other regions who were loyal to him. Many centuries later, European settlers in North America slowly "cleansed" the land of most Native Americans with the tacit consent of the state. The most notorious twentieth century instance of ethnic cleansing was the Nazi attempt to exterminate Europe's Jews during the 1930's and 1940's. In the early 1970's, Idi Amin of Uganda "cleansed" that country of East Indians so that indigenous Africans could take over their land and businesses. In the 1980's and 1990's, Serbians in the former Yugoslavia tried to "cleanse" territory that they were claiming for Serbian Christians by driving out Muslim citizens.

Dallas L. Browne

See also: Annhilation of racial and ethnic groups; Genocide: physical; Holocaust; Indian Removal Act.

Ethnic enclaves

Significance: Ethnic enclaves are isolated communities, free from contact from the majority population, that are usually intended to maintain customs and traditions that are under attack by outsiders. Enclaves are usually created by groups that feel oppressed by outside forces.

Ethnic enclaves are territories inhabited by a distinct group of people who are separated from the dominant population by differences in language, religion, social class, or culture and who are frequently subjected to prejudice and discrimination. An ethnic group has a shared history based on a sense of difference from others resulting from several factors, including a unique set of experiences (such as being enslaved or defeated in a war), skin color or other physical differences (such as height), or geography.

Reasons for Formation

Enclaves are established for two major reasons. Some are found in nations and among groups where a distinct sense of injustice exists between peoples. This sense of discrimination prevents communication and results in isolation and a sense of inferiority within the minority group. The dominant group persecutes persons deemed

Patrons examine the produce at a store in San Francisco's Chinatown. Early Chinese immigrants formed ethnic enclaves such as this to lessen the effects of discrimination.

inferior who then withdraw into isolated communities to protect themselves from attack. Enclaves can also be built because of a sense of ethnic superiority, or ethnocentrism. In this case, one group sees itself as being far superior to any others and deliberately separates itself from the rest of society. This self-imposed isolation results from the view that the way of life being lived by group members should not be contaminated by "inferior" outsiders.

Ethnic enclaves result from the failure of groups to accommodate, acculturate, or assimilate. Accommodation is a reduction of conflict among groups as they find ways of living with one another based on mutual respect for differences. Groups maintain their differences but agree to live with one another. In places where enclaves develop, only physical separation lessens conflict: Groups continue to hate and discredit one another but geography keeps them apart. Acculturation, meaning taking over some of the attitudes and beliefs of the other group, fails to take place in these situations because contact between different peoples is rare, and they stick to their traditional values. Instead of becoming more alike, as would be true under the process of assimilation, the groups become more and more different. A common culture fails to develop, and frequently misunderstandings and miscommunication can lead to violent conflicts. It is as if each group lives in a different world, with memories, sentiments, feelings, and attitudes that are totally unknown to the other. The more divergent peoples are or become, the more difficult assimilation will be. This situation is evident among the peoples of southeastern Europe, especially in areas of the former Yugoslavia, such as Bosnia, Croatia, and Serbia. It is also true in African states such as Burundi, Nigeria, and the Union of South Africa.

In a few situations, enclaves develop as a defense against attacks by physically or numerically superior outsiders. If the group does not retreat and separate from the dominant society, it will be annihilated. In this case, cutting off the community from contact with others serves the function of preserving traditions, customs, and beliefs. Most often, this is done by withdrawing into the wilderness beyond the reach of the persecutors. In the United States in the 1840's, members of the Church of Jesus Christ of Latter-day Saints (Mormons) adopted this strategy to save themselves from mob attacks in the East. Brigham Young, the successor to the group's founder Joseph Smith, deliberately chose to settle his people by the Great Salt Lake, then part of Mexico, because it seemed far enough away from the United States that no one would bother them. The Mormons lived in this isolated area free from contact with others well into the 1880's and preserved their distinct religious beliefs.

Development of the Concept

The concept of ethnic identity and ethnic enclaves developed in the 1800's, though different words and phrases such as "immigrant group," "foreign stock," and "race" were used in place of "ethnic." The term "ethnic" was first used by social scientists in the 1920's to differentiate the supposedly less fervent attachments based on language and history in comparison to the supposedly more fundamental biological attachments based on racial inheritance. Many social scientists were interested in the question of how people of different linguistic and historical traditions would become part of modern, specifically American, society. Robert Ezra Park of the University of Chicago developed a theory of intergroup relations based on an inevitable process of contact, competition, accommodation, and, finally, full assimilation. As group members moved upward in the American class system, they would gradually lose their ethnic attachments and ultimately be accepted as true citizens. The more different groups were from the white, Anglo-Saxon, majority, however, the longer and more difficult the process would be (as in the case of American Indians and African Americans). Gunnar Myrdal, the great Swedish sociologist, supported this view in his classic *An American Dilemma* (1944), a study of race relations in the United States. Park's analysis of assimilation has been mostly accepted by sociologists, though Milton Gordon, in *Assimilation in American Life* (1964), pointed out that assimilation takes much longer than has been assumed and is frequently marred by conflict and disorder. Most sociologists and historians writing on the subject since then have agreed with Gordon and have detailed the difficulties experienced by various American ethnic groups. Most observers have agreed that retreating into enclaves is sometimes necessary for group survival but always makes cooperation between groups more difficult. *Leslie V. Tischauser*

Core Resources

Nathan Glazer and Daniel Patrick Moynihan's *Beyond the Melting Pot: The Negroes, Puerto Ricans, Jews, Italians, and Irish of New York City* (Cambridge, Mass.: MIT Press, 1963) is a classic study of the long-term persistence of ethnic identities in the United States. Milton M. Gordon's *Assimilation in American Life* (New York: Oxford University Press, 1964) outlines the factors involved in the process of assimilation. Martin N. Marger's *Race and Ethnic Relations: American and Global Perspectives* (Belmont, Calif.: Wadsworth Press, 1985) surveys ethnic problems from a worldwide perspective.

See also: Accommodationism; Assimilation: cultural and structural; Assimilation theories; Chinatowns; Enclave economies; French Canadians; Internal colonialism; Little Havana; Little Italies; Little Tokyos.

Racial and Ethnic Relations in America

Categorized List of Entries

CHILDHOOD CANCER:

A Nursing Overview

CHILDHOOD CANCER:

A Nursing Overview

Susan K. Maul-Mellott RN, PhD
Assistant Professor
University of Texas Health Science Center
School of Nursing at Houston

Jeanette N. Adams RN, MSN
Assistant Professor
University of Texas Health Science Center
School of Nursing at Houston

Jones and Bartlett Publishers, Inc.
Boston/Monterey

Copyright © 1987 by Jones and Bartlett Publishers, Inc. All rights reserved. No part of the material protected by this copyright notice may be reproduced or utilized in any form, electronic or mechanical, including photocopying, recording, or by any information storage and retrieval system, without written permission from the copyright owner.

Editorial offices: Jones and Bartlett Publishers, Inc., 23720 Spectacular Bid, Monterey, CA 93940.
Sales and customer service offices: Jones and Bartlett Publishers, Inc., 20 Park Plaza, Boston, MA 02116.

Printed in the United States of America
10 9 8 7 6 5 4 3 2 1

Library of Congress Cataloging-in-Publication Data

Maul-Mellott, Susan K.
  Childhood cancer.

  Includes index.
  1. Tumors in children. 2. Tumors in children — Nursing.
I. Adams, Jeanette, RN. II. Title. [DNLM: 1. Neoplasms
— in infancy & childhood. 2. Neoplasms — nursing.
WY 156 M449c]
RC281.C4M38 1987   618.92'992   86-27767

ISBN: 0-86720-381-1

Production Services: Editing, Design & Production, Inc.

Production Editor: Lilliane Chouïnard

Interior Design: Maria Karkucinski

Illustrations: Asterisk Group

Photo Credits: Figs. 2-1, 2-2, 4-8   Photographed by Terri Ingalls
                Fig. 4-9   Len Shalansky

Figure 3-1 is reproduced by permission of the American Cancer Society.
Figure 5-3 is reproduced by permission of Smithers Medical Products, Inc.

The selection and dosage of drugs presented in this book are in accord with standards accepted at the time of publication. The authors and publisher have made every effort to provide accurate information. However, research, clinical practice, and government regulations often change the accepted standard in this field. Before administering any drug, the reader is advised to check the manufacturer's product information sheet for the most up-to-date recommendations on dosage, precautions, and contraindications. This is especially important in the case of drugs that are new or seldom used.

This book is dedicated to the person who is among the most influential in my life. This nurse graduated from Shady Side Hospital in Pittsburgh, PA, in 1942, served in the Army Nurse Corps during World War II, and dedicated her life to helping others. This nurse died in 1981 after a brief bout with cancer. Without her love and encouragement, my career and eventually this book would not have been possible. This book is therefore dedicated to the memory of my mother, Bernice Moody Sandbach.

Susan

And to my mother, Sybil Bishop Nolan, whose love and life taught me the essence of caring for others. Her experience with cancer serves to help others cope triumphantly, as she did.

Jeanette

ALSO OF INTEREST

CANCER NURSING: Principles and Practice
Susan L. Groenwald, RN, MS

After over 8 years in development, there is finally a text that provides comprehensive coverage of oncology from a nursing perspective. With over 40 top
cancer nursing experts as contributors, CANCER NURSING fills the need for an
up-to-date text for students or health professionals involved in the care of
individuals diagnosed with cancer.

A variety of approaches is used to accomplish the editor's goals providing
the most comprehensive review of cancer nursing available. Common clinical
manifestations of cancer are presented in depth. The most striking feature of the
book is the depth provided on the basic science principles and theories that
underlie the care of individuals with cancer. Designed primarily for the specialist
in cancer nursing, this book will be a necessary resource for students and faculty
of undergraduate and graduate oncology courses, clinicians involved in the care
of individuals with cancer, and researchers concerned with issues related to
cancer nursing.

1987, ISBN: 0-86720-351-X, c.a. 1000 pp., cloth

Available directly from the publisher or your local bookseller.

As the number of children living with cancer increases dramatically, so does the likelihood that they will be encountered by nurses and other health-care providers practicing in a variety of settings—general and specialty hospitals, community health clinics, home health services, pediatricians' offices, schools and colleges, sports medicine clinics, and industrial settings. This book will assist these health-care providers to update their knowledge of pediatric oncology in order to comprehensively and knowledgeably plan and implement care for these children and their families.

Growth and development are emphasized throughout the book as the foundations upon which care of a pediatric client and family are based. Various environmental, cultural, and socioeconomic influences, and how they impact the needs of this population, are discussed. Content regarding *specific treatment modalities,* including newly developed *adjunctive therapies,* is presented and indexed for quick reference. Relevant *nursing considerations,* based on comprehensive assessment of the data, are highlighted with specific developmental suggestions. Each chapter is summarized by a listing of the chapter's *Key Points.*

As a care planning guide, this book will prove to be particularly valuable through the use of the *Yellow Pages,* which is a categorization of resource information, various national community resources, and care planning and teaching ideas. It is the authors' intent to improve the quality of care for children with cancer with this useful reference.

CONTENTS

6

ADJUNCTIVE THERAPIES: KEYS TO SURVIVAL 125

7

FAMILY AND INFLUENTIAL OTHERS: WHAT HAPPENS TO THEM? 149

☐ 10

AFTER THE CURE 197

YELLOW PAGES 219

tung

eyes

glasses

mouth

cheaks

nose

ears

hair

every thing you need to
have a happy face!

1

CONSIDERATIONS IN CARING FOR CHILDREN

INTRODUCTION

When assuming a position on a pediatric oncology unit for the first time, a nurse faces a challenge that he or she probably has never encountered before. The magnitude of such a position looms as an iceberg before a sailor. As the new pediatric oncology nurse begins to work with the children with cancer and their families, a major discovery takes place. The nurse rapidly discovers that the experience gained in nursing school was only the tip of the iceberg. There is so much to be learned beyond nursing school, so much hidden from the view of the registered nurse at the basic level. The effects of treatment, the impact of cancer on the child and the family, and the long-term sequelae of childhood cancer, are all factors that influence the nurse when planning care for the child. Thus, there is the need for a compact resource about pediatric oncology nursing — a resource that presents information about the entire child, the family, and the disease. This book has been developed to act as such a resource.

Care of the child with cancer is a complex, overwhelming, but rewarding experience. It takes a basic knowledge of pediatric nursing, of the child's growth and development, and of pediatric oncology nursing, as well as a large amount of compassion, caring, and willingness to share a part of oneself with others. As a result of this experience, the pediatric oncology nurse will grow personally and professionally. She will develop memories and friendships that she will carry with her for the rest of her life.

Cancer is the second leading cause of death in children. In 1983, cancer accounted for 11% of childhood deaths. This percentage, however, is misleading, as the cancer death rate for young men and women has been dropping steadily since 1962. These decreased numbers can be attributed to earlier detection, as well as to better treatments for many types of childhood cancer (American Cancer Society, 1986). The dropping death rate means an increasing number of active patients and long-term survivors, which creates larger and more widespread nursing concerns.

Childhood cancer was first reported in the literature in 1876 by Duzan. At that time, 182 deaths were reported for the period between 1832 and 1875. In the United States in the early 1900s, the United States Death Registration System was established, and by 1933 all of the then 48 states contributed to the system. Even with this registration system, it was not until after World War II that childhood cancer was recognized as a leading cause of death in children under 15 years of age (Fochtman and Foley, 1982).

Current treatment for cancer was slow to develop. Surgery had been the main treatment until recent years. Radiation therapy was added to surgery as a treatment in the 1920s. The use of chemotherapy with pediatric oncology patients did not emerge until the early 1950s (Fochtman and Foley, 1982). Multimodal therapy for childhood cancer is now well established and will be discussed in detail in the following chapters.

HIGH-LEVEL WELLNESS

A current concept in the field of health is "high-level wellness." This concept was identified by Dunn (1977) as the ability of a person to function at the highest level possible in a given environment. According to Dunn, wellness is a continuum on which the individual moves toward a higher level of functioning (Fig. 1-1). The continuum measures not only the physical aspects of a person's wellness, but also other dimensions of wellness, such as the emotional–mental, social, and spiritual dimensions (Fig. 1-2). Therefore, an individual can be at a higher level of wellness in one dimension than in others. This concept illustrates effectively the need for an individualized interdisciplinary team approach with each child being treated for cancer.

Low
Level

High
Level

FIG. 1-1. Functioning continuum

TEAM CONCEPT

The interdisciplinary team approach utilizes different members of the health team based on the needs of the child and family. The child and family are at the center of any team (Fig. 1-3). The child must be aware of the diagnosis and must be an active participant in the care. If the truth is hidden from the child, any level of trust in others may be shattered if the child should learn about the disease by accident — other children may be overheard, a member of the team may "slip" and say something to the child, or the child may simply read the name of the hospital on the building. The family is the core in which the child functions and thus serves as a great support to the child and significant others.

Other major members of the team include the nurse and the physician. In many cases the physician will remain the major member of the team whether the child is an inpatient or an outpatient. In most institutions the nursing personnel will vary depending on where the patient is being treated.

There is no better place than here to emphasize the importance of communication. It is essential for inpatient and outpatient nurses to communicate with each other concerning the needs of the child and the family. The inpatient nurses are able to observe the child 24 hours a day, which gives them more insights concerning the child than the outpatient nurses may have. On the other hand, outpatient nurses see the child in a more natural state, coming from home or school.

The clinical nurse specialist is the vital link between these groups of nurses. She has access to the patient and family on both an inpatient and outpatient basis, and she can coordinate the care of the child, as well as facilitate communication between all the team members.

Other members of the team who participate

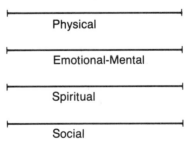

Physical

Emotional-Mental

Spiritual

Social

FIG. 1-2. Dimensions of wellness.

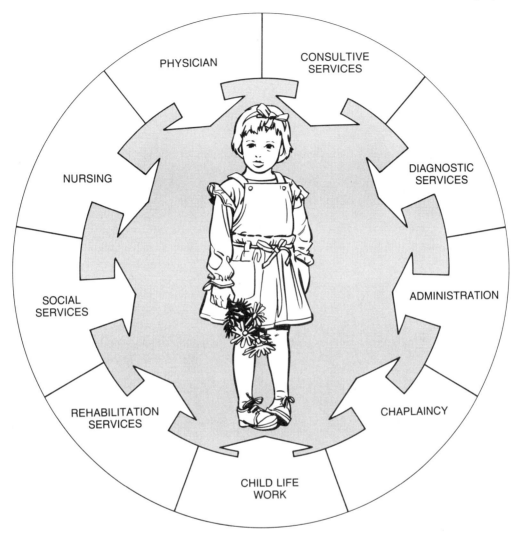

FIG. 1-3. Team approach.

[From Dr. Jan van Eys, Chairman, Dept. of Pediatrics, M. D. Anderson Hospital, Houston, TX]

on both an inpatient and outpatient basis include the psychologist, the social worker, the child life worker, the dietitian, the chaplain, the occupational therapist, and the physical therapist. Some members of the team should function more either on an inpatient or on an outpatient basis, and each member should participate with the team based on the needs of the child. Many hospitals have schoolteachers who communicate with the child's hometown teacher in order to keep the child current with school work. On an outpatient basis, the school nurse, the teacher, the local physician, community nurses, and other community agencies may be involved with the team. The specific roles of these team members in the case of the child with cancer will be further discussed throughout the chapters that follow.

NORMAL GROWTH AND DEVELOPMENT

To fully understand the different types of childhood cancer and their effects on the child and on the family, a nurse needs a working knowledge of normal growth and development during childhood. A nurse also must be able to understand the normal child in order to understand how the child with cancer can be helped to cope with this illness. Growth and development, as explained by developmental theorists, as well as the development of body image and play, are such important topics that they deserve a complete discussion.

Traditionally, discussions of growth and development utilize standard age groupings: infant (0 – 1 year); toddler (1 – 2 years); preschool (3 – 5 years); school-age (6 – 11 years); and adolescent and young adult (12 – 21 years). Growth and development are considered as a unit since they are simultaneous, ongoing processes. *Growth* means an increase in the number and size of cells, measured quantitatively in terms of height, weight, and the like. *Development* refers to the increase in skills resulting from mastery of a series of smaller tasks. *Maturation,* which is often considered along with growth and development, is described as aging, or the increase in competence and adaptability that allows the child to function at a higher level. Both development and maturation are qualitative changes that occur along with the quantitative growth changes.

Ordinarily, growth and development occur as an orderly, sequential process, progressing in three directions. Development proceeds first from the general to the specific. For example, an infant makes general "cooing" sounds before language develops; gross motor activities, such as walking, precede the fine motor activities, such as fastening buttons. The second direction is cephalocaudal, or head-to-toe. Infants gain control of their head and neck muscles before they gain control of the trunk and extremities. The third direction is proximodistal, or near-to-far. The infant, for example, will reach for an object before the fingers have developed the control to hold the object.

During the process of growth and development, children pass through successive stages. Each stage is affected by the preceding stage, and it will affect the stage to follow. There are critical periods in development when an environmental event will have a maximum effect on the process. There seems to be an opportune time to learn a skill. Crawling, for example, is learned by the infant at approximately 6 months of age. Crawling can be learned at a later time, but the child will encounter more difficulty mastering it. There is no fixed or steady pace of development. Instead, there are periods of accelerated and decelerated growth, such as during an adolescent growth spurt. Factors that are known to influence the growth and development of a child include heredity, environment, illness, and the child's unique individuality.

Four developmental theorists are frequently quoted throughout the literature: Sigmund Freud, Erik Erikson, Jean Piaget, and Lawrence Kohlberg. Their theories are outlined in Table 1-1 to provide an overview of the developmental process.

FREUD'S THEORY OF PSYCHOSEXUAL DEVELOPMENT

Sigmund Freud defined the child's development in terms of sexuality. He described the newborn child as having powerful instinctual drives, based on desires for pleasure and physical gratification, called *libido.* Libido is satisfied by stimulation of various parts of the body at certain periods in life (Whitehurse & Vasta, 1977). During the course of development, the libido operates from the oral, anal, phallic, and genital areas (Teung, 1982).

In the *oral stage* (birth to 1 year), the mouth is the principal site of gratification, and the infant's libido needs are satisfied through sucking.

According to Freud, overindulgence in sucking can lead to dependence and optimism in the adult, whereas frustration of sucking needs can lead to suspiciousness and pessimism.

In the *anal stage* (1 to 3 years), the anal region becomes the source of gratification. Toilet training is a source of conflict in this stage. The child may "hold back" stool, or "let it go," in order to gain control over the parents. If toilet training is early and harsh, the child may grow up to have patterns of aggressiveness and miserliness; if it is delayed and easy, the child may develop patterns of generosity as an adult.

In the *phallic stage* (3 to 5½ years), the genital area is the source of gratification. The boy focuses on his penis, while the girl focuses on her clitoris. The child also focuses on the parent of the opposite sex as an object of his or her erotic wishes. This is commonly called the Oedipus complex. Failure to resolve this conflict successfully through identification with the parent of the same sex may lead to sexual uncertainty, narcissism, and guilt.

The *latency stage* (5½ years to puberty) is a period during which the libido is dormant. No part of the body derives sexual satisfaction during this period because of the repression of sexual feelings from the phallic stage. This dormancy allows the child to form relationships with children of similar age and sex.

In the *genital stage* (at puberty) the sexual impulses break through again, and the genital zone becomes once again the site of gratification. The youth must have successfully completed all the previous stages before this stage can be reached and normal adult sexual choices can be undertaken.

ERIKSON'S THEORY OF PSYCHO-SOCIAL DEVELOPMENT

Erikson describes development as the progress through defined psychosocial stages, each of which requires specific tasks to be mastered for successful and healthy progression to and throughout adulthood (Gohsman, 1981). Erikson describes eight stages of psychosocial development; the first five stages occur during childhood, and the last three stages occur during adulthood.

Erikson believes the child in infancy establishes either a sense of trust or a sense of mistrust. If the child's needs are met consistently, he or she develops a sense of trust in others and himself. Any deviation from the usual that does not have a pleasurable outcome leads toward a sense of mistrust (Scipien, 1986; Teung, 1982). Erikson proposes that an infant develops mistrust when basic needs are not met or there is a lack of trust-promoting experiences.

In the toddler stage, the child strives to establish a sense of autonomy and to avoid shame and doubt, and to gain self-control without losing self-esteem. During this stage, the child begins to learn to control his or her behavior. The toddler has quick mood changes and wants and needs to be assertive, but is often afraid to be. The toddler needs sympathetic guidance and graduated support. If the child is led repeatedly to believe that his or her actions are unacceptable or ineffective, shame and self-doubt will emerge. A strong sense of trust developed in the previous stage, however, allows the child to try again.

The preschooler is faced with the tasks of learning initiative and avoiding a sense of guilt, since at this stage the child begins to develop a conscience. Physical and social worlds are eagerly explored by the preschooler, who is intrusive, asks endless questions, makes many noises, and is constantly exploring the environment both physically and intellectually. Guilt easily develops due to the limits that must be placed on the child, who feels that many actions are unacceptable to the people he or she is trying to please. Since the superego is developing, the child also may disapprove of his or her own actions. These feelings are often carried over into the child's dreams and fantasies.

TABLE 1-1. THEORIES OF CHILD DEVELOPMENT

	Infant (0–1 yr)	Toddler (1–2 yrs)	Preschool (3–5 yrs)	School Age (6–11 yrs)	Adolescent (12–21 yrs)
Freud Psychosexual Development	Oral stage	Anal stage	Phallic stage	Latency period	Genital stage
Erikson Psychosocial Development	Trust vs mistrust	Autonomy vs shame and doubt	Initiative vs guilt	Industry vs inferiority	Identity vs role diffusion
Piaget Cognitive Development	Sensorimotor phase Reflexes (0–1 mo) Primary circular reactions (1–4 mo) Secondary circular reactions (4–8 mo)	Coordination of secondary schemata (8–12 mo) Tertiary circular reactions (12–18 mo) Inventions of new means (18–24 mo)	Preconceptual phase	Intuitive thought (4–7 years) Phase of concrete operations (7–11 years)	Phase of formal operations
Kohlberg Moral Development	Preconventional level Stage 1 Punishment and obedience	Stage 2 Gain rewards from others	Conventional level Stage 1 Interpersonal harmony Approval of others	Stage 2 Law and order Established rules	

The school-age child combines all the previously learned skills and strives toward a sense of industry and away from a sense of inferiority, concentrating on those skills that will be needed to function in an adult world. The child focuses on reality and wider social interactions. The threat of failure can lead the child to a sense of inferiority and inadequacy.

The adolescent has the task of developing a sense of identity and avoiding role confusion. The adolescent identifies with others, such as heroes, rock groups, group leaders, and so on, in an attempt to establish a personal identity while striving to become separate from his or her family and its value system. Attitudes and behaviors become unpredictable as the adolescent tries to establish his or her own value system. There is a strong preoccupation with body image, and role confusion develops from the many behaviors and roles the adolescent has to choose from and from the rapid changes occurring in his or her self-perception.

The young adult proceeds to the stage of intimacy versus isolation in which there is the task of developing love and friendship with others. Most of the adult years are spent in the stage of generativity (productivity and satisfaction), rather than stagnation (lack of productivity).

The final adult stage, however, is one Erikson calls integrity versus despair. Here the adult is either happy with life (integrity) or disturbed by the lack of meaning in life and a dread of dying (despair).

PIAGET'S THEORY OF COGNITIVE DEVELOPMENT

Piaget's theory is concerned with the order of change in the child's intellectual functioning, rather than in the mastery of skills. Piaget proposes that an interaction with the environment can either be assimilated into an existing structure or that the structure can accommodate the new event. He further believes that the child's cognitive abilities are constructed by the child in step-by-step interactions with the environment.

In Piaget's theory, the first of five developmental phases is the *sensorimotor phase* (birth to 2 years). In this phase, the child learns to relate to the environment using motor skills. Piaget describes six successive stages the child progresses through during this phase. In the first stage (birth to 1 month), the child uses reflexes to perceive the environment. During the second stage (1 to 4 months), the child's perceptions of events center around the body. In the third stage (4 to 8 months), the child begins to acknowledge the external environment. From 8 to 12 months, the child begins to develop the concept of means–end relationships. The means–end relationship is constantly being applied during the 12 to 18-month period, which leads to the sixth stage (19 to 24 months), when the child begins to interpret experiences by mental image. By this time, object permanence has emerged (Teung, 1982; Whitehurst, 1977).

The next phase, the *preconceptual phase,* occurs from 2 to 4 years of age. During this phase, the child is largely egocentric. All the events of the child's life revolve around the child, and he assumes others understand what he is saying and what he is thinking. Play becomes the means by which the child adapts (Teung, 1982; Whitehurst, 1977).

The phase of *intuitive thought* (4 to 7 years) is an extension of the previous phase. The child is still subjective, but the egocentric nature is beginning to diminish. Thought processes tend to focus on one idea at a time, rather than form a chain of ideas (Teung, 1982).

During the phase of *concrete operations* (7 to 11 years), the child begins to expand widely his cognitive abilities. During this phase the child can classify (a geranium and a rose are both flowers), can conserve (two glasses have the same amount of milk even though they are shaped differently), can order items (arranging them according to size), can communicate socially (alter rules so others can play a game), and can understand reversibility (understands that a clay animal was made from a ball of clay). The child has a good understanding of the relationship of parts to a whole, the hierarchy of classes, and systems of classification. The child also begins to reason inductively (Teung, 1982; Whitehurst, 1977).

In the last phase, *formal operations* (beginning at 11 years of age), the child uses rational thinking that is deductive and futuristic. A child in this phase systematically analyzes all the possible answers to a problem (Teung, 1982; Whitehurst, 1977).

KOHLBERG'S THEORY OF MORAL DEVELOPMENT

Kohlberg postulates three levels, each consisting of two stages, which the child passes through during moral development (Murray and Zenterr, 1979; Kolbe, 1981). Kohlberg proposes that these stages are universal regardless of cultural conditions. The *preconventional level* begins with the toddler in stage one. During stage one, the toddler is functioning on the basis of punishment and obedience. The toddler is egocentric and focuses all actions in terms of the self. In stage two of the preconventional level, young preschoolers are still egocentric, but are beginning to consider occasionally how their actions may affect others.

The second level is called the *conventional level*. The school-age child at stage one of this level bases action on the approval of others. The child in this stage tries to conform to group norms and is very aware of the feelings of others. Stage two brings about the desire for established rules from people in authority. Law and order are valued, and decisions are made based on guilt and fear. Some adults do not progress past this stage (Kolbe, 1981).

The third level is called the *postconventional level*. During stage one of the third level, the person tries to gain the respect of an individual or a community by developing a morality of contracts, individual rights, and democracy. In stage two, the person develops a morality based on self-respect and respect for others.

Although these theories address different aspects of development, they all occur simultaneously and, thus, are interrelated, as can be demonstrated in the following discussion.

ADOLESCENT DEVELOPMENT

Adolescence is a unique age. The development of the adolescent is divided into three phases, early adolescence (12 to 13 years old), middle adolescence (14 to 16 years old), and late adolescence (17 to 19 years old) (Nelms, 1981). In early adolescence, identity begins to change as the adolescent becomes more assertive, seeks more independence, spends less time with the family, and relies less on family members for approval and acceptance. Adolescents in this age group also are insecure, seem self-centered and egocentric, and exhibit behavior changes, as they begin to experiment with their own belief systems.

Adolescents in the middle phase are moving toward a new identity, which is determined largely by their peers. Adolescents in this phase strive to be like their friends and to avoid isolation. When with peers, adolescents are free to explore a variety of behaviors and appearances, which allows them to prove themselves through appearance and high-risk behaviors, and to develop their own beliefs and individuality.

During late adolescence, new identity becomes well established. Adolescents in this group are gradually losing dependency on the peer group and thus become aware of their own strengths and weaknesses. Adolescents in this phase make choices about their futures, their educations, and their occupations. Independence increases as the adolescent makes more and more decisions, but full independence is rarely achieved during this phase.

BODY IMAGE

As with other growth and developmental aspects, the child's body image also follows an orderly, sequential path as the child grows. Body image is defined as the mental picture a person has of his or her body. It includes the person's perception of bodily functions, sensations, and mobility. There is a constant, but gradual, change as the child grows (Griffiths, 1980).

Newborns have a global, diffuse image of their bodies. Infants come to know their bodies through tactile and kinesthetic sensations, visual perceptions, and self-generated actions. The two body parts of particular importance to the infant are the mouth and the hands. By utilizing these body parts, the infant can explore the body and the environment.

Toddlers try to discover who they are in relation to their environment, and how to manage the environment and the body. The toddler does not have a sense of defined body boundaries. Feces, for example, are perceived as a viable part of the child; thus, toilet training can be psychologically difficult for the child.

The preschooler is busy exploring the environment. During this stage, the child's interest changes from body processes to body surfaces. The area of the body of special interest to the child this age is the genital area. Preschoolers are frequently found fondling their genitals. Depending on parental attitudes, the child's images of the body and its parts will vary. The child may feel that the genitalia are clean or dirty, pleasing or repulsive, good or bad, loved or disliked, and all of these feelings can be carried over into the adult years.

The school-age child begins to perceive specific body parts. At this age a child can apply concrete cognitive concepts to the parts of the body, which are viewed in terms of their uses and sensations. The early school-age child (8 to 9 years old) views the body as a hollow organ filled with food at intervals and emptied at other times, whereas the skin is viewed as holding the body together, protecting everything inside. Peer acceptance becomes an important aspect of the school age child's body image. This need for peer acceptance intensifies as the child reaches the age of adolescence.

An important focus of adolescents' attention is their developing sexual characteristics and growth spurt. They become quite aware of others' opinions and are highly sensitive to any physical impairment or body disfigurement.

PLAY

Play develops similarly to the developmental aspects already discussed. Play is a child's work. Through play children can rearrange the world to suit their needs, and they receive much self-satisfaction from the mastery of these experiences.

Play is utilized by children in many ways. Imaginative play is used by the child to assimilate reality and strive toward self-realization. It is used as a way to control stress and to express, in an acceptable form, that which cannot be expressed otherwise. Play is used by children as a means to master anxiety, as enjoyment, as a

form of communication, and as an attempt to master the environment. How a child plays, however, varies depending upon his or her age and development (Table 1-2) (Teung, 1982).

The infant is stimulated through eye contact, verbal interactions, and touch. Infants like games with simple movements and music. "Peek-a-boo" games allow the infant to gain a sense of trust and confidence that parents will reappear after having been gone. "Pat-a-cake" and "bye-bye" games begin to involve the infant as an active participant in the play, and games such as "This little pig" and "How big?" enhance the infant's awareness of the body. Both active toys, such as busy boxes, and passive toys, such as soft stuffed animals, are appropriate toys. During this stage of solitary play, there is no preference for playmates of the same or opposite sex. In fact, since play is self-centered and individualistic, physical aggression is common when another child is around. The purpose of the infant's play is simply to learn more about himself, and interference from others is not tolerated.

In infancy, the child's play is based initially on stimuli presented by someone else. Play stimuli should be presented based on the child's development from head to toe and from the center of the body outward. Play behaviors become rituals to the child, and consistency in these play rituals becomes important.

The toddler begins to utilize parallel play (children play along side of each other, but not together). When toddlers do interact, fighting is common as one toddler attempts to take toys away from the other. The toddler needs activities such as playing with pull toys to foster the mastery of mobility. The toddler also loves being read to and told stories; favorite stories often are requested frequently. (Sounds and names of objects are learned easily when they come from a story). A toddler has a short attention span and will move from one play experience to another after a brief time interval. Because of this short attention span and the

TABLE 1-2. PLAY DEVELOPMENT

	Social Nature of Play	Activities	Toys
Infant	Solitary play	Peek-a-boo Pat-a-cake Bye-bye This little pig How big?	Crib devices Busy box Stuffed animals
Toddler	Parallel play	Story telling Reading to child Finger paint Water play	Pull toys Stacking toys Hammer toys
Preschooler	Cooperative play	Finger paint Water play Hide and seek Simon says Dress up Story telling Reading to child Games played to music	Tricycle Wagon Push/pull toys Balls Dolls Blocks Large wooden puzzles Scene toys (hospital, dollhouse)
School-age	Cooperative play → Competitive play	Hobbies Crafts Competitive sports Musical instruments Tag, hopscotch Jump rope Clubs	Board games Puzzles Books Records
Adolescent	Competitive play → Adult play	Parties Dances Listening to music Reading Sports "Sex" games (spin the bottle, post office)	Chess Backgammon Electronic games Pool Ping-Pong

toddler's new mobility, the child must be closely supervised, and a safe play environment is a necessity. Toys with small removable parts that could be easily swallowed should be avoided. Because the toddler strives for a sense of autonomy and mastery over stressful situations, water play and finger painting are acceptable ways to express frustration.

During the preschool years, the child begins to move from parallel play to cooperative play. Playmates begin to become "helpers," and the preschooler wants to be with others, as well as to play alone from time to time. Toys such as tricycles and push/pull toys, which utilize the muscles in the extremities, are important for this age group, and finger painting and water play continue to be important activities. Fantasy and make-believe also are an integral part of the preschooler's play. It is through make-believe that the preschooler begins to model roles of significant adults. Preschoolers also use play to combine reality and imagination through the use of stories and environmental toys, such as doll houses, hospitals, and farms. Group games, especially those that involve music, are enjoyed by the preschooler. Games enable the child to learn new skills and to take turns.

The early school-age child (6 to 8 years old) is involved in cooperative play, which proceeds to group and competitive play. During early school-age, the child strives to be with others of the same age and sex and is willing to postpone immediate gratification of needs. As competitive play develops, others are seen as partners, and acceptable behaviors for winning and losing develop. Board games that enhance a child's eye – hand coordination and fine motor control, such as Candyland and Mousetrap, are well liked by children of this age. In older school-age children, games of chance and skill, such as Monopoly and Checkers, should be offered. The school-age child has a strong urge to win and enjoys choosing games to play. Hobbies and collections begin to interest the child at this time. Today baseball cards have given way to stickers, which are easily traded. Crafts are also of interest now, and competitive sports take on increasing importance. Other play activities enjoyed by this age group include puzzles, records, reading books, coloring, and drawing. Musical instruments also create an interest for the school-age child, but the amount of interest of the child may differ from that of the parent, which frequently results in battles over practice of an instrument. As the school-age child adds more importance to activities with others outside the family, other group activities develop. Scouting and other formal clubs are frequently a means of gaining independence from adults. Other activities of common interest to this group include tag, hopscotch, jump rope, and gymnastics.

During adolescence, group activities, such as parties and dances, take on increasing importance. During early adolescence, peers of the same sex attend activities together, and dating usually begins toward the end of this period. Play activities become more and more like those of adults. Games such as chess, which require patience and concentration, become popular. As heterosexual relationships develop, so do beginning sexual games, such as "spin-the-bottle" and "post office". Despite these group activities, the adolescent still requires time alone to form an identity of his own.

This development of play is important to the health care worker, since play can be utilized to help the child cope with illness, as will be discussed in the next chapter.

BOOK OVERVIEW

It is important to maintain this knowledge of normal growth and development throughout any discussion of childhood cancer. With cure rates increasing, more children are surviving their disease and can become productive adults if normal growth and development is facilitated. The World Health Organization (WHO) defines health as "a state of complete physical, emotional, and social wellbeing, not merely the absence of disease or infirmity." The WHO further describes optimal health as "the attainment by people of the highest possible level of health" (Bedworth & Bedworth, 1978). It is important for all who are involved with the child to strive for this level of optimal health throughout the treatment process. Each of the following chapters will emphasize the growth and developmental aspects of the child that influence the child's ability to obtain an optimal level of health and well-being.

As the reader progresses through the remainder of this book, the developmental and team concepts will be emphasized and re-emphasized as dictated by the topics being discussed. The common types of childhood cancer will be discussed in terms of their pathology, occurrence, primary sites, presenting signs and symptoms, usual treatment, and survival rates. Treatment modalities, such as chemotherapy, radiation, and surgery, will be expanded upon, as will hospitalization and adjunctive therapies. The latter half of the book turns toward the psychosocial needs of the child, the family, and significant others. Coping methodologies, cultural norms, community support systems, and re-entry into the school and community are all topics that will be addressed. The last chapters discuss the needs of the child and the family when death becomes imminent or, if the child survives, the long-term effects of cancer and its treatment. Death is a difficult, but necessary, topic to discuss in relation to the child with cancer. Unfortunately, in the past large numbers of children have not survived their cancer, so statistics are not available yet on possible long-term sequelae.

The authors hope that through the use of this text the reader may develop a well-rounded approach to the care of the child with cancer. With the physical and psychosocial needs of the child and the family being addressed, the nurse can form a basis for a nursing care plan tailored to each patient. Through this holistic approach, the child will benefit whether he is in the nurse's care for 1 day, 1 week, 1 month, or longer.

KEY POINTS

- Care of the child with cancer is a complex, overwhelming, but rewarding experience.
- Cancer is the second leading cause of death in children.
- The high-level wellness continuum allows a person to function at the highest level possible in a given environment.
- High-level wellness contains physical, emotional–mental, social, and spiritual dimensions.
- The child and the family are the center of the interdisciplinary team of health-care workers.
- The nurse must understand the normal child in order to understand how the child with cancer can cope with this chronic illness.
- Growth and development occur as an orderly, sequential process.
- Developmental theorists frequently quoted are Sigmund Freud (psychosexual development), Erik Erikson (psychosocial development), Jean Piaget (cognitive development), and Lawrence Kohlberg (moral development).
- Adolescence is a unique age that progresses through three phases of development, while incorporating principles from previous stages of growth and development.
- Knowledge of the development of body image and the use of play is important in dealing with children with cancer.
- It is important for all who are involved in treating children with cancer to strive for a level of optimal health throughout the treatment process.

REFERENCES

American Cancer Society. (1986). CA: *A Cancer Journal for Clinicians, 34,* 24.

Bedworth, D., and Bedworth, A. (1978). *Health education: a process for human effectiveness* (pp. 26–27). New York: Harper & Row.

Dunn, H. (1977). *High level wellness* (pp. 4–5). Thorofare, NJ: Charles B. Slack.

Fochtman, D., and Foley, G. (1982). *Nursing care of the child with cancer.* Boston: Little, Brown and Company.

Gohsman, B. (1981). The hospitalized child's need for mastery. *Issues in Comprehensive Pediatric Nursing, 5,* 67–76.

Griffiths, S. (1980). Changes in body image caused by antineoplastic drugs. *Issues in Comprehensive Nursing, 4,* 17–28.

Kolbe, L., *et al.* (1981). Propositions for an alternate and complementary health education paradigm. *Health Education, 12,* 29.

Murray, R., and Zenter, J. (1979). *Nursing assessment and health promotion through the life span.* Englewood Cliffs, NJ: Prentice-Hall.

Nelms, B. (1981).What is a normal adolescent? *MCN, 6,* 402–406.

Scipien, G., Barnard, M., Chard, M., Howe, J. and Phillips, P. (1986). *Comprehensive pediatric nursing.* New York: McGraw-Hill.

Steele, S. (1983) *Health promotion of the child with long-term illness* (p. 18). East Norwalk: Appleton-Century-Crofts.

Teung, A. (1982). *Growth and development: a self-mastery approach* (p. 35). East Norwalk: Appleton-Century-Crofts.

Whaley, L., and Wong, D. (1982). *Nursing care of infants and children* (p. 47). St. Louis: C. V. Mosby.

Whitehurst, G., and Vasta, R. (1977). *Child behavior* (p. 13). Boston: Houghton Mifflin Co.

When Well 9 years

the
cub scout

in the hospitail.

Oh no!

Sick

2

EFFECTS OF ILLNESS, HOSPITALIZATION, AND SURGERY

INTRODUCTION

Any illness causes a crisis for the patient, the family, and significant others, especially when the patient is a child. Children constantly are attempting to master new skills and tasks. To add a set of tasks as large as those that accompany a chronic illness such as cancer often delays, or even stops, the normal development of a child. In this chapter we will discuss by age groups the effects of a chronic illness on a child's development, including the effects of hospitalization and surgery. The traditional age groups of infant (0 to 1 year), toddler (1 to 2 years), preschool (3 to 5 years), school age (6 to 11 years), and adolescent or young adult (12 to 21 years) will be utilized throughout the discussion.

It is difficult to separate the effects of illness and the effects of hospitalization on the child. An attempt will be made to do just that, however, since many children with cancer are being treated as outpatients. The effects of any illness on a child will be discussed first, followed by the specific effects of cancer and the effects of hospitalization. Comments on helping the child to cope with hospitalization, the use of play, surgery and its effects on the child, and, finally, the effects of pain and methods for its relief are also presented.

EFFECTS OF ILLNESS ON THE CHILD

The way that a child perceives illness is based on the child's age and past experiences with illness, the responses of the family members, the onset, nature, and extent of the illness, the amount of limitation the illness causes, the treatment, and the prognosis. Other factors include environmental conditions, culture, seasons such as holidays, sex, intelligence level, and ordinal position of the child.

Research dating back as far as 1951 demonstrates two theories held by children about the cause of illness. Before 10 years of age children usually perceive illness as punishment. After 10 years of age the "germ theory" is the general framework for the cause of illness. Studies also demonstrate that multiple causality of illness is not understood until the child is approximately 12 years old (Wood, 1983).

ILLNESS AS PUNISHMENT

Studies completed by Gips and Gellert (cited in Wood, 1983) demonstrated that younger children blamed outside forces for their illness, and older children blamed themselves. Wood determined that whether or not children blame themselves for their illness was not a factor of age but rather of gender; males hold this belief more than females. Young children frequently blame their parents for the lack of protection from illness. Young children also interpret illness as punishment for bad thoughts. For example, a young child may wish a parent harm while being spanked. When illness occurs the child feels guilty about those thoughts and believes the illness is a punishment for such thoughts. Isolation of the child often is perceived as further punishment (Steele, 1983). Parents can contribute to this misconception of illness as punishment by innocently saying, "You had better stop that or you'll get hurt and have to go see the doctor and get a shot." Comments such as this increase the child's fantasies about the cause of illness and injury. Varma (cited in Wood, 1983) further suggests that hospitalization before 3 years of age may affect a child's later perceptions of illness as being punitive in nature, even though the child may not consciously remember the experience.

GERM THEORY

Children who believe in the germ theory have various levels of understanding about the theory. In the Wood study (1983) the children's predominant concept was that the very presence of viruses or bacteria caused immediate illness. They had no understanding of normal flora or germs, and an incomplete understanding of the concept of "host defenses." Because of such beliefs, the child often feels helpless when confronted with an illness.

OTHER DEVELOPMENTAL PERCEPTIONS

Adolescents may perceive illness as a threat to their body image. Illness causes dependence, lack of control, separation from peers, and interruption of daily routines. These factors influence the development of the adolescent, who is

striving for independence and identity. Frequently, adolescents experience regression and depersonalization due to their illnesses.

Infants rarely perceive changes of any significance in their body functions. As the child grows and gains control of various body functions, loss of these functions alters the child's self-image. It is frustrating to the child, for example, when a leg cast is applied after the child learns to crawl, walk, or run. In addition, the preschooler has a high fear of mutilation. Illnesses that involve the genital area are frequently associated with fears of castration.

The way that a child perceives illness affects the way that a child perceives the treatment of the illness. The child understands illness better when there is physical evidence of it, such as diarrhea or vomiting. The intensity of the symptoms also affects the child's response. However, the intensity of the treatment is not always consistent with the child's perception of the treatment. In a child's mind, often a Band-Aid is all that's needed to fix a cut, even if the cut is severe.

Many treatments force a child's mind to become very active and to form fantasies. Imagery and relaxation often help to dispel those fantasies. Painful treatments are often misunderstood by the child, who seldom sees the need to have more pain inflicted than the illness itself creates. Shots are a good example of such treatments. If continued treatments disrupt a child's socialization, the child can develop poor perceptions of the treatment. The child therefore needs help to understand the relationship of the treatment to the illness and to be prepared for the treatments so that he or she perceives them accurately and tolerates them better.

THE CHILD WITH CANCER

The effect of cancer on the child often can become overwhelming. Brodie (1974) has shown that a child with cancer has more overall anxiety than a healthy child. Bluebond-Langer (1978) demonstrated that even if children aren't told, most children are aware of the seriousness of their illness. Research also has found that if children can be allowed to express their anxieties about their diseases, they are better able to internalize and accept the extent of the illness (De Christopher, 1981).

Weisman (1979) observes that patients and families who are coping with the crisis of cancer are at high risk for anxiety and worry about 2 to 3 months after the initial diagnosis. Lederer (1952) feels that another time of high anxiety for the child and family is during the beginning of treatment, when the patient is entering into the unknown or partially understood.

There are periods of body image changes for any child with cancer. The first phase is during the diagnosis period (Griffiths, 1980). The child can no longer trust how his or her body will operate and function. The body becomes disorganized and seems a threat to the child's integrity. Negative feelings about the entire body may exist if the disease is not located in one body part, but rather is dispersed throughout the body as with leukemia. The second phase is when the child and the family are told of the child's prognosis. Children with a poor prognosis have more devastating alterations in their body images than do children with a good prognosis, because they are affected by the threat of death and separation.

Much work has been done on the effect of cancer on the adolescent patient. Kellerman and colleagues (1980) studied the effect of chronic illness on the adolescent's anxiety levels, self-esteem, and locus of control. A group of normal adolescents was compared with a group of adolescents with chronic illnesses. Kellerman found no significant differences between the healthy adolescents and the chronically ill adolescents in terms of their trait anxiety (the stable component of personality resistant to situational fluctuation) and their self-esteem. Kellerman concluded, however, that a diagnosis of certain types of serious or chronic diseases was associated with a reduction of the adolescent's sense of control over the future as it related to his or her health.

In a second study Kellerman found that ill adolescents stated that their freedom and popularity were frequently disrupted by their disease. Female adolescents felt more of an impact from their disease in this respect than males felt. In all chronically ill adolescents the higher the impact of the illness, the higher the anxiety and the lower their self-esteem. Specifically, adolescents with cancer reported that most of their problems were due to the treatment, which frequently was perceived as worse than the disease; the treatments created general problems as well as affected their body image. These adolescents reported greater illness-related disruption of body image and schooling than did the healthy adolescents. They also expressed more illness-induced family disruption than did adolescents with other illnesses (Zeltzer, 1980).

Hayes (1980) stated that patients in an Adolescent Oncology Unit at Roswell Park Memorial Institute were concerned about their futures, their loss of independence, and their fear of rejection. Frequently used defense mechanisms were denial, intellectualizing, and overcompensation as means to cope with their fears.

In an observational study at the Young Adult Program at the Center for Attitudinal Healing, Dunlop (1982) identified six major problem areas specific to adolescents with cancer. The first problem area is uncertainty about the future. Adolescents with this problem may develop "I don't care" attitudes, resentment toward well friends, avoidance of returning to school or job, or wheelspinning behavior, where there is planning but nothing is carried out. The second problem area is identification with the illness and the sick role. When this problem develops the adolescent values the dependency, attention, and power resulting from the illness. The patient may even try not to get well in order to retain security derived from the sick role. A third problem area is negative risk taking. The most common negative risks used by adolescents include the use of drugs and the deliberate avoidance of treatments. These negative risk behaviors allow the adolescent to exert some control over his or her life.

Fourth in the problem areas identified by Dunlop is that, to the adolescent, illness and death are unexpected life events. Having had little preparation for these events, the adolescent cancer patient knows no way to communicate about them. Factors that determine the adolescent's success in coping with these events include previous experiences, family communication patterns, belief systems, and support systems. The fifth problem area is independence – dependence conflicts with parents. These conflicts are intensified and complicated by the adolescent's development of cancer, and the more independent the adolescent was before the diagnosis of cancer, the more difficult it will be for him or her to accept dependency. The resulting frustration is frequently expressed as moodiness, secretiveness, resentfulness, and out and out rages and attacks. The last problem area identified by Dunlop is that of the adolescent feeling different. Physical changes due to the illness and treatment cause anxiety. Frequently social isolation occurs when friends stay away because they don't know what to say, and often the adolescent will develop feelings of worthlessness, anger, depression, and frustration.

One aspect of body image affected by cancer and frequently "forgotten" in terms of adolescents, is sexuality. The treatment of cancer may cause permanent secondary changes that are not easy for the adolescent to accept. The female may have the development of her secondary sex characteristics altered to include delayed menarche or amenorrhea. Males may

become sterile due to the effect of the treatments on the testes. These changes not only affect the adolescent's body image but also the ability to have sexual intercourse, the ability to carry or father a child, and the affections of a sexual partner.

Other results of cancer treatment that affect body image include alopecia, weight fluctuations, and disfiguring surgery. These problems are discussed at other points in this book.

THE EFFECTS OF HOSPITALIZATION ON THE CHILD

Hospitalization affects children of different ages in many ways. It creates the threat of the strange and unknown, the possibility of surprise, loss of control, additional tasks for children to master, and long-term effects for the child. Petrillo and Sanger (1980) state eleven concerns of the child who requires hospitalization: an imperfect body; the degree of illness to require hospitalization; threatened or real separation; spending time with unfamiliar people; difficulty maintaining contact with siblings and peers; possible painful procedures; feelings of guilt toward self or parents for hospitalization; unfamiliar routines and environment; placement of parents in a helpless role; the need for the child to be in a dependent role; and the need to relate to health professionals who may appear frightening.

In the 1950s, Robertson identified a three-staged process for the hospitalized child: protest; despair; and finally detachment. Conclusions from other studies in this area include: (1) Hospitalization does tend to have negative effects; (2) the effects seem to be the greatest between the ages of 7 months and 5 years; (3) illness itself appears to be disturbing; (4) hospitalization for over 1 week that occurs under 5 years of age appears to have very long-term effects; and (5) many children are not disturbed by the hospitalization experience (King, 1981;

Nadler, 1983; Vernon, Foley, Sipowitz, and Schulman, 1965). Since the literature demonstrates different effects of hospitalization at different stages, these effects must be examined developmentally.

DEVELOPMENTAL EFFECTS OF HOSPITALIZATION

For the *infant,* hospitalization means a change which affects patterns of feeding, sleeping, and elimination. Painful procedures cause displeasure in the infant. Maternal–infant bonds may be disrupted, and the mother's ability to care for the child after hospitalization can be at risk. Without a predictable environment the infant may not trust that his or her needs will be met. The nurse must also remember that separation anxiety peaks at about 9 months.

The *toddler's* perception of the hospitalization experience is based on the effects on the child. Separation anxiety and regression are the most common responses seen to stress. The child's fantasy substitutes for the lack of a knowledge base. The toddler has no sense of time and wants all his or her needs met now, if not sooner. The toddler has a great fear of abandonment, and the crib becomes a prison; the very sense of security and belonging are threatened. Robertson's three stages of reactions to hospitalization are most evident with this age group if the parent is not present with the child in the hospital. The protest phase may last for hours to days, with the toddler crying and screaming for his mother. During this phase very little can be done to comfort the child. The second stage of despair brings the child to a state of distrust and anger, which may result in thumbsucking, masturbation, and fingering of the lips or locks of hair. The child no longer resists attempts to comfort him or her. During the third stage of denial or detachment, the child passively accepts support measures and ceases to care. The mother is ignored during the visit. The child's happy disposition is often mis-

interpreted by staff as a "positive" adjustment.

The *preschool*-age child views hospitalization and intrusive procedures as punishment and with a sense of guilt. The child may respond with frustration, despair, and social withdrawal. Feelings of distrust, anger, and rage may be directed toward others. The preschooler, however, can tolerate separation and a strange environment better than the toddler, and also is more willing to postpone immediate gratification. This patient needs trust and truthfulness, however. For the older preschooler, age-appropriate teaching can be done 1 to 2 days in advance of hospitalization. The child will respond to appropriate limits of behavior if the reasons for the limits are understood in advance.

Hospitalization for the *school-age* child means separation from family and peers, resulting in depression and anger. The stimulation of school and play activities is missed. Most children in this age group tolerate procedures well if explanations are given in advance. Nonsexual intrusive procedures such as ear exams are tolerated best by this age group. School-age children wish to live up to adults' expectations, and thus develop a sense of industry.

Confinement, dependency, fear of effects to body image, and boredom are problems faced by the hospitalized *adolescent.* Typically the adolescent has a strong need and desire to be in control. Since this is not always possible, mood swings are common. The adolescent may express hostility, feelings of helplessness or being trapped, and humiliation, or he or she may react passively. The adolescent may want to act as he or she feels and at the same time act as an adult.

EFFECTS OF HOSPITALIZATION ON SLEEP

An important aspect of hospitalization is its effect on sleep. Hagemann (1981) conducted studies on the duration and disruption of night sleep. Sleep during the first night of hospitalization was shorter than usual. This was due to either delayed onset of sleep or early termination of sleep, which resulted in a loss of REM (rapid eye movement) sleep. This loss is significant since subsequent effective adoptive behaviors and mood are thought to be affected by adequate amounts of REM stage sleep. The most common cause of sleep deprivation was a delay of onset due to late routines, restlessness from being in a new and strange environment, noise, and a normal resistance to sleep intensified by the hospitalization.

Hagemann found that sleep disruptions more commonly occurred from external causes than internal causes. External causes such as routine nursing care measures occurred later in the sleep pattern and were of short duration. Internal causes such as pain and other physiological discomforts occurred early in the sleep pattern and were of longer duration. Arousal from internal causes was found most frequently in children with a history of previous hospitalizations, and when hospitalization was due to their medical condition. Disturbances due to internal causes suggest that these children were sleeping lighter, and that physiological discomfort interfered with achieving a restful sleep. This further suggests that acutely ill children may have more sleep disruptions from physical discomfort. If placed in an intensive care unit or a unit with high nighttime activity, arousal due to external causes will also increase. It can therefore be further suggested that this loss of sleep of the acutely ill child may have a serious effect on the child's mood and ability to adapt.

LONG-TERM ILLNESS AND HOSPITALIZATION

Long-term illnesses such as childhood cancer are often associated with periods of hospitalization for treatments, surgery, infections, and progressive disease. Problems that are observed during the hospitalization of the child with cancer include: fluctuations of weight; gastro-

intestinal side-effects of chemotherapeutic medications; infections of many types; bleeding tendencies; central nervous system problems, including seizures; peripheral neuropathies; brain damage; hearing problems; emotional liability; behavior and socialization problems; fear of dying; and many others.

Because separation and abandonment are the biggest fears of the hospitalized child with cancer, parents should be encouraged to stay with the child as much as possible. Isolation should be utilized only when absolutely necessary. The young child cannot cope well with the threat of separation that accompanies the isolation process.

Knafl, Deatrick, and Kodadek (1982) conducted a study of working parents with acutely and chronically ill hospitalized children. When the children were acutely ill, the visiting patterns of the mothers and fathers differed. The mothers had more flexible work schedules and thus were with their children more often, from 8 to 24 hours a day. The fathers visited their children more often on their way to and from work. Parents who referred to the hospitalization in negative ways focused on the disruption and the exhaustion it produced. Even parents who adjusted to the routine described hospitalization as a major change causing a loss of normal routines and a time of physical exhaustion.

With the chronically ill child, hospitalization frequently is prescheduled. This allows the parents time to rearrange work and home schedules, thus producing less household disruption. Factors that influence the visiting patterns of these parents include travel time, finances, the child's expectations and needs, and the parents' perceptions of the importance of the treatments the child is receiving. In the Knafl study, admission, surgery, and discharge were rated as the most important times to be with the child. While several families in the study shared the responsibility for being with the child, the mother still had the primary responsibility. Also, if the family lived close to the hospital, the visiting was more frequent. Visiting patterns were also related to the child's level of development. The parents reported that as the children got older they would verbalize specific requests and expectations in terms of their parents' visitations. With adolescents the amount of parental visitation was based on the adolescent's expectations and previous experiences with hospitalization. In nine out of ten cases, however, the parents would have preferred to spend more time visiting with their hospitalized child.

COPING WITH HOSPITALIZATION

In helping a child to cope with hospitalization, an essential aspect is truthfulness. A child benefits from truthful discussions of the illness and the progress being made. Not only does this explain the reason for the hospitalization, but it also establishes a trusting relationship with the health professional. This trusting relationship is necessary in order to help the child deal with the illness.

A trusting relationship is especially important with the hospitalized adolescent with cancer. The adolescent's general emotional reaction to hospitalization depends on a wide variety of factors, among the most important of which are the adolescent's self-confidence, trust in parents and health professionals, anxiety displayed by others in regard to the illness, preparation for hospitalization, support from the family and health professionals during the hospitalization, and the way in which painful procedures are handled.

Parents and selected health professionals play a large role in the information-gathering process of the hospitalized adolescent. Craft (1981) examined the preferences of 40 adolescents and their parents at a midwestern medical center and teaching hospital. Of these adolescents, 23 had a chronic illness. Both the adolescents and their parents felt that health professionals should provide information on medications, marriage, and childbearing.

Other results of the study suggest that the older the adolescent, the more likely the selection of the health professional rather than the parent as the information provider. These findings also suggest that when topics such as cause, seriousness, symptoms, and length of diagnosis were being discussed, the adolescents wanted the emotional support provided by their parents and appreciated their presence. This study indicated that the adolescent's preference for an information provider may not be the same as the parental preference. The nurse must act to determine the preferences at time of admission and must work to facilitate communication between the parents and the adolescent. Primary nursing provides patients and parents with a consistent nurse with whom a trusting relationship can be developed.

One method of providing information about cancer and training in coping skills for the adolescent and parent is the "I Can Cope" approach (see Yellow Pages for availability of the "I Can Cope" kit). Developed in 1977 for the American Cancer Society, this technique utilizes a 2-day retreat during which parents and adolescents spend time together and apart. The retreat begins with a relaxation exercise, after which the "I Can Cope" concept is introduced, and the program proceeds from there. Topics covered include learning about cancer, coping with daily health problems, expressing feelings, learning to like yourself, living with limits, and possible resources. When this approach was utilized by the University of Iowa Hospitals and Clinics, it was found to be very beneficial by the participants in helping them to cope with illness and hospitalization.

DEVELOPMENTAL MASTERY OF HOSPITALIZATION

Just as the effects of illness and hospitalization vary according to the age of the child, so do the child's attempts at mastery. For the infant, when the basic physiologic and psychological needs are met, the hospital environment and the home environment become consistent with one another. A primary nurse can provide the infant with a consistent caregiver who can meet the infant's oral needs, develop trust, stimulate sensory and nervous system development, and provide opportunities for mastery of significant developmental tasks.

Toddlers need to have their parents involved with their care, as they need the consistency the parents can provide. A primary nurse and consistent staffing also help the toddler to cope with hospitalization. When the parent must leave the child, an item of the parent's should be left with the child. The toddler then begins to realize that the parent is going to return. Familiar objects belonging to the child, such as a favorite doll or blanket, also should be brought to the hospital as a form of security for the child. Games such as peek-a-boo should be used to teach the child that when people and objects go away they will come back. The toddler has no sense of time, therefore explanations should be given that focus on stable events in the child's day. An example of such an explanation would be, "You may go to the playroom after lunch," or, "Your mommy will be back after your nap." The child's day should be structured as closely as possible to the home routine, especially the child's toilet training routine. Similarities in the child's routine allow for consistency and trust to develop.

Preschoolers may feel that the hospitalization is a punishment for something they did. Every effort must be made to help the child to understand the reason for the hospitalization. This can be accomplished through stories, drawings by the child, using body outline charts, coloring books, hospital equipment, and the like. Procedures and events such as tests and surgery must be explained to the child in terms of how it will help the child. Dolls and stuffed animals can be used by children to help them express their feelings about what is happening. The child should always be encouraged and praised for his or her efforts. The child should also be encouraged to accomplish as much as possible of his or her own care, which gives the child a sense of control and accomplishment and attempts to dispel any fears of body mutilation or castration the preschooler may have.

School-age children are willing to help with their own care and want to know what everything is and how it works. This child should be allowed to play with the hospital equipment both before and after procedures are acccomplished, if possible. Children at this age love being a "big brother" or "big sister" to someone who is new to the hospital setting. This type of peer relationship should be encouraged.

The hospitalized adolescent has a need for privacy, participation in treatment, recreational opportunities with peers, opportunities to discuss what is happening to and around him or her, and maintenance of contact with family and peers from outside the hospital environment. The adolescent must be involved in decisions about his or her care. If possible, hospitalizations should be scheduled around special events, school days, and work schedules. The adolescent should receive praise and respect for his or her ability to exert some control over the care. When adolescents are involved in the planning, their needs for independence and control are at least partially met, and they are likely to be more compliant with the care provided. Other attempts to allow the adolescent to exert some control and provide normality would be to encourage the patient to wear street clothes rather than a hospital gown and to follow routines similar to the ones at home, such as showering at night rather than in the morning.

SELF-CARE

Some form of self-care has been mentioned with almost every age group. Lum and colleagues (1978) found that when patients are encouraged to take part in their own care, they experience an increase in knowledge and a decrease in anxiety. The literature also supports the idea that patients will follow through with self-care more readily when they feel their concerns are understood, when they are taught about their illness and treatment, and when they are encouraged to participate in planning their own care (Lauer, 1978).

Dorothea Orem developed a self-care theory of nursing. According to Orem, self-care is exercised in order to sustain life and health, to recover from disease and injury, and to cope with the effects of disease and injury. When demands to accomplish these goals are made upon the individual (demands for self-care), there is an attempt to meet these demands by decision-making and action-taking (self-care agency) (cited in Eichelberger, et al., 1980). Children learn responsible self-care when they are allowed to choose from alternatives, take action, and evaluate consequences. Children also learn about self-care from the behaviors they see in parents and other caretakers. Well children utilize self-care on a continual basis with the help of their parents. When the child becomes ill, self-care can continue at various levels, with the demands of self-care being met by the child along with the parent or the nurse. Decisions about who will meet the child's needs must be negotiated among all the parties involved, with the goal of returning self-care to the child as soon as possible.

ENVIRONMENTAL CONSIDERATIONS

The environment in the hospital needs to be altered to meet the needs of the child. Most hospitals are designed on an adult level. Sinks and toilets that are built at an adult height are just one example. Most of the beds are not low enough for young children to crawl in and out of easily. Although there is little that can be done about these standard hospital features, the remainder of the hospital environment can be altered to be more suitable for children. Children with cancer need to be able to express themselves. That is one part of the environment that can and must be altered.

The environment can be made to look ap-

pealing to children by putting up appropriate wallpaper and pictures. One hospital in the southwestern United States has had the walls on the pediatric unit painted with giraffes, zebras, and so on. Children who were patients at the time of the painting added pictures of animals, such as turtles, to the lower portion of the walls. Several of the ceilings, such as over the treatment tables, are also painted with pleasing pictures.

Other environmental factors also can be added to allow for expression of feelings by the children. Bulletin boards can be placed at the head of each bed so that the child has a space where personal pictures and messages can be displayed. Chalk boards or other special walls, on which the children are free to write whatever they wish, can be built. Walls in the corridors or waiting rooms can be used to display the artwork of the patients. In some hospitals volunteer departments have coordinated newspapers designed and made by the children. These papers may be sent to children who are outpatients, who are on maintenance therapy, or who recently went off therapy.

Other environmental considerations include a playroom and a kitchen. These areas are necessary to (1) promote family interactions outside of the patient's room; (2) establish some normalcy in the child's environment; and (3) allow the child a nonthreatening environment in which interactions with other children can occur. Space also should be provided for parents to sleep, for siblings to visit, and for a schoolroom on the pediatric unit. Nursing personnel can play a vital role as nursing consultants to the architects and hospital administrators during renovation, or creation, of such a unit.

THE USE OF PLAY

All the above environmental considerations involve play with the child. It is through the use of play that children learn about the world around them. Prugh and coworkers (1954) noted that play or fantasy can help professionals to understand how children interpret illness and hospitalization and how they cope with the illness. Projective techniques such as drawings, play therapy, and puppet play, allow children to express their feelings about what is going on around them. The professional must take into consideration the developmental process of play discussed in Chapter 1 when utilizing play in the care of the child.

PLAY AND PREPARATION FOR PROCEDURES

Play is a very useful technique to prepare children for procedures, surgery, and other happenings in a hospital. Providing concrete experiences through play prior to a procedure or surgery supports a child's sense of security, because the child then will know what to expect. Parents may feel that the preparation itself will create or increase the fears that a child may have about the upcoming event. However, the child who does not have accurate information about a procedure will fantasize about the event, and the fantasies may be more frightening than the actual event. The child's response to a procedure or a situation depends on how the event is perceived, not on what is actually happening. Therapeutic play thus helps the child to perceive, as well as to adjust to, the reality of the procedure. Having play as an outlet, the child's aggressive feelings about the procedure may be expressed and resolved along with unfounded fears and fantasies.

The choice of when to prepare a child for a procedure depends on the age and developmental level of the child. If a child is prepared too early, too much time is left for the patient to create fantasies and to activate fears. If the preparation is given in too short a time prior to the procedure, the child does not have time to prepare defenses adequately. The answer to this problem should be determined through a team effort. The team should consist of the doctor, the nurse, the parent, and the child. For pre-school children the parents usually know how their child reacts to stressful situations and how far in advance he or she wants to be told about upcoming events. Sensory preparation, *i.e.,* what the child will feel, see, hear, and smell, is as important as the information provided about the procedure or surgery itself.

In theory, preparation of the child parallels that of the adult, except that the parents must also receive the preparation. The nurse must assess the knowledge base of both the parent and the child before the teaching begins. Ideally, an environment free from interruptions and distractions, such as television or toys, should be selected for the teaching. The facts about the procedure should be related to the family at the child's level of understanding. Sometimes parents wish to be informed about the procedure first so they can help explain it to the child. Questions should be encouraged from both the child and the parents. The explanation should be broken down into small steps that are understandable to the child. Concrete examples should be used to provide a "picture" to the child of what is actually going to happen. Visual aids are valuable resources for this purpose. If the child is old enough, have him or her explain or demonstrate what has been taught. This will help the nurse to evaluate the teaching and to identify areas that need to be clarified or re-emphasized.

Visual aids used during the teaching can be developed by the nurse, or there are many commercial products available to meet the needs of the child. Shaver has designed a book for children who are patients at a pediatric oncology clinic (see Yellow Pages). Cancer treatments such as intravenous chemotherapy, bone marrow aspirations, radiation therapy, EEG, EKG, fingersticks, and so on, are explained in the book. Books and pamphlets concerning every aspect of hospitalization, cancer, and its treatment are available from commercial sources such as Centering Corporation (see Yellow Pages).

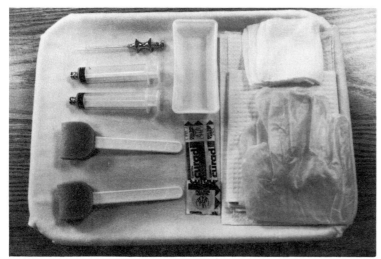

Play bone marrow tray contents:
Tray
Sterile gloves
Sterile drapes
Sponges
Betadine tub
Two syringes
Bone marrow needle
Bandaid

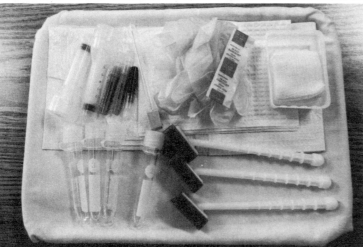

Play lumbar puncture tray contents:
Tray
Sterile gloves
Sterile drapes
Sponges
Betadine tub
Syringe
Needle
Four specimen tubes
Lumbar puncture needle
Bandaid

FIG. 2-1. Play trays (for procedures).

Many of the needed visual aids, however, can be developed easily by the nurse to meet the individual needs of the patient. If the child is to undergo a bone marrow aspiration or a spinal tap the nurse can utilize a "play tray" of equipment designed for these procedures (Fig. 2-1). The child should be allowed to perform the procedure under adult supervision on a doll. This not only allows the child to view and feel the equipment utilized, but also to express feelings about the procedure in a nonthreatening environment. Adequate time should be allowed so that the child is not rushed to complete the experience. The assistance of the child life worker can be a big asset here.

If the child is to undergo surgery, dolls can be used to demonstrate to the child what will actually happen during the operation (Fig. 2-2). If the child is to have an exploratory laparotomy, for example, before the teaching session begins the nurse can make an incision on the doll's abdomen, suture it together, and apply a dressing. During the teaching the nurse then can point out what the child's "stomach" will look like after the surgery. This type of visual aid is also effective with surgery resulting in radical alterations of body image, such as amputations. The patient is thus prepared before the event for what actually will be done. The surgery on the dolls should be as realistic as possible and show what will actually happen to the child. If the child will have a nasogastric tube, the doll also should have one. Then after the surgery or the procedure when the NG is discontinued for the child, it can be discontinued for the doll. In many communities there are organizations such as doll clubs that could furnish the hospital with cloth dolls for teaching purposes.

FIG. 2-2. Dolls used for preop teaching:
Left — laparotomy.
Right — amputation.

FIG. 2-3. Special sign for procedures/collections.

Written material such as booklets and pamphlets, and even coloring books, can be developed by a unit or institution to illustrate common procedures. A simple board game similar to such games as "Candy Land" can be developed by the staff. Puppet shows are also useful. If the nursing staff is creative, they can develop many visual aids needed for this type of play.

OTHER EXAMPLES OF THERAPEUTIC USES OF PLAY

Play allows the child to participate in the care and can be utilized throughout hospitalization and treatment. If the child is receiving a certain treatment, such as a 24-hour urine collection, special signs can be created that the child can color and then place at the head of the bed so that all can see it (Fig. 2-3). A drawing of an old-fashioned gas pump (Fig. 2-4) can be used to promote needed weight gain. As a child gains weight the gas pump can be "filled up" until the desired weight is reached. This way the entire team can visualize the child's progress and give positive feedback. Another therapeutic play idea is a picnic held outside on hospital property. The amount of food consumed by the patients actually increases when it's fun to eat.

To encourage ambulation a "Walk the Hall Club" can be established by drawing a simple calendar on a sheet of paper and posting it at the child's bedside along with a box of stars (Fig. 2-5). Every time the child walks a certain distance, a star is placed on that day on the calendar. Again, everyone can see the progress the child is making. This calendar and stars idea can be expanded and used for meals eaten, breathing treatments taken, exercises completed, and so on.

One example of a therapeutic play technique was utilized with 10-year-old Cindy. Cindy had a brain tumor that was treated successfully, but the size of the original tumor was so great that there was residual brain damage. As a result of the tumor, Cindy could not perform simple

FIG. 2-4. "Gas pump" to measure weight gain

physical tasks well such as brushing her hair, bathing herself, or using eating utensils to feed herself. A bare tree was drawn and placed on the wall in her room (Fig. 2-6). Every time Cindy did a "small task" such as brushing her hair, she placed a leaf on the tree. When a larger task, such as walking down the hall and back, was accomplished, Cindy placed a flower near the tree. The leaves and flowers were dated, and the tasks completed were listed on them. As the tree became full of leaves, everyone, including Cindy, could see a very definite improvement in Cindy's skills.

USE OF DIVERSIONARY PLAY

Since play is such an intregal part of all children's lives, they should be encouraged to par-

SUNDAY	MONDAY	TUESDAY	WEDNESDAY	THURSDAY	FRIDAY	SATURDAY
		1 ★	2 ★ ★	3 ★ ★ ★	4 ★ ★ ★	5 ★ ★ ★ ★
6 ★ ★ ★ ★ ★	7	8	9	10	11	12
13	14	15	16	17	18	19
20	21	22	23	24	25	26

FIG. 2-5. Walk the Hall Club calendar.

ticipate in play even when mobility is limited. Beds can be wheeled into the hall and to the playroom. Many hospitals now employ child life workers to be with the children and help them express themselves through age-appropriate play. Music and art specialists also are being seen in hospitals in increasing numbers, and many hospitals show films or videotapes in playrooms or lobbies. Parties can be planned by volunteer departments to provide entertainment for the children. Petting zoos can bring animals to the units for children to pet and touch.

Hospitalized children can participate in seasonal events too. Pumpkin-carving contests are appropriate at Halloween. The children and their families can be involved actively in helping to decorate the nursing unit at Christmastime. Every spring there is the Houston Livestock Show and Rodeo. Children, families, and staff at one hospital all dress up in their best "western duds" for a few days that week. June is typically a "wedding" month. Why not have a "pretend" wedding? The staff could dress up, and at the end of the day a reception could be held, with all the children and families invited to attend.

So much can be done through the use of play to foster the child's development and adaptation to the illness. All that is needed is a little imagination and creativity on the part of the staff.

SURGERY AND ITS EFFECTS ON THE CHILD

Surgery has different effects on a child than it has for an adult. While many of the actual nursing treatments, such as preoperative preparation, dressing changes, coughing, and deep breathing are similar, many of the possible psychosocial problems are unique to the child.

PREOPERATIVE CARE

In a study of 33 school-aged children hospitalized for a surgical procedure, Tesler and Savedra (1981) found that before surgery the dominant coping strategy used by the children was precoping or orienting behavior. This type of coping behavior finds the child attempting to gain information to accurately assess the situation. The child may ask questions, actively explore the environment, or simply sit quietly and observe what is going on around him. Other coping mechanisms displayed include cooperating behavior during blood drawing, resistive behavior during painful procedures, and attempts at controlling the situation.

The child who is going to have surgery must know why, where, how, and what will happen to him. Studies have shown that the anxiety of the child and parents has been reduced effectively through the use of preparation programs. Studies also have shown that anxiety in the mother correlates positively with anxiety in the preschool child. When the mother's fears are reduced, the child's fears also are reduced substantially (Schreier and Kaplan, 1983).

Especially with the child with cancer, the nutritional status and needs of the patient must be assessed preoperatively. The child who has lost weight prior to the surgery due to preoperative therapy may need to improve his or her nutritional status before surgery can be done. Tube feedings and hyperalimentation are frequently utilized for this purpose. A central line for hyperalimentation can be placed to provide nutritional support both preoperatively and postoperatively.

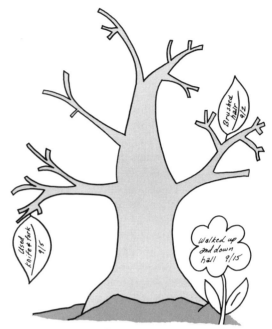

FIG. 2-6. Motivation tree.

When the child goes to surgery, a familiar item or toy should be allowed to accompany the child. This helps to reduce the strangeness and to provide some security. The preschool and school-aged child are developing a sense of modesty and should be allowed to wear their underpants to surgery. These underpants can be removed with less anxiety and trauma after the child is asleep in the operating room.

TYPES OF SURGERY

While children with cancer occasionally have needs for the same types of surgery performed on healthy children, such as the removal of tonsils and adenoids, hernia repair, and appendectomies, surgery is usually related to the malignant disease. Types of surgery vary from local biopsies of lesions, to exploratory laparatomies, to pelvic extenterations. The purposes of the surgery may be to remove all or part of a tumor, to obtain a specimen for examination by a pathologist, to determine the extent of the disease, to remove metastatic disease, or to relieve symptoms.

POSTOPERATIVE CARE

In most hospitals pediatric patients go to the recovery room following surgery. The immediate postoperative period is one of three stressful periods during a child's hospitalization (Vernon, 1965). The trauma of separation from the parent at such a traumatic time compounds the child's anxiety and can make a child very uncooperative while in the recovery room. Des, Bushong and Crumrine (1977) conducted a study in which parents were allowed into the recovery room. Eighty-eight percent (88%) of the parents felt their presence helped their child. Maul (1984) surveyed two groups of parents (one preoperatively and one postoperatively) and a group of recovery room nurses concerning their feelings about parents in the recovery room. Over 50% of the parents felt they should be in the recovery room continuously, and 25% felt they should be there at frequent intervals. Of the nurses over 50% felt the parents should be there at least at frequent intervals or continuously. If parents are not currently allowed in the recovery room in an institution, revision of such a policy should be considered.

Regardless of the type of surgery, immediately postoperatively most children use inactive behavior as a coping strategy. Upon return from surgery children tend to sleep a lot or lie quietly still. Then they attempt to control behavior in order to control their stress. Children should be allowed to alter situations, if possible, because it affords them a sense of mastery over the environment. Children frequently will use television as a means to screen out unwanted stimuli from the environment.

Because many pediatric oncology patients who undergo surgery previously have received therapy for their disease, they face special problems postoperatively. Both chemotherapy and radiation therapy create side-effects such as immunosuppression and gastrointestinal problems, which will be discussed in later chapters. Postoperatively the pediatric oncology patient may be susceptible to slow healing, wound dehiscence, delayed return of peristalsis, infection, bleeding, anemia, and nutritional problems.

Of particular impact postoperatively to children with bone cancer are the effects of amputation. Any type of amputation creates a change in the child's body image. Children who undergo an amputation generally go through four stages: (1) impact; (2) retreat; (3) acknowledgment; and (4) reconstruction. The impact stage brings despair, discouragement, and passive acceptance. In this retreat stage the child undergoes acute grief as the reality of the amputation sets in. The child may exhibit anxiety, tension, sleep disturbance, anorexia, weight loss, fear, guilt, anger, or withdrawal. During this stage many children experience feelings of helplessness and lowered self-esteem. The child now needs to have everyone place emphasis on his or her many strengths. Before the patient can move on to the next stage, there must be acceptance of the loss of the body part and acknowledgment that there is no hope of retrieving it. The child in the acknowledgment stage demonstrates a willingness to get involved in the care of the amputation site. The child also may demonstrate hostility toward others who are considered "normal." Usually before moving out of this stage, the child is wearing a prosthesis, has accepted being "different," and has realized that this change is permanent. During the reconstruction phase the child tries to reach the maximum rehabilitation potential that is possible.

Shifting occurs among the various phases, and progression is not necessarily steady. Rusk (cited in Walters, 1981) has established six classes (levels) of rehabilitation. Class I is *full restoration*, in which the child is not disabled despite the handicap. Class II is *partial restora-*

tion, in which the child functions well but must modify physical activity. Class III is *self-care plus*. In this class the child is disabled but can carry out the normal activities of daily living, including going to school. Class IV is *self-care minus*. These children are severely disabled and need help with activities of daily living and with ambulation. Class V is *cosmetic plus*, wherein the child cannot ambulate but has a prosthesis for cosmetic and psychological reasons and is independent in a wheelchair. Class VI is *not feasible*. These children do not have a prosthesis and must be taught to do as much as possible from a wheelchair.

PAIN

A child with cancer may encounter pain in all phases of the illness. Pain may come from treatments and procedures that are necessary to diagnose and manage the disease. Generally this pain is of less intensity and duration than pain that is a direct result of the disease. Pain from treatment may be related either to the disease process or to psychological factors.

Children react individually to pain. Psychological, social, and cultural factors influence how and when children will react to the sensations they experience. The child's fear and anxiety level, developmental level, past experiences, expectations, and conception of pain are all psychological factors that influence pain. Social and cultural factors include the child's learned behaviors and parental attitudes, since parents and society teach children how to react to the pain stimulation. A classic study by Zborowski (cited in Teung, 1982) regarding cultural influences on the response to pain found that there were similar reactions to pain manifested by members of different ethnocultural groups, but that the members did not necessarily reflect similar attitudes to pain. Zborowski found that Italian and Jewish patients tended to reflect a future-oriented sense of apprehension and anxiety in relation to the symptomatic meaning of

pain. "Old American" patients were concerned with the incapacitating aspects of pain, but the future still was viewed optimistically. Irish patients viewed the pain as a self-fulfilling prophecy (Teung, 1982). In a study of negroes' and northern Europeans' perceptions of pain, Chapman and Jones found that skin pigmentation did not contribute to the difference in pain sensitivity and pain tolerance (cited in Teung, 1982). A study by Maskey and Spear supported this finding with their results, which demonstrated no significant differences in the pain response between white and black medical students of the same sex (cited in Teung, 1982).

Based on these factors that influence the reactions to pain, clearly it becomes difficult to define pain, but the literature is filled with just such attempts. Bonica describes pain as "becoming progressively more severe and finally developing into violence, boring, relentless, intolerable, agonizing suffering, which soon demoralizes the victim and prevents him/her from eating, resting or sleeping" (Rankin, 1980). Sternbach defines pain as "an abstract concept which refers to (1) a personal, private sensation of hurt; (2) a harmful stimulus which signals current or impending tissue damage; and (3) a pattern of responses which operate to protect the organism from harm" (Rankin, 1980).

But perhaps the best definition is Margo McCaffery's. According to McCaffery (1980), pain defies definition. But she does offer this operational definition: "Pain is whatever the experiencing person says it is, existing whenever he says it does." This definition is applicable to any age group, sex, culture, or race.

STAGES OF PAIN

Matthews and colleagues (1973) have described three stages of the progression of pain in the patient with cancer. The first or *early-stage* pain follows surgery for diagnosis and treatment of a primary lesion. Pain in this stage is short and temporary, resembling acute pain. *Intermediate-stage* pain occurs when there are cancer recurrences or metastasis, or postoperative contraction of scars and nerve entrapment. The pain may subside as in the earlier stage, or it may persist and require palliative methods of control, such as radiation, chemotherapy, neurosurgery, and analgesics. *Late-stage* pain occurs when treatment methods no longer affect the progress of the disease. The patient may be more anxious and depressed as the pain becomes overwhelming and continuous, and as death becomes imminent. Late-stage pain is similar to chronic or intractable pain, and treatments for the relief of the pain become ineffective. Attempts to control late-stage pain are made through the use of neurosurgery, nerve blocks, psychotropic drugs, and narcotic analgesics.

SIGNS AND SYMPTOMS OF ACUTE PAIN

Usually a child experiencing acute pain will demonstrate some visible sign of that pain, whether the child can verbalize or not. The child may perspire, may have an increased cardiac rate or higher blood pressure, or look pale. In addition the child may cry, moan, tense the skeletal muscles, or rub or guard the painful part. There are other responses to pain that are not as visible as these or as readily associated with pain. Many times a child minimizes expressions of pain so that he or she appears to be a "good patient." This is often encouraged by both the family and health professionals. Often these actions are misinterpreted as the child having little or no pain at all. Also, children may become so fatigued from lack of sleep due to pain that they don't even have the energy to cry. Progressive pain may also result in depression and decreased self-esteem, which may lower the expression of pain. Symptoms of pain the child might exhibit include anorexia, nausea and vomiting, weight loss, anger, hostility,

increased irritability, or decreased social interaction and recreational participation (Rankin, 1980).

Expression of pain will vary with each developmental level. The infant generally expresses pain through crying. The toddler expresses pain nonverbally through clenched teeth, rocking and rubbing, or through aggressive behavior such as kicking, biting, and yelling. A child at this age level cannot describe the pain or its location, but may be able to say that it hurts. The preschooler can begin to describe the pain and can be encouraged to locate the pain by pointing to the part of the body that hurts. School-age children can describe their pain, but may be reluctant to do so. They may fear rejection or a shot, or even may be trying to protect their parents. Adolescents may view pain as a weakness and be reluctant to express it.

MANAGING PAIN

Research has demonstrated that "doctors and nurses who do not hesitate to medicate adults for pain connected with surgery, burns, or other trauma, do not medicate children as frequently for the same problems" (McGuire, 1982). Many nurses and doctors feel that children do not require pain medication and, in fact, that infants do not even feel the pain. It is now thought, however, that an infant can perceive pain before the myelinization of the nerve fibers has been completed. It is also thought that the younger the child, the lower the tolerance of pain (McGuire, 1982).

Numerous methods to relieve pain in the child with cancer include medications, massage, therapeutic touch, measures to decrease anxiety, distraction, relaxation techniques and self-hypnosis, medication, surgery, radiation, and chemotherapy. The methods chosen will depend on the type and extent of pain, the extent of the disease, and the particular child and family. Table 2-1 offers tips for managing pain in children.

TABLE 2-1. TIPS TO MANAGING A CHILD'S PAIN

1. Know how a child's age and developmental level affect his perception and description of pain.
2. Know how the child communicates pain.
3. Observe the child for restlessness, decreasing or increasing activity, loss of appetite, clinging, and whining.
4. Develop a trusting relationship.
5. Tell the child that the medicine will make him feel better, and reinforce this when it does.
6. Medicate the child early, before the pain becomes intense.
7. Avoid "shots" when possible.
8. Use relaxation and other techniques to decrease anxiety.
9. Don't let the child talk you out of the medicine if you feel he or she needs it.
10. Beware of adolescents' fears of addiction.
11. Get the parents involved.
12. Have parents bring in the child's favorite toys, games, and books.
13. Be honest with the child about whether a shot or procedure will hurt.
14. Follow a painful experience with a pleasant one.

Adapted from McGuire, L. & Dizard, S. (August, 1982). Managing pain in the young patient. **Nursing 82,** 54–55.

ANALGESICS

The most common method utilized to control a child's pain is through the use of analgesics. Not every patient will require the use of narcotics to control the pain. Each child must be assessed individually for the type (acute or chronic) and extent (mild to severe) of the pain he or she is experiencing. There are three levels of analgesia that can be achieved with medication. The three levels correspond to the levels of mild, moderate, and severe pain, and each has distinct medications. The most effective single analgesic for mild to moderate pain is aspirin. Aspirin does affect platelet function, however, and should be avoided if the child is being treated actively with chemotherapy or radiation. When combinations of drugs are utilized for moderate pain, aspirin and codeine or oxycodone can be utilized. There is an addictive and synergistic effect between these drugs.

Drugs of this type include Ascodeen (aspirin and codeine) and Percodan (aspirin, phenacetin, caffeine, and oxycodone). These drugs are not recommended for use with severe chronic pain. While codeine and oxycodone are narcotics and produce analgesia similar to that of low-dose morphine, they do not produce the same increasing analgesia with increasing dosage. One double-blind crossover, single-dose study of commercially available analgesics for use with moderate cancer pain documented the effectiveness of aspirin. Aspirin was more effective than Ponstel, Talwin, Tylenol, Datril, phenacetin, or codeine (Lipman, 1980).

Narcotics are usually the drugs of choice with severe chronic pain. Although narcotics demonstrate no significant difference among themselves in terms of potency and side-effects, they differ significantly in duration of action. When the patient has chronic pain, drugs with a longer duration are the drugs of choice. Drugs commonly utilized with chronic pain include hydromorphone (Dilaudid), levorphanol (Levo-Dromoran), meperidine, methadone, morphine, and oxymorphone (Numorphan). Of these drugs the longest duration (6 to 8 hours) can be achieved through the use of levorphanol tartrate and methadone.

Methadone and continuous-drip morphine have been used recently with increasing frequency. Methadone has been demonstrated to produce changes in behavior in children with irretractable pain within 24 hours after the first dose and has proven to be effective with pain relief at home, as well as in the hospital. Table 2-2 lists the characteristics of methadone and its recommended dosage.

Although the use of continuous-drip morphine as a method of pain control has been used mostly with adults, one study conducted at Ohio State University in Columbus and the University of Washington in Seattle demonstrated effective use of continuous drip morphine with children. This study included as their sample eight children who had not received adequate

TABLE 2-2. CHARACTERISTICS OF METHADONE AND RECOMMENDED DOSAGES

Synthetic opiate-type narcotic
Actions similar to morphine
Main site of detoxification: liver
Patient has relatively clear sensorium
Absorbed well from GI tract
Oral therapeutic levels greater than other narcotics
Effects last 6–8 hr
Less expensive (oral form) than other oral narcotics
Mild withdrawal syndrome when used for pain control
Hazard for accumulation effects in body
Side-effects: nausea, vomiting, dizziness, dry mouth, euphoria, depression, may lower seizure threshold
Pediatric Analgesic dosage = 0.7 mg/kg/24 hr   in 4–6
                          or   doses
                    20 mg/m²/24 hr   (oral or
                                       Sub Q)

Adapted from Martinson, I., et al. (March 1982). Nursing care in childhood cancer: Methadone. **American Journal of Nursing,** 433.

relief with other oral and parenteral narcotics. Pain relief with continuous-drip morphine was adequate for one of the children, but complete for the other seven. Other studies on this method of administration of morphine with adults have demonstrated that patients receiving a continuous drip of morphine require considerably less drug than patients receiving morphine by the IM or PRN routines (Boyer, 1982).

Of major concern to patients, families, and health professionals are the issues of tolerance to and dependency on narcotics used for pain control. Studies have demonstrated that patients with cancer who suffer from chronic pain *do not* experience tolerance to a drug and *do not* require increases in dosages of the narcotics. Dependency also has been shown *not* to be a significant problem with the treatment of pain due to physical origin in cancer patients (Lipman, 1980).

A third type of analgesic in use are oral cocktail mixtures. The use of these cocktail mixtures began in the late 19th century in London. In 1952 Brompton's Hospital in London published "Brompton's cocktail." In the 1970s Brompton's cocktail was being called the analgesic of choice in advanced cancer pain by leading physicians in Europe and North America. However, recent studies have demonstrated that Brompton's cocktail has no advantage over morphine in pain control (Lipman, 1980).

Currently various pain cocktails are being utilized. All of them are mixtures of varying amounts of the following ingredients: morphine or methadone, cocaine or amphetamine, sugar or honey, 90% to 98% alcohol or gin, and chloroform water. If the cocktails are made with morphine they are administered every 3 to 4 hours; if they are made with methadone they are administered every 6 to 8 hours (Muller and Pelczynski, 1982).

There has been much criticism and controversy over the ingredients used in these cocktails. One argument is that cocaine does not have an additive effect to the other narcotic analgesic used. Also the restlessness, agitation, confusion, and hallucination seen as side-effects of cocaine raise questions about the use of this drug in the mixture. Methadone can produce respiratory problems due to large amounts accumulating in the plasma over time. Although alcohol is part of the cocktail, it offers no pharmacological or therapeutic advantage, but it may allow the use of less narcotic. Chloroform water was originally added for its medicinal taste, however, chloroform has been identified as a carcinogen and has been removed from the American GRAS list of agents generally regarded as safe for use in drugs, food, and cosmetics. Because of these controversies, two major cancer centers in England, St. Christopher Hospice in London and Sir Michael Sobel House in Oxford, now only use aqueous solutions of morphine as their primary narcotic analgesic (Muller and Pelczynski, 1982).

No matter which drug is utilized, the nurse must first assess the patient for the nature and extent of the pain. Once the need for an analgesic is determined, the patient should be started with a high dose and then titrated downward. This breaks the pain cycle and allows the patient some relief from the pain. A PRN medication routine should be avoided. This type of routine allows pain to return and the pain cycle to begin all over again. One of the most important points is to remain in close contact with the child and the family, who can help assess the pain level and relief. Family members have a large influence over the child's perception of pain. By demonstrating to the child and the family that you are concerned about the pain, you help to relieve some of their anxiety and tension.

THERAPEUTIC TOUCH

One method of decreasing pain is therapeutic touch. Illness is viewed as an imbalance of the energy flows within the patient; the energy patterns are believed to be blocked, congested, or sluggish. Therapeutic touch is said to be effective through the intentional and specified interactions between the vital energy fields of the nurse and the patient (Boguslawski, 1980). Acute pain can be relieved within minutes, and the relief will last for several hours. Patients with chronic pain often can experience relief for as long as a week. After therapeutic touch the patient generally feels more relaxed. Feelings of peace, orderliness, and caring may be communicated to the patient by the nurse.

Variations of the therapeutic touch technique can be utilized through simple relaxation techniques and massage. Anxiety also can be controlled through the use of relaxation and distraction techniques. Sally, a 7-year-old, was crying in pain one day after her surgery. The nurse calmed the child and taught her to do relaxation of all her muscles. After attempting the relaxation techniques, the child fell asleep and rested quietly. The communication aspect and the one-to-one attention alter the child's pain perceptions, and may account for some of the effectiveness of these techniques.

RADIATION, CHEMOTHERAPY, AND SURGERY

Radiation and chemotherapy frequently decrease the child's pain by reducing the tumor size. A smaller tumor presses on fewer nerves and organs, as there will be less pain. Surgery may be necessary to extract all or part of the tumor to relieve some pain and pressure.

NEUROSURGICAL INTERVENTIONS

Neurosurgical interventions are utilized with chronic, intractable pain in an attempt to offer some relief for the patient. These interventions interrupt the nerve pathways at three different levels (Terzian, 1980). The first level of nerve pathways is referred to as the *first-order neuron.* This system is peripheral in that the pain is transmitted by delta type A and type C fibers from nerve receptors located in the skin throughout the body.

The second level is referred to as the *second-order neuron* and is located in the dorsal horn of the gray matter in the brain. This level represents the cord level neurons. The *third-order neurons* are located in the thalamus, where the pain sensations are relayed into deeper regions of the brain.

Interventions differ with each level. At the first-order neuron level, nerve blocks with local anesthesia or neurolytic agents are often used. The effects from the nerve blocks last for hours if local anesthetics are used, or up to weeks or months if neurolytic agents such as alcohol, phenol, or saline are used. Neurolytic nerve blocks are utilized when neurosurgery is contraindicated. Side-effects of nerve blocks include headache, numbness, and paresthesia, but these are usually minor and transient. Surgical intervention at this level consists of the use of a neurectomy, rhizotomy, and sympathectomy. Neurectomy is the surgical interruption of the peripheral nerve. Two problems with this type of surgery are that it is difficult to isolate just one nerve and that peripheral nerves do regenerate. A posterior rhizotomy consists of severing the posterior roots as they enter the spinal cord. This type of surgery is utilized for pain in the thoracic and lumbar regions of the spinal cord. A sympathectomy is the removal of the sympathetic ganglia at various points along the sympathetic chain.

Another method to relieve pain at this level is electrical stimulation through transcutaneous, percutaneous, or permanent implant methods. With the transcutaneous method (sometimes referred to as TENS) a battery-powered stimulator sends electrical impulses to the body through electrodes attached to the skin. The main side-effect of this method is skin irritation (Meyer, 1982). This method has been shown to be effective in 25% of cases of chronic intractable pain. An example is Candy, a 14-year-old with osteosarcoma who complained of chronic back pain. After the electronic stimulator was placed at the area of pain on her back, Candy was relieved of pain for extended periods of time when the stimulator was used. With percutaneous stimulation a needle electrode is implanted into the painful peripheral nerve. This method has proven to be successful 50% of the time. When it is successful the patient is a candidate for a permanent peripheral nerve implant. With this permanent method an electrode and a receiver are implanted surgically in the body and are activated by an external transmitter carried by the patient. This method also is effective about 50% of the time (Terzian, 1980).

At the second-order neuron level, surgical interventions such as cordotomy or tractotomy are utilized. A cordotomy is the interruption of the lateral spinothalamic tract within the spinal cord. The disadvantage of cordotomy is that the level of anesthesia drops after a few months and the pain returns. A tractotomy is the interruption of the spinothalamic tract in the medulla or mesencephalon in the brain. This procedure has a high morbidity and mortality rate, however, so it is not frequently done.

Neurosurgical interventions at the third-order neuron level are reserved for patients who have severe intractable pain that has not been relieved by other methods. The two interventions at this level include stereotactic thalamotomy and electrical stimulation. The stereotactic thalamotomy interrupts the spinothalamic tract at the thalamus, producing an absence of pain and temperature sensation on the side opposite to and below the level of the lesion. One problem with this method is that although pain relief is immediate, it diminishes over time. With electrical stimulation at this level, the electrodes are surgically implanted with a receiver and the patient controls the stimulation with an external transmitter. Relief from pain with this method is more complete and long-lasting than with the surgery method.

Although none of the above methods of pain control are foolproof and complete, the patient's need for relief, even for a short period of time, demands the use of any method that provides such relief. It is up to the nurse to be the child's advocate and work with the physician to choose a method of pain control that may offer some relief based on the ongoing assessment of the child.

CONCLUSION

This chapter has discussed the various aspects of illness, hospitalization, and surgery for all children including those with cancer. Aspects of pain control in children have also been considered. Utilization of information presented in this chapter will help to assure that children and their families receive the best care possible.

KEY POINTS

- All aspects of illness and hospitalization must be examined from the child's developmental perspective.
- Before 10 years of age, children view illness as punishment.
- After 10 years of age, children believe in the germ theory as the cause of illness.
- The child with cancer suffers from the effects of illness, as well as the effects of chronic illness.
- Hospitalization has damaging emotional effects on children.
- Robinson has defined three stages of emotional process for the hospitalized child: (1) protest; (2) despair; and (3) detachment.
- Truthfulness is a very important aspect of coping with hospitalization.
- The child's attempts at mastery of hospitalization will vary according to the age of the child.
- Some form of self-care is important.
- The environment in the hospital should be altered to meet the needs of the child.
- Play helps professionals understand how children interpret and cope with their illness and hospitalization.
- Preoperative teaching is very important for both the child and the family.
- Postoperatively the child with cancer faces special problems due to previous chemotherapy and radiation therapy.
- Children react individually to pain, and differently than adults.
- Even infants can experience pain.
- Avoid PRN medication routines for pain relief.
- Remain in close contact with the child and the family.

REFERENCES

Bluebond-Langer, M. (1978). *The private worlds of dying.* Princeton: Princeton University Press.

Boguslawski, M. (1980). Therapeutic touch: a facilitator of pain relief. *Topics in Clinical Nursing, 82,* 27–37.

Boyer, M. (1982). Continuous drip morphine. *American Journal of Nursing, 82,* 602–604.

Brodie, B. (1974). Views of healthy children toward illness. *American Journal of Public Health, 64,* 1156–1159.

Craft, M. (1981). Preferences of hospitalized adolescents for information providers. *Nursing Research, 30,* 205–211.

DeChristopher, J. (1981). Children with cancer: their perceptions of the health care experience. *Topics in Clinical Nursing, 3,* 9–19.

Des, T., Bushong, M., and Crumrine, R. (1977). Parents in pediatric RR. *AORN, 26,* 266–273.

Dunlop, J. (1982). Critical problems facing young adults with cancer. *Oncology Nursing Forum, 9,* 33–38.

Eichelberger, K., *et al.* (1980). Self-care nursing plan: helping children to help themselves. *Pediatric Nursing, 6,* 9–13.

Fisher, S. (1983). The psychosexual effects of cancer and cancer treatment. *Oncology Nursing Forum, 10,* 63–68.

Fochtman, D., and Foley, G. (Eds.). (1982). *Nursing care of the child with cancer.* Boston: Little, Brown and Company.

Gohsman, B. (1981). The hospitalized child and the need for mastery. *Issues in Comprehensive Pediatric Nursing, 5,* 67–76.

Gorovitz, J., and Shore M. (1983). Meeting the psychological needs of hospitalized adolescents: a look at England. *Children's Health Care, 11,* 154–159.

Griffiths, S. (1980). Changes in body image caused by antineoplastic drugs. *Issues in Comprehensive Pediatric Nursing, 4,* 17–27.

Hagemann, V. (1981). Night sleep of children in a hospital. Part I, sleep duration. *Maternal-Child Nursing Journal, 10,* 127–142.

Hansen, B., and Evans, M. (1981). Preparing a child for procedures. *MCN, 6,* 392–397.

Hayes, V. (1980). The adolescent unit: a holistic approach to cancer management. *Oncology Nursing Forum, 7,* 9–12.

Kellerman, J., *et al.* (1980). Psychological effects of illness in adolescents I: anxiety, self-esteem, and perception of control. *Journal of Pediatrics, 97,* 126–131.

King, J., and Ziegler, S. (1981). The effects of hospitalization on children's behavior: a review of the literature. *Children's Health Care, 10,* 20–28.

Knafl, K., Deatrick, J., Kodadek, S. (1982). How parents manage jobs and a child's hospitalization. *MCN, 7,* 125–127.

Lauer, P., Murphy, S., Powers, M. (1982). Learning needs of cancer patients: a comparison of nurse and patient perceptions. *Nursing Research, 31,* 11–16.

Lederer, H. (1952). How the sick view their world. *Journal of Social Issues, 8,* 14–16.

Lincoln, L. (1978, Summer). Effects of illness and hospital procedures on body image in adolescents: a review of the literature. *Maternal-Child Nursing Journal, 7,* 55–60.

Lipman, A. (1980). Drug therapy in cancer pain. *Cancer Nursing, 3,* 39–46.

Lum, J., *et al.* (1978, November/December). Nursing care of oncology patients receiving chemotherapy. *Nursing Research, 27,* 340–346.

Martinson, I., *et al.* (1982). Nursing care in childhood cancer: methadone. *American Journal of Nursing, 82,* 432–435.

Matthews, G., *et al.* (1973). Cancer pain and its treatment. *Seminars in Drug Treatment, 3,* 45–52.

Maul, S. (1984, January/February). The child with cancer, the parent, and the recovery room: a desirable combination? *Journal of Pediatric Oncology Nursing, 1,* 33.

McCaffery, M. (1980). Understanding your patient's pain. *Nursing '80, 10,* 26–31.

McGuire, L. and Dizard, S. (1982). Managing pain in the young patient. *Nursing '82, 12,* 52–55.

Meyer, T. (1982). TENS relieving pain through electricity. *Nursing '82, 12,* 57–59.

Muller, R. and Pelczynski, L. (1982). You can control cancer pain with drugs, but the proper way may surprise you. *Nursing '82, 12,* 50–57.

Nadler, H. (1983). Art experience and hospitalized children. *Children's Health Care, 11,* 160–164.

Nilsen, J. (1982, March). Nursing care in childhood cancer: adolescence. *American Journal of Nursing, 82,* 436–439.

Petrillo, M., Sanger, S. (1980). *Emotional care of hospitalized children* (2nd ed.). Philadelphia: Lippincott.

Prugh, D., *et al.* (1954). A study of the emotional reactions of children to hospitalization and illness. *American Journal of Orthopsychiatry, 23,* 70–106.

Rankin, M. (1980). The progressive pain of cancer. *Topics in Clinical Nursing, 2,* 57–73.

Schreier, and Kaplan, D. (1983). The effectiveness of a preoperation preparation program in reducing anxiety in children. *Children's Health Care, 11,* 142–147.

Steele, S. (1983). *Health promotion of the child with long-term illness.* East Norwalk: Appleton-Century-Crofts.

Terzian, M. (1980). Neurosurgical interventions for the management of chronic intractable pain. *Topics in Clinical Nursing, 2,* 75–88.

Tesler, M. and Savedra, M. (1981). Coping with hospitalization: A study of school-aged children. *Pediatric Nursing, 7,* 35–38.

Teung, A. (1982). *Growth and development: a self-mastery approach.* East Norwalk: Appleton-Century-Crofts.

Teyber, E, and Littlehales, D. (1981). Coping with feelings: seriously ill children, their families, and hospital staff. *Children's Health Care, 10,* 58–62.

Vernon, D., Foley, J., Sipowitz, R. and Schulman, J. (1965). *The psychological responses of children to hospitalization and illness.* Springfield, IL: Thomas.

Vipperman, J., and Rager, P. (1980). Childhood coping: how nurses can help. *Pediatric Nursing, 6,* 11–18.

Walters, J. (1981, July). Coping with a leg amputation. *American Journal of Nursing, 81,* 1349–1352.

Weisman, A. (1979). *Coping with cancer.* New York: McGraw-Hill.

Welch, D. (1981). Waiting, worry, and the cancer experience. *Oncology Nursing Forum, 8,* 14–18.

Wood, S. (1983). School aged children's perceptions of the causes of illness. *Pediatric Nursing, 9,* 101–104.

Zeltzer, L., *et al.* (1980). Psychologic effects of illness in adolescence II: impact of illness in adolescents—crucial issues and coping styles. *Journal of Pediatrics, 97,* 132–138.

3
TYPES OF CHILDHOOD CANCERS

INTRODUCTION

Approximately six thousand new cases of childhood cancer are diagnosed annually. Childhood cancer will affect those six thousand children plus an undetermined number of family members, friends, neighborhoods, and communities. Despite the small percentage of all children involved, cancer is of importance to nurses and others in the health field who work with children.

More and more children diagnosed as having various types of cancer will become long-term survivors; in fact, over half of these children will be cured of the disease (Klopovich and Cohen, 1984). Thus childhood cancer has become a chronic childhood illness. On the negative side the cancer diagnosis carries with it the threat of death; in fact, cancer is the second leading cause of death in children and the primary cause of death from disease (ACS, 1985). As is discussed throughout this book, the diagnosis of cancer poses many unique problems and challenges to the affected child and family that can seriously hinder psychosocial, cognitive, and, of course, physical growth and development.

There are important differences between childhood and adult cancer. The most common cancers of adults, including lung, breast, colorectal, and skin, are uncommon in children. Children develop malignancies of rapidly growing body systems, such as the reticuloendothelial system, the central nervous system, and connective tissue. Another factor is that childhood cancer is usually a highly malignant disease that has a significant impact on a growing and developing individual with immature organ systems. On the positive side, however, is the point that generally children tolerate even aggressive therapies well. The high remission and cure rate for acute lymphocytic leukemia is one example of the success of multimodal therapy in this childhood cancer. Table 3-1 summarizes the types of childhood cancer listed in order of greatest incidence. This chapter will discuss the common cancers in childhood, outlining disease characteristics, epidemiology, symptomatology, diagnostic procedures, treatment, prognosis, and current investigative work pertaining to each. Generally childhood cancer is treated utilizing multi-chemotherapeutic agents and multitreatment modalities (Chapters 2, 4, and 5). The reader is referred to information in these other chapters related to each cancer and treatment type that is appropriate to the assessment of and care planning for these children and their families.

LEUKEMIA

Leukemia is the most common malignancy found in children. Two broad classifications of

TABLE 3-1. INCIDENCE OF CHILDHOOD CANCER

Site	Rate per Million	Total (%)
Leukemias	33.6	30.2
Central nervous system (brain)	20.7	18.6
Lymphomas	15.1	13.6
Sympathetic nervous system (Neuroblastoma)	8.6	7.7
Soft tissue (rhabdomyosarcoma)	7.1	6.5
Kidney (Wilms' tumor)	6.8	6.1
Bone	5.1	4.6
Retinoblastoma	3.0	2.6
Liver	1.3	1.2
Other	9.9	8.9
Total	111.1	100.0

Adapted from Silverberg and Lutea (1983).

there are two types of

leukemia exist, acute and chronic with subgroups within each of these categories. Chronic leukemia is uncommon in childhood. This discussion will focus on acute leukemia. The most prevalent type of acute leukemia is *acute lymphocytic leukemia* (ALL), which comprises almost 70% of all childhood leukemia. Using immunological markers, ALL is further subdivided into phenotypic subgroups: T-cell, approximately 25%; pre-B-ALL, 26%; B-cell, 2%; and non-T, non-B or common ALL, approximately 67% (Pullen, et al., 1983). A classification based on blast cell morphology and cytochemical staining has been in use since 1976. This morphologic classification divides the lymphoblasts into three types: L1, 73% of the cases; L2, 24%; L3, less than 2% (Lichtman and Siegel, 1983).

About 15% of children who are diagnosed with leukemia have *acute non-lymphocytic leukemia* (ANLL). Although symptomatology is similar, response to treatment and prognosis varies from the typical favorable course of ALL. This will be discussed further in the following subsections.

EPIDEMIOLOGY

For every 100,000 children, 6 new cases of ALL occur annually. The peak age at diagnosis is 4 years, with a slightly higher rate of occurrence in males (Lichtman and Siegel, 1983). Approximately 90% of the cases are found in white children. Children with Down's syndrome have a 20 times greater incidence of ALL than the general population.

Although a number of proven causes of leukemia are known, e.g., ionizing radiation, benzene exposure, and some cancer chemotherapeutic agents, most cases develop in patients where no etiologic cause can be determined. It is of interest that rates of occurrence of leukemia in different countries are remarkably similar, in contrast to marked differences in the incidence of many other types of tumors (Greenwald and Greenwald, 1983).

There are important differences in the occurrence of ALL in white and black children. In terms of incidence, white children are affected about twice as frequently as black children. The survival rates are generally poorer in black children, with a significantly smaller remission rate, shorter duration of remission, and shorter survival. A greater number of the *acute non-lymphocytic leukemia* (ANLL) cases has been reported to occur among black children, although some authors maintain that the percentage of this unfavorable cell type is similar for blacks and whites (Haddy, 1982).

CLINICAL PICTURE AND DIAGNOSIS

Regardless of cell type the typical presentation of the child with leukemia results from the reduction of the number and function of hematopoietic cells. Symptoms of anemia such as malaise, fatigue, and anorexia, therefore, often are present. Signs of thrombocytopenia include gingival, cutaneous, or nasal bleeding. Lack of mature white blood cells predisposes the child to infection — fever in conjunction with signs of a specific infection site such as skin or respiratory system often are indications of infection. Rapid cell division and accumulation of blast cells in the lymphatic system, liver, spleen, or testes causes enlargement of these organs and can be a presenting symptom. Bone and joint pain may also occur)(Lichtman and Siegel, 1983).

Regarding diagnosis of ALL, complete blood counts document anemia and thrombocytopenia in most patients. The granulocyte picture may be variable, with approximately 50% having a white blood cell count (WBC) less than 25,000. The WBC count may be depressed or very high, which is relatively uncommon (Klopovich and Cohen, 1984). Bone marrow aspiration reveals suppression of normal cells and the presence of blasts or immature cells. A spinal tap is usually done; however, less than 10% of all cases show central nervous system (CNS) involvement at diagnosis (Klopovich and Cohen, 1984). A CT scan of suspected involved organ systems or biopsy, particularly testicular biopsy, may be indicated depending on the clinical picture. Blood chemistry evaluation usually reveals high uric acid levels due to the presence of cellular waste products, and blood or exudate culture may demonstrate bacterial growth if infection is present.

In ANLL the presenting symptomatology is similar, as are diagnostic findings. A slightly higher percentage (15%) of patients present with CNS involvement (Klopovich and Cohen, 1984).

PROGNOSIS

Analysis of survival and mortality statistics from various cancer centers nationwide has established six individual factors that are significant in predicting remission duration and survival for ALL. These are the initial WBC, nodal enlargement, age, hemoglobin, sex, and platelet count. Sex continues to be an important prognostic factor even in the prolonged remission period, whereas the other factors lose their prognostic value after 2 years of continuous complete remission (CCR). The most favorable prognosis exists for those who have an initial WBC of less than 10,000 and are between 3 and 7 years of age; almost 90% of these children remain in CCR for 4 or more years past diagnosis. Approximately 50% of all patients fall into an intermediate group and (1) are less than 3 years of age or greater than 7, with an initial WBC of less than 10,000, or (2) are any age with an initial WBC between 10,000 and 50,000. About 65% of this group survive 4 years past diagnosis. In the poor prognosis group, the initial WBC is greater than 50,000; the median survival in this group is under 2 years. Specifically those in the infant age group and adolescents with other poor prognostic factors such as high WBC or CNS involvement, form subsets with a particularly poor prognosis. Sex differences exist with males generally surviving for shorter periods, primarily due to the occurrence of testicular relapse. Ethnic differences have been mentioned; blacks generally have shorter remission periods and greater incidence of relapse when compared to whites of similar prognostic and treatment groups, and even when availability of medical care is excluded as a factor. Finally the group of children with CNS involvement at diagnosis also form a poor prognostic category (Miller, 1982). In addition to the fact that many children with ANLL form a subgroup with a poorer prognosis, many unfavorable prognostic factors, including ethnic group, are more often present in these patients than in those with ALL (Haddy, 1982).

The primary reason for identifying significant prognostic criteria is to identify those children at high risk for early treatment failure, relapse, and death. Generally children in these poor prognostic groupings are treated more aggressively than those in favorable and intermediate prognostic groups. Research continues to be undertaken as to the success of more intensive treatment in these children with a poorer prognosis. Children in the favorable prognostic groups are more often treated less intensively than those with ANLL without compromising effectiveness. This approach results in reduction of both toxicity and delayed side-effects for the child who is likely to become a long-term survivor (Miller, 1982).

TREATMENT

Treatment of ALL is aimed at the eradication of leukemia blast cells based on the theory that this will allow for regrowth of normal cells. Apparently ALL is highly responsive to therapy, as is indicated by the dramatic improvement in remission rates and long-term survival with the widespread use of multiagent chemotherapy. Treatment is based on the principles of (1) obtaining a complete remission, (2) early use of CNS prophylaxis, (3) maintaining remission with combination chemotherapy, (4) providing intensive supportive care, and (5) tailoring therapy to prognostic factors based on the individual child's status. Although there are various effective protocols combining chemotherapeutic agents, most protocols consist of three basic phases.

Induction therapy refers to the initial attempt to effect remission, i.e., an absence of leukemia cells from the bone marrow and peripheral blood. Ninety-five percent of children with ALL achieve an initial complete remission in a period of 4 to 6 weeks when treated with a combination of vincristine, prednisone, cyclophosphamide, L-asparaginase and daunomycin (Miller, 1982). There are differing opinions regarding the efficacy of therapy with only three of these drugs (vincristine, prednisone, and either L-asparaginase or daunomycin). Proponents maintain that a similar remission rate is obtained with less toxicity (Lichtman and Siegel, 1983).

Consolidation or intensification therapy has as its goal the further reduction of the leukemic cell burden. Controversy exists whether this phase of therapy is necessary. It does seem to improve the outlook for those children with poor prognostic factors and to enhance the remission rate for those in the intermediate prognostic group due to age and initial WBC count. This protocol consists of an aggressive regimen including dexamethasone, vincristine, doxorubicin, L-asparaginase, cyclophosphamide, cytosine arabinoside, 6-thioguanine, and intrathecal methotrexate. This multidrug administration is begun either immediately after remission or in the third month of the maintenance phase of therapy (Lichtman and Siegel, 1983).

Maintenance therapy is a crucial part of therapy for ALL, prolonging the period of remission. Most protocols continue maintenance therapy for 30 to 36 months. The goal of this phase is to maintain control, to prevent the potential problem of drug-resistant clones of cells from developing, and to minimize the impact of immediate and long-term side-effects. Many agents and schedules of administration can be used employing the drugs mentioned above; however, most regimens include oral 6-mercaptopurine given on a daily basis and methotrexate given weekly (Klopovich and Cohen, 1984). As mentioned previously, careful monitoring and intense supportive therapy are important components of this stage. Various adjunctive therapies may be used at this stage, if needed, including blood component therapy and nutritional support. It is also at this phase of therapy that experimental or investigational methods may be used, such as bone marrow transplant in selected patients, usually those with a poor prognosis.

Central nervous system prophylaxis is one of the most important advances in treatment of childhood ALL. Eradication of disease theorized present in the CNS at diagnosis is the focus of this treatment. The blood–brain barrier effectively inhibits the action of most chemotherapeutic agents, resulting in "sanctuary" sites in which leukemia cells can proliferate. To prevent this problem intrathecal administration of chemotherapeutic drugs and cranial irradiation are used. Without CNS prophylaxis over 50% of affected children will relapse quickly with bone marrow involvement following identification of CNS disease (Miller, 1982). Research is in progress regarding the most effective and least toxic treatment. It appears that the smallest effective dose of cranial irradiation is necessary, in addition to intrathecal methotrexate administration. One successful regimen includes 2400 rads of cranial irradiation and five doses of intrathecal methotrexate. Some centers are investigating intensive initial intrathecal methotrexate followed by injection at 2 month intervals throughout the maintenance phase (Klopovich and Cohen, 1984). As discussed in detail in Chapter 10, delayed toxic effects from both intrathecal administration and cranial irradiation are increasingly being documented and include abnormal CT scan, impaired school performance, and rare leukoencephalopathy. Alternative approaches such as fractionated radiotherapy and changes in intrathecal methotrexate schedules are currently being investigated (Miller, 1982).

Similar to CNS relapse testicular relapse is also common. As children experience prolonged remission and cure, attention is being paid to the possible benefit of elective testicular biopsy and treatment of occult testicular leukemia. One series reports an incidence of occult testicular leukemia of 8.5%, for which they recommend bilateral testicular irradiation and a 2-year course of intensive systemic therapy. Sterility is irreversible with this treatment, but hormone production and sexual performance remain intact. Prophylactic treatment has not been advocated due to the long-term effects and the fact that the risk of relapse is not as great as that with CNS disease (Kolopvich and Cohen, 1984). In terms of other potential sanctuary sites, namely liver, spleen and kidneys, prophy-

lactic irradiation has not been shown to enhance survival and does increase morbidity (Lichtman and Siegel, 1983).

The treatment of acute non-lymphocytic leukemia is less successful than for ALL with a 70% to 75% remission induction rate. Until very recently remission duration has been 9 to 16 months. Current research is predicting an increased long-term survival rate of 56%, particularly for patients under 18 years.

Induction therapy for ANLL is usually comprised of cytosine arabinoside and daunomycin. Severe marrow *dysfunction* occurs and many patients require two inductions to obtain remission. Additional aggressive treatment with these drugs may continue as consolidation and maintenance therapy. Many other drugs may be employed, however, notably 5-azacytadine, 6-thioguanine, N-AMSA, and VP-16. Since the course of therapy is not yet well documented, some patients are treated for as little as 12 months or as much as several years. CNS relapse is a frequent complication; thus CNS prophylaxis is now considered routine.

Because of the poor prognosis for ANLL, early treatment with bone marrow transplant was considered if an human leukocyte antigen (HLA) identical donor was available (see Chapter 6 for a discussion of bone marrow transplantation. More aggressive chemotherapy and supportive therapy may result in a better prognosis for this group of children. Since bone marrow transplant poses risks and necessitates a matched donor, it may not continue to be the preferred treatment for ANLL as the effectiveness of other forms of treatment for ANLL improve (Klopovich and Cohen, 1984).

Treatment failure normally indicates an unfavorable prognosis. Successive remissions have been achieved, however, with intensive therapy. Usually these remissions are short-lived and extensive toxic effects occur. The decision to pursue newer modalities depends on many factors, such as the child's clinical status, previous therapy and complications, organ dysfunction, parental and patient wishes, and prognosis (Miller, 1982).

BRAIN TUMORS

Central nervous system tumors are the second most common childhood malignancy.

EPIDEMIOLOGY

Most of these tumors occur in the infratentorial region of the brain (51.2%), with others occurring in the supratentorial region and the spinal cord. Only 30% of adult brain tumors occur in the infratentorial area. Childhood brain tumors represent 9% to 20% of all childhood tumors and do not vary in incidence between white and black children, but are more common in males. The most common age for these tumors is between 5 and 10 years of age, but they can occur at any age (van Eys, 1984).

Table 3-2 classifies childhood brain tumors by location. The emphasis of this section will be on infratentorial tumors since their incidence is so high. Medulloblastomas and astrocytomas each account for 30% of all childhood tumors. Ependymomas, the most frequent fourth ventricular tumors, account for 12%, while optic

TABLE 3-2. BRAIN TUMORS IN CHILDREN

Infratentorial Tumors
  Cerebellar and fourth ventricle
    Astrocytoma
    Medulloblastoma
    Ependymoma
  Brain stem
    Brain stem glioma
Supratentorial Tumors
  Hemispheres
    Astrocytoma
    Sarcoma
    Meningioma
  Midline
    Craniopharyngioma
    Optic glioma
    Pinealoma
    Ependymoma
Spinal Cord Tumors
  Ependymoma
  Astrocytoma

From van Eys, J. (1984).

pathway gliomas account for only 5% of these tumors (McDonald, 1983).

There is no known cause for brain tumors. A developmental origin is suspected in children. In some of these tumors chromosome defects have been demonstrated. Chemical and viral etiologies have not been found in humans, but can be demonstrated in laboratory animals (McDonald, 1983). A significantly lower incidence of brain tumors has been found in black African children living in Uganda and Nigeria, suggesting a possible environmental influence (Haddy, 1982).

CLINICAL PICTURES AND DIAGNOSIS

Medulloblastomas occur in the cerebellum at the midline and expand into the fourth ventricle and other areas of the brain, as well as to the spinal cord. They cause ventricular obstruction, which leads to increased intracranial pressure (Maul, 1984).

Astrocytomas vary in terms of location, size, rate of growth, and degree of differentiation. These tumors are either cystic or solid and often occur in the cerebellum (Maul, 1984).

Brain stem gliomas are usually slow growing astrocytomas or glioblastomas that are located in the center of the brain stem.

Ependymomas are usually found in the fourth ventricle and are composed of the ependymal cells that line the ventricles. There are various grades of this tumor that are classified according to the cell differentiation. These tumors also cause increased intracranial pressure from obstruction of the ventricles (Maul, 1984).

Most of the symptoms that create the clinical picture of a child with a brain tumor are generalized in nature. It is difficult to assess the condition of a child with a brain tumor because of the lack of communication skills, the vagueness of symptoms, and the commonality of the symptoms. Many young children have visual problems, for example, or are clumsy, have problems in school, and so on. Also initial symptoms may be associated with other problems such as other childhood diseases, especially cerebral palsy, seizure disorders, and meningitis or head trauma. Psychosocial experiences also can produce similar symptoms. It is common in childhood for there to be one or more of the following: a regression or halt in development; deterioration in school performance; irritability; lack of attentiveness; an unusual degree of unpredictability in behavior and in changes in responsiveness; loss of sphincter control; disturbances in previous patterns of sleeping and eating; and other behavioral problems.

The generalized signs and symptoms produced by brain tumors result from increased intracranial pressure, whereas localized symptoms can result from pressure of the tumor or enlarged ventricle on other structures or from destruction of the neuropathways. Cerebral edema may develop, causing the obstruction of the flow of cerebrospinal fluid, resulting in hydrocephalus.

The generalized symptoms resulting from increased intracranial pressure vary according to the age of the patient and the location and growth rate of the tumor. In infants the anterior fontanelle may appear full and tense while the child is in an upright position. The infant's eyes may exhibit the sunset phenomenon (deviate downward) and the split sutures may prevent a cracking sound when percussed (Maul, 1984).

Headaches are the most common sign and symptom of increased intracranial pressure. In very young children and infants, headaches may be expressed as irritability. The headache can be so severe that it awakens the child in the morning. Young children also exhibit head holding, head rolling, rocking, and anorexia. Vomiting (often projectile) frequently accompanies the morning headaches and is not preceded by nausea.

Impaired vision is another symptom of increased intracranial pressure. Optic pathways may be interfered with. Papilledema may develop but the resulting vision problems are intermittent. Visual problems may not be readily apparent in young children, since they are naturally hyperopic until approximately 9 years of age.

Seizures rarely occur early in the course of the disease. They often tend to be of focal origin, but some are psychomotor or generalized in character. When seizures do occur they generally indicate that the tumor involves the temporal lobes of the brain or that herniation has occurred. Herniation also presents with large pupils that are nonreactive to light, decorticate posturing, Cheyne–Stokes respiration, and a decreased level of consciousness progressing to coma.

Focal neurologic effects also will be present depending on the location of the tumors. Supratentorial tumors with hemisphere locations can present with seizures, but clinically it is difficult to determine the type of tumor present. Supratentorial tumors with midline locations have the most insidious onset. These tumors can present with personality changes or endocrine changes, optic pathway interference may occur, and increased intracranial pressure may develop.

Increased intracranial pressure is an early symptom with infratentorial tumors. Vomiting and headaches are seen as a result, as are disturbances of gait and balance. Spinal cord tumors that are intramedullary create symmetrical muscle weakness and atrophy. Spinal cord tumors that are extramedullary cause specific nerve root effects.

Diagnosis is often difficult, as mentioned earlier, due to the many possible diagnoses based on these symptoms. Radiological studies are relied upon for diagnosis since many of these tumors are surgically inaccessible. If there is adequate radiologic demonstration of the tumor, a tissue diagnosis is not necessary for treatment. Standard diagnostic skull films are useful to document increased intracranial pressure. These films can demonstrate suture separation, specific bony erosions, and increased digital markings. In young children a brain tumor need not be present, however, for digital markers to be prominent.

Computerized tomography (CT) of the brain is the diagnostic tool of choice. A contrast-enhanced study must be done with all children who are suspect to avoid missing small lesions. This method of diagnosis has replaced the use of other radiologic exams since it is noninvasive, safe, painless, highly accurate, effective, and can be done on an outpatient basis.

Lumbar puncture is usually avoided. If a large amount of fluid is extracted, or if the fluid continues to leak out of the puncture site, there can be a shift in the intracranial contents and herniation may develop. When spinal fluid is obtained it must be examined for presence of malignant cells, a culture must be obtained, and a chemical evaluation must be done. Protein is elevated in about $\frac{1}{3}$ of the cases. Rarely a low glucose level will be found.

PROGNOSIS AND TREATMENT

The treatment and prognosis of the different types of central nervous system tumors vary with each type of tumor, so these two categories will be discussed together following the general principles of treatment.

Surgical treatment is the treatment of choice, but cure by this treatment alone is rare. Many tumors are inaccessible to surgery or can only partially be removed. Surgery is utilized for diagnostic purposes, therefore, as well as to remove a tumor and for decompression and debulking of the tumor.

Radiotherapy is the second most frequently used treatment with brain tumors, although long-term effects of such treatment to the central nervous system can be very costly. On a short-term basis cerebral edema often develops, and corticosteroids are often required. On a long-term basis endocrine abnormalities are common, as are EEG disturbances. Other effects of radiotherapy on children are discussed in Chapter 5 and Chapter 10.

Chemotherapy has not proven to be as effective with brain tumors as it is with other types of childhood tumors. Several reasons for this include the blood–brain barrier problem and the slow growth rate of some brain tumors. The optimal route of administration also differs with different types of brain tumors, and tolerance to the chemotherapy may be low due to the side-effects of the radiation therapy. Common drugs used in different protocols include single agents such as methotrexate, carmustine (BCNU), and steroids, and combinations of drugs such as methotrexate, oncovin, prednisone, and procarbazine which are used in the MOPP protocol (Klopovich and Cohen, 1984).

CEREBELLAR ASTROCYTOMA

This type of tumor comprises only approximately 20% of all pediatric intracranial tumors. A 5-year survival rate of 75% has been obtained after complete surgical removal of the tumor. If only partial removal is possible, the 5-year survival rate falls to 56%. Surgery is the treatment of choice for this type of tumor since is it often cystic and the cerebellum can tolerate a lot of surgery and trauma before a loss of function occurs. Radiotherapy and chemotherapy are not indicated with this tumor. Even if it does reoccur after surgery or is only partially removed, the tumor is slow growing and can be treated with further surgical intervention at a future date.

MEDULLOBLASTOMA

This tumor is the most commonly seen CNS tumor in children, with 80% of all cases occurring before the age of 15. If the disease is confined to the posterior fossa at diagnosis, the prognosis is better than if metastasis has occurred. Prognosis is poorer in younger children and in boys. Late recurrences occur, but a 10-year survival rate is associated with cure. Currently there is only a 5-year survival rate of 35%, however, and a 10-year survival rate of 25%.

Total resection of the tumor is the first attempted treatment. But since this tumor rapidly metastasizes throughout the cerebellum and the spinal cord, all patients receive radiotherapy. Generally patients receive approximately 4500 rads over the entire brain, 5500 rads to the tumor bed, and 3500 to 4500 rads to the spinal column. Controversy exists over the benefit of chemotherapy. Some studies have found no improvement in prognosis; others report significant improvement. No set regimen is recommended but combinations of vincristine, CCNU, methotrexate, BCNU and MOPP protocols are commonly being utilized.

BRAIN STEM GLIOMA

This tumor occurs primarily in children between 3 and 8 years of age and accounts for 10% to 15% of all pediatric brain tumors. The prognosis is poor, with a median survival rate of 15 months with no radiation to 47 months with therapy. There is a reported 5-year survival rate of 20 to 30% (van Eys, 1984). Due to the location of this tumor in the brain stem, surgery is difficult to impossible. As a result radiation is the treatment of choice. The radiation is administered only to the brain stem, at a dose of 5000 to 6000 rads. The use of chemotherapy is controversial and unclear. Drugs such as methotrexate, vincristine, and CCNU have been utilized without much increase in survival rate.

EPENDYMOMAS

This tumor can occur anywhere in the brain or the spinal cord, but in children it is most often seen in the fourth ventricle. It represents 9% of all brain tumors and 24% of intraspinal tumors.

The prognosis rate varies from study to study with the 5-year survival rate reported to be from 15% to 60%. The prognosis will vary depending on the patient's age, the degree of malignancy of the tumor, and the treatment utilized.

Treatment of these brain tumors also varies from study to study. Total removal by surgery is difficult and rarely curative. Radiation therapy is given either locally or to the total craniospinal axis. The benefits of each type of radiotherapy are controversial. Chemotherapy is utilized basically if the tumor reoccurs. Drugs that may be effective include BCNU, CCNU, and methotrexate. There is debate about whether even to treat these tumors, although survival has been prolonged through radiotherapy.

OTHER TUMORS

There are many other types of brain tumors that occur less frequently. The prognosis and treatment will vary with each specific tumor, but the general principles of surgery, radiotherapy, and chemotherapy apply to all. Overall, the prognosis of these other brain tumors is not good.

LYMPHOMA

Lymphomas as a group account for a relatively low rate of incidence, making them the third most common cancer in childhood. They are a significant type of malignancy in practice in that many Hodgkin's disease patients, in particular, become long-term survivors. These cancers of the lymphatic system have for a long time been thought to have an infectious etiology, and viruses have been found to be associated with Hodgkin's disease and Burkitt's lymphoma, a non-Hodgkin's lymphoma type. Research is still underway to determine etiology; genetic and environmental factors also are being considered. Although cancers of the lymph share a common site of origin, the most common lymphoma, Hodgkin's disease, does vary from other lymphomas. This section therefore will discuss Hodgkin's disease separately, followed by non-Hodgkin's lymphoma.

HODGKIN'S DISEASE

EPIDEMIOLOGY

This type of lymphoma is primarily a disease of the second decade of life, continuing to be frequent in the young adult age group. The disease is rare in children under 5, but does occur in infants and young children. Boys are more commonly affected in the early years by a 3–4 to 1 ratio, although the incidence in girls begins to increase in the preteen period. After age 12 the sex ratio has been shown to change to a preponderance of females. There are indications of racial and socioeconomic differences. The clinical course of black children has been found to be unfavorable in some cancer centers, for example, although other centers have found black patients to show no unusual characteristics. At a southwestern cancer center, Mexican–American children comprised 19% of those treated and had an accelerated course of the disease compared to whites (Sullivan, et al., 1984). In contrast to the clinical course, incidence rates appear to be similar in whites and nonwhites and this seems to hold true cross culturally (Haddy, 1982). A South American study reported high rates of Hodgkin's disease in Brazilian children living in poor socioeconomic conditions. Socioeconomic conditions could, of course, be closely linked to data on racial or ethnic differences.

CLINICAL PICTURE AND DIAGNOSIS

The most common presenting symptom in the majority of children with Hodgkin's disease is painless cervical adenopathy, with or without associated fever. Approximately half of these cases manifest mediastinal involvement as well. The typical constellation of symptoms includes anorexia, malaise, and lassitude. Weight loss may occur. The disease is categorized into four stages, which will be discussed later, but the presence of these clinical signs adds a "B" designation to the stage determined. The fever pattern is variable with approximately 30% of the cases showing a moderate intermittent temperature elevation of 2° to 3°F above normal. The typical recurrent and relapsing fever in adults, known as Pel–Ebstein, is rare in children, as are night sweats. Pruritus is uncommon but may occur in adolescents with significant mediastinal disease (Haddy, 1982; Bakemeier, et al., 1983).

Diagnosis involves various imaging techniques, including x-ray, sonography and CT scanning, blood testing, and direct surgical evaluation. X-ray of the chest and lymphangiography are done routinely to detect mediastinal involvement, as well as the involvement of pelvic and para-aortic nodes. Ultrasound is a useful and noninvasive means of evaluating abdominal and neck areas for masses and later to determine response to therapy. Computerized tomography may be done to more precisely evaluate questionable mediastinal node enlargement and lung or pleural masses. It is not as useful in abdominal scanning as lymphangiogram or ultrasound. Nuclear scanning may be used in the child who is sensitive to radiopaque dyes or whose large pulmonary or mediastinal masses contraindicate lymphangiogram. This procedure (gallium scanning) has been shown to be particularly useful in evaluating obscure or recurrent disease, since gallium citrate has an affinity for lymphomas, particularly Hodgkin's tissue (Sullivan, et al., 1984).

Hematologic examination usually uncovers leukocytosis and a mild normocytic, normochromic anemia. Elevated serum alkaline phosphatase may be present when blood chemistries are analyzed. High gamma globulin levels are common. Finally bone marrow biopsy usually is done as part of the preliminary workup, although the failure to demonstrate Reed–Sternberg cells is common and does not rule out Hodgkin's.

The staging designation depicted in Figure 3-1 is as follows: Stage I disease is confined to one lymph node group; stage II disease occurs on only one side of the diaphragm; stage III disease involves nodes bilaterally affected, usually including the spleen (which is considered a node for staging); and stage IV disease is a disseminated process involving many body sites including the lung, liver, bone marrow, CNS, and others (Sullivan, et al., 1984).

The staging process is vital to successful treatment and obtaining the best prognosis for each child with Hodgkin's disease. Precise anatomic staging enables the provision of appropriate therapy for the extent of the disease. Also comparison of the effectiveness of treatment among children with similar disease pictures is enhanced, which has important research implications.

Surgical procedures are used for comprehensive anatomic staging. Biopsy of the largest and most central node in an enlarged node group is usually the procedure of choice and will reveal the presence of R–S cells in an individual with Hodgkin's disease (Bakemeier, et al., 1983). The operative procedure that best defines precise anatomic involvement is a staging celiotomy. This procedure is performed on all newly diagnosed patients over 5 years old who do not have obvious stage IV disease. There are some additional benefits to the procedure, aside from the accurate diagnostic picture it affords. One positive aspect of doing the celiotomy is the careful evaluation of the spleen, which is involved in 30% to 40% of the patients with stage I and stage II disease. For the female child the staging celiotomy provides an opportunity to reposition the ovaries to minimize exposure should pelvic radiation be required at a later time.

Usually the operation consists of splenectomy, liver biopsy, and removal of representative lymph nodes done though a midline inci-

sion. While the patient is in surgery a wedge biopsy is obtained from the iliac crest for bone marrow examination. Recovery from surgery includes management of ileus due to bowel manipulation and overcoming the potential for fulminate infection related to splenectomy. This threat of infection lasts through the lifetime of a child having had a splenectomy, with 10% of the children in a sample of 200 developing a serious infection up to 20 years postsplenectomy. Prophylactic antibiotic therapy is usually administered postoperatively to guard against this life-threatening complication (Sullivan, et al., 1984).

PROGNOSIS

The outcome for the child with Hodgkin's disease varies directly with both clinical staging at diagnosis and histological characteristics of the tissue type. Definitive cure is the outlook for more than 90% of those children with stage I and II, A or B (with or without constitutional symptoms). Stage III disease continues to have a favorable prognosis approaching 90%, while stage IV patients with disseminated disease have only a 50% survival rate (Sullivan, et al., 1984).

TREATMENT

Following staging a treatment plan is based on the stage and other considerations such as age and sex. Involved field radiotherapy is the indicated therapy in the first, most favorable, stage. In stages I and II with small mediastinal node involvement, treatment includes "mantle," or neck and mediastinal radiotherapy. If mediastinal involvement is significant, radiotherapy is administered along with combination chemotherapy. Stage III disease requires both radiation and chemotherapy; stage IV necessitates combination chemotherapy with optional radiotherapy for large masses.

Some modifications are made for the developing child. For example, splenectomy may be

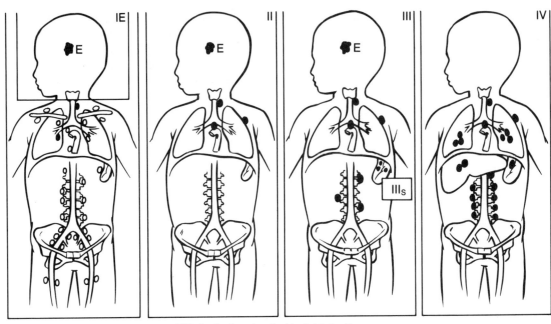

FIG 3–1. Staging in Hodgkin's disease.

Stage		Substage
Stage I	Single node region	I
	Single extralymphatic. Organ/site	I (E)*
Stage II	Two or more node regions, same side of diaphragm	II
	Single node region + localized single extralympatic. Organ/site	II (E)
Stage III	Node regions both sides of diaphragm	III
	± Localized single extralymphatic	III (E)
	Organ/site: Spleen, both	III(E)
		III (ES)
Stage IV	Diffuse involvement extralymphatic	
	Organ/site ± node regions	IV
All stages divided	Without weight loss/fever/sweats	A
	With weight loss/fever/sweats	B

*E = extranodal; S = spleen involved.

[Adapted from Bakemeier, Zagers, Cooper, and Rubin (1983)]

omitted in patients under 5 years, or radiotherapy may be delayed until age 8 or more to prevent growth retardation. Multiple agent chemotherapy is used consistently for stage I and stage II patients with unfavorable characteristics and for all stage III and stage IV patients. Depending on the cancer center, many regimens are used and are summarized in Table 3-3.

The use of several chemotherapeutic agents (MAC) (Table 3-3) sandwiched around a course of involved field radiotherapy is a typical treatment (see Chapters 4 and 5). Surgical intervention is not used generally as a treatment modality in children with Hodgkin's except for the initial staging, biopsies, and splenectomy, due to its disfiguring effects on the growing child and the efficacy of chemotherapy. Some new approaches include investigation of different combinations of chemo- and radiotherapy and the use of the MOPP protocol with extended field radiotherapy following surgical staging, which results in a projected 91% survival rate for all stages (Sullivan, et al., 1984).

NON-HODGKIN'S LYMPHOMA

Third in frequency of occurrence of childhood tumors, about 60% of all lymphomas are of the non-Hodgkin's type. Most classification systems agree in the separation of non-Hodgkin's into two morphologically different groupings, nodular and diffuse, which are further divided into various cell types. Other methods of classification exist; of note is the system in use at St. Jude's Hospital, which differentiates tumors by anatomical site of presentation (Klopovich and Cohen, 1984). For the purposes of this discussion, non-Hodgkin's types as a group and Burkitt's lymphoma will be the main considerations.

EPIDEMIOLOGY

The peak incidence occurs in the 7 to 11 age group: Burkitt's lymphoma shows a slight variation with peak incidence in 5- to 9-year-olds. There is a relatively low incidence of non-Hodgkin's in the adolescent age group but a gradual rise in numbers of adult cases. A male predominance is demonstrated in children with about a 3 : 1 ratio, while the reverse is true for adults. In terms of geographic distribution, Burkitt's lymphoma is most common in Africa, representing 50% of all malignant tumors in African children. According to many worldwide comparisons, it appears that the lower socioeconomic groups have a higher occurrence of non-Hodgkin's; in the United States, however, the mortality rates are higher in high population areas, particularly in the higher education and income levels (White and Siegel, 1984). In terms of race, while the most common tumor in black Africans is Burkitt's lymphoma, this tumor is uncommon in white or black American children. In the United States little difference is seen based on racial characteristics (Haddy, 1982).

Several etiologic theories have been investigated implicating viruses, genetic or constitutional factors, and radiation-related factors. Non-Hodgkin's has been reported increasingly as a secondary malignancy following multimodal treatment of Hodgkin's disease. Other potential associations include primary immunodeficiency syndromes, immunosuppression, anticonvulsant therapy, and certain connective tissue diseases (White and Siegel, 1984).

CLINICAL PICTURE AND DIAGNOSIS

The typical presentation of the child with non-Hodgkin's lymphoma is one of acute onset of symptoms and rapid progression. Approximately 80% of the cases are thought to have disseminated disease at diagnosis. The abdomen is the most frequent presenting site (from 23% to 46% of the cases). Lymph node involvement is frequent, as well as direct extension to surrounding structures. The most common initial symptom is pain, either localized to the abdomen or referred to other sites. Other symptoms include vomiting, anorexia, diarrhea,

TABLE 3-3. MULTIAGENT CHEMOTHERAPY PROTOCOLS FOR HODGKIN'S DISEASE

MAC (multiagent chemotherapy) Doxorubicin Prednisone Procarbazine Vincristine Cyclophosphamide	CVPP CCNU Vinblastine Procarbazine Prednisone
A-COPP Doxorubicin Prednisone Vincristine Cyclophosphamide Prednisone Procarbazine	ABVD Doxorubicin Bleomycin Vinblastine B-CAVe Bleomycin CCNU Doxorubicin Vinblastine
MOPP HN₂ Vincristine Prednisone Procarbazine	ABDIC Doxorubicin Bleomycin CCNU Prednisone

Adapted from Sullivan, M., Fuller, L., and Butler, J. (1984).

weight loss, ascites, distention, palpable mass, fever, and paraplegia. An "acute" abdomen can result from intestinal obstruction. Abdominal tumors may be localized and can be resected completely in some cases (White and Siegel, 1984).

Approximately one third of childhood non-Hodgkin's occur in the nodal areas above the diaphragm in the neck, axilla, or mediastinum. Symptoms include those of tracheal compression with coughing, wheezing, increasing dyspnea, and malaise. Pleural effusions and other pressure-related symptoms can occur, such as superior vena cava syndrome. This disease picture usually represents a tumor that is rapidly progressive with frequent metastasis. When head and neck regions are involved, there is significant risk of CNS involvement.

The remainder of cases involve peripheral lymph nodes and extranodal sites such as lung, bone, and soft tissue. Symptoms are related to the specific site involved and are usually the result of pressure on adjacent organs and structures.

The African Burkitt's lymphoma often involves the jaw, an early sign being the loosening of the teeth. The maxilla is more usually involved and this may result in exophthalmos. In America Burkitt's and non-Hodgkin's lymphomas often present in the abdomen (White and Siegel, 1984).

Diagnosis is based on a complete history and thorough physical examination to rule out other possible diseases. Imaging studies are done that provide information regarding diagnosis and the extent of the disease and provide a baseline for monitoring disease progression. Gallium scanning is usually successful due to the predilection of lymphoma tissue for gallium; this is often combined with ultrasound. Bone marrow aspiration is routinely done, particularly to rule out ALL. A spinal tap is important to determine CNS involvement and will also be indicated at intervals during the treatment phase. Routine blood studies, culture when indicated, and biopsy when feasible are also indicated (White and Siegel, 1984).

STAGING AND PROGNOSIS

There is no uniform staging system in use for non-Hodgkin's lymphoma. The Children's Cancer Study Group separates the disease into favorable and unfavorable prognostic groupings (Table 3-4). The extent of the disease has been found to be of significance in predicting prognosis (White and Siegel, 1984).

In general the presence of CNS involvement or infiltration of the bone marrow at the time of diagnosis are considered poor prognostic signs. For Burkitt's lymphoma the single most important factor has been demonstrated to be the initial size of the tumor burden. Correlates of tumor burden such as lactic dehydrogenase (LDH) and uric acid levels have been found to be significant predictors, as are age and Epstein–Barr virus antibodies. Relapse generally carries a poor prognosis, unless the original treatment course was inadequate (White and Siegel, 1984).

With combined treatment the 3-year survival rate is 50% to 80% for children with non-Hodgkin's lymphoma. The aggressive regimen LSA_2L_2 (discussed below) has demonstrated a particular improvement in prognosis for children with intra-abdominal lesions, even when metastasis is present. With the use of this regimen even children with advanced disease appear to have a better than 50% chance of cure (Klopovich and Cohen, 1984).

TREATMENT

The multimodal treatment plan is based on the following principles: (a) early and rapid reduction in the tumor burden, (b) systemic treatment even if apparent localized disease, (c) CNS prophylaxis to eliminate the site of relapse. Many centers are now tailoring treatment to individual histologic types, rather than using a uniform protocol for all children with non-Hodgkin's lymphoma. Gasparini and colleagues (1983) suggest that Burkitt's lymphoma, in particular, be considered a separate grouping. Surgery is important to the diagnostic phase and in the treatment of localized dis-

TABLE 3-4. PROGNOSTIC FACTORS IN NON-HODGKIN'S DISEASE

Favorable	Unfavorable
Localized abdominal disease	CNS involvement at diagnosis
	Bone marrow infiltration at diagnosis
Burkitt's Lymphoma	
Decreased tumor burden	Large tumor burden

ease. Many centers also are beginning to employ a "second look" procedure to evaluate residual tumor bulk more accurately and to plan more effectively further therapy (Wollner, et al., 1980). Radiation (a previous mainstay of therapy) is used primarily for reduction of bulk disease and local symptom control, chemotherapy having become the primary treatment modality. In Burkitt's lymphoma radiotherapy has been shown to have little effect on bulk disease, possibly due to the rapid doubling time of this cell type (White and Siegel, 1984).

The chemotherapeutic regimen most widely used is the 10 drug protocol LSA_2L_2. In most cases this intensive regimen includes a staging surgery, radiation therapy during induction, and a combination of drugs in an induction, consolidation, and maintenance schedule. The drugs are cyclophosphamide, vincristine, prednisone, methotrexate, daunomycin, cytosine arabinoside, thioguanine, L-asparaginese, BCNU, and hydroxyurea. Following the original surgery a second look laparotomy is included for all children with gross residual intraabdominal disease. (Wollner, et al., 1980)

Other less demanding regimens have been compared favorably with LSA_2L_2, particularly for some histologic types. Found to be similarly effective in general is a regimen including cyclophosphamide, intrathecal methotrexate, vincristine, prednisone (COMP) and radiotherapy, although stratified analysis has found it to be less effective for lymphoblastic lymphoma (3-year survival of 27% versus 76% for LSA_2L_2), but more effective for nonlymphoblastic (56% survival versus 29%). Another regimen using vincristine, doxorubicin, prednisone, 6-mercaptopurine, L-asparaginase, and intrathecal methotrexate with both cranial and tumor site

radiation, has been shown to obtain an 86% relapse-free survival in a sample of mediastinal lymphoblastic lymphoma cases. Murphy and colleagues questioned the importance of radiation therapy and CNS prophylaxis. They randomized the use of radiation therapy, obtaining 2-year survival rates of 55% (White and Siegel, 1984).

Similar concerns have been addressed in dealing with Burkitt's lymphoma; combination protocols have been shown to be more effective than single-agent regimens. Drugs shown effective and used in these regimens include cyclophosphamide, vincristine, methotrexate, prednisone, cytosine arabinoside, and doxorubicin, including CNS prophylaxis with methotrexate (White and Siegel, 1984).

NEUROBLASTOMA

Tumors of the sympathetic nervous system, arising from neural crest tissue rank fourth in frequency of incidence in childhood, and are the third most common solid tumors. They are highly malignant tumors with complex hormonal activity, which can cause a variety of symptoms. This malignancy has the highest reported incidence of spontaneous regression, although spontaneous maturation into a benign ganglioneuroma also can occur.

EPIDEMIOLOGY

Incidence is reported as 1 in 10,000 to 40,000 infants, with a peak occurrence at 2 years of age. Neuroblastoma rarely occurs in children over 6 years. Genetic factors may play a role in the occurrence of this malignancy. A greater likelihood of disease in more than one sibling, as well as the association of neuroblastoma with other hereditary disorders, lends support to this theory (Putman, et al., 1983). Ethnic differences seem to exist; for example, the incidence of neuroblastoma is somewhat lower in black children, although no significant differences have been found regarding outcome (Haddy, 1982).

SYMPTOMS AND DIAGNOSIS

Because of the numerous sites of origin of the primary tumor and the symptoms related to frequent metastatic lesions, few pediatric tumors present with the range of symptoms found in neuroblastoma. Seventy percent of the tumors arise in the abdomen; about half of these originate in the adrenal gland and half in the other ganglia of the viscera. Thus abdominal pain and palpable mass with or without tenderness are typical presenting signs. Related digestive disturbances may also occur, such as anorexia and vomiting. An increase in abdominal girth or pressure-related spinal cord compression may be noted. The other 30% of tumors originate in cervical, thoracic, or pelvic side chains, which cause pressure-related symptoms such as ptosis, respiratory distress, dysphagia, or problems with defecation or urination. Metabolic symptoms caused by excessive amounts of catecholamines include hypertension, diaphoretic episodes, and irritability. Diarrhea and hypercalcemia are possible signs, thought to be related to production of an intestinal peptide. Since up to 70% of patients present with metastasis, constitutional signs may occur such as weight loss, fever, fatigue, and pain (Voute, 1984).

Diagnosis is based on hematologic, biochemical, and radiologic studies. Anemia and infiltration of the bone marrow commonly are seen. Excessive catecholamine excretion is found in tests of 12- or 24-hour urine samples. To determine location and size of primary metastatic lesions, skeletal survey, chest X-ray, and often an inferior vena cavogram are done.

Also used to delineate tumor location are CT scanning, ultrasound, and radioisotope studies. Staging of the tumor and any metastatic involvement is based on these diagnostic tests and is essential for effective treatment planning. Typically used staging designations are:

I.   Tumor confined to origin
II.   Tumor extends beyond origin but does not cross the midline
III. Tumor extends beyond midline; bilateral involvement of regional lymph nodes
IV.   Remote disease indicating metastatic spread
IV-S. Criteria for stage II except that remote disease present in the liver, skin, or bone marrow (excluding bone) (Evans et al., Staging system, cited in Voute, 1984)

An international staging system using a TNM classification has been developed for neuroblastoma, as for other pediatric tumors, in an attempt to standardize classification. With this system clinical or surgical assessment is made of tumor size and location, node location, and metastasis.

PROGNOSIS

Several factors are important in predicting prognosis for the child with neuroblastoma. Histologic type, that is a well-differentiated cell type, is associated with a favorable prognosis. Age at diagnosis varies inversely with survival, with infants under 6 months having the most favorable outcome. Stage at diagnosis definitely influences prognosis with stages I and II patients, particularly in the younger age groups, experiencing a more favorable response. In stage IV patients a different trend is noted—patients over 8 years old seem to do better than those in the 1 to 8 year range, although they have a prolonged at risk period before being considered long-term survivors. Site of origin is also important, with cervical, thorax, and pelvic tumors (approximately 30%)

showing a better prognosis. Finally catecholamine secretion has been associated with prognosis. Nonsecretors (approximately 5% of the cases) appear to have a poorer prognosis (Ibid).

Stage I children generally have an excellent prognosis with complete surgical excision. Stages II and III patients continue to have a good prognosis, dependent on the interaction of the various prognostic factors — age, histologic type, and site of origin. Advanced stage patients continue to have a poor prognosis of an approximately 5% 10-year survival rate (Klopovich and Cohen, 1984).

Spontaneous regression has been documented with this tumor more than any other. It is most common in children under 2 years, and the process remains unclear.

TREATMENT

For stage I patients, complete excision of the tumor is optimal and usually curative. In patients over 2 years subsequent radiotherapy is recommended if excision is incomplete. For stage II patients no further treatment is warranted following complete surgical excision and determination of normal postoperative urinary catecholamines. If catecholamine excretion is increased postoperatively the child may profit from chemotherapy. If excision of tumor and nodes is not possible or is not complete, radiotherapy followed by chemotherapy is selected as a treatment plan.

For stage III patients surgical excision, if feasible, is followed by local radiotherapy and then chemotherapy. In stage IV the resectable tumor is removed, and the residual is treated by radiotherapy. Chemotherapy is the foundation of treatment to obtain remission although long-term survival is unlikely. Stage IV-S treatment is controversial. Some centers use surgical resection, when feasible, low-dose radiation to the liver, and short-term chemotherapy. At other centers surgical removal with biopsy of liver to confirm the diagnosis is followed by small doses of chemotherapy, and a second-look operation after a few months of treatment. Protocols in use at present include combinations of vincristine, cyclophosphamide, doxorubicin, cisplatin, and VM-26; high-dose melphalan and autologous bone marrow transplant have also been used (Voute, 1984; Klopovich and Cohen, 1984).

In regard to recurrence of neuroblastoma or the development of a second malignancy, Dannecker and colleagues (1983) conducted a review of the literature to determine the frequency of late recurrence. In their review 18 cases were reported in which periods from 4 to 15 years of tumor-free survival had been documented. Puberty was the time of relapse in all but 2 of these cases. There was a high incidence of stage IV disease at recurrence and an associated poor prognosis. The authors concluded that followup on children with neuroblastoma who are survivors should perhaps be considered past puberty, perhaps with determinations of urinary catecholamines, keeping in mind that this late recurrence seems to be a relatively rare event.

RHABDOMYOSARCOMA

Rhabdomyosarcoma is the most common soft tissue sarcoma of childhood and is the seventh most common childhood tumor. Overall it accounts for 4% to 8% of all childhood malignancies and 5% to 15% of the solid tumors. It is a highly malignant type of cancer, and about 20% of the patients present with metastatic disease. The Intergroup Rhabdomyosarcoma Study (IRS) was created by physicians to examine the results of treatment and to attempt to improve the prognosis.

EPIDEMIOLOGY

This tumor commonly occurs in early childhood and adolescence. The annual incidence in the United States is 4.5 per million in white children and 1.3 per million in black children

**TABLE 3-5. INCIDENCE OF
RHABDOMYOSARCOMA BY SITE**

Orbit	9%
Other head and neck sites	34%
Trunk	15%
Retroperitoneum	3%
Genitourinary tract	21%
Extremities	18%

under the age of 15 (3 : 1 ratio). After the age of 15 the rate in black children exceeds that of white children. It occurs in males and females in a ratio of 1.4 : 1.

Sites of occurrence are according to age ranges. The younger age group accounts for 70% of the patients and has primary sites occurring in the head and neck areas and in the genitourinary tract. Peak incidence occurs between 2 and 5 years of age. In adolescents the primary sites are the head and neck extremities and the testes. Incidence by site occurs as indicated in Table 3-5.

The etiology of rhabdomyosarcoma is unknown. Various sources do indicate an increased frequency of congenital anomalies, however, as well as a possible link to environmental factors, a possible genetic predisposition, and a possible link to the effects of therapy for another tumor.

CLINICAL PICTURE AND DIAGNOSIS

The presenting signs and symptoms depend on the location of the tumor and any metastases. Generally the tumor presents as an asymptomatic mass that is usually discovered by the patient or the parent. The primary focus of the following discussion will be placed on the head and neck area, since this area accounts for 43% of the occurrences of this disease. The other sites will be discussed briefly.

The head and neck region is divided into the specific areas where the tumor presents. If it occurs in the orbital region, the child may have swelling, proptosis, discoloration, and limitation of ocular motion. Tumors in the other areas of the head and neck may also cause swelling, airway obstruction, dysphagia, epistaxis, pain, discharge from sinuses, hoarseness, and chronic otitis media. Tumors located in the nasopharynx, nasal cavity, paranasal sinuses, and the middle ear may also invade the central nervous system creating facial palsies, respiratory distress and paralysis, and meningeal symptoms.

Tumors in the genitourinary tract may present with urinary tract symptoms, such as hematuria and urinary frequency and retention, and with urethral, vaginal, and other perineal masses. Tumors presenting in the extremities, the trunk, and the retroperitoneal regions simply present with enlarging asymptomatic masses.

When metastasis occurs, it is spread through the lymphatic and hematogenous systems. Sites of metastases may be far from the original area of presentation. Metastatic sites include the lung, bone, bone marrow, lymph nodes, brain, spinal cord, heart, and breast.

Multiple diagnostic procedures are utilized to determine the extent of disease for staging, treatment determination, and a data base for future comparison. Biopsy of the lesion is utilized for a definitive diagnosis. Other diagnostic evaluations routinely done include a complete blood count, urinalysis, chest X-ray, CT scans of the area and adjacent structures, bone marrow biopsy, bone and liver scans, and a cerebrospinal fluid exam if the tumor is in the head and neck region.

After the extent of disease has been determined, the patient's disease is clinically staged according to the criteria developed by the Intergroup Rhabdomyosarcoma Study. This classification is based upon the extent of the disease, including regional lymph nodes, and the extent of disease after initial surgery. Table 3-6 demonstrates this classification system.

PROGNOSIS

As the classification progresses from group I to group IV, the prognosis worsens significantly. A picture of the prognosis of this disease can be created by examining the incidence of cases in each group: group I, 16%; group II, 26%; group III, 40%; and group IV, 18%. Over half of the cases occur in groups III and IV, unfortunately, where the prognosis is poor.

The prognosis is based on several factors. A good prognosis occurs when there is localized disease at diagnosis (group I), favorable histology, early symptoms with little chance to spread, and with an age between 1 and 7 years at diagnosis.

Recurrent disease occurs mostly during the first 2 years following diagnosis. If the disease recurs at the primary site the prognosis remains good; however, metastatic disease signals a poor prognosis.

TREATMENT

Treatment consists of a combination of surgery, radiation, and chemotherapy. There are three goals of surgery: (1) To provide tissue for diagnosis; (2) to remove the tumor; and (3) if this is not possible, to reduce the tumor size as much as possible. Surgery may result in permanent disfigurement, depending on the location of the tumor.

Radiation therapy is used to treat the primary disease as well as any metastasis. Patients in group I who have had their disease totally excised through surgery do not receive this treatment modality. The radiation is administered in doses of 4000 to 6000 rads, depending on the tumor site and the age of the child.

Chemotherapy is utilized to eradicate any microscopic disease that may be present. Patients in all groups receive this therapy. Multiple chemotherapeutic agents are also utilized to reduce the tumor to enable a more complete surgical removal of the tumor. Chemotherapeutic agents currently being utilized include actinomycin D, vincristine, cyclophosphamide, and doxorubicin.

TABLE 3-6. STAGING SYSTEM, INTERGROUP RHABDOMYOSARCOMA STUDY

Group I	Localized disease, completely resected
	Regional nodes not involved
	   Confined to muscle or organ of origin
	   Contiguous involvement—infiltration
	      outside the muscle or organ of origin, as
	      through fascial planes; totally resected

Group II	Regional disease
	   Grossly resected tumor with microscopic
	      residual disease; no evidence of gross
	      tumor; no clinical or microscopic evidence
	      of regional node involvement
	   Regional disease, completely resected
	      (regional nodes involved completely
	      resected with no microscopic residual)
	   Regional disease with involved nodes
	      grossly resected, but with evidence of
	      microscopic residual

Group III	Incomplete resection or biopsy with gross residual disease
Group IV	Metastatic disease present at onset

WILMS' TUMOR (NEPHROBLASTOMA)

Wilms' tumor is the most common renal tumor and the fifth most common pediatric cancer; it is a highly malignant embryonal cancer that forms in the kidney. Wilms' tumor is an example of the success of chemotherapy to treat cancer, showing a change in survival from 8% with surgery alone to 50% with postoperative radiation, to over 90% with surgery and chemotherapy (Putman, 1983).

EPIDEMIOLOGY

The incidence of Wilms' tumor in children under 15 is 7.5 per million annually for whites and 7.8 per million annually for blacks. The average age at diagnosis is $3\frac{1}{2}$ years; with 90% of the patients under 7 at diagnosis. The worldwide incidence seems consistent with the above figures with no apparent environmental or racial influences; however, girls are affected approximately twice as often as boys.

There are interesting suspected hereditary influences. A hereditary form appears to account for about 40% of the cases. It is transmitted as an autosomal dominant and is associated with all bilateral tumor involvement. Additionally, Wilms' tumor is associated with other congenital anomalies such as sporadic aniridia, in which one of three cases will develop Wilms'. Other suspected associations include hemihypertrophy and genitourinary anomalies (Putman, 1983).

SYMPTOMS AND DIAGNOSIS

An abdominal mass is the usual presenting sign in an otherwise healthy-appearing child. Often the parent has noticed either an enlarging abdomen or has discovered the mass accidentally. About a third of the patients complain of abdominal pain. Hematuria may occur, as well as nonspecific complaints of fever, malaise, constipation, or anorexia. Hypertension is frequently present on examination.

Diagnosis is made by physical examination, laboratory studies, and radiologic and serographic studies. Examination of the abdomen reveals a unilateral, smooth, nontender firm mass. Indicated lab tests include complete blood count, urinalysis, urinary catecholamines, blood urea nitrogen, and creatinine and liver function, which are helpful in preoperative evaluation of baseline values. Bone marrow infiltration is rare, in contrast to its common occurrence in neuroblastoma. Intravenous Pyelography (IVP) and chest X-ray are important in determining the presence of the tumor, the functional ability of the other kidney, and lung metastasis. Many centers also use ultrasound if radiographic information is questionable and to determine any spread of the tumor. Skeletal survey is not usually indicated since bone metastasis is rare. Staging is a vital aspect of treatment planning and is based on the diagnostic workup, surgical evaluation, and histologic type.

PROGNOSIS

Results of various studies have indicated the important nonfavorable prognostic factors to be presence of hematogenous spread at diagnosis, histologic type (anaplasia or sarcomatous), and lymph node involvement. Other factors of less importance but also nonfavorable include tumor size and operative spillage, invasion of other blood vessels, and extension of tumor within the abdomen. Without metastasis (stages I, II, and III), projected survival is approximately 83%, while those with metastasis range from 30% to 60% depending on areas of involvement. Generally younger children have more favorable cell types and less incidence of metastasis (Belasco, 1984).

TREATMENT

Surgical management is an important component of the treatment plan. Staging is determined by surgical evaluation, with any residual tumor marked for followup and radiotherapy. If the tumor is unilateral, nephrectomy will often accomplish complete excision. If the upper pole of the kidney is involved, an adrenalectomy may be required. Recovery from surgery is usually prompt and complete with a low incidence of postoperative complications.

Radiation and chemotherapy are used in addition to surgery with varying frequency, depending on the clinical picture and staging. Radiation may be used postoperatively to shrink large tumors thereby facilitating removal. Preoperative irradiation also has been thought to possibly decrease the incidence of intraoperative rupture and tumor spillage. Postoperative radiation for patients with stages II and III, and for stage IV patients even with pulmonary metastasis, is done to offer protection against local recurrence. Lung metastasis is also often treated with radiation (DiAngio, 1984).

Research is currently being conducted to evaluate the effectiveness of single agent and combination chemotherapy, both adjuvant to radiotherapy and as substitutes for irradiation. The use of actinomycin D and vincristine has improved survival rates. In advanced disease combination therapy has been shown to be more effective than single agent therapy. Clinical trials are underway to document a regimen adding doxorubicin as superior to the two-drug regimen of actinomycin D and vincristine (Putnam, et al., 1983).

In the 5% of children with bilateral disease, aspects of treatment include excision of tumor(s) as totally as possible while preserving functional renal tissue or nephrectomy of most involved kidney. This is followed by actinomycin D and vincristine, with doxorubicin or radiation added if residual tumor shrinkage does not occur. Second-look surgery with additional tumor resection is done in 2 to 3 months, after tumor shrinkage has occurred. In some cases renal transplantation or dialysis may be needed for long-term management (Belasco, 1984).

Until recently recurrent disease had been thought to herald a poor prognosis. Improved results have been obtained for these children with multimodal therapy. Remission has been demonstrated in 20% to 50% of these patients (Belasco, 1984).

BONE TUMORS

Bone tumors constitute only 5% of all childhood malignancies, with the majority occurring in adolescence. The two most common bone tumors in childhood are osteosarcoma and Ewing's sarcoma.

OSTEOSARCOMA

EPIDEMIOLOGY

Osteosarcoma occurs basically in the ends of the long bones, but can occur in any bone. It is more commonly found in males than females, but occurs equally in the black and caucasian races. The most common ages of occurrence are between 10 and 25 years of age. The tumor consists of large spindle cells that arise from the bone-forming mesenchymal cells and is characterized by the production of malignant osteoid (new bone that has not undergone calcification). The most common sites of occurrence of osteosarcoma are the distal femur, the proximal tibia, and the proximal humerus.

CLINICAL PICTURE AND DIAGNOSIS

The presenting sign is usually a visible, painful mass. It occurs weeks to months before a diagnosis is made. Frequently trauma to the site occurs causing pain and swelling, which in turn leads to the diagnosis of the tumor. There is no association between the trauma and the occurrence of the tumor, however.

Diagnostic studies include radiographs of the site and a metastatic work up. The most common sites for the metastasis to occur include other bones (10%) and the lungs (90%). Biopsy confirms the diagnosis.

PROGNOSIS

The prognosis is greater than a 50% 5-year survival. Ten years ago there was a 5-year survival rate of 20%. This improvement is due to the combination of early detection and resection of pulmonary metastases, adjunctive chemotherapy, and better supportive care.

TREATMENT

Osteosarcoma is a radioresistant tumor; therefore treatment focuses on chemotherapy and surgery. The most common surgery utilized is amputation of the affected limb above the joint. Several other types of surgery are utilized at some of the major cancer centers. Limb salvage

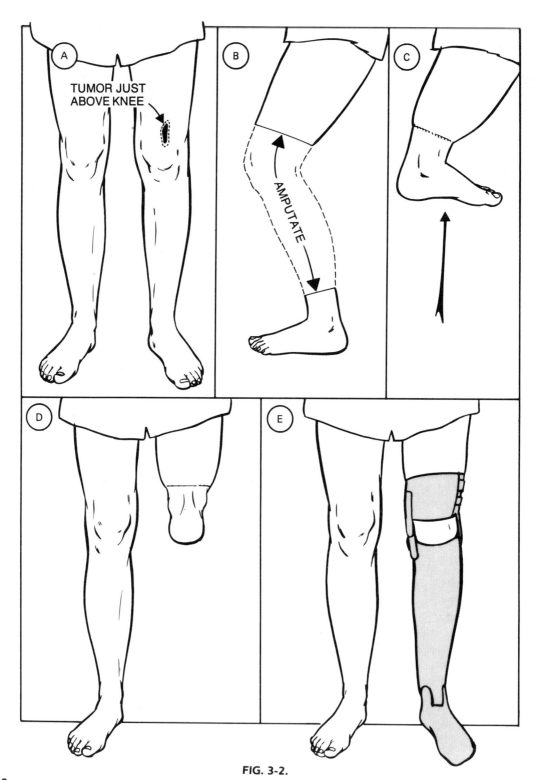

A

TUMOR JUST
ABOVE KNEE

B

AMPUTATE

C

D

E

FIG. 3-2.

is being attempted whereby the involved area is surgically resected after several courses of chemotherapy, replaced by a prosthetic rod, and then followed by more chemotherapy. Another type of surgery under investigation is the rotationplasty or "turn-about" operation. The leg is amputated above the knee; the lower portion (the amputated part) is further amputated above the ankle and then reattached to the patient's leg (Rosen, 1984) (Fig. 3-2). This allows the foot to serve as an anchor for the prosthesis.

Multiagent chemotherapy has been utilized both pre- and postoperatively since 1972. This is the main reason for the improved prognosis rate. The chemotherapeutic agents commonly used include high-dose methotrexate with citrovorum rescue, doxorubicin, cisplatin, vincristine, and cyclophosphamide.

EWING'S SARCOMA

EPIDEMIOLOGY

This bone tumor occurs most often in the bones of the trunk (pelvis, scapula, ribs) or in the midshaft of long bones such as the femur. It occurs most often in early adolescence; however, unlike osteosarcoma, it is extremely rare in black children. Ewing's sarcoma also differs from osteosarcoma in that it does not produce osteoid. Ewing's sarcoma also differs histologically; it appears as a group of small, round cells.

CLINICAL PICTURE AND DIAGNOSIS

The major symptoms of Ewing's sarcoma are similar to that of osteosarcoma, i.e., swelling and pain. Fever may also be present, as well as a high WBC and an elevated Erythrocyte Sedimentation Rate.

Diagnosis includes radiographic studies of the affected limb, a bone scan, metastatic survey, and biopsy. All of this is necessary since Ewing's sarcoma metastasizes through hematogenous spread to the lungs and other bones. Biopsy is used for definitive diagnosis.

PROGNOSIS

Prognosis is determined by tumor site and whether metastasis is present. If the tumor originates in the long bones, the prognosis is better than if it originates in the pelvis or sacrum. If the child is free of metastasis at diagnosis, there is a 3-year survival rate of approximately 60%. If metastasis is present at diagnosis, however, the median disease-free survival rate is 75 weeks. Those who develop metastasis later have only approximately a 37-week disease-free survival rate.

TREATMENT

Surgery is utilized to excise the tumor if possible. In most cases an amputation is not performed due to the radiosensitivity of this tumor. Usually 4000 to 6000 rads of radiation therapy are given to the primary site over a period of 4 to 6 weeks. Radiation therapy is also applied to any metastatic sites. Chemotherapeutic agents commonly utilized include vincristine, actinomycin D, cyclophosphamide, 5-fluorouracil, doxorubicin, and BCNU.

RETINOBLASTOMA

Retinoblastoma is a tumor that arises from the retina of one or both eyes. It is a malignant

◀ **FIG. 3-2.** Rotationplasty. The child is first diagnosed with a tumor above the knee (A). Following several courses of chemotherapy, the leg is then amputated above and below the knee (B). The foot and heel joint are attached in a backwards fashion at the upper amputation site (C). After healing, the patient is ready for a below the knee prosthesis (D). The patient then has a functional, movable "knee" joint with a prosthesis attached (E).

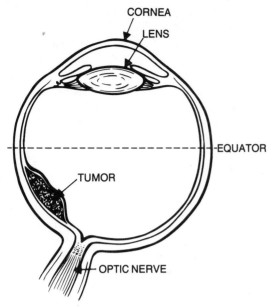

FIG. 3-3. Retinoblastoma.

congenital tumor that can be successfully treated.

EPIDEMIOLOGY

Retinoblastoma occurs in approximately 1 out of 23,000 births. It is more prevalent in whites than blacks, but there is a $2\frac{1}{2}$ times greater peak mortality in blacks than in whites. Retinoblastoma is usually diagnosed by the age of 2 years, but the tumor is probably present at birth. It is rare for the tumor to be diagnosed after the age of 6 years, but it has been diagnosed at birth. There is a 5% association with other congenital defects, particularly mental retardation (Metz, 1983).

In over 90% of the cases with this tumor there is no family history of the disease. In only approximately 6% of the cases is there a dominant autosomal gene involved. Even if the occurrence is sporadic, there is a risk of transmission to offspring. Therefore, siblings and offspring of retinoblastoma patients need re-

peated examinations during the first 2 years of life in order to detect possible tumors at an early age.

Retinoblastoma arises from the posterior portion of the retina, but spreads readily within the eye (Fig. 3-3). It occurs bilaterally 30% of the time, usually in cases of hereditary retinoblastoma. It also metastasizes outside the eye along the optic nerve and to the cranial cavity. Distant spread occurs through the bloodstream to the bone, lungs, and liver. The tumor may even outgrow its blood supply resulting in necrosis and the formation of calcium deposits (Tapley, 1984).

CLINICAL PICTURE AND DIAGNOSIS

Since the child is so young at time of diagnosis, the parents are usually the first to notice a problem with the child. The most common presenting sign is the "cat's eye reflex," which is present when the tumor fills the eye to the point where the pupil is whitened by the underlying tumor. Other signs include strabismus (especially if the tumor develops in the macula), a red and painful eye with or without glaucoma (indicates extensive disease), and limited vision or loss of vision (occurs with massive bilateral tumor) (Tapley, 1984).

The diagnostic workup is conducted in an attempt to define the extent of the disease in the eye and to exclude metastases, especially in the central nervous system. Since the tumor occurs bilaterally in 30% of the cases, both eyes must be examined. This examination takes place under general anesthesia using direct and indirect ophthalmoscopy, thus assuring a widely dilated pupil. The mass that is seen will be projecting generally into the vitreous and be a creamy pink color with extensive surface vascularization (Tapley, 1984).

Computerized tomography is used to determine the extent of the tumor. It is the most sensitive tool utilized for diagnosis and staging. It can demonstrate bilateral involvement, bone destruction, nerve involvement, and intracranial extension of the lesion. Biopsy of the tumor is contraindicated, since it may lead to tumor spread and orbital involvement. However, a sample of aqueous humor is extracted and then examined by the lab to determine if the lactic acid dehydrogenase levels are elevated. This test is most accurate if the fluid is fresh (not frozen) and free of blood cells. Other diagnostic tools used for staging include lumbar puncture to determine cerebral spinal fluid involvement, a complete blood count, and SMA-12. Brain, bone and liver studies must be conducted if the disease is advanced (Metz, 1983).

After initial diagnosis the tumor is classified into one of five groups based on the number and size of the tumors and their locations. This staging is then utilized to plan the treatment. Table 3-7 lists the various groups or stages. The prognosis for each group refers to the amount of useful vision and not to survival rates.

PROGNOSIS

Prognosis is concerned not only with useful vision as previously discussed, but also with survival rates. Both depend upon the stage of the tumor at the time of diagnosis. Untreated retinoblastoma is generally fatal. Treatment increases the survival rate from 0 to approximately 80%, varying with the extent of the disease and treatment, but the prognosis for patients with metastasis is very poor (Tapley, 1984).

Retinoblastoma patients are predisposed to second tumors, the most common being osteosarcoma. This appears to be the case particularly if originally the child had bilateral retinoblastoma.

TREATMENT

The aggressiveness of treatment depends upon the stage of the disease at the time of diagnosis. The use of enucleation surgery is the treatment

TABLE 3-7. STAGING FOR RETINOBLASTOMA

Group I
Very favorable prognosis*
  Solitary tumor, less than 4 disc diameters in size at or behind the equator
  Multiple tumors, none over 4 disc diameters in size at or behind the equator

Group II
Favorable prognosis
  Solitary tumor, 4 to 10 disc diameters in size at or behind the equator
  Multiple tumors, 4 to 10 disc diameters in size behind the equator

Group III
Doubtful prognosis
  Any lesion anterior to the equator
  Solitary tumors larger than 10 disc diameters behind the equator

Group IV
Unfavorable prognosis
  Multiple tumors, some larger than 10 disc diameters
  Any lesion extending anterior to the ora serrata

Group V
Very unfavorable prognosis
  Massive tumors involving over half the retina
  Vitreous seeding

*Prognosis refers to the probability of preserving useful vision, not to survival rate.

of choice for groups IV and V patients. In groups I, II, and III, irradiation may be adequate. When the eye is surgically removed, approximately 10 to 15 mm of the optic nerve must also be removed since this is the main route for spread of the tumor.

Radiation therapy is utilized for all groups of patients in various circumstances. In groups I, II, and III, when there is unilateral disease and no enucleation is performed, radiation is given to the retina through a lateral portal at a dose of 3500 to 4500 rads in 3 to 4 weeks at a rate of 3 doses per week. All of the patients are reexamined under anesthesia 4 to 6 weeks after therapy is completed. For any of the groups, if there is a residual tumor at the cut end of the optic nerve once the eye is enucleated, radiation therapy to the intracranial portion of the optic nerve is indicated. If the tumor extends into the ora serrata or if there is vitreous seeding, a 1000 to 1500 rad tumor dose is given through an anterior portal. If the tumor is bilateral, generally the eye with the greatest involvement is enucleated and radiation therapy is delivered to the other eye in an attempt to save some vision. If the bilateral tumor is diagnosed early and both eyes contain small tumors, both eyes may be irradiated instead of the use of enucleation (Metz, 1983).

During the radiation treatment the child must be immobilized by either sedation or an immobilizing cast. The chapter on radiation (Chapter 5) discusses immobilization techniques to be utilized with children.

If the total radiation dose does not exceed 5000 rads in 5 weeks, the possibility of radiation sequelae is minimal; however, radiation cataracts may develop and can be removed as any cataract. For infants a complication of radiation therapy to this area is a possible growth-retarding effect on the bones in the orbital region. If the patient is under 2 years of age at the time of irradiation, a facial asymmetry may develop. Radiation therapy has also been responsible for the late appearance of orbital osteogenic sarcoma and rhabdomyosarcoma (Tapley, 1984).

Chemotherapy by itself is ineffective as a treatment for retinoblastoma. Drugs which have proven effective in various combinations include nitrogen mustard, triethylenemelamine (TEM), actinomycin D, 5-flourouracil, cyclophosphamide, vincristine, and doxorubicin. Combination chemotherapy is also utilized to treat extraocular disease. Combinations of vincristine-cyclophosphamide-intrathecal methotrexate or vincristine-cyclosphosphamide-doxorubicin are frequently used (Metz, 1983).

OTHER TUMORS

Several other tumors occur in childhood; however, their incidence is so infrequent that they do not warrant discussion here. If a child presents at an institution with a tumor such as a liver tumor, a melanoma, an ovarian tumor, or with histiocytosis X, any of the references at the end of this chapter can be consulted for information concerning that disease. The principles of treatment and the psychosocial aspects of these diseases are similar to those discussed thus far. The remainder of this book will address aspects of the care of the child with cancer and the family or significant others.

CONCLUSION

This chapter has presented information about the most common types of childhood cancer. Various aspects of each malignancy have been covered including the specific disease characteristics, epidemiology, symptomatology, common diagnostic procedures, treatment, prognosis, and current investigational work being done in the area. This discussion serves as a resource to the practicing health professional in the planning and implementation of care to meet the needs of children with various types of cancer and their families.

KEY POINTS

- Six thousand new cases of childhood cancer are diagnosed annually.
- Childhood cancers are treated utilizing multichemotherapeutic agents and multi-treatment modalities.

LEUKEMIA

- Leukemia is the most common malignancy found in children, and the most common acute leukemia is acute lymphocytic leukemia (ALL).
- Diagnosis of ALL documents anemia and thrombocytopenia, variable granulocytes, altered WBC, and suppression of normal cells and the presence of blasts or immature cells in the bone marrow.
- Most favorable prognosis for ALL is an initial WBC less than 10,000, and the child being between 3 and 7 years of age.
- Treatment of leukemia is divided into three phases — induction, consolidation, and maintenance — utilizing multiagent chemotherapy and central nervous system prophylaxis.
- Treatment of acute non-lymphocytic leukemia is less successful than of ALL; bone marrow transplant is frequently the treatment of choice, given a suitable donor.

BRAIN TUMORS

- Most childhood brain tumors occur in the infratentorial region of the brain.
- Most symptoms of a brain tumor are generalized in nature so that initial symptoms may be associated with other childhood diseases. Common initial symptoms are increased intracranial pressure, headaches, impaired vision, nausea, and vomiting.
- Surgical treatment is the treatment of choice, with the use of radiotherapy as secondary. Chemotherapy has not proven to be effective.

HODGKIN'S DISEASE

- Most common presenting symptom is painless cervical adenopathy with or without associated fever.
- The disease is categorized into four stages with a favorable prognosis for stages 1 to 3.
- Treatment varies with each stage but utilizes radiotherapy and chemotherapy.

NON-HODGKIN'S LYMPHOMA

- The abdomen is the most frequent site.
- Most common initial symptom is pain, either localized to the abdomen or referred to other sites.
- One third of the lymphomas can occur above the diaphragm resulting in tracheal compression, coughing, wheezing, increasing dyspnea, and malaise.
- African Burkitt's lymphoma usually involves the jaw.
- Treatment consists of surgery for diagnostic purposes, radiotherapy for debulking the tumor mass, and chemotherapy regimens.

NEUROBLASTOMA

- Numerous sites of origin with frequent metastatic lesions are common.
- Typical presenting symptoms are abdominal pain and a palpable mass.
- Diagnosis is categorized into 5 stages with stages 1 and 2 having the most favorable diagnosis.
- Treatment varies with disease stage, but usually consists of surgical removal followed by radiotherapy and possible chemotherapy.

RHABDOMYOSARCOMA

- Sites of occurrence vary with age; the tumor usually presents as an asymptomatic mass.
- Disease is categorized into four groups, with a significant decrease in prognosis from groups I to IV.
- Treatment consists of a combination of surgery, radiotherapy, and chemotherapy.

WILMS' TUMOR

- An abdominal mass is the usual presenting sign.
- Disease is categorized into 5 stages with good prognosis for stages I to III.
- Treatment consists of surgical excision, followed by radiation and chemotherapy.

OSTEOSARCOMA

- Presents with a visible, painful mass.
- Treatment consists of surgical excision and chemotherapy since the tumor is radioresistant.

EWING'S SARCOMA

- Major symptoms are swelling and pain.
- The presence of metastasis decreases prognosis significantly.
- Tumor is very radiosensitive so radiotherapy is primary treatment with surgical excision, if possible, and the use of chemotherapy.

RETINOBLASTOMA

- Parents are usually the first to notice a problem with the child, with the most common presenting sign of the "cat's eye reflex."
- Tumor occurs bilaterally in 30% of the cases.
- Disease is categorized into five groups with a good prognosis following treatment.
- Treatment consists of radiotherapy for all stages and enucleation for groups IV and V.
- Retinoblastoma patients are predisposed to secondary tumors, especially osteosarcoma.

REFERENCES

American Cancer Society. (1985). *Cancer facts and figures* (p. 19). New York: American Cancer Society.

Bakemeier, R., Zagers, G., Cooper, R., and Rubin, P. (1983). The malignant lymphomas: Hodgkin's disease and non-Hodgkin's lymphoma, multiple myeloma, and macroglobulinemia. In: P. Rubin (Ed.), *Clinical oncology: a multidisciplinary approach* (6th ed., pp. 346–369). New York: American Cancer Society.

Belasco, J., Chatten, J., and D'Angio, G. (1984). Wilms' tumor. In: W. Sutow (Ed.), *Clinical pediatric oncology* (3rd ed., pp. 588–621). St. Louis: C. V. Mosby.

Dannecker, G., Leidig, E., Treuner, J., and Niethammer, D. (1983). Late recurrence of neuroblastoma: a reason for prolonged followup? *American Journal of Pediatric Hematology/Oncology, 5,* 271–274.

Gaddy, D. (1982). Nursing care in childhood cancer update. *American Journal of Nursing, 82,* 416–421.

Gasparini, M., Lombardi, F., Gianni, C., Lattuada, A., Rilke, F., and Fossati-Bellani, F. (1983). Childhood non-Hodgkin's lymphoma: prognostic relevance of clinical stages and histologic subgroups. *American Journal of Pediatric Hematology/Oncology, 5,* 161–171.

Greenwald, E., and Greenwald, E. (1983). *Cancer epidemiology.* New York: Medical Examination Publishing Company.

Gustafsson, E., and Kreuger, A. (1983). Sex and other prognostic factors in acute lymphoblastic leukemia in childhood. *American Journal of Pediatric Hematology/Oncology, 5,* 243–250.

Haddy, T. (1982). Cancer in black children. *American Journal of Pediatric Hematology/Oncology, 4,* 285–292.

Hardin, K. (1980). Solid tumors in children. *Issues in Comprehensive Pediatric Nursing, 4,* 29–47.

Klopovich, P., and Cohen, D. (1984). An overview of pediatric oncology for the adult oncology nurse. *Oncology Nursing Forum, 11,* 56–63.

Lichtman, M., and Siegel, G. (1983). The leukemias. In: P. Rubin (Ed.), *Clinical oncology: a multidisciplinary approach* (6th ed., pp. 370–390). New York: American Cancer Society.

Maul, S. (1984). Childhood brain tumors: a special nursing challenge. *MCN, 9,* 123–129.

McDonald, J., Salazer, O., Rubin, P., Lapham, L., and Bakemeier, R. (1983). Central nervous system tumors. In: P. Rubin (Ed.), *Clinical oncology: a multidisciplinary approach* (6th ed., pp. 262–278). New York: American Cancer Society.

Metz, H., Salazar, D., and Rubin, P. (1983). Tumors of the eye. In: P. Rubin (Ed.), *Clinical oncology: a multidisciplinary approach* (6th ed., pp. 280–294). New York: American Cancer Society.

Miller, D. (1982). Acute lymphoblastic leukemia. In: C. Tebbi (Ed.), *Major topics in pediatric and adolescent oncology.* Boston: G. K. Hall Medical Publishers.

Nesbit, M., Robinson, L., and Dehner, L. (1984). Round-cell sarcoma of bone. W. Sutow (Ed.), *Clinical pediatric oncology* (3rd ed., pp. 516–537). St. Louis: C. V. Mosby.

Pochedly, C. (1975). *Clinical management of cancer in children.* Acton: Publishing Sciences Group.

Pories, W., Murinson, D. and Rubin, P. (1983). Soft tissue sarcoma. P. Rubin (Ed.), *Clinical oncology: a multidisciplinary approach* (6th ed., pp. 308–324). New York: American Cancer Society.

Pullen, D. J., Crist, W., Falletta, J. M., Boyett, J. M., Roper, M., Dowell, B., Van Eys, J., Humphrey, G. B., Head, D., Brock, B. L., Blackstock, R., Metzgar, R. S., and Cooper, M. D. (1983). Pediatric oncology groups classification protocol for acute lymphocytic leukemia (ALINC 13): immunologic phenotypes and correlation with treatment results. In: S. B. Murphy and J. R. Gilbert (Eds.), *Leukemia research: advances in cell biology and treatment* (pp. 221–239). New York: Elsevier North-Holland.

Putman, T., Cohen, H., and Constine, L. (1983). Pediatric solid tumors. P. Rubin (Ed.), *Clinical oncology: a multidisciplinary approach* (6th ed., pp. 392–427). New York: American Cancer Society.

Rosen, G. (1984). Spindle-cell sarcoma–osteogenic sarcoma. In: W. Sutow (Ed.), *Clinical pediatric oncology* (3rd ed., pp. 684–709). St. Louis: C. V. Mosby.

Rubin, P., Evarts, C., and Boros, L. (1983). Bone tumors. P. Rubin (Ed.), *Clinical oncology: a multidisciplinary approach* (6th ed., pp. 296–306). New York: American Cancer Society.

Silverberg, E., and Lutea, J. (1983). A review of American cancer society estimates of cancer cases and deaths. *CA-A Cancer Journal for Clinicians, 33,* 2–25.

Sullivan, M., Fuller, L., and Butler, J. (1984). Hodgkin's disease. In: W. Sutow (Ed.), *Clinical pediatric oncology* (3rd ed., pp. 416–451). St. Louis: C. V. Mosby.

Tapley, N., Strong, L., and Sutow, W. (1984). Retinoblastoma. In: W. Sutow (Ed.), *Clinical pediatric oncology* (3rd ed., pp. 539–558). St. Louis: C. V. Mosby.

van Eys, J. (1984). Malignant tumors of the central nervous system. W. Sutow (Ed.), *Clinical pediatric oncology* (3rd ed., pp. 516–537). St. Louis: C. V. Mosby.

Voute, P. (1984). Neuroblastoma. W. Sutow (Ed.), *Clinical pediatric oncology* (3rd ed., pp. 559–587). St. Louis: C.V. Mosby.

4

CHEMOTHERAPY

INTRODUCTION

Childhood cancers are usually treated with a combination of chemotherapy, radiation therapy, and surgery. Chemotherapy is by far the most common method of treatment. As a result of chemotherapy, however, the child often feels "sicker" for varying lengths of time. In order to understand the use of chemotherapy, its effect on the child, and what nursing can do to minimize the effects of such treatment, an examination of the mechanisms of action of the drugs at the cellular level, the methods of infusion, and the side-effects of these drugs will be presented along with considerations regarding the growth and development of the child.

CELL CYCLE

Cells progress through five phases of development: M phase; G_1 phase; G_0 phase; S phase; and G_2 phase. The M phase is when the single parent cell divides into two daughter cells. The cell then progresses into the G_1 phase. In this phase the cell is basically dormant. The cells in this phase either undergo ribonucleic acid (RNA) protein synthesis or they move into the G_0 phase, which is a resting phase (Fig. 4-1). Cells can remain in this G_0 phase for long periods of time or until stimulated to reenter the active cell cycle. After the RNA protein synthesis occurs in the G_1 phase, the cells move into

the S phase. This is a metabolically active phase during which DNA is made. Cells in this phase are very susceptible to chemotherapy. The cells then move into the G_2 phase where again they become relatively dormant. During this phase the cell undergoes some RNA and protein production in preparation for the division that occurs in the M phase, as the cycle repeats itself. Cancer cells lack growth control and thus do not remain in the G_0 or the resting phase. Cancer cells grow very rapidly and quickly progress through the remaining phases.

ANTINEOPLASTIC DRUGS

Antineoplastic drugs kill cancer cells in one of two ways. The first group of these drugs are known as cell-cycle nonspecific (CCNS) drugs. These drugs kill cells in all phases of the cell cycle, including the G_0, or resting phase. The second group of drugs are the cell-cycle specific (CCS) drugs. These drugs work only in specific phases of the cell cycle and do not kill cells in the G_0 phase. Some anticancer drugs are both CCNS and CCS, depending on their dose and schedule of administration.

Tumors progress through three growth rates. Initially the cells grow slowly, then they become vascularized and begin rapid logarithmic or log-stage growth. In this period the cancerous cells are dividing rapidly. The cells eventu-

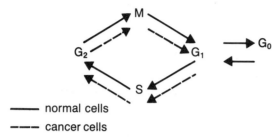

—— normal cells

- - - cancer cells

FIG. 4-1. Normal vs. tumor cell cycles.

ally slow in their reproduction and reach a plateau stage. CCNS drugs are useful at this stage. They kill the resting cells as well as cells in the active cycle. These drugs not only debulk the tumor, causing shrinkage or stasis of the tumor and lessening of symptoms, but they also may effect remission and disappearance of all signs of the cancer. CCS drugs are best utilized during the rapid division or log-stage. These drugs do not produce the amount of hematologic, immunologic, or mucous membrane toxicity that the CCNS drugs often cause. Both CCS and CCNS drugs are utilized during maintenance therapy in order to inhibit a significant regrowth of the tumor and thus prevent clinical relapse.

Drugs are utilized singularly and in combinations. This allows for cells that are in different phases of the cycle to be killed at any given time. Unfortunately, cancer cells are not selectively killed by these agents. Rapidly growing normal cells in a child's body are also susceptible. The most common normal cells that are so affected include those of the bone marrow, hair follicles, oral mucosa, and the entire gastrointestinal (GI) tract.

Based on all of these considerations, chemotherapy for a child with cancer is selected by the physician, who must take into consideration the effect of the drug on the specific cancer cells and the side-effects of that drug, as well as the size of the child and his or her tolerance to the chemotherapy regimen. Not all drugs cause the same side-effects. Some side-effects are dose and schedule dependent. Many of the drugs

react differently with people of different ages, and children are no exception.

Each type of cancer that is treated with chemotherapy has its own protocol, which may vary with each institution. A protocol is a picture or schema of the plan of care. In the case of a child with cancer, the protocol can contain all the components of treatment or simply the chemotherapy routine. Any radiotherapy, bone marrow aspirations, lumbar punctures, or surgery may be included in the overall schema. An example of a protocol is presented in Figure 4-2. Using this protocol it can be seen that a patient will receive methotrexate (MTX) and vincristine (VCR) at the first, second, ninth, and tenth weeks, L-asparaginase (L-ASP) for 5 days between the fourth and fifth weeks, and surgery at the seventh week. Intrathecal methotrexate will be given at the third and eleventh weeks.

Protocols are established by various groups. The National Cancer Institute (NCI) in Washington, DC has developed study programs throughout children's cancer centers that are members of NCI. These study programs offer well-organized, systematic studies with large enough numbers of subjects to achieve statistical significance. The childhood cancer centers involved in the study program are organized into three major groups: The Children's Cancer Study Group (CCSG); Cancer and Leukemia Group B (pediatric section) (CALGB); and the Pediatric Oncology Group (POG). More than two hundred hospitals or medical centers are members of these groups. Studies undertaken by these groups can be national studies, such as the National Wilms' Tumor Study, where all the groups utilize the same protocol, or there may be studies developed at the group or institutional levels.

These protocols or studies utilize drugs in various stages of their development. Drugs progress through three phases of trials on humans before they become commercially available. In phase I trials the main objective is

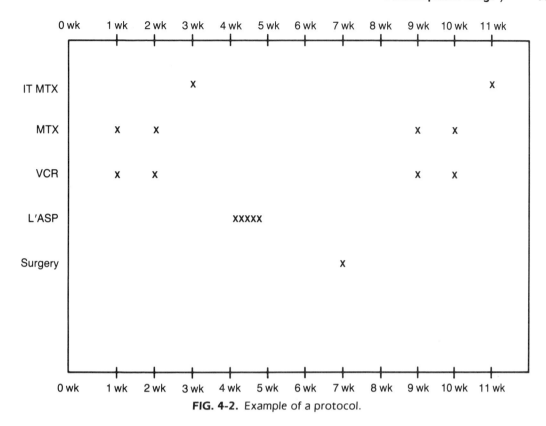

FIG. 4-2. Example of a protocol.

to establish a maximum tolerated dose of a drug on a given schedule and route of administration. By doing this the investigators determine the toxicity patterns of the drug and whether the toxicity is predictable, tolerable, and reversible. In phase II trials the investigators determine what antitumor activity, if any, the drug has for humans. In other words, they determine the types of cancer that are affected by the drug. In phase III trials the drug is tested to determine if it has any value in relation to other potential treatments. The investigators determine into which combination of drugs and protocols this drug will fit best.

Drugs utilized in these protocols and studies are categorized. Categories include alkylating agents (CCNS), antimetabolites (CCS), antibiotics (CCS), nitrosureas (CCNS), vinca alkaloids (CCS), hormones, miscellaneous drugs, and investigational agents. The alkylating agents are a group of drugs that prevent cancer cell division by causing cross-linkage of deoxyribonucleic acid (DNA) strands in the nuclei of the cells, resulting in the breakdown of chromosomal materials. Examples of these drugs include cyclophosphamide (Cytoxan) and nitrogen mustard. The antimetabolites interfere with the function of naturally occurring substances such as nucleic acid, thus inhibiting the synthesis of DNA or RNA. Examples of this group of drugs include methotrexate, 6-mercaptopurine, and cytarabine (Cytosar).

Antibiotics are grouped together not by their mechanisms of action, but rather by their common sources of plants, bacteria, and fungi. Some antibiotics interfere with the synthesis of cellular proteins. Others specifically attack DNA either by inhibiting its synthesis or by damaging preformed DNA and disrupting its repair mechanisms. Examples of the antibiotics include actinomycin D, bleomycin, and doxorubicin (Adriamycin).

The nitrosureas are highly lipid-soluble and can easily cross the blood–brain barrier, which makes them effective in the treatment of brain tumors. Carmustine (BCNU) is an example of a nitrosurea. The vinca alkaloids are derived from the *Vinca rosea* plant and are effective against lymphomas. These drugs include vincristine and velban. There are five types of hormones that are used as chemotherapeutic agents: corticosteroids (including prednisone), androgens (including testolactone), estrogens (including diethylstilbestrol), antiestrogens (including tamoxifen), and the progestins (including medroxyprogesterone). The miscellaneous and investigational drugs have a variety of mechanisms of action and include such drugs as cisplatin, L-asparaginase, procarbazine, AMSA (methanesulfon-M-anisidide), and VP-16 (etoposide).

PEDIATRIC NURSING CONSIDERATIONS

Although nurses must know the dosage, route, and side-effects of the chemotherapeutic agents that are administered to their patients, this information is readily available in other textbooks. There are several nursing considerations, however, which are of special significance when working with children.

Certain antineoplastic drugs have special considerations for the pediatric patient. While the drugs are utilized with both adult and pediatric oncology patients, some of the patterns of side-effects in children may differ. L-asparaginase is one such drug. Children are less likely than adults to require discontinuation of this drug due to side-effects; when discontinuation does occur the primary cause in children is hy-

persensitivity reactions. In adults common causes for discontinuation of therapy include impaired renal function, lethargy, confusion, depression, and personality disorders. However, a new strain of L-asparaginase, the *Erwinia* strain, has been shown to be equally effective as the older *E. coli* strain, yet seems to cause fewer allergic and neurotoxic reactions. The danger of anaphylaxis for both forms is markedly decreased if the drug is given intramuscularly.

Doxorubicin and daunorubicin are cardiotoxic in both adults and children; however, children appear to be at an equivalent or even greater risk to develop cardiac damage as a result of receiving these drugs. Cisplatin has toxic effects similar in adults and children, but children appear to be more likely to develop hypomagnesemia than adults. No data is available on the optimal dose of intrathecal methotrexate in children under 3 years of age. Suggested doses are 6 mg for patients less than 1 year of age, 8 mg for those between 1 and 2 years of age, and 10 mg for 2-year-olds. Normally 12 mg per injection is given to patients between 3 and 60 years of age. If these dosages are not followed, the risk of neurotoxicity complications, such as encephalopathy is increased in children. When they are given the drug intravenously, children under 15 years of age have been shown to have lower plasma concentrations than adults after a 6-hour infusion, which is associated with the less severe toxicity in the child. Pulmonary toxicity consisting of a cough, fever, dyspnea, and patchy bibasilar infiltrates on chest X-ray has been demonstrated mostly in children and young adults receiving standard dose methotrexate for remission-maintenance therapy.

METHODS OF INFUSION

The method of infusion chosen for the pediatric patient is also a special consideration for the pediatric oncology nurse. Invasive devices such as intravenous cannulas pose a threat to all cancer patients. The risk of infection in compromised patients such as children with cancer increases when intravenous devices are utilized. Studies have been conducted that compare the use of steel cannulae, such as butterfly needles, with the use of Teflon cannulae. In several studies steel needles have demonstrated a lower incidence of infectious complications than plastic catheters. Other studies have demonstrated a low risk of infection for both cannulae, a high incidence of phlebitis with the Teflon catheter, and a high incidence of infiltration with the steel needle. These studies predict fewer complications with the Teflon catheter, but only if it is left in place no longer than 24 hours. Studies also have demonstrated that the use of antibiotic ointments to decrease the incidence of infectious complications were of little benefit (Knobf, 1982).

It is not realistic to expect to change a child's IV every 24 hours. Children do not have enough veins in good condition, especially after extensive chemotherapy, to change the site so frequently. A nurse must also consider the emotional impact on the child that such frequent intrusive procedures would produce. The steel needle would be best utilized, therefore, for the child who is not critically ill. It poses less infection-related problems than the Teflon catheter.

Besides the type of cannula to be utilized, the nurse must also consider the placement site of the IV. The developmental level of the child must be a consideration. A child who is 12 months old is at the stage of learning to walk and developing gross motor skills. To put an IV in this child's foot would hinder the child's developmental process and possibly jeopardize the patency of the IV. Other sites and developmental levels to consider include the placement of the IV in the scalp of the 4-month old child who is trying to turn over for the first time, or the placement of the IV in the hand of the child

who is attempting to develop fine motor control. When there are no other sites available, however, the developmental level must be considered secondary to the patency of an IV. A 21-gauge needle should be utilized in most children. In the neonate and infant up to the age of 46 weeks, scalp veins are frequently used. The infant can move the hands freely and also can be easily handled by others with the IV in the scalp.

INDWELLING CENTRAL VENOUS CATHETERS

Several new approaches to the administration of chemotherapy have developed in the major cancer treatment centers. Indwelling central venous catheters are one such approach. The catheters are generally either a Broviac or a Hickman catheter. The Broviac catheter is the smaller lumened, with an internal diameter of 1.0 mm, whereas the Hickman catheter has an internal diameter of 1.6 mm. These catheters are designed to administer long-term chemotherapy infusions, total parenteral nutrition, blood products, or antibiotics, as well as to obtain frequent blood samples, and to monitor central venous pressure (Vogel, 1983). The catheter is inserted into the external jugular vein or the cephalic vein through subcutaneous tunnel from the abdominal area (Fig. 4-3). The catheter is anchored subcutaneously by a single Dacron cuff (Anderson, 1982). This procedure has two benefits: (1) The insertion site through the skin is away from the opening into the bloodstream (the benefit being that if the insertion site should become infected, the infection will not be introduced immediately into the vascular system); and (2) by placing the insertion site dressing on the child's abdomen, the child's development is not interrupted by the IV site. The child can still walk, crawl, roll over, and use the hands without interference from the IV site. One also must consider the child's body image, especially if the catheter is to remain in place after discharge.

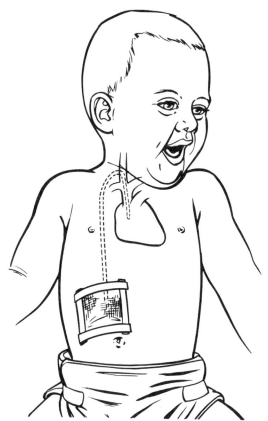

FIG. 4-3. Catheter inserted via subcutaneous tunnel originating in the abdomen.

One problem of these IV lines is that the Broviac catheter's internal diameter is not large enough for the administration of blood products and antibiotics, and for drawing blood. With only one central venous catheter, some institutions use the line for multiple purposes. With this employment of the CV line, the TPN or hyperalimentation infusions often were getting off of the scheduled infusion rate. The Fred Hutchinson Cancer Research Center in Seattle, WA began using a double-lumen Hickman catheter for their bone marrow transplant patients. These catheters consist of a fusion of the Broviac catheter and the Hickman catheter (Fig. 4-4). The hospital utilizes the Broviac catheter for the patient's total parenteral nu-

trition and the Hickman catheter for all other uses. They have made use of the double-lumen catheters with over 150 patients, including children, with some remaining in place over 100 days post-bone marrow transplant. The only criterion is that the vein be large enough to accommodate the catheter (Anderson, 1982).

VASCULAR ACCESS GRAFTS

Another new approach practiced in several institutions includes the use of vascular access grafts made of Dacron or polytetrafluoroethylene. The grafts are inserted under local anes-

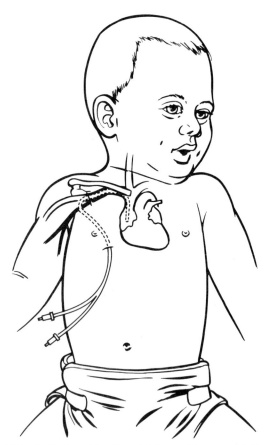

FIG. 4-4. Combination Hickman/Broviac Catheter.

thesia into either the upper arm or the groin area. Grafts to the groin area are usually reserved for mastectomy patients, thus not frequently needed for children. The grafts are sutured to the artery, then run subcutaneously in a straight line or a loop to a vein to be sutured in place (Fig. 4-5). A bruit or "thrill" can be heard and felt over the graft area if the graft is patent and thrombosis has not occurred. There must be a 2-week waiting period between the time of insertion and its first use. This allows for the swelling, edema, and ecchymosis to subside (Schulmeister, 1982). A tourniquet is not needed when inserting the IV, and only 21- or 23-gauge steel needles should be used. There will be a back-flow pressure, so the nurse must have the infusion ready to go. When discontinuing the IV, mild pressure should be applied for at least 5 minutes. Tourniquets or hard pressure may obstruct the arterial blood flow. These grafts may be utilized up to 4 times a day, with infusions usually of less than 8 hours duration. Repeated punctures in one area or punctures with larger than a 21-gauge needle will weaken the graft (Schulmeister, 1982). These grafts are useful to start an IV in a child with poor veins.

Depending on the age of the child, the child or the family should be taught how to care for the graft. The child may resume showers, baths, and swimming after the incision site has healed. The graft site must be assessed every day to check for changes in texture, color, and temperature, and for a pulsation to indicate proper functioning. The child must be instructed to tell the family or the nurse if there is any tingling or numbness present. Pressure over the graft site can be avoided by wearing nonrestrictive clothing and by not carrying heavy objects with the grafted arm (Schulmeister, 1982).

INTRAARTERIAL CHEMOTHERAPY

Another approach currently being practiced in some institutions is intraarterial chemother-

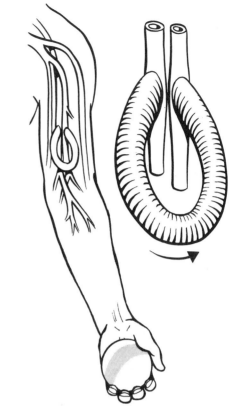

FIG. 4-5. Vascular access graft.

apy. This approach is the "infusion of antineoplastic drugs through a catheter in a major artery directly into a tumor" (Johnston, 1981). Tumors that receive this form of treatment are usually localized and inoperable and are found in the liver, head, neck, or bones. With this approach the tumor receives a high concentrated dose of the chemotherapeutic drug before it is diluted by the blood or metabolized by the liver or kidneys, which also results in lower systemic levels of the drug and fewer side-effects. Most catheters are inserted using angiographic techniques with the child being hospitalized for approximately 3 to 5 days. After the chemotherapy is completed, the catheter is removed and the child is discharged until the next treatment. Some patients receive long-term intraarterial chemotherapy. In these cases, a Si-lastic catheter may be placed surgically. The catheter remains in place and the child is treated as an outpatient while using portable infusion pumps. Problems that may occur with all intraarterial catheters include displacement of the catheter tip, chemotherapy infusion to the wrong organ, a tear in the arterial wall resulting in pain during infusion, embolus or thrombus, and catheter occlusion (Johnston, 1981).

OTHER INFUSION METHODS

Additional approaches being employed in hospitals throughout the country include long lines placed in the anticubital fossa instead of central lines, and portable infusion pumps for chemotherapy at home. Portable infusion pumps allow the child freedom from IV poles, allowing more freedom to move about. There are many varieties of portable pumps commercially available. An example of one type of pump is pictured in Figure 4-6.

All of these approaches are an attempt to enhance the effective administration of chemotherapy and to decrease the trauma of intravenous treatments. Whereas most of the approaches were developed for adults, they have been adapted easily to the pediatric patient. They aid the child by allowing freedom of movement and continued development similar to other children at that age level.

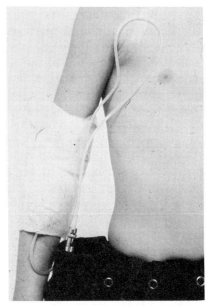

FIG. 4-6. Portable infusion pump.

therapy are those of the bone marrow, the hair follicles, and the gastrointestinal tract. Side-effects commonly observed include: (1) extravasation; (2) nausea and vomiting; (3) stomatitis; (4) alopecia; and (5) bone marrow depression resulting in anemia, leukopenia, and thrombocytopenia. Table 4-1 reviews these side-effects and several possible interventions. While there are standard nursing care plans for all of these side-effects, additional considerations must be examined when the patient is a child.

SIDE-EFFECTS

Whether the child is in the hospital or at home, the chemotherapy the child receives causes side-effects. Some degree of the toxicities are dose related. The degree of side-effects from any given antineoplastic agent also varies with the individual characteristics of the patient who receives the drug. As stated previously, the normal cells most often affected by the chemo-

EXTRAVASATION

One of the most important considerations is that of possible extravasation of the chemotherapeutic agent. Many of these drugs cause severe tissue damage when they infiltrate into the surrounding area. (See Fig. 4-7.) This becomes particularly important in the pediatric patient due to mobility of the child, the IV placement site, and the developmental process that the child is experiencing. Just because a child has a form of

TABLE 4-1. SIDE-EFFECTS OF CHEMOTHERAPY

Side Effects	Interventions
Extravasation	Establish a protocol in your institution See Table 4-2 for sample protocol
Nausea and vomiting	Give antiemetics (prescribed) (Table 4-3) Avoid spicy and greasy food Make tray attractive Environment should encourage age-appropriate distractions Utilize relaxation techniques, hypnosis, and systematic desensitization
Stomatitis	Discontinue flossing when WBC drops to between 15,000 and 10,000 Discontinue use of toothbrush when platelet count drops between 10,000 and 5,000 Provide mouth care every 4 hr around the clock (every 2 hr for severe stomatitis) Process of giving oral care is more important than actual agents used Lemon-glycerine swabs are not generally accepted as being effective Milk of magnesia may be utilized, but it has a drying action and an unpleasant taste (does soften and sooth tissues)—if utilized, swab in mouth and leave on for 15–20 min before rinsing mouth Hydrogen peroxide has a good foaming and cleaning effect—Utilize a solution of one part hydrogen peroxide to four parts saline (use solution immediately since hydrogen peroxide decomposes rapidly in water and when in contact with mucous membranes)—Rinse with water and saline; caution—hydrogen peroxide can break down new tissue and may irritate tongue and buccal mucosa Avoid commercial mouthwashes Utilize toothettes or foam sticks to stimulate gums and palate (avoid flavored toothettes) Power spray devices may remove debris and stimulate oral tissues Waterpicks are useful to remove food and particles between patient's teeth, but does not remove plaque effectively Utilize local anesthetics (lidocaine 2%) prior to meals (15 ml/3 hr) Anesthetic sprays may be damaging to inflamed mucosa Bland diet should be served at room temperature Cold and liquid foods are tolerated well
Alopecia	Scalp tourniquets or cooling of the scalp with ice may be used to decrease blood flow to the hair follicles during intravenous chemotherapy infusion Scalp tourniquets can be either a tubing tourniquet or a pneumatic tourniquet Reassure child that hair will return Encourage child to wear a scarf or hat Fit child for a wig prior to loss of hair Expose child to other children without hair
Myelosuppression Anemia	Blood transfusions (prescribed) Iron preparations (prescribed)
Thrombocytopenia	Platelet transfusion (prescribed) Assess for bleeding (petechiae, oral hemorrhage, bruising) Avoid injections if possible Stool softeners (prescribed) Avoid taking rectal temperature
Leukopenia	Assess for signs and symptoms of infection 0–2 hr Broad-spectrum antibiotics (prescribed) Good perineal care Avoid plastic or rubber pants Meticulous oral care Avoid rectal temps, suppositories, enemas, bladder catheterization, if possible Granulocyte transfusion (prescribed) Avoid crowds
Anaphylatic reactions	Apply ice to infusion area and elevate site Stop IV infusion Maintain airway Give epinephrine and other medications as prescribed (Table 4-7) Anaphylatic tray at bedside during infusion

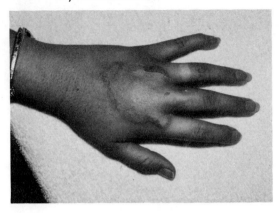

FIG. 4-7. Damage from extravasation.

cancer, he or she does not stop developing physically or emotionally. Children must still learn to walk, learn fine and gross motor skills, and so on. Not only must the nurse consider the child's developmental level when placing the IV, he or she also must consider the child's body movements that might dislodge the IV. For example if the IV is placed in a 12-month-old child's foot, the nurse must remember that the child will continually try to stand and walk using that foot. This may dislodge the IV and cause infiltration of the fluid that is being infused. The nurse must check for a return blood flow prior to giving any chemotherapy administration, but with children this is not always possible due to the size, number, and condition of the child's veins. If extravasation should occur, it should be handled by the protocol that has been established at your institution (see Table 4-2 for a sample protocol). When extravasation occurs, the child may complain of a stinging or burning sensation, the site will become swollen, and there will be no blood return. The nurse must continually observe the child for these signs of extravasation. Children may be crying and screaming throughout the entire procedure, not just at the time of extravasation. Younger children may not be able to speak and verbally tell you of the stinging or burning.

How an extravasation will affect a child's development depends on several factors. Most important to consider is the age of the child, and secondly, the location of the extravasation. Extravasations that are located in the anticubital fossa may cause contractures for a child of any age. If the extravasation occurs in the foot of a twelve-month old child who is trying to walk, however, the child's development may be delayed. If it occurs in the foot of a five-year old, the child has already learned to walk, so gross motor development will not be as delayed as with the younger child. With the adolescent the appearance of the extravasation and its remaining scar may cause disruption to the adolescent's body image to a greater degree than for a toddler with the same extravasation.

NAUSEA AND VOMITING

Nausea and vomiting have been identified by patients, families and health-care providers as being caused by most chemotherapeutic agents. Morren and colleagues (1979) found gastrointestinal upset in 83% of the chemotherapy patients in his study. Of the various studies reviewed for this chapter, the majority of the patients experienced nausea or vomiting in each study before or after the antiemetic treatment. The termination of therapy has been attributed to the effects of nausea and vomiting by patients even though they knew that the chemotherapy was controlling their disease.

TABLE 4-2. EXTRAVASATION PROCEDURE EXAMPLE

1. Stop infusion, but leave needle in place
2. Inject 5 ml sodium bicarbonate (5 mEq) via indwelling needle; then remove needle
3. Inject Solu-Cortef 100 mg subcutaneously into infiltrated area
4. Apply hydrocortisone cream (1%) to area, followed by a sterile 4×4 dressing
5. Apply ice pack for 24 hours

Adapted from Swartz, A. (1979).

Despite all of this attention to nausea and vomiting in the nursing literature, several factors are evident: (1) There is no truly effective antiemetic for use with adults receiving chemotherapeutic agents; (2) much of the therapy for the nausea and vomiting does not have a documented scientific basis; and (3) experimentation with means other than the conventional antiemetic drugs is being undertaken in order to determine a more effective means to control these side-effects.

Nausea and vomiting occur when the emetic center of the brain, located in the medulla, is stimulated by one of several factors, usually neurologic stimuli from several pathways. Two areas of the medulla are affected. One area receives stimulation from afferent fibers from the pharynx, the gastrointestinal tract, the heart, the cerebral cortex, or the vestibular apparatus. The other area is the chemoreceptor trigger zone (CTZ). Chemicals, drugs, or toxic substances in the blood activate the CTZ. It has been shown that there are dopamine receptors in the CTZ and that certain prostaglandins can induce nausea and vomiting. Other factors (both psychological and physiological) are believed to influence nausea and vomiting, including the patient's anxiety level, the type of chemotherapeutic agent, the time of administration, the patient's food intake, the activity level, the amount of sleep before and after chemotherapy, the conditioning effect of previous treatment, and the patient's environment.

One study of nausea and vomiting with children receiving chemotherapy without use of antiemetics demonstrated that no chemotherapeutic agents were found that never or always produced nausea and vomiting. In fact most patients' symptoms fluctuated widely. The conclusion from this particular study is that nondrug variables influence chemotherapy-associated nausea and vomiting in children (Zeltzer et al., 1984).

Medications to control vomiting in children

and infants not receiving chemotherapy rarely are used. They often mask the symptoms diagnostic of potentially serious diseases such as intestinal obstruction. The antiemetics are used extensively with pediatric patients who are receiving chemotherapy however. Table 4-3 examines several of the antiemetics discussed in the literature as having some effectiveness in altering nausea and vomiting resulting from chemotherapy. Pediatric dosages and other pediatric considerations are included.

No matter which antiemetic drug is administered, there are several pediatric considerations that must be examined. Side-effects are common to almost all of the antiemetics discussed. One such side-effect is that central nervous system acting antiemetics may contribute, in combination with viral illnesses, to the development of Reye's syndrome. Several of the antiemetics that have hepatotoxic potential, such as trimethobenzamide (Tigan) may unfavorably alter the course of Reye's syndrome. The extrapyramidal symptoms that the drugs produce may be confused with central nervous system signs of an undiagnosed primary disease besides Reye's syndrome, such as encephalopathies, which could also be responsible for the nausea and vomiting (Physician's Desk Reference, 1985). The nurse must therefore be careful when assessing the cause of the patient's vomiting, and not just assume that the vomiting is due to chemotherapy.

Extrapyramidal reactions are common to almost all of the antiemetics discussed. The symptoms vary according to the degree of severity of the reaction that the patient experiences. Several of the varied symptoms include dystonia, torticollis, dysphasia, oculogyric crisis, akathisia, gait disturbances, restlessness, jaw spasm, muscle spasm, tremors, and even Parkinson-like symptoms. The Parkinson symptoms are effectively treated with anti-Parkinson drugs, a reduction in the antiemetic drugs, or cessation of the drug altogether (Physician's Desk Reference, 1985). This reaction is

TABLE 4-3. COMMON ANTIEMETIC DRUGS

Adult Dose	Pediatric Dose	Considerations	Side-Effects
	Prochlorperazine (Compazine)		
10 mg every 4 hr IM, PO 25 mg suppository every 12 hr	Do not use in children <20 lb or <2 yr old. PO or Suppository 20–29 lb: 2½ mg 1 or 2 times/day (not to exceed 7.5 mg/day) 30–39 lb: 2½ mg 2 or 3 times/day (not to exceed 10 mg/day). 40–85 lb: 2½ mg 3 times/day or 5 mg 2 times/day (not to exceed 15 mg/day) IM 0.06 mg/lb Give deep IM	Do not use after pediatric surgery More prone to develop extrapyramidal reactions Use lowest effective dosage Contraindicated in bone marrow depression Do not mix with any other solution in a syringe Protect from light	Possible restlessness, excitement, drowsiness, blurred vision, skin reaction, hypotension, leukopenia, agranulocytosis, cholestatic jaundice, extrapyramidal (neuro-muscular) reactions
	Chlorpromazine (Thorazine)		
25 mg every 4–6 hr IM, PO 50–100 mg suppository every 6–8 hr	Do not use in children <6 mo old PO ¼ mg per lb every 4–6 hr Suppository ½ mg per lb every 6–8 hr IV/IM ½ mg per lb every 6–8 hr Maximum dosage: Up to 5 yr (50 lb) Not over 40 mg/day 5–12 yr (50–100 lb) Not over 75 mg/day IV: Dilute to at least 1 mg/1ml. Give 1 mg every 2 min	Contraindicated in bone marrow depression. No use of alcohol with this drug due to additive effects and hypotension. Duration of activity following IM may last up to 12 hr. Inject slowly (deep IM, upper, outer buttocks)	Drowsiness, jaundice, hematological disorders, agranulocytosis, hypotension, fainting, dizziness, extrapyramidal (neuro-muscular) reactions, allergic reactions
	Trimethobenzamide HCl (Tigan)		
PO 250 mg every 6 hr Suppository 200 mg every 6 hr IM 200 mg TID or QID IV Not recommended for IV use	PO 30–39 lb: 1 or 2 100 mg capsules TID or QID. >90 lb: 250 mg capsules TID or QID Suppository (200mg) <30 lb: ½ 100 mg suppository TID or QID 30–90 lb: ½–1 100 mg suppository TID or QID >90 lb: 1 suppository (200 mg) TID or QID IM Not for use in children IV Not recommended for IV use	Do not use with premature infants or newborns IM may cause pain, stinging, burning, redness and swelling at IM site Give deep IM	Extrapyramidal reactions, drowsiness, hypersensitivity, hypotension following IV administration, blood dyscrasias, blurred vision, coma, convulsions, depression, diarrhea, dizziness, disorientation, headache, jaundice, muscle cramps

TABLE 4-3. COMMON ANTIEMETIC DRUGS (continued)

Adult Dose	Pediatric Dose	Considerations	Side-Effects
		Thiethylperazine (Torecan)	
<u>PO</u> 10 mg 1 to 3 times/day <u>IM</u> 2 ml (20 mg) 1 to 3 times/day <u>Suppository</u> 10 mg 1 to 3 times/day	Appropriate dosage has not been determined in children	IV route is contraindicated due to hypertension Do not use in children <12 yr of age	Convulsions, extrapyramidal reactions, dizziness, headache, fever, restlessness, drowsiness, dryness of mouth and nose, blurred vision, tinnitus, peripheral edema of arms, hands, face, blood dyscrasias, hypotension, allergic reactions, hyperpyrexia
		Droperidol (Inapsine)	
0.5 mg to 2.5 mg 30 to 60 min before infusion and every 4 to 6 hr IM or IV for premedication <u>IM</u> 30 to 60 min prior to operation	Do not use in children <2 yr No dosage for nausea/vomiting, for premedication, or for induction of anesthesia. 2 to 12 yr: 1.0 to 1.5 mg/20 to 25 lb	Protect from light Potentiates other central nervous system depressants	Hypotension, drowsiness, extrapyramidal reactions, restlessness, hyperactivity, anxiety, dizziness, chills, tachycardia, hallucinations
		Metoclopramide hydrochloride (Reglan)	
10 mg IV to increase gastric emptying 2 to 4 mg/kg IV every 2 hr for control of nausea/vomiting	<6 yr: 0.1 mg/kg IV 6 to 14 yr: 2.5 to 5 mg IV to increase gastric emptying None given for control of nausea/vomiting	Do not use with epileptics Give IV injections over 1 to 3 minutes No information in PDR on relief of nausea/vomiting Low doses (10 to 20 mg) proven ineffective with nausea/vomiting Abstention from eating for 8 hr helps	Drowsiness, extrapyramidal reactions, (more frequent in children and young adults), restlessness, diarrhea, anxiety, lassitude, fatigue, dizziness
		Promethazine (Phenergan)	
12.5 to 25 mg IM or IV every 4 hr 25 mg PO or suppository then 12.5 to 25 mg every 4 to 6 hr	<12 yr: Not to exceed ½ adult dose (IM or IV) 25 mg PO or suppository then 12.5 to 25 mg every 4 to 6 hr (Adjust for age and weight of child, and severity of nausea/vomiting.	Give deep IM Additive effects with alcohol or other central nervous system depressants Use with caution in bone marrow depression Do not give intra-arterial injection For IV, give in concentration ≤25 mg per ml and at a rate not to exceed 25 mg/min Deep IM route is preferred to IV administration Alter dose of barbiturates and analgesics	Hallucinations, convulsions, sudden death, extrapyramidal reactions, leukopenia, agranulocytosis, drowsiness, fatigue, blurred vision, hypotension, hypertension, dizziness, fainting, urticaria

(Table continues on next page)

TABLE 4–3. COMMON ANTIEMETIC DRUGS (continued)

Adult Dose	Pediatric Dose	Considerations	Side-Effects
Dexamethasone (Decadron)			
10 mg IV 4 to 8 mg PO	0.75 to 9.0 mg/day PO, IM, IV depending on specific disease entity	Do not use when patient has systemic fungal infection For diabetes, peptic ulcer, give IV slowly over 5 min	Fluid and electrolyte disturbances, musculoskeletal, gastrointestinal, dermatologic, neurological, endocrine, ophthalmic, metabolic, tingling, myalgias, malaise, minimal side effects
Methylprednisolone (steroid)			
250 mg IV every 4 hr	None given	Only administer by IV Do not use when patient has systemic infection, diabetes, or peptic ulcer Give over 10 to 20 min Use within 48 hr of mixing	Generalized swelling, facial rash, weakness, lethargy, myalgias, euphoria, minimal side effects
Tetrahydrocannabinol (THC)			
20 mg/m^2 every 3 hr PO	None given	Depression, anxiety, and paranoia are intensified Age influences person's response Accurate dose of natural THC is impossible Can intensify phantom pain May potentiate effects of sedatives Not physiologically addicting	Euphoria, increased appetite, sedation, dizziness, postural hypotension, spatial disorientation, reddened eyes, dry mouth, tachycardia, bronchodialation, angina, transient panic reaction, impaired immediate recall and perceptual coordination

particularly important to look for in children who have brain tumors, or those who use crutches to ambulate, since these patients are affected easily by this type of reaction. Infants who are learning to walk also must be observed closely.

Other common reactions include hypotension and the potentiation of the effects of other CNS depressants, analgesics, and sedatives the patient may be receiving (Physician's Desk Reference, 1985). To combat the hypotensive effect of these drugs, the child should remain in bed with the side rails up for at least one half

hour after administration, particularly if given the drug parenterally. Also if the child is receiving a CNS depressant, analgesic, or sedative in addition to the antiemetic, as mentioned above, the nurse must be aware of potential enhancement effect. It is the nurse's responsibility to inform the physician of this potential, to inform the patient and the family of the potential enhancement of the drug, and to inform coworkers of signs and symptoms to look for.

Drugs mentioned in the literature as useful antiemetics include diazepam (Valium), domperidone, droperidol (Inapsine), fluphenazine plus nortriptyline, levomepromazine, trimethobenzamide (Tigan), Reglan, and nabilone (Maxwell, 1982). The investigations of these drugs in the literature all have one major point in common: They do not study the effectiveness of the drugs as antiemetics on pediatric populations. Therefore as nurses we must be aware that if these drugs are used with our pediatric patients to control nausea and vomiting due to chemotherapy, the patient, the family, the physician, other health-team members, and ourselves are treading uncharted, untested territory in regard to these drugs. The potential side-effects in children are unknown, and the patient must be under continual observation to determine if there are any adverse reactions.

One antiemetic drug not discussed so far has a great impact on the pediatric/adolescent patient both in the inpatient and the outpatient setting. This drug is known as tetrahydrocannabinol, as delta-9-tetrahydrocannabinol, as THC, and as marijuana. In 1839 marijuana was introduced into western medicine, but in 1937 its use was prohibited in the United States by federal law. In the 1960s, however, marijuana's best-known component, THC, was synthetically produced. Recent research with this synthetically produced component has demonstrated its effective antiemetic use. Double-blind studies have been attempted to study the effects of this drug (Seipp, 1980). A common problem encountered by several of these studies is that the double-blind study design is not maintained. The patients and nurses are able to correctly determine which drug the patient is receiving due to the side-effects of THC. Another common problem with these studies is the attitude of the nursing staff and the patients. Using marijuana is against the principles of many adults. One 60-year old woman was removed from a study because "she admitted that she had violated her moral and ethical code by using a bad drug like 'marijuana'" (Andrysiak, 1979). When a double-blind study design

by Seipp and colleagues (1980) was not maintained, they investigated the attitudes of the nurses and their inability to maintain the double-blind study design. The nurses who participated in the study had anxiety and apprehension about the adequacy of the staff to make observations of the patients' behavior, about their ability to manage patients who were "hallucinating from the drugs," and about actual "pot smoking" on the unit and its effects on other patients. After 1 year of conducting this study, eighteen of the original twenty nurses responded to a followup survey. Adequate staffing was the only problem that had emerged during the 1-year study.

These studies were conducted on adult patients. The responses of both the patients and the staff may be different when pediatric or adolescent patients are studied. Studies of this type currently are being conducted in various institutions. The use of marijuana is being documented at much younger ages than even a few years ago. It is easier for the adolescent and younger child to obtain the drug illegally; the drug-use crisis in our school systems is common knowledge. Based on the current social use of this drug by the pediatric/adolescent age group, medical use with this age group should be more easily accepted. In fact large numbers of cancer patients are experimenting with marijuana on their own, in and out of the hospital. Nurses must be aware of the effects of and the proper usage of the drug. Sharing information about marijuana or about sources of such information does not mean that the nurse condones its use. The nurse simply can give the patient information about the drug that will enable the patient and the family to make up their own minds regarding its use. Even though THC is legally distributed to most community hospitals and cancer treatment centers, large numbers of cancer patients are still getting it illegally (Rovinski, 1983).

Marijuana can be smoked or ingested. Smoking avoids the possible side-effect of intestinal absorption. It is suggested that the patient inhale, hold the breath for 10 seconds, exhale, and then wait 50 seconds before repeating the process. The patient should use only as much as is needed for emetic control and not feel that the entire cigarette must be smoked each time. The peak effect occurs in 10 minutes and lasts for about 2 hours (Rovinski, 1983).

Some people find that smoking the marijuana is too harsh; it burns their throats and causes coughing spells. These people can add $\frac{1}{8}$ cup of finely ground marijuana to a brownie recipe. The drug must be sautéd in butter before being added to the mix, as it is ineffective in its raw form. The peak effect from this method occurs in about 1 hour and may last up to 6 hours (Rovinski, 1983). For patients nauseated by chocolate, THC works very well in ginger snaps. This form is especially palatable to young children.

While antiemetics are the major component of attempts to control nausea and vomiting, they are frequently ineffective. Other methods of control have been investigated to supplement antiemetic therapy. A study conducted at Temple University Health Science Center examined several factors that may influence the degree of nausea and vomiting. The first finding was that "no matter what dietary adjustments or alterations were made, none seemed to make any difference in the degree of nausea and vomiting." What they found regarding foods is that: (1) Patients may view some foods as sick foods and some as reward foods; (2) foods presented to the patient consistently during the nausea and vomiting period may be associated with that period; (3) avoiding spicy or greasy foods was helpful; (4) the appearance of the meals was important; and (5) foods that patients crave may be tolerated well (Scogna, 1979). All of these findings have pediatric implications. Every child has his or her favorite foods (*i.e.*, hot dogs), which he or she gets as rewards (*i.e.*, ice cream), and foods the child gets only when he's sick (*i.e.*, tea, soup, toast). If a

kitchen facility or a cafeteria, or some other source of food is available, the patient, the parents, and the nurse should take advantage of this opportunity to fix the child the type of food that is desired. The child should not always be given the same food or favorite foods during or immediately following the chemotherapy, nausea, and vomiting experience. The child may associate the food with the nausea and vomiting experience, and may "learn" to experience more nausea and vomiting when the food is presented. The study also demonstrated that the patient's subjective attitude about the effectiveness of the therapy, the average number of hours of sleep before a treatment, and the adjustment in activity levels 24 hours pre- or posttherapy had no influence on the degree of nausea and vomiting the patient experienced (Scogna, 1979).

Attempts to control the patient's environment have also been studied in attempts to control nausea and vomiting. Attempts to control the environment include discarding disagreeable sights and smells, plus psychogenic and conditioning factors, and focusing the patient on something other than the chemotherapy and its side-effects. Some studies advocate the use of multipatient rooms that provide an opportunity for patient interaction. Others report that multipatient rooms are too stressful. Some studies report less nausea and vomiting if the patient is seated rather than lying down during the infusion (Grant, 1982). For pediatric patients the environment should offer age-appropriate distractions. Many children benefit from watching cartoons on TV, from playing games by themselves or with others, or from sleeping. The child-life worker can be a valuable resource in providing stimulation and distraction for these pediatric patients. Adolescents may simply wish to listen to their favorite radio station or tape, or visit with their peers. Popular headphones and portable stereo units are frequently seen on the units. Many children prefer to have their chemotherapy infusions covered by paper

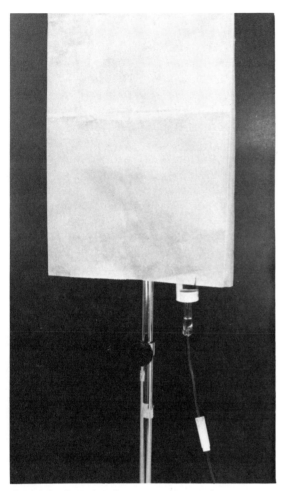

FIG. 4-8. Covering for chemotherapy bag.

bags or "cloth bag covers" (Fig. 4-8) since the site of the chemotherapy infusion bag itself sometimes causes nausea and vomiting.

Relaxation techniques and hypnosis have also been utilized to attempt to decrease nausea and vomiting. This is particularly true with anticipatory vomiting. Nausea and vomiting experienced by one in four patients prior to receiving chemotherapy is probably a learned response to the treatment. Systematic desensitization utilizes relaxation as a counterconditioning stimulus to take the place of the stimulus of the nausea and vomiting. Sometimes the stimulus is simply driving to the hospital for the chemotherapy treatments. One such relaxation technique, the Jacobsonian progressive deep-muscle relaxation technique, was utilized in a study by Morrow and Morrell (1982). In this technique the patients learn progressive relaxation of the muscles of their hands, forearms, forehead, eyes, mouth, tongue, upper back and shoulders, chest, and stomach. The procedure takes approximately 20 minutes to complete. The investigators found that this technique, when taught to the patients away from the hospital, was more effective in reducing anticipatory nausea and vomiting than the combination of counseling and no other treatment. Systematic desensitization was also found to reduce the severity and duration of the anticipatory nausea, if it occurred at all, and in the reduction of the severity but not the duration of the vomiting, if it occurred. Relaxation and hypnosis have also been studied in the control of postchemotherapy side-effects, with some success (Burish, 1981).

STOMATITIS

Equally disturbing to the patient, but not occurring until some time after the infusion has been completed, is stomatitis. Stomatitis refers to the ulcerative lesions in the mouth and oral pharynx. These lesions develop from 5 to 14 days after exposure to the chemotherapeutic drug and last for 4 to 10 days. Drugs that can cause stomatitis include actinomycin D (Dactinomycin), daunorubicin, bleomycin, doxorubicin (Adriamycin), methotrexate, and fluorouracil (5-Fu). The cases of stomatitis vary from mild to severe forms. The mild form is a generalized inflammatory reaction with mild erythema, edema along the mucocutaneous junction of the lip, dryness of the mouth, and a burning sensation of the lips. Severe stomatitis is characterized by hemorrhagic ulcerations of the oral mucosa, concomitant pain, low-grade fever, possible secondary infection, and dysphagia. Salivary gland activity also decreases, producing less saliva and increased saliva viscosity.

One study reported in an article by Ostchega (1980) states that 39% of adults and 90% of children with malignancies below the neck developed mild to severe stomatitis following chemotherapy. The oral mucosa's rate of mitosis is highest in children, which explains why they have more oral problems than adults. Due to this rapid rate of mitosis and cell growth, in children the first signs of oral deterioration often appear within 2 or 3 days after the chemotherapy.

Another interesting development is the fact that the patient's WBC count often correlates with the oral problems since they have basically the same cell renewal rates. The immunosuppressed patient is more susceptible to disease, and infections may develop without the usual signs and symptoms. Mouth lesions provide infectious organisms with an easily accessible port of entry into the patients' systems. Infections may develop from a variety of organisms, with gram-negative organisms being one of the chief groups. With the patient's oral secretions decreased (gram-negative bacteria are thus not washed into the esophagus), and with the use of antibiotics (antibiotics disturb the interbacterial balance), the gram-negative bacteria can flourish (Ostchega, 1980).

Fungal infections are a second group of infectious organisms. The infection caused by fungus is called candidiasis, moniliasis, or thrush. Subacute thrush appears as cream-colored, flaky, loose plaque covering a bright red, inflamed mucosa. Chronic thrush presents with dry, red, buccal mucosa, patches of plaque, and a swollen, red, shiny, dry, cracked tongue. When thrush occurs in the upper gastrointestinal system in small children in diapers, it is common for a fungal dermatosis to also occur. Viral infections such as herpetic stomatitis or herpes simplex virus also occur. These viral infections present with a yellowish-brown, easily wiped away membrane, causing severe pain. The vesicles may extend out of the mouth and over the lips (Daeffler, 1980).

Assessment is the one nursing action above all others that is vital for the prevention of stomatitis and its complications. The child who is to receive chemotherapy *must* have an adequate assessment made of his or her mouth *prior* to receiving the drugs *and* on a daily basis afterwards. The areas to be assessed include the lips, the tongue, the palate, the gingival tissue, and the mucous membranes. The nurse should examine the areas for moisture, color, texture, and the presence or absence of debris. The nurse should also determine if the child's teeth have erupted on schedule, if dental caries are present, if the child is a nose or mouth breather, if he or she can eat, and if any routine care for the teeth and mouth has been conducted. If the child has any mouth problems, a dentist should be consulted prior to the onset of chemotherapy. After chemotherapy has begun, no dental work can be accomplished due to the patient's resultant immunosuppression (Ostchega, 1980). After adequate oral assessment has been completed prechemotherapy, the child and the family must develop a schedule of oral care that will become routine prior to the development of any oral complications. This routine must also be carried through after the chemotherapy, between courses, and even after the treatments are completed. Routine care prior to chemotherapy should consist of brushing the child's teeth at least twice daily. It is preferable to brush after each meal and snack, but this is not often feasible. Toothbrushing removes plaque from the teeth, the tongue, and the gums and also stimulates the gingival tissues to maintain tone and prevent circulatory stasis. Children need to use smaller toothbrushes that are soft and yet have handles long enough for the child to hold easily. Toothbrushes should be replaced when they become frayed, often as frequently as every 2 to 3 months. Flossing is the most effective means of removing plaque from between the teeth. The child should be taught to floss the teeth daily with an unwaxed floss. The child must be taught to floss correctly since improper flossing may be injurious to the gums. Children may find it hard to control the floss, but they can be taught to tie the ends together to form a 10-inch circle for easier handling. Whenever brushing or flossing is not possible due to thrombocytopenia the child should be taught at least to rinse the mouth with water or another solution.

If the child's WBC count drops or stomatitis develops, mouth care must be altered. When the child's platelet count drops to between 15,000 and 10,000, flossing should be discontinued. Brushing with a toothbrush should be discontinued when the platelet count drops to between 10,000 and 5,000 (Ostchega, 1980). This does not mean that mouth care should be discontinued altogether. To the contrary, mouth care is even more essential at this critical point in the child's care. As the child feels more sick or in more pain or discomfort due to the stomatitis, he or she is less likely to cooperate with mouth care. This is when the nurse plays a major role in the child's care. The child (if old enough) and the family can be taught to carry out the mouth care themselves, although the nurse is always responsible for the care and for assuring that it is done. Often the child will not allow the nurse to do the mouth care; the family, however, must not be overtaxed with the responsibility for all the child's care. If at all possible the nurse should do the mouth care at night to allow the family some rest and to assure that a good job of cleansing the mouth is done. The literature does not support just one type of oral care; however, a few basic measures are standard. If the patient has any dental apparatus it should be removed. Children may have partial plates for tooth spacing if teeth have been shed too early due to decay, accidental

loss, or other reasons. They may also have braces, retainers, or night spacers. All of these devices should be removed. Wires from braces should also be removed if the WBC drops because they may cause bleeding and further deterioration of the gums (Bruya, 1975). (A summary of interventions for stomatitis can be found in Table 4-1).

One consideration for pediatric nurses who use irrigation equipment and cleansing agents such as hydrogen peroxide, is that depending on the age of the child, he or she may be very frightened of the equipment or of the effect of the hydrogen peroxide or other agents used. Adequate teaching prior to implementation of this care is an absolute must with the pediatric patient and family. It will assure more cooperation and compliance on the part of the child and assure a quicker resolution of any oral problems.

Several difficulties are apparent with the use of viscous lidocaine. The drug causes numbness of the tongue and the mouth that may interfere with the pharyngeal stage of swallowing and may cause the patient to bite the tongue or cheek. The taste is unpleasant to some patients. The patient's sensitivity to the heat of food may be impaired. Also the drug has systemic effects on the cardiovascular system and the central nervous system. As a result, the Physicians' Desk Reference (1985) recommends limiting the use of this drug to 15 ml (300 mg) every three hours. This limits the amount of the drug to 120 ml or less every 24 hours. This is especially important in children, and the nurse must stress to the parents and the child the importance of limiting the intake of this drug since in most cases the child will probably not understand why he or she cannot continually utilize this drug to maintain a numbness in the mouth.

Cold and liquid foods are usually tolerated well. Liquids that children tolerate well include popsicles, snow cones, fruitades, carbonated beverages, mild malts, and milk shakes. The child's favorite liquid can be frozen and made into popsicles. Instant breakfasts are not only tolerated well, but provide necessary calories and nutrients. Dietary supplements may be added to the fruitades to increase the nutrients that the child receives. Vegetables such as cucumbers, and fruits such as watermelon and grapes, are often less aggravating than fruit juices. If the patient cannot or will not consume the amount of nutrients that are required to promote healing of the oral mucosa, the patient may require other methods of feeding. These methods include a nasogastric (NG) feeding tube, a gastrostomy or jejunostomy feeding tube, or a hyperalimentation line. Any method of nutritional support chosen must depend on the nutritional needs of the child, the condition of the child, the age of the child, and the amount of stress that the method will produce for the child. In many cases the child may tolerate any method other than the NG tube, which may further irritate an already irritated oropharynx.

ALOPECIA

Another side-effect that occurs days after the chemotherapy infusion is completed is alopecia. Although this side-effect is not physically painful, it can be emotionally painful for anyone. The emotional distress is only partially alleviated by the use of a wig or scarf.

Hair growth is cyclic as is the growth of all cells. Each hair grows at a slow, steady, independent rate. Hair grows in three phases. The first and longest phase is called the *anagen* phase. This phase of active growth lasts for approximately 3 to 7 years; approximately 90% of a person's hair is in this active phase. The second phase is the *catagen* or involution/transitional phase. This phase involves involution of the hair root, lasts only for a few days, and involves less than 1% of the hairs. The last phase is the *telogen* phase, or the dormant phase. This phase lasts for approximately 3 months,

involves 10% of the hairs, and ends when the old hair is shed and new hair is regenerated and anagen begins. Hairs on other parts of the body, such as pubic hair and eyebrows, have a shorter anagen phase, and most of the hairs are in the telogen phase (Maxwell, 1980; Kennedy, 1983).

Chemotherapy works on the hair follicle cells in one of two ways, depending on the dose of the drug and the type of drug. Each hair follicle has a bulbous base of mitotically active matrix cells that move up in rows to the upper bulb and elongate vertically. The hairs are forced upward and then emerge at the skin. Chemotherapeutic drugs attack the hair follicle cells during the mitotic cycle of the matrix cells in the bulb. If the chemotherapeutic drugs are given in small doses, they decrease the size of the bulb, thus causing a constriction of the hair shaft. The constriction moves up as the hair grows, and then breaks off easily once it has come through the scalp. The root remains in the scalp, already recovered from the effects of the chemotherapy and again actively functioning. Larger doses of chemotherapeutic drugs cause the bulb to atrophy completely. The hair then comes out either (1) by falling out spontaneously, or (2) following a disturbance such as combing or washing. Only the hairs in the anagen phase are affected by the chemotherapeutic drugs. The 10% of hairs in the telogen phase will remain in place. Alopecia is not affected by a familial tendency to baldness. Baldness is not hair loss, but rather a reduction of the hair follicle size from large and coarse to very small and fine. Drugs that can cause alopecia include cyclophosphamide (Cytoxan), methotrexate, 5-fluorouracil (5-Fu), vinblastine, vincristine, VM-26, VP-16, actinomycin D, and doxorubicin (Adriamycin). Cyclophosphamide, actinomycin D, doxorubicin, and vincristine produce moderate to marked alopecia; the other drugs produce only mild effects. The use of doxorubicin results in alopecia in more than 80% of the patients treated with 60 to 75 mg/m² and in approximately 100% of the patients treated with cumulative doses of 180 to 315 mg/m² of body surface area. Complete hair loss usually occurs within 21 days (Lovejoy, 1979; Welch, 1980).

Investigators have attempted to decrease the amount of alopecia that occurs either by cooling the scalp with ice or by applying a tourniquet around the head. These two methods have been attempted with various devices. Both of these methods are based on the principle of reducing blood flow, or the occlusion of the blood flow to the hair follicle cells while the drug levels are high. This principle is feasible since the main blood supply to the scalp is located subcutaneously and can be occluded by external pressure or constricted by cold. Since skin cells are slow to progress through the cell cycle, they are able to sustain the blood supply loss for a period of time before necrosis occurs.

Several studies have demonstrated that the use of a tourniquet device can minimize the effect of alopecia (Lovejoy, 1979; Welch, 1980). Scalp tourniquets are applied when the drug levels are at their peak and remain in place as long as possible. If the drugs are given by IV push, there are immediate peak plasma levels that then taper off. The scalp tourniquet should be applied at the time of administration of the drugs and left in place for 20 minutes. If the drugs are given by IV infusion, the scalp tourniquet should be applied when the plasma levels are the highest and left on until 10 minutes after the infusion is complete. The tourniquet should remain in place for no longer than 20 minutes. Scalp tourniquets *should not* be utilized with children with leukemia or lymphoma, because the malignant cells are throughout the blood and lymph systems. Children with other types of cancer that can metastasize to or originate in the scalp should also not use these methods.

Two methods of applying a tourniquet to the scalp have been studied. One method is through the use of a tubing tourniquet. This simply can be two Penrose drains, or some other tubing, tied together. This type of scalp tourniquet is not recommended for two reasons. First, the pressure on the underlying tissue cannot be controlled and is not homogeneous. Also there is a high probability of compression damage to the underlying nerves resulting from this method. The second method is through the use of a pneumatic tourniquet (Fig. 4-9). This method employs a scalp sphygmomanometer. These pnuematic tourniquets should have cuff pressures set so that they do not exceed the patient's perioperative systolic pressure by much more than 70 mm Hg. This level has been chosen based on several studies on operative systolic blood pressure and nerve conduction. This tourniquet is recommended because the amount of pressure utilized can be controlled, uniform pressure can be applied to the underlying tissues, and there is less probability of nerve compression and nerve damage (Lovejoy, 1979; Welch, 1980). This technique may be difficult to use on young children who will not sit still for the 20 minutes needed. Also children may feel uncomfortable from the pressure on their head. Although most of the studies stated that the patients did not experience dizziness, syncope, or headaches, they did experience a sensation of the head feeling tightly squeezed and of numbness (Maxwell, 1980). One study by Lovejoy (1979) demonstrated that adults tolerated the scalp tourniquets for up to 10 minutes. After that time some patients become increasingly aware of time. These feelings may be intolerable for the child. None of these studies reviewed were conducted on a pediatric population, so that how children will tolerate this procedure has not been documented in the literature.

The second method for attempting to control alopecia is through the cooling of the scalp. The cooling technique is used because it constricts the blood vessels of the scalp, thus decreasing the amount of the drug that reaches the hair follicles. Another principle of this technique is

FIG. 4-9. Scalp tourniquet.

that the cooling should reduce the cell uptake of the drug. Studies using this technique have had varying success rates. Studies have utilized crushed ice with 70% of patients experiencing less than 70% hair loss, a cryogel pack technique (Table 4-4) with 45% experiencing no significant hair loss and 35% experiencing only minor loss, and a "Chemocap" cooling device (Table 4-5) with only a minimal number of patients experiencing no alopecia.

The difficulties found with these cooling techniques on children are similar to those that would be encountered with the scalp tourniquet. Complaints from patients include the coldness of the scalp, the weight of the caps, and the fact that the caps are "uncomfortable."

Children are also difficult to contain in a bed, and often resist lying still for over an hour.

No matter which, if any, method is used to decrease alopecia, some hair will be lost, and the child's body image will suffer. Hair loss is very tragic for children, especially the adolescent. The child must be reassured that the hair will return after the course of chemotherapy has been completed. It may return curlier, a different texture, or a slightly different color.

Meanwhile the child can utilize several methods to help cope with the changed body image. Many children wear scarves or hats to cover the thin patches of hair. Some of these children will only take their hats off when they sleep, and some children with scarves do not even do that. Children can be fitted for wigs that resemble the real hair. The wigs should be fitted prior to any hair loss so that color, length, and style can be duplicated as accurately as possible. Resources must be explored for obtaining wigs or financial assistance since a good wig can be

TABLE 4-4. CRYOGEL PACK TECHNIQUES

1. The patient wets his/her hair.
2. Protectors made from gauze and cotton wool are applied over the ears.
3. The head is covered by a wet crepe bandage, which reduces the amount of trapped air under the cap and improves conduction.
4. The cooled cap is then placed over the bandaged scalp 15 minutes before the treatment and left in place for at least 30 minutes afterward (approximately 50 to 60 minutes total).
5. The patient is made comfortable on a bed, with the back and head well supported with pillows. A blanket is available if required.
6. The research nurse remains with the patient until the procedure is completed.

TABLE 4-5. CHEMOCAP TECHNIQUES

1. Precool scalp for 10 minutes with cap (wetting of the hair may be utilized to improve conduction).
2. Ten minutes prior to the infusion, remove cap for 30 seconds to apply scalp tourniquet; reapply cap.
3. Leave cap and tourniquet in place for 30 minutes after infusion is complete (a total of 60–80 min).

quite costly. Exposure to other children without hair is also helpful for the child. "Bald is beautiful" posters also say that having no hair is really OK.

MYELOSUPPRESSION

An additional side-effect that occurs a period of time after the chemotherapy infusion is completed, is myelosuppression, or bone marrow depression. This condition results in anemia (decreased red blood cells), leukopenia (decreased white blood cells), and thrombocytopenia (decreased platelets).

ANEMIA

With anemia the child does not produce adequately functioning red blood cells, or adequate red blood cells are destroyed by chemotherapy. Anemia can also result not only from insufficient production of adequate RBCs, but also from excessive bleeding. The child may experience an increased heart rate and respirations, acid-base alterations, weakness, and fatigue. Other symptoms of anemic children include pallor, listlessness, constipation, anorexia, poor feeding, and "bad" behavior. If the anemia is severe any activity, including eating or walking, is a chore. The child uses all available energy just trying to exist. The anemic child should be encouraged to rest prior to meals and at frequent intervals throughout the day.

Another cause of anemia could be nutritional. Iron deficiency anemia develops slowly, over time, as not enough iron is supplied in the diet and the body's iron stores are depleted. This type of anemia is most prevalent in all children between 6 months and 3 years of age and during the adolescent growth spurt. It has also been found in increasing numbers in school-age children. When a child is receiving chemotherapy, he or she may also experience iron deficiency anemia.

Correction of the anemia depends on the cause. Moderate anemia is defined as a hemoglobin below 6 to 7 mg/dl, and severe anemia is defined as a hemoglobin of 2 to 3 mg/dl. The point at which a child should be transfused varies with the child's condition and the cause of anemia. For chronic blood loss the patient should receive packed red blood cells, since blood volume is usually normal. Iron deficiency is common with chronic blood loss, so the patient must also be treated with iron supplementation (see Table 4-6 for Iron Precautions). A child with acute blood loss should receive a transfusion of whole blood to replace the cellular components as well as the blood volume.

THROMBOCYTOPENIA

Thrombocytopenia may be the cause of the bleeding that leads to the child becoming anemic. When a child's platelet count drops to below 25,000 per mm^3 he or she may require a platelet transfusion. This is especially true if the child has petechiae or a bleeding tendency. If a patient's platelet count reaches approximately 9,000 mm^3, he or she is susceptible to oral hemorrhage, especially after oral trauma such as toothbrushing. As a child's platelet count falls, he or she will bleed more easily and for longer periods of time before clotting occurs. The child also may bruise for no reason at all. Bleeding may occur from the gums or the nose or, as

TABLE 4-6. IRON PRECAUTIONS

To reduce gastric irritation, give iron shortly after meals.
Avoid large amounts of milk (interferes with absorption).
Iron can be taken with juice.
Supplements can be taken in the form of chewable tablets, nonchewable tablets, liquids, or drops.
Teeth may be temporarily stained (can attempt to avoid this by using a dropper or straw and by rinsing mouth and brushing teeth afterwards).
Stools may turn black, and constipation may develop.
Accidental ingestion may result in hemorrhage and death.
The entire course of medicine must be taken, even after symptoms disappear.

petechiae, anywhere on the skin. The bleeding may be an intermittent oozing or it may appear as blood clots that continuously form, break away, and then form again. This type of bleeding is seen frequently in children as nosebleeds.

Nose picking and epistaxis are common in childhood. Over 90% of nosebleeds in all children are in the anterior nasal septum and stop spontaneously with pressure. These children also bleed easily from the posterior nasal septum, which does not respond well to pressure and may require packing. When a nosebleed occurs the child should be positioned in a sitting position and instructed to breathe through the mouth. Direct, firm pressure should be applied for 2 to 10 minutes from the lateral side of the nose against the septum. If bleeding does not stop, the nose can be packed by a doctor. A form of petroleum jelly should be applied to the nasal mucosa after the bleeding stops to prevent crusting of blood.

Measures should be taken to avoid trauma to the child with low platelets, although a child often finds it impossible to avoid cuts, bumps, bruises, and falls. If the child is an outpatient and the platelet count is low, he or she should not be allowed to participate in contact sports, to ride bikes or skate boards, to climb on playground equipment, and so on. An inpatient should not be allowed to do "wheelies" with wheel-chairs, run up and down halls, ride the IV poles and the like. The child should avoid excessive nose blowing or frequent sneezing. This may be difficult if the child has a cold or allergies.

If thrombocytopenia is severe the nurse may need to alter the child's care. Injections should be avoided if possible. Mild pressure should be applied after injections, venipunctures, and fingersticks. Bruising may result if too much pressure is applied. Stool softeners can be given the patient to help prevent constipation and straining, although laxatives are only a last resort in the school-age child. Parents are first encouraged to include more roughage and high-resi-

due foods in the child's diet, and to increase the oral fluid intake. If the child cannot or will not eat or take in adequate fluids, however, laxatives should be used. Laxatives are *never* used with infants. Rectal temperatures and attempts to remove any impaction should be avoided. The nurse also must assess the child's skin, stools, urine, gums, vomitus, sputum, and nasal secretions every 4 hours for bleeding. Sedation may be required if the child has severe thrombocytopenia and the activity level cannot be adequately quieted to avoid bleeding. Any adolescent female should be assessed for her menstrual history, beginning with the 10-year-old female. The physician should be informed if the child is having a menstrual period and a pad count should be maintained.

LEUKOPENIA

Leukopenia also may be a cause of altered activity of the child. The granulocytes are the white blood cells that protect against bacterial infections. A common term for granulocytes is "poly" or polymorphonuclear cells. When the granulocytopenia reaches a severe level of 1,000 granulocytes per mm³, gram-negative bacterial infection becomes a threat. The nurse can calculate a child's absolute granulocyte count by using the following formula:

Absolute granulocyte count =
$$\frac{\% \text{ granulocytes} \times \text{total WBC count}}{100}$$
(See Fig. 4-10 for a sample hematology lab slip.)

If the child's granulocyte count becomes low while the child is still receiving chemotherapy, treatment is frequently stopped. Since pus will not form without granulocytes, a localized infection is difficult to diagnose and it could become a systemic infection very rapidly. The nurse must therefore observe the child frequently for changes in status. The nurse should look for any redness or pain, malaise, decrease in the level of alertness, a dry non-

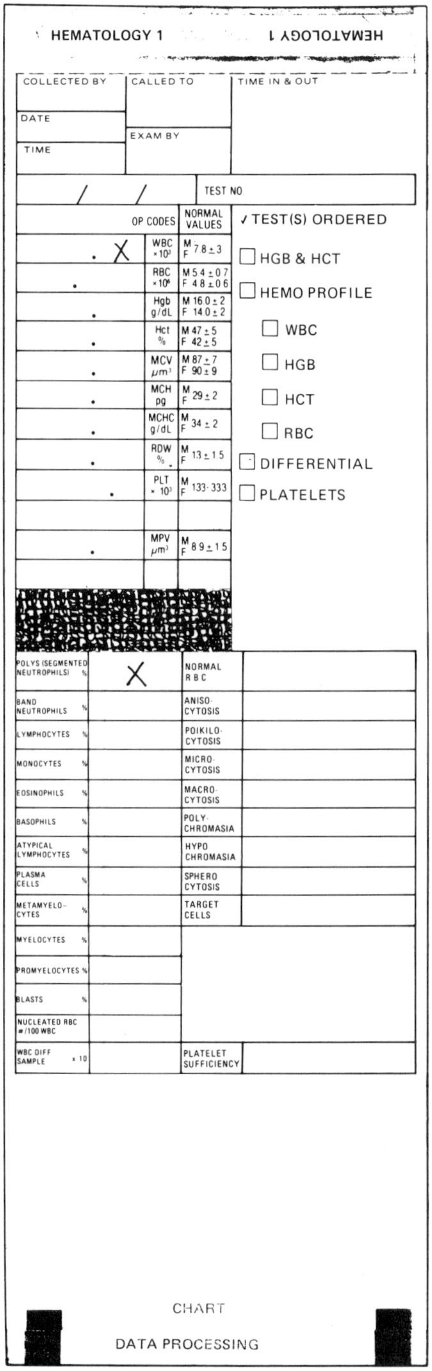
HEMATOLOGY 1

COLLECTED BY	CALLED TO	TIME IN & OUT
DATE	EXAM BY	
TIME		

/ / TEST NO

	OP CODES	NORMAL VALUES	✓ TEST(S) ORDERED
. X	WBC ×10³	M F 7.8 ± 3	☐ HGB & HCT
.	RBC ×10⁶	M 5.4 ± 0.7 F 4.8 ± 0.6	☐ HEMO PROFILE
.	Hgb g/dL	M 16.0 ± 2 F 14.0 ± 2	☐ WBC
.	Hct %	M 47 ± 5 F 42 ± 5	☐ HGB
.	MCV μm³	M 87 ± 7 F 90 ± 9	☐ HCT
.	MCH pg	M F 29 ± 2	☐ RBC
.	MCHC g/dL	M F 34 ± 2	☐ DIFFERENTIAL
.	RDW %	M F 13 ± 1.5	☐ PLATELETS
.	PLT × 10³	M F 133-333	
.	MPV μm³	M F 8.9 ± 1.5	

POLYS (SEGMENTED NEUTROPHILS) %	X	NORMAL RBC	
BAND NEUTROPHILS %		ANISOCYTOSIS	
LYMPHOCYTES %		POIKILOCYTOSIS	
MONOCYTES %		MICROCYTOSIS	
EOSINOPHILS %		MACROCYTOSIS	
BASOPHILS %		POLYCHROMASIA	
ATYPICAL LYMPHOCYTES %		HYPOCHROMASIA	
PLASMA CELLS %		SPHEROCYTOSIS	
METAMYELOCYTES %		TARGET CELLS	
MYELOCYTES %			
PROMYELOCYTES %			
BLASTS %			
NUCLEATED RBC #/100 WBC			
WBC DIFF SAMPLE × 10		PLATELET SUFFICIENCY	

CHART

DATA PROCESSING

FIG. 4-10. Hematology lab slip.

productive cough without rales or other signs of consolidation, and fever greater than 38.6°C (101.5°F).

Gram-negative bacteria are the most common causes of infection in these children. Any child who has a fever of 38.6°C should be examined for signs of an infection, which should be assumed to be bacterial until proven otherwise. The child should be started on broad-spectrum antibiotics after cultures have been obtained. The specific type and number of antibiotics will vary with each institution's policy. Once the site of infection and the causative organism have been identified, the antibiotic of choice for that organism should be given. In many cases the site of infection cannot be identified, nor can the causative organism. These patients should continue to be treated with broad-spectrum antibiotics. The antibiotics most frequently used are an aminoglycoside such as gentamicin and a cephalosporin such as cephalothin. Carbenicillin is sometimes added to the combination therapy if the child is at high risk for *Pseudomonas* organisms. The antibiotics are administered for a minimum of 7 to 10 days. Contagious diseases are isolated, while reverse isolation is not utilized in many hospitals because it has been found to be ineffective (Donovan, 1976; Potter, 1981).

Common sites of bacterial infections include the skin, the bloodstream, the perineal/perianal area, the bladder and kidneys, the respiratory tract, and the mouth (Donovan, 1976). This has many implications for nursing, especially when a child is the patient. Perineal care becomes especially important with both the child in diapers, and the child with diarrhea. Skin breakdown and diaper rashes in the perineal area are very common in young children. These areas can become infected easily. The nurse should keep the diaper area dry, clean, and aerated. Thick diapers should be used to help drain away the wetness. Plastic or rubber pants should not be used since they keep the area wet and warm. The perineal/perianal area should be cleansed with water and a mild soap with each diaper change. If powder is used, it should be used sparingly. Caldesene powder is especially good to use since it is an antifungal and antibacterial powder. Corn starch should be avoided since clumping occurs and provides a growth medium for fungus.

Stomatitis, discussed earlier in this chapter, provides an accessible portal for infection, as do teething and shedding of teeth. Thus oral care must be meticulously undertaken. Prior to any type of skin puncture, the skin should be prepared with an antibacterial agent such as Betadine. IV sites should be checked frequently for signs of infection and IV site care should be given every 24 hours. Rectal thermometers, suppositories, and enemas should be avoided since perirectal abscesses may develop. These lesions are painful and life-threatening. The treatment for these abscesses includes the use of antibiotics, cleansing the area with antibacterial solutions and water with perineal squirt bottles or sitz baths, and heat therapy. Bladder catheterization should be avoided, if possible. If catheterization is inevitable, Foley catheter care must be given at least twice a day. Above all, meticulous hand washing between care of every patient is one of the most important functions a nurse can do to help prevent infection.

Fungal infections are a second type of common infections. The sites of a fungal infection in a child may be as obvious as thrush or a fungal diaper rash, or as difficult to diagnose as a systemic fungal infection. An infection caused by a fungal organism commonly is seen in patients whose white blood cell count is below 200 mm. The drug of choice for most systemic fungal infections is amphotericin B, but it is so toxic that it is only given to the patient when the diagnosis of a fungal infection is confirmed. Side-effects include fever, chills, hypotension, nausea, vomiting, headaches, nephrotoxicity, and severe hypokalemia (Ostchega, 1980; Potter, 1981).

Viral infections also are seen in the child who is granulocytopenic. The herpes group of viruses are the most serious viral infections in children with cancer. These include herpes zoster, herpes simplex, varicella (chickenpox), and cytomegalovirus. A continuous infusion of Ara-A (cytosine arabinoside) for a 5-day period is the treatment of choice for confirmed cases, even though it causes further bone marrow depression. Live virus vaccines such as the polio and measles vaccines should be avoided by all children receiving immunosuppressive therapy. Siblings should also avoid these immunizations. Patients who are receiving corticosteroids as part of their therapy are very susceptible to severe viral infections. If the pediatric oncology patient is exposed to others with known viral infections, passive immunization with plasma or zoster immune globulin may be attempted.

Should a child become severely granulocytopenic, a granulocyte transfusion may be necessary. Many of the children who need this WBC transfusion have already received transfusions of other blood products. This increases the chances of the child's possible reaction to the WBC transfusion. If a reaction does occur, the child will experience fever, chills, urticaria, and severe respiratory distress, which may lead to a respiratory arrest.

Children receiving outpatient therapy and their parents must be taught to monitor blood counts weekly. A study by Harder and Hatfield (1972) demonstrated that patients can safely monitor their blood counts by having them done at a local laboratory. The investigators also found that this personal involvement raised the patients' self-esteem, strengthened the nurse–patient relationship, and returned a small portion of control to the patients' lives. This sort of involvement by the adolescent patient will help him or her to master the developmental task of independence for which all adolescents are striving. The school-age child and the adolescent should understand the significance of the weekly blood counts, which will allow them even more of an opportunity to participate in their own care.

The child who is an outpatient when granulocytopenia occurs must be cautious about the environment. Crowds should be avoided at times when the granulocyte count is low. Places to avoid include shopping centers, movie theaters, birthday parties, and sometimes even school. If a child in the patient's class becomes ill, especially with a viral disease such as chickenpox, the teacher must inform the child, the parents, and the school nurse so that appropriate action can be taken. The school nurse also should be kept informed of the weekly blood counts. Other common problems such as insect bites, lice, and so on, also may cause problems for the granulocytopenic child. If the child scratches hard enough to break the skin, organisms have a convenient portal for entry into the child's system. Parents (and children) should watch for any of these signs and symptoms and should be taught preventive measures to take.

ANAPHYLACTIC REACTIONS

A sixth side-effect occurs fairly rapidly after exposure to chemotherapeutic agents or other antigens. These anaphylactic reactions range from a mild irritation (a local reaction) to anaphylactic shock (a systemic reaction), which may be fatal. These reactions occur not only to chemotherapeutic agents such as L-asparaginase, but also to common antigens found in antibiotics (*i.e.*, penicillin, cephalosporin, tetracycline, and others), other drugs (*i.e.*, aspirin, tranquilizers, benzocaine), biologicals (*i.e.*, antitoxins, vaccines, gamma globulin, insulin), diagnostic agents (*i.e.*, IVP dye, gallbladder dye), foods (*i.e.*, eggs, milk, nuts, seafood), and insect stings. Any history of allergies increases the chance of new reactions. Approximately 10% to 20% of the pediatric population has been estimated to have allergies. Foods are the most common allergens in infancy, whereas envi-

ronmental factors are the leading causes in childhood. If there is any suspicion of a previous reaction to a substance, another agent should be substituted, remembering that cross-reactions can occur between drugs that are chemically related. Repeated exposure to an antigen increases the likelihood of an allergic reaction. The severity of the reaction will depend upon the patient's degree of hypersensitivity and the amount of antigen absorbed, its rate of absorption, and the route of administration. For these reasons oral medications are safer than intravenous medications. The child's level of growth and development, however, also influence the form of the drug the child can tolerate. Not all children can swallow pills, and not all medications come in an oral liquid form. Any patient with a history of allergies should be observed carefully for at least 10 to 20 minutes after receiving a drug. Also children who do have allergies should be encouraged to wear medic-alert tags, in case they ever become unconscious and need medications.

When the body is exposed repeatedly to the same antigen, the immune system may overreact. The antigens react with the immunoglobin IgE attached to mast cells and basophils. The mast cells and basophils release the chemical mediators histamine, SRS-A (slow-reacting substance), and bradykinin, which all affect the pulmonary and vascular systems. Large amounts of histamine can cause bronchospasm, vasodilation, and increased capillary permeability. SRS-A, a lipid substance, is similar to histamine in that it also stimulates intense bronchoconstriction. It differs from histamine, however, in that it is not inhibited by antihistamines. The peptide substance bradykinin produces vasodilation and increased capillary permeability. When histamine and bradykinin work together, a profound vascular collapse occurs, resulting from fluid leaving the intravascular space and leaking into the interstitial spaces. As a result of these physiological changes, allergic reactions take place at the local or systemic levels (Harmon, 1980).

Local reactions are similar to insect bite reactions in which only a limited area is involved. The area will be swollen, red, and itching. Ice should be applied to the area and the site should be elevated, if possible. If the reaction is not controlled, an antihistamine such as diphenhydramine (Benadryl; 25 to 50 mg) is administered either PO or IV. If the local reaction is severe, epinephrine (0.2 to 0.5 ml subcutaneously) may be given with diphenhydramine.

When anaphylaxis occurs the symptoms are systemic and magnified. The child's skin feels hot and itchy all over, with urticaria and diffuse erythema. These reactions are followed quickly by stridor, dysphagia, and dyspnea. The patient may complain of feeling as if the tongue is swelling and filling up the mouth. Bronchospasm, wheezing, and laryngeal spasm develop. Vascular collapse occurs resulting in severe hypotension, decreased consciousness, tachycardia, and diminished urine output. The vascular collapse can occur at any time in this process.

As soon as any of the generalized signs becomes evident, the IV infusion should be stopped and the doctor notified immediately. Maintaining the patient's airway is the top priority. The child's respiratory status, pulse, and blood pressure must be assessed. Oxygen, intubation equipment, and emergency drugs should be readily available (Table 4-7).

Anaphylactic shock is frightening to anyone, but particularly so to a child who may not understand what is happening anyway. Parents also tend to have a panic reaction as their child's breathing becomes more difficult before their very eyes. In order to help prevent such reactions, the nurse must have a complete history of the patient.

Another precaution for the nurse is the use of an anaphylactic tray. This tray consists of all the first-line materials to be used should a reaction occur; it should be taken to the patient's room whenever a drug known to have severe hyper-

TABLE 4-7. ANAPHYLACTIC DRUGS

Epinephrine (5 ml of 1 : 10,000 or 0.5 ml of 1 : 1,000 solution on hand)
  0.01 mg/kg (1 : 1,000 strength) up to 0.5 ml every 20 minutes
  Causes bronchodilation, reduces laryngeal edema, and raises blood pressure
Isotonic saline or plasma
  Increases intravascular volume
Dopamine, norepinephrine, and isuprel
  In a 5% D5W solution
  Pressor agents
Solu-Cortef, Solu-Medrol, or steroids
  Decreases capillary permeability and maintains intravascular volume
  Steroids stabilize mast cells and prevent further release of histamine, SRS-A, and bradykinin
Aminophylline
  250–500 mg in 100 ml 5% D5W by continuous drip over 20 minutes
  Prolongs bronchodilation

sensitivity reactions (such as L-asparaginase) is being given. The nurse also should notify a physician who is on the unit that the drug is being given, and ask the physician if it would be possible to remain on the unit for approximately 20 to 30 minutes in case such a reaction occurs.

CHILD AND FAMILY TEACHING

The child and the family must be aware of the effects and risks of the chemotherapy being administered. In many cases the age of the child dictates that the parents be the ones who receive the education about the drugs and their side-effects. But frequently the preschool-age child is ready to learn about the disease and its treatment. Informed consent has typically been obtained from the parent without the child being present or signing the document. Evidence is increasing which not only documents that teaching to obtain consent is often forgotten, but also that the child, when given information about his or her health care, becomes more compliant with the care (Igoe, 1980; Dodd, 1982). Many institutions now require an assent form from the child, truly involving the child in the care.

Prominent studies in the literature demonstrate that information given during the informed consent procedure, as mentioned above, is not retained very well. There appear to be several factors involved: patients and their families may simply not fully understand the risks involved in the chemotherapy; they may feel a need to "do something now" to help the child; the stress of hearing the diagnosis of cancer renders people unable to understand more than one half of what is presented to them; and a study reported by Perin (1981) demonstrated that the readability of five consents was equivalent to material written at upper division college or graduate level. Another important factor is that when multiple side-effects are present, instructions for managing them are so numerous that they become confusing to patients and their families (Harder, 1983). All these factors have led to the development of "primers," "chemotherapy fact sheets," and other devices to be utilized by nursing staff after the informed consent is obtained, to meet the needs of the patient and family through continual review of the drug information and management of side-effects. Studies undertaken by Harder (1983) and by Satterwhite, Pryor, and Harris (1980) demonstrate that most patients do read and follow the instructions printed in educational material. In fact these and several other studies have found improved adherence to regimens, higher levels of functioning, shorter hospital stays, and fewer readmissions as a result of patient education. This knowledge about what to expect also increases the patient's sense of independence.

The child and the parents must be educated about the chemotherapy at the time consent is obtained, prior to the chemotherapy, and during the infusion, and education should be reinforced between treatments. The actions of the drugs, why multiple drugs are necessary, and the side-effects of the drugs and their management must all be taught, and the child must be an active participant in this education. Methods of instruction will naturally vary with the age and developmental level of the child. Some of the most important factors of the teaching are evaluation, reinforcement, and correction of wrong information.

CONCLUSION

If these principles are followed, the chemotherapeutic course for each child will progress with less complications for everyone involved in the child's care. The patient, the family, and the nurse must work together to make the chemotherapy experience the least traumatic and damaging to the child as possible. The nurse is the key that unlocks the door to the knowledge and care that makes this possible.

KEY POINTS

- The pediatric oncology nurse must be aware of how the cell cycle functions and how the antineoplastic drugs affect the cycle.
- The pediatric oncology nurse must understand how protocols are developed, and how their use affects the patient.
- Pediatric oncology nurses must utilize principles of growth and development when considering nursing actions for their patients.
- The pediatric oncology nurse must be aware of how the side-effects of the chemotherapy regimen affect children and of the appropriate nursing actions to be undertaken by the nurse, the patient, and the family.
- The pediatric oncology nurse must continually educate the child and the family about the treatment, the side-effects, and other considerations of the chemotherapy regimen.

REFERENCES

Anderson, M., Aker, S., and Hickman, R. (1982). The double-lumen Hickman catheter. *American Journal of Nursing, 82*, 272–274.

Andrysiak, T., Carroll, R., and Ungerleider, J. (1979). Marijuana for the oncology patient. *American Journal of Nursing, 79*, 1396–1398.

Berry-Opersteny, D., and Heusinkveld, K. (1983). Prophylactic antiemetics for chemotherapy-associated nausea and vomiting. *Cancer Nursing, 6*, 117–123.

Bingham, C. (1978). The cell cycle and cancer chemotherapy. *American Journal of Nursing, 78*, 1201–1205.

Bruya, M., and Madeira, N. (1975). Stomatitis after chemotherapy. *American Journal of Nursing, 75*, 1349–1352.

Burish, T., and Lyles, J. (1981). Effectiveness of relaxation training in reducing adverse reactions to cancer chemotherapy. *Journal of Behavior Medicine, 4*, 65–68.

Chow, M., Durand, B., Feldman, M., and Mills, M. (1979). *Handbook of Pediatric Primary Care.* New York: John Wiley & Sons.

Daeffler, R. (1980). Oral hygiene measures for patients with cancer. I. *Cancer Nursing, 3*, 347–356.

Daeffler, R. (1980). Oral hygiene measures for patients with cancer. II. *Cancer Nursing, 3*, 427–432.

Daeffler, R. (1981). Oral hygiene measures for patients with cancer. III. *Cancer Nursing, 4*, 29–35.

Dean, J., Salmon, S., and Griffith, K. (1979). Prevention of doxorubicin-induced hair loss with scalp hypothermia. *New England Journal of Medicine, 301*, 1427–1429.

DeWalt, E., and Haines, A. (1969). The effects of specified stressors on healthy oral mucosa. 22–27.

Dodd, M. (1982). Cancer patient's knowledge of chemotherapy: Assessment and informational interventions. *Oncology Nursing Forum, 9*, 39–44.

Dodd, M., and Mood, D. (1981). Chemotherapy: Helping patients to know the drugs they are receiving and their possible side effects. *Cancer Nursing, 4*, 311–318.

Donovan, M., and Pierce, S. (1976). *Cancer Care Nursing.* New York: Appleton-Century-Crofts.

Grant, M. (1982). Environmental influences on the occurrence of chemotherapy-associated nausea and vomiting. *Oncology Nursing Forum, 9*, 50–51.

Griffiths, S. (1980). Changes in body image caused by antineoplastic drugs. *Issues in Comprehensive Pediatric Nursing, 4*, 17–27.

Harder, L. (1983). Primers assist patients in managing chemotherapy side effects. *Oncology Nursing Forum, 10*, 74–76.

Harder, L., and Hatfield, A. (1982). Patient participation in monitoring myelosuppression from chemotherapy. *Oncology Nursing Forum, 9*, 35–37.

Harmon, A., and Harmon, D. (1980). Anaphylaxis sudden death anytime. *Nursing 80, 10*, 40–43.

Hart, C., and Rasmussen, D. (1982). Patient care evaluation: A comparison of current practice and nursing literature for oral care of persons receiving chemotherapy. *Oncology Nursing Forum, 9*, 22–27.

Hunt, J., Anderson, J., and Smith, I. (1982). Scalp hypothermia to prevent adriamycin-induced hair loss. *Cancer Nursing, 5*, 25–31.

Johnston, S., and Patt, Y. (1981). Caring for the patient on intra-arterial chemotherapy: Are you ready? *Nursing 81, 11*, 108–112.

Kennedy, M., Packard, R., Grant, M., Padilla, G., Presant, C., and Chillar, R. (1983). The effects of using chemocap on occurrence of chemotherapy-induced alopecia. *Oncology Nursing Forum, 10*, 19–24.

Knobf, M., (1982). Intravenous therapy guidelines for oncology practice. *Oncology Nursing Forum, 9,* 30–34.

Levitt, D. (1980). Cancer chemotherapy. *RN, 43,* 53–56.

Levitt, D. (1980). Cancer chemotherapy, Part 2. *RN, 43,* 57–60.

Levitt, D. (1980). Cancer chemotherapy, Part 3. *RN, 43,* 51–54.

Levitt, D. (1980). Cancer chemotherapy, Part 4. *RN, 43,* 33–37, 112.

Levitt, D. (1981). Cancer chemotherapy, Part 5. *RN, 44,* 56–59.

Levitt, D. (1981). Cancer chemotherapy, Part 6. *RN, 44,* 69–72.

Lovejoy, N. (1979). Preventing hair loss during Adriamycin therapy. *Cancer Nursing, 2,* 117–121.

Maxwell, M. (1980). Scalp tourniquets for chemotherapy-induced alopecia. *American Journal of Nursing, 80,* 900–903.

Maxwell, M. (1982). Research with antiemetics for cancer chemotherapy: problems and possibilities. *Oncology Nursing Forum, 9,* 11–16.

Morran, C. (1979). Incidence of nausea and vomiting with cytotoxic chemotherapy: A prospective randomized trial of antiemetics. *British Medical Journal, 1,* 1323–1324.

Morrow, G., and Morrell, C. (1982). Behavioral treatment for the anticipatory nausea and vomiting induced by the cancer chemotherapy. *The New England Journal of Medicine, 307,* 1476–1480.

Muss, H., White, D., Michielutte, R., Richards, F., Cooper, M., Williams, S., Stuart, J., and Spurr, C. (1979). Written informed consent in patients with breast cancer. *Cancer, 43,* 1549–1556.

Ostchega, Y. (1980). Preventing and treating cancer chemotherapy's oral complications. *Nursing 80, 10,* 47–52.

Passos, J., and Brand, L. (1966). Effects of agents used for oral hygiene. *Nursing Research, 15,* 196–202.

Perin, G. (1981). Promoting informed consent. *Topics in Clinical Nursing, 2,* 61–65.

Physicians' Desk Reference. (1985). Oradell: Medical Economics Company.

Potter, S. (1981). Critical infections in the pediatric oncologic patient. *Nursing Clinics of North America, 16,* 699–706.

Pryor, A. (1978). Cancer chemotherapy in children. *Issues in Comprehensive Pediatric Nursing, 3,* 46–59.

Rovinski, C. (1983). Therapeutic use of noninvestigational marijuana in cancer care. *Cancer Nursing, 6,* 141–144.

Satterwhite, B. (1980). What to do when Adriamycin infiltrates. *Nursing 80, 10,* 37.

Satterwhite, B., Pryor, A., Harris, M. (1980). Development and evaluation of chemotherapy fact sheets. *Cancer Nursing, 3,* 277–283.

Schulmeister, L. (1982). Vascular access grafts in cancer chemotherapy. *American Journal of Nursing, 82,* 1388–1389.

Scogna, D., and Smalley, R. (1979). Chemotherapy-induced nausea and vomiting. *American Journal of Nursing, 79,* 1562–1564.

Seipp, C., Chanh, A., Shiling, D., and Rosenberg, S. (1980). In search of an effective antiemetic: a nursing staff participates in marijuana research. *Cancer Nursing, 3,* 271–276.

Swartz, A. (1979). Chemotherapy extravasation management. *Cancer Nursing, 2,* 405–407.

Toal, D. (1980). Tumor cell kinetics and cancer chemotherapy. *American Journal of Nursing, 80,* 1802–1804.

Vogel, T., and McSkimming, S. (1983). Teaching parents to give indwelling C. V. catheter care. *Nursing 83, 13,* 55–56.

Welch, D., and Lewis, K. (1980). Alopecia and chemotherapy. *American Journal of Nursing, 80,* 903–905.

Zeltzer, L., Lebaron, S., and Zeltzer, P. (1984). A prospective assessment of chemotherapy related nausea and vomiting in children with cancer. *American Journal of Pediatric Hematology/Oncology, 6, Spring,* 5–16.

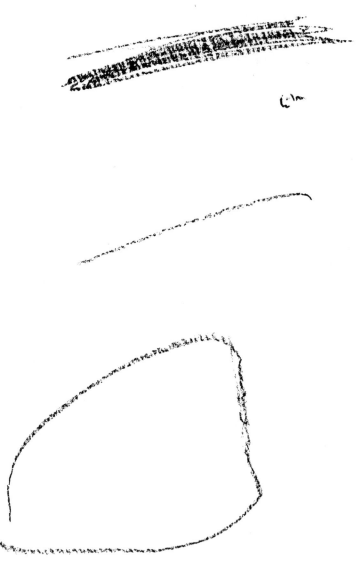

5

RADIATION

ANITA REDNER, RN, MS
Radiation Therapy Staff Nurse
New England Medical Center

INTRODUCTION

Children who receive radiation and their families undergo a unique experience that has many implications for nurses who care for them. The purpose of this chapter is threefold: (1) To review the basic concepts of radiation therapy in the treatment of pediatric cancer; (2) to familiarize nurses with the overall radiation treatment experience for the child and family; and (3) to review the occurrence and management of acute and long-term side-effects of radiation on the growing and developing child.

RADIATION AS A TREATMENT MODALITY

Radiation has been used to treat cancer since the turn of this century. Along with surgery and chemotherapy, radiation therapy is a major modality for cancer treatment. Radiation therapy, also referred to as radiotherapy, therapeutic radiology, and XRT, may be used to cure, to control the progression of, or to palliate cancer.

Radiation therapy, similar to surgery, is used primarily for local and regional control of cancer. Surgery and radiation therapy are used in complementary ways to achieve the best possible local control of the cancer, as well as the best cosmetic and functional results. When these two modalities are used in combination, radiation is more effective in destroying micro-scopic tumors, whereas surgery treats bulky tumor masses more effectively (Levene and Harris, 1982). Radiation therapy may also be combined with chemotherapy, which is used for systemic control of cancer. Radiation therapy most often is used in combination with surgery and chemotherapy in aggressive multimodality regimes for treating pediatric cancers. Increased cure and survival rates for many pediatric cancers have resulted from these combined treatment approaches.

Despite the common usage of radiation to treat pediatric cancer, nurses are often unfamiliar with basic concepts that underlie its use. Radiation also is misunderstood and feared by many people, including both lay persons and some health professionals. An understanding of what radiation is, what effects it has on normal cells and cancer cells, and how it is delivered enables nurses to dispel misconceptions and base their nursing interventions on fact.

NATURE AND SOURCES OF RADIATION

In a simplified model of the atom, electrons (negatively charged) orbit around a central nucleus that contains protons (positively charged) and neutrons (no charge). Atoms of the same element the nuclei of which have the same number of protons but a different number of

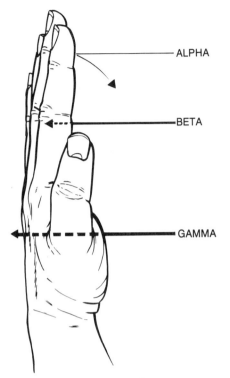

ALPHA

BETA

GAMMA

FIG. 5-1. Types of radiation.

neutrons are called *isotopes.* Some isotopes that occur naturally are *stable isotopes,* while others that occur naturally or are produced artificially are *unstable isotopes,* or *radioisotopes.* As the nuclei of these unstable isotopes decay, radiation of varying energies may be emitted.

The three types of radiation emitted from radioisotopes are alpha, beta, and gamma radiation. *Alpha radiation* is not used therapeutically due to its poor penetrating abilities. *Beta radiation* has greater penetrating abilities and is often emitted from therapeutic internal radiation sources. *X-rays* and *gamma rays* are bundles of electromagnetic energy, or photons, that have even greater penetrating abilities and range than beta radiation (Fig. 5-1). External radiation therapy treatments commonly make use of X-rays and gamma rays.

EFFECT OF RADIATION ON NORMAL AND CANCER CELLS

When living cells are exposed to radiation, a sequence of events takes place which ultimately results in biological effects. Radiation can produce *ions* by freeing electrons from the atoms it passes through in a process called ionization. When radiation interacts with molecules of living cells, physical changes take place due to the process of ionization. Further chemical reactions that occur both within the cell and in the extracellular environment ultimately result in cell damage or cell death. These effects are due primarily to disruptions in DNA, such as single- or double-strand breaks. Cells exposed to radiation during the time of cellular division are more vulnerable to damage. Although both normal and cancer cells are affected in this way by radiation, they have different mechanisms for such functions as repair and renewal of cell populations.

Tissues considered to be most sensitive to the effects of radiation exposure include such rapidly proliferative tissues as the bone marrow, skin, gastrointestinal epithelium, and the gonads. Tumors also exhibit varying degrees of radiosensitivity, as indicated in Table 5-1. Many other factors also are involved in whether a particular tumor will ultimately be radiocurable.

Normal tissue responses to radiation include acute, intermediate, and late effects. *Acute effects* result from cellular damage to rapidly proliferating tissues such as the bone marrow, skin, and epithelial lining of the gastrointestinal and genitourinary tracts. These effects occur during or immediately following a course of radiation therapy. *Subacute or intermediate effects* result from radiation damage to more slowly proliferating tissues. They occur after completion of the treatment course. *Late effects* may also occur months to years after exposure to radiation. The mechanism of these effects is unknown,

Patient size and mobility are also important factors to be considered.

but it is believed to be due to effects on small blood vessels (Bloomer and Hellman, 1975).

PRINCIPLES OF PLANNING AND DELIVERY OF RADIATION THERAPY

The goal of radiation therapy is to achieve maximum tumor control with a minimum amount of damage to surrounding normal tissue. Choices of the appropriate volume of tissues to be irradiated, radiation dose, and number and frequency of treatments, are based on this treatment goal (Fig. 5-2).

Treatment fields or *ports* are planned to encompass the tumor areas and any adjacent tissue or regional lymph nodes that are either known to be involved with tumor or are at high risk for tumor involvement. Several technical considerations can minimize normal tissue damage. For example, treatment is delivered from several different angles, or *multiple fields.* The treatment course may also include plans to narrow fields *(boost or cone-down)* and deliver higher doses to the actual tumor or postoperative tumor site. Treatment plans sometimes call for the use of lead blocks, which, when placed between the machine and patient prior to each treatment, shield certain vital organs in the treatment fields, such as the lungs, kidneys, and liver.

The unit *rad* (radiation *a*bsorbed *d*ose) is used to describe the amount of radiation delivered to the tumor. The choice of total dose of radiation is based on the dose necessary to achieve tumor

TABLE 5-1. EXAMPLES OF SENSITIVITY OF COMMON PEDIATRIC TUMORS TO RADIOTHERAPY

HIGH SENSITIVITY
Germ cell
Hodgkin's disease
Non-Hodgkin's lymphoma
Leukemic infiltrates
Wilms' tumor
Retinoblastoma
Neuroblastoma
Rhabdomyosarcoma

MILD TO LOW SENSITIVITY
Osteosarcoma
Other bone and soft tissue sarcomas
Malignant melanomas
Malignant gliomas

Adapted from Fochtman, D. and Foley, G. (1982). **Nursing Care of Children with Cancer** (p. 184). Boston: Little, Brown, & Co.

control in relationship to that which can be tolerated by surrounding normal tissues. The total dose of radiation is divided or *fractionated* into smaller doses given on a regular basis to allow for normal tissue recovery. A typical treatment course involves 4 to 5 weekday treatments over the course of 2 to 6 weeks. The total dose of radiation may vary from 1000 to 3000 rad for palliation, to as high as 6000 to 7000 rad for palliation or potential cure.

The treatment machine to be used is chosen on the basis of how appropriate the radiation beam is in relation to characteristics such as the size and mobility of the patient and the location and size of the tumor.

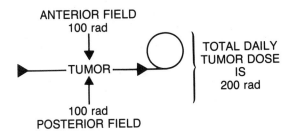

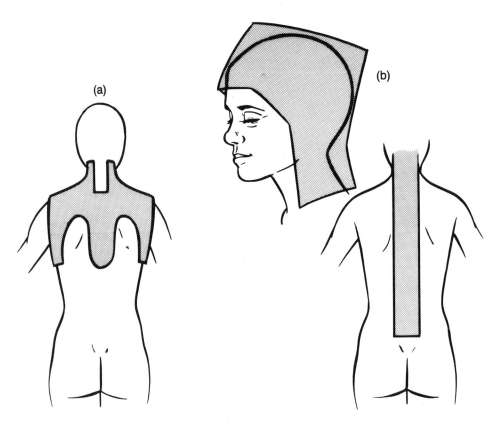

FIG 5-2. Radiation field selection. Radiation therapy is usually administered from several different angles, or multiple fields. This technique allows a high dose of radiation to be delivered to the tumor, while it minimizes the amount of damage to normal tissues the radiation passes through. In the example shown, half of the daily tumor dose is delivered from an anterior field (100 rad); the other half is delivered from a posterior field (100 rad). The total daily dose to the tumor is 200 rad. Treatment fields, or ports, are planned to encompass the tumor areas and any adjacent tissue or regional lymph nodes either known to be involved with tumor or at high risk for tumor involvement. Some examples of commonly used fields include: (a) a "mantle" field for treatment of Hodgkin's disease, and (b) a field encompassing the whole brain and craniospinal axis, used to treat children with ALL.

The first generation of radiation treatment machines, the *kilovoltage machines,* delivered relatively low energy X-rays with the maximum dose delivered to the skin surface. Often this was insufficient to provide adequate deep tumor dosage and caused severe skin reactions. These machines are still being used, but only to treat superficial lesions.

Megavoltage machines produce more penetrating, higher energy radiation with maximum effects below the skin surface and less skin damage. *Cobalt-60 machines* (1.25 million electron volts) are widely used megavoltage machines. The radioactive source of a Cobalt-60 machine is exposed at the time of treatment to permit the emission of gamma rays. It is otherwise shielded by heavy metal. *Linear accelerators* and the less commonly used *Betatrons* (4 – 45 million electron volts) produce higher energy X-rays from a process of accelerating electrons rather than by exposing a radioactive source. Many of these high energy X-rays can penetrate deeper than the gamma rays produced by the Cobalt-60 machines.

THE RADIATION THERAPY COURSE AND THE RADIATION THERAPY TEAM

A typical sequence of events in a radiation therapy department includes an initial consultation

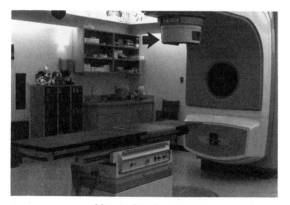

Linear Accelerator

TABLE 5-2. THE RADIATION THERAPY TEAM

Radiation oncologist (radiation therapist)—an M.D. trained and board-certified in the medical specialty of radiation oncology

Radiation oncology nurse—a professional nurse specializing in the nursing care of persons receiving radiation therapy; education and training may include concentration in oncology nursing

Radiation therapy technologist (RTT)—an individual trained and certified in the administration of radiation therapy

Radiation dosimetrist and radiation physicist—individuals responsible for assisting with treatment planning design and calculation of radiation dosage; physicists are also responsible for calibration and maintenance of radiation machines and radiation safety; education ranges from dosimetry education/certification to Ph.D. in physics and certification

The team includes receptionists, administrative and office staff. It may also include social workers, nutritionists, and other health-care professionals.

with the radiation oncologist, a separate visit for treatment planning, a series of daily treatments, and routine followup appointments. In the course of these visits the child and family meet and interact with a wide variety of department personnel (Table 5-2).

INITIAL CONSULTATION

Initial contact with the child and family is usually made by the radiation oncologist, or radiation therapist, a physician trained and board-certified in this specialty. After reviewing the child's medical history, X-rays, other diagnostic tests, and pathology slides provided by the referring physician, the radiation oncologist performs appropriate physical exams. After discussion with other physicians, he or she is then able to discuss a proposed plan of treatment, including anticipated acute and long-term side effects, with the family. If the radiation oncologist initially sees the hospitalized child as an inpatient, the radiation oncology nurse may also visit and invite the child and the parents to tour the department. Otherwise the nurse meets and interacts with the child and family in the department.

TREATMENT PLANNING

Treatment planning also referred to as *simulation* or *localization,* generally takes place on a subsequent visit. With a special diagnostic X-ray machine called a *simulator,* the radiation oncologist uses fluoroscopy to help to delineate the specific areas to be treated or blocked from radiation treatment. The radiation therapy technologist assists the radiation oncologist to place small lead wires on the skin and, in some instances, to instill contrast media into areas (*e.g.,* the bladder) that must be visualized on X-ray. The technologist and radiation dosimetrist or physicist also make detailed measurements of the involved areas of the body. Information from the simulation is later processed, often by computer, by the radiation physicist to produce a treatment plan that includes all of the technical data needed for delivering daily treatments to the patient (Levene and Harris, 1982).

During the treatment planning session, the child lies on the X-ray table of the simulator, which resembles a conventional X-ray machine. In order to plan accurate treatment fields a variety of immobilization techniques may be used. Sedation or anesthesia may be required for a child who is too young or too irritable to lie still for the duration of a simulation session, which may last from one half hour to over an hour. (see "Special Considerations for Treatment Planning and Daily Treatments" below).

The radiation oncologist and other members of the planning team must periodically leave the simulation room and enter an adjoining room in order to perform fluoroscopy and to take some permanent simulation X-ray films. The team can monitor the child at all times through a window or on a television monitor and can hear and speak with the child through an intercom. Parents can remain with the child if they wear lead aprons for their protection.

Except for any possible discomfort secondary to the child's position or to instillation of contrast media, there is no discomfort associated with simulation. As with any diagnostic X-rays, these cannot be seen, heard, smelled, or felt. The X-ray table and machine are slowly moved into various positions in an effort to line up appropriate fields. The lights in the room may be switched off periodically to allow the team to accurately visualize a grid of light that shines on the child's skin in a "simulation" of the proposed treatment fields. At the end of the session the technologist uses these lighted areas as a guide to place either temporary or permanent markings on the skin to delineate the treatment fields.

Temporary skin dyes are used in some departments to outline the borders and centers of the treatment fields. These remain on the skin throughout the treatment course, and should not be washed off or touched up in any way. They can eventually be washed off with gentle, repeated use of soap and water or baby oil. Permanent skin markings also are placed in the corners and centers of the fields by gently

Mickey Mouse greets children as they come for radiation treatment.

pricking the skin with a needle and placing a small drop of indelible ink at that spot to make a small permanent freckle or "tattoo." These permanent markings are necessary for the child's physicians to be able to reproduce the exact placement of the treatment fields in case future treatments are needed or if complications occur in these areas. Some departments use permanent markings exclusively because they require no special care to maintain and are less noticeable during the course of treatment, but their permanence is troubling to some people. The types of markings are discussed with the child and the parents prior to the simulation.

Snapshots of the child's treatment positions are often taken during the treatment planning session as a guide for the technologists who will be giving daily treatments. They are placed in the radiation therapy record, along with the radiation oncologist's prescription for the fields to be treated and the treatment plan. The prescription and treatment plan indicate the treatment fields, the number of total treatments and how often they are to be given, and the daily and total dosage of radiation to be given to each field. A variety of technical details also are included for the technologists to follow to ensure that daily treatments are accurate.

Unless treatment is to be given on an emergency basis, the treatment course does not begin on the same day as treatment planning. Several days are often necessary to complete the treatment plan and to make other technical arrangements.

DAILY TREATMENTS

Daily treatments are quicker than the treatment planning session. They are given by radiation therapy technologists, who are trained and certified in this field. The technologists help the child to lie on an X-ray table in the exact positions that were used during the simulation. Once again the room lights may be turned on and off, and the table and machine may be moved, as the technologists reproduce the position(s) the child was in for the simulation. Each treatment field is exposed, then set up and treated. Because the technologists must leave the room to deliver each treatment, they observe the child at these times with a television monitor and an intercom. The treatment (which cannot be seen or felt) takes from 1 to 5 minutes per field, depending on the treatment machine. Most machines make some noise when the treatment is delivered. Children also might notice a harmless ozone odor during treatment. In some instances the machine moves while the treatment is in progress.

The radiation oncologist is often present on the first day of treatment, and when any significant changes are made, to observe that the setup is satisfactory. He or she is not necessarily present for most daily treatments, however, unless a problem arises. The technologist takes an extra few minutes to take an X-ray film of each field on the first day of treatment, when any change is made in the location of a field, and at least once a week thereafter so that the radiation oncologist can compare these to the original simulation films. This ensures accurate treatment and is simply one of the many quality control checks built into each radiation therapy department. Double-checks of the treatment plan, the technologists' recording of the daily treatments, and the physicists' calculations are also made on a regular basis.

Depending on the child's condition and family situation, a child may receive treatment on an inpatient or an ambulatory basis. The radiation therapy team makes every effort to assist a family to make an appropriate choice and provides support services in conjunction with other members of the child's health-care team.

ON-TREATMENT VISITS

During the course of daily treatments, the radiation oncologist and nurse see the child on a formal basis once a week. At this time they assess the child's weight, general condition, and the presence of acute side-effects, and comfort measures are prescribed if necessary. In addition to these formal sessions, the services of the radiation oncologist and nurse generally are available at any time, by telephone or in person, if problems or concerns arise. A formal session is held at the end of the entire treatment course for discussion and instructions for care until the first followup visit.

FOLLOWUP VISITS

Regular followup is essential for evaluation and management of the tumor, side-effects of treatment, and the child's general condition. Followup appointments often are made in conjunction with the other services the child receives (*e.g.,* surgery or medical oncology) for convenience and comprehensive care. After an appropriate disease-free interval, monthly or bimonthly followup appointments are usually changed to annual visits.

OCCURRENCE AND MANAGEMENT OF ACUTE SIDE-EFFECTS

GENERAL CONCEPTS

Acute side-effects result from radiation to rapidly proliferating normal tissues. The severity of acute effects is related to the daily dosage and the period of time over which the total dosage is delivered, which may be modified by the radiation oncologist and individual patient factors (Cassady, 1982).

Most acute side-effects are site-specific. The extent of the affected area(s) depends on the size, location, and arrangement of the treatment fields. Acute side-effects are also cumulative: Symptoms occur when sufficient normal cell destruction has taken place. Many acute side-effects are therefore not evident immediately, may worsen as treatment progresses, and

may continue for several weeks after treatment is completed. Unless otherwise noted, these concepts apply to all of the following discussions of acute side-effects.

Children are believed to possess a tolerance for the acute effects of radiation equal or superior to adults, with more rapid recovery of normal tissues (Simone, et al., 1982; Cassady, 1982). Some special considerations for treatment are necessary, however, due to the unique physiology of children and the use of aggressive multimodality treatment. Children have greater nutritional needs for growth and development, for example, and therefore may be less able to tolerate the nutritional impairments and possible weight loss that accompany some acute reactions to radiation therapy. Careful observation and nutritional interventions are required.

With regard to acute effects of multimodality treatment, surgical wounds located within radiation fields do not necessarily exhibit reduced ability to heal (Cassady, 1982). Interactions with chemotherapy may occur, however, including: (1) the recall phenomenon, a dramatic reappearance of a radiation reaction in a previously irradiated child, precipitated by administration of chemotherapeutic agents such as actinomycin D or Adriamycin; (2) radiation-induced alteration of chemotherapy drug metabolism resulting in enhanced toxicities; and (3) additive toxicities of combined modalities such as concurrent radiation and chemotherapy-induced mucositis (Simone, et al., 1982). Children who receive both modalities therefore require very careful monitoring.

Patient management begins with careful observation for expected side-effects and accurate assessment of their severity based on the child's treatment plan. Any nurse who cares for a child receiving radiation therapy should report the occurrence of side-effects to the radiation therapy team so that specific care instructions can be prescribed and possible treatment adjustments made.

TABLE 5-3. RADIATION SIDE-EFFECTS/INTERVENTIONS

Side-Effects	Suggested Interventions

Skin Reaction	Preventive Skin Care for radiation sites includes:
	Avoiding trauma
	  Mechanical: Wear loose, lightweight clothes of nonirritating fabrics
	    Avoid rubbing, scratching, or taping the skin
	    Wear protective clothing if exposed to strong wind
	    (For adolescents) avoid shaving axillary hair if axilla is in the field; electric razor
	      only for facial shaving if face is in the field
	  Chemical: Avoid all cosmetics, perfumes, powders, lotions or creams, deodorants,
	      and medications (unless prescribed) to the skin; swimming permitted if
	      washable skin marks are not used
	  Thermal: Avoid the use of cold (e.g., ice bags)
	    Wear warm clothing in cold temperatures
	    Avoid the use of heat (e.g., hot water bottles, heating pads)
	  Ultraviolet: Wear protective clothing, wide-brimmed hat when exposed to the sun
	    Avoid the use of sunlamps

Erythema	Light dusting of nonmedicated cornstarch to relieve itch
Dry desquamation (dryness, scaling, itching)	**Light** application of prescribed, hydrophilic skin lubricant several times a day (e.g., Aquaphor, A and D Ointment); do not apply directly before daily treatment; no cream containing alcohol or heavy metals should be prescribed
Moist desquamation (erythema, localized pain, sloughing, weeping of serious exudate)	Stop treatment temporarily Keep open to air if possible Gently irrigate with normal saline or normal saline/hydrogen peroxide in low concentration If necessary, dress according to need: debridement—adherent (e.g., wet to dry) dressing; protection/drainage—nonadherent layered dressing. Secure dressings without taping the skin
Fatigue	Use measures to conserve energy: help child to pace/modify usual daily activities; encourage rest periods, especially directly after daily treatments Improve nutrition and hydration
Increased intracranial pressure	Monitor neurological signs Administer steroids (if prescribed)
Bone marrow depression	Monitor blood counts, signs of infection, and bleeding Preventive measures as indicated for infection and bleeding (see Chap. 4 on chemotherapy) Supportive measures as indicated Possible breaks in treatment
Alopecia	Use gentle care of hair and scalp; mild shampoo if allowed Loose, nonirritating head coverings: scarves, hats Wear wig when scalp has recovered from acute skin reaction For patchy hair loss, use surrounding hair or scarf to cover bald spots
Eye irritation	Gently cleanse eyes with warm normal saline if drainage present Artificial Tears if prescribed Eyepatch may be helpful; secure **without** tape in treatment field
Nasal mucosal irritation	Gently cleanse around nostrils if drainage present Use normal saline nasal spray or drops if prescribed Use humidifier/room vaporizer

(Table continues on next page)

TABLE 5-3. RADIATION SIDE-EFFECTS/INTERVENTIONS *(continued)*

Side-Effects	Suggested Interventions
Ear pain/blockage	Administer anesthetic ear drops
Decreased saliva/thick saliva; taste alterations; dental disease; mucositis	Refer to dentist familiar with radiation therapy prior to starting treatment; include full set of X-rays, cleaning, treatment of any existing dental disease; any necessary extractions should be followed by several weeks to allow for healing prior to starting treatment Use regular gentle tooth cleaning Use physiologic mouth rinses (e.g., normal saline, possibly with baking soda) Use fluoride trays (prescribed) Use artificial saliva or mineral rinses (prescribed) Avoid trauma to oral tissues: thermal—avoid hot foods, smoking; mechanical—avoid foods that are hard or coarse, avoid overvigorous mouth care; chemical—avoid acidic juices, spices, alcohol, alcohol-containing mouthwashes
Pharyngitis	Serve soft, bland, nonspicy foods; foods that coat the mucosa Use topical analgesics (e.g., viscous lidocaine, Aspergum if permitted) Use P.O. analgesics
Hoarseness	Encourage child to whisper instead of talk when possible to conserve voice
Indigestion: nausea; vomiting	Use psychological interventions (e.g., distraction) Nutrition: Serve simple, bland foods and cold vs. hot foods; electrolyte-containing liquids if vomiting; avoid eating or drinking 1–2 hours before and after treatment Environment: Maintain an environment free of noxious stimuli; have child sit in front seat of car if driving for treatments; schedule treatments outside of rush hours, if possible; rest in a comfortable position; fresh air Use antiemetics before treatment and at regular intervals after treatment Use antacids for indigestion
Diarrhea	Nutrition: Serve low-residue, bland, nongreasy foods and electrolyte-containing fluids Avoid stimulants (tea, coffee, chocolate), foods that are too hot or cold, milk or milk products (except yogurt); if child is lactose-intolerant: Lact-aid may be added to milk Rectal care: Use gentle rectal care, sitz baths, creams if prescribed; change diaper frequently Antidiarrheals: As prescribed; use regularly if diarrhea is chronic Environment: Become aware of available restrooms along the route to/from treatments for "emergency" stops
Cystitis	Increase PO fluids Obtain urinalysis, culture, and sensitivity to rule out infection Use urinary analgesics (prescribed) Acidify urine (prescribed)

The following section of this chapter is a review of acute side-effects of radiation therapy, (suggested interventions for which are for easy reference in Table 5-3). Although management of side-effects is always based on the same principles, each radiation oncologist or team has preferred interventions. Management also must be individualized for each child's situation. The information in this section is intended therefore as a general guide.

SKIN REACTIONS

The highly proliferative epithelial cells respond rapidly to radiation. Although skin reactions are normal and temporary reactions to be expected from treatment, they can be uncomfortable. Certain factors affect their degree and severity. For example, when radiation is delivered to areas where skin surfaces are in contact with each other, such as the axilla, the risk of skin reaction is increased. Other factors that place the child at higher risk for skin reactions are fair complexions, preexisting skin inflammations, and prior or concomitant chemotherapy.

FATIGUE

Fatigue is another common side-effect and is often misinterpreted by family members as a sign of disease progression. The causes of fatigue are not well understood. Proposed causes include the release of waste products from destruction of cells into the bloodstream and higher energy demands imposed on the patient by increased cellular repair processes (Yasko, 1982). Others suggest that multiple factors related to aggressive multimodality treatment, compounded by the rigors of daily travel, increase the fatigue level. Whatever the cause, progressive fatigue may limit the child's involvement in usual daily activities.

BONE MARROW DEPRESSION

Because bone marrow cells respond rapidly to radiation, bone marrow depression may occur. Distribution of active bone marrow in children is more widespread than in adults, whose active bone marrow is limited to centrally located bones such as the sternum and pelvic bones. Radiation treatment plans that include large areas of active bone marrow in children there-fore necessitate careful observation of peripheral blood counts (Moss, 1979). Children receiving bone marrow-depressing chemotherapy are also at greater risk for this complication.

INCREASED INTRACRANIAL PRESSURE

Inflammation of brain cells and resulting edema caused by cranial radiation may be manifested by neurological symptoms sometimes misinterpreted as a worsening of the underlying disease. Signs and symptoms of increased intracranial pressure such as headache, nausea with or without vomiting, changes in mental status, and other neurological signs and symptoms may occur (Yasko, 1982).

ALOPECIA

Damage to hair follicles can result in hair loss in treatment fields on any part of the body. Cranial radiation often results in temporary scalp hair loss. Mantle fields used in the treatment of Hodgkin's disease and some head and neck fields may also cause temporary loss of scalp hair. The situation is often complicated by chemotherapy-induced alopecia, discussed in Chapter 4.

RADIATION TO THE HEAD AND NECK

Radiation to the head and neck can result in a variety of acute side-effects that may affect not only the child's appearance, but important physical and social functions such as eating and talking as well. Discomfort, physical complications, impaired nutrition and its sequelae, and social isolation may result. Irritation of the eyelids and conjunctivae may cause excessive tearing with later occurrence of dryness and thick drainage with crusting. Similarly the nasal mucosa respond with increased, followed by decreased, thickened secretions. Edema of the eustachian tube or middle or inner ear secondary to radiation can cause pain or a blocked sensation (Yasko, 1982).

Temporary or permanent damage to the salivary glands may result in a decreased quantity of, altered, or more viscous saliva, which makes eating, tasting, swallowing, and talking difficult. Since saliva also serves to protect the teeth from decay, decreased function can result in dental caries in the absence of meticulous dental care. More serious dental complications may occur in children who undergo radiation if they do not receive adequate treatment of preexisting dental disease. Children who are to receive radiation that may affect the mouth should therefore see a dentist prior to receiving any radiation treatments. Dentists who care for children receiving radiation therapy should be familiar with the ramifications of radiation in general and with the child's individual treatment plan.

Taste alterations may result from radiation damage to the taste buds and may be compounded by changes in taste perception secondary to the cancer itself, to chemotherapy, or to salivary changes. These alterations include unpleasant tastes of certain foods, a metallic taste unrelated to food, or a decrease in the ability to taste, especially sweets. Taste alterations may be temporary or permanent. (Yasko, 1982).

The epithelial cells of mucous membranes throughout the body are highly radioresponsive. Children are thought to have a greater, more rapid ability to restore mucous membrane integrity (Cassady, 1982), but the additive effects of chemotherapy are a common problem. In the mouth radiation-induced mucositis at first manifests as dry, inflamed tissues, progressing to development of a whitish-yellow membrane fixed to the tissues and eventual ulceration. As with stomatitis related to chemotherapy, infection and hemorrhage are possible complications (Yasko, 1982).

PHARYNGITIS, HOARSENESS, ESOPHAGITIS

Pharyngitis may occur with radiation fields that involve head and neck lesions, cervical spine lesions, the craniospinal axis, and mantle fields. Temporary hoarseness and esophagitis also may occur. Increased mucous secretions cause some children to have problems with gagging and may lead to vomiting.

INDIGESTION, NAUSEA, AND VOMITING

Inflammation from destruction of epithelial cells that line the esophagus, stomach, or intestines may cause indigestion, nausea, and vomiting. Subsequent stimulation of vomiting centers in the brain may occur from cellular waste products that are released (Yasko, 1982). Environmental factors such as the daily drive for treatments may contribute to these problems. As with chemotherapy, radiation-induced nausea and vomiting may also have a strong psychogenic component.

Nausea and vomiting may occur from 1 to 6 hours after treatment and are continuous in nature (Yasko, 1982). They are often less severe than symptoms induced by chemotherapy, however, and usually respond to conservative measures. Also children seem to tolerate radiation to the gastrointestinal tract better than adults (Simone, et al, 1982; Cassady, 1982). Unlike most side-effects of radiation, nausea and vomiting often occur after the first treatment, if they are to happen, and may lessen during the course of treatments. The problems generally disappear shortly after completion of the treatment course.

DIARRHEA

Destruction of highly proliferative epithelial cells that line the small and large intestines results in ulceration of intestinal mucosa with impaired digestion and absorption. Fluid and electrolyte disturbances also may occur, along with lactose intolerance and perirectal skin irritation.

Diarrhea usually does not occur until 2 or more weeks after the start of radiation. It is therefore usually not necessary to prescribe dietary alterations as a preventive measure for diarrhea at the start of the treatment course. Dietary alterations should be made with regard to the child's current bowel habits. Some children have problems with constipation following surgery, for example, and constipation is a frequent problem with toilet training. Starting a preventive low-roughage diet 1 to 2 weeks in advance of possible radiation-induced diarrhea may lead to more severe constipation problems.

CYSTITIS

Cystitis may result from inflammation of the epithelial lining of the bladder. Since the symptoms are virtually identical to those of a urinary tract infection, culture and urinalysis should be made to rule out this possibility.

OCCURRENCE AND MANAGEMENT OF SUBACUTE SIDE-EFFECTS

Subacute effects of radiation result from damage to more slowly dividing normal tissues. They are related to the radiation dose, the volume of irradiated tissue, and the organs receiving radiation (Cassady, 1982). Interactions with chemotherapeutic agents may increase the severity of subacute effects.

Some examples of subacute effects include radiation pneumonitis, pericarditis, nephritis, and hepatitis, all of which are thought to be related to a subacute or chronic endothelial vasculitis. These affects commonly occur from 4 to 12 weeks after radiation, but may occur 6 months later (i.e., pericarditis). Severity of these effects also may be augmented by admin-

istration of various chemotherapeutic agents. Medical management often includes the use of steroids (Cassady, 1982).

Another pediatric subacute reaction noted with moderate frequency is the additive effect of prior radiation on cyclophosphamide (Cytoxan)-induced hemorrhagic cystitis, which sometimes necessitates changing to another chemotherapeutic agent (Cassady, 1982). Subacute myositis is sometimes noted about 6 to 8 weeks following radiation to an extremity and may cause some local symptoms, which generally resolve in several weeks (Cassady, 1982).

The child and family may be upset by the late emergence of subacute effects and may misinterpret them to mean progression of disease. Families therefore, should be informed that these symptoms may occur. They also should be instructed as to how to identify and report relevant symptoms to their health-care providers. Close followup and collaboration and communication between services, particularly radiation oncology and medical oncology, are necessary. Nurses who work with children who have received radiation within the preceding 6 months should always consider the possibility of subacute radiation effects in the presence of unexplained symptoms.

OCCURRENCE AND MANAGEMENT OF LONG-TERM SIDE-EFFECTS

As described earlier, the goal of radiation therapy is to deliver a dose of radiation capable of destroying the cancer with the least possible impairment of surrounding normal tissues. In children this problem is compounded by the potential future growth and development of normal tissues. Many children have the potential for a more normal lifespan, the very length of which increases the possibility of developing long-term complications. Thus, the concept of benefit versus risk is a major consideration in planning radiation therapy for children.

The extent and degree of long-term side effects are related primarily to the total radiation dose and the size of the daily radiation fraction (Cassady, 1982), but also may depend on a number of factors related to the way the radiation is delivered, the age of the child at the time of radiation treatment, and the use of other treatment modalities. Radiation oncologists attempt to minimize the chances of long-term side effects without sacrificing tumor control by employing modern and exact planning and delivery techniques. Careful followup of children who have received radiation therapy is necessary, and preventive and remedial measures for functional or cosmetic impairments are sometimes possible.

Perhaps the two most commonly expressed concerns of parents whose children are to receive radiation therapy are about damage to the reproductive organs or the brain. Gonadal dysfunction can result from radiation to the ovaries and testes. (Cassady, 1982; Fochtman, 1982). Radiation oncologists are aware of the radiation dose and fractionation capable of causing sterility and possible failure to develop secondary sexual characteristics (Cassady, 1982). Variables such as the radiation technique, the age of the child, and the use of other modalities, especially chemotherapy, however, often make it difficult to generalize about exact causes and effects of gonadal dysfunction. In conjunction with other services treating the child, the radiation therapy team must apprise the family of possible gonadal effects on the individual child and help to guide them toward future considerations and counseling.

Breast development may be disrupted by radiation to the chest in preadolescent girls, resulting in agenesis or poor development of the breast (Cassady, 1982; Fochtman, 1982). Mammoplasty is a possible corrective procedure for these young women.

Radiation to the CNS may result in a variety of problems, including a wide spectrum of possible intellectual impairments, leukoencephalopathy, and radiation myelitis (Cassady, 1982; Fochtman, 1982; Simone, 1982). The brain is considered more sensitive to the effects of radiation during the first 3 to 4 years of life, when myelinization is incomplete. Most central nervous system (CNS) impairments are related to concurrent administration of certain chemotherapeutic agents, especially intrathecal and systemic high-dose methotrexate and/or actinomycin D (Cassady, 1982). Continued neurologic followup of a child who has received CNS irradiation, especially in conjunction with chemotherapy, is indicated. Performance evaluations are also important, as remedial programs may be instituted for the child with learning disabilities.

Radiation also can cause retardation of bone growth, resulting in decreased stature or limbs of varying lengths. Various asymmetries thus may result, prompting radiation oncologists to attempt to create symmetry in planning treatment fields in a child (Cassady, 1982; Fochtman, 1982; Simone, 1982). Improper treatment for Wilms' tumor, for example, may result in a structural scoliosis because of uneven radiation across the vertebral bodies. Decreased soft tissue or muscle bulk as a result of radiation may compound the problem by creating a secondary or acquired scoliosis (Simone, et al., 1982). Orthopedic followup is often necessary.

Many other site-specific long-term effects are possible (Cassady, 1982; Fochtman, 1982; Morrow and Wilson, 1981; Simone, 1982). Radiation to the head and neck may result in failure of teeth to erupt or other dental complications, or may cause decreased salivary function. Radiation to the lens of the eye may result in cataract formation that may or may not be visually significant. Possible impairments of endocrine function include hypothyroidism and a decrease in pituitary hormones, including growth hormones. Also possible are respiratory, genitourinary, and cardiovascular effects. Long-term radiation-induced gastrointestinal problems that include esophageal stricture, bowel obstruction, fistula formation, chronic enteritis, and malabsorption also may be related to the use of chemotherapeutic agents such as actinomycin D and doxorubicin (Adriamycin) (Cassady, 1982).

Children appear to be more susceptible than adults to development of a radiation-induced second malignancy later in life (Cassady, 1982; Fochtman, 1982; Morrow and Wilson, 1981). Certain organs (*e.g.,* the thyroid) appear to be at greater risk, and a genetic predisposition seems likely, as children with certain disorders (*e.g.,* retinoblastoma) seem particularly prone to second tumor development. As with other long-term side-effects, other variables such as the child's age, use of chemotherapy, duration of followup, and radiation treatment technique are thought to be related to development of second malignancies. It is hoped that improved radiation therapy techniques with higher energy machines will decrease the risk of this development (Simone, et al., 1982).

A further discussion of long-term effects of cancer treatment can be found in Chapter 10.

PATIENT MANAGEMENT

EDUCATION, MONITORING, AND SUPPORT

The complexity of the radiotherapy experience, particularly when viewed within the context of aggressive multimodality treatment, heightens the need for comprehensive family education. Although the radiation oncologist provides information about the treatment plan and side-effects, the radiation oncology nurse usually takes primary responsibility for assessing and meeting the family's learning needs.

ORIENTATION

The family may be invited to visit the radiation therapy department prior to the treatment

Pediatric Waiting Room

planning session. Some parents benefit from a separate tour and a more detailed orientation session prior to their child's visit. This is helpful in preparing them to participate actively in later orienting their child. Parents can be provided with written and verbal information about radiation therapy in general, as well as their child's individual treatment plan, anticipated side-effects, and ways to monitor and manage these side-effects. The nurse also can review the radiation experience and clinical procedures. A tour can be arranged to introduce the parents to their child's care providers and to acquaint them with the physical layout of the department and the stimulation and treatment rooms and machines. At this time the nurse can help the parents and technologists to discuss what role the parents will play during the simulation and treatment sessions. Although some departments prefer not to have parents present during these procedures, most departments will make individual decisions about the extent of parental presence and involvement. Well-prepared parents can be of enormous assistance, in many instances, to both the radiation team and the child by being present in the planning and treatment areas.

The nurse and parents can describe the radiation therapy department and procedures to the child in a separate orientation tour geared to the child's individual needs and learning abilities. Many departments use models or dolls to help explain what the child might experience. An introduction to the technologists, a chance to look at planning and treatment areas, and opportunities to try out the X-ray table and immobilization devices, as well as the television and intercom monitors, can be included in a child's tour. Some departments also respond to requests for siblings, grandparents, or other significant family members or friends to make short tours of the department at some point in the child's treatment course.

Identification and correction of common misconceptions about radiation treatment are important considerations for child and family education, particularly in light of the negative social views about radiation that are prevalent. Fears that the child or his clothing will become "contaminated" with radioactivity are common, as are such comic book and cartoon concepts as being "zapped with rays." A familiar example of this is the Incredible Hulk, the fictional character who was transformed into his menacing shape by exposure to radiation. Adults and children respond favorably to explanations comparing the more familiar diagnostic X-rays with those used for treatment.

INTERPRETING THE TREATMENT PLAN

The radiation oncology nurse also can interpret the often confusing radiation therapy plan in understandable terms. Size and placement of the treatment fields is a common cause for concern, particularly since marked areas often appear to be larger than expected, or appear to encompass areas that would not seem to require treatment (e.g., the lower back as part of the treatment field for a tumor in the abdomen). Concerns are also often expressed about the possibility of radiation damage to critical structures near the marked treatment areas (e.g., the eye). Reinforcement of the radiation oncologist's explanations about the exact areas

to be treated and blocked, and the rationale for and explanation about multiple fields are often necessary. Because some machines have the ability to rotate around the child, only one field of two opposing fields may be marked on the skin (e.g., in treatment to the abdomen via anterior and posterior fields, the marks need to be placed only on the abdomen; technologists can set up the posterior field using the anterior marks as a guide). The child and parents need to understand the exact location of treatment fields in order to take appropriate care of the skin.

Parents and children benefit from knowing the exact number of treatments planned, and many children enjoy marking off their progress on a calendar or chart. They should be prepared, however, for possible changes in the treatment plan. Such changes may be based on new information, tumor response, patient tolerance, or change in patient status, and should always be explained by the radiation oncologist. Breaks in treatment due to side-effects such as low blood counts are also common. Although delays in a long course of treatment are disappointing (and, if overlong, not desirable), parents and children can be reassured that missed treatments often can be made up without the need to add extra treatments.

ONGOING TEACHING AND SUPPORT

The formal introductory and weekly sessions with the radiation oncologist and nurse were described earlier. Ongoing informal assessment of the child's and family's physical and emotional responses to treatments are made by all members of the radiation therapy team. Referrals to services such as nutritional and dental often are necessary, and social service is consulted to help the family to deal with the enormous practical, social, emotional, and financial burdens that a long course of daily treatments can impose. The child's radiation therapy plan

"Ribbon Tree"

celebrate the completion of treatment with department staff who have worked with them, but also provides closure to a significant experience in their lives. Siblings, grandparents, or friends may be invited to an "end of radiation therapy" party.

SPECIAL CONSIDERATIONS FOR TREATMENT PLANNING AND DAILY TREATMENTS

In order to plan and deliver accurate treatment, a variety of immobilization techniques as well as sedation or anesthesia may be used.

IMMOBILIZATION TECHNIQUES

The child and parents are prepared in advance of the simulation for the use of immobilization techniques, particularly since some children might view these mistakenly as punishment measures. Safety and comfort are primary considerations in deciding which immobilization techniques will be used. Soft straps, sandbags, or pillows are sometimes sufficient to immobilize the child but more often, custom-made body casts or molds are made prior to the simulation. The ALPHA CRADLE® Patient Immobilization System, which utilizes a lightweight styrofoam base and interior that can be comfortably molded by the child's body in a few minutes, is one example of an appropriate immobilization device (Fig. 5-3).

Any immobilization method must be continually reassessed for the child's comfort and safety, and appropriate modifications must be made. Since the treatment table is often raised far off the floor, immobilization serves a dual purpose by also protecting the child from a possible fall. The possibility of accidental aspiration while in the treatment position also must be assessed; the child must be monitored, and suction equipment must be readily available.

and progress also must be communicated to other services involved in the child's care, including inpatient staff who care for the hospitalized child and school and community health nurses who care for the child at home.

The impact of treating children in primarily adult departments cannot be underestimated. Many departments acknowledge the different needs and sensitivities of children and adults and set aside separate waiting rooms or areas specifically for children and their families. Toys, books, games, and wall decorations in waiting rooms and treatment areas provide a more familiar, warmer atmosphere.

Departments may mark the end of a child's treatment course with a party. This not only gives the child and family an opportunity to

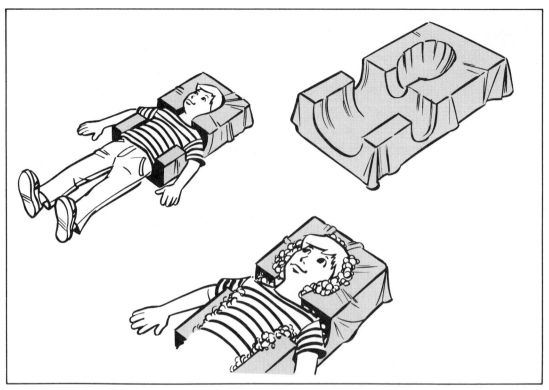

FIG. 5-3. Styrofoam Alpha Cradle Patient Immobilization System.

Since large areas of the body must be exposed sometimes for accurate planning and treatment, the child's need for warmth, particularly if he or she is very young or very ill, also must be recognized and managed. Lamps that radiate some heat near exposed areas can be used with caution, and other areas can be covered with a blanket. The child should be encouraged to express any discomforts or fears associated with immobilization.

SEDATION OR ANESTHESIA

Infants, toddlers, and any child who is too anxious or irritable to lie still for the duration of the treatment planning session may require sedation or anesthesia. Depending on the child's age and medical condition, sedation with an agent such as chloral hydrate or DPT [a mixture of meperidine (Demerol), promethazine (Phener-

gan), and chlorpromazine (Thorazine) given IM or PO] may be sufficient, but for some children, particularly toddlers, general anesthesia is necessary. A pediatric anesthesia team administers the anesthetic and monitors the child throughout the treatment and recovery period. Appropriate monitoring and emergency equipment must be on hand when any child is sedated or anesthetized. The treatment planning team attempts to perform the simulation as quickly as possible, an endeavor that may be complicated by the addition of extra personnel and equipment into the simulation room. Parents may not be allowed in the simulation room when a child is sedated or anesthetized, in which case they benefit from encouraging reports of the progress being made in the simulation room.

Because treatment sessions usually are shorter than treatment planning, sedation or anesthesia considerations are different. Sedation with agents such as chloral hydrate and

DPT has the advantage of easy administration and the need for less sophisticated monitoring during treatment and recovery. But daily sedation can cause the child to be sleepy for a good part of every day, a situation considered undesirable in a course of treatments lasting weeks. Also the onset and quality of the sedative effect may be variable, resulting in delays and difficulties in treatment.

Alternatively short-acting general anesthetics not requiring intubation can be administered on a daily basis by a pediatric anesthesia team. Methohexital (Brevitol; P.R.) or ketamine (IV or IM) are commonly used agents. Pretreatment administration of atropine and close monitoring throughout treatment and recovery are necessary when these agents are used. Advantages include quick and less variable effect, rapid recovery, and little or no adverse effects on the child during the rest of the day. If the child does not have a line for central venous access, however, the need for a patent IV or repeated IM injection sites can be troublesome.

The need for daily sedation or anesthesia does not preclude the child receiving daily radiation treatments on an outpatient basis, particularly if the parents are reliable, and supported. Many parents are upset about having their child receive daily anesthesia and require accurate information about the technical necessity for this measure. Sometimes daily anesthesia eventually can be discontinued as either the child's condition improves or he or she becomes more accustomed to the radiation therapy department and treatment routine. The importance of the child's accurate positioning is so great, however, that this decision is made with great care by the radiation therapy team.

SCHEDULING

In most radiation therapy departments the technologists are in charge of establishing a schedule of daily treatments for their patients. Treatments are given generally at the same

Pediatric Recovery Room

time daily throughout the treatment course. Technologists often will set aside more time in their schedules to treat a child to accommodate either the unpredictable behavior of an awake child or the requirements of daily sedation or anesthesia.

Children who require sedation or anesthesia are scheduled for early morning treatment, since they must remain NPO after midnight. Otherwise technologists try to accommodate the scheduling needs of the child and family. Consideration is given to the child's and siblings' normal daily schedule, parents' work schedules, and transportation arrangements. Changes in scheduling are made to coordinate the child's visits to other services when necessary.

MAINTENANCE OF A SUPPORTIVE ATMOSPHERE IN THE TREATMENT ROOM

Consistent assignment of one or more empathetic technologists who work with pediatric patients facilitates the development of a trusting relationship. An understanding technologist may discern fears or discomforts that a child has not expressed. Children who are bothered by the need to expose themselves for treatment, particularly adolescents, are reassured by the technologists' efforts to limit exposure and to restrict admittance to the treatment room to necessary personnel. The awake, immobilized child benefits from reassurance by the technologist that things are going well.

Many departments make individual decisions about how much parents can participate in daily treatment sessions. Some children benefit from their parents' presence in the treatment area during setups and from hearing their parents over the intercom, especially early in the course of treatments. The radiation oncology nurse can serve as the child's support when it is not possible or appropriate for parents to be present.

Many children enjoy taking toys or security blankets with them into the treatment room. Parents should be reassured that these will not become radioactive or interfere with their child's treatment.

CONCLUSION

Increasing numbers of children with cancer are likely to receive radiation therapy, often as part of aggressive multimodality treatment. Understanding what ionizing radiation is, how it affects living tissues, and how it is planned for and delivered to children can help nurses share the radiation experience with pediatric patients and their families. The radiation therapy team can manage acute and long-term effects of treatment on growing and developing children, with their individual needs and abilities, only in close collaboration with others involved in the children's care.

KEY POINTS

- Radiation therapy is primarily used for **local and regional control of cancer.**
- X-rays or gamma rays given off by radiation therapy machines are capable of damaging and destroying cancer cells by a complex series of reactions. Since normal cells are also damaged by radiation, **the goal of radiation therapy is to achieve maximum tumor control with a minimum amount of damage to surrounding normal tissues.**
- A typical sequence of experiences in a radiation therapy department include: an initial consultation with a radiation oncologist, a separate visit for treatment planning, a series of daily treatments, and routine followup appointments. Members of the **radiation therapy "team"** include radiation oncologists, radiation oncology nurses, radiation therapy technologists, radiation dosimetrists and physicists, receptionist and administrative staff, and other health-care professionals.
- In order to plan and deliver accurate treatment, a variety of **immobilization techniques** may be used. Either **sedation or anesthesia** also may be used for very young children. Special considerations are necessary to maintain a safe, supportive environment when these techniques are used.
- **Normal tissue responses to radiation include acute, intermediate, and late effects.** Although children generally tolerate the acute effects better than adults, late effects are of more concern. The appearance and severity of normal tissue effects depend on many factors, and preventive measures or adjustments in treatment are often necessary. Nursing management includes self-care teaching, observation, communication, and specific therapeutic measures.
- **Patient management** includes orientation of the patient and family to the radiation therapy department, interpretation of the treatment plan, special regard for scheduling and transport needs, maintenance of a supportive atmosphere in the planning and treatment areas, and ongoing teaching and support.

REFERENCES

Bloomer, W. D., and Hellman, S. (1975). Normal tissue responses to radiation therapy. *New England Journal of Medicine, 293,* 80–83.

Cassady, J. R. (1982). Radiation therapy. In K. J. Welch, (Ed.), *Complications of pediatric surgery: Prevention and management,* (pp. 416–426). Philadelphia: W. B. Saunders.

Fochtman, D., Ferguson, J., Ford, N., and Pryor, A. (1982). The treatment of cancer in children. In D. Fochtman and G. V. Foley (Eds.), *Nursing care of the child with cancer* (pp. 219–224). Boston: Little, Brown and Company.

Hassey, K. H., and Rose, C. M. (1982). Altered skin integrity in patients receiving radiation therapy. *Oncology Nursing Forum 9,* 44–49.

Levene, M. B., and Harris, J. R. (1982). Overall principles of cancer management: Radiation therapy. In *Cancer: A manual for practitioners* (6th ed.; pp. 52–53). Boston: American Cancer Society, Mass. Div.

Morrow, M. and Wilson, H. L. (1981). Children with cancer: A developmental approach. In L. B. Marino (Ed.), *Cancer nursing* (pp. 458–459). St. Louis: C. V. Mosby.

Moss, W. T., Brand, W. N., and Battifora, H. (Eds.). (1979). *Radiation oncology: Rationale, technique, results* (5th ed., p. 636). St. Louis: C. V. Mosby.

Simone, J. V. (1982). Principles of pediatric oncology. In S. K. Carter, E. Gladstein, and R. B. Livingston (Eds.), *Principles of cancer treatment* (pp. 157–158). New York: McGraw-Hill.

Simone, J. V., Cassady, J. R., and Filler, R. M. (1982). Cancers of childhood. In V. T. Devita, S. Hellman, S. A. Rosenberg (Eds.), *Cancer: Principles and practice of oncology* (pp. 1257–1258). Philadelphia: J. B. Lippincott.

Yasko, J. M. (1982). *Care of the client receiving external radiation therapy* (pp. 134, 150–151, 153, 166, 179). Reston, VA: Reston Publishing.

6

ADJUNCTIVE THERAPIES: KEYS TO SURVIVAL

INTRODUCTION

In the increasingly complex experience that cancer treatment has become, the hallmarks of treatment, radiation, surgery, and chemotherapy have been joined by significant additional therapies. These adjuvant therapies may be predominantly supportive, such as hyperalimentation or self-hypnosis, or they may be aimed at cure, for example, bone marrow transplantation or biological response modifier therapy. This chapter will consider treatments that have been proven effective or appear to have the most promise for treatment of childhood cancer. The final section also will consider the most frequently sought unproven methods in order to acquaint the reader with this sensitive topic. This chapter will depart from the usual format of this book in that, under each subheading, the treatment briefly will be discussed as to its usual indications, procedural aspects, and complications. The reader is referred to pertinent discussions in other chapters for the developmental aspects regarding nutrition, invasive therapies, grief responses of families, and so on.

SUPPORTIVE THERAPIES

This section will describe those often used components of cancer treatment that have become essential in helping the oncology patient to survive aggressive cancer therapies. Since most treatments for cancer remain nonspecific, normal tissues and function are usually disturbed or damaged in the course of treatment. Frequently the hematological and gastrointestinal systems are affected due to the body's response to chemo- and radiotherapy (see Chaps. 4 and 5). Additionally the trauma of the cancer experience, both disease and treatment related, has been documented as causing emotional distress, which may, in turn, contribute to ongoing physical distress. Therefore three types of supportive therapies will be addressed— nutritional therapy, blood component therapy, and behavioral therapy.

HYPERALIMENTATION

The widespread use of hyperalimentation, or total parenteral nutrition (TPN), is a relatively recent addition to multimodal cancer therapy. Concern over the possibility of augmenting tumor growth, and the technical difficulties associated with maintenance of an infection-free intravenous line in the past precluded the use of TPN in combating malnutrition in cancer patients. Research in the last 10 to 20 years, however, has shown that tumor growth did not occur as a result of TPN (Lum and Gallagher-Allred, 1984; Hushen, 1982). Rather insuring adequate caloric and protein intake by TPN effected improved nutritional status and even weight gain, increased tolerance of chemotherapy, radiotherapy, and surgical intervention, and improved immunologic status. Additionally most patients report emotional benefits of an improved physical appearance and energy level resulting from TPN (Hushen, 1982).

INDICATIONS

Both the disease and its treatment can result in a need for TPN. The caloric demand of a tumor or toxic gastrointestinal effects due to drug therapy can cause nutritional imbalance. Pedi-

atric populations are particularly vulnerable due to the increased metabolic demands of children and the psychological influences of disease on their willingness to eat. Improved techniques and equipment have made the use of TPN feasible in many more patients than heretofore. Many cancer centers and general hospitals have developed criteria for the use of this therapy.

In pediatric populations long-term hyperalimentation has been used with success for a variety of conditions including pseudo-obstruction syndrome, Crohn's disease, and short bowel syndrome, as well as for intractable vomiting or malnutrition resulting from chemotherapy (Parfitt and Thompson, 1980). Although there is no evidence that intravenous hyperalimentation affects the ultimate outcome of childhood malignancy, it is known that rates of complication and duration of survival are favorably affected by its use (Culbert and Pickering, 1984).

PROCEDURE

Patients are considered for TPN using criteria developed by an interdisciplinary staff. Although specifics may vary slightly, consideration is usually based on (1) extent of weight loss, (2) the documentation of low serum protein, (3) the existence of lack of immunologic competence, and (4) diagnostic and prognostic data. TPN is not used usually as a routine measure, nor is it instituted or maintained in the hopelessly ill patient (Rapp, et al., 1976). For the benefit of maximum support it is considered optimal that a patient identified as needing TPN can be started on it preceding oncologic therapy.

After determining the patient's suitability for hyperalimentation, the appropriate mechanism is evaluated. The Hickman catheter frequently is used. It is placed by the physician infraclavicularly through the subclavian vein to the mid superior vena cava (Fig. 6-1). A chest X-ray is taken immediately to check catheter

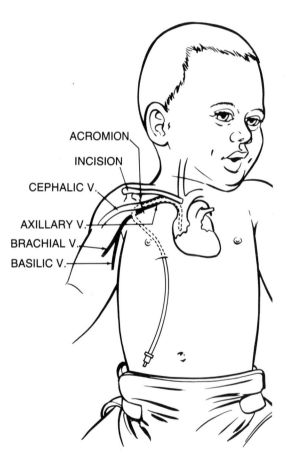

ACROMION

INCISION

CEPHALIC V.

AXILLARY V.

BRACHIAL V.

BASILIC V.

FIG. 6-1. Placement of Hickman catheter.

location and to rule out potential complications such as pneumothorax, hemothorax, and malposition of the catheter (Appleby, 1983) (see Chap. 4). With verification of correct placement, TPN solution orders are written by the physician based on the child's weight, disease and treatment characteristics, and fluid and electrolyte picture. A number of preparations are in common usage. Generally glucose (25% to 50%) and amino acids (approximately 4.25%) are included, with additional vitamins, minerals, and trace elements added as needed by the patient (Bussey, 1984) (Table 6-1). Usually a beginning solution is started at a slow rate in order to ensure pancreatic response to the increased glucose load (Appleby, 1983).

Careful monitoring of the child receiving TPN is important. Areas of concern include fluid and electrolyte balance, infection control, and maintenance of the subclavian line. In terms of fluid and electrolyte balance, a determination of urine sugar and acetone is necessary every 6 hours to assess excessive excretion of the highly concentrated glucose solution. When reported to the physician, elevation of urine sugars will frequently result in an order to slow the rate of the TPN solution in an attempt to decrease renal spilling of glucose. In some cases, regular insulin may be added to the TPN bag. In an effort to prevent sepsis great care is taken in the dressing and tubing changes. In many cancer centers and larger hospitals a team may be responsible for all patients on hyperalimentation, or specified nursing personnel may be assigned to these patients. Generally it is considered best to reduce to a minimum the number of staff handling the infusion system. In most hospitals dressings and tubing are changed by the team or specified person 3 times weekly, unless the dressing becomes soiled, wet, or loose. Patients with draining wounds, tracheostomies, or radiation sites near the catheter site need closer surveillance. Enterostomal therapists may be able to apply collection bags over a fistula, for example, to prevent con-

TABLE 6-1. STANDARD CENTRAL VEIN (CV) SOLUTION

Each liter bag contains
　Crystalline amino acids
　Dextrose
　Sodium
　Potassium
　Magnesium
　Calcium
　Phosphate
　Acetate
　Chloride

Trace element additives
　Zinc
　Copper
　Manganese
　Chromium
　Nitrogen

Vitamins
　B Complex with C, A, D, E — once weekly
　B Complex with C — twice weekly
　Cyanocobalamin, 100 mcg — once weekly
　　(contraindicated in patients receiving methotrexate)
　Phytonadione, 10 mg — once weekly
　　(contraindicated in patients receiving warfarin)

tamination of the catheter site and dressing (Rapp, et al., 1976). Additionally these patients may need dressings that are waterproof in contrast to the often used elastoplast dressings (Appleby, 1983). Routine measures such as checking vital signs every 4 hours, observations of the surrounding area for inflammation, handwashing, and screening visitors are all necessary precautions, and frequently will be already in place due to the patient's general medical condition. Blood cultures usually are done for temperature elevations, but every attempt is made to discover other potential sources of infection prior to removing the catheter.

In regard to maintenance of the subclavian line, most units advocate restriction of the use of the line to the administration of nutritional substances. This means that the line is not used for medications, central venous pressure monitoring, or blood drawing (Rapp, et al., 1976;

TABLE 6-2. KEY CONCERNS IN THE CARE OF THE CHILD RECEIVING TPN

Concern	Nursing Action
Fluid and electrolyte balance	Urine sugar and acetone determination q 6 hr, evaluation of I & O, blood chemistry assays, careful regulation of flow rate
Infection control	Aseptic dressing change at regular intervals and as necessary loosening or soiling of dressing
	Periodic aseptic tubing change, as specified by unit policy
	Reduction in numbers of persons handling TPN line
	Prevention of contamination from draining wounds, tracheostomies, etc.
	Careful observation of site, patient's general status, including vital signs
	Careful handwashing for all including the patient
	Screening visitors, attendants
	Blood cultures for temperature elevations
Maintenance of line patency	Restrict use to nutritional products only
	Declotting protocol implemented by trained personnel
	Heparinize for TPN free intervals
	Use of electronic pumping for consistency in rate
	Connections taped securely

Appleby, 1983). Due to the existence of special Intravenous Hyperalimentation (IVH) teams in most hospitals, clogging of the line is a problem handled by the IVH nurse. Irrigation with various solutions, including urokinase and streptokinase, is usually successful in declotting the catheter (Ryan and Gough, 1984). When hyperalimentation fluids are given on an intermittent basis — such as on a 12-hour schedule prior to discharge, or if interrupted for short periods for passes, school, and so on — irrigation of the catheter is required to keep the line open. This is done in most institutions with a dilute solution of heparin on an every day or every shift basis. The key concerns in the care of a child receiving TPN are summarized in Table 6-2.

For most patients receiving hyperalimentation, the administration of concurrent fat emulsions is necessary. Total parenteral nutrition fluids do not supply essential fatty acids. Frequently this is a prominent nutritional deficiency in patients malnourished due to cancer or its treatment. Additionally fat emulsions are an important source of calories (Hutchison,

1982). A typical solution used is Intralipid, which is a 10% fat emulsion supplying 1.1 calories per ml. Twenty percent fat emulsions are beginning to be used more widely for greater caloric administration (Appleby, 1983).

In terms of administration, fat emulsions are best given through an electrically controlled pump piggybacked into TPN tubing. No filter should be used because emulsified particles are too large to pass through most IV filters. Care must be taken that piggyback sites and all connections are taped securely. Although it is possible to administer fat emulsions peripherally, due to their isotonicity, the site should be checked frequently for phlebitis and swelling (Hutchison, 1982). The usual dosage for children is 250 ml per day, with the maximum being 4 gm/kg of ideal body weight, at a rate not to exceed 1 gm/kg over 4 hours. The first administration should be started gradually at a rate of 0.1 ml/min for 10 minutes to children under 12, who need to be observed for dyspnea, cyanosis, headache, flushing, nausea, vomiting, chest and back pain, and allergic reaction (Hutchison, 1982).

COMPLICATIONS

Complications arising from the use of TPN, a hypertonic, high-solute solution, include fluid and electrolyte imbalance, which may result in congestive heart failure. Monitoring urine sugar, acetone, and fluid intake and output at 4-hour intervals will help prevent this occurrence. The high glucose concentration predisposes the child to infection and sepsis. Careful monitoring of vital signs and catheter site will help in prevention or early detection. Although it is not common, thrombophlebitis of the subclavian vein may occur and is characterized by temperature elevation, pain at the insertion site, or edema of the neck, arm, or catheter site (Rapp, et al., 1976). Long-term data are not fully available regarding total growth hormone suppression, poor bone formation, and emotional difficulties that may be experienced while on long-term TPN (Parfitt and Thompson, 1980).

Complications or adverse reactions that may arise from lipid infusion include initial infusion allergic reactions and an unpleasant taste during the infusion. Due to the incompatibility of lipids with many electrolyte or drug solutions, lipids usually are clamped off during administration of other solutions to guard against precipitation. Specific compatibilities should be checked if lipids must be infused concurrently with other solutions besides TPN (Hutchison, 1982).

GOING HOME ON HYPERALIMENTATION

As TPN is used increasingly to maintain nutrition for specific periods of time, oncology staffs frequently are considering the feasibility of administering TPN at home. Several cancer centers and children's hospitals have instituted home hyperalimentation programs, delineating the skills and understanding needed by the children and parents to manage this procedure at home. According to a New York survey, in 1982 42% of the patients initiated on home parenteral nutrition had some form of malignancy (Konstantinides, 1985). Criteria for selection of patients and families who can be maintained at home vary from institution to institution, but generally include inability of the gastrointestinal tract to maintain adequate nutritional status, metabolic stability, intellectual and psychosocial readiness to manage the home treatment plan, the existence of adequate family and community support networks, local resources for the hyperalimentation solution equipment, and physician and visiting nurse backup. To prepare the child and family for discharge, a step-by-step teaching plan is instituted that progresses to the family's assumption of total responsibility for the hyperalimentation line. Whenever feasible the hyperalimentation administration schedule is altered gradually to fit into a 12-hour time frame, allowing the child maximum freedom during the day, with the fluid being given during the evening and night (Konstantinides, 1985; Parfitt and Thompson, 1980). Some settings include a "dry run" prior to returning home, which entails the family's stay at a local motel where they are on their own with the child but must check in daily with the hospital (Parfitt and Thompson, 1980). Following a successful dry run, the family returns home with the backup of local medical, nursing, and pharmaceutical services, continued contact with the cancer center, and periodic evaluation regarding the hyperalimentation therapy. The cost of this form of nutritional support usually can be reimbursed through third party payers except for a deductible fee; however, most insurers require prior approval. This is an expensive therapy, with estimates ranging from $55,000 to $70,000 per year, as calculated in one institutional setting for adult patients. This figure includes the solution cost supplies, home nursing visits, and clinical followup (Konstantinides, 1985). Medicaid coverage may be available but varies from state to state. In general, restrictive policies and low

TABLE 6-3. BLOOD COMPONENT THERAPY

Blood Components	Indications	Complications
Red blood cells	Anemia	Immediate
Packed red blood cells	Hypovolemia	Hemolytic reaction
Fresh		Febrile reaction
Frozen		Allergic reaction
Leukocyte poor		
Irradiated		Delayed
		Infections
Whole blood		Hemolytic reaction
(Infrequent usage)		Iron deposition
Fresh		Suppression of erythropoiesis
Frozen		Electrolyte disturbances
Irradiated		Antibody formation
Platelets		
Fresh	Acute bleeding	Allergic reaction
Pooled or single donor	Prevention of bleeding	Febrile reaction
White blood cells	Presence of serious infection	Febrile reaction
Fresh	in neutropenic patient	Allergic reaction
		Respiratory distress syndrome
Other		
Coagulation factors	Hepatic dysfunction	
	Chemotherapy toxicities	
Vitamin K	Post-long-term antibiotics	
	hepatic dysfunction	

reimbursement rates make Medicaid an inadequate source of funding (Curtiss, 1983).

BLOOD COMPONENT THERAPY

A frequently used tool in the supportive care of the child with cancer is the use of blood components. This is due partly to the lengthened survival time for these children and the use of more aggressive treatment modalities, and partly to the refinement of blood component administration. Testing mechanisms are now used widely, for instance, to detect hepatitis B to decrease exposure to that potential hazard. Other infectious agents, however, are not routinely screened for, such as cytomegalovirus, Epstein–Barr virus, hepatitis A, non-A and non-B hepatitis, and toxoplasmosis (Culbert and Pickering, 1984). The occurrence of acquired immune deficiency syndrome (AIDS) among various population groups, including transfusion recipients, can now be more effectively prevented with the use of a reliable screening test. Immunodeficiency predisposes the AIDS patient to opportunistic infection, which is of particular significance in the already vulnerable cancer patient (Boland and Gaskill, 1984). Besides the potential for transmission of infection, the continued possibility of antigenic reaction makes transfusion therapy less than invariably safe, despite vast improvement in providing for compatibility between donor and recipient. Every transfusion has the possible result of jeopardizing all later transfusions or any future bone marrow transplantation. Therefore most medical experts recommend keeping transfusion to a minimum and not utilizing a potential bone marrow donor as a blood component donor until after transplantation (Culbert and Pickering, 1984). Each component will be briefly discussed in terms of its indications, techniques for administration, and complications (see Table 6-3).

Erythrocyte Therapy

INDICATIONS

Red blood cell (RBC) replacement is indicated when an increased oxygen-carrying capacity of the blood is required, as in correction of a hypovolemic state. If the child with anemia has coexisting problems, however, which can be managed nutritionally, by eliminating certain drug agents, or by treating a chronic infection, these methods should be tried prior to transfusion therapy. A thorough evaluation of the need for transfusion is needed. Experience with patients who are Jehovah's Witnesses has indicated that a conservative policy of RBC transfusion may be adequate. Many of these patients survive with hemoglobins of 2.5 to 4.0 gm/100 ml (Culbert and Pickering, 1984).

When need has been determined, the etiology of the deficit in oxygen-carrying capacity will determine the component used. Packed red cells usually are preferred, except in the case of massive or uncontrolled bleeding, in which case whole blood or fresh frozen plasma with packed red cells would be the treatment of choice. The packed cells may be frozen (particularly if autotransfusion has been anticipated), centrifuged, and leukofiltered. For children with repeated febrile reactions, leukocyte-poor RBCs may be used (Bahu, 1983). Frozen packed RBCs appear to pose the least problems and yield a more refined product, but may be more costly and difficult to store (Culbert and Pickering, 1984).

PROCEDURES

The type and rate of administration either of packed cells or whole blood will be determined by the individual situation. In the case of anemia, for example, 10 ml of packed red blood cells/kg of body weight should raise the hematocrit by about 10 points (Hazinski, 1984). Care must be taken to ensure compatibility of the transfusion, following accepted nursing practice and unit policy. Care also must be taken in administration not to use electronic pumping equipment if it damages RBCs. A major responsibility after the initiation of red blood cell replacement is the monitoring of the child for possible adverse reactions. Immediate reactions include the rare hemolytic reaction characterized by chills, fever, pain at needle site, nausea and vomiting, and progressive shock with renal failure. As a precaution against these reactions, blood should be started at a slow drip rate for the first 20 minutes or 50 ml, and personnel should stay with the patient. Should a hemolytic reaction occur, the transfusion should be stopped immediately, the intravenous line should be maintained, and the physician should be contacted immediately. Close monitoring and treatment for shock may be necessary. Both the donor transfusion and a urine sample from the patient must be saved for testing (Waley and Wong, 1983). One additional precaution that can be taken for the severely immunosuppressed patient is the irradiation of the unit to be administered. A 1500 rad dose of radiation will eliminate significant lymphocyte contamination of any component preparation, which is important in the prevention of a graft versus host response in these immunosuppressed patients (Culbert and Pickering, 1984).

COMPLICATIONS

In addition to hemolytic reactions, febrile reactions and allergic reactions are common problems. Both necessitate close monitoring and discontinuance of the transfusion. For febrile reactions acetaminophen or salicylates may be given prophylactically. Children who tend toward allergic reactions may be given antihistamines for prophylaxis. Should wheezing and signs of laryngeal edema occur during an allergic reaction, epinephrine may be used. Hypothermia also may occur if blood is not allowed to warm to room temperature (less than 1 hour) before transfusion. Finally air emboli might occur if blood is given through a pump (Bahu, 1983).

There are a variety of delayed reactions that can occur days or weeks following the transfusion. These include hepatitis, malaria, syphilis, cytomegalovirus, and bacterial infections, delayed hemolytic reaction, iron deposition, suppression of erythropoiesis, electrolyte disturbances, and antibody formation from multiple transfusions (Waley and Wong, 1983). Already mentioned in the section on blood component therapy, Acquired immune deficiency syndrome has also occurred. The incubation period is unknown and may be months to years. The early symptoms are typically nonspecific, but repeated, perhaps overwhelming, infections eventually occur (Boland and Gaskill, 1984). Although this is a significant and frequently fatal complication of blood transfusion, only a small proportion of AIDS cases has been linked to blood transfusion (CDC, 1983). Recent Advances in screening for the HTLV-III virus associated with AIDS substantially diminish this risk.

Platelet Replacement

INDICATIONS

The child with cancer frequently has difficulty with thrombocytopenia. Decreased production of platelets due to malignant invasion of the bone marrow or suppression due to chemo- or radiotherapy may occur. An increase in the consumption of platelets also can occur as a result of hemorrhage, immune destruction, splenic sequestration or destruction, or disseminated intravascular coagulation. Both to treat an acute bleeding episode when thrombocytopenia is a factor, or as a preventive measure

when the platelet count is low, platelet replacement may be indicated. Institutions vary as to the use of transfusion for prophylaxis when platelet counts fall to a predetermined low, or only when indicated for active bleeding (Culbert and Pickering, 1984).

PROCEDURE

Since young platelets appear to be most effective in shortening bleeding time, collection of platelets from suitable donors is best done immediately prior to transfusion. Most hospitals use plasma – platelet – phoresis, or continuous flow, centrifugation techniques. These techniques allow multiple units to be harvested from a single donor, thereby decreasing the foreign platelet antigenic exposure. In addition, frequent collections can be made from a pool of known tissue-typed donors, often family members, without ill effects to the donor. Again it must be noted that anticipation of bone marrow transplant should preclude the use of possible bone marrow donors.

Techniques that would allow autotransfusion of platelets through the availability of prolonged frozen storage are being developed; currently it is usually preferable to give platelets immediately, with a brief storage period at room temperature, for the most prompt effect on clotting. Platelets are administered intravenously at a dosage usually calculated as 1 unit per 5 kilograms, to a maximum of 10 units (Culbert and Pickering, 1984). As with whole blood or packed red cells, careful monitoring for immediate and delayed adverse reactions is necessary. Precautions concerning the administration of blood products, according to correct nursing practice and unit policy, must be taken to safeguard the child requiring platelet transfusion (Bahu, 1983).

COMPLICATIONS

The complications discussed previously under erythrocyte replacement, such as allergic and febrile reactions, can still occur with platelet transfusion although the refinement of plasma-platelet-phoresis makes these reactions somewhat less likely. With each transfusion from a random donor, however, the effectiveness of future transfusions is endangered due to the problem of sensitization (Culbert and Pickering, 1984). Since platelet survival can be shortened by fever or sepsis, close monitoring in the post-transfusion period is important (Bahu, 1983). A platelet count may be obtained 1 hour following the transfusion (Masoorli and Piercy, 1984).

Granulocyte Replacement

INDICATIONS

Due to intensive chemotherapy, tumor invasion of bone marrow, or overwhelming infection, low white blood cell counts are frequently a problem in children with cancer. At counts lower than 100/ml, patients are very vulnerable for overwhelming bacterial sepsis. Antibiotic therapy is of limited usefulness in patients with such marked neutropenia. Although still somewhat experimental, granulocyte replacement may be attempted in situations of very low granulocyte counts in patients with infections (Culbert and Pickering, 1984).

Limiting the effectiveness of granulocyte replacement are the short life span (about 6 hours) of white cells and the technical difficulties associated with collection of a sufficient number of cells to be beneficial to the recipient. In the past patients with chronic granulocytic leukemia with exceedingly high white counts were used as donors; however, rare incidence of bone marrow engraftment of these cells, or graft versus host reactions, occurred in some immunosuppressed individuals. The use of normal donors is more widely advocated, with prior preparation of the donor using agents to increase the number of circulating granulo-cytes. Two of these agents are dexamethasone and etiocholanolone. An additional precaution is to collect the white cells in vessels containing hydroxethel-starch (Hes) (Culbert and Pickering, 1984).

PROCEDURE

Various leukophoresis techniques based on the principle of harvesting and concentrating leukocytes have been developed. It is theorized that some filtration procedures cause alterations in white cell morphology and function; thus, large numbers of cells must be given to demonstrate an effect in the white blood cell count of the recipient.

Generally red cells and 80% of the plasma component of blood are removed. Transfusions should be administered as promptly as possible and no more than 24 hours after collection. Often the patient is premedicated with oral diphenhydramine and acetaminophen, and vital signs are taken every 30 minutes to monitor allergic reactions (Masoorli and Piercy, 1984).

COMPLICATIONS

Due to the fact that most children needing granulocyte replacement have been transfused previously with other blood products, reactions are common. Usually such adverse responses include fever, chills, and urticaria during infusion. A severe respiratory distress syndrome also can occur, as can graft versus host response in immunodeficient patients (Culbert and Pickering, 1984).

Other Blood-Related Therapies

In the bleeding child, other coagulation factors besides platelets may be required. Particularly in the case of prolonged broad-spectrum antibiotic therapy or hepatic dysfunction, vitamin K deficiency may occur. Other coagulation factors, namely factors II, VII, IX, and X, are vitamin K dependent and the patient thus may also be deficient in them. Deficiencies can be treated with intravenous or intramuscular administration of vitamin K. If advanced hepatic failure has occurred, replacement of these other coagulation factors may be needed. Some chemotherapeutic agents may contribute to deficiencies; for example, L-asparaginase interferes with protein synthesis (Culbert and Pickering, 1984).

BEHAVIORAL TECHNIQUES

The use of behavioral techniques such as hypnosis, designed to alter the consciousness of the sick person, dates back to ancient times. Until recently practitioners of such techniques were often viewed as quacks however, who had little scientific credibility (Daley and Greenspun, 1981). Research-based investigation into behavioral techniques (*e.g.*, hypnosis and imagery) has begun recently to establish their use as valuable adjunctive therapies for some patients. These noninvasive techniques have minimal risks and potential for benefit in many children. In pediatric oncology imagery and self-hypnosis have been used with demonstrated positive effects for the reduction of emesis and treatment-related pain control (Zeltzer, et al., 1983; Kellerman, et al., 1983; Olness, 1981; Cotanch, et al., 1985). Despite such evidence of effectiveness, noninvasive techniques are underutilized, according to a survey of 29 cancer center nursing staffs (Hockenberry and Bologna-Vaughn, 1985). In a different context the psychotherapy method used by the Simontons at the Cancer Counseling and Research Center (Fort Worth, TX) utilizes behavioral techniques to help the patient explore the psychological factors that affect tumor growth. The center advocates behavioral techniques as self-help for the patient to use in addition to standard medical treatment. The Ameri-

can Cancer Society has studied the Simonton treatment and has concluded that there is no evidence that any objective benefit results from this treatment for cancer (ACS, 1982). The proponents of the use of imagery, muscle relaxation, and hypnosis emphasize, however, that as a supportive treatment for symptom control these techniques have a definite place in the treatment plan for those children who benefit (Olness, 1981; Fox, 1982, Cotanch, 1985).

INDICATIONS

Research to date generally has shown a measurable benefit from the use of behavioral methods to treat chemotherapy-induced emesis and the pain and anxiety associated with cancer treatment, *e.g.*, bone marrow aspiration, lumbar punctures, and chemotherapeutic injections. Anticipatory nausea and vomiting also have been significantly reduced using these behavioral interventions (Redd and Hendler, 1984). In data gathered to date, it appears that children of both sexes from the ages of 5 to 11 seem to learn and use imagery with great ease (Olness, 1981). Also the earlier in the course of the disease the child is exposed to these techniques, the more likely it is that the techniques will be successful in controlling pain or vomiting (Olness, 1981). Behavioral interventions also often result in a snowball effect; many patients use them to alleviate other types of discomfort, such as insomnia, and to enhance their sense of personal control (Redd and Hendler, 1984).

PROCEDURE

It is emphasized by those who are using both hypnosis and imagery that only persons with formal training in hypnotherapy should help children in the use of these techniques (Daley and Greenspun, 1981; Olness, 1981). Each child needs to be approached as an individual. The therapist spends time interacting with the child to establish rapport and to determine what type of imagery will work best. Patients are given an explanation of hypnosis and taught an initial induction technique such as eye fixation or hand levitation. Then suggestions for progressive muscular relaxation are given, including the use of slow, rhythmic breathing. The child is instructed to visualize or experience being in a favorite or special place. The images vary depending on the particular choice the child makes regarding the special place. When deep relaxation is observable, posthypnotic suggestions are given related to a heightened sense of well-being and reduction of discomfort. The child is encouraged to achieve mastery over fear of a procedure or adverse symptom.

Children are encouraged to practice these imagery exercises themselves and frequently practice prior to a procedure with reinforcement from the therapist later during the actual procedure. Using this process with a sample of adolescents, Kellerman and colleagues (1983) found that the 16 patients who agreed to use hypnosis achieved significant reductions in distress as measured before and after the initiation of hypnosis. Olness (1981) uses a variety of images depending on the patients' wishes. In switch imagery, for example, the child visualizes switches for parts of the body. The child imagines then that the switches are being "turned off," thereby eliminating sensation and controlling pain. In Olness's study of 25 pediatric patients, 19 demonstrated substantial symptom relief using imagery exercises. Cotanch and coworkers (1985) further used the child's involvement of "all the senses" in the fantasy. Verbal suggestions are made by the therapist to increase awareness of physical sensation, followed by specific suggestions related to the child's feelings posthypnosis. The suggestion is made that the child will feel safe, for example, helped by the antiemetic and able to drink cold liquids when he or she is awakened. In their sample of 20 children, Cotanch and coworkers found that children in the hypnosis group experienced a statistically significant re-

duction in postchemotherapy emesis. These children also reported being less bothered by chemotherapy than those in the control group and had a greater oral intake in the 24 hours following chemotherapy.

Frequent practice by the child or adolescent is associated with more rapid development of symptom control. Although school-aged children seem most amenable to the use of imagery, adolescents can use the technique effectively if given more time to learn it. Reinforcement in group sessions is considered helpful in retaining the imagery skills (Olness, 1981). Some therapists have had success teaching the techniques to parents or family members. Although little scientific data has been reported, family members have been found to learn the techniques easily and have benefited themselves from feeling more involved in the treatment. Also the effectiveness of imagery can thus be sustained at home or in the clinic when the therapist is not available (Redd and Hendler, 1984).

COMPLICATIONS

No complications are specified in the literature on this technique. The investigators mentioned the care that should be taken regarding recommendations to use imagery exercises to activate an immunologic response against the disease. Although some patients choose to practice imagery, it is important that they do not feel that a failure in their imagery is responsible for any treatment failure (Olness, 1981; Fox, 1982). Psychologically the child could experience guilt and distress if the burden of the effectiveness of disease treatment rested on the effectiveness of the imagery exercises being attempted.

ADJUNCTIVE TREATMENT MODALITIES

There are many new components of multimodal cancer therapy, some still under investigation. The two most widely investigated — bone marrow transplantation and the use of biological response modifiers, that is, immunotherapy and interferons — will be discussed in this section. It is important to recognize that many children experiencing these therapies have failed the more conventional therapies. There is accordingly the element of desperate hope that this new treatment will bring about cure. Also media attention regarding these therapies may have brought about false hope and misinformation. These are pertinent considerations in the care of patients undergoing adjunctive therapies.

BONE MARROW TRANSPLANTATION

Bone marrow transplantation (BMT) is a relatively new component of multimodal cancer therapy. This technique currently is being investigated for its efficacy in the treatment of acute leukemia and other malignancies, as well as aplastic anemia and severe immunodeficiencies. The purpose of BMT for acute leukemia is the eradication of the disease. This is attempted through the administration of supralethal chemotherapy and subsequent rescue of the recipient with transplanted new marrow. Another theorized benefit is the control of acute leukemia through an immunologic antileukemic effect of the transplanted marrow (Wiley, et al., 1983).

Research begun as early as the late 1800s has led to the current approach, which is the use of BMT for patients with acute lymphocytic leukemia (ALL) who have relapsed and other leukemia patients, particularly those with acute non-lymphocytic leukemia (ANLL), whose prognosis is poor. Some studies comparing transplantation both in relapse and in remission indicate superior results obtained with patients in remission (Johnson, 1981).

Three types of transplants are possible in humans. These are allogeneic, in which donor and recipient belong to the same species; iso-

geneic or syngeneic, in which donor and recipient are genetically identical; and autologous, in which donor and recipient are the same individual. Autologous transplants are obviously superior in terms of eliminating the pre- and posttransplant problems of donor selection and graft versus host disease. For patients with acute leukemia, however, a potential serious disadvantage is the contamination of the marrow with malignant cells, even in patients who are in clinical remission. Some success has been noted with this technique in patients with lymphoma, but those with ALL were found to do less well than those who received syngeneic transplants (Spruce, 1983). For the most part then, BMT in its most common usage for pediatric cancer patients involves allogeneic or, when feasible, isogeneic techniques (Table 6-4).

INDICATIONS

Usual indications for BMT are ALL after a first relapse, ANLL, and other non-neoplastic diseases such as aplastic anemia and immunodeficiency syndromes. In some centers bone marrow transplant may be employed in children following intensive chemotherapy and immunosuppression. When this situation is anticipated, as in solid tumor therapy, autologous transplant can be planned. Of critical concern is the donor selection process and timing of the transplant, whether the patient is in relapse or remission.

PROCEDURE

Besides clinical indications, the critical determinant of whether to use BMT is the availability of a suitable donor. The discovery of the human leukocyte antigen (HLA), locus on the sixth chromosome, and an antigen, the mixed lymphocyte culture (MLC), has greatly improved this process. It is believed that there are other determinants of histocompatibility due to the fact that, despite HLA matching, a number

TABLE 6-4. BONE MARROW TRANSPLANT TECHNIQUES

	Types	
	Autologous	Allogeneic
Purpose	Nonleukemic patients —to allow use of large amounts of chemotherapy in order to kill the tumor Leukemic patients —to allow use of large amounts of chemotherapy in order to kill leukemic cells in the bone marrow and throughout the body	Leukemic or aplastic anemia patients —to allow use of large amounts of chemotherapy and total body irradiation in order to kill leukemic or aplastic cells in the bone marrow and the body and replace it with nonleukemic or nonaplastic bone marrow
Donor marrow	Patient's own marrow	Matched donor for ABO typing Human lymphocyte antigen (HLA) Mixed lymphocyte culture (MLC)
Chemotherapy	Varies	Piperazinedione or Cytoxan —given for approximately 2–4 days
Total Body Irradiation	None	6 doses
Blood Products	Irradiated	Irradiated
IVH	Yes	Yes
Isolation	Good handwashing, masks, sterile linen, private room, and bath	Complete reverse isolation, sterile linen, private room, and bath
Antibiotics	IV antibiotics	Oral antibiotics IV antibiotics Creams to all body orifices
Aspiration	Prior to beginning of chemotherapy or while in remission Done under general anesthesia with multiple sticks Pressure dressing to area Marrow is frozen and stored	Day of transplant Done under general anesthesia with multiple sticks Pressure dressing to area
Transplant	As a blood transfusion ≈ 50cc IVP	As a blood transfusion ≈ 50cc IVP
Complications	Not as severe No graft versus host reactions Immunosuppression Nutritional problems Infection Side-effects of chemotherapy Hypocalcemia ⎱ Hypokalemia ⎰ Individualized Hyponatremia Reintroduction of malignant cells	Graft versus host reaction Immunosuppression Nutritional problems Skin problems Infection Side-effects of chemotherapy Side-effects of irradiation (mucocytitis, paratitis, diarrhea, loss of appetite) Hypocalcemia ⎱ Hypokalemia ⎰ Individualized Hyponatremia

TABLE 6-5. NURSING CONSIDERATIONS IN GRAFT VERSUS HOST DISEASE

Signs and Symptoms	Nursing Care
Acute GVHD	Mild
Skin	Lubricate with oil base lotion, use antihistamines and steroid creams
Erythema	Frank desquamation
Maculopapular eruption	Sterile protective techniques, debridement, coverage of affected areas with
Desquamation	Betadine/NS impregnated gauze and antimicrobial creams.
Liver	Observe for jaundice, bleeding
Elevated liver enzymes, bilirubin	Protective measures for itching, decrease risk of injury
Gastrointestinal	Careful I & O, weigh qd, good rectal care
Diarrhea	
Chronic GVHD	Physical therapy, oil based lotions, sun protection
Skin	
Increased pigmentation, thickening, contractures, conjunctivitis, photosensitivity	
Liver	Enzyme replacement, monitoring
Liver dysfunction, coagulopathy	
Gastrointestinal	Antidiarrheal medications, dietary modification, may require TPN
Malabsorption, chronic diarrhea	
Musculoskeletal	Encourage range of motion, physical therapy
Arthritis	
Pulmonary	Encourage activity to preserve function, prevent infection
Shortness of breath, dyspnea on exertion, cough	
Immune system	Teaching regarding infection, careful monitoring, antibiotic therapy, support
Opportunistic infection	

Cogliano-Shutta, N., Broda, E. and Gress, J. Bone marrow transplantation. NCNA, 20(1) 49–65)

of transplants still result in graft rejection or graft versus host disease (GVHD). Generally siblings are the most likely source of a match with a 25% chance of being compatible; parents, extended family, or unrelated persons usually are not compatible donors. Although transplant from incompatibly matched donors has been done, the risks of rejection and GVHD are increased significantly (Wiley, et al., 1983).

Preparation of the recipient includes an analysis of general health status, including physiologic, psychologic, and bacteriologic parame-

ters. Open discussion with the family, the child, and a multidisciplinary team is an important aspect. An in depth nursing assessment is done, particularly regarding past coping experiences and outcomes. When a decision to proceed is made, a conditioning regimen is begun. This may vary with each cancer center, but preparation generally includes a low bacterial diet, oral, nonabsorbable antibiotics to sterilize the gastrointestinal tract, Bactrim prophylaxis against *pneumocystis carinii* pneumonia, high-dose chemotherapy (usually with cyclophosphamide), and total body irradiation (TBI). (If autologous transplant is performed, some elements of the conditioning treatment would be unnecessary, *e.g.*, TBI and high-dose chemotherapy.) TBI and chemotherapy are started several days before isogeneic or allogeneic transplantation and usually take place in protective isolation. TBI is given following chemotherapy as a single dose of 1000 rad or in up to 8 fractionated doses totaling approximately 1320 rad. The use of fractionated TBI is being evaluated to determine if it reduces the potential for pulmonary toxicity (Wiley, et al., 1983).

The donor is hospitalized for 2 to 3 days. A medical evaluation regarding general health and suitability for anesthesia is done. On the day of the transplant the donor undergoes multiple bone marrow aspirations under general anesthesia. Usually the posterior iliac crests are used, although anterior crests and other sites may be required. Each aspiration involves only a small volume to avoid dilution with peripheral blood, so a number of aspirations are needed to harvest the required 400 to 800 cc of marrow.

After filtering to remove bone chips and fat globules, the marrow suspension, usually approximately 50 cc, is placed in a blood transfusion bag and administered intravenously, either by IV drip or push. The recipient may be premedicated with Tylenol and Benadryl if there is a history of previous transfusion reactions.

During and after transfusion the recipient is monitored closely for pulmonary embolism and fluid overload. Continuing close supervision and intensive supportive care are necessary until hematologic self-sufficiency occurs, usually within 6 to 8 weeks. Protective isolation is continued until the neutrophil count reaches a predetermined level (500 at UCLA Medical Center) (Wiley, et al., 1983). A much longer period of up to 1 year may be required to regain normal marrow function. Susceptibility to infection, bleeding, and anemia frequently necessitate the use of blood products. These blood components are irradiated to inactivate immunologically competent cells, which helps to avoid potential graft versus host reaction (Cogliana-Shutta, et al., 1985). Laminar air flow environments are being studied currently for their effectiveness.

COMPLICATIONS

Major complications following transplantation involve the occurrence of rejection of the donor graft by the recipient and acute or chronic graft versus host disease, in which the infused lymphoid cells in the graft reject the recipient. Despite donor–recipient matching, the frequency of graft versus host disease is 70%, with a 25% mortality rate (Spruce, 1983). The appearance of manifestations of acute GVHD can occur as early as 7 days or as late as 150 days after transplantation, and consist of involvement of skin, liver, intestinal tract, and lymphoid system (Dicke, et al., 1983).

Chronic GVHD has become a major complication in those who survive 150 days. As many as one third of these patients may be affected (Spruce, 1983). Most of them have had acute GVHD and manifest extensive symptomatology, with skin, liver, gastrointestinal, musculoskeletal, pulmonary, and immune system dysfunctions. In terms of progression of symptoms, untreated patients manifest deterioration of status to post-Karnovsky performance status and death. Treatment involves corticosteroid therapy and the use of cyclophosphamide, which modifies or permanently arrests the course of GVHD (Dicke, et al., 1983). A summary of signs, symptoms, and nursing considerations for both acute and chronic GVH are presented in Table 6-5. Although the incidence of GVHD overall has not appreciably changed, the severe form of the disease and resulting mortality appear to have decreased. It is interesting to note, however, that the occurrence of GVHD seems to have an antileukemic effect. This presents a unique paradox in treatment, that is, no GVHD, less risk of fatal infection, but greater risk of recurrence of leukemia (Johnson, 1981). Prevention of GVHD has been attempted with the use of small weekly doses of methotrexate, the immunomodulating agent cyclosporin A (CSA), and through the removal of immunocompetent T-cells from the donated marrow (Wiley, et al., 1983; Tutschka, et al., 1983). Research is ongoing as to the efficacy of these and other methods to reduce the incidence of the significant problem of GVHD in allogeneic transplantation.

Other problems that face the post-transplant patient include interstitial pneumonia and complications from the conditioning regimen. Incidence of interstitial pneumonia has been reported to be as high as 40% to 50% of allogeneic transplant patients who survive more than 30 days post-transplant, with a mortality of 60% to 70%. Cytomegalovirus (CMV) is isolated as the associated organism in one half of the cases (Wiley, et al., 1983; Tutschka, et al., 1983). *Pneumocystis carinii* pneumonia had been previously problematic for these patients, but prophylactic use of Bactrim has diminished this problem. Complications from the conditioning regimen may occur post-transplant and include mucositis, nausea and vomiting, diarrhea, inappropriate antidiuretic hormone secretion, nephropathy, and heart failure (Wiley, et al., 1983). All patients are at high risk for bacterial and fungal infections in the period 3 to 4 weeks post-transplantation. With improved therapy the mortality rate, however, is low.

Late sequalae of BMT have been identified. These include cataracts, which developed in over 50% of the patients followed for more than 2 years, effects on the growth process from total body irradiation, and diminished fertility (Wiley, et al., 1983). The psychological effects of intensive treatment and isolation may be significant and include long-term effects of isolation and body image disturbances. Long-term followup and counseling usually is recom-

mended. The economic impact is sizeable with the average cost of transplant being between $60,000 and $80,000. A hospital stay of 30 to 60 days usually is required. Third party payment varies—financial arrangements and funding information are usually explored on a case-by-case basis (Wiley, et al., 1983).

BIOLOGICAL RESPONSE MODIFIER THERAPY

Biological response modifiers are factors or approaches that modify the interaction between the malignant process and the host. Usually this interaction is influenced to bring about a therapeutic benefit. Although clinical trials have produced variable results, it is widely held that there is a relationship between tumor and host that can be modified, either by affecting the host's response or the tumor cells. The various types of immunotherapy and interferon are both examples of biological response modifiers (Scogna and Schoenberger, 1982) (Fig. 6-2).

Immunotherapy

Immunotherapy has become a recognized component of multimodal therapy. In most centers, it involves the initial use of cytoreduction chemotherapy to reduce the tumor burden. This is followed by the immunotherapy manipulations, which have as their goal the improvement of patient survival (Murphy and Hersh, 1980). The use of immunotherapy in acute leukemia has been attempted due to (1) the documented success of experimental trials in animals, (2) relapse and death of many patients with leukemia following chemotherapy-induced remissions, and (3) the promising results reported by Mathé in a 1969 study (cited in Murphy and Hersh, 1980). Although in its early stages of development, human immunotherapy has been added to the chemotherapeutic regimen in patients with certain leukemias to

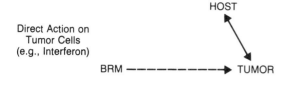

Direct Action on
Tumor Cells
(e.g., Interferon)

Enhancement of
Host Response
(e.g., BCG, MER)

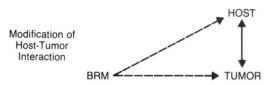

Modification of
Host-Tumor
Interaction

FIG. 6-2. *Biological response modifiers:
Theorized mechanisms of action.*

improve the efficacy of the chemotherapy and decrease the concurrent immunosuppression in treated patients. In addition to maintaining immunologic competence, the aim of this therapy is to support the capacity of the immune system to destroy residual leukemia cells (Murphy and Hersh, 1980).

INDICATIONS

According to Mahoney and Starling (1981) in a review of research using immunotherapy in acute childhood leukemia, the bulk of the clinical trials have failed to demonstrate a beneficial effect, although an increased median survival time has been frequently observed. These authors propose that in children with acute myelogenous leukemia, however, immunotherapy may be indicated in view of the generally poor long-term prognosis associated with this disease.

Another important indication may be the immunorestoration of impaired host defense mechanisms, which are the result of both the disease process and intensive chemotherapy. In some studies a decrease in the incidence of fatal infections observed in patients maintained on immunotherapy has been attributed to this immunorestoration (Murphy and Hersh, 1980).

Research is currently underway that may demonstrate the use of the potential capacity of the human immune system to be tumoricidal in vitro, and at tumor sites other than the skin. The success of immunotherapy against dermal deposits has been noted using local immunotherapy with the bacillus of Calmette–Guérin (BCG) or other antigens (LoBuglio, 1980).

PROCEDURE

The original local immunotherapy using BCG is primarily administered using application of BCG with scarification. Treatment areas include axilla, groin, and other areas when needed. In melanoma the site treated is that of the primary disease, for example. The areas to be treated are cleansed, and BCG liquid is applied to the skin by spreading it with a sterile gloved finger. The tine, a multipronged grid, is pressed firmly into the skin through the liquid. BCG is then reapplied and a small hair dryer on a cool setting is used to dry each site. Careful skin care and observation for local inflammatory reactions are important interventions (Carroll, 1978).

Newer techniques include the cloning of more specific antibodies in the treatment of T-cell lymphoma and leukemia. In one study seven of eight patients had measurable tumor responses although there were not complete responses to mouse hybridoma monoclonal antibody. Dosages and dose schedule were developed over the course of the study. It was found that slow IV infusion of antibody over 4 to 6 hours on a biweekly schedule was most effective (DiJulio and Bedigian, 1983).

COMPLICATIONS

Side-effects vary with the immunotherapeutic agent, dose, and route. Generally side-effects with BCG are mild and include pruritis, fever, chills, flaring at previous injection sites, and occasional lymphadenopathy. In one report only 1% of patients had to discontinue therapy due to toxicity. With methanol-extraction residue of BCG (MER) similar side-effects are possible and occasionally severe systemic complications may occur. Immunotherapy in children generally is well tolerated, however (Mahoney and Starling, 1981). Unlike surgery, radiation, and chemotherapy, immunotherapy attacks cancer cells specifically and does not damage normal cells.

With monoclonal antibodies, careful monitoring to detect allergic reaction and renal function abnormalities is important. Infection is also a possible complication, although infection is an ever-present threat with this type of patient (DiJulio and Bedigian, 1983).

Interferon

Interferon is a naturally occurring protein that is not itself an antiviral agent. It has been found to inhibit the growth of viruses. Theoretically, it is believed to act by initiating DNA-directed RNA synthesis and protein synthesis. The rate of growth of a new protein molecule is depressed. The antitumor effect may thus be the combined or exclusive result of inhibition of tumor virus replication, cell transformation by a virus, or inhibition of tumor growth through the effects of the immune system (McAdams, 1980; Scogna and Schoenberger, 1982).

INDICATIONS

Interferon has been studied for its efficacy in a number of human cancers including breast cancer, lymphoma, multiple myeloma, prostate cancer, and ovarian cancer. Although research is currently underway, positive response has been noted in many patients studied. The evidence is not yet complete regarding efficacy in childhood cancer, but in preliminary research on patients in Finland with a variety of cancers, including leukemia and lymphoma, patients who were treated with interferon had an acute antitumor effect. Also interferon seemed to interact positively with chemotherapeutic agents. Research has been inhibited by a lack of available pure interferon and the difficulty and cost of production. Recombinant DNA methods for producing interferon are under study for their efficacy. It is likely that the cost of production will be greatly reduced by these methods (Merigan, 1982).

In a different study, Arvin and colleagues (1982) noted that in a randomized double-blind placebo controlled study of 44 children with cancer and varicella, interferon had an antiviral effect against the varicella virus. When interferon was administered early in the course of the disease, the patients given interferon had fewer days of formation of new lesions, reduced dissemination of the disease, and decreased incidence of complications.

PROCEDURE

In most clinical trials interferon has been administered by intramuscular or subcutaneous injection. The substance reaches the circulatory system within 5 to 8 hours of intramuscular injection, and within 8 to 10 hours when injected subcutaneously. Repeated injections every 12 hours maintain the serum level. The course of treatment and dosage is variable depending on patient characteristics, cancer site, and so on. Interferon is known to be only minimally cleared by the kidney and the liver; it penetrates poorly into respiratory, central nervous system, and eye tissues. Since this substance is still being studied, and particularly without demonstrated effects in children, its use should be carefully monitored and governed by a research protocol.

COMPLICATIONS

Side-effects have included fever, particularly after initial doses, nausea, vomiting, myalgia, and chills. Lassitude and malaise and local reactions have occurred with subcutaneous administration (Mayer and Smalley, 1983; Scogna and Schoenberger, 1983). Of greater importance is the marrow suppressive effect, which reverses rapidly once therapy is discontinued (Scogna and Schoenberger, 1983; McAdams, 1980).

UNPROVEN METHODS

The American Cancer Society periodically updates its publication, *Unproven Methods of Cancer Management,* with methods that are purported to cure cancer. People with cancer and their families may become interested in these unproven methods for many reasons. Some of these include fear of and ignorance regarding cancer and its treatment and hope for a painless, sure cure (Isler, 1974). It would be impossible to outline all of the known methods here, but this section will describe briefly those that are most controversial or widely used. The reader is referred to the Yellow Pages and the above-mentioned publication for more detailed information. Two research studies will be cited at the conclusion of this section which estimate the prevalence and rationale for knowledge and use of alternative therapies in pediatric oncology populations.

CLASSIFICATION OF UNPROVEN REMEDIES

DEVICES

This method includes electrical gadgets, diathermy and hyperthermia machines, and charms. Machines have been promoted by various inventors, bearing their names, such as the Hubbard E. Meter, Drown Radio Therapeutic Instrument, or the Dotto Electronic Reactor (Howard-Ruben and Miller, 1983). Some types of faith healing may use various implements or equipment.

METABOLIC THERAPIES

These methods for treatment of cancer exist in abundance. Advocates of metabolic cancer therapies propose that cure is attained through supporting the individual's vital forces and defense mechanisms, minimizing carcinogen intake, promoting excretion of toxic waste, and developing a positive mental outlook (Howard-Ruben and Miller, 1983).

An example of a metabolic regimen is the "grape cure," which calls for strict adherence to an exclusive diet of grapes for a specific period followed by gradual introduction of other foods, megavitamins, and mineral therapy. Other types of dietary prescriptions include the use of herbal and medicinal teas, certain vegetable juices, and high colonic coffee enemas. Megavitamins may be administered to patients in addition to drug products. Research into potential links between cancer and vitamins is ongoing. This aspect appears significant in that numerous theories regarding the protective qualities of certain vitamins and carcinogenic enhancing qualities of others have been developed. However, as yet, no definitive cause and effect relationship has been established between a particular vitamin and human cancer. The vitamins that have received the most attention and study are vitamins A, C, D, and E. Although the studies regarding vitamins C and E suggest their anticarcinogenic properties in animals, research attempting to replicate an increased survival time in humans treated with high-dose vitamin C is unsupported. Vitamin A has been proven to be anticarcinogenic in animal studies, but its toxicity in large doses remains a problem in conducting clinical trials of its effectiveness in humans (Shamberger, 1982).

DRUGS, VACCINES, AND ENZYMES

These substances comprise a third group of unproven methods. The most famous among these biological therapies are the drugs Krebiozen and Laetrile. Federal investigation of Krebiozen found it to be composed of small amounts of creatinine and mineral oil and to have no demonstrable anticancer effect (Isler, 1974). Laetrile has been the object of much publicized social and legal controversy since its promotion in the 1950s by Ernest Krebs, Jr., son of its discoverer, Ernest Krebs, Sr. The predominant ingredient of Laetrile, amygdalin, had been determined too dangerous for human use by the senior Krebs; however, his son reintroduced it as a cancer cure. The promotion of the product has over the years become the crusade of various groups, chief among them the John Birch Society. The use of the drug became an issue involving personal freedom of choice. Also the fact that Laetrile was made from a variety of organic products attracted individuals who were against chemical additives and drugs. Assertions have been made that the production and sale of this relatively inexpensive to make compound have been a profitable venture for a few key promoters. Most individuals who use Laetrile are pressured into purchasing, in addition, a multitude of other products at premium prices, including vitamins, enzymes, special supplements, and so on. The widespread advertising of Laetrile as "safe" had been based primarily on its classification as a vitamin, despite the fact that the substance fails to meet the criteria for a vitamin and has been rejected as a vitamin by the National Nutrition Consortium and others (Lerner, 1981). Laetrile has been studied by the FDA and the National Cancer Institute and has failed consistently to show reproducible benefit (Howard-Ruben and Miller, 1984). The NCI study, a retrospective analysis of human experiences with Laetrile, found only 68 Laetrile-treated cases evaluable. Of these 68 cases, 6 demonstrated improvement in their cancer at the time of treatment with Laetrile.

A further problem is the potential toxicity of the substance. Amygdalin contains 6% cyanide by weight. Usually the largest portion of the cyanide component is excreted through the intestines following an ingested dose. If Laetrile is taken with any one of a number of foods containing beta-glucosidase, however, much larger amounts of cyanide can be released. There have been documented cases of cyanide poisoning following accidental ingestion of Laetrile tablets (Lerner, 1981). Following such reports the FDA widely distributed information about the drug's toxicity. Related to the issue of toxic effects, a study done in a major cancer center found that approximately one fourth of the patients interviewed were unaware of Laetrile toxicity (Pendergrass and Davis, 1981).

USE OF UNPROVEN METHODS

Regarding the frequency of the use of alternative or unproven therapies, in a study of 106 patients, one in twenty children received some alternative form of cancer therapy (Pendergrass and Davis, 1981). This reported level of use excluded the category "faith healer," however, since the researchers felt that the parents' interpretation of the term was broad and the reported usage was a falsely high estimate. An important set of implications drawn from this study was an analysis of factors that cause parents to choose an alternative form of treatment. Of utmost influence was the failure of conventional therapy to control the disease. Related to this failure, many parents sought unproven methods to minimize pain or to reduce the trauma of invasive procedures. Unproven methods that were easy to use, such as oral versus injectable, were sought in this situation. Lastly some parents tended to turn to alternative forms of therapy when they felt dissatisfied with their role in their child's care. Highly technical hospital procedures can make the parent feel isolated and helpless, while some alternative methods include important roles for the parent, for example, diet modification therapies, which enhance the parents' feelings of control (Pendergrass and Davis, 1981).

Similar findings were documented in another major cancer center, with a level of usage of alternative therapies reported as less than 10% (Copeland, et al., 1983). No patients or parents reported the use of Laetrile. A significant number of parents expressed the need for more information regarding their child's cancer treatment. It can be inferred that, as noted in the Pendergrass study, parents tended to consider alternative therapies when they were dissatisfied with their perceived involvement in their child's care. The parents' perceived lack of information regarding treatment may be seen as related to a need to feel more involved in the experience, and this could influence the choice of alternative therapies.

In the Copeland study almost 50% of the sample was Hispanic; there were some noteworthy differences between the two cultural groups — Anglo and Hispanic. The Hispanic parents wanted more information about alternative therapies from the medical staff. In addition, they reported feeling less willing to approach their physicians. This factor may have contributed to a lack of a sense of participation in the treatment regimen. Non-English speaking respondents also were more likely to express a desire to have the treatment plan explained again. Although limited in their ability to generalize to other populations or cultural groups, these findings indicate that those of other cultural groups may be more likely to turn to alternative therapies. This may occur because of a perception of exclusion due to language barriers and a feeling of reluctance to approach the physician with questions.

To summarize the general area of the use of unproven drugs, two research studies document that the actual level of use is relatively small. A substantial number of parents are unaware of drug toxicities, however. Furthermore those who do choose alternative therapies tend to do so when conventional therapies have failed or as an attempt to relieve pain. Most parents who used unproven methods in these samples maintained their involvement with traditional medical treatment. The investigators do note, however, that there may be an unknown number of families outside the mainstream of conventional medicine who are using unproven methods exclusively (Copeland, et al., 1983). Again it appears there is some relation between the parents' feeling of being involved and adequately informed and their tendency to consider the use of unproven methods.

CONCLUSION

This chapter has covered the range of supportive therapies, adjunctive treatment modalities, and the most frequently encountered unproven methods. An overview of the rationale, indications, procedural implications, and common side-effects have been presented. The role of supportive and adjunctive therapies is becoming increasingly important in the complex treatment for cancer. The use of unproven methods also merits the consideration of health professionals in the total care of the child and family with cancer, both from the point of view of counseling and because of the potential physiological impact on the child.

KEY POINTS

- Supportive therapies, particularly hematologic and nutritional ones, are frequently used to enhance survival of the child with cancer. "Curative" therapies then can be administered for their maximum effect.

- Behavioral techniques have been demonstrated in recent research to reduce the incidence and intensity of treatment-related problems, particularly nausea, vomiting, and procedural pain. Some patients have chosen to use imagery techniques as a direct cancer-killing therapy, but scientific documentation of this usage is not conclusive.

- Bone marrow transplantation is an important technique usually used with patients with ALL who have relapsed on conventional therapy, or with other types of leukemia patients, such as those with ANLL, with unfavorable prognoses. Problems of rejection, graft versus host disease, and infection may need to be addressed during the post-transplant course.

- Biological response modifiers are relatively new additions to cancer therapy and hold promise for the future. Interferon and various immunotherapy agents have been given for various types of cancers with some success. Side-effects are generally mild. A great advantage is the specificity of these treatments for malignant cells, sparing normal cells.

- Unproven methods are used by families of children with cancer, although the level of usage seems relatively low among those families followed in cancer centers. A perception of lack of involvement in the treatment plan and progression of the child's disease despite conventional treatment are associated with the use of unproven methods. Lack of information regarding potential toxicities of these therapies and the desire to better understand the conventional treatment protocol is a problem expressed by many parents.

REFERENCES

American Cancer Society (1982). Unproven methods of cancer management: O. Carl Simonton, M.D. *Ca-Cancer Journal for Clinicians, 32,* 59–61.

Appleby, L. (1983). Initiation, maintenance and termination of total parenteral nutrition. *Journal of the National Intravenous Therapy Association, 6,* 31–35.

Arvin, A., Kushner, J., Feldman, S., Baehner, R., Hammond D., and Merigan, I. (1982). Human leukocyte interferon for the treatment of varicella in children with cancer. *New England Journal of Medicine, 306,* 761–765.

Bahu, G. (1983). Administering blood safely, *American Operating Room Nurses Journal, 37,* 1073–1100.

Boland, M., and Gaskill, T. (1984). Managing AIDS in children. *Maternal Child Nursing Journal, 9,* 384–389.

Bussey, H. (1984). Components of total parenteral nutrition solutions. *Journal of the National Intravenous Therapy Association, 7,* 209–213.

Carroll, R. (1978). BCG immunotherapy by the tine technique: the nurse's role. *Cancer Nursing, 1,* 241–246.

Centers for Disease Control (1983). Update: AIDS. *Morbidity and Mortality Weekly Reports, 32,* 465.

Cogliana-Shutta, N., Broda, E., and Gress, J. (1985). Bone marrow transplantation. *Nursing Clinics of North America, 20,* 49–65.

Copeland, D., Silverberg, Z., and Pfefferbaum, B. (1983). Attitudes and practices of families of children in treatment for cancer. *American Journal of Pediatric Hematology/Oncology, 5,* 65–71.

Cotanch, P., Hockenberry, M., and Hermann, S., (1985). Self hypnosis as anti-emetic therapy in children receiving chemotherapy. *Oncology Nursing Forum, 12,* 41–46.

Culbert, S., and Pickering, L. (1984). Physiologic support. In W. Sutow, D. Fernback, and T. Vietti (Eds.), *Clinical pediatric oncology* (3rd. ed., pp. 267–302). St. Louis: C. V. Mosby.

Curtiss, F. (1983). Third party reimbursement for home parenteral nutrition and IV therapy. *Journal of the National Intravenous Therapy Association, 6,* 193–197.

Daley, T., and Greenspun, E. (1981). Stress management through hypnosis. D. Sutterly and G. Donnelly (Eds.), In *Coping with stress: A nursing perspective* (pp. 225–231). Rockville, MD: Aspen.

Dicke, A., Kanojia, M., and Zander, A. (1983). Allogeneic bone marrow transplantation in hematologic disorders. *Cancer Bulletin, 35,* 23–28.

DiJulio, J., and Gedigan, J. (1983). Hybridoma monoclonal antibody treatment of T-cell lymphomas: Clinical experience and nursing management. *Oncology Nursing Forum, 10,* 22–27.

Fox, B. (1982). Psychogenic etiology and prognosis of cancer: Current status of theory. In (Eds.), A., Christ and D., Flomenhaft, Childhood cancer: Impact on the family (pp. 3–29). New York: Plenum Press.

Hazinski, M. (1984). *Nursing care of the critically ill child,* pp. 90–104, St Louis: C. V. Mosby.

Hockenberry, M., and Bologna-Vaughn, S. (1985). Preparation for intrusive procedures using non-invasive techniques in children with cancer: State of the art versus new trends. *Cancer Nursing, 8,* 97–102.

Howard-Ruben, J. and Miller, N. (1984). Unproven methods of cancer management, part II: Current trends and implications for patient care. *Oncology Nursing Forum, 11,* 67–73.

Hushen, S. (1982). Questioning TPN as the answer. *American Journal of Nursing, 82,* 852–854.

Hutchison, M., (1982). Administration of fat emulsions. *American Journal of Nursing, 82,* 275–77.

Isler, C. (1974). The fatal choice: Cancer quackery, *RN, 37,* 55–59.

Kellerman, J., Zeltzer, L., Ellenberg, L., and Dash, J. (1983). Adolescents with cancer. *Journal of Adolescent Health Care, 4,* 85–90.

Konstantinides, N. (1985). Home parenteral nutrition: A viable alternative for patients with cancer. *Oncology Nursing Forum, 12,* 23–29.

Lerner, I. (1981). Laetrile: A Lesson in Cancer Quackery. *Ca-Cancer Journal for Clinicians, 31,* 91–95.

Lobuglio, A. (1980). Approaches to human immunotherapy. In A. LoBuglio (Ed.), *Clinical immunotherapy* (Vol. II, pp. 1–4). New York: Marcel Decker, Inc.

Lum, L., and Gallager-Allred, C. (1984). Nutrition and the cancer patient: A cooperative effort by nursing and dieticians to overcome problems. *Cancer Nursing, 7,* 469–474.

Mahoney, D., and Starling, D. (1981). Immunotherapy in acute leukemias. *The American Journal of Pediatric Hematology/Oncology, 3,* 409–418.

Masoorli, S., and Piercy, S. (1984). A lifesaving guide to blood products. *RN, 47,* 32–37.

Mayer, D., and Smalley, R. (1983). Interferon: Current status. *Oncology Nursing Forum, 10,* 14–19.

McAdams, C. (1980). Interferon: The penicillin of the future. *American Journal of Nursing, 80,* 714–718

Merigan, T. (1982). Interferon—The first quarter century. *Journal of the American Medical Association, 248,* 2513–2516.

Miller, N., and Howard-Ruben, J. (1983). Unproven methods of cancer management, part I: Background and historical perspectives. *Oncology Nursing Forum, 10,* 46–52.

Murphy, S., and Hersh, E. (1980). Human leukemia. In A. Lobuglio (Ed.), *Clinical immunotherapy.* New York: Marcel Decker.

Olness, K. (1981). Imagery (self hypnosis) as adjunct therapy in childhood cancer. *American Journal of Pediatric Hematology/Oncology, 3,* 313–321.

Parfitt, D., and Thompson, V. (1980). Pediatric home hyperalimentation: Educating the family. *Maternal Child Nursing Journal, 5,* 196–202.

Pendergrass, T., and Davis, S. (1981). Knowledge and use of alternative cancer therapies in children. *American Journal of Pediatric Hematology/Oncology, 3,* 339–345.

Rapp, M., Hilkmeyer, R., Copeland, E., and Dudrick, S. (1976). Hyperalimentation. *Nursing '76, 39,* 1–8.

Redd, W., and Hendler, C. (1984). Learned Aversions to Chemotherapy Treatment. *Health Education Quarterly, 10,* Special Supplement, Spring, 57–65.

Ryan, J., and Gough, J. (1984). Complications of central venous catheterization for total parenteral nutrition: Role of the nurse. *Journal of the National Intravenous Therapy Association, 7,* 29–35.

Scogna, D., and Schoenberger, C. (1982). Biological response modifiers: An overview and nursing implications. *Oncology Nursing Forum, 9,* 45–49.

Shamberger, R. (1982). Vitamins and cancer: Current controversies. *Cancer Bulletin, 34,* 150–153.

Spruce, W. (1983). Bone marrow transplantation: Major problems and future directions. *American Journal of Pediatric Hematology/Oncology, 5,* 301–306.

Spruce, W. (1983). Bone marrow transplantation: Use in neoplastic disease. *American Journal of Pediatric Hematology/Oncology, 5,* 287–293.

Tutschka, P., Beschorner, W., Hess, A., and Santos, C. (1983). Cyclosporin-A to prevent graft versus host disease. *Blood, 61,* 318–325.

Waley, L., and Wong, D. (1983). *Nursing care of infants and children* (2nd ed., pp. 1338–1376). St. Louis: C. V. Mosby.

Wiley, F., and Decuir-Whalley, S. (1983). Allogeneic bone marrow transplantation for children with acute leukemia. *Oncology Nursing Forum, 10,* 49–53.

Zeltzer, L., Kellerman, J., Ellenberg, L., and Dash, J., (1984). Hypnosis for the reduction of vomiting associated with chemotherapy and disease in adolescents with cancer. *Journal of Adolescent Health Care, 4,* 77–84.

7

FAMILY AND INFLUENTIAL OTHERS — WHAT HAPPENS TO THEM?

INTRODUCTION

Families can and do cope effectively with the crisis of childhood cancer. The process will vary with individual characteristics of families that experience this crisis. Of importance are the coping resources and mechanisms of the family; the characteristics and developmental levels of the family members; the environmental factors influencing the family (both human and material); the unique course of the child's illness, and the family's interpretation of the cancer experience and its meaning to their lives. This chapter will focus on the family and the significant others who play a crucial role in the process of managing the crisis of childhood cancer. A brief introduction to coping behavior of the adult and the child will furnish a background for consideration of individual members' special needs and responses.

Variations in the nuclear family that may affect the stress response or coping response of the family are presented. The influence of the developmental level, particularly in regard to well siblings, also is discussed. The various roles extended family and community factors play in the experience and the ways these supports can be used by the family are also considered. Each section of this chapter will present helpful nursing strategies that are effective in supporting the family's constructive coping efforts.

THEORIES OF COPING BEHAVIOR

Members of families bring different levels of coping skills to a crisis. Commonalities in the coping process for all family members, regardless of age and developmental level, and the specific adaptations made by adult and child family members, are useful to consider when planning nursing support.

Coping is a process encompassing cognitive, emotional, and behavioral activities that are used to deal with a threat situation. Coping behaviors are skills learned by individuals through past experience and experimentation. This process is always a dynamic one, with new information and new challenges being balanced by existing resources and skills. In some instances people may be temporarily or permanently overwhelmed by the demands placed upon them and suffer coping failure. The ability to cope is not an innate skill, but one that is learned; therefore, the individual can improve coping efforts by learning and practicing more constructive coping behaviors.

The first step in the coping process is an appraisal of the threat situation (Fig. 7-1). Usually this involves a thought process in which the implications of the crisis, including its meaning for the individual and for significant others, are considered. Upon learning that their child has cancer, parents will immediately assign a value

149

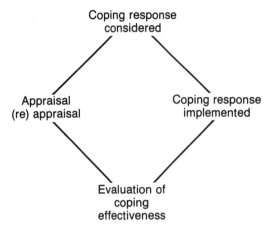

Coping response
considered

Appraisal   Coping response
(re) appraisal   implemented

Evaluation of
coping
effectiveness

FIG. 7-1. A model of coping behavior.

to the crisis, usually a negative one. They almost automatically anticipate the loss of the child, long-term pain and suffering, and the enormous financial burden, as these are commonly associated with cancer in the United States.

The belief system and cultural context of the individual will affect this appraisal process. In cultures where physical attractiveness is highly prized, for example, in the American and some Middle Eastern societies, the implication of weight loss and alopecia may have more influence than in others where performance or intellectual capacity are more desired traits.

The individual then considers the amount of control he or she can exert over the stressor. In other words, there is an acknowledgment of the fact that a crisis exists; now what can be done about it? At this point some crises can be resolved immediately—for example, putting out a fire in a wastebasket—by direct action on the part of the person. Parental response such as taking the newly diagnosed child to a specialist may be less direct, perhaps, but is perceived as helpful. Another example of a healthy response at this point might be a child's denial of the truth of the diagnosis, indicating a capacity for control of the stress by not letting it into one's consciousness. Short-term denial by parents

and children is a common and constructive response that gives people time to gather their resources for coping.

Another consideration in this initial control step is the appraisal of potential resources for managing the crisis. Parents may think of the availability of the extended family members to care for well children. Siblings may reach out to a favorite friend or an animal. Both parents and siblings may recognize a need for more information to better deal with the situation.

Following this appraisal of possible control mechanisms, the individual usually is prepared to implement a selected coping response. The action taken at this point will be influenced by the previous processes and by past experience. Each member of the family brings a set of learned responses to the crisis that probably will be attempted if those responses have been successful in the past. This is a common time for a parent to express a feeling of being overwhelmed. Most families have not had to deal with a crisis of this magnitude and are initially at a loss for a model of successful management of such a situation. In a later section the support of other parents in the same situation will be considered as one valuable avenue of constructive action.

For many families implementation of coping behavior may be a trial and error period. Nevertheless, some common strategies have been observed as useful to confront a major crisis. Hamburg and Adams (1967) studied parents of children diagnosed as having leukemia. They found that a method used by many of the parents in this crisis situation was the seeking of information pertinent to the diagnosis, new responsibilities, the treatment plan, and ways of preparing to grieve. Although certainly not an all-encompassing coping strategy, the seeking of information can be a powerful strategy for each member of the family. In this regard Chesler and Barbarin (1984) found that parents in their sample identified the problems of being excluded from their child's care and the failure of the health-care professionals to acknowledge them as knowledgeable partners in their child's care to be most bothersome to them. Related to acquiring information many families find it reassuring to learn and practice new skills and to rehearse possible alternative outcomes. Examples of these coping strategies include a parents developing skill in nasogastric tube feeding techniques or the management of hyperalimentation therapy in preparation for discharge. In addition to learning these skills, a well-prepared parent will want to anticipate possible problems and solve these potential difficulties in advance so that immediate action can be taken if the need arises.

Some families have discovered that finding meaning in the stress experience has been a constructive coping strategy. Examples of this are families who make a practice of reaching out to new families facing the diagnosis. The national Candlelighters Foundation, a support group of parents of children with cancer, sprang from such a context. A final example of a very helpful coping strategy is seeking and receiving emotional support from others. For some the ability to accept support is a natural process; for other individuals a crisis situation influences their ability to rely on or be supported by others.

The preceding discussion focused on examples of coping behaviors that promote effective management of the crisis situation. Not all families consistently use constructive behaviors. The classic defense mechanisms such as repression, denial, projection, and so on, may be used exclusively or may be used intermittently with consciously applied cognitive and behavioral strategies. In addition, families may use tension-relieving strategies — drinking or drugs, eating, sleeping, crying, and the like — as their primary or secondary responses.

Coping behavior is usually followed at some point by a reappraisal of the situation and an assessment of the effectiveness of the coping behavior. This step will usually lead to continu-

ation of the use of successful coping strategies and attempts to change those that are ineffective. In the evaluation of a family's coping responses, this last step is a key point to keep in mind. Successful management of the crisis is the desired outcome, and families may achieve this goal in a multitude of ways. Constructive coping is best judged by its efficacy; what appears to be unhealthy coping may be, in actuality, a family's best possible response to the crisis for them at that time.

Miller (1983) proposes some outcomes indicating successful coping that are useful in directing the attention of the health-care provider to the results of the coping efforts. She has identified five criteria for effective coping in a study of chronically ill adults, which seem to be generally applicable to family members and pediatric patients:

1. Uncomfortable feelings (anxiety, fear, grief) contained
2. Hope generated
3. Self-esteem enhanced
4. Relationships with others maintained
5. State of wellness maintained or improved

CHARACTERISTICS OF FAMILIES COPING UNDER THE STRESS OF CANCER IN THEIR CHILD

Studies of families of children with cancer, based on projective and objective measures and interviews, report commonalities in effective coping behavior. Strategies reported as being the "strongest and most viable sources for survival and mastery" of the experience of childhood cancer included spouse or significant other support, religious belief or belief in a fundamental meaning of life, and honesty with the children when responding to their questions (Spinetta and Deasy-Spinetta, 1981). In their research these investigators have developed a Family Adjustment Scale, which assesses family coping behavior in six categories that the family unit should meet:

1. The emotional needs of the patient
2. The emotional needs of the siblings
3. The emotional needs of the mother
4. The emotional needs of the father
5. The medical needs of the patient
6. The day-to-day needs of family members

This scale is used by the health team caring for the family and is correlated with psychometric measurement of the family adjustment pattern. This instrument was found to be valid in measuring the family's overall adjustment and thus may prove to be helpful in care planning and predictive intervention with these families.

In other research Battle (1975) reports a range of family feelings including guilt, sorrow, panic, inadequacy, and embarrassment, which occur with the diagnosis of chronic illness. To cope with these feelings demands the family's management of several identified conflicts in various domains of family function. Among these are the tasks of dealing with strained marital relationships; difficulties in everyday care of the affected child including frequent trips to a hospital or clinic; difficulties in supporting siblings' reactions and behaviors; and difficulties in dealing with community agencies. Teyber and Littlehales (1981) note that these feelings and problems are pervasive and are seldom resolved fully at any stage of the child's illness. Parenting competence may diminish under the onslaught of such demands. At the same time the affected child and siblings continue to expect and need parenting and gratification of their needs, just as they did prior to the illness.

CHARACTERISTICS OF CHILDREN'S COPING PATTERNS

Before discussion of the adaptations made by chronically ill children and their siblings, the underlying development of coping behavior in children must be considered. Vipperman and Roger (1980) have defined a maturational program of childhood coping behaviors based on cognitive, emotional, and behavioral development. Developing a sense of trust in caretakers and environment, infants learn primarily through motor activity that may be goal oriented or impulsive tension release. Examples include body rocking, toy manipulation, avoidance of undesirable stimuli, and crying to bring attention to their needs.

Toddlers continue to learn through sensorimotor means. In addition, as they develop a sense of autonomy and independence, they begin Piaget's stage of preoperational thought. This makes them capable of higher level coping responses than the generalized responses exhibited in infancy. Some commonly seen behaviors in response to stress include separation anxiety, regression, and aggression. Additionally some toddlers engage in fantasy and are able actively to play out tension-producing experiences in an attempt to master them. Seeking to establish a sense of initiative, preschoolers continue their cognitive development in the preoperational area. They continue to cope through the use of fantasy and "acting out." They are also capable of a host of self-care skills. They strive to retain control over care situations by such diverse methods as aggressive protest, withdrawal, or regression. Being innately curious, experimentation and exploration are common and may be used as coping strategies.

Having achieved a certain degree of autonomy and independence, the school-age child strives for a sense of industry. Capable of higher thought processes, the use of concrete operations is characteristic at this stage. Although various defense mechanisms will continue to be used, including aggression and regression, the school-age child will often attack a problem using a more cognitive approach. A child at this age seeks explanations and understanding in order to control the situation. An increasing knowledge base will help the child to understand body functions and disease processes. Motor activity continues to be an outlet for tension as in the past. In the adolescent, cognitive problem solving continues to be used and is strengthened by the ability to conceptualize. At this stage the adolescent strives for identity and is characterized by abstract thought processes, or formal operations. As in each of the other age groups, defense mechanisms continue to be used, now including rationalization and intellectualization. Although capable of higher order intellectual processes, the adolescent may resort to negativistic behavior similar to the toddler, or very egocentric behavior typical of toddlers and preschoolers, in frustrating or stressful situations. The coping processes of the child increase in range and complexity with age and are facilitated by advancing cognitive, motor, and social skills (Vipperman and Roger, 1980).

PARENTS COPING WITH CANCER IN THEIR CHILD

In recent years the outlook for pediatric cancer patients has improved vastly. For many children, cure is now a realistic hope. But this cure brings with it a tremendous long-term demand on parental resources. The chronic nature of the illness, together with the still common fear of the terminal potential of cancer, brings about a host of parental feelings and behaviors. Common parental feelings include anxiety, denial, anger, guilt, and fear (Battle, 1975). Guilt is particularly difficult to manage. In our society parents hold primary responsibility for their children's well-being and care. Parents are likely to respond to a catastrophic illness in their child with guilt related to a feeling of responsibility for having caused or allowed it to happen (Ross, 1980). Guilt can be an almost incapacitating emotion. The helpless inadequacy engendered by guilt feelings temporarily

may cause a lack of confidence and inability to make decisions (Ross, 1980).

Of particular note are parental responses differentiated by sex. For many reasons much of the burden of the child's everyday care frequently falls on the mother. In a study of two-parent families in which both parents were working, it was more likely that the mother rearranged work schedules or missed work to be with the child than the father (Knafl, et al., 1982). In addition to work-related problems and the resentment and emotional tension such a situation evokes, the mother frequently experiences particular feelings of guilt when she shoulders this responsibility for the child's care virtually alone. Some mothers can identify the resentment that this feeling of sole responsibility can induce. Spinetta and Deasy-Spinetta (1981) interviewed parents and noted one mother who verbalized her feeling of "being dumped on." When she and her husband began to communicate more effectively, they realized that while she felt resentful over the heavy burden of care she bore, he felt left out of his child's life. This may be the situation frequently when one parent, mother or father, assumes the largest share of responsibility and the parents do not communicate well.

In an interesting presentation of case studies from her practice with families of chronically ill children, Donna Wong (1980) has identified the "empty mother syndrome." This is described as the occurrence of a "dead feeling," a response to the death of a child after long years of caring for that child. While identifying the sorrow and loss felt by all family members, the mother is particularly at risk due to the likelihood that she has been the primary caretaker throughout the long illness. Suddenly, if the illness is terminal, she no longer has this special mothering role. Often over time she may have postponed her career, failed to maintain social relationships, and in some cases may have even grown distant from her spouse and other children. Wong noted differences in the regrets expressed by the mothers and the fathers. Fathers missed things they did with the child who had died, while mothers missed everything about the child. "Pining" for the child was the common response, as well as an estranged feeling from the remainder of the family, whom she may have felt were not grieving as deeply as she.

Fathers' responses to chronic illness in their child often have been assumed to be similar to mothers' responses (McKeever, 1981). Two reasons for this assumption are the less frequent presence of fathers on a regular basis as attendants to their hospitalized child and a misperception of the father's role as peripheral in regard to emotional or illness-related issues. Whatever the reason, there is a lack of documented evidence regarding fathers' responses, however, it has been noted that fathers receive less support than mothers since they are often less available to interact with health professionals (McKeever, 1981). In a small sample of fathers of chronically ill children, five areas of paternal concern were identified. The first was the lack of communication with health professionals, with both lack of emotional support and lack of factual knowledge identified as problems. Secondly, in the realm of life-style, career advancement, and so on, a majority of fathers felt that their children's illnesses had had adverse effects on their career advancement and mobility. In addition most fathers rarely participated in social, political, or athletic activities in the community. In the area of daily involvement with their ill child, most fathers were involved to a significant degree; some shared the responsibility for the child's care equally with their wives. McKeever points out that there have been contradictory findings in this regard, with some studies showing a detached father who avoids the daily care of his chronically ill or handicapped child. There is a need for more research in this area. In terms of coping mechanisms, it appears that fathers are less likely than mothers to share their concerns with others. There was little involvement reported in mutual help groups, for instance. It

may be society's expectation that men will not need outlets such as emotional support from others; on the other hand, their lack of involvement may simply reflect a lack of time to engage in such activities. Finally, fathers, more often than mothers, expressed concern about the future, including the long-term impact of the illness experience on the well siblings (McKeever, 1981).

To close this general discussion of parental responses, it can be concluded that the parents of the chronically ill child are a population at risk. They frequently suffer from feelings evoked by their child's illness, with guilt being a particularly painful and incapacitating response. Also their personal roles and career aspirations may have to be put aside intermittently or permanently during the child's illness. Very real concerns about the child's treatment regimen and the ability of the child to live independently in the future as an adult are common. The financial burden has a great impact on parents' perceptions and management capabilities, which is a subject to be discussed later in this chapter.

STRESSORS FOR NONTRADITIONAL FAMILIES

Many types of families other than the traditional nuclear family exist in American and other societies. Variations on this structure have become increasingly common in the present social context, and may include single-parent and divorced families, stepfamilies, and families undergoing separation or experiencing troubled marital relationships. In addition to the parental stresses and responses described previously, these atypical families are under particular stress, with possibly limited resources.

In a study published in 1981, Ellison stated the following: "In the 1980s, as many as 40% of the children in this country will spend part of their childhood living in a single parent family." With this expected frequency it becomes increasingly likely that chronically ill children such as children with cancer will be among these. The single-parent family usually faces additional problems in an effort to cope with illness of one of the child members. These problems include financial aspects, the possible inability of the single parent to accommodate work schedules to the child's needs, particularly if he or she is hospitalized, and lack of the range of resources for emotional support of the single parent, the ill child, and other healthy children in the family. As in traditional families, guilt, sorrow, and grief are usually experienced; these feelings may be compounded by residual problems relating to the single-parent status (divorce or death) and guilt over the inability to devote more attention to the ill child. On the other hand the single parent may have established an extremely close relationship with the child or children (Engebretson, 1982).

Despite a high divorce rate, many Americans marry and remarry. An increasingly frequent situation therefore is the stepfamily, or blended family. Though there may be two parents, the problems of stepfamilies can also be significant and predate the illness of one of the children. Some structural differences characteristic of the stepfamily include: It is born of many losses; family members have different histories and expectations; the parent–child relationship precedes that of the new couple; legal relationships are nonexistent or ambiguous; financial arrangements may assume emotional overtones; and there are additional relations and ex-relations (Engebretson, 1982). When these potential problem areas are coupled with the crisis of childhood cancer, many problems can surface that will compromise the family's ability to cope effectively.

Intervention with these atypical families, as with the two-parent family, is based on thoughtful assessment of the family's unique assets and deficits. Health personnel must also be aware of legal custody, support, and visitation arrangements (Coucouvanis and Solomons, 1983). It is often assumed that the parent staying with the child has the legal authority to

sign consent forms, for example. This may not always be the case. It is important to consider the social stigma these families may experience. The nurse encouraging participation in unit activities and parents' groups may need to provide extra support and encouragement for them to participate with or feel accepted by other parents. They may need particular assistance from social services regarding alimony or insurance coverage. Child care for healthy siblings may present more of a problem due to lack of availability of family members to help, or due to emotional unwillingness to help because of difficulties in the past. If support groups or local church or community organizations offer such services, referral will be helpful. There may be a local chapter of Parents Without Partners or the Stepfamily Association of America to which these families also can be referred.

In terms of long range planning and followup, recognition and anticipation of problems need attention. Little research has been done on the long-range consequences of single parenting and step-parenting on the child, but primary preliminary investigation points to a somewhat higher incidence of lowered academic achievement and the increased influence of peer relationships on these children (Ellison, 1981). Chapter 9 will address particular problems chronically ill children often have in the school setting related to their illness. The combined risk of changes in family structure and chronic illness merits careful consideration and planning.

CULTURAL VARIATIONS

In the coping model presented at the beginning of this chapter, it was noted that the appraisal phase of the coping response is influenced by the family and individual cultural context. As each individual matures into adulthood, values and beliefs which are the accepted norms of his or her cultural group gradually are incorporated. Thus during the appraisal phase the individual assesses a crisis in terms of the value system held from childhood. Cultural beliefs and practices can influence the implementation of coping behaviors as well.

Although there has not been extensive research in this area, some studies have been done of the responses of parents from various cultural groups to cancer in their child (Spinetta, 1984). It was found that Mexican families, for example, when contrasted with American families, generally were less open with their children about knowledge of the illness and treatment efforts, less reliant on spouse support and more reliant on extended family support, more sustained through the experience by their belief in the meaning of life and, finally, more passive and fatalistic regarding treatment and cure. Many of the same factors were present in the Vietnamese family. Additionally, the Vietnamese community frequently makes use of a spokesperson in interactions with those outside their group. It is important that initial medical discussions include this chosen representative. The participative decision-making process, increasingly used with American families, is another area of contrast. Rather than appreciating the physician's honesty in presenting alternatives, the family from the Vietnamese cultural group may interpret this as lack of confidence and credibility (Spinetta, 1984).

It can be seen from beginning work in the area of cultural variability that much more research needs to be done. In order to effectively plan to care for these families, the primary nurse should gather as much background information about the cultural group as possible. The local or nearest embassy for that country is a helpful resource, as are nationals of the country who are visiting or employed in the United States. The public library has a vast array of reading material available. The major hazard in gleaning this information is that generalizations will be made and acted upon without verifying that the general information about a culture applies to the individual family in question.

The second step then in providing culturally sensitive care is to elicit specific information from the family regarding their values, beliefs, life-style, health practices, and so on. A pioneer in transcultural nursing, Madeline Leininger, calls this process of gathering information a cultural assessment and maintains that it should be a part of the data gathered and used in planning. She proposes that, along with physical assessment data, cultural assessment be an essential part of the data base (Leininger, 1985). Unless a family member or the health professional is fluently bilingual, an interpreter should be obtained. Besides obvious variables of the affected child and family, such as diet preferences, habits, usual health care practices, and so on, it is important to discover the family's emotional response to the disease experience and their coping resources. A crucial point to discuss is the extent to which information has been or will be communicated to the child. An example is the Arab culture, in which the father is believed to be the head of the household and the ultimate decision-maker. The child is seen as one who must be protected from harm. The family may feel that open communication about the illness is not in the child's best interest, much like the response noted in the Mexican families studied by Spinetta. Since this will deviate from the usual approach of the staff, careful consideration of this aspect needs to be undertaken so as to meet child, family, and staff needs.

Conflict frequently arises over the use of traditional medical practices or folk medicine. Many hospital and treatment teams have assumed a more tolerant posture and allow a family to continue folk medical treatments, unless they are harmful or contraindicated by the cancer treatment itself. The use of a medicine man, or trembler, for the native American (American Indian), or the drinking of herbal teas, are examples of folk practices that are not contraindicated by any concurrent medical treatment. When efforts are made to accommodate these folk beliefs, families are helped to feel more at ease and less pressured into certain modes of cancer treatment. Although more definitive research is needed regarding compliance postdischarge, it may be that collaboration between folk healers and "modern medicine" may enhance compliance with the prescribed regimen.

Variations in health-care practices are also found among members of various religious groups. Jehovah's Witnesses furnish the most striking example of illness-related beliefs that may pose difficulties for cancer care providers. Since this group is prohibited by their religion from receiving blood and blood products, their treatment has presented challenges to physicians, nurses, and other health team members. Formerly Witnesses were refused treatment in some areas because of their unwillingness to accept blood in the event of emergency or as supportive care. Many cancer centers now are modifying their approach to include careful monitoring, the use of a blood substitute (Fluosol-DA), and vigorous use of other preparations such as albumin, immune globulins, platelets, and intraoperative salvage, whenever these are acceptable to the family (Dixon and Smalley, 1981).

SUPPORT STRATEGIES

A key concept in considering how to best care for the family facing childhood cancer is embodied in the word "support." The cancer crisis is personal and unique to the particular family situation. Nursing's most useful intervention is support — the physical and emotional "girding up" of the family for their fight. The analogy to battle readiness is a helpful one in the sense that, while those behind the lines can supply ammunition, elements of survival, care for the injured, encouragement, and so on, the battle cannot be fought by anyone but the soldier. So the family must ultimately face and manage the crisis alone, assisted by the many faceted types of support offered by the health-care team.

Once the commitment to provide support is made, many kinds of activities follow which will be outlined in this section. Basically these strategies can be classified into four groups of related tasks: (1) Assisting the family to assess the crisis in terms of their resources to deal with it; (2) assisting the family to implement selected coping behaviors; (3) assisting the family to evaluate the effectiveness of the actions; and (4) assisting the family to plan and try out alternative strategies for dealing with practical problems.

ASSESSING THE CRISIS

Keeping in mind the usual shock and grief reactions that follow knowledge of the diagnosis of cancer, the nurse will be sensitive to clues indicating the family's receptiveness to information. Indications of readiness for the task of discovering the impact that the cancer experience, including its treatment, will have on the family may include a request for information by family members about drug side-effects or the timing of events in the protocol. For example, Jennifer, an 11-year-old with lymphoma, and her family spent a few days after their initial discovery of her diagnosis talking in hushed voices among themselves. The questions they asked at this point revolved around hospital procedure or diagnostic tests. In conversations with the parents, the nurse assessed them still to be experiencing both denial and grief responses, indicated by their vacillation between hope for a second diagnostic test result to be negative and talking about their daughter as if they had already lost her. After a time the primary nurse, who had been gently providing small amounts of information related to the chemotherapy regimen, was asked the name and action of the antiemetic. This was interpreted as a signal that a certain degree of acceptance had occurred, and that the family was ready to gather information needed to more actively cope with Jennifer's care.

The question of providing information is a pivotal one in client care planning and intervention. When a person is in a crisis state, perception of outside events may be distorted. Therefore information presented at this time may be missed completely or may be misinterpreted. In a discussion of avoiding communication blocks, Johnson (1980) pinpoints common problems that occur with "high risk" parents, i.e., those who have high-risk children. The first problem is *too little information.* This occurs when the family has been given scanty or generalized information. Parents under stress usually find generalizations inadequate and instead desire specific information. In addition to information about the risk situation, parents who were interviewed by Johnson complained that they needed information about related aspects, such as the child's development, behaviors, and functional ability. Thus parents of children with cancer actively seek out the latest blood count results, expected drug side-effects, and the anticipated time for returning to school. These details are important for realistic planning regarding how best to cope and what help from outside sources will be needed.

Parents in this study noted that the most stressful communication problem occurred when *conflicting information* was given by different professionals. Johnson suggests that nurses and others establish exactly what the family has been told and what "they have been told last," so as to guard against giving conflicting information. For parents who are particularly anxious or highly critical it may be best to select one professional to communicate with them. Primary nursing has much to offer in the way of such a consistent approach.

Another problem that parents observed was the provision of *too much information.* Usually this occurred when an overwhelming amount was presented at once, since over time most parents agreed they wanted as much information as possible. During an acute period such as a hemorrhagic episode because of thrombocytopenia, information related to the crisis will be desired most, whereas parents usually will not

be receptive to information regarding school attendance or growth and development at this particular time.

A final group of communication problems identified by these parents included *information given to the wrong person at the wrong time, in the wrong place, or using the wrong format.* The first three occur frequently in crisis situations as anxious health professionals communicate significant details to an aunt who is relieving a tired mother, or to one parent rather than both. The wrong time and place become potential hazards when there are few private places for parents to have conferences, or little time budgeted for discussion. The last area mentioned by these parents, wrong format, is a common problem because of reliance on oral communication even when this is inappropriate to achieve the desired result (Johnson, 1980). For example, Heather's parents were so excited that their daughter was to be discharged that they paid little attention to oral instructions regarding supplemental feedings and insertion of an NG tube. At home they realized their lack of knowledge and felt they would have benefited from written instructions and even diagrams of the procedure.

In a large-scale study of 201 parents in 6 cancer centers, a structured 6-week educational program "Coping with Childhood Cancer" was implemented and evaluated (Wallace, et al., 1984). Although the authors acknowledge the educational efforts for the parents of the oncology patient, a needs assessment in one institution revealed the parents' lack of information in many areas. An effective way to provide information might be a structured course, with the use of a text and self-testing as well as group testing. Additionally, the participants reported the positive benefits of support and group camaraderie. More research into the area of formal, group approaches to both parent and patient education about cancer could document this as an important adjunct to the traditional one-to-one method often utilized.

IMPLEMENTING COPING BEHAVIOR

In the appraisal step a preliminary examination of the family's resources for coping will have been initiated. In this next phase the family can be helped further to define and try out coping strategies. As has been mentioned, individuals and families tend to use coping strategies that have proved useful in the past. If the family has not had previous experience with an over-whelming demand such as cancer, they may be at a loss for coping strategies. The nurse, medical social worker, child-life worker, and others may all be helpful in problem solving with the family about coping behaviors that have been used successfully by other families and might be workable in their situation. The role of mutual help groups for parents has been recognized by many authors as valuable in this regard (Pochedly, 1983). A survey of parents in one institution found the need for support groups ranked as high as the need for information among the mothers of cancer patients, with fathers preferring an educationally focused group (Wallace, et al., 1984). In some hospitals special groups for parents spring up, sometimes without professional assistance. In one large cancer center gathering together informally to do the laundry provides a meeting place. Telephone numbers are often exchanged, and essential support is given and received. Community dining rooms (when available) lend an informal, relaxed environment for a sharing of feelings and experiences. Formal organizations such as the Candlelighters and groups sponsored by the American Cancer Society and Leukemia Society provide a more structured mechanism for support as well as many other tangible services, which will be discussed in the last section of this chapter.

Maintaining relationships with the careproviders is a task parents perceive to be of utmost importance. Support from caregivers is helpful, and most parents report positive feelings about the competency and concern of the staff. Prob-lems do occur, however. Chesler and Barbarin (1984) identified three demographic factors about parents of children with cancer which correlated significantly with perceived problems with the medical staff. These were the age of the child at diagnosis, the parent's level of education, and the child's experience of a relapse. The family of the older child and the child having a relapse were significantly more likely to perceive difficulty in their interactions with the staff. The difficulties primarily were in the areas of providing support for the parents' and child's needs, providing information, and providing competent care. These findings point to some families, such as those whose child is experiencing a relapse, having special support needs as they attempt to cope.

Helpful support interventions used by pediatric oncology nurses include tangible encouragement for constructive coping efforts, the provision of guidance, and well-thought-out advice. For instance, parents can be helped to plan vacations, and occasional leisure activities around the medical needs of the affected child or perhaps away from the child (McKeever, 1981). In the hospital, respite from a long night caring for the child can be offered by a sensitive nurse. Perhaps by arranging an hour of time the nurse can be available to be with that child exclusively, the parents can leave together for breakfast. Parents who are "veterans" of the long-term management of a child with many needs, when contrasted to parents of acutely ill children, have been found to be more adept at pacing themselves (Knafl, et al., 1982). Parents in the cited study observed that they had learned to discriminate when it was important to be with the child, and when they and the child could tolerate separation. Although this was a study of families of ill children in which both parents worked, the principle illustrated applies to other types of families as well. Nurses can help parents to learn to pace themselves.

An area of coping that presents particular problems for many parents is that of discipline.

Guilt feelings, realistic concern over the child's health status, and the natural desire to make the child's life as happy as possible, contribute to a reluctance to enforce preillness rules of behavior. Seriously ill children report this change in parental expectations to be anxiety producing. They imagine that they must be going to die or that their parents no longer care about them (Spinetta and Deasy-Spinetta, 1981). Parents often need help in defining realistic expectations of their child's behavior, which has been changed by the disease process, and in knowing how the identified limits will be enforced. Parents usually are very receptive to suggestions from health personnel and other parents, particularly after a period of time at home where an ill, manipulative, frightened child has made chaos of family life. When individual limits are set and subsequently maintained, praise for the parent and the child is in order. James, a 4-year-old with ALL, is a good example. Prior to and during a second hospitalization for treatment, his behavior had regressed to that of a negativistic toddler. Refusing to eat or to go to the playroom, he insisted on watching television all day sitting on his mother's lap. Also he began fighting the taking of his medications, spitting them out at whoever offered them. Together with his mother and the child-life worker, a chart was drawn up scheduling James's day. He was awarded stars for cooperative behavior and eating some of each meal. He achieved privileges based on the number of stars per day over a minimum amount of time and had a planned TV time with his mom in the afternoon. Using this structure his behavior improved markedly, and the strain on his mother was vastly reduced.

The acquisition of skills and knowledge function as constructive coping strategies for most parents. As parents acquire skills and increase their competence in the care of their child, it is important to reward these efforts with praise and recognition. Planning instructional modules with some built-in incentives for progress is helpful. Often there are natural incentives in

that discharge becomes feasible as the parents' coping skills increase. Learning to change a sterile dressing and maintain a hyperalimentation line, for example, prior to discharge on home hyperalimentation therapy is a must. Public recognition of a family's efforts by other parents, perhaps an announcement in the parent group or in a newsletter when a family is making progress, can serve as an incentive for them as well as for other families.

Finally it would be remiss to ignore the vast array of printed material available in both the lay and professional literature regarding the cancer experience and how to survive it. For reference many of these materials are indexed in the Yellow Pages of this book. Although referring families to reading material would hardly be an effective single instructional strategy, in conjunction with other approaches such as formal instruction, demonstration, discussion, and active participation, it can be valuable and is easily accessible to the parents.

In summary the nurse assists families to use coping behavior through direct and indirect means. Encouragement and praise for successes and support during failures consistently are important. In addition, parents can be helped to acquire skills and knowledge that will expand their resources for coping and increase their confidence.

EVALUATING COPING EFFECTIVENESS

It has often been said, "It's results that count," and this is certainly true of coping behavior. As discussed in the introduction to the coping process, it is helpful to have established criteria for determining success of coping efforts. Many people will be able to identify their own success empirically and will remark, "We are doing better now," or, "Last week's discussion in the parent group helped us work through some discipline problems we were having with John." Some families need assistance with this step. The criteria established by Miller (1983) as listed earlier in this chapter will help them to assess their progress.

Since these are perhaps long-range outcomes, a helpful intervention is to assist families to identify intermediate criteria that will indicate their progress. For example Betsy's father was having a difficult time resolving guilt feelings over his divorce from Betsy's mother the year before the child was diagnosed. He erroneously felt that the disease might not have occurred or might have been diagnosed earlier had his wife not been under so much pressure in the single-parent role. Maintaining his own self-esteem and handling the guilt feelings were long-range goals; they seemed almost unachievable to him. With help identifying a short-range accomplishment that meant progress toward that end, however, he was able to congratulate himself on his ability to share his feelings with the parent group. He was relieved to find that fathers from intact families had similar guilt feelings. Next he set out to understand his daughter's diagnosis more completely. Upon achieving that goal he could see that the vague symptomatology preceding Betsy's initial diagnosis was a common occurrence and a typical cause of delay in diagnosing children with lymphoma.

A significant point to keep in mind is that progress must be measured in terms of a family's chosen criteria, not those of health professionals. The family may identify vastly different goals for successful coping. These goals merit respect, and although nurses can make suggestions of other, "more constructive," goals these must ultimately be the family's decision. It is important to encourage the parent to complete the step of evaluating effectiveness. Often the very families who are most unsuccessful in their coping efforts are the most reluctant to take on any new tasks. They may be hesitant to do this necessary step of looking at the results of their efforts. Scott's family is a good example of this problem. Scott, a 16-year-old with osteogenic sarcoma, was physically and emotionally sapped by two courses of preoperative cisplatin

when he was hospitalized for an infection. His appetite was affected by the fads common in adolescence, as well as by chemotherapy-related nausea, and was poor. He had lost 10 pounds in the last month. His parents were very concerned about this problem and recognized the potential implications of malnutrition for their son's recovery from surgery. As a result of their concern, they began alternately to try to accommodate Scott's particular food likes and nag him about his poor food intake. Every meal became a battle with Scott eating less and less of even favorite foods. Soon other areas of family relationships began to suffer, including the parents' support for each other. His mother finally became receptive to the idea of a planning conference between the parents, Scott and his sister, his primary nurse, the social worker, the physician, and the nutritionist to evaluate Scott's nutritional status. In the conference it became clear that Scott's parents had felt too overwhelmed by anxiety and frustration to step back and look at the outcome of their attempts to make Scott eat. Together with the health team and Scott, a few new approaches were planned, such as more extensive use of supplements (milk shakes and frozen desserts, for example) and an occasional pass to join friends for dinner. It was further decided that maintenance of Scott's normal weight plus or minus 5 pounds would be the long-term desired outcome, with an intermediate goal of regaining 1 pound per week. Scott's case illustrates the importance of the evaluation phase and the planning of alternatives.

PLANNING ALTERNATIVES

A valuable skill in the coping process is that of planning alternatives. The most efficient use of this skill would be to anticipate the possible failure of some of the coping strategies and to plan alternatives from the start. More often alternatives are considered when plan A fails, as was the case in the previous situation regarding Scott. When this happens it is important for the nurse to keep in mind that a failure of sorts has occurred and that the patient and family may feel demoralized and frustrated by that experience. Intensive encouragement and praise for any constructive efforts will help the family maintain confidence in their coping capability.

In summary support strategies comprise a vital portion of total client care. Activities that function as support range from direct assistance in care, listening, and sharing, to more indirect assistance in the form of gently guiding the family in the identification of their own coping style and implementation of selected strategies. In a comprehensive program aimed at the total family, cancer services at North Memorial Medical Center provides an ongoing family-centered program in a retreat setting. This program is a multifaceted presentation focusing on helping families to cope with the cancer diagnosis and the rigors of living with cancer (Johnson and Norby, 1981). Such programs may pioneer the development of comprehensive support and training for the coping process required to meet the demands of this illness.

SIBLINGS OF THE CHILD WITH CANCER

The siblings of an ill child have been termed the "forgotten grievers" (Zelauskas, 1981, p. 45) and the "families' forgotten other child" (Craft, 1979, p. 297). Until recently, with the focus of concern on the overwhelming task of promoting survival for the affected child, all other members of the family suffered from a relative lack of attention and research documentation. This was particularly true for well siblings. With vast improvements in survival rates, the perspective has broadened to more appropriately encompass the entire family. When siblings began to be studied, it was found that in many cases they were less adjusted than their ill brother or sister, with the potential for severe long-term consequences. One sibling's comment aptly describes the feelings of neglect and anger generated by the experience of such an illness in the family: "If you're the sick one,

everybody cares. If you're the brother or sister, they don't give a hoot" (Zelauskas, 1981). As a result the well child may be frightened of these feelings, experience guilt, reflect the parents' anxieties, and resent the special attention received by the ill child. It is important for health professionals to more accurately identify and provide for the needs of the well siblings. As Spinetta notes, "In its attempts to keep marital relationships alive . . . and to help the children with cancer cope with and master their illness, the medical team should not ignore the needs of those persons who will in most cases live the longest with memories . . . the siblings of children with cancer" (Spinetta and Deasy-Spinetta, 1981.

COMMON FEELINGS AND BEHAVIORS

The usual situation at the time of diagnosis is one of family separation, with well siblings being boarded out to relatives or friends. This situation contributes to a feeling of rejection in the well children. Often they are uninformed for as long as several weeks. The child with cancer becomes the central figure in the family's life. The well child normally has to sacrifice parental attention and involvement in outside activities, as well as assume additional responsibilities, depending on the age of the child. Additionally, this well sibling may notice physical changes in the cancer patient — hair loss, weight loss, or amputation. This combination of experiences leads to many feelings. Fear and anger are typical. In a cyclic fashion enhanced by the phenomenon of sibling rivalry, anger often gives rise to guilt feelings and resentment. The parent and the ill child may become targets of these angry feelings. When preferential treatment and variable rules for conduct are applied by the parent to the affected child, these feelings are intensified. (Kramer, 1981).

Alternatively the well child may turn guilt and angry feelings inward, resulting in destructive impulses and behaviors such as withdrawal, school difficulties, and generalized behavior problems (Kramer, 1981). In studies of siblings of children with cancer it was found that, as a group, siblings were less "adjusted" than the affected child, as determined by a battery of psychometric tests, (Spinetta and Deasy-Spinetta, 1981). It is particularly notable that siblings' scores worsened when other family members, including the ill child, were doing well. One explanation for this is that the scoring reflected the adequately met emotional needs of the other family members. In times of crisis such as when pain increases, or in times of remission, the emotional needs of the ill child and parents tended to be met by each other and health personnel, friends, and so on, who rally around for support. In contrast the well sibling is often left out of the crucial decision making or worry of the crisis periods. When "all is well" during remission or good response to treatment, the parent and ill child again turn their concern to the business of living. The parent may not realize the unanswered questions and worries the well child may continue to have (Spinetta and Deasy-Spinetta, 1981). In some cases parents and ill children enter a state of near denial between clinic visits or when in remissions. While there is not yet enough research documentation on the siblings, it seems plausible that they evidence a different pattern of reaction and many unresolved feelings which do not allow them the break of a denial period. The above research indicates that, for whatever reason, siblings often do less well than the ill child.

DEVELOPMENTAL CONSIDERATIONS AND DIFFERENCES

A number of studies indicate that the age of the well sibling has an influence on the type of response seen. The following discussion of developmental levels will trace the response noted in the well sibling as a function of age.

The infant sibling is most affected by illness in the family. Due to heightened dependency needs of infants and their attachment to the parents, particularly the mother, a parent's preoccupation with the sick child can be particularly devastating. The required separations from the parent–caretaker(s) threatens the achievement of the developmental task for this age, the development of trust (Kramer, 1981).

At the toddler stage the task of developing autonomy is of utmost concern to the child and parent. The newly emerging independence is tenuous at best, alternating with clinging behaviors and dependence. Separation during this time can retard the toddler's progress toward autonomy. At this cognitive level the child is unable to understand the reason for the separation and may interpret the parents' behavior as lack of love or punishment (Kramer, 1981). Preschoolers (similar to toddlers) continue to move toward establishing independence and initiative in exploring the environment. In studies of the effect of a sibling's experience with cancer on this age group, these children viewed their parents as psychologically more distant from them than did the patients. Further in terms of self-concept and attitudes toward parental responsiveness, the well siblings indicated significantly less adaptive responses than did the patients (Spinetta and Deasy-Spinetta, 1981). Since preschoolers are naturally egocentric, as are toddlers, they are emotionally and cognitively unable to understand the need for parental separation.

The school-age child's world is expanding beyond the family to include school and extracurricular activities. Although cognitively more capable of understanding separation and the legitimate needs of the ill sibling, the well child still feels neglected. The restriction of many of the family's usual activities — for example, sports, scouting, church — generates feelings of resentment. School performance changes in many cases, and the child may miss many opportunities for social and intellectual growth (Kramer, 1981).

In school-age and adolescent siblings, Spinetta and Deasy-Spinetta (1981) found perception of greater psychological distance from parents and increased perception of conflict in contrast to affected children. Adolescents who were affected by cancer showed more directly illness-related concerns, whereas adolescent siblings had concerns that surfaced in many aspects of their lives. This may be partially explained by the tendency of the adolescents' parents, when threatened by the loss of the sick child, to place undue restrictions on the well teenager. Since the task at this age focuses on the achievement of independence from parental authority, anger and acting out behavior may complicate the situation (Kramer, 1981). In a study of the effects of a death on adolescent siblings, approximately one third of the sample reported contemplating suicide, and two thirds noted worsening of their study habits, which in most cases caused poorer grades (Balk, 1983). This study was conducted with adolescents, the majority of whose siblings had died suddenly from accidental causes. It could be hypothesized that the long-term strain of the cancer experience could generate these same behaviors and feelings in well siblings, regardless of the outcome of the illness.

HELPFUL SUPPORT STRATEGIES FOR SIBLINGS

With this delineation of both general responses common to all ages and specific developmental considerations, planning and intervention directed at the specific needs of well siblings is beginning to take place. Research and clinical experience indicate that key principles are open communication and sibling involvement. Beginning with the explanation of the diagnosis, honesty and inclusion of the sibling should be fostered. Most clinicians agree that all children of any age should be told the name of the diagnosis—that it is cancer. For the young child the initial information can be broadened and deepened as cognitive abilities increase; it is necessary, therefore, to re-explain

frequently, offering repeated opportunities for questions or exploration of previously explained issues. How to tell the child is often a major concern of the parents. Parents should be told that displays of their natural feelings and concerns, such as crying, and so on, are appropriate responses and help the well child to realize the seriousness of the situation. Support from health professionals, even utilizing role play, may help especially anxious parents not to lose control of their emotions completely, as this may unduly frighten the well sibling (Kramer, 1981). The parent can be helped to select only essential information to discuss at the beginning with provisions for followup information based on the well children's ages and understanding. For example it may be explained that the diagnosis is a form of cancer, and that a long period of treatment and trips to the hospital can be foreseen. As with any sensitive subject, such as sex, and death, the child's own questions will cue the parent to his or her readiness to be given more information.

After the initial information has been given, siblings need to be updated, particularly if separated from their parents and the ill child. Family conferences are helpful, as is bringing the siblings to clinic and the hospital when feasible. There are currently materials suitable for both the affected child and the well sibling, which have been indexed in the Yellow Pages of this book. These include feeling oriented and informational materials.

Although communication with the infant, toddler, or preschooler is essential, it needs to be accomplished with different approaches. Verbal communication and some written materials read to the child may be helpful, depending on the individual sibling. In addition play therapy—both structured and unstructured—is useful. If he or she is allowed to see and manipulate equipment, to use dolls and puppets representing family members and hospital personnel and materials designed for tension release, the well but anxious sibling can be helped to cope much as the ill child is helped in these ways (Zelauskas, 1981). For the child this age, particularly, supporting the parent in finding time to spend at home or in activities with the well child is important. The issue of quality time for the well children of any age is a crucial one. Health personnel can influence parents to direct needed attention to these "other children" through information, counseling, and the provision of respite from the sick child's care. Problem solving with the parent and child regarding resources, such as neighborhood friends who could take the carpool for a week so that the siblings can get to lessons, tutors, Scouts, and the like, or a relative to stay with the sick child while the parent(s) take the others to a movie, will measurably benefit the entire family.

Another key issue, that of sibling involvement, is influenced by developmental level, but nevertheless is feasible to some degree for all ages. Parental participation has been found to decrease anxiety and guilt. It follows that sibling participation similarly can promote positive coping (Kramer, 1981). Comforting and preparing a meal or a drink, or helping to distract with a game or a story are within the range of most siblings. If the family is to learn a home-care treatment, older siblings can be included in the instruction and will serve as valuable back up.

When distance or the family's particular situation preclude siblings' physical presence, either at the hospital, the clinic, or at home, keeping in touch becomes particularly important. Lines of communication can be kept open with letters, phone calls, or tapes. Parents can be counseled to positively reinforce the well siblings' help in any of these ways. Tangible support such as knitting a cap, researching needed information, developing a favorite recipe, or donating blood or blood components can all be support activities that will help the affected child and the "well" one. Involvement decreases alienation and promotes a positive

concept of the self. By using these methods, healthy siblings can be prevented from becoming emotionally damaged by the cancer experience.

A final area of concern is that of counseling parents regarding the needs of their healthy children. It is understandable that the focus of attention is on the affected child. Sometimes through thoughtful questions asked by a nurse, however, the parents will recognize or share their concerns about their other children. They can be counseled to be particularly sensitive to the needs of well siblings at greatest risk: those undergoing concurrent stresses of their own (starting school, moving); those already having a poor relationship with the ill child or the parent(s); and those with lessened or ineffective coping strategies (limited communication abilities, few outlets). Intervention in these and other situations involving healthy siblings can help to minimize the negative impact of the illness experience on them (Taylor, 1980).

COMMUNITY SUPPORT SERVICES FOR THE FAMILY

EXTENDED FAMILY AND FRIENDS

The support of the extended family, both local and distant, and friends often has been noted to play a major role in the coping process. In a study of perceived sources of support for families with cancer, parents indicated friends and relatives to be third and fifth, respectively, of greatest helpfulness (Morrow, et al.,1983). Caplan (1964) notes how helpful assistance with everyday tasks can be — tasks such as doing the shopping, washing a load of laundry, or fixing the nightly meal. These tasks often are performed by friends and relatives, in addition to their giving valuable emotional support.

On the negative side both friends and neighbors can be thoughtless and serve as an additional source of anxiety for the family. Some families experience the withdrawal of friends;

relatives may criticize parents for believing medical information, or pressure them to seek unproven treatment methods (Fife, 1980). For some parents these stresses and the crises related to the disease come at the same time that work and social ties are most strained. Satisfaction and support from these sources can thus be limited in their ability to offset some of the negative influences of well-meaning but negative comments from extended family and friends.

Families may need advice and assistance in dealing with problems posed by these friends and relatives when their support is less than helpful. Information regarding the disease process and treatment is helpful to dispel myths, and families easily can be supplied with such information to share with others. In most cases an open response to questions is the most successful approach; anticipation of the family's concerns will prepare them for that experience. When feasible extended family members or very close friends could be included in family conferences about the child's progress and treatment plans. Their participation in receiving updated, accurate information will relieve the parents of the burden of acting as liaison or informant between the cancer treatment facility and concerned others.

MUTUAL HELP GROUPS

The valuable support offered by other families of children with cancer has been well documented in the literature. Mutual help groups can provide emotional support and promote positive coping behavior. In addition to the empathy and understanding another parent can offer, the ability of a person who has been through a crisis to offer such support to another is in itself a positive statement. It helps the newly suffering parent to realize that coping with this overwhelming crisis is possible. Modeling of successful coping behavior is one of the most useful roles played by members of mutual help groups (Adams, 1979).

The arisal of cancer-related support groups, as groups in other disease-related categories, is a relatively recent phenomenon. Although mutual support is not a new concept, the organization of a group effort toward this purpose is relatively new. Usually organized groups have grown out of parents' personal experiences — the loss of a child or a perceived gap in the services provided to families. Those who have studied the self-help/mutual help phenomenon theorize that these groups have sprung up spontaneously when the needs of individuals were not matched with an available and accessible professional service (Gussow and Tracy, 1978). Also many professionals have observed the unique type of support offered by someone "who's been there and knows" (Pochedly, 1983).

There are many mutual help groups for parents of children with cancer in existence at national, state, and local levels. The functions of the groups differ. Most offer some degree of emotional support, either on a one-to-one basis or through group meetings. Education of the members on various aspects of cancer treatment, care needs, and the like, often is provided. Many groups have become formalized on a state or national level and, as such, depending on locale, offer assistance with housing, temporary child care, meals, and so on. Some members of such groups are active socially and politically in trying to influence the passage of related legislation or obtain funds for research. Examples of these groups are the Candlelighters, the Society of Compassionate Friends, PALMS (Parents Against Leukemia and Other Malignancies), and the Leukemia Society. For more details and the addresses of these and other community services, see the Yellow Pages of this book. The services of the American Cancer Society, a national nonprofit educational and service organization, are also listed. In localities where formalized groups do not exist, interested parents with hospital staff encouragement may want to start one. The organizations listed in the Yellow Pages can furnish information on that process as well. Referral of parents to such a group will usually be an important step in their progress toward coping successfully with their child's needs and the family's needs related to the cancer experience.

FINANCIAL AND OTHER ASSISTANCE

One very obvious stress factor in a family's cancer experience is the economic impact of the illness and related costs. A major influence on the coping process concerns the family's resources; frequently the financial burden exceeds the resources. In an overview of cancer costs, Baird (1981) notes that individual patient costs have been estimated to range up to $35,000 per family, a figure representing about one sixth of the total health-care costs in the United States. Although much of this financial strain is shared by third party payers, a 20% share of a hospital bill figuring in the thousands is still a sizeable amount for most American families.

In addition to and probably far exceeding these direct costs are the contributing costs not directly brought about by the disease but closely related. For example transportation to and from a medical center, hotel and meals for family members, special foods for the ill child, and wig, cap, and clothing purchases related to change in body size due to illness, are some of these indirect costs. In a study carried out at an oncology center in the midwest, seventy families of children with cancer kept careful records and found that their "out of pocket," primarily nonreimbursable costs, including lost income, totaled $453.74 per month (Lansky, 1979). Already under emotional stress, many families are additionally burdened by these economic stresses.

There are some avenues for assistance for these families. As already mentioned insurance companies assume some of these costs. Crippled Children's Services may be applicable in some states; some families qualify for Medicaid help with some of the costs. State and county

hospitals underwrite many costs for those who cannot pay or must pay on a sliding scale. Private and governmental research grants may finance drug costs if the child is on an experimental protocol. In New Hampshire the Cancer Commission helps with unmet costs when there is no other alternative for payment (Lansky, 1979).

Many of the indirect costs are offset by social programs, kindly relatives and neighbors, and voluntary organizations. The American Cancer Society offers a range of services, including equipment for loan. The Leukemia Society helps with blood replacement. Mutual help groups may help in tangible ways with transportation, recycling medical equipment, wigs, and so on, or by providing temporary child care.

Legislation is being proposed continually that would assist families with catastrophic illness costs. In addition various procompetition bills, prepayment plans, and the use of diagnosis related groups (DRGs) may change the financial realities in long-term cancer care in the future. Home-care reimbursement is a subject of much controversy. Although various studies have demonstrated that cost containment can occur through more home-based care, many third party payers have yet to adequately reimburse home-care services (Baird, 1981). Hospice care for the terminally ill child also is being evaluated as a cost-effective alternative to hospital-based care. Finally the development of more effective educational and training programs to better prepare families for successful home care of their ill member is a viable and economically sound alternative to in-hospital care. Various demonstration projects are underway to evaluate this approach more fully (Baird, 1981).

CONCLUSION

This chapter has presented an overview of the coping process with consideration of adaptations made by individuals of different developmental stages, social contexts, and cultural groups. The specific problems faced by parents and siblings were explored, with supportive interventions proposed. The broader extended family and community were discussed regarding the positive support and potential negative impact they could have on the family's coping process. The role of mutual help groups in the illness experience and their positive value in modeling coping behavior and in providing needed services were presented. Finally the cost of cancer care, both direct and indirect, and possible financial resources for the family were discussed.

KEY POINTS

- The coping process includes cognitive, emotional, and behavioral components.
- Useful long-term coping strategies employed by families of children with cancer include:
  - Acquiring information about the disease, its treatment, and expected problems
  - Learning new skills
  - Rehearsing for alternative outcomes
  - Finding meaning in the cancer experience
  - Reaching out to others for emotional support
- Criteria for evaluating results of successful coping behavior include the ability to handle uncomfortable feelings, to remain hopeful, and to maintain self-esteem and relationships with others.
- There are commonalities of coping behavior in families of children with cancer based on the success in meeting each family member's emotional needs, as well as the medical and emotional needs of the patient.
- Children's use of coping behavior is dependent upon age and developmental level, with regression and physical activity being behaviors common to most developmental stages.
- Parents coping with cancer in their child frequently report feelings of anxiety, denial, anger, guilt, and fear.
- Additional stressors for parents include the financial burden and related sacrifices in personal and professional realms.
- Nontraditional families may encounter problems in their coping efforts related to diminished resources or lack of available support.
- Cultural differences do exist in family coping behavior and may necessitate planning culturally sensitive interventions.
- Appropriate support efforts for families coping with cancer include interventions designed to assist with:
  - Assessing the crisis
  - Implementing coping behavior
  - Evaluating the effectiveness of coping behavior
  - Making alternative plans when coping behavior has failed to meet family goals

- The needs of well siblings are receiving increasing attention. Recent research has shown that, without intervention, well siblings may cope less well than the ill child.
- A range of community support services is often available to the family for tangible support, including financial and emotional support.
- Mutual help groups provide a unique type of support, which can positively influence the coping process.

REFERENCES

Adams, J. (1979). Mutual help groups: Enhancing the coping ability of oncology clients. *Cancer Nursing, 2,* 95–98.

Baird, S. (1981). Economic realities in the treatment and care of the cancer patient. *Topics in Clinical Nursing, 2,* 67–80.

Balk, D. (1983). Effects of sibling death on teenagers. *Journal of School Health, 53,* 14–18.

Battle, C. (1975). Chronic physical disease: Behavioral aspects. *Pediatric Clinics of North America, 22,* 525–531.

Caplan, G. (1964). *Principles of preventive psychiatry.* New York: Basic Books.

Chesler, M. and Barbarin, O. (1984). Relating to the medical staff: How parents of children with cancer see the issues. *Health and Social Work, 9,* 49–64.

Coucouvanis, J., and Solomons, H. (1983). Handling complicated visitation problems of hospitalized children. *MCN, 8,* 131–134.

Craft, M. (1979). Help for the family's neglected "Other child." *American Journal of Maternal Child Nursing, 4,* 297–300.

Dixon, J. L., and Smalley, M. G. (1981). Jehovah's Witnesses: The surgical/ethical challenge. *Journal of the American Medical Association, 246,* 2471–2472.

Ellison, E. (1981). Social behavior and psychosocial adjustment of single and two parent children. *Western Journal of Nursing Research, 3,* 283–299.

Engebretson, J. (1982). Stepmothers as first time parents: Their needs and problems. *Pediatric Nursing, 8,* 387–390.

Fife, B. (1980). Childhood cancer is a family crisis: A review. *Psychosocial and Mental Health Studies, 18,* 29–34.

Gussow, Z., and Tracy, G. (1978). The role of self help clubs in adaptation to illness and disability. *Nursing Digest, 6,* 23–31.

Hamburg, D., and Adams, J. (1967). A perspective on coping behavior. *Archives of General Psychiatry, 17,* 277–284.

Johnson, J., and Norby, P. (1981). We Can Weekend: A program for cancer families. *Cancer Nursing, 4,* 23–28.

Johnson, S. H. (1980). Avoiding communication blocks with high risk parents. *Issues in Comprehensive Pediatric Nursing, 4,* 61–72.

Knafl, K., Deatrick, J., and Kodadek, S. (1982). How parents manage jobs and a child's hospitalization. *MCN, 7,* 125–127.

Kramer, R. F. (1981). Living with childhood cancer: Healthy siblings perspectives. *Issues in Comprehensive Pediatric Nursing, 5,* 155–165.

Lansky, S. (1979). Childhood cancer: Non-Medical costs of the illness. *Cancer, 43,* 403.

Leininger, M. (1985). Transcultural care: Diversity and universality, a theory of nursing, *Nursing and Health Care, 6,* 209–212.

McKeaver, P. (1981). Fathering the chronically ill child. *MCN, 6,* 124–128.

Miller, J. (1983). *Coping with chronic illness.* Philadelphia: F. A. Davis.

Morrow, G., Hoagland, A., and Morse, I. (1983). Sources of support perceived by parents of children with cancer: Implications for counseling. *Patient Counseling and Health Education, 4,* 36–39.

Pochedly, C. (1983). *Cancer in children: Reasons for hope.* Port Washington, NY: Ashley Books, Inc.

Ross, J. (1980). Childhood cancer: The parents, the patients, the professionals. *Issues in Comprehensive Pediatric Nursing, 4,* 7–16.

Spinetta, J., and Deasy-Spinetta, P. (Eds.) (1981). *Living with childhood cancer.* St. Louis: C. V. Mosby.

Spinetta, J. (1984). Measurement of family function, communication and cultural effects, *Cancer Supplement, 53,* May 15, pp. 2330–2337.

Taylor, S. (1980). Siblings need a plan of care, too. *Pediatric Nursing, 6,* 9–13.

Teyber, E., and Littlehales, D. (1981). Coping with feelings: Seriously ill children, their families and hospital staff. *Children's Health Care, 10,* 58–62.

Vipperman J., and Roger, P. (1980). Childhood coping: How nurses can help. *Pediatric Nursing, 6,* 11–18.

Wallace, M., Bakke, A. H., and Pendergrass, T. (1984). Coping with childhood cancer: An educational program for parents with cancer. *Oncology Nursing Forum, 11,* 30–35.

Wong, D. (1980). Bereavement: The empty mother syndrome. *MCN, 5,* 385–388.

Zelauskas, B. (1981). Siblings: The forgotten grievers. *Issues in Comprehensive Pediatric Nursing, 5,* 45–52.

8

DEATH, ALWAYS A THREAT . . . SOMETIMES A REALITY

JOANN WALSH, RN, BSN, MA
Pediatric Oncology Clinical Coordinator
Children's Hospital at Stamford

INTRODUCTION

American Cancer Society (1982) statistics indicate that 50% of all children diagnosed with cancer will survive 5 years or longer when they receive treatment at a pediatric cancer center. This fact provides the basis of hope for families of children with cancer. On a more personal level for an individual family, however, the reality remains that their child might not survive, regardless of what the statistics portend.

Cancer survival rates are improving each year, but there is increasing concern about occurrence of secondary malignancies and other life-threatening complications. This means the threat of impending death may diminish, but it will never go away. The word "cure" still must be used cautiously, especially when discussing prognosis with families.

The prevailing attitude of most people is that the diagnosis of cancer means eventual, if not immediate, death. Most families are hesitant to put aside their fear and accept the premise that their child might live a full life. The family's anticipatory grieving begins the day their child is diagnosed with cancer. Their grief not only includes their fear of loss through death, but also grief over the loss of the child's health. The possibility of their child's death is particularly painful to accept. As parents they expected their child would outlive them. Also they believed they could protect their child from harm. Although there are many other reasons for grieving, these causes are paramount because they make the parents feel powerless.

Anticipatory grieving can be helpful when it challenges the family to mobilize all its strengths and resources to provide optimal support for the child and for each family member. Many parents have commented that they have reorganized their priorities in life once the diagnosis has been made. Recognizing their own strengths and resources will be extremely valuable to parents who must manage the period of their child's illness, which in unfortunate circumstances can include the final days of his or her life.

CULTURAL INFLUENCES

Methods of dealing with the terminal phase of illness and death vary according to the cultural background of the family. The issues and challenges death raises for the child, the family, and the medical team are best addressed in the context of the family's culture and community. The child's attitudes about death evolve primarily from family beliefs and, secondarily, from experiences learned in the community. For the family and the child, family beliefs and support from outside are keys to coping with this all-encompassing experience. It is within its own cultural experience that a family must continue to live as they grieve. Health-care providers must use caution not to overgeneralize, but instead to use the cultural information that follows as a frame of reference for nursing assessment.

Two generations ago dying and death were household events. Though there is a movement again to support dying at home, most Americans currently die in a hospital. Since hospitals ordinarily do not encourage children as visitors, there is little opportunity for them to be around the dying. Children's only firsthand experience with death usually is the death of a pet or the funeral of an elderly relative. They learn about death indirectly through observing their parents' grief reactions, through talking with their parents, and by watching television. In time children learn their parents' views on life and death and begin to internalize them as their own. It is therefore critical that professionals attempt to understand families' philosophies of life and death in order to help them to maximize their coping abilities (Spinetta, 1979).

Decisions about whether or not to tell a child he or she is dying, how to prepare for impending death, the choice of where a child should die, and final care of the body are all closely influenced by culture. In making these decisions families who have gradually begun to shed cultural traditions may find themselves in conflict with grandparents or other community members who strongly advocate that traditions be honored. Other families will fall back on abandoned traditions in an effort to find comfort and to elicit support from their community. In both cases the impact of heritage is significant.

HISPANIC FAMILIES

It is common in Mexico for most people to die at home. Yet in a study by Kalish and Reynolds (1976), only 54% of Mexican–Americans indicated they would choose to die at home. Further investigation showed that Mexican–Americans would choose to protect others, particularly children, from the unpleasantness of death whenever possible. In the United States they have a choice; in Mexico often there is no other alternative. In addition the large families and the cramped living quarters of many Mexican–Americans add problems to caring for the dying at home. Many of these families generally are satisfied with keeping their dying child in the hospital provided the parents can be with the child, food can be brought in, and group visits by family members is permitted.

Hispanic families are primarily Roman Catholic. The services of a priest are important to most of them. If hospitalization has removed them from their community and their parish priest, it is important that a hospital chaplain or a local priest be contacted to support the family and perform the necessary rituals. A grieving parent may not have the wherewithal to arrange for a priest so it is helpful when a hospital staff member can offer to facilitate the visit.

CHINESE AND JAPANESE FAMILIES

The family of Chinese or Japanese ethnic groups also are likely to choose the hospital setting for their dying child. According to Kakikawa (1984) in her paper presented at the Third International Conference on Cancer Nursing, most Japanese cancer patients die in a hospital because the diagnosis is withheld from the patient and because the care is viewed as too complex for family management. For others this practice may be related to a belief in the presence of spirits of death. Keeping spirits of death away from the home is important. Incense and noise are practices commonly used to deter the spirits of death.

BLACK FAMILIES

As with Hispanic cultures the role of the church is significant in the black community and is particularly apparent around the time of death. As suggested in black spirituals, death is a positive symbol for liberation from social injustice and exploitation. It is in this respect a sad but welcome event. Church members are extended family for most blacks. There may be much weeping and singing, but it should be understood that "we weep because we care, not because we despair" (Kalish & Masambu, 1976). Their presence at the bedside is both helpful and respectful.

MIDDLE AND NEAR EASTERN FAMILIES

Middle and Near Eastern families usually are adamant that their children not be told they are dying. Often they insist that not even the diagnosis of cancer be revealed. They fear that knowing the truth might cause the child to give up his or her struggle to live. Parents feel personally responsible to keep hope alive. For example, an Arab Muslim family is not expected to plan for death or to give up hope even under the gravest circumstances; either is considered to defy the will of Allah (Meleis, 1981). In a setting where honesty with patients is valued, this approach is particularly difficult to work around. Many parents take the responsibility of shielding their child by rarely leaving the child unattended and by insisting that only they provide interpretation to the child of what is going on around him.

To foster and respect the ethnic or religious practices of a family, the hospitalized dying child should be permitted a private room. This practice is not meant to hide the situation from other patients; rather it is a courtesy to provide privacy to the family in its grief and to give it the freedom to carry out traditional behaviors. Carrying out these rituals or behaviors during this time may be essential to successful coping after the child dies.

CHILDREN'S CONCEPTIONS OF DEATH

Healthy children gradually develop a concept of death. Research is inconclusive about how early this process begins, but by understanding a child's cognitive and psychosocial development inferences can be drawn. There is evidence that seriously ill children may develop a concept of death earlier or sooner than the healthy child. Table 8-1 demonstrates the development of death concepts in children.

According to Piaget, the thought process is apparent by the age of 2; mental imagery is developed, and verbal skills are progressing (Ginsberg and Opper, 1969). There are indications that the preschooler thinks death means something that does not move and is not forever; that is, an immobile (dead) object is capable of moving again sometime later. About age 5 death begins to be personified in forms such as "the killer monster" or "the bogeyman." Nightmares might occur or the child might express the need to sleep near parents or brothers and sisters. This vivid fantasy also manifests itself in violent play activities such as "car crashes" or cowboys and Indians.

Because the preschooler experiences the fear of dying as separation from those who care for him physically and emotionally, the most effective support for the child is the presence of those he or she needs and loves. Parents verbally can support their small children by promising to stay with them and by assuring them they will not be alone. Hospitals can help by allowing parents to stay at the bedside of their child. In some situations even pets or favorite toys can provide the needed sense of security.

At age 6 or 7 the child enters Piaget's concrete operational phase (Ginsberg and Opper, 1969). Reasoning and logic begin to apply to objects physically present, and questions are

TABLE 8-1. DEATH CONCEPTS IN CHILDREN

Approximate Age	Piaget's Level of Cognitive Development	Concept of Death	Characteristic Behavior
2–6 yr	Preoperational	Immobile, does not move Reversible Personified	Has nightmares Wants to sleep near other family members Talks about a "killer monster" or "bogeyman" Play activities include violence—"car crashes" Play scripts include "You can't move, you're dead" or "Now you're alive again"
6–12 yr	Concrete operational	Painful Permanent In the future, happens to old people	Fears pain may lead to death Curious about the physical details of death: body decomposition, cemeteries, coffins, etc. Questions what happens after death
Over 12 yr	Formal operational	End of human experience Personalized, internalized	Begins developing personal philosophy of life and death Denies anxiety and vulnerability by taking risks

answered through observations, even questions about death. At this point a child begins to suspect that death is permanent. Curiosity about the details of death may seem morbid. Cemeteries, burials, coffins, and causes of death are of investigative interest. Kay was a 6-year-old in the terminal phase of leukemia. As trips to the clinic became more and more frequent, she began commenting on the cemetery that she had to pass by. Questions changed from "Who takes care of the cemetery?" to "Are there children in the cemetery besides old people?" Eventually she asked to be driven through the cemetery.

Beginning at age 9 or 10 the child gradually begins to distinguish death from "going away" to understanding what biologic death is and to wonder what happens after death. Though the permanence of death is firmly established in a 9- or 10-year old's mind, it does not involve a personal fear. The fear of pain and bodily harm is more prevalent. Ten-year old Chris's immediate response to being told his leg needed to be amputated because of a life-threatening tumor was, "But how will I walk?" and "Will the doctors keep it (the surgery) from hurting?"

Language may not necessarily reflect the child's level of understanding (Hostler, 1978). When the school age child asks if he is dying he may be questioning whether he is safe and whether someone will protect him from being hurt. This is a question parents should be prepared to deal with. In some relationships the child might ask this question of a particular health-team member. Unless requested or approved by the parent to answer in the affirmative, it is appropriate to divert the question back to the child by asking what he or she means (Solnit and Green, 1963).

According to Piaget, formal operational development occurs during adolescence (Ginsberg and Opper, 1969). The capacity for abstract thinking and deductive reasoning becomes well integrated. Death is conceptualized as the end of the human experience and for the first time fear of one's own death is experienced. At this time denial helps the adolescent cope with the recognized vulnerability and anxiety over the possibility of death. In its extreme denial may lead to risk-taking behavior such as drug ingestion, fast driving, or reckless motorcycling. Similarly the adolescent who refuses chemotherapy may be denying vulnerability. For example Jay's response to his parents' attempts to persuade him to comply with his chemotherapy was, "Who needs it?"

Many adults find it difficult to broach the subject of death with their children. Adolescents are in many respects adults, so it is not unusual to find them evading the issue of death and dying in conversation. Their sense of loss is manifested in their behavior, however, by depression, withdrawal, or activities to complete unfinished business. If parents can convey an openness about discussing death, many adolescents will take advantage of the time to prepare themselves, their families, and their friends for the inevitable future.

Some parents find comfort in believing their child never knew he or she was dying. One could speculate that perhaps in these situations the child was comforted too because he kept the "secret." He kept his parents from knowing he knew he was dying. Children sometimes do choose to protect their parents from their painful situation. Someone needs to be available with whom the child can discuss fears, however, or isolation will prevent the child's needs from being met.

THE FAMILY EXPERIENCING DEATH OF A CHILD

The breadth of hope is diminished once curative treatment is stopped. The expectation of a full future is abandoned. Parents who are ready for this phase of their child's illness turn toward emphasizing the quality of life remaining. Hope continues but is aimed at day-to-day events, such as fulfillment of a last wish, a visit by a special friend, the end of pain.

Some children do very well for several months after curative therapy is stopped. Their disease may progress slowly, allowing them new freedom from medications and doctors. It is important to discuss this possibility with parents, because it may confuse them and lead them to wonder about the original diagnosis. Miracle treatments may be attempted to assure this continued grace period. The flame of hope may start to flicker again only to be quenched by the eventual downhill course of events.

The family's need to communicate becomes more important as death moves closer. Their ability to communicate often diminishes at this time, however. Fear and physical and emotional fatigue become real obstacles to communication. Often a health-team member can facilitate communication between parents, and between parents and children, who seem isolated from one another. Sometimes a family meeting can be the format for alleviating these obstacles and getting feelings and concerns out in the open.

Other children in the family should be included in discussions, if possible, for they have questions and fears too. Sometimes a child-life worker or other staff member can successfully engage a frightened, withdrawn brother or sister. Siblings may be experiencing guilt feelings because at one time they wished their brother or sister was dead, or because they may be pleased their parents will have more time to spend with them again. To share these feelings and to know other people have similar thoughts can help relieve their burden of guilt. Sibling support is useful throughout the child's illness, but it can become extremely helpful at this point.

Books on death and dying for children and parents are useful tools to facilitate communication and to open up discussions between child, parents, and siblings. Many books are available, such as those listed in Tables 8-2 and 8-3.

TABLE 8-2. BOOKS TO HELP CHILDREN UNDERSTAND DEATH

Brown, M. W. (1958). The Dead Bird. Reading, Massachusetts: Childrens Addison-Wesley Publishing Co.

Coutant, H. (1974) First Snow. New York: Random House.

Crawford, C. (1974). Three-Legged Race. New York: Harper & Row.

DePaola, T. (1973). Nana Upstairs and Nana Downstairs. New York: Penguin.

Fassler, J. (1971). My Grandpa Died Today. New York: Human Sciences Press.

Koch, R. (1975). Goodbye Grandpa. Minneapolis: Augsburg Publishing House.

Lee, V. (1972). The Magic Moth. New York: Seabury Press.

Miles, M. (1971). Annie and The Old One. Boston: Little & Brown.

Saint-Exupery, A. (1943). The Little Prince. New York: Harcourt Brace.

Silverstein, S. (1964). The Giving Tree. New York: Harper & Row.

Slote, A. (1973). Hang Tough Paul Mather. Philadelphia: J. B. Lippincott.

Smith, D. (1973). A Taste of Blackberries. New York: Thomas Crowell.

Viorst, J. (1972). The Tenth Good Thing About Barney. New York: Atheneum.

White, E. B. (1952). Charlotte's Web. New York: Harper & Row.

Williams, M. (1958). The Velveteen Rabbit. New York: Doubleday.

TABLE 8-3. BOOKS FOR PARENTS

Arnstein, H. (1960). What to Tell Your Children. Indianapolis: Bobbs Merrill.

Grollman, E. (1967). Explaining Death to Children. Boston: Beacon Press.

Grollman, E. (1976). Talking About Death. Boston: Beacon Press.

Jackson, E. (1965). Telling a Child About Death. New York: Hawthorne.

Stein, S. (1972). About Dying. New York: Walker & Co.

Wolf, W. (1973). Helping Your Child to Understand Death. Springfield: C. Thomas.

DEATH IN THE HOSPITAL

As soon as therapy is stopped, several issues must be addressed. Most important among these issues is to determine where the child will die, and then to determine who will be involved in the child's care. Family members usually will consider their child's wishes as to where the last days should be spent. When a child wants to go home, a significant number of parents might decide to grant the child's request. After bringing the child home, however, some of these families find they are unable to cope with the situation, and the child returns to the hospital. More frequent reasons for parents choosing hospitalization are better management of the illness or the effects on the family. With staff counseling and support, parents usually can convince their child to accept the necessity of remaining in the hospital when this is in the best interest of the family as a whole.

The primary caretaker usually has been selected by the child over the course of the illness. Most frequently this person is the mother or father or both. If both parents take responsibility, their mutual support of each other can have a positive effect on the care of their child. For the single parent to provide a similar measure of care for the child, the support of a friend or relative may be needed. Parent support groups become a welcome source of strength and comfort at this time.

If the parents are separated or divorced and both want to share in the experience, they should agree to cooperate to provide a loving atmosphere for the child. They should plan to avoid engaging in conflict near the child to assure a positive measure of care. The parents might need professional support in order to accomplish this goal.

Separated, divorced, or remarried parents may feel a renewed sense of guilt about having abandoned their original family relationship. Friends, relatives, and health-care team members can be supportive by emphasizing that what the parents had done for themselves, as well as for their child, was what they thought was best at the time. In cases where a parent has remarried, the new spouse can be an additional reinforcer.

When a family chooses to remain with a child in the hospital, it is important that the staff assure them that measures for pain relief and comfort will be provided. Intrusive measures should be eliminated as much as possible. Touching and talking to their child are comforts that all parents readily can offer. The parents might also be encouraged to assume responsibility for physical care, such as bathing and feeding, if they desire. Small children frequently insist their parents provide these aspects of care.

The most important role for the nurse at this final stage is to be available to the family. By listening to the family, staff members will discover what is needed most — whether it is assurance that their child is comfortable, someone with whom to share reminiscent moments, or clarification of what a doctor has said. Listening is a most valuable tool, and the staff must allow themselves time to use it. If the nurse also listens closely to the child, his or her needs will become readily apparent. The child's needs are demonstrated verbally and nonverbally. Behavioral cues, particularly through play and fantasy, are common ways the child communicates needs.

DEATH AT HOME

When a family chooses to take their child home to live until death occurs, it is important that they understand the child can be rehospitalized at any time. Some families are only willing to embark on home care when they are assured that this option remains.

Ida Martinson has written extensively on home care for dying children. Her manual on home care (Table 8-4) provides a wealth of information for parents and medical staff. When both child and family want the child to be at home, and the family is able to manage care with support from nurses and physicians, there is no reason to deny this option (Martinson, 1980).

Many communities now have hospice programs, which assist with home care and provide the family with emotional support. Other communities have visiting nurses trained to assist with home care. Because community agencies often have not worked with dying children, it is helpful if care is coordinated with the hospital or clinic pediatric nurse before a visiting nurse begins work with the family. Discharge planning is imperative. A hospital visit by the visiting nurse before the child's discharge might be arranged to meet the family and to discuss the necessary care with the staff. The staff may offer "tips" about the child they have learned during the course of the illness that may make the child's home care easier to manage. It is important that the child and family do not feel abandoned by the staff they have come to know and trust

If a family is not linked with a home-care agency, they will need medical consultation

TABLE 8-4. BOOKS FOR NURSING STAFF

Arnold, J. and Gemma, P. (1983). A Child Dies: A Portrait of Family Grief. Rockville: Aspen Systems Corporation.

Burton, L. (1974). Care of the Child Facing Death. Boston: Routledge & Kegan Paul.

Easson, W. (1977). Dying Child: The Management of the Child or Adolescent Who Is Dying. New York: C. Thomas.

Gyulay, J. (1978). The Dying Child. New York: McGraw Hill.

Langner, M. (1978). The Private Worlds of Dying Children. Princeton: Princeton University Press.

Martinson, I. (1976). Home Care for the Dying Child. New York: Appleton-Century-Croft.

Mitchell, M. (1967). Child's Attitude Toward Death. New York: Schocken.

Reed, E. (1970). Helping Children with the Mystery of Death. Nashville: Abington Press.

Sahler, O. (1978). The Child and Death. St. Louis: C. V. Mosby.

available 24 hours a day. A local hospital may be able to provide this service. Often a family physician becomes the resource person. The family must know they can call the designated person at any time.

For the family at home with their child it is important that signs of imminent death be discussed. Plans also should be made as to who to call first in the event of death. Many families will make funeral arrangements. Having solved these problems ahead of time eliminates the need to make such decisions at the moment of death, when grief may be acute.

The dying child will gradually withdraw from those around him or her. The need for visitors is past and parents may not want others to encroach on the remaining valuable time they have to spend with their child. If the child is hospitalized a "no visitors" sign may be posted to ensure privacy. If the child and family are home someone should be appointed to answer the phone or accept visitors at the door.

Whether or not a child is home, extended family or friends can take responsibility for some household activities, child care, food preparation, or care of pets. Even small children in the family may want to assume some special responsibilities. Regardless of age there should be something they can do so that they feel that they are participating in, and not just observing, this family event. A cooperative effort is often key to making home care possible and will enhance the family's coping process after death has occurred.

ENHANCING COPING EFFORTS

When the child dies the family becomes the primary focus of the health team. The qualities most needed to support the surviving family are the same as those needed to support the dying child: love, compassion, courage, endurance, humor, and humility (Duda, 1982). With supportive approaches the family will know they are cared for. Caring can be shown through a touch on the shoulder, praying with the family

if that is their wish, or by just sitting with them. Even tears are appropriate if they do not interfere with what needs to be done.

Parental responses will vary widely at the moment of death. Crying, wailing, angry outbursts, and clinging to the child are not unusual. Acute grief cannot be consoled but will subside. Some parents may choose to hold or rock their child as their last attempt to say goodbye. Some mothers may want to help bathe and dress their child before they leave the hospital or before calling the funeral director. Some parents may cope by slowly packing the child's belongings and organizing their exit from the hospital. Others may not even want to go back into the child's room.

The most difficult time for families is not necessarily at the time of death or at the funeral. In fact, the most difficult period can be afterwards, when family and friends have left and the activity has quieted down (Biebel, 1981). Because of this it may be helpful for someone from the health team to call a family several weeks after the death. Health-team members have been significant in the life of the family up to this time; the loss of their support is felt by most families.

Similarly the support given by other families in the hospital and clinic may have been significant. Some families remain in contact with each other after their children die. Parent groups organized around children with cancer, such as Candlelighters, can continue to be supportive to parents. Who can better understand a parent's loss than someone who has had the same experience?

Some communities offer support groups for the bereaved. They not only provide a caring environment in which to share one's experience, but also provide insight into symptoms and management of grief. Other support resources include the community family physician who knew the child and the family's religious community.

It is important that families be informed of support resources even if they feel they are doing fine. Parents experience grief at different times and in varying intensities. A resource given at one point may be invaluable at a future point. Families also should be alerted that they may be less emotionally available to and tolerant of their surviving children, so that the children also may be in need of outside support (Sahler & Friedman, 1981).

HELPING THE HELPERS

Nurses who practice in pediatric oncology have obviously choosen a specialty that requires skill at supporting two opposing forces; life and death. Initial interventions with the child and the family are aimed at maintaining life and all its experiences. At some point in time, the focus might switch to supporting the same family through the process of death. Having chosen this field a nurse must then make other choices: to remain objective and detached or to become subjective and involved; to encourage independency or allow dependency; to focus on the quantity or on the quality of life (Benoliel, 1973). Experienced clinicians will be more adept at making choices that enhance coping than will be beginning practitioners. Most likely a nurse has been prepared for these times through personal experience in this setting.

Previous experience with families is not the only way to learn to cope in the pediatric oncology setting, however. Coping is partially based on a personal philosophy of life and death. Until one closely analyzes one's own values and beliefs about life and death, inner conflicts can be expected to reoccur and dissatisfaction with some medical decisions and situations will continue. Books such as those listed in Table 8-4 can be a help to nurses working with these patients and their families.

Coping can be enhanced by one's thought processes, behaviors, and personal relationships (Willis, 1979). Some nurses cope by imagining themselves in their patient's situations to determine what is the most helpful thing they could do for them. Others might project themselves into the future by thinking of what they are going to do after work or on the weekend. Still others might accept a situation as a valuable learning experience and enter into it with enthusiasm. Most people use thought processes to cope with stressful situations, but they remain unaware of what these processes are and how they benefit from them.

It is easy to reorganize specific behaviors to enhance coping. Jogging or other regular physical exercise are widely accepted as stress-reducing activities. Drinking alcohol and smoking also are behaviors aimed at reducing stress, although they are not recommended to promote good physical health. Reading an enjoyable book, listening to music, or going to a movie are pastimes many people choose to use to relax after a stressful day.

Sharing relationships is another means of enhancing one's ability to cope. Having one or more friends to confide in about personal matters as well as a network of friends with whom social activities are shared is important to retain a healthy outlook on life. Even nursing departments can foster relationships by "buddying" their new employees with unit nurses to strengthen the support that is always needed in a new work situation.

An inability to cope can lead to depression or grief. Somatic complaints such as insomnia, physical exhaustion, irritability, headaches, weight changes, alcohol abuse, or isolating behavior can each be a sign of depression or grief. Colleagues exhibiting any of these behaviors should not be ignored. Rather they should be encouraged to speak about their feelings. Staff support meetings or an informal get together after work can be formats to facilitate group sharing. These functions are particularly helpful soon after the death of a child when caregivers may feel especially emotionally drained. It is important that staff members not lose concern for those they work with.

Nursing departments also should be responsible for supporting nurses in this specialty. Orientation or in-service programs should address the child's concept of death, the grief process, and coping techniques for the nurse working with grief and stress. Nurses need a good understanding of these issues both to provide better care and to know how to sustain themselves in this work environment. In addition nursing managers should be open to changes in work schedules when a nurse is having a difficult time coping with a patient assignment or the work day in general. A change in patient assignment, a rotation to the outpatient setting, an extra coffee break, an extra day off, or a leave of absence for a vacation are all creative ways to help alleviate stress. These special considerations may prevent a nurse from leaving this specialty entirely.

In summary, a nurse's source of renewal comes from within, through personal beliefs and thoughts, as well as from outside, through the people that fill one's life and through activities. Nursing managers and colleagues must be supportive of each other to develop a staff that not only cares for patients and families, but also cares for each other.

CONCLUSION

While death is not always imminent, it is a subject that is always thought of when a child is diagnosed with cancer. The child and family must be supported through the entire illness, from diagnosis through removal from treatment or through the dying process. Staff members must also be supported so that they may remain as valuable assets for the child and family, both today and in the future.

KEY POINTS

- The family's cultural background and family values, including religious practices, must be acknowledged and respected.
- These influences provide the foundation for the family's coping abilities.
- The child's age, maturity, and cognitive ability must be considered.
- Children of varying ages have different needs and fears, which must be assessed prior to developing a plan of support.
- Nursing care must address the needs of both patient and family during the terminal phase of illness and the family's needs at the time of death and immediately following death.
- The aim should be to eliminate as much confusion as possible during this stressful event.
- Nursing staff must examine their own coping processes and behaviors.
- Nursing administration must consider its role in enhancing nurses' coping skills.

REFERENCES

American Cancer Society. (1982). *Facts and figures.* New York: American Cancer Society.

Biebel, D. (1981). *Jonathon. You left too soon.* Nashville: Thomas Nelson.

Duda, D. (1982). *A guide to dying at home.* Sante Fe: John Muir Publications.

Ginsberg, H. and Opper, S. (1969). *Piaget's theory of intellectual development: An introduction.* Englewood Cliffs, NJ: Prentice Hall.

Hostler, S. (1978). The development of the child's concept of death. In O. J. Sahler (Ed.), *The child and death* (pp. 1–25). St. Louis: C. V. Mosby.

Kakikawa, F. (March, 1984). Present status of terminal care in Japan. In *Proceedings of the 3rd International Conference on Cancer Nursing* (pp. 46–54). Melbourne, Australia.

Kalish, R. A. and Masambu, J. (1976). Death and bereavement: The role of the black church. *Omega* 7:25. pp. 23–34.

Kalish, R. A. and Reynolds, D. K. (1976). *Death and ethnicity: A psychocultural study.* Los Angeles: University of Southern California Press.

Martinson, I. (June, 1980). Home Care for the Child with Cancer. In *Proceedings of the First National Conference for Parents of Children with Cancer* (pp. 86–93). Bethesda, MD: National Institute of Health.

Meleis, A. (1981). The Arab American in the health care system. *AJN, 81,* 1174.

Solnit, A. and Green, M. (1963). Pediatric management of the dying child, II: A study of the child's reaction to the fear of dying. In A. Solnit & S. Provence (Eds.), *Modern Perspectives in Child Development* (pp. 217–228). New York: International Universities Press.

Spinetta, J. (1979). *Talking with children with a life threatening illness.* Bethesda, MD.: National Cancer Institute.

9

SCHOOL AND EDUCATION: GETTING ON WITH LIFE

INTRODUCTION

Those who work with children with cancer are engaged in something of a juggling act. On the one hand the immediate question of survival mandates a focus on treatment and life-support activities. On the other hand, the dramatic improvement in survival rates for these children, combined with recent research on the long-term adjustment of cancer survivors, has alerted health professionals to the need to consider the future for these children. Overprotection to the point of stifling cognitive, emotional, and social development, will not serve the long-range needs of those living with childhood cancer. As Van Eys (1977) observes, "For a child to be cured, he has to view the world with anticipation and with eagerness to learn what his peers are learning."

This chapter will explore the non-illness-related experiences of the child with cancer, particularly the school experience. The influence of school and related activities as a socializing force in the lives of children and as changed by a child's chronic illness will be presented. Social and legislative trends in the education of handicapped and health-impaired children, particularly the impact of PL 94-142 (the Education for All Handicapped Children's Act) will be discussed. Finally selected model programs designed to facilitate the reentry of the chronically ill child into school will be reviewed.

SCHOOL DAYS

COMPONENTS OF NORMAL GROWTH AND DEVELOPMENT

School is a constant in the lives of most children aged 6 to 17 in any modern, industrialized society. Its influence on a child's developing personality cannot be overestimated. While early childhood forms the basis for lifelong interpersonal, emotional, and, to some extent, cognitive and physical development, the school experience certainly shapes major cognitive and social directions for the developing individual.

School can be viewed as an arena for the acquisition of knowledge and skills. The pride of achieving reading and arithmetic skills continues to be important to most first graders regardless of their health status. Goal attainment is a regular feature of the school day, as specific tasks are accomplished. Although children learn to start and finish tasks, follow directions, and improve through criticism at home, the classroom provides an objective atmosphere that helps refine these abilities.

In addition the development of peer relationships and interpersonal skills is a direct outgrowth of the school's socializing influence. Most children first become members of clubs, first play team sports, and first work toward a cooperative goal within the curricular or extra-curricular context. Friendships are formed that extend beyond the boundaries of a school building — these friendships can last a lifetime. The feedback a child receives about his or her behavior from peers is vastly different and per-haps ultimately more influential on personality development than that received from parents, siblings, or other relatives. Thus the emotional and social impact of school is a significant force in a child's development.

School further serves as both practice and preparation for the future. The acquisition of cognitive and technical skills is important in preparation for career development and activi-ties of daily living. The refinement of social and interpersonal skills are likewise essential ones in the job market, home, and social settings. Underlying these skills are feelings of confi-dence and increased self-esteem that enable a young adult to venture into the world to estab-lish a career, a home, and a family. Experiences at school and at home serve to maintain and reinforce this sense of self-esteem and self-con-fidence.

There is another significant dimension of the school experience that influences the child's development. The regular achievement and long-range planning required in the school set-ting validate the future for children. The acqui-sition of skills and mastery of complex princi-ples are aimed toward preparing the child for the larger arena of life. In this way participation in school reinforces the fact of the future for all children. It affirms the probability of living to use the skills gained. Kleinberg (1982) notes in *Educating the Chronically Ill Child*, "School work represents normality for children and its con-tinued role in their lives is a signal that hope is not lost, that they may, in fact, continue to live for many months or years to come." For those children who cope with life-threatening illness, this sense of hope for the future is vital. Many of these children will live to be adults. As their chances for survival increase, so does their need to prepare for adulthood through the school experience.

IMPLICATIONS OF CHRONIC ILLNESS

For chronically ill children, including those with childhood cancer, many aspects of their disease and treatment influence their ability to progress academically. Frequent hospitaliza-tions and clinic visits may result in absences from school. School attendance is a major fac-tor in "keeping up." Cairns and colleagues (1982) report that in one institution treating children with cancer, a group of newly diag-nosed children missed an average of 41 school days or 2 months in the year they were diag-nosed. In this group the rate of absences con-tinued to remain high for 3 years after diag-nosis or throughout the treatment period. In their work with school-age children with cancer, Spinetta and Deasy-Spinetta (1981) also found absenteeism to be a significant problem. The pressure of making up missed work may pose an additional burden on these students.

Also physical health problems may compro-mise school performance. For example impair-ments such as nausea or anemia create difficul-ties even when the child is able to attend school. Low platelet counts related to disease or chemo-therapy effects may trigger bleeding episodes and preclude participation in certain activities, such as contact sports. Another treatment-re-lated side-effect, immunosuppression, causes susceptibility to infection, which becomes a major concern if outbreaks of childhood dis-eases, such as chickenpox, measles, or influ-enza, occur. Noticeable physical changes such as weight gain or loss, alopecia, mouth lesions, or nausea and vomiting may subject the child and classmates to anxiety. Mobility can be a significant problem for the child using crutches or a prosthesis or simply experiencing fatigue. Changing classes in junior and senior high school may present problems. Residual effects of therapy such as diminished hearing due to cisplatin administration will necessitate special consideration or the need for special diets or timing of meals.

Many of these physical problems apply to children with cancer regardless of age or school level. However, the type of experience the child may have and the types of accommodations the child will need vary with grade level, type of school setting, and many other factors.

Elementary level children are primarily concerned with basic cognitive and social skills. In many school settings they stay in a central classroom with perhaps one or two class changes for specialty areas, such as music or physical education. In some parts of the country, however, this system is giving way to team teaching with a few teachers. Nevertheless one teacher usually is responsible for the monitoring of the child's progress and for much of the child's formal instruction. At this level the child with cancer has interaction with one or two groups of classmates and one primary teacher. Early elementary grade students may be hampered by illness since the skills taught are basic ones which lay the foundation for later grades. On the other hand interaction with only a few teachers and groups of classmates limits the number of relationships the child and family must maintain during illness-related interruptions.

Although body image and self-esteem are vital considerations at any age, peer pressure is not yet a major force and physical changes are usually accepted. Adults in the school environment may be needed to support both the affected child and classmates in this process. Differences are often treated with curiosity, particularly if handled constructively. A blunt comment by another young child may be interpreted, however, as ridicule by the vulnerable cancer patient. Specific suggestions for preparation of elementary grade classmates for the ill child's return will be presented later in this chapter.

The *secondary level* presents a different set of problems. New influences include the socialization process of junior and senior high school and the developmental characteristics of adolescence. The adolescent with cancer frequently attempts to minimize his or her differences to the point of denial or avoidance of their implications. Spinetta and Deasy-Spinetta (1981) found that some adolescents and their parents gave the school only minimal information. Difficulties with scheduling of classes, mobility impairment, and the need for interaction with several teachers may result in major school-related problems for the teenager with cancer. The situation becomes a vicious cycle, with school-related difficulties undermining self-esteem, which is already compromised by the existence of physical differences (alopecia, weight loss or gain, fatigue). Due to the mechanics of operating the larger secondary school, policies may create special problems, particularly when communication is poor. For example the adolescent wearing a hat in class can be embarrassed when a teacher, unaware of the illness, requires the hat to be removed (NCI, 1980). The pressures of completion of graduation requirements necessary for college entrance or entry into the job market are usual concerns of healthy adolescents. Chronically ill young adults share these burdens, but may face additional obstacles, both disease related and society related. Whether or not to disclose the disease history — particularly if in a remission state — is a decision the individual must make. The choice will depend on many factors, including the awareness of exclusion from certain jobs or scholarship programs if the illness history is made known (Koocher, 1981).

INTERPERSONAL AND PSYCHOSOCIAL CONSIDERATIONS

In preliminary studies of children with various types of malignancies, some documentation of a higher than expected incidence of school phobia was reported. Lansky and coworkers (1975) noted an incidence of 10% in a study of

100 children being cared for in an urban oncology center. Compared to an estimated annual incidence of 1.7% in the general school-age population, this finding was attributed to fear of separation, particularly from their mother. However, the children studied were having school-related problems. More recently, Spinetta and Deasy-Spinetta (1981) noted that students in their clinic population attended school willingly. This study involved all school-age children with cancer in the clinic service.

PEER RELATIONSHIPS

An important facet of the school experience, interpersonal relationships can provide both a support and a challenge for the student with cancer. Peers are a valuable source of friendship, camaraderie, and understanding. Ill children desire normal peer interaction just as their healthy counterparts do. However, obstacles to the achievement of successful relationships occur because of attitudes of the child's friends and emotional constraints imposed by the child on him or herself. Peer-induced problems include lack of understanding and ignorance, which may result in teasing, hostility, or lack of consideration for the ill child's needs or feelings (Cunningham, 1983).

One major cause of difficulty in interrelationships with those outside the child's immediate family is the widespread lack of current knowledge regarding cancer on the part of the general population. Fear and myth continue to be frequent responses of the uninformed to the news that a neighbor has cancer. Out of this fear grows an awkwardness in daily interaction, a feeling of not knowing what to say, leading to avoidance. This experience of being "shunned" is common to both adult and pediatric cancer patients, although the degree to which it occurs varies depending on the individual, the family, and the general awareness of the community (Mullan, 1984). If shunned by friends and their parents, the child with cancer

will feel alienated and thus be inhibited from reaching out to others. The child's friends may also be shielded from contact with the child affected by cancer because of their parents' mistaken belief that emotional involvement with a sick child will be detrimental to a healthy child.

TO TELL OR NOT TO TELL

The issues of what to tell and whom to tell are a source of conflict for some families. If they choose the route of open communication about the illness, the child and the family must be prepared for some surprising reactions, even from close friends. Parents of children with cancer report reactions of anger, pity, fear, embarrassment, and complete avoidance (Fife, 1980). These responses filter down to the child, making school and social interactions a potentially difficult arena. Open communication affords an opportunity for the maximum amount of support and understanding to help the child and others deal with their feelings. In most cases accurate knowledge dispels or lessens fear. Open disclosure diminishes the threat of alienation of the child, if received constructively. Children frequently withdraw when the truth cannot be faced by others, including their parents (Fife, 1980).

If the child and parents opt for limited disclosure, a different set of pros and cons is involved. Discussing the diagnosis only among the family and close friends is an approach used by some families. A child with leukemia was describing this situation when he said, "My mom told me not to tell, because then the others will treat me like a regular kid" (Adams, 1978). The benefit to this family was that special treatment, good or bad, was not given to their child. Families may tell school officials that the child has "anemia" or a blood disease, for instance, rather than leukemia. Junior and senior high school students, who interact daily with several teachers and classes of students, may be reluctant to discuss their disease history. These adolescents want to avoid being singled out as different, so they may opt for not discussing their disease. There are hazards to this approach. If health problems develop school officials must intervene without basic knowledge of the child's or adolescent's status. The student may be disciplined or penalized for unavoidable behavior, such as an inability to participate fully in physical education. Friends and classmates may ostracize the student because of a lack of understanding. For example Jill (aged 12) had lymphoma and became fatigued during PE, causing her team to do poorly in an intramural competition. The response from her teammates was anger over her failure to play hard, and they concluded mistakenly that she was a poor sport.

Peer relationships can be supportive to the child with cancer. Due to ignorance and miscommunication, however, these relationships sometimes challenge the interpersonal skills of all concerned, as they attempt to achieve a state of closeness despite fear of involvement. As the general public becomes more informed about cancer, many of these problems will subside. In one study the expected incidence of teasing and problems with social interaction were not substantiated (Spinetta and Deasy-Spinetta, 1981). This may indicate that the school children and staff are becoming better informed in some areas. It also may reflect better preparation of children with cancer, equipping them to handle potentially sensitive issues.

CHILD RELATED PROBLEMS AND CONCERNS

The child with cancer continually faces the inner conflict created by the disease. The cancer cannot be ignored, for once diagnosed it becomes a major part of the child's life. On the other hand if the cancer becomes the overwhelming concern, other important facets of the child's life are usually neglected. A balance must be maintained, both within the child and within significant others, as to what must be done to maintain physical health without sacri-

ficing social and emotional health. Reintegration into the school setting is essential for social and emotional health although, at times, it poses risks to physical health. Reentry is not always an easy process, even when the return to school is eagerly anticipated. As discussed, the prevailing ignorance and superstition of the public, constraints because of the child's physical status, and the fears and anxieties of the parents as well as the child, are all factors which influence the success of the school experience.

In a major investigation of the school-aged child with cancer, it was demonstrated that pediatric cancer patients differed significantly from their classmates in certain school activities. Difficulties with attendance, concentration on schoolwork, a higher rate of learning disabilities, and lowered energy levels were major problems that kept these children from achieving at optimal levels. Emotionally these children were less likely to reach out to others, to initiate activities, to engage in new activities, or to express their feelings (Spinetta and Deasy-Spinetta, 1981).

In a study of 20 school-aged children with leukemia and 20 healthy school-aged children, Scungio (1983) found that leukemic children demonstrated significantly lower self-concepts than did the healthy children. The affected group also rated themselves lower on intellectual and school status, appearance, popularity, and happiness than did the healthy children. The children with leukemia participated in significantly fewer social activities than did the healthy children. The affected children participated in many more nonsocial activities, such as clinic visits, which was a significant change from their pre-illness life-style. Finally a significant positive correlation was demonstrated between the children's self-concepts and the time spent in social activities; a strong negative relationship was found between self-concept and the time spent in nonsocial activities. The author concluded that to help the leukemic child develop and adjust to the disease process, caregivers must help the child devote maximal efforts to quality living.

A poor self-concept can negatively influence school performance. Considering the combined influences of a diminished physical health, the stresses posed by a demanding treatment regimen, and increased emotional turmoil, the child with cancer is at risk for an unsuccessful school experience. Recent work has uncovered the additional potential for delayed cognitive effects of disease and treatment. A detailed discussion of this topic can be found in Chapter 10.

TEACHER AND ADMINISTRATIVE CONCERNS

Many of the problems arising from myths about cancer and lack of information affecting the general population likewise affect the responses of teachers and school administrators to the student with cancer. Integrating this child into the classroom has been viewed as an acute stress experience for the teacher (Spinetta, 1981). Many programs for teachers include little information on this topic. As previously mentioned there have been marked changes in the treatment and survival of the child with cancer. These factors contribute to the possibility that most teachers are unprepared on the basis of their education or personal experience to interact with this child. In a study of 82 participants in a seminar for educators of students with cancer, a majority of teachers were found to be lacking in information about cancer treatment, side-effects, and the actual prevalence of cancer in children. School nurses in this sample, although better informed than teachers, nevertheless indicated that less than one fourth of them were aware of the frequency of the diagnosis of cancer in children, and over one third erroneously attributed behavioral problems to chemotherapy side-effects (Ross, 1984).

The National Cancer Institute's booklet *Students with Cancer: A Resource for the Educator*

(1980) addresses teacher concerns. These include the need to consider personal feelings regarding life-threatening illness and the issue of death. Even when teachers have had some preparation, a student with cancer in the classroom can be "emotionally demanding and time consuming."

School administrators face the challenge of adapting policies and procedures to the special needs of this child. The family may make unrealistic demands on the school and teacher. As Spinetta (1981) observes, "The school is an educational and not a paramedical institution." The approach needed is one that helps assure teachers and other school personnel that the illness-related needs of the child are being well met, freeing the school to focus on its area of expertise — education.

The school nurse plays a key role in the reintegration of the child into the school setting. As the school-based health resource, this nurse is in the position to act as a liaison between the treatment facility and the school, interpreting the complexities of the disease process while remaining cognizant of the realities in the school setting. In one study school nurses were surveyed to determine how they perform this role and what they perceive as the needs of the child with cancer in the school (Moore and Triplett, 1980). In a Midwestern sample school nurses were found to be poorly informed regarding the special needs of the school-aged child with cancer. However, there was widespread recognition of their direct responsibility to serve as a resource person for school staff, to keep up to date on the student's condition, and to maintain a trustful relationship with the student. The survey demonstrated that the psychosocial needs of these students often went unrecognized. Of particular significance was the finding that the majority of the nurses who had actually cared for a child with cancer felt uninformed about the illness, its treatment, and its special needs. Many had received information from parents or students, and not from the child's physician, a hospital-based nurse, or a cancer center. In a replication of the study using a different geographical area, the results were similar. With 118 respondents from 225 school nurses in a Southwestern urban school district, the majority (67%) concurred that they served as a resource for members of the school staff and teachers. Whereas the actual number of school nurses who had had experience with a child with cancer (32 out of 118, or 27%) was relatively small, these nurses felt adequately informed and felt they could manage without help. As in the Midwestern group, however, aspects of psychosocial needs were unrecognized or unmet. Anticipating the student's feeling of rejection due to the disease or changes in appearance, for example, and intervention to support peers after a student's death, were not identified by a majority of school nurses as actions they would take. Finally the referral system was lacking, with only approximately 40% having received information from the child's physician or cancer center staff (Adams, 1983).

From these studies it appears that school nurses can be helped in their perceived role as resource, as well as caregiver, by a more specific, better organized referral system. In-service education also may be helpful in alerting school nurses to concerns typical of children and adolescents with cancer. As mentioned earlier the improvement in survival rates and vast changes in therapy have brought about a new group of chronically ill students. As with the general public, school staffs and others not working intimately with these children and families may lack current knowledge regarding cancer and its treatment, which will hinder the reintegration of these children into school and community.

The role of the school nurse in this area is an increasingly important one. Moreover the nurse is the member of the school staff most likely to be approached by child, parent, and teacher for assistance and information. Rustia and colleagues (1984) noted that parents of handicapped children often exchanged information with school nurses, but that in many cases this information, such as side-effects of medications, was not relayed to the classroom teachers. Mechanisms are needed in many school settings for the formal transfer of important information about the child.

With these considerations in mind the remainder of this chapter will focus on the social, legal, and educational mechanisms that are developing and, together with innovative hospital-based programs, are attempting to alleviate some of the difficulties faced by this child's re-entry into school.

SOCIAL AND LEGISLATIVE INFLUENCES

A major influence on the school lives of chronically ill children was the Education for All Handicapped Children's Act of 1975 (Table 9-1). This legislation ensured that institutions of public education provide a suitable program for all children, regardless of health status. Children with cancer are under the designation, "other health impaired," which entitles them to the safeguards and benefits established for children needing special education. Under the law each child is assured an individualized educational program within the least restrictive environment (Kleinberg, 1982). This legislation requires that a school district must provide

TABLE 9-1. FEATURES OF THE EDUCATION FOR ALL HANDICAPPED CHILDREN'S ACT OF 1975

Primary guarantees
   Individualized educational placement
   Education in the least restrictive environment
Benefits to the health-impaired child
   Free education assured
   Homebound instruction provided
   In-hospital instruction provided
   Parental input into planning
   Physical modification of the school setting as needed
     (ramps, elevators, classroom seating changes, etc.)

for the education of a chronically ill child with whatever physical or curricular means deemed reasonable under the law. The provision of homebound teachers and hospital-based schooling, when considered most appropriate for the child's needs, is one feature of this act. Parental involvement in the formulation of the individualized program is guaranteed by this legislation, plus a case-finding program to identify health-impaired children.

This legislation cannot remove social or emotional barriers to a child's education, but it does guarantee access to the educational system and its resources. In response to this legislation educational preparation for teachers and new subspecialty areas of hospital teachers and special education teachers have emerged to better meet the needs of this group of children. Technological advances such as educational television with hookups to home, school, and hospital, have also been developed through grants and are indirect results of this legislation.

Because of this and related legislation requiring the removal of architectural barriers and discrimination in employment of handicapped persons and a growing awareness of the needs and rights of the handicapped, social practices are changing. The visibility of those with handicaps has been increased by media coverage, significantly altering the attitude of the general population, who have become more tolerant and understanding in this area. The American Cancer Society and other voluntary organizations that concern themselves with cancer patients and families have mounted educational and social programs. Although myths and superstition remain, the outlook is changing. Hopefully the children affected by cancer in the future will not have to waste so much of their limited energy on changing the negative attitudes of those around them regarding either their right or their capacity to prepare for a productive life. (Fig. 9-1).

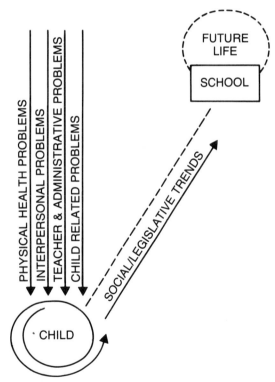

FIG. 9-1. School experience of the child with cancer.

REENTRY: SMOOTHING THE WAY

The importance of the school experience in normalizing the life of the child with cancer has been discussed. Making the return to school a successful process must be a long-range goal in the nursing plan for each child treated for cancer. An initial step is the encouragement of continuation of school activities within the hospital setting.

THE HOSPITAL TEACHER

Hospital-based teachers are available in most cancer centers, general hospitals, and children's hospitals. Under the Education for All Handicapped Children's Act, provision for appropriate education of health-impaired children is assured. School districts have instituted hospital-based schools to meet the needs of children hospitalized for periods of 3 weeks or more, or for chronically ill children requiring repeated hospitalizations. Although the facilities and services provided in different hospital settings vary, the principles behind this instruction are the same, governed by law and institutional policy. Usually a teacher(s) from the public school district is assigned to the pediatric unit of the hospital. One-to-one or group instruction may be used, depending on the child's need and medical status and on the available facilities in the unit. Teachers in these settings are governed in their practice by the policies and procedures of both their school district and the hospital. Children in the school or in one-to-one instruction are monitored for their progress, usually completing work assigned to them by their usual teacher in the community, whenever this is feasible. Ideally the child's work is sent with them to the hospital, or the hospital teacher contacts the community school teacher for appropriate lesson plans and homework. Since this type of schooling is very restrictive in terms of environment and opportunity for socialization, its use is appropriate only on a temporary basis, with the ultimate goal being the return of the child to some form of grouped school placement (Kleinberg, 1982). It serves as an initial step in providing for the continuity of the child's education, however, and offers a limited potential for socialization.

Technology has aided the educational process in many ways, and use of teleteaching through telephone hookup, closed circuit television, and computer programs supplements both home-based and hospital programs (Kleinberg, 1982). This type of programming enlarges the world for the child and helps the student to retain skills already acquired in school.

A cooperative relationship between the primary or staff nurse and the hospital teacher is vital to the success of this program. Since school is normally a scheduled part of a child's day, most hospital schools attempt to have a regular school day of a few hours. The unit staff members reinforce this by scheduling mealtimes and treatments around school, and by firmly encouraging school attendance whenever feasible. Sam, an 8-year-old second grader with a brain tumor, had been doing well in school at home, but when a new course of chemotherapy made him very nauseous, he became reluctant to attend school in the hospital. He used the possibility of vomiting as his reason and, even with antiemetic administration, postponed going to the schoolroom every morning. His frequent tardiness became cause for concern and the hospital teacher contacted nursing personnel. In a conference with Sam and the hospital teacher, the nurse was able to convince Sam to try regular attendance, assuring him that if a vomiting episode occurred, he could hurry back to his room. Soon Sam was involved in his school activities with few problems with vomiting.

THE HOMEBOUND TEACHER

For children ready to be discharged but not yet physically able to return to school, a homebound program is provided by law. As with the hospital-based program, a teacher is assigned from the local school district. Certification of need is required, which is initiated by the child's physician. Due to the length of time needed to process requests for homebound instruction, prompt communication when this type of need is anticipated is crucial to steady school progress. The child's physical stamina and educational needs, as well as teacher workload, will determine frequency of the teacher's visits. Cooperation between the local school and the homebound teacher is very important to provide for as much continuity as possible. Even more restrictive in terms of socialization opportunities, homebound instruction serves as a short-term effort to prevent the child from falling too far behind (Kleinberg, 1982).

With cooperative efforts hospitalized children can have a school experience. Programs within the home and hospital setting are not the ideal long-term solution for most children with cancer, but they do serve to prepare these children for reentry to their usual school setting.

PLANNING FOR RETURN TO SCHOOL

The next step in the transition process is discussion with the child and parent about the return to school. Topics for discussion include when the child might be medically ready to reenter school, how the child plans to handle classmates' questions, and suggestions for the parents regarding communication with the school (Wear and Blessing, 1976).

Another step that can be taken at this time is the process of certifying the child for special education services. Physician verification of the medical status is necessary to establish the presence of a handicapping condition (Bryan, 1980). The hospital teacher and medical social worker also are instrumental in this process. Initiating the process prior to discharge will help to prevent unnecessary delay in verifying the child's eligibility for needed services. Once a referral is made the school district will be able to determine the most appropriate setting to meet the learning objectives for the child. For example Lisa — an 11-year-old with ALL — was discharged with low WBC and platelet counts, but was eager to continue her schooling so as not to fall behind in sixth grade. The use of a homebound teacher temporarily helped her keep up so that she could return at grade level when her counts reached safer levels.

REENTRY PROGRAMS

Many hospitals, particularly cancer centers and other chronic illness-related facilities, have provided model programs to ease the transition for the chronically ill child while attempting to meet educational and emotional needs of those within the school setting. A structured referral system combined with orientation of the school staff and classmates of the child are usual features of such programs.

As a basic guideline the American Cancer Society has developed a handbook for the educator, which is listed in the Yellow Pages. Basic information to include in any reentry program is presented in this booklet. For example it is helpful to designate one person — a teacher, school nurse, counselor, or administrator — as liaison between the school, the student, the family, and the treatment center. This is an important consideration for junior and senior high school students because they come in contact with a large number of teachers, students, and administrators in the course of a day.

The initial communication may be in the form of a telephone conference or a visit. School personnel are prepared for changes in the child's appearance, if applicable, and are encouraged to ask questions. Written followup is helpful. The Wisconsin Cancer Center sends a letter to the teacher as well as a checklist of essential current information prepared at the time of discharge (Wear and Blessing, 1976).

Secondly a team conference including teachers, the school nurse, a member of the treatment center staff, family member(s), and the student should be scheduled to disseminate information and plan as a team each semester or school year. At Riley Hospital for Children in Indianapolis, such a conference is held to present factual information about cancer (REACH, 1983). Periodic conferences are held at least yearly, as mandated by PL 94-142, or more often if necessary. Thirdly an orientation program for classmates is helpful in anticipating problems and answering questions. This orientation can include an exploration of feelings regarding illness in general and cancer in

TABLE 9-2. CHARACTERISTICS OF REENTRY PROGRAMS

Orientation of child with cancer and family
Designated liaison between hospital and school
   Nurse/social worker
Detailed referrals from cancer center
   Telephone conference
   Written contact
Team conferences
   Initial
   Periodic
Orientation program
   School staff
   Classmates
Evaluation of effectiveness
   Student and family responses
   Teacher, administrator, school nurse responses
   Student attendance

particular, as well as a discussion of pertinent information about the specific student's type of cancer and treatment.

Consent of the student and family is obtained prior to discussing details about the illness. Sachs (1980) describes a 13-year old with leukemia who was adamant about wanting to be the one to inform his classmates, saying, "Tell them to ask Jack when he gets back." Respecting his wishes, his return to school plan included a presentation for school officials and teachers, with a kit for the teachers to later augment explanations to the children after Jack's return. A science unit or assignments about cancer can be prepared by the teacher or class, in conjunction with a visit from treatment center personnel, to discuss current methods or equipment. The Riley program provides an additional session of "medical play" for elementary grade classmates. Besides providing information about disease, the American Cancer Society suggests that the usual social and medical concerns need to be addressed, such as the student's exposure to communicable disease, the possibility of medical crises, and the need for routine health screening. A final note is to emphasize to school personnel and classmates that cancer is not contagious and isolation of the student is not necessary or desirable (NCI, 1980).

An evaluation phase is an important component of any program. Responses from school personnel and classmates can be elicited and compared with the actual experience of reentry as reported by the child and the family. Also the subsequent school experience, including the occurrence of excessive absenteeism or special problems, is assessed in many programs (REACH, 1983). The important components in a reentry program are summarized in Table 9-2.

CONCLUSION

This chapter has explored the importance of schooling and educational experiences to the growth and development of all children, including those with chronic illnesses. Trends in social and legislative mandates on the education of these children have been traced with emphasis on the assurances made to health-impaired children under the Education for All Handicapped Children's Act of 1975. Particular problems encountered by chronically ill children, particularly those with cancer, have been cited. Finally innovative programs for reentry have been described, with the essential components outlined. The nurse in the hospital caring for the child with cancer should be aware of this information. With programs such as these in mind, nursing interventions can be designed to achieve the goal of return to the most "normal" life possible for this child. In every case this will include some sort of educational experience, which will have to be adapted to individual needs and set within the least restrictive environment possible. When placed in the forefront of planning considerations, the following key points will enhance the possibility of "truly curing" the child with cancer (Van Eys, 1979).

KEY POINTS

- School is a normal, highly influential force in the lives of children.
- When self-esteem is threatened, as in chronic illness, the school experience becomes even more critical.
- Under PL 94-142 every child, regardless of health status, is guaranteed appropriate state funded schooling.
- With attention to special needs and flexibility in scheduling, even seriously ill children can continue their educational process.
- The goal of return to school is a powerful motivator and instills a feeling of hope in the pediatric cancer patient and family.
- Planning must begin early in the initial diagnostic/treatment phase to prevent delay in school return when the child is physiologically stable.
- With education of the general public and the specific school population, most problems related to school reentry can be anticipated, prevented, or solved.
- A team approach involving those in medicine, nursing, social work, various therapy disciplines, and education has been used with success in pilot programs across the country.
- Child and family input into planning the return to school, as well as assessment of the success of the process, are vital parts of any reentry program.
- Only by ensuring the continuity of this important part of a child's life, and simultaneously meeting disease-related and emotional needs, can a truly cured child emerge from the treatment of cancer.

REFERENCES

Adams, J. (1983). School nurse survey: Perceptions of school nurses regarding the needs of students with cancer. University of Texas, Houston, unpublished manuscript.

Adams, J. (1978). Simulation gaming as a nursing intervention for children with leukemia. Master's Thesis, University of Texas School of Nursing.

Bryan, E. (1980). Use of medical information in school planning. *Journal of School Health, 50,* 259–61.

Cairns, N., Klopovich, P., Hearne, E., and Lansky, S. (1982). School attendance of children with cancer. *Journal of School of Health, 52,* 152–155.

Fife, B. (1980). Childhood cancer as a family crisis: A review. *Journal of Psychosocial Nursing and Mental Health Services, 18,* 29–34.

Kleinberg, S. (1982). *Educating the chronically ill child.* Rockville, MD: Aspen.

Koocher, G., and O'Malley, J. (1981). *The Damocles syndrome: Psychosocial consequences of surviving childhood cancer.* New York: McGraw Hill Book Co.

Lansky, S., Lowman, J., Vats, T., and Gynlay, J. (1975). School phobia in children with malignant neoplasms. *American Journal of Diseases of the Child, 129,* 42–46.

McNair, F., (1980). At-home rehabilitation of pediatric cancer patients: A team approach. *5,* 50–55.

Moore, I. and Triplett, J. (1980). Students with cancer: A school nursing perspective. *Cancer Nursing, 3,* 265–270.

Mullan, F. (1984). Re-entry: The educational needs of the cancer survivor. *Health Education Quarterly, 10,* Special Supplement, 88–93.

National Cancer Institute (1980). *Students with cancer: A resource for the educator.* NIH Publication No. 80-2086, Bethesda, MD.

REACH (1983). *Re-entry education about classmate's hospitalization.* James Whitcomb Riley Hospital for Children, Indianapolis, IN.

Ross, J. (1984). Resolving the non-medical obstacles to successful school re-entry for children with cancer. *Journal of School Health, 54,* 84–86.

Rustia, J., Hartly, R., Hansen, G., Shutte, D., and Spielman, L. (1984). Redefinition of school nursing practice: Integrating the developmentally disabled. *Journal of School Health, 54,* 58–61.

Sachs, M. (1980). Helping the child with cancer go back to school. *Journal of School Health, 50,* 328–331.

Scungio, J. (1983). The relationship between self concept and social activities of leukemia and healthy children. University of Alabama, Birmingham, unpublished manuscript.

Spinetta, J., and Deasy-Spinetta, P. (Eds.) (1981). *Living with childhood cancer* (pp. 153–168). St. Louis: C. V. Mosby.

Van Eys, J. (1977). What do we mean by the truly cured child? In J. Van Eys (Ed.) *The Truly Cured Child* (pp. 79–96). Baltimore: University Park Press.

Wear, E. and Blessing, P. (1976). Child and cancer: Facilitating the return to school. In B. Peterson and C. Kellogg (Eds.), *Current practice in oncologic nursing* (pp. 222–230). St. Louis: C. V. Mosby.

10

AFTER THE CURE

INTRODUCTION

The problem of the long-term survivor has arisen in the field of pediatric oncology. Albeit welcome, the long-term survival of the child with cancer creates substantial difficulties for the child and family. As survival rates improve health professionals will be confronted increasingly with the task of helping a young adult to rebuild his or her life following the "holocaust" of an experience with cancer. This chapter will address these concerns by considering the timing of cessation of therapy, the recurrence of disease or a new incidence of malignancy, and the steadily increasing list of delayed effects found to occur in long-term survivors. Finally ways in which caregivers can help the child and the family to prepare for cure, while anticipating and managing possible problems, will be presented.

OFF THERAPY

For the child who has spent interminable hours waiting in clinics, being punctured and radiated, feeling nauseous and coping with baldness, the end of the treatment protocol symbolizes a return to some semblance of normal living. The parent likewise eagerly anticipates this benchmark of success and hope. Criteria for cessation of active treatment varies with cancer site, type of protocol, and complicating factors. The child's response to therapy for example, whether in a first or subsequent remission of disease, has a bearing on the timing of discontinuance of therapy. (See Chapter 3 for a more detailed discussion of treatment protocols, their duration, and criteria for cessation by specific cancer site.)

FAMILY IMPACT

When cessation occurs most families are both apprehensive and jubilant. Sam, aged $6\frac{1}{2}$, and his parents eagerly anticipated the date of his last IV and intrathecal methotrexate course and planned a party for the unit and the staff the following week. Spirits were high and Sam's anticipation of starting school was only slightly dampened by his continued baldness. A month later, however anxiety had so consumed this family that a counseling session was planned to help them to cope with their conflicting emotions. The psychologist observed that it was typical for families to experience elation and dread at this point. The security of the treatment regimen and the faith established during the $3\frac{1}{2}$ years of close surveillance and active treatment of the child were hard to relinquish.

In a followup study of long-term survivors

conducted by Koocher (1981), many parents reported a peak of anxiety at the end of active treatment. This stressful period was as brief as 10 days for a Wilms' tumor patient, contrasted with several years for one patient with leukemia; of note is that this surprised most of the parents since they did not expect anxiety at this phase of therapy. One possible explanation is the realization by the parents that they now have the primary responsibility for the care of their sick child, as opposed to the shared responsibility of the intensive treatment period.

In a study conducted to determine the psychosocial responses to terminating chemotherapy, results suggested that negative reactions may be a normal emotional response (Lewis and LaBarbera, 1983). Frequent responses reported by parents whose children had recently terminated chemotherapy included strong feelings of anxiety, fears of relapse, uncertainty over proper treatment, and negative feelings regarding losing contact with hospital personnel and other parents. The authors go so far as to suggest that absence of these "normal" negative feelings and fears may indicate parental inability to accept the "danger of the child's disease [which] may well interfere with appropriate aftercare." Caregivers may need to emphasize to them the possibility that they may feel stressed at unexpected times.

Even during the relative freedom of the off-therapy period, monitoring continues. Depending on the cancer site and the child's medical status, frequency of clinic visits ranges from monthly to yearly. Diagnostic monitoring may continue, including spinal taps and bone marrows, although less often than in the active treatment phase. The increased interval between clinic visits demands a well-informed patient and family who are alert for potential problems. The topic of patient education has been covered in Chapter 4, and information regarding resources for patient and family education are listed in the Yellow Pages of this book.

An interesting emotional phenomenon occurs during both periods of remission and cessation of therapy. Reports of "near denial" of the illness have been documented by those who work closely with these families. Spinetta and Deasy-Spinetta (1981) report that adolescents in particular may allow themselves to forget about the illness between clinic visits. This option may not be possible for those patients with visible impairments such as alopecia, surgical scars, radiation markings, or a prosthesis. To a lesser degree parents report that periods of relative health or freedom from intensive treatment may serve as a break from thinking constantly about the disease, but that the knowledge of it cannot be totally denied (Spinetta and Deasy-Spinetta, 1981).

One possible outcome of the less extensive contact with oncology staff during a period of long-term remission is that infrequent and brief visits may predispose the parent and child not to confront important concerns. If there are no signs of recurrence at checkup, the accompanying relief might distract the parent or patient from asking about other health risks, such as sexual activity, smoking, or school-related problems. Clinicians have recently begun to confront the implications of "adaptive denial," in which the cancer survivor truly believes that all is well and takes health risks such as missing checkups, smoking, or engaging in unprotected sexual activity (Koocher, 1981). In this regard Dunlop (1982) identifies the taking of "negative risks" as possible signals for help in coping with their distress. When the use of drugs or other escape mechanisms were part of the young adult's previous life-style, posttreatment use may not be danger signals, but rather part of the individual's coping style. The obvious risks attendant on these behaviors can be confronted directly. On the other hand, when a previous nonuser initiates these behaviors, caregivers should be alert to the individual's need for tension release and help in choosing more constructive coping strategies. Jean, a 17-year-old girl with Hodgkin's disease, had reported in her history that she disliked drug use and hoped she would not need to use analgesics on a regular basis. During a clinic visit while Jean was in remission, her mother confided that she had noted signs of alcohol use and was worried at the change in Jean's behavior. Inviting Jean to attend the teen group, the social worker brought up drug use in a hypothetical adolescent case study. As the group analyzed possible reasons for drug use, Jean shared her experiments with alcohol as a way of relating to her peer group. Two of the other teens shared similar feelings and the ways they had learned to cope with the alienation they felt from former friends due to their illness. Some of the veterans of the group commented that the immediate benefits of alcohol were not worth risking a complication or an interaction with drug therapy for their disease.

RECURRENCE OF DISEASE

For long-term survivors who later succumb to cancer, a recurrence of the original disease in the interval of 5 to 9 years postdiagnosis is the usual cause. In the period of 10 to 19 years postdiagnosis, mortality is often related to a second primary neoplasm or to complications such as organ failure or infection (Koocher, 1981).

Why second tumors occur is unknown, just as the etiology of the primary cancer remains a mystery in most cases. Risk factors hypothesized to play contributing roles include environmental toxins, viral or radiation exposure, and genetic factors, all of which may have existed in the patient at one time, theoretically predisposing the individual to the first cancer episode. Subsequent treatment with carcinogenic substances such as radiation and certain chemotherapeutic agents may then pose added long-term hazards (Koocher, 1981).

In general the frequency of second tumor occurrence is estimated to be approximately 20 times greater than the expected tumor rate for the general population. It appears that the risk increases over time, peaking between 15 and 19 years after initial diagnosis and declining after that. When related to radiation therapy, new tumors nearly always occur in previously irradiated sites. It is important to note that many (approximately 40%) of these tumors are benign (Koocher, 1981).

Relapse after elective cessation of therapy is of course a matter of serious concern to parents, the child, and the treatment team. It has been felt that for most individuals the likelihood of a response to therapy decreases following each relapse. In a study of 125 relapses of ALL, however, another remission was achieved in 91% of treatment courses. In addition multiple subsequent relapses, aggressively treated, demonstrated an approximately 90% success rate (Reaman et al., 1980). The authors suggest that the possibility of achieving successive remissions in relapsed ALL patients may be better than previously thought and may justify a more aggressive treatment. In a small study of individuals with secondary osteogenic sarcoma, formerly felt to be a cancer with a very poor prognosis as a secondary neoplasm, indications were that successful response and remission was a realistic expectation justifying an optimistic and aggressive approach (Pillay, et al., 1983).

For families who counted themselves among the survivors, late recurrence of disease or the development of a new tumor is an extremely traumatic event. The very real fear that hope for cure has been lessened and a decrease in the perception of control have been identified as particularly distressing to the parents. Also the parents can no longer feel they belong to the "successful" group. Treatment plans become more individualized, again lessening the feeling of control they had under the familiar protocol. For the child and the family, revisions will need to be made in the thinking, planning, and communicating that is done about the illness. Krulik (1982) notes that parents in her study, for instance, realized the change in developmental status that had occurred in their children in the years since the initial diagnosis.

TABLE 10-1. DELAYED EFFECTS OF TREATMENT

System Affected	Manifestations	Predisposing Factors
Central nervous system	Learning disabilities Neuropathies Seizure disorders Growth retardation	Methotrexate intrathecally Irradiation Vincristine therapy
Musculoskeletal	Atrophy, fibrosis Scoliosis, kyphosis Amputation Growth retardation	Irradiation Surgical intervention Malnutrition
Gastrointestinal	Chronic enteritis Cirrhosis	Chemotherapeutic agents Irradiation
Renal	Hemorrhagic cystitis Nephritis	Irradiation Certain chemotherapeutic agents (cyclophosphamide)
Respiratory	Interstitial pneumonia Pulmonary fibrosis	Cyclophosphamide, methotrexate, tetrametylene dimethanesulfonate, bleomycin, mitomycin nitrosoureas
Cardiovascular	Congestive heart failure Chronic pericarditis	Doxorubicin Mediastinal radiation
Sensory	High-frequency hearing loss Taste changes	Aminoglycoside antibiotics Cisplatin Various chemotherapeutic agents Irradiation of oral cavity
Hematopoietic	Immune system alterations Chronic bone marrow suppression	Irradiation Chemotherapy

Reproductive	Ovarian suppression
	Temporary or permanent
	  azoospermia
	Mutagenicity
		Irradiation
		Various chemotherapeutic
		  agents

Cognitive function	Learning disabilities Memory deficit Distractability Decreased verbal ability and IQ scores	Cranial radiation Intrathecal drugs

Psychosocial	Uncertainty about future
	Sick role assumption
	Negative risk-taking
	Independence/dependence conflicts
	Fear of illness/death
	Stigmatized as
	  different
		Illness experience
		Continuing public
		  ignorance about cancer

Perhaps a child who was a toddler during the diagnostic and active treatment period, has a late recurrence during the school-age or adolescent period. Different communication about the illness, as well as different areas of concern, will prevail. This period with its characteristic problems has been called the midstage and presents challenges different from those at the diagnosis and earlier treatment stages.

DELAYED EFFECTS OF TREATMENT

Adverse somatic effects to the child with cancer who is undergoing treatment result from cellular damage and a combination of host, disease, or treatment factors. As discussed previously in this book, treatment for cancer damages both tumor cells and normal cells. Normal cells can in some cases repair themselves, reversing the ill effects of disease or treatment. In other instances damage and disability result. The most long-term or disabling of these effects will be discussed and are summarized in Table 10-1.

Damage to the *central nervous system,* often occurring in children treated with cranial radiation or intrathecal drug administration, has been reported in the literature with estimates ranging from 20% to 40% of samples of children followed for periods of 5 years or more (Oliff and Levine, 1982). Leukoencephaly—characterized by subtle and overt symptomatology such as dementia, paresis, and seizures—may occur in as many as 15% of patients receiving cranial radiation, intrathecal medications, or both (Jaffe, 1984). Learning problems and seizure disorders are other potentially significant neurological outcomes. Learning disabilities will be discussed under delayed cognitive effects. Growth retardation is thought to be related to effects on the hypothalamic pituitary axis causing impairment in pituitary function. However some research (Wells, et al., 1983) indicates that while growth hormone secretion may be temporarily affected, and while irradiated children show decreases in height gains during treatment, the slowing of growth appears to be temporary. Thus delayed effects of cranial irradiation on the long-term aspects of growth are thought to be minimal.

The *musculoskeletal system* can be affected in an obvious way, such as amputation, or less directly through changes in tissue or bone brought about by chemotherapy, radiation, or damage from the disease itself. Radiation specifically may cause atrophy, underdevelopment, or fibrosis of muscles in the irradiated area. Curvature of the vertebral column also can result, causing scoliosis or kyphosis. The latter may be manifested particularly in the growing child (under 6 or during pubescence), particularly following unilateral abdominal or vertebral radiation. Dental problems also may occur, including shortening of roots, multiple caries, and abnormalities in alignment (Wells, et al., 1983). (For more specifics regarding long-term effects of radiation therapy, see Chapter 5.)

An important aspect of musculoskeletal delayed effects is that they are usually highly visible defects. Although one would anticipate that adjustment to such residual deformity would be difficult, Koocher (1981) found in his retrospective study of long-term survivors of childhood cancer that there was no significant correlation between the degree of physical impairment and long-term psychological adjustment.

Another musculoskeletal delayed effect that has been briefly mentioned is growth retardation. Various theories related to decreased production of growth hormone, in the case of cranial irradiation, and damage to the epiphysial portion of a long bone have been advanced. Research indicates that growth rate does slow during radiation therapy, but that most children seem to "catch up" after therapy ceases (Wells, et al., 1983; Jaffe, 1984). It is important to consider, however, the total status of the child who is receiving radiation or chemotherapy. Such a child may be malnourished, below average weight percentile for age, and experience intermittent periods of loss of appetite and potential for infection. Given such negative factors catch up growth may not occur as expected. In addition the impact of a malnourished appearance is itself a visible effect of both disease and therapy, which sometimes becomes a long-term psychological effect.

The *gastrointestinal system* may be chronically affected by both chemotherapy and radiotherapy. Chronic enteritis has resulted from radiotherapy due to the formation of areas of fibrosis or ulceration throughout the gastrointestinal tract. Again the total dose of radiation administered to this area seems to be the major influence on the development of late toxicities. Some chemotherapeutic agents implicated as hepatotoxins are methotrexate, aminopterin, chlorambucil, cytosine arabinoside, daunomycin, and doxorubicin. In the case of methotrexate, the schedule and duration of therapy has been shown to have a bearing on the development of fibrosis — lower dosage, daily and oral regimens being more likely to result in this complication than higher dose, intermittent therapy (Oliff and Levine, 1982).

Radiation therapy may cause chronic disease of the *renal system* such as chronic cystitis, nephritis, and hypertension, particularly if there is concurrent administration of actinomycin D (Jaffe, 1984). Chemotherapeutic agents are also nephrotoxic, notably 6-mercaptopurine, cisplatin, and BCNU. Additionally, cyclophosphamide therapy may cause both acute and chronic hemorrhagic cystitis, and long-term fibrosis and contraction of the bladder (Oliff and Levine, 1982).

The *respiratory* and *cardiovascular systems* also may suffer late effects following certain drug and treatment protocols. Radiation, infection, or surgery to resect metastatic lung lesions may cause chronic respiratory problems. Exposure to cyclophosphamide, methotrexate, bleomycin, mitomycin-C, and the nitrosourea group of drugs may result in chronic pulmonary problems, including interstitial pneumonia and pulmonary fibrosis (Greene and Fergusson, 1982). Periodic examination with pulmonary function studies and thorough clinical assessment should be carried out. In terms of cardiovascular effects, doxorubicin is a cardiotoxic as well as antineoplastic agent. Cardiac effects that include congestive heart failure appear to be related to the cumulative dosage. Patients who have received doses in excess of 600 mg/M^2 experience a sharp increase in the incidence of heart failure; however, heart failure also has occurred in cases of low dosage, and has not occurred in other cases of very high dosage. Children receiving doxorubicin therapy therefore should be monitored regularly by echocardiogram, EKG, and careful clinical observation. The predictive value of such testing has not been completely determined — endomyocardial biopsy and cardiac catheterization are the most reliable predictors, but are costly, require specialized treatment facilities, and are invasive techniques (Oliff and Levine, 1982). Other long-term cardiovascular effects include pericarditis following radiation therapy to the mediastinum, and occlusive arterial disease occurring at the site of radiation therapy (Oliff and Levine, 1982).

In terms of *sensory impairment*, a potential long-term effect is high-frequency hearing loss. There are a variety of drug agents, notably the aminoglycoside antibiotics, that are known to be ototoxic. In the group of antineoplastic drugs, CDP (cisplatinum, or cisplatin), effective against a variety of childhood tumors, is usually the causative agent. For this reason baseline and periodic audiograms are commonly performed to assess the child's hearing acuity. Impairment seems to be related to dose and age. In a prospective study by McHaney and colleagues (1983) bilateral, high-frequency hearing loss occurred in 88% of the sample, with increasing impairment varying directly with increasing dosage. For most of these children only very high dosages were found to impair hearing in the main frequency range for everyday communication. At any dosage or frequency range, the degree of hearing loss was inversely related to age (McHaney, et al., 1983). This finding was thought to be related to an increased susceptibility of less mature cochlear and vascular systems to CDP ototoxicity, leading clinicians to expect the greatest effect to be on the infant.

Testing methods for this age group are inadequate at present for thorough evaluation. The investigators also studied the sample further to note any reversibility of the hearing loss. It was concluded that the impairment was permanent. Implications include delays in speech and language acquisition for the young child and potential related school difficulties for all ages. Careful monitoring with the use of remediation, changes in classroom seating, and hearing aids may be indicated.

The long-term effects on the *hematologic system* include alterations in the immune system and compromised bone marrow function. These effects occur most commonly following extensive radiation therapy, particularly to marrow-containing bones. The total dose required to produce this result is theorized to be between 3000 and 5000 rad, with the extent of damage dependent upon the volume of marrow involved, age at the time of radiation, and concurrent administration of other marrow toxic agents. The use of alkylating agents can also bring about prolonged marrow suppression. Busulfan has been shown to cause marrow aplasia for a prolonged period both experimentally in animal studies and in humans with chronic myelogenous leukemia (Oliff and Levine, 1982).

In the area of *sexual and reproductive function,* many implications merit consideration for long-term survivors. Since this is a relatively new area being studied, research into reproductive patterns is limited. Some survivors have married and reproduced, however, so preliminary information is available.

It is known that the ovary and testis are sensitive to both radiation and some chemotherapeutic agents. It is theorized that pubescent boys and girls are most vulnerable to effects on the *reproductive system*. A study conducted on samples of prepubescent girls did not show the ovarian suppression noted in girls who had begun menses (Greene and Fergusson, 1982). In males it has been found that while some low dosages of radiation produce only temporary azoospermia, high dosages (1000 rad) may result in permanent sterility. Likewise chemotherapy often produces an abrupt, dose-related, and possibly reversible suppression of spermatogenesis. Of additional concern is the danger of mutagenicity to sperm during therapy — low dosages of radiation have been shown to be related to genetic abnormalities of the sperm (Kaempfer, et al., 1983).

Because of these concerns Koocher (1981) included an assessment of marriage and reproductive status in an extensive followup of long-term survivors from the Sidney Farber Institute. Of the sample who were 21 and older, approximately 50% were married. In interviews with the cancer survivors and their spouses, the two problems most often discussed were the survivor's ability to conceive children and the sexual relationship. It was felt that most sexual concerns were culturally related to expectations regarding appearance and performance in the sexual role. Most couples felt they had resolved these concerns with open communication. Related to this is the fact that in this sample the more severe the physical limitations in women, the less chance of their being married, while this was not true of males (Koocher, 1981).

Regarding reproduction 75% of the married group had children. Some of the spouses did report being more "lump conscious" and taking their children to the doctor more often for various reasons because of a fear of the possibility of cancer. Nevertheless the children were reported to be developing normally (Koocher, 1981) and to be without serious health problems.

It should be noted that in addition to the potential for sterility and genetic effects related to potentially mutagenic influences of radiation and chemotherapy, some cancer therapies which include surgery may cause permanent sterility or reduced fertility; pelvic exenteration and unilateral and bilateral testicle removal are obvious examples.

Because of the above considerations, some

cancer centers have initiated the availability of sperm banking. People most interested in this option are those in the 17 to 35 age group at the time of diagnosis, although younger patients may be interested. Kaempfer and colleagues (1983) note that parents or staff should not assume lack of interest or concern regarding future reproductive potential in the adolescent male patient. In contrast to the young adult or older male, the adolescent may have less interest in the detailed financial or contractual information such as storage facilities and potential legal ramifications, and in many cases, leave such arrangements to the parents. A casual, nonthreatening discussion about concepts of lowered fertility or infertility and reassurance as to potency will best serve his immediate needs. Information regarding the time requirements for collection prior to chemotherapy or radiotherapy will be of importance in decision making. If a decision to elect sperm banking is made, a relaxed and private collection mechanism must be arranged. In one large medical center it was the influence of one 16-year old's inquiry about the possibilities of sperm banking that brought about the offering of this option as standard practice to male adolescent oncology and bone marrow candidates. The majority of patients who elected to store reported an increased trust in caregivers because their concern was taken seriously (Kaempfer, et al., 1983).

Long-term *cognitive* effects recently have received attention. In a review of the literature, Jaffe (1984) reports that although there have been conflicting reports on the occurrence of neuropsychiatric abnormalities in long-term cancer survivors, recent evidence suggests that there are long-term cognitive sequelae of cranial irradiation, particularly in the younger age groups at the time of therapy. The cognitive skills that appear to be most affected are quantitative, memory, and motor skills. Fergusson (1981) concludes from a review of studies in this area that the combination of irradiation

and methotrexate used on the central nervous system during early stages of neurologic development produce measurable intellectual impairment in some children. Maturity of the developing brain, as well as concurrent treatment with other agents, may affect the toxicity and resulting cognitive and neurologic effects. Although the mechanism is poorly understood, the damage seems to be age-related, with younger children showing the greatest effects. Some of these effects include distractability, memory deficits, decreased verbal performance, and lowered IQ scores (Pfefferbaum-Levine, et al., 1984). Because of these data on long-term treatment effects, monitoring of cognitive development will be a necessary aspect of the followup care for long-term survivors.

Cognitive development and success in educational or vocational training are important components of adult life. As discussed in Chapter 9, the child's return to school is a continuing concern and merits recognition as a priority in care planning. Together with this concern must go careful planning to develop an individualized program that will accommodate any cognitive or sensory impairment and resultant learning disabilities. Meadows and coworkers (1980) state that for some survivors learning disabilities seem to be related to specific areas of functioning such as auditory perception, attention span, and short-term memory. The use of teaching strategies aimed at reducing the impact of these learning problems should become an integral part of the individualized educational program (IEP) for the affected child.

At the time of diagnosis of learning problems or the encountering of school-related difficulties, it is important to recognize that this may represent another period of frustration and anger for the child and the parents. The relief related to long-term survival may thus be dampened by the knowledge that a new set of problems has arisen. Anger at the health team that provided the treatment may occur and needs to be accepted by health professionals as a normal reaction. The nurse or other health team member needs to shift the focus to planning special learning techniques that will be effective in helping the child to attain his or her individual potential. Remedial classes and tutoring or placement in a special education program may be appropriate courses of action. Parents may need assistance in these arrangements, and medical certification of problems is required (Fergusson, 1981). Fifteen-year-old Mindi illustrates this situation well. Treated for ALL from the age of 5 to $8\frac{1}{2}$, she had shown excellent treatment response and had been off treatment for approximately 6 years. Although coming in regularly for followup, her rosy health picture had distracted clinic personnel from probing into her school and social life. Mindi was attending school but was generally just getting by. She was going from one near-failure to another in high school, after being an average student in grammar school and junior high. Mindi's parents initiated a conference with the social worker because the teenager was threatening to drop out of school. Interviews with both Mindi and school staff revealed a frustrated adolescent who had withdrawn from friends, ate alone at lunch, failed to bring homework or progress reports home and, in general, was clinically depressed. An educational diagnostician found that learning difficulties existed, related to memory deficits and a mild hearing impairment, which partially explained her behavior. Special tutoring and a change in classroom seating were arranged, as well as frequent conferences between teachers, Mindi, and her parents, to more carefully monitor her progress. The remainder of that sophomore year was a difficult time of adjustment, with many resentful feelings aired both by Mindi and her father. However, with her mother's encouragement, Mindi joined the chorus at school the next fall and began to be more interested in school activities. Although she missed too much school in the previous year to stay at grade level, she made steady progress and remained in school, a much happier adolescent.

PSYCHOSOCIAL EFFECTS

Dunlop (1982) identified six major areas of concern to the young adult with cancer, in her work at the Center for Attitudinal Healing. Although this population was predominantly still actively being treated for their cancer, the six areas seem appropriate age-related concerns for survivors. The cancer diagnosis becomes an ever present reality, regardless of cure status, and affects psychosocial functioning. The areas of concern include uncertainty about the future, identification with illness or the sick role, taking negative risks, facing illness and death as potential unexpected life events, independence–dependence conflicts with parents, and the stigma of being different.

For the cancer survivor avoidance of planning for the future is not unusual. Returning to school or getting a job may be indefinitely postponed. Fear of relapse may prompt this behavior (Dunlop, 1982). Also there are real problems associated with seeking employment. Many cancer patients encounter discrimination simply on the basis of their disease history (Kolberg, 1983). This may be particularly true for the adolescent or young adult who has no history of successful work performance to use to convince a potential employer. The usual reasons cited for not hiring a former cancer patient include concern over health insurance coverage, decreased productivity, excessive sick leave or absenteeism, disability payments, and the potential for death (Koocher and O'Malley, 1981). Even when a survivor has a job, reports of being denied a promotion or advanced training are noted. In a study of persons with cancer in California, 84% of those returning to blue collar jobs reported on-the-job discrimination. Types of discrimination included demotion, denial of advancement, and reduction of benefits (King, 1984). In addition some individuals experience avoidance and stressful interaction with other employees. To counter the arguments given for not hiring cancer patients, the National Cancer Institute studied two sets of employees who had cancer histories and found that measures of employee absenteeism, turnover, and job performance were all within normal limits. The study documented that discrimination does exist, however. The United States military disqualifies applicants with a cancer history, (King, 1984). In this particular followup of survivors, approximately half reported work-related problems, including discrimination based on their cancer history and what they felt was the necessity for deception about their disease with the employer and coworkers. Of importance here is the fact that cancer patients, similar to those with other handicaps, are protected by affirmative action legislation and have recourse to free legal assistance through the United States Department of Labor (King, 1984).

Illness identification and adoption of sick role behavior is a potential problem that is more evident in the acute active treatment phase than when in remission or long-term survival. Some young persons fuse identities with the role of cancer patient, however, and may continue to adopt the sick role even over the long term (Dunlop, 1982).

The occurrence of negative risk-taking can be potentially destructive long-term behavior both in the active and remission phases of treatment. Risk-taking per se is a common behavior in the adolescent. Negative risk-taking includes behaviors such as the use of drugs, avoidance of treatment or checkups, failure to maintain nutrition, and unprotected sexual activity. Possibly even more than in the active treatment phase, some of these behaviors may occur in an attempt to deny or minimize the reality of the cancer diagnosis in the period following pronouncement of "cure." Without careful monitoring negative risks such as these

and others can certainly have long-term consequences. Dunlop observes that much of this type of behavior may be the need to risk relapse in order to test control and is best dealt with through patience, understanding, and time (Dunlop, 1982).

Illness and death are unexpected events in childhood. When illness occurs, particularly in the period of adolescence or early adulthood, the normal conflict over independence intensifies. Illness renders the adolescent and young adult dependent on others. Despite their best intentions parents often become protective under the threat of harm to their "child," robbing the young adult of previously gained independence and decision-making ability. Resentful feelings on the part of the young adult may result. On the other hand parents may resent the perceived or real dependency of the child resulting from the illness experience. A vicious cycle of conflict can ensue, sometimes spilling over into the area of treatment and long-term followup. In most states the patient is considered legally responsible to consent or deny treatment after the age of 18 (Dunlop, 1982). Legal accountability may not resolve emotional conflicts, however, or issues such as control of the treatment plan of a "sick" young adult.

Samuel illustrates this point. At 19, he refused a forequarter amputation of his shoulder and right arm for osteogenic sarcoma. As a music lover Samuel played piano in a local band and felt the amputation would severely limit his capabilities. He lived with his father, who was adamant that every avenue be used to obtain a "cure." Logical arguments and emotional pleas from the father failed to change Samuel's mind, and the surgeon cancelled the procedure that had been scheduled on the father's authority. Hurt by what he described as his son's suicidal behavior, the father would not listen to explanations of alternative treatment plans. He began to visit his son in the hospital less often, stating it was too painful an experience. A family conference with the nursing staff, physician, and social worker could not bring the two together, and Samuel left the hospital to begin his outpatient treatment with the issue unresolved. Although health professionals continued to provide emotional support for both people, the relationship became increasingly strained. Finally Samuel moved out on his own, he and his father both missing the strength they could have gained from each other.

The last area identified in Dunlop's work is the problem of "being different." As Dunlop observes, "Being different is a deeply felt social and physical experience. Prolonged illness separates the young adult from peers and activities" (1982). Even in the remission phase, individuals with cancer may have obvious differences in body weight, loss of limb or hair, surgical scars, and so on, or less obvious but perceived differences in the fact that they have been diagnosed and treated for a potentially life-threatening illness. In many cases young adults reinforce others' views of them as different by becoming withdrawn or reluctant to reach out to others.

There is some indication that preillness feelings of self-esteem and self-concept may influence the adjustment made "after the cure." Individuals who already have attained a positive self-image and confidence in relationships with others may perhaps be more able to accommodate changes in body image, for instance, without developing a negative self-concept. Others who have been ill since early childhood, have matured within the context of a stigmatizing experience which has influenced the development of personal confidence by limiting their life experiences. Research is needed in this area to delineate those who cope successfully with a long-term illness experience and emerge confident and positive about themselves as people, of whom there are certainly many. The level of knowledge that exists now seems to indicate

that the perception of being different can pose real obstacles to development. We are only beginning to identify effective ways of helping these long-term survivors overcome these obstacles.

PREPARATION FOR CURE

In a symposium devoted to exploring the issue of the truly cured child in pediatric oncology, Dr. Jan Van Eys made the following observation: "We have achieved in pediatric oncology a respectable number of biological cures. . . . But do we have a truly cured child, a child who is mentally healthy and who can function at an age-appropriate level in society?" (1977) In discussing the issue further he specified that the environment of the child must be conducive to normal development in order to achieve the above optimal outcome — that is, a child who is mentally healthy and able to function age-appropriately. The environment is the one created by parents and family as well as the whole of the experiences encountered throughout the illness and treatment period. In this regard families and caregivers are both responsible for furnishing an environment that provides a mechanism for development and growth. Approaches that focus on this goal will be the content of the remainder of this chapter. The reader should keep in mind the various givens of the disease and treatment situation, constraints imposed by the family or child, and the limits perceived by caregivers, which have been discussed throughout this book.

Although the variables that enhance normal development are many, Van Eys pinpoints three factors of special significance to children being cured of cancer (Van Eys, 1977). First is the possession of sensorimotor equipment that is as normal as possible. This aspect relates to the minimization and early detection of the toxic effects of disease and treatment. Secondly the environment must allow progression for the child's skills and understanding. Latitude to practice skills and achieve ever-increasing levels of independent function are vital in this regard. Lastly normal development is made possible by a self-image that allows positive social interaction. The psychosocial aspects of disease impact and coping behavior are important considerations in development of this self-image.

Although most parents and health-team members would agree with the need for these three components, the problem becomes implementation of both an in- and out-of-hospital life-style that allows for their achievement. In the first instance the treatment plan itself or attendant complications may preclude an outcome that includes normal sensorimotor equipment. As greater concern for the long-term quality of the life being saved becomes a central issue, health professionals are assessing more carefully the risk or benefit derived from various therapies. Consideration of the use of less extensive radiation, for example, or lowering dosages of chemotherapy to minimal yet effective levels are becoming frequent research questions. Alertness of caregivers to the possibilities regarding toxicities is, of course, of extreme importance in order to minimize damage or begin early remediation to lessen the ultimate deleterious effects. When alternative plans can be made, as in sperm banking to assure future reproductive capability, those actions are certainly warranted. Further in the case of long term followup attention to the risk of second malignancy is being recognized as a matter for concern. In a sample of individuals with osteogenic sarcoma as a second primary cancer, the observation was made that close followup was not occurring at the time the second tumor emerged; greater alertness by parents and physicians may have brought about earlier referral and diagnosis. Since these authors (Pillay, et al., 1983) and others emphasize the need for a more optimistic and aggressive approach to second malignancies in long-term survivors, earlier diagnosis and treatment become even more important.

NORMALIZATION OF CHILDHOOD

The second and third components proposed by Van Eys, which are progression of development and a positive self-image, involve the normalizing of an abnormal environment. Few would deny the difficulties faced by the child with cancer and his or her family. The stress on the every day functioning of the family is tremendous and is an experience vastly different from a normal childhood. Managing to care effectively for the physical and emotional needs of this child, generated by the cancer and its treatment, becomes an all-consuming task for most families. As predictable as the shock phase following diagnosis, the initial period of treatment justifiably focuses on the question of survival. However, for many, this overwhelming issue of survival and conquering illness remains the primary concern well into the treatment and remission phase. Health professionals must intervene to help the family to balance their emphasis on illness-related issues with an equal emphasis on growth and wellness. Although it is essential not to deny the cancer experience for the child, as it is part of his or her reality, so it is vital not to focus so totally on it that other important components of living and developing are excluded. At each state of development critical concepts are synthesized and tasks accomplished. Failure to proceed in this step-by-step fashion, although not precluding eventual attainment of that particular skill, will lengthen and distort the process for the child. Within the context of normal psychosocial, cognitive, and sensorimotor development, some progress on the part of the child needs to be maintained despite the illness. To illustrate this some considerations for each age group are discussed and summarized in Figure 10-1.

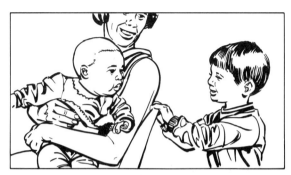

Infant
and
toddler

Damage to developing CNS

Lack of opportunity to practice
motor, interpersonal skills

Separation related anxieties

Preschooler

Damage to developing CNS

Lack of interaction with other
children

Lack of cognitive stimulation

Feelings of guilt

Deception regarding disease

School-aged
child

Lack of cognitive abilities

Absence from school

Diminished social interaction

Parental overprotection/lack
of discipline

Adolescent

Perceived alienation of peers

Compromised intellectual/
physical well being

Absence from school

Anxiety/uncertainty about
future

Parental overprotection/lack
of expectation

Negative risk-taking behavior

FIG. 10-1. Threats to normal childhood for the child with cancer.

INFANCY

The period of infancy is considered by most clinicians to be a vulnerable and important time in a child's life — a time when separations, traumas, and physical and emotional stresses are best avoided. Although cancer is not common in the infant age group, it does occur. Some researchers feel that children whose cancer is discovered in infancy or early childhood, whose treatment is short, who do not have relapses, and whose families are supportive, have the best psychological prognosis (Koocher and O'Malley, 1981). Nevertheless in regard to "normalizing" childhood the period of infant development does pose many concerns for those who care for the child with cancer. Delayed effects resulting from the impact of disease, radiation, or chemotherapy on the developing central nervous system are an important consideration. In general both the frequency and severity of toxic effects appear to be inversely related to age (Fergusson, 1981). Lack of opportunity to practice the skills usually learned at this time, such as sitting, crawling, standing, feeding self with finger foods, and so on due to immobility, fatigue, or restraint, will slow the child's developmental progress. Emotionally, separation from parents and traumatic, painful procedures are potentially damaging experiences with results that are as yet largely undocumented.

For these reasons, caretakers must intervene to provide normal developmental experiences, even in the face of apparently more pressing physical care needs. Opportunities can be integrated into daily routines. A clean and safe area on the floor can be arranged for supervised crawling practice, for instance, and restraints can be released periodically to allow manipulative play with both hands. Crib toys and mobiles can be used to provide stimulation. Parent involvement is naturally enthusiastically recommended. It is most meaningful if in addition to helping to hold the infant for treatments or to coax the child to take a bottle, the parent is encouraged and praised for playing and teaching the child new skills.

TODDLERS

The often negativistic demeanor of toddlers makes this a difficult time for hospitalization. The introduction or maintenance of a cancer protocol, with its frequent medication and treatment administration, is particularly demanding for a child this age. As with the infant significant delayed effects are potential problems for the toddler. Maintaining physical well-being, particularly adequate nutrition, is vital for physical and psychosocial progress. Psychomotor skills continue to develop and are refined when opportunities are available.

Provision for opportunities to practice skills may take planning and ingenuity. Family and health personnel will be dealing with a normally independent toddler whose efforts to "do it myself" can lengthen mealtimes or keep X-ray personnel waiting. Riding a tricycle in the hospital or at home with depressed platelet counts may have to be temporarily postponed, but should be reinstituted as soon as it is medically feasible. Intravenous lines and drainage devices can be transported to the playroom. Screening for beginning problems with sensorimotor abilities should be part of the treatment and followup routine. Setting limits on behavior and disciplining the child in the family's usual manner are essential components of "normal" childrearing that need to be continued.

PRESCHOOLERS

Both at home and in the hospital, the preschool child is probably most frustrated by an unstimulating environment. The child with cancer is at times confined physically or emotionally to a narrow sphere of experience. The pain and fear of this illness experience, if not checked, can dominate the preschooler's reality due to guilt feelings and the active imaginings of this age group. For this reason special interventions to enlarge the child's world, be it in the hospital or at home, need to be implemented. Television is an obvious tool but should be used with specific objectives in mind. Most hospitals and locales have children's programming available that can be especially useful when coupled with discussion or educational programs used by the parent, nurse, or preschool teacher. Contact with other children is an important part of the normal preschooler's experience and should be maintained as much as is medically feasible — periods of immunological suppression can be handled with tape recordings, letters, cards, and phone calls from playmates. Curiosity about the hospital and the child's own disease process may offer perfect opportunities for open discussion of these matters, suited to the child's understanding and added to as cognitive ability increases. Interestingly in a study of long-term survivors the variable of when the child was told about the illness was shown to be significant in long-term adaptation (Koocher and O'Malley, 1981). Children told within 1 year of diagnosis, or who were diagnosed in infancy and told before age 6, had a better overall adjustment than those who were informed later or who were self-informed (*i.e.*, learned of diagnosis other than from parent or physician).

SCHOOL AGE AND ADOLESCENCE

As discussed in more detail in Chapter 9, school-age and adolescence periods have particular significance when changed by an illness experience, due to the impact of these developmental states on future planning. Although the physical influences of the malignant process and treatment are important variables during this period and affect the child's energy level and cognitive ability to assimilate new information, it is probably the emotional consequences of the illness, the treatment, or others' responses that can be most devastating. Being

unlike peers, unable to participate in usual school, sports, or social activities, or perceiving the fear or rejection of others, the school-aged or adolescent child may be inhibited in trying new situations. Coupled with the parents' tendency to overprotect their child, these factors may seriously hamper developmental progress.

Scheduling a child in school and other activities with as structured a day as possible, is helpful for in-hospital children. Hospital school activities, unit activities such as parties or field trips, and regular meal and self-care times are all components of normalizing the hospital day (Volz, 1981). Just as in the home setting, most children behave better and feel more secure with consistency. Also for the in-hospital child, many cancer centers and other hospitals have peer group and social events that all children on the unit are encouraged to attend. The establishment of a pediatric or adolescent unit newspaper is a device used by many to help inpatients contribute to their experience in the hospital, share feelings, and learn new skills and information.

In addition to these types of activities, however, it is important to encourage the child's or adolescent's continued involvement with friends and school activities within the home community. Actively listening to discussions of school activities and special friends, as well as encouraging them to keep in touch, is an important consideration for nurses and other health professionals. Planning for the homecoming dance or attending a movie with a friend are important to many teens and should be allowed at home or in hospital as much as is physically feasible. Expectations that self-care activities, such as getting dressed and accomplishing usual chores around the house, will continue in a normal manner maintains consistency in the environment and tells the child that "life goes on."

Parents may need assistance in this process of letting life go on. As their ill child matures, it is difficult for them to give serious consideration to preparation for puberty, setting realistic behavioral limits, or enforcing academic expectations, unless they have hope for the child's eventual recovery. Health personnel and others in the community may share in this hope, or as with many in our society, persist in the belief that cancer is a death sentence. Sometimes health professionals as well as parents and the child with cancer must evolve a system of future planning, exploring every available avenue for development despite active opposition from others who are less informed.

Limit-setting and enforcing usual expectations are normal activities for parents and those who work in pediatrics. This becomes a particular problem for parents of the chronically ill or critically ill. When a child is in pain or fearful, or has recently survived a crisis, adults have a natural tendency to spare the child more pain or anxiety. Misbehavior on the child's or adolescent's part may draw indulgence instead of criticism from parents who are grateful to see them feeling well enough to misbehave. Over the long term, this type of attitude is confusing to these children. Many interpret lack of limits as lack of love or concern (Spinetta and Deasy-Spinetta, 1981). For many families this failure to impose behavioral limits indicates the lack of belief in the child or adolescent's future. Such families need intervention to work through their hopelessness in a realistic manner. Meanwhile they can be helped to recognize that most children feel more secure with parental control. Also enforcing limits helps prevent or minimize some very real problems with sibling resentment (see Chapter 7).

The question of dating and developing intimate relationships is usually an area of particular concern. Koocher and O'Malley (1981) found that the aspect of intimacy and sexual functioning was a common worry among cancer survivors and their partners. Schmale and colleagues (1983) report that young adults, even as much as 12 years after treatment, felt as though they were "sitting on a powder keg and waiting for it to go off." Schmale questions how often and to what extent this uncertainty affects the survivor's life and relationships. A related concern is whether to openly disclose information about the disease or to withhold it. Some adolescents and young adults opt to tell only close family and friends. A consequence of this approach is that casual dating and friendships that arise may be overshadowed by the hidden cancer diagnosis. Should a casual relationship become a deeper one, the cancer survivor then must confront the need to inform the partner, not knowing what the outcome will be for the future of the relationship. As for any adolescent or young adult, questions of mate and career assume significance — these normal challenges are compounded by the individual's cancer history.

IMPLICATIONS FOR HEALTH PROFESSIONALS

The task for those who work with children with cancer is to prepare the child physically, emotionally, and socially for the future while sustaining that child through the rigors of the present. To achieve this overall goal, five components of the task can be identified.

ENHANCE GROWTH AND DEVELOPMENT OF THE CHILD

In ways specified throughout this book, every effort must be made to treat the child with a regard to future development. Parents often need assistance in maintaining an image of the future, particularly during times of crisis. Health professionals can convey that the future is a viable reality by their concern for long-term effects of treatment as well as for school or social problems. Health professionals will not convey false hope, of course, in the case of a child with a poor prognosis. With increasing success in achieving remission even in those who have relapsed, however, it is appropriate to maintain hope in the present in most cases.

To enhance the child's developmental progress, it must be assumed that growth and development are being periodically monitored. To do this in a consistent manner it is important to use some assessment tool mutually acceptable to unit or cancer center staff that can be included in the child's permanent file for future reference. The Denver Development Screening Test (DDST) or the Bayley Scale are two such instruments that are widely used. Both also serve to assist both parents and health professionals in anticipating the skills the child will be acquiring. In this way opportunities can be planned for "practice." Eight-month-old Lynn was being treated for neuroblastoma and was in the hospital for the third time in the 60 days postdiagnosis. When her physical condition began to improve, her primary nurse administered the DDST and found that her fine motor-adaptive development was better than expected for her age. She could pick up her small objects with a neat pincer motion. Together with Lynn's mother and the dietitian, plans were made to include finger foods on her tray to encourage this phase of her development. Her nutritional intake increased as a result, and beginning steps toward independence were taken.

For school-age children and adolescents, implementation of appropriate actions to take must be consistent on the nursing unit. The nursing kardex can be used to note developmentally appropriate actions. For example Erikson's identified crisis for school-aged children (industry versus inferiority) could be noted. Then specific activities designed to promote a sense of industry could be planned and integrated into the everyday routine. School activities would, of course, be one example, as well as writing a submission for the unit newspaper, totaling the intake and output record, or graphing white blood count tests. Running errands and helping out with younger children, when the child's condition permits, are other things school children normally do that could be worked into the hospital routine. As various tasks are mastered, and periodically with readmission, these ideas can be reevaluated and changed.

MONITOR FOR DELAYED EFFECTS

Baseline assessments of sensorimotor abilities and cognitive abilities, if feasible, are necessary for comparison with later periodic evaluation. Regular examination of vision and hearing, neurological function, cardiac function, and so on, are and should be features of every research protocol, particularly for young children and those receiving maximal dosages who seem to be at higher risk. The specific systems monitored will be influenced by the type of treatment. Health teaching of child and parents and close cooperation with school personnel are useful adjuncts to cancer center evaluations in terms of consistency of followup.

McCalla (1985) describes a multidisciplinary approach to the identification and intervention for adverse late effects. At the National Cancer Institute, a late effects team was established. This team was led by a pediatric oncologist and was coordinated by a pediatric nurse practitioner. The team determined guidelines for assessment of the child's medical and psychological status and work or educational situation. Neuropsychologic assessment includes various intelligence, attention, visual-motor coordination, behavioral, and personality measures. Ongoing discussion with an assigned social worker and child psychiatrist to analyze these realms of function are performed. Using this information, the late effects team recommends interventions, which are discussed with the child and parents along with significant other persons in the family, community, or school situation.

Monitoring for recurrence of malignancy, either as relapse or a new primary cancer, should be a priority for the primary-care provider. Often in long-term survival situations, the family returns to their personal physician or pediatrician for routine followup and episodic care that is not related to the initial cancer treatment. Communication with the cancer center regarding timing of delayed effects and recurrent cancers will keep this local health-care provider as current as possible and make followup examinations more effective. It is important that the patient and family recognize their responsibility for followup throughout the patient's life span.

REHABILITATE OR REMEDIATE TO GAIN NEEDED SKILLS

When adverse effects from therapy or disease are noted, or if in the normal course of treatment the child becomes unable to "keep up" with peers, prompt referral for remediation is indicated. As discussed in Chapter 9, children with cancer are covered under the education for All Handicapped Children's Act of 1975. Services provided that may be needed are tutoring, special educational experiences, and physical accommodations in the school setting. Since the process of certifying the child as health-impaired may take time, early referral is important.

Additionally it continues to be important for cancer center personnel, school staff, and private physicians to monitor the long-term survivor's psychosocial as well as physical function. Assessment of the child's and parents' perceptions of these vital aspects of life are justifiably included in each followup visit. Some centers have focused on this aspect to the extent of research study on school and other components of long-term adjustment (Spinetta and Deasy-Spinetta, 1981; Koocher and O'Malley, 1981).

EDUCATE OTHER HEALTH PROFESSIONALS AND LAY COMMUNITY

The child with cancer who becomes a long-term survivor has many battles yet to face. The ignorance of the public regarding cancer in general, and long-term survival in particular, can pose significant obstacles to these individuals. Discrimination in school and work settings has already been discussed. The more subtle withdrawal of friends or lack of social contact also occurs far too frequently.

The American Cancer Society and many other groups devoted to the goal of informing the public about cancer have done much to change the negative impact of a cancer diagnosis. It remains a priority task, however, as long as the myth and misinformation persist. Each person who works with these children recognizes every day the continuing store of misinformation that often affects the well-being of the cancer survivor and family.

For these reasons those who work in cancer centers and other health facilities that treat these children and are informed, must formally and informally endeavor to educate those who are not informed. Speaking to interested community groups, publicizing the positive facets of cancer treatment as well as the negative ones, and recognizing the success in cancer treatment, are ways informed health providers can shape more positive attitudes.

SUPPORT EACH OTHER

There are few aspects of nursing that require more emotional reserve, in addition to technical expertise, than pediatric oncology. Recognizing this fact, it is nevertheless important to note that in many cancer centers, often because of various supportive services, job satisfaction is high and turnover is low in this demanding specialty. As in many other patient-care settings, the positive benefits of combining talents toward the goal of effective approaches have resulted in not only better care for patients' families, but a more supportive environment for the staff. In a general hospital setting such an atmosphere will often exist when the staff is committed to achieving it. However there may be a greater tendency to neglect the acute support needs of those caring for pediatric oncology patients when such patients are not commonly seen.

It is important to note the problems that are often encountered in this specialty practice. As noted by Van Eys (1977) ". . . the challenges of nursing the patient who might die are so great that it is hard to nurse a patient who might live. The emotional and physical investment in the care of the patient is so great that the caregiver has to protect himself. . . . After all, the care that we are asked to give is overwhelming." He maintains that for this reason we sometimes find it harder to prepare the child for the future and more difficult to believe in and focus on the truly cured child, because that requires such an investment of self. The risks to the caregiver's emotional health are ever present; these children might not be among the survivors and the pain of losing them, after commitment to them, is so great. Certainly in addition to the commitment to the children themselves is the intense involvement that often occurs with the families. This level of involvement exposes the health-care giver to disappointment and frequently makes him or her a target for the family's anger. These are additional emotional stresses.

Most settings that specialize in oncology have established support mechanisms such as rap groups and individual counseling services. General hospitals frequently have such services, although they may not be geared to the unique conflicts faced in the oncology area. Staff can informally meet these support needs for each other. Also unit staffs can encourage their administrators to provide more formal assistance. Continuing education is of help as well in assisting personnel on a general pediatric unit to feel more knowledgeable and confident in the care of this specialized patient and family. Community and national resources also are available to nurses, and many of these are listed in the Yellow Pages, including the local units of the American Cancer Society and the Association of Pediatric Oncology Nurses.

CONCLUSION

In conclusion this chapter has focused on the cured childhood cancer patient's special needs and risks. Various delayed effects of aggressive cancer treatment and the potential for secondary malignancy were presented. A developmental approach to normalizing childhood for these children in order that they will be prepared to be truly cured survivors, has been described, with specific suggestions given. Finally the components of the responsibilities of caregivers toward those children who survive have been explored. Throughout it has been the author's premise that all pediatric oncology patients must be treated in a way that maximizes their developmental capacity. Only then can we adequately meet the future needs of those, now becoming a majority, who will become long-term survivors.

KEY POINTS

- The impact of elective cessation of therapy can be positive and negative.
- Parents and patients are often surprised by the degree of anxiety they feel at the end of the treatment protocol.
- Longer intervals between checkups in the period following cessation of therapy often predisposes the family to a "near denial" of the illness, with potentially serious consequences.
- Health-care providers must remain vigilant and explore physical and psychosocial well-being at each return visit.
- Late recurrence of disease can occur in the period 5 to 9 years postdiagnosis.
- Mortality for the cancer patient who has been free of disease for 10 to 19 years postdiagnosis is often related to a second primary neoplasm.
- Somatic delayed effects due to treatment for cancer involve many body systems and appear to be directly related to site and dosage.
- Cognitive delayed effects involve memory, learning, and perception and appear to be inversely related to age at time of treatment.
- The impact of the cancer experience on psychosocial development includes such consequences as avoidance of future planning, sick role adoption, negative risk-taking, independence–dependence conflicts, the feeling of being different, and the reality of facing illness and death.
- To better prepare pediatric oncology patients for cure, the focus must be on normalizing an abnormal childhood.
- At each age group careful monitoring and planning can be effective in promoting "normal" developmental progress.
- Health professionals who work with children with cancer have the responsibility to:
  - Enhance growth and developmental progress
  - Monitor for delayed effects
  - Rehabilitate or remediate to gain skills
  - Educate others
  - Support each other
- To produce a truly cured child, the complexities of cancer treatment must take second place to preparing that child for living well in the future.

REFERENCES

Dunlop, J. (1982). Critical problems facing young adults with cancer. *Oncology Nursing Forum, 9,* 33–38.

Fergusson, J. (1981). Cognitive late effects of treatment for acute lymphocytic leukemia in childhood. *Topics in Clinical Nursing, 2,* 21–29.

Greene, P., and Fergusson, J. (1982). Nursing care in childhood cancer: Late effects of therapy. *American Journal of Nursing, 82,* 443–446.

Inati, A., Sallen, S., Cassady, J., Hitchcock-Bryan, S., Clavell, L., Belli, J. and Sollee, N. (1983). Efficacy and morbidity of central nervous system prophylaxis in childhood acute lymphoblastic leukemia: Eight years' experience with cranial irradiation and intrathecal methotrexate. *Blood, 61,* 297–302.

Jaffe, N. (1984). Late sequelae of cancer therapy. In W. Sutow, D. Fernbach, and T. Vietti (Eds.), *Clinical Pediatric Oncology* (pp. 810–824). St. Louis: C. V. Mosby.

Kaempfer, S., Hoffman, S., and Wiley, F. (1983). Sperm banking: A reproductive option in cancer therapy. *Cancer Nursing, 6,* 31–38.

King, M. (1984). After cancer: Trouble on the job. *Cancer News,* Autumn, p. 14.

Kolberg, R. (1983, July 24). Cancer survivors often encounter discrimination. *Houston Chronicle,* Section 3, p. 4.

Koocher, G., and O'Malley, J. (1981). *The Damocles syndrome: Psychosocial consequences of surviving childhood cancer.* New York: McGraw Hill Book Co.

Krulik, T. (1982). Helping parents of children during the midstage of illness. *Cancer Nursing, 5,* 441–445.

Lewis, S., and La Barbera, J. (1983). Terminating chemotherapy: Another stage in coping with childhood leukemia. *The American Journal of Pediatric Hematology/Oncology, 5,* 33–37.

McCalla, J. (1985). A multidisciplinary approach to identification and remedial intervention for adverse late effects of cancer therapy. *Nursing Clinics of North America, 20,* 117–130.

McHaney, V. A. Thidadoux, G., Hayes, F., and Green, A. (1983). Hearing loss in children receiving cisplatin chemotherapy. *Journal of Pediatrics, 102,* 314–317.

Meadows, A., Krejmas, N., and Belasco, J. (1980). Medical cost of cure: Sequelae in survivors of childhood cancer. In J. Van Eys and M. P. Sullivan (Eds.), *Status of curability of childhood cancer* (pp. 263–275). New York: Raven Press.

Orliff, A., and Levine, A. (1982). Late effects of antineoplastic therapy. In A. Levine (Ed.), *Cancer in the young* (pp. 732–750). New York: Masson Publishing USA.

Pfefferbaum-Levine, B., Copeland, D., Fletcher, J., Ried, H., Jaffe, N., McKinnon, W. (1984). Neuropsychologic assessment of long-term survivors of childhood leukemia. *The American Journal of Pediatric Hematology/Oncology, 6,* 123–127.

Pillay, R., Graham-Pole, J., Novak, L., Kurczynski, E., and Yulish, B. (1983). Successful treatment of osteogenic sarcoma developing as a second cancer in childhood. *American Journal of Pediatric Hematology/Oncology, 5,* 103–105.

Reaman, G., et al. (1980). Improved treatment results in the management of single and multiple relapses of acute lymphoblastic leukemia. *Cancer, 45,* 3090–3094.

Schmale, A., et al. (1983). Well being of cancer survivors. *Psychosomatic Medicine, 45,* 163–169.

Spinetta, J., and Deasy-Spinetta, P. (Eds.) (1981). *Living with childhood cancer.* St. Louis: C. V. Mosby.

Van Eys, J. (Ed.) (1977). *The truly cured child* (pp. 82–89). Baltimore: University Park Press.

Volz, D. (1981). Time structuring for hospitalized school aged children. *Issues in Comprehensive Pediatric Nursing, 5,* 205–210.

Wells, R., et al. (1983). The impact of cranial irradiation on the growth of children with acute lymphocytic leukemia. *American Journal of Diseases of Children, 137,* 37–39.

APPENDIX

YELLOW PAGES

Resources for Children with Cancer and Their Families

I. NATIONAL ORGANIZATIONS

AMERICAN CANCER SOCIETY (ACS)
Description: National voluntary organization with aims of research, education and patient services.
Services include: counseling, equipment, dressings, transportation and other which vary by location.

Address National: American Cancer Society
National Headquarters
777 Third Avenue
New York, NY 10017
(212) 371-2900

Local in all states, most cities

NATIONAL INSTITUTES OF HEALTH (NIH)
Description: Subsection of U.S. Dept. of Health, and Human Services. National Cancer Institute is the specific related agency. Services include information and publication on a wide range of cancer topics for the public and professionals. A new service, PDQ (Physician Data Query) is a computerized database of current diagnostic, treatment and prognostic information available to the practicing physician in the community.
Cost: Usually free, or bulk rates.

Address: Office of Cancer Communications
NCI Bldg. 31, Room 10A18
Bethesda, MD 20205

THE LEUKEMIA SOCIETY
Description: National and local organization for support of patients and families with leukemia and related disorders. Services include financial assistance, counseling.

Address National: Leukemia Society of America, Inc.
211 E. 43rd Street
New York, NY 10017
(212) 573-8484

Also Local Chapters

ASSOCIATION FOR CARE OF CHILDREN'S HEALTH (ACCH)
Description: National organization dealing with health care issues for acute and chronically ill children and families. Interdisciplinary health professionals and lay members. Local chapters.

Address National: Association for Care of Children's Health
3615 Wisconsin Avenue
Washington, DC 20016
(202) 244-1801

Also Local Affiliates

II. MATERIALS

Source: American Cancer Society (ACS)
Title: You Have A Student With Cancer, 1980.
Description: For school personnel, includes feelings on cancer, info about cancer, hints about contact while child absent, on return, etc.
Cost: Free

Source: ACS
Title: I Can Cope
Description: Kit includes tape cassettes and information related to an 8 week course for those with cancer and their families. Course emphasizes factual information and coping strategies as well as resource information.
Cost: $18.00
Courses taught in various local ACS Chapters are free.

Source: ACS
Title(s): Nursing In-Service Educational Program on Nursing Management of Childhood Cancer, 1979
A Cancer Source Book for Nurses, 1975
Parent's Handbook on Leukemia, 1977
Description: All booklets for health professionals/families/patients regarding the impact of the cancer diagnosis, problems encountered and resources to contact. In Parent's Handbook, good section on "Telling: Why and How" for child and siblings.

Source: ACS
Title(s): Dealing With Pain—A Handbook for Persons With Cancer and Their Families, 1983
Questions and Answers About Pain Control: A Guide for People With Cancer and Their Families 1983
Description: These booklets are specifically about pain and pain control—helpful for older children, parents.
Title: Parent's Handbook on Leukemia 1977
Description: Definitions, medications, protocols, emotional aspects, common problems are discussed for the lay person.
NOTE: ACS locals will distribute a flyer listing all their educational books, films, pamphlets, etc.

Source: NIH
Title: Young People With Cancer: A Handbook for Parents (NIH Publication #80-2378)
Description: Discusses cancer, treatment, outlook, emotional aspects and ways of coping; lists resources.
Cost: Free

Source: NIH
Title: The Leukemic Child (NIH No. 81-863, 1981)
Description: Chronicle of parental response to the diagnosis and treatment of leukemia. Written by a parent and includes sections on the disease, hospitalization and death.

Source: NIH
Title: Students With Cancer: A Resource for the Educator
Description: Considers cancer, treatment, prognosis, and ways teachers and schools can help in lay terms. Gives resources for additional information.
Cost: Free

Source: NIH
Title: Maintaining a Normal Life
Coping with Cancer — A Resource for the Health Professional
Eating Hints
Radiation Therapy & You
Description: These booklets deal with psychosocial aspects and life-style implications of the cancer experience. Helpful for parents and families as well as for health professionals.
Cost: Free

Source: W. B. Saunders, Co.
Title: You and Leukemia: A Day at a Time by Lynn Baker, M.D.
Description: A highly readable guide to leukemia for children aged 10 and up. Good explanations of diagnostic tests, various treatments, as well as the emotional response to the chronic disease process.

Address: Available from publisher or local bookstore

Source: Leukemia Society
Title: Emotional Aspects of Childhood Leukemia: A Handbook for Parents by J. Spinetta, P. Deasy-Spinetta, F. Kung, and D. Schwartz
Description: Emotional issues facing the family are covered including the impact of diagnosis, hospitalization, school adjustment, siblings' feelings, death of the child, and resources.

Source: ACS
Title: Cancer Nursing News
Description: Newsletter for nurses working with children with cancer — full of ideas, resource information, etc.

Source: Candlelighters Foundation
Title: **Candlelighters Foundation Bibliography and Resource Guide**
Description: Annotated listing of over 500 books, articles, audiovisuals, and re-
source organizations on childhood cancer, medical support, effects on family, long-
term survivors, death and bereavement.
Cost: $1.00

Address: Candlelighters Foundation
Suite 1011
2025 Eye St., NW
Washington, DC 20006

Source: Association for Care of Children's Health
Title(s):   **The Chronically Ill Child and Family in the Community**
For teenagers: **Your Stay in the Hospital**
Preparing the Child for Repeated or Extended Hospitalization
When Your Child Has a Lifethreatening Illness
Description: Pamphlets for families and health professionals that help in dealing
with psychosocial issues related to the child with cancer. This organization has many
other related materials.
Cost: Some free, some nominal cost, bulk rates

Title: ACCH; Selected Books and Pamphlets on Chronic Illness and Handicaps
Description: A bibliography list of materials

Source: BOOKWORM Children's Books
Title: Variety of children's books, ranging from dealing with death, specific handicaps, sibling relationships in story books.
Description: Books are annotated and grouped by age categories as well as topic
categories. Helpful for referral information for families, or as source for purchasing
books.

Address: BOOK-WORM
1740 N. Hermitage
Chicago, IL 60622
(312) 486-3586 or 486-8236

Source: Fred Rogers' Media
Title: Death of a Goldfish
Talking with Young Children About Death
Description: First film, Death of a Goldfish is for use with young children; the second
is for adults.
Cost: For rent or sale.

Address: Toni Gray
Marketing Services
Family Communication
4802 Fifth Avenue
Pittsburgh, PA 15213

Source: Centering Corporation
Description: Various booklets, pamphlets, and audiovisual programs on topics of children's death, chronic illness, and many other subjects appropriate for both children and adults.
Cost: Varies with each booklet.

Source: Centering Corporation
Title: **Patient Education Series**
Description: 15 booklets in a series: Breathe Big (inhalation therapy); Catscan, Diabetic Dips, ECG, EEG, Endo-Proctoscopes, Fractures & X-ray, IV, IVP, Tumors, Radiation, Spinal Tap, Surgery, Tonsils,
Cost: Individually — $.65 each
All 15 books — $9.75

Address: Centering Corporation
P.O. Box 3367
Omaha, NB 68103-0367

Source: Aplastic Anemia Foundation of America (AAFA)
Title: **Families Coping with Hospital Life**
Description: A 12-page booklet to help parents and friends of those leukemia and aplastic anemia patients who must undergo bone marrow transplants. It offers advice on handling changes in family life, working with the health-care team, and dealing with emotions such as anger and fear.
Cost: Single copies available

Address: AAFA
P.O. Box 22689
Baltimore, MD 21203

Source: For challenged kids by Mattel, Inc.
Title: **Dolls with Disabilities**
Description: These 19-inch soft-sculptured dolls are designed to help children with disabilities develop a self-image. Handicaps include a boy who is a one-legged skier, a boy in a wheelchair, a girl with leg braces and canes, a ballerina who wears hearing aids, and a visually impaired girl with a cane and guide dog.
Cost: $40 to $45 each

Address: For Challenged Kids by Mattel, Inc.
5959 Triumph St.
Commerce, CA 90840
(800) 227-3800

Source: Smithers Medical Products, Inc.
Title: **Alpha Cradle Patient Immobilization System, Inc.**
Description: Patient immobilization system which utilizes a lightweight styrofoam base and interior that can be completely molded by the child's body in a few minutes. Samples of materials are available upon request.

Address: Smithers Medical Products, Inc.
5192 Darrow Road
Hudson, OH 44236
(216) 650-0151

III. FACILITIES

HOSPICE

Source: National Hospice Organization
131A Dolly Madison Boulevard
McClean, VA 22101
(703) 356-6770

Association of Community Cancer Centers
11-600 Nebel Street, Suite 201
Rockville, MD 20852
(301) 984-9496

LIVING ARRANGEMENTS

Source: Ronald McDonald Houses
Description: Homelike atmosphere for children who are seriously ill and their families; lodging provided at reasonable cost; some locations may provide activities, other services.
National Address: Mr. A. L. Jones
Ronald McDonald House Coordinator
c/o Golin Communications, Inc.
500 N. Michigan Avenue
Chicago, IL 60614
(312) 836-7100

CAMPS

Source: Camp Brochure
Title: Sky High Hope Camp
Description: Week-long residential camp for children with leukemia or other childhood cancers. Treatment and medication can be continued.
Cost: $50/child (1982)
Address: 2430 E. Arkansas Avenue
Denver, CO 80210
Title: Sundrops Oncology Camp
Address: Childscope
Box 837
Broken Arrow, OK. 74013
NOTE: Additional camps listed periodically in Candlelighters Newsletter, or contact Candlelighters or the local American Cancer Society; Candlelighters will send listing of all camps for $0.50.

IV. SUPPORT (Chronic and Terminal Illness)

NAME:	DESCRIPTION:

Make Today Count
1137 Colusa Avenue
Berkeley, CA 94707
	Local chapters
	  Newsletters
	  Local groups

SHANTI 218 S. Sixth Street Burlington, IA 52601	Support, counseling, medical and legal advice
Shanti Nilaya P.O. Box 2396 Escondido, CA 92025	
Hanuman Foundation Dying Project P.O. Box 2228 Taos, NM 87571 (505) 758-1181	Newsletter, free consultation by phone
Candlelighters Foundation Suite 1011 2025 Eye St., N.W. Washington, DC 20006	Also local chapters
Center for Attitudinal Healing 19 Main Street Tipsuron, CA 94920 (415) 435-5022 and Center for Attitudinal Healing 2818 West T.C. Jester Houston, TX 77018 (713) 688-1734	Support, group counseling

V. SUPPORT (Parent)

Source: Candlelighters
Description: National organization of parents whose children have or have had cancer; many local chapters (some with different names). Services include information, social activities for parents, siblings, mutual help, outreach, etc. —may vary by locality
National Organization: Candlelighters Foundation
              2025 Eye St., N.W., Suite 1011
              Washington, DC 20006
              (202) 659-5136 (day) or (202) 544-1696

VI. INFORMATION

Source: Cancer Information Service
Description: Toll free telephone inquiry system which supplies information about cancer and cancer related resources. Rapid access to latest information resources; written information often available. Calls are confidential, multilingual in some areas. Telephone: Call the number for your State. For areas not listed below, call 1-800-638-6694.

Alabama: 1-800-292-6201
Alaska: 1-800-638-9066
California: 1-800-252-9066
(From Area Codes 213, 619, 714, and 805 only)
Colorado: 1-800-332-1850
Connecticut: 1-800-922-0824
Delaware: 1-800-523-3586
District of Columbia (and suburban Maryland and Virginia): 202-636-5700
Florida: 1-800-432-5953
Georgia: 1-800-327-7332
Hawaii: Oahu: 524-1234; Neighbor Islands: Call collect
Illinois: 800-972-0586
Kentucky: 800-432-9321
Maine: 1-800-225-7034
Maryland: 1-800-492-1444
Massachusetts: 1-800-952-7420
Minnesota: 1-800-582-5262

New Hampshire: 1-800-225-7034
New Jersey (Northern): 800-223-1000
New Jersey (Southern): 800-523-3586
New York State: 1-800-462-7255
New York City: 212-794-7982
North Carolina: 1-800-672-0943
North Dakota: 1-800-328-5188
Ohio: 1-800-282-6522
Pennsylvania: 1-800-822-3963
South Dakota: 1-800-328-5188
Texas 1-800-392-2040
Vermont: 1-800-225-7034
Washington: 1-800-552-7212
Wisconsin: 1-800-362-8038

NOTE: Can also call 1-800-4-CANCER for up-to-date information from the National Cancer Institute.

VII. INFORMATION (unproved methods)

Source: ACS
Title: Unproved Methods of Cancer Management
Description: Booklet outlining all major types of unproved methods in current usage, with details of proposed effectiveness and ACS stand.
Note: Local chapters also furnish information and will provide speakers in this topic. Another source is the Fraud Division of the AMA.

VIII. SERVICES (Financial Assistance)

Cancer Care, Inc.
One Park Avenue
New York, NY 10016

United Way
801 N. Fairfax
Alexandria, VA 22314

Crippled Children's Services
Contact: Department of Human Resources under Health and Human Resources in your State.

ALSO: see ACS
       see Leukemia Society

Source: Home Nutritional Support, Inc.
Programs: Home Parenteral Nutrition
Home Enteral Nutrition
Home Antibiotic/Fluid Therapy
Description: Programs provide "in-hospital" monitoring and intervention at home.
Cost: Varies with service; many services covered by third party payers.

Address: Home Nutritional Support, Inc.
       238 Passaic Avenue
       Fairfield, NJ 07.006
       (800) 631-0415
NOTE: Many home care agencies are being developed. The local Cancer Society, or the local hospital discharge department could help with specific agencies in specific localities.

IX. SERVICES (at home care)

American Continue Care
(AH Supply Corp.)
1450 E. Alton Avenue
Irvine, CA 92714
(714) 754-2300

Home Nutritional Support, Inc.
238 Passaic Avenue
Fairfield, NJ 07006
(800) 631-0415

Comprehensive Cancer Centers
Recognized by the National Cancer Institute

ALABAMA

Lurlee Wallace Tumor Institute
University Station
619 South 19th Street
Birmingham, AL 35294
Phone: (205) 934-5077

CALIFORNIA

Los Angeles County-University of Southern Califor-
nia Comprehensive Cancer Center
2025 Zonal Avenue
Los Angeles, CA 90033
Phone: (213) 224-7008
UCLA-Jonsson Comprehensive Cancer Center
924 Westwood Boulevard, Suite 650
Los Angeles, CA 90024
Phone: (213) 825-5268

CONNECTICUT

Yale Comprehensive Cancer Center
Yale University School of Medicine
333 Cedar Street
New Haven, CT 06510
Phone: (203) 432-4122

DISTRICT OF COLUMBIA

Vincent T. Lombardi Cancer Research Center
Georgetown University Medical Center
3800 Reservoir Road, N.W.
Washington, DC 20007
Phone: (202) 625-7066
Howard University Cancer Research Center
College of Medicine
Washington, DC 20059
Phone: (202) 745-1406
Howard University Cancer Center
Department of Oncology
2041 Georgia Avenue, N.W.
Washington, DC 20060
Phone: (202) 636-7697

FLORIDA

Comprehensive Cancer Center for the State of
Florida
University of Miami School of Medicine
1475 N.W. 12th Avenue
Miami, FL 33136
Phone: (305) 547-7707

ILLINOIS

Illinois Cancer Council
36 S. Wabash Avenue, Suite 700
Chicago, IL 60603
Phone: (312) 346-9813
Northwestern University Cancer Center
Ward Memorial Building
303 East Chicago Avenue
Chicago, IL 60611
Phone: (312) 226-5250
University of Chicago Cancer Research Center
905 East 59th Street
Chicago, IL 60637
Phone: (312) 947-6386
University of Illinois
P.O. Box 6998
Chicago, IL 60680
Phone: (312) 996-6666
Rush-Presbyterian-St. Luke's Medical Center
1753 West Congress Parkway
Chicago, IL 60612
Phone: (312) 942-6642

MARYLAND

Johns Hopkins Comprehensive Cancer Center
600 N. Wolfe Street
Baltimore, MD 21205
Phone: (301) 955-8822

MASSACHUSETTS

Sidney Farber Cancer Institute
44 Binney Street
Boston, MA 02115
Phone: (617) 732-3555

MICHIGAN

Michigan Cancer Foundation
110 East Warren Avenue
Detroit, MI 48201
Phone: (313) 833-0710

MINNESOTA

Mayo Comprehensive Cancer Center
200 First Street, S.W.
Rochester, NM 55901
Phone: (507) 284-3311 or 284-8964

NEW YORK

Columbia University Cancer Center/Institute of
    Cancer Research
Hammer Health Sciences Center
701 W. 168th Street
New York, NY 10032
Phone: (212) 694-6900
Memorial Sloan-Kettering Cancer Center
1275 York Avenue
New York, NY 10021
Phone: (212) 794-6561
Roswell Park Memorial Institute
666 Elm Street
Buffalo, NY 14263
Phone: (716) 845-5770

NORTH CAROLINA

Duke University
Comprehensive Cancer Center
P.O. Box 3814
Durham, NC 27710
Phone: (919) 684-2282

OHIO

Ohio State University Comprehensive Cancer Center
410 W. 12th Avenue
Columbus, OH 43210
Phone: (614) 422-5022

PENNSYLVANIA

The Fox Chase Cancer Center
7701 Burholme Avenue
Philadelphia, PA 19111
Phone: (215) 728-2490
University of Pennsylvania Cancer Center
578 Maloney Building
3400 Spruce Street
Philadelphia, PA 19104
Phone: (215) 662-3910

TEXAS

The University of Texas System Cancer Center
M.D. Anderson Hospital and Tumor Institute
MD 920
6723 Bertner Avenue
Houston, TX 77030
Phone: (713) 792-6000

WASHINGTON

Fred Hutchinson Cancer Research Center
1124 Columbia Street
Seattle, WA 98104
Phone: (206) 292-2930

WISCONSIN

The University of Wisconsin Clinical Cancer Center
600 Highland Avenue
Madison, WI 53792
Phone: (608) 263-8610